P9-BZF-905

PAGE 38 | **ON THE ROAD**

YOUR COMPLETE DESTINATION GUIDE
In-depth reviews, detailed listings
and insider tips

TOP EXPERIENCES MAP **NEXT PAGE**

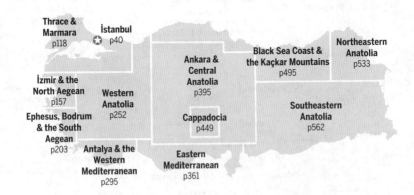

Thrace & Marmara p118

İstanbul ✪ p40

İzmir & the North Aegean p157

Western Anatolia p252

Ephesus, Bodrum & the South Aegean p203

Antalya & the Western Mediterranean p295

Ankara & Central Anatolia p395

Cappadocia p449

Eastern Mediterranean p361

Black Sea Coast & the Kaçkar Mountains p495

Northeastern Anatolia p533

Southeastern Anatolia p562

PAGE 667 | **SURVIVAL GUIDE**

YOUR AT-A-GLANCE REFERENCE
How to get around, get a room,
stay safe, say hello

THIS EDITION WRITTEN AND RESEARCHED BY

James Bainbridge

Brett Atkinson, Jean-Bernard Carillet, Steve Fallon, Will Gourlay,
Virginia Maxwell, Brandon Presser, Tom Spurling

❯ Turkey

ROMANIA
Bucharest
Sevastopol

BLACK SEA
(KARADENİZ)

BULGARIA
Burgas

Kapikule
Edirne
Kırklareli

GREECE
Ipsala Tekirdağ Çorlu İstanbul
Keşan
Gelibolu
Gallipoli
Peninsula Lapseki
Çanakkale Bandırma
Troy
(Truva)
Ayvacık
Assos Edremit Balıkesir
Lesvos
Ayvalık
Bergama Pergamum
Chios
Aliağa
Yeni
Foça
Çeşme
İzmir Sardis
Odemis
Selçuk
Kuşadası Aydın Nazilli
Priene
Ephesus
Didyma Milas
Güllük
Bodrum Gökova
(Akyaka)
Kos Marmaris

Sea of
Marmara
Darıca
Yalova
Gemlik
İznik
Bursa
Uludağ
(2543m)
Eskişehir
Kütahya
Afyon
Uşak
Manisa
Çivril
Hierapolis/
Pamukkale
Afrodisias
Yatağan
Muğla
Ortaca
Dalaman
Fethiye
Ölüdeniz
Patara
Beach
Megiste
Lycian
Way

The Bosphorus
The Dardanelles

Kocaeli
(İzmit)
Adapazarı
Bolu
Sakarya River
Gordion
Polatlı

Cide
İnebolu
Sinop
Amasra
Zonguldak
Karabük
Safranbolu
Kastamonu
Tosya Osmancı
Gerede Kurşunlu
Çankırı
Ilgaz
Çorum
Sungurlu
Hattu
Yoz
Ankara
Kırıkkale

Kırşehir

Akşehir
Eğirdir
Gölü
Beyşehir
Gölü
Isparta
Beyşehir
Burdur
Denizli
Çavdır
Termessos
Perge Aspendos
Antalya
Kemer
Finike
Olympos
Side
Alanya
Anamurium Anamur

Göreme
Nevşehir
Derinkuyu
Aksaray
Cappadocia Yahya
Niğde

Tuz Gölü
(Salt Lake)

Konya
Ereğli
Karaman
Akseki
Kırobası
Uzuncaburç
Silifke
Olukbaşı
Kızkalesi

Adana
Tarsus
Mersi
(İçel)

Lefkoşa/
Lefkosia
(Nicosia)

CYPRUS

Crete

MEDITERRANEAN SEA
(AKDENİZ)

Ikaria
Samos
Kaş
Kos

Ani
Eerie ruins of a former
Armenian capital (p552)

Cappadocia
Surreal fairy chimneys
and cave dwellings (p449)

Sumela Monastery
Cliff-face monastery
surveys valleys (p516)

Nemrut Dağı (Mt Nemrut)
Giant stone heads litter
a mountain (p583)

Konya
Dervishes whirl at the
Mevlâna Festival (p438)

ELEVATION

3000m
2500m
2000m
1500m
1000m
700m
500m
200m
100m
0

18
TOP
EXPERIENCES

Crossing Between the Continents

1 In İstanbul, you can climb aboard a commuter ferry (p78) and flit between Europe and Asia in less than an hour. Every day, a flotilla of boats take locals up the Bosphorus and over the Sea of Marmara, sounding their sonorous horns as they go. Morning services share the waterways with diminutive fishing boats and massive container ships, all accompanied by flocks of wildly shrieking seagulls. At sunset, the tapering minarets and Byzantine domes of the Old City are thrown into relief against a dusky pink sky – it's the city's most magical sight.

Cappadocia

2 The hard-set honeycomb landscape looks sculpted by a swarm of genius bees. The truth – the cooling effects of a major volcanic eruption – is only slightly less cool. Humans have also left their mark here in the frescoes of colourful Byzantine churches or in the bowels of complex underground cities. These days, Cappadocia (p449) is all about good times; fine wine, fine food and five-star caves; trail rides, valley hikes and hot-air ballooning. There's enough to keep you buzzing for days. Uçhisar Castle, Uçhisar (above)

HOLGER LEUE

Ephesus

3 Undoubtedly the most famous of Turkey's ancient sites and considered the best-preserved ruins in the Mediterranean, Ephesus (p205) is a powerful tribute to Greek artistry and Roman architectural prowess. A stroll along the marble-coated Curetes Way provides myriad photo opportunities, but the true *pièce de résistance* is the Terraced Houses complex, offering incredible insight into the daily lives of the city's elite through vivid frescoes and sophisticated mosaics.

Lycian Way

4 Acclaimed as one of the top 10 long-distance walks in the world, the Lycian Way (p29) follows well-laid and signposted paths for 500km between Fethiye and Antalya. This is the Teke peninsula, birthplace of the ancient (and mysterious) Lycian civilisation. The route leads through pine and cedar forests in the shadow of mountains rising almost 3000m, and past villages, stunning coastal views and an embarrassment of ruins at such ancient cities as Pınara, Xanthos, Letoön and Olympos. Walk it in sections unless you have a lot of time and stamina. Rock-cut tomb, Fethiye (below)

MICHAEL ZEGERS/PHOTOLIBRARY

Kebaps

5 Just about anything you can poke a şiş (skewer) at will be an essential component of some Turkish towns' proprietary kebap. They're made with cubed meat, minced meat, aubergine (eggplant), plums and chestnuts. But the most famous regional variation – the Adana kebap – keeps it nice and simple: minced beef or lamb is mixed with powered red pepper, grilled on a skewer and served with sliced onions dusted with sumac (a slightly acidic local herb) and barbecued tomatoes. *Afiyet olsun* (bon appétit)!

HANAN ISACHAR

Sultanahmet Park, İstanbul

6 History resonates when you stand in this garden between the Blue Mosque (p49) and Aya Sofya (p45). Edifices built for the glorification of God and powerful men – not necessarily in that order – these two buildings remind beholders of the city's Byzantine and Ottoman heritage. Book-ended by the Roman-era Hippodrome and a modern-day tourist enclave where remnants of the Great Palace of Byzantium provide decorative flourishes, the park offers more than peerless photo opportunities – it visually reinforces İstanbul's claim to be the greatest city in the world.

Sumela Monastery

7 The improbable cliff-face location of the Sumela Monastery (p516) is more than matched by the surrounding verdant scenery. Gently winding roads leading to the monastery twist past rustic riverside fish restaurants, and the progress of travellers is often pleasantly hindered by flocks of fat-tailed sheep being guided to fresh pastures. The last few kilometres afford a couple of tantalising glimpses across pine-covered valleys to Sumela's honey-coloured walls, and the final approach by foot is best accompanied by a soundtrack from local musicians.

JEAN-BERNARD CARILLET

Hamams (Turkish Baths)

8 At most of the traditional hamams in Turkey all the extras are on offer: bath treatments, facials, pedicures and so on. But we recommend you stick with the tried and true – a soak and a scrub followed by an elective pummelling. The world (and your body) will never feel quite the same again. For a truly atmospheric experience, seek out a soak in a centuries-old hamam in Antalya's atmospheric old quarter or in historic Sultanahmet, İstanbul. Cağaloğlu Hamamı, İstanbul (left)

İZZET KERIBAR

Patara Beach

9 Patara (p329) boasts Turkey's longest sand beach, a chunk of the Lycian Way long-distance footpath, and has some of the most extensive ruins in the region. The Mediterranean town was also the principal port for ancient Lycia. Still not convinced? St Nicholas (better known as Santa Claus) was born here in the 4th century, and saints Paul and Luke changed boats here while on their third mission from Rhodes to Phoenicia. Or so it says in Acts 21:1-2.

Practising Your Turkish

10 Getting a grasp on basic Turkish is pretty straightforward as most sounds are similar to those made by speakers of English. Kick off your fledgling Turkish vocabulary by ordering from menus featuring lots of tasty regional variations. In restaurants, tea shops and bus stations, always take the time to accept heartfelt invitations to chat over a glass of çay. Remember that travel is not a race, and those leisurely times you spend trying to converse with the immensely welcoming locals will emerge as highlights of your trip.

Ani

11 Ani (p552) is a truly exceptional site. Historically intriguing, culturally compelling and scenically magical, this ghost city floating in a sea of grass looks like a movie set. Lying in blissful isolation right at the Armenian border, the site exudes an eerie ambience. Ani was completely deserted in 1239 after a Mongol invasion, but before that it was a thriving city and a capital of both the Urartian and Armenian kingdoms. The ruins include several notable churches, including the imposing Church of St Gregory and the Church of the Redeemer, as well as a cathedral built between the years 987 and 1010. Church of the Redeemer ruins, Ani (above)

Nemrut Dağı (Mt Nemrut)

12 One man's megalomania echoes across the centuries atop Nemrut Dağı's (p583) exposed and rugged summit. A gently emerging sunrise coaxes stark shadows from the mountain's giant sculpted heads, and as dawn breaks the finer details of the immense landscape below are gradually added. Huddling against the chill of a new day, a warming glass of çay (tea) could not be more welcome. And when your time on the summit is complete, don't miss the graceful Roman bridge crossing the nearby Cendere River.

Gallipoli Peninsula

13 The narrow stretch of land (p130) guarding the entrance to the much-contested Dardanelles is a beautiful area, where pine trees roll across hills above Eceabat's back-packer hangouts and Kilitbahir's castle. Touring the peaceful countryside is a poignant experience: memorials and cemeteries mark the spots where young men from far away fought and died in gruelling conditions. The passionate guides (p131) do a good job of evoking the futility and tragedy of the Gallipoli campaign, one of WWI's worst episodes. Kilitbahir Castle, Gallipoli Peninsula (right)

HOLGER LEUE

Safranbolu

14 Listed for eternal preservation by Unesco in 1994, Safranbolu (p411) is Turkey's prime example of an Ottoman town brought back to life. Domestic tourists descend here full of sentiment to spend a night or two in half-timbered houses that look torn from the pages of a children's storybook. And the magic doesn't end there. Sweets and saffron line the cobblestone alleyways as artisans and cobblers ply their centuries-old trades beneath medieval mosques. When the summer storms light up the night sky, the fantasy is complete.

IZZET KERIBAR

Kırkpınar Oil Wrestling

15 In late June or early July, the northern city of Edirne (p119) fills with beefy *pehlivan* (wrestlers) from across Turkey, along with crowds who come to watch this centuries-old sport (p122). There's a festival atmosphere outside the riverside stadium, with families picnicking on the grass and stalls springing up. Inside, olive oil–soaked hopefuls, from *baş* (first class) contestants to prepubescent whippersnappers, try to get a grip on their opponents' slippery sinews and topple them. Hands go down opponents' shorts, where it's easier to get a hold.

TOLGA BOZOGLU/EPA/CORBIS

Pamukkale

17 Famed for its intricate series of calcite shelves and crowned by elaborate Roman ruins, the 'Cotton Castle' – a bleach-white mirage by day and alien ski slope by night – is one of the most unusual treasures in Turkey. Gingerly tiptoe through the crystal travertines and when you reach the top, reward yourself with a refreshing dunk in the ancient pool amid toppled columns and dramatic friezes. See p279.

Whirling Dervishes

16 Join Rumi's Sufi brethren and whirl your heart's intent. Today devotees and other aspirants converge on Konya (p438), the birthplace of the poet and philosopher priest, Rumi, and home to the remarkable Mevlâna Museum, a site of crackling energy and a beacon for tolerance in the Muslim world. December sees a major surge in tourism for the annual Mevlâna Festival (3 to 17 December; p443), a colourful celebration of love for the great unseen that defies all non-belief.

Gület Cruising

18 Known locally as a blue voyage (*mavi yolculuk;* p318), a cruise lasting four days and three nights on a *gület* (traditional wooden sailing boat) along the western Mediterranean's Turquoise Coast is the highlight of many a traveller's trip to Turkey. This trip will have you exploring isolated beaches and watching sunsets. To be away from it all, out at sea and (usually) away from the internet, is a treat not often savoured nowadays. A moored *gület,* Bodrum Peninsula (above)

welcome to
Turkey

A richly historical land with some of the best cuisine you will ever taste, one of the world's greatest cities and scenery from white-sand beaches to soaring mountains.

An Epic History

When you set foot in Türkiye (Turkey), you are following in the wake of some remarkable historical figures. Ottoman sultans used to luxuriate in İstanbul's Topkapı Palace, surrounded by fawning courtiers, harem members, eunuchs and riches from an empire stretching from Budapest to Baghdad. Centuries earlier, Byzantine Christians cut cave churches into Cappadocia's fairy chimneys and hid from Islamic armies in underground cities.

At other points over the millennia, the Hittites built Hattuşa's stone walls on the Anatolian steppe, Romans coursed down the Curetes Way at Ephesus (Efes), whirling dervishes gyrated with Sufi mysticism, and the mysterious Lycians left ruins on Mediterranean beaches. Turkey has hosted A-list history-book figures including Julius Caesar, who famously 'came, saw and conquered' near Amasya, and St Paul, who criss-crossed the country.

Cultural Depth

Of course, Turkey's current inhabitants are just as memorable. The extroverted Turks have most in common – out of all their varied neighbouring countries, from Azerbaijan to Bulgaria – with their hot-blooded southern European neighbours. They're also, understandably, proud of their heritage, and full of information (though we can't vouch for its accuracy) about subjects from kilims (flat-weave rugs) to the Aya Sofya's floating dome. Turkey's long history has given it a profound depth of culture. Immersing yourself in that culture is as simple as soaking in a Seljuk or Ottoman hamam, eating a kebap and tasting influences brought along the Silk Road, or visiting the ancient ruins scattering the fields, bays and mountains.

Landscapes & Activities

The greatest surprise for first-time visitors to Turkey, with its stereotypes of kebaps, carpets and moustachioed hustlers in the bazaar, is the sheer diversity found between its Aegean beaches and eastern mountains. In İstanbul, you can cruise – on the Bosphorus as well as through markets and nightclubs – in a Westernised metropolis offering equal parts romance and overcrowded insanity. In holiday spots such as Cappadocia and the southwestern coasts, mix trekking, horse-riding and water sports with meze savouring on a panoramic terrace. Then there are the less-frequented eastern quarters, where honey-coloured outposts overlook the plains of ancient Mesopotamia, and weather-beaten relics add lashings of lyricism to mountain ranges.

It's hardly surprising Turkey has attracted so many folk over the centuries. Come and discover their legacy for yourself.

need to know

Currency
» Türk Lirası (Turkish lira; TL)

Language
» Turkish

When to Go

İstanbul
GO Apr-May, Sep

Eastern Anatolia
GO May-Jun, Sep

Cappadocia
GO May, Sep-Oct

Aegean
GO May-Jun, Sep

Mediterranean
GO Apr, Sep-Oct

Desert, dry climate
Warm to hot summers, mild winters
Mild to hot summers, cold winters

High Season
(Jun–Aug)
» Prices are highest
» Expect crowds and book ahead at hot spots
» Christmas–New Year is also a busy, expensive period
» Hot weather throughout the country

Shoulder Season (May)
» Fewer crowds
» Most businesses are open and prices drop
» September is also shoulder season
» Warm, spring temperatures likely, especially in the southwest

Low Season
(Oct–Apr)
» Few travellers
» Accommodations in tourist areas may close
» Expect discounts of 20% or more
» October is autumn; spring starts in April
» Kurban Bayramı holiday occurs

Set Your Budget

Budget (per day) at least
TL50
» Dorm bed: TL15-25
» Rooms and dorms often include breakfast
» Take night buses and trains to skip accommodation costs

Midrange (per day) at least
TL100
» Double room in a midrange hotel: TL75-175
» Eateries serving alcohol are generally more expensive
» Buses and trains often work out cheaper than hire cars

Top end (per day) at least
TL300
» Main course in a top-end restaurant: >TL17.50
» You can pick up flights for the same as, or less than, buses

Money

» ATMs are widely available. Credit cards are accepted by most businesses in cities and tourist areas.

Visas

» To stay for up to 90 days, you can buy a visa at the airport.

Mobile Phones

» SIM cards are cheap and widely available, although your phone must be unlocked. After about a month, the network will block your phone.

Driving/ Transport

» Drive on the right; the steering wheel is on the left side of the car. Buses are fast and efficient; trains are generally slow.

Websites

» **Lonely Planet** (www.lonelyplanet. com/turkey) Info, bookings and forum.

» **Turkey Travel Planner** (www.turkey travelplanner.com) Useful travel info.

» **Turkish Cultural Foundation** (www. turkishculture.org) Culture and heritage.

» **Go Turkey** (www. goturkey.com) Official tourism portal.

» **Hürriyet Daily News** (www. hurriyetdailynews. com) Turkish news.

» **All About Turkey** (www.allaboutturkey. com) Multilingual introduction.

Exchange Rates

Australia	A$1	TL1.37
Canada	C$1	TL1.47
Europe	€1	TL1.97
Japan	¥100	TL1.74
New Zealand	NZ$1	TL1.09
UK	UK£1	TL2.37
USA	US$1	TL1.50

For current exchange rates see www.xe.com.

Important Numbers

In this book, local codes are listed under the names of locations.

Turkey country code	☑90
International access code from Turkey	☑00
Ambulance	☑112
Fire	☑110
Police	☑155

Arriving in Turkey

» **İstanbul Atatürk & Sabiha Gökçen International Airports**
Havaş Airport Bus To Taksim every 30 minutes (TL10 to TL13)
Airport Shuttle Seven or eight a day to Taksim or Sultanahmet (€10)
Light rail From Atatürk to Zeytinburnu, then tram to centre (TL3)

» **Big İstanbul Bus Station**
Light rail To Aksaray, and tram to centre (TL3)
Bus To Taksim Sq or Eminönü (TL1.50)
Taxi 20/30 minutes to Sultanahmet/Taksim Sq (TL25/30)
See also p111.

ISLAM & RAMAZAN

On the whole, Islam is a moderate presence in Turkey. In İstanbul and the west there are as many bars as mosques and it is sometimes easy to forget you are in an Islamic country. The one time of year when Westerners do need to temper their behaviour is Ramazan, the holy month when Muslims fast between dawn and dusk. Ramazan currently falls in the summer.

If you aren't a fasting Muslim, don't go to an *iftar* (evening meal to break fast) tent for a cheap feed.

Don't eat, drink or smoke in public during the day.

Cut the locals some slack; waiters and others might be grumpy if they are fasting in hot weather.

Don't dress provocatively; Muslims have to give up sex for the month.

if you like...

Bazaars

Centuries ago, Seljuk and Ottoman traders travelled the Silk Road, stopping at caravanserais to do business. The tradition is alive and so is haggling in Turkey's labyrinthine bazaars, where locals and tourists converge to buy gear ranging from carpets to mosque alarm clocks.

Grand Bazaar, İstanbul Hone your bargaining skills in the city's original and best shopping mall, with 4000-plus shops (p60)

Urfa Bazaar With its narrow alleyways, shady courtyards and proximity to Syria, Urfa's bazaar has a Middle Eastern flavour (p576)

Kapalı Çarşı, Bursa Explore the silk and shadow-puppet shops in this heritage labyrinth, far removed from more-touristy markets (p262)

Wait a minute, we're supposed to haggle! True to Monty Python's *Life of Brian,* bagging a carpet can be an entertaining, theatrical process, entailing repeat visits and gallons of çay (p675)

Spice Bazaar, İstanbul Jewel-like *lokum* (Turkish delight) and colourful pyramids of spices provide eye candy at the fragrant bazaar (p61)

Hamams

Hamams are also known as Turkish baths, a name coined by the Europeans who were introduced to their steamy pleasures by the Ottomans. With their domed roofs, they combine elements of Roman and Byzantine baths. Go for a massage or just soak in the calming atmosphere.

Sefa Hamamı, Antalya Retaining many of its Seljuk features, this restored 13th-century Seljuk gem is found in Kaleiçi (Old Antalya) between Ottoman houses and the Roman harbour (p352)

Cağaloğlu Hamamı, İstanbul Patrons have been getting soapy and steamy at the city's most beautiful hamam, near the Aya Sofya, since 1741 (p84)

Traditional Turkish contortionism You may feel truly pummelled if you've asked for 'the works', but many masseurs actually let foreigners off lightly; you might see towel-wrapped Turks getting literally walked over

Sokollu Mehmet Paşa Hamam, Edirne Mimar Sinan designed this 16th-century beauty, facing the famous Three-Balcony Mosque (p122)

Beaches

Sun-seekers will find themselves swimming in options when deciding where to recline by the 'wine-dark sea' (in the words of Homer). Turkey is surrounded by the Mediterranean, the Aegean, the Black Sea and the Sea of Marmara. This being a country lathered in history, sunbathers can contemplate the Greek myths that took place on the Turkish coast.

Patara Visitors once came for the temple and oracle of Apollo, but today sun-seekers and sea turtles prefer the 20km of white sand (p329)

Kabak Take a steep tractor ride down to the Mediterranean beach community (p325)

Aegean islands A Greek monastery overlooks Bozcaada's Ayazma beach, and you might have Gökçeada's beaches to yourself (p145)

Pamucak Close to Kuşadası and Selçuk, but significantly less developed, Pamucak's wide expanse of delta river sand is one of the southern Aegean's least crowded beaches (p220)

» The remote beach at Kabak (p325) is flanked by dramatic cliffs

TIM BARKER

Museums

In a country marked by great dynasties, from Hittite hill men to Ottoman sultans, museums are a regular sight. Every self-respecting town has a museum to preserve its local history, ranging from dusty collections of prehistoric fragments to innovative, interactive centres.

İstanbul As well as the likes of the Museum of Turkish & Islamic Arts, with carpets fit for palaces, check out less-obvious sights such as Santralİstanbul, a former power station (p83)

Museum of Health, Edirne The museum of Ottoman medicine occupies a mental hospital where patients were treated using music therapy (p123)

Göreme Open-Air Museum Only in Cappadocia could a valley of rock-cut Byzantine churches be called a museum (p452)

Museum of Anatolian Civilisations, Ankara Sheds light on the ancient civilisations that warred and waned on the surrounding steppe (p397)

Ottoman diorama A must-have feature for Turkish museums, with moustachioed mannequins enacting daily life in an Ottoman household (p412)

Cities

Turks are a regionalist bunch; they will invariably tell you their town's *en çok güzel* (the most beautiful). In fact, with one notable exception, Turkey doesn't do cities as well as it does mountains and beaches, but there are some worthwhile places to experience urban Turkey.

İstanbul Today's megacity was once the capital of empires; you can't blame the İstanbullus for thinking their city is still the centre of the world (p40)

İzmir The former city of Smyrna is right on the Aegean; ferries travel along the seafront, with its holiday atmosphere (p183)

Antalya The gateway to the Turkish Riviera, and both classically beautiful and stylishly modern in its own right (p349)

Edirne Turkey's northernmost city is not a major stop on the tourist circuit, leaving you to enjoy the stunning Ottoman mosques with the locals (p119)

Antakya (Hatay) The site of the biblical Antioch is distinctively Arabic (p388)

Boutique Hotels

From half-timbered Ottoman mansions to Greek stone houses, Turkey's architectural gems are increasingly being converted into small, one-off hotels. These distinctive properties offer a local experience with a stylish twist.

Cappadocia Take up residence in a fairy chimney and experience troglodyte living with luxurious features such as a cave hamam (p456)

Alaçatı More than 100 stone Greek houses in this Aegean village have been converted into boutique digs; options include a former olive warehouse and windmills (p196)

Asude Konak, Gaziantep There are boutique hotels in wild southeastern Anatolia too – evening meals in the courtyard are one of the attractions at this 19th-century townhouse (p568)

Ottoman Anatolia Safranbolu and Amasya – with rocky bluffs and, overlooking the latter, Pontic tombs – are idyllic settings for their many hotels in Ottoman piles (p413)

Kaleiçi A smattering of boutique hotels adds further charm to Antalya's Roman-Ottoman old quarter (p352)

>> The Library of Celsus at Ephesus (p209) held 12,000 scrolls in niches around its walls

IZZET KERIBAR

History

Turks are proud of their long, eventful history, and it's easy to share their enthusiasm at the country's mosques and palaces, ruins and museums. Just wander through a bazaar or eat a kebap and you'll get a sense of history; both contain influences introduced by Silk Road traders.

İstanbul Every acre of this former capital of empires exudes a sense of its historic significance, particularly in Sultanahmet among the Topkapı Palace et al (p45)

The Dardanelles On one side is Troy, with a replica Trojan Horse; on the other, the Gallipoli Peninsula saw a bloody WWI campaign (p130)

North Aegean There's living history in the communities descended from Turkmen nomads and from people displaced by the population exchange between Turkey and Greece (p169)

Christianity The Islamic country has a rich Christian past; check out Cappadocia's rock-cut Byzantine monasteries, and the northeastern valleys' medieval Georgian churches (p484)

Ruins

On the list of what makes Turkey one of the world's greatest travelling destinations, its ruins compete with kebaps for first place. Whether in a city centre or atop a craggy cliff, the country's relics bring out the historical romantic in you.

Ephesus The best-preserved classical city in the eastern Mediterranean (p205)

Pergamum The Asclepion was ancient Rome's pre-eminent medical centre and the theatre is a vertigo-inducing marvel (p177)

Armenian Eastern Anatolia's Armenian ruins include a 10th-century church on an island and Ani, the former capital (p552)

Kekova A sunken city and Lycian tombs lie on the Mediterranean seabed (p342)

Obscure sites Hiding in every corner of Turkey are seldom-visited, overgrown ruins, where it might be just you, the wind and the caretaker

Nemrut Dağı Atop Mt Nemrut are the remains of statues – mostly their heads – built by a megalomaniac pre-Roman king (p583)

Activities

With its beautiful and diverse terrain, ranging from mountain ranges to beaches, Turkey is a prime spot for outdoor activities. Whether you try an extreme sport for the first time or just take a gentle stroll, be sure to reward yourself with some çay and baklava, or Efes beer and meze.

Trekking Opportunities range from half-day wanders in Cappadocia to 500km Mediterranean trails (p28)

Diving Swim over ancient amphoras and, off the Gallipoli Peninsula, a WWI shipwreck (p30)

Water sports On the Aegean and Mediterranean coasts, windsurfing, kiteboarding, canoeing and waterskiing are among the fun on offer (p30)

Adventure sports Eastern Anatolia offers adrenaline-pumping activities including white-water rafting and mountain walking (p29)

Canyoning The 18km-long Saklıkent Gorge near Fethiye is Turkey's top spot for canyoning (p327)

Skiing Ski resorts across the country include Cappadocia's Erciyes Dağı and Bursa's Uludağ (p31)

If you like... flamboyant architecture
Dolmabahçe Palace (p75) and Divriği's doorways (p438) won't disappoint

If you like... obscure ancient civilisations
Seek out Hattuşa (p422) and the Phrygian Valley (p270)

Landscape

Apart from a toe sticking into Europe, Turkey is part of Asia, so it should come as no surprise that its landscapes are varied and stunning. With ancient ruins and bucolic villages dotting the rural areas, taking in the natural scenery couldn't be more pleasant.

Cappadocia The fairy chimneys and *tuff* valleys are best explored on foot or horseback (p449)

Northeastern Anatolia Mountains and rugged scenery including Turkey's highest peak, Mt Ararat (5137m; p560)

Amasra to Sinop A great drive takes you past Black Sea beaches and green hills (p499)

Behramkale The hillside village has dreamy views of the Aegean coast (p165)

Lake Van A 3750-sq-km lake surrounded by snowcapped mountains (p609)

Bozburun Peninsula Raw Mediterranean coast, riddled with coves and pine forests (p303)

Nemrut Dağı Mountain-top stone heads gaze at the Anti-Taurus Range (p583)

Ala Dağlar National Park Waterfalls crash down limestone cliffs in the Taurus Mountains (p481)

Food & Drink

Turkey has epicurean indulgence nailed, from street snacks to gourmet restaurants with panoramic terraces. Not only does every region offer local dishes, you can sample them in individualistic eateries; the culinary siblings of the country's boutique hotels. You'll also never be short of places to toast your trip in style.

Balıkçı Ayvalık's fishermen's association runs one of the best fish restaurants on the Aegean (p170)

Cihangir Artists and trustafarians chill outside bars and cafes in this fashionable İstanbul neighbourhood (p96)

Doyuranlar Gözleme On the Gallipoli Peninsula, a great example of the family-run eateries that offer fresh fare and a bucolic atmosphere (p138)

Ziggy's Named after the David Bowie song, Ürgüp's stylish restaurant has killer views of the Cappadocian moonscape (p476)

Western Mediterranean A beverage by the sea is just the thing at the end of a hot Turkish day, and towns like Ölüdeniz and Patara have some alluring hang-outs (p323)

month by month

Top Events

1 **Oil wrestling,** June

2 **Walking,** October

3 **Music festivals,** July

4 **Ski season,** December

5 **Nevruz,** March

January

The dead of winter. Even İstanbul's streets are empty of crowds, local and foreign, and snow closes eastern Anatolia's mountain passes and delays buses.

New Year's Day

A surrogate Christmas takes place across the Islamic country, with the usual decorations, exchange of gifts and greeting cards. Christmas and New Year are an exception to the low season; prices rise and accommodation fills up.
1 January

March

As in the preceding months, you might have sights to yourself outside the country's top destinations, and you can get discounts at the accommodation options that open their doors.

Nevruz

Kurds and Alevis celebrate the ancient Middle Eastern spring festival with much jumping over bonfires and general jollity. Banned until a few years ago, Nevruz is now an official holiday with huge parties, particularly in Diyarbakır, that last well into the morning.
21 March

Çanakkale Deniz Zaferi

Turks descend on the Gallipoli (Gelibolu) Peninsula and the town across the Dardanelles to celebrate what they call the Çanakkale Naval Victory. The busloads of people make it a good time *not* to visit the area!
18 March

April

The beginning of the tourist shoulder season follows the arrival of spring. It's not a great time to get a tan in northern Turkey, but you can enjoy balmy, breezy weather in the southwest.

Anzac Day, Gallipoli Peninsula

The WWI battles for the Dardanelles are commemorated again, this time with more emphasis on the Allied soldiers. Antipodean pilgrims sleep at Anzac Cove before the dawn services; another busy time on the peninsula.
25 April

International İstanbul Film Festival

For most of the month, the wonderful vintage cinemas on and around Beyoğlu's İstiklal Caddesi host a packed program of Turkish and international films and events, with cheap-as-çay tickets available. An excellent crash course in Turkish cinema, but book ahead.
www.iksv.org/film

International İstanbul Tulip Festival

The city's parks and gardens are resplendent with tulips, which originated in Turkey before being exported to the Netherlands during the Ottoman era. Unsurprisingly, multicoloured tulips are often planted to resemble the Turks' cherished 'evil eye'.
Late March to early April

May

Another good month to visit. The shoulder

season continues, with attendant discounts, but spring is going strong and the Aegean and Mediterranean beaches are seriously heating up.

International Giresun Aksu Festival

The historic, hazelnut-producing Black Sea town hails fecundity and the new growing season with boat trips to Giresun Island, concerts, traditional dance performances and other open-air events.
Four days from May 20

Ruins, Mosques, Palaces & Museums

In İstanbul and at famous sights such as Ephesus (Efes), this is your last chance until September to have a look at the main attractions without the crowds, which can become almost unbearable at the height of summer.

June

Summer brings the high tourist season to Turkey. Until the end of August, expect sizzling temperatures, unbudging hotel prices and crowds at sights – avoided by visiting early, late or at lunchtime.

Cherry Season

June is the best month to gobble Turkey's delicious cherries, which Giresun introduced to the rest of the world. On the Sea of Marmara, Tekirdağ's Kiraz Festivalı (Cherry Festival) in June celebrates the juicy wonders.

Kafkasör Kültür ve Sanat Festivalı, Artvin

Join the crush at the *boğa güreşleri* (bloodless bull-wrestling matches) at the Caucasus Culture & Arts Festival, held in a pasture near the northeastern Anatolian mountain town.
Last weekend in June

Historic Kırkpınar Oil Wrestling Festival, Edirne

In a sport dating back 650 years, *pehlivan* (wrestlers) from across Turkey rub themselves from head to foot with olive oil and grapple.
Late June or early July

July

This month and August turn the Aegean and Mediterranean tourist heartlands into sun-and-fun machines, and temperatures peak across the country. The blue skies bring out the best in the hot-blooded Turkish personality.

Kültür Sanat ve Turizm Festivalı, Doğubayazıt

The Kurdish town between Mt Ararat (Ağrı Dağı) and the romantic İshak Paşa Palace hosts its Culture and Arts Festival, allowing you to immerse yourself in Kurdish heritage through music, dance and theatre performances.
June or July

Music Festivals

Turkey shows its European side at a string of summer music jamborees; including İstanbul, İzmir and Bursa's highbrow international festivals, Aspendos Opera & Ballet Festival, plus multiple pop, rock, jazz and dance music events in İstanbul and other cities.
June to July

August

Even at night, the weather is hot and humid; pack sun cream and anti-mosquito spray. Walking and activities are best tackled early in the morning or at sunset.

Cappadocian Festivals

Two festivals take place in the land of fairy chimneys (rock formations). A summer series of chamber music concerts are held in the valleys and, between the 16th and 18th, sleepy Hacıbektaş comes alive with the annual pilgrimage of Bektaşi dervishes.
www.klasikkeyifler.org

Bodrum International Ballet Festival

The 15th-century Castle of St Peter, as well as housing the Museum of Underwater Archaeology, is an atmospheric location for the two-week festival, which features Turkish and international ballet and opera performances.
www.bodrumballetfestival.gov.tr

September

Ahh...the heat and crowds lessen, and prices start to drop. Accommodation and tourist activities, such as boat trips, begin winding down for the winter.

Diving

The water is warmest between May to October and you can expect water temperatures of 25°C in September. Turkey's scuba diving centres are Kuşadası and Ayvalık on the Aegean, and Marmaris and Kaş on the Mediterranean.

International İstanbul Biennial

The city's major visual-arts shindig, considered to be one of the world's most prestigious biennials, takes place from mid-September to mid-November in odd-numbered years. In 2009, it featured 120 projects by 70 artists from 40 countries. www.iksv.org

October

Autumn is truly here and many accommodation options have locked their doors for the winter. Good weather can't be guaranteed in İstanbul, but you can enjoy fresh, sunny days along the Mediterranean and Aegean.

Walking

The weather in eastern Anatolia has already become challenging by this time of year, but in the southwest, autumn and spring are the best seasons to enjoy the scenery without too much sweat on your brow. www.trekkinginturkey.com

Akbank Jazz Festival

From late September to mid-October, İstanbul celebrates its love of jazz with this eclectic line-up of local and international performers. Marking its 20th anniversary in 2010, the festival also took place in Ankara, İzmir, Eskişehir and Gaziantep (Antep). www.akbanksanat.com

Antalya Golden Orange Film Festival

Held in early October, Turkey's foremost film event features screenings, a parade of stars in cars and the obligatory controversy. At the award ceremony in Aspendos, the Golden Orange, nicknamed the Turkish Oscar, is awarded to filmmakers. www.altinportakal.org.tr

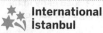

November

Even on the coastlines, summer is a distant memory. Rain falls on İstanbul and the Black Sea, and eastern Anatolia is ensnarled in snow.

Windsurfing

In Turkey's windsurfing centre, Alaçatı, it's the end of the season, which begins in mid-May and sees the protected Aegean bay host the Windsurf World Cup in August. Many of the eight resident schools close from early November. www.alacati.de

Karagöz Festival, Bursa

Five days of festivities and performances celebrate the city's Karagöz shadow-puppetry heritage, with local and international puppeteers and marionette performers.

Efes Pilsen Blues Festival

Between early October and early November, American blues twangers tour nationwide, from İstanbul to Gaziantep. www.pozitif-ist.com

December

Turks fortify themselves against the cold with hot çay and kebap-induced layers. Most of the country is chilly and wet or icy, although the western Mediterranean is milder and hill walking there is viable.

Ski Season

Hit the slopes at the beginning of the ski season at half a dozen resorts across the country – including Cappadocia's Erciyes Dağı (Mt Erciyes) and Uludağ, near Bursa. December to April

Snow in Anatolia

If you're really lucky, after skiing on Erciyes Dağı, you could head west and see central Cappadocia's fairy chimneys looking even more magical under a layer of snow. Eastern Anatolia is also covered in a white blanket, but temperatures get brutally low.

itineraries

Whether you've got six days or 60, these itineraries provide a starting point for the trip of a lifetime. Want more inspiration? Head online to lonelyplanet.com/thorntree to chat with other travellers.

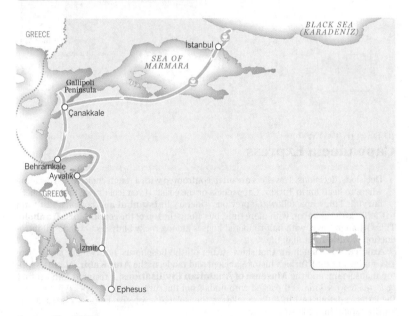

One to Two Weeks
Classic Turkey

Most first-time visitors to Turkey arrive with two ancient names on their lips: **İstanbul** and Ephesus. You'll need at least three days in the continent-straddling megacity to even scrape the surface of its millennia of history. Without a doubt, the top three sights are the **Aya Sofya**, **Topkapı Palace** and **Blue Mosque** but there's a sultan's treasury of other sights and activities, including a **cruise** up the Bosphorus to the Black Sea (Karadeniz), the **nightlife** around the heaving İstiklal Caddesi and the **Grand Bazaar**'s 4000-plus shops.

You can head straight to **İzmir**, near Ephesus, on the ferry and train, but if you have time, meander via the **Gallipoli Peninsula**, most pleasantly reached on the ferry and bus via **Çanakkale**. An afternoon tour of the poignant battlefields, still haunted by ghosts of the WWI campaign, is a memorable experience. The north Aegean is rich in ruins and you could climb the hill to the Temple of Athena at **Behramkale**, but you may prefer to relax in tumbledown **Ayvalık** and save your energy for glorious **Ephesus**, the best-preserved classical city in the eastern Mediterranean.

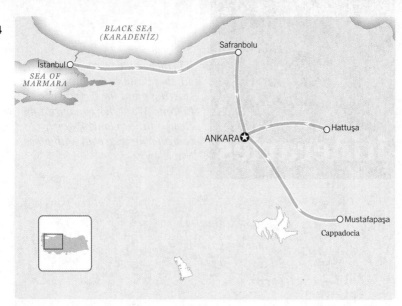

10 Days to Two Weeks
Cappadocia Express

> Decisions, decisions. Travellers are often confronted with a tough choice when deciding where to head for in Turkey: Cappadocia or the coast. If you feel drawn to the former's fairytale landscape, follow the previous itinerary in **İstanbul** and hop on a fast train to the Turkish capital or, with more time, bus along the top of the country to **Safranbolu**. This Ottoman town, with half-timbered houses among rocky bluffs, is a wonderful introduction to rural Anatolian life.

Ankara is no match for that show-stealer on the Bosphorus, but two key sights here give an insight into Turkish history, ancient and modern: the **Anıt Kabir**, Atatürk's hilltop mausoleum, and the **Museum of Anatolian Civilisations**, a restored 15th-century *bedesten* (covered market) packed with finds from the surrounding steppe. Tying in with the latter, a detour east of Ankara takes in the isolated, evocative ruins of **Hattuşa**, the Hittite capital in the late Bronze age.

Leave three days to explore **Cappadocia**, where there are valleys of fairy chimneys (rock formations) and rock-cut churches with Byzantine frescoes, underground cities and horse-riding to get through. You also need to leave time to just sit and appreciate the fantastical landscape in çay-drinking villages such as **Mustafapaşa**, with its stone-carved Greek houses and stone grapevine on the 18th-century church.

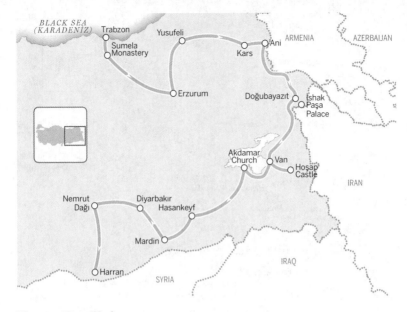

Three to Four Weeks
Eastern Delights

❭ Head south from buzzing Trabzon to **Sumela Monastery**, which peers down on a forested valley from its rockface. The onward route is best tackled by car to appreciate the
scenery, particularly the valleys of medieval **Georgian churches** after Erzurum. Around
the rafting and trekking centre of **Yusufeli**, the drive is one of Turkey's most scenic, heading over mountains, through gorges and past crumbling castles.

Ani is the star attraction of Russian-influenced **Kars**; once a thriving Armenian capital, it's now a field strewn with magnificent ruins next to the border of modern Armenia.
Next, head south to the predominantly Kurdish town of **Doğubayazıt**, nicknamed 'doggy
biscuit' by travellers on the hippie trail. Six kilometres uphill from town, the almost impossibly romantic **İshak Paşa Palace** surveys the plains near the Iranian border.

Further south is **Van**, on the southeastern shore of a vast, mountain-ringed lake. Make
sure you eat lots of the famously tasty local *kahvaltı* (breakfast) because there are numerous sights to get through, including the 10th-century **Akdamar church**, the sole in-
habitant of an island in Lake Van (Van Gölü), and the recently restored **Hoşap Castle**.
Heading west, don't miss **Hasankeyf**, with its rock-cut castle by the Tigris River, and
honey-coloured **Mardin**, overlooking the roasting Mesopotamian plains.

Head northwest and enter the Byzantine city walls at **Diyarbakır**, the heartland of
Kurdish culture, then climb **Nemrut Dağı** (Mt Nemrut) to see the gigantic stone heads.
Finish near the Syrian border in **Harran**, which hosted Abraham in 1900 BC and is one
of the oldest continuously inhabited spots on earth.

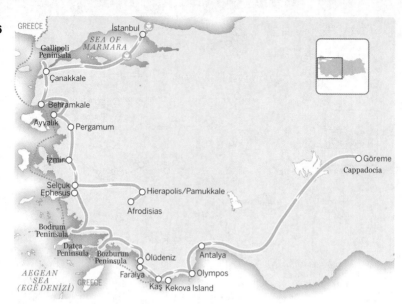

Three to Four Weeks
Palm Trees & Fairy Chimneys

❭ If you have a kind boss, you don't have to choose between Cappadocia's wavy valleys and the coast's white-sand beaches – prepare to spend many hours on buses and check out both areas. Follow our first itinerary, plus, to see some of Turkey's most awe-inspiring Roman ruins, stop in **Pergamum**, the empire's pre-eminent medical centre, and climb the hill to the **acropolis**.

After **Ephesus**, take a day trip from your base at **Selçuk** to the travertines and ruins of **Hierapolis** at Pamukkale. The brilliant white terraces can be dizzying in the midday sun, but swimming among submerged marble columns in the **Antique Pool** will restore your cool. Nearby **Afrodisias** is at least as impressive and less crowded – the only other people among the soaring colonnades might be archaeologists.

Returning to the coast, head along the chichi **Bodrum Peninsula** or the **Datça** and **Bozburun Peninsulas**, where the mountain towns and fishing villages are best explored by scooter. Continuing southeast, beautiful **Ölüdeniz** is the spot to paraglide over the Mediterranean or lie low on a beach towel. You're now within kicking distance of the 509km-long **Lycian Way**. Hike for a day through superb countryside to overnight in heavenly **Faralya**, overlooking Butterfly Valley, and further inroads into the trail will definitely top your 'next time' list.

Continuing along the coast, have a pit stop at laid-back **Kaş**, its pretty harbourside square alive nightly with the hum of friendly folk enjoying the breeze, views, boutique browsing and a beer or two. One of Turkey's most beguiling boat trips departs from here, taking in the sunken Byzantine city at **Kekova Island**. From Kaş, it's a couple of hours to **Olympos**, where you can spend a few days unwinding at the beach tree houses.

Back in the city, **Antalya**'s Roman-Ottoman quarter, Kaleiçi, is worth a wander against the backdrop of a jaw-dropping mountain range. Next, drag yourself away from the beach and catch the bus north to claim your cave in **Göreme**. This travellers' hang-out is the most popular base in Cappadocia, a surreal moonscape dotted with often-phallic tuff cones. The famous formations line the roads to sights including the rock-cut fres-coed churches of **Göreme Open-Air Museum** and the Byzantine underground cities at **Kaymaklı** and **Derinkuyu**.

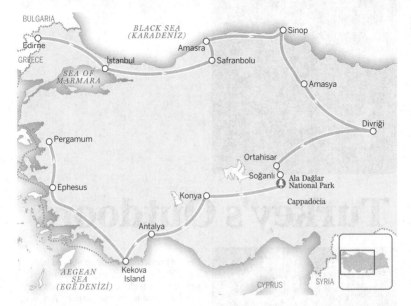

Four Weeks
Anatolian Circle

⟩ This trip only leaves out eastern Anatolia, a mission in itself, and takes in obscure gems as well as prime sights, including **Edirne**'s Selimiye Camii. The 16th-century mosque is the finest work of the great Mimar Sinan. Next, spend a few days among more mosques, palaces and some 13 million folk in **İstanbul**, former capital of the Ottoman and Byzantine empires, before heading east to **Safranbolu**, with its winding streets of Ottoman mansions. From here, turn north to **Amasra**, which is a low-key Black Sea port town, but more importantly the beginning of the drive to **Sinop** through rugged hills.

South of Samsun, **Amasya** matches Safranbolu with its Ottoman houses, as well as having Pontic tombs, a castle and less of a tourist industry. Heading south, pause in Sivas and detour up a mountain valley to **Divriği**, an Alevi town that offers a taste of eastern Anatolia. The 800-year-old, Unesco-protected **Ulu Cami** mosque and hospital complex has stone doorways with intricate carvings.

The next stop, **Cappadocia**, is wholeheartedly back on the beaten track. However, instead of joining the rest on a tour bus or hot-air balloon, explore the fairy chimneys and cave churches by **walking** or **horse-riding**. Göreme and Ürgüp are the usual bases, but you could stay in a less-touristy village such as **Ortahisar**, with its craggy castle.

South of central Cappadocia, see rock-cut churches without the worst of the crowds in **Soğanlı**, where Byzantine monastic settlements occupy two valleys. If you really want to get away from it all, head into the **Ala Dağlar National Park** for some of Turkey's most breathtaking scenery in the Taurus Mountains (Toros Dağları).

You're now fit for the journey across the hazy plains to **Konya**, a convenient stop en route to the Mediterranean and the birthplace of the Mevlâna (whirling dervish) order. The turquoise-domed **Mevlâna Museum**, containing the tomb of the order's 13th-century founder, is an enduring symbol of Turkey.

When you glimpse the glittering Med, follow the coastal part of the previous itinerary. You won't have time to stop everywhere if you want to sunbathe and hit the hamam – **Antalya**'s Seljuk Sefa Hamam is a good one – so pick some highlights, such as the ruins at **Kekova Island**, **Ephesus** and **Pergamum**.

Turkey's Outdoors

Western Mediterranean

The Turquoise Coast offers the widest array of activities, including sea-kayaking, boat trips, diving, two waymarked walking trails, canyoning, rafting and paragliding.

Cappadocia

Excellent for a half- or full-day hike, with a surreal landscape of curvy valleys and fairy chimneys. There are also mountain-walking opportunities, horse-riding, and skiing on Erciyes Dağı (Mt Erciyes).

Eastern Anatolia

Head to the eastern wilds, especially the northern part, for serious adrenaline fixes – mountain walking, white-water rafting, skiing, snowboarding and snowshoeing.

South Aegean

Bring your swimming trunks to the more-popular stretch of the Aegean, where operators in spots like Bodrum offer boat trips galore and water sports including diving and waterskiing.

Need a break from monuments and historic sites? You've come to the right country. Turkey offers a wide array of activities, from the hair-raising to the serene. You want to shoot down a river in a raft? Swim over archaeological remains? Tackle challenging summits? Explore the countryside on horseback? No problem, it's all here.

And Turkey's outdoor pursuits don't stop there. Active travellers from aspiring kayakers to dedicated skiers will find superb playgrounds. Good safety standards can be expected whatever activity you choose, provided you stick to reputable operators who employ qualified, English-speaking staff.

The good thing about Turkey is that epicurean indulgences are never far away. After all that exertion, few things could be better than gobbling up some baklava or relaxing in a hamam. The thrill of the outdoors, good food and well-being: what a great combination.

Walking & Trekking

Walking in Turkey is increasingly popular among both Turks and travellers, and a growing number of local and foreign firms offer walking holidays here; a few are listed on p687 and p695. The country is blessed with numerous mountains, from the Taurus ranges in the southwest to the Kaçkars in the northeast, which all provide fabulous hiking opportunities. Hiking is also the best way to visit villages and sights rarely seen by holidaymakers, and it will give you a taste of life in rural Turkey.

SADDLE UP!

Cappadocia is Turkey's top spot for horse-riding, with numerous good riding tracks criss-crossing the marvellous landscapes. Outfits including Cappadocia's own horse whisperer (p456) are ready to take you on guided rides, ranging from one-hour jaunts to week-long, fully catered treks. The best thing about riding here is that you can access terrain you can't get to otherwise – a wise (and ecofriendly) way to escape the crowds.

Hiking options range from challenging multiday hikes, including Mt Ararat (Ağrı Dağı), Turkey's highest summit and a possible location of Noah's Ark, to gentle afternoon strolls, such as in Cappadocia.

More information on hiking in Turkey is available at www.trekkinginturkey.com.

Safety Advice

» Bar a couple of well-known and well-maintained trails, most trails are not signposted and it's recommended to hire a guide.

» Weather conditions can fluctuate quickly between extremes, so come prepared and check out the local conditions before setting off.

Day Walks

For half- or full-day walks, Cappadocia is unbeatable, with a dozen valleys that are easily negotiated on foot, around Göreme and the Ihlara Valley (p484). These walks, two to eight hours in length with minor gradients, are perfectly suited to casual walkers and even families. The fairy chimneys are unforgettable, and walking is the best way to do the landscapes and sights justice – and discover areas that travellers usually don't reach. After all, there aren't many places in the world where you can take a walk along a string of ancient, rock-cut churches set in a lunar-like landscape.

Waymarked Trails

Turkey has two iconic long-distance trekking routes: the Lycian Way and the St Paul Trail. You don't have to walk these trails in their entirety; it's easy to bite off a small chunk. The routes are best tackled in spring or autumn, and www.trekkinginturkey.com has pages on both.

Lycian Way

Chosen by the *Sunday Times* as one of the world's 10 best walks, the Lycian Way is about 500km long and extends between Fethiye and Antalya, partly inland, partly along the coast of ancient Lycia, via Patara, Kalkan, Kaş, Finike, Olympos and Tekirova. Highlights include stunning coastal views, pine and cedar forests, laid-back villages, ruins of ancient cities, Mt Olympos and Baba Dağ. Kate Clow, who established the trail, describes it in detail in the walking guide *Lycian Way*.

St Paul Trail

The St Paul Trail is also 500km long, from Perge, 10km east of Antalya, to Yalvaç, northeast of Eğirdir Gölü (Lake Eğirdir). Partly following the route walked by St Paul on his first missionary journey in Asia Minor, it's more challenging than the Lycian Way, with more ascents. Along the way you'll pass canyons, waterfalls, forests, a medieval paved road, Eğirdir Gölü, Roman baths and an aqueduct, and numerous quaint villages.

St Paul Trail, by Kate Clow and Terry Richardson, describes the trail in detail.

Mountain Walks

Turkey is home to some seriously good mountain walking.

Mt Ararat (p560) Turkey's highest mountain, the majestic and challenging 5137m Mt Ararat, near the Armenian border, is one of the region's top climbs and can be tackled in three days (but preferably four). You'll need to be cashed up and patient with all the bureaucracy (a permit is mandatory). To acclimatise, start with nearby 4053m Süphan Dağı (p611).

The Kaçkars (p520 and p542) In eastern Anatolia, the Kaçkars are increasingly popular with Europeans. They offer lakes, forests and varied flora, at altitudes ranging from 2000m to 3937m. There are more than 30 possible routes, ranging from a few hours to several days, notably the multiday Trans-Kaçkar Trek. For more info, read www.trekkinginturkey.com's Kaçkars page, www.kackarlar.org or *The Kaçkar – Trekking in Turkey's Black Sea Mountains* (Kate Clow and Terry Richardson).

HIKER'S DILEMMA: ARARAT OR KAÇKARS

Zafer Onay, a trekking guide based in Doğubayazıt (p560), guides hikers on Mt Ararat and in the Kaçkars. 'Mt Ararat is a great climb, but landscapes in the Kaçkars are more scenic; they form a range, which means you can expect more diversity. It's more colourful, you can see wildflowers and, if you're lucky, you can spot bears and ibex. Birdwatching is also an option in the Kaçkars.'

Cappadocia Southern Cappadocia has a few good mountain walks, including 3268m Mt Hasan (p486) and the Taurus Mountains (Toros Dağları) in Ala Dağlar National Park (p481).

» Kuşadası and Bodrum, south Aegean (p224)
» Marmaris and Kaş, western Mediterranean (p299 and p337)
» Ayvalık, north Aegean (p171)

Water Sports

Lounging on a white-sand beach is certainly tempting, but there are many opportunities to dip your toes in the sea.

Scuba Diving

OK, the Red Sea it ain't, but where else in the world can you swim over amphoras and broken pottery from ancient shipwrecks? Turkey also offers a wide choice of reefs, drop-offs and caves. The waters are generally calm, with no tides or currents, and visibility averages 20m (not too bad by Mediterranean standards). Pelagics are rare, but small reef species are prolific. Here you can mingle with groupers, dentex, moray eels, sea breams, octopus and parrot fish, as well as the occasional amberjack, barracuda and ray. You don't need to be a strong diver; there are sites for all levels of proficiency. For experienced divers, there are superb expanses of red coral to explore (usually under 30m of water).

The standard of diving facilities is high, and you'll find professional dive centres staffed with qualified instructors who speak English. Most dive centres are affiliated with internationally recognised dive organisations. Compared to other destinations in the world, diving in Turkey is pretty cheap, and it's also a great place to learn. Most dive companies offer introductory dives for beginners and reasonably priced open-water certification courses.

While it is possible to dive all year, the best time is May to October, when the water is at its warmest (you can expect up to 25°C in September).

Top Dive Spots

The following have a deserved reputation for fine scuba diving:

Sea Kayaking & Canoeing

Look at the map of Turkey. See the tortuous coastline in the western Mediterranean part of the country? So many secluded coves, deep blue bays, pine-clad mountains, islands shimmering in the distance, laid-back villages... Paddling is the best way to experience the breathtaking scenery of the aptly named Turquoise Coast, and to comfortably access pristine terrain.

Another draw is that you can disembark at places that are not accessible by road – ideal if you want to find your own slice of paradise. Adding excitement to the journey, you might see flying fish and turtles, and if you're really lucky you might even come across dolphins frolicking around your kayak.

Day trips are the norm, but longer tours can be organised with overnight camping under the stars on deserted beaches. They should include transfers, guides, gear and meals.

Highlights

Kekova Sunken City (p342) This magical spot, with Byzantine ruins partly submerged 6m below the sea, perfectly lends itself to a sea-kayaking tour from Kaş. This superb day excursion, suitable for all fitness levels, allows you to glide over underwater walls, foundations and mosaics submerged by 2nd-century earthquakes, clearly visible through crystal-clear waters.

Patara (p330) Canoeing trips on the Xanthos River offer a unique opportunity to glide past jungle-like riverbanks and discover a rich ecosystem, with birds, crabs and turtles. The prospect of ending your journey on splendid Patara beach adds to the appeal.

Canyoning

Canyoning is a mix of climbing, hiking, rappelling, swimming and some serious jumping or plunging – down waterfalls, river gorges and water-polished chutes in natural pools. Experience is not usually necessary, but water confidence and reasonable fitness are an advantage. Expect adventure centres offering canyoning to provide wetsuits, helmets and harnesses, and outings to be led by a qualified instructor. The 18km-long **Saklıkent Gorge** (p327), southeast of Fethiye, features jumps, leaps in natural pools, scrambling over rocks and rappelling.

White-Water Rafting

It's important to choose an operator that has the experience, skills and equipment to run a safe and exciting expedition. Stick to the more reputable ones. Your guide should give you a comprehensive safety talk and paddle training before you launch off downstream. The best rafting spots:

Çoruh River (p542) Come to Yusufeli from May to July for fantastic white-water rafting; and come as soon as possible, as the area is slated to be flooded by a dam. Thanks to rugged topography and an abundance of snowmelt, the iconic Çoruh River offers world-class runs with powerful Class II to V rapids to get the blood racing. An added thrill is the breathtaking scenery along the sheer walls of the Çoruh Gorge. Trips generally last three hours.

Barhal and İspir Rivers (p542) Also near Yusufeli, the fainter of heart can take a mellow but equally scenic float trip on these tributaries of the Çoruh.

Çamlıhemşin (p521) Gentler rapids and impressive scenery.

Zamantı River (p481) In Cappadocia's Ala Dağlar National Park.

Saklıkent Gorge (p327) An 18km-long gorge near Fethiye.

Köprülü Kanyon (p360) In the western Mediterranean, near Antalya.

Windsurfing & Kitesurfing

Part of windsurfing's 2010 world cup was held in Alaçatı (p201) on the Çeşme Peninsula, and it's no wonder. With constant, strong breezes (around 16 to 17 knots) and a protected 500m-long and 400m-wide shallow area with calm water conditions from mid-May to early November, this is a world-class destination for windsurfers. It's also an ideal place to learn the sport, with a wide array of classes available. The area is a prime spot for kitesurfing, too. For more information check out www.alacati.de.

Winter Sports

Turkey is not just a summer destination. It's still little known outside Turkey that winter sports are widely available here, notably excellent skiing (*kayak* in Turkish).

Skiing

Don't get us wrong; it ain't the Alps, but powder junkies will be genuinely surprised at the quality of the infrastructure and the great snow conditions from December to April.

Whether you're a seasoned *kayakcı* (skier) or a novice standing in snow for the first time, there are options galore. Most ski resorts have been upgraded in recent years and now feature good facilities, including hotels equipped with saunas, hamams and even indoor pools. Best of all, prices are considerably lower than at Western European resorts and the vibe is unpretentious and family-oriented.

Locals form a significant portion of the clientele, though Russians, Germans and vacationers from the Middle East account for a growing share of the crowd. Off the slopes there's a thriving nightlife. Ski

---

PARAGLIDING

Picture yourself, comfortably seated, gracefully drifting over the velvety indigo of the sea, feeling the caress of the breeze... Paragliding from the slopes of Baba Dağ (1960m) in Ölüdeniz (p322), which has consistently excellent uplifting thermals from late April to early November, is top notch. For beginners, local operators offer tandem flights, for which no training or experience is required. You just have to run a few steps and the rest is entirely controlled by the pilot, to whom you're attached with a harness. Parasailing is also available, and Kaş (p337) is also popular among paragliders.

DO YOU WANNA GÜLET?

For a boat trip along the Aegean or Mediterranean coast, there are endless possibilities, ranging from day trips – out of pretty much everywhere with a harbour, from Ayvalık in the north Aegean all the way around the coast to Alanya in the eastern Mediterranean – to chartering a graceful *gület* (wooden yacht; p319) for a four-day cruise around beaches and bays. The most popular *gület* route is the trip from Kale (near Olympos) to Fethiye (or vice versa), although aficionados say the route between Marmaris and Fethiye is prettier.

resorts are some of Turkey's most liberal spots, with clubs and licensed bars (steaming mulled wine!).

Most hotels offer daily or weekly packages that include lift passes and full board. Rental of skis, boots and poles is available, as is tuition, though English-speaking instructors are hard to find.

Resorts

Palandöken The biggest and most renowned ski resort (p539), on the outskirts of Erzurum.

Sarıkamış (p556) The low-key resort near Kars is the most scenic of the lot, surrounded by vast expanses of pines. It's famous for its reliable snow pack and sunny skies. Snowboarders are also catered for.

Tatvan (p608) On the slopes of Nemrut Dağı (the one near Van).

Uludağ (p270) Near Bursa.

Davraz Dağı (p293) Near Eğirdir.

Erciyes Dağı (Mt Erciyes; p491) Above Kayseri.

Other Sports

Cross-country skiing is popular in Sarıkamış, with a network of groomed tracks that snake around the forest. Snowshoeing is available in Cappadocia, Sarıkamış and Mt Ararat.

regions at a glance

İstanbul

History ✓✓✓
Nightlife ✓✓✓
Shopping ✓✓✓

History
The megacity formerly known as Constantinople and Byzantium was the capital of a series of empires, all of which left their mark. The Aya Sofya, a church turned mosque turned museum, is the most famous remnant of the Byzantine Empire and Ottoman landmarks include the Blue Mosque and Topkapı Palace. Everywhere you turn on the hilly streets, history looks back at you.

Nightlife
Beyoğlu is an exhilarating melting pot where anything goes after dark. Between the dusk and dawn calls to prayer, up-for-it crowds swirl through rooftop bars, pedestrian precincts and clubs on the Bosphorus. From Sultanahmet's sights and accommodation, wander over the Galata Bridge – where you don't have to be a troll to duck under the bridge for a sundowner – then grab a nargileh (traditional waterpipe) or an Efes beer and join the party.

Shopping
The city's bazaars are justly famous: the Grand Bazaar, with more than 4000 shops; the arty Arasta Bazaar's carpet and ceramics stores; and the Spice Bazaar, for all your Turkish Viagra needs. There are markets and malls galore, including Kadıköy's food market on the Asian side, and the Wednesday market in the streets around Fatıh Mosque. Central neighbourhoods range from bohemian Çukurcuma, which specialises in antiques and collectables, to Tünel/Galata for avant-garde fashion.

p40

Thrace & Marmara

History ✓✓
Battlefields ✓✓✓
Architecture ✓

History
Turkey's northwest corner is famous for the Gallipoli Peninsula, site of the WWI battles, and Edirne, capital of the Ottoman Empire before Constantinople. Gökçeada island's Greek heritage can still be felt, and an 18th-century Transylvanian prince lived in Tekirdağ.

Battlefields
Over 100,000 soldiers died on the now-tranquil Gallipoli Peninsula, a pilgrimage site for Australians, New Zealanders and Turks. Touring the memorials, battlefields and trenches that dot the beaches and hills is simply heart-wrenching.

Architecture
Edirne's Ottoman gems include Selimiye Mosque, one of the finest works of the great architect Mimar Sinan. There's an interesting walk uphill from Gelibolu harbour, past mosques and tombs, and Gökçeada's hilltop villages, with the tumbledown Greek houses, like time capsules.

p118

İzmir & the North Aegean

History ✓✓✓
Village Life ✓✓
Food ✓✓

History

Troy, the sight of the famous military trick, is near the top of Turkey's Aegean coast. The hilltop ruins of Pergamum are also renowned, plus there are numerous less-visited sights and some living history: echoes of the population exchange with Greece and descendents of Turkmen nomads.

Village Life

The southern Aegean can keep its flashy resorts. In laid-back spots such as Bozcaada island, the Biga Peninsula, Behramkale, Ayvalık and Bergama, life has kept its alluringly slow rural pace. The changing seasons and weekly markets are still the main events.

Food

This is the place to try Aegean *balık* (fish) and rakı (aniseed brandy) on a seafront terrace, while avoiding the worst seaside tourist prices. There's even a saying about one town's pescetarian excellence: 'rakı, *balık,* Ayvalık'.

p157

Ephesus, Bodrum & the South Aegean

History ✓✓✓
Nightlife ✓✓✓
Sun & Surf ✓✓

History

Romans once bustled along the Curetes Ways at Ephesus, Turkey's most visited ruins. Less frequented relics of Aegean history include Didyma, where the Temple of Apollo was once the world's largest temple after Selçuk's Temple of Artemis; and eerie Priene, a hilltop Ionian city.

Nightlife

The tourist machine humming between Bodrum's palm trees has created a mean nightlife, with waterfront bar-clubs making the most of the town's twin bays. Another sexy spot for a sundowner is Türkbükü, summer playground of İstanbul's jet set.

Sun & Surf

The southern Aegean is renowned as Turkey's Côte d'Azur with good reason. Beatific smiles beam on the yachts cruising its coastline; and the beaches in and around Bodrum are excellent for sunning, swimming and water sports.

p203

Western Anatolia

History ✓✓✓
Ruins ✓✓✓
Craftwork ✓✓

History

With its mosques and museums, Bursa was the Ottoman capital before Constantinople. The Byzantines also left their mark, and the Phrygian Valley's rock-hewn monuments survive from the distant Phrygian days. More recently, vibrant Eskişehir has become one of Turkey's 'Anatolian Tiger' economic boomtowns.

Ruins

At Hierapolis, you can bathe among fluted marble columns. Ruins that promise to be 'the new Ephesus' are Sagalassos, a ruined Pisidian-Hellenistic-Roman city backed by sheer rock, and Afrodisias, with the grandeur of a classical city.

Craftwork

İznik is famous for its tiles; the floral beauties, a trademark of Ottoman architecture, are still made here. Porcelain-producing Kütahya is similarly inclined, and in Bursa's markets you can buy Karagöz shadow puppets and Bursa silk.

p252

Antalya & the Western Mediterranean

History ✓✓✓
Beaches ✓✓✓
Ruins ✓✓✓

History
The Turquoise Coast's coves and valleys are layered with history. Even its two waymarked paths, the Lycian Way and St Paul Trail, namecheck historical folk who passed through. Lycian sepulchres and sarcophagi litter the Teke peninsula.

Beaches
Patara, Turkey's longest beach, is home to nesting sea turtles and Lycian ruins; the hippy favourite Olympos is famed for its 'tree house' accommodation and naturally occurring flames of Chimaera. For solitude, take a tractor down to Kabak's cliff-flanked beach.

Ruins
Over three millennia after the Lycian civilisation first appeared, its trademark funerary monuments nestle in spectacular spots such as Xanthos and Pınara. Other gems include Antalya's Roman-Ottoman antique quarter and Knidos, the Datça Peninsula's Dorian port city.

p295

Eastern Mediterranean

History ✓✓
Food ✓✓
Christian Sites ✓✓✓

History
'Open-air museums' are a Turkish speciality; the one in Karatepe-Aslantaş National Park features the ruins of a summer retreat for neo-Hittite kings. History has a fairytale quality here. Maiden's Castle seemingly floats offshore, and hydra-headed Typhon held Zeus captive in the Chasm of Heaven.

Food
In addition to its Mediterranean fish restaurants, this Arab-spiced area has a culinary centre in Antakya (Hatay). Influences from nearby Syria are seen in the lemon wedges and mint accompanying kebaps and local specialities.

Christian Sites
The early Christian and Old Testament sites in Tarsus include St Paul's ruined house, where pilgrims drink from the well. Paul and Peter both preached in Antakya (the biblical Antioch), and St Thecla, patron saint of teachers, fasted in the grotto near Silifke.

p361

Ankara & Central Anatolia

History ✓✓
Architecture ✓✓
Ruins ✓✓✓

History
The whirling dervishes first swirled here, Atatürk began his revolution, Alexander the Great cut the Gordion knot and King Midas turned things to gold. Julius Caesar uttered his famous line: *'Veni, vidi, vici'* ('I came, I saw, I conquered').

Architecture
Amasya and Safranbolu are in the grip of 'Ottomania', with boutique hotels occupying their half-timbered, black-and-white houses – right down to the *gusül-hane* (cupboard bathroom). Konya's turquoise-domed Mevlâna Museum is a Turkish icon and Seljuk caravanserais dot the steppe.

Ruins
Hattuşa was the Hittite capital, and stone stars explode above the doors of Divriği's 780-year-old mosque complex. There are Pontic tombs in the cliffs above Amasya and, last but certainly not least, Gordion's Phrygian tomb might be the world's oldest wooden structure.

p395

Cappadocia

History ✓✓
Hiking ✓✓
Caves ✓✓✓

History

Cappadocia was a refuge for Byzantine Christians, who carved monastic settlements into the rock, left frescoes on the cave walls and hid from Islamic armies in underground cities. You can see all these relics, and relive the area's equine history on horseback.

Hiking

This is one of Turkey's best regions for going walkabout, with options ranging from gentle saunters through the dreamy valleys to serious missions. South of leafy Ihlara Valley, 3628m Mt Hasan and the Ala Dağlar National Park are both challenging.

Caves

Cappadocia's *tuff* cliff faces and surreal fairy chimneys (rock formations) are riddled with caves. Some are occupied by centuries-old churches, others by full-time cave-dwellers. Many are open for guests to sample the troglodyte lifestyle.

p449

Black Sea Coast & the Kaçkar Mountains

History ✓✓✓
Hiking ✓✓✓
Scenery ✓✓✓

History

Anatolia's north coast was once the Kingdom of Pontus, and the Ottoman Greeks tried to create a post-WWI Pontic state here by ousting the local Turks. Impressive ruins include Sumela, the Byzantine monastery clinging to a cliff face, and Trabzon's 13th-century Aya Sofya church.

Hiking

Stretching 30km, and climbing past forested valleys, passes, plateaus and lakes to jagged peaks and glacial faces, the Kaçkar Mountains are one of Turkey's top destinations for serious trekkers. Our tips are Şenyuva, where TV is banned, and Firtina Valley.

Scenery

The Kaçkar Mountains and coastline west of Sinop offer some of Turkey's most rugged, least discovered, scenery. The winding road from Amasra to Sinop – both quiet Turkish coastal towns – is the country's answer to California's Hwy 1.

p495

Northeastern Anatolia

History ✓✓✓
Outdoor Activities ✓✓✓
Slow Travel ✓✓✓

History

Romantic relics are squirreled away here, a legacy of the area's position near four borders. Ani is the former Armenian and Urartian capital; medieval Armenian and Georgian churches and castles are found nearby; and İshak Paşa Palace is straight out of *Thousand and One Nights*.

Outdoor Activities

There's a raft of activities – quite literally in the case of the white-water rafting and trekking centre Yusufeli, which a new dam may soon flood. Hikers can head to Mt Ararat and local sections of the Kaçkar Mountains, and snow bunnies to Palandöken and Sarıkamış.

Slow Travel

To enjoy the mountainous countryside at a mellow pace, explore the *yaylas* (mountain valleys) northeast of Artvin. Nestling in the landscape are villages, ruins, traditional wooden houses and a Caucasian ambiance.

p533

Southeastern Anatolia

History ✓✓✓
Food ✓✓✓
Architecture ✓✓✓

History

This area is rich with memories of past civilisations. An Armenian king built Lake Van's island church and a Commagene megalomaniac erected the statues atop Mt Nemrut. Most poignantly, a new dam will likely submerge the historic, honey-coloured village of Hasankeyf.

Food

With Kurdish and Arabic influences, the area's cuisine is a knockout. Top places to try local dishes are Gaziantep, with the planet's tastiest pistachio baklava, and Şanlıurfa, home of the Urfa kebap.

Architecture

History has left stunning buildings throughout the region, including the Mor-gabriel and Deyrul Zafaran monasteries, which rise mirage-like from their rocky surroundings. Mystery-shrouded Şanlıurfa, Mardin's brown labyrinth of lanes, and basalt-walled Diyarbakır and are also worth a visit.

p562

Look out for these icons:

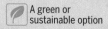

TOP CHOICE Our author's recommendation   A green or sustainable option   FREE No payment required

On the Road

İstanbul

POP 13 MILLION

Best Places to Stay

» Marmara Guesthouse (p87)
» Hotel Empress Zoe (p87)
» Four Seasons Istanbul at the Bosphorus (p91)
» 5 Oda (p90)
» Hotel İbrahim Paşa (p87)

Best Places to Eat

» Çiya Sofrası (p98)
» Hatay Has Kral Sofrası (p93)
» Develi (p95)
» Karaköy Güllüoğlu (p94)
» Karaköy Lokantası (p95)

Why Go?

Some ancient cities are the sum of their monuments. But others, such as İstanbul, factor a lot more into the equation. Here, you can visit Byzantine churches and Ottoman mosques in the morning, shop in chic boutiques during the afternoon and party at glamorous nightclubs through the night. In the space of a few minutes you can hear the evocative strains of the call to prayer issuing from the Old City's tapering minarets, the sonorous horn of a crowded commuter ferry crossing between Europe and Asia, and the strident cries of a street hawker selling fresh seasonal produce. Put simply, this marvellous metropolis is an exercise in sensory seduction like no other.

Ask locals to describe what they love about İstanbul and they'll shrug, give a small smile and say merely that there is no other place like it. Spend a few days here, and you'll know exactly what they mean.

When to Go

İstanbul

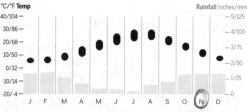

April Sunshine and breezes usher in the colourful International İstanbul Tulip Festival.

June to July Atmospheric venues host the International İstanbul Music Festival.

September Heat disperses and locals enjoy the season for *levrek* (bluefish), a favourite local fish.

History

BYZANTIUM

The first historically significant settlement here was founded by Byzas, a Megarian colonist. Before leaving Greece, he asked the Delphic oracle where to locate his new colony and received the enigmatic answer: 'Opposite the blind'. When Byzas and his fellow colonists sailed up the Bosphorus in 657 BC, they noticed a small colony on the Asian shore at Chalcedon (modern-day Kadıköy). Looking left, they saw the superb natural harbour of the Golden Horn (Haliç) on the European shore. Thinking, 'Those people in Chalcedon must be blind', they settled on the opposite shore, on the site of Lygos, and named their new city Byzantium.

Byzantium submitted willingly to Rome and fought its battles for centuries. But it finally got caught out supporting the wrong side in a civil war. The winner, Septimius Severus, razed the city walls and took away its privileges in AD 196. When he relented and rebuilt the city, he named it Augusta Antonina.

CONSTANTINOPLE

Another struggle for control of the Roman Empire determined the city's fate for the next 1000 years. Emperor Constantine pursued his rival Licinius to Augusta Antonina, then across the Bosphorus to Chrysopolis (Üsküdar). Defeating his rival in 324, Constantine solidified his control and declared the city the 'New Rome'. He laid out a vast new city to serve as capital of his empire and inaugurated it with much pomp in 330.

Constantine died in 337, just seven years after the dedication of his new capital, but the city continued to grow under the rule of the emperors. Theodosius I ('the Great'; r 379–95) had a forum built on the present site of Beyazıt Sq, while his son Theodosius II built his self-titled walls in 413 when the city was threatened by the marauding armies of Attila the Hun. Flattened by an earthquake in 447 and hastily rebuilt within two months, the Theodosian Walls still surround the Old City today.

Theodosius II died in 450 and was succeeded by a string of emperors, including the ambitious Justinian (r 527–65). Three years before taking the throne, Justinian had married Theodora, a strong-willed former courtesan. Together they further embellished Constantinople with great buildings, including the famous Aya Sofya,

built in 537. Justinian's building projects and constant wars of reconquest exhausted his treasury and his empire. Following his reign, the Byzantine Empire would never again be as large, powerful or rich.

Much of ancient Constantinople's building stock remains, including churches, palaces, cisterns and the Hippodrome. In fact, there's more left than most people realise. Any excavation reveals ancient streets, mosaics, tunnels, water and sewage systems, houses and public buildings buried beneath the modern city centre.

Ottoman sultan Mehmet II, who became known as Fatih (meaning 'the Conqueror'), came to power in 1451 and immediately departed his capital in Edirne, aiming to conquer the once-great Byzantine city.

In four short months, Mehmet oversaw the building of Rumeli Hisarı (the great fortress on the European side of the Bosphorus) and also repaired Anadolu Hisarı, built half a century earlier by his great-grandfather Beyazıt I. Together these fortresses controlled the strait's narrowest point.

The Byzantines had closed the mouth of the Golden Horn with a heavy chain to prevent Ottoman boats from sailing in and attacking the city walls on the northern side. Not to be thwarted, Mehmet marshalled his boats at a cove (where Dolmabahçe Palace now stands) and had them transported overland by night on rollers, up the valley (present site of the Hilton Hotel) and down the other side into the Golden Horn at Kasımpaşa. Catching the Byzantine defenders by surprise, he soon had the Golden Horn under control.

The last great obstacle was provided by the city's mighty walls on the western side. No matter how heavily Mehmet's cannons battered them, the Byzantines rebuilt the walls by night and, come daybreak, the impetuous young sultan would find himself back where he'd started. Finally, he received a proposal from a Hungarian cannon founder called Urban who had come to help the Byzantine emperor defend Christendom against the infidels. Finding that the Byzantine emperor had no money, Urban was quick to discard his religious convictions and instead offered to make Mehmet the most enormous cannon ever seen. Mehmet gladly accepted and the mighty cannon breached the walls, allowing the Ottomans into the city. On 28 May 1453 the final attack began and by the

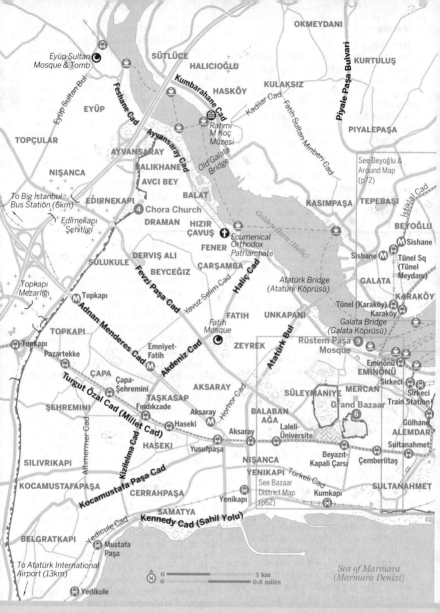

OKMEYDANI

KURTULUŞ

Eyüp Sultan
Mosque & Tomb

SÜTLÜCE

HALICIOĞLU

Piyale Paşa Bulvarı

KULAKSIZ

Kumbarahane Cad

HASKÖY

Kadılar Cad

Fatih Sultan Minberi Cad

PIYALEPAŞA

EYÜP

Feshane Cad

Eyüp Sultan Bul

Rahmi
M Koç
Müzesi

Ayvansaray Cad

Old Galata
Bridge

TOPÇULAR

AYVANSARAY

BALIKHANE

AVCI BEY

See Beyoğlu &
Around Map
(p72)

NİŞANCA

BALAT

KASIMPAŞA

TEPEBAŞI

İstiklal Cad

To Big İstanbul
Bus Station (6km)

EDİRNEKAPI

4 Chora Church

DRAMAN

HIZIR
ÇAVUŞ

BEYOĞLU

Edirnekapı
Şehitliği

Golden Horn (Haliç)

Ecumenical
Orthodox
Patriarchate

Sishane

DERVİŞ ALİ

FENER

Sishane

Tünel Sq
(Tünel
Meydanı)

SULUKULE

BEYCEĞİZ

ÇARŞAMBA

GALATA

Topkapı
Mezarlığı

Fevzi Paşa Cad

Yavuz Selim Cad

Haliç Cad

Atatürk Bridge
(Atatürk Köprüsü)

KARAKÖY

Topkapı

Adnan Menderes Cad

FATİH

UNKAPANI

Tünel (Karaköy)
Karaköy

TOPKAPI

Fatih
Mosque

Galata Bridge
(Galata Köprüsü)

Topkapı

Pazartekke

Emniyet-
Fatih

Akdeniz Cad

ZEYREK

Atatürk Bul

Rüstem Paşa
Mosque

9

ÇAPA

Çapa-
Şehremini

TAŞKASAP

AKSARAY

EMİNÖNÜ

Eminönü

Sirkeci

ŞEHREMİNİ

Turgut Özal Cad (Millet Cad)

Fındıkzade

SÜLEYMANİYE

MERCAN

Sirkeci
Train Station

Altınmermer Cad

Aksaray

Horhor Cad

Grand Bazaar

5

Haseki

BALABAN
AĞA

Gülhane

HASEKİ

Kızılelma Paşa Cad

Aksaray

Laleli-
Üniversite

Beyazıt-
Kapalı Çarşı

ALEMDAR

Yusufpaşa

Çemberlitaş

Sultanahmet

SİLİVRİKAPI

Kocamustafa Paşa Cad

NİŞANCA

Türkeli Cad

SULTANAHMET

KOCAMUSTAFAPAŞA

CERRAHPAŞA

YENİKAPI

See Bazaar
District Map
(p62)

Kumkapı

Yenikapı

SAMATYA

Kennedy Cad (Sahil Yolu)

BELGRATKAPI

Yedikule Cad

Mustafa
Paşa

To Atatürk International
Airport (13km)

N

0   1 km
0   0.6 miles

Sea of Marmara
(Marmara Denizi)

Yedikule

İstanbul Highlights

1 Uncover the secrets of
opulent **Topkapı Palace** (p54)

2 Marvel at one of the
world's great skylines from a
rooftop bar (p100)

3 Kick up your heels at
one of İstanbul's boisterous
meyhanes (taverns; p97)

4 Admire the extraordinary
Byzantine mosaics and

frescoes at the **Chora Church**
(p67)

5 Take a **ferry trip** along the
mighty Bosphorus or up the
fascinating Golden Horn (p78)

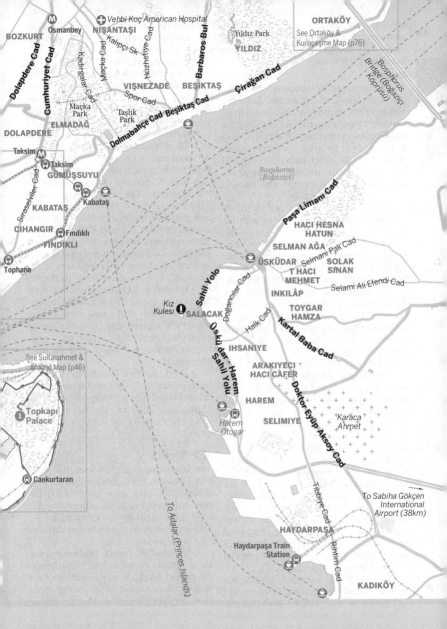

⑥ Join the crush and lose yourself in the labyrinthine **Grand Bazaar** (see boxed text, p70)

⑦ Contemplate the cutting edge at a new **contemporary art gallery** (see boxed text, p75)

⑧ Enjoy a tea and nargileh (waterpipe) with the locals at a traditional **çay bahçesi** (tea garden; p99)

⑨ Explore the busy shopping streets around the Spice Bazaar, making sure not to miss the diminutive but gorgeous **Rüstem Paşa Mosque** (p61)

evening of the 29th the Turks were in complete control of the city. The last Byzantine emperor, Constantine XI Dragases, died fighting on the walls.

İSTANBUL

Seeing himself as the successor to great emperors such as Constantine and Justinian, Mehmet the Conqueror at once began to rebuild and repopulate the city. He chose the conspicuous promontory of Seraglio Point as the location for his ostentatious palace, Topkapı, and he also repaired and fortified Theodosius' walls. İstanbul was soon the administrative, commercial and cultural heart of his growing empire.

The building boom Mehmet kicked off was continued by his successors, with Süleyman the Magnificent and his architect Mimar Sinan (p78) being responsible for an enormous amount of construction. The city was endowed with buildings commissioned by the sultan and his family, court and grand viziers; these include the city's largest and grandest mosque, the Süleymaniye (1550). Later sultans also added mosques, and in the 19th century numerous palaces were built along the Bosphorus, among them Dolmabahçe.

As the Ottoman Empire grew to encompass the Middle East and North Africa as well as half of Eastern Europe, İstanbul became a fabulous melting pot of nationalities. On its streets people spoke Turkish, Greek, Armenian, Ladino, Russian, Arabic, Bulgarian, Romanian, Albanian, Italian, French, German, English and Maltese.

However, what had been the most civilised city on earth in the time of Süleyman eventually declined along with the Ottoman Empire, and by the 19th century İstanbul had lost much of its former glory. Nevertheless, it continued to be the 'Paris of the East' and, to affirm this, the first great international luxury express train, the famous *Orient Express,* connected İstanbul and the French capital in 1883.

The post-WWI campaign by Mustafa Kemal (Atatürk) for national salvation and independence was directed from Ankara. In founding the Turkish Republic, Atatürk decided to leave behind the imperial memories of İstanbul and set up his new government in Ankara, a city that could not be threatened by gunboats. Robbed of its status as the capital of a vast empire, İstanbul lost much of its wealth and glitter. The city's streets and neighbourhoods decayed,

its infrastructure was neither maintained nor improved and virtually no economic development occurred.

The city stayed this way until the 1990s, when a renaissance took place. Since this time, public transport has been upgraded and continues to be improved, suburbs have been reinvigorated and parklands now line the waterways. When İstanbul won the right to become the European Capital of Culture in 2010, other ambitious projects were undertaken and many major buildings have benefited from painstaking restoration.

İstanbul's cultural transformation is just as marked. The seedy dives of Beyoğlu have been replaced by funky cafes, bars and studios, transforming the suburb into a bohemian hub. Galleries such as İstanbul Modern, Santralİstanbul, the Pera Museum and the Sakıp Sabancı Müzesi have opened, showcasing Turkey's contemporary art to the world. The live-music scene in the city has exploded, making İstanbul a buzzword for creative, energetic music with a unique East-West twist. And a new generation of artisans is refining and repositioning the city's traditional crafts industries – making for exciting and unexpected shopping experiences.

In short, Turkey's bid to join the EU is underpinned by the fact that these days its beloved İstanbul is a cosmopolitan and sophisticated megalopolis that has reclaimed its status as one of the world's truly great cities.

◉ Sights

The Bosphorus strait, between the Black and Marmara Seas, divides Europe from Asia/Anatolia. On its western shore, European İstanbul is further divided by the Golden Horn into the Old City (aka the historic peninsula) in the south and the New City in the north.

At the tip of the historic peninsula is Sultanahmet, the centre of İstanbul's Unesco-designated World Heritage Site. It's here that you'll find most of the city's famous sites, including the Blue Mosque (Sultan Ahmet Camii), Aya Sofya and Topkapı Palace (Topkapı Sarayı). The adjoining area, with hotels to suit all budgets, is actually called Cankurtaran (*jan*-kur-tar-an), although if you say 'Sultanahmet' most people will understand where you mean.

Up the famous Divan Yolu boulevard from Sultanahmet you'll find the Grand

Bazaar (Kapalı Çarşı). To its north is the Süleymaniye Mosque, which graces the top of one of the Old City's seven hills, and further on are the Western Districts. Downhill from the bazaar is the Golden Horn, home to the bustling transport hub of Eminönü.

Over Galata Bridge (Galata Köprüsü) from Eminönü is Beyoğlu, on the northern side of the Golden Horn. This is where you'll find some of the best restaurants, shops, bars and nightclubs in the city. It's also home to Taksim Sq, the heart of 'modern' İstanbul.

The city's glamour suburbs include Nişantaşı and Teşvikiye, north of Taksim Sq, and the suburbs lining the Bosphorus, especially those on the European side. However, many locals prefer to live on the Asian side. Üsküdar and Kadıköy are the two Asian hubs, reachable by a short ferry ride from Eminönü or a drive over Bosphorus Bridge.

İstanbul's otogar (bus station) is at Esenler, about 10km west of the city centre. The city's main airport, Atatürk International Airport, is in Yeşilköy, 23km west of Sultanahmet; a smaller airport, Sabiha Gökçen International Airport, is 50km southeast. The two main train stations are currently Haydarpaşa station near Kadıköy on the Asian side and Sirkeci station at Eminönü.

SULTANAHMET & AROUND

It's not surprising that many visitors to İstanbul never make it out of Sultanahmet – after all, few cities have such a concentration of sights, shops, hotels and eateries within easy walking distance.

Aya Sofya   MUSEUM
(Map p46; ☎0212-522 0989; Aya Sofya Meydanı, Sultanahmet; adult/under 6yr TL20/free, official guide 45min TL30-50; ⊙9am-6pm Tue-Sun May-Oct, to 4pm Nov-Apr, upper gallery closes 15-30 min earlier) Called Sancta Sophia in Latin, Haghia Sofia in Greek and the Church of the Divine Wisdom in English, this extraordinary building is İstanbul's most famous monument.

Emperor Justinian had the Aya Sofya built as part of his effort to restore the greatness of the Roman Empire. It was completed in 537 and reigned as the greatest church in Christendom until the Conquest in 1453. Mehmet the Conqueror had it converted into a mosque and so it remained until 1935, when Atatürk proclaimed it a museum. Ongoing restoration work (partly Unesco funded) means that the dome is always filled with scaffolding, but not even this can detract from the experience of visiting one of the world's truly great buildings.

On entering his great creation for the first time almost 1500 years ago, Justinian exclaimed, 'Glory to God that I have been judged worthy of such a work. Oh Solomon! I have outdone you!'. Entering the building today and seeing the magnificent domed ceiling soaring heavenward, it is easy to excuse his self-congratulatory tone.

As you walk into the inner narthex (Map p49), look up to see a brilliant mosaic of Christ as Pantocrator (Ruler of All) above the third and largest door (the Imperial Door). Once through this door the magnificent main dome soars above you. Supported by 40 decorated ribs, it was constructed of special hollow bricks made in Rhodes from a unique light, porous clay; these rest on huge pillars concealed in the interior walls, which creates an impression that the dome hovers unsupported.

The curious elevated kiosk screened from public view is the Sultan's loge. Ahmet III (r 1703–30) had it built so he could come in, pray and leave again unseen, thus preserving the imperial mystique. The ornate library, on the west wall, was built by Sultan Mahmut I in 1739.

In the side aisle to the northeast of the Imperial Door is the weeping column, with a worn copper facing pierced by a hole. Legend has it that putting one's finger in the hole can lead to ailments being healed if the finger emerges moist.

The large 19th-century medallions inscribed with gilt Arabic letters are the work of master calligrapher Mustafa İzzet Efendi, and give the names of God (Allah), Mohammed and the early caliphs Ali and Abu Bakr.

Mosaics

From the floor of Aya Sofya, 9th-century mosaic portraits of St Ignatius the Younger (c 800), St John Chrysostom (c 400) and St Ignatius Theodorus of Antioch are visible high up at the base of the northern tympanum (semicircle) beneath the dome. A seraph (winged biblical angel) is just to their east. Next to the three saints, but seen only from the upstairs east gallery, is a portrait of Emperor Alexandros. In the apse is a wonderful mosaic of the Madonna and Child; a nearby mosaic depicts the archangel Gabriel.

Sultanahmet & Around

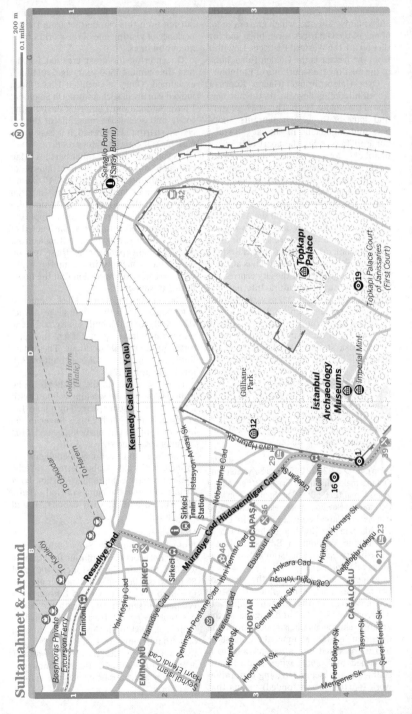

200 m
0.1 miles

Golden Horn
(Haliç)

To Üsküdar

To Harem

To Kadıköy

Bosphorus Private
Excursion Ferry

Seraglio Point
(Saray Burnu)

Kennedy Cad (Sahil Yolu)

Topkapı
Palace

Topkapı Palace Court
of Janissaries
(First Court)

19

Imperial Mint

Istanbul
Archaeology
Museums

Gülhane
Park

İstasyon Arkası Sk

Tava Hatun Sk

12

Sirkeci
Train
Station

Nobethane Cad

Erdoğan Sk

29

Gülhane

16

1

39

Reşadiye Cad

EMİNÖNÜ

Eminönü

SİRKECİ

35

Sirkeci

Hamidiye Cad

Yalı Köşkü Cad

Muradiye Cad Hüdavendigar Cad

İbni Kemal Cad

46

46

HOCAPAŞA

Ebussuut Cad

Ankara Cad

Hükümet Konağı Sk

Cağaloğlu Yokuşu

21 23

CAĞALOĞLU

Şehinşah Postane Cad

Aşirefendi Cad

HOBYAR

Cemal Nadir Sk

Cağaloğlu Yokuşu

Tasvir Sk

Ferdi Gökçay Sk

Şeref Efendi Sk

Mengene Sk

Köprücü Sk

Hocahanı Sk

Seyhatislam Hayri Erandi Cad

 İSTANBUL

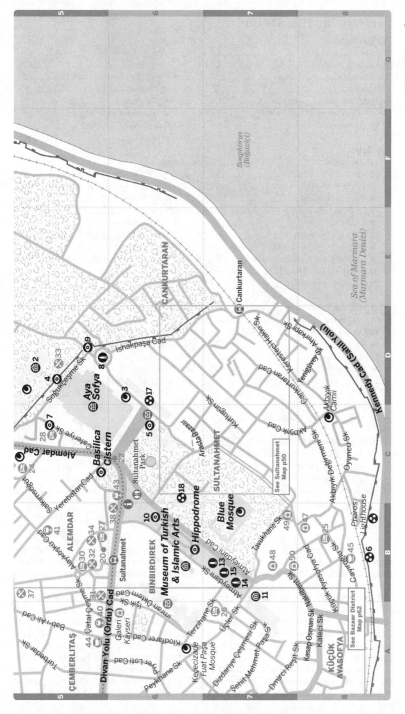

Bosphorus
(Boğaziçi)

Sea of Marmara
(Marmara Denizi)

CANKURTARAN

Kennedy Cad (Sahil Yolu)

Cankurtaran

Akbıyık
Camii

Phanos
Lighthouse

Ishakpaşa Cad

Aya
Sofya

Basilica
Cistern

Alemdar Cad

Sultanahmet
Park

Museum of Turkish
& Islamic Arts

Hippodrome

Blue
Mosque

See Sultanahmet
Map p50

SULTANAHMET

ALEMDAR

Sultanahmet

BINBIRDIREK

ÇEMBERLİTAŞ

Divan Yolu (Ordu) Cad

KÜÇÜK
AYASOFYA

See Bazaar District
Map p62

Sultanahmet & Around

Top Sights

- Aya Sofya ... C5
- Basilica Cistern ... C5
- Blue Mosque ... B7
- Hippodrome ... B6
- İstanbul Archaeology Museums ... D4
- Museum of Turkish & Islamic Arts ... B6
- Topkapı Palace ... E4

Sights

1 Alay Köşkü ... C4
2 Aya İrini ... D5
3 Aya Sofya Tombs ... D6
4 Ayasofya Konakları ... D5
5 Baths of Lady Hürrem ... C6
6 Bucoleon Palace ... B8
7 Caferağa Medresesi ... C5
8 Fountain of Sultan Ahmet III ... D5
9 Imperial Gate, Topkapı Palace ... D5
10 Kaiser Wilhelm's Fountain ... B6
11 Marmara University Republican Museum ... B7
12 Museum of the History & Science of Technology in Islam ... C3
13 Obelisk of Theodosius ... B7
14 Rough-Stone Obelisk ... B7
15 Spiral Column ... B7
16 Sublime Porte ... C4
17 Sultanahmet Archaeological Park ... D6
18 Tomb of Sultan Ahmet I ... C6
19 Topkapı Ticket Office ... E4

Activities, Courses & Tours

20 Ambassador Hotel Spa Center ... B5
21 Cağaloğlu Hamamı ... B4
22 İstanbul Vision City Sightseeing Bus Ticket Stand ... C6
Urban Aventures ... (see 34)

Sleeping

23 Agora Life Hotel ... B4
24 Cheers Hostel ... C5
25 Emine Sultan Hotel ... B8
26 Hotel İbrahim Paşa ... A7
27 Hotel Nomade ... B5
28 Ottoman Hotel Imperial ... C5
29 Sirkeci Konak ... C3
30 Tan Hotel ... B5

Eating

31 Çiğdem Pastanesi ... B5
32 Karadeniz Aile Pide & Kebap Sofrası ... B5
33 Karakol Restaurant ... D5
34 Khorasani ... B5
35 Konyali Lokantasi ... B2
36 Paşazade ... B3
37 Sefa Restaurant ... B5
38 Tarihi Sultanahmet Köftecisi Selim Usta ... B6
39 Ziya Şark Sofrası ... C4

Drinking

40 Cosy Pub ... A5
Hotel Nomade Terrace Bar ... (see 27)
41 Kybele Cafe ... B5
42 Set Üstü Çay Bahçesi ... F2
43 Sultan Pub ... C6
44 Türk Ocağı Kültür ve Sanat Merkezı İktısadi İşletmesı Çay Bahçesi ... A5
45 Yeni Marmara ... B8

Entertainment

46 Hojdapaşa Art & Culture Center ... B3

Shopping

47 Cocoon ... B8
48 Khaftan ... B7
49 Mehmet Çetinkaya Gallery ... B7
50 Nakkaş ... B7

The upstairs galleries house the most impressive of Aya Sofya's mosaics and mustn't be missed. They can be reached via a switchback ramp at the northern end of the inner narthex. The magnificent *Deesis Mosaic (The Last Judgement)* in the south gallery dates from the early 14th century. Christ is at the centre, with the Virgin Mary on the left and John the Baptist on the right.

At the apse end of the southern gallery is the famous mosaic portrait of Empress Zoe (r 1028–50), who had three husbands and changed this mosaic portrait with each one. The portrait of the third Mr Zoe, Constantine IX Monomachus, survives because he outlived the empress.

To the right of Zoe and Constantine is another mosaic depicting characters with less-saucy histories: in this scene Mary holds the Christ child, centre, with Emperor John (Johannes) Comnenus II (the Good) to the left and Empress Eirene (known for her charitable works) to the right. Their son Alexius, who died soon after this portrait was made, is depicted next to Eirene.

As you leave the museum from the narthex, make sure you turn and look up above the door to see one of the church's finest late-10th-century mosaics. This shows Constantine the Great, on the right, offering Mary, who holds the Christ child, the city of Constantinople; Emperor Justinian, on the left, is offering her Aya Sofya.

On the opposite side of Aya Sofya Meydanı are the **Baths of Lady Hürrem** (Haseki Hürrem Hamamı), built as Aya Sofya's hamam from 1556 to 1557. Designed by Sinan, the hamam was commissioned by Süleyman the Magnificent in the name of his wife Hürrem Sultan, known to history as Roxelana. The hamam has recently undergone an extensive restoration and is once again functioning as a traditional bathhouse.

FREE **Aya Sofya Tombs**　　　　TOMBS
(Aya Sofya Türbeleri; admission free; ☺9am-7pm) Part of the Aya Sofya complex but entered via Kabasakal Caddesi, these tombs are the final resting places of five sultans and their families. Each of the buildings has ornate interior decoration. Mehmed III's tomb dates from 1608 and is adorned with particularly beautiful İznik tiles; Selim II's tomb was built in 1577 and features stunning calligraphy; Murad III's tomb dates from 1599 and sports gorgeous coral-coloured İznik tiles; and the tiny tomb of the children of Murad III has simple but incredibly beautiful painted decoration. The fifth building is Aya Sofya's original baptistry, converted to a mausoleum for sultans İbrahim and Mustafa I during the 17th century; it is currently closed for restoration.

Blue Mosque　　　　MOSQUE
(Sultan Ahmet Camii; Map p46; Hippodrome, Sultanahmet) With his eponymously named mosque, Sultan Ahmet I (r 1603–17) set out to build a monument that would rival and even surpass the nearby Aya Sofya in grandeur

Aya Sofya

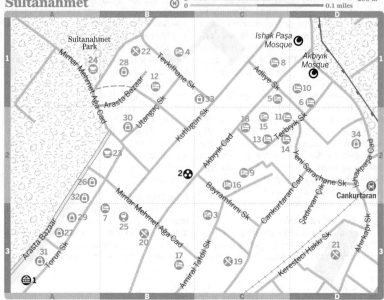

and beauty. Today it's more widely known as the Blue Mosque.

The mosque's architect, Mehmet Ağa, managed to orchestrate the sort of visual wham-bam effect with the mosque's exterior that Aya Sofya achieved with its interior. Its curves are voluptuous, it has six minarets and the courtyard is the biggest of all of the Ottoman mosques. The interior has a similarly grand scale: the blue tiles that give the building its unofficial name number in the tens of thousands, there are 260 windows and the central prayer space is huge.

To best appreciate the mosque's design, enter the complex via the Hippodrome (p51) rather than from Sultanahmet Park. Once inside the courtyard, which is the same size as the mosque's interior, you'll appreciate the building's perfect proportions.

The mosque is such a popular attraction that admission is controlled so as to preserve its sacred atmosphere. Only worshippers are admitted through the main door; tourists must use the south door.

Inside, the stained-glass windows and İznik tiles lining the walls immediately attract attention. Although the windows are replacements, they still create the luminous effects of the originals, which came from Venice. You will also see immediately why

the Blue Mosque, constructed between 1606 and 1616, more than a millennium after Aya Sofya, is not as daring as its venerable neighbour: four huge 'elephant's feet' pillars hold up the dome, a less elegant but sturdier solution to the problem of support.

The tile-encrusted **Tomb of Sultan Ahmet I** (donation expected; ⊙9.30am-4.30pm), the tomb of the Blue Mosque's great patron, is in a separate building on the north side facing Sultanahmet Park. Ahmet, who had ascended to the imperial throne aged 13, died one year after the mosque was constructed, aged only 27. He rests here with a dozen or so children (his decedents), powerful evidence that wealth and privilege didn't make the imperial family immune from tragedy.

Great Palace Mosaic Museum   MUSEUM
(Büyüksaray Mozaik Müzesi; Map p50; ☑0212-518 1205; Torun Sokak, Sultanahmet; admission TL8; ⊙9am-6pm Tue-Sun Jun-Oct, to 4.30pm Nov-May) When archaeologists from the University of Ankara and Scotland's St Andrews University dug at the back of the Blue Mosque in the mid-1950s, they found a mosaic pavement dating from early Byzantine times (c AD 500). Covered with wonderful hunting and mythological scenes and emperors' portraits, the pavement was part of

a triumphal way that led from the Byzantine emperor's Great Palace (which stood where the Blue Mosque now stands) down to the harbour of Bucoleon to the south. It is now displayed *in situ* in this museum, where there are informative panels documenting the floor's rescue and renovation.

Other 5th-century mosaics were saved when Sultan Ahmet I had an *arasta* (row of shops) built on top of them. The **Arasta Bazaar** now houses numerous carpet and ceramic shops that provide rental revenue for the upkeep of the Blue Mosque.

Enter the Great Palace Mosaic Museum from Torun Sokak behind the mosque and the Arasta Bazaar.

Hippodrome   PARK
(Atmeydanı; Map p46) The Byzantine emperors loved nothing more than an afternoon at the chariot races, and the Hippodrome was their venue of choice. In its heyday, the rectangular arena consisted of two levels of galleries, a central spine, starting boxes and the semicircular end known as the sphendone.

The Hippodrome was the centre of Byzantine life for 1200 years and of Ottoman life for another 400-odd years. The Byzantines supported the rival chariot teams of 'Greens' and 'Blues', which had separate political connections. Support for a team was akin to membership of a political party and a team victory had important effects on policy. A Byzantine emperor might lose his throne as the result of a post-match riot.

Ottoman sultans also kept an eye on activities in the Hippodrome. If things were going badly in the empire, a surly crowd gathering here could signal the start of a disturbance, then a riot, then a revolution. In 1826 the slaughter of the corrupt janissary corps (the sultan's personal bodyguards) was carried out here by the reformer Sultan Mahmut II (r 1808–39). And in 1909 there were riots here that caused the downfall of Abdül Hamit II and the rewriting of the Ottoman constitution.

Despite the fact that the Hippodrome could have ended up being the scene of their downfall, Byzantine emperors and Ottoman sultans outdid one another in beautifying it, adorning it with statues from the far reaches of the empire. Unfortunately, only a handful of these statues remains. Chief among the thieves responsible for their disappearance were the soldiers of the Fourth Crusade, who sacked Constantinople, supposedly a Christian ally city, in 1204.

Near the northern end of the Hippodrome, the stone gazebo with a mosaic-covered dome interior is **Kaiser Wilhelm's**

Two Days

With only two days, you'll need to get cracking! On day one, visit the **Blue Mosque**, **Aya Sofya** and the **Basilica Cistern** in the morning and follow our **walking tour** of the **Grand Bazaar** in the afternoon. Enjoy dinner somewhere in Beyoğlu, followed by a nargileh (water pipe) in Tophane.

Day two should be devoted to **Topkapı Palace** and the **Bosphorus**. Spend the morning at the palace, then board one of the private excursion boats at Eminönü for a **Bosphorus cruise**. Afterwards, walk up through Galata to **İstiklal Caddesi**, have a drink at a **rooftop bar** and enjoy dinner at a **meyhane** (tavern).

Four Days

Follow the two-day itinerary, and on your third day visit the **İstanbul Archaeology Museums** in the morning and the **Süleymaniye Mosque** in the afternoon. For dinner, sample the succulent kebaps at **Develi** or **Zübeyir Ocakbaşı**. Day four should be devoted to a **Golden Horn cruise**; on your way back from Eyüp get off at Ayvansaray and walk uphill to visit the Byzantine mosaics and frescoes at the **Chora Church**. Back in Sultanahmet, shop for souvenirs at the **Arasta Bazaar** before hitting the bar, restaurant and club scenes on the other side of Galata Bridge.

Fountain. The German emperor paid a state visit to Abdül Hamit II in 1901, and presented this fountain to the sultan and his people as a token of friendship.

The immaculately preserved pink granite Obelisk of Theodosius, the oldest monument in İstanbul, was carved in Egypt during the reign of Thutmose III (r 1549–1503 BC) and erected in the Amon-Re temple at Karnak. Emperor Theodosius (379–95) had it brought from Egypt to Constantinople in AD 390. The original obelisk was cut down for transit – the top segment was placed on the ceremonial marble base Theodosius had made. Look for the carvings of Theodosius, his wife, sons, state officials and bodyguards watching the chariot action from the *kathisma* (imperial box).

South of the obelisk is a strange column rising out of a hole in the ground. Known as the Spiral Column, it was once part of a golden basin supported by three entwined serpents cast to commemorate the victory of the Hellenic confederation over the Persians at Plataea. It stood in front of the temple of Apollo at Delphi from 478 BC until Constantine the Great had it brought to his new capital city around AD 330. Historians suspect the bronze serpents' heads were stolen during the Fourth Crusade.

Little is known about the 4th-century Rough-Stone Obelisk, except that in 869 an earthquake toppled the bronze pine cone from its top, and that it was clad with sheets

of gilded bronze by Constantine VII Porphyrogenitus (r 913–59), an act commemorated in the inscription in its base. Its bronze plates were ripped off during the Fourth Crusade, but you can still see the boltholes where they would have been attached.

Note the original ground level of the Hippodrome at the base of the obelisks and column, some 2.5m below ground.

The Marmara University Republican Museum (admission free; ⊙10am-6pm Tue-Sun), at the southern end of the Hippodrome, is a handsome example of Ottoman Revivalism, a homegrown architectural style popular in the late 19th century. Its collection of original prints by Turkish artists is displayed here, and the building has good toilet facilities.

Museum of Turkish & Islamic Arts
MUSEUM

(Türk ve İslam Eserleri Müzesi; Map p46; ☑0212-518 1805; Atmeydanı Sokak 46, Sultanahmet; admission TL10; ⊙9am-4.30pm Tue-Sun) This impressive museum is housed in the palace of İbrahim Paşa, built in 1520 on the western side of the Hippodrome.

İbrahim Paşa was Süleyman the Magnificent's close friend and brother-in-law. Captured by Turks as a child in Greece, he was sold as a slave into the imperial household in İstanbul and worked as a page in Topkapı, where he became friendly with Süleyman, who was the same age. When his friend became sultan, İbrahim was in turn made chief falconer, chief of the royal bedchamber and grand vizier. This palace was bestowed on him by Süleyman the year before he was given the hand of Süleyman's sister, Hadice, in marriage.

The fairy tale didn't last, alas. İbrahim's wealth, power and influence on the monarch became so great that others wishing to influence the sultan became envious, chief among them Süleyman's wife, Roxelana. After a rival accused İbrahim of disloyalty, she convinced her husband that İbrahim was a threat and Süleyman had him strangled in 1536.

Inside, you'll be wowed by one of the world's best collections of antique carpets and some equally impressive manuscripts and miniatures. Labels are in both Turkish and English.

The coffee shop in the lovely green courtyard of the museum is a welcome refuge from the press of crowds and touts in the area.

Basilica Cistern   HISTORIC BUILDING
(Yerebatan Sarnıcı; Map p46; ☎0212-522 1259; www.yerebatan.com; Yerebatan Caddesi 13, Sultanahmet; admission TL10; ☺9am-7.30pm) When those Byzantine emperors built something, they certainly did it properly! This extraordinary cistern, built by Justinian in 532, is a great place to while away half an hour, especially during summer when its cavernous depths stay wonderfully cool.

Like most sites in İstanbul, the cistern has a colourful history. Known in Byzantium as the Basilica Cistern because it lay underneath the Stoa Basilica, one of the great squares on the first hill, it was used to store water for the Great Palace and surrounding buildings. Eventually closed, it seemed to have been forgotten by the city authorities some time before the Conquest. Enter scholar Petrus Gyllius, who was researching Byzantine antiquities in 1545 and was told by locals that they could obtain water by lowering buckets in their basement floors. Some were even catching fish this way. Intrigued, Gyllius explored the neighbourhood and discovered a house through whose basement he accessed the cistern. Even after his discovery, the Ottomans (who referred to the cistern as Yerebatan Sarayı) didn't treat the underground palace with the respect it deserved and it became a dumping ground for all sorts of junk, as well as corpses. It has been restored at least three times.

The cistern is 65m wide and 143m long, and its roof is supported by 336 columns arranged in 12 rows. It once held 80,000 cu metres of water, pumped and delivered through nearly 20km of aqueducts.

Constructed using columns, capitals and plinths from ruined buildings, the cistern's symmetry and sheer grandeur of

GREAT PALACE OF BYZANTIUM

Constantine the Great built this palace soon after he founded Constantinople in AD 324. Successive Byzantine leaders left their mark by adding to it, and the complex eventually consisted of hundreds of buildings enclosed by walls and set in terraced parklands stretching from the Hippodrome over to Aya Sofya and down the slope, ending at the sea walls and the Bucoleon Palace. The palace was finally abandoned after the Fourth Crusade sacked the city in 1204, and its ruins were pillaged and filled in after the Conquest, becoming mere foundations for much of Sultanahmet and Cankurtaran.

Various pieces of the Great Palace have been uncovered – many by budding hotelier 'archaeologists' – and an evocative stroll exploring the Byzantine substructure is a great way to spend an afternoon. The mosaics in the **Great Palace Mosaic Museum** (Map p50) once graced the floor of the complex and you can also walk past remnants of the **Bucoleon Palace** (Map p46) and **Magnaura Palace** (Map p50).

Great Palace excavations at the **Sultanahmet Archaeological Park** (Map p46) on Kabasakal Caddesi, southeast of Aya Sofya, have been ongoing since 1998 but had stalled when this book went to print due to controversy about some of the excavations being subsumed into a new extension of the neighbouring luxury Four Seasons Hotel.

For more information, check out www.byzantium1200.com, which has 3-D images that bring ancient Byzantium to life, or purchase a copy of the lavishly illustrated guidebook *Walking Through Byzantium: Great Palace Region,* which was also produced as part of the Byzantium 1200 project.

conception is quite extraordinary. Don't miss the two columns in the northwestern corner supported by upside-down Medusa heads, or the column towards the centre featuring a teardrop design.

Walking on the raised wooden platforms, you'll feel water dripping from the vaulted ceiling and may catch a glimpse of ghostly carp patrolling the water. Lighting is atmospheric and the small cafe near the exit is certainly an unusual spot to enjoy a cup of çay.

FREE **Little Aya Sofya**   MOSQUE
(Küçük Aya Sofya Camii, SS Sergius & Bacchus Church; Map p62; Küçük Aya Sofya Caddesi; donation requested) Justinian and Theodora had this building constructed some time between 527 and 536, just before Justinian built Aya Sofya. It was named after the two patron saints of Christians in the Roman army. Its dome is architecturally noteworthy and its plan – that of an irregular octagon – is unusual. Like Aya Sofya, its interior was originally decorated with gold mosaics and featured columns made from fine green and red marble. The mosaics are long gone, but the impressive columns remain. The church was converted into a mosque by the chief white eunuch Hüseyin Ağa around 1500; his tomb is to the north of the building.

After being listed on the World Monuments Fund (www.wmf.org) register of endangered buildings, this gorgeous example of Byzantine architecture has recently been restored and is looking terrific. There's a tranquil *çay bahçesi* in the forecourt.

After visiting Little Aya Sofya, go north up Şehit Mehmet Paşa Sokak and back up the hill to see the diminutive but truly beautiful **Sokollu Mehmet Paşa Mosque**, designed by Sinan in 1571.

Topkapı Palace   PALACE
(Topkapı Sarayı; Map p46 & p56; ☎0212-512 0480; www.topkapisarayi.gov.tr/eng; admission palace TL20, Harem TL15; ☺9am-6pm Wed-Mon, Harem closes 5pm) This opulent palace complex is the subject of more colourful stories than most of the world's royal residences put together. It was home to Selim the Sot, who drowned after drinking too much champagne; İbrahim the Mad, who lost his reason after being imprisoned for 22 years by his brother Murat IV; and the malevolent Roxelana (p631), a former concubine who became the powerful consort of Süleyman the Magnificent. And they're just three among a long progression of mad, sad and downright bad Ottomans who lived here between 1453 and 1839.

Mehmet the Conqueror started work on the palace shortly after the Conquest in 1453 and lived here until his death in 1481. Subsequent sultans lived in this rarefied environment until the 19th century, when they moved to ostentatious European-style palaces such as Dolmabahçe, Çırağan and Yıldız that they built on the shores of the Bosphorus. Mahmut II was the last sultan to live in Topkapı.

A visit to Topkapı requires at least three hours, but preferably longer. If you are short on time see the Harem, the Treasury and the rooms around the İftariye Baldachin. Buy your ticket to the palace at the main ticket office just outside the gate to the second court; tickets to the Harem are available at the ticket box outside the Harem itself. Guides to the palace congregate next to the main ticket office. A one-hour tour will cost you €10 per person if you're in a largeish group; you'll need to negotiate a price if you're in a small group or by yourself. Alternatively, an audioguide costs TL10 (plus an extra TL10 for the Harem). These are available at the booth just inside the turnstile entrance to the second court.

Before you enter the Imperial Gate (Bâb-ı Hümâyûn) of Topkapı, take a look at the ornate structure in the cobbled square near the gate. This is the Fountain of Sultan Ahmet III (Map p46), built in 1728 by the sultan who loved and promoted tulips so much that his reign was dubbed the 'Tulip Era'.

First Court

Topkapı grew and changed with the centuries, but the palace's basic four-courtyard plan remained the same. The Ottomans followed the Byzantine practice of secluding the monarch from the people: the first court was open to all; the second only to people on imperial business; and the third and fourth only to the imperial family, VIPs and palace staff.

As you pass through the great Imperial Gate behind Aya Sofya, you enter the First Court, known as the Court of the Janissaries. On your left is the Byzantine **Aya İrini** (Hagia Eirene, Church of the Divine Peace; Map p46), commissioned in the 540s by Justinian to replace an earlier church that had occupied this site. The building here is almost exactly as old as Aya Sofya. It's only usually opened for concerts during the International İstanbul Music Festival, but there is some talk of it being used as a Museum of Byzantium in the future. Next to Aya İrini is the Karakol restaurant, a much better option for lunch than the Konyalı restaurant in the Fourth Court. A little bit further on, to the left, is a path leading to the Imperial Mint (Darphane-I Amire), where temporary exhibitions are sometimes held, and to the İstanbul Archaeology Museums.

Second Court

The Middle Gate (Ortakapı or Bâb-üs Selâm) leads to the palace's Second Court, which was used for the business of running the empire. Only the sultan and the *valide sultan* (mother of the reigning sultan) were allowed through the Middle Gate on horseback. Everyone else, including the grand vizier, had to dismount. The gate was constructed by Süleyman the Magnificent in 1524.

To the right after you enter are models of the palace. Beyond them, in a nearby building, you'll find a collection of imperial carriages.

The Second Court has a beautiful, park-like setting. Topkapı is not based on a typical European palace plan (one large building with outlying gardens) but, instead, is a series of pavilions, kitchens, barracks, audience chambers, kiosks and sleeping quarters built around a central enclosure.

The great Palace Kitchens are to your right (east) and on the left (west) side is the ornate Imperial Council Chamber, also called the Dîvân-ı Hümayûn. The Imperial Divan (council) met in the Imperial Council Chamber to discuss matters of state while the sultan eavesdropped through a grille high on the wall at the base of the Tower of Justice (Adalet Kulesi) in the Harem. Behind the Imperial Council Chamber is the Inner Treasury, which was being renovated when this book was being researched.

The entrance to the palace's most famous sight, the Harem, is beneath the Tower of Justice.

Harem

If you decide to tour the Harem – and we highly recommend that you do so – you'll need to purchase a dedicated ticket; these are available from the ticket office outside the Harem's entrance.

As popular belief would have it, the Harem was a place where the sultan could engage in debauchery at will (and Murat III did, after all, have 112 children). In reality, these were the imperial family quarters, and every detail of Harem life was governed by tradition, obligation and ceremony. The word 'harem' literally means 'private'.

The women of Topkapı's Harem had to be foreigners, as Islam forbade enslaving Muslims. Girls were bought as slaves (often having been sold by their parents at a good price) or were received as gifts from nobles and potentates.

On entering the Harem, the girls would be schooled in Islam and Turkish culture and language, as well as the arts of make-up, dress, comportment, music, reading and writing, embroidery and dancing. They then entered a meritocracy, first as ladies-in-waiting to the sultan's concubines and children, then to the sultan's mother and finally – if they showed sufficient aptitude and were beautiful enough – to the sultan himself.

Ruling the Harem was the *valide sultan*. She often owned large landed estates in her own name and controlled them through black eunuch servants. Able to give orders directly to the grand vizier, her influence on the sultan, on the selection of his wives and concubines and on matters of state, was often profound.

The sultan was allowed by Islamic law to have four legitimate wives, who received the title of *kadın* (wife). He could also have as many concubines as he could support – some had up to 300, although they were not all in the Harem at the same time. If a sultan's wife bore him a son she was called *haseki sultan;* if she bore him a daughter she was called *haseki kadın.* The Ottoman dynasty did not observe the right of the first-born son to the throne, so in principle the throne was available to any imperial son. Each lady of the Harem struggled to have her son proclaimed heir to the throne, which would assure her own role as the new *valide sultan.*

Although the Harem is built into a hillside and has six levels, only a dozen or so of the most splendid rooms can be visited, all of which are on one level. Interpretive panels in Turkish and English have been placed along the self-guided tour route.

Highlights of the tour include the narrow Courtyard of the Black Eunuchs, the Courtyard of the Concubines & the Sultan's Consorts, the Apartments of the Valide Sultan, the grand Imperial Hall, the ornate Privy Chambers of Murat III and Ahmet I, the Fruit Room and the Twin Kiosk/Apartments of the Crown Prince.

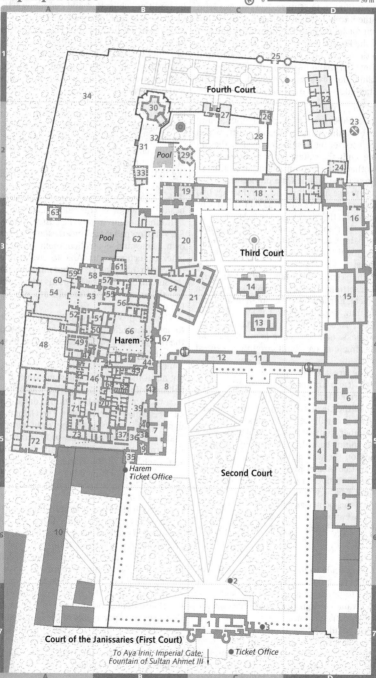

0 ————————————— 50 m

ISTANBUL

Fourth Court

34

30

27

26

23

22

32

31

Pool

29

33

19

18

17

Third Court

63

16

Pool

62

20

24

59

58

57

61

60

54

53

51

56

64

14

15

52

50

66

21

13

48

49

65 67

Harem

44

12

11

46

8

6

71

LI

70

39

72

73

37 36

40

7

4

35

Harem
Ticket Office

Second Court

5

10

2

1

3

To Aya İrini; Imperial Gate;
Fountain of Sultan Ahmet III

● *Ticket Office*

Third Court

If you enter the Third Court after visiting the Harem you should head for the main gate into the court and enter again to truly appreciate the grandeur of the approach to the heart of the palace. This main gate, known as the Gate of Felicity or Gate of the White Eunuchs, was the entrance into the sultan's private domain.

Just inside the Gate of Felicity is the Audience Chamber, constructed in the 16th century but refurbished in the 18th century. Important officials and foreign ambassadors were brought to this kiosk to conduct the high business of state. Seated on divans whose cushions were embroidered with over 15,000 seed pearls, the sultan inspected the ambassadors' gifts and offerings as they were passed through the small doorway on the left.

Right behind the Audience Chamber is the pretty, multidomed Library of Ahmet III, built in 1719.

To the right of the Audience Chamber (ie on the opposite side of the Harem exit) are the rooms of the Dormitory of the Expeditionary Force, which now house rich collections of imperial robes, kaftans and uniforms worked in silver and gold thread. Next to the Dormitory of the Expeditionary Force is the Treasury. See the following section for details of its collection.

Opposite the Treasury on the other side of the Third Court is another set of wonders: the holy relics in the Suite of the Felicitous Cloak, nowadays called the Sacred Safekeeping Rooms. These rooms constitute a holy of holies within the palace. Only the chosen few could enter the Third Court, but entry into the Suite of the Felicitous Cloak was for the chosen of the chosen, and then only on ceremonial occasions.

In the entry room to the Sacred Safekeeping Rooms, notice the carved door from the Kaaba in Mecca and the gilded rain gutters from the same place. To the left, a room contains the Prophet Mohammed's footprint in clay, the rod of the Prophet Moses and the sword of the prophet David.

Also in the Third Court are the Quarters of Pages in Charge of the Sacred Safekeeping Rooms, where the palace school for pages and janissaries was located. These days the building hosts temporary exhibitions.

Treasury

With its incredible collection of precious objects, and its simply breathtaking views from a balcony terrace, the Treasury is a highlight of a visit to the palace. The building itself was constructed by Mehmet the Conqueror in 1460 and has always been used to store works of art and treasure. In the first room, look for the jewel-encrusted sword of Süleyman the Magnificent and the Throne of Ahmet I, inlaid with mother-of-pearl and designed by Mehmet Ağa, architect of the Blue Mosque. In the second room, the tiny Indian figures, mainly made from seed pearls, are well worth seeking out.

After passing through the third room and having a gawk at the enormous gold

and diamond candlesticks, you will come to a fourth room and the Treasury's most famous exhibit – the Topkapı Dagger. The object of the criminal quest in the 1964 movie *Topkapı*, it features three enormous emeralds on the hilt and a watch set into the pommel. Also here is the Spoonmaker's Diamond (Kaşıkçı Elması), a teardrop-shaped 86-carat rock surrounded by several dozen smaller stones. First worn by Sultan Mehmet IV (r 1648–87) at his accession to the throne in 1648, it is the world's fifth-largest diamond. It is called the Spoonmaker's Diamond because it was originally found in a rubbish dump in Eğrıkapı and purchased by a street pedlar for three spoons.

Fourth Court

Pleasure pavilions occupy the northeastern part of the palace, sometimes called the Tulip Garden or Fourth Court. A late addition to Topkapı, the Mecidiye Köşkü was built by Sultan Abdül Mecit (r 1839–61). Beneath it is the Konyalı restaurant.

Up the stairs at the end of the Tulip Garden are three of the most enchanting buildings in the palace, joined by a marble terrace with a beautiful pool. Murat IV (r 1623–40) built the Revan Kiosk from 1635 to 1636 after reclaiming the city of Yerevan (now in Armenia) from Persia. In 1639 he constructed the Baghdad Kiosk, one of the last examples of classical palace architecture, to commemorate his victory over that city. Notice the superb İznik tiles, the mother-of-pearl and tortoiseshell inlay, and the stained-glass windows.

Jutting out from the terrace is the golden roof of the İftariye Baldachin, the most popular happy-snap spot in the palace grounds. İbrahim the Mad built this small structure in 1640 as a picturesque place to break the daily Ramazan fast.

At the west end of the terrace is the Circumcision Room (Sünnet Odası), used for the ritual that admits Muslim boys to manhood. Built by İbrahim in 1640, the outer walls of the chamber are graced by particularly beautiful tile panels.

Soğukçeşme Sokak   HISTORIC AREA

(Map p46) Soğukçeşme Sokak (Street of the Cold Fountain) runs between the Topkapı Palace walls and Aya Sofya. In the 1980s the Turkish Touring & Automobile Association (TTAA) acquired all of the buildings on the street and decided to demolish most of them to build nine re-creations of the prim

Ottoman-style houses that had occupied the site in the previous two centuries.

A vitriolic battle then played out on the pages of İstanbul's newspapers, with some experts arguing that the city would be left with a Disney-style architectural theme park rather than a legitimate exercise in conservation architecture. The TTAA eventually got the go-ahead (after the intervention of no less than Turkey's president) and in time opened all of the re-created buildings as Ayasofya Konakları, one of the first boutique heritage hotels in the city. Conservation theory aside, the colourful buildings and cobbled street are particularly picturesque and worth wandering past.

Caferağa Medresesi HISTORIC BUILDING
(Map p46; ☑0212-513 360; Caferiye Sokak; admission free; ☺8.30am-7pm) This lovely little *medrese* (seminary), tucked away in the shadows of Aya Sofya, was designed by Sinan on the orders of Cafer Ağa, Süleyman the Magnificent's chief black eunuch. Built in 1560 as a school for Islamic and secular education, today it is home to the Turkish Cultural Service Foundation, which runs workshops in traditional Ottoman arts such as calligraphy, *ebru* (traditional Turkish marbling) and miniature painting. Some of the arts and crafts produced here are for sale and there's a small cafe/*lokanta* (eatery serving ready-made food) in the courtyard.

Gülhane Park PARK
(Gülhane Parkı; Map p46) Once the park of the Topkapı Palace, shady Gülhane Park is now a popular relaxation spot for locals rather than sultans. It's particularly pretty in late March and early April, when the thousands of tulip bulbs planted to celebrate the International İstanbul Tulip Festival come into bloom. On the western edge of the park is the Museum of the History of Science and Technology in Islam (admission TL5; ☺9am-4.30pm Wed-Mon), which is housed in the former palace stables. At the far (northern) end of the park is the wonderful Set Üstü Çay Bahçesi (p98), an outdoor tea garden with superb views over the Bosphorus. Although relatively pricey, there are few better places in the city to enjoy a pot of tea.

To the left of the south exit is a bulbous kiosk built into the park wall. Known as the Alay Köşkü (Parade Kiosk), this is where the sultan would sit and watch the periodic parades of troops and trade guilds commemorate great holidays and military victories. It's now home to the İstanbul

headquarters of the Ministry of Culture and Tourism.

Across the street from the Alay Köşkü (not quite visible from the Gülhane gate) is an outrageously curvaceous rococo gate leading into the precincts of what was once the grand vizierate, or Ottoman prime ministry, known in the West as the Sublime Porte. Today the buildings beyond the gate hold various government offices.

İstanbul Archaeology Museums
MUSEUMS
(Arkeoloji Müzeleri; Map p46; ☑0212-520 7740; Osman Hamdi Bey Yokuşu, Gülhane; admission TL10; ☺9am-6pm Tue-Sun May-Sep, to 4pm Oct-Apr) It may not pull the number of visitors that flock to nearby Topkapı, but this superb museum complex shouldn't be missed. It can be reached easily by walking down the slope from Topkapı's First Court, or by trudging up the hill from the main gate of Gülhane Park. Allow at least two hours for your visit.

The complex is divided into three buildings: the Archaeology Museum (Arkeoloji Müzesi), the Museum of the Ancient Orient (Eski Şark Eserler Müzesi) and the Tiled Kiosk (Çinili Köşk). These museums house the palace collections, formed during the 19th century by archaeologist and artist Osman Hamdi Bey (1842–1910) and added to greatly since the republic was proclaimed. Excellent interpretive panels are in both Turkish and English.

The first building on your left as you enter is the Museum of the Ancient Orient. Overlooking the park, it was designed by Alexander Vallaury and built in 1883 to house the Academy of Fine Arts. It displays Anatolian pieces from Hittite empires and pre-Islamic items collected from the Ottoman Empire.

A Roman statue of the god Bes greets you as you enter the Archaeology Museum on the opposite side of the courtyard. Turn left and walk into the dimly lit rooms beyond, where the museum's major treasures – sarcophagi from the Royal Necropolis of Sidon – are displayed. Osman Hamdi Bey unearthed these sarcophagi in Sidon (Side in modern-day Lebanon) in 1887 and in 1891 persuaded the sultan to build this museum to house them.

In the first room you will see a sarcophagus that is Egyptian in origin, but which was later reused by King Tabnit of Sidon; his mummy lies close by. Also here is a beautifully preserved Lycian Sarcophagus made from Paros marble and dating from the end of the 5th century. Note its beautifully rendered horses, centaurs and human figures. Next to this is the Satrap Sarcophagus, with its everyday scenes featuring a provincial governor.

After admiring these, pass into the next room to see the famous marble Alexander Sarcophagus, one of the most accomplished of all classical artworks. It's known as the Alexander Sarcophagus because it depicts the Macedonian general and his army battling the Persians. (It was actually sculpted for King Abdalonymos of Sidon, not Alexander, though.) Truly exquisite, it is carved out of Pentelic marble and dates from the last quarter of the 4th century BC. One side shows the Persians (long pants, material headwear) battling with the Greeks. Alexander, on horseback, sports a Nemean Lion's head (the symbol of Hercules) as a headdress. The other side depicts the violent thrill of a lion hunt. Remarkably, the sculpture has remnants of its original red-and-yellow paintwork.

At the end of this room the Mourning Women Sarcophagus also bears traces of its original paintwork. Its depiction of the women is stark and very moving.

The rooms beyond house an impressive collection of ancient grave cult sarcophagi from Syria, Lebanon, Thessalonica, Ephesus and other parts of Anatolia.

After seeing these, turn back and walk past Bes to room 4, the first of six galleries of statues. Look for the Ephebos of Tralles in room 8 and the exquisite head of a child from Pergamum in room 9.

The annexe behind the main ground-floor gallery is home to a Children's Museum. While children will be bored stiff with the dioramas of early Anatolian life, they will no doubt be impressed by the large-scale model of the Trojan Horse, which they can climb into. Beside the Children's Museum is a fascinating exhibition entitled 'In the Light of Day', which focuses on the archaeological finds that have resulted from the city's huge Marmaray transport project. The exhibition continues downstairs, where there is also an impressive gallery showcasing Byzantine artefacts.

If you have even a passing interest in İstanbul's rich archaeology, don't miss the mezzanine level showcasing 'İstanbul Through the Ages'. After seeing the displays here you can appreciate how much of the ancient city remains covered.

The last of the complex's museum buildings is the gorgeous Tiled Kiosk of Sultan Mehmet the Conqueror. Thought to be the oldest surviving nonreligious Turkish building in İstanbul, it was built in 1472 as an outer pavilion of Topkapı Palace and was used for watching sporting events. It now houses an impressive collection of Seljuk, Anatolian and Ottoman tiles and ceramics.

BAZAAR DISTRICT

Crowned by the city's first and most evocative shopping mall – the famous Grand Bazaar – the bazaar district is also home to two of the grandest of all Ottoman buildings, the Süleymaniye and Beyazıt Mosques.

Grand Bazaar   BAZAAR

(Kapalı Çarşı, Covered Market; Map p66; www.kapalicarsi.org.tr; ⊙8.30am-7.30pm Mon-Sat) This labyrinthine and chaotic bazaar is the heart of the Old City and has been so for centuries. No visit to İstanbul would be complete without a stop here.

Starting as a small masonry *bedesten* (covered market) built during the time of Mehmet the Conqueror, the bazaar grew to cover a vast area as neighbouring shopkeepers put up roofs and porches (so that commerce could be conducted comfortably in all weather). Finally, a system of locked gates and doors was provided so that the entire minicity could be closed up tight at the end of the business day. Today, the bazaar has 16 *hans* (caravanserais), 64 lanes, mosques, banks, a police station, restaurants, workshops and more than 2000 shops, making it a world within itself.

When here, make sure to peep through doorways to find hidden *hans* and to take every side street to dig out tiny boutiques and workshops. Visit shops, drink too much çay, compare price after price and try your hand at the art of bargaining. Allow at least three hours for your visit; some travellers spend three days.

Beyazıt Square   SQUARE

Sultan Beyazıt II (r 1481–1512) specified that an exceptional amount of marble, porphyry, verd-antique and rare granite be used to decorate the Beyazıt Mosque (Beyazıt Camii; Map p62), which was built between 1501 and 1506 and is the focal point of this landmark square. Though officially called Hürriyet Meydanı (Freedom Sq), İstanbullus know it simply as Beyazıt. Under the Byzantines this was the Forum of Theodosius, the largest of the city's many forums, built by the emperor in AD 393. Today, the square is backed by the impressive portal of İstanbul University.

Süleymaniye Mosque   MOSQUE
(Süleymaniye Camii, Mosque of Sultan Süleyman the Magnificent; Map p62; Prof Sıddık Sami Onar Caddesi) The Süleymaniye crowns one of the seven hills dominating the Golden Horn and provides a magnificent landmark for the entire city. It was commissioned by the greatest, richest and most powerful of the Ottoman sultans, Süleyman the Magnificent (r 1520–66), and was the fourth imperial mosque built in İstanbul.

Although it's not the largest of the Ottoman mosques, the recently restored Süleymaniye is certainly the grandest. It was designed by Mimar Sinan (see boxed text, p78), the most famous and talented of all imperial architects. Although Sinan described the smaller Selimiye Camii in Edirne as his best work, he chose to be buried here in the Süleymaniye complex, probably knowing that this would be the building by which he would be best remembered. His tomb is just outside the mosque's walled garden in the northern corner.

Inside, the mosque is breathtaking in its size and pleasing in its simplicity. There's little decoration except for some fine İznik tiles in the *mihrab* (niche indicating the direction of Mecca); gorgeous stained-glass windows done by one İbrahim the Drunkard; and four massive columns, one from Baalbek, one from Alexandria and two from Byzantine palaces in İstanbul.

The *külliye* (mosque complex) of the Süleymaniye, which is outside the walled garden, is particularly elaborate, with the full complement of public services: soup kitchen, hostel, hospital, *medrese*, hamam etc. Today the soup kitchen, with its charming garden courtyard, houses the Darüzziyafe Restaurant, a lovely place to enjoy a cup of tea. Lale Bahçesi, located in a sunken courtyard next to Darüzziyafe, is a popular hang-out for uni students, who come here to chat, drink çay and indulge in nargilehs. The former *medrese* now houses a library and a raft of simple eateries serving *fasulye* and *pilav* (beans and rice).

Near the southeast wall of the mosque is its cemetery, home to the **tombs** (◷9am-7pm Tue-Sun) of Süleyman and Roxelana. The tilework in both is superb.

Şehzade Mehmet Mosque   MOSQUE
(Şehzade Mehmet Camii, Mosque of the Prince; Map p62; Şehzadebaşı Caddesi, Kalenderhane) Süleyman the Magnificent commissioned Sinan to design the Şehzade Mehmet Mosque in memory of his son Mehmet, who died of smallpox at the age of 22. It was completed in 1548 and is noteworthy for its delicate minarets and attractive garden setting.

Rüstem Paşa Mosque   MOSQUE
(Rüstem Paşa Camii, Mosque of Rüstem Paşa; Map p62; Hasırcılar Caddesi) Hidden in the middle of the busy Tahtakale district to the west of the Spice Bazaar, this little-visited mosque is an absolute gem. Built in 1560 by Sinan for the son-in-law and grand vizier of Süleyman the Magnificent, it is a showpiece of the best Ottoman architecture and tile work, albeit on a small scale.

At the top of both sets of entry steps, there's a terrace and the mosque's colonnaded porch. You'll immediately notice the panels of İznik tiles set into the mosque's facade. The interior is covered in similarly gorgeous tiles and features a lovely dome, supported by four tiled pillars.

The preponderance of tiles was Rüstem Paşa's way of signalling his wealth and influence to the world, with İznik tiles being particularly expensive and desirable. It may not have assisted his passage into the higher realm, though, because by all accounts he was a loathsome character. His contemporaries dubbed him Kehle-i-Ikbal ('Louse of Fortune') because even though he was found to be infested with lice before his marriage to Mihrimah (Süleyman's favourite daughter), this did not prevent his marriage or his subsequent rise to great fame and fortune. He is best remembered for plotting with Roxelana to turn Süleyman against his favourite son, Mustafa. They were successful and Mustafa was strangled in 1553 on his father's orders.

The mosque is easy to miss because it's not at street level. Look for the stairs on Hasırcılar Caddesi, or to the left of the ablutions block on the side street.

Spice Bazaar   BAZAAR
(Mısır Çarşısı, Egyptian Market; Map p62; ◷8am-7pm Mon-Sat) This bustling marketplace was constructed in the 1660s as part of the New Mosque complex, with rents from the shops going to support the upkeep of the mosque and its charitable activities. It was called

Bazaar District

400 m
0.2 miles

Galata Bridge (Galata Köprüsü)

Resadiye Cad

Eminönü

See Sultanahmet & Around Map p46

Turyol Bosphorus Ferry

Köşkü Cad

Hamidiye Cad

Şeyhül Islam Hayri Efendi Cad

Şehirmşah Postane Cad

HOBYAR

18

29

36

Yalı

7

EMİNÖNÜ

YENİ CAMİ MEYDANI

Yenicami Meydanı Sk

Tahmis Sk

15

11

35

32

Çiçek Pazarı Sk

Çeşnici Sk

Tarakçı Cafer Sk

Bezciler Sk

Golden Horn (Haliç) Ferries

Eminönü Bus Stand

Spice Bazaar

Mahmutpaşa Yokuşu

SURURİ

19 30

Hasırcılar Cad

31 33

Alaçahamam Cad

Sabuncuhanı Sk

Çarkçılar Sk

TAYAHATUN

Sobacılar Cad

Rüstem Paşa Mosque

23

Sobacılar Sk

Marpuççular Sk

Tornruk Sk

TAHTAKALE

Vasıf Çınar Cad

Pşirkçı Yokuşu

MERCAN

See Grand Bazaar Map p66

Kutlucular Cad

Prof Cemil Bilsel Cad

Uzunçarşı Cad

Ağızlıkçı Sk

Havancı Sk

Nargileci Sk

Çökelik Sk

Mercan Cad

Çakmakçılar Yokuşu

SARIDEMİR

Ragıp Gümüşpala Cad

Siyavuşpaşa Sk

Fuat Paşa Cad

Kible Çeşme Cad

Kepenekçi Saburhanesi Sk

Hayriye Hanım Sk

DEMİRTAŞ

Fetvayokuşu Sk

Süleymaniye Cad

Süleymaniye Mosque

12

İstanbul University

Besim Ömer Paşa Cad

Namahrem Sk

Şemsettin Sk

Mimar Sinan Cad

10

Ayşe Kadın Hamamı Sk

Süleymaniye İmareti Sk

24

27

21

Kirazlı Mescit Sk

Oluk Sk

Süleymaniye Cad

Yoğurtçuoğlu Sk

Tavanlı Çeşme Cad

Vefa Cad

Sarı Beyazıt Cad

Müşküle Sk

MOLLA HÜSREV

KÜÇÜKPAZAR

Hacı Kadın Cad

Darülhadis Sk

Melekşah Sk

Hızır Külhanı Sk

Vefa Türbesi Sk

Himmet Sk

Katip Çelebi Cad

Cemal Yener Tosyalı Cad

SÜLEYMANİYE

Darülelham Sk

Veznecıler Cad

22

VEFA

Azep Askeri Sk

Revani Çelebi Sk

KALENDERHANE

Dede Efendi Cad

Şehzade Mehmet Mosque

Fevziye Cad

BALABAN AĞA

6

İbadethane Sk

Zeyrek Cad

İtfaiye Cad

Kendiri Cad

Atatürk Bul

Suyolu Sk

Sarachane Park

KALENDERİYE

Şehzadebaşı Cad

Gençtürk Cad

1

To Sur. Ocakbaşı (400m)

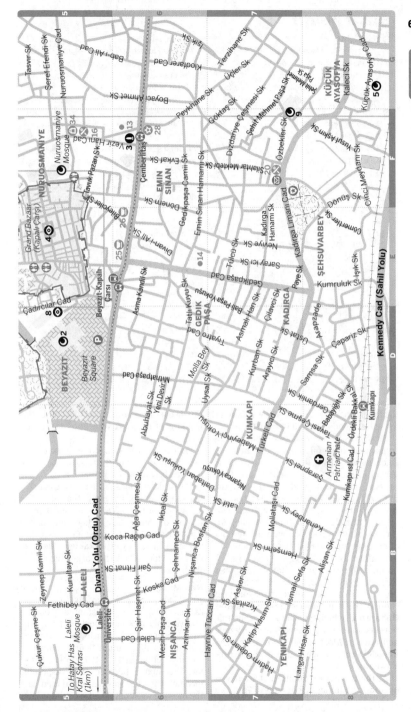

KÜÇÜK
AYASOFYA

NURUOSMANİYE

Nuruosmaniye
Mosque

Grand Bazaar
(Kapalı Çarşı)

EMİN
SİNAN

ŞEHSUVARBEY

KADIRGA

Beyazıt-Kapalı
Çarşı

BEYAZIT

Beyazıt
Square

GEDİK
PAŞA

Kennedy Cad (Sahil Yolu)

KUMKAPI

Armenian
Patriarchate

Kumkapı

Divan Yolu (Ordu) Cad

LALELİ

Laleli
Mosque

Laleli-
Üniversite

NİŞANCA

YENİKAPI

To Hatay Has
Kral Sofrası
(1km)

Taşvir Sk

Şeref Efendi Sk

Bab-ı Ali Cad

Nuruosmaniye Cad

Boyacı Ahmet Sk

Işık Sk

Kılodfarer Cad

Terzihane Sk

Üçler Sk

Peykhane Sk

Göktaş Sk

Dizdariye Çeşmesi Sk

Şehit Mehmet Paşa Sk

Şehit Mehmet
Paşa Sk

Kaleci Sk

Küçük Ayasofya Cad

Yusuf Aşkın Sk

Özbekler Sk

Tavuk Pazarı Sk

Bileyciler Sk

Yeşil Han Cad

Çemberlitaş

Emin Sinan
Mescidi Sk

Silahtar Mektebi Sk

Evkat Sk

Denem Sk

Gedikpaşa Camii Sk

Emin Sinan Hamamı Sk

Kadırga
Hamamı Sk

Kadırga Limanı Cad

Dönüş Sk

Civici Meydanı Sk

Cömertler Sk

Divan-ı Ali Sk

Asma Kandil Sk

Gedikpaşa Cad

Tülcü Sk

Neviye Sk

Saray İçi Sk

Paye Sk

Kumruluk Sk

Işık Sk

Çadırcılar Cad

Tatlı Kuyu Sk

Balı Paşa Yokuşu

Asmalı Han Sk

Çilavcı Sk

Ustat Sk

Ayazpaşa

Çaparız Sk

Ördekli Bakkal Sk

Tiyatro Cad

Molla Bey
Sk

Kurban Sk

Arayıcı Sk

Samsa Sk

Gerdanlık Sk

Babayiğit Sk

Abuhayat Sk

Yeni Devir
Sk

Uysal Sk

Mabeyinci Yokuşu

Türkeli Cad

Tavaşı Çeşme Sk

Mithatpaşa Cad

Nişanca Yokuşu

Sarapnel Sk

Kenanbey

Mollataşı Cad

Dalbaban Yokuşu Sk

Latif Sk

Hemşehri Sk

Alişan Sk

Zeynep Kamil Sk

Kurultay Sk

Şair Fıtnat Sk

Ağa Çeşmesi Sk

Koca Ragıp Cad

İkbal Sk

Şehnameci Sk

Nişanca Bostan Sk

Asker Sk

Kızıltaş Sk

İsmail Sefa Sk

Çukur Çeşme Sk

Fethibey Cad

Şair Haşmet Sk

Koska Cad

Laleli Cad

Mesih Paşa Cad

Azimkar Sk

Hayriye Tüccarı Cad

Hadım Odaları Sk

Katip Kasım Sk

Langa Hisar Sk

İSTANBUL

the Egyptian Market because it was famous for selling goods shipped in from Cairo.

As well as *baharat* (spices), nuts, honeycomb and olive-oil soaps, the bustling spice bazaar sells truckloads of *incir* (figs), *lokum* (Turkish delight) and *pestil* (fruit pressed into sheets and dried) – try the highly regarded **Malatya Pazarı** (shop 44) if you want to take home some dried fruit or nuts, and **Ucuzcular Baharat** (shop 51) if you're after spices. Although the number of shops selling tourist trinkets increases annually, this is still a great place to stock up on edible souvenirs, share a few jokes with the vendors and marvel at the well-preserved building. Make sure you visit shop 41, the atmospheric **Mehmet Kalmaz Baharatçı**, which specialises in henna, potions, lotions and the sultan's very own aphrodisiac. Most of the shops offer vacuum packaging, which makes it easy to take souvenirs home.

At the time of research, the bazaar was opening on Sundays from 8am to 7pm, but shopkeepers were unsure as to whether this would continue. Ask your hotel for an update.

On the western side of the market there are outdoor produce stalls selling fresh foodstuffs from all over Anatolia. Also here is Hasırcılar Caddesi, a narrow street selling spices and other goods that are often a fraction of the price of equivalent products in the Spice Bazaar. Look out for the flagship store of the most famous coffee purveyor in Turkey, **Kurukahveci Mehmet Efendi**, which is on the corner nearest to the bazaar.

New Mosque   MOSQUE
(Yeni Cami; Map p62; Yenicami Meydanı Sokak, Eminönü) Only in İstanbul would a 400-year-old mosque be called 'New'. The New Mosque was begun in 1597, commissioned by Valide Sultan Safiye, mother of Sultan Mehmet III (r 1595–1603). Safiye lost her august position (and disposable income) when her son the sultan died, and the mosque was completed six sultans later

in 1663 by Turhan Hadice, mother of Sultan Mehmet IV.

In plan, the New Mosque is much like the Blue and Süleymaniye Mosques, with a large forecourt and square sanctuary surmounted by a series of semidomes crowned by a grand dome. The interior is richly decorated with gold, coloured İznik tiles and carved marble, and has an impressive *mihrab*.

In the courtyard near the Spice Bazaar is the **tomb of Valide Sultan Turhan Hadice**. Buried with her are no fewer than six sultans, including her son Mehmet IV.

Galata Bridge   LANDMARK
(Map p62) Nothing is quite as evocative as walking across Galata Bridge. At sunset, when Galata Tower is surrounded by the silhouettes of shrieking seagulls and the mosques atop the seven hills of the city are thrown into relief against a soft red-pink sky, the surrounds are spectacularly beautiful. During the day, the bridge carries a constant flow of İstanbullus crossing between Beyoğlu and Eminönü, a line of hopeful anglers trailing their lines into the waters below, and a constantly changing procession of street vendors hawking everything from fresh-baked *simit* (sesame seed–coated bread rings) to Rolex rip-offs.

Underneath the bridge, fish restaurants and cafes on its lower level serve drinks and food all day. Come here to inhale the evocative scent of apple tobacco wafting out from the nargileh cafes and to watch the passing parade of ferry traffic plying the waters. The eateries below the bridge are much of a muchness (and that's not much at all), but the cafes are wonderful spots to enjoy a tea or late-afternoon beer.

This bridge was built in 1994 to replace an iron structure dating from around 1910, which in turn had replaced three earlier structures. The 1910 bridge was famous for its seedy fish restaurants, teahouses and nargileh joints that occupied the dark recesses beneath its roadway, but it had a major flaw: it floated on pontoons that blocked the natural flow of water and kept the Golden Horn from flushing out pollution. In 1992 the iron bridge was damaged by fire and the remnants were dragged up the Golden Horn; you pass them on the ferry trip to Eyüp.

Note that the bridge is sometimes the location for a scam whereby a shoeshiner drops his brush in front of a tourist, who helpfully bends over to pick it up. The tourist is then offered a shoeshine by the grateful recipient – unfortunately, the service never turns out to be for free.

WESTERN DISTRICTS
Broadly described as the district between the city walls and the Bazaar District, this area was once dotted with the churches of Byzantium. While most of the churches have been converted to mosques, and many of the houses are tumbledown or have been razed for ugly apartment blocks, a few hours' exploration will give you a taste of workaday İstanbul. There are several sights worth visiting if you have the time, and the Chora Church is an absolute must-see for all visitors to İstanbul.

Aqueduct of Valens   LANDMARK
(Map p62; Atatürk Bulvarı) Rising majestically over the traffic on busy Atatürk Bulvarı, this limestone aqueduct is one of the city's most distinctive landmarks. Commissioned by Emperor Valens in AD 373, it was part of an elaborate system linking over 400km of water channels, some 30 bridges and over 100 cisterns within the city walls, making it one of the greatest hydraulic engineering achievements of ancient times.

Molla Zeyrek Mosque   MOSQUE
(Molla Zeyrek Camii, Church of the Pantocrator; Map p62; İbadethane Sokak) Originally part of an important Byzantine sanctuary comprising two churches, a chapel and a monastery, the Zeyrek mosque is now in a deplorable state of disrepair, which has led to it being listed on the World Monument Fund's register of endangered buildings. At the time of research it was closed to the public while restoration work was being undertaken.

The monastery is long gone and the northernmost church is derelict, but the southern church, built by Empress Eirene before her death in AD 1124 (she features in a mosaic at Aya Sofya with Emperor John Comnenus II) was saved by being converted into a mosque and still has some features intact, including a magnificent mosaic floor.

The Ottoman building to the east of the mosque houses the Zeyrekhane restaurant, which has a cafe terrace with glorious Golden Horn and Old City views.

After you've visited Zeyrek, a pleasant 15-minute walk uphill through the

ISTANBUL

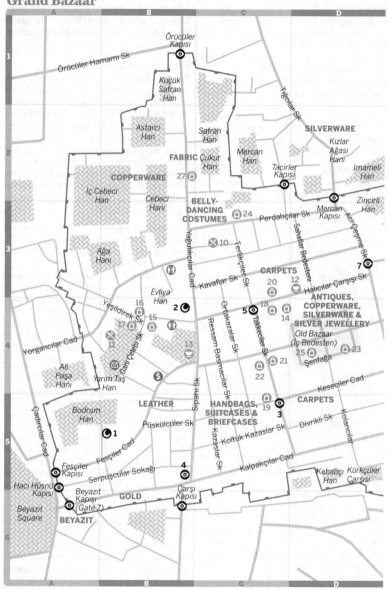

residential streets will bring you to the Fatih Mosque – the best time to do this is on a Wednesday, when the sprawling Fatih Çarşamba Pazarı (Fatih Wednesday Market), the city's best open-air market, is held in the streets surrounding the mosque.

Fatih Mosque   MOSQUE

(Fatih Camii, Mosque of the Conqueror; Map p42; Fevzi Paşa Caddesi, Fatih) This mosque, 750m northwest of the historic Aqueduct of Valens, was the first great imperial mosque to be built in İstanbul. Set in extensive

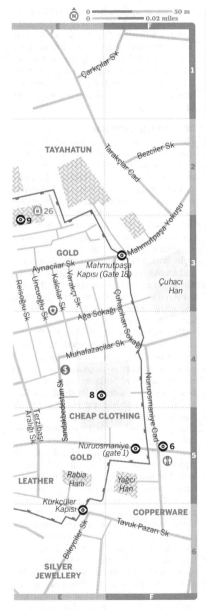

built it burned down in 1782. What you see today dates from the reign of Sultan Abdül Hamit I (r 1774–89).

The much-visited **tomb of the Conqueror** (⊙9.30am-4.30pm Tue-Sun) is in the cemetery behind the mosque, though Mehmet is actually buried under the *mimber* (pulpit) in the mosque itself.

Chora Church   MUSEUM
(Kariye Müzesi; Map p42; ☎0212-631 9241; Kariye Camii Sokak, Edirnekapı; admission TL15; ⊙9am-6pm Thu-Tue Apr-Sep, to 4.30pm Oct-Mar) İstanbul has more than its fair share of Byzantine monuments, but few are as drop-dead gorgeous as the Chora Church. The fact that it's tucked away in the little-visited Western Districts of the city means that many visitors overlook it, but we counsel you not to do the same.

grounds, the mosque complex was enormous and included 15 charitable establishments – religious schools, a hospice for travellers, a caravanserai and more. The mosque was finished in 1470 but was destroyed by an earthquake; after being re-

The church was originally known as the Church of the Holy Saviour Outside the Walls, but what you see today is not the first church-outside-the-walls on this site. This one was built in the late 11th century, and underwent repairs, restructuring and conversion to a mosque in the succeeding centuries. Virtually all of the interior decoration dates from 1312 and was funded by Theodore Metochites, a poet and man of letters who was auditor of the treasury under Emperor Andronikos II (r 1282–1328). One of the museum's most wonderful mosaics, found above the door to the nave in the inner narthex, depicts Theodore offering the church to Christ.

The mosaics, which depict the lives of Christ and Mary, are simply stunning. Look out for the Deesis (Christ in Majesty), which shows Christ and Mary with two donors: Prince Isaac Komnenos and Melane, daughter of Mikhael Palaiologos VIII. This is under the right dome in the inner narthex. On the dome itself is *Genealogy of Christ,* a wonderful depiction of Jesus and his ancestors. On the narthex's left dome is a serenely beautiful mosaic of Mary and the child Jesus surrounded by her ancestors.

In the nave are three mosaics: of Christ; of Mary and the child Jesus; and of the Dormition (Assumption) of the Blessed Virgin – turn around to see the latter as it's over the main door you just entered. The 'infant' being held by Jesus is actually Mary's soul.

To the right of the nave is the Parecclesion, a side chapel built to hold the tombs of the church's founder and his relatives, close friends and associates. It is decorated with frescoes depicting Old Testament scenes.

The Chora is one of the city's best museums and deserves an extended visit. On leaving, we highly recommend sampling the unusual Ottoman menu at the Asitane restaurant, which is in the basement of the next-door Kariye Oteli. Alternatively, a simple *peynirli tost* (toasted cheese sandwich) and glass of çay can be enjoyed at the Kariye Pembe Köşk in the plaza overlooking the museum.

You can see a smaller but similarly wonderful display of Byzantine mosaics at the nearby Church of Theotokos Pammakaristos (Fethiye Camii & Müzesi, Church of the All-Praised Mother of God; admission TL5; ☺9am-4.30pm Thu-Tue), built between 1292 and 1294.

The best way to get to this part of town is to catch the Golden Horn (Haliç) ferry from Eminönü to Ayvansaray and walk up the hill along Dervişzade Sokak and Şişhane Caddesi following the remnants of Theodosius II's land walls. From Şişhane Caddesi, veer left into Vaiz Sokak just before you reach the steep stairs leading up to the ramparts of the wall, then turn sharp left into Kariye Sokak and you'll come to the Chora Church.

BEYOĞLU & AROUND

The suburb of Beyoğlu (*bay*-oh-loo) rises from the shoreline north of Galata Bridge, and incorporates both Taksim Sq and the grand boulevard, İstiklal Caddesi. In the mid-19th century it was known as Pera and acknowledged as the 'European' quarter of town. Diplomats and international traders lived and worked here, and the streets were showcases for the latest European fashions and fads. European-style patisseries, restaurants, boutiques and embassies were all built following the European architectural styles of the day. It even had telephones, electric lights and one of the first electric tramways in the world, the Tünel.

However, all this changed in the decades after the republic was formed. Embassies moved to the country's new capital, Ankara, the glamorous shops and restaurants closed, the grand buildings crumbled and Beyoğlu took on a decidedly sleazy air. Fortunately the '90s brought about a rebirth and Beyoğlu is once again the heart of modern İstanbul, ground zero for galleries, cafes and boutiques. Here, hip new restaurants and bars open almost nightly, and the streets showcase cosmopolitan Turkey at its best. Put simply, if you miss Beyoğlu, you haven't seen İstanbul.

The best way to get a feel for this side of town is to spend an afternoon or day exploring by foot. If you're based in Sultanahmet, catch the tram to Kabataş and the connecting funicular up to Taksim Sq. Then work your way down İstiklal Caddesi, exploring its many side streets along the way. At the foot of the boulevard is Tünel Sq; follow Galipdede Caddesi downhill and you will be able to explore the historic neighbourhood of Galata before walking across Galata Bridge to Eminönü, from where you can catch a tram, or walk, back up to Sultanahmet. All up it's a walk of at least two hours from Taksim Sq – but dedicating a full day will be more rewarding.

Galata Tower
LANDMARK

(Galata Kulesi; Map p72; Galata Meydanı, Galata; admission TL10; ⏰9am-8pm) Originally constructed in 1348, this tower was the highest point in the Genoese fortifications of Galata and has been rebuilt many times. It has survived several earthquakes, as well as the demolition of the rest of the Genoese walls in the mid-19th century. Though the view from its vertiginous panorama balcony is spectacular, we suggest enjoying this over a drink on the terrace of the Anemon Galata hotel opposite, rather than paying the inflated entry fee here.

İstanbul Modern
MUSEUM

(İstanbul Modern Sanat Müzesi; Map p72; ☎0212-334 7300; www.istanbulmodern.org; Meclis-i Mebusan Caddesi, Tophane; adult/student/under 12yr TL14/7/free; ⏰10am-6pm Tue, Wed & Fri-Sun, to 8pm Thu) The İstanbul Modern is the big daddy of a slew of newish, privately funded art galleries in the city. Its stunning location on the shores of the Bosphorus and its extensive collection of Turkish 20th-century art make it well worth a visit. The icing on the cake is provided by a constantly changing and uniformly excellent program of exhibitions by local and international artists in the exhibition galleries on the ground floor.

There's also a well-stocked gift shop, a cinema that shows art-house films and a stylish cafe-restaurant with superb views of the Bosphorus.

İstiklal Caddesi
BOULEVARD

(Independence Ave; Map p72) In the late 19th century, this major street was known as the Grande Rue de Pera, and it carried the life of the modern city up and down its lively promenade. It's still the centre of İstanbullu life, and a stroll along its length is a must. Come between 4pm and 8pm daily – especially on Friday and Saturday – and you'll see İstiklal at its busiest best.

About halfway along İstiklal Caddesi is the Galatasaray Lycée, founded in 1868 by Sultan Abdül Aziz (r 1861–76) as a school where students were taught in French as well as Turkish. Today it's a prestigious public school.

Close by is the Cité de Pera building, home to the famous Çiçek Pasajı (Flower Passage). When the *Orient Express* rolled into Old İstanbul and promenading down İstiklal Caddesi was all the rage, the Cité de Pera building was the most glamorous address in town. Built in 1876 and deco-

rated in Second Empire style, it housed a shopping arcade as well as apartments. As Pera declined, so too did the building, its stylish shops giving way to florists and then to *meyhanes,* where enthusiastic revellers caroused the night away. In the late 1970s parts of the building collapsed; once rebuilt, the passage was 'beautified' and its raffish charm was lost. These days locals bypass the touts and mediocre food on offer here, and make their way behind the passage to one of İstanbul's most colourful and popular eating precincts, Nevizade Sokak.

Next to the Çiçek Pasajı you'll find Şahne Sokak and Beyoğlu's Balık Pazar (Fish Market), with stalls selling fruit, vegetables, pickles and other produce. Leading off the Balık Pazar you'll find the neoclassical Avrupa Pasajı (European Passage), a small gallery with marble paving and shops selling tourist wares and some antique goods; as well as the Aslıhan Pasajı, a two-storey arcade bursting at the seams with secondhand books.

Pera Museum
MUSEUM

(Map p72; ☎0212-334 9900; www.peramuzesi. org.tr; Meşrutiyet Caddesi 65, Tepebaşı; adult/student & child over 12yr/child under 12yr TL7/3/free; ⏰10am-7pm Tue-Sat, noon-6pm Sun) If, like many travellers, you've seen reproductions of the famous Osman Hamdi Bey painting *The Tortoise Trainer* and would love to see the real thing, this is the place to do it. The painting is part of the museum's wonderful collection of Orientalist paintings, which occupies the 3rd floor. Other floors host permanent exhibitions of Kütahya tiles and ceramics, Anatolian weights and measures and top-notch temporary exhibitions.

Taksim Square
LANDMARK

(Map p72) The symbolic heart of modern İstanbul, this busy square is named after the stone *taksim* (reservoir) on its western side, once part of the city's old water-conduit system. The *taksim* is now home to the unassuming Taksim Republic Art Gallery (Taksim Cumhuriyet Sanat Galerisi; admission free; ⏰variable).

The square is in no way a triumph of urban design – in fact, it's a chaotic mess. On its western side, the İstiklal Caddesi tram circumnavigates the Cumhuriyet Anıtı (Republic Monument), created by an Italian architect-sculptor team in 1928. It features Atatürk, his assistant and successor İsmet İnönü, and other revolutionary leaders.

On the square's northern side is a hectic bus terminus and on its eastern side is the

START **ÇEMBERLİTAŞ
TRAM STOP**
FINISH **SAHAFLAR
ÇARŞISI**
DISTANCE **1KM**
DURATION **3 HOURS**

Walking Tour
Grand Bazaar

❯ Visitors are often overwhelmed by the bazaar's labyrinthine layout and vociferous touts, but if you follow this walking tour you should enjoy your visit.

Start at the tram stop next to the tall column known as ① **Çemberlitaş**, which was erected by order of Emperor Constantine to celebrate the dedication of Constantinople as capital of the Roman Empire in 330. From here, walk down Vezir Han Caddesi and you will soon come to the entrance to the ② **Vezir Han**, a *han* (caravanserai) built between 1659 and 1660 by the Köprülüs, one of the Ottoman Empire's most distinguished families. Five of its members served as Grand Vizier (*Vezir*) to the sultan, hence its name. In Ottoman times, this *han* would have offered travelling merchants shelter and a place to do business. While in the city the merchants and their entourages would have slept and eaten upstairs and conducted their business downstairs; their animals (mainly camels and horses) would have been quartered in the courtyard and

the merchants' goods would have been stored and sold on the upper levels. Though gold manufacturers still work here, the *han* is in a sadly dilapidated state, as are the many (some experts say hundreds) of similar buildings dotted throughout the district. Look for the *tuğra* (crest) of the sultan over the main gateway.

Continue walking down Vezir Han Caddesi until you come to a cobbled pedestrianised street on your left. Walk along this until you come to the ③ **Nuruosmaniye Mosque**, commissioned by Mahmut I in 1748. In front of you is one of the major entrances to the Grand Bazaar, the Nuruosmaniye Kapısı (Nuruosmaniye Gate, Gate 1), adorned by another sultan's seal. The brightly lit street in front of you is Kalpakçılar Caddesi, the busiest street in the bazaar. Originally named after the *kalpakçılars* (makers of fur hats) who had their stores here, it's now full of jewellers, who pay up to US$80,000 per year in rent for this high-profile location. Start walking down the street and then turn right and take the marble stairs down to the **4** **Sandal Bedesten**, a 17th-century stone warehouse featuring 20 small domes. This warehouse has always been used for the storage and sale of fabric, although the current range of cheap textiles on sale couldn't be more different to the fine *sandal* (fabric woven with silk) that was sold here in the past.

Exit the Sandal Bedesten on its west (left) side, turning right into Sandal Bedestenı Sokak and then left into Ağa Sokak, which takes you into the oldest part of the bazaar, the **5** **Cevahir (Jewellery) Bedesten**, also known as the Eski (Old) Bedesten. This has always been an area where precious items are stored and sold, and these days it's where most of the bazaar's antique stores are located. Slave auctions were held here until the mid-19th century.

Exiting the *bedesten* from its south door, walk down to the first cross-street, Halıcılar Çarşışı Sokak, where popular shops including Abdulla Natural Products and Derviş are located. Also here is a good spot for a tea or coffee, **6** **Etham Tezçakar Kahvecı**.

Walking east (right) you will come to a major cross-street, Kuyumcular Caddesi (Street of the Jewellers). Over the bazaar's history, most silversmiths working in the bazaar have been of Armenian descent and most goldsmiths have been of Arabic or Aramaic descent – this is still true to this day. Turn left and walk past the little kiosk in the middle of the street. Built in the 17th century and known as the **7** **Oriental Kiosk**, it now houses a jewellery store but was once home to the most famous *muhallebici* (milk pudding shop) in the district. A little way further down, on the right-hand side of the street, is the entrance to the pretty **8** **Zincirli (Chain) Han**, home to one of the bazaar's best-known carpet merchants – Şişko Osman. Back on Kuyumcular Caddesi, continue walking and then turn sharp left into Perdahçılar Sokak (Street of the Polishers). Walk until you reach Terlikçiler Sokak, where

you should turn left. This charming, known for its marble *sebils* (public dr fountains) and shops selling kilims (pile, woven rugs). Turn right into Zenneciler Sokak (Street of the Clothing Sellers) and you will soon come to a junction with another of the bazaar's major thoroughfares, Sipahi Caddesi (Avenue of the Cavalry Soldiers). **9** **Şark Kahvesi**, a traditional coffee house, is right on the corner. Turn left into Sipahi Caddesi and walk until you return to Kalpakçılar Caddesi, the street with all of the jewellery shops. Turn right and exit the bazaar from the **10** **Beyazıt Kapısı** (Beyazıt Gate, Gate 7). Turn right again and walk past the market stalls to the first passage on the left, and you will find yourself in the **11** **Sahaflar Çarşısı** (Old Book Bazaar), which has operated as a book and paper market since Byzantine times. At the centre of its shady courtyard is a bust of İbrahim Müteferrika (1674–1745), who printed the first book in Turkey in 1732. From here, you can exit to Beyazıt Sq and make your way down Divan Yolu Caddesi to Sultahnamet or north along the walls of İstanbul University to the Süleymaniye Mosque (p61).

Many visitors choose to combine a visit to the Grand Bazaar with one to the Spice Bazaar (p61) at Eminönü. If you are keen to do this, backtrack through the bazaar to the Mahmutpaşa Kapısı (Mahmutpaşa Gate, Gate 18) and follow busy Mahmutpaşa Yokuşu all the way down the hill to the Spice Bazaar. Along the way you will pass one of the oldest hamams in the city, the Mahmutpaşa Hamamı (now converted into a shopping centre). This street and the streets to the west of the Spice Bazaar (collectively known as Tahtakale) are the busiest mercantile precincts in the Old City. This is where locals come to buy everything from wedding dresses to woollen socks, coffee cups to circumcision outfits – a wander around here (as opposed to the touristy streets around Sultanahmet) will give you a taste of the real İstanbul.

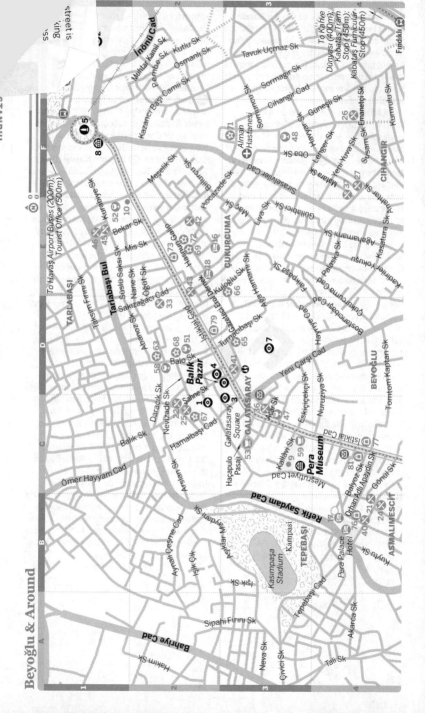

STANBUL

Beyoğlu & Around

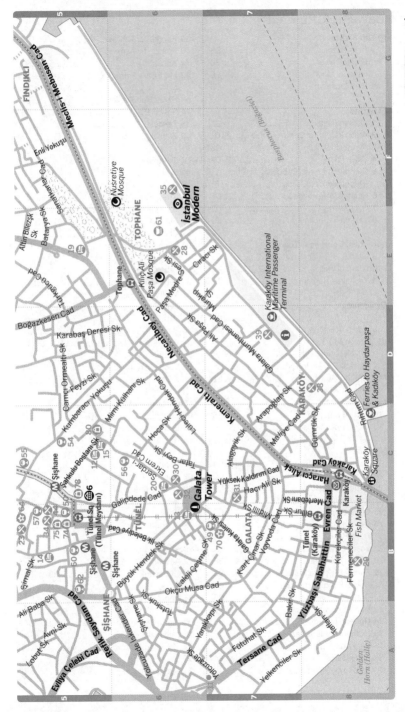

FINDIKLI

Meclis-i Mebusan Cad

Enli Yokuşu

Altın Bilezik Sk
Batarya Sk
Sarayarkası Cad

Türkücü Cad

Boğazkesen Cad

Karabaş Deresi Sk

Camcı Ormeatlı Sk

Feyzi Sk

Kumbaracı Yokuşu

Mimi Kulhanı Sk

Lüleci Hendek Cad

Hoca Sk

Nusretiye
Mosque

TOPHANE

35

61

Istanbul
Modern

Kılıç Ali
Paşa Mosque

Tophane

Serdar-ı Ekrem Cad

Ali Paşa Sk

Paşa Medresi Sk

Serçi Sk

28

Ciracı Sk

Murakıp Sk

Necatibey Cad

Kemeraltı Cad

Galata Mumhanesi Cad

39

Karaköy International
Maritime Passenger
Terminal

KARAKÖY

Arapoğlan Sk

Mahiye Cad

Gümrük Sk

38

Rıhtım Cad

Ferries to Haydarpaşa
& Kadıköy

Bosphorus (Boğaziçi)

Şişhane
55
Şehkulu Bostanı Sk
54
80
15
12
556
30
20
Galipdede Cad
78
6
TÜNEL
(Tünel Meydanı)
Tünel Sq
64
57
34
75
14
23
50
Şişhane
62
Şişhane

Talat Beyn Sk

Galata
Tower

Alageyik Sk

Yüksek Kaldırım Cad

Hacı Ali Sk

31

GALATA

Kart Çınar Sk

Midilli Sk

Galata Kulesi Sk

49

70

Voyvoda Cad

Bilfur Sk

Mertebanı Sk

Tünel
(Karaköy)

Küçük Çeşme Sk

Karaköy

Evren Cad

Fish Market

29

Karaköy
Square

Haraçcı Alısk

Karaköy Cad

İlk Belediye Cad

Büyük Hendek Cad

Okçu Musa Cad

Laleli Çeşme Sk

Tütsülük Sk

Yanıkkapı Sk

Şimal Sk

Ali Baba Sk

Avni Sk

Lobut Sk

Evliya Çelebi Cad

Refik Saydam Cad

ŞİŞHANE

Yolcuzade İskender Cad

Şişhane Sk

Okçu Musa Cad

Fütühat Sk

Yüzbaşı Sabahattin
Evren Cad

Bakir Sk

Kürekçiler Cad

Fermeneciler Sk

Tersane Cad

Yelkenciler Sk

Tırhan Sk

Golden
Horn (Haliç)

recently renovated **Atatürk Cultural Centre**. In the middle of the square is an entrance to both the metro and the funicular tram running down to Kabataş.

Askeri Müze MUSEUM
(Military Museum; ☑0212-233 2720; Vali Konağı Caddesi, Harbiye; adult/student TL4/1; ⊙9am-5pm Wed-Sun) For a rousing experience, present yourself at this little-visited museum 1km north of Taksim.

The museum is spread over two very large floors. On the ground floor are displays of medieval weapons and armour, military uniforms, and glass cases holding battle standards, both Turkish and captured. There's also a huge diorama of the Conquest, complete with sound effects. The upper floor has displays on WWI and the War of Independence, including a Çannakale diorama.

The easiest way to get to the museum is to walk up Cumhuriyet Caddesi from Taksim Sq. This will take around 20 minutes. Alternatively, take any bus heading up Cumhuriyet Caddesi from Taksim Sq. Try to visit in the afternoon so that you can enjoy the concert given by the Mehter (the medieval Ottoman Military Band), which takes place between 3pm and 4pm most days.

BEŞIKTAŞ, ORTAKÖY & KURUÇEŞME

Dolmabahçe Palace PALACE
(Dolmabahçe Sarayı; ☑0212-236 9000; www.dolmabahce.gov.tr; Dolmabahçe Caddesi, Beşiktaş; adult/child TL20/1; ⊙9am-4pm Tue-Wed & Fri-Sun Mar-Sep, 9am-3pm Oct-Feb) These days it's fashionable for critics influenced by the less-is-more aesthetic of the Bauhaus masters to sneer at buildings such as Dolmabahçe Palace. Enthusiasts of Ottoman architecture also decry this final flourish of the imperial dynasty, finding that it shares more in common with the Paris Opera than Topkapı Palace. But whatever the critics may say, this 19th-century imperial residence is a clear crowd favourite.

Less is more was certainly *not* the philosophy of Sultan Abdül Mecit, who, deciding that it was time to give lie to talk of Ottoman military and financial decline, decided to move from Topkapı to a lavish new palace on the shores of the Bosphorus. For a site he chose the *dolma bahçe* (filled-in garden) where one of his predecessors, Sultan Ahmet I, had built an imperial pleasure kiosk surrounded by gardens. In 1843 Abdül Mecit commissioned architects Nikoğos and Garabed Balyan to construct an Ottoman-European palace that would impress everyone who set eyes on it. Construction was completed in 1856. Traditional Ottoman palace architecture was rejected in favour of a European-style building with neobaroque and neoclassical decoration. Eschewing pavilions, the building turns in on itself and all but ignores its splendid Bosphorus views.

The palace, which is set in well-tended gardens and entered through an ornate gate, is divided into two sections: the over-

---

CONTEMPLATE THE CUTTING EDGE

We reckon that the recent trend for İstanbul's family business dynasties to endow private art galleries is the best thing to hit the city since the tulip bulb arrived. Suddenly, İstanbul has a clutch of world-class contemporary art museums to add to its already impressive portfolio of major tourist attractions. No wonder it was named a European Capital of Culture in 2010.

The first cab off the rank was the **Proje4L/Elgiz Museum of Contemporary Art** (Elgiz Çağdaş Sanat Müzesi, İstanbul; ☑0212-290 2525; www.elgizmuseum.org; B Blok, Beybi Giz Plaza, Meydan Sokak, Maslak; ⊙10am-5pm Wed-Fri, 10am-4pm Sat), closely followed by **İstanbul Modern** (p69) in Tophane and the **Pera Museum** (p69) off İstiklal Caddesi. And let's not forget the privately endowed universities, which are joining the fray with style and loads of substance – the **Sakıp Sabancı Müzesi** (p81) on the Bosphorus and **Santralİstanbul** (p83) on the Golden Horn are the two most prominent, but there are others as well. Many have become venues for the **International İstanbul Biennial** (www.iksv.org/english/biennial), held between September and early November in odd-numbered years.

All of this is great news for the visitor, who can see world-class exhibitions in drop-dead-gorgeous surrounds complete with stylish gift shops and quality cafes. Some are even free – and you gotta love that.

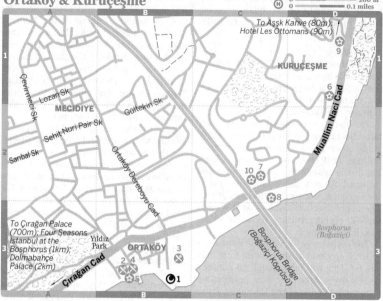

Ortaköy & Kuruçeşme

the-top *Selamlık* (ceremonial suites) and the slightly more restrained Harem-*Cariyeler* (Harem and concubines' quarters). Both are visited on a compulsory – and unfortunately rushed – guided tour.

At the end of your tour, make sure you visit the Crystal Palace, with its fairy-tale-like conservatory featuring etched-glass windows, crystal fountain and myriad chandeliers. There's even a crystal piano

and chair. It's next to the aviary on the street side of the palace.

The tourist entrance to the palace is near the ornate clock tower built by Sultan Abdül Hamit II from 1890 to 1894. There's an outdoor cafe near here with premium Bosphorus views and dirt-cheap prices (yes, really).

Ortaköy   NEIGHBOURHOOD
(Middle Village; Map p76) This charming waterside suburb embraces a jumble of Ottoman buildings renovated as stylish boutiques and eateries. On balmy nights the restaurants, bars and cafes on and around the teeny cobbled square by the water overflow with locals enjoying a drink or meal while indulging in some of the city's best people-watching.

Right on the water's edge, the decorative **Ortaköy Mosque** (Ortaköy Camii, Büyük Mecidiye Camii) is the work of Nikoğos Balyan, one of the architects of Dolmabahçe Palace. A strange mix of baroque and neoclassical influences, it was designed and built for Sultan Abdül Mecit III from 1853 to 1855. With the modern Bosphorus Bridge looming behind it, the mosque provides the classic photo opportunity for those wanting to illustrate İstanbul's 'old-meets-new' character.

Try to time your visit for Sunday, when the bustling street market fills the cobbled lanes. Do as the locals do and come for brunch, then pick through the market's beaded jewellery, hats and other trinkets before heading home to avoid the late-afternoon traffic crush.

To get here from Sultanahmet, catch the tram to Kabataş and then bus 22, 25E or 30D; from Taksim Sq, catch bus DT2, 40, 40T or 42T (get off at the Ortaköy or Kabataş Lisesi bus stop). Be warned that traffic along Çirağan Caddesi is almost always congested, so bus and taxi trips here can be excruciatingly slow.

ASIAN SHORE

Although most of İstanbul's noteworthy sights, shops, bars and eateries are on the European side of town, many locals prefer to live on the Asian (aka Anatolian) shore, citing cheaper rents and a better standard of living. For others, the best thing about living in or visiting this side of town is the scenic ferry ride between the continents.

ÜSKÜDAR

Üsküdar (*oo*-skoo-dar) was founded about two decades before Byzantium, and was originally called Chrysopolis. The Ottomans called it Scutari. Unwalled and therefore vulnerable, it became part of the Ottoman Empire at least 100 years before the Conquest.

Today Üsküdar is a bustling working-class suburb with a handful of important Ottoman mosques that attract visitors. If coming to Üsküdar from Sultanahmet, catch the ferry from Eminönü. This runs every 15 to 30 minutes (depending on the time of day) between 6.35am and 11pm. Dentur–Avrasya ferry services also operate between Beşiktaş (from beside the Deniz Müzesi) and Üsküdar. Ferries start at 6.25am and run every 20 to 30 minutes until 1am.

Mosques   MOSQUES

Judging that Scutari was the closest point in İstanbul to Mecca, many powerful Ottoman figures built mosques here to assist their passage to Paradise. Every year a big caravan set out from here, en route to Mecca and Medina for the Haj, further emphasising the suburb's reputation for piety.

As you leave Üsküdar dock, the main square, Demokrasi Meydanı (currently being redeveloped as part of the massive Marmaray transport project), is right in front of you. Its northeastern corner is dominated by the Mihrimah Sultan Mosque, some-

times referred to as the İskele (ferry dock) Camii. This mosque was designed by Sinan for Süleyman the Magnificent's daughter and built between 1547 and 1548.

South of the square is the Yeni Valide Mosque (Yeni Valide Camii, New Sultan's Mother Mosque). Featuring a wrought-iron 'birdcage' tomb in its overgrown garden, it was built by Sultan Ahmet III from 1708 to 1710 for his mother Gülnuş Emetullah. East of the square is the Ağa Mosque (Ağa Camii).

West of the square, overlooking the harbour, is the charming Şemsi Paşa Mosque (Şemsi Paşa Camii). Designed by Sinan and built in 1580 for Grand Vizier Şemsi Paşa, its modest size and decoration reflect the fact that its benefactor occupied the position of grand vizier for only a couple of months under Süleyman the Magnificent. Its *medrese* has been converted into a library and there's a popular *çay bahçesi* on its southern side.

The Atik Valide Mosque (Atik Valide Camii; Çinili Camii Sokak) is another of Sinan's works, and is considered by many experts to be among his best designs. It was built for Valide Sultan Nurbanu, wife of Selim II (The Sot) and mother of Murat III, in 1583. Nurbanu was captured by Turks on the Aegean island of Paros when she was 12 years old, and went on to be a successful player in the Ottoman court. Murat adored his mother and on her death commissioned Sinan to build this monument to her on Üsküdar's highest hill.

The nearby Çinili Mosque (Çinili Camii, Tiled Mosque; Çinili Camii Sokak) is unprepossessing from the outside, but has an interior made brilliant with İznik tiles, the bequest of Mahpeyker Kösem (1640), wife of Sultan Ahmet I and mother of sultans Murat IV and İbrahim (r 1640–48).

To find the Atik Valide and Çinili Mosques, walk up Hakimiyet-i Milliye Caddesi until you get to the traffic circle. Continue up Dr Fahri Atabey Caddesi for about 1km until you get to little Sarı Mehmet Sokak, on your left. From here you'll spot the minarets of Atik Valide Mosque. To get to the Çinili Mosque from the Atik Valide Mosque, walk east along Çinili Camii Sokak for about 300m, after which it turns north and runs uphill. The Çinili Mosque is about 200m further on. All up it's about a 25-minute walk to the Çinili Mosque from the main square.

KADIKÖY

If you've got a spare few hours, you may want to explore Kadıköy, the site of the city's

THE GREAT SINAN

Sultan Süleyman the Magnificent's reign (r 1520–66) is known as the golden age of the Ottoman Empire, but it wasn't only his codification of Ottoman law and his military prowess that earned him respect. Süleyman's penchant for embellishing İstanbul with architectural wonders had a lot to do with it – however, he couldn't have done this without Mimar Sinan, Turkey's best-known and greatest architect. Together they perfected the design of the classic Ottoman mosque.

Born in 1497, Sinan was a recruit to the *devşirme* (the annual intake of Christian youths into the Ottoman army), becoming a Muslim (as all such recruits did) and eventually taking up a post as a military engineer in the corps. Süleyman the Magnificent appointed him the chief of the imperial architects in 1538. He designed a total of 321 buildings, 85 of which are still standing in İstanbul.

Most Sinan-designed mosques have a large forecourt with a central *şadırvan* (ablutions fountain) and domed arcades on three sides. On the fourth side stands the mosque, with a two-storey porch. The main prayer hall is covered by a large central dome rising much higher than the two-storey facade, and surrounded by smaller domes and semidomes.

İstanbul's superb **Süleymaniye Mosque** is the grandest and most visited work of Sinan's, so if you only have time to visit one of Sinan's masterpieces, make it this one. The **Atik Valide Mosque** in Üsküdar is similar to the Süleymaniye in many ways, most notably in the extent of its outbuildings. The much smaller, tile-encrusted **Rüstem Paşa Mosque** and **Sokollu Mehmet Paşa Mosque** are both exquisite, well rewarding anyone who makes the effort to see them.

Sinan didn't only design and construct mosques. The **Çemberlitaş Hamamı** is also one of his works, giving you a perfect excuse to blend your architectural studies with a pampering session. He also designed the **Baths of Lady Hürrem** and the **Caferağa Medresesi**.

Sinan's works survive in other towns of the Ottoman heartland, particularly Edirne (p119), the one-time capital of the empire.

first colony (originally called Chalcedon). Although there's nothing to show of its historic beginnings and there are no headline sights, Kadıköy is worth visiting for its fabulous fresh produce market and the presence of one of İstanbul's best eateries, Çiya Sofrası. The market is south of the ferry dock, and Çiya is close to its centre, as is Baylan Pastanesi, a great spot for coffee and cake.

Kadıköy and the affluent suburbs stretching southeast to Bostancı are the Asian side's entertainment hubs. For alternative culture, head to **Kadife Sokak** to check out its independent cinema, grunge boutiques, tattoo studios and hugely popular bars. And to see the wealthy at play, cruise down **Bağdat Caddesi**, which is full of shops, restaurants and cafes.

To the north of Kadıköy is the neoclassical **Haydarpaşa Train Station**, resembling a German castle. In the early 20th century when Kaiser Wilhelm of Germany was trying to charm the sultan into economic and military cooperation, he presented the station as a small token of his respect. Today there's talk of transforming it and its surrounds into a high-rise recreation and trade precinct. Ferries travelling between Kadıköy and Karaköy usually make a quick stop here.

To get to Kadıköy from Sultanahmet, hop on the ferry from Eminönü, which runs every 15 to 20 minutes (depending on the time of day) between 7.30am and 8.40pm. The last ferry back to Eminönü is at 8.20pm.

From the ferry terminal at Karaköy (the Beyoğlu side of Galata Bridge) services run from 6.15am every 10 to 30 minutes (depending on the time of day) until 11.30pm. The last ferry back to Karaköy is at 11.30pm.

A ferry service also operates from Beşiktaş (catch it from beside the Deniz Müzesi), starting at 7.15am and running every half-hour until 9.15pm. The last ferry back to Beşiktaş is at 8.45pm.

🏃 Activities

Ferry Cruises

During the 18th and 19th centuries the Bosphorus and Golden Horn were alive with *caïques* (long, thin rowboats), their oars dipping rhythmically into the currents as they carried the sultan and his courtiers from palace to pavilion, and from Europe to Asia. The *caïques* are long gone, but in their place are the sleek speedboats of the moneyed elite and the much-loved public ferries used by the rest of İstanbul's population. A trip on one of these ferries – whether it be the short return trip to Kadıköy or Üsküdar, on which you cross from Europe to Asia and back again, or one of the longer trips detailed below – is an essential activity while you are in İstanbul.

Bosphorus Ferry CRUISE
Divan Yolu and İstiklal Caddesi are always awash with people, but neither is the major thoroughfare in İstanbul. That honour goes to the mighty Bosphorus strait, which runs from the Sea of Marmara (Marmara Denizi) to the Black Sea (Karadeniz), located 32km north of the city centre. In modern Turkish, the strait is known as the Boğaziçi or İstanbul Boğazı (from *boğaz*, meaning throat or strait). On one side is Asia; on the other, Europe.

Departure Point: Eminönü
Hop onto a boat on the Eminönü quay. You can choose between İstanbul Deniz Otobüsleri's (İDO's) Public Excursion Ferry, which carries passengers on a return trip along the length of the Bosphorus, or you can opt for a shorter trip to Rumeli Hisarı and back on a private excursion boat. See Getting There & Away (p82) for details.

It's always a good idea to arrive 30 to 45 minutes or so before the scheduled departure time so as to be sure of getting a seat with a view. The Asian shore is to the right side of the ferries as they make their way up the Bosphorus, Europe is to the left.

As you start your trip, you'll see the small island and tower of Kız Kulesı on the Asian side near Üsküdar. This squat tower is one of the city's most distinctive landmarks. In ancient times, a predecessor of the current 18th-century structure functioned as a tollbooth and defence point; the Bosphorus could be closed off by means of a chain stretching from here to Seraglio Point. More recently, the tower featured in the 1999 Bond film *The World is Not Enough*.

On the European shore, you'll pass grandiose Dolmabahçe Palace. In his travelogue *Constantinople in 1890,* French writer Pierre Loti described this and the neighbouring Çırağan palace as 'a line of palaces white as snow, placed at the edge of the sea on marble docks', a description that remains as accurate as it is evocative.

Beşiktaş to Kanlıca
After a brief stop at Beşiktaş the ferry sails past Çırağan Palace (now the Çırağan Palace Hotel Kempınski) and the Ortaköy Mosque. Towering over the mosque's minarets is the huge Bosphorus Bridge, opened in 1973 on the 50th anniversary of the founding of the Turkish Republic. Under the bridge on the European shore is the green-and-cream-coloured Balyan Usta Yalı, built in the 1860s by architect Sarkis Balyan. Balyan built his *yalı* (wooden summer mansion built next to the water) here so as to enjoy an unimpeded view of the imposing Beylerbeyi Palace (Beylerbeyi Sarayı; ☑0216-321 9320; Abdullah Ağa Caddesi, Beylerbeyi; adult/student TL10/1; ☺9.30am-4pm Tue, Wed & Fri-Sun Mar-Sep, to 3pm Oct-Feb), which he designed for Sultan Abdül Aziz on the opposite shore. Look for its two whimsical marble bathing pavilions on the shore, one of which was for men, the other for the women of the Harem. The ferry doesn't stop here, but you can visit another time by catching bus 15 from Üsküdar and getting off at the Çayırbaşı stop.

Past the suburb of Çengelköy on the Asian side is the imposing Kuleli Military School, built in 1860 and immortalised in Irfan Orga's wonderful memoir *Portrait of a Turkish Family*. Look for its two 'witchhat' towers.

Almost opposite Kuleli on the European shore is Arnavutköy, a suburb boasting a number of well-preserved *yalıs*. One of İstanbul's most famous *köfte* (meatball) restaurants, Köfteci̇ Ali Baba

---

HAVE YOUR SAY

Found a fantastic restaurant that you're longing to share with the world? Disagree with our recommendations? Or just want to talk about your most recent trip?

Whatever your reason, head to lonelyplanet.com, where you can post a review, ask or answer a question on the Thorntree forum, comment on a blog, or share your photos and tips on Groups. Or you can simply spend time chatting with like-minded travellers. So go on, have your say.

İSTANBUL ACTIVITIES

(http://koftecialibaba.net; Bebek-Arnavutköy Caddesi 69; köfte TL6, beans TL4; ⊙10am-11pm), is located on the main square near the ferry dock. On the hill above Arnavutköy are buildings formerly occupied by the **American College for Girls**. Its most famous alumna was Halide Edib Adıvar, who wrote about the school in her 1926 autobiography *Memoir of Halide Edib*.

Arnavutköy runs straight into the glamorous suburb of **Bebek**, famous for chic cafes such as **Mangerie** (www.mangerie bebek.com; 3rd fl, Cevdetpaşa Caddesi 69; salads TL25-34, burgers TL33-35, noodles TL30-32), **Lucca** (www.luccastyle.com; Cevdetpaşa Caddesi 51b; pastas TL20, burgers TL25) and **Divan Brasserie** (Cevdetpaşa Caddesi 28b; salads TL17-25, sandwiches TL19-29, pastas TL20-29). It also has a branch of **Starbucks** (30 Cevdetpaşa Caddesi) with a fabulous terrace overlooking the water. As the ferry passes, look out for the mansard roof of the **Egyptian consulate**, an art nouveau minipalace built by the last khedive of Egypt, Abbas Hilmi II. It's just south of the waterside park. In the park itself is the Ottoman Revivalist–style Bebek Mosque.

Opposite Bebek is **Kandilli**, the 'Place of Lamps', named after the lamps that were lit here to warn ships of the particularly treacherous currents at the headland. Among the many *yalıs* here is the small **Kırmızı Yalı** (Red Yalı), constructed in 1790; a little further on is the long, white **Kıbrıslı Mustafa Emin Paşa Yalı**.

Next to the Kıbrıslı Yalı are the Büyük Göksu Deresi (Great Heavenly Stream) and Küçük Göksu Deresi (Small Heavenly Stream), two brooks that descend from the Asian hills into the Bosphorus. Between them is a grassy, shady delta, which the Ottoman elite thought just perfect for picnics. Foreign residents, who referred to the place as 'the sweet waters of Asia', would often join them. If the weather was good, the sultan joined the party – and did so in style. Sultan Abdül Mecit's version of a picnic blanket was the rococo **Küçüksu Kasrı** (☎0216-332 3303; Küçüksu Caddesi; admission adult/student TL4/1; ⊙9.30am-4pm Tue, Wed & Fri-Sun Mar-Sep, to 3pm Oct-Feb), constructed from 1856 to 1857. You'll see its ornate cast-iron fence, boat dock and wedding-cake exterior from the ferry. To visit, get off the ferry at Kanlıca and catch bus 11H or 15F.

On the European side, just before the **Fatih Bridge** (Fatih Köprüsü), the majestic structure of **Rumeli Hisarı** (Fortress of

SEEING THE DERVISHES WHIRL

The brotherhood called the Mevlevi follows a mystical form of Islam that uses allegorical language to describe a love for God, and is famous for its meditative *sema*, a whirling ceremony that represents a union with God.

The Mevlevi are guided by the teachings of Celaleddin Rumi, known as Mevlâna (Our Guide). Born in 1207, Rumi was a brilliant student of Islamic theology who became profoundly influenced by Şemsi Tebrizi, a Sufi (Islamic mystic) disciple.

The Mevlevi order was outlawed by Atatürk in the 1920s as part of his reforms, but in the early 1950s the Turkish government recognised the tourist potential for 'whirling' and the Konya Mevlâna Festival was born. The whirling dervish 'performance' is a growing attraction for visitors to Turkey, but the Mevlevi order is still technically outlawed here.

You can see the dervishes whirl in a number of spots around İstanbul but, frankly, most of them are little more than tourist shows. The best option is usually to go to the **Galata Mevlevihanesi** (Map p72; ☎0212-245 4141; Galipdede Caddesi 15, Tünel), where *semas* have been held for centuries (in recent years mainly for the benefit of tourists).

When this book went to print the Mevlevihanesi was closed for restoration and so was not hosting *semas* – check the boards outside for updates. There is also a one-hour tourist performance at the **Hodjapaşa Art & Culture Center** (Map p46; ☎0212-511 4626; info@hodjapasha.com; tickets adult/under 15yr TL40/25; ⊙7.30pm Wed & Fri-Mon) in a converted 550-year-old hamam near Eminönü.

Remember that the ceremony is meant to be a religious one – by whirling, the adherents believe that they are attaining a higher union with God – so don't talk, leave your seat or take flash photographs while the dervishes are spinning.

Europe; ☑0212-263 5305; Yahya Kemal Caddesi 42; admission TL3; ⊘9am-4.30pm Thu-Tue) looms over a pretty village of the same name. Mehmet the Conqueror had Rumeli Hisarı built in a mere four months during 1452 in preparation for his planned siege of Constantinople. For its location he chose the narrowest point of the Bosphorus, opposite **Anadolu Hisarı** (Fortress of Asia), which had been built by Sultan Beyazıt I in 1391. In doing so, he was able to control all traffic on the strait, thereby cutting off the city from resupply by sea. Just next to the fortress is a clutch of cafes and restaurants, the most popular of which is **Sade Kahve** (☑212-358 2324; www.sadekahve.com; Yahya Kemal Caddesi 36; breakfast plates TL15; ⊘8am-10pm), a favourite weekend brunch spot for İstanbullus. To get to Rumeli Hisarı, get off the ferry at Yeniköy or Sarıyer (further on) and catch bus 25E back towards town. This bus stops at Emirgan as well as at Rumeli Hisarı before terminating at Kabataş.

Almost directly under the Fatih Bridge on the Asian side is the **Köprülü Amcazade Hüseyin Paşa Yalı**. Built right on the water in 1698, it's the oldest *yalı* on the Bosphorus and was undergoing a long-overdue renovation when this book was being researched. Directly under the bridge on the European side is the huge **Palace of İmer Faruk Efendi**, built in the late 19th century and once home to the grandson of Sultan Abdül Aziz, and to his wife Sabiha Sultan, daughter of Mehmet VI. When the sultanate was abolished in 1922, Mehmet walked from this palace onto a British warship, never to return to Turkey.

Kanlıca to Yeniköy

Past the bridge, still on the Asian side, is the charming suburb of **Kanlıca**, famous for its rich and delicious yoghurt, which can be sampled at the two cafes in front of the ferry stop or on the boat itself. This is the ferry's third stop, and if you so choose, you can stop and explore before reboarding the boat on its return trip. From here you can also catch a ferry across to Emirgan or Bebek on the European side and return to town by bus.

High on a promontory above Kanlıca is **Hıdiv Kasrı** (Khedive's Villa; ☑0216-413 9644; www.beltur.com.tr; Çubuklu Yolu 32, Kanlıca; admission free; ⊘9am-10pm), an art nouveau villa built by the last khedive of Egypt as a summer residence. Restored after decades of neglect, it now functions as a **restaurant**

(mains TL10-20.50) and **garden cafe** (tosts TL4-4.50, cake TL6). The villa is an architectural gem, and the extensive garden is superb, particularly during the International İstanbul Tulip Festival in April. To get here from the ferry stop, turn left into Halide Edip Adivar Caddesi and then turn right into the second street (Kafadar Sokak). Turn left into Haci Muhittin Sokağı and walk up the hill until you come to a fork in the road. Take the left fork and follow the 'Hadiv Kasrí' signs to the villa's car park and garden.

Opposite Kanlıca on the European shore is the wealthy suburb of **Emirgan**. It's well worth visiting for the impressive **Sakıp Sabancı Müzesi** (Sakıp Sabancı Museum; ☑0212-277 2200; http://muze.sabanciuniv.edu; Sakıp Sabancı Caddesi 42; exhibition admission varies; ⊘10am-6pm Tue, Thu, Fri & Sun, to 10pm Wed & Sat), which hosts world-class travelling exhibitions. The museum is also home to one of the city's most glamorous eateries, **Müzedechanga** (☑0212-323 0901; www.changa-istanbul.com; mains TL22-40; ⊘10am-1am Tue-Sun), with an interior designed by the fashionable Autoban partnership and a terrace with sweeping Bosphorus views. If you're after a simpler snack, there's a branch of the popular chain eatery **Sütiş** (Sakıp Sabancı Caddesi 1; ⊘6am-1am) opposite the ferry dock. It has outdoor seating and a delicious all-day breakfast menu.

Yeniköy to Sarıyer

North of Emirgan is **Yeniköy**, on a point jutting out from the European shore. This is the ferry's next stop. First settled in classical times, Yeniköy later became a favourite summer resort, evidenced by **Sait Halim Paşa Yalı**, the lavish 19th-century Ottoman *yalı* of the one-time grand vizier. Look for its two small stone lions on the quay. On the opposite shore is the suburb of **Paşabahçe**, famous for its glassware factory.

Originally called Therapeia for its healthy climate, the little cove of **Tarabya** to the north of Yeniköy on the European shore has been a favourite summer watering place for İstanbul's well-to-do for centuries, although modern development has sullied some of its charm. For an account of Therapeia in its heyday, read Harold Nicholson's 1921 novel *Sweet Waters*.

North of the village are some of the old summer embassies of foreign powers. When the heat and fear of disease increased in the warm months, foreign ambassadors and their staff would retire to these palatial residences, complete with lush gardens. Such residences extended north to the village of Büyükdere, which is also notable for its churches and for the Sadberk Hanım Müzesi (☎0212-242 3813; www.sadberkhanim muzesi.org.tr; Piyasa Caddesi 27-29, Büyükdere; admission TL7; ☺10am-5pm Thu-Tue), named after the wife of the late Vehbi Koç, founder of Turkey's foremost commercial empire. There's an eclectic collection here, including beautiful İznik and Kütahya ceramics, Ottoman silk textiles, and Roman coins and jewellery. The museum is a 10-minute walk from the next ferry stop, at Sarıyer.

Sarıyer to Anadolu Kavağı

After stopping at Sarıyer, the ferry sails on to Rumeli Kavağı, known for its fish restaurants. After a short stop here it then crosses the strait to finish the journey at Anadolu Kavağı. Once a fishing village, the local economy here now relies on the tourism trade, and the main square is full of mediocre restaurants and their pushy touts. Perched above the village is the ruins of Anadolu Kavağı Kalesi (Yoros Kalesi), a medieval castle that originally had eight massive towers in its walls. First built by the Byzantines, it was restored and reinforced by the Genoese in 1350 and later by the Ottomans. To get here, it's a 25-minute walk up steep Caferbaba Sokağı. From the ruins there are great views of the Black Sea.

If you decide to travel back to town by bus rather than ferry, catch bus 15A to Beykoz or Kanlıca from the main square and then transfer to bus 15 to Üsküdar or E-2 to Taksim.

Getting There & Away

There are numerous ways to explore the Bosphorus. Most people take the Bosphorus Public Excursion Ferry (one way/return TL15/25), which leaves Eminönü at 10.30am year-round. There are usually extra services at noon and 1.30pm from mid-April to October. These ferries depart from the Boğaz İskelesi (Bosphorus Public Excursion Ferry Dock) at Eminönü and stop at Beşiktaş, Kanlıca, Yeniköy, Sarıyer, Rumeli Kavağı and Anadolu Kavağı. The journey takes 90 minutes each way; return services leave Anadolu Kavağı at 3pm (year-round) and at 4.15pm and 5pm (6pm on Saturday) from mid-April to October. From mid-June to early August, a sunset cruise (TL20) leaves Eminönü on Saturday evenings at 7.15pm and returns from Anadolu Kavağı at

10pm. Check www.ido.com.tr for timetable and fare updates, as these often change. Options for returning to town by bus or exploring by bus along the way were mentioned previously in the text.

Another option is to buy a ticket on a private excursion boat. Although these only take you as far as Anadolu Hisarı and back (without stopping), the fact that the boats are smaller means that you travel closer to the shoreline and so can see a lot more. The whole trip takes about 90 minutes and tickets cost TL10. Turyol (☎0212-512 1287; www. turyol.com) boats leave from the dock on the western side of Galata Bridge (next to where the fish sandwiches are sold) every hour from 11am to 6pm on weekdays and every 45 minutes or so from 11am to 7.15pm on weekends. Boats operated by other companies leave from near the Boğaz İskelesi.

Bus tickets cost TL1.50 per leg.

Golden Horn Ferry   CRUISE

Most visitors to İstanbul know about the Bosphorus cruise, but not too many have heard about the Haliç (Golden Horn) trip. Until recently, this stretch of water to the north of Galata Bridge was heavily polluted and its suburbs offered little to tempt the traveller. All that's changing these days, though. The waters have been cleaned up, beautification works are under way along the shores, and impressive museums and galleries are opening in the Haliç suburbs. Spending a day hopping on and off the ferry and exploring will give you an insight into a very different – and far less touristy – İstanbul.

Departure Point: Eminönü

These ferries start in Üsküdar on the Asian side, but take on most of their passengers at the Haliç İskelesi (Golden Horn Ferry Dock) on the far side of Galata Bridge at Eminönü. The iskele (jetty) is behind a car park next to the Storks jewellery store. The ferry then sails underneath the Atatürk Bridge and stops at Kasımpaşa on the opposite side of the Golden Horn. This area is where the Ottoman imperial naval yards were located, and some of the original building stock is still evident.

Fener

The next stop is on the opposite shore, at Fener. This area is the traditional home of the city's Greek population, and although few Greeks are resident these days, a number of important Greek Orthodox sites are located here. The prominent red-brick building on the hill is the Greek Lycée of the Fener (Megali School, Great School), the oldest house of learning in İstanbul. The school has been housed in Fener since before the Conquest – the present building dates from 1881.

Closer to the shore, to the left of the ferry stop and across Abdülezel Paşa Caddesi, is the Ecumenical Orthodox Patriarchate (Map p42; ☎0212-531 9670; www.ec-patr.org; Sadrazam Ali Paşa Caddesi, Fener; donation requested; ⊙9am-5pm). The compound is built around the historic Church of St George, which dates from 1730. Every Sunday morning, Greek Orthodox pilgrims come here for the Divine Liturgy.

To the right of the ferry stop, in the waterside park, is the attractive Gothic Revival Church of St Stephen of the Bulgars (Sveti Stefan Church; Mürsel Paşa Caddesi 85, Fener). This cast-iron church was constructed in Vienna, then shipped down the Danube and assembled here in 1871. Unfortunately, it's not normally open to visitors.

If you're hungry, Fener is home to the most famous işkembecisi (tripe soup venue) in the city: Tarihi Haliç İşkembecisi (☎0212-534 9414; www.haliciskembecisi.com; Abdülezel Paşa Caddesi 315, Fener; ⊙24hr). Locals swear by the hangover-fighting properties of işkembe and often make late-night pilgrimages here. It's on the main road opposite the ferry stop.

Fener to Sütlüce

The ferry passes Balat, on the western shore, and then passes between the derelict remains of the original Galata Bridge before stopping next at Hasköy on the opposite shore, home to the fascinating Rahmi M Koç Müzesi (Map p42; ☎0212-369 6600; www.rmk-museum.org.tr; Hasköy Caddesi 5, Hasköy; adult/student & child TL11/6; ⊙10am-5pm Tue-Fri, to 7pm Sat & Sun). Founded by the head of the Koç industrial group to exhibit artefacts from İstanbul's industrial past, this museum is as popular with children as it is with adults and is well worth a visit. It's directly to the left of the ferry stop.

The next stop is Ayvansaray on the opposite shore, from where you can walk to visit the Chora Church or the Church of Theotokos Pammakaristos. You'll see the remains of Theodosius II's massive land walls running up the hill to the right (north) of the ferry dock. The ferry then crosses under the Haliç Bridge to Sütlüce. Art-lovers should

consider getting off here and catching bus 36T, 47, 47Ç or 47E to Bilgi Üniversitesi, home to Santralİstanbul (☎0212-311 7809; www.santralistanbul.org; Kazım Karabekır Caddesi 2/6, Eyüp; adult/over 65yr & under 13yr/student TL7/5/3; ⊙10am-8pm Tue-Sun). Housed in a converted power station, it's one of the best contemporary art galleries in the city. Check the website for what's on. Also here is a branch of Starbucks, a köfte kiosk and the excellent Tamirane (☎0212-311 7309; www.tamirane.com; sandwiches TL12-19, pastas TL14-23; ⊙11am-midnight Mon-Thu, 11am-2am Fri, 10am-2am Sat, 11am-9pm Sun), a bar/cafe/club that's known for its delicious food, well-priced drinks and popular open-buffet Sunday brunch (TL36), when live jazz is performed.

If you're keen to make your way back to Taksim from here, the gallery provides a free shuttle bus leaving every 20 minutes (30 minutes on weekends) from midmorning to 10.30pm.

Eyüp

The ferry's last stop is across the water in Eyüp. This conservative suburb is built around the Eyüp Sultan Mosque & Tomb (Map p42; Eyüp Sultan Camii & Türbe; Camii Kebir Sokak, Eyüp; ⊙tombs 9.30am-4.30pm), one of the most important religious sites in Turkey. The tomb houses the remains of Ayoub al-Ansari (Eyüp Ensari in Turkish), a friend of the Prophet's who fell in battle outside the walls of Constantinople while carrying the banner of Islam during the Arab assault and siege of the city from 674 to 678. The mosque built next to his tomb was where the Ottoman princes came for their coronations – it was levelled by an earthquake in 1766 and the present mosque was built in its place. The mosque is a popular place for boys to visit on the day of their circumcision and is always busy on Fridays and on religious holidays. To get here, cross the road from the ferry stop and walk up İskele Caddesi, the main shopping street, until you reach the mosque.

After visiting the mosque and tomb, many visitors head north up the hill to enjoy a glass of tea and the wonderful views on offer at the Pierre Loti Cafe (☎0212-581 2696; Gümüşsuyu Balmumcu Sokak 1, Eyüp; ⊙8am-midnight), where the famous French novelist is said to have come for inspiration. To get here, walk out of the mosque's main gate and turn right. Walk around the complex (keeping it to your right) until you see a set of stairs and a steep cobbled path winding uphill through the Eyüp Sultan Mezarlığı (Cemetery of the Great Eyüp), a burial ground to many important Ottoman figures. Alternatively, a *teleferik* (cable car; TL1.50 each way from 8am to 11pm) travels from the waterfront to the top of the hill.

Getting There & Away

Haliç ferries leave Eminönü every hour from 7.45am (10.45am on Sundays) to 8pm (9pm on Sunday); the last ferry returns to Eminönü from Eyüp at 7.45pm (8.45pm on Sunday). The ferry trip takes 35 minutes and costs TL1.50 per leg. Check www.ido.com.tr for timetable and fare updates.

If you wish to return by bus rather than ferry, then 36E, 44B, 99 and 399B travel from outside the ferry stop at Eyüp via Balat and Fener to Eminönü. Buses 39 and 39B travel via Edirnekapı to Beyazıt, allowing you to stop and visit the Chora Church on your way back.

To return to Taksim from Hasköy or Sütlüce by bus, catch the 36T or 54HT. For Eminönü, catch bus 47, 47Ç or 47E.

Bus tickets cost TL1.50 per leg.

Hamams

A visit to a hamam is a quintessential Turkish experience. We've listed five here – three tourist hamams in historic buildings, one modern hamam that is known for its fantastic massages, and the city's best gay hamam. The tourist hamams are pricey and their massages generally are short and not particularly good, but you'll be in gorgeous historic buildings that offer separate squeaky-clean baths for males and females – weighing up these facts and deciding whether or not to go is up to the individual. For the best bath and massage (by a mile) go to the Ambassador Hotel Spa Center. For a total pampering experience, head to one of the luxe five-star hotel spas in the city – the Ritz Carlton, Hotel Les Ottomans and Four Seasons Istanbul at the Bosphorus all have excellent spas offering indulgent hamam treatments.

Cağaloğlu Hamamı   HAMAM
(Map p46; ☎0212-522 2424; www.cagaloglu hamami.com.tr; Yerebatan Caddesi 34; bath, scrub & massage TL78-98; ⊘men 8am-10pm, women to 8pm) Built in 1741, this is the city's most beautiful hamam. Its baths each have a large *camekan* (reception area) with private, lockable cubicles where it's possible to have a nap or a tea at the end of your bath.

There's a pleasant cafe as well as a shop selling quality olive-oil soap and other hamam accessories.

Çemberlitaş Hamamı   HAMAM
(Map p62; ☎0212-522 7974; www.cember litashamami.com.tr; Vezir Hanı Caddesi 8, Çemberlitaş; bath, scrub & soap massage TL55; ⊘6am-midnight) Designed by Sinan in 1584, this gorgeous hamam has a splendid original *camekan* in the men's section and a recently restored/rebuilt one in the women's section. As well as an array of bath treatments, there are facials and oil massages on offer. Tips are included in the prices and there's a discount for ISIC holders.

Gedikpaşa Hamamı   HAMAM
(Map p62; ☎0212-517 8956; www.gedikpasaham ami.com; Hamam Caddesi 65-67, Gedikpaşa; bath, scrub & soap massage TL50; ⊘men 6am-midnight, women to 11pm) Another Ottoman-era choice, the Gedikpaşa Hamamı has been operating since 1475. Its interior isn't as beautiful as those at Cağaloğlu and Çemberlitaş, but services are slightly cheaper and there's a small swimming pool.

Ambassador Hotel Spa Center   HAMAM
(Map p46; ☎0212-512 0002; www.hotelambas sador.com; Ticarethane Sokak 19, Sultanahmet; bath, scrub & soap massage TL75, bath, scrub & soap & oil massage TL98-118, remedial & aroma-therapy massage TL49-118; ⊘noon-11pm Mon-Fri, noon-midnight Sat & Sun) Located in a modern hotel just off Divan Yolu, this small spa might lack atmosphere, but its bath and massage packages are excellent and you get the pretty (but small) hamam all to yourself. The Turkish massage treatment gives you the same package that you get in the big hamams (bath, scrub and soap massage), but we recommend paying the extra and having the oil massage as well. You can also book the hamam for private use (TL40 per person per hour).

Yeşildirek Hamamı   HAMAM
(Map p72; ☎0212-297 7223; Tersane Caddesi 74, Azapkapı; bath with/without massage TL30/20; ⊘6am-9pm) Located at the base of the Atatürk Bridge, this is the city's best gay hamam (men only). It's spacious, well maintained and has all the traditional trappings. Be discreet.

⮞ Courses

Note that prices for courses are often set in euros or US dollars rather than Turkish lira.

Caferağa Medresesi HANDICRAFTS
(Map p46; ☑0212-528 0089; www.tkhv.org; Caferiye Sokak, Sultanahmet) This gorgeous building is the home of the Turkish Cultural Services Foundation, which runs courses for locals and travellers in techniques such as calligraphy, miniature painting, *ebru*, binding and glass painting. Courses are organised into 2½-hour sessions one day per week over three months, and occasionally there are sessions held over shorter periods; contact the foundation for prices and availability.

Cooking Alaturka COOKING
(☑0212-458 5919; www.cookingalaturka.com; Akbıyık Caddesi 72a, Cankurtaran; cooking classes per person TL130) Owner Eveline Zoutendijk established the first cooking school (see also Eating, p91) in İstanbul in 2002, and after moving to these purpose-designed premises in Sultanahmet in 2008 she now runs hands-on Turkish cooking classes that are highly regarded. The delicious results are enjoyed over a five-course lunch with drinks. Cash only.

İstanbul Culinary Institute
COOKING, WALKING TOURS
(Enstitü; Map p72; ☑212-251 2214; www.istanbul culinary.com; Meşrutiyet Caddesi 59, Tepebaşı) This bustling operation offers a range of cooking classes as well as two half-day walking tours, one focusing on street food (US$60) and the other visiting the Spice Bazaar and Beyoğlu Fish Market (US$70). If you need the tour to be conducted in English, specify this when booking.

İstanbul Food Workshop COOKING
(www.istanbulfoodworkshop.com; Yıldırım Caddesi 111, Fener) A three-hour Turkish cooking

class/market visit costs TL100 to TL145 per person, or you can take a six-hour Turkish and Ottoman cooking class plus a market visit (TL160 to TL235 per person).

Turkish Flavours COOKING
(Map p46; ☑532 218 0653; www.turkishfla vours.com; Apartment 3, Vali Konağı Caddesi 14, Nişantaşı) As well as running excellent foodie tours of the Spice Bazaar and Kadıköy markets, which include a huge lunch at award-winning Çiya Sofrası (€125 per person), Selin Rozanes conducts small-group cooking classes in her elegant Nişantaşı home (€80 per person). The results of your labours are enjoyed over a four-course lunch with drinks. If requested, the course can focus on a kosher Sephardic menu.

Tours

Note that most tour companies in İstanbul set their charges in euros rather than in Turkish lira.

İstanbul Vision City Sightseeing Bus
BUS TOUR
(Map p46; ☑0212-234 7777; www.plantours. com; one-day ticket adult/student & 6-12yr/under 6yr €20/15/free) This is a hop-on-hop-off double-decker bus service with multi-language recorded commentary. Ticket booths are opposite Aya Sofya and in Taksim Sq. The full circuit takes 90 minutes, or you can get on and off the bus at six stops around town (note that buses only run four times per day from November to March and nine times per day from April to October). Expect traffic congestion on the Beyoğlu section.

İSTANBUL FOR CHILDREN

Children of all ages will enjoy the gadget-filled **Rahmi M Koç Müzesi** (p83) in Hasköy. The spooky **Basilica Cistern** (p53), with its upside-down heads on columns, is also usually a hit. Older children will enjoy the ferry trip down the Bosphorus, particularly if it's combined with a visit to the fortress of **Rumeli Hisarı** (p85) – but beware of the steep stairs here, which have no barriers. On **Büyükada** and **Heybeliada** (p115), two of the Princes' Islands, you can hire bikes or circle the island in a *fayton* (horse-drawn carriage), which is lots of fun.

If you're staying in Sultanahmet, there's a good playground in Kadırga Park, near Little Aya Sofya. If you're staying in Beyoğlu, there's one right at the water's edge, next to the Fındıklı tram stop – very scenic, but be sure to watch your toddlers carefully!

If you need to resort to bribery to ensure good behaviour, there's a toyshop area in Eminönü. The biggest and best shop here is **Ekincioğlu Toys & Gifts** (Map p62; ☑0212-522 6220; Kalçın Sokak 5). And there's a small shop in Beyoğlu: **İyigün Oyüncak** (Map p72; ☑0212-243 8910; İstiklal Caddesi 415).

İstanbul Walks   WALKING & CULTURAL TOURS
(Map p72; ☎0212-292 2874; 5th fl, İstiklal Caddesi 53, Beyoğlu; www.istanbulwalks.net; walking tours adult/student & over 65yr/under 12yr €20/16/free) Specialising in cultural tourism, this small company offers a large range of guided walking tours conducted by knowledgeable English-speaking guides. Tours concentrate on the city's various neighbourhoods, but there are also tours to major monuments including Aya Sofya, Topkapı Palace and the İstanbul Archaeology Museums. Of note are its excellent tour of the Grand Bazaar (€20) and the 'Dining Out in a Turkish Way' evening (€60), in which participants are taken to a traditional teahouse, an *ocakbaşı* (grill house), an *işkembecisi*, a *meyhane* and a nargileh cafe.

Urban Adventures   WALKING & CULTURAL TOURS
(Map p46; ☎0212-512 7144; www.urbanadventures.com; 1st fl, Ticarethane Sokak 11, Sultanahmet; all tours €25) Run by the reputable tour company Intrepid, this program of city tours includes a four-hour walk around Sultanahmet and the Bazaar District; another around İstiklal Caddesi in Beyoğlu; and an evening spent enjoying dinner with a local family in their home plus visiting a teahouse for tea, a nargileh and a game of backgammon.

★★ Festivals & Events

During the warmer months İstanbul is buzzing with arts and music events, giving the visitor plenty of options when it comes to entertainment. Most of the big-name arts festivals are organised by the İstanbul Foundation for Culture & Arts (☎0212-334 0700; www.iksv.org/english; Sadi Konuralp Caddesi 5, Şişhane). Tickets to most events are available from Biletix (www.biletix.com). Headline events:

April

International İstanbul Film Festival
                    FILM FESTIVAL
(www.iksv.org/film/english) Held in the first half of the month, the program includes retrospectives and recent releases from Turkey and abroad.

International İstanbul Tulip Festival
                    FLOWER FESTIVAL
The city's parks and gardens are planted with over nine million tulips that come into bloom in late March or early April each year.

June

Efes Pilsen One Love   MUSIC FESTIVAL
(www.pozitif-ist.com) This two-day music festival held at Santralİstanbul features international headline acts playing everything from punk to pop, electronica to disco.

International İstanbul Music Festival
                    MUSIC FESTIVAL
(www.iksv.org/muzik/english) The city's most famous arts festival presents a feast of classical music and opera.

July

International İstanbul Jazz Festival   MUSIC FESTIVAL
(www.iksv.org/caz/english) The number-one jazz festival in town is an intriguing hybrid of conventional jazz, electronica, world music and rock.

September

International İstanbul Biennial
                    ARTS FESTIVAL
(www.iksv.org/bienal/english) The city's major visual-arts shindig takes place between September and November in odd-numbered years.

Akbank Jazz Festival   MUSIC FESTIVAL
(www.akbanksanat.com) This boutique event in September and October features an eclectic lineup of local and international artists.

November

Efes Pilsen Blues Festival   MUSIC FESTIVAL
(www.pozitif-ist.com) This long-running event tours nationally and stops for a two-day program in İstanbul.

🛏 Sleeping

Every accommodation style is available in İstanbul. You can live like a sultan in a world-class luxury hotel, doss in a friendly hostel dorm, or relax in a well-priced boutique establishment.

Hotels reviewed here have rooms with private bathroom and include breakfast in the room price. Exceptions are noted in the reviews. All prices given are for high season and include the KDV (*katma değer vergisi;* value-added tax). During low season (October to April, but not around Christmas or Easter) you should be able to negotiate a discount of at least 20% on the price. Before you confirm any booking, ask if the hotel will give you a discount for cash payment (usually 5% or 10%), whether a pick-up from the airport is included (it often is if you stay more than three nights) and whether there are discounts for extended stays. Book ahead from May to September and for the period in June when the Grand Prix is being held.

Note that all hotels in İstanbul set their prices in euros, and we have listed them as such here.

SULTANAHMET & AROUND

The Blue Mosque (Sultan Ahmet Camii) gives its name to the quarter surrounding it. This is the heart of Old İstanbul and is the city's premier sightseeing area, so the hotels here and in the adjoining neighbourhoods to the east (Cankurtaran), south (Küçük Aya Sofya) and northwest (Binbirdirek, Çemberlitaş, Alemdar and Cağaloğlu) are supremely convenient. The area's only drawbacks are the number of carpet touts and the lack of decent bars and restaurants. Note, too, that some of the hotels in Cankurtaran can be noisy – late at night the culprits are the hostels and bars on Akbıyık Caddesi, which play loud music; early in the morning your sleep may be disturbed by the sound of the call to prayer issuing from the Akbıyık Camii behind Adliye Sokak.

TOP **Marmara Guesthouse** PENSION €€
CHOICE (Map p50; ☎0212-638 3638; www.marmaraguesthouse.com; Terbıyık Sokak 15, Cankurtaran; s €35-55, d €45-60; ❄ @) There are plenty of family-run pensions in Sultanahmet, but few can claim the Marmara's levels of cleanliness and comfort. Charming manager Elif Aytekin and her family live on site and go out of their way to make guests feel welcome. There's a vine-covered terrace with sea views, a light-filled breakfast room and a book exchange. Rooms have comfortable beds with feather duvets, double-glazed windows and safe boxes; some even have sea views. A gem.

Hotel Empress Zoe BOUTIQUE HOTEL €€€
(Map p50; ☎0212-518 2504; www.emzoe.com; Adliye Sokak 10, Cankurtaran; s €80, d €120, ste €140-245; ❄) Named after the feisty Byzantine empress whose portrait adorns the gallery at Aya Sofya, this fabulous place is owned and managed by American Ann Nevans and her sister Cristina, who really know their stuff when it comes to running a boutique hotel. All rooms and suites are individually and charmingly decorated and there's a gorgeous flower-filled garden where breakfast is served. The rooftop

lounge-terrace is a perfect spot for a sunset drink.

Hotel İbrahim Paşa BOUTIQUE HOTEL €€€
(Map p46; ☎0212-518 0394; www.ibrahimpasha.com; Terzihane Sokak 5, Binbirdirek; standard r €99-175, deluxe r €129-235; ❄ @) We have no doubt that İbrahim Paşa would have approved of this exemplary boutique hotel that borrows his name. Successfully combining Ottoman style with contemporary decor, it offers comfortable rooms, high levels of service, gorgeous ground-floor common areas and a terrace bar with views of the Blue Mosque.

Osman Han Hotel HOTEL €€
(Map p50; ☎0212-458 7702; www.osmanhanhotel.com; Çetinkaya Sokak 1, Cankurtaran; s €45-75, d €50-110; ❄ @) With only seven rooms and an extremely pleasing decor, the Osman Han can almost claim boutique status – its low prices and lack of a bar are the only barriers. Amenity levels are high – rooms have minibar, tea/coffee facilities, satellite TV and rain-shower/antistress showerheads in the bathroom. The pretty breakfast room and terrace have views of the Sea of Marmara and the minarets of the Blue Mosque.

Sarı Konak Oteli BOUTIQUE HOTEL €€€
(Map p50; ☎0212-638 6258; www.istanbulhotelsarikonak.com; Mimar Mehmet Ağa Caddesi 42-46, Cankurtaran; r €69-139, ste €129-249; ❄ @) The Sarı Konak is a truly classy joint. Its spacious deluxe rooms are beautifully decorated with soothing colour schemes, top-notch linens and attractive prints, embroideries and etchings on the walls; the standard rooms are considerably smaller, but are just as attractive; and the suites are total knockouts – perfect for families. Guests enjoy relaxing on the roof terrace with its Sea of Marmara and Blue Mosque views, but are equally partial to hanging out in the downstairs lounge and courtyard.

Hanedan Hotel HOTEL €€
(Map p50; ☎0212-516 4869; www.hanedanhotel.com; Adliye Sokak 3, Cankurtaran; s €30-40, d €40-60; ❄ @) Pale lemon walls and polished wooden floors give the Hanedan's rooms a light and elegant feel, as do the white marble bathrooms and firm beds covered with crisp white linen. A pleasant roof terrace overlooks the sea and Aya Sofya. Those travelling with children will be thrilled with the spacious and well-priced family rooms (€70 to €90), one of which has a sea view.

Hotel Alp Guesthouse HOTEL €€

(Map p50; ☑0212-517 7067; www.alpguesthouse. com; Adliye Sokak 4, Cankurtaran; s €35-55, d €55-70; ❄) The Alp lives up to its location in Sultanahmet's premier small-hotel enclave, offering a range of attractive and well-equipped rooms at remarkably reasonable prices. Rooms have four-poster beds with white linen; wooden floorboards scattered with rugs; and extras such as satellite TV. The best rooms are at the front of the building. The roof terrace is lovely, with great sea views and comfortable indoor and outdoor set-ups. There's wi-fi but no internet station.

Hotel Peninsula HOTEL €

(Map p50; ☑0212-458 6850; www.hotelpeninsula.com; Adliye Sokak 6, Cankurtaran; s €30-40, d €30-55; ❄) The hallmarks here are friendly staff, comfortable rooms and bargain prices – a winning combination. There's a terrace with sea views and comfortable hammocks, and a breakfast room with indoor and outdoor tables. The same owners operate the equally impressive but slightly more expensive and comfortable **Hotel Grand Peninsula** (Map p50; ☑0212-458 7710; www.grandpeninsulahotel.com; Çetinkaya Sokak 3; s €35-50, d €45-80; ❄ @), a short walk away.

Hotel Şebnem HOTEL €€

(Map p50; ☑0212-517 6623; www.sebnemhotel.net; Adliye Sokak 1, Cankurtaran; s €50-70, d €65-100; ❄ @) Simplicity is the rule at the Şebnem, and it works a treat. Rooms have wooden floors, good bathrooms, satellite TVs and comfortable beds. Framed Ottoman prints provide a touch of class. The large terrace upstairs has views over the Sea of Marmara (as do the more expensive double rooms), and downstairs rooms face onto a pretty private courtyard garden. Breakfast is good here, too.

Metropolis Hostel HOSTEL €

(Map p50; ☑0212-518 1822; www.metropolishostel. com; Terbıyık Sokak 24, Cankurtaran; dm €14-17, d with/without bathroom €60/40; ❄ @) This friendly place is located in a quiet street far enough away from noisy Akbıyık Caddesi that a good night's sleep is the rule rather than the exception. There are only 52 beds in total (seven dorms and seven doubles); all rooms have air-conditioning and one of the dorms is for females only. Add to all of this clean shared bathrooms, lockers in all dorms and a rooftop terrace with sea views and you have the recipe for a really terrific hostel stay.

Cheers Hostel HOSTEL €

(Map p46; ☑0212-526 0200; www.cheershostel. com; Sultan Camii Sokak 21, Alemdar; dm €11-20, d with/without bathroom €60/40; @) Tucked into a quiet street near Aya Sofya, this recently opened hostel is generating great word of mouth. And no wonder – there's one shower and toilet for every five guests (all new and impeccably clean) and the dorms are bright and airy. The only downside is the lack of air-conditioning in the larger dorms: they get very hot in summer. There's an indoor bar and entertainment area on the top floor and a small terrace on the street.

Tan Hotel HOTEL €€€

(Map p46; ☑0212-520 9130; www.tanhotel.com; Dr Emin Paşa Sokak 20, Alemdar; s €79-109, d €79-129; ❄ @) This well-run hotel in an excellent location just off Divan Yolu is a showcase of understated modern style and high-level service. Rooms are generously sized and bathrooms are excellent (all have jacuzzis). There's even a terrace bar sporting excellent views of the Blue Mosque, Aya Sofya and the Sea of Marmara. The breakfast buffet is one of the best around.

Agora Life Hotel BOUTIQUE HOTEL €€€

(Map p46; ☑0212-526 1181; www.agoralifehotel. com; Kadınlar Hamamı Sokak, Cağaloğlu; s €69-129, d €79-209, ste €199-259; ❄ @) Opened in 2010, this charming hotel in a quiet cul-de-sac around the corner from the Cağaloğlu Hamamı isn't aiming for hip hotel credentials, instead focusing on service and quiet elegance as its signatures. There are plenty of amenities in the rooms, and the rooftop terrace has a simply extraordinary view. Opt for standard room 103, which has a balcony complete with Aya Sofya view, or one of the deluxe or suite rooms – the Santa Sophia suite is sensational.

Emine Sultan Hotel HOTEL €€€

(Map p46; ☑212-458 4666; www.eminesultan. com; Kapıağası Sokak 6, Cankurtaran; s €70-85, d €105-120; ❄ @) Solo female travellers and families will feel particularly at home at the Emine Sultan. Manager Özen Dalgın is as friendly as she is efficient, and the rest of the staff (mainly family members) follow her lead. Rooms have a pretty cream-and-pink decor; all come with satellite TV/DVD and squeaky-clean bathrooms. A delicious breakfast is served in an upstairs room overlooking the Sea of Marmara and the roof terrace overlooks the Blue Mosque.

Sirkeci Konak HOTEL €€€
(Map p46; ☑0212-528 4344; Taya Hatun Sokak 5, Sirkeci; r €150-340; ▓@▨) This terrific hotel overlooking Gülhane Park offers large and well-equipped rooms with extras such as tea- and coffee-making equipment, satellite TV, quality toiletries and luxe linen. There's also a wellness centre with pool, gym and hamam in the basement – a rarity on this side of town. Top marks go to the complimentary walking tours, afternoon teas and Anatolian cooking lessons.

Hotel Nomade BOUTIQUE HOTEL €€€
(Map p46; ☑0212-513 8172; www.hotelnomade. com; Ticarethane Sokak 15, Alemdar; s €85, d €100-120; ▓) Chic surrounds and reasonable pricing don't often go together, but the Nomade bucks the trend. Just a few steps off busy Divan Yolu, this hotel's 16 small rooms and three suites have great bathrooms, stylish bedlinen and satellite TV. With one of the best roof-terrace bars in town (smack-bang in front of Aya Sofya) and a decidedly designer vibe, this place is about as hip as Sultanahmet gets.

Ottoman Hotel Imperial HOTEL €€€
(Map p46; ☑0212-513 6150; www.ottomanhotel imperial.com; Caferiye Sokak 6, Sultanahmet; s €90-180, d €120-210; ▓@) This four-star choice is in a wonderful location just outside the Topkapı Palace walls. Rooms are decorated with Ottoman-style objets d'art and have high levels of service, comfort and amenity – opt for one with an Aya Sofya view or in the rear annexe. No roof terrace, but there's a lovely rear garden with restaurant and bar instead.

Sultan Hostel HOSTEL €€
(Map p50; ☑0212-516 9260; www.sultanhostel. com; Akbıyık Caddesi 21, Cankurtaran; dm €9-16, d without bathroom €42-48, d with bathroom €48-56; @) Always packed to the rafters with backpackers, the Sultan should only be considered if you're young, don't care too much about creature comforts and are ready to party. There's a clean shower and toilet for every eight guests and an array of dorms, the cheapest of which sleeps 26 and has air-conditioning. The next-door **Orient International Hostel** (Map p50; ☑0212-518 0789; www.orienthostel.com; Akbıyık Caddesi 13, Cankurtaran; dm €11-15, s without bathroom €25-30, d without bathroom €35-40, s with bathroom & air-con €50-55, d with bathroom & air-con €80-90; @) is similar, though its breakfast isn't as generous

and its large dorm is dark and musty (the rooftop bar here is better, though).

Also recommended:

Hotel Ararat HOTEL €€
(Map p50; ☑0212-516 0411; www.ararathotel. com; Torun Sokak 3, Cankurtaran; r €40-110; ▓@) The Ararat is tiny but its charming host Haydar Sarigul and cosy rooftop terrace-bar in the shadow of the Blue Mosque make it a popular choice.

Hotel Uyan İstanbul HOTEL €€
(Map p50; ☑0212-518 9255; www.uyanhotel. com; Utangaç Sokak 25, Cankurtaran; s €50-60, d standard/deluxe €75/130; ▓@) The Uyan offers comfortable and attractive rooms with a good range of amenities. The elegant decor nods towards the Ottoman style, but never goes over the top – everyone will feel comfortable here.

Four Seasons Hotel İstanbul
 LUXURY HOTEL €€€
(Map p50; ☑0212-638 8200; www.foursea sons.com; Tevkifhane Sokak 1, Sultanahmet; r €300-490; ▓@) Known for its service (extraordinary), history (deliciously disreputable), location (right in the heart of Old İstanbul) and rooms (wow).

Tulip Guesthouse HOSTEL €
(Map p50; ☑0212-517 6509; www.tulipguest house.com; Terbıyık Sokak 15, Cankurtaran; dm €10-12, s €35, d with/without bathroom €45/35; ▓@) This unassuming place doesn't have features such as a rooftop terrace, but it's clean and offers the cheapest dorm bed prices around. There's a small breakfast room with sea views.

Agora Guesthouse HOSTEL €€
(Map p50; ☑0212-458 5547; www.agoraguest house.com; Amiral Tafdil Sokak 6, Cankurtaran; dm €12-17, s €60, d €70-80; ▓@) Worth considering for its comfortable bunk beds (all with lockers underneath) and clean, modern bathrooms. Drawbacks: an inadequate number of showers and toilets and a lack of natural light in the basement dorms.

BEYOĞLU & AROUND

Most visitors to İstanbul stay in Sultanahmet, but Beyoğlu is becoming a popular alternative. Stay here to avoid the touts in the Old City, and because buzzing, bohemian Beyoğlu has the best wining, dining and shopping in the city. Unfortunately there isn't the range or quality of accommodation options here that you'll find in Sultanahmet –

the exception being an ever-increasing number of stylish apartment and suite hotels. These often command spectacular Bosphorus and Golden Horn views – something you sometimes pay for by having to climb six or seven floors of stairs.

Getting to/from the historical sights of Old İstanbul from Beyoğlu is easy: you can either walk across Galata Bridge (approximately 45 minutes), or catch the Taksim Sq–Kabataş funicular and tram.

Note that when this book was being researched, the Pera Palace Hotel (www.pera palace.com) was nearing the end of a long restoration that will see it once again claim the title as the city's premier historic hotel.

TOP CHOICE 5 Oda
BOUTIQUE HOTEL €€€

(Map p72; ☎0212-252 7501; www.5oda. com; Şahkulu Bostan Sokak 16, Galata; s €115-130, d €125-140; ❋@) The name means 'Five Rooms', and that's exactly what this seriously stylish suite hotel in bohemian Galata is offering. A great deal of thought has gone into the design here – each suite has an equipped kitchen unit, lounge area with satellite TV, custom-designed furniture, large bed with good reading lights, black-out curtains to ensure a good night's sleep, and windows that open to let in fresh air. The location is convenient as well as characterful, and the owners go out of their way to make guests feel at home.

Witt İstanbul Hotel
BOUTIQUE HOTEL €€€

(Map p72; ☎0212-293 1500; www.wittistanbul. com; Defterdar Yokuşu 26, Cihangir; ste €160-390; ❋@) Just up the hill from the Tophane tram stop in the trendy suburb of Cihangir, this stylish place has 17 suites with fully equipped marble kitchenettes, seating areas with flat-screen satellite TVs, CD/DVD players, king-sized beds and huge bathrooms. Some suites look over to the Old City and the penthouse suites have private terraces with a panoramic view of the Bosphorus. There's a lobby bar and 24-hour reception.

Anemon Galata
HISTORIC HOTEL €€€

(Map p72; ☎0212-293 2343; www.anemonhotels. com; cnr Galata Kulesi Sokak & Büyük Hendek Sokak, Galata; s €128-150, d €150-175; ❋@) Located on the attractive square that surrounds Galata Tower, this wooden building dates from 1842 but has been almost completely rebuilt inside. Individually decorated rooms are extremely elegant, featuring ornate painted ceilings, king-sized beds and

antique-style desks. Large bathrooms have baths and marble basins. Best of all is the restaurant, which boasts one of the best views in the city. Request a room with a view.

Ansen 130 Suites
BOUTIQUE HOTEL €€€

(Map p72; ☎0212-245 8808; www.ansensuites. com; Meşrutiyet Caddesi 70, Şişhane; r €119-189; ❋@) The Şişhane neighbourhood has become the most fashionable pocket of town in recent times, something that the Ansen's owners anticipated when they restored this handsome five-story historic building in 2003. The suites are large and exceptionally well set up, with work desk, satellite TV and lovely bathroom; some also have an equipped kitchenette and Golden Horn view. There's a popular Italian restaurant on the ground floor.

İstanbul Apartments
APARTMENT €€

(Map p72; ☎0212-249 5065; www.istanbulapt. com; Tel Sokak 27, Beyoğlu; d €70-80, tr €85-95, q €110-120; ❋@) Located in a quiet side street off İstiklal Caddesi, this well-run operation offers eight apartments sleeping between two and six people. Each has a small living room with equipped kitchenette, couch, dining table and satellite TV, as well as one or two bedrooms with comfortable beds and good-sized bathrooms. Antique rugs, objets d'art, paintings and textiles are used as decorations throughout the building. There's a washing machine and dryer for communal use.

Marmara Pera
HOTEL €€€

(Map p72; ☎0212-251 4646; www.themarmara hotels.com; Meşrutiyet Caddesi 1, Tepebaşı; standard r €79-129, superior r €119-169; ❋@⬛) This slick little sister of the landmark Marmara hotel in Taksim Sq opened in 2004 and has been a popular choice ever since. Rooms are smallish but well appointed and the location is excellent. Stand-out amenities include one of the best restaurants in the city (Mikla; see p95), a rooftop pool bar with spectacular views, and a 24-hour fitness centre. It's worth paying extra for a room on a higher floor with sea view. Breakfast isn't included in the room price.

World House Hostel
HOSTEL €€

(Map p72; ☎0212-293 5520; www.worldhouse istanbul.com; Galipdede Caddesi 117, Tünel; dm €10-14, d with bathroom €50; @) Many of İstanbul's hostels are impersonal hulks with junglelike atmospheres, but this place near Galata Tower is small, friendly and calm. Best of all is the fact that it's close to

Beyoğlu's restaurant, bar and club scene, but not *too* close – it's possible to grab a decent night's kip here. The four-, six-, eight- and 14-bed dorms are clean and light and there's a cheerful cafe on the ground floor.

Büyük Londra Oteli   HISTORIC HOTEL €€
(Map p72; ☑0212-245 0670; www.londrahotel. net; Meşrutiyet Caddesi 53, Tepebaşı; unrenovated s €35-60, unrenovated d €50-80, renovated s/d €75/85; ☀) The highlight of the 1892 Büyük Londra is its wonderfully preserved lounge, which has barely been touched since it hosted well-heeled passengers fresh off the *Orient Express*. We love the ruffled curtains dangling with tassels, the decorated mouldings, the deep maroon carpets and the bar. The gilded staircase, complete with mammoth Bohemian crystal chandelier, leads up to the rooms...and this, folks, is where our enthusiasm falters. Some of the rooms are musty and worn (very *Addams Family*). Book one that's been recently renovated – these have air-con and are comfortable.

Also recommended:

Eklektik Guest House   BOUTIQUE HOTEL €€€
(Map p72; ☑0212-243 7446; www.eklektikgalata. com; Kadrıbey Cıkmazi 4, Galata; r €95-125; ☀@) This gay-owned-and-managed place offers a great location, eight individually decorated rooms and friendly service.

**İstanbul Holiday
Apartments**   APARTMENT €€€
(☑0212-251 8530; www.istanbulholidayapart ments.com; apt per night €115-260, minimum stay 3 or 7 nights; ☀) These handsome apartments in locations including Galata, Taksim and Kabataş sleep between one and seven people and are perfect for city sojourns of three days or more.

Mısafir Suites   BOUTIQUE HOTEL €€€
(Map p72; ☑0212-249 8930; www.misafirsuites. com; Gazeteci Erol Dernek Sokak 1, Taksim; ste per night €135-200; ☀@) This suite hotel offers seven stylish rooms sleeping two or three people. All windows are double-glazed, meaning that, despite the close proximity of İstiklal Caddesi, getting a good night's sleep isn't a problem.

BEŞIKTAŞ, ORTAKÖY & KURUÇEŞME

TOP CHOICE **Four Seasons İstanbul at the Bosphorus**   LUXURY HOTEL €€€
(☑212-381 4000; www.fourseasons.com/bospho rus; Çırağan Caddesi 28, Beşiktaş; s €320-540, d €380-570, ste €600-18,000; P☀@☀) This

recently opened hotel incorporates an Ottoman men's guesthouse called the Atik Paşa Konak, which was built around the same time as Çırağan palace. The interiors and new wings were designed by fashionable İstanbullu architect Sinan Kafadar. It's difficult to overpraise this place – service is exemplary, rooms are wonderfully comfortable and the setting on the Bosphorus is truly magical. Add to this its excellent spa and fitness centre, restaurant, marble terrace (complete with bar/cafe) and huge outdoor pool overlooking the Bosphorus and you are left with a package that's almost impossible to improve upon.

✖ Eating

İstanbul is a food-lover's paradise. Teeming with affordable fast-food joints, cafes and restaurants, it leaves visitors spoiled for choice when it comes to choosing a venue. Unfortunately, Sultanahmet has the least impressive range of eating options in the city. Rather than eating here at night, we recommend crossing Galata Bridge and joining the locals in Beyoğlu and the Bosphorus suburbs. Absolutely nothing can beat the enjoyment of spending a night in a *meyhane* on Nevizade Sokak or in the Asmalımescit quarter (both in Beyoğlu), or dining at one of the swish restaurants on the Bosphorus.

If you are planning to take a ferry trip on the Golden Horn or upper reaches of the Bosphorus, we have listed dining recommendations in the Ferry Cruises (p78) section.

Note that if we've included a telephone number in the review, it means you should book ahead.

For a good local foodie website, check İstanbul Eats (http://istanbuleats.com).

SULTANAHMET & AROUND

Cooking Alaturka   ANATOLIAN €€€
(Map p50; ☑0212-458 5919; www.cookingala turka.com; Akbıyık Caddesi 72a, Cankurtaran; set lunch or dinner TL50; ☺lunch Mon-Sat & dinner Mon-Sat by reservation) This great little restaurant is run by Dutch-born foodie Eveline Zoutendijk, who both knows and loves Anatolian food. She serves a set four-course menu that changes daily according to what produce is in season and what's best at the local markets. Eveline says that she aims to create a little haven in the midst of carpet-selling frenzy and she has indeed done this. There's even a range of Turkish cooking

utensils and products for sale – great stuff! Don't get it confused with the touristy fish restaurant on the rooftop of the Hotel Ala-turka at the other end of the steet.

Ziya Şark Sofrası   ANATOLIAN €€
(Map p46; www.ziyasark.com.tr; Alemdar Caddesi 28, Alemdar; pides TL11-14, kebaps TL13.50-23.50)
A relatively new branch of a well-respected Aksaray eatery, Ziya is located on the busy road between Eminönü and Sultanahmet but doesn't seem to get the custom it deserves (locals eat here but tourists don't – or didn't before we published this review). The food here is fresh and well cooked, the decor is cheerful and the service is friendly. It's one of the best eating options in the area, albeit with an alcohol-free policy.

Paşazade   ANATOLIAN €€
(Map p46; ☑0212-513 3601; Cafariye Sokak, Hocapaşa; meze TL6-12, mains TL13-23) Advertising itself as an *Osmanlı mutfağı* (Ottoman kitchen), Paşazade has been attracting rave reviews from tourists staying in the hotels around Sirkeci – and we think they've had it to themselves for long enough. Well-priced Ottoman dishes are served in the attractive streetside restaurant or on the rooftop terrace, which has a great view. Portions are large, the food is delicious and service is attentive. Bravo.

Teras Restaurant   RESTAURANT €€€
(Map p46; ☑0212-638 1370; Hotel Armada, Ahırkapı Sokak, Cankurtaran; meze TL7-16, mains TL24-37)
The chef at this upmarket hotel restaurant came up with a clever idea when he devised his Turkish degustation menu (TL68). Three courses of 'İstanbul cuisine' feature and are complemented by an excellent wine list. You can also order from the à la carte menu – the fish is particularly good. Book a terrace table with a Blue Mosque view.

Balıkçı Sabahattin   SEAFOOD €€€
(Map p50; ☑0212-458 1824; www.balikcisabahattin.com; Seyit Hasan Koyu Sokak 1, Cankurtaran; mains TL25-60; ☺noon-midnight) This is the only restaurant in Sultanahmet that locals from other parts of town will visit, drawn by the reputation of Mr Sabahattin, the 'Fisherman' owner. The limited menu of meze and fish here is excellent, though service can be harried. You'll dine in a wooden Ottoman house or under a leafy canopy in the garden.

Çiğdem Pastanesi   CAFE €
(Map p46; Divan Yolu Caddesi 62a) Çiğdem Pastanesi has been serving locals since 1961

and it's still going strong. The *ay çöreği* (pastry with a walnut, sultana and spice filling) is the perfect accompaniment to a cappuccino, and the *su böreği* (lasagnelike layered pastry laced with white cheese and parsley) goes wonderfully well with a cup of tea or fresh juice.

Hafız Mustafa Şekerlemeleri   CAFE €
(Map p62; Hamidiye Caddesi 84-86, Eminönü; ☺7.30am-11pm) Choosing between the delicious baklava, tasty *börek* (filled pastry) or indulgent *meshur tekirdağ peynir helvası* (a cheese-based sweet prepared with sesame oil, cereals and honey or syrup) is the challenge that confronts customers at this popular place in Eminönü. You can enjoy your choice with a glass of tea in the upstairs cafe.

Also recommended:

Sefa Restaurant   LOKANTA €
(Map p46; Nuruosmaniye Caddesi 17, Cağaloğlu; mains TL6.50-16; ☺7am-5pm) Locals highly rate this place, found on the way to the Grand Bazaar. Try to arrive early for lunch because many of the dishes run out by 1.30pm.

Konyalı Lokantası   LOKANTA €€
(Map p46; Mimar Kemalettin Caddesi 5, Sirkeci; soups TL5-8, porsiyon TL8-17, kebaps TL12-17; ☺closed Sun) The bustle of the Eminönü docks is replicated inside this popular *lokanta* every lunchtime, when crowds of shoppers, workers and commuters pop in here to choose from the huge range of soups, *böreks,* kebaps and stews on offer.

Khorasani   OCAKBAŞI €€
(Map p46; www.khorasanirestaurant.com; Ticarethane Sokak 39-41, Alemdar; meze TL6-8, kebaps TL16-28) Here, the meat plays second fiddle to the surrounds, which are extremely attractive. The chef hails from Antakya, and the kebap style is that of southeastern Anatolia.

Yeşil Ev Courtyard Cafe   CAFE €€
(Map p50; www.yesilev.com.tr; Kabasakal Caddesi, Sultanahmet; sandwiches TL10-14, salads TL10-17, cheese platter TL20) The charming rear courtyard of this Ottoman hotel between the Blue Mosque and Aya Sofya is a perfect spot to enjoy a drink or light lunch in summer.

Karakol Restaurant   INTERNATIONAL €€€
(Map p46; ☑0212-514 9494; www.karakolrestaurant.com; First Court, Topkapı Palace; sandwiches TL19-22, salads TL20-26, mains

The cheapest way to enjoy fresh fish from the waters around İstanbul is to buy a *balık ekmek* (fish sandwich) from a boatman. Go to the Eminönü end of Galata Bridge (Map p62) and you'll see bobbing boats tied to the quay. In front of each boat, men tend to a cooker loaded with fish fillets. The quick-cooked fish is crammed into a quarter loaf of fresh bread and served with salad and a squeeze of lemon. It will set you back a mere TL4 or so.

Other simple fishy snacks are on offer at **Fürreyya Galata Balıkçısı** (Map p72; fish soup TL5, fish sandwich TL5), a cute hole-in-the-wall cafe near Galata Tower or at the ramshackle **Furran Balıkçısı** (Map p72), an open-air fish restaurant next to the Fish Market at Karaköy. Here you can order a serve of freshly caught fish (TL6 to TL14) and have the cooks grill it to perfection over coals. Look for the plastic furniture and bright red tablecloths.

TL20-35; ⊙10am-6pm year-round, to 10pm summer) The food here is average, but the location is wonderful and you can order a beer or a glass of wine. The menu features international and Turkish dishes. Book for dinner only.

Tarihi Sultanahmet Köftecisi Selim Usta KÖFTECI €€
(Map p46; Divan Yolu Caddesi 12, Alemdar; köfte, beans & salad TL16) Locals flock here to grab a quick snack of the signature *köfte* served with white beans, pickled chillies and salad.

Karadeniz Aile Pide & Kebap Sofrası PIDECI €
(Dr Emin Paşa Sokak 16; pides TL7-10; ⊙6am-11pm) This long-timer next to Tan Hotel serves a delicious *mercimek* (lentil) soup and is also a favourite for its pide (Turkish pizza).

BAZAAR DISTRICT

TOP CHOICE **Hatay Has Kral Sofrası**
ANATOLIAN €€
(☑0210-534 9707; www.hatayhaskralsofrasi.com; Ragıb Bey Sokak 25, Aksaray; pides TL10-12, kebaps TL18-20, stews TL13-18, tuzdas TL35-50) It may be a bit difficult to find, but this sensational *sofrası* ('table') serves the best southeastern Anatolian cuisine in the Old City and is well worth the trek from Sultanahmet or Beyoğlu. The mezes are as unusual as they are spicy, and the mains are total knockouts – if there are two or more of you try the *tuzda tavuk* or *tuzda kuzu* (chicken or lamb covered in a salt crust, slow-cooked in the oven and then theatrically cracked open at the table). The kebaps and desserts are just as good – don't leave without sampling the *paşa kebap* (minced lamb with pine nuts and cheese) and the cheesy *künefe* (layers of kadayıf cemented together with sweet cheese, doused in syrup and served hot). To get here, catch the tram to Aksaray, walk down Adnan Mendenes Caddesi past the Valide Sultan Mosque and continue following the disused tramline past a small divided park. When you reach a second small park, turn right and walk slightly uphill. Take the first street on the left and the restaurant is a short way down on the left-hand side of the road. No alcohol.

Hamdi Et Lokantası KEBAPÇI €€
(Hamdi Meat Restaurant; Map p62; ☑0212-528 8011; www.hamdirestorant.com.tr; Kalçın Sokak 17, Eminönü; meze TL4-12, kebaps TL15-22) An İstanbullu favourite since 1970, Hamdi's phenomenal views overlooking the Golden Horn and Galata are matched by great kebaps and a bustling atmosphere. Unfortunately, service levels have fallen in recent years. Book online as far ahead of your meal as possible and request a spot on the terrace.

Sur Ocakbaşı OCAKBAŞI €€
(http://surocakbasi.net; İtfaiye Caddesi 27, Zeyrek; kebaps TL12-22) Indulge in some top-notch people-watching while enjoying the grilled meats at this popular place in the shadow of the Aqueduct of Valens. The square here is always full of locals having a gossip or doing their daily shop, and tourists were a rare sight before Anthony Bourdain filmed a segment of *No Reservations* here and blew the place's cover. Try the mixed kebap plate, the *içli köfte* (deep-fried lamb and onion meatballs with a bulgur coating) and the *çiğ köfte* (meat pounded with spices and eaten raw).

Havuzlu Restaurant LOKANTA €€
(Map p66; Gani Çelebi Sokak 3, Grand Bazaar; porsiyon TL6-16, kebaps TL16-18; ⊙11.30am-5pm Mon-Sat) There are few more pleasant experiences than parking one's shopping bags and enjoying a meal at the Grand Bazaar's best eatery. A lovely space with a vaulted ceiling and ornate central light-fitting, Havuzlu serves up tasty and reliable *hazır yemek* (ready-made food) and freshly grilled kebaps to hungry hordes of tourists and shopkeepers. It also has a clean toilet, something quite rare in the bazaar.

Bab-ı Hayat ANATOLIAN €
(Map p62; www.babihayat.com; Mısır Çarşısı 47, Eminönü (Spice Bazaar); pides TL7-8, kebaps TL9-14; ⊙11am-7pm Mon-Sat) It took seven months for a team headed by one of the conservation architects from Topkapı Palace to restore and decorate this vaulted space over the eastern entrance to the Spice Bazaar. The result is an atmospheric setting in which to enjoy unadorned Anatolian dishes. Enter through the Serhadoğlu fast-food shop.

Zeyrekhane RESTAURANT €€
(Map p62; www.zeyrekhane.com; İbedethane Arkası Sokak 10, Zeyrek; sandwiches TL11-15, salads TL12-18, mains TL19.50-35; ⊙closed Mon) This restaurant in the restored former *medrese* of the Zeyrek Molla Mosque also has an outdoor garden and terrace with magnificent views of the Golden Horn and Süleymaniye Mosque. It serves everything from *croque monsieurs* and club sandwiches to *mantı* (Turkish ravioli). The fact that it sells alcohol makes it a great spot for a sunset drink, too.

Zinhan Kebap House at Storks KEBAPÇI €€
(Map p62; ☑0212-512 4275; www.zinhanrestaurant.com; Ragıpgümüşpala Caddesi 2-5, Eminönü; mezes TL5-6, pides TL10-13.50, kebaps TL15-23) Zinhan's regal position next to Galata Bridge is one of the best in the city. Its top-floor roof terrace offers sensational views, good mezes (try the *haydari*, a yoghurt dip made with roasted aubergine (eggplant) and garlic; and *kısır*, a salad of bulgur, parsley and tomato paste), adequate kebaps and extremely comfortable surrounds. Book ahead and request a table with a view.

Fes Cafe CAFE €€
(Map p62; Ali Baba Türbe Sokak, Nuruosmaniye; sandwiches TL12-15, salads TL15-18, pasta TL15-18; ⊙closed Sun) A chic cafe hidden in a charming street just outside the Grand Bazaar's Nuruosmaniye Gate, Fes is a wonderful place

to try Turkish coffee (served on a silver tray with a glass of water and piece of Turkish delight). It's also a good spot for a casual lunch.

Tarihi Süleymaniyeli Kuru Fasulyeci Erzıncanli Ali Baba FASULYECI €
(Map p62; www.kurufasulyeci.com; Prof Sıddık Sami Onar Caddesi 11, Süleymaniye; fasulye & pilav TL6) Join the crowds of hungry locals at this long-time institution in the former *kütüphanesi medrese* (theological-school library) of the Süleymaniye Mosque. It has been dishing up its spicy signature *fasulye* (Anatolian-style haricot beans cooked in a spicy tomato sauce) dish for more than 80 years. Try it with *ayran* (yoghurt drink). Next-door **Ali Baba Kanaat Lokantası** is almost a carbon copy.

Also recommended:

İmren Lokantası LOKANTA €
(Map p62; Kadırga Meydanı 143, Kadırga; porsiyon TL4-7, kebaps TL8-9.50) This tiny neighbourhood *lokanta* is well off the tourist trail but is worth the walk. It serves excellent, dirt-cheap dishes such as peppery lamb *guveç* (stew) or *musakka* (baked aubergine and mincemeat).

Burç Kebap OCAKBAŞI €€
(Map p66; off Yağulıcılar Caddesi, Grand Bazaar; kebaps TL7-18; ⊙8am-7pm Mon-Sat) The *üsta* (master chef) at this simple place presides over a charcoal grill where choice cuts of southeastern Turkey–style meats are cooked. You can claim a stool or ask for a *dürüm* (wrapped in bread) kebap to go.

WESTERN DISTRICTS
Asitane OTTOMAN €€€
(www.asitanerestaurant.com; Kariye Camii Sokak 6, Edirnekapı; starters TL12-18, mains TL26-42) This elegant restaurant next to the Chora Church serves the city's most authentic Ottoman cuisine (dating from 1539), such as baked melon stuffed with minced ham and beef, rice, herbs, almonds and pinenuts. The chefs here have tracked down recipes from the imperial kitchens of the Topkapı, Edirne and Dolmabahçe Palaces, which they prepare using original ingredients and cooking methods. Lunch here is as delicious as it is unique.

BEYOĞLU & AROUND
⎡TOP⎤ **Karaköy Güllüoğlu** BAKLAVACI €
CHOICE (Map p72; Rıhtım Caddesi, Katlı Otopark Altı, Karaköy; porsiyon TL2.75-5.50; ⊙8am-7pm Mon-Sat) The Güllü family opened its first

baklava shop in Karaköy in 1949, and it has been making customers deliriously happy and dentists obscenely rich ever since. Go to the register and pay for a glass of tea and *porsiyon* (portion) of baklava (*fıstıklı* is pistachio, *cevizli* is walnut and *sade* is plain). You then queue to receive a plate with two or three pieces, depending on the type you order. The *börek* (TL4 to TL4.50) here is also exceptionally fine.

Zübeyir Ocakbaşı
OCAKBAŞI €€

(Map p72; ☎212-293 3951; www.zubeyirocakbasi. com; Bekar Sokak 28; meze TL4-6, kebaps TL10-20) Every morning, the chefs at this popular *ocakbaşı* prepare the fresh, top-quality meats to be grilled over their handsome copper-hooded barbecues that night: spicy chicken wings and Adana kebaps, flavoursome ribs, pungent liver kebaps, and well-marinated lamb *şiş kebaps* (roasted meat on a skewer). Their offerings are known throughout the city, so booking a table is essential.

Karaköy Lokantası
LOKANTA/MEYHANE €€

(Map p72; ☎212-292 4455; Kemankeş Caddesi 37, Karaköy; meze TL6-10, porsiyon TL7-12, grills TL11-16; ⊙closed Sun) This family-run *lokanta* opposite the International Maritime Passenger Terminal has a gorgeous tiled interior that was designed by the wildly fashionable Autoban Design Partnership. The dishes are tasty and well priced, and service is friendly and efficient. It functions as a *lokanta* during the day, but at night morphs into a popular *meyhane*, with slightly higher prices and some streetside tables. If you're here for lunch, drop in to Karaköy Güllüoğlu for dessert and sample their deservedly famous baklava.

Antiochia
ANATOLIAN €€

(Map p72; ☎0212-292 1100; www.antiochiacon cept.com; Minare Sokak 21, Asmalımescit; meze TL6-9, mains TL12-19; ⊙closed Sun) Dishes from the southeastern city of Antakya (Hatay) are the speciality at this recently opened restaurant in fashionable Asmalımescit. Sit inside or in the quiet pedestrianised street to sample meze plates featuring salads dominated by wild thyme, pomegranate syrup, olives, walnuts, hot pepper and tangy home-made yoghurt. The choice of kebaps is equally unusual and delicious.

Mikla
MODERN TURKISH €€€

(Map p72; ☎0212-293 5656; www.miklarestau rant.com; Marmara Pera hotel, Meşrutiyet Caddesi 15, Tepebaşı; appetisers TL24-36, mains TL44-71; ⊙closed Sun) Local celebrity chef Mehmet Gürs is a master of perfectly executed Mediterranean cuisine, and the Turkish accents he employs make his food truly memorable. Extraordinary views and luxe surrounds complete the experience. In summer, request a table on the terrace.

İstanbul Modern Cafe
MODERN TURKISH €€€

(Map p72; ☎0212-249 9680; Meclis-i Mebusan Caddesi, Tophane; pizza TL18-27, pasta TL18-32, mains TL26-50; ⊙10am-midnight Mon-Sat, to 6pm Sun) An 'industrial arty' vibe and great views over the water to the Old City (when there is no moored cruise ship in the way) make the cafe at the İstanbul Modern Gallery a perfect choice for lunch. Pasta is home-made, pizzas are Italian style and the service is slick. You don't need to pay the gallery fee if you are only here for lunch – there's a side entrance. Book ahead to snaffle a table on the terrace.

9 Ece Aksoy
MEYHANE €€€

(Map p72; ☎212-245 7628; www.dokuzeceaksoy. com; Otelier Sokak 9, Tepebaşı; mains TL18-35, mixed meze plates TL18-36) The cool jazz on the soundtrack suits the warm-toned casual interior of this modern *meyhane*. The

---

KING OF KEBAPS

Turkey's signature dish is undoubtedly the kebap. Turks adore anything cooked on a skewer, and if asked where they would love to celebrate a special event, they will often nominate the Samatya branch of **Develi** (☎0212-529 0833; Gümüşyüzük Sokak 7, Samatya; mains TL12-25), a longstanding favourite nestled in the shadow of Theodosius' Great Wall. The succulent kebaps here come in many guises and often reflect the season – for instance, the *keme kebabi* (truffle kebap) is only served for a few weeks each year. Prices here are extremely reasonable for the quality of food that is on offer, and the service is exemplary. Catch a taxi (the trip should only cost TL12 or so from Sultanahmet) or the train from Sirkeci or Cankurtaran. It's close to Koca Mustafa Paşa station. Exit the train station and walk north uphill – Develi is ahead on a plaza filled with parked cars.

chef/host here is a true believer in the superiority of local and organic produce, and uses this to make her flavoursome dishes. Don't miss the mezes – they're sensational.

Canım Ciğerim İlhan Usta ANATOLIAN €€
(Map p72; ☎0212-252 6060; Minare Sokak 1, Asmalımescıt; 5 skewers TL11) The name means 'my soul, my liver', and this small place behind the Ali Hoca Türbesi specialises in a set meal of grilled liver served with herbs, *ezme* (spicy tomato sauce) and grilled vegetables. If you can't bring yourself to eat offal, fear not – you can substitute liver with lamb or chicken. No alcohol.

Sofyalı 9 MEYHANE €€
(Map p72; ☎0212-245 0362; Sofyalı Sokak 9, Asmalımescıt; mezes TL2.50-10, mains TL13-25; ☉closed Sun) Tables here are hot property on Friday and Saturday night, and no wonder. This great little place on the city's most happening street serves up good *meyhane* food and makes everyone feel welcome. Most guests stick to mezes rather than ordering mains – make your choice from the waiter's tray and don't feel obliged to accept any that are put down on the table beforehand.

Kahvedan CAFE-BAR €€
(Map p72; www.kahvedan.com; Akarsu Caddesi 50, Cihangir; sandwiches & wraps TL10-18, pastas TL10-18, mains TL12-30; ☉9am-2am Mon-Fri, 9am-4am Sat & Sun) This expat haven serves dishes such as bacon and eggs, French toast, *mee goreng* and falafel wraps. Owner Shellie Corman is a traveller at heart, and knows the importance of things such as free wi-fi, decent wine by the glass, keen prices and good music. There's a happy hour every Tuesday from 8pm to 11pm.

Medı Şark Sofrası KEBAPÇI €€
(Map p72; Küçük Parmak Kapı Sokak 46a; kebaps TL9-25) This excellent *kebapçı* off İstiklal Caddesi specialises in meat dishes from the southeastern region of Turkey, which are served with the house speciality of *babam ekmek* ('my father's bread'). It's known for its Adana and *beyti* kebaps, which are perfectly accompanied by a glass of *ayran* (no alcohol is served).

Hacı Abdullah LOKANTA €€€
(Map p72; www.haciabdullah.com.tr; Sakızağacı Caddesi 9a; meze TL10.50-23, mains TL16-42) This İstanbul institution (established in 1888) serves a good range of meze and *hazır yemek*. There's no alcohol, but the array of delicious desserts well and truly compensates.

Doğa Balık SEAFOOD €€€
(Map p72; ☎0212-243 3656; www.dogabalik.com; 7th fl, Villa Zurich Hotel, Akarsu Yokuşu Caddesi 36, Cihangir; meze TL12-24, mains TL26-60) There's something awfully fishy about this place – and the locals love it. On the top floor of a modest hotel in Cihangir, Doğa Balık serves fabulously fresh fish in a dining space with wonderful views across to the Old City.

Kafe Ara CAFE €€
(Map p72; Tosbağ Sokak 8a, Galatasaray; mains TL14-20) Named after its owner, legendary local photographer Ara Güler, whose works adorn the walls and who holds court here most days, this casual cafe is set in a converted garage but also has tables and chairs spilling out into a wide laneway opposite the Galatasaray Lycée. It serves an array of well-priced paninis, salads and pastas. No alcohol.

Fasulı Lokantası FASULYECI €€
(Map p72; www.fasuli.com.tr; İskele Caddesi 10-12, Tophane; beans & rice TL11.50) There are two types of *fasulye* (bean dishes) served in Turkey: Anatolian style Erzincan beans cooked in a spicy tomato sauce, and Black Sea–style beans cooked in a red gravy full of butter and meat. This light, airy *lokanta* next to the nargileh joints in Tophane serves its beans Black Sea style, and they are quite delicious.

Also recommended:

Zencefil VEGETARIAN €€
(Map p72; ☎0212-243 8234; Kurabiye Sokak 8, Taksim; mains TL7-13; ☉closed Sun) This popular vegetarian cafe is comfortable and quietly stylish. Try the daily and weekly specials, all of which come with home-baked bread and herb butter. Note that when this book was being researched there was talk of the restaurant moving to a nearby location.

Saray Muhallebicisi MUHALLEBICI €
(Map p72; ☎0212-292 3434; İstiklal Caddesi 173, Beyoğlu) This *muhallebici* (milk-pudding shop) is owned by İstanbul's mayor, no less. It's been dishing up its range of over 30 puddings since 1935.

Galata Konak Patisserie Cafe PATISSERIE €
(Map p72; www.galatakonakcafe.com; Hacı Ali Sokak 2/2, Galata) After checking out the

MEYHANES – THE BIGGEST PARTY IN TOWN

If you only have one night out on the town when you're in İstanbul, make sure you spend it at a *meyhane* (Turkish tavern). On every night of the week, *meyhanes* such as Sofyalı 9, Alem, 9 Ece Aksoy and Karaköy Lokantası are full of groups of chattering locals choosing from the dizzying array of meze and fish dishes on offer, washed down with a never-ending supply of rakı (aniseed brandy). On Friday and Saturday nights, *meyhane* precincts such as Nevizade and Sofyalı Sokaks literally heave with people and are enormously enjoyable places to be.

Traditional *meyhanes* often host musicians playing *fasıl*, a lively local form of gypsy music. One of the best *meyhanes* in town is **Despina** (📞0212-247 3357; Açıkyol Sokak 9, Kurtuluş; dinner incl drinks TL50), which was established back in 1946 and is known for its excellent music. It's way off the tourist track in the suburb of Kurtuluş, on the eastern shore of the Golden Horn – ask your hotel to organise a taxi. Other options are **Cumhuriyet** (Map p72; 📞0212-293 1977; Sahne Sokak 4; set menu limited/unlimited TL55/65) in Beyoğlu's Balık Pazar (Fish Market); **Alem** (Map p72; 📞0212-249 6055; Nevizade Sokak 8-10, Beyoğlu; set menu incl all drinks TL55; ⊙10am-2am, live music 8pm-midnight); **Demeti** (Map p72; 📞0212-244 0628; Şimşirci Sokak 6, Cihangir; set menu limited/unlimited TL55/65; ⊙closed Sun); and **Kokosh by Asmali** (Map p72; 📞0212-293 2547; www.asmalikokosh.com; Meşrutiyet Caddesi 83c, Tepebaşı; set menu incl drinks TL90; ⊙closed Sun, Mon & summer), opposite the historic Pera Palace Hotel.

If you eat at a *meyhane* where there's live music make sure you tip the musicians when they play at your table, as they work for tips rather than salary. Between TL5 to TL10 for each person at the table is about right. And note that the difference between a limited and an unlimited menu is usually to do with the range of alcoholic drinks on offer.

---

pastries and cakes on sale in the ground-floor patisserie, make your way up the stairs or take the lift to the roof terrace cafe, which has a fabulous view.

Güney Restaurant   LOKANTA €€
(Map p72; Kuledibi Şah Kapısı 6, Galata; soups TL3, porsiyon TL3.50-8; ⊙closed Sun) You'll be lucky if you can fight your way through the crowds of hungry locals to claim a lunchtime table at this bustling *lokanta* opposite Galata Tower.

Konak   ANATOLIAN €€
(Map p72; www.konakkebap.com; İstiklal Caddesi 259, Galatasaray; pides TL7-9, kebaps TL8-15) Eateries on İstiklal are often dreadful, but this long-time favourite bucks the trend. It serves excellent kebaps and pides; try the delectable *İskender kebap* (döner kebap on fresh pide and topped with savoury tomato sauce and browned butter). There's another branch near Tünel.

Helvetia Lokanta   LOKANTA €
(Map p72; Sümbül Sokak; soup TL5, porsiyon TL5-9; ⊙8am-10pm Mon-Sat, 8am-11am Sun) This hip *lokanta* is popular with locals (particularly of the vegetarian variety), who pop in here for fresh, tasty and cheap-as-chips soups, salads and bean dishes.

ORTAKÖY & KURUÇEŞME

Eateries on and around the Golden Mile (along Muallim Naci and Kuruçeşme Caddesis in Ortaköy and Kuruçeşme) can get pricey, and if you're on a tight budget you should probably limit yourself to brunch – like most young locals do. On weekends, the stands behind the Ortaköy Mosque do brisk business selling *gözlemes* (savoury pancakes) and *kumpir* (baked potatoes filled with your choice of sour cream, olive paste, cheese, chilli or bulgur).

Aşşk Kahve   CAFE €€
(Map p76; Muallim Naci Caddesi 64b, Kuruçeşme; brunch TL10-25; ⊙closed Mon winter) The city's glamour set loves this garden cafe to bits, and its weekend brunches are an institution. Go early to snaffle a table right at the water's edge. It's accessed via the stairs behind the Macrocenter. To get here from Sultanahmet catch the tram to Kabataş and then bus 22 or 25E to Kuruçeşme.

House Cafe   INTERNATIONAL €€€
(Map p76; İskele Sq 42, Ortaköy; breakfast platter TL24, sandwiches TL15-26, pizzas TL17.50-27.50, mains TL16.50-29.50; ⊙9am-1am Mon-Thu, to 2am Fri & Sat, to 10.30pm Sun) This casually chic cafe is one of the best spots in town

for Sunday brunch. A huge space right on the waterfront, it offers a good-quality buffet spread for TL45 between 10am and 2pm. Food at other times can be disappointing, though that doesn't deter the locals, who flock here every weekend.

Banyan
ASIAN €€€

(Map p76; ☑0212-259 9060; www.banyanrestau rant.com; 3rd fl, Salhane Sokak 3, Ortaköy; mains TL25-42) The Asian fusion dishes served at this stylish eatery are pleasant, but it's the extraordinary view of Bosphorus Bridge and Ortaköy Mosque that set this place apart. Book a table on the terrace.

ASIAN SHORE

ÜSKÜDAR

Kanaat Lokantası
LOKANTA €€

(Ahmediye Meydanı; soup TL4-5, porsiyon TL6-10, kebaps TL9-13) This barnlike place near the ferry terminal has been serving up competent *hazır yemek* since 1933, and is particularly fancied for its desserts. Its understated but pleasing decor features framed photographs of old street scenes. You'll find it in the street behind the Ağa Mosque.

KADIKÖY

TOP CHOICE Çiya Sofrası
LOKANTA €€

(www.ciya.com.tr; Güneşlibahçe Sokak 43; meze plate TL5-12, porsiyon TL6-14, desserts TL3-8) This is the best *lokanta* in the city. We love the simple modern interior and ever-friendly staff, and we adore the food – everything from the delicious self-service vegetarian meze spread to the *perde pılavı* (chicken, rice and almonds encased in pastry) and *katmer fıstık şeker hamun kaymak* (sweet pistachio flaky pastry with clotted cream). Next-door Çiya Kebapçı is owned and run by the same people, and is just as impressive. To get here from the ferry terminal, cross the main street and enter the streets given over to the produce market on the right-hand (southern) side of Söğutlüçeşme Caddesi; Çiya is in here. No alcohol.

🍷 Drinking

It may be the biggest city in a predominantly Islamic country, but let us assure you that İstanbul's population likes nothing more than a drink or three. If the rakı (aniseed brandy)-soaked atmosphere in the city's *meyhanes* isn't a clear enough indicator, a foray into the thriving bar scene around Beyoğlu will confirm it.

Alternatively, you can check out the alcohol-free, atmosphere-rich *çay bahçe-*

sis or *kahvehanes* (coffee houses) dotted around the Old City. These are great places to relax and sample that great Turkish institution, the nargileh, accompanied by a cup of *Türk kahve* (Turkish coffee) or çay. It will cost around TL2 for a tea, TL6 for a Turkish coffee and TL10 to TL15 for a nargileh at all of the places listed here.

SULTANAHMET & AROUND

Set Üstü Çay Bahçesi
TEA GARDEN

(Map p46; Gülhane Park, Sultanahmet; ⊙10am-11pm) Locals adore this terraced tea garden and every weekend can be seen parading arm-in-arm through Gülhane Park to get here. Follow their example and enjoy a pot of tea and a *tost* (toasted sandwich) while enjoying spectacular water views. No nargileh.

Yeni Marmara
NARGILEH CAFE

(Map p46; Çayıroğlu Sokak, Küçük Ayasofya; ⊙8am-midnight) This cavernous teahouse is always packed with locals playing backgammon, sipping çay and puffing on nargilehs. The place has bags of character, featuring rugs, wall hangings and low brass tables. In winter a wood stove keeps the place cosy; in summer patrons sit on the rear terrace and look out over the Sea of Marmara.

Derviş Aile Çay Bahçesi
TEA GARDEN

(Map p50; Mimar Mehmet Ağa Caddesi, Sultanahmet; ⊙9am-11pm Apr-Oct) Locations don't come any better than this. Directly opposite the Blue Mosque, the Derviş' comfortable cane chairs and shady trees beckon patrons in need of a respite from the tourist queues.

Cafe Meşale
TEA GARDEN

(Map p50; Arasta Bazaar, Utangaç Sokak, Sultanahmet; ⊙24hr) Generations of backpackers have joined locals in claiming a stool and enjoying a çay and nargileh here. In the summer months there's live Turkish music between 8pm and 10pm every evening. You'll find it in the sunken courtyard behind the Blue Mosque and next to the Arasta Bazaar.

Türk Ocaği Kültür ve Sanat Merkezi İktisadi İşletmesi Çay Bahçesi
TEA GARDEN

(cnr Divan Yolu & Bab-ı Ali Caddesis, Çemberlitaş; ⊙8am-midnight, later in summer) Tucked into the rear right-hand corner of a shady Ottoman cemetery, this popular tea garden is a perfect place to escape the crowds and relax over a tea and nargileh.

Hotel Nomade Terrace Bar
BAR

(Map p46; Ticarethane Sokak 15, Alemdar; ⊙noon-11pm) The intimate terrace of this boutique hotel overlooks Aya Sofya and the Blue Mosque. Settle down in a comfortable chair to enjoy a glass of wine, beer or freshly squeezed fruit juice. The only music that will interrupt your evening's reverie is the Old City's signature sound of the call to prayer.

Kybele Cafe
BAR-CAFE

(Map p46; Yerebatan Caddesi 35, Alemdar; ☻3pm-1am) The lounge bar at this charming but vaguely eccentric hotel is chock-full of antique furniture, richly coloured rugs and old etchings and prints, but its signature style comes courtesy of the hundreds of colourful glass lights hanging from the ceiling.

Sofa
BAR-CAFE

(Map p50; Mimar Mehmet Ağa Caddesi 32, Cankurtaran; ☻11am-11pm) Ten candlelit tables beckon patrons into this friendly bar-cafe just off Akbıyık Caddesi. There's a happy hour between 5pm and 6.30pm each day, and a decidedly laid-back feel.

Sultan Pub
PUB

(Map p46; Divan Yolu Caddesi 2; ☻9.30pm-1am) This local version of Ye Olde English Pub has been around for decades. The 30-to-40ish crowds come for spectacular sunsets on the rooftop terrace or peerless people-watching from the sun-drenched streetside tables. The Cosy Pub, up the road at number 66, is similar.

BAZAAR DISTRICT

Lale Bahçesi
TEA GARDEN

(Map p62; Sifahane Sokak, Süleymaniye; ☻9am-11pm) In a sunken courtyard that was once part of the Süleymaniye *külliye*, this charming tea garden is always full of students from the nearby İstanbul University, who come here to spend a lazy hour or two on cushioned seats alongside a pretty fountain. In winter the students huddle inside the atmospheric kilim (pileless woven rug)-clad *medrese*. The nargilehs here are among the cheapest in town.

Erenler Çay Bahçesi
TEA GARDEN

(Map p62; Yeniçeriler Caddesi 36/28; ☻9am-midnight, later in summer) Set in the leafy courtyard of the Çorlulu Ali Paşa Medrese, this nargileh joint is always full of students from nearby İstanbul University doing their best to live up to their genetic heritage and develop a major tobacco addiction.

İlesam Lokalı
TEA GARDEN

(Map p62; Yeniçeriler Caddesi 84; ☻8am-midnight, later in summer) This club in the court-

Tea and nargileh go together like Posh and Becks. And the best setting in which to try out this particularly magic combo is the traditional *çay bahçesi* (tea garden), of which İstanbul has many. These *çay bahçesis* are where the locals go to practice *keyif*, the Turkish art of quiet relaxation. To emulate them, follow the smell of apple tobacco to the following faves.

» Derviş Aile Çay Bahçesi (p98)
» Erenler Çay Bahçesi (p99)
» Lale Bahçesi (p99)
» Tophane Nargileh (p99)

yard of the Koca Sinan Paşa Medrese was formed by the enigmatically named Professional Union of Owners of the Works of Science and Literature. Fortunately, members seem happy for strangers to infiltrate their ranks. After entering the gate to Koca Sinan Paşa's tomb, go past the cemetery – it's the second teahouse to the right.

BEYOĞLU & AROUND

There are fewer *çay bahçesis* on this side of Galata Bridge, but lots more bars.

The most popular bar precincts are on or around Balo Sokak and Sofyalı Sokak, but there are also a number of sleek bars on roof terraces on both sides of İstiklal – these have fantastic views and prices to match.

TOP CHOICE Tophane Nargileh
NARGILEH CAFE

(Map p72; off Necatibey Caddesi, Tophane; ☻24hr) This atmospheric row of nargileh cafes behind the Nusretiye Mosque and opposite the Tophane tram stop is always packed with trendy teetotallers, and is a fabulous place to come after a meal. Follow your nose to find it – the smell of apple tobacco is incredibly enticing.

TOP CHOICE Mikla
BAR

(Map p72; www.miklarestaurant.com; Marmara Pera Hotel, Meşrutiyet Caddesi 15, Tepebaşı; ☻from 6.30pm Mon-Sat summer only) It's worth overlooking the sometimes uppity service at this rooftop bar to enjoy what could well be the best view in İstanbul. After your drink, move downstairs to the restaurant (see p95).

Leb-i Derya
BAR-RESTAURANT

(Map p72; www.lebiderya.com; 6th fl, Kumbaracı Yokuşu 57, Tünel; ☻4pm-2am Mon-Thu, to 3am

ROOFTOP REVELRY

The ritzy superclubs along the Bosphorus are where the city's Botoxed and blinged set glams up and gets down, but their high prices can put some people off. Fortunately, there's an equally glamorous but much cheaper entertainment alternative that we can recommend: investigating the city's vibrant rooftop bar scene.

İstanbul's sensational skyline and wonderful waterways provide the perfect backdrop for a rapidly growing number of rooftop bars in Beyoğlu. Most offer spectacular views; some also provide live music, morphing into dance clubs after midnight. They rarely levy cover charges and their dress codes are relatively relaxed, though you should don the best your suitcase has to offer. Drinks average between TL15 to TL20.

The best of a rapidly growing crop include **360**, **5 Kat**, **Mikla**, **X Bar**, **Leb-i Derya** and **Leb-i Derya Richmond**.

Fri, 10am-3am Sat, to 2am Sun) Ask many İstanbullus to name their favourite watering hole and they're likely to nominate this unpretentious place. On the top floor of a dishevelled building off İstiklal, it has wonderful views across to the Old City and down the Bosphorus, meaning that seats on the small outdoor terrace or at the bar are highly prized. There's another, more upmarket branch in the Richmond Hotel on İstiklal Caddesi that has even better views.

360
BAR-RESTAURANT

(Map p72; www.360istanbul.com; 8th fl, İstiklal Caddesi 311, Galatasaray; ☺noon-2am Mon-Thu & Sun, 3pm-4am Fri & Sat) İstanbul's most famous bar, and deservedly so. If you can score one of the bar stools on the terrace you'll be happy indeed – the view is truly extraordinary. The place morphs into a club after midnight on Friday and Saturday.

X Bar
BAR-RESTAURANT

(Map p72; www.xrestaurantbar.com; 7th fl, Sadı Konuralp Caddesi 5, Şişhane; ☺9am-midnight Sun-Wed, to 4am Thu-Sat) High culture meets serious glamour on the top floor of the İstanbul Foundation for Culture and Arts (İKSV) building. Our meals here haven't been worth their hefty price tags, so we suggest limiting yourself to a sunset aperitif or two – the Golden Horn view is simply extraordinary.

Public
BAR-RESTAURANT

(Map p72; Meşrutiyet Caddesi 84, Şişhane; ☺noon-midnight) The best thing to occur in Şişhane since the arrival of the metro, this bar/restaurant/nightclub is operated by highly professional owners who also run a successful cafe in Bebek, meaning that the city's glam set (most of whom live in that Bosphorus suburb) loves it to bits.

Mavra
BAR-CAFE

(Map p72; Serdar-ı Ekrem Caddesi 31a, Galata; ☺9am-2am Mon-Fri, to 4pm Sat & Sun) Serdar-ı Ekrem Caddesi is one of the most interesting streets in Galata, full of ornate 19th-century apartment blocks, avant-garde boutiques and laid-back cafes and bars. Mavra is a bit of everything – during the day it functions as a cafe and at night it reinvents itself as a hip bar.

Papillon
BAR

(Map p72; 4th fl, Balo Sokak 31; ☺4pm-late) A classic example of the drinking dens found on Beyoğlu's top floors, this laid-back hangout feels more like someone's living room than a bar. Beanbags, pot plants, mirrorballs and psychedelic decor are scattered across two floors. The drinks are cheap, too. Head down Balo Sokak past the James Joyce Irish pub, take the steps on the left just before the 'Balo' and 'Haydar Rock Bar' signs, and climb all the way to the top; it gets going after 10pm.

5 Kat
BAR-RESTAURANT

(Map p72; www.5kat.com; 5th fl, Soğancı Sokak 7, Cihangir; ☺10am-1.30am) This İstanbul institution is a great alternative for those who can't stomach the style overload at 360 and the like. In winter, drinks are served in the boudoir-style bar; in summer, action moves to the outdoor terrace. Both spots have great Bosphorus views.

Otto
BAR

(Map p72; www.ottoistanbul.com; Sofyalı Sokak 22, Asmalımescit; ☺11am-2am) Smack-bang in the centre of the Sofyalı party precinct, Otto is a good choice if you want a quick drink before moving onto dinner at one of the Asmalımescit restaurants. Its other branches at Santralİstanbul in Sütlüce (open 10am to 2am Monday to Thursday and to 4am Friday and Saturday; take the Golden Horn Ferry to Sütlüce, see p83) and at Şehbender Sokak 5 (open 11am to 2am Monday to Saturday), next to Babylon (p102) in Tünel, are known for their live music (particularly jazz).

Badehane
BAR

(Map p72; General Yazgan Sokak 5, Tünel; ⊘9am-2am) This tiny unsigned watering hole is a favourite with locals. On a balmy evening the laneway is crammed with chattering, chain-smoking artsy types sipping a beer or three; when it's cold they squeeze inside.

Haco Pulo
TEA GARDEN

(Map p72; Passage ZD Hazzopulo, İstiklal Caddesi; ⊘9am-midnight) There aren't nearly as many traditional teahouses in Beyoğlu as there are in atmospheric Old İstanbul, so this one is treasured by the locals. Set in a delightfully picturesque cobbled courtyard, it's stool-to-stool 20- to 30-somethings on summer evenings. Walking from İstiklal Caddesi through the skinny arcade crowded with offbeat shops adds to the experience. No nargileh.

Perla Kallâvi Nargileh Cafe
NARGILEH CAFE

(Map p72; 4-6 fl, Kallâvi Sokak 2; ⊘10am-2am) Follow the scent of apple tobacco to this nargileh cafe occupying the top three floors of an ornate building on İstiklal Caddesi (enter from the side street). It's inevitably full of young people (including plenty of women) enjoying a glass of tea and a bubbling pipe in the welcoming indoor spaces or on the small terrace with its Sea of Marmara views.

Kahve Dünyasi
CAFE

(Meclis-i Mebusan Caddesi, Tütün Han 167, Tophane; ⊘7.30am-9.30pm) The name means 'coffee world', and this new coffee chain has the local world at its feet. The secret of its success lies with the huge coffee menu, decent snacks, reasonable prices, delicious chocolate spoons (yes, you read that correctly), comfortable seating and free wi-fi. The filter coffee is better than its espresso-based alternatives. It's near the Kabataş tram. There's another branch in Nuruosmaniye Caddesi in Cağaloğlu, near the Grand Bazaar. Neither branch offers nargileh.

Also recommended:

Atölye Kuledıbı
BAR-CAFE

(Map p72; www.atolyekuledibi.com; Galata Kulesi Sokak 4, Galata; ⊘10am-midnight Mon-Fri, to

2am Fri & Sat) Great music (sometimes live) and a welcoming atmosphere characterise this bohemian place near Galata Tower.

KeVe
BAR-RESTAURANT

(Map p72; Tünel Geçidi 10, Tünel; ⊘8.30am-2am) Located in a plant-filled belle-époque arcade, atmospheric KeVe is invariably full of 30- to 40-somethings enjoying a drink before kicking on to an exhibition-opening along İstiklal.

Club 17
GAY & LESBIAN

(Map p72; Zambak Sokak 17, Taksim; cover charge Fri & Sat incl 1 drink TL10; ⊘11pm-4am Sun-Thu, to 5.30am Fri & Sat) Aggressive techno music and a jam-packed interior are the hallmarks of this popular gay bar.

Bigudi Cafe
GAY & LESBIAN

(Map p72; 4th & 5th fl, Balo Sokak 20, Beyoğlu; ⊘pub 2pm-2am daily, club midnight-4am Fri & Sat) The pub admits gay men, but the arty terrace club, where lipstick lesbians outnumber trucker-butch types, is resolutely off limits to nonfemales.

☆ Entertainment

There's an entertainment option for everyone in İstanbul. With its array of cinemas and almost religious devotion to all forms of music, it's rare to have a week go by when there's not a special event, festival or performance scheduled. In fact, the only thing that you can't do in this town is be bored.

The best nightclubs are clustered in what is known as the 'Golden Mile' between Ortaköy and Kuruçeşme on the Bosphorus. To visit any of the venues on this sybaritic strip you'll need to dress to kill and be prepared to outlay loads of lira – drinks start at TL20 for a beer and climb into the stratosphere for imported spirits or cocktails. Booking the restaurants at these venues is a good idea, because it's usually the only way to get past the door staff – otherwise you'll be looking at a lucky break or a tip of at least TL100 to get the nod. Venues are busiest on Friday and (especially) Saturday nights, and the action doesn't really kick off until 1am or 2am.

The Beyoğlu clubs are cheaper, and relatively attitude free. They don't have the same wow factor, though.

For an overview of what's on in town make sure you pick up a copy of *Time Out İstanbul* and check out the **Biletix** (www. biletix.com) website. You can buy tickets for most events either through Biletix or at the venue's box office. Biletix outlets are found in many spots throughout the city, but the most convenient for travellers is at the İstiklal Kitabevi (İstiklal Caddesi 55, Beyoğlu; ☺10am-10pm). Alternatively, it's easy to buy your ticket by credit card on Biletix's website and collect the tickets from either Biletix outlets or from the venue before the performance.

Nightclubs
BEYOĞLU & AROUND

Araf
CLUB
(Map p72; 5th fl, Balo Sokak 32; no cover charge) Grungy fun central for English teachers and Turkish-language students, who shake their booties to the in-house band and swill the cheapest club beer in town.

Ghetto
CLUB
(Map p72; www.ghettoist.com; Kalyoncu Kulluk Caddesi 10; ☺closed summer) This three-storey club behind the Çiçek Pasajı has a bold postmodern decor and an interesting musical program featuring local and international acts. Check the website for schedules and cover charges.

Dogzstar
CLUB
(Map p72; www.dogzstar.com; Kartal Sokak 3, Galatasaray; cover charge TL5; ☺closed Sun) It's a three-storey affair, but the compact size (300 persons max) makes for an acoustic powerhouse. The owners altruistically give the collected cover charges to performers and also charge reasonable drink prices and provide a terrace for cooling off in summer.

Love Dance Point
GAY & LESBIAN
(www.lovedp.net; Cumhuriyet Caddesi 349, Harbiye; ☺11.30pm-4am Wed, to 5am Fri & Sat) The major player in the city's gay club scene, Love is now in its 10th year and shows absolutely no sign of having its star wane. Here, gay anthems meet hard-hitting techno and Turkish pop, making for one hell of a party. Straights can occasionally be spotted on the dance floor.

ORTAKÖY & KURUÇEŞME

Crystal
CLUB
(Map p76; ☎0212-261 1988, ext 2; www.clubcrystal.org; Muallim Naci Caddesi 65, Ortaköy; adult/student TL35/25; ☺midnight-5.30am Fri & Sat) Crystal is home to the city's techno aficionados, who come to appreciate sets put together by some of the best DJs from Turkey and the rest of Europe. There's a great sound system, a crowded dance floor and a lovely covered garden.

Reina
CLUB
(Map p76; ☎0212-259 5919; www.reina.com.tr; Muallim Naci Caddesi 44, Kuruçeşme; cover charge weekends TL50, weekdays free; ☺summer only) This is İstanbul's most famous nightclub. It's where Turkey's C-list celebrities congregate, the city's nouveaux riches cavort and an occasional tourist gets past the doorman to ogle the spectacle and the magnificent Bosphorus view.

Sortie
CLUB
(Map p76; ☎212-327 8585; www.sortie.com.tr; Muallim Naci Caddesi 141, Kuruçeşme; cover charge Fri & Sat TL50, Mon-Thu & Sun free; ☺summer only) Sortie has long vied with Reina as the reigning queen of the Golden Mile, nipping at the heels of its rival dowager. It pulls in the city's glamour-pussies and poseurs, all of whom are on the lookout for the odd celebrity or tabloid fodder.

Supperclub
CLUB
(Map p76; ☎212-261 1988; www.supperclub.com; Muallim Naci Caddesi 65, Kuruçeşme; no cover charge; ☺summer only) With an all-white decor and a location close to the Bosphorus, Supperclub has an unmistakable resort feel. Customers lounge or dine in oversized beach beds in lieu of tables and chairs, enjoying the atmospheric lighting, live shows, imported DJ talents and highly creative cuisine.

Also recommended:

Anjelique
CLUB
(Map p76; ☎0212-327 2844; www.istanbuldoors.com; Salhane Sokak 10, Ortaköy; no cover charge; ☺summer only) Right on the waterfront, and very glam – wear your Jimmy Choos and make a reservation.

Blackk
CLUB
(Map p76; ☎0212-236 7256; www.blackk.net; Muallim Naci Caddesi 71, Kuruçeşme; no cover charge; ☺7.30pm-4am Fri & Sat Nov-Apr) This ultrafashionable supper club is divided into three areas – club, resto-lounge and Levendiz Rom (Gypsy) *meyhane*. The club relies on its giant mirror ball for the wow factor, but both the resto-lounge and *meyhane* have great Bosphorus views.

Live Music
BEYOĞLU & AROUND

Babylon
ECLECTIC
(Map p72; ☎0212-292 7368; www.babylon.com.tr; Şehbender Sokak 3, Tünel; cover charge varies; ☺9.30pm-2am Tue-Thu, 10pm-3am Fri & Sat,

closed summer) Babylon devotes itself almost exclusively to live performances, and the eclectic program often features big-name international acts. DJ chill-out sessions are in the restaurant/lounge behind the concert hall. Buy tickets at the box office (open 10am to 6pm) opposite the venue.

Munzur Cafe & Bar   TURKISH FOLK
(Map p72; www.munzurcafebar.com, in Turkish; Hasnun Galip Sokak 21, Beyoğlu; ⊙1pm-4am, music from 9pm) Seventeen years old and counting, this bar has arguably the best singers' line-up in the street and also hosts expert *bağlama* (lute) players. It brings in diverse customer groups trying to connect to the lyrics of the songs.

Nardis Jazz Club   JAZZ
(Map p72; ☑0212-244 6327; www.nardisjazz.com; Galata Kulesi Sokak 14, Galata; cover charge varies; ⊙8pm-1am Mon-Thu with sets at 9.30pm & 12.30am, 8pm-2am Fri & Sat with sets at 10.30pm & 1.30am, closed summer) Just downhill from Galata Tower, this venue – run by jazz guitarist Önder Focan and his wife Zuhal – is where real jazz aficionados go. It's small, so you'll need to book if you want a decent table.

Jolly Joker Balans   ECLECTIC
(Map p72; ☑0212-251 7762; www.jollyjokerbalans. com; Balo Sokak 22; admission varies; ⊙from 10pm Wed-Sat, closed summer) The gig-goers among the lively multinational crowd enjoy the city's best locally brewed beer (the caramel brew) and gravitate towards the upstairs bi-level performance hall, which features a balcony with glass floors.

Eylül   TURKISH FOLK
(Map p72; Gazeteci Erol Dernek 2, Çukurcuma; ⊙2.30pm-4am, music from 8.30pm) This place is popular with students and young İstanbullus wanting to listen to the musical strains of their Anatolian homeland. Until the music starts, you'll think you've walked into a Turkish-rock bar.

Roxy   ECLECTIC
(Map p72; ☑0212-249 1283; www.roxy.com.tr; Aslan Yatağı Sokak 5, Taksim; cover charge TL25, student TL5-10; ⊙10pm-4am Fri & Sat, closed summer) It's been going since 1994, but bright young things still flock to this dance-and-performance space off Taksim Sq. Expect anything from retro to rap, hip hop to jazz fusion and electronica to anthems.

Toprak   TURKISH FOLK
(Map p72; www.toprakturkubar.tr.gg/ANA-SAYFA. htm; Hasnun Galip Sokak 17a, Beyoğlu; ⊙4pm-

4am, show from 10pm) The tables here are arranged facing the performance area (as in a music hall); all the better to soak in the singers' pathos.

ORTAKÖY & KURUÇEŞME

İstanbul Jazz Center   JAZZ
(Map p76; ☑0212-327 5050; www.istanbuljazz. com; Salhane Sokak 10, Ortaköy; ⊙from 7pm, live sets 9.30pm & 12.30am Mon-Sat, closed summer) Affectionately known as JC's, this is the city's best-known jazz club. Big-name international acts regularly play Friday and Saturday nights – check the web for details. There are set dinner menus costing TL40 to TL60, or you can order à la carte.

Cinemas
İstiklal Caddesi, between Taksim and Galatasaray, is the heart of İstanbul's *sinema* (cinema) district, so you can simply cinema-hop until you find something you like. The only cinema close to Sultanahmet is the Şafak Sinemaları at Çemberlitaş. Foreign films are mostly shown in English with Turkish subtitles, but double-check at the box office in case the film has *Türkçe* (Turkish) dubbing, which sometimes happens with blockbusters and children's films.

If possible, buy your tickets a few hours in advance; depending on the venue, tickets cost between TL10 and TL14 – many places offer reduced rates before 6pm, to students, and all day once a week (usually Wednesday).

Citylife Cinema   CINEMA
(www.citylifecinema.com; 6th fl, City's Nişantaşı Mall, Teşvikiye Caddesi 162, Nişantaşı) In a new-ish shopping mall on the main street in the fashionable shopping suburb of Nişantaşı.

Finansbank AFM Fitaş   CINEMA
(Map p72; Mayadrom Akatlar Alışveriş Merkezi, İstiklal Caddesi 24-26, Beyoğlu)

Rexx   CINEMA
(www.rexx-online.com; Sakızgülü Sokak 20-22, Kadıköy) From the ferry dock, walk straight ahead up Söğütlüçeşme Caddesi, turn right into General A Gündüz Sokak and then ask someone to show you the way to the Rexx Sinemaları or, if that doesn't work, Kadife Sokak (the cinema is at its northern end).

Şafak Sinemaları   CINEMA
(Map p62; Divan Yolu 134, Çemberlitaş)

Sport
There's only one spectator sport that really matters to Turks: football. Eighteen teams

104

İSTANBUL

NIGHTLIFE RIP-OFFS

Foreigners, especially single foreign males, are targets for a classic İstanbul rip-off that works like this:

You're a single male out for a stroll in the afternoon or evening. A well-spoken, well-dressed Turk strikes up a conversation and recommends a bar or nightclub. As he seems like a nice guy, you agree to accompany him to one of these places. You enter, sit down and immediately several women move to your table and order drinks. When the drinks come, you're presented with a huge cheque – TL500 isn't unusual. It's a mugging and if you don't pay up, scary-looking guys will suddenly appear, take you into the back office and raid your wallet. If you don't have enough cash, they may even escort you to an ATM so that you can withdraw funds.

A variation is a single foreign male having a drink and a meal in a restaurant or bar. Several Turkish friends sitting nearby strike up a conversation, then suggest you all take a taxi to another venue. In the taxi, they forcibly relieve you of your wallet. Occasionally, these guys will pretend to be policemen, accosting you on a back street, roughing you up and taking your wallet in the process.

How do you avoid such rip-offs? As many Turks are generous, hospitable, curious and gregarious, it's difficult to know whether an invitation is genuine (as it most often is) or the prelude to a mugging. Tread carefully if there's any reason for suspicion. As for nightclub recommendations, take them from a trusted source, such as this book. Avoid any bar or nightclub in Aksaray (the city's red light district) and steer clear of Beyoğlu's back streets late at night.

from all over Turkey compete from August to May, and three of the top teams – Fenerbahçe, Galatasaray and Beşiktaş – are based in İstanbul. Each season runs between August and May. The top team of the first division plays in the European Cup.

Matches are usually held on weekends, normally on a Saturday night. Almost any Turkish male will be able to tell you which is the best match to see. Tickets are sold at the clubhouses at the *stadyum* (stadium) or through Biletix, and usually go on sale between Tuesday and Thursday for a weekend game. Open seating is reasonably priced; covered seating – which has the best views – can be expensive. If you miss out on the tickets you can get them at the door of the stadium, but they are usually outrageously overpriced.

🔒 Shopping

If you love shopping you've come to the right place. Despite İstanbul's big-ticket historic sights, many travellers come here and find the highlight of their visit was shopping, particularly searching and bantering for treasures in the city's atmospheric bazaars. The best of these are the Grand Bazaar and Arasta Bazaar, which specialise in carpets, jewellery, textiles and ceramics.

For Turkish musical instruments, check out the shops along Galipdede Caddesi,

which runs between Tünel Sq and Galata Tower in Beyoğlu. For designer fashions, head to the upmarket shopping area of Nişantaşı, and for avant-garde fashion go to Serdar-ı Ekrem Caddesi in Galata. Antique hunters should wander through the streets of Çukurcuma in Beyoğlu.

Come energised, come with maximum overdraft and – most importantly – come with room in your suitcase.

SULTANAHMET

Cocoon RUGS, TEXTILES

(Map p46; www.cocoontr.com; Küçük Ayasofya Caddesi 13, Sultanahmet) There are so many rug and textile shops in İstanbul that choosing individual shops to recommend is incredibly difficult. However, we had no problem whatsoever in singling out this pair of shops. Felt hats, antique costumes and textiles from Central Asia are artfully displayed in one store, while rugs from Persia, Central Asia, the Caucasus and Anatolia adorn the other. There's a third shop in the Arasta Bazaar (Map p50) and a small shop selling felt objects in the Grand Bazaar (Map p66).

Jennifer's Hamam TEXTILES, SOAP

(Map p50; www.jennifershamam.com; 135 Arasta Bazaar, Sultanahmet) Run by Canadian Jennifer Gaudet, this lovely shop stocks hamam items including towels, shawls, robes and *peştemals* (bath wraps) produced on old hand looms or motor looms. It also sells natural soaps, *keses* (coarse cloth mittens used for depilation) and Rosense products (natural rose hand and body products from Isparta).

Mehmet Çetinkaya Gallery RUGS

(Map p46; www.cetinkayagallery.com; Tavukhane Sokak 7) When rug experts throughout the country meet for their annual shindig, this is one of the places where they come to check out the good stuff. There's a second shop in the Arasta Bazaar and one at the Four Seasons İstanbul at the Bosphorus hotel.

Yılmaz İpekçilik TEXTILES

(Map p50; Ishakpaşa Caddesi 36; ⊙9am-9pm Mon-Sat, 3-9pm Sun) Hand-loomed textiles made in a family-run factory in Antakya are on sale in this out-of-the-way shop. Good-quality silk, cotton and linen items at reasonable prices make it worth the short trek.

Khaftan ART, ANTIQUES

(Map p46; www.khaftan.com; Nakilbent Sokak 33) Owner Adnan Cakariz sells antique Kütahya and İznik ceramics to collectors and museums here and overseas, so you can be sure that the pieces he sells in his own establishment are top notch. Gleaming Russian icons, delicate calligraphy (old and new), ceramics, Karagöz puppets and contemporary paintings are all on show in this gorgeous shop.

İstanbul Handicrafts Market HANDICRAFTS

(İstanbul Sanatlar Çarşısı; Map p50; Kabasakal Caddesi, Sultanahmet) Set in the small rooms surrounding the quiet, leafy courtyard of the 18th-century Cedid Mehmet Efendi Medresesi, this handicrafts centre is unusual in that local artisans work here and don't mind visitors watching them. It's a hassle-free place to purchase calligraphy, embroidery, glassware, miniature paintings and ceramics.

Nakkaş RUGS, JEWELLERY

(Map p46; Mimar Mehmet Ağa Caddesi 39) As well as pricey rugs and jewellery, Nakkaş stocks an extensive range of ceramics made by the well-regarded İznik Foundation. One of the reasons the place is so beloved of tour groups is the beautifully restored Byzantine cistern that's in the basement – make sure you have a peek.

İznik Classics & Tiles CERAMICS

(Map p50; Arasta Bazaar 67 & 73, Sultanahmet) İznik Classics is one of the best places in town to source hand-painted collector-item ceramics made with real quartz and using metal oxides for pigments. Admire the range in the two shops and gallery in the Arasta Bazaar, in its Grand Bazaar (Map p66) store or at 17 Utangaç Sokak in Cankurtaran. For a less-expensive range of Kütahya ceramics, check out **Ceramic Art Gallery** (Map p50; Arasta Bazaar 43, Sultanahmet; www.ceramicpalace.com) nearby.

BAZAAR DISTRICT

TOP CHOICE Design Zone JEWELLERY, HANDICRAFTS

(Map p62; www.designzone.com.tr; Alibaba Türbe Sokak 21, Nuruosmaniye; ⊙closed Sun) Contemporary Turkish designers show and sell their work in this attractive boutique. Look out for the superstylish jewellery created by owner Özlem Tuna and unique collectables such as the handcrafted hamam-bowl sets. The varied stock caters to all budgets.

Yazmacı Necdet Danış TEXTILES

(Map p66; Yağlıkçılar Caddesi 57, Grand Bazaar; ⊙8.30am-7.30pm Mon-Sat) Fashion designers and buyers from every corner of the globe know that when in İstanbul, this is where to come to source top-quality textiles. It's crammed with bolts of fabric of every description – shiny, simple, sheer and sophisticated – as well as *peştemals,* scarves and clothes. Next-door **Murat Danış** is part of the same operation.

Derviş TEXTILES, SOAP

(Map p66; www.dervis.com; Keseciler Caddesi 33-35, Grand Bazaar; ⊙8.30am-7.30pm Mon-Sat) Gorgeous raw cotton and silk *peştemals* share shelf space here with traditional Turkish dowry vests and engagement dresses. If these don't take your fancy, the pure olive-oil soaps and beautiful felt-and-silk shawls are sure to step into the breach. There's another store at Halıcılar Caddesi 51.

Abdulla Natural Products TEXTILES, SOAP

(Map p66; Halıcılar Caddesi 62, Grand Bazaar; ⊙8.30am-7.30pm Mon-Sat) Be sure to keep your luggage allowance in mind when entering this stylish shop. It sells handmade woollen throws from eastern Turkey, top-quality cotton bed and bath linen, and beautifully packaged olive-oil soap.

Ak Gümüş HANDICRAFTS

(Map p66; www.ak-gumus.com; Keseciler Caddesi 68-70, Grand Bazaar; ⊙8.30am-7.30pm Mon-Sat) Specialising in Central Asian tribal arts, this and its associated two stores stock an array of felt toys and hats, as well as

TURKISH DELIGHT

Ali Muhiddin Hacı Bekir was the most famous of all Ottoman confectioners. He came to İstanbul from the mountain town of Kastamonu in 1777 and opened a shop in the Old City where he concocted delicious boiled sweets and the translucent jellied jewels known to Turks as *lokum* and to the rest of the world as Turkish Delight. His products became so famous throughout the city that his sweet-shop empire grew, and his name became inextricably linked in the minds of İstanbullus with authentic and delicious *lokum*. Today, locals still buy their *lokum* from branches of the business he began over two centuries ago.

The flagship store of **Ali Muhiddin Hacı Bekir** (Map p62; www.hacibekir.com.tr/eng) is located at Hamidiye Caddesi 83, Eminönü, near the Spice Bazaar. There are also stores on İstiklal Caddesi (Map p72) and in the produce market at Kadıköy.

A more recent family dynasty has been established at **Herşey Aşktan** (Map p72; www.herseyasktan.com; Meşrutiyet Caddesi 79, Tepebaşı), opposite Pera Palace Hotel. Its delicious *lokum* can be packaged in decorative boxes, creating a perfect gift to take home to friends and family.

As well as enjoying *sade* (plain) *lokum*, you can buy it made with *cevizli* (walnut) or *şam fıstıklı* (pistachio), or flavoured with *portakkallı* (orange), *bademli* (almond) or *roze* (rose water). Ask for a *çeşitli* (assortment) to sample the various types.

jewellery and other objects made using coins and beads.

Phebus
JEWELLERY

(Map p66; Şerifağa Sokak 122, Cevahir Bedesten, Grand Bazaar; ⊗8.30am-7.30pm Mon-Sat) Enter this tiny shop to see the owner creating his attractive gold jewellery, much of which references Byzantine designs. You can choose something from the stock or have a piece custom made.

Dhoku
KILIMS

(Map p66; Takkeciler Sokak 58-60, Grand Bazaar; ⊗8.30am-7.30pm Mon-Sat) One of a new generation of rug stores in the Bazaar, Dhoku (meaning 'texture') designs and sells contemporary kilims featuring attractive modernist designs. The same people run **EthniCon** (www.ethnicon.com) opposite.

Muhlis Günbattı
TEXTILES

(Map p66; Perdahçılar Sokak 48, Grand Bazaar; ⊗8.30am-7.30pm Mon-Sat) One of the most famous stores in the Grand Bazaar, Muhlis Günbattı specialises in *suzani* (needlework) fabrics from Uzbekistan. These spectacularly beautiful bedspreads and wall hangings are made from fine cotton embroidered with silk. There's another store opposite the Four Seasons Hotel in Sultanahmet.

Şişko Osman
RUGS

(Fatty Osman; Map p66; www.siskoosman.com; Zincirli Han 15, Grand Bazaar; ⊗9am-6pm Mon-Sat) The Osmans have been in the rug business for four generations and their

popularity has seen their original shop triple in size. The range and customer service here are certainly hard to beat.

Sofa
ART, JEWELLERY

(Map p62; Nuruosmaniye Caddesi 85, Cağaloğlu; ⊗closed Sun) As well as its eclectic range of prints, ceramics, calligraphy and curios, Sofa sells contemporary Turkish art and books. The range of jewellery made out of antique coins and 24-carat gold is lovely.

Vakko İndirim
CLOTHING

(Map p62; Yenicamii Caddesi 1/13, Eminönü; ⊗closed Sun) This remainder outlet of İstanbul's most glamorous department store should be on the itinerary of all bargain hunters. Top-quality men's and women's clothing is sold here for a fraction of its original price.

BEYOĞLU & AROUND

Doors
CLOTHING

(Map p72; www.umitunal.com; Ensiz Sokak 1b, Tünel; ⊗9am-8pm Mon-Sat, noon-6pm Sun) Local fashion designer Ümit Ünal is rapidly acquiring an international profile, with stores in New York, Hong Kong and London stocking his striking pieces. His women's clothes, which use natural fabrics in muted colours, are best described as wearable art. Prices are surprisingly reasonable considering the originality and quality on offer.

Tezgah Alley
CLOTHING

(Map p72; Terko 2 Caddesi, off İstiklal Caddesi; ⊗closed Sun) Put your elbows to work fighting your way to the front of the *tezgah* (stalls) in this alley, which are heaped with T-shirts, jumpers, pants and shirts on offer for a mere TL3 to TL6 per piece. Turkey is a major centre of European clothing manufacturing, and the items here are often factory run-ons from designer or high-street-chain orders.

SIR CERAMICS
(Map p72; www.sircini.com; Serdar Ekrem Sokak 66, Galata; ☺closed Sun) Ceramics produced in İstanbul can be very pricey, but the attractive hand-painted plates, platters, bowls and tiles sold at this small atelier are exceptions to the rule.

Artrium ART, JEWELLERY
(Map p72; Tünel Geçidi 7, Tünel; ☺closed Sun) This Aladdin's cave is crammed with antique ceramics, Ottoman miniatures, maps, prints and jewellery.

Lale Plak MUSIC
(Map p72; Galipdede Caddesi 1, Tünel; ☺closed Sun) This long-standing magnet for music aficionados is crammed with CDs in every genre, including jazz, Western and Turkish classical, Turkish folk and electronica.

Mephisto MUSIC
(Map p72; ☎0212-249 0687; İstiklal Caddesi 197, Beyoğlu; ☺9am-midnight) If you manage to develop a taste for local music while you're in town, this popular store is the place to indulge it. As well as a huge CD collection of Turkish popular music, there's a select range of Turkish folk, jazz and classical music.

BEŞIKTAŞ, ORTAKÖY & KURUÇEŞME
The shops around fashionable W Hotel near Dolmabahçe Palace are among the most glamorous in the city. Marni, Chloé, Marc Jacobs and Jimmy Choo are just a few of the labels that draw the city's moneyed elite here to shop.

Haremlique TEXTILES
(www.haremlique.com; Şair Nedim Bey Caddesi 11, Akaretler; ☺closed Sun) This local business, found among the international labels sold in the area around W Hotel, sells top-drawer bedlinen and bathwares.

❶ Information
Bookshops
The following shops specialise in English-language publications:

Galeri Kayseri (Divan Yolu 11 & 58, Sultanahmet; ☺9am-9pm) Fiction and glossy books set in or about İstanbul.

Homer Kitabevi (Yeni Çarşı Caddesi 28, Galatasaray; ☺10am-7.30pm Mon-Sat, 12.30-7.30pm Sun) Great range of Turkish fiction and nonfiction.

İstanbul Kitapçısı (İstiklal Caddesi 379, Beyoğlu; ☺10am-6.45pm Mon-Sat, noon-6.45pm Sun) Books on İstanbul, plus a great selection of maps, prints, postcards and music.

Pandora (Büyükparmakkapı Sokak 8b; ☺10am-8pm Mon-Wed, to 9pm Thu-Sat, 1-8pm Sun) Great fiction and travel sections, as well as loads of books about Turkey.

Robinson Crusoe (İstiklal Caddesi 389, Beyoğlu; ☺9am-9.30pm Mon-Sat, 10am-9.30pm Sun) Novels and nonfiction.

Dangers & Annoyances
İstanbul is no more nor less safe a city than any large metropolis, but there are a few dangers worth highlighting. Some İstanbullus drive like rally drivers, and there is no such thing as a generally acknowledged right of way for pedestrians. As a pedestrian, give way to cars, motorcycles and trucks in all situations, even if you have to jump out of the way. Bag-snatching is only a slight problem, especially on Galipdede Sokak in Tünel and on İstiklal Caddesi's side streets. Lastly – and probably most importantly – you should be aware of the long-standing nightlife scam targeting male visitors. What could possibly go wrong, you ask? See boxed text, p104, for the low-down.

Emergency
Ambulance (☎112)

Fire (☎110)

Police (☎155)

Tourist police (☎0212-527 4503; Yerebatan Caddesi 6, Sultanahmet) Across the street from the Basilica Cistern.

Media
The monthly English edition of *Time Out İstanbul* (TL5) has a large listings section and is the best source for details about upcoming events – you can pick it up at the airport, at newspaper booths in Sultanahmet and at the bookshops listed in this section.

The Guide: İstanbul (TL6.50) is published bimonthly and includes a comprehensive listings section.

Medical Services
Although they are expensive, it's probably best to visit one of the private hospitals listed here if you need medical care when in İstanbul. Both accept credit-card payments and charge around TL180 for a standard consultation.

Alman Hastanesi (German Hospital; Map p72; ☎0212-293 2150; www.almanhastanesi.com.tr; Sıraselviler Caddesi 119, Taksim; ☺8.30am-6pm Mon-Fri, to 5pm Sat) A few hundred

THE MARMARAY PROJECT

Marmaray (www.marmaray.com) is an ambitious public transport project aimed to relieve İstanbul's woeful traffic congestion. Its name comes from combining the name of the Sea of Marmara, which lies just south of the project site, with *ray*, the Turkish word for rail. Plans show the Sirkeci–Halkalı rail line, which presently follows the coast to Yeşilköy near the airport, going underground at Yedikule and travelling to underground stations at Yenikapı and Sirkeci. From Sirkeci it will travel some 5km in a new tunnel being built under the Bosphorus to another underground station on the Asian side at Üsküdar. From there it will come to ground level at Söğütlüçeşme, about 2km east of Kadıköy, where it will connect with the Gebze Anatolian rail line.

The original completion date was to be 2010, but the deadline has been extended to October 2013, and it may take even longer. Some of this delay has been due to archaeological finds that have been made during excavation work. Basically, Old İstanbul is built on layer upon layer of history. No sooner had workmen commenced digging when they found an ancient port and bazaar in Üsküdar and a 4th-century Byzantine harbour in Yenikapı. Diggers were replaced by brushes, and archaeologists have been at work ever since – to find out more about their discoveries, visit the excellent 'In the Light of Day' exhibition on show at the İstanbul Archaeology Museums (p59).

metres south of Taksim Sq on the left-hand side, this hospital has eye and dental clinics and English-speaking staff.

Vehbi Koç American Hospital (Amerikan Hastanesi; Map p42; ☑0212-444 3777; Güzelbahçe Sokak 20, Nişantaşı; ☺24hr emergency department) About 2km northeast of Taksim Sq, this hospital has English-speaking staff and a dental clinic.

Money

ATMs are everywhere in İstanbul and include those conveniently located next to Aya Sofya Meydanı in Sultanahmet and all along İstiklal Caddesi in Beyoğlu.

The 24-hour *döviz bürosus* (exchange bureaux) in the arrivals hall at Atatürk International Airport offer rates comparable to those offered by city bureaux. Other exchange bureaux can be found on Divan Yolu in Sultanahmet, near the Grand Bazaar and around Sirkeci station in Eminönü.

Post

İstanbul's central PTT (post office; Map p46) is a couple of blocks southwest of Sirkeci Train Station.

There's a convenient PTT booth (Map p46) on Aya Sofya Meydanı in Sultanahmet and there are PTT branches in the basement of the law courts (Map p46) on İmran Öktem Caddesi in Sultanahmet; on Yeni Çarşı Caddesi off Galatasaray Sq (Map p72); near Galata Bridge in Karaköy (Map p72); and in the southwestern corner of the Grand Bazaar (Map p66).

You can send parcels at the central post office, or parcels less than 2kg at other PTT branches (but not at the booth in Sultanahmet).

Telephone

If you are in European İstanbul and wish to call a number in Asian İstanbul, you must dial ☑0216, then the number. If you are in Asian İstanbul and wish to call a number in European İstanbul dial ☑0212, then the number. Don't use the area codes if you are calling a number on the same shore.

Tourist Information

The Ministry of Culture & Tourism operates the following tourist information offices:

Atatürk International Airport (☺24hr) Booth in international arrivals area. Can supply a city map and a transport map.

Elmadağ (Map p72; ☺9am-5pm Mon-Sat) In the arcade in front of the İstanbul Hilton Hotel, just off Cumhuriyet Caddesi, about a 10-minute walk north of Taksim Sq. Due to relocate to the Atatürk Cultural Centre on Taksim Sq when the renovation there is completed.

Karaköy International Maritime Passenger Terminal (Map p72; Kemankeş Caddesi, Karaköy; ☺9am-5pm Mon-Sat)

Sirkeci Train Station (Map p46; ☺8.30am-5pm) Will close or relocate at some stage due to Marmaray transport works.

Sultanahmet (Map p46; ☑0212-518 8754; ☺8.30am-5pm) At the northeast end of the Hippodrome.

ⓘ Getting There & Away

İstanbul is the country's foremost transport hub.

Air

Atatürk International Airport (IST; Atatürk Havalimanı; ☑0212-465 5555; www.ataturkair

port.com) Located 23km west of Sultanahmet. The *dış hatlar* (international terminal) and *iç hatlar* (domestic terminal) are side by side.

FACILITIES There are car-hire desks, money-exchange offices, a pharmacy, ATMs and a PTT in the international arrivals hall and a 24-hour supermarket on the walkway to the metro. The **left-luggage service** (per suitcase per 24hr TL15-20; ⊙24hr) is to your right as you exit customs.

Sabiha Gökçen International Airport (Sabiha Gökçen Havalimanı; SAW; ☑0216-585 5000; www.sgairport.com) Located 50km east of Sultanahmet, on the Asian side of the city, and popular with cut-price European carriers.

FACILITIES There are car-hire desks, exchange offices, a pharmacy, a minimarket and a PTT here.

For details of international flights to and from İstanbul, see p683. For information on flights from İstanbul to other Turkish cities, see p689.

Boat

KARAKÖY

The **Karaköy International Maritime Passenger Terminal** (Map p72) is just near Galata Bridge.

YENİKAPI

Yenikapı (Map p62) is the dock for the **İstanbul Deniz Otobüsleri** (İDO; www.ido.com.tr) fast ferries across the Sea of Marmara to Bursa, Yalova and Bandırma (from where you can catch

a train to İzmir). These carry both passengers and cars.

Bus

The city's main bus station for both intercity and international routes is the **Big İstanbul Bus Station** (Büyük İstanbul Otogarı; ☑0212-658 0505; www.otogaristanbul.com). Called simply the 'otogar', it's in the western district of Esenler, about 10km northwest of Sultanahmet.

The easiest way to get to the otogar is to catch the tram from Sultanahmet to Aksaray and then connect with the Light Rail Transit (LRT) service, which stops at the otogar on its way to the airport – all up a half-hour trip costing only TL3. If you're going to Beyoğlu, bus 830 leaves from the centre of the otogar every 15 minutes between 5.50am and 8.45pm, taking about an hour to reach Taksim Sq (TL1.50). Bus 910 leaves for Eminönü every 15 to 25 minutes between 6am and 8.45pm; the trip takes approximately 50 minutes (TL1.50). A taxi to Sultanahmet costs approximately TL25 (20 minutes); to Taksim Sq it's TL30 (30 minutes).

Excluding holiday periods, you can usually come to the otogar, spend 30 minutes comparing prices and departure times to destinations outside İstanbul, and be on your way within the hour. There's no easy way to find the best fare; you have to go from one office to another asking prices and inspecting the buses parked around the back. If you plan to leave sooner rather than later, make sure you ask about departure times as well as fares. Touts will be happy to sell you a

SERVICES FROM İSTANBUL'S OTOGAR

DESTINATION	FARE (TL)	DURATION (HR)	DISTANCE (KM)
Alanya	83	16	860
Ankara	39-49	6	450
Antalya	71	12½	740
Bodrum	83-95	12½	860
Bursa	25	4	230
Çanakkale	42	6	340
Denizli (for Pamukkale)	60	12	665
Edirne	16	2½	235
Fethiye	65	12	820
Göreme	50-60	11	725
İzmir	56-66	8	575
Kaş	70	12	1090
Konya	54	10	660
Kuşadası	67	9	555
Marmaris	83	12½	805
Trabzon	50	18	1110

cheap fare on a bus leaving in four hours' time, but in the meantime several buses from other companies offering similar rates could have seen you on your way.

There's a much smaller otogar at **Harem** (Map p42; ☎0216-333 3763), south of Üsküdar and north of Haydarpaşa Train Station. If you're arriving in İstanbul by bus from anywhere in Anatolia (the Asian side of Turkey) and your bus stops here first, it's always quicker to get out and take the car ferry to Sirkeci/Eminönü (ferry from 7am, then every half-hour until 9.30pm daily; TL1.50). If you stay on the bus until the Big Otogar, you'll add at least an hour to your journey (and then you'll still have to travel into town). If, however, your bus stops at a private bus station and the driver asks if you want to take a service into Taksim, it will be faster to continue on the original bus to the otogar if you're heading towards Sultanahmet.

For details of international bus services, see p685.

Car & Motorcycle

The E80 Trans-European Motorway (TEM) from Europe passes about 10km north of Atatürk International Airport, then as Hwy 02 takes Fatih Bridge across the Bosphorus to Asia, passing some 1.5km north of Sabiha Gökçen International Airport. This will be your main route for getting to and from İstanbul, but try to avoid rush hours (7am to 10am and 3pm to 7pm Monday to Saturday) as the traffic is nightmarish and the Bosphorus bridges come to a standstill.

If you want to hire a car for your travels, we recommend you hire it from either of the airports on your way *out* of İstanbul, minimising the amount of time you'll need to spend navigating İstanbul's manic roads in an unfamiliar vehicle.

Train

At the time of writing, all trains from Europe were terminating at **Sirkeci Train Station** (Sirkeci Garı; Map p46; ☎0212-520 6575), but this will change as works on the Marmaray project proceed. Outside the station's main door there's a convenient tram that runs up the hill to Sultanahmet or the other way over the Golden Horn to Kabataş, from where you can travel by funicular rail up to Taksim Sq.

Trains from the Asian side of Turkey and from countries east and south currently terminate at **Haydarpaşa Train Station** (Map p42; ☎0216-336 4470), on the Asian shore close to Kadıköy. Ignore anyone who suggests you should take a taxi to or from Haydarpaşa. The ferry between Karaköy and Kadıköy is cheap and speedy; taxis across the Bosphorus always get stuck in traffic. Tickets for trains leaving from Haydarpaşa Train Station can also be purchased from Sirkeci Train Station. Note that as part of the Marmaray project, Haydarpaşa Train Station is scheduled to

INTERNATIONAL TRAIN SERVICES TO/FROM İSTANBUL

For timetable and fare updates, and to check details of when these services depart European destinations on their return trips, go to www.tcdd.gov.tr.

From Sirkeci Train Station

All the following services are express trains. The fares quoted are for a seat (cheapest) to a single couchette (most expensive). Note that at the time of research, the leg between Cerkezkoy and Sirkeci involved a bus transfer due to Marmaray works.

DESTINATION	TRAIN	FARE	DEPARTS	ARRIVES	DURATION (HR)
Belgrade, Serbia	Bosfor/Balkan Ekspresi	€49-109	10pm daily	8.12pm	22
Bucharest, Romania	Bosfor Ekspresi	€38.80-136	10pm daily	5.09pm	19
Sofia, Bulgaria	Bosfor Ekspresi	€20-55	10pm daily	12.40pm	15
Thessaloniki, Greece	Dostluk/Filia Ekspresi	€26-89	8.30am & 9pm daily	10.02pm & 8.30am	11½

From Haydarpaşa Train Station

A ticket for the Trans-Asya train from Haydarpaşa station to Tabriz in Iran costs €352. It departs Wednesday at 11.55pm and arrives in Tabriz 66½ hours later, at 8.20pm on Saturday. The fare quoted is for a 1st-class couchette (the only option available). Note that to get to Syria, you will need to take a train from Gaziantep (Antep) to Aleppo as the *Toros Espress* from İstanbul is no longer operating. See p687 for details.

close and services will move to a new station currently being built in Sögütlüçeşme, near Üsküdar.

Major domestic train services departing Haydarpaşa:

4 Eylül Mavi (Malatya via Ankara, Kayseri & Sivas)

Doğu Ekspresi (Kars via Ankara, Kayseri, Sivas & Erzurum)

Güney Ekspresi (Kurtalan via Ankara, Kayseri, Sivas, Malatya & D iyarbakır)

İç Anadolu Mavi (Adana via Konya)

Meram Ekspresi (Konya)

Pamukkale Ekspresi (Denizli via Eğirdir)

Vangölü Ekspresi (Tatvan via Ankara, Kayseri & Malatya)

There are six services between İstanbul and Ankara: the Baskent, Cumhuriyet, Fatih, Boğazıçı, Anadolu and Ankara Expresses.

❶ Getting Around
To/From the Airport

ATATÜRK INTERNATIONAL AIRPORT

Light Rail Transit (Sultanahmet 50min, Taksim Sq 85min) The easiest and cheapest option. From the arrivals hall, follow the 'Rapid Transit' signs down the escalators and turn right to the LRT station. Travel six stops to Zeytinburnu (TL1.50), where you can connect with a tram (TL1.50) that takes you directly to Sultanahmet and then continues to Kabataş, where you change to a funicular (TL1.50) to go to Taksim Sq. LRT services depart every 10 minutes or so from 5.40am until 1.40am.

Airport Shuttle (www.istanbulairportshuttle. com; per person €10) Eight shuttles per day between the airport and Sultanahmet or Taksim. These can be slow – book ahead and allow lots of time before your flight.

Havaş Airport Bus (☑0212-244 0487; www. havas.com.tr; TL10; 40min) Runs between the airport and Cumhuriyet Caddesi near Taksim Sq. Buses leave the airport every 30 minutes from 4am until 1am.

Taxi A taxi to Sultanahmet or Taksim Sq should cost around TL35, more if there's heavy traffic.

SABIHA GÖKÇEN INTERNATIONAL AIRPORT

Havaş Airport Bus (☑0212-444 0487; www. havas.com.tr; TL13; 1hr) Travels between the airport and Cumhuriyet Caddesi near Taksim Sq. These depart the airport every 30 minutes between 4am and midnight, and thereafter when flights land.

Airport Shuttle (www.istanbulairportshuttle. com; per person €10) Runs seven shuttles per day between the airport and Sultanahmet or Taksim. These can be slow – book ahead and allow lots of time before your flight.

İstanbul Elektrik Tramvay ve Tünel (İETT) is responsible for running public buses, funiculars and historic trams in the city. Its excellent website (www.iett.gov.tr) has useful timetable and route information in Turkish and English. Metro, tram and Light Rail Transit (LRT) services are run by İstanbul Ulaşım (www.istanbul -ulasim.com.tr), and the ferries are run by İstanbul Deniz Otobüsleri (İDO; www.ido.com.tr).

Taxi A taxi to Sultanahmet will cost around TL90, to Taksim Sq TL80. The cost will be higher if there's heavy traffic.

İETT Bus Bus number E3 travels between the airport and the Levent 4 metro station (TL1.50), where you can connect with the metro to Taksim Sq (TL1.50), and then the funicular (TL1.50) and tram (TL1.50) to Sultanahmet, but the trip will take hours. The buses depart between 7am and 10.40pm.

Boat

The most enjoyable and efficient way to get around town is by ferry. **İDO** (☑0212-444 4436; www.ido.com.tr) has timetable information or you can pick up a printed timetable at any of the ferry docks. *Jetons* (transport tokens) cost TL1.50 and it's possible to use the İstanbulkarts (see boxed text, p112) on all routes.

The main ferry docks are at the mouth of the Golden Horn (Eminönü, Sirkeci and Karaköy) and at Beşiktaş, a few kilometres northeast of Galata Bridge, near Dolmabahçe Palace. There are also busy docks at Kadıköy and Üsküdar on the Asian (Anatolian) side. Ferries travel many routes around the city, but the following routes are those commonly used by travellers.

Beşiktaş–Kadıköy Every 30 minutes from 7.45am to 9.15pm.

Eminönü–Anadolu Kavağı Take the Boğaziçi Özel Gezi (Bosphorus Excursions Ferry); between one and three services per day.

Eminönü–Kadıköy Approximately every 15 to 20 minutes from 7.30am to 9.10pm.

Eminönü–Üsküdar Approximately every 20 minutes from 6.35am to 11.30pm.

Kabataş–Kadıköy–Kınalıada–Burgazada– Heybeliada–Büyükada Take the Adalar (Princes' Islands) ferry; approximately every hour from 6.50am to 9pm.

Karaköy–Haydarpaşa Approximately every 20 minutes from 6.10am to 11.30pm.

Karaköy–Kadıköy Approximately every 20 minutes from 6.10am to 11.30pm.

Üsküdar–Eminönü–Kasımpaşa–Fener–Hasköy–Ayvansaray–Sütlüce–Eyüp Take the Haliç ferry; approximately every hour from 10.30am to 7.45pm.

Note: at the time of writing, the Eminönü *iskeles* were being upgraded, which may lead to changes in which ferry line leaves from which *iskele*.

Dolmuş

Dolmuşes are privately run minibuses working defined routes. As a short-term visitor to the city, you won't have much, if any, cause to use them.

Public Transport

BUS

İstanbul's bus system is extremely efficient. The major bus stations are at Taksim Sq, Beşiktaş, Aksaray, Rüstempaşa-Eminönü, Kadıköy and Üsküdar. Most services run between 6.30am and 11.30pm. Destinations and main stops on city bus routes are shown on a sign on the kerbside of the *otobüs* (bus) or on the electronic display at its front.

İETT (www.iett.gov.tr) buses are run by the city and you must have a ticket (TL1.50) before boarding. You can buy tickets from the white booths near major stops or from some nearby shops for a small mark-up (look for 'İETT *otobüs bileti satılır*' signs). Think about stocking up on a supply to last throughout your stay in the city, or buying an İstanbulkart. Blue private buses regulated by the city, called Özel Halk Otobüsü, run the same routes; these accept cash (pay the conductor) and transport cards.

FUNICULAR RAILWAY

The Tünel was built in the late 19th century to save passengers the steep walk from Karaköy up the hill to İstiklal Caddesi in Beyoğlu. The three-minute service still runs today from 7am to 9pm Monday to Friday (from 7.30am on weekends), every five or 10 minutes, and the fare is TL1.

A new funicular railway runs through a tunnel from the Bosphorus shore at Kabataş, where it connects with the tram, up the hill to the metro station at Taksim Sq. The three-minute service runs around every three minutes and costs TL1.50.

LIGHT RAIL TRANSIT (LRT)

An LRT service connects Aksaray with the airport, stopping at 16 stations including the otogar along the way. Services depart every 10 minutes or so from 5.40am until 1.40am and cost TL1.50, no matter how many stops you travel. There are plans to eventually extend this service to Yenikapı.

METRO

A modern metro system connects Şişhane, near Tünel Sq in Beyoğlu, and Atatürk Oto Sanayi in Maslak, the city's financial centre. Unfortunately, it's not possible to travel between the two points in one trip – one metro runs between Şişhane and Taksim Sq; another runs between Taksim and Levent 4, stopping at Osmanbey, Şişli, Gayrettepe and Levent en route; and a third runs between Levent 4 and Atatürk Oto Sanayi, stopping at Sanayi Mahallesi and İTÜ Ayazağa. The full trip takes 30 to 40 minutes. Services run every five minutes or so from 6.15am to 12.30am Monday to Thursday, from 6.15am to 1am on Friday and Saturday and from 6.30am to 12.20am on Sunday. Tickets cost TL1.50.

Works are currently underway to extend the Taksim–Şişhane route over the Golden Horn via a new metro bridge and under the Old City to Yenikapı via stops at Unkapanı, and

TRANSPORT CARDS

If you're in town for a week or so, it makes sense to purchase one of the electronic transport cards that were introduced in 2009. These can be used on the city's ferries, İETT buses, Light Rail Transit (LRT), trams, metro and funiculars:

İstanbulkart Similar to London's Oyster Card, Hong Kong's Octopus Card and Paris' Navigo, the İstanbulkart offers convenience and a slight discount on fares. The cards can be purchased (TL10) and recharged at machines at ferry docks, metro stations and bus stations. They're simple to operate: as you enter a bus or pass through the turnstile at a ferry dock or metro station, swipe your card for entry and the fare will automatically be deducted from your balance.

beşiBiryerde Card Named after traditional Turkish jewellery consisting of five pieces of gold, this nonrechargeable five-fare card costs TL7.50 and is available from machines and ticket booths at ferry docks, metro stations, some tram stops and bus stations.

Note that at the time of writing, both cards were proving hard to access. Ideally, they should be available for purchase and recharging at machines at ferry docks, metro stations and bus stations. Ask your hotel for an update on their status, price and availability.

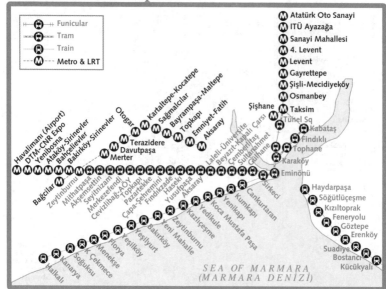

Şehzadebaşı. It will then connect with the LRT to Aksaray and with a transport tunnel that's being built under the Bosphorus as part of the Marmaray project. This tunnel will include a metro connection between Yenikapı, Sirkeci, Üsküdar and Sögütlüçeşme.

TRAIN

İstanbul has two *banliyö treni* (suburban train lines). The first rattles along the Sea of Marmara shore from Sirkeci Train Station, around Seraglio Point to Cankurtaran (Sultanahmet), Kumpapı, Yenikapı and a number of stations before terminating past Atatürk International Airport at Halkalı. The second runs from Haydarpaşa Train Station to Gebze via Bostancı. Though decrepit, the trains are reliable (nearly every half-hour) and cheap (TL1.50). Note that services will be suspended at some point so that works can be completed on the Marmaray project.

TRAM

An excellent *tramvay* (tramway) service runs from Zeytinburnu (where it connects with the airport LRT) to Sultanahmet and Eminönü, and then across Galata Bridge to Karaköy (to connect with the funicular to Tünel) and Kabataş (to connect with the funicular to Taksim Sq). Trams run every five minutes or so from 6am to midnight. Tickets cost TL1.50. There's also a line from Zeytinburnu to Bağcılar, but tourists have little or no need to use this.

A quaint antique tram rattles its way up and down İstiklal Caddesi in Beyoğlu daily, beginning

its 15-minute journey just outside the Tünel station and travelling to Taksim Sq, stopping in front of the Galatasaray Lycée en route. Tickets aren't available on board – you'll need to purchase a *jeton* (TL1.50) from the Tünel station.

Taxi

İstanbul is full of yellow taxis. The flagfall is TL2.50 and the rate per km is TL1.50. There are no evening surcharges.

Taxi rates are very reasonable – from Sultanahmet to Taksim Sq will cost around TL12; ignore taxi drivers who insist on a fixed rate as these are much higher than you'd pay using the meter. Double-check the money you give the driver, too: drivers have been known to insist they were given a TL5 note for payment, when they were really given TL20.

Few of the city's taxis have seatbelts. If you take a taxi over either of the Bosphorus bridges it is your responsibility to cover the toll. The driver will add this to your fare.

As far as tipping goes, locals usually round up the fare to the nearest 0.5TL.

AROUND İSTANBUL

If you're staying in İstanbul for a while you may want to consider taking a day trip to the Princes' Islands, a peaceful antidote to the hustle and bustle of the big city.

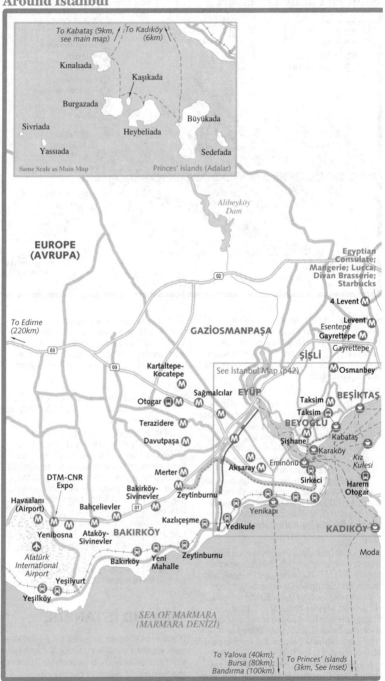

To Kabataş (9km, see main map)
To Kadıköy (6km)

Kınalıada

Kaşıkada

Burgazada

Sivriada

Heybeliada

Büyükada

Yassıada

Sedefada

Same Scale as Main Map

Princes' İslands (Adalar)

Alibeyköy Dam

EUROPE (AVRUPA)

Egyptian Consulate;
Mangerie; Lucca;
Divan Brasserie;
Starbucks

02

4 Levent Ⓜ

Levent Ⓜ
Esentepe
Gayrettepe Ⓜ
Gayrettepe

To Edirne (220km)

03

GAZİOSMANPAŞA

ŞİŞLİ

03

Kartaltepe-Kocatepe

See İstanbul Map (p42)

Ⓜ Osmanbey

Otogar ⓂⓂ

Sağmalcılar Ⓜ

EYÜP

Taksim Ⓜ

BEŞİKTAŞ

Terazidere Ⓜ

Taksim

BEYOĞLU

Davutpaşa Ⓜ

Ⓜ

Şişhane Ⓜ

Kabataş

Karaköy

Kız Kulesi

Merter Ⓜ

Ⓜ

Aksaray Ⓜ

Eminönü

Bakırköy-Sivinevler Ⓜ

Zeytinburnu

Sirkeci

Harem Otogar

DTM-CNR Expo

Bahçelievler

01

Ⓜ

Kazlıçeşme

Yenikapı

KADIKÖY Ⓞ

Havaalanı (Airport)
Ⓜ

Ⓜ Ⓜ

Ataköy-Sivinevler

Ⓜ

BAKIRKÖY

Yedikule

Moda

Yenibosna

Ⓐ
Atatürk International Airport

Bakırköy

Yeni Mahalle

Zeytinburnu

Yeşilyurt

Yeşilköy

SEA OF MARMARA (MARMARA DENİZİ)

To Yalova (40km);
Bursa (80km);
Bandırma (100km)

To Princes' Islands
(3km, See Inset)

Princes' Islands

Most İstanbullus refer to the Princes' Islands as Adalar ('The Islands'). The group lies about 20km southeast of the city in the Sea of Marmara and makes a great destination for a day's escape, particularly as the ferry ride here is so enjoyable.

In Byzantine times, refractory princes, deposed monarchs and others who had outlived their roles were interned on the islands (rather like Abdullah Öcalan, the ex-PKK leader, marooned today on İmralı Island in the Sea of Marmara). A ferry service from İstanbul was started in the mid-19th century and the islands became popular summer resorts with Pera's Greek, Jewish and Armenian business communities. Many of the fine Victorian villas built by these wealthy merchants survive today.

You'll realise after landing that there are no cars on the islands, something that comes as a welcome relief after the traffic mayhem of the city. Except for the necessary police, fire and sanitation vehicles, transport is by bicycle, horse-drawn carriage and foot, as in centuries past.

All of the islands are extremely busy during the summer, particularly on weekends, so we recommend avoiding a Sunday visit.

There are nine islands in the group and the ferry stops at four. Year-round there are 15,000 permanent residents scattered across the six islands that are populated, but numbers swell to 100,000 or so during the summer months when İstanbullus – many of whom have holiday homes here – come here to escape the city heat.

⦿ Sights & Activities

The ferry's first stop is **Kınalıada**, a favourite holiday spot for İstanbul's Armenian population. It is sprinkled with low-rise apartments, all sporting red tiled roofs and oriented towards the water. The island has a few pebble beaches, a modernist mosque and an Armenian church to the left of the ferry station.

The second stop, **Burgazada**, has always been favoured by İstanbullus of Greek heritage. Sights include a hilltop chapel, mosques, a synagogue, a handful of restaurants and the home of the late writer Sait Faik, now a modest **museum** (☉9am-noon & 2-5pm Mon-Fri, to 1pm Sat). Frankly, neither island offers much reward for the trouble of getting off the ferry.

İSTANBUL PRINCES' ISLANDS

In contrast, the charming island of **Heybeliada** (Heybeli for short) has much to offer the visitor. It's home to the Turkish Naval Academy, which was founded in 1773 and is seen to the left of the ferry dock as you arrive. It also has several restaurants and a thriving shopping strip with bakeries and delicatessens selling picnic provisions to day trippers, who come here on weekends to walk in the pine groves and swim from the tiny (but crowded) beaches. The island's major landmark is the hilltop **Haghia Triada Monastery** (☑0216-351 8563). Perched above a picturesque line of poplar trees in a spot that has been occupied by a Greek monastery since Byzantine times, this building dates from 1894 and has an internationally renowned library. The monastery functioned as a Greek Orthodox school of theology where priests were trained until 1971, when it was controversially closed on the government's orders. You may be able to visit if you call ahead.

Heybeliada has a couple of hotels, including the **Merit Halki Palace**, which is perched at the top of Rafah Şehitleri Caddesi and commands wonderful views over the water. The delightful walk up to this hotel passes a host of large wooden villas set in lovingly tended gardens. There are many lanes and streets leading to picnic spots and lookout points off the upper reaches of this street. To do this walk, turn right as you leave the ferry and make your way past the waterfront restaurants and cafes to the plaza with the Atatürk statue. From here walk up İşgüzar Sokak, veering right until you hit Rafah Şehitleri Caddesi.

If you don't feel like a walk (this one's uphill but not too steep), you can hire a bicycle from one of the shops in the main street or a *fayton* (horse-drawn carriage) to take you on a tour of the island. A *küçük tur* (25-minute tour) costs TL30, a *büyük tur* (one-hour tour) TL40. Some visitors choose to spend the day by the **pool** (weekdays/weekends TL50/60) at the Merit Halki Palace, but most locals swim at the beaches around the island; however, it pays to check the cleanliness of the water before you join them.

The largest island in the group, **Büyükada** ('Great Island'), shows an impressive face to visitors arriving on the ferry, with gingerbread villas climbing up the slopes of the hill and the bulbous twin cupolas of the Splendid Otel providing an unmistakable landmark.

The **ferry terminal** is a lovely building in the Ottoman kiosk style dating from 1899. Inside, there's a pleasant cafe with an outdoor terrace. There are eateries serving fresh fish to the left of the ferry terminal, next to an ATM.

In 2010, the **Islands Museum** opened in the former Büyükada Primary School, one of a slew of cultural projects undertaken as part of İstanbul's European Capital of Culture program. Exhibits document the heritage of the Princes' Islands.

The island's main tourist attraction is the Greek **Monastery of St George**, in the saddle between Büyükada's two highest hills. To get here, walk from the ferry straight ahead to the clock tower in İskele Meydanı (Dock Sq). The shopping district (with cheap eateries) is to the left along Recep Koç Sokak.

Bear right onto 23 Nisan Caddesi, then head along Çankaya Caddesi up the hill to the monastery; when you come to a fork in the road, veer right. The enjoyable walk, which takes at least one hour, takes you past a long progression of impressive wooden villas set in gardens. About a quarter of the way up on the left is the **Büyükada Kültür Evi**, a charming spot where you can enjoy a tea or coffee in a garden setting. The house itself dates from 1878 and was restored in 1998.

After 40 minutes or so you will reach a reserve called 'Luna Park' by the locals. The monastery is a 25-minute walk up an extremely steep hill from here. As you ascend you will sometimes see pieces of cloth tied onto the branches of trees along the path – each represents a prayer, mostly offered by female supplicants who are visiting the monastery to pray for a child.

When you reach the monastery, there's not a lot to see. A small and gaudy church is the only building of note, but there are fabulous panoramic views from the terrace, as well as a small restaurant. From here it's possible to see all the way to İstanbul, as well as over to the nearby islands of Yassıada and Sivriada.

Bicycles are available for rent in town, and shops on the market street can provide picnic supplies, although food is cheaper on the mainland.

Just off the clock tower square and opposite the Splendid Otel you'll find a *fayton* stand. Hire one for a long tour of town, the hills and shore (one hour, TL55) or a shorter tour of the town only (TL22). It costs TL20 to be taken to 'Luna Park'. A shop just near the *fayton* stand hires out bicycles.

✕ Eating

Unfortunately, restaurants on the islands are unremarkable and pricey, particularly those overlooking the water near the ferry terminals.

HEYBELIADA

Mavi Restaurant   SEAFOOD €€€
(www.mavirestaurant.net; Yali Caddesi 29; mains TL14-40; ⊙24hr) This fish restaurant on the main waterfront promenade is popular with locals and has loads of outdoor seating.

BÜYÜKADA

Yücetepe Kır Gazinosu
Restaurant   ANATOLIAN €€
(Monastery of St George; mains TL9-11; ⊙daily Apr-Oct, weekends only Nov-Mar) Simple but appetising food is served at the outdoor tables here. It even sells alcohol.

Kiyi Restaurant   SEAFOOD €€€
(Çiçekli Yali Sokak 2; mains TL22; ⊙summer only) This ramshackle place is a favourite of big-city food critics. Start with the mezes (there are plenty of options) and then opt for some simply grilled or fried locally caught fish. To get here, walk left from the ferry terminal alongside the water, passing the row of restaurants and then turning around the bend.

Club Mavi   ANATOLIAN €€€
(clubmavi.com/ada/ada.html; Büyüktur Yolu 12; mains TL20-30; ⊙summer only) This hotel restaurant is in a pine grove on a bluff on the quiet side of the island – taking a *fayton* here and back is an enjoyable part of the experience. The food takes second place to the view, which is spectacular.

Sofrada Restoran   LOKANTA €€
(Isa Çelebi Sokak 10; porsiyon TL8-14) Near the *fayton* park and clock tower, this place

serves up simple dishes including *mücver* (zucchini fritters), köfte and *karniyarik* (aubergine stuffed with minced meat). You won't find a cheaper meal than this on the island.

ℹ Getting There & Away

In summer, ferries run to the islands every day between 6.50am and 9pm, departing from the Adalar İskelesi ferry dock at Kabataş, opposite the tram stop. The most useful departure times for day trippers are 8.30am, 9.20am, 10.10am, 10.40am and 11.35am Monday to Saturday and 8.30am, 9am, 9.30am, 10am, 11am and noon on Sunday, but timetables change, so check www.ido.com.tr beforehand.

The ferry returns from Büyükada at times including 4pm, 4.45pm, 5.45pm, 6.30pm and 7.40pm Monday to Saturday and 3.15pm, 4.30pm, 5.05pm, 5.45pm and 6.15pm on Sunday, stopping at Heybeliada en route to Kabataş. The last ferry of the day leaves Büyükada at 7.40pm (9pm on Sunday). The trip costs TL3 to the islands, and the same for the return trip; legs between the islands cost TL1.50.

Note that the ferries seem dangerously overcrowded on summer weekends; time your trip for weekdays or make sure you board the vessel and grab a seat at least half an hour before departure unless you want to stand the whole way.

The ferry steams away from Kabataş and after 20 minutes makes a quick stop at Kadıköy on the Asian side before making its way to the first island, Kınalıada. It's not uncommon to see dolphins on this leg of the trip (25 minutes). After this, it's another 10 minutes to Burgazada, another 15 minutes again to Heybeliada and another 10 minutes to Büyükada.

Many day trippers stay on the ferry until Heybeliada, stop there for an hour or so, and then hop on a ferry to Büyükada, where they have lunch and spend the rest of the afternoon.

You can also take a fast catamaran from Eminönü or Kabataş to Bostancı on the Asian shore, then another from Bostancı to Heybeliada and Büyükada, but you save little time and the cost is much higher.

Thrace & Marmara

Best Places to Stay

» Gallipoli Houses (p137)
» Hotel Kervansaray (p141)
» Zeytindali Hotel (p146)
» Hotel Crowded House (p138)
» Hotel Endorfina (p126)

Best Places to Eat

» Melek Anne (p125)
» Doyuranlar Gözleme (p138)
» İlhan Restaurant (p130)
» Liman Restaurant (p139)
» Zindanaltı Meyhanesi (p125)

Why Go?

Although much of Turkey's European sliver is distinctively Balkan, the area lies at the heart of Turkish identity. On the Gallipoli (Gelibolu) Peninsula, contemporary Turkey's national consciousness was forged in the bloody WWI campaign; along with a sense of nationhood for Australia and New Zealand, and the Atatürk (Mustafa Kemal) legend. Today, the Aegean breeze ruffling the pines belies the battles that took place here. Edirne was the capital of the Ottoman Empire before Mehmet the Conqueror (Mehmet Fatih) took Constantinople (İstanbul), and the Tunca River flows past mosque and palace complexes. The city's 650-year-old Historic Kırkpınar Oil Wrestling Festival recalls the days of Ottoman-Byzantine clashes.

Overlooking the Dardanelles from the Anatolian side, studenty Çanakkale is a good urban hang-out. Gökçeada island, with windblown beaches and tumbledown Greek villages perched above its central valley, is one of the best-kept secrets in the entire Aegean.

When to Go

Edirne

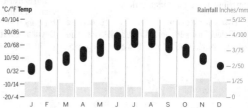

May Fields of vivid red poppies carpet Gökçeada island.

Late June/early July Oily Goliaths grapple at the Historic Kırkpınar Oil Wrestling Festival, Edirne.

September Autumn on the Gallipoli Peninsula.

Edirne

📞 0284 / POP 136,000

Despite being European Turkey's largest settlement outside İstanbul, Edirne is (unwisely) disregarded by all but a handful of travellers, who come to enjoy its stunning mosques. The city was the Ottoman capital for almost a century, and many of its key buildings are in excellent shape. You can enjoy mosques as fine as almost any in İstanbul – without the crowds you have to fight through by the Bosphorus. However, Edirne is hardly a backwater; with the Greek and Bulgarian frontiers a half-hour's drive away, it's a bustling border town. The streets are crowded with foreigners, locals,

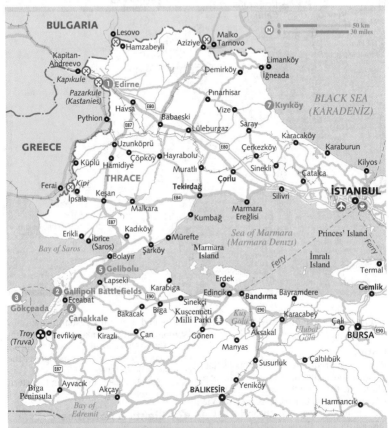

Thrace & Marmara Highlights

❶ Marvel at the floating dome in master architect Mimar Sinan's **Selimiye Camii** (p120), one of Edirne's great Ottoman mosques

❷ Walk through the blood-soaked past and peaceful present of the **Gallipoli battlefields** (p131)

❸ Enjoy the rugged landscape and the eerily out-of-time Greek atmosphere in villages on the remote island of **Gökçeada** (p145)

❹ Watch the slippery fun at Edirne's annual **Historic Kırkpınar Oil Wrestling Festival** (p122)

❺ Feast on fish and add a Turkish flag to the 'Flag Father Tomb' in **Gelibolu** (p128), home to one of the peninsula's better war museums

❻ Catch some live music among students and 'beer bongs' in vibrant **Çanakkale** (p140)

❼ Cool off in the gin-clear waters of the Black Sea at the fishing village of **Kıyıköy** (p126)

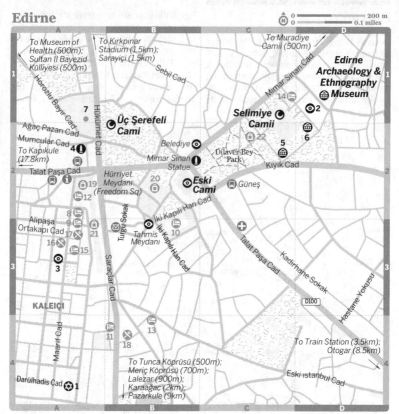

and the occasional uniformed parade from the military garrison.

History

Emperor Hadrian made Hadrianopolis (later Adrianople) the main centre of Roman Thrace in the early 2nd century AD. The settlement was an important stop on the Via Ignatia linking Rome with İstanbul. In the mid-14th century the nascent Ottoman state began to grow in size and power. In 1363 its army crossed the Dardanelles, skirted Constantinople and captured Adrianople, which the Ottomans made their capital.

For a century, Edirne was the city from which the Ottoman sultan launched campaigns in Europe and Asia. When the time was ripe for the final conquest of the Byzantine Empire, Mehmet the Conqueror set out for Constantinople from here.

When the Ottoman Empire collapsed after WWI, the Allies handed Thrace to the Greeks and declared Constantinople (now İstanbul) an international city. In the summer of 1920 Greek armies occupied Edirne, only to be driven back by forces under the command of Atatürk. The Treaty of Lausanne (1923) ceded Edirne and eastern Thrace to the Turks.

⊙ Sights & Activities

Selimiye Camii   MOSQUE
(Selimiye Mosque) Great Ottoman architect Mimar Sinan (see boxed text, p78) designed Edirne's grandest mosque (1569–75) for Sultan Selim II (r 1566–74). The mosque is smaller but more elegant than Sinan's Süleymaniye Camii in İstanbul, and it is said that he considered this to be his finest work. Lit up at night, the complex is a spectacular sight.

Enter the mosque through the courtyard to the west, as the architect intended, rather than through the terraced park or

Edirne

the subterranean row of shops to the south. You don't need to buy a plastic bag for your shoes from the ladies in the courtyard.

The broad, lofty dome – at 31.3m, marginally wider than that of İstanbul's Aya Sofya – is supported by eight unobtrusive pillars, arches and external buttresses, creating a surprisingly spacious interior. As they only bear a portion of the dome's weight, the walls are sound enough to hold dozens of windows, the light from which brings out the interior's colourful calligraphic decorations.

The delicately carved marble *mimber* (pulpit), with its conical roof of İznik tiles, and the *şadırvan* (ablutions fountain) beneath the central prayer-reader's platform are particularly exquisite.

Part of the Selimiye's striking effect comes from its four 71m-high minarets, which Sinan fluted to emphasise their height. Each tower also has three *şerefes* (balconies), Sinan's respectful nod, perhaps, to his predecessor, the architect of the Üç Şerefeli Cami.

Medreses   MUSEUMS

(Selimiye Camii) The *medrese* (seminary) in the southern corner of the Selimiye complex houses the Selimiye Foundation Museum (Selimiye Vakıf Müzesi; ☏212 1133; admission free; ⊙9am-5pm Tue-Sun), with displays cov-

ering the restoration of the mosque, metalwork, İznik tiles and seminary education. The *medrese* in the eastern corner houses the Turkish & Islamic Arts Museum (Türk İslam Eserleri Müzesi), which was being renovated when we visited.

Edirne Archaeology & Ethnography Museum   MUSEUM

(Edirne Arkeoloji ve Etnografya Müzesi; ☏225 1120; admission TL3; ⊙9am-5pm Tue-Sun) Facing a garden of janissary gravestones behind the Selimiye Camii, this museum focuses on local history and traditional products, with displays covering embroidery, textiles, calligraphy and jewellery. The Ottoman technique of lacquering wood, cardboard and leather was developed in Edirne. There are several reconstructions of Ottoman houses, including bridal and circumcision rooms.

The archaeological section features exhibits from prehistory, with finds from the Macedonian Tower and the Taşlıcabayır tumulus near Kırklareli to the east. The terracotta sarcophagi (6th century BC) from Enez (Aenus) in southwest Thrace; the 1st- and 2nd-century terracotta figures; and the bronze figures from a millennium earlier are exquisite. The grounds contain all kinds of jars, sculptures, menhirs (standing stones), a dolmen and a Roman tomb.

SLIP-SLIDING AWAY IN EDİRNE

One of the world's oldest and most bizarre sporting events, in which muscular men, naked except for a pair of heavy leather shorts, coat themselves with olive oil and throw each other around, takes place annually in late June/early July in northern Edirne. It's called the **Tarihi Kırkpınar Yağlı Güreş Festivali** (Historic Kırkpınar Oil Wrestling Festival).

The origins of this oleaginous contest go back 6½ centuries to the early days of the Ottoman Empire. Shortly before the conquest of Edirne in 1363, Sultan Orhan Gazi sent his brother Süleyman Paşa with 40 men to conquer the Byzantine fortress at Domuz in Rumelia, the European part of the Ottoman Empire. The two-score soldiers were all keen wrestlers, and after their victory challenged each other to bouts. Two of them were so evenly matched that they fought for days without any clear result, until both of them finally dropped dead. When the bodies were buried under a nearby fig tree, a spring mysteriously appeared. The site was given the name Kırkpınar ('40 Springs'), in the wrestlers' honour.

The original Kırkpınar is now the village of Samona, just over the border in Greece; the annual three-day contest has been held outside Edirne since the birth of the republic. Wrestlers, who are classed not by weight but by height, age and experience, compete in 13 categories – from *minik* (toddler) to *baş* (first class) – and dozens of matches take place simultaneously in the Sarayiçi stadium. Bouts are now capped at 30 or 40 minutes, after which they enter 'sudden death' one-fall-wins overtime. When all the fights are decided, prizes are awarded for gentlemanly conduct and technique, as well as the coveted and hotly contested *başpehlivan* (head wrestler) title.

You can buy tickets to the wrestling from **Biletix** (www.biletix.com) for about TL30. Transport and accommodation fill up fast around the festival.

For more information visit **Kırkpınar Evi** (Kırkpınar House; ☑212 8622; www.kirkpinar.com; ⊙10am-noon & 2-6pm), with displays about oil wrestling, or check out its website and www.turkishwrestling.com.

Üç Şerefeli Cami   MOSQUE

(Three-Balcony Mosque) With its four strikingly different minarets, the Üç Şerefeli Cami dominates Hürriyet Meydanı (Freedom Sq). The name refers to the three balconies on the tallest minaret. The second-tallest minaret has only two.

It was built between 1437 and 1447 in a design halfway between the Seljuk Turkish-style mosques of Konya and Bursa and the truly Ottoman style, which would later reach its pinnacle in İstanbul. In the Seljuk style, smaller domes are mounted on square rooms, whereas here the 24m-wide dome is mounted on a hexagonal drum and supported by two walls and two massive hexagonal pillars. The designs under the domes and central *şadırvan* in the partially covered courtyard – another innovation that came to be standard – are fantastic.

Sokollu Mehmet Paşa Hamam   HAMAM

(wash & massage TL30; ⊙for men 7am-10pm, for women 10am-6pm) Across the street from the Üç Şerefeli Cami, Mimar Sinan designed this atmospheric hamam for Grand Vizier Sokollu Mehmet Paşa in the 16th century.

Makedonya Kulesi   LANDMARK

Southwest of the hamam stands the restored **Macedonian Tower**, part of the city fortifications dating back to Roman times. Around its base, recent excavations have uncovered parts of the old city wall, a necropolis and the remains of a Byzantine church. Artefacts and smaller finds can be seen in the Edirne Archaeology & Ethnography Museum.

Eski Cami   MOSQUE

The **Old Mosque** (1403–14) exemplifies one of the two classic mosque styles used by the Ottomans in their earlier capital, Bursa. Like Bursa's Ulu Cami, the Eski Cami has rows of arches and pillars supporting a series of small domes. Inside, there are striking red, white and black geometric patterns on the domes, and a marvellous *mimber;* huge calligraphic inscriptions cover the walls.

Kaleiçi   HISTORIC AREA

The Kaleiçi area, framed by Saraçlar Caddesi, Talat Paşa Caddesi, the railway line and the Tunca River, was the original medieval town, with narrow streets laid out on a grid plan. You could start exploring by walking south from the tourist office along Maarif Caddesi, which takes you past some fine examples of ornate wooden houses with attractive Edirnekari woodwork and finishes at Edirne's derelict Great Synagogue (Büyük Sinagog; 1906). Cumhuriyet Caddesi, running perpendicular to Maarif Caddesi, is another interesting street with wooden houses.

NORTH OF THE CENTRE

TOP CHOICE Museum of Health MUSEUM
(Sağlık Müzesi; ☎224 0922; admission TL10; ⊙9am-5.30pm) Part of the Sultan Bayezid II Külliyesi complex, this museum has scooped European tourism awards for its illustrations of the therapy and teaching that took place here. One of the most important Ottoman hospitals, it operated from 1488 to 1909, and music therapy was employed from 1652 – when mentally ill people were still being burnt alive in Europe. A 10-piece band played different 'modes' to treat ailments from paralysis to palpitations. Because all healing work was carried out in one room (the şifahane – healing room), the hospital required fewer staff. This created the first centralised hospital system. The sound of water was also used, and the gurgling fountain in the high-ceilinged hall is certainly soothing after a long walk from the centre.

The museum continues into the medrese, where dioramas cover aspects of Ottoman medicine, including a cauterisation – a popular operation – and the development of antidotes (coaxing a viper to bite a chicken).

Approach via the Ottoman Yalnızgöz Köprüsü (Lone Eye Bridge; 1570) over the Tunca River. Buses to Yenimaret ('Y.Maret') from opposite the tourist office pass the complex (TL1, 10 minutes); a taxi costs about TL7.

Sultan II Bayezid Külliyesi MOSQUE
Standing in splendid isolation north of the centre, this mosque complex was undergoing renovations at the time of writing. Ottoman architect Hayreddin built it for Sultan Bayezid II (r 1481–1512) between 1484 and 1488. In style, the mosque lies midway between the Üç Şerefeli and Selimiye models: its large prayer hall has one large dome, similar to the Selimiye, but it also has a courtyard and fountain, like the earlier Üç Şerefeli. The interior has a rough, almost unfinished feel to it.

The extensive complex includes a tabhane (travellers hostel), bakery, imaret (soup kitchen), tımarhane (asylum), medrese and darüşşifa (hospital).

Sarayiçi HISTORIC AREA
The Inner Palace is actually an island that was once the private hunting reserve of the Ottoman sultans. Today it's the site of the famous Kırkpınar oil wrestling matches.

Near the modern stadium, which is flanked by uberbutch başpehlivan (champions) in bronze, stands the Adalet Kasrı (Justice Hall; 1561), a stone tower with a conical roof that dates from the time of Süleyman the Magnificent. In front of it are two square columns: on the Seng-i Hürmet (Stone of Respect) to the right, people would place petitions to the sultan, while the Seng-i İbret (Stone of Warning) on the left displayed the heads of high-court officers who had managed to dis the sultan.

Behind the Justice Hall is the small Fatih Köprüsü (Conqueror Bridge; 1452). Across it and on the right is a sombre Balkan Wars memorial; straight ahead and to the left are the scattered ruins of Edirne Sarayı (Edirne Palace), part of which are being restored. Begun by Sultan Murat II in 1450, the palace once rivalled İstanbul's Topkapı Palace in size and luxury, though you'd be hard-pressed to visualise it nowadays.

To get here, walk north along Hükümet Caddesi and cross the Tunca River on Saraçhane Köprüsü (Saddler's Bridge); or head north on Mimar Sinan Caddesi and Saray Yolu, and cross the river on Saray Köprüsü (Palace Bridge; 1560). Alternatively, it's a scenic 1km walk along the road to the north of the river from the Sultan Bayezid II complex.

Muradiye Camii MOSQUE
A 15-minute walk northeast of Selimiye Mosque along Mimar Sinan Caddesi brings you to the Muradiye Mosque, built for Sultan Murat II and topped with an unusual cupola. Note the massive calligraphy on the exterior. Built between 1426 and 1436, it once housed a Mevlevi (whirling dervish) lodge. The mosque's T-shaped plan, with twin eyvans (vaulted halls) and fine İznik tiles, is reminiscent of Ottoman work in Bursa.

The small cemetery on the east side contains the grave of Şeyhülislâm Musa Kâzım Efendi, the Ottoman Empire's last chief Islamic judge, who fled the British occupation of İstanbul after WWI and died here in 1920.

SOUTH OF THE CENTRE

To reach the quiet south from the centre, follow Saraçlar Caddesi under the railway line and cross the **Tunca Köprüsü**, an Ottoman stone humpback bridge dating back to 1615, and the equally graceful **Meriç Köprüsü** (1847). The area around the bridges is packed with restaurants, tea gardens and bars, all great places to come for a drink or a meal in warm weather. The best ones are those on the southern side of the Meriç River, which offer perfect sunset river vistas.

A taxi back to the centre costs TL7; a horse and cart, TL10.

🛌 Sleeping

Most of Edirne's budget and midrange hotels are on Maarif Caddesi.

Selimiye Taşodalar

TOP CHOICE

BOUTIQUE HOTEL €€

(☎212 3529; www.tasodalar.com.tr; Selimiye Arkası Hamam Sokak 3; s/d from €80/100; ❄@) Occupying a historic Ottoman mansion, the 'Stone Rooms' could not be in a choicer spot: next to Selimiye Mosque and the 14th-century Sultan Selim Saray Hamam. Some of the nine rooms' bathrooms are disappointing, and a few pieces of kitsch feel out of place in the Ottoman interiors, but antiques and cedar furniture abound. Room 104 has an attractive mirrored dresser, and kingly 109 has a closed balcony overlooking the mosque. The hotel has an in-house restaurant and a pleasant tea garden.

Efe Hotel BOUTIQUE HOTEL €€

(☎213 6166; www.efehotel.com; Maarif Caddesi 13; s/d TL85/125; ❄@) The Efe is a stylish choice, with a lobby filled with antiques and curios, and paintings, photos and prints in the corridors. The 22 bright little rooms are well equipped and the hotel features the English Pub, open from September to May, and the flashy Patio bar-restaurant.

Hotel Rüstempaşa Kervansaray HISTORIC HOTEL €€

(☎212 6119; www.edirnekervansarayhotel.com; İki Kapılı Han Caddesi 57; s/d TL60/120; ❄) Just south of the Eski Cami, this 75-room hotel occupies a 16th-century *han* (caravanserai), built for Süleyman the Magnificent's grand vizier Rüstempaşa. Its inner courtyard of-

fers a romantic setting for breakfast; the rooms, reached via narrow stone steps and long corridors, are of a good size but are airless and underwhelming.

Tuna Hotel HOTEL €€

(☎214 3340; fax 214 3323; Maarif Caddesi 17; s/d TL60/85; ❄) The 'Danube' is a dependable choice, from its comfortable maroon rooms with small TV to the modest breakfast spread, served in a small courtyard by the back annexe.

Otel Açıkgöz HOTEL €

(☎213 1944; hotelacikgoz@acikgoz.com; Tüfekçiler Çarşısı 54; s/d TL50/70; P❄) Apart from its slightly out-of-the-way location, the 'Open Eye' is one of Edirne's best deals. Behind its unprepossessing exterior, set back from the pedestrianised main drag, its 35 rooms tick all the boxes without flourish, with small fridges and TVs.

Saray Hotel HOTEL €€

(☎212 1457; www.edirnesarayhotel.com, in Turkish; Eski İstanbul Caddesi 28; s/d TL45/80; ❄) Beneath its huge orange sign, the 'Palace' is a modest, 44-room business hotel with a 'who's who' of oil wrestlers hanging at the entrance. It often fills up, so book ahead.

Park Hotel HOTEL €€

(☎225 4610; parkotel@isnet.net.tr; Maarif Caddesi 7; s/d TL65/120; ❄) The rooms here, with glass-fronted showers, are much pleasanter than suggested by the scruffy-looking reception area. The large 1st-floor lounge even fits in a massage chair, and a restaurant and pub adjoin the hotel.

Hotel Aksaray PENSION €€

(☎212 6035; Alipaşa Ortakapı Caddesi 8; s/d/tr excl breakfast TL40/75/90, s/tr without bathroom TL30/80; ❄) The rooms in this building are cheap but not particularly good value, with less-than-spotless bathrooms despite the smell of bleach. Although it sports a ceiling fresco, the ground-floor room next to reception is noisy at night.

🍴 Eating

There's a wide assortment of eateries along Saraçlar Caddesi. The riverside restaurants south of the centre are more atmospheric, but most open only in summer and are often booked solid at weekends.

The city's dish of choice is *Edirne ciğeri*, which is thinly sliced calf's liver deep fried and eaten with crispy fried red chillies and yoghurt.

TOP CHOICE Melek Anne   CAFE €

(☑213 3263; Maarif Caddesi 18; mains TL6) Occupying a 120-year-old house, there's an arty feel to 'Mama Angel's' green and purple furniture and outdoor area with beanbags. A good range of home cooking is offered throughout the day, including breakfast plus vegetarian and chicken dishes.

Zindanaltı Meyhanesi   MEYHANE €€

(☑212 2149; Saraçlar Caddesi 127; meze TL5, mains TL9) Choose your meze, such as spicy *patlıcan* (eggplant/aubergine), and mains, including a *karışık* (mixed) plate with *köfte* (meatballs) and *şiş* kebap (roast skewered meat) among other goodies, and head to the roof terrace. The wooden-fronted building is a popular spot with views of the pedestrianised main drag.

Niyazi Usta   KEBAPÇI €€

(☑213 3372; Alipaşa Ortakapı Caddesi; ciğeri TL9) If you're ready to try Edirne-style calf's liver, head to this bright, modern and spotlessly clean eatery. There's a smaller branch on the far side of the florist.

Lalezar   MODERN TURKISH €€

(☑223 0600; Karaağaç Yolu; mains TL9-20) The best riverside option on the way to Karaağaç, Lalezar has a bilingual menu with dishes ranging from pide (Turkish-style pizza) to pasta, including the spicy *içli köfte* (stuffed meatball) starter. The grounds are a delight, and some choice tables are set on raised platforms among the trees.

Penaltı   CAFE €

(Alipaşa Ortakapı Caddesi; mains TL6.50) Its walls hung with photos of soccer stars, 'Penalty' snack bar is the local tip for Turkish *kahvaltı* (breakfast). Not-so-inspiring burgers are also available.

🍷 Drinking & Entertainment

Tea gardens cluster around the Mimar Sinan statue in the city centre, and there's a row of bars between the two bridges south of the centre.

Café Pena   BAR

(Alipaşa Ortakapı Caddesi 6) Decorated with film posters and Americana in its outside courtyard and multiple upstairs rooms, Pena attracts a lively, young crowd (and that's just the staff). Draft beer, cocktails and fancy coffees are on offer.

London Café   BAR

(Saraçlar Caddesi; mains TL5) This unexpected pleasure on two floors serves non-Turkish staples such as pasta and sandwiches, but its raison d'être is the dispensing of booze.

Patio   BAR-RESTAURANT

(Aziziye Sokak 5; mains TL15) The staff are slightly too cool for *okul* (school), but local kids come to this stylish, sanitised spot to drink jazzy cocktails and east Western fare. Trees grow in the partly covered courtyard and the soundtrack is chill-out.

🛍 Shopping

Traditional Edirne souvenirs include *meyve sabunu* (fruit-shaped soaps) scented with attar of roses, and *badem ezmesi* (marzipan).

Ali Paşa Covered Bazaar   BAZAAR

(off Saraçlar Caddesi) Mimar Sinan designed this atmospheric bazaar in 1569.

Bedesten   MARKET

(off Talat Paşa Caddesi) Across a little wooden bridge from the Eski Cami, this market dates from 1418.

Selimiye Arastası   MARKET

(Selimiye Arcade) Also known as Kavaflar Arastası (Cobblers' Arcade), this is below Selimiye Mosque.

Keçecizade   FOOD & DRINK

(Saraçlar Caddesi 50) Branches throughout the centre, including one opposite the post office, sell *lokum* (Turkish delight) and *badem ezmesi*.

ℹ Information

Banks are found in the area around the tourist office.

Araz Döviz (Ali Paşa Bazaar, Talat Paşa Caddesi; ⊙9am-7pm Mon-Sat) One of the only places to change cash and travellers cheques on Saturdays.

Post office (PTT; Saraçlar Caddesi) The only place to change money on Sundays.

Sky Internet Cafe (Turgu Sokak; per hr TL2; ⊙8.30am-2am)

Tourist office (☑213 9208; Talat Paşa Caddesi; ⊙9am-6pm) Very helpful, with English-language brochures and city map.

ℹ Getting There & Around

Bus & Dolmuş

Edirne's otogar (bus station) is 9km southeast of the centre on the access road to the E80. For more information on nearby Bulgarian and Greek border crossings, see p685. A dolmuş is a minibus that stops anywhere along its prescribed route.

ÇANAKKALE (TL30, four hours) Regular buses.

İSTANBUL (TL10, 2½ hours) Frequent buses, but demand is high so book ahead.

KAPIKULE (TL5, 25 minutes) Dolmuşes run to this Bulgarian border crossing, 18km northwest, from outside Şekerbank, opposite the tourist office on Talat Paşa Caddesi.

KEŞAN Hourly minibuses (TL12, 1½ hours), run by **Güneş** (☎213 2105; Kadirhane Sokak), leave from the company's office northwest of the hospital. A cheaper service (TL7, 2½ hours) leaves from the otogar.

PAZARKULE The nearest Greek border post is 9km southwest of Edirne. Catch a dolmuş (TL1, 20 minutes) straight there from near the tourist office, or change in Karaağaç.

UZUNKÖPRÜ (TL7, one hour) Güneş minibuses to Keşan stop here, as does the cheaper service from the otogar (TL4, 1¾ hours).

Car

The toll from Edirne to İstanbul on the E80 is under TL10. You can hire a vehicle from **Turizm Rent A Car** (☎214 8478; Talat Paşa Caddesi) for about €60 per day for a small car.

Train

Edirne train station is 4km southeast of the Eski Cami. To get to the station from the centre, dolmuşes and city buses travelling southeast on Talat Paşa Caddesi, including bus 3, pass Migros supermarket – you should get off here and walk down İstasyon Caddesi. A taxi costs around TL10.

İSTANBUL (TL10, four to 6½ hours) The *Edirne Ekspresi* leaves Edirne at 7.30am and 4pm, and the *Bosfor Ekspresi* leaves at 3.50am. From İstanbul, the former service leaves at 8.30am and 3.15pm, and the latter at 10pm.

EUROPE The *Bosfor Ekspresi* leaves Edirne at 2.32am for Bucharest (Romania).

Uzunköprü
☎0284 / POP 39,100

About 63km southeast of Edirne on the E87/ D550, the farming town of Uzunköprü (Long Bridge) sits on the banks of the Ergene River. Amazingly, the 1392m-long Ottoman bridge (1426–43), after which the town is named, is still standing with all of its 174 arches intact. It remains on the town's main access road from the north, an impressive feat after nearly six centuries of continuous use.

🛈 Getting There & Away

Uzunköprü is the border crossing town on the rail line connecting İstanbul with Greece; the

Dostluk-Filia Ekspresi leaves for Thessaloniki at 1.20am, and for İstanbul at 4am. The station is 4km north of town – if you take an Edirne-bound bus from the station by the bridge, ask the driver to drop you off, or take a taxi (TL7).

Kıyıköy
☎0288 / POP 2500

One of European Turkey's handful of settlements on the Black Sea, Kıyıköy (formerly Salmidesos) is a popular getaway for İstanbullus, but can be just as easily reached from Thrace. Come here for the sandy **beach**, north of the village, where you can hire pedal-boats and meander around the river mouth; the remains of the 6th-century **Kıyıköy Castle** (Kıyıköy Kalesı); and the **market** on Tuesday.

TOP CHOICE Hotel Endorfina BOUTIQUE HOTEL €€ (☎388 6364; www.hotelendorfina.com; Manastır Üstü; half-board per person TL150; @☀) The main reason to visit Kıyıköy is to stay at this boutique hotel, found on a bluff above the main beach and river, and with a fantastic terrace. Rooms are in white cubes, each with a private balcony or terrace, and it's a cosmopolitan İstanbul outpost, from its contemporary architecture to the excellent managers. Activities, a fish restaurant and pick-ups from Saray are added attractions.

The best of the basic pensions are **Midye Pansiyon** (☎388 6472; s/d excl breakfast TL40/80), just east of the main square; the cliff-top **Deniz Feneri** (☎388 6073; d TL100), at the eastern end of the village; and **Necip Usta Pansiyon** (☎388 6068; d TL50), above the main beach.

Accommodation fills fast in the summer, but there are many *ev pansiyonus* (pensions in private homes), where the owners' starting prices are typically TL50 for a double or twin. There are two just before Son Tango restaurant, and one on the road indicated by the 'Ender Pansiyon' sign. You can also camp by both beaches.

The village is full of restaurants and cafes. As well as at most of the previously mentioned accommodation options, you can eat at **Son Tango** (☎388 6283; mains TL10), a good choice for breakfast; **Marina** (☎388 6058; mains TL10), where dishes include *mantı* (Turkish ravioli), *köfte* and breakfast; and **Kösk** (☎0536 475 8169; mains TL15), with good meze and fish. All have terraces with prime sundowner potential.

There's one direct bus a day from İstanbul (TL17, three hours) at 4pm year-round, and to İstanbul from Kıyıköy at 8am and 12.15pm. Alternatively, buses run every two to three hours to/from Saray (TL5, 30 minutes), 30km southwest, which is linked to İstanbul (TL14, 2½ hours, hourly), Tekirdağ (TL9, 1½ hours, regular) and Edirne (TL13, two hours, twice daily).

Tekirdağ
☑0282 / POP 138,000

Famous for its grapes – used to produce wines and rakı (aniseed brandy) – and cherries, Tekirdağ overlooks an attractive bay on the northern shore of the Sea of Marmara. It's not worth a trip in itself, but the city makes a reasonable pit stop en route to/from Greece or the Gallipoli Peninsula. Once known as Rodosto, it has interesting architecture, including some lovely old wooden *yalı* (seafront mansions), and three diverse museums. Tekirdağ is also known for its gypsy musicians, who entertain drinkers and diners on and around the waterfront promenade.

The small **tourist office** (☑261 1698; ⊙9am-6pm Mon-Fri year-round, 10am-7pm Sat & Sun Jun-Sep) is near the *iskele* (jetty).

◉ Sights

Waterfront   SEAFRONT
This is the most pleasant part of the city, with a long promenade running round the bay, centred on the *iskele* and nearby playground, tea gardens, bars and restaurants.

Rákóczi Museum   MUSEUM
(Rakoczi Müzesi; ☑263 8577; Hikmet Çevik Sokak 21; admission TL3; ⊙9am-noon & 1-5pm Tue-Sun) This unusual museum is devoted to Prince Ferenc (Francis) II Rákóczi (1676–1735), the courageous leader of the first Hungarian uprising against the Habsburgs between 1703 and 1711. Forced into exile, the Transylvanian eventually turned up in Turkey and was given asylum by Sultan Ahmet III; he settled in Tekirdağ in 1720 and lived here until his death. In 1906 Rákóczi's remains were returned to Kassa in Hungary (now Košice in Slovakia), along with the interior fittings from the house. Between 1981 and 1982, however, these were painstakingly reproduced and put on display in a surprisingly informative museum that is something of a pilgrimage site for visiting Magyars.

The three floors contain portraits, weapons, kitchen equipment, ceramics and even a water well. The finest room is the 2nd-floor reception, with stained-glass windows, walls painted with Hungarian folk motifs, and a chair made by the good prince himself. Look out for the writing room of Kelemen Mikes (an 18th century Transylvanian essayist); his fictitious letters to an imaginary aunt in Constantinople described life in the exiled court. To get here from the *iskele,* walk or catch a dolmuş (TL1) west along the waterfront for about 1km until you see the large wooden Namık Kemal House above you. The museum is further up the slope on the left.

Tekirdağ Museum   MUSEUM
FREE (Tekirdağ Müzesi; ☑261 2082; Barbaros Caddesi; ⊙9am-5pm Tue-Sun) From the Rákóczi Museum, walk 100m east, past ramshackle wooden mansions, to reach the town museum. Housed in a fine late-Ottoman building, it contains finds from several local tumuli (burial mounds) and from a site at Perinthos (Marmara Ereğlisi). The most striking exhibits are the marble chairs and the table set with bronze bowls from the Naip tumulus dating back to the early 5th century BC; and a wonderful pottery brazier in the form of a mother goddess from the Taptepe tumulus (4300 BC). Also interesting are the poignant inscriptions from a number of Roman gravestones translated into English. Read them and weep; they are timeless.

Namık Kemal House   MUSEUM
FREE (Namık Kemal Evi; Namık Kemal Caddesi 9; ⊙8.30am-noon & 1-5pm Mon-Fri, 9.30am-3.30pm Sat) In a gingerbreadlike wooden house, this small ethnographical museum is dedicated to Tekirdağ's most famous son, who was born nearby. A nationalist poet, journalist and social reformer, Kemal (1840–88) had a strong influence on Atatürk, who called him 'the father of my ideas'. The two-storey house is beautifully restored; don't miss the music room, the kitchen with its Turkish utensils, and the beautiful coffered ceilings. Climb the steps at the east end of the *köfte* restaurants; it's on the far right-hand side of the square.

Rüstem Paşa Külliyesi   MOSQUE
(Mimar Sinan Caddesi 19) Heading downhill to the waterfront from Namık Kemal House, this small, square mosque is on the right. The great Mimar Sinan designed it in 1546.

THREE CHEERS FOR RAKI

Turkey's unofficial national drink is rakı (pronounced rah-*kuh*), an aniseed-flavoured distillation not unlike French pastis. Like the latter, it is drunk with water and ice, but unlike the French tipple, which is an appetiser, rakı is often consumed with food.

Turkey is the world's third-largest producer of grapes, a high percentage of which are grown around Tekirdağ. About a third of these grapes are consumed fresh, but much of the remainder goes into making rakı.

It's a long, complicated process, involving fresh grapes or well-preserved raisins that are mashed, shredded, mixed with water and steamed. Next, anise is added and the product goes through a double-distillation process. It is then watered down to an alcoholic strength of about 45% and aged for between 60 and 75 days. The most common brand is Yeni Rakı (New Rakı), but arguably the best is Tekirdağ Rakısı, which has a distinctive flavour thanks to the artesian water it uses from Çorlu, a town to the northeast of Tekirdağ. Turks drink what they call *aslan sütü* ('lion's milk', possibly because of the milky white it turns when water is added) with anything, but it's best with cold meze, white cheese and melon, and fish.

Orta Camii MOSQUE
Turn left at the top of the steps at the east end of the *köfte* restaurants and head uphill to find this brown stone mosque (1855) with a single minaret.

Hüseyin Pehlivan MONUMENT
At the bottom of the hill, below the Rüstem Paşa Külliyesi, this chunky statue commemorates another famous Tekirdağan, a great oil wrestler (1908–82).

✯ Festivals & Events
Tekirdağ's red-letter event is the **Kiraz Festivali** (Cherry Festival) in early June, a week-long orgy of cherry gobbling and judging, as well as music concerts and oil-wrestling matches.

🛏 Sleeping
Golden Yat Hotel HOTEL €€
(☎261 1054; www.goldenyat.com, in Turkish; Yalı Caddesi 42; s/d/tr/ste from TL80/120/150/200; ❄) With golden bedspreads and red carpets, this 54-room hotel is the best option by the harbour. Rooms are shipshape, if slightly overpriced, and you won't forget the views from the eyrie-like 5th-floor breakfast room in a hurry.

Rodosto Hotel HOTEL €€
(☎263 3701; info@rodostohotel.com; İskele Caddesi 34; s/d TL80/120; ❄) The Rodosto, the only other accommodation on the waterfront, has been left in the wake of Golden Yat Hotel. Rooms are old, gloomy and tired, but the staff are a friendly bunch, and solo travellers can save money with the boxy 'economy single' (TL45).

🍴 Eating
Buses often pause for lunch in Tekirdağ, pulling up opposite the promenade at the row of restaurants serving *Tekirdağ köftesi*, a spicy version of *köfte*, eaten with rice and peppers. Alternatively, grab a *balık ekmek* (fish kebap, TL3.50) across the road on the waterfront.

Meşhur Köfteci Ali Usta KÖFTECI €
(☎261 1621; Atatürk Bulvarı 24; mains TL10) With four branches in the area, the 'Famous Master Ali Köfte Restaurant' serves a good range of dishes, including four types of *köfte*.

ℹ Getting There & Away
Buses for İstanbul (TL15, 2½ hours), Edirne (TL12, two hours), Eceabat (TL27, three hours) and Çanakkale (TL30, 3½ hours) stop at the otogar and along the waterfront.

Gelibolu
📞0286 / POP 29,000
The pretty little harbour town of Gelibolu is not the same as Gallipoli. It's the largest town on the peninsula and has the same name, but is almost 50km from the main battlefield sites. However, if you do fall victim to confusion and get off the bus early, or you arrive from Lapseki on the ferry across the Dardanelles, you'll find Gelibolu to be a very pleasant spot. Just about everything you'll need – hotels, restaurants, banks, stalls selling seashell ashtrays – is clustered around the harbour.

☉ Sights

Gallipoli War Museum
MUSEUM

(Gelibolu Savaş Müzesi; ☏566 1272; Sahil Yolu; admission TL2.50; ☺9am-noon & 1-6pm Tue-Sun) On the main road into town, this museum gets top marks for presentation; from the sandbags and barbed wire outside to the displays before, above and even below you under glass. The artefacts do a good job of evoking the human cost of the campaign, ranging from a letter home on pink paper to photos of the excavations and dedications carried out in the present day.

FREE Piri Reis Museum
MUSEUM

(Piri Reis Müzesi; ☺8.30am-noon & 1-5pm Fri-Wed) Overlooking the harbour walls, this stone tower is all that remains of the Greek settlement of Callipolis, which gave the present town and peninsula their name. Inside, the small museum honours the swashbuckling admiral and cartographer Piri Reis (1470–1554), whose statue stands in the harbour on the way to the ferry pier. He is celebrated for his *Kitab-i-Bahriye* (Book of the Sea), which contains detailed information on navigation and very accurate charts of ports in the Mediterranean. But the fruit of his life's work, dating back to 1513, was the first known map to show the Americas in their entirety. There's a large, shallow well and an upstairs chamber displaying copies of Reis' famous maps.

Shrine of Ahmed-i Bican Efendi
MONUMENT

The road from the Piri Reis Museum veers uphill, passing several military buildings. After about 800m, this pretty shrine is above the road in a small park to the left.

Tomb of Mehmed-i Bican Efendi
TOMB

(Mehmed-i Bican Efendi Turbesi; admission free; ☺24hr) Across the road from the park is this grand tomb. Bican was the author of *Muhammadiye,* a commentary on the Quran.

Hallac-i Mansur Türbesi
TOMB

(Tomb of Hallac-i Mansur; admission free; ☺24hr) Return to the other side of the park and continue along the road to this landmark, which looks more like a mosque than a tomb.

TOP CHOICE Bayraklı Baba Türbesi
TOMB

(Flag Father Tomb; admission free; ☺24hr) Turn right at Hallac-i Mansur Türbesi onto Fener Yolu (Lighthouse St) and begin walking out to the headland. A short distance on the left you'll see flag-lined steps leading down to this tomb. It contains the mortal remains of one Karaca Bey, an Ottoman standard bearer who, in 1410, ate the flag in his keeping piece by piece rather than let it be captured by the enemy. When his comrades asked where the flag was and he told them, they refused to believe him. Karaca duly split open his stomach to prove his actions – and a legend was born. The tomb is decked out with hundreds of Turkish flags; the attendant will sell you one to add to the collection.

Azebler Namazgah
MOSQUE

(Soldiers' Open-Air Prayer Area; admission free; ☺24hr) At the end of the headland, which was once the site of the 14th-century Gelibolu Fort, this outdoor mosque is on the right of the tea garden and lighthouse. The unusual, vaguely Mogul-looking mosque (1407) has a white marble *mihrab* (niche indicating the direction of Mecca) and *mimber.*

French Cemetery
CEMETERY

(admission free; ☺24hr) Return to the main road and continue downhill. On the left a tall modern bell tower marks this cemetery from the Crimean War (1854–56) – what the French call the Guerre d'Orient. It houses the bones of 11 Senegalese soldiers who died in the Gallipoli campaign and were buried here between 1919 and 1923.

Saruca Paşa Türbesi
TOMB

(Tomb of Saruca Pasa; admission free; ☺24hr) Next to the French Cemetery is this tomb of a late-14th-century Ottoman military hero.

Hamzakoy
BEACH

The road continues down to the resort part of town, which has a thin strip of rough sandy beach and a small cafe.

FREE Deniz Kuvvetleri Kültür Park
PARK

(Sea Forces Culture Park) You can walk back to the centre around the bottom of the headland, along the beach past fisherpeople and cafes. En route, this small park is full of spent torpedoes, mines, and even a tiny submarine standing on end.

🛏 Sleeping & Eating

Otel Hamzakoy
RESORT €€

(☏566 8080; www.hamzakoyotel.com; Hamzakoy; s/d TL60/100) Despite the temperamental wi-fi, aged showers and unappetising breakfasts, this pink block is much more pleasant than its crumbling exterior

---

suggests. Inside it's light and airy, and the rooms have small balconies with sea views. It's 2km north of the harbour, with a cafe-bar on the beach just opposite.

Oya Hotel HOTEL €
(☑566 0392; Miralay Şefik Aker Caddesi 7; r TL60-70, ste TL90) With something of a nautical theme, Oya is a little old and grubby but is the best of Gelibolu's central options, which are mostly found near the Piri Reis Museum.

TOP CHOICE İlhan Restaurant RESTAURANT €€
(☑566 1124; Liman; mains TL15) The best of Gelibolu's harbourside restaurants, where you can tuck into local *sardalya* (sardines) cooked in a clay dish. Friendly İlhan is right on the *iskele*, with both sea and harbour views. There's a wide range of delicious fish and meze on the menu, which is available in English.

❶ Getting There & Away

The otogar is 500m southwest of the harbour, past the war museum on the main road to Eceabat.

ECEABAT (TL5, 50 minutes) Hourly minibuses run from the ferry pier, and continue to Kilitbahir (TL5, one hour).

EDİRNE (TL25, three hours, hourly)

İSTANBUL (TL35, 4½ hours)

LAPSEKİ The ferry (per person TL2, motorbikes TL8, cars TL20, 30 minutes) leaves every hour on the hour, in either direction.

Gallipoli (Gelibolu) Peninsula

☑0286

For a millennium, the slender peninsula that forms the northwestern side of the Dardanelles, across the strait from Çanakkale, has been the key to İstanbul: any navy that could break through the strait had a good chance of capturing the capital of the Eastern European world. Many fleets have tried to force open the strait, but most, including the mighty Allied fleet mustered in WWI, have failed.

Antipodeans and many Britons won't need an introduction to Gallipoli. The peninsula is the backbone of the 'Anzac legend' – created when an Allied campaign to knock Turkey out of WWI and open a relief route to Russia turned into one of the greatest fiascos of the war. By the end of the campaign 130,000 men were dead, a third from Allied forces and the rest Turkish.

Today the Gallipoli battlefields are peaceful places, covered in brush and pine forests. But the battles fought here nearly a century ago are still alive in many memories, both Turkish and foreign, especially in those of Australians and New Zealanders, who view the peninsula as a place of pilgrimage. The Turkish officer responsible for the defence of Gallipoli was one Mustafa Kemal – the future Atatürk – and the Turkish victory is commemorated in Turkey on 18 March. The big draw for foreigners, though, is Anzac Day (25 April), when a dawn service marks the anniversary of the Allied landings, attracting thousands of travellers from Down Under and beyond.

The most convenient base for visiting the Gallipoli battlefields is Eceabat on the western shore of the Dardanelles, although Çanakkale, on the eastern shore, has a wider range of accommodation and restaurants, and a more vibrant nightlife.

The southern third of the peninsula is given over to a national park. Even if you're not well up on the history, it's still worth visiting for the area's rugged natural beauty.

History

Not even 1500m wide at its narrowest point, the Strait of Çanakkale (Çanakkale Boğazı), better known as the Dardanelles or the Hellespont in English, has always offered the best opportunity for travellers – and armies – to cross between Europe and Asia Minor.

King Xerxes I of Persia forded the strait with a bridge of boats in 481 BC, as did Alexander the Great a century and a half later. In Byzantine times it was the first line of defence for Constantinople, but by 1402 the strait was under the control of Sultan Bayezid I (r 1390–1402), which allowed his armies to conquer the Balkans. Mehmet the Conqueror fortified the strait as part of his grand plan to conquer Constantinople (1453), building eight separate fortresses. As the Ottoman Empire declined during the 19th century, Great Britain and France competed with Russia for influence over this strategic sea passage.

In a bid to seize the Ottoman capital, then First Lord of the Admiralty Winston Churchill organised a naval assault on the strait early in 1915. In March a strong Franco-British fleet tried to force them without success. Then, on 25 April, British, Australian, New Zealand and Indian troops landed on Gallipoli, and French troops landed near Çanakkale. Turkish and Allied troops fought desperately, devastating one another. After nine months of ferocious combat but little headway, the Allied forces withdrew.

The outcome at Gallipoli was partly due to bad luck and leadership on the Allied side, and partly due to reinforcements to the Turkish side brought in by General Liman von Sanders. But a crucial element in the defeat was that the Allied troops landed in a sector where they faced Lieutenant Colonel Mustafa Kemal.

A relatively minor officer, the future Atatürk had managed to guess the Allied battle plan correctly when his commanders did not, and he stalled the invasion in spite of bitter fighting that wiped out his regiment (see Chunuk Bair, p135). Although suffering from malaria, Kemal commanded in full view of his troops throughout the campaign, miraculously escaping death several times. At one point a piece of shrapnel hit him in the chest, but was stopped by his pocket watch. His brilliant performance made him a folk hero and paved the way for his promotion to *paşa* (general).

The Gallipoli campaign lasted until January 1916, and resulted in a total of more than half a million casualties, of which 130,000 were deaths. The British Empire saw the loss of some 36,000 lives, including 8700 Australians and 2700 New Zealanders. French casualties numbered 47,000 (making up over half the entire French contingent); 8800 Frenchmen died. Half the 500,000 Ottoman troops were casualties, with almost 86,700 killed. Despite the carnage, the battles here are often considered the last true instance of a 'gentleman's war', with both sides displaying respect towards their enemy.

☞ Tours

Many people visit Gallipoli on a guided tour, which is the best way to see a lot in a short amount of time. The usually very-well-informed guides can explain the battles as you go along, answer questions and even help you locate a specific gravesite. The recommended tour providers generally offer five- or six-hour afternoon tours, including transport by car or minibus, guide and picnic lunch. It's best to take the tour from Eceabat as it typically costs TL45, as opposed to TL60 from Çanakkale. Tours do not cover

the less-visited sites at Cape Helles and the more northerly Suvla Bay; to do that, you have to hire a guide for a private tour, which costs over TL100 even if you have your own vehicle. Condensed tours from İstanbul are available, but these can be exhausting as they involve visiting the battlefields straight after a five-hour bus ride.

The best agencies in Eceabat and Çanakkale:

Crowded House Tours   TOUR

(☑814 1565; www.crowdedhousegallipoli.com) Based at Hotel Crowded House in Eceabat (p138), and normally led by the indefatigable Bülent 'Bill' Yılmaz Korkmaz, these tours are among the most informative and popular on the peninsula. Also on offer is a morning snorkelling tour (TL30, including transportation and equipment) to a WWI shipwreck at North Beach, and private tours. One- and two-day packages involve a transfer from accommodation in İstanbul to the otogar, then a night in Eceabat before the tour.

TJs Tours   TOUR

(☑814 3121; www.anzacgallipolitours.com) Based at TJs Hotel (p139) in Eceabat, this agency also offers some quality guides such as Graham 'Ibrahim', and private tours.

Hassle Free Travel Agency   TOUR

(Map p142; ☑213 5969; www.hasslefreetour.com) Operates tours out of Anzac House Hostel (p143) in Çanakkale, as well as longer packages lasting up to 15 days. Its tour costs €40 but includes lunch in a restaurant.

Trooper Tours   TOUR

(Map p142; ☑0212-516 9024; www.troopertours.com) Represented in Çanakkale by Yellow Rose Pension (p143), Trooper offers a range of tours, starting and finishing in İstanbul or Kuşadası and lasting from one to nine days (€99 to €729).

Battlefield Sites

Gallipoli National Historic Park (Gelibolu Yarımadası Tarihi Milli Parkı) encompasses 33,500 hectares of the peninsula and all of the significant battle sites. There are several different signage systems in use: normal Turkish highway signs; national park administration signs; and wooden signs posted by the Commonwealth War Graves Commission. This can lead to confusion because the foreign and Turkish troops

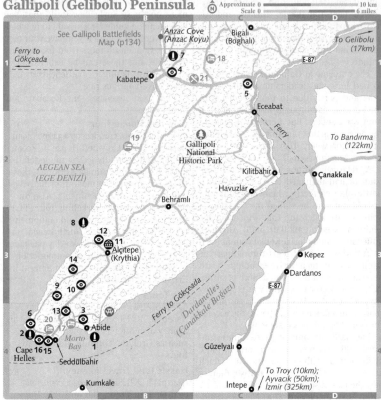

THRACE & MARMARA

used different names for the battlefields, and the park signs don't necessarily agree with those erected by the highway department. We've used both English and Turkish names.

There are currently three dozen Allied war cemeteries in the national park, with about another 20 Turkish ones. The principal battles took place on its western shore, around Anzac Cove (Anzac Koyu), 12km northwest of Eceabat, and in the hills east of the cove.

The peninsula is a fairly large area to tour, especially without your own transport; it's over 35km as the crow flies from the northernmost battlefield to the southern tip of the peninsula. If time is tight or you're touring by public transport, head to Anzac Cove or Lone Pine and Chunuk Bair first.

For extra information, head to **Kilye Bay Information Centre** (Kilye Koyu Ana Tanıtım Merkezi; Map p132; admission free; ⏰9am–noon & 1–5pm). Popular with Turkish visitors, this modern centre includes an information centre with interactive displays, exhibition areas, a memorial, cinema, library and cafeteria. It's about 3km north of Eceabat, some 200m off the İstanbul highway.

Also recommended is the **Kabatepe Information Centre & Museum** (Kabatepe Müzesi ve Tanıtma Merkezi; Map p132; admission TL3; ⏰9am–1pm & 2–6pm), roughly 1km east of the village of Kabatepe. This older centre has a good collection of artefacts, although Kilye Bay is stronger on background information. Inside are old blood-stained uniforms, rusty weapons, bullets welded together, and other battlefield finds, including the skull of a luckless Turkish soldier with a bullet lodged in the forehead. The photos and correspondence are particularly touching, including one from an understated Englishman who wrote, 'I hope the next show will be better,' and another soldier's last letter, in which he

THRACE & MARMARA GALLIPOLI (GELIBOLU) PENINSULA

reassures his mother: 'I don't want underwear. I have money.'

Northern Peninsula

(Map p132) About 3km north of Eceabat, the road to Kabatepe heads west into the park past the Kilye Bay Information Centre. We describe the sites in the order most walkers and motorists are likely to visit them.

Kabatepe Village (Kabatepe Köyü)

(Map p132) The small harbour here was probably the object of the Allied landing on 25 April 1915. In the predawn dark it is possible that uncharted currents swept the Allies' landing craft northwards to the steep cliffs of Arıburnu – a bit of bad luck that may have sealed the campaign's fate from the start. Today there's little in Kabatepe except for a campground, cafe and dock for ferries to Gökçeada island (p145).

The road uphill to Lone Pine (Kanlısırt) and Chunuk Bair begins 750m northwest of the Kabatepe Information Centre & Museum. Anzac Cove is another 3km north.

Anzac Cove (Anzac Koyu)

(Map p134) Heading northwest from the information centre, it's 3km to Beach (Hell Spit) Cemetery. Before it, a rough track cuts inland to Lone Pine (1.5km) and, across the road from the car park at the cemetery, another track heads inland to Shrapnel Valley Cemetery and Plugge's Plateau Cemetery.

Following the coastal road for another 400m from the turn-off, or taking the footpath from Beach Cemetery past the WWII bunker, brings you to Anzac Cove, beneath and just south of the Arıburnu cliffs, where the ill-fated Allied landing began on 25 April 1915. Ordered to advance inland, the Allied forces at first gained some ground but later in the day met with fierce resistance from the Ottoman forces under the leadership of Mustafa Kemal, who had foreseen where they would land and disobeyed an order to send his troops further south to Cape Helles. After this failed endeavour, the Anzacs concentrated on consolidating and expanding the beachhead while awaiting reinforcements.

In August of the same year a major offensive was staged in an attempt to advance beyond the beach up to the ridges of Chunuk Bair and Sarı Bair. It resulted in the battles at Lone Pine and The Nek, the bloodiest of the campaign, but little progress was made.

Another 300m along is the Arıburnu Sahil Anıtı (Arıburnu Coastal Memorial), a moving Turkish monument with Atatürk's famous words of peace and reconciliation, spoken in 1934:

> To us there is no difference between the Johnnies and the Mehmets...You, the mothers, who sent your sons from faraway countries, wipe away your tears; your sons are now lying in our bosom...After having lost their lives in this land, they have become our sons as well.

Just beyond the memorial is Arıburnu Cemetery and, 750m further north, Canterbury Cemetery. Between them is the Anzac Commemorative Site (Anzac

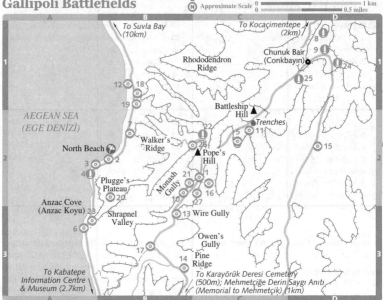

Tören Alanı), where dawn services are held on Anzac Day. Look up and you can easily make out the image in the sandy cliff face nicknamed 'the Sphinx' by young 'diggers' (Aussie infantrymen) who had arrived from Australia via Egypt.

Less than 1km further along the seaside road on the right-hand side are the cemeteries at **No 2 Outpost**, set back inland from the road, and **New Zealand No 2 Outpost**. The **Embarkation Pier Cemetery** is 200m beyond the New Zealand No 2 Outpost on the left.

Towards Lone Pine

(Maps p132 & p134) Return to the Kabatepe Information Centre & Museum and follow the signs just under 3km uphill for Lone Pine.

En route, the first monument you come to, **Mehmetçiğe Derin Saygı Anıtı** (Map p132) on the right-hand side of the road about 1km from the junction, is dedicated to the 'Mehmetçik' (Little Mehmet, the Turkish 'tommy' or 'digger') who carried a Kiwi soldier to safety.

Another 1200m brings you to the **Kanlısırt Kitabesi** (Bloody Ridge Inscription; Map p134), which describes the battle of Lone Pine from the Turkish viewpoint.

Lone Pine (Kanlısırt)

(Map p134) Lone Pine, 400m uphill from Kanlısırt Kitabesi, is perhaps the most moving of all the Anzac cemeteries. Australian forces captured the Turkish positions here on the afternoon of 6 August 1915, and 7000 men died, in an area the size of a soccer field, in just four days. The trees that shaded the cemetery were swept away by a fire in 1994, leaving only one: a lone pine planted from the seed of the original solitary tree, which stood here at the beginning of the battle and gave the battlefield its name. Reforestation of the park is proving successful.

The tombstones carry touching epitaphs and the cemetery includes the grave of the youngest soldier to die here, a boy of just 14. The remains of trenches can be seen just behind the parking area.

From here, it's another 3km up the one-way road to the New Zealand Memorial at Chunuk Bair.

Johnston's Jolly (Kırmızı Sırt) to Quinn's Post

(Map p134) Progressing up the hill from Lone Pine, the ferocity of the battles becomes more apparent; at some points the trenches are only a few metres apart. The order to attack meant certain death to those who fol-

Gallipoli Battlefields

◎ Sights

lowed it, and virtually all did as they were ordered on both sides.

The road marks what was the thin strip of no-man's land between the two sides' trenches, as it continues to the cemeteries **Johnston's Jolly** (Kırmızı Sırt), 200m on the right beyond Lone Pine, **Courtney's & Steele's Post**, roughly the same distance again, and **Quinn's Post**, 100m uphill. Almost opposite Quinn's Post is the **Yüzbaşı Mehmet Şehitliği** (Captain Mehmet Cemetery).

57 Alay (57th Regiment) & Kesikdere Cemeteries

(Map p134) About 1km uphill from Lone Pine, across the road from the statue of a Mehmet, is the **cemetery** and monument for the Ottoman 57th Regiment, which was led by Mustafa Kemal, and sacrificed by him to halt the first Anzac assaults. The

cemetery has a surprising amount of religious symbolism for a Turkish army site, as historically the republican army has been steadfastly secular. The statue of an old man showing his granddaughter the battle sites represents Hüseyin Kaçmaz, who fought in the Balkan Wars, the Gallipoli campaign and at the fateful Battle of Dumlupınar during the War of Independence. He died in 1994, aged 111, the last surviving Turkish Gallipoli veteran.

Down some steps from here, the Kesikdere Cemetery contains the remains of another 1115 Turkish soldiers from the 57th and other regiments.

Sergeant Mehmet Monument (Mehmet Çavuş Anıtı) & The Nek

(Map p134) About 100m uphill past the 57th Regiment Cemetery, a road goes west to the Sergeant Mehmet Monument, dedicated to the Turkish sergeant who fought with rocks and his fists after he ran out of ammunition, and The Nek. It was at The Nek on the morning of 7 August 1915 that the 8th (Victorian) and 10th (Western Australian) Regiments of the third Light Horse Brigade vaulted out of their trenches into withering fire and were cut down before they reached the enemy line, an episode immortalised in Peter Weir's film *Gallipoli*.

Baby 700 Cemetery & Mesudiye Topu

(Map p134) About 200m uphill on the right from the access road to The Nek is the Baby 700 Cemetery and the Ottoman **cannon** called the Mesudiye Topu. Named after its height above sea level in feet, Baby 700 was the limit of the initial attack, and the graves here are mostly dated 25 April.

Düztepe & Talat Göktepe Monuments

(Map p134) The Düztepe Monument, uphill from the Baby 700 Cemetery, marks the spot where the Ottoman 10th Regiment held the line. Views of the strait and the surrounding countryside are superb. About 1km further on is a **monument** to a more recent casualty of Gallipoli: Talat Göktepe, chief director of the Çanakkale Forestry District, who died fighting the devastating forest fire of 1994.

Chunuk Bair (Conkbayırı) & Around

(Map p134) At the top of the hill, some 500m past the Talat Göktepe Monument, turning right at the T-junction takes you east to the **Suyatağı Anıtı** (Watercourse Monument). Having stayed awake for four days and nights, Mustafa Kemal spent the night of 9–10 August here, directing part of the counterattack to the Allied offensive. Further south is **Kemalyeri** ('Kemal's Place') at Scrubby Knoll, his command post, and the road back to the Kabatepe Information Centre & Museum.

Back at the T-junction, turn left for Chunuk Bair, the first objective of the Allied landing in April 1915, and now the site of the **Chunuk Bair New Zealand Cemetery and Memorial** (Conkbayırı Yeni Zelanda Mezarlığı ve Anıtı).

As the Anzac troops made their way up the scrub-covered slopes on 25 April, Mustafa Kemal, the divisional commander, brought up the 57th Infantry Regiment and gave them his famous order: 'I am not ordering you to attack, I am ordering you to die. In the time it takes us to die, other troops and commanders will arrive to take our places'. The 57th was wiped out, but held the line and inflicted equally heavy casualties on Anzac forces below.

Chunuk Bair was also at the heart of the struggle for the peninsula from 6 to 10 August 1915, when some 30,000 men died on this ridge. The peaceful pine grove of today makes it difficult to imagine that blasted wasteland, when bullets, bombs and shrapnel mowed down men as the fighting went on day and night. The Anzac attack from 6 to 7 August, which included the New Zealand Mounted Rifle Brigade and a Maori contingent, was deadly, but the attack on the following day was of a ferocity which, according to Mustafa Kemal, 'could scarcely be described'.

To the east a side road leads to the Turkish **Chunuk Bair Mehmet Memorials** (Conkbayırı Mehmetçik Anitları), five giant tablets, like the fingers of a hand praying to god, with Turkish inscriptions describing the battle.

Southern Peninsula

(Map p132) Fewer travellers visit the southern peninsula, where there are more British, French and Turkish memorials than Anzac sites. During low-season weeks, it's a good place to escape the traffic and tour groups, although the Çanakkale Şehitleri Anıtı in particular is becoming increasingly popular with Turkish groups.

From Kabatepe it's about 12km to the village of **Alçıtepe**, formerly known as Krithia. A few metres north of the village's main intersection is the **Salim Mutlu War Museum** (admission TL1; ☺8am-8pm), a

hodgepodge of rusty finds from the battlefields, giving a sense of just how much artillery was fired. Past the souvenir stands, the more-ambitious **Gallery of the Gallipoli Campaign** (admission TL3; ☺8am-8pm) takes a more illustrative approach, with photos and artefacts enhanced by mockups, dioramas and sound effects. At the main intersection, a sign points right to the Turkish **Sargı Yeri Cemetery** (1.5km), with its enormous statue of 'Mehmet' and solid **Nuri Yamut Monument**; take the first left for the **Twelve Tree Copse** (2km) and **Pink Farm** (3km) cemeteries.

From Pink Farm, the road passes the **Lancashire Landing Cemetery**. Turn right 1km before Seddülbahir village for the **Cape Helles British Memorial**, a commanding stone needle honouring the 20,000-plus Britons and Australians who perished in this area and have no known graves. The initial Allied attack was two-pronged, landing on 'V' Beach at the tip of the peninsula as well as Anzac Cove. **Yahya Çavuş Şehitliği** (Sergeant Yahya Cemetery) remembers the Turkish officer who led the resistance to the Allied landing here, causing heavy casualties. **'V' Beach Cemetery** is visible 500m downhill.

Seddülbahir is a sleepy farming village with a few pensions and restaurants, a war museum and the ruins of an Ottoman/Byzantine fortress overlooking a small harbour.

North of the village, the road divides; the left fork leads to the **Skew Bridge Cemetery**, followed by the **Redoubt Cemetery**. Turn right and head east, following signs for Abide or Çanakkale Şehitleri Anıtı (Çanakkale Martyrs' Memorial) at Morto Bay, and you'll pass the **French War Memorial & Cemetery**. French troops, including a regiment of Africans, attacked Kumkale on the Asian shore in March 1915 with complete success, then re-embarked and landed in support of their British comrades-in-arms at Cape Helles, where they were virtually wiped out. The French cemetery is rarely visited but is quite moving, with rows of metal crosses and five white concrete ossuaries each containing the bones of 3000 soldiers.

The **Çanakkale Şehitleri Anıtı** (Çanakkale Martyrs' Memorial), also known as the Abide monument, is a gigantic four-legged, almost-42m-high stone table that commemorates all the Turkish soldiers who fought and died at Gallipoli. It's

GALLIPOLI UNDER THREAT

It seems a world away from the early 1980s, when Australian film director Peter Weir spent two days scampering over the hills of the Gallipoli Peninsula and saw not a living soul. The numbers of visitors have grown by leaps and bounds since then and they're not just foreigners. Since 2004, when 81 students from the 81 provinces in Turkey made the patriotic pilgrimage to where national hero Mustafa Kemal led their nation to victory, *belediyes* (town and city councils) from Edirne to Van have been sending their citizens in by the busload. According to Turkish official sources, domestic visitors numbered two million in 2007, up from between 400,000 and 500,000 five years before.

This increased popularity has made conservation of the national park particularly challenging, and many people feel that the local government and park administration don't always handle the situation effectively. In recent years the flow of bus and coach traffic has become extremely heavy, particularly around the most-visited Turkish cemeteries and monuments. Supposed 'improvements' such as car parks and road-widening schemes have caused considerable damage to some areas, most shockingly at Anzac Cove. The beach there is now little more than a narrow strip of sand.

Crowds of travellers turn up for the dawn Anzac Day memorial service, one of the most popular events in Turkey for foreign visitors, and almost a rite of passage for young Australians in particular. In 2005 more than 20,000 people came to mark the 90th anniversary of the Gallipoli landings, and this overwhelmed the peninsula's modest infrastructure. Just as many people are expected in 2015, the 100th anniversary; tours and cruises are already being marketed. Local operators estimate that about 5000 people visit around Anzac Day. Traffic still reaches all-day jam proportions the day before, some people coming in from as close as Çanakkale don't always make the service in time, and many bed down at the Anzac Commemorative Site to be sure that they do make it.

Some 50,000 Turks turn up on 18 March to celebrate what they call the Çanakkale Naval Victory (Çanakkale Deniz Zaferi), when Ottoman cannons and mines succeeded in keeping the Allied fleet from passing through the Dardanelles in 1915. It's easier to appreciate Gallipoli's poignancy and beauty at almost any other time than its around this event and Anzac Day, and many visitors find their emotional experience completely different if they take the time to explore at leisure away from the crowds.

surrounded by landscaped grounds, including a rose garden planted to commemorate the 80th anniversary of the conflict in 1995.

🛏 Sleeping & Eating

There are some good accommodation options inside the park itself, but most are around Seddülbahir and can be tricky to get to without your own transport.

TOP CHOICE Gallipoli Houses   BOUTIQUE HOTEL €€
(Gelibolu Evleri; ☑814 2650; www.gallipoli.com.tr; Kocadere Köyü; s/d half-board from €70/90; ✲) In a village among open fields, this guesthouse has three rooms in the main stone house and seven more in equally attractive annexes. A calm atmosphere pervades the property from the classical music–soundtracked reception to the stylishly decorated rooms. The home-cooked breakfasts and dinners are innovative and

copious, and packed lunches are available. We love the views of the battlefields and sights, as well as the stars, from the rooftop terrace. The Belgian owner is a history buff and can answer just about any question you may have on the campaign.

Pansiyon Helles Panorama   PENSION €
(☑862 0035; hellespanorama@hotmail.com; s/d without bathroom TL25/55) Just west of the centre of Seddülbahir, this welcoming guesthouse has seven rooms and a lovely garden. The 'panorama' part of the name refers to the views from the balconies of both Çanakkale Şehitleri Anıtı and the Cape Helles British Memorial.

Hotel Kum   HOTEL €€€
(☑814 1455; www.hotelkum.com; s/d/tr/ste half-board TL110/180/225/275, 4-person caravan TL30; ☉Apr-Oct; ✲ ✲) The military brass stay here before dawn services. Kum's

rooms occupy clean, two-storey blocks between lawns, with a beach 50m away. The rooms don't have a lot of character, but they have terraces, and Kum is in a good, central location on the quiet side of the peninsula.

Abide Motel
PENSION €€

(☏862 0010; motelabide@hotmail.com; Morto Bay; s/d TL45/90) Undergoing a renovation when we visited, Abide has basic rooms and a big terrace restaurant, set in scruffy grounds near the French Cemetery.

Mocamp
PENSION €€

(☏862 0056; www.seddulbahirmocamp.com; Seddülbahir; s/d/tr TL75/100/130) This lime-green building is not the best deal on the peninsula, but its nine spacious rooms are a notch above the usual pension fare, with blue-tiled bathrooms, and it has a tranquil location next to 'V' Beach Cemetery.

TOP CHOICE Doyuranlar Gözleme
LOCAL €

(☏814 1652; mains TL6) Recommended by locals, Doyuranlar serves *gözleme* (savoury pancakes), *köfte, menemen* (a type of omelette) and breakfast, and you can munch on peppery greens as they are planted next to your table. Look out for the '*Gözleme, ayran, çay*' sign on the Eceabat–Kabatepe road.

ℹ Information
Information Centres

For good general information, head to Kilye Bay Information Centre (p132) and Kabatepe Information Centre & Museum (p132).

Further Information

Gallipoli Battlefield Guide (Çanakkale Muharebe Alanları Gezi Rehberi) An excellent bilingual (and most historically accurate) reference book by Gürsel Göncü and Şahin Doğan, available at some bookshops in Çanakkale and Eceabat.

Gallipoli: A Battlefield Guide By Australians Pam Cupper and Phil Taylor.

Defeat at Gallipoli Using letters and diaries, Peter Hart and Nigel Steel tell the soldiers' stories.

Gallipoli Peninsula National Historic Park Guide Map (Gelibolu Yarımadası Tarihi Milli Parkı Kılavuz Harita) Park information centres sell this very detailed map.

Visit Gallipoli (www.anzacsite.gov.au)

Gallipoli Association (www.gallipoli-association.org)

Many accommodation options in Eceabat and Çanakkale screen at least one of the following every night.

Gallipoli Peter Weir's 1981 film is an easy way to get an overview of the campaign.

Gallipoli (Gelibolu) A 2005 documentary by Tolga Örnek.

Gallipoli: The Fatal Shore Harvey Broadbent's documentary is quite dated (1987), but includes interviews with veterans of the campaign.

ℹ Getting There & Around

With your own transport, you can easily tour the northern battlefields in a day. Trying to do both the northern and southern parts of the peninsula is possible within one day, provided you get an early start. Touring by public transport is tricky; dolmuşes serve only a few sites and villages. The most important group of monuments and cemeteries, from Lone Pine uphill to Chunuk Bair in the northern peninsula, can be toured on foot.

FERRY You can cross the Dardanelles between Çanakkale and Eceabat or Kilitbahir on the peninsula.

TAXI Drivers in Eceabat will run you around the main sites for about TL100, but they take only two to 2½ hours, and few speak English well enough to provide a decent commentary. An organised tour (p131) is a better idea.

Eceabat
☏0286 / POP 5500

Just over the Dardanelles from Çanakkale, Eceabat (Maydos) is a small, easygoing waterfront town with the best access of any main centre to the main Gallipoli battlefields. It's especially attractive to those who don't fancy the hustle and bustle of Çanakkale. Ferries dock by the main square (Cumhuriyet Meydanı), which has hotels, restaurants, ATMs, a post office, bus company offices, and dolmuş and taxi stands.

Like most of the peninsula, Eceabat is swamped with students and tour groups over weekends from 18 March to mid-June, and again in late September.

🛏 Sleeping

TOP CHOICE Hotel Crowded House
HOSTEL €

(☏814 1565; www.crowdedhousegallipoli.com; Hüseyin Avni Sokak 4; dm/s/d TL15/45/60; ❉ @) Recommended by readers, this gem of a backpackers occupies a four-storey building just off the main square. The 24 comfortable, spick-and-span rooms and three dormitories edge Crowded House towards 'boutique backpacker' territory, as do the ground-floor bar and mezzanine breakfast area. Best of all is the welcome and professional service offered by Ringo and the guys.

Hotel Boss
BUSINESS HOTEL €

(☎814 1464; www.heyboss.com; Cumhuriyet Meydanı 14; s/d TL40/70; ✳@) This narrow building's pale yellow facade hides a cool, compact hotel, with a black-and-white reception and some of Eceabat's best rooms. The helpful staff speak a little English and it may appeal to travellers who want to forego staying at a backpackers.

TJs Hotel
HOSTEL €

(☎814 3121; www.anzacgallipolitours.com; Cumhuriyet Meydanı 5a; dm TL15, r per person TL25-50; ✳@) Overlooking the main square, TJs has rooms to suit every budget, from basic rooms and dorms to 'hotel' rooms with air-con and balconies. The long corridors are rather institutional and on our visit the service was somewhat shambolic, but the 5th-floor bar with its Ottoman-style decor is fabulous.

Aqua Boss Hotel
HOTEL €

(☎814 2864; İstiklal Caddesi 91; s/d TL35/60; ✳) This cavernous stone building on the waterfront, 50m south of Liman Restaurant, is a kooky affair starting with the birds flitting between the beams in its entrance hall. With 40 rooms and a fitness centre, it's like being a guest in a decaying country mansion.

Hotel Boss II
HOTEL €

(☎814 2311; Mehmet Akif Sokak 70; r from TL40; ✳) A fallback option if the backpackers and other Boss hotels are full, with basic but clean rooms and wooden bungalows. It's a 15-minute walk southwest of the centre.

✕ Eating

⬛TOP⬛ Liman Restaurant
CHOICE
SEAFOOD €€

(☎814 2755; İstiklal Caddesi 67; mains TL10) At the southern end of the main waterfront strip, the 'Harbour' is Eceabat's best restaurant, offering excellent meze and fish dishes. The covered terrace is a delight in all weather and the service is a notch above that of its neighbours'.

Maydos Restaurant
INTERNATIONAL €€

(☎814 1454; İstiklal Caddesi; mains TL8-15) Maydos' waterfront terrace, with views across the Dardanelles, is popular among locals. The varied menu focuses on meat, from steak to stroganoff, but there are five salads and a range of meze (TL3.50 to TL12). With a good list of wines and rakı, the only drawback is its location, 500m south of the centre.

Meydan Lokantası
LOKANTA €

(☎814 1357; kordon; mains TL7) One of the waterfront eateries serving simple fare to power tour groups through the battlefields, Meydan offers relatively good service and dishes including the recommended *tavuk şiş* (roast chicken kebap).

Boğaz
SEAFOOD €

(Cumhuriyet Meydanı; kebaps TL3) Between Hotel Boss and TJs Hotel, this fishmongers does a good line in *balık ekmek* (fish kebaps); a good way to sample local sardines.

⬛ Drinking

Boomerang Bar
BAR

(Cumhuriyet Caddesi 102) With boomerangs and yin yangs painted on the walls, along with photos of Anzac Day parties, this beach shack is the best place for a beer if you don't fancy crossing the Dardanelles. Past the tourist office at the town's north entrance.

Kafe'e'
CAFE

(Cumhuriyet Caddesi 72; ◷9am-10pm) Entered through Eceabat Cultural Centre or the neighbouring internet cafe, this cafe has sweeping views of the Dardanelles. Drinks, including beer and çay, and board games available.

ⓘ Information

Tourist office (Cumhuriyet Caddesi 72; ◷8am-5pm) Erkan in the neighbouring internet cafe speaks English.

ⓘ Getting There & Away

ÇANAKKALE **Gestaş** (☎444 0752; www.gestas denizulasim.com.tr) ferries cross the Dardanelles in both directions (TL2, car TL23, 25 minutes) every hour on the hour between 7am and midnight, and roughly every two hours after that.

GELİBOLU Hourly buses or minibuses (TL5, 50 minutes) are available.

KABATEPE In summer there are several dolmuşes daily to Kabatepe ferry dock (TL2.50, 15 minutes) on the western shore of the peninsula; in winter they meet the ferries. The dolmuşes can drop you at the Kabatepe Information Centre & Museum, 750m southeast of the bottom of the road up to Lone Pine and Chunuk Bair.

KİLİTBAHİR Dolmuşes frequently run down the coast (TL1.50, 10 minutes).

İSTANBUL Buses leave hourly (TL38, five hours).

Kilitbahir

Just across the Narrows from Çanakkale and accessible by ferry, Kilitbahir (Lock of the Sea) is a tiny fishing harbour dominated by a massive **fortress** (admission TL3; ☉8am-5pm Tue-Sun winter, to 7.30pm summer). Built by Mehmet the Conqueror in 1452 and given a grand seven-storey interior tower a century later by Süleyman the Magnificent, the castle is well worth a quick look around. Climb the rail-less staircase onto the walls if your nerves will stand it (people suffering from heart disease, hypertension and vertigo are warned not to do so and you'll soon see why).

At the end of one of the castle walls, the **Sarı Kule** (admission TL1) houses a small war museum, and overlooks the **Namazgah Tabyası** (Namazgah Redoubt), a mazelike series of 19th-century defensive bunkers.

The small, privately run ferry to/from Çanakkale (per person TL1.50, car TL18, 20 minutes) can carry only a few cars and waits until it is full before departing. From the ferry, dolmuşes and taxis run to Eceabat and Gelibolu, as well as to the Turkish war memorial at Abide, although you may have to wait for them to fill up.

Çanakkale

☏ 0286 / POP 86.600

The liveliest settlement on the Dardanelles, this sprawling harbour town would be worth a visit for its sights, nightlife and overall vibe even if it didn't lie opposite the Gallipoli Peninsula. The sweeping waterfront promenade heaves in the summer months, and the sizeable student population means there's always something happening in the bars and streets.

Çanakkale is also a good base for visiting the ruins at Troy (p159) and has become a popular destination for weekending Turks. During the summer, try to plan your visit for midweek.

◉ Sights

Military Museum   PARK, MUSEUM

(Askeri Müze; ☏ 213 1730; Çimenlik Sokak; museum admission TL4; ☉9am-5pm Tue, Wed & Fri-Sun; ℗) A park in the military zone at the southern end of the quay houses the Military Museum, also known as the Dardanelles Straits Naval Command Museum (Çanakkale Boğaz Komutanliği Deniz Müzesi). It's free to enter the park, which is open every day and is dotted with guns, cannons and military artefacts.

A sea-facing late-Ottoman building contains informative exhibits on the Gallipoli battles and some war relics, including fused bullets that hit each other in mid-air. Apparently the chances of this happening are something like 160 million to one, which gives a chilling idea of just how much ammunition was being fired.

Nearby is a replica of the **Nusrat minelayer** (Nusrat Mayın Gemisi), which played a heroic role in the sea campaign. The day before the Allied fleet tried to force the straits, Allied minesweepers proclaimed the water cleared. At night the *Nusrat* went out and picked up and relaid loose mines. Three Allied ships struck the *Nusrat*'s mines and were sunk or crippled.

Mehmet the Conqueror built the impressive **Çimenlik Kalesi** (Meadow Castle) in 1452, and Süleyman the Magnificent repaired it in 1551. The cannons surrounding the stone walls are from French, English and German foundries. Inside are some fine paintings of the battles of Gallipoli.

Archaeology Museum   MUSEUM

(Arkeoloji Müzesi; ☏ 217 6565; 100-Yil Caddesi; admission TL5; ☉8am-5pm; ℗) Just over 1.5km south of the otogar, just off the road to Troy, is the Archaeology Museum, also called the Çanakkale Museum (Çanakkale Müzesi).

The best exhibits here are those from Troy (p159) and Assos (p165), although the finds from the tumulus at Dardanos, an ancient town some 10km southwest of Çanakkale, are also noteworthy. There's quite a bit on display in the small garden.

Dolmuşes heading down Atatürk Caddesi towards Güzelyalı or Troy will drop you off near the museum for TL1.

Clock Tower   LANDMARK

The five-storey Ottoman *saat kulesi* (clock tower) near the harbour was built in 1897. It was paid for by an Italian consul and Çanakkale merchant who left 100,000 gold francs in his will for this purpose.

TOP CHOICE Trojan Horse   MONUMENT

Along the waterfront promenade north of the main ferry pier, don't be surprised to see this much-larger-than-life model, as seen in the movie *Troy* (2004). The model of the ancient city and information displays beneath it are better than anything you'll find at Troy.

Korfmann Library   LIBRARY

(Korfmann Kütüphanesi; ☏ 213 7212; Tifli Sokak 12; admission free; ☉10am-6pm Tue-Sat) Housed in a 19th-century former school in the old town, this library, opposite the Tifli Mosque, was the bequest of the late Manfred Osman Korfmann (1945–2005), archaeological director at Troy from 1988 to 2003. It contains 6000 volumes on history, culture, art and archaeology.

Yalı Hamam   HAMAM
(Çarşı Caddesi 5; ☺men 6am-11pm, women 8am-6pm) In this 17th-century hamam, the full works costs TL30. The women's entrance is just around the corner on Hapishane Sokak.

WWI Cannons   MONUMENT
(Cumhuriyet Meydanı) The inscription on this monument reads: 'Mehmets (Turkish soldiers) used these cannons on 18 March 1915 to ensure the impassability of the Çanakkale Strait'.

Çanakkale Pot   MONUMENT
Behind the WWI cannons is an oversized copy of this 19th-century style of pot, which is slowly regaining popularity.

✯✯ Festivals & Events
Çanakkale is almost unbearably overcrowded around the following events.

Çanakkale Naval Victory   COMMEMORATION
(Çanakkale Deniz Zaferi) Turks celebrate this day on 18 March.

Anzac Day   COMMEMORATION
Australians and New Zealanders descend on the Gallipoli Peninsula to mark this day, on 25 April (see boxed text, p137).

🛏 Sleeping
Çanakkale has hotels to suit all budgets, except on Anzac Day, when rip-offs and price-jacking abound. If you intend to be in town around 25 April, book well in advance and check prices carefully.

[TOP CHOICE] Hotel Kervansaray
BOUTIQUE HOTEL €€
(☎217 8192; www.otelkervansaray.com; Fetvane Sokak 13; s/d/tr TL90/140/170; ❄@) Çanakkale's only real boutique hotel lays on plenty of Ottoman touches, in keeping with the restored house it occupies (once owned by an early-20th-century judge). The 19 rooms have a dash of character without being overdone. The ones with showers are in the main historical building; the rest (with bathtubs) are across the inviting courtyard and garden, in a new annexe sympathetic to the red-brick original.

Maydos Hotel   HOTEL €€
(☎213 5970; www.maydos.com.tr; Yalı Caddesi 12; s/d from TL50/90; ❄@) This relatively swish hotel, with 36 town-facing, waterfront and internal rooms, is a calm retreat from the studenty mayhem outside, although noise could intrude on boisterous nights. Brown sofas and objets d'art adorn the reception, and we love the breezy bar-restaurant.

Anzac Hotel   HOTEL €
(☎217 7777; www.anzachotel.com; Saat Kulesi Meydanı 8; s/d/tr €35/45/60; ❄@) The Kervansaray's three-star sister is a great deal, with an unbeatable position by the clock tower and strait views across Çanakkale's rooftops. There's a mezzanine cafe, rooms have satellite TV, safe and minibar, and staff are well informed.

Hotel Artur   HOTEL €€
(☎213 2000; www.hotelartur.com; Cumhuriyet Meydanı 28; s/d from TL80/120; ❄@) A modish town-centre escape, Artur has 32 rooms on four floors and a nicely designed lobby, littered with white sofas and decorative art. The trendy Café Ka restaurant is next door. The only drawback is the lift, which starts from the top of some steps.

Hotel Akol   HOTEL €€€
(☎217 9456; www.hotelakol.com.tr; Kayserili Ahmet Paşa Caddesi; s/d/ste TL150/200/370; ❄❄) A short trot from the Trojan Horse, this tower – studded with orange balconies – is much easier on the eyes once you've gone through its revolving door. Antique furniture dots the classical-themed lobby, and the 138 rooms are small but comfortable. There's a roof bar and the service lives up to the Akol's best-in-town reputation.

Hotel Helen Park   HOTEL €
(☎212 1818; www.helenhotel.com; Tekke Sokak 10; s/d €40/60; ❄) Newer but the same price as the nearby Hotel Helen, the Park's 16 rooms have muted colour schemes, pleasantly decorated bathrooms and flat-screen TVs. The buffet breakfast takes place in the reception area, overlooking a quiet street.

Çanak Hotel   HOTEL €€
(☎214 1582; www.canakhotel.com; Dibek Sokak 1; s/d TL70/120; ❄@) This excellent mid-range option is tucked just off Cumhuriyet Meydanı, with a stunning roof bar and games room, and a skylit atrium connecting the floors. Some of the 52 smart but low-key rooms have balconies.

Çanakkale

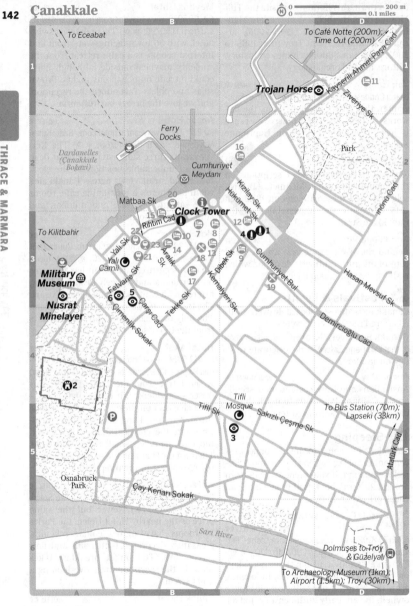

Otel Anafartalar HOTEL €€
(☎217 4454; www.hotelanafartalar.com.tr; İskele Meydanı; s/d TL75/125; ❉@) A big pinkish block with 71 rooms in a prime location near the ferry docks, the Anafartalar has fine views of the strait if you can bag a front

room with balcony. The carpets and bedspreads could do with an upgrade, though.

Efes Hotel PENSION €
(☎217 3256; www.efeshotelcanakkale.com; Fetvane Sokak 5; s/d excl breakfast TL40/50; ❉) An excellent choice for couples and lone women,

the friendly Efes has a feminine touch that's lacking in other budget options. Flowery bedding features in the cheerful rooms, and small balconies overlook the fountain in the back garden. There's no wi-fi, but internet cafes are nearby. Breakfast costs an extra TL5.

Yellow Rose Pension HOSTEL €
(📞217 3343; www.yellowrose.4mg.com; Aslan Abla Sokak 5; dm/s/d/tr/q TL20/30/50/70/90; 🅿 @) Found on a quiet, central street, this is good value, with a monumental TV in the lounge, four floors of small rooms and dorms, and surprisingly effective garden-hose showers. The tiled floors and smell of disinfectant makes things feel rather spartan, but there's a kitchen and staff are very helpful.

Anzac House Hostel HOSTEL €
(📞213 5969; www.anzachouse.com; Cumhuriyet Meydanı 59; dm/s/d without bathroom & excl breakfast TL17/25/40; @) Within rucksack-lugging distance of the ferry terminal, Anzac House has traditionally been the backpacker's digs of choice in Çanakkale (breakfast is extra, at TL10). Upstairs, despite the colourful doors and window frames, facilities such as the lines of shower booths in the bathrooms are uninviting. Nonetheless, the staff are helpful and Hassle Free Travel Agency is based here.

✖ Eating

The waterfront is lined with licensed restaurants. For cheaper fare, street stalls along the *kordon* (waterfront promenade) offer corn on the cob, mussels and other simple items, and Matbaa and Fetvane Sokaks are home to many soak-up-the-Efes eateries. A local speciality is *peynir helvası,* a dessert made with soft white village cheese, flour, butter and sugar and served natural or baked.

Anafartalar Kebap KEBAPÇI €€
(📞214 9112; İskele Meydanı; mains TL10; ⊙8am-11.30pm) With glass walls and low tables in a covered courtyard in front of the hotel of the same name, Anafartalar is quieter and better value than the nearby fish restaurants. The pide and İskender kebab (döner kebap on fresh pide, with tomato sauce, browned butter and yoghurt) are both excellent.

Café Notte RESTAURANT -BAR €€
(📞214 9112; Kayserili Ahmet Paşa Caddesi 40; mains TL12; ⊙8am-11.30pm) In the heart of the trendier northern waterfront strip, this cool bar-bistro has a cosmopolitan menu and cocktails (TL10); we found the White Russians to be better than the Margaritas. Fajitas and fish and chips are on offer, as are simpler eats such as pizzas and sandwiches (TL4 to TL10).

Gülen Pide KEBAPÇI, PIDECI €€
(📞212 8800; Cumhuriyet Bulvarı 27; kebaps TL9-19; ⊙11am-10.30pm) Locals recommend this *kebapçı* (kebab restaurant) strip, and Gülen is a good choice with a clean, white-tiled floor and an open kitchen producing pide

and *lahmacun* (Arabic-style pizza; TL2.50 to TL8.50).

Gülen Pizza
INTERNATIONAL €

(Hükümet Sokak; pizzas from TL6) On the other side of the park from Gülen Pide, this place serves all the pizza classics.

Çonk Coffee
CAFE €

(Kemalyeri Sokak; snacks TL2.50) Old coins and cameras adorn this friendly cafe, which serves Turkish coffee, sandwiches and *tost* (toasted sandwiches).

Drinking & Entertainment

Çanakkale has a frenetic bar and club scene, catering to a local student crowd and, in season, marauding young Aussies and Kiwis. Many venues have regular live music, and most of the busiest places are clustered around Matbaa and Fetvane Sokaks.

Benzin
BAR-CAFE

(Eski Balıkhane Sokak 11; ☎) This waterfront bar-cafe done out in 1960s decor is a relaxing spot for a drink and a bite (pizzas TL8 to TL12.50) but gets packed at the weekend.

Time Out
LIVE MUSIC

(Kayserili Ahmet Paşa Caddesi; beer TL6) A rock club of the stylish (rather than dingy) variety, with pictures of Elvis et al, outside tables and a barman who plays sets.

Hedon Club
LIVE MUSIC

(Yalı Caddesi 41; beer TL7) This informal little club is a good place for a beer, and it's an intimate venue, with two floors of tables overlooking the stage. There's sometimes a cover charge.

Makkarna Bistro
BAR

(Matbaa Sokak 8; beer TL6) One of the drinking dens on this buzzing pedestrianised lane, Makkarna serves cocktails and the traditional Turkish 'beer bong' (TL15).

Han Bar
BAR

(Fetvane Sokak 26) Upstairs in the 19th-century Yalı Han, this is a popular hangout where DJs play. The outside gallery overlooks an equally popular courtyard tea garden.

Information

Çanakkale is centred on its harbour, with a PTT (Post, Telegraf, Telefon) booth, ATMs and public phones right by the docks, and hotels, restaurants, banks and bus offices all within a few hundred metres.

Araz Internet (Fetvane Sokak 21; per hr TL1.50; ⊗9am-midnight) Internet access in the centre.

Çanakkale.com.tr (www.canakkale.com.tr) A good source of information.

Tourist office (☎217 1187; Cumhuriyet Meydanı; ⊗8am-7pm Jun-Sep, 8.30am-5.30pm Oct-May) Some 150m from the ferry pier, with brochures and bus timetables.

❶ Getting There & Away

Air

Turkish Airlines (www.thy.com) flies to/from İstanbul (TL85, 55 minutes) three times a week. A Turkish Airlines shuttle bus (TL7) links central Çanakkale with the airport, 2km southeast; otherwise a taxi costs about TL10.

Bus

Çanakkale's otogar is 1km inland of the ferry docks, beside a large Carrefour supermarket, but most buses pick up and drop off at the bus company offices near the harbour. If you're coming from İstanbul, hop on a ferry from Yenikapı to Bandırma and then take a bus to Çanakkale. It's easier than trekking out to İstanbul's otogar for a direct bus.

Ankara (TL45, 10 hours, regular)
Ayvalık (TL25, 3½ hours, hourly)
Bandırma (TL20, 2½ hours, hourly)
Bursa (TL30, 4½ hours, hourly)
Edirne (TL30, 4½ hours, regular)
İstanbul (TL35, six hours, regular)
İzmir (TL35, 5½ hours, hourly)

Car

Car parks throughout the centre charge TL3 per hour.

Dolmuş

Troy Dolmuşes to Troy (TL4, 35 minutes, hourly) leave on the half-hour between 9.30am and 4.30pm (7pm in summer, and less frequently at weekends) from a station at the northern end of the bridge over the Sarı River, and drop you by the ticket booth. Coming back, hourly dolmuşes leave on the hour between 7am and 3pm (5pm in summer).

Gelibolu Take the ferry to Eceabat (or Kilitbahir) and pick up a minibus; or take a bus or minibus from Çanakkale otogar to Lapseki (TL5, 45 minutes) and then take the ferry across the Dardanelles.

Boat

Bozcaada See p164.
Eceabat See p139.
Gökçeada See p147.
Kilitbahir See p139.

Gökçeada

🎵 0286 / POP 8600

Just north of the entrance to the Dardanelles, rugged, sparsely populated Gökçeada (Heavenly Island) is one of only two inhabited Aegean islands belonging to Turkey. Measuring 13km from north to south and just under 30km from east to west, it is by far the nation's largest island. Gökçeada is a fascinating place, with some dramatic scenery packed into a small area, and a Greek feel to it throughout. It's a great place to escape to after visiting Gallipoli.

Gökçeada was once a predominantly Greek island called Imbros. During WWI it was an important base for the Gallipoli campaign; indeed, Allied commander General Ian Hamilton stationed himself at the village of Aydıncık (then Kefalos) on the island's southeast coast. Along with its smaller island neighbour to the south, Bozcaada (p160), Gökçeada was retained by the new Turkish Republic in 1923 but was exempted from the population exchange. However, in the 1960s when the Cyprus conflict flared up, the Turkish government put pressure on local Greeks, who numbered about 7000, to leave; today only a few hundred pensioners remain.

Gökçeada's inhabitants mostly earn a living through fishing, sheep- and cattle-rearing, farming the narrow belt of fertile land around Gökçeada town, and tourism. Apart from its semideserted Greek villages, olive groves and pine forests, the island boasts fine beaches and craggy hills. Unlike Bozcaada, it is a rare example of an Aegean island that hasn't been overtaken by tourism and, because it is a military base, will hopefully stay that way.

◎ Sights & Activities

TOP CHOICE Greek villages   HISTORIC AREA
Heading west from Gökçeada town, you'll pass Zeytinli (Aya Theodoros) after 3km, Tepeköy (Agridia), another 7km on, and Dereköy (Shinudy), another 5km west. All were built on hillsides overlooking the island's central valley to avoid pirate raids. Many of the houses are deserted and falling into disrepair, particularly at Dereköy, which is reminiscent of the Mediterranean ghost town of Kayaköy (p323). However, thanks to a couple of inspired accommodation options, Zeytinli and Tepeköy are discovering the benefits of small-scale tourism, and both are worth a visit. Tepeköy is absolutely gorgeous, surrounded by green-grey scree-covered hills, with views over valleys and a large reservoir, plus a dash of Greek heritage in its main square and taverna. Its Greek church is also picturesque; apparently this is the only settlement in Turkey that does not have a mosque.

Kaleköy   SEAFRONT, RUINS
Although the views are dented by the presence of the military, the Gökçeada Resort Hotel and a large yacht marina, Kaleköy (formerly Kastro) exudes an infectious seaside contentment. Above the tiny public beach and rocks are a hillside old quarter, a lovely whitewashed former Greek church and the remains of an Ottoman-era castle. The coastline between Kaleköy and Kuzulimanı forms a sualtı milli parkı (national marine park).

THRACE & MARMARA GÖKÇEADA

Gökçeada

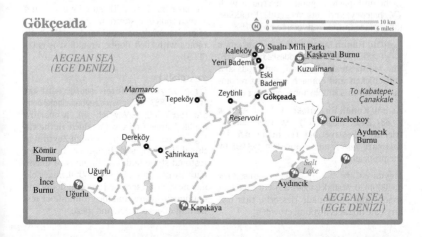

Beaches
BEACHES

The sand beach at Aydıncık is the best on the island, and is adjacent to Tuz Gölü (Salt Lake). Further west on the stunningly picturesque southeast coast, there are smaller beaches at Kapıkaya and Uğurlu.

Windsurfing
WINDSURFING

Aydıncık beach and Tuz Gölü, respectively offering flat water and waves, are popular for windsurfing and kitesurfing. Ice Angels (http://iceangels-club.com; ⊙May-Sep) offers equipment rental (per hour/day TL20/50) and tuition (one hour from TL40).

⭐ Festivals & Events

During the Yumurta Panayırı (Egg Festival) in the first week of July, many former Greek inhabitants return to the island, along with the Orthodox Patriarch of İstanbul.

🛏 Sleeping & Eating

The old-fashioned *ev pansiyonu*, which has virtually died out elsewhere, is still alive and kicking on Gökçeada. It's not unusual for locals to approach and offer you a spare room in their house, for considerably less than the prices charged by pensions and hotels.

GÖKÇEADA TOWN

Restaurants are clustered around the main square.

Otel Taşkın
HOTEL €

(☎887 3266; www.taskinotel.com, in Turkish; Zeytinli Caddesi 3; s/d TL30/60) In the quiet backstreets southwest of the main square, Hotel Flood has a brown-tiled exterior (including a mosaic of a *gület* – a wooden yacht) and spacious, good-value rooms with TV, balcony and lots of light. Breakfast takes place in the front courtyard.

🌿 Gül Hanım Mantı Evi
LOKANTA €

(☎887 3773; Atatürk Caddesi 23; mains TL6) The *mantı* steals the show, but moussaka and chicken and spinach are also recommended at this simple home-cooking eatery.

Asmalı Konak Birhanesi
CAFE-BAR €

(☎887 2469; mains TL7) At this female-friendly side-street bar, the menu includes calamari, *köfte*, meze, and fish netted by the proprietor.

Meydanı Café
PATISSERIE €

(☎887 4420; Atatürk Caddesi 35) For excellent snacks and shop-made desserts, this big, airy cafe attracts a young crowd.

KALEKÖY

Club Masi Hotel
BOUTIQUE HOTEL €€

(☎887 4619; www.hotelmasi.com; Eski Bademli; r TL125-175; ❄@≋) Located above the Gökçeada–Kaleköy road, the country cousin of İstanbul's Hotel Masi has stylish, modern rooms with some of the island's best views. The terrace, with its outdoor pool, jacuzzi, sun loungers and bar, gazes at Kaleköy castle and the Aegean.

Kalimerhaba Motel
PENSION €

(☎887 3648; erayda@msn.com; Barbaros Caddesi 28; s/d TL50/70; ❄) On Kaleköy's waterfront, Kalimerhaba has some of Gökçeada's smartest, cleanest budget rooms, entered from a big, light reception and vine-covered terrace.

Kale Otel
PENSION €

(☎887 4404; www.kalemotel.com; Barbaros Caddesi 34; s/d excl breakfast TL40/70; ❄) Light filters through the Castle's flimsy curtains more readily than the hot water comes from its taps, but the downstairs area is perfect for lounging on the waterfront. The Dağınık family is welcoming, if rather late-rising, and the Turkish breakfast (TL5) is delicious.

Yukarı Kaleköy
AREA

For a sundowner with million-dollar views over the bay and hills, climb to Yukarı Kaleköy (Upper Kaleköy) and Yakamoz Motel's terrace restaurant; then continue past it, following the signs to Poseidon Pansiyon, to the bar-cafe below the castle.

AYDINCIK

Şen Camping
CAMPGROUND €

(☎898 1020; s/d TL30/60, camping per person excl breakfast TL7) With sun loungers and a reed-roofed restaurant, beachfront Şen offers camping on sand, and small, basic rooms with tiled floors. Breakfast is extra (TL5).

ZEYTİNLİ

TOP CHOICE Zeytindali Hotel
BOUTIQUE HOTEL €€€

(☎887 3707; www.zeytindalihotel.com; s/d TL160/200; ⊙May-Oct; ❄) A narrow cobbled street (leave your vehicle in the village car park) winds up through Zeytinli to this delightfully stylish 16-room hotel in a restored stone building. Rooms are imaginatively decorated in a style that mixes old and new, with varnished wooden floors and antique furniture, and the ground-floor restaurant offers seafood and meze.

TEPEKÖY

Barba Yorgo PENSION €
(☎887 3592; www.barbayorgo.com; r per person TL35; ☺May-Sep) Accommodation at this unique establishment, run by the eponymous (and gregarious) Greek 'Papa George', is in a few properties – including two rooms above the central taverna and a lovingly restored village house overlooking the valley 200m away, with wooden floors, sparrows in the rafters and a glowering mountain right out back just begging for a morning scramble.

Tavern MEYHANE €€
(Cumhuriyet Meydanı; mains TL10-15; ☺May-Sep) The host of Barba Yorgo also runs the film-set-worthy village restaurant, where you can sample above-average meze, eat wild boar (a no-no elsewhere in Turkey) and drink the house-made retsina wine.

UĞURLU

Mavi Su Resort RESORT €€
(☎897 6090; www.mavisuresort.com; s/d TL75/120; ❄@) If you really want to get away from it all, the Blue Water, with 35 rooms and suites, is for you. South of town, the resort is just before Uğurlu, which is about as far as you can get from anything on Gökçeada. The rooms are some of the island's best, and the lovely long garden stretches virtually into the sea.

Gül Pansiyon PENSION €
(☎897 6144; s/d TL30/60) By far the newest option in the village, the friendly Rose Pension overlooks the grassy central square. It has bright rooms with small, clean bathrooms and a restaurant (*köfte* TL7) on its covered veranda.

Shopping

Gökçeada is committed to becoming the first Turkish community to produce only organic foodstuffs; at present its 120,000 trees produce an annual 2000 tonnes of oil, most of which is organic. At the forefront of this endeavour is Elta-Ada (☎887 3287; www.elta-ada.com.tr), a farm that produces organic olive oil, dairy products (soft white cheeses, yoghurt and butter) and assorted fruits and vegetables. Shops around the main square in Gökçeada town sell organic fruit, vegetables and produce, including Elta-Ada's kiosk (Cumhuriyet Meydanı; ☺8am-9pm summer), opposite the Pegasus Otel, and Ekozey (Atatürk Caddesi), near Gül Hanım Mantı Evi. If you visit Gökçeada in May/June, don't miss its organic black cherries.

❶ Information

The ferry docks at Kuzulimanı, but facilities such as an internet cafe, taxis, bank, ATMs and post office are found inland at Gökçeada town, where most of the island's population lives.

Tourist office (☎887 2800; Cumhuriyet Meydanı; ☺10am-8pm Jun-Sep) In a kiosk on Gökçeada town's main square.

Websites See www.gokceada.com and www.gokceada17.net.

❶ Getting There & Away

Check departure times, because they do change.

GALLIPOLI PENINSULA Gestaş (☎444 0752; www.gestasdenizulasim.com.tr) runs daily ferries to/from Kabatepe (per person TL2, cars TL20, 1½ hours) on the western side of the peninsula, leaving the mainland at 10am, 3pm and 7pm and departing the island at 7.15am, noon and 5pm. Tickets are also valid for the Eceabat–Çanakkale ferry, so you don't have to pay again to cross the strait.

ÇANAKKALE Ferries run at weekends, leaving Çanakkale (per person TL2, cars TL23, two hours) at 9am on Friday and 5pm on Sunday, and returning from Gökçeada at 6pm on Friday and 7pm on Sunday.

❶ Getting Around

BUS & DOLMUŞ Ferries dock at Kuzulimanı, where buses and dolmuşes should be waiting to drive you the 6km to Gökçeada town (TL1.50, 15 minutes), or straight through to Kaleköy, 5km further north (TL2.50, 25 minutes). A bus runs between Kaleköy, Gökçeada and Kuzulimanı roughly every hour; it doesn't always stick to the timetable, but is generally reliable for catching the ferry.

CAR Gökçeada Rent-A-Car (☎218 2869; Atatürk Caddesi, Gökçeada town; per day TL80) The only petrol station is 2km from Gökçeada town centre on the Kuzulimanı road.

TAXI You can taxi from Gökçeada town to Kaleköy (TL7, 5 minutes), Kuzulimanı (TL14, 10 minutes), Zeytinli (TL10, 10 minutes), Tepeköy (TL13, 20 minutes) and Uğurlu (TL25, 30 minutes).

Bandırma

☎0266 / POP 111,000
An undistinguished 20th-century *beton-ville* (concrete city), the port town of Bandırma marks the junction between ferries across the Sea of Marmara from İstanbul and İzmir-bound trains. Taking a ferry from central İstanbul to Bandırma is a quick and pleasant way to get to Anatolia, or to the Gallipoli Peninsula via Çanakkale.

The otogar is 2km uphill from the ferry terminal, out on the main highway and served by *servis* (shuttle buses). The train station is next to the ferry terminal.

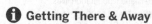 Getting There & Away

BUS Bandırma is midway between Bursa (TL15, two hours, 115km) and Çanakkale (TL20, 2¾ hours, 195km).

CAR The major rental companies do not have offices here, so you may want to bring a car from İstanbul. A local company, if you are planning a short trip, is **Viraj Rentacar** (☏718 2102; virajoto kiralama@hotmail.com; Mehmetçik Caddesi 29).

FERRY There are at least two daily fast ferries that are run by **İstanbul Deniz Otobüsleri** (İDO; ☏455 6900; www.ido.com.tr; per pedestrian/car/passenger TL32/125/27), connecting Bandırma with İstanbul's Yenikapı docks (two hours). It's a comfortable service, with assigned seats, refreshments available, a business-class lounge and a lift for disabled passengers.

TRAIN There are daily express trains to/from İzmir (TL17, six hours), leaving at 4pm/2.20pm. Apart from Tuesday, there are also services at 9.50am/9.25am, and these trains coordinate with the ferry to/from İstanbul.

Acropolis, Pergamum (p176)
Take in the classical splendour of Pergamum's acropolis, one of Turkey's most impressive ancient sites

149

TO THE GLORY OF GOD AND IN LOVING MEMORY OF 7000 AUSTRALIAN SOLDIERS WHO FOUGHT ON GALLIPOLI IN 1915 AND THOSE, NO KNOWN GRAVES, AND 1700 MEN. BURIED WHOSE GRAVES ARE NOT RECORDED IN OTHER AREAS OF THE PENINSULA. BUT WHO FELL IN THE ANZAC AREA AND HAVE NO KNOWN GRAVES, AND ALSO OF 960 AUSTRALIANS AND 252 NEW ZEALANDERS WHO FIGHTING ON GALLIPOLI IN 1915 INCURRED MORTAL WOUNDS OR SICKNESS AND FOUND BURIAL AT SEA.

THEIR NAME LIVETH
FOR EVERMORE

1. Ölüdeniz (p322)

Enjoy the sheltered bay and lush national park by day and party through the night

2. Bozcaada (p160)

This idyllic, epicurean island in the Aegean is perfect for relaxing with a glass of wine

3. Carpets (p650)
Turkey's carpets are the product of a textile-making tradition that has developed over centuries

4. Library of Celsus, Ephesus (p205)
The best-preserved ruins in the Mediterranean, Ephesus is a tribute to Greek and Roman prowess

5. Lone Pine Australian cemetery, Gallipoli (p134)
Lone Pine is perhaps the most moving of the Anzac cemeteries, marking the loss of 7000 men

IZZET KERIBAR

2

4

1. Hierapolis, Pamukkale (p280)
Visitors can bathe amid the World Heritage–
listed ruins of Hierapolis

2. Aya Sofya, İstanbul (p45)
One-time church, mosque and now museum,
this is İstanbul's most famous monument

3. Lycian tombs, Kaleköy (p343)
Kaleköy is home to the ruins of ancient Simena

4. Castle of St Peter, Bodrum (p235)
Erected by the Knights Hospitaller in 1437

MZJ/IMAGEBROKER

3

154

1. Turkish delight (p106)
Jewel-like *lokum* (Turkish delight) was created by Ottoman confectioner Ali Muhiddin Hacı Bekir

2. Spice Bazaar, İstanbul (p61)
As well as spices, this bustling market sells nuts, honeycomb, olive-oil soaps, *incir* (figs) and more

3. Cherry-juice vendor
Turkey's delicious cherries were introduced to the rest of the world by the historic town of Giresun, which means 'cherry' in Greek

SEONG JOON CHO

KIMBERLEY COOLE

4. Blue Mosque, İstanbul (p49)
The blue interior tiles of Sultan Ahmet Camii number in their tens of thousands, giving rise to its unofficial title, Blue Mosque

5. Shops in Kaleiçi, Antalya (p349)
Rummage through the wares in the antique quarter of Kaleiçi, which translates to 'within the castle'

DALLAS STRIBLEY

Selimiye Camii, Edirne (p120)
The magnificent interior of Ottoman architect Mimar Sinan's grandest mosque

İzmir & the North Aegean

Why Go?

The quieter northern section of Turkey's Aegean coast is the ideal destination for anyone who wants to relax in the sun – without getting stuck on the beach. There are beaches, of course – such as those on Bozcaada – but the hills and peninsulas are also rich in history and culture. There's the remains of Troy, hilltop ruins in Bergama and Behramkale, and, around the latter, communities descended from Turkmen nomads.

Perhaps the most poignant piece of local history is the population exchange between Turkey and Greece. In spots such as Ayvalık and Bozcaada town, you might hear elderly people chatting in Greek as you wander through the picturesque old Greek quarter.

The local city, İzmir, is a laid-back place with plenty of sights around its bazaar and waterfront. It's also the gateway to the Çeşme Peninsula, where Alaçatı offers the greatest concentration of the region's many boutique hotels.

Best Places to Stay

» Biber Evi (p166)
» Alaçatı Taş Otel (p198)
» Hünnap Han (p168)
» Foçantique Boutique Hotel (p182)
» Annette's House (p169)

Best Places to Eat

» Balıkçı (p170)
» Cafe Agrilia (p199)
» Sakız (p189)
» Sandal Restaurant (p163)

When to Go

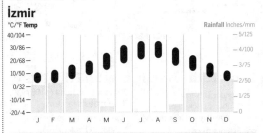

İzmir

June Bozcaada's wine festival is on the viticultural Aegean island.

July International İzmir Festival brings music and dance to the region.

September Windsurf and *gület* cruise on the Çeşme Peninsula without crowds.

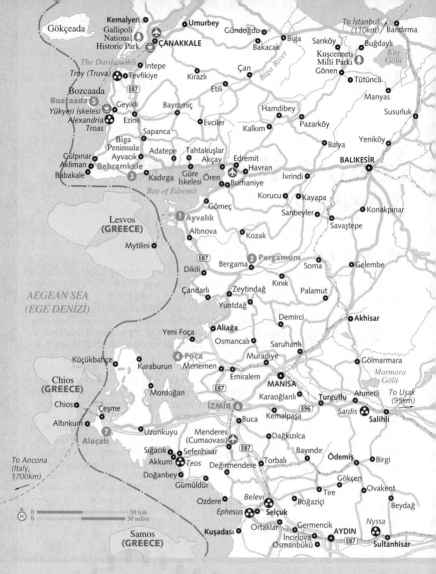

İzmir & the North Aegean Highlights

1 Wander the crumbling, atmospheric backstreets of the old town in **Ayvalık** (p169)

2 Explore the ruins of the Roman Empire at **Pergamum** (Bergama; p174), one of the country's finest ancient sites

3 Climb Behramkale's cobbled streets to the amazing **Temple of Athena** (p166) with its glorious sea views

4 See where the Turks holiday in **Foça** (p181), an amiable seaside town straddling two bays

5 Relax on the beach and sample the local vino on the idyllic, epicurean island of **Bozcaada** (p160)

6 Hunt for bargains in **İzmir's** (p187) chaotic bazaar before retiring to the waterfront for a sunset drink

7 Windsurf by day and fine-dine by night in **Alaçatı** (p198), the region's favourite boutique bolt hole

Troy (Truva) & Tevfikiye

☑0286

It has to be said, if it wasn't for the name – and its legendary associations – these ruins would be one of Turkey's many forgotten, overgrown sites. Of all the ancient centres in Turkey, the remains of the great city of Troy are among the least impressive. Unlike at Aegean archaeological wonders like Ephesus (p205) and Pergamum (p174), you'll have to use a great deal of imagination to reconstruct the city's former splendour. Still, for history buffs and fans of Homer's *Iliad,* it's an important site to tick off the list – and the wooden horse is fun. Troy is a popular destination for weekending school parties; try to visit midweek.

History

The first people lived here during the early Bronze Age. The cities called Troy I to Troy V (3000–1700 BC) had a similar culture, but Troy VI (1700–1250 BC) took on a different Mycenae-influenced character, doubling in size and trading prosperously with the region's Greek colonies. Archaeologists argue over whether Troy VI or Troy VII was the city of King Priam who engaged in the Trojan War. Most believe it was Troy VI, arguing that the earthquake that brought down the walls in 1250 BC hastened the Achaean victory.

Troy VII lasted from 1250 BC to 1000 BC. An invading Balkan people moved in around 1190 BC, and Troy sank into a torpor for four centuries. It was revived as a Greek city (Troy VIII, 700–85 BC), then as a Roman one (Novum Ilion; Troy IX, 85 BC to AD 500). Before eventually settling on Byzantium, Constantine the Great toyed with the idea of building the capital of the eastern Roman Empire here. As a Byzantine town, Troy didn't amount to much.

The Fourth Crusaders sometimes claimed that their brutal behaviour in Turkey was justified as vengeance for Troy, and when Mehmet the Conqueror visited the site in 1462 he, in turn, claimed to be laying those ghosts to rest. After that, the town simply disappeared from the records.

⊙ Sights

Ruins of Troy   RUINS

(☑283 0536; per person TL15; ⊙8.30am-7pm May-15 Sep, to 5pm mid-Sep–end Apr) Souvenir shops straggle along the road between Hotel Hisarlık and the ruins. You can pick up illustrated guidebooks here or at the on-site shop. Guides are available for tours (€50, 1½ hours); inquire at the hotel or ticket booth, or contact Mustafa Askin through his website (www.thetroyguide.com) in advance.

The first thing you see as you approach the ruins is a huge replica of the city's most potent symbol – and the means of its legendary demise – a wooden horse. The Trojan horse model was built by the Ministry of Tourism and Culture. You can climb up inside and admire the views through windows in the horse's sides (which presumably didn't feature in the original Greek design).

The Excavations House, near the base of the horse, was used by earlier archaeological teams, and today holds models and superimposed pictures to give an idea of what Troy looked like at different points in its history, as well as information on the importance of the Troy myth in Western history. Outside is the small Pithos Garden, with a collection of oversized storage jars and drainage pipes.

Although the site is still confusing, the circular path around the ruins has signboards to help you understand what you're seeing.

As you approach the ruins, take the stone steps up on the right. These bring you out on top of what was the outer wall of Troy VIII/IX, from where you can gaze on the fortifications of the east wall gate and tower of Troy VI.

Go back down the steps and follow the boardwalk to the right, between thick stone walls and up a knoll, from where you can look at some original (as well as some reconstructed) red-brick walls of Troy II/III. The curved protective roof above them is the same shape and height as the Hisarlık mound before excavations began in 1874.

Continue following the path, past the northeast bastion of the heavily fortified city of Troy VI, the site of a Graeco-Roman Troy IX Temple of Athena and, later, the walls of Troy II/III. You can make out the stone foundations of a megaron (building with porch) from the same era.

Next, beyond traces of the wall of Early/Middle Troy (Troy I south gate) are more remains of megarons of Troy II, inhabited by a literal 'upper class' while the poor huddled on the plains.

The path then sweeps past Schliemann's original trial trench, which was cut straight through all the layers of the city. Signs point out the nine city strata in the trench's 15m-high sides.

Troy (Truva)

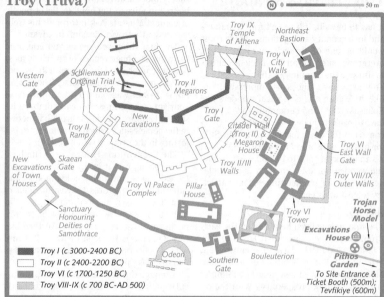

Just round the corner is a stretch of wall from what is believed to have been the two-storey-high Troy VI **Palace Complex**, followed by traces from Troy VIII/XI of a **sanctuary** to unknown deities. Later, a new sanctuary was built on the same site, apparently honouring the deities of Samothrace. Eventually, the path passes in front of the Roman **Odeon**, where concerts were held, and, to the right, the **Bouleuterion** (Council Chamber), bringing you back to where you started.

🛏 Sleeping & Eating

Most visitors stay in Çanakkale (p140) and visit Troy on a day trip. However, the village of Tevfikiye, 1km from the ruins, makes a pleasant change from the hassle of Çanakkale.

Varol Pansiyon　　　　　　　PENSION €
(☎283 0828; s/d TL40/70) Overlooking a lush garden behind the village shop in Tevfikiye, Varol is clean, lovingly cared for and homely. Rooms are of a decent size, and guests can use the kitchen.

Hotel Hisarlık　　　　　　　HOTEL €
(☎283 0026; www.thetroyguide.com; s/d/tr €25/35/50) This basic but comfortable hotel is run by local guide Mustafa Askin's family.

Some 500m from the ruins, it's a good spot for watching country life once the coaches have disappeared. The restaurant, which serves Turkish home cooking, is ideal for energising yourself before or after a Trojan tour.

ℹ Getting There & Away

DOLMUŞ See p144 for services to/from Çanakkale.

TOUR The travel agencies we've listed in Çanakkale and Eceabat (see p131) offering afternoon tours of the Gallipoli battlefields also offer morning trips to Troy (around TL60 per person); worth considering if you want a guided tour of both sites at an affordable rate.

Bozcaada

🕿0286 / POP 2700

Beautiful little Bozcaada. The second of Turkey's two inhabited Aegean islands (the other is Gökçeada), it's the sort of place where you arrive planning to spend a night and wind up wishing you could stay forever. That's seemingly what happened to the İstanbullus who are steadily filling Bozcaada town with boutique hotels and restaurants. Nonetheless, it's still one of the Aegean's prettiest small towns, with a warren of picturesque, vine-draped old houses and cobbled streets huddling beneath a huge medieval fortress.

Windswept Bozcaada (formerly Tenedos) has always been known to Anatolian oenophiles for its wines, and vineyards still blanket its sunny slopes (see boxed text, p163). The island is small (about 5km to 6km across) and easy to explore. Lovely unspoilt sandy beaches line the coast road to the south.

Be warned that outside the school-holiday period (mid-June to mid-September) many businesses shut down; some, particularly eating and drinking options, open their doors at weekends and on Wednesdays, when a market fills the main square.

◉ Sights

Fortress
FORTRESS

(admission TL1.50; ◷10am-1pm & 2-6pm) Although Bozcaada is a place for hanging out rather than doing anything specific, there is one official tourist attraction: Bozcaada town's impressive castle. It dates to Byzantine times, but most of what you see are later Venetian, Genoese and Ottoman additions. Inside the double walls are traces of a mosque, ammunition dumps, a barracks, an infirmary and Roman pillars.

Beaches
BEACH

The best beaches – Ayana, Ayazma, Sulubahçe and Habbele – straggle along the southwest coast, although Tuzburnu to the east is also passable. Ayazma is by far the most popular and best equipped, boasting several cafes (offering the usual Turkish fare) as well as a small, abandoned Greek monastery uphill.

Bozcaada Local History Museum
MUSEUM

(Bozcaada Yerel Tarih Müzesi; ☑0532 215 6033; Lale Sokak 7; adult/child TL5/3; ◷10am-8pm late May-Sep) A treasure trove of island curios – maps, prints, photographs, seashells and day-to-day artefacts. Next door, a small private gallery sells island scenes.

Church
CHURCH

(20 Eylül Caddesi) The church, in the old Greek neighbourhood to the west of the fortress, is sadly rarely open.

⌷ Sleeping

BOZCAADA TOWN

The locals are hot on the İstanbullu incomers' Gucci heels in the accommodation game. Headscarf-wrapped ladies may greet you at the *iskele* (pier) and offer you their spare room; if not, wander through the old

DISCOVERING TROY

Until the 19th century, many historians doubted whether Troy was a real place at all. One man who was convinced of its existence – to an almost obsessive level – was the German businessman Heinrich Schliemann (1822–90), who in 1871 received permission from the Ottoman government to excavate a hill near the village of Hisarlık, which archaeologists had previously identified as a possible site for the city. This was to be no slow, forensic excavation, however. Schliemann was more of an eager treasure hunter than a methodical archaeologist and he quickly tore open the site, uncovering the remains of a ruined city, which he confidently identified as the Troy of Homeric legend; and a great cache of gold artefacts, which he named, with typical understatement, 'Priam's Treasure'. These discoveries brought Schliemann world fame, but also greater scrutiny of his slapdash approach, prompting criticism and revealing that not all of his findings were quite as he presented them.

In his haste, Schliemann had failed to appreciate that Troy was not a single city, but rather a series of settlements built successively, one on top of the other, over the course of about 2500 years. Subsequent archaeologists have identified the remains of nine separate Troys, large sections of which were damaged during Schliemann's hot-headed pursuit of glory. Furthermore, it was soon established that his precious treasures were not from the time of Homer's Troy (Troy VI), but from the much earlier Troy II.

Schliemann's dubious attitude towards archaeological standards continued after the excavation when he smuggled part of 'Priam's Treasure' out of the Ottoman Empire. Much of it was displayed in Berlin, where it was seized by invading Soviet troops at the end of WWII. Following decades of denials about their whereabouts, the treasures were eventually found hidden away in the Pushkin Museum in Moscow, where they remain while international wrangles over their true ownership continue.

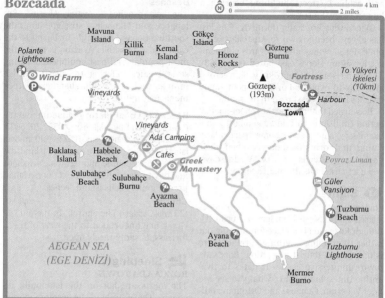

Greek quarter west of the castle and an offer will be forthcoming. Apart from Hotel
İskele, the following are located in the fast-
gentrifying old Greek neighbourhood.

Kale Pansiyon   PENSION €€
(☑697 8617; www.kalepansiyon.net, in Turkish;
s/d TL50/100) With commanding views
from the top of town, the family-run Kale
has 14 simple but fastidiously clean rooms
and a terrace on the lane for breakfast. Of
its two houses, the one on the right has
better bathrooms; light wooden floors and
kilims are found throughout.

Otel Kaikias   BOUTIQUE HOTEL €€€
(☑697 0250; www.kaikias.com, in Turkish; s/d
TL175/230; ☒) Overlooking a tiny seaside
square near the castle, this artful hotel is
an attraction in itself – from the reception's
plant ceiling to the antiques and artefacts,
such as a bookcase of flaking tomes behind
protective glass. Outside the main building
and across the cobbles is the restaurant-
bar, with its wooden decks and verandah.

Otel Ege Bozcaada   HOTEL €€€
(☑697 8189; www.egehotel.com; r TL180; ☒) A
19th-century primary school now turned
into a cavernous hotel with 35 attractively
furnished rooms, each with the name of a
poet, and an extract of their verse, engraved

on the door. The top-floor rooms have balconies with views of the fort. Off season,
rooms are also available as singles (TL80).

Ergin Pansiyon   PENSION €€
(☑697 0038; www.erginpansiyon.com, in Turkish; s/d TL40/80; ☒) The delicious Turkish
breakfast served in a courtyard, and the
rooftop terrace with its castle view, almost
make up for Ergin's rooms. The decorative
disasters include mixing green walls and
orange blankets, but it is nonetheless one of
Bozcaada town's cheaper options.

Hotel İskele   BOUTIQUE HOTEL €€
(☑697 0087; www.bozcaadaiskeleotel.com, in
Turkish; per person TL80; ☒) At the southern
end of the harbour, clearly visible from
the ferry, this blue-and-white hotel has 12
rooms, six facing the castle across the water, and a fish restaurant. The rooms are
quirkily decorated with shells, objets d'art
and, occasionally, antique furniture and
balconies.

Kaptan Aynar   EV PANSIYONU €
(☑697 8042; s/d TL30/60) Below Ergin
Pansiyon, this slightly tired modern
house has three spare rooms with beds
of varying comfort, a washing machine
and a sunny little garden. Breakfast is not
provided.

SOUTHWEST & EAST COASTS

Güler Pansiyon PENSION €€
(📞 697 8454; guleradaotel@hotmail.com; Tuzburnu Yolu Üzeri; s/d TL50/100) Although a little aged, this farmhouse, located about 2.5km south of town on the Tuzburnu road, has an authentic island feel and a beautiful setting. Eleven simple rooms open onto a verandah overlooking a vineyard, with a private beach at the far end. The Gülers are friendly folk and the wine is a good tipple.

Ada Camping CAMPGROUND €
(📞 697 0442; senayalir@mynet.com; Eski Kule Mevkii; per person TL15) This well-equipped camp site, 200m inland from Sulubahçe beach, has a kitchen, a barbecue and tents for hire (per person TL20).

✗ Eating

Check the price of fish before ordering. There have been complaints from travellers about the exorbitant costs in some restaurants.

TOP CHOICE Sandal Restaurant SEAFOOD €€€
(📞 697 0278; Alsancak Sokak; mains TL20-25; ⊙lunch & dinner; 🛜) Major reasons to visit Sandal, with its blue-and-white colour scheme and seating on a cobbled lane, are its service – the waiter was former Turkish president Turgut Erzal's manservant – and its fresh fare. The mixed meze plate (TL20) is bread-moppingly good, featuring lashings of olive oil.

Lodos SEAFOOD €€€
(📞 697 0545; Çinar Çarşi Caddesi; mains TL20; 🛜) Everything at this decade-old restaurant is spot on: the seascapes decorating its 120-year-old walls create the feel of a bijou

fisherman's cottage; the menu explains dishes such as *deniz börülcesi* (black-eyed peas that grow in tidal areas) and shrimp casserole; and the service is equally thoughtful.

Ada Café CAFE €€
(📞 697 8795; Çinar Çeşme Sokak 4; mains TL8-17.50, 35cl wine from TL14; ⊙8.30am-midnight May-Sep) The İstanbul-born owners, Melih and Semra, have thrown themselves wholeheartedly into island life, running this popular cafe, which serves as an unofficial tourist information point. There is a good range of breakfast choices plus hot and cold meze; the house speciality is red poppy-based products, including cordial and dessert.

Koreli SEAFOOD €€
(📞 697 8098; Yali Caddesi 12; mains TL15) In business since 1967, this harbourside restaurant near Hotel İskele clearly knows what it's doing, and roars with regulars who come for meze and seafood such as calamari and octopus.

Café at Lisa's CAFE €€
(📞 697 0182; Kurtulus Caddesi; mains TL15;🛜) Behind Hotel İskele, this charming cafe in an old bakery is run by Lisa, an Australian who also publishes the local rag (so is very au fait with island goings-on). It's a great place for breakfast – Lisa's omelettes are legendary – as well as cake and Western mains such as pizza.

Gülüm Ocakbaşı OCAKBAŞI €€
(📞 697 8567; Sakarya Sokak 5; mains TL12; ⊙lunch & dinner) Next to Tüketim Market, this *ocakbaşı* (grill house) serves a wide range of Turkish classics, including kebaps, *köfte* (meatballs) and pide (Turkish-style pizza).

FINE WINE

Bozcaada has been one of Turkey's great wine-growing regions since ancient times, when enormous quantities of wine were used to fuel the debauchery at festivals for Dionysus, the Greek god of wine. Nobody is quite sure why, but some magical alchemy of the island's climate, topography and soil make-up perfectly suits the growing of grapes. The island's four main winemakers are Corvus, Talay, Ataol and Yunatçılar.

Corvus (www.corvus.com.tr; Çinar Çarşi Caddesi), which has a shop next to Lodos restaurant, is the work of the famous Turkish architect Reşit Soley. Its wines such as Karga, named after the island's many crows, and Zeleia Vasilaki have impressed wine critics internationally.

The **Talay shop** (www.talay.com.tr; Cumhuriyet Meydanı), behind the ATMs on the main square in Bozcaada town, offers tastings of its reds, whites and rosés (TL9 to TL25). You can also visit the winemaker's fermentation tanks, behind the Ziraat Bankası.

If travelling in June, try to coincide with the annual **Wine Festival**, which offers free tastings, tours of the wine houses and lectures on the processes of viticulture.

Ali Baba
CAFE €

(☑697 0207; Ayazma Plajı; mains TL5) One of the eateries at Ayazma beach, readers rate Ali Baba for its food – with simple dishes on offer such as *köfte* and tasty *gözleme* (savoury pancake) – and its casual atmosphere, although this extends to the toilets' cleanliness.

Tüketim Market
FOOD MARKET €€

(Alsancak Sokak 20; ⊗8am-1am high season, 9am-9pm low season) Around 50m from Sandal Restaurant, with fresh bread and fruit, cheeses and meats – great for getting up a picnic.

🍷 Drinking

Bakkal
CAFE

(Lale Sokak) Opened by an İstanbullu restaurateur, this super-cool cafe serves Corvus wine (glass TL8), smoothies, espressos and delectable sandwiches (TL18 to TL25). Seating is at little tables on the lane or inside, among products such as De Cecco pasta and organic skin toner.

Bar Ali
BAR-RESTAURANT

(Çınar Çarşı Caddesi; ⊗8am-4am high season) The waterfront seating area overlooks the fortress, and, festooned with cushions, beanbags and deckchairs, is the place to wind down at the end of the day. Inside there's a more formal area where you can tuck into wines and cheese, plus a mezzanine with comfy leather chairs.

Polente
BAR

(Yali Sokak 41; ⊗8pm-2am; 🛜) Polente, off the main square, plays an eclectic mix of music, including Latin and jazz, and attracts an equally eclectic mix of locals and visitors (mostly 20- and 30-somethings).

ℹ Information

MONEY **Ziraat Bankası** (Cumhuriyet Meydanı) This branch and other ATMs are on the main square in Bozcaada town, near the PTT.

INTERNET ACCESS **Captain Internet Kafe** (Çınar Çarşi Caddesi; per hr TL2; ⊗9.30am-11pm)

TOURIST INFORMATION **Information booth** (İskele Caddesi) In addition to this wooden hut near the *iskele,* you can pick up a map from some of the accommodation and cafes, including Ada Café (see p163).

ℹ Getting There & Away

BOAT **Gestaş** (☑444 0752; www.gdu.com. tr) ferries run daily to Bozcaada from Yükyeri İskelesi (Yükyeri harbour; 30 minutes; return per person/car TL3/40), 4km west of Geyikli, south of Troy, leaving the mainland at 10am, 2pm and 7pm and departing the island at 7.30am, noon and 6pm. Hydrofoils also sail from Çanakkale (55 minutes; per person TL10) on Wednesday and Saturday, leaving at 9am and returning at 6pm. It's worth checking departure times, as they do change.

BUS Hourly dolmuşes link Çanakkale otogar (bus station) with Geyikli (TL7.50) via Ezine, with connections to Yükyeri İskelesi (TL1.50). Dolmuşes meet the ferry from Bozcaada and run to Geyikli and to Ezine (TL4), from where there are services to Çanakkale and destinations to the south such as Behramkale/Assos and Gülpınar.

ℹ Getting Around

BICYCLE You can hire mountain bikes (one hour/day TL10/25) at **İskele Sancak Café** (☑0532 443 8999; İskele), on the right when you disembark from the ferry.

DOLMUŞ Hourly dolmuşes (minibuses) leaves from near the *iskele* in Bozcaada town to Ayazma beach (TL4). In the summer, more-frequent dolmuşes also serve Ayazma via Ada Camping and Sulubahçe beach, and there's a service to Polente *feneri* (lighthouse) on the west coast for watching sunset.

TAXI A taxi from Bozcaada town to Ayazma costs TL20-23.

WALKING To walk from Bozcaada town to Ayazma takes about 1½ hours.

Biga Peninsula
☑0286

With your own transport, the isolated Biga Peninsula, with its assorted, all-but-forgotten ruins, makes a good day trip. You can go by public transport too, but be prepared for lots of waiting at hot roadsides.

ALEXANDRIA TROAS

Ten kilometres south of Geyikli lie the ruins of **Alexandria Troas** (☑0532 691 3754; Dalyan köyü), scattered around the village of Dalyan.

After the collapse of Alexander the Great's empire, Antigonus, one of his generals, took control of this land, founding the city of Antigoneia in 310 BC. Later, he was defeated in battle by Lysimachus, another of Alexander's generals, who took the city and renamed it in honour of his late commander. After a period of Roman occupation, during which St Paul passed through, an earthquake eventually destroyed much of the city.

The site is undeniably atmospheric, with its great grass-strewn ruins, but also rather confusing, with little in the way of clear signage. Much of the site remains buried and excavations are ongoing, but there are some wonderful relics to see, such as stone arches and crystal-clear inscriptions. Archaeological finds so far include a theatre, temple, necropolis, nymphaeum (shrine for water nymphs), stadium, aqueduct, church and five odeons.

To get to Dalyan by bus or dolmuş from Çanakkale otogar (TL10), you have to change in Ezine and Geyikli.

GÜLPINAR

Gülpınar is a one-street farming village south of Geyikli, with few services beyond a petrol station and some shops selling picnic provisions. However, it was once the ancient city of **Khrysa**, famous for its 2nd-century-BC Ionic temple to Apollo – and for its mice. An oracle had told Cretan colonists to settle where 'the sons of the earth' attacked them. Awaking to find mice chewing their equipment, they decided to settle here and built a temple to Smintheion (Lord of the Mice). The 5m-tall cult statue of the god, of which only a fragment remains, had marble mice carved at its feet.

The ruins of the **Apollon Smintheion** (admission incl museum TL5; ☉8am-5pm) lie 300m down a side road at the bottom of the village (look for the brown sign on the right if you're coming from the north). Wonderful reliefs and column drums with illustrated scenes from the *Iliad,* which recounts the Apollo Smintheon priest Chryse's feud with Agamemnon, were found amid the ruins. On display in the site's **museum** (☉6am-2pm Aug & Sep), they are the earliest temple friezes depicting scenes from the Trojan war.

To get to Gülpınar by bus or dolmuş from Çanakkale otogar (TL9), you have to change in Ezine. From Gülpınar there are buses to Babakale (TL1.50, 15 minutes) and to Behramkale (TL3, one hour).

BABAKALE (LEKTON)

From Gülpınar, a road heads 9km west past a few coastal developments to Babakale, the westernmost point of mainland Turkey. The village's harbour is being expanded, but otherwise it's a sleepy place that seems almost overawed by the 18th-century **fortress**.

The fort was built to combat pirates and is notable for being the last Ottoman castle built in present-day Turkey. There's

not much else to look at, beyond views of Lesvos and Bozcaada over the water, but it's a pleasant place to unwind for a day or two.

Above the harbour, the **Uran Hotel** (☏747 0218; s/d TL40/80; ❄) has simple but sea breeze-fresh rooms with tiny bathrooms and small balconies overlooking the castle and sea. There's also a delightful terrace and a good and reasonably priced **fish restaurant** (mains TL15). Try the speciality, *kalamar* (squid).

There are buses from Gülpınar (TL1.50, 15 minutes) and daily services from Ezine (TL7, two hours).

Behramkale & Assos
☏0286

Behramkale and Assos are two separate parts of the same settlement: an old hilltop Greek village spread out around the ruins of an ancient temple to Athena (Behramkale); and, at the bottom of the steep hill, a former working harbour with a small pebble beach, where the old stone buildings and warehouses have been transformed into hotels and fish restaurants (Assos). They make a fine combination, but try to avoid visiting on weekends and public holidays from the beginning of April to the end of August, when tourists pour in by the coach load.

Locals often refer to the two areas as Assos *liman* (harbour) and *köyü* (village). There are few facilities other than an ATM and pharmacy in Behramkale. Wi-fi is not universally available in accommodation, but many eating and drinking options have networks.

History

The Mysian city of Assos was founded in the 8th century BC by colonists from Lesvos, who later built its great temple to Athena in 530 BC. The city enjoyed considerable prosperity under the rule of Hermeias, a one-time student of Plato who also ruled the Troad and Lesvos. Hermeias encouraged philosophers to live in Assos, and Aristotle himself lived here from 348 to 345 BC, and ended up marrying Hermeias' niece, Pythia. Assos' glory days came to an abrupt end with the arrival of the Persians, who crucified Hermeias and forced Plato to flee.

Alexander the Great drove the Persians out, but Assos' importance was challenged by the ascendancy of Alexandria Troas to the north. From 241 to 133 BC the city was ruled by the kings of Pergamum.

St Paul visited Assos briefly during his third missionary journey, walking here from Alexandria Troas to meet St Luke before taking a boat to Lesvos.

In late-Byzantine times the city dwindled to a village. Turkish settlers arrived and called the village Behramkale. Only the coming of tourism revived its fortunes.

⊙ Sights & Activities

Temple of Athena RUINS
(☏217 6740; admission TL5; ⊘8am-7.30pm) Right on top of the hill in Behramkale village is this 6th-century BC Ionic temple. The short tapered columns with plain capitals are hardly elegant, and the concrete reconstruction hurts more than helps, but the site and the view out to Lesvos are spectacular and well worth the admission fee.

Villagers set up **stalls** all the way up the hill to the temple, touting local products from bags of dried herbs or mushrooms to linen.

Hüdavendigar Camii MOSQUE
Beside the entrance to the temple, this 14th-century mosque is a simply constructed Ottoman mosque – a dome on squinches set on top of a square room – built before the Turks had conquered Constantinople and assimilated the lessons of Sancta Sophia. It's one of just two remaining Ottoman mosques of its kind in Turkey (the other is in Bursa).

Other Ruins RUINS
Scramble down the hill from the temple, or walk along the road to Assos, to find the **necropolis**. Assos' sarcophagi (from the Greek, 'flesh-eaters') were famous. According to Pliny the Elder, the stone was caustic and 'ate' the flesh off the deceased in 40 days. Other ruins include the remains of a late-2nd-century-BC **theatre** and **basilica**.

Ringing the hill are stretches of the **city walls** of medieval Assos, which are among the most impressive medieval fortifications in Turkey.

🛏 Sleeping

Where you sleep depends on whether you prefer the picturesque and lively Assos harbour (even if the interiors of the lovely stone houses are often something of a letdown), or the more peaceful and atmospheric Behramkale village.

In high season, virtually all the hotels around the harbour insist on *yarım pansiyon* (half-board), though you could try negotiating.

BEHRAMKALE

TOP CHOICE **Biber Evi** BOUTIQUE HOTEL €€€
(☏721 7410; www.biberevi.com; s TL200-230, d TL240-270; ✳) This 150-year-old stone house was restored over the course of three and a half years by Lütfi, a former theatre director and a cultivator of the noble *biber* (pepper). There are almost 100 varieties of chilli in the garden; they appear in everything from jams and relishes to, figuratively, the tiles in the six rooms' bathrooms – modern versions of the Ottoman *gusülhane* (cupboard bathroom), featuring underfloor heating. The bar is well stocked with single malts, the terrace has views of the temple and coast, and the extensive breakfasts and gourmet dinners also demonstrate care and creativity. Bookings need to be for at least two nights.

Eris Pansiyon PENSION €€
(☏721 7080; www.erispansiyon.com; s/d incl tea TL70/120) Set in a stone house with pretty gardens at the eastern end of the village, past Ehl-i Keyf restaurant and some small galleries, this American-run guesthouse has three pleasant, peaceful rooms. Afternoon tea, featuring home-made cake, is served on a terrace with spectacular views over the hills, and there's a library and book exchange.

Dolunay Pansiyon PENSION €€
(☏721 7172; s/d TL50/100; ✳) In the centre of the village on the main square, the Dolunay is a homely affair with six spotless, simple rooms set around a pleasant courtyard. There's also a pretty terrace with sea views where you can have a scenic breakfast.

Old Bridge House BOUTIQUE HOTEL €€
(☏721 7100; www.oldbridgehouse.com.tr; s/d TL100/200, bungalow s/d TL60/120; ✳≈) Offering smart rooms and spacious bungalows with small bathrooms, this option is no longer such a travellers' hang-out since it changed hands. However, the staff are very accommodating and the property is being developed. It's near the Ottoman bridge to the north of Behramkale, looking up at the temple and village.

Assos Konuk Evi PENSION €€
(☏721 7081; s/d/tr from TL60/80/100; ✳≈) Hidden at the top of the village, overlooking the sea from a bluff 200m up, this guesthouse has not been as lovingly restored as some of Behramkale's other options. Nonetheless, it's a notch above the village pensions and there's a shady courtyard.

Tekin Pansiyon
PENSION €€

(☎721 7099; assostekinpansiyon@hotmail.com; s/d TL50/100; ✴) One of the first pensions you pass, the Tekin's rooms are entered from a wooden balcony. It doesn't go beyond the basic pension requirements, and the rooms face away from Behramkale's panormaic views, but the little tables on the balcony overlook village goings-on.

ASSOS

Çakır Restaurant and Yelken Camp offer accommodation in wooden huts (s/d half-board from TL60/100).

Hotel Kervansaray
HOTEL €€

(☎721 7093; www.assoskervansaray.com; s/d with sea view TL120/140; ✴✴) A 19th-century acorn store, the cavernous Kervansaray offers fun and games including outdoor and indoor pools, a sauna and jacuzzi. This hotel's smart rooms, which overlook the central hall or the sea, have small bathrooms and plasma-screen TVs concealed in wooden cases; some have balconies. Across the lane, the Kervansaray Butik Otel charges the same prices and offers similar rooms.

Yıldız Saray Hotel
PENSION €€

(☎721 7025; www.yildizsaray-hotels.com; s/d/f TL80/120/200; ✴) Though some of its bedding looks rather '70s, the Star Palace's colourful carpets and walls hoist it above the realm of village pensions. Three rooms open onto an upstairs terrace and two have a fireplace. The family apartment with two doubles and a jacuzzi bath is good value, and breakfast is served on a fantastic floating platform. The owners also operate another hotel, just east along the coast at Kadırga.

Dr. No Antik Pansiyon
PENSION €

(☎721 7397; dr.noantikpansiyon@hotmail.com; s/d TL35/70; ✴) A Bond villain's hideaway it ain't, but this friendly budget option's rickety rooms are passable – apart from the slightly offensive green colour scheme. Breakfast is served downstairs in the restaurant with its covered outside seating.

Hotel Behram
HOTEL €€

(☎721 7016; hotelbehram@yahoo.com; s/d TL70/120; ✴ @) This seafront hotel's rooms are enlivened by colourful bedspreads and curtains. There's a creeping sense of decay in reception, but, on the plus side, an open-air restaurant right by the water.

✖ Eating & Drinking

In contravention of the way these things usually work, the settlement at the bottom of the hill is actually the 'posh' part of town, where prices, if not standards, are higher than at the top. Be sure to check the cost of fish and bottles of wine before ordering.

BEHRAMKALE
Biber Evi Restaurant
RESTAURANT €€€

(☎721 7410; mains TL30; ☺dinner; 🛜) Small parties only, book ahead to dine at this boutique hotel (see p166), which uses ingredients fresh from its kitchen gardens. Dishes include slow-roasted lamb or goat and fish. The multi-talented chef, Lütfi, came third in a nationwide meze competition with his cured tuna.

Panorama Restaurant
RESTAURANT €€

(☎721 7037; mains TL10) The views at good-natured Mehmet and family's restaurant certainly live up to its name. Dishes include a range of meat feasts, plus mezes such as *börülce* (black-eyed peas), stuffed pumpkin flowers and *avcı boreği* (hunter's *börek;* pastry filled with meat or cheese).

Mantı & Börek Evi
LOKANTA €

(☎721 7050; mains TL7; ☺8am-7pm) Serving *mantı* (Turkish ravioli), *avcı boreğı* and a good range of mezes, this *lokanta* (eatery serving ready-made food) has a small terrace overlooking the main square. It's one of the only eateries on the hill offering beer.

Aile Çay Bahçesi
TEA GARDEN €

(tea TL0.75, soft drinks TL2; 🛜) For a coffee or Coke on the main square, this place has a pleasant shaded terrace offering attractive views. It serves *gözleme* (TL4) good enough to gobble.

ASSOS
Uzunev
SEAFOOD €€

(☎721 7007; mains TL15-20; ☺lunch & dinner) Uzunev is considered the best fish restaurant in town, and has pleasant tables on the terrace and seafront. Try the succulent speciality, sea bass à l'Aristotle (steamed in a special stock), or the delicious seafood meze (TL10). In high season after 10pm, it metamorphoses into a disco-bar.

Çakır Restaurant
SEAFOOD €€

(☎721 7048; mains TL10-15) Past Hotel Kervansaray, the Çakýr brothers' restaurant is one of the laid-back hang-outs overlooking a pebble beach and rickety wooden platforms above the water. You can pick meze and mains such as *kalamar* and *köfte* from the fridge.

Yelken Camp BAR
(📞721 7433; 🛜) Just before Çakır, Yelken is a good spot for a sundowner with a thatched bar, colourful sofas and music to soundtrack your wave watching.

ℹ Getting There & Away

ÇANAKKALE Regular buses run from Çanakkale (TL10, 1½ hours) to Ayvacık, where you can pick up a dolmuş to Behramkale (TL3, 20 minutes). Some dolmuşes make a second stop down in Assos (TL4) in summer, but some don't, obliging you to switch to the shuttle service.

In low season, dolmuşes run less frequently. Try to get to Ayvacık as early in the day as you can to catch a dolmuş to Behramkale. If you miss the last one, Ayvacık has a couple of hotels, or a taxi to Behramkale will cost around TL25 to TL30.

BİGA PENINSULA Dolmuşes run to Behramkale from Gülpınar (TL3, one hour).

BAY OF EDREMİT In the summer, dolmuşes connect Behramkale with Küçükkuyu (TL4, one hour); otherwise a taxi costs TL40-45.

ℹ Getting Around

SHUTTLE In summer, there's a shuttle service throughout the day between Behramkale and Assos (TL1, every 30 minutes). In winter, dolmuşes occasionally run between Assos and Behramkale (TL7.50).

Ayvacık

📞0286 / POP 7600

Heading to or from Behramkale you may have to transit Ayvacık, which has a big **Friday market** where women from the surrounding villages sell fruit, vegetables and baskets. Those in long satiny overcoats or brightly coloured headscarves are the descendants of Turkmen nomads who settled in this area.

Ayvacık is famous for its diminutive carpets, and some 20 villages and Turkmen communities in the region still produce them. Two kilometres out of Ayvacık, opposite the Total garage on the main road to Çanakkale, is the **Doğal Boya Arıştırma ve Geliştirme Projesi** (Dobag; Natural Dye Research & Development Project; 📞712 1274; ⊙9am-6pm), which was set up in 1982 to encourage villagers to return to weaving carpets from naturally dyed wool. The prices charged by the village women, who sporadically display their handiwork here,

are cheaper than those found in big-city bazaars. The great majority of carpets are exported, and the prices are not extravagant considering what goes into the process; every stage – shearing, carding, spinning, weaving, knotting and dyeing – is done by hand. The upstairs exhibition hall may be empty out of season, but there are a few displays and some coffee table books for sale. Phone ahead to organise a village tour.

ℹ Getting There & Away

Regular buses run to/from Çanakkale (TL10, 1½ hours). There are also regular buses or dolmuşes to Ayvacık from Ezine, Behramkale and Küçükkuyu.

Bay of Edremit

Some 4km east of Behramkale, there are camp sites and several hotels right on the lengthy beach at Kadırga – firmly package-holiday territory. Twenty kilometres further on, the road meets the highway, which runs east along the north shore of the Bay of Edremit.

Turn left here, towards Ayvacık, and head 4km northwest into the hills to reach the village of Yeşilyurt, set among pine forests and olive groves. The many restored houses' yellow stone walls have been beautifully enhanced by red brick and wood, and the village offers plenty of boutique hotels and restaurants.

Back on the coastal highway, you could pause in Küçükkuyu to inspect the **Adatepe Zeytinyağı Museum** (📞0286 752 1303; ⊙9am-7pm), housed in an old olive-oil factory and explaining the process of making olive oil.

From Küçükkuyu, head 4km northeast into the forested hills to visit the pretty village of Adatepe, a cluster of restored stone houses below a lizard-like rock formation. The area is great for walking, with waterfalls, plunge pools for swimming and, near the falls at Başdeğirmen, a Roman bridge. At the top of Adatepe you'll find the blissfully tranquil **Hünnap Han** (📞0286 752 6581; www.hunnaphan.com; s/d half-board TL190/250), a restored country pile with traditionally decorated rooms, a lovely garden and stone courtyard.

Buses stop in Küçükkuyu, which has Metro and Truva offices, every hour en route to Çanakkale (TL15) and İzmir (TL25). A taxi from Küçükkuyu to Adatepe or Yeşilyurt costs TL10. In the summer, dolmuşes run to Behramkale (TL4, one hour); otherwise a taxi costs TL40 to TL45.

The road continues east, past a string of holiday villages, hotels and second-home developments aimed at domestic tourists. Just before Güre İskelesi, follow the brown signpost and head 2.5km north into the hills to find the **Etnografya Galerisi** (Ethnographic Gallery; ☑0266 387 3340; admission TL2; ☺8am-8pm) in Tahtakuşlar village. Exhibits such as a domed tent give an insight into the local villages inhabited by descendents of Turkmen people who moved here in the 15th century.

Demre Tour, based in Akçay, 10km west of Edremit, runs **jeep safaris** (☑0266 384 8586; incl lunch TL50, incl night in a Turkmen tent & three meals TL125; ☺Jun-Sep) in Mount Ida National Park (Kazdağı Milli Parkı).

There is a good lunch stop near the seafront in Akçay. Turn right off the main street just after Ömür Lokanta to find the multicoloured **Zeyyat Lokanta** (mains TL10; ☺8am-10pm), which has outside seating and dishes up home-cooking such as *balık* (fish) with peppers.

A new airport is set to open at Edremit, with Atlasjet flights.

Ayvalık

☑0266 / POP 36,000

At first glance, there would appear to be little remarkable about the seaside resort and fishing town of Ayvalık (the name means 'Quince Orchard'). Though pleasantly free of pushy touts, its seafront resembles a number of others along this stretch of coast, with a harbour filled with excursion boats, a palm-tree-lined waterfront and fish restaurants. Back from the front, however, a charmingly crumbly old Greek village provides a kind of outdoor museum. Horses and carts clatter down cobbled lanes lined with picturesque shuttered houses – some restored, many left to decay. The whole place has an appealingly tumbledown feel to it, with life proceeding at torpor pace; headscarf-wearing women hold court from their doorsteps, dogs sleep at the roadside, and the shadows slowly grow in the Aegean sunshine.

Olive-oil production is the traditional business around here, and is still thriving, with lots of shops selling the end product. The broken chimney next to Tansaş super-

market in the town centre belongs to a now-abandoned olive-oil factory. Ayvalık is also well known as a gateway to local islands, including Alibey, just offshore, and Lesvos, Greece.

⊙ Sights & Activities

Old Town   HISTORIC AREA

There are few specific sights but Ayvalık's old town is a joy to wander around, with its maze of cobbled streets lined with wonderfully worn-looking Greek houses. You can pick up a map with information about sights, including the former Greek Orthodox churches (see boxed text, p172), at Tarlakusu Gurmeko (see p171). There are plans to turn the broken-chimneyed former olive-oil factory just northwest of the cafe into a local museum.

Markets   MARKET

Thursday sees one of the region's largest and most vibrant markets, and stalls seem to fill the whole town. Seek out the **köy pazarı** (village market), which takes place next to the main **pazar yeri** (bazaar). A daily **fish market** (Balık Pazarı) also takes place on the front next to the terminal for the ferry to Alibey (p173).

Cruises   CRUISE

(per person incl lunch TL20) In addition to the dive sites (see boxed text, p171) and summer ferries to Lesvos (see p172), cruises head around the bay's islands, including Alibey, and stop here and there for swimming, sun-bathing and walking. They generally depart at 11am and return by 6.30pm. Jale Tour (see p172) also cruises to Assos (TL40), leaving at 10.30am and returning by 7.30pm.

Beaches   BEACH

There are a number of good, sandy beaches a few kilometres to the south. Sarımsaklı Plaj (Garlic Beach) is the most famed and will inevitably be the most crowded, as this is package-holiday territory. Stay on the bus a bit longer until you reach Badavut to the west and you'll find some quieter stretches.

🛏 Sleeping

TOP CHOICE **Annette's House**   PENSION €€

(☑312 5971; www.annetteshouse.com; Neşe Sokak 12; per person TL45; @) On a quiet square (Thursdays excepted, when it's the site of the village market), this is an oasis of calm and comfort. The personable Annette, a retired teacher from Germany, presides over the eight charming rooms

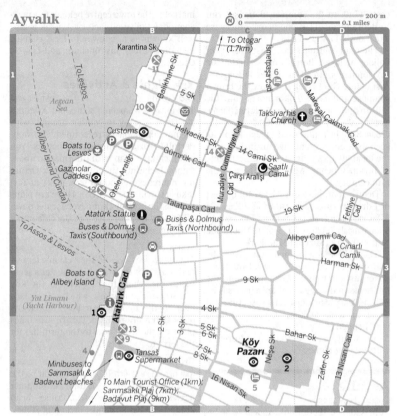

where modernity meets traditional decor, with white floors emphasising the colourful carpets. There are two singles and a garden flat, which has its own slice of the pleasantly shady garden. If you are after breakfast, it costs an extra TL10.

Kelebek Pension PENSION €€
(☑312 3908; www.kelebek-pension.com; Mareşal Çakmak Caddesi 108; s/d/tr TL50/80/120; ❄) Winning praise from readers and building a good reputation around the Aegean, this seven-room pension is owned by the English- and German-speaking Kıray family. The quaint, white-and-blue building has a terrace for breakfast in the fresh air.

Taksiyarhis Pension PENSION €€
(☑312 1494; www.taksiyarhispension.com; Mareşal Çakmak Caddesi 71; per person without bathroom TL35; ❄) Rooms of all shapes and sizes fill a 120-year-old Greek house behind the eponymous church. It has bags of character, with a vine-shaded terrace, exposed wooden beams and a jumble of cushions, rugs and handicrafts. Travellers are well catered for with a communal kitchen and a book exchange. Breakfast costs TL10 extra.

Bonjour Pansiyon PENSION €€
(☑312 8085; www.bonjourpansiyon.com; Fevzi Çakmak Caddesi, Çeşme Sokak 5; s/d without bathroom TL50/90; ❄) In a 300-year-old mansion that housed the French embassy in the early 1900s, this has a faded grandeur to it, with aged furniture and antique knick-knacks filling every corner. You receive a terrific welcome and an excellent buffet breakfast in the courtyard. The 12 rooms are immaculately presented, although most share bathrooms and some of the beds could use an upgrade.

✗ Eating

TOP CHOICE Balıkçı SEAFOOD €€
(☑312 9099; Balıkhane Sokak 7; mains TL17; ☾dinner) The waterfront 'Fisherman'

restaurant, run by a local association of fishermen and marine environmentalists, is the perfect place to grab a rakı (aniseed brandy) and understand the expression 'rakı, *balık,* Ayvalık'. The staff happily talk you through the meze and fish, explaining which catches are less boney and so on. After that, settle into the tiled terrace or sit inside for a better view of the Turkish troubadours, who get a singalong going from 8.30pm onwards.

Tarlakusu Gurmeko   CAFE €€
(☏312 3312; Cumhuriyet Caddesi 53; ⊙8.30am-8.30pm; 🛜) Run by a clued-up couple from İzmir, this cafe sells a range of teas and coffees, including good cappuccino (TL4.50). If you enjoy your cup, you can buy a bag of beans or leaves from the shop. Nibbles include cookies, brownies, soup, salads, cheese plates and *börek* (TL3.50).

Deniz Kestanesi   SEAFOOD €€€
(☏312 3262; Karantina Sokak 9; mains TL15; ⊙10am-midnight) Perhaps the smartest restaurant in town, and certainly one of the most expensive (although it's better value than Şehir Kulübü), the 'sea urchin' is a very stylish indoor/outdoor affair. It's right on the waterfront, with wooden floors, high ceilings, leather chairs and great views of Alibey's twinkling lights. Meat dishes are available in addition to meze (TL6 to TL14) and *balık* including bass, bream, shark and mullet.

Hatipoğlu Pastaneleri   PATISSERIE €
(Atatürk Caddesi 12; tea/Turkish coffee TL1/2; ⊙7am-1am; ❄) With a great selection of traditional Turkish puds, pastries and cakes, this friendly patisserie makes a terrific breakfast or tea stop. Try the Ayvalık speciality, *lok* (sponge oozing honey; TL3), and go on, add a scoop of *dondurma* (ice cream).

Deniziçi Cafeterya   BAR-CAFE €
(☏312 1537; Gazinolar Caddesi 1; pizzas TL6-9; ⊙8am-12.30am; 🛜) The Sea Café serves light meals and snacks including pizzas, *kalamar* and burgers. Just west of White Knight Café, in among the pricey fish restaurants, it's a perfect spot for a sundowner.

🍷 Drinking & Entertainment

White Knight Café   BAR
(☏312 3682; Cumhuriyet Meydanı 13; beer TL4; ⊙9am-2am; 🛜) Popular cafe by the statue of Atatürk, overseen by Ahmet and his British wife, Anthea. The vibe is mellow, except

DIVING OFF AYVALIK

The waters around Ayvalık are famed among divers for their red coral. However, as most of it grows at depths of between 30m and 42m, reaching it is not an activity for beginners. Dive companies in Ayvalık can organise trips to see the coral and its attendant marine life, including moray eels, grouper, octopus and sea horses. One of the best is the **Korfez Diving Center** (☏0532 266 3589; www.korfezdiving.com; ⊙Mar-Nov), which moors its boat by the fish market. A day's diving costs TL80 and dive courses are TL500.

GHOSTS FROM THE PAST

Walking the quiet backstreets of Ayvalık, it is difficult to appreciate you are passing the remains of one of the most traumatic events in Turkey's history – the great population exchange that took place after the creation of the Turkish state (see p634).

The early 1920s hold mixed memories for the town. Pride over its role in the Turkish War of Independence – it was here that the first shots were fired – is tempered by what happened afterwards. The Ottoman Greeks, who made up the majority of the population, were forced to abandon the land of their birth and relocate to the Greek island of Lesvos, while the Turks from that island were, in turn, compelled to start new lives in Ayvalık. Despite the enormous distress this must have caused, the Ayvalık-Lesvos exchange is nonetheless regarded as one of the least damaging episodes of the period. The reasons why the exchange caused less tumult than many others had much to do with the proximity of the two communities, which enabled people from both sides to continue visiting their former homes – mixed though their emotions must have been during those trips. Furthermore, both communities were involved in the production of olive oil, and so would have found much that was familiar in the other.

Today, whispers from the past are everywhere. Some elderly locals can speak Greek and many of the town's former Greek Orthodox churches remain standing, albeit converted into mosques. The Ayios Ioannis, which in 1923 became the Saatlı Camii ('Clock Mosque', so named for its clock tower), still serves as a church for Ayvalık's expat community on Sunday mornings. The former Ayios Yioryios is today the Çınarlı Camii, named after the *çınar* (plane trees) that grew here, of which one remains. One of the grandest of all the old Greek churches, the Taksiyarhis, was never converted. However, it no longer functions as a church either, but rather sits empty and forlorn, waiting to be renovated at some unspecified future date.

when major football matches are shown, and it sells English-language magazines and previous-day newspapers.

Studio Organic   CINEMA, CLASS
(☑312 3312; Cumhuriyet Caddesi 53) The studio above Tarlakusu Gurmeko cafe offers a cinema club (TL2) on Friday evening, plus night classes – yoga on Mondays, drawing on Tuesdays, photography on Tuesdays and Thursdays, and tango and salsa on Wednesdays.

ⓘ Information

C@fein Cafe Net (Cumhuriyet Meydanı; per hr TL1.50; ☺8.30am-midnight) Internet access on the main square.

Post office (Atatürk Caddesi) At the northern end of town on the main street.

Tourist office Main branch (☑312 2122; Yat Limanı Karşısı; ☺8am-noon & 1-5pm Mon-Fri); Kiosk (Yat Limanı; ☺Jun-Sep) The main tourist office is beyond the yacht marina, but in high season you can get information from the kiosk on the waterfront south of the main square.

ⓘ Getting There & Away
Boat

LESVOS From May to September, boats sail daily except Sunday to Lesvos, Greece (passenger one way/return €40/50, car €60/70, 1½ hours) at 5pm, and to Ayvalık on the same days at 8.30am. From October to May, boats sail to Lesvos at the same time on Tuesday, Thursday and Saturday, and to Ayvalık on the same days.

Note that times do change and you *must* make a reservation (in person or by telephone) 24 hours before departure. When you pick up your tickets, bring your passport.

For information and tickets, contact **Jale Tour** (☑331 3170; www.jaletour.com; Gümrük Caddesi 24).

Bus

BERGAMA It is possible to make a day trip to Bergama (TL7, 1¾ hours, 45km). Hourly Bergama buses leave the otogar between 8am and 7pm and drive slowly south through town, so you can jump on at the main square.

ÇANAKKALE Coming from Çanakkale (TL13, 3¼ hours, 200km, five a day) smaller companies may drop you on the main highway, from where you'll have to hitch to the centre. Larger companies, such as Ulusoy, provide *servis* shuttles to their offices in the centre.

EDREMİT Regular dolmuşes go from Ayvalık otogar (TL6, one hour).

İZMİR There are hourly buses to/from İzmir (TL15, three hours, 150km).

Car

BERGAMA The inland route to Bergama, via Kozak, is much more scenic and only marginally slower than the coast road, winding through idyllic pine-clad hills. Backtrack north towards Gömeç then turn right.

🛈 Getting Around

Bus & Dolmuş

TOWN CENTRE Dolmuş taxis (white with red stripes running around them) serve the town centre, stopping to put down and pick up passengers along a series of short set routes. You can catch them at the main square. Destinations include Armutçuk, 1km to the north of town; fares are typically TL1.50.

OTOGAR Ayvalık *belediyesi* (town) buses (TL1.50 to TL3) run through town between the otogar and the main square.

SOUTH *Belediyesi* buses continue from the main square to the tourist office and the beaches around Sarımsaklı. Minibuses (TL1.50 to TL2) also depart for the beaches from beside the Tansaş supermarket sign south of the main square.

Car

Navigating Ayvalık old town's fiendishly narrow lanes can be an extremely stressful experience. You'd be better off parking at one of the car parks along the waterfront. They generally cost TL6/10 per day/night. Accommodation options in the old town generally only have one or two parking spaces; these are hot property and there is a danger your car will get scratched by another vehicle.

Taxi

A taxi from the otogar to the town centre costs TL6.

Alibey Island

Named after a hero of the Turkish War of Independence, Alibey Island, known to the locals as Cunda, lies just offshore, facing Ayvalık across the water. It's linked to the mainland by a causeway and is generally

regarded as a quieter extension of Ayvalık itself, with residents of both communities regularly shuttling back and forth between the two. Accessible both by dolmuş taxi and the more pleasant option of the ferry, the island makes for a fine day trip from Ayvalık.

The ferry will drop you at a small quay, in front of which is a long line of fish restaurants. Behind these sits a small, distinguished-looking town made up of old (and in parts rather dilapidated) Greek stone houses. As with Ayvalık, the people here were compelled into a population exchange in the early 1920s; in this instance with Muslims from Crete.

Just to the right of the ferry stop is the town's main square. There are ATMs on the seafront and an information board with maps in the car park at the eastern end of the esplanade. Behind the square is a small tourist market with stalls selling jewellery and other trinkets.

One of the most famous relics of the town's Greek past, the **Taksiyarhis church** (not to be confused with the church of the same name in Ayvalık), perches on a small hill, just inland from the tourist market. Though it avoided being turned into a mosque, the church suffered severe damage during an earthquake in 1944, and today stands in picturesque decrepitude. Inside are some faded and rather forlorn-looking frescoes.

The nicest parts of the island are west, where there are good beaches for sunbathing and swimming, and to the north, much of which is taken up by the **Pateriça Nature Reserve**. This has good walking routes and, on the north shore, the ruins of the Greek **Ayışığı Manastırı** (Moonlight Monastery).

🛏 Sleeping

Prices are high on Alibey and the options are not as attractive or as professionally

---

FAST FOOD – AYVALIK STYLE

Ayvalık may have made its name as an olive-oil producer, but these days it's better known throughout Turkey for a rather less refined culinary offering – *Ayvalık tost* ('Ayvalık toast'). The town's take on fast food is essentially a toasted sandwich, crammed with all manner of ingredients, including cheese, *sucuk* (spicy veal sausage), salami, pickles and tomatoes. These goodies are, of course, lathered in ketchup and mayonnaise (unless you specifically request otherwise). It's available at cafes and stalls throughout town, but **Avşar Büfe** (Atatürk Caddesi, Tanşas Yanı; ☺24hr high season, 7am-3am low season) and the surrounding eateries are good places to take the *tost* challenge. *Tost* typically costs just TL3.50 (or TL2.50 for just cheese), but take note – it's a fast-food feast in a sandwich.

run as Ayvalık's pensions, so we recommend visiting on a day trip.

Ada Kamping CAMPGROUND
(☎327 1211; www.adacamping.com; Alibey Adası; camp site per person TL15, caravan/bungalow per person TL50/70; ☺Apr-Nov) This large, well-equipped camping ground lies 3km to the west of town. The air-conditioned bungalows are simple but spotless, although the caravans and the grounds are a little worn-looking. The site boasts its own beach and waterside restaurant (mains TL15), plus a kitchen for guest use.

Zehra Teyze'nin Evi PENSION
(☎327 2285; Namik Kemal Mahallesi 7; s/d TL80/140; ✹) This pension occupies a shuttered house right beside the Taksiyarhis church, although its interior and proprietors are not as inspiring as its picturesque facade.

✖ Eating & Drinking

Lal Girit Mutfağı MUTFAK
(☎327 2834; Altay Pansiyon Yanı 20; meze TL6, beer TL6; ☺dinner) At this *mutfak* (restaurant serving home cooking) and local hangout Emine serves delicious *Girit* (Cretan) dishes learnt from her grandmother, including *peynirli kabak* (courgette with feta cheese). If you buy some fish on the seafront (about TL10), she will cook it for you.

Ada Restaurant SEAFOOD
(☎327 1928; Sahil Boyu 27; meze TL6-12, mains TL10; ☺lunch & dinner) With a point-and-pick counter and plenty of outside tables, this fish restaurant is near the eastern end of the line of interchangeable eateries on the seafront. Locals recommend it for Zeynep's cooking.

Lezzet Diyarı SEAFOOD
(☎327 1016; Çarşı Caddesi 17; mains TL20; ☺1pm-11pm) Even by Turkish standards, the fridge in this small blue-and-white restaurant is heaving with meze. Hot dishes include Aegean staples such as octopus casserole.

Taş Kahve BAR-CAFE
(Sahil Boyu 20; tea TL0.50, beer TL5; ☺7am-midnight) From the card players and swooping swallows inside to the children tearing around outside, this is Alibey's favourite venue to catch up on town gossip.

ℹ Getting There & Away

BOAT Boats to Alibey Island (June to early September, TL4, 15 minutes, every 15 minutes) leave from a quay behind the tourist kiosk just off the main square in Ayvalık.

CAR & DOLMUŞ On the other side of the road, you can pick up a dolmuş taxi across the causeway to the island (TL2, 20 minutes). They run between 6am and midnight, and drop off at the eastern end of Alibey esplanade, where there's also a car park (TL4).

TAXI These typically cost TL25 between the island and central Ayvalık.

Bergama (Pergamum)

☎0232 / POP 58,200

As Selçuk is to Ephesus, so Bergama is to Pergamum; a small, workaday market town that's become a major stop on the tourist trail because of its proximity to some remarkable ruins – in this instance Pergamum, site of the Asclepion, ancient Rome's pre-eminent medical centre. The Asclepion and the fantastic acropolis don't attract as many visitors as Ephesus, giving Bergama a more laid-back, friendly feel than its tourism-savvy southern counterpart. As a result, many visitors end up falling for this town where classical splendour overlooks slow-paced everyday life.

There has been a town here since Trojan times, but Pergamum's heyday was during the period between Alexander the Great and the Roman domination of all Asia Minor, when it was one of the Middle East's richest and most powerful small kingdoms.

History

Pergamum owes its prosperity to Lysimachus, one of Alexander the Great's generals, who took control of much of the Aegean region when Alexander's far-flung empire fell apart after his death in 323 BC. In the battles over the spoils Lysimachus captured a great treasure, estimated at over 9000 gold talents, which he entrusted to his commander in Pergamum, Philetarus, before going off to fight Seleucus for control of Asia Minor. But Lysimachus lost the battle and was killed in 281 BC, whereupon Philetarus set himself up as governor.

Philetarus, a eunuch, was succeeded by his nephew Eumenes I (263–241 BC), who was in turn followed by his adopted son, Attalus I (241–197 BC). Attalus declared himself king, expanding his power and forging an alliance with Rome.

During the reign of Attalus' son, Eumenes II (197–159 BC), Pergamum achieved its greatest glory. Rich and powerful, Eumenes founded a library that would in time rival that of Alexandria, Egypt, then the world's

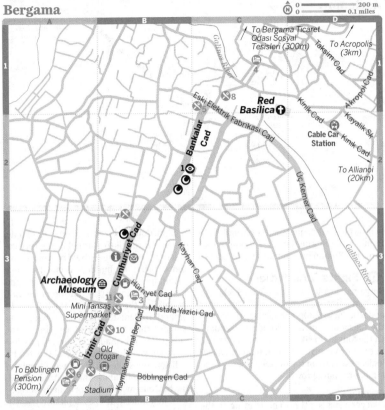

Bergama

◎ Top Sights

Archaeology Museum	B3
Red Basilica	C1

◎ Sights

1	Hacı Hekim Hamamı	B2

⊟ Sleeping

2	Gobi Pension	A4
3	Hotel Anıl	B3
4	Odyssey Guesthouse	C1

⊗ Eating

5	Çiçeksever	C1
6	Kervan	A4
7	Köy Evi	B3
8	Paksoy Pide	C1
9	Simge Pastanesi ve Simit Dünyasi	A4
10	Yanikoğlu Supermarket	B4
11	Zıkkım	B3

greatest repository of knowledge. He also added the Altar of Zeus to the buildings already crowning the acropolis, built the 'middle city' on terraces halfway down the hill, and expanded and beautified the Asclepion. Inevitably, much of what the Pergamese kings built hasn't survived the ravages of the centuries (or the acquisitive enthusiasm of Western museums), but what has is impressive, dramatically sited and well worth visiting.

Eumenes' brother Attalus II kept up the good work but under his son, Attalus III, the kingdom began to fall apart again. With no

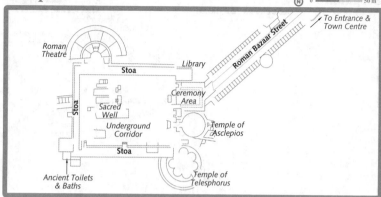

Roman Theatre

Stoa

Library

Roman Bazaar Street

To Entrance & Town Centre

Stoa

Sacred Well

Ceremony Area

Underground Corridor

Temple of Asclepios

Stoa

Ancient Toilets & Baths

Temple of Telesphorus

heir, Attalus III bequeathed his kingdom to Rome, and the kingdom of Pergamum became the Roman province of Asia in 129 BC.

Sights & Activities

Bergama's attractions open from 8.30am to 6.30pm daily between June and September and 8.30am to 5.30pm in low season (except the museum, which is closed on Monday). Of the four main sights, only the museum is in the town centre. The two main archaeological sites are on top of steep hills, several kilometres out of town.

Acropolis
RUINS

(Akropol; admission TL20) The road up to the acropolis winds 5km from the Red Basilica to a car park (TL3) at the top, with some souvenir and refreshment stands nearby. If you're planning to walk to the site, take plenty of water as you won't be able to stock up on the way. A short cut shaves a couple of kilometres from the walk; opposite the Red Basilica, take Mahmut Şevket Paşa Sokak, the narrow lane between Aklar Gıda groceries and a carpet shop, which leads to the Lower Agora. Take care as the path is steep and not always clearly marked.

A line of rather faded (and in some places completely obliterated) blue dots marks a suggested route around the main structures, which include the **library** as well as the marble-columned **Temple of Trajan**, built during the reigns of the emperors Trajan and Hadrian and used to worship them as well as Zeus. It's the only Roman structure surviving on the acropolis, and its foundations were used as cisterns during the Middle Ages.

Immediately downhill from the temple, descend through the tunnel to the vertigo-inducing, 10,000-seat **theatre**. Impressive and unusual, its builders decided to take advantage of the spectacular view, and conserve precious space on top of the hill, by building the theatre into the hillside. In general, Hellenistic theatres are wider and rounder than this, but at Pergamum the hillside location made rounding impossible and so it was increased in height instead.

Below the stage is the ruined **Temple of Dionysus**, while above the theatre is the **Altar of Zeus**, which was originally covered with magnificent friezes depicting the battle between the Olympian gods and their subterranean foes. However 19th-century German excavators were allowed to remove most of this famous building to Berlin, leaving only the base behind.

Piles of rubble on top of the acropolis are marked as palaces, including that of **Eumenes II**, and you can also see fragments of the once-magnificent defensive **walls**.

To escape the crowds and get a good view of the theatre and Temple of Trajan, walk downhill behind the Altar of Zeus, or turn left at the bottom of the theatre steps, and follow the sign to the *antik yol* (antique street). Ruins, including gymnasiums, sprawl down the hill to a building on the site of the **Middle City** protecting part of a peristyle court and some fantastic **mosaic floors**; look for the grotesque faces at the far end. With sights beyond including the **Lower Agora**, from here you could ruin hop back to the foot of the hill, taking the short cut suggested in the opposite direction.

Asclepion
RUINS

(Temple of Asclepios; admission/parking TL15/3) An ancient medical centre, the Asclepion was founded by Archias, a local who had been cured at the Asclepion of Epidaurus (Greece). Treatments included mud baths, the use of herbs and ointments, enemas and sunbathing. Diagnosis was often by dream analysis.

Pergamum's centre came to the fore under Galen (AD 131–210), who was born here and studied in Alexandria, Greece and Asia Minor before setting up shop as physician to Pergamum's gladiators. Recognised as perhaps the greatest early physician, Galen added considerably to knowledge of the circulatory and nervous systems, and also systematised medical theory. Under his influence, the medical school at Pergamum became renowned. His work was the basis for Western medicine well into the 16th century.

The Asclepion is 2km uphill from the town centre as the crow flies (but it's a winding road), signposted from Cumhuriyet Caddesi just north of the tourist office and PTT. A second road runs from Böblingen Pension, southwest of town. It's closed to motorists and we don't recommend walking it, as it passes through a large military base; if you do, be off it by dusk and don't take photos.

A Roman **bazaar street**, once lined with shops, leads from the entrance to the centre, where you'll see the base of a column carved with snakes, the symbol of Asclepios (Aesculapius), god of medicine. Just as the snake sheds its skin and gains a 'new life', so the patients at the Asclepion were supposed to 'shed' their illnesses. Signs mark a circular **Temple of Asclepios**, a **library** and, beyond it, a **Roman theatre**.

You can take a drink from the **Sacred Well**, although the plastic tube out of which the water flows doesn't look particularly inviting, and pass along the vaulted underground corridor to the **Temple of Telesphorus**, another god of medicine. Patients slept in the temple hoping that Telesphorus would send a cure or diagnosis in a dream. The names of Telesphorus' two daughters, Hygeia and Panacea, have passed into medical terminology.

Soft drinks are available from the stalls by the Asclepion car park, albeit at a premium.

Red Basilica
RUINS

(Kınık Caddesi; admission TL5) The cathedral-sized Red Basilica was originally a giant temple to the Egyptian gods Serapis, Isis and Harpocrates, built in the 2nd century AD. It's still an imposing-looking place, though rather scattered and battered-looking these days. Be careful as you make you way around as several sections of the basilica's high walls are severely damaged.

During its pagan pomp, this must have been an awe-inspiring place. In his Revelation, St John the Divine wrote that this was one of the seven churches of the Apocalypse, singling it out as the throne of the devil. Look for a hole in the podium in the centre, which allowed a priest to hide and appear to speak through the 10m-high cult statue. The building is so big that the Christians didn't convert it into a church but built a basilica inside it. The most intact section, the southern rotunda, was used for religious and cult rituals; once covered in marble panels, it is now just red brick.

Along with the glass-topped northern rotunda, the curious red flat-brick walls of the large, roofless structure are visible from midway down the roads to the acropolis and town centre. You can easily walk to the Red Basilica, or stop your taxi there on your way to/from the acropolis.

Archaeology Museum
MUSEUM

(Arkeoloji Müzesi; ☎631 2884; Cumhuriyet Caddesi; admission TL5) Right in the centre of town, the Archaeology Museum boasts a

Acropolis

small but substantial collection of artefacts, including Greek, Roman and Byzantine gravestones, busts and pillars. Most interestingly, it features a collection of statues from the 4th century BC that formed part of the so-called 'Pergamum School' when sculptors, breaking with the more grotesque and stylised traditions of previous centuries, first began to represent the gods as recognisably human with expressive features. Other finds from the surrounding sites include a smashed Roman tablet listing city laws, discovered at the Lower Agora on the acropolis.

Look out too for the scale replica of the Altar of Zeus (the original is in Berlin) and, in the main hall, finds from the nearby, and quite probably doomed, site of Allianoi (see p179). The ethnography gallery focuses on the crafts and customs of the Ottoman period with dioramas representing folk dancing and carpet weaving.

Hacı Hekim Hamamı   HAMAM
(Cumhuriyet Caddesi; ⊙6am-11pm) Situated near the Kulaksız Cami, this 16th-century hamam charges TL40 for the full works.

🛏 Sleeping

The most handsome, if rather tumbledown, part of town is around the northern end of Cumhuriyet Caddesi.

⌐TOP⌐ Odyssey Guesthouse   PENSION €
⌐CHOICE⌐ (⌂631 3501; www.odysseyguesthouse. com; Abacıhan Sokak 13; dm TL15, s/d from TL35/40, s/d without bathroom from TL25/35) This 180-year-old house is full of crannies, corners and character, which the friendly proprietor Ersin has emphasised with a well-stocked book exchange and a copy of Homer's *Odyssey* in every room. Up top is a kitchenette for guest use and a terrace with views of the Red Basilica; this is where guests staying in the budget annex also have their breakfast (which costs an extra TL7).

Gobi Pension   PENSION €
(⌂633 2518; www.gobipension.com; İzmir Caddesi 18; s/d TL40/65, s/d without bathroom TL25/45; @🌣) On the main road behind a shady terrace draped in greenery, this is a great family-run place with 12 bright, breezy rooms, including recently renovated options and more basic affairs. Those at the front have double glazing to keep the traffic noise out and those at the back overlook a garden; some have balconies. It's well set up for travellers, with a kitchen, laundry

service and help on hand from English-speaking Mustafa.

Hotel Anıl   HOTEL €€
(⌂632 6352; www.anilhotelbergama.com; Hatuniye Caddesi 4; s/d/tr TL70/100/130; 🌣) The Anıl has a central location, and winning views of the acropolis from its third and fourth floors. Rooms are comfortable and well equipped, though their turquoise furniture is as shocking as the pink exterior. The fifth-floor restaurant only opens at the height of summer.

Böblingen Pension   PENSION €
(⌂633 2153; dincer_altin@hotmail.com; 3 Sokak 2; s/d TL30/60, s/d without bathroom TL25/50; 🌣@) Behind its flaking yellow exterior – among pine trees on the side of the Asclepion hill, south of the centre – the Böblingen's 13 rooms are a little old, but spotless. Those round the back are vaguely musty but well kitted out with mod cons. With its big balconies, the shipshape pension is helmed by the English-speaking Dinçer and family, who also offer dinner (TL15).

Efsane Hotel   HOTEL €€
(⌂632 6350; www.efsanehotelbergama.com; Atatürk Bulvarı 82; s/d/tr TL55/90/110; 🌣🌣) Just north of the otogar, Efsane is the same standard as its sister operation, Hotel Anıl, but prices are lower because of its out-of-town location.

🍴 Eating

⌐TOP⌐ Kervan   FAMILY RESTAURANT €€
⌐CHOICE⌐ (⌂633 2632; İzmir Caddesi; mains TL12) Next to Gobi Pension, Kervan is popular among locals for its large outdoor terrace and excellent food. The menu features a good range of kebaps, pide, *çorba* (soup) and, for dessert, *künefe* (syrup-soaked dough and sweet cheese sprinkled with pistachios).

Köy Evi   LOKANTA €
(Village House; Galinos Caddesi 12; mantı TL5; ⊙10am-7.30pm) This is a fabulous family-run place with cosy seating inside or out in the courtyard. The home-cooked dishes change daily, but typically include stuffed peppers, *mantı* and *patlıcan* kebap (meat grilled with aubergine).

Bergama Ticaret Odası
Sosyal Tesisleri   RESTAURANT €€
(⌂632 9641; Ulucamii Mahallesi; mains TL15; ⊙9am-midnight) To reach this restaurant, follow the road 300m up the hill behind Odyssey Guesthouse and it's in the park on

the left. It's one of the only eateries in Bergama that serves alcohol and its outdoor terrace, garden and hall-like dining room have sweeping views of town. There's nothing jaw-dropping on its meze trolley, but it attracts a steady trickle of diners. Do not visit late, as the surrounding streets are not Bergama's most salubrious neighbourhood.

Sağlam Restaurant
RESTAURANT €€

(☑667 2003; Yeni Otogat Yanı; mains TL12; ⊙11.30am-3pm & 6pm-midnight) This Bergama favourite has moved out of town to the Opet garage by the otogar. Despite the proximity of the petrol pumps, it has a pleasant dining environment and an unlimited buffet. Beer, meze, pide and kebabs are also offered.

Simge Pastanesi ve Simit Dünyasi
PATISSERIE €

(İzmir Caddesi; baklava & ice cream TL4; ⊙24 hrs) For a coffee and cake between sights, Simge serves all manner of pastries and baklava. Along with the neighbouring Simgecan Pastanesi, run by the same family, it's considered the best patisserie in town.

Paksoy Pide
PIDECI €

(İslamsaray Mahallesi; pide TL3.50-5.50) Pint-sized Paksoy is clean and patronised by locals. Watch the chef rolling and flipping the pide classics in front of the oven.

Zıkkım
CAFE-BAR €

(Cumhuriyet Caddesi; mains TL5-9; ⊙10.30am-1am) With shady garden seating just off the main road, Zıkkım makes a welcome midtown pit stop, offering cheap *köfte* and salads (white-bean salad TL3.50).

Bergama Sofrası
LOKANTA €

(☑631 5131; Bankalar Caddesi 44; köfte TL7) Sit outside next to the hamam or inside the diner-like interior, with its clean surfaces and open kitchen under bright lights. The vegetables, chips and soup look rather stewed by the evening, but meat dishes such as spicy *köfte* are freshly cooked.

Çiçeksever
CAFE €

(Bankalar Caddesi; mains TL7) In a good area for small eateries, Çiçeksever serves simple dishes such as pide and *çorba*.

Market
MARKET

(⊙8am-6pm) Bergama has a bustling Monday market, which stretches from the old otogar past the Red Basilica. It's great for fresh fruit and veg. Böblingen Caddesi and the area around the old bus station are good for picnic-hunting. Cheese, olives, fresh bread and dried fruit are all sold.

Yanikoğlu Supermarket
SUPERMARKET

(İzmir Caddesi; ⊙8am-midnight) A supermarket stocking all the essentials.

İZMIR & THE NORTH AEGEAN BERGAMA (PERGAMUM)

ALLİANOİ

In 1998 local farmers made an exciting discovery in the Valley of Kaikos at Allianoi, 20km east of Bergama – the remains of a Roman spa and asclepion, among the oldest and best preserved yet found. A fine statue of Aphrodite on display in the Bergama museum (p177) came from Allianoi.

Unfortunately, the archaeological site is now a centre of controversy. The Valley of Kaikos is the proposed site of the new Yortanlı Dam – already built, although not yet open – which will bring vital water reserves to the region, but also submerge Allianoi under 17m of water. The archaeologists in charge of the site started a petition to save it, and the opening of the dam had been delayed when we visited, but it looks to be a losing battle. Although the majority of the site remains unexcavated, it seems likely the dam will eventually open, albeit not before the site has been surrounded by a wall and covered with a layer of (hopefully) protective clay – essentially re-burying the site (and the problem) in the hope that future generations might be able to come up with a solution.

Bulldozers have already caused damage to the site and archaeologists are working to uncover and rescue what they can. For more information, visit www.europanostra.org/allianoi.

To visit you need to obtain a permit from the Archaeology Museum in Bergama. The museum is reluctant to issue permits, but you may be able extract one if you can demonstrate you are an archaeologist or have a particular reason for visiting Allianoi.

There is no bus service, but you could try taking the infrequent bus from Bergama to Paşaköy (TL5, 45 minutes), which can drop you at the turn-off to Paşaka, and then walk the 1km to Allianoi. Returning to Bergama is tricky – you can only try hailing a passing bus. A taxi here from Bergama costs TL50 to TL60.

❶ Information

Modern Bergama lies spread out either side of one long main street, along which almost everything you'll need can be found, including hotels, restaurants, banks, the PTT and museum.

Tourist office (☑631 2851; Hükümet Konağı, Cumhuriyet Caddesi; ⊙8.30am-noon & 1-5.30pm) Just north of the museum, it offers little more than a sketch map, although the board outside has useful information such as bus and minibus times.

❶ Getting There & Away

Bus

Bergama's *yeni* (new) otogar lies 7km from the centre, at the junction of the İzmir-Çanakkale highway and the main road into town. Between 6am and 7pm, a free *servis* bus shuttles between there and the *eski* (old) otogar in the town centre. Outside these hours you will have to take a taxi (about TL20). Some buses from Çanakklale drop you at the junction near the otogar, from where you can walk to the bus station and pick up the *servis* (despite what taxi drivers may tell you).

ANKARA TL50, eight to nine hours, 480km, nightly

AYVALIK TL7.50, 1¼ hours, 60km, every hour

İSTANBUL (via Bursa) TL50, 11 hours, 250km, nightly with additional morning services in high season

İZMİR TL10, two hours, 110km, every 45 minutes

Dolmuş

In the early morning and evening, half-hourly dolmuşes to Ayvalık and Çandarlı leave from the old otogar; in between, they leave from the new otogar.

❶ Getting Around

Bergama's sights are so spread out that it's hard to walk round them all in one day. The Red Basilica is over 1km from the tourist office, the Asclepion is 2km away and the acropolis is over 5km away.

BUS Between 6am and 7pm, half-hourly buses run through town between the old otogar and the market area (TL1.50), 200m past the Red Basilica at the foot of the road up to the acropolis.

CABLE CAR The cable car (one-way/return TL6/12) runs between the acropolis and the market area mentioned above.

TAXI A convenient option is to book a 'city tour'. From the centre to the Asclepion, basilica and acropolis, with 30 minutes at the first two sights and an hour at the latter, should cost around TL50. Taxis wait around some of the mosques and the otogars. Individual fares from the taxi rank near Köy Evi are about TL7 to the Asclepion, and TL15 to the acropolis.

Çandarlı

☑0232

The small and tranquil resort town of Çandarlı (ancient Pitane) sits on a peninsula jutting into the Aegean, 33km southwest of Bergama. It's dominated by a small but stately 14th-century restored Genoese **castle** (admission free; ⊙24hr Jul & Aug), which is normally closed outside high season, and has a sandier beach than some of its neighbours.

Local tourism fills most of the pensions in high summer. From late October to April/May it's pretty much a ghost town.

Shops, internet cafes and the PTT are in the centre, 200m behind the seafront. The castle, pensions and restaurants line the seashore. Market day is Friday.

🛏 Sleeping

Most of the hotels and pensions lie west of the castle, facing a thin strip of coarse sand.

Otel Samyeli   HOTEL €€
(☑673 3428; www.otelsamyeli.com, in Turkish; Sahil Plaj Caddes; s/d/tr TL40/80/120; ❄) In the middle of the bay, Otel Samyeli has simple, spotless and cheerful rooms – number 11, a triple, has a sofa and a sea view – and a seafront fish restaurant (mains TL15). Reserve in advance (a week in summer).

Emirgan Beach Hotel   HOTEL €
(☑673 2500; www.otelsamyeli.com; Sahil Plaj Caddesi; s/d TL40/60; ❄) Operated by the same owners as Otel Samyeli, the Emirgan is 150m to the west and right on the beach. It's older than Samyeli but has more character, with long white balconies leading to the quiet rooms.

🍴 Eating

For fresh fruit, the daily *çarşı* (market), in the shadow of the town mosque, is a good place to replenish. There's a also a Tanşas supermarket, and ice cream stalls on the seafront east of the castle.

Köşem Lokantası   LOKANTA €
(☑673 2132; PTT Sokak 3; mains TL4-9; ⊙10am-10pm) A big hit at lunchtime with workers from the nearby supermarket and beyond, this *lokanta* serves a plethora of eats including pide, *köfte*, İskender kebap and daily specials. It's 200m behind Otel Samyeli on the left, across the main road from the park.

Deniz Restaurant   SEAFOOD €€
(☑673 3124; Sahil Plaj Caddesi; mains TL12; ⊙11am-11pm) With tables right on the sea-

front, the 'Sea Restaurant' is friendly and good value, serving all the usual meze and fish dishes plus meat options.

Drinking & Entertainment

Pitaneou Cafe-Bar
BAR
(Sahil Plaj Caddesi; beer TL4) A popular hang-out with pleasant tables under vines on the seafront. Snacks are available.

Musti Bar
BAR
(Sahil Plaj Caddesi; beer TL4) On the seafront one block west of the castle, Musti is Çandarlı's main dancing hotspot in season.

🛈 Getting There & Away

Frequent buses run between Çandarlı and İzmir (TL11.50, 1½ hours) via Dikili (TL3, 15 minutes). At least six dolmuşes run daily to and from Bergama (TL4, 30 minutes).

Yeni Foça
☎ 0232 / POP 3470

This small resort town set around a harbour boasts a strip of coarse beach, and a wealth of crumbling Ottoman mansions and old Greek stone houses. Long discovered by second-home hunters, Yeni Foça now has its fair share of modern monstrosities alongside the aged marvels. Nevertheless, it's a pleasant place to laze away a day or two. There are some more secluded beaches to the south towards Foça (Eski Foça).

There are newer choices, but the traditionally styled Otel Naz (☎814 6619; www.nazotel.com; Sahil Caddesi 113; s/d TL40/80) is a seafront stalwart. It has large, quite attractively decorated rooms. A pizza restaurant and bar were being built when we visited.

In an attractive one-storey stone building, Kıvanç Café & Restaurant (☎814 7857; Sahil Caddesi 67; mains TL10) offers a good mix of meat and fish dishes, including chicken *şiş* (recommended), pizzas and pide. Seating is on the covered terrace or underneath a fat palm tree by the beach.

The town has a PTT, internet cafe and ATMs. Buses leave every half-hour to İzmir (TL10, 1¾ hours) and every three hours to Foça (TL4). Taxis to Foça cost around TL40.

Foça
☎ 0232 / POP 13,300

If Çandarlı is too quiet and Kuşadası (in the southern Aegean) too noisy, Foça could be just the ticket. Sometimes called Eski Foça (Old Foça) to distinguish it from its newer neighbour (Yeni Foça) over the hill, the happy-go-lucky holiday town hugs twin bays and a small harbour. Graceful old Ottoman-Greek houses line a shoreline crowded with fishing boats and overlooked by a string of restaurants and pensions.

The town is the site of ancient Phocaea, which was founded before 600 BC and flourished during the 5th century BC. During their golden age, the Phocaeans were great mariners, sending swift vessels powered by 50 oars into the Aegean, Mediterranean and Black Seas. They were also keen colonists, founding Samsun on the Black Sea, as well as towns in Italy, Corsica, France and Spain.

More recently, this was an Ottoman-Greek fishing and trading town. It's now a prosperous, middle-class Turkish resort, with holiday villas gathering on the outskirts and a thin, dusty beach with some swimming platforms. There are some more secluded beaches to the north towards Yeni Foça.

Foça's seafront is divided into two bays by a peninsula, at the tip of which sits Beşkapılar castle. To the north is the Küçük Deniz (Small Sea), which is the most picturesque part of town, comprising a harbour filled with small fishing vessels, a long esplanade (where people fish), a line of restaurants and pensions and a small beach.

The Büyük Deniz (Big Sea) to the south is a more no-nonsense place with just a couple of restaurants. This is where the town's excursion boats and big fishing vessels moor.

The otogar is just inland from the Büyük Deniz. Heading north from here, with the Büyük Deniz on your left, takes you through the centre of town to the Küçük Deniz. You will pass the tourist office, the PTT and banks, before reaching the harbour after around 350m. Continue north along the Küçük Deniz's right-hand (eastern) side to find the pensions.

⊙ Sights & Activities

Ancient Phocaea Ruins
FREE
RUINS
Little remains of the ancient Ionian city: a ruined theatre, remains of an aqueduct near the otogar, an *anıt mezarı* (monumental tomb), 7km east of town on the way to the İzmir highway on the left, and traces of two shrines to the goddess Cybele.

Temple of Athena
RUINS
In recent years, the townsfolk made this exciting discovery above the outdoor

sanctuary of Cybele. The site was found to contain, among other things, a beautiful griffin and a horse's head believed to date to the 5th century BC. Excavations are undertaken there every summer; visits will be possible by the end of 2012.

Beşkapılar
FORTRESS

If you continue past the outdoor sanctuary of Cybele, you'll come to the city walls and the partially rebuilt Beşkapılar (Five Gates) castle, built by the Byzantines, repaired by the Genoese and the Ottomans in 1538–39, and clearly much restored since.

Dışkale
FORTRESS

Guarding the town's southwestern approaches, the 17th-century Dışkale (External Fortress) is best seen from the water (on a boat trip) as it's inside a military zone.

Boat Trips
CRUISE

Between late April and early October, boats leave daily at about 11am from both the Küçük Deniz and Büyük Deniz for day trips around the outlying islands with various swim stops en route, returning for about 6.30pm. Most visit Siren Rocks (see boxed text, p181'), and typically cost TL25 including lunch and tea.

Belediye Hamamı
HAMAM

(☑812 1959; 115 Sokak 22; ⊙8am-midnight) Treatments cost TL15 to TL30 at this tourist-friendly hamam.

🛏 Sleeping

There are camping grounds on the coast north of Foça.

TOP CHOICE Foçantique Boutique Hotel
BOUTIQUE HOTEL €€€

(☑812 7616; www.focantiquehotel.com; Küçük Deniz Sahil Caddesi 54; r standard/deluxe TL250/290, ste TL525) Foça's top choice for comfort and style, lying at the far, quiet end of Küçük Deniz. Guides Inci and Alemdar have lovingly restored the 19th-century Greek stone house; the 10 beautifully decorated rooms feature an eclectic mix of antiques and curios, such as Turkmen dresses. The four-person suite has twin and double rooms, two washing machines in the bathroom, and an open-plan kitchen and living room with balcony.

Hotel Grand Amphora
HOTEL €€

(☑812 3930; www.hotelgrandamphora.com; 206 Sokak 7; s/d/tr TL75/100/120; ✻ ⌨) Not quite as grand as the name would suggest, this is nonetheless the only hotel in town with

a pool (albeit small), and it's good for sun-soaking on the sunloungers. Rooms are small but comfortable.

Siren Pansiyon
PENSION €

(☑812 2660; www.sirenpansiyon.com; 161 Sokak 13; s/d TL30/50) The English-speaking, helpful Remzi's justifiably popular pension, a short walk from the seafront, is a spotless and good-value choice. Some of the doors needed a spot of oil and the place was starting to look aged when we visited, but a renovation was planned. The roof terrace with kitchen is a highlight. Breakfast costs an additional TL7.

İyon Pansiyon
PENSION €€

(☑812 1415; www.iyonpansion.com; 198 Sokak 8; r TL90) Readers rate İyon, where eight simple rooms open onto a courtyard below a blue bridge, which links two terraces with views of the hills. There are sea views from an upstairs room and the reception/breakfast area. A renovation was underway when we visited; we hope they remove the wallpaper covering the ancient stone walls upstairs.

🍴 Eating

Foça has a decent Tuesday market, which is a good place to stock up for a picnic. There are also various grocery stores.

Fokai Restaurant
RESTAURANT €€

(☑812 2186; 121 Sokak 8; mains TL8-20; ⊙10am-midnight) Above the cafe at the Beşkapılar castle end of the Büyük Deniz seafront, Fokai is recommended by readers and locals alike. Its busy waiters dart around the attractively decorated dining room and large terrace. Dishes range from pizza to (underwhelming) chicken casserole – you're safest with fish.

Çarşı Lokantası
LOKANTA €€

(☑812 2377; Küçük Deniz Caddesi 18; mains TL8-18) This *lokanta* on the lane behind Neco Café & Bar is the best place in town for lunch. A mixed plate (with meat) typically includes *köfte*, stew, *kalamar* and half a dozen vegetables and starches, sprinkled with herbs and spices by the friendly Mesut. Treat yourself to a pudding with ice cream; you won't regret it.

Akaryum Restaurant
RESTAURANT €€

(☑812 6191; Sahil Caddesi 46; mains TL12-20) Locals recommend the Aquarium, one of the fish-focused restaurants on the eastern side of the Küçük Deniz. The packed menu and fridge fit in the full gamut of fish and meat dishes, and even include *crepes*.

Foça's offshore islands provide some of the last remaining homes to the endangered Mediterranean monk seal, once common throughout the region. There are thought to be fewer than 400 left in the world, so you shouldn't bank on seeing one. Thankfully, much of Foça's offshore area is now a protected zone, the extent of which was increased in 2007. For more information on the Mediterranean monk seal, contact the Ankara-based **SAD-AFAG (Underwater Research Society-Mediterranean Seal Research Group;** 0312 443 0581; www.sadafag.org), which oversees protection programs on the coast.

The seals' habit of basking on rocks and their wailing plaintive cries are believed to have been the inspiration for the legend of the Sirens, as featured in Homer's *Odyssey*.

Living on rocky islands, the sirens were strange creatures, half-bird, half-woman. They used their beautiful, irresistible singing voices to lure sailors towards their perilous perches, where the ships would be dashed against the rocks, and the sailors killed. Odysseus supposedly only managed to resist their entreaties by having himself lashed to his ship's mast.

Appropriately enough, one of the seals' favourite modern basking spots is the Siren Kayalıkları (Siren Rocks) on Orak Island, just off Foça's shore, although these days it is the seals' lives, rather than those of local sailors, that are in danger.

Harika Köfte Evi KÖFTECİ €
(812 5409; Belediye Karşısı; mains TL8) In addition to four types of *köfte* – reputedly the best in town – the Wonderful Köfte House serves *çorba* and *tavuk şiş* (roast skewered chicken kebap).

Palmiye CAFE €
(Cumhuriyet Meydanı) A popular choice for breakfast, right on the main square next to the Küçük Deniz, with *simit* (sesame seed-coated bread rings), *tost,* olives and orange juice on offer.

 Drinking

Dip Bar BAR-CAFE
(Sahil Caddesi 3; beer TL6) One of the Küçük Deniz's cooler hang-outs, Dip is popular for the traditional Turkish activities of backgammon and smoking despite its smart blue cushions. You get four different nibbles with your beer.

Keyif BAR-CAFE
(Sahil Caddesi 42a; beer TL6) Slightly funkier than the nearby Neco Café & Bar – it's got a glitter ball – Keyif offers both Western music and live Turkish performers; dancing has been known to take place inside.

ℹ Information

Fokai 2 Internet Café (194 Sokak; per hr TL1.50; 8.30am-midnight) Just off the main square.

Tourist office (/fax 812 1222; Cumhuriyet Meydanı; 8.30am-noon & 1-5.30pm Mon-Fri,

10am-7pm Sat Jun-Sep) Very helpful, with lots of brochures.

ℹ Getting There & Around

Bus

İZMİR & MENEMEN Between 6.30am and 9.15pm (11pm in summer) half-hourly buses run to İzmir (TL8, 1½ hours, 86km), passing through Menemen (for connections to Manisa).

BERGAMA Take the bus to Menemen/İzmir, jump off on the highway and flag down any bus heading north.

YENİ FOÇA Three to five city buses run daily to/from Yeni Foça (TL4, 30 minutes, 22km); the timetable is in the otogar. These buses pass the pretty, small coves, beaches and camping grounds north of Foça.

Car

If you're staying in the area for a few days you could hire a car from **MNB Oto Kiralama** (812 1987; www.mnbrentacar.com; 123 Sokak 6; one day TL85), behind the police station on the Büyük Deniz.

İzmir

 0232 / POP 2.7 MILLION

If it wasn't for the fire that ravaged İzmir in 1922, Turkey's third-largest city might attract as many visitors as that place on the Bosphorus. As it is, the views on the *kordon* (seafront) – known locally as *birinci* (first) *kordon,* while Cumhuriyet Bulvarı is *ikinci* (second) *kordon* – are of miles of houses and high rises, overlooking the ferries

İZMİR & THE NORTH AEGEAN

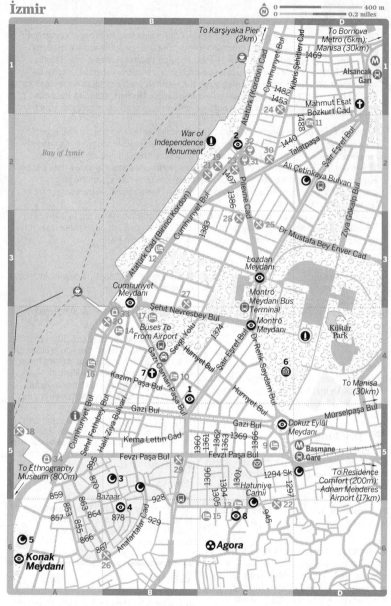

criss-crossing the bay. Inland, although buzzing Alsancak is a pleasantly leafy area, roads such as Fevzi Paşa Bulvarı are dirty ribbons of tarmac. This leads past the crowded modern bazaar to Basmane, a once-affluent area where the *pavyons* (clubs),

which used to host great Turkish singers, are now sleazy nightspots.

But these drawbacks are merely cosmetic. Spending a night or two in this cosmopolitan city is one of the best things you can do in urban Turkey. With its Levantine and

İzmir

Jewish heritage (see boxed text, p186), İzmir is proudly distinct from the rest of Turkey; indeed, its fellow countrymen sometimes still regard İzmiris with a degree of suspicion. That's certainly not to say there aren't Turkish flags aplenty between the palms, but İzmir does have a liberal, laid-back feel. During Ramazan, when some bars in İstanbul and elsewhere close, it's business as usual in the countless watering holes on the balmy *kordon*.

Indeed, at the water's edge the city comes into its own. İzmir owes a huge debt to its late mayor, Ahmet Piristina, who managed to overturn a remarkably ill-conceived plan to build yet another highway – right along the seafront. Snatched from development's claws, the *kordon* is now one of the city's main attractions – a wide, pleasant esplanade that provides many sunset-watching opportunities.

History

İzmir was once Smyrna, a city founded by colonists from Greece some time in the early part of the 1st millennium BC. Over the next 1000 years it would grow in importance as it came under the influence of successive regional powers: first Lydia, then Greece, and finally Rome. By the 2nd century AD it was, along with Ephesus and Pergamum, one of the three most important cities in the Roman province of Asia. Under Byzantine rule, however, its fortunes declined as the focus of government turned north to Constantinople. Things only began to look up again when the Ottomans took control in 1415, after which Smyrna rapidly became Turkey's most sophisticated commercial city.

After the collapse of the Ottoman Empire at the end of WWI, the Greeks invaded, but were eventually expelled following fierce fighting, which, along with a subsequent fire, destroyed most of the old city. The day that Atatürk recaptured Smyrna (9 September 1922) marked the moment of victory in the Turkish War of Independence, and it is now the biggest local holiday. The events of 1922 are commemorated in the rather top-heavy monument gracing the waterfront.

◉ Sights

Kordon & Alsancak   SEAFRONT, NEIGHBOURHOOD

Very much the symbol of the new İzmir, this long boulevard has over the past decade been transformed into as fine a waterfront area as you'll find on this coast. The *kordon*'s (largely) pedestrianised confines are now home to a great selection of bars and restaurants that attract droves of people at the end of the day to watch the picture-perfect sunsets. Inland, the Alsancak district has also undergone much restoration in recent years and is now the focus of the city's nightlife.

Konak Meydanı   SQUARE

On a pedestrianised stretch of Cumhuriyet Bulvarı, this wide plaza, named after the Ottoman **government mansion** (*hükümet konağı*), pretty much marks the heart of the city; signs pointing to the centre simply say 'Konak'. It's the site of a late Ottoman **clock tower** (*saat kulesi*) built in 1901 to mark the 25th anniversary of Sultan Abdül

COSMOPOLITAN İZMİR

Between the early 17th and early 20th centuries İzmir had one of the Ottoman Empire's largest populations of Levantines. This international expat community was drawn here when İzmir was one of the empire's principal trading hubs, and its influence can still be seen. Areas such as Bornova, northeast of the centre, have whole streets of Levantine houses, which reveal the various nationalities' different temperaments. French- and British-built houses have open balconies, as their owners didn't mind being glimpsed from the street, whereas the more-conservative Italians had closed balconies and the Greeks had no balconies. Visit www.levantineheritage.com for more information. Levantine sights in the centre include:

Alsancak train station (Ziya Gökalp Bulvarı) The 19th-century station is colonial in style, with stained glass windows and a steam train outside.

St John's Church (Ziya Gökalp Bulvarı) This Anglican-Episcopal church was consecrated in 1902.

Jackson's (☑422 6045; Gazi Kadınlar Sokak 17; mains TL12; ☺lunch & dinner) This restaurant was a British consular residence; the rack behind the bar was used for displaying china.

Apikam (city museum & archive; ☑293 3900; Şair Eşref Bulvarı 1; ☺8.30am-5.30pm Mon-Sat) Formerly a fire station, built by the British in 1923, it has displays on İzmir's history and a courtyard cafe.

Konak Pier (Atatürk Caddesi) Gustave Eiffel, who designed Paris' famous tower, also designed the site of today's shopping centre in 1890.

Konak clock tower Designed by the Levantine French architect Raymond Charles Père.

Sen Polikarp church (Saint Polycarpe; Vali Kazım Dirik Caddesi)

İzmir's Levantine community is fast disappearing, but it still has a sizeable Jewish community, mostly in Alsancak, and it is possible to tour of some of the city's beautiful old **synagogues** (guided tours €35). The tours usually take in some of the restored synagogues in Karataş, the Old Jewish Quarter; including the **Bet Israel**, which has a museum on its upper floor, and lies near the **Asansör** (☺7.30am-midnight), an elevator built in 1907 to enable trade between Karataş and the Turkish Halil Rifat Paşa neighbourhood – the alternative is 155 steps. At the foot of the lift, a plaque marks the typical old İzmir house where **Darío Moreno**, the late Jewish singer of *Canım İzmir* (My dear İzmir), was born. Other highlights include the three Ottoman-style synagogues on Havra Sokak in the bazaar, the remainder of nine that used to stand here. To arrange a tour, call the tourist office (p191).

Hamit II's coronation. Its ornate Orientalist style may have been meant to atone for Smyrna's European ambience. Beside it is the lovely Konak Camii, dating from 1755, which is covered in Kütahya tiles.

Agora
RUINS

(Agora Caddesi; admission TL3; ⏱8.30am-7pm, to 5.30pm Sat; P) The ancient Agora, built for Alexander the Great, was ruined in an earthquake in AD 178, but rebuilt soon after by the Roman emperor Marcus Aurelius. Colonnades of reconstructed Corinthian columns, vaulted chambers and arches give you a good idea of what a Roman bazaar must have looked like. Later, a Muslim cemetery was built on the site and many of the old tombstones can be seen around the perimeter of the Agora. Ask for the free brochures, which give a good introduction. The site's entered on the south side, just off Gazi Osman Paşa Bulvarı.

Archaeology Museum
MUSEUM

(Arkeoloji Müzesi; ☎489 0796; Bahri Baba Parkı; admission TL8; ⏱8.30am-5pm Tue-Sun) At the southern end of Konak Meydanı, the traffic returns with a vengeance, but over the road is Turgutreis Parkı; and, on the hill above the park (not signposted but visible from the road), İzmir's archaeology and ethnography museums. Across the road from the white 'Sağlık Bakanlığı' (Ministry of Health) hospital building, a path leads to the museums through the left side of the park.

The Archaeology Museum is a little dry in places, but contains a fine collection of remnants from the local region: Greek statuary and amphoras, Byzantine oil lamps and a beautifully decorated sarcophagi from the Çeşme Peninsula.

FREE Ethnography Museum
MUSEUM

(Etnografya Müzesi; ☎489 0796; ⏱8.30am-6.30pm Tue-Sun) More interesting than the neighbouring Archaeology Museum, the Ethnography Museum occupies the former St Roche Hospital. This lovely old four-storey stone building houses colourful displays (including dioramas, photos and information panels) demonstrating local arts, crafts and customs. You'll learn about everything from camel wrestling, pottery and tin-plating to felt-making, embroidery and the art of making those curious little blue-and-white 'evil eye' beads (see boxed text, p192). Other exhibits include weaponry, woodwork and illustrated manuscripts.

Fatih Camii
MOSQUE

(Birleşmis Milletler Caddesi) Above the museums, this reconstructed, blue-tiled mosque has a small tea garden with a view down the hill, and a beautiful interior. The tiles inside show the difference between İznik designs (see p256 along the base of the walls) and more-colourful, vibrant İzmir tiles with large, flowing motifs (above the windows and on the domed ceiling).

Kemeraltı Bazaar
BAZAAR

(⏱8am-5pm) İzmir's version of a Turkish bazaar may be disappointingly unexotic if you've never visited one before. Much of what goes on sale here is aimed squarely at the domestic market – pots and pans, socks, wedding dresses, clocks etc, albeit enlivened here and there with more-intriguing items, such as water pipes, beads and leather goods (a local speciality). The architecture is no great shakes, with the exception of the Kızlarağası Han.

What the bazaar certainly does have, however, is atmosphere. It can, to put it mildly, get rather busy. The streets are narrow and the people are many. It's a great place to get lost for a couple of hours – and with alleys intertwining here, there and everywhere, it's pretty much guaranteed that will happen. When it all gets too much, you can revive yourself at one of the numerous cafes. Anafartalar Caddesi rings the main bazaar area and is its principal thoroughfare.

Kızlarağası Han
BAZAAR

(Kemeraltı Bazaar; ⏱8am- 5pm) This restored caravanserai (1744) is like a much smaller, calmer version of İstanbul's famous Covered Bazaar. The market is touristy, with many items from the far end of the Silk Road (China), but good for a wander. There's a cafe in the courtyard, where merchants once tethered their camels.

Hisar Camii
MOSQUE

(Kemeraltı Bazaar) The interior of the city's largest mosque (1592) is quintessentially İzmiri. The blue-and-gold motifs on the domed ceiling are simpler and less Oriental than classic Ottoman designs. Also look out for the roses and grapes carved along the bottom of the women's gallery and the designs on the stone staircase.

Kültür Park
PARK

Much of the inland centre of town, between Alsancak and Basmane, was heavily damaged in the 1922 fire, and is now taken up by the Kültür Park. The park injects a little greenery into the city and attracts strolling couples and joggers – who have their own dedicated track. Specific attractions include a 50m parachute tower, an amusement park, some contemporary sculptures on the west side of the pond, and exhibition halls for events including the International İzmir Festival.

Museum of History & Art   MUSEUM
(Tarih ve Sanat Müzesi; ☑445 6818; Kültür Park; admission TL3; ⊙8.30am-6.30pm Tue-Sun) Containing three separate departments (Sculpture, Ceramics and Precious Artefacts), this museum gives a good overview of the region's artistic heritage. Look out for the 2nd-century-AD high relief of Poseidon and Demeter from the Agora, the late Neolithic anthropomorphic vase, and the cute sitting Aphrodites from the Roman period.

FREE Atatürk Evi   HISTORIC BUILDING
(Atatürk Caddesi; ⊙9am-noon & 1-5.15pm Tue-Sun) During İzmir's 19th-century heyday the *kordon* was lined with stately offices and fine houses. Most of these have long since vanished, but this building gives an idea of what the homes of the wealthy would have looked like. Atatürk stayed here between 1930 and 1934 whenever he visited the city.

Kadifekale   FORTRESS
(Rakım Elkutlu Caddesi) Following its sacking by Lydia in the 6th century BC, Smyrna would have to wait another couple of centuries before being refounded, by Alexander the Great. He chose a secure site on Kadifekale (Mt Pagus), southeast of the modern city centre, erecting the fortifications that still crown the hill. The view from the 'Velvet Fortress' is magnificent, especially just before sunset. You may see Kurdish women, migrants from southeastern Anatolia, hard at work on horizontal carpet looms.

Bus 33 from Konak will carry you up the hill. We don't recommend walking in either direction, especially later in the day, as the surrounding neighbourhood is notoriously rough. Tourists have been attacked there.

Şıfalı Lux Hamam   HAMAM
(☑445 2209; Anafartalar Caddesi 660; bath & massage from TL30; ⊙8am-10pm for men, 7am-6pm for women) This clean hamam has a lovely domed and marble interior.

Mask & Costume Museum   MUSEUM
This museum, which will feature hundreds of pieces including Atatürk's death mask, is set to open in 2010.

✦ Festivals & Events

From mid-June to mid-July the annual International İzmir Festival offers performances of music and dance in Çeşme and Ephesus as well as İzmir (in the Kültür Park). Check www.iksev.org for programme and ticket information.

🛏 Sleeping

İzmir's waterfront is dominated by large high-end business hotels, which fill up quickly during the summer trade shows, while inland are more budget and midrange options, particularly around Kemeraltı Bazaar and Basmane train station. Here and there, you'll find a few boutique hotels, the trend having reached İzmir in the past few years.

BAZAAR & BASMANE

1294 Sokak and 1296 Sokak, just southwest of Basmane train station, boast many options occupying restored Ottoman houses. However, this is an unsalubrious area after dark, and, although the hotels' facades are often attractive, their interiors are generally grungy and uninviting. Readers have had bad experiences here. If you want a budget hotel, we recommend heading instead to 1368 Sokak, east of the station.

TOP CHOICE Konak Saray Hotel   BOUTIQUE HOTEL €€
(☑483 7755; www.konaksarayhotel.com; Anafartalar Caddesi 635; s/d TL60/90; ☀@) One of İzmir's best-value options, the Konak Saray occupies a beautifully restored old Ottoman house that's been transformed into a superior hotel. A hit with readers, its 27 modern rooms, although a touch small, have mini-bars, plasma-screen TVs and soundproofing to keep the bazaar noise out. There's also a great top-floor restaurant. With Agora views, the new Agora branch of Konak Saray will charge the same prices.

Otel Antik Han   BOUTIQUE HOTEL €€
(☑489 2750; www.otelantikhan.com; Anafartalar Caddesi 600; s/d €45/65; @) This restored Ottoman building, built in 1851, is one of İzmir's few historic hotels, with pleasant (if in places a little threadbare) rooms with plasma-screen TVs and minibars. The tranquil courtyard is a world away from the hustle and bustle of the bazaar outside.

Residence Comfort   APARTMENT €€
(☑425 9503; www.comfortresidence.com; Gaziler Caddesi 206; s/d from €55/70; ☀P) Recommended by readers, this Basmane branch of

the chain has 25 large suites with carpeted, open-plan kitchens and living rooms. Winning touches include plasma-screen TVs, breakfast left at your door and washing machines in the senior suites, although they overlook busy Gaziler Caddesi. The location is a drawback, but all west-bound buses go to Konak Pier.

Grand Zeybek Hotel
HOTEL €€

(☏441 9590; www.grandzeybekhotels.com; 1368 Sokak 5-7, Basmane; s/d TL50/100; ✳@) Despite the name, this isn't grand at all, but, along with its three sister hotels on the same street, it's one of Basmane's safer options. The plain old Hotel Zeybek (TL40/80) is across the street.

Güzel İzmir Oteli
HOTEL €

(☏483 5069; www.guzelizmirhotel.com; 1368 Sokak 8; s/d TL40/70) The Good İzmir Hotel's rooms are basic and small, but it's close to the train station and bus offices. With a woman working in the bright reception, it has a more reputable air than Basmane's many pay-by-the-hour operations.

ALSANCAK & SEAFRONT

North of Gazi Bulvarı is safer and pleasanter, although the hotels here are firmly in midrange and top-end territory.

MyHotel
BOUTIQUE HOTEL €€€

(☏445 5241; www.myhotel.com.tr; Cumhuriyet Bulvarı 132; s/d €80/110; ✳@) A sort of business/boutique affair, MyHotel is superstylish, with glass floors, an über-cool lobby bar and clean minimalist (if a touch dark) rooms. It's near the seafront but doesn't have sea views.

Hotel Yaman
HOTEL €€

(☏421 1287; www.hotelyaman.com; 1440 Sokak 19; s/d €45/60; ✳) In an ideal location near the cafes and bars around Kıbrıs Sehitleri Caddesi, the no-frills Yaman is a good-value option for a short stay. However, the maid didn't visit our room during the days we spent there.

Swissôtel Grand Efes
HOTEL €€€

(☏414 0000; www.swissotel.com.tr; Gazi Osman Paşa Bulvarı 1; s/d €140/160; P✳@≋) The five-star luxury-business Grand Efes is the biggest player in town, occupying a prime location overlooking Cumhuriyet Meydanı and the bay. The rooms are as generically luxurious as you'd expect, with flat-screen TVs, large beds and elegant leather and steel furniture, although you might have to

look out of the window (or take a trip up to the Sky Bar) to remind yourself which city you're in. Also boasts an excellent restaurant and spa.

Hilton İzmir
HOTEL €€€

(☏497 6060; www.hilton.com; Gazi Osman Paşa Bulvarı 7; s/d €115/135; P✳@≋) Reputedly the tallest building on Turkey's Aegean coast, the Hilton literally stands above the competition. The public rooms luxuriate in grey marble, and there are fabulous views from its well-appointed bedrooms, restaurants and bars, as well as good facilities, including health club, pool, tennis and squash courts.

Otel Kilim
HOTEL €€€

(☏484 5340; www.kilimotel.com.tr; Atatürk Caddesi; s/d TL125/165; ✳@) There are better options on the seafront, but they tend to cost more. Beyond Kilim's brown-and-cream reception, its rooms are blandly comfortable, with nice touches such as glass-fronted minibars, plasma-screen TVs, big shower heads and black-and-white photos of İzmir. Half a dozen rooms face the sea; the others have good side views.

İzmir Palas Oteli
HOTEL €€

(☏465 0030; www.izmirpalas.com.tr; Atatürk Caddesi; s/d from TL120/165; P✳) Established in 1927 and rebuilt in '72, the 138-room Palas is rather boxy on the outside, and businesslike and bland within, but very comfortable with the conveniences you'd expect for the price, and a reasonable restaurant, Deniz. Its biggest boon is its seafront location and sweeping views of the bay.

✗ Eating

The place to be seen on a romantic summer's evening is the sea-facing *kordon*. Though you pay for the location – most restaurants have outside tables with views of the bay – some serve excellent food. On and around Kıbrıs Şehitleri Caddesi in Alsancak, you lose the sunset views but gain on atmosphere; try in particular 1453 Sokak.

For fresh fruit and veg, freshly baked bread and delicious savoury pastries, head for the canopied market, just off Anafartalar Caddesi.

TOP CHOICE Sakız
MODERN TURKISH €€

(☏484 1103; Şehit Nevresbey Bulvarı 9a; mains TL12-22; ⊙noon-2pm & 7.30-10pm Mon-Sat) With a wooden terrace and red-and-white tablecloths, Sakız is a cut above the usual rakı-*balık*-bill restaurants. Its fresh meze *balık kokoreç* (fish intestines) and *köz patlıcan* (smoked aubergine with tomatoes and peppers) are recommended; the unusual mains include sea bass with asparagus and stir-fried fish with artichoke. For lunch, choose between 35 vegetarian dishes (10 on Saturday).

Damla Restaurant
AEGEAN €€€

(☑464 6655; 1407 Sokak 8; mains from TL30; ☉lunch & dinner) A local secret in a quiet part of Alsancak, Damla's dishes include perfectly cooked *dana pirzola* (steak) and *bonfile şiş* (beef kebap). It's a great place to try local specialities such as *şevketi bostan,* a vegetable root, served as a meze or with lamb between February and April; and fresh *taze börülce* beans.

Reyhan
PATISSERIE €

(☑444 7946; Dr Mustafa Bey Enver Caddesi 24; cheesecake TL6.75) An İzmir institution for generations, this patisserie is serious about sweet stuff, with a professional taster and headset-wearing waiters. Only fruit in season is used in decadent delights such as strawberry cheesecake and almond-cream cake with pineapple and almonds.

Balık Pişiricisi
SEAFOOD €

(☑464 2705; Atatürk Caddesi 212; mains TL20; ☉noon-10.30pm) The queues of diners on the street and waiters galloping from table to table reveal much about this fish restaurant. Though simple and modern, it has a reputation for good seafood at reasonable prices. Try the speciality, *dil şiş* (grilled sole).

Café de Bugün
CAFE €

(☑425 8118; Atatürk Caddesi 162; sandwiches TL6-11, filter coffee TL4) You can watch the ferries come and go through the big window at this fancy cafe in the *Bugün* (Today) newspaper building. With a long list of coffees, smoothies and wraps, it's good for lunch. An acoustic guitarist plays here on Wednesdays from 8pm.

Deniz Restaurant
SEAFOOD €€€

(☑464 4499; Atatürk Caddesi 188; mains from TL17; ☉11am-11pm) İzmir's premier fish restaurant is still going strong, offering dishes such as fish paella as well as the odd kebap, but it's expensive even by fish eateries' standards. Try the house speciality, *tuzda balık* (fish baked in a block of salt that's broken at your table; suitable for three or four people). Expect your fellow diners to be in their best party frocks.

Kırım Ciğ Börek
BÖREKÇİSİ €

(off Birleşmis Milletler Caddesi; börek TL1.50-2; ☉8am-2pm Tue-Sun) This little booth in a working-class neighbourhood churns out the best *çiğ* (cooked using the 'raw' method) *börek* for miles around. Will your favourite be *peynirli* (cheese) or *kıymalı* (minced meat)? To reach it, walk up the steps across the main road from Fatih Camii.

Kırçiçeği
KEBAPÇI €€

(☑464 3090; Cumhuriyet Bulvarı; kebaps TL11-18; ☉24 hrs) This local chain is pricey but worth it for the great pide (TL8) – including *ıspanaklı peynirli* (cheese and spinach) and *kuşbaşılı kaşarlı* ('bird's head'; the bits of meat supposedly resemble birds' heads) – and kebaps. The *ayran* (yoghurt drink) brand, Eker, from Bursa, is not widely available.

Sir Winston Tea House
CAFE €

(☑421 8861; Dr Mustafa Bey Enver Caddesi 20; sandwiches TL13, tea TL4-8) On a street known for its cafes, this is one of the best, serving dozens of teas, hot and cold coffees, good salads and pastas. There's shady seating outside. A new branch is opening opposite Sakız.

Asansör
RESTAURANT €€

(☑261 2626; Darío Moreno Sokağı; mains TL15-30; ☉9am-midnight) Housed at the top of an early 20th-century elevator (see boxed text, p186), the location is İzmir's best, loved by both readers and local couples. In addition to the stunning panoramic views, it makes a cool refuge in summer, well away from the main tourist trail. A range of meat dishes is joined by pastas and salads; if you can't afford them, try the smaller cafe opposite (sandwiches TL5 to TL8.50, open same hours) or come for a beer (TL6). It's about 2km from the town centre.

7/A
CAFE €

(☑465 0072; 1379 Sokak 7/A; mains TL8.50-16) This new cafe is winning plaudits from locals for its *zeytinyağlı tabağı* (olive-oil plate) and *ev mantısı* (house *mantı*), although some of the portions could be larger. At the beginning of a pedestrianised walkway, it has great people-watching potential.

Tuğba
CONFECTIONER €

(Gazi Osman Paşa Bulvarı 56, Çankaya; ☉8.30am-11pm) Power up for a visit to the bazaar with dried fruit, nuts, baklava and Turkish delight. There's an Alsancak branch at the southern end of Kıbrıs Şehitleri Caddesi.

%100
RESTAURANT, CAFE €€€

(☑441 5593; Konak Pier, Atatürk Caddesi; mains TL22) More casual than its neighbours at the tip of the shopping centre, %100 serves sushi, salads, pasta, steaks, kebaps, fish and good pizza. There are views up and down the coast, a long drinks menu including cocktails (TL20) and chilled beats in the background.

Mennan
PATISSERIE €

(899 Sokak 30; cornet TL3.50) This cafe in the bazaar is known for its excellent home-made ice cream.

Rıza Aksüt
PATISSERIE €

(863 Sokak 66; cake TL3; ✻) In the Baş Durak area of the bazaar, try the *peynir tatlısı* (sponge dessert made with cheese), preferably *kaymaklı* (with cream), at this dessert shop.

Drinking & Entertainment

The locals start their evening's entertainment with a stroll along the *kordon*, which is also good for a sundowner on the seafront. Things get steadily trendier and livelier the further north you go. The row of bars around Balık Pişiricisi Restaurant is particularly popular; Alinda Café Bar and neighbouring Café Melanie stage live music and beers cost about TL7. Alsancak plays host to the city's hottest nightlife, particularly in the clubs and bars on side streets such as Sokaks 1482 and 1452/Gazi Kadınlar.

Jackson's (see boxed text, p186) has a salsa night on Monday, and tango/milonga on Thursday.

Aksak Lounge
BAR

(1452 Sokak 10) In a typical İzmir mansion with high ceilings, balconies and a courtyard garden, Aksak attracts a cultured crowd to its jazz nights on Tuesday and Sunday.

Tyna
BAR

(Ali Çetinkaya Bulvarı 5; beer TL4) The outside tables are hot property at this pizzeria on a small square. Most just come for a beer; pizzas cost TL6. Across Ali Çetinkaya Bulvarı, Eko is also popular for a drink *en plein air*.

Kybele
CLUB

(Gazi Kadınlar Sokak; admission TL20; ☺Fri & Sat) Rock bands entertain the dancefloor in this small club occupying an old İzmir house with stone walls and ornate decor.

Cine Bonus
CINEMA

(www.cinebonus.com.tr, in Turkish; Konak Pier, Atatürk Caddesi; adult TL12.50) Five screens; films in English with Turkish subtitles.

Shopping

İzmir's shopping scene spans all sections of the market – from the bazaar, with its crowded intensity, its haggling and its old-world commercial exuberance, to the Konak Pier shopping centre, a bright, shiny, modern mall jutting out over the water and filled with big-name chains. The former offers atmosphere and plenty of (sometimes unwanted) human interaction, the latter air-conditioned sterility and hands-off deference – take your pick.

Dösim (Cumhuriyet Bulvarı 115) is geared towards tourists and its prices are a little high, but the quality is dependable and it stocks a wide range of items – from slippers to necklaces (from TL50).

The branch of **Remzi Kitabevi** (Konak Pier, Atatürk Caddesi) has a large selection of English-language books for both adults and children.

ⓘ Information

Banks, ATMS, internet cafes and wi-fi networks are found all over the centre.

İzmir Döviz (☑441 8882; Fevzi Paşa Bulvarı 75, Çankaya; ☺8am-7pm Mon-Sat) Money changer where no commission is charged.

Post office The main PTT is on Cumhuriyet Meydanı.

Tourist office (☑483 5117; 1344 Sokak 2) Inside the ornately stuccoed İl Kültür ve Turizm Müdürlüğü building just off Atatürk Caddesi. Has English-, German- and French-speaking staff.

Dangers & Annoyances

Like any big city, İzmir has its fair share of crime. However, the main tourist routes are fairly safe, with the notable exceptions of the Kadifekale

---

TRAVEL CARDS

İzmir has two travel cards, covering bus, metro and ferry, and available at stations, piers and shops with the Kent Kart sign:

» **Kent Kart** (City Card) You pay a TL5 deposit when you buy this and put credit on it. When you use the card TL1.55 is debited from it, then every journey you make for the next 90 minutes is free.

» **Üç-beş** (three-five) This card with three credits, each valid for a single journey, costs TL5.75.

THE EVIL ALL-SEEING EYE

However short your trip to Turkey, you can't fail to notice the famous 'evil eye' watching you wherever you go. This age-old superstition is still remarkably persistent throughout Turkey; the beads, pendants and other artefacts emblazoned with the eye are made as much for the local market as for tourists.

In a nutshell, certain people are thought to carry within them a malevolent force that can be transmitted to others via their eyes. Charms, resembling eyes, known as *nazar boncuk*, are used to reflect the evil look back to the originator.

The majority of the evil-eye production takes place in the Aegean region, and many shops in Kemeraltı Bazaar sell them.

neighbourhood and the area around Basmane train station, which is something of a red-light district – lone women should take special care. Do not enter Kemeraltı Bazaar after dark, and be alert to pickpockets and thieves there during the day.

Getting There & Away

Air

There are many flights to İzmir's **Adnan Menderes Airport** (455 0000; www.adnanmenderesairport.com) from European destinations; see also p684.

Turkish Airlines (484 1220; www.thy.com; Halit Ziya Bulvarı 65) offers direct flights from İstanbul (both airports), Adana, Ankara, Antalya, Diyarbakır, Erzurum, Gaziantep, Kayseri Kars, Malatya, Samsun, Sivas, Trabzon and European destinations. Other airlines serving İzmir include:

Atlasjet (www.atlastjet.com)

Izair (www.izair.com.tr)

Onur Air (www.onurair.com.tr)

Pegasus Airlines (www.flypgs.com)

Sun Express (www.sunexpress.com.tr)

Bus

İzmir's mammoth otogar lies 6.5km northeast of the city centre. For travel on Friday or Saturday to coastal towns to the north of İzmir, buy your ticket a day in advance; in the high season, two days in advance. Tickets can also be purchased from the bus companies' city-centre offices, mostly found at Dokuz Eylül Meydanı in Basmane.

Long-distance buses and their ticket offices are found on the lower level; regional buses (eg Selçuk, Bergama, Manisa, Sardis etc) and their ticket offices are on the upper level. City buses and dolmuşes leave from a courtyard in front of the lower level.

Short-distance buses (eg the Çeşme Peninsula) leave from a smaller local bus terminal in Üçkuyular, 6.5km southwest of Konak. They now pick up and drop off at the otogar as well.

Details of daily bus services to important destinations are listed in the table, p193.

Train

Most intercity services arrive at **Basmane Garı**, although **Alsancak Garı** is being vamped up and is set to receive more trains. For northern or eastern Turkey, change at Ankara.

ANKARA There are daily trains to/from Ankara (TL27, 15 hours), leaving in both directions at at 5.50pm and 7.45pm and travelling via Eskişehir (TL21, 11 hours).

BANDIRMA There are daily trains to/from Bandırma (TL17, six hours) at 2.20pm/4pm. Apart from on Tuesday, there are also services at 9.25am/9.50am, and these trains coordinate with the ferry to/from İstanbul.

MANİSA Every day but Tuesday, there are six trains to/from Manisa (TL3-7.50, 1¾ hours).

SELCUK Six daily trains travel to Selcuk, leaving between 8am and 7pm (TL4.75, 1½ hours).

Getting Around

To/From the Airport

The airport is 18km south of the city on the way to Ephesus and Kuşadası.

BUS On the hour every hour, buses 200 and 202 runs between both arrivals terminals and the Swissôtel (formerly Efes Otel) via Üçkuyular; 204 runs between both arrivals terminals and the otogar via Bornova metro. Both cost two credits (see boxed text, p191).

SHUTTLE Hourly Havaş buses (TL10, 30 minutes) leave from Gazi Osman Paşa Bulvarı near the Swissôtel between 3.30am and 11.30pm; and to the Swissôtel from domestic arrivals, leaving 25 minutes after flights arrive.

To/From the Bus Stations

If you've arrived at the main otogar on an intercity bus operated by one of the larger bus companies, a free *servis* shuttle is provided to the centre, normally Dokuz Eylül Meydanı. If you arrive on a local bus, you can catch a dolmuş (TL1.75, 25 minutes) that runs every 15 minutes between the otogar and both Konak and

Basmane Garı, or you can take buses 54 and 64 (every 20 minutes) to Konak or 505 to Bornova metro (every 30 minutes). Passes (see boxed text, p191) can be bought at the bus stop.

To get to the otogar, the easiest way is to buy a ticket on an intercity bus at Dokuz Eylül Meydanı and take the bus company's *servis*. However, if you're catching a local bus from the otogar (eg to Salihli), take the metro to Bornova then pick up bus 505.

To get to Üçkuyular bus station, catch bus 554 or 169 from the Konak bus terminal.

Boat

The most pleasant way to cross İzmir is by **ferry** (☺6.40am-11.40pm). Roughly half-hourly timetabled services, with more at the beginning and end of the working day, link the piers at Karşıyaka, Bayraklı, Alsancak, Pasaport, Konak and Göztepe. *Jetons* (transport tokens) cost TL3 each.

Bus

City buses lumber along the major thoroughfares, although bus stops are infrequent. Montrö Meydanı, by the Kültür Park, is a major terminal or transfer point. Routes 86 and 169 run down Şair Eşref Bulvarı then pass Montrö Meydanı, the bazaar and Agora (and serve the same route in reverse after terminating in Balçova, past Üçkuyular in southwest İzmir); 269 runs down Talatpaşa Bulvarı and Cumhuriyet Caddesi to Konak Meydanı. See the boxed text on p191 for information about passes.

Car

Large international car-hire franchises, including Budget, Europcar, Hertz, National Alamo and Avis, and smaller companies have 24-hour desks at the airport, and some have an office in town.

Green Car (☑446 9060; www.greenautorent. com; Mithatpaşa Caddesi 57) This local company is one of the largest in the Aegean region.

Metro

İzmir's **metro** (☺6.30am-11.30pm; jeton TL1.80) is clean and quick. There are currently 10 stations running from Üçyöl to Bornova via Konak, Çankaya and Basmane, although there are plans to expand the network.

Taxi

You can either hail a taxi or pick one up from a taxi stand or from outside one of the big hotels. Fares start at TL3.75 then cost TL0.30 per 100m. Make sure the meter is switched on.

Around İzmir

MANİSA

☑0236 / POP 282,000

Backed by mountains, the modern town of Manisa was once the ancient town of

SERVICES FROM İZMİR'S OTOGAR

DESTINATION	FARE (TL)	DURATION (HR)	DISTANCE (KM)	FREQUENCY (PER DAY)	VIA
Ankara	38	8	550	hourly	Afyon
Antalya	40	7	450	hourly	Aydın
Bergama	10	2	110	frequent	Menemen
Bodrum	25	3¼	286	every 30min in high season	Milas
Bursa	25	5	300	hourly	Balıkesir
Çanakkale	35	6	340	hourly	Ayvalık
Çeşme	12	1¾	116	frequent	Alaçatı
Denizli	21	3¼	250	hourly	Aydın
Foça	8	1½	86	frequent	Menemen
İstanbul	45	9	575	hourly	Bursa
Konya	30	8	575	every 2 hours	Afyon
Kuşadası	15	1¼	95	frequent	Selçuk
Manisa	8	1	45	frequent	Sarnıc
Marmaris	35	4	320	hourly	Aydın
Salihli	10	1½	90	frequent	Sardis
Selçuk	8	1	80	frequent	Belevi

Magnesia ad Sipylus. The early Ottoman sultans left Manisa many fine mosques, but retreating Greek soldiers wreaked terrible destruction during the War of Independence. The main reasons to visit are to inspect the mosques and the finds from Sardis in the museum, or to take in the Mesir Şenlikleri festival.

◉ Sights & Activities

Of Manisa's many old mosques, the **Muradiye Camii** (1585), the last work of the famous architect Mimar Sinan, has the most impressive tile work. The adjoining building, originally constructed as a soup kitchen, is now **Manisa Museum** (⌕231 3685; admission TL3; ☺9am-noon & 1-5pm Tue-Sun), which houses some fine mosaics from Sardis.

More or less facing the Muradiye, the **Sultan Camii** (1522) features some gaudy paintings. The **hamam** (⌕232 3347; admission TL15; ☺10am-9pm) next door has separate entrances for men and women. Above the town centre is the **Ulu Cami** (1366), ravaged by the ages and not as impressive as the view from its hillside perch.

✸ Festivals & Events

If you're able to visit during the four days around the spring equinox, you can catch the **Mesir Şenlikleri**, a festival in celebration of *mesir macunu* (power gum).

According to legend, over 450 years ago a local pharmacist named Müslihiddin Celebi Merkez Efendi concocted a potion to cure Hafza Sultan, mother of Sultan Süleyman the Magnificent, of a mysterious ailment. Delighted with her swift recovery, the queen mother paid for the amazing elixir to be distributed to the local people.

These days townsfolk in period costumes re-enact the mixing of the potion from sugar and 40 spices and other ingredients, then toss it from the dome of the Sultan Camii. Locals credit *mesir* with calming the nerves, stimulating the hormones and immunising against poisonous stings.

ⓘ Getting There & Around

It's easiest to get to Manisa by half-hourly bus from İzmir (TL8, 50 minutes, 30km), although trains also run (see p192). From Manisa, buses to Salihli pass Sardis (TL5, one hour). To get to Manisa's historic mosques, take a dolmuş from in front of the otogar to Ulu Parkı (TL1).

SARDİS (SART)

Sardis was once the capital of the wealthy Lydian kingdom that dominated much of the Aegean before the Persians arrived. Its ruins, 90km east of İzmir, make a particularly worthwhile excursion.

Sardis was near the Pactolus River, which carried specks of gold that the Lydians collected with fleece sieves. Croesus (595–546 BC) was a king of Lydia, and coinage seems to have been invented here; hence the phrase 'rich as Croesus'. Sardis became a great trading centre partly because its coinage facilitated commerce.

The then-Persian town was sacked during a revolt in 499 BC. After the Persians, Alexander the Great took the city in 334 BC and embellished it even more. An earthquake brought down its fine buildings in AD 17, but it was rebuilt by Tiberius and developed into a thriving Roman town. The end for Sardis came soon after Tamerlane visited in 1401 in his usual belligerent mood.

The ruins of Sardis are scattered around the village of Sartmustafa in a valley overshadowed by a craggy mountain range.

◉ Sights

Ruins of Sardis   RUINS
(admission TL3; ☺8am-5pm, to 7pm high season)
The most extensive ruins lie at the eastern end of the village, immediately north of the road. Information panels dot the site.

You enter the site along a **Roman road**, past a well-preserved **Byzantine latrine** and, backing onto a synagogue, rows of **Byzantine shops**, which belonged to Jewish merchants and artisans. Some of the buildings have been identified from inscriptions and include a restaurant, an office, a hardware store, and shops belonging to Sabbatios and Jacob, an elder of the synagogue.

Turn left from the Roman road to enter the **havra** (synagogue), impressive because of its size and beautiful decoration: fine geometric mosaic paving and coloured stone on the walls.

Beside the synagogue is the grassy expanse of what was once the hamam and gymnasium. This complex was probably built in the 2nd century AD and abandoned after a Sassanian invasion in 616.

Right at the end is a striking two-storey building called the **Marble Court of the Hall of the Imperial Cult**, which, though heavily (and unattractively) restored, gives an idea of the former grandeur of the building. Behind it you'll find an ancient **swimming pool** and rest area. Look out also for the Roman altar with two Roman eagles on either side and lions back-to-back.

Across the road from the enclosed site, continuing excavations have uncovered a stretch of the **Lydian city wall** and a **Roman house** with painted walls right on top of an earlier Lydian residence.

Temple of Artemis   RUINS
(admission TL3; ⊘8am-5pm) A sign points south down the road beside the tea houses to the Temple of Artemis, just over 1km away. Today, only a few columns of the once-magnificent but never-completed building still stand. Nevertheless, the temple's plan is clearly visible and very impressive. Next to it is an **altar** used since ancient times, refurbished by Alexander the Great and later by the Romans. Clinging to the southeastern corner of the temple is a small brick **Byzantine church**.

As you head back to İzmir, look to the north of the highway and you'll see a series of softly rounded **tumuli**, the burial mounds of the Lydian kings.

❶ Getting There & Away
Half-hourly buses to Salihli (TL10, 1½ hours, 90km) leave from İzmir otogar, and pass Sartmustafa. You can also catch dolmuşes to Sartmustafa (TL1, 15 minutes, 9km) from the back of Salihli otogar.

You should be able to hail a bus heading along the highway from Salihli to Manisa (TL5, one hour), making it possible to visit both Manisa and Sardis in the same day.

ÇEŞME PENINSULA

The Çeşme Peninsula is İzmir's summer playground, which means that it can get very busy with Turkish tourists at weekends and during the school holidays. The main places to visit are Çeşme itself, a family-oriented resort and transit point for getting to the Greek island of Chios; and Alaçatı, a much more upmarket affair whose central core of old Greek stone houses holds a multitude of boutique hotels and high-end restaurants. Alaçatı Surf Paradise (see boxed text, p201) and Pırlanta Beach are respectively windsurfing and kitesurfing hotspots.

Çeşme
☎0232 / POP 21,300
Çeşme, an unremarkable but pleasantly authentic port town and holiday resort, makes a reasonable base for a few days on the Peninsula – especially when travelling

to or from Chios, 8km away across the water. Inevitably, it's popular with weekending İzmiris and can get busy during the school holidays, when prices rise accordingly.

◉ Sights & Activities

FREE Çeşme Castle   FORTRESS
(Cumhuriyet Meydanı) The Genoese fortress, whose dramatic walls dominate the town centre, was built in 1508 and repaired by Sultan Beyazıt, son of Sultan Mehmet the Conqueror (Mehmet Fatih), to defend the coast from attack by pirates. Later, the Rhodes-based Knights of St John of Jerusalem also made use of it. The battlements offer excellent views of Çeşme, and it's good to walk around inside – under arches, up and down steps, and through towers with exhibits on subjects including the area's naval history.

Çeşme Museum   MUSEUM
(Çeşme Müzesi; admission TL3; ⊘9am-7pm Tue-Sun) Housed in the castle's Umur Bey tower, this museum displays archaeological finds from nearby Erythrae.

Statue of Cezayirli Gazi Hasan Paşa
                    MONUMENT
Facing İskele Meydanı, with its back to the fortress, is a statue of this great Ottoman admiral (1714–90), who was sold into slavery but became a grand vizier. He is shown accompanied by a lion; he famously brought one to Turkey from Africa.

Orthodox Church of Ayios Haralambos   CHURCH
(İnkılap Caddesi) North of the castle, this imposing but redundant 19th-century church is used for temporary exhibitions of arts and crafts during the summer months.

Beach   BEACH
At the far northern end of the waterfront esplanade is a small, sandy beach.

Boat Trips   CRUISE
From late May to September, gülets (traditional Turkish wooden yachts) offer one-day boat trips to nearby Black Island, Donkey Island and Wind Bay, where you can swim and snorkel. Browse the waterfront to compare prices and negotiate; they should cost around TL20 to TL30, including lunch. Boats usually leave around 10am and return around 5pm.

Hamam   HAMAM
(☎712 5386; Bağlar Çarşı Caddesi 11; wash & massage TL40; ⊘10am-11pm Jun-Sep) Past the

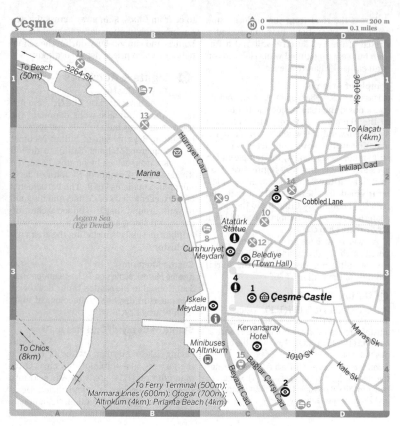

Kervansaray Hotel is a restored hamam from the 18th-century with a dome and marble interior. Bathing is mixed and peştamals (hamam bath towels) are used.

🛏 Sleeping

Barınak Pansiyon
PENSION €
(☎712 6670; 3052 Sokak 58; s/d TL30/50; ❄) Next to Sahil Pansiyon (which is traditionally a good choice, but was closed for renovations when we visited town), Barınak has spacious, spotless yellow rooms with good bathrooms and some funky *nazar boncuk* (see boxed text, p192) sheets. There is a little terrace for breakfast and the helpful proprietor, Suat, speaks some English.

Rıdvan Otel
HOTEL €€
(☎712 6336; www.ridvanotel.com; Cumhuriyet Meydanı 11; s/d TL60/100; ❄) Next to the seafront Ertan Otel, the Rıdvan's 36 rooms are slightly clinical, but their balconies over-

look the sea or the castle and main square. Photos of old İzmir abound, and there's a branch of Özüt (cafe) on the ground floor with seating on the square.

Hotel Doga Garden
RESORT €€€
(☎712 6839; www.cesmehoteldogagarden.com; 1005 Sokak 17; r TL150; ❄ ▨) This friendly little resort is often colonised by tour groups in the summer, but you might have its poolside bar-restaurant to yourself in the low season. The rooms are quite pleasant and it could be a reasonable option in the winter, when prices plummet (s/d TL40/60).

Alim Pansiyon
PENSION €
(☎712 6971; tamerakpinar@hotmail.com; 1021 Sokak 3; s/d TL30/60) South of the centre on the way to the ferry terminal, the Alim has basic rooms and the proprietors are fairly friendly. Breakfast costs an additional TL7.

Çeşme

✖ Eating

The most touristy restaurants are all along the waterfront and specialise mainly in fish and seafood – and have menus in various languages. For cheaper, more locally oriented places, head to İnkılap Caddesi.

Rumeli   PATISSERIE €
(İnkılap Caddesi; ⊗8am-8pm) Occupying an Ottoman stone house, this 65-year-old *pastane* (patisserie) sells great ice cream (TL1.50 per scoop) from its side window, and stocks all manner of local jams, pickles and preserves.

Pasifik Otel Restaurant   SEAFOOD €€
(☑712 1767; Tekke Plajı Mevkii 16; mains TL10-15; ⊗noon-midnight) If you fancy a walk and some fish, head to this hotel restaurant, at the far northern end of the seafront, where you can enjoy a great fish casserole on seating overlooking a small beach.

İmren Lokantası Restaurant RESTAURANT €€
(☑712 7620; İnkılap Caddesi 6; mains TL15; ⊗noon-9pm) Çeşme's first restaurant, opened back in 1960, is set in a bamboo-roofed atrium with a fountain and plants. It's famous locally for its traditional, high-quality Turkish food, including stews.

Patika Restaurant & Café-Bar RESTAURANT €€
(☑712 6357; Cumhuriyet Meydanı; mains TL12; ⊗3pm-midnight) Overlooking the square, with a cute, two-table balcony, Patika serves standard meat and fish dishes. Between 9pm and 4am daily, Turkish music is performed on the small stage. Alcohol is not served.

Star Restaurant   INTERNATIONAL €€
(☑712 9444; Ertürk Sokak 3; mains TL10-30) This Norwegian-Turkish-owned restaurant offers cosmopolitan surprises such as Hawaiian pizza and pasta carbonara alongside the gamut of steaks and *lahmacun* (Arabic-style pizza). The tables on the leafy cobbled square next to the church are perfect for whiling away an afternoon.

Ekol Restaurant   LOKANTA €€
(☑712 9077; Kutludağ Sokak 16; mains TL12-25) Recommended by locals, this popular lunch spot is good for a basic feed. The diverse menu offers casseroles and curry, steaks and stroganoff, although not all dishes are always available. Mezes include the recommended *patlican* (aubergine) and tomatoes, and the house speciality *kabak çiçeği dolması* (stuffed courgette flowers).

Rıhtım Restaurant   SEAFOOD €€
(☑712 7433; Balıkçı Barınağı Karşısı; mains TL11-30) One of the touristy fish restaurants on the waterfront, Rıhtım's fish fridge and wine rack are particularly well stocked. The large dining room, proudly displaying huge empty bottles of Metaxa (a Greek spirit), has more personality than the neighbouring places.

🍷 Drinking & Entertainment

Star Restaurant has cocktails on the menu and a disco-bar upstairs; head to Patika Restaurant & Café-Bar for live Turkish music.

No Problem Bar   EXPAT BAR
(☑712 9411; Çarşı Caddesi 14; beer TL5; ⊗9am-midnight; 🛜) Decorated with British souvenir towels, this expat hang-out offers tastes of Blighty such as a full English breakfast (TL10), pub quiz (8pm Monday) and book exchange.

❶ Information

The **tourist office** (☑/fax 712 6653; İskele Meydanı 4; ⊗8.30am-noon & 1-5.30pm Mon-Fri), ferry and bus ticket offices, banks with ATMs, restaurants and hotels are all within two blocks of Cumhuriyet Meydanı, the main square near the waterfront with the inevitable Atatürk statue.

Sahil Net (Hürriyet Caddesi; per hr TL2; ⊗9am-1am) Internet access.

ⓘ Getting There & Away

Bus

You have to transit İzmir to travel between Çeşme and most places (and transit Çeşme to get to other parts of the peninsula). Çeşme otogar is almost 1km south of Cumhuriyet Meydanı, although you can pick up dolmuşes in town.

İSTANBUL TL50, 11 hours; there are morning and evening services with Metro; in the summer other companies offer additional buses.

İZMİR Buses run every 15 minutes to İzmir's main otogar (TL12, 1¾ hours) and the city's smaller, western Üçkuyular terminal (TL10, 1½ hours, 85km).

ANKARA Same details as İstanbul.

Dolmuş

ILICA & ALAÇATI Dolmuşes (TL3.50) leave every five minutes in summer, half-hourly in winter, from the corner of İnkılap Caddesi and 2052 Sokak.

ALTINKUM Dolmuşes (TL3.50) leave half-hourly from Çeşme otogar, and pick up on the main street 20m south of the tourist office.

Ferry

As times (and destinations) change every year, check the websites listed below.

CHIOS Ferries sail to/from the nearby Greek island (one way/return €25/40, car €70/120, 1½ hours), once or twice a day between mid-May and mid-September. Outside that period, ferries sail to Chios on Friday and Saturday and return on Saturday and Sunday. Tickets can be bought direct from **Ertürk** (☑712 6768; www.erturk.com.tr; Beyazıt Caddesi 6; ⊗9am-7.30pm); you don't need to purchase your ticket in advance unless you have a car.

ANCONA Between May and September, ferries sail on Thurdays to Ancona, Italy (single €215 to €505, car €260, 60 hours), coming back on Saturdays. Tickets can be bought direct from **Marmara Lines** (☑712 2223; www.marmara lines.com; Turgut Özal Bulvarı 13D).

Taxi

ALAÇATI To Alaçatı centre costs about TL35.

Around Çeşme

PIRLANTA BEACH & ALTINKUM

Southwest of Çeşme, the aptly named **Pırlanta (Diamond) Beach** is good for kitesurfing (as well as windsurfing). Two companies rent equipment here; **Adrena-line Sports** (☑0541 803 9733; www.adrenaline sports.com.tr; ⊗May-Sep) also offers tuition.

Back on the main road from Çeşme, turn right to reach the increasingly built-up resort of **Altınkum**, which boasts a series of delightful sandy coves. There's a cafe with sunloungers on a clean beach with turquoise water right where the dolmuşes stop.

Half-hourly dolmuşes run from Çeşme to Altınkum (TL3.50) via Pırlanta Beach (TL2.50).

Alaçatı
☑0232

A few kilometres southeast of Çeşme lies Alaçatı, which, until 10 years ago, was a largely forgotten backwater of old, tumble-down Greek stone houses. In 2001, however, Zeynep Öziş turned one of these *taş* (stone) buildings into an upmarket boutique hotel. It was a huge success, soon spawning a host of imitators (now more than 100). Over the past few years Alaçatı has seen a restoration boom, with new holiday homes shooting up on its outskirts, and seemingly every house in its historic centre taken up by a hotel, a high-end restaurant or an art gallery. The centre is now more like Ibiza than an Aegean village in the summer; chill-out compilations are never far from earshot and flashy İstanbullus outnumber elderly locals.

If you're not claustrophobic, the hordes of well-heeled İstanbullus and İzmiris give the main street, Kemalpaşa Caddesi, a lively, buzzing feel during the summer. If you are, or if country calm seems more appealing than mingling with Turkey's trend-setters, the best times to visit are spring and autumn. It's a great place to wander, even if there are no sights as such, just a general feeling of contented well-to-do-ness.

🛏 Sleeping

Prices drop sharply out of season, although most hotels (and restaurants) open only from mid-May to mid-October and for Christmas and New Year. Reservations are essential in the high season. For more boutique hotels, visit www.charmingalacati.com.

TOP CHOICE **Alaçatı Taş Otel** BOUTIQUE HOTEL €€€ (☑716 7772; www.tasotel.com; Kemal-paşa Caddesi 132; s/d incl afternoon tea from €125/155; ❄❄) The acorn from which the mighty oak grew, the Taş, a former olive warehouse at the bottom of the main street, was Alaçatı's first boutique hotel. Under the dynamic owner, Zeynep, it's still setting the standard in its gorgeous rooms overlooking a walled garden and large swimming pool. The seven rooms have an elegant simplicity, with no TVs; the poolside afternoon teas are more lavish, featuring freshly baked cakes. Open year-round.

İncirliev   BOUTIQUE HOTEL €€€
(☑716 0353; www.incirliev.com; Mahmut Hoca Sokak 3; r incl afternoon tea from €130; ✳) This rebuilt 100-year-old Greek house is named after the fig tree in its garden – under which guests feast on the legendary breakfasts, featuring jams made by the charming Osman (with some help from the Aegean sun). The eight rooms, including one in the former stable and a white room with a French bed, artfully mix mod cons, rugs and antiques.

Değirmen Otel   BOUTIQUE HOTEL €€€
(☑716 6714; www.alacatidegirmen.com, in Turkish; Değirmen Sokak 3; s/d TL100/180; ✳) Taking fancy to a whole new level, the Mill Hotel occupies four converted windmills on a small hill near the main entrance to town. Rustic in feel but beautifully decorated, the eight circular rooms, some with circular beds or wooden spiral staircases, are arranged around a first-floor pool and terrace restaurant.

Sailors Hotel Meydan   BOUTIQUE HOTEL €€€
(☑716 8765; www.sailorsotel.com; Kemalpaşa Caddesi 66; r €120; ✳) One of four Sailors properties in Alaçatı, this hotel occupies an old Greek house on the main square, above a buzzing streetside cafe (see boxed text, p199) with a strong smell of good coffee. Rustic but refined, the blue-and-white rooms have closed balconies.

✕ Eating

There are few better places to eat in the whole north Aegean than Alaçatı, although you have to pay for the privilege. Of the dozens of restaurants that have opened in the past decade, the vast majority are gourmet affairs aimed at the smart set, with mains typically starting at around TL18. Many restaurants close for lunch, when everyone heads to the beach, and open only at weekends (if at all) in low season.

Six new restaurants will have opened at Alaçatı marina by the time this book is published, including a branch of Şifne's excellent fish restaurant, Ferdi Baba.

 Cafe Agrilia   GOURMET RESTAURANT €€€
(☑716 8594; Kemalpaşa Caddesi 75; mains TL18-41; ☻breakfast, dinner) A stalwart

---

TALAT ERBOY: OWNER OF ZEYTIN VS.

Talat Erboy is a member of the Alaçatı-Çeşme Slow Food convivium and owner of **Zeytin Vs.** (Olives Etc.; ☑716 0320; Kemalpaşa Caddesi 95), which sells 'ethnic Aegean' olive and olive-oil products, including soaps and body oils.

Local Food

Artichokes are very famous in this area and I love them with olive oil as a meze.

Hidden Spot

Hicimemiş is just five minutes' walk from the main square but it's very quiet and unspoilt, with preserved old stone houses and traditional Turkish cafes. Plenty of antique shops are opening there.

Favourite Activity

There's a good cycling route to Ovacık, where you can find lots of wineries.

Best Beach

If you drive to the end of the road past the windsurfers you get to Alaçatı Beach, a 1km-long sandy beach that's always calm. If the wind blows suddenly then I'll go to Ilıca Beach near the Sheraton.

Favourite Cafe

During the winter many of my friends meet at **Orta Kahve** (☑716 8765; www.sailorsotel.com; Kemalpaşa Caddesi 66; mains TL15) to drink tea and coffee and gossip when business is slow.

Long before Alaçatı became the boutique getaway so beloved of the İstanbul jet set, the town was a windsurfer's paradise. Its strong, consistent northerly winds – blowing at a steady 16 to 17 knots – make it a big hit with the surfing community. Alaçatı Surf Paradise is now generally recognised as one of the prime destinations outside Europe for windsurfing, on a par with the likes of Dahap in Egypt.

'The wind comes from the land to the sea, leading to few waves and flat water, which is easy for beginners and fun for pros – it's a sideshore wind,' explains Ali Palamutcu of Myga Surf City, one of the schools at Alaçatı Surf Paradise. 'You can touch the sea floor and walk, so it feels secure and comfortable to learn.'

Sadly, although Alaçatı might still be just another Aegean backwater if the surfers hadn't discovered it, the windsurfing beach has suffered in recent years. The construction of a marina cannibalised 1km of the beach, reducing it to 2km and leading to fears for the surfers' safety with boats motoring past. The road there is now lined with large new houses, which are part of the ongoing Port Alaçatı residential development.

The İzmir Association of Architects has tried three times to stop the Port Alaçatı development in the courts. It's a prominent example of worries over the prospects for Alaçatı as its tourist machine continues to hum. The town will not become the next Bodrum or Fethiye; the Ministry of Tourism has demarcated the whole peninsula as an upscale tourism destination, and houses with more than two storeys are banned in Alaçatı. However, with the Alaçatı Preservation Society and the Alaçatı Tourism Society both defunct, there are concerns that the quality of service offered to visitors may suffer if development continues unchecked. 'The genie is out of the bottle and we're trying to squeeze it back in,' says one hotelier.

The latest affront to the windsurfing community is the new footpath from town, which runs through the middle of Alaçatı Surf Paradise. It has angered some, but Ali Palamut-

that's 100% Alaçatı – both elegant and relaxing. From the melt-in-your-mouth, home-smoked beef starter to mains such as *granyoz* (a type of wild sea bass) on a bed of asparagus and cherry tomatoes, the food is unusual and delicious. Agrilia has moved, and now occupies a former olive-oil factory beyond the bottom of Kemalpaşa Caddesi, with a high ceiling and courtyard.

Su'dan Restaurant
RESTAURANT-BAR €€€

(☎716 7797; Mithat Paşa Caddesi 22; mains TL28-42; ◷9am-1pm & 7-11pm) This five-year-old restaurant-bar in Hicimemiş (see boxed text, p199) is a stylish temple to the culinary arts; the former gambling den is adorned with a red vintage fridge and basins of fruit and ice. The work of obsessive foodie Leyla, the menu includes stuffed courgette flowers with home-made salsa verde, chocolate mousse with wild mulberries, and apple and basil vodka. On the same street, Su'dan Palas (double from €125) occupies a 19th-century Greek building.

Kaptan'nın Yeri
SEAFOOD €€

(☎716 8030; Garaj İçi; fish TL15; ◷9am-midnight) One of the first eateries below the car park, the Captain's Place is one of the cheapest spots to eat good fish in Alacatı. In addition to fresh catches from the fish market such as calamari and sardines, the smoked aubergine meze is recommended.

Yusuf Usta Ev Yemekleri
LOKANTA €

(☎716 8823; Zeytinci İş Merkezi 1; mains TL8) With most of the town's restaurants specialising in contemporary cuisine, it's nice to go somewhere where the dishes (and prices) remain traditional. On the ring road near the main entrance to Alaçatı, its TL3 salad bar and *bain marie* with meat and vegetable mains are popular at lunchtime.

Rasim
MODERN TURKISH €€

(☎716 8420; Kemalpaşa Caddesi 54; mains TL15-30; ◷11am-11pm) Just above the main square, this decades-old restaurant serves hearty Turkish fare such as köfte and fish soup – both recommended.

Café Eftalya
CAFE €

(Cami Arkası Sakarya 3; gözleme TL6) In the line of cafes next to the mosque, Eftalya's gözleme, packed with cheese and greens, is a hearty breakfast choice. Home-made lemonade, meat-filled çiğ börek and mantı are also available.

201

cu displays the upbeat attitude you would expect of a windsurfer, saying the path will increase the centre's circulation of customers. 'It's becoming an ironic bay, with some people living a very expensive lifestyle and other people just coming for the windsurfing – but everyone I see is very positive, rich or not.'

For now, windsurfing continues largely unhindered, with the main season running from mid-May to the beginning of November (many operators close outside that time). The Windsurf World Cup takes place here in August. With seven schools at Alaçatı Surf Paradise (and one across the bay), more than 5000 people start windsurfing here every year.

ASPC and Myga are the largest operators. English-speaking instructors are normally available at the following centres, as are kitesurf boards. Hiring boards for longer periods lowers daily rates.

ASPC (Alaçatı Surf Paradise Club; 716 6611; www.alacati.info) This Turkish-German operation offers good courses and high-quality equipment, charging €40 to €65 for a package (board, wetsuit, harness and shoes) for one day. Booking ahead lowers the daily rates. JP/Neil Pryde, Tabou/Gaastra and, for beginners, Tabou Coolrider/Gaastra Freetime boards are available. A starter course consisting of five hours (10 hours for three students or more) across three days costs €180.

Myga Surf Company (716 6468; www.myga.com.tr) Myga has a range of equipment, charging €45 to €75 for a package for one day. It also hires out paddle boards. A five-hour starter course (7½ hours for two students, 10 hours for three or more), which can be spread across a few days, costs €185.

Active Alaçatı Windsurf Centre (716 6383; www.active-surf.com) Recommended by readers, Active charges €40 to €50 for a package for one day. A starter course offering a similar amount of instruction to those above costs €204.

Ciğerci Hasan STREET FOOD €
(Mektep Caddesi; köfte TL4-8) Downhill from Âlâ, this *ciğerci* (liver *köfte* salesman) sells the goods, seasoned with fresh thyme and served with cumin, onions and tomatoes.

Drinking & Entertainment

At central bars such as 15 Eylül, Efes is not available and bottles of imported beer costing over TL10 are offered instead. Cafe Agrilia hosts a tango night on Saturday. In summer, the İstanbul mega-club Babylon (www.babylon.com.tr) organises regular beach parties.

Gizem Café BAR-CAFE
(Cumhuriyet Meydanı; beer TL6) Although its prices follow the Alaçatı trend and shoot up at the height of summer, 'Mystery Café' is one of the best-value places for a drink.

Âlâ BAR-RESTAURANT
(Mektep Caddesi; beer TL8) With tables on the thoroughfare leading from Kemalpaşa Caddesi to the mosque, this new bar-restaurant occupies a former bakery.

Getting There & Around

BICYCLE ASPC (see boxed text, p201) rents out mountain bikes (one day/week from €10/60).

BUS Metro has an office by the car park, selling tickets to nationwide destinations (normally via İzmir).

CAR You can rent cars from **Işıltı** (716 8514; Uğur Mumcu Caddesi 16; one day TL70).

DOLMUŞ Frequent dolmuşes run to/from Çeşme (TL3.50, 10 minutes, 9km) and İzmir (TL12, one hour, 75km). Between mid-May and November, dolmuşes run to/from Alaçatı Surf Paradise (TL2), which is 4km south of town on the western side of the *liman* (harbour).

Sığacık

0232

More remote and much less spoilt than many coastal towns, Sığacık is a pretty port village, clustered around a crumbling 16th-century castle. With no beach, there's not much to do here except stroll the picturesque waterfront, take a boat trip and watch the fishermen returning with their catch. Tranquil and peaceful, it's only marred by a new marina and two nearby resorts.

Sığacık is also famous for its fish, particularly *kalamar* and *barbun* (red mullet). If you haven't yet indulged in Turkey's wonderful fresh fish, now might be the time.

İZMİR & THE NORTH AEGEAN SIĞACIK

🛏 Sleeping & Eating

To find Sığacık's pensions, head towards the harbour then follow the waterfront promenade to the right beside the city walls.

With a nice family feel and spacious, attractive rooms, **Teos Pansiyon** (📞745 7463; www.teospension.com; 126 Sokak 14; d TL100; 🏶) is good value. Sofas, sea views and big white beds all feature. You can buy fresh fish from the market and ask the obliging family to cook it for you.

Around 60m beyond the Teos at the far end of the bay, the basic rooms at **Sahil Pansiyon** (📞745 7199; 127 Sokak 48; s/d TL25/40) are only let down by their aged bathrooms; breakfast costs an extra TL7.50.

One of the touristy restaurants on the harbour, the **Liman** (📞745 7011; Liman Meydanı 19; mains TL15) doesn't disappoint with its fresh fish and seafront views.

For cheaper eats and a genuine welcome, cut inland to the French-Turkish **Tekne Restaurant** (📞745 7421; Şadırvaniçi; pide TL5; ⏱8.30am-midnight), with tables in a delightful old courtyard behind Burg Pansiyon.

ℹ Getting There & Away

ÇEŞME You have to travel via İzmir.

İZMİR Take a bus or dolmuş to Seferihisar from İzmir's Üçkuyular otogar (p192; TL4.50, 50 minutes, every 30 minutes). From Seferihisar, half-hourly dolmuşes run to Sığacık (TL1.50, 10 minutes, 5km).

Akkum & Teos

📞0232

Two kilometres over the hill from Sığacık is **Akkum**. A protected cove, it used to attract windsurfers in their thousands in summer but has been eclipsed by Alaçatı (see boxed text, p201). Today, it's quieter and cheaper than Alaçatı and has larger waves.

Of its two smooth, sandy beaches, Büyük Akkum has the better facilities – windsurfing, sea kayaking and diving equipment and instruction are available – but Küçük Akkum is likely to be quieter.

Before Akkum, turn left to reach the scattered **ruins** at Teos, 5km from Sığacık: primarily a few picturesque fluted columns, left over from a temple to Dionysus and re-erected amid grass and olive groves. Teos was once a vast Ionian city, and you can roam the fields in search of other remnants (including a theatre used for Dionysian festivals). It's a good place to come for a picnic.

🛏 Sleeping & Eating

There are pensions just after the Teos turn-off and camp sites further on, although we recommend staying in Sığacık instead.

On the road to the ruins, 1km from the turn-off, is **Teos Park**, a forestry department picnic grove. Here you can buy snacks and cold drinks to enjoy beneath shady pine trees overlooking the sea.

Above Küçük Akkum, **Yakamoz** (📞745 7599; 3216 Sokak 8; mains TL18) has a great terrace, serving seafood and Turkish classics as well as international dishes such as English breakfasts and fajitas.

ℹ Getting There & Away

BICYCLE Bikes are generally available at Sığacık's pensions.

DOLMUŞ In summer, frequent dolmuşes run to Teos from Seferihisar (TL2, 20 minutes) via Sığacık and Akkum.

TAXI A taxi from Sığacık to Akkum costs about TL6; a return trip to Teos (including waiting time) costs about TL20.

Ephesus, Bodrum & the South Aegean

Best Places to Stay

» Kempinski Barbaros Bay (p251)

» Maçakızı (p248)

» Casa Dell'Arte (p250)

» Su Otel (p239)

Best Places to Eat

» Bağarası (p244)

» Fish Market (p241)

» Selçuk Köftecisi (p216)

» Kaplan Dağ Restorant (p219)

Why Go?

There's a mighty good reason why humans have been fighting over the lands along the south Aegean for 4000 years – it's one of the hemisphere's most serenely scenic strips of grove-studded coastline (oh, and it has its strategic marine advantages too). Travellers got wise to the region's virtues several decades ago, and now the breezy Bodrum Peninsula is a veritable vacation magnet that lures crowds of jetsetters hoping to score a slice of paradise. Although development has been rapid here, its embrace is by no means complete.

Long before holiday homes dotted the landscape, the south Aegean featured an impressive constellation of ancient cities and temples; homages to mythic gods and goddesses. So rich is the region's archaeological record that modern structures are matched one-for-one by stunning reminders of a bygone era.

Ultimately, the blend of classical remains and turquoise beachscapes has proven to be quite the winning combination; this is one of Turkey's most visited regions.

When to Go

Selçuk

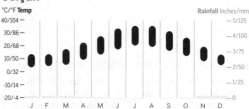

May & June Sun and cool breezes make it the perfect time to swing by.

July & August Join the all-night party in Bodrum or the cruise crowds at Ephesus.

September & October See the region's ruins sans oppressive heat.

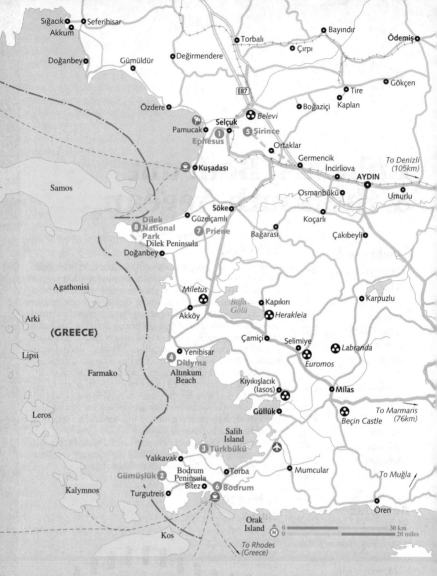

Ephesus, Bodrum & the South Aegean Highlights

1 See how the Romans lived at **Ephesus** (p205), the Med's best-preserved ruins

2 Savour fresh seafood and a chilled-out hipster vibe in **Gümüşlük** (p245)

3 Strap on your heels and oversized sunglasses for posh **Türkbükü** (p248)

4 Stare sky-high at the soaring temple ruins of stunning **Didyma** (p229)

5 Sip fruit wine in the hillside village of **Şirince** (p218), set amid orchards

6 Dine stylishly and dance wildly in party town, **Bodrum** (p234)

7 Roam the remarkable but less-visited ruins of **Priene** (p226), where ivory-white columns hide among trembling tree trunks

8 Snap your camera on windswept capes then swim in the crystal coves of **Dilek National Park** (p226)

History

The Mycenaean and Hittite civilisations were the earliest recorded along the south Aegean. From 1200 BC, Ionians fleeing Greece established themselves in the area along the coast and founded important cities at Ephesus, Priene and Miletus. South of Ionia was mountainous Caria where the great King Mausolus' tomb, the Mausoleum of Halicarnassus, became one of the Seven Wonders of the Ancient World. Caria was also home to Herodotus, the 'Father of History'. Roman Ephesus prospered with rich trade and commerce, becoming the capital of Asia Minor. The city also attracted a sizeable Christian population. St John settled here with the Virgin Mary, where he is said to have written his gospel. In the 15th century the Knights of St John briefly captured the area now called Bodrum, before the Ottoman forces took over.

Ephesus (Efes)

The best-preserved classical city in the eastern Mediterranean, if not all of Europe, Ephesus (☎892 6010; admission/parking TL20/3; ⌚8am-6.30pm May-Oct, 8am-4.30pm Nov-Apr) is *the* place to get a feel for what life was like in Greco-Roman times. In its heyday, Ephesus was the grand capital of the Roman province of Asia and boasted over 250,000 inhabitants. A fertility avatar of the goddess Artemis was heavily worshipped here, and fervent devotees constructed a temple in her honour – the biggest on earth, in fact, which later become of one of the Seven Wonders of the Ancient World. Today, 18% of the former city has been unearthed for the public after almost 150 years of excavations.

History
EARLY LEGEND

According to legend, Androclus from Ionia was constantly under attack by Dorian invaders from the north. He decided to find a new location to protect his people in a far-off land. So, he packed up his things and visited the oracle of Delphi in order to figure out where to found his new settlement. The oracle told him rather cryptically (as usual) that he would found his new town thanks to three elements: 'the fish, the fire and the boar'.

Androclus left present-day Greece, set out on the Aegean Sea and landed on the west coast of Asia Minor (present-day Tur-

key). After a long journey the famished Androclus and his crew rested on the shore and cooked a freshly caught fish. The fish was so incredibly fresh that it jumped out of the pan, toppled over the coals and set the nearby forest on fire. A boar, hidden behind some bushes, got frightened and bolted across the beach while trying to make a swift escape. Androclus chased the boar through the brush, and in the exact place that he killed the creature (near the current location of the ruins of the Temple of Artemis) he founded the city of Ephesus.

ARTEMIS

Androclus and his Ionian followers arrived in Asia Minor in the 10th century BC, but they were not the first people to settle the land. Several centuries earlier the Leleggians chose the coastal region as their home. At the centre of the Leleggians' religious practices was the mother and fertility goddess Cybele. When the Ionians arrived, they peacefully integrated with the local tribes and incorporated the Leleggians' cult beliefs into their own, and the Artemis of Ephesus emerged – a unique Artemis that symbolised fertility rather than the hunt. The devotees of Artemis constructed a temple in her honour, which, because of its great beauty and size, would eventually inspire one of the Seven Wonders of the Ancient World.

CROESUS & THE PERSIANS

By 600 BC, the Temple of Artemis and Ephesus' bustling port were attracting huge sums of money from merchants and religious devotees. This quickly aroused the envy of King Croesus of Lydia, who promptly attacked the city. The Ephesians, who had neglected to build defensive walls, stretched a rope from the Temple of Artemis to the town, a distance of 1200m, hoping to win the goddess' protection. Croesus responded to this quaint defensive measure by giving some of his famous wealth for the completion of the temple. But he destroyed Ephesus and relocated its citizens inland to the southern side of the temple, where they built a new city.

Neglecting (or perhaps forbidden) to build walls, the Ephesians were forced to pay tribute to Croesus' Lydia and, later, to the new regional masters, the Persians. They later joined the Athenian confederacy, but eventually fell back under Persian control.

In 356 BC the Temple of Artemis was destroyed in a fire set by Herostratus, who

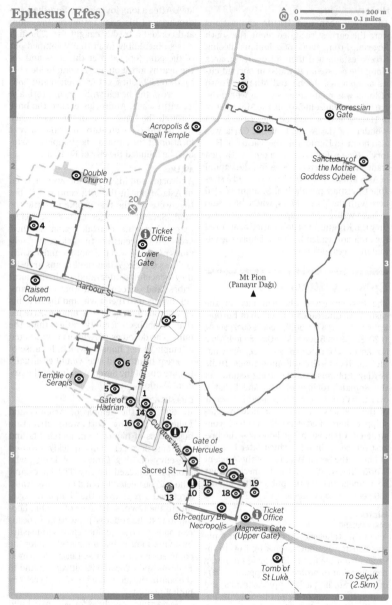

claimed to have done it to get famous, proving that modern society has no monopoly on a perverted sense of celebrity.

The Ephesians planned a grand new temple, the construction of which was well under way when Alexander the Great arrived in 334 BC. Much impressed, Alexander offered to pay for the cost of construction in return for having the temple dedicated to himself. The Ephesians declined his offer, saying tactfully that it was not fitting for one god to make a dedication to another.

Ephesus (Efes)

When finished, the temple was recognised as one of the Seven Wonders of the Ancient World.

LYSIMACHUS & THE ROMANS

After Alexander the Great's death, Ionia came under the control of Lysimachus, one of his generals. When the harbour started to fill with silt, Lysimchus forced the Ephesians to move and built what we now see as Ephesus, in the strategic position between the two hills.

Little survives of Lysimachus' city, although at one time it had a defensive wall almost 10km long. A prominent square tower, nicknamed 'St Paul's Prison', also survives on a low hill to the west (which is commonly believed to be a crude lighthouse).

Roman Ephesus was the capital of Asia Minor and its population rapidly grew to around 250,000. (Side note for comparison: the current population of Kuşadası is a wimpy 30,000.) Successive emperors vied with one another to beautify the city and it drew immigrants from all around the empire. Despite the fame of the cult of Diana, Ephesus soon acquired a sizeable Christian congregation. St John supposedly settled here with the Virgin Mary, and St Paul lived in the city for three years (probably in the AD 60s).

THE END

Despite efforts by Attalus II of Pergamum, who rebuilt the harbour, and Nero's proconsul, who dredged it, the harbour continued to silt up. Emperor Hadrian tried diverting the Cayster, but eventually the sea was forced back to Pamucak. Malarial swamps began to form, the port quickly lost its viability, and the influx of Christians meant a swift drop in funds generated by tributes to Diana. Ephesus was on the decline, and by the 6th century, when the Emperor Justinian was looking for a site to build a basilica for St John, he chose Ayasuluk Hill in Selçuk instead.

☉ Sights

The best way to navigate a path through Ephesus is to start at the Magnesia Gate in Upper Ephesus and work your way downhill along the Curetes Way, through the Library of Celsus, past the lower agora and out along the Harbour St. You'll find the best photo ops in the morning when the sun is behind you.

Upper Ephesus   RUINS

Like any city in the ancient world, the first structure to welcome visitors was always a bathhouse; in Ephesus' case it was known as the **Varius Baths**. Baths were placed at all of a city's main entrances, as it was customary to wash oneself clean of any harmful agents acquired during the arduous journey. But baths were also a social place, like a hamam, where friends and new acquaintances would hang out, scrub themselves clean and even get massages.

Fresh as a daisy? Good. Now it's time to move into the city's legislative district, which was anchored by a large square known as the **Upper Agora**. It was here that politicos would get together to share the latest news and spread gossip – kinda like an ancient version of Twitter. Although it may be hard to imagine now, the entire agora was once filled with polished marble, and there was the small **Temple of Isis** in the middle. Grand columns used to flank the legislative agora, but they were struck down and 'recycled' into other structures by marauding Christians several centuries later. Notice the archways in the distance – these were storage houses where locals preserved their food.

Walking towards the theatre, eagle eyes will spot bits of terracotta piping once used to funnel water throughout the city. The 5000-seat theatre up ahead was known as the **Odeon** and was primarily used for municipal meetings. Marble seats and carved ornamentation suggest that the theatre was quite magnificent in its time.

Further on, two of the six original Doric columns mark the entrance to the very ruined remains of the **Prytaneum** (town hall) and city treasury. A giant statue of Artemis once stood here in all of her fertile glory: fused legs, huge breast and welcoming arms extending out from her body. Her hands have been missing for centuries – scholars believe that they were crafted out of gold. The Prytaneum was also home to the **Temple of Hestia Boulaea**, where the 'life of the city', or eternal flame, was guarded and tended to by vestal virgins.

A side street known as the **Sacred Street** led to the city's **Asclepion**, or hospital. Doctors were considered missionaries of the god Asclepius and his daughter Hygieia. Asclepius' symbol was the snake (hence the plethora of 'pharmacy' symbols etched into the stone) because it could shed its skin and renew itself. Also, it was known early on that snake venom had curative powers. In ancient times, hospitals were more than just a place where physical ailments were cured. It is believed that Greek and Roman medicine approached health in a holistic fashion – the brain and body were closely connected.

Nearby is the ruined **Temple of Domitian**, named after Domitian (r AD 81–96), who was known as quite a cruel ruler. He expelled St John to Patmos and executed his own nephew for taking an interest in Christianity. A temple in his honour was ordered at his request, and after his death it was promptly demolished.

The **Pollio Fountain** and **Memius Monument** only begin to hint at the lavish fountains that covered the ancient capital. The sound of trickling water was believed to have curative powers ('expendable' water was also a sign of great wealth).

Curetes Way
RUINS

Named for the semi-gods who helped Lena give birth to Artemis and Apollo, the **Curetes Way** was the Champs Élysées of Ephesus, with rows of popular shops selling incense and silk, and pedestals displaying statues of honoured citizens (usually doctors). Be sure to pause at the top of the street before walking down – this vantage

point clearly illustrates how much excavation has been done, and how much there is left to go (the entire Curetes Way was once buried under six-metre mounds of earth). Now is a good time to imagine the throngs of surrounding tourists in white togas and leather sandals that clicked on the marble floors as they walked by.

The **Trajan Fountain**, halfway down the boulevard, was erected to honour the eponymous emperor during a royal visit. The statue of Trajan himself was three times the size of the actual man, and water would flow underneath spilling out onto the main street to clean it. The inscription on the fountain reads: 'I have conquered it all, and it's now under my foot' (the round sphere under the ruined giant foot is meant to represent the earth, which proves that Romans knew the world was round!)

After the fountain are the famous **men's latrines** and **brothel** just beyond (often daintily dubbed the 'love house'). The latrines were another sociable spot in the city – even if you had a private bathroom at home you would often come to the public toilets to shoot the shit with your friends (sorry, we had to say it). Many of the wealthy elite had a membership to the latrines, and would mark their seat of choice (notice the graffiti-ed 'P' – no pun intended). Eavesdrop on a guided tour to find out the logistics of ancient bum washing...

The brothel was a windowless structure where working prostitutes would earn their keep. Unsurprisingly, the brothel is quite close to the port, making it easily accessible to hungry sailors after spending months at sea. Prostitution was considered to be quite a normal profession; in fact many historians are surprised that the structure is so small considering the size of the city. Oh, and contrary to popular belief, there was no 'love tunnel' connecting the library and the whorehouse.

You can't miss the impressive Corinthian-style **Temple of Hadrian**, Ephesus' second-most famous attraction after the library. However, unlike the library, the temple is known for its intricate decorative details, not its sheer size. Every inch was coated in some sort of pattern – the temple's first arch features Tyche, the goddess of chance, and Medusa and her trademark snake-hair ward off evil spirits on the second arch. After passing the first arch, look up and into the temple's left corner. There's a relief of a man on a horse chasing a boar, which represents the mythic founding of the city. At shoulder-height you'll spot backwards swastikas representing the Meander River (which brought great amounts of silt into the harbour, ending Ephesus' life).

Terraced Houses
RUINS

(Yamaç Evleri; admission TL15) Across from the Temple of Hadrian is the entrance to the magnificent Terraced Houses. It's a crying shame that the off-putting admission fee will deter many people from visiting, because we *highly* encourage you spend your time and dime to check it out. A walk through the covered complex will offer visitors a chance to appreciate the luxury in which the elite of the Roman world lived. Seven homes are currently on display, and the first – measuring over 900 square metres – is the largest. All of the homes had running water (hot and cold!), not to mention lavish mosaics and frescoes adorning almost every flat surface. At the time of research, twenty-two types of marble had been found from all over the former Roman Empire. Before exiting, take a good look at one of the doorframes to get an idea of how short humans used to be.

Library of Celsus
RUINS

Celsus Polemaeanus was the Roman governor of Asia Minor early in the 2nd century AD. According to an inscription in Latin and Greek on the side of the front staircase, his son, Consul Tiberius Julius Aquila, erected this library in his father's honour after the governor's death in 114. Celsus was buried under the western side of the library.

The library held 12,000 scrolls in niches around its walls, making it the third-largest library in the ancient world after Alexandria and Pergamum. A 1m gap between the inner and outer walls protected the valuable books from extremes of temperature and humidity. The library was originally built as part of a complex, and architectural sleight of hand was used to make it look bigger than it actually is: the base of the facade is convex, adding height to the central elements; and the central columns and capitals are larger than those at the ends.

Niches on the facade hold statues representing the Virtues: Arete (Goodness), Ennoia (Thought), Episteme (Knowledge) and Sophia (Wisdom). The library was restored with the aid of the Austrian Archaeological Institute and the originals of the statues are in Vienna's Ephesus Museum.

Marble Street
RUINS

The city's third main street, the Marble Street, carved a wide artery from the library to the theatre, though at the time of research this road was closed to visitors due to continuing excavations. Instead, tourists must walk through the city's **Lower Agora** – a 110-sq-metre space that once had a massive colonnade and functioned as a textile and food market.

After exiting the agora you'll reach the **Great Theatre**, reconstructed by the Romans between AD 41 and AD 117. The first theatre on the site dated from the Hellenistic city of Lysimachus, and many features of the original building were incorporated into the Roman design, including the ingenious shape of the *cavea* (seating area), capable of holding 25,000 people: each successive range of seating up from the stage is pitched more steeply than the one below, thereby improving the view and acoustics for spectators in the upper seats.

Archaeologists often glean a rough estimate of a city's size by multiplying its theatre's capacity by ten; thus, Ephesus is believed to have been a capital with roughly 250,000 inhabitants.

Harbour Street
RUINS

Ephesus' fourth and final grand boulevard, Harbour Street, also known as Arcadia, was once the grandest street in Ephesus, a legacy of the Byzantine emperor, Arcadius (r AD 395–408). In its heyday, water and sewerage channels ran beneath the marble flagstones and 50 streetlights lit up its colonnades. For many, this vast marble avenue was their first vision of the lavish capital after getting cleaned up at the **Harbour Baths**. Today, an extra-high column marks what would have been the water's edge at the end of the arcade.

After exiting the Lower Gate, you'll see the remains of the **Gymnasium of Vedius** (2nd century AD) on your way back to the main road. The vast gymnasium once had exercise fields, baths, toilets, covered exercise rooms, a swimming pool and a ceremonial hall. A bit further along is the **Stadium**, dating from the same period. The Byzantines removed most of its finely cut stones to build the castle on Ayasuluk Hill.

Information

While guesthouses in Selçuk will lend you books to guide you through Ephesus, and mediocre **audio guides** (TL10) are available in a multitude

EPHESUS FROM THE AIR

If you fancy getting an elevated perspective on the famous ruins, Sky and Sea Adventures (☎892 2262; www.skyltd.com.tr; flights from €50) offer trips in a two-seater microlight out of Selçuk Airport, just east of Ephesus. Your journey will take you up above Selçuk, taking in all of Ephesus' principal sights, before heading out to the coast for a sky-high gawp at the more modern attractions of Kuşadası.

of languages, we highly recommend hiring a guide to show you around. A good guide can really bring the ruined city to life as (s)he reveals some of the fascinating intricacies of ancient times that will undoubtedly remain hidden if you visit on your own. Ask around before visiting – it's best to book ahead as the good guides get snatched up first. Small group tours can be a more affordable option for budgetarians – make sure to sniff out a few tour options before deciding on the itinerary that suits your interests best. We do not recommend hiring one of the 'guides' loitering around the site entrances.

Allow around 1½ to two hours to do Ephesus justice, and tack on an extra 45 minutes to see the incredible Terraced Houses (which cost an additional TL15 per person). It's best visited early in the day or late in the afternoon to avoid the harsh midday heat, as the sun reflects off the marble and stones. Consider bringing water with you and don't forget to use the restrooms before entering; there are no facilities within the site.

In the height of summer Ephesus can be a very crowded place, with busloads of visitors pouring in. But, in a way, all those people do at least make it easier for you to visualise it as a proper, working metropolis.

ⓘ Getting There & Away

If you plan on spending the night near Ephesus, you have the choice between landlocked Selçuk just a few kilometres up the road, or sea-facing Kuşadası just a bit further on. But don't bother searching for complimentary lifts to Ephesus from your hotel – local law explicitly forbids this. Instead you'll have to take a taxi, private vehicle or join up with an organised tour.

Ephesus has two entry points, located roughly 3km apart. If you're getting dropped off, ask to be let off at the upper entrance (the Magnesia Gate) so that you can walk downhill to the other entry/exit. We don't recommend walking to

Ephesus from Selçuk – while the first 20 minutes are easy enough, the last part is an uphill climb along an unshaded stretch of highway.

Frequent Pamucak and Kuşadası minibuses pass the Ephesus turn-off (TL4, five minutes, 3km), leaving you with a 20-minute walk to the ticket office at the Lower Gate. A taxi from Selçuk should cost about TL15.

Around Ephesus

If you've joined up with a tour group to visit Ephesus, chances are high that you'll also be taken to one or both of the following places, which orbit the impressive ruins only a couple kilometres away.

◉ Sights

Meryemana (Mary's House)

HISTORIC BUILDING

(☎894 1012; admission per person/car TL12.50/5; ◷8am-7pm May-Oct, to 4.30pm Nov-Apr) Believers say that the Virgin Mary came to Ephesus with St John towards the end of her life (AD 37–45). In the 19th century, nun Catherina Emmerich of Germany had visions of Mary at Ephesus, although she had never visited the place herself. Using her descriptions, clergy from İzmir discovered the foundations of an old house on the wooded slope of Bülbül Dağı (Mt Coressos), not far from Ephesus. The ruins have been dated to around the 6th century AD, albeit with some earlier elements, possibly from the 1st century. Pope Paul VI unofficially authenticated the site during a visit in 1967 and it quickly became a place of pilgrimage.

The tiny chapel is usually mobbed by coach parties. Note the pale red line on the side of the chapel after you exit – everything under the line is part of the original foundation. There are information panels in various languages, but if you are interested in why over a million people visit here each year, we recommend *Mary's House* by Donald Carroll, which traces the extraordinary history of the site over 2000 years. A small shop also sells brochures and booklets (€3).

To Muslims, Mary is Meryemana, Mother Mary, who bore İsa Peygamber, the Prophet Jesus. Below the chapel, a 'wishing wall' is covered in rags: visitors tie bits of cloth (or paper, plastic and cruise-ship stickers – in fact anything at hand) to a frame and make a wish.

Mass is held at 7.15am Monday to Saturday (evening service at 6.30pm), and at

10.30am on Sunday. A special service to honour Mary's Assumption is held in the chapel every 15 August. Note that 'appropriate dress' is required to enter.

If you want refreshments, head for **Café Turca** (Meryemana Evi; mains TL4-10 ☺breakfast, lunch & dinner) at the entrance. Otherwise, the site is a great spot for a picnic – it's cool, verdant and full of birdsong.

The site lies 8.5km from Ephesus' Lower (northern) Gate and 7km from the Upper (southern) Gate. There's no dolmuş service so you'll have to hire a taxi – around TL50 return from the otogar (bus station). Prices are negotiable, or take a tour.

FREE **Grotto of the Seven Sleepers** RUINS
If you're heading from Meryemana to Ephesus you'll pass the road leading to the Grotto of the Seven Sleepers. According to legend, seven persecuted Christians fled Ephesus in the 3rd century AD and took refuge in a cave on the northeastern side of Mt Pion. Agents of their persecutor, Emperor Decius, found the cave and sealed it. Two centuries later an earthquake brought down the wall, awakening the sleepers who proceeded to amble into town for a meal. Finding all their old friends long dead, they concluded that they had undergone some sort of resurrection. When they died they were buried in the cave and a cult following developed.

The grotto is actually a Byzantine-era necropolis with scores of tombs cut into the rock. It lies around 200m from the car park (1.5km from Ephesus); follow the well-trodden path up the hill.

It's not worth a special trip, as there's not a great deal to see, but the shady, kilim-covered shacks serving *ayran* (yoghurt drink) and *gözleme* (savoury pancake) nearby make a good spot for a bit of R&R after sweaty Ephesus.

Selçuk
☑0232 / POP 27,280

As the gateway to Ephesus and the keeper of one of the Seven Wonders of the Ancient World, Selçuk comes as a surprise to most tourists. This quiet town is set along a snaking stack of stout foothills and acts more as a weighstation for the throngs of passers-through rather than a vibrant tourist hub. That said, it's still a pleasant place to base oneself for a few days of sightseeing – evenings are atmospheric as locals mill about amongst the backlit minarets and soaring

aqueduct ruins. There's a vast collection of pensions here, and they cater mostly to independent travellers on budgets.

◉ Sights

If your itinerary allows it, try to split up Selçuk's sights over a couple of days, as the swarms of daytrippers (especially in summer) can be maddening. Note that the citadel looming over the town is closed to visitors.

FREE **Temple of Artemis** RUINS
(Artemis Tapınağı; ☺8.30am-5.30pm) Ephesus used to earn fabulous sums of money from pilgrims paying homage to the Ephesian fertility avatar of Artemis. The Temple of Artemis, at the western end of Selçuk, was in its day the largest in the world, eclipsing even the Parthenon at Athens, and thus earning a spot on the list of the Seven Wonders of the Ancient World. Today, you're more likely to wonder where it all went. Only one of its original 127 columns remains, often as not topped by a stork's nest; a poignant testament to the transitory nature of human achievement. Still, it's a lovely tranquil place, the enormous pillar giving you some indication of the vast size of the temple.

Ephesus Museum MUSEUM
(☑892 6010; Uğur Mumcu Sevgi Yolu Caddesi; admission TL5; ☺8.30am-6.30pm summer, to 4.30pm winter) This excellent museum houses a striking collection of artefacts recovered from the ancient city. The first gallery is dedicated to finds from the Terrace Houses of Ephesus, including scales, jewellery and cosmetic boxes. This is also where you'll find the famous effigy of Priapus, the Phallic God, as seen plastered on every postcard from İstanbul to Antakya. No doubt to avoid offending delicate sensibilities, it's displayed inside a darkened case. Press the light to see him illuminated in all his rampant glory.

The other display areas hold collections of coins, funerary goods, and plenty of statuary. There's an entire room dedicated to sculpted representations of Eros, and an enormous (and slightly creepy looking) head and arm of the Emperor Domitian that once formed part of a 7m-high statue. Look out for the exquisitely carved multi-breasted marble statues of an egg-holding Artemis, which have become icons of the city.

The final room, near the entrance, holds an interesting exhibition based on the exca-

EPHESUS, BODRUM & THE SOUTH AEGEAN

Selçuk

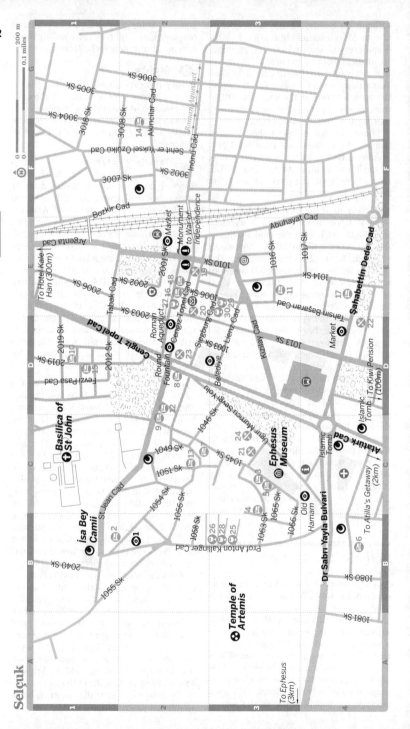

200 m
0.1 miles

Basilica of St John

İsa Bey Camii

Temple of Artemis

Ephesus Museum

To Ephesus (3km)

To Atilla's Getaway (2km)

To Kiwi Pension (100m)

To Hotel Kale Han (300m)

Old Hamam

Dr Sabri Yayla Bulvarı

Şahabettin Dede Cad

Atatürk Cad

Islamic Tomb

Eski Izmir Cad

Bozkır Cad

Argenta Cad

Cengiz Topel Cad

St Jean Cad

Fevzi Paşa Cad

Tabak Cad

Siegburg Cad

Lienz Cad

Tahsin Başaran Cad

Abuhayat Cad

Şehit er Yüksel Özülkü Cad

İnönü Cad

Akıncılar Cad

Prof Anton Kallinger Cad

Uğur Mumcu Sevgi Yolu

Roman Aqueduct

Round Fountain

Monument to War of Independence

Market

Market

Ironman Aqueduct

3005 Sk
3006 Sk
3018 Sk
3004 Sk
3008 Sk
3007 Sk
3002 Sk
2001 Sk
2002 Sk
2003 Sk
2906 Sk
2019 Sk
2012 Sk
2040 Sk
1049 Sk
1051 Sk
1054 Sk
1055 Sk
1056 Sk
1058 Sk
1063 Sk
1065 Sk
1066 Sk
1080 Sk
1081 Sk
1046 Sk
1045 Sk
1003 Sk
1010 Sk
1009 Sk
1013 Sk
1014 Sk
1016 Sk
1017 Sk
9090 Sk

vations of a gladiators' cemetery discovered in 1993. Displays describe the gladiators' weapons, detail their training regimes and cheerfully catalogue the various gruesome injuries they suffered. Also worth a mention is the frieze from Hadian's Temple; note the four heroic Amazons with their breasts cut off. Eagle eyes will spot the cross on the bust of Augustus.

It's best to visit the museum after touring the ruins, but try to get here early to avoid the overwhelming cruise crowds who rush through the museum before being carted back to their ship.

Basilica of St John   HISTORIC BUILDING
(St Jean Caddesi; admission TL5; ⊙8.30am-6.30pm summer, to 4.30pm winter) St John is said to have come to Ephesus twice: once between AD 37 and AD 48 with the Virgin Mary, and again in AD 95 towards the end of his life, when he wrote his gospel on Ayasuluk Hill. A 4th-century tomb was believed to house his remains, so in the 6th century Emperor Justinian (r 527–65) erected a magnificent church, the Basilica of St John, on top of it.

Earthquakes and marauders turned the site into a heap of rubble until a century ago when restoration began; virtually all of what you see now is restored. In its day it was considered a near-marvel and attracted thousands of medieval pilgrims. Even today it still draws busloads of 'holy site' tourists during the season. Look out for the information panel with a plan and drawing, which gives a very good idea of the building's once-vast size – as do the old marble steps and monumental gate.

İsa Bey Camii   MOSQUE
(St Jean Caddesi) At the foot of Ayasuluk Hill is the imposing and beautiful İsa Bey Camii, built in 1375 by the Emir of Aydın in a post-Seljuk/pre-Ottoman transitional style. There's a bust of İsa Bey diagonally opposite. The mosque is usually open to visitors, except at prayer times. Leave your shoes at the door and remember to cover up properly. Interesting sidenote: the ornate carpets inside were donated by locals.

Roman Aqueduct   RUINS
Running east–west intermittently along Namık Kemal Caddesi and İnönü Caddesi are the impressive remains of a Roman and Byzantine aqueduct, which serve today as a handy nesting place for storks. Eggs are laid in March, and the birds stay right through to end of September. Mood-lighting accents the stone ruins in the evenings, making it quite an atmospheric and romantic place to dine.

Çamlık Steam Locomotive Museum

MUSEUM

(📞894 8116; Köyü Selçuk; admission TL5; ⊙8am-7pm summer, to 5pm winter) Trainspotters will delight in this open-air museum, a few kilometres from central Selçuk on the Aydın road. The attractively landscaped site has over 30 steam locomotives, some as old as the 1887 C-N2 from the UK, and most of which are free to climb on. Atatürk had his headquarters here and kept his special white train at this station during Aegean manoeuvres. A small gallery space honours the memory of Atatürk with countless photos, portraits, newspaper articles and an antique desk.

Çetin Museum

MUSEUM

(📞894 8116; Köyü Selçuk; admission TL3; ⊙9am-5pm) Located 300m beyond the roundabout for Pamucak and Kuşadası, this small museum details Anatolian life in the 1950s with a costumed doll collection and folk-dancing exhibit. And although it's curated in an uninspiring hangar, it makes for a cheery stop for those with some extra time on their hands.

Crisler Library

NOTABLE BUILDING

(📞892 8317; www.crislerlibraryephesos.com; Prof Anton Kallinger Caddesi 40; admission TL5; ⊙9am-5pm Mon-Fri) Although not technically a 'sight', the Crisler Library is a wonderfully calm haven for those interested in learning more about Ephesus and the region's rich history. The library is the result of a bequest from a distinguished American biblical scholar, archaeologist and Harvard graduate, B Cobbey Crisler. Proving to be a terrific source of information on ancient, classical, biblical and Islamic history, it also boasts a lecture program, conference facilities, a well-stocked bookshop and a very informal cafe.

🛌 Sleeping

Competition between Selçuk's many pensions is intense, and the standard of service and value offered by these places is higher here than perhaps anywhere else. Most of the accommodation caters to budget and midrange travellers; high-end visitors (and travellers seeking a spot of sand with their Ephesus visit) should consider staying in Kuşadası instead. Mom-and-pop-shop digs is the name of the game here, so expect a high quality of service, free breakfast, air-conditioning, home-cooked meals (at decent prices) in the evenings, free use of bicycles, free internet access and discounts on local tours. Most pensions offer laundry for TL15 per load.

Jimmy's Place

HOTEL €€

(📞892 1982; www.jimmysplaceephesus.com; 1016 Sokak 19; d/ste from €30/70; ❄@☎) Smack in the centre of the action and just a stone's throw from the bus station, Jimmy's Place is an inviting spot with five spacious floors of neatly renovated rooms (especially the deluxe ones). Jimmy and his staff are eager to please, offering a variety of services including an informal and highly informative travel service (check out the wall full of photocopied brochures detailing the region's sights and activities) and a gut-busting breakfast that includes all-important filter coffee. There's a carpet store in the back if you feel so inclined. The hotel also manages a private swimming pool situated in an ivy-clad cloister just two blocks down the road.

Akay Hotel

HOTEL €€

(📞892 3172; www.hotelakay.com; 1054 Sokak 7; s/d from €35/55; ❄@☎) Hand-cut stone foundations, white walls and inviting green doors wrap around friendly Akay's two wings of accommodation. The 'old wing' is a bit of a misnomer now that everything's been freshly refurbished with laminate faux-wood flooring and tastefully simple decor. Newer rooms have polished dark-wood floors and sit around an inviting turquoise pool and patio. Did we mention the friendly owners? Ria, of Swiss extraction, will do everything in her power to make you feel at home. A-la-carte dinners (mains TL12 to TL15) are served on the relaxing roof terrace.

Homeros Pension

PENSION €

(📞892 3995; www.homerospension.com; 1048 Sokak 3; s/d/tr TL45/70/105; ❄@) On a quiet alley, Homeros has a dozen rooms spread over two houses, all imprinted with the quirky character of the welcoming and kind-hearted owner, Derviş. A carpenter, he is responsible for most of the traditional-style furniture, which lends itself well to the plethora of hanging textiles (literally every surface is covered by some sort of colourful costume or quilt). Both buildings have roof terraces with good views. Belly-filling traditional dinners (TL15) are the norm, as are complimentary glasses of homemade wine in the evenings. There are TL5 discounts if you're willing to share a bathroom.

Barım Pension

PENSION €

(📞892 6923; barim_pansiyon@hotmail.com; 1045 Sokak 34; s/d TL35/60; ❄️@) Twelve inviting rooms sit behind the unforgettable facade – a huge work of wire art replete with figurines and camels. The two friendly brothers that own the pension are metalworkers, and have outfitted much of the 140-year-old stone house with their art. Breakfasts are served in the adorable stone cloister tucked away in the back amid dangling vines and potted shrubs.

Atilla's Getaway

HOSTEL €

(📞892 3847; www.atillasgetaway.com; Acarlar Köyü; dm/s/d incl half-board TL35/40/45; ❄️@🏊) The most unique accommodation option in Selçuk by far, Atilla's is a chilled-out backpackers 'resort' located 2.5km south of the city centre. Run by the eponymous Atilla, a sociable Turkish-Australian, the hostel has tonnes of little perks like an amoeba-shaped pool framed by classical statues, a buzzing bar, volleyball court, handy travel office, and regular shuttle service to Selçuk centre. Air-conditioning in the private rooms will set you back an extra TL7 per night (per room) – the basement dorms are fan only.

Hotel Bella

HOTEL €€

(📞892 3944; www.hotelbella.com; St Jean Caddesi 7; s/d from TL60/80; ❄️@) This popular midranger has a dozen small rooms that have clearly benefited from a designer's touch. Ottoman rugs and trinkets abound – most of the lobby has been converted into a carpet-cum-jewellery shop. Evening dinners on the fantastic roof terrace will set you back a cool TL20.

Nilya

HOTEL €€

(📞892 9081; www.nilya.com; 1051 Sokak 7; s/d/ ste TL100/165/210; ❄️) One of the more tasteful and subdued options in town, Nilya is situated down a quiet side street with great views over the lush floodplain. Rooms are outfitted with traditional crafts, antiques and colourful drapery, and the central courtyard is a calm place with shady trees, lanterns and a trickling fountain.

Naz Han

PENSION €€

(📞892 8731; www.nazhan.net; 1044 Sokak 2; r €60-80; ❄️@) Situated beside Hotel Bella, this little charmer lives up to its name ('naz' means 'coy') with an adorable-but-overpriced collection of antique-clad rooms. Set in a 100-year-old Greek house, the accommodation is arranged around a quaint courtyard filled with artefacts and antiques. A small roof terrace grants views over Selçuk's scenic surrounds. The owners sell homemade olive oil grown on an orchard in nearby Şirince.

Hotel Pension Nazar

HOTEL €

(📞892 2222; www.nazarhotel.com; 2019 Sokak 14; d €30-50; ❄️🍴@) Completely overhauled a few years ago, Nazar offers top-of-the-line pension accommodation. The 13 rooms are big, clean and comfortable. Air-con is available in the superior rooms, and superb home-cooked meals are served on the roof terrace for a reasonable €7. There's also a pool set in a courtyard-garden and an ever-friendly welcome from the owner, Osman.

Alihan Guesthouse

PENSION €

(📞892 9496; www.alihanguesthouse.com; 1045 Sokak 34; r with shower per person TL25; ❄️) Spick and span with gleaming wood following a recent renovation, this is a cheery little place, just up the hill from the park, presided over by the keen-to-please Isa, his wife Melissa, and Sheila the dog. It's a mishmash of styles but is informal and cheap.

Hotel Kale Han

HOTEL €€

(📞892 6154; www.kalehan.com; Atatürk Caddesi; s/d from TL100/140; ❄️@🏊) Recognised by its faux-castle facade, Hotel Kale Han is a solid option in the midrange price bracket. Black-and-white photographs and a modest collection of antiques give the welcoming interior a certain old-home charm. Try for a room in the second building out back – it's more removed from the highway. Even if you're not staying at the hotel, it's worth swinging by the lovely indoor restaurant. Collector plates adorn the wooden beams overhead and guests are invited to plunk out a tune on the old piano.

Vardar

PENSION €

(📞892 4967; www.vardar-pension.com; Şahabettin Dede Caddesi 9; s/d from TL25/40; ❄️@) Sparkling clean and popular with Asian tourists, Vardar ticks all the boxes in the budget category with simple rooms adorned by Turkish kilim (pileless woven rug) and a lovely roof terrace offering fleeting views of Mary's House in the distance.

Australia & New Zealand Guesthouse

HOSTEL €

(📞892 6050; www.anzguesthouse.com; 1064 Sokak 12; dm/s/d from TL15/30/50; ❄️@) Although it's but a faint flicker of the vibrant backpacker base it once was, ANZ is still a characterful spot with a labyrinth of small bedrooms arranged rather haphazardly around an intimate, petal-strewn courtyard. International flags add an extra splash of colour, as do the embroidered cushions and tapestries in the indoor chill-out room. The dorms are perfectly fine, though the bathrooms are two flights of stairs away. Breakfast costs an extra TL7.50.

Nur Pension   PENSION €
(Ali's Place; ☑892 6595; www.nurpension.com; 3004 Sokak 20; dm/s/d TL20/35/50; ❄ ﹫) Past the train station in a lonelier part of town. Competitively priced. Rooms are small but clean.

Ürkmez Hotel   PENSION €
(☑892 6312; www.urkmezhotel.com; Namık Kemal Caddesi 20; s/d €35-38; ❄ ﹫) Neat and tidy with lots of smiles.

Kiwi Pension   PENSION €
(☑892 4892; www.kiwipension.com; 1038 Sokak 26; r with/without bathroom TL68/40; ❄ ﹫ ✉) Clean and tasteful option in a residential block. Run by the friendly Alison.

Tuncay Pension   PENSION €€
(☑892 6260; www.tuncaypension.com.tr; 2015 Sokak 1; s/d €25/35-50; ❄) Friendly owners, funky courtyard, rather overpriced.

Canberra Hotel   HOTEL €
(☑892 7688; www.canberraephesus.com; s/d/tr €25/35/45; ❄ ﹫) Generic wallpaper coats comfy-but-tiny rooms. Roof deck has Astroturf and great views.

Wallabies Hotel   HOTEL €
(☑892 3204; www.wallabieshotel.net; Cengiz Topel Caddesi 2; r TL50; ❄) Close-up aqueduct views are the big drawcard, especially during stork season.

Hotel Antik   HOTEL €
(☑892 1265; www.efesantikhotel.com; Atatürk Caddesi 4; s/d TL25/50; ❄ ﹫) Upside: simple, cheap and clean. Downside: chatterbox owner.

✖ Eating

Selçuk isn't overflowing with inspiring options, but you'll do just fine at any of the joints listed below. Most pensions also churn out home-cooked meals in the evenings at very reasonable prices.

Selçuk Köftecisi   KÖFTECI €
(Şahabettin Dede Caddesi; mains TL6-9; ⏰breakfast, lunch & dinner) Yes, you've heard it all before: 'this place has the best *köfte* (meatballs)!', but this time it's actually true. This family-run spot has been churning out bullet-sized meatballs since 1959, and although it's rather monopolised by tour groups, we still highly recommend stopping by. Rumbling bellies should order two portions of the veal *köfte*, as the dish sizes are on the small side. Be sure to save room for the scrumptious Temple of Artemis dessert – a pudding flavoured with almonds, vanilla and *tahin* (sesame seed pulp).

Ejder Restaurant   ANATOLIAN €€
(Cengiz Topel Caddesi 9/E; mains TL7-17; ⏰breakfast, lunch & dinner) Run by a welcoming husband-and-wife team (Mehmet does the meat, his wife the veg), this popular restaurant is a firm favourite with travellers for its delicious dishes (try chicken *şiş* or the sizzling Anatolian meat platter) and atmospheric setting under the arches of the Roman Aqueduct. While waiting for your meal, ask to see the 25 tomes of comments left by diners – everyone leaves a note, their signature and a small memento (a metro ticket from their hometown, a foreign coin etc – we even found a parking ticket and human hair!). Careful perusers will find an autograph from the late Steve Irwin.

Sişçi Yaşarın Yeri   KÖFTECI €
(Atatürk Caddesi; mains from TL6; ⏰breakfast, lunch & dinner) This small stall on the main road is hugely popular with those in the know for its delicious *köfte* and kebaps. Sadly, Yaşar has passed away, but his son is continuing the tradition. Although rather hidden away, there's a small, shaded seating area around the back with a few tables.

St John's Café   MEDITERRANEAN €
(www.stjohn-cafe-ephesus.com; Uğur Mumcu Caddesi 4/C; mains TL5-7; ⏰breakfast, lunch & dinner; ☎) Welcoming owners and top-notch coffee are the big draws at the welcoming li'l cafe. Down your cuppa with a special *künefe* dessert from Antioch or taste-test the zesty homemade hummus.

Kebab House Mehmet & Alibaba   KEBAPÇI €€
(1047 Sokak 4-A; mains TL5-16; ⏰breakfast, lunch & dinner; ☎) Covered in testimonials from contented customers, this friendly and informal joint dishes out tasty Turkish fare. The smiley owners are eager to please and are happy to educate the uninitiated palate with a variety of local treats such as Adana kebap. Complimentary coffee and yoghurt sides are the norm.

Eski Ev
ANATOLIAN €

(Old House Restaurant; 1005 Sokak 1/A; mains TL6-11; ⊘breakfast, lunch & dinner) With tables set in a little courtyard shaded by grapefruit and pomegranate trees, this intimate place spins tasty Turkish dishes amid decorated lanterns, bird cages and wicker chairs. Try the appetising speciality 'Old House Kebap' served sizzling on a platter.

Market
FOOD MARKET

(Şahabettin Dede Caddesi; ⊘9am-5pm winter, 8am-7pm summer) Every Saturday, Selçuk holds a fantastic market behind the bus station. With its fresh fruit, veg, cheese and olives, it's a great place to stock up for a picnic. There's a similar market behind the train station on Wednesdays.

🍷 Drinking

If you're looking for a party then you better head to Kuşadası. In Selçuk there are two small clusters of bars – one on Prof Anton Kallinger Caddesi, the other in the town centre on Siegburg Caddesi.

Destina Cafe & Bar
BAR-CAFE

(Prof Anton Kallinger Caddesi 24; ⊘10am-3am) Situated on a residential street, Destina bustles with a young local crowd that gathers around candlelit tables in the charming outdoor garden. Inside, mod music wafts through the air as furious games of backgammon are played on white leather sofas. Head to the hidden chill-out room in the back and grab a stool upholstered in snazzy animal print.

Amazon
BAR-CAFE

(Prof Anton Kallinger Caddesi 22; ☎) Although billed as a restaurant, we much prefer Amazon as a drinking spot. With some of the most refined decor in town, this sociable place has an African hunting-lodge vibe inside, and the outdoor seating, just across the road, boasts views of one of the Seven Wonders of the Ancient World (hey, it's not every restaurant that can say that).

Anton
BAR-CAFE

(Prof Anton Kallinger Caddesi) Although the brusque service starkly contrasts the inviting blue-and-white Med-inspired facade, Anton is still a congenial place for a late-night drink. Enjoy a beer in the back courtyard surrounded by Roman busts and decorative murals.

Denis Café
BAR

(Cengiz Topel Caddesi 20; ⊘10am-2am) Right in the middle of town, this welcoming spot has distinct *oda*-inspired decor (traditionally luxurious, elegant, sumptuous); the perfect spot to puff on a nargileh (water pipe).

Pink
PUB

(Siegburg Caddesi 24; ⊘10am-2am Sun-Thu, 10am-3am Fri & Sat) The oldest drinking establishment in Selçuk, it's referred to as a cafe, looks like a pub, but functions as a bar-cum-nightclub. Ask Mesut, the eager bartender, to demonstrate some magic tricks.

Sky Bar
PUB

(Siegburg Caddesi 24; ⊘10am-2am Sun-Thu, 10am-3am Fri & Sat) Just up the block from Pink, this popular pub-style spot is usually crowded with football-watching locals.

ℹ Information

There are banks with ATMs and foreign exchange offices along Cengiz Topel and Namık Kemal Caddesis.

Selçuk Hospital (☑892 7036; Dr Sabri Yayla Bulvarı)

Tourist office (www.selcuk.gov.tr; Agora Caddesi 35; ⊘8am-noon & 1-5pm summer, Mon-Fri winter)

ℹ Getting There & Around

Bus & Dolmuş

Recent improvements in the region's transportation infrastructure mean that it's fairly easy to link up with the other major sights in the south Aegean without having to switch buses in undesirable junction towns like Aydın and Söke during the summer months. Buses run from Selçuk direct to İzmir (TL8, one hour) every 40 minutes from 6.30am to 9pm (less frequent in winter). If you ask in advance your bus can usually drop you at the junction road that leads to İzmir's airport (it'll be a 2km walk or a TL10 taxi from there). There are three daily buses in summer connecting Selçuk to Bodrum (TL25, 3¼ hours); two during the quieter months. Two direct buses reach Denizli (TL25, 4½ hours) daily. You'll usually have to make a brief switch in Denizli, Aydın or Bodrum to reach destinations along the Mediterranean such as Fethiye and Antalya. Direct buses link Selçuk to İstanbul (TL45-50, 10 hours) via Bursa; there are at least three nightly departures and one during the day at 11.30am.

Dolmuşes run to Kuşadası (TL4, 30 minutes) and Pamucak (TL2.50, 10 minutes) every 20 minutes from 6.55am to 10pm during the summer months (shorter hours in winter). The last minibus back from Kuşadası is at midnight in high season and 8pm during the slower months. There are no buses to Söke.

The easiest way to access the ruins at Priene, Miletus and Didyma is to rent a car (figure TL80 plus petrol per day) or join up with a guided tour. Tours do not run everyday.

Taxi

Note that the town of Selçuk has put a ban on free rides to Ephesus, so you must take a taxi or join up with a tour. Taxi rides around town cost TL5 and it's about TL120 to Izmir airport (try to bargain). Figure TL15 to Ephesus and TL50 (return) to the House of Mary.

Train

At the time of research there were no trains running to Denizli, though this may change in the future. Five trains run daily from Selçuk to İzmir (TL4.75, 45 minutes). Services start at 6.25am and finish at 7.20pm. There is a connection between the train and a ferry service in the town of Bandırma that links İzmir to İstanbul. You are not guaranteed a seat, even if you purchase a ticket in advance.

Şirince

📞 0232 / POP 960

Secreted high in the inland hills among wild orchards and rolling groves, Şirince is a scenic little village dotted with a dollhouse collection of stone-and-stucco houses. The area was probably settled when Ephesus was abandoned, but what you see today mostly dates from the 19th century. The story goes that a group of freed Greek slaves moved here in the 15th century and called the village Çirkince (Ugliness) to deter others from following. The name was changed to the more honest Şirince (Pleasantness) in the 1920s during the founding of the new republic.

Before Atatürk's republic, Şirince was a larger town inhabited by Ottoman Greeks. The current villagers, who moved here from Salonica during an exchange of populations in 1924, are ardent fruit farmers who also make and sell an interesting assortment of wines (TL10 to TL20). Flavours range from raspberry and peach to the trendier black mulberry and pomegranate.

Şirince is by no means the 'undiscovered gem' as usually marketed in other guidebooks. In fact, it's the village's widely known reputation for authenticity that has marked the start of its demise. During the day, souvenir shops run the entire length of the main street as vendors try to lure you in using a smattering of catcalls in different languages. Visitors who ignore this and stay the night (at a stiff premium, of course) will be well rewarded with the chance to see the real village after the tour buses have gone.

◉ Sights & Activities

If you're trying to avoid the crowds then it's best to visit in the evening when the droves of daytrippers have long retreated from the mountains – 3pm is about the busiest time of day. Şirince's charm lies in its subtleties, so your time is best spent simply ambling around the crooked cobbled lanes and admiring the adorable architecture.

The ruined **Church of St John the Baptist** (⊙8am-8pm summer, 8.30am-6.30pm winter) is of limited interest. Faded frescoes adorn the walls, which date back to Byzantine times. Funds are scarce, so restorations have yet to turn the space into more than a sanctuary for cawing birds. Check out www.societyofephesus.com if you're interested in learning more about the structure.

🛏 Sleeping

Şirince is a captive market, and room rates can be ludicrously inflated for what you get.

Nişanyan House   BOUTIQUE HOTEL €€€
(📞898 3208; www.nisanyan.com; r TL215-275, cottage TL275; ❄@) The brainchild of 'small hotel' connoisseur Sevan Nişanyan (known around Turkey for his guide to boutique sleeps), this elegant manor house may look like it's a restored ruin, but it's actually a modern structure that's been expertly designed to mimic the village's natural rustic charm. Faded frescoes adorn the walls and black-and-white photographs hang over wooden sleigh-beds. Sip your welcome drink (made from local mulver flowers) in the quaint library or enjoy the views of the cracked terracotta tiles and crumbling chimneys of the village houses below.

Güllü Konak   BOUTIQUE HOTEL €€€
(📞898 3131; www.gullukonak.com; Şirince Köyü 44; r TL340-420, ❄@) Set in two gorgeous stone-and-stucco manses, this endearing boutique enclave features over a dozen spacious rooms and a pristine private garden. The decoration hints at cottage living without being oppressive – perfect for all tastes. Too bad it's overpriced...

Kırkınca Pansiyon   BOUTIQUE HOTEL €€
(📞898 3133; www.kirkinca.com; s/d TL130/250; ❄) Just up the hill opposite the bazaar, the Kırkınca has boutique aspirations with its clutch of stone terraces and 250-year-old

abodes. They've all been very elegantly done up with a mixture of quality bespoke modern fixtures and restored antiques. Some of the rooms have four-poster beds and one even has its own mini-hamam. The main building has a shaded roof terrace with views of the town and countryside.

İstanbul Pansiyon
PENSION €€

(📞898 3189; www.istanbulpension.com; İstiklal Mah 13; d TL150; ❄) Believe it or not, the five rooms at this inviting li'l inn are set in a converted stable. But you'd never know it – Yeliz, the kind owner, has done a wonderful job of providing all the modern comforts (there's hip leather headboards!) while maintaining the structure's rustic village charm.

✗ Eating

Artemis Şirince Şarap Evi Restaurant
ANATOLIAN €€

(📞898 3240; www.artemisrestaurant.com; mains TL9.50-28; ⊗breakfast, lunch & dinner) Artemis is housed in former Greek school, set right by the village entrance. It's a hulk of a restaurant that overlooks the surrounding valley and offers the best village views of any establishment in town. The interior has old stoves and darkened floorboards, while outside there's a large terrace and garden. It looks very grand and touristy, but it's actually a great place for a bite, and the prices are pretty reasonable. You can also come here just for a drink – the *oda*-style lounge inside is a charming spot for a tea break.

Şirincem Restaurant & Cafe
ANATOLIAN €€

(📞898 3180; mains TL7-14; ⊗breakfast, lunch & dinner) Situated across the way from the palatial Artemis Restaurant, this quaint village-style option is tucked under a thicket of shade-baring trees. Ali, the soft-spoken owner, is a fruit farmer by day and kindly dotes on his customers in the evening. Be sure to try the stewed meat platter – a popular local dish. Wash down your Anatolian staples with a glass of locally produced fruit wine (a nice assortment of red and white wines are also available if fruit wines aren't your thing).

🔒 Shopping

These days almost every house on the village's main street has been transformed into a storefront selling a variety of local wares, namely fruit wine. Ask to sample your wine of choice before making the purchase – it's not everyone's cup of tea – some of the fla-

vours taste a bit too much like cough syrup. Other shops sell olive oil, soaps and leather goods, usually crafted locally (it's best to ask). It's worth stopping by **Demetrius of Ephesus** (Şirince Köyü 26), a local artisan who crafted most of the jewellery and trinkets for the movie *Troy* – you'll know you're in the right place when you see the photo of Brad Pitt hanging above the cash register.

ℹ Getting There & Away

Minibuses (TL2.50) leave Selçuk for Şirince every 30 minutes in summer, and every hour in winter.

Tire & Kaplan

📞0232

Pleasant as Selçuk is, no one could call it undiscovered. However, it's possible to make a straightforward day trip into the Aegean hinterland, which will give you a fascinating insight into less-touristy Turkey. You can do this by dolmuş, but it really works best if you hire a car.

At the base of the Bozdağler Mountains and surrounded by farmland, Tire hosts a very popular **Tuesday market**, which has become a frequent stop for tour groups in recent years. Trade begins at 8.30am with a special market prayer over the loud speaker, and traders start carting their goods away around sunset.

If you can't make it to Tire on a Tuesday, it's still worth coming through to explore the small cluster of felt-darning workshops. There are only three felt makers left in the region; they practise the traditional craft using a blend of teased cotton and wool. At **Keçeci** (📞512 2391; www.tireconkece.com; ⊗8.30am-7.30pm Mon-Sat), the owner will gladly show you the design-making process. First a pattern is created, then patted down with water, three layers of cotton are added, then more water, and the concoction is pressed for a full hour.

Before leaving Tire, make sure you drive up into the neighbouring hills for a meal under festive gourds and dried leaves at **Kaplan Dağ Restorant** (📞512 6652; www.kaplandag.com; mains TL10-12; ⊗1-9.30pm Tue-Sun) in the tiny hamlet of Kaplan. The restaurant has amazing views over the inland plains, however it's mostly known throughout the region for their (yeah, you guessed it) *köfte*. Waiters have mastered the art of carrying out an enormous wooden platter of scrumptious homemade mezes – try the locally grown herbs with a glass of special blackberry juice. Reservations on Tuesdays and weekends are essential.

❶ Getting There & Away

There are hourly minibuses to Tire from Selçuk (TL6). A cab ride from Tire to Kaplan costs TL15 (there is no dolmuş service).

Pamucak

☑ 0232

Once a malaria-infested swamp and a veritable no-go zone between Selçuk and Kuşadası, Pamucak is now a scenic sandy cove flanked by pine-studded hillocks. Located 7km west of Selçuk, the area is only minimally developed, with a small handful of beachfront hotels and nothing more. Without teams of resort staff to mop up the daily detritus, parts of the beach do get a little litter-strewn at times, but the wide swaths of sand usually mean relative privacy even when crowds of Turkish families flock to the seaside on weekends. From February to March, the estuary wetlands (a 15-minute walk from the beach) attract flamingos.

The most pleasant accommodation option in the area is **Dereli** (☑ 893 1205; www.dereli-ephesus.com; Pamucak Plaj; d TL70-100) with its stash of beach-facing bungalows that line the shimmering sand behind a row of chubby palms. Campgrounds (TL15 per person) are also available.

❶ Getting There & Away

Minibuses run every half-hour from Selçuk (TL2.50, 10 minutes, 7km) in summer and every hour in winter. To/from Kuşadası, go to Selçuk first. The dolmuşes roll by Dereli – you can ask the driver to let you off at the gate to Ephesus if you so choose.

Kuşadası

☑ 0256 / POP 54,660

The fourth busiest cruise port in the entire Mediterranean, Kuşadası has shed its fishing-village roots in order to become the official gateway to Ephesus. Most tourists will only spend twenty minutes in town, which is about the time it takes to disembark from an ocean liner. But those who are able to stick around and explore will find that the friendly city is actually quite fun.

You won't get much in the way of Turkish culture beyond the trademark hospitality (although you'll find some, if you're prepared to seek it out). Instead you'll have free reign over a decent, if oft-crowded beach, and some of the coast's headiest nightlife – think Irish pubs, happy hours, singalongs, tribute acts and swaying discos. Now, if that sounds like a bit too much, then you're better off basing yourself in the quieter confines of sleepy Selçuk nearby.

◎ Sights & Activities

Kuşadası's town has a small artificial beach, but the area's most famous stretch of sand, and the primary focus for the majority of its package holiday visitors, is **Kadınlar Denizi** (Ladies Beach), 2.5km south of town and served by dolmuşes running along the coastal road. It's nice enough but packed with big hotels and woefully inadequate for the high summer crowds. The coast south of Kadınlar Denizi has several small beaches, each backed by big hotels.

In town, the main formal attraction is the minor stone **fortress** that occupies most of **Güvercin Ada** (Pigeon Island), a small island connected to the mainland by a causeway. Its main hall hosts exhibitions of handicrafts and there are a few coops on stilts for the eponymous pigeons, but the fortress' main appeal is as a strolling route – it's particularly popular with local courting couples who secret themselves among the battlements and canoodle.

East of the island are the cruise ship docks and, handily situated immediately to the south, the main **bazaar** area. This is a strictly tourist-oriented place – cheap leather jackets, knock-off designer bags, carpets, jewellery etc – but you'll rarely be harassed by vendors.

It's possible to use Kuşadası as a base for exploring much of the region. The town has numerous tour operators and travel agents offering trips to all the major local attractions, including Ephesus (full day with lunch for €45) and 'PMD' (Priene, Miletus, Didyma; €50), as well as further afield to Pamukkale (€45).

🛏 Sleeping

Kuşadası is chock-a-block with hotels and more are being erected all the time. Most of the accommodation in the heart of the city either belongs to the pension or business-hotel category. For something more resorty, try exploring the bays extending north and south of the centre.

Hotel Ilayda
BUSINESS HOTEL €€

(☏614 3807; www.hotelilayda.com; Atatürk Bulvarı 46; s/d TL70/120; ✳@) Once referred to by locals as 'the hospital' for its Soviet-inspired facade, Ilayda has benefited from its recent refurbishment, and the results have placed this seaside option at the top of our list. Although the rooms are small, savvy designer touches and smooth lines have shaped the limited space in a very inspired way; the floor-to-ceiling windows with their unobstructed beach views also do a great deal to help. The central location, good in-house restaurant and record-low price tag make Ilayda unbeatable.

Atlantique Holiday Club
RESORT €

(☏633 1320; www.atlantiqueclub.com; Karaova Mevkii Sahil Setileri; per person incl full board from €35; ✳✳@) Though you may be quick to snicker at an all-inclusive option, consider this: for the price of a backpacker's pad downtown you get the amenities of a seaside resort (swimming pools, tennis courts and a private beach), a clean room with crisp white furnishings, and three buffet-style meals per day. Sure, it's not the Ritz, but a deal like this – at a friendly and vibrant establishment, no less – is a guilt-free option that's pretty much impossible to pass up. It's located 7km south of the city centre and easily accessible by dolmuş No 6.

Club Caravanserai
HISTORIC HOTEL €€

(☏614 4115; www.kusadasihotelcaravanserail.com; Atatürk Bulvarı 2; s/d/ste €65/85/150; ✳) This grand 17th-century caravanserai is one of the town's unmistakeable landmarks. Yards of neon illuminate the battlements in the evening, and during the day the looming stone structure is the subject of countless photographs. Giant boulder-like stairs lead guests up to the second storey where rooms are sprawled out along the generous inner courtyard. Rooms are appointed with authentic Ottoman decorations, from hand-crafted rugs to ornate drapery. Kitschy 'Turkish nights' are often held down below.

Villa Konak
BOUTIQUE HOTEL €€

(☏612 6318; www.villakonakhotel.com; Yıldırım Caddesi 55; s €30-60, d €40-70; ✳@✳) Hidden away from the hubbub in the old quarter of town is the Villa Konak, a restored 140-year-old stone house. The charming rooms are have been attractively done up with the odd Orientalist flourish that are reminiscent of a bygone era. Lodging is arranged around a large, rambling courtyard-garden complete with pool, ancient well, scattered Roman ruins and shady magnolia trees. It's a peaceful spot, with a tea parlour and a lofted library nook.

Charisma
LUXURY HOTEL €€€

(☏618 3266; www.charismahotel.com; Akyar Mevkii 5; s/d/ste €165/220/850; ✳@✳) A looming marble hulk covered in tinted blue windows (the owners also run a marble quarry), Charisma has upped the ante in the top-end category. Located north of the city centre on a private patch of pebbly sand, this rambling campus features swish leather furnishings in the lobby and a swanky wood-beamed veranda that leans over the crashing waves out back. Rooms are arranged in two shimmering towers; every guest gets a sea view, though the beige carpeting feels a bit dated. Quiet Charisma seems most popular with an older American crowd.

Kısmet
LUXURY HOTEL €€€

(☏618 1290; www.kismet.com.tr; Gazibeğendi Bulvarı 3; s/d/ste €99/129/339; ☺Apr–mid-Nov; ✳@✳) About as big a contrast to the town's core constituency as you can get, the Kısmet is a grand affair that feels distinctly oriental in style. Located at the northern end of town, the hotel occupies a sprawling property owned by a descendant of the last sultan; manicured gardens abound. Rooms are simple and some – painted in a pale, coffee-stained-teeth colour – could use a bit of a facelift, but everyone gets a balcony with lovely views of the sea or bustling town.

Hotel Stella
PENSION €

(☏614 1632; www.hotelstellakusadasi.com; Bezirgan Sokak 44; s/d TL35/70; ✳✳@) Right in the heart of the city on a rather hilly street, Hotel Stella promises a friendly welcome and a selection of tidy rooms with sea-and-city views. Discounts are available for longer stays.

Liman Hotel
PENSION €€

(Mr Happy's; ☏614 7770; www.limanhotel.com; Kıbrıs Caddesi, Buyral Sokak 4; s/d €25/38; ✳@) Presided over by the aptly named 'Mr Happy' (AKA the more tongue-twisterly Hasan Degirmenci), Liman Hotel is a stalwart of the local budget scene. It occupies one of the best positions of any pension, right near the seafront, and some of the 17 rooms have excellent sea views. There's a great terrace where breakfast (included),

Kuşadası

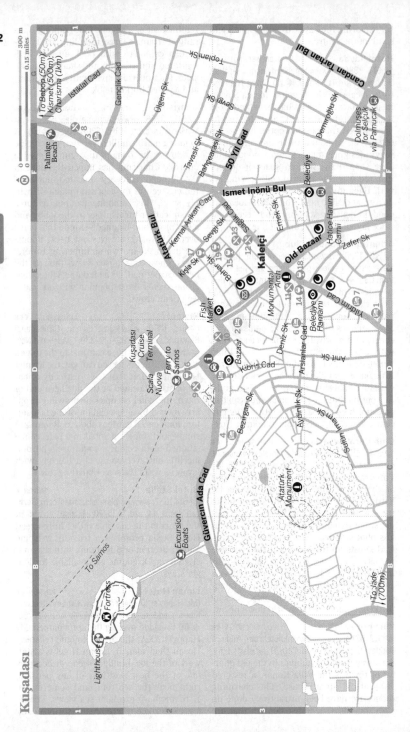

Kuşadası

dinner (optional extra) and the obligatory belly dancing evenings are laid on. Extras include a library and free maps.

Sezgin Hotel Guest House   HOSTEL €
(☎614 4225; www.sezginhotel.com; Arsanlar Caddesi 68; s/d €25/30; ❄ ♨ @) Budgetarians get a lot for their money here: large wood-panelled rooms, comfortable beds, armchairs, TVs, fridges and small balconies overlooking a compact garden and pool. The owner, Sezgin, is friendly and helpful and organises regular special events, including Turkish-style barbecues and belly dancing.

Cennet Pension   PENSION €
(☎614 4893; www.cennetpension.com; Yıldırım Caddesi 69; s/d TL40/60; ❄) Another pleasant option in the city's old quarter, Cennet is run by a Turkish-German couple who preside over a small stash of prim rooms and a gorgeous rooftop terrace with perhaps the best views in all of Kuşadası. The bathrooms could use some major sprucing up...

✖ Eating

The town's prime dining location is down by the picturesque marina but competition keeps bills down. Always ask the price of seafood and wine before you order it.

For the cheapest options, it's simple: head inland. The Kaleiçi, the old part of Kuşadası behind the post office, has some atmospheric dining rooms as well as a few cheap and cheerful joints.

Ferah   SEAFOOD €€€
(☎614 1281; İskele Yanı Güvercin Parkı İçi; mains TL15-25; ⏰lunch & dinner) The tables sit directly on the water's edge, making it a great place to watch the setting sun, passing yachts and towering cruise ships. Simply put, the food at Ferah is exquisite; succulent mezes tempt the palate, as do finely prepared seafood mains. Grab a bottle of rakı and a handful of dear friends and you've got yourself a very memorable evening.

Bebop   INTERNATIONAL €€
(☎618 0727; www.bebopjazzclub.com; mains from TL9; ⏰lunch & dinner) Located within the marina, Bebop kinda feels like a resort, 'cept for the fact that there's no accommodation. Come in the morning and stay for dinner – there's a spacious dining area and a tantalising swimming pool with a halo of beach chairs. Jazz beats (oftentimes live) float through the air late in the evening.

Değirmen Restaurant   LOCAL €€
(www.degirmenltd.com; Davutlar Yolu 4km, Saraydamları Mevkii; snacks & mains TL2-20; ⏰lunch & dinner) A veritable village-themed amusement park about 10km south of the city centre, Değirmen's gourmet safari sits on a sprawling acreage with views of the Dilek Peninsula. Pack a picnic using the latest crops in the quaint farmers' market, or enjoy a relaxed meal in the on-site restaurant amid Ottoman handicrafts.

Planet Yucca   INTERNATIONAL €€
(☎612 0769; Sağlik Caddesi 56; mains TL12-26; ⏰lunch & dinner) Billed rather bizarrely as a 'Mexican-Chinese-Turkish Restaurant', Planet Yucca really does make an earnest effort to be a veritable UN of cuisine. The lively and faithful clientele is a mix of continents as well. The menu competes with the Encyclopaedia Brittanica in length, so it's best to stick with the line-up of Turkish dishes for satisfying results. Free taxi pickups sweeten the deal.

Saray   INTERNATIONAL €€€
(☎0544 921 6224; Bozkurt Sokak 25; mains TL15-35; ⏰breakfast, lunch & dinner) Enjoying a dedicated following among both locals and expats, the Saray shows two different faces to the world. Outside is a rather refined

GETTING WET IN KUŞADASI

Culture is all very well, and the ruins of Ephesus and the like undeniably impressive and evocative, but sometimes you just want to slide down a big tube filled with water. The opportunity for a bit of wet-and-wild adventure is provided at **Adaland** (☎618 1252; www.adaland.com; Çamlimanı Mevkii; adult/child TL40/30; ☺10am-6pm May-Oct), Europe's largest water park, with dozens of chutes, slides, river rides and pools, as well as a newly opened sea park, home to a variety of marine life. Adaland is just north of Kuşadası near Pamucak.

For something a little more worthy, you can learn to scuba-dive – or if you've already learnt, just go for a dive – with the **Aquaventure Diving Center** (☎612 7845; www.aquaventure.com.tr; Miracle Beach Club, Kadınlar Denizi; ☺8am-6pm), by Ladies' Beach, which offers PADI open water courses for €250 and reef dives from €30. Staff can arrange a pick-up from most of the major hotels.

courtyard, all shady trees, candlelight and linen, while inside, particularly later in the evening, it can be a bit more happy hour and singalong. The menu is a typical Kuşadası calling-all-ports affair – Chinese, Indian, Mexican, fish and chips etc – but with some decent Turkish choices, and several vegetarian options. Wednesday is 'Turkish Night' – don't show up if you're allergic to kitsch.

Köfteci Ali
KÖFTECI €
(Arsanlar Caddesi 14; mains TL5; ☺24hrs summer, 9am-midnight winter) Situated near the entrance of Bar St, ready to hoover up the early morning post-club traffic, this simple street booth does some terrific spicy wrapped pide kebaps. The chances are high that you'll be served by Ali himself, who sleeps just four hours a night in the summer season.

Cimino
ITALIAN €€
(Atatürk Bulvarı 56/B; mains TL5-19; ☺lunch & dinner) A place to meet-and-eat locally, this mellow bistro-cum-café serves good cappuccinos and mainly Italian-style fare. It's opposite the seafront and plays good jazz music.

Kazim Usta Restaurant
SEAFOOD €€€
(☎614 1226; Liman Caddesi 4; meze TL5-12, mains TL15-30; ☺breakfast, lunch & dinner) Opposite the tourist office, this venerable establishment founded way back in 1950 is considered the top fish restaurant in town, and has capitalised on its reputation by overcharging. The sumptuous fish soup is a speciality. If you want a table on the waterfront, reserve at least a day in advance.

Drinking & Entertainment

Nightlife in Kuşadası can be easily divided into three sections. The centre of the town's tourist nightlife is the infamous **Barlar**

Sokak (Bar St), which could honestly be renamed Irish St, as pretty much every bar is now dedicated to the Emerald Isle. Locals tend to prefer the **Kaleiçi** part of town (also known as 'old town') for their evenings of revelry. Bars and clubs in this district are positioned in a variety of charming stone houses and courtyards. If you're looking to kick things up a notch (and drain your wallet at lightning speed), your third option is the cluster of giant entertainment complexes along **Cape Yılancı**, slightly south of the city centre. During the day these compounds function largely as private beaches; at night the attention turns to the elegantly furnished bars, dance platforms and stages set right over the water. Live bands are the norm, performing jazz, Latin and funk, and al-fresco discos go on till the early hours.

Jade
CLUB
(www.jadebeachclub.com; Yılancı Burnu Mevkii; admission weekday/weekend TL25/30) Like Raina in İstanbul, Jade is the most famous entertainment complex in town. Like a genie that grants infinite wishes, this sprawling compound offers virtually every type of vacation accoutrement: a swimming pool, volleyball net, beachside lounge chairs, dance floors, bars and a concert stage; there's even an exotic tranny cabaret show if you feel so inclined...

Orient Bar
LIVE MUSIC
(www.orientbar.com; Kaleiçl Kışla Sokak 14 & 17) Situated in a cosy stone structure in the heart of Kaleiçi, Orient Bar offers up a fun evening of live music where, by the end of the evening, everyone's singing along in tipsy revelry. Grapevines dangle from the lattice roof, so you're feeling peckish just reach up and snatch some fruit. Extra li'l touches

- like framed portraits on the wall and teeny treasure chests that carry your bill – make this spot particularly memorable.

Bizim Meyhane
MEYHANE

(Kişla Sokak) With low beams, stone walls and plenty of dangling musical instruments, this place looks more barn than bar. Run by a sister and brother who sing and play their own tunes, Bizim is atmospheric, infectious and fun. Join the locals tossing back the rakı.

Biraver
PUB

(Liman Caddesi) Located at the cruise port's Scala Nuova shop, Biraver is the most popular spot in town for beer-toting locals. The homemade draught brews are surprisingly good.

Akdeniz
BAR

(Arsanlar Caddesi 1; ☺Apr-Oct) With its elevated position overlooking the entrance to Bar St, this is a perfect spot to watch the dolled up crowds emerge for the evening's raucousness. The bar itself is shaded by a tall tree and is rather peaceful. There's also an attached restaurant (not bad) and apartment-hotel.

Jimmy's Irish Bar
PUB

(Barlar Sokak 8; ☺Apr-Nov) Jimmy's is still one of the biggest names in town, partly because it has the handiest position at the entrance to the street. For all of its mass-market, karaoke, 'hey, where you from?' faults, this can be a good place to meet other travellers (so long as you can hear what they're saying; it's very loud). The giant satellite dish on the roof beams in the compulsory football matches.

Another Bar
BAR

(Tuna Sokak 10) Converted from an old citrus orchard, Another Bar has tables and stools dotted among the remaining trees and a large, central palm. There's also a large screen and a dance floor.

❶ Information

There are several banks with ATMs on Barbaros Hayrettin Bulvarı.

Özel Kuşadası Hastanesi (☏613 1616; Anıt Sokak, Turkmen Mahallesi) Excellent private hospital 3km north of the centre on the Selçuk road. Has English-speaking doctors.

Post office (Barbaros Hayrettin Bulvarı 23-25; ☺8.30am-12.30pm & 1.30-5.30pm Mon-Sat winter, 8am-midnight daily summer)

Tourist office (İskele Meydanı, Liman Caddesi; ☺8am-noon & 1-5pm Mon-Fri) Near the wharf where the cruise ships dock, about 60m west of the caravanserai. It doesn't have a lot of information, although it can provide up-to-date maps.

❶ Getting There & Away

Boat

All Kuşadası travel agents sell tickets to the Greek island of Samos.

From 1 April to 31 October, boats depart daily from Kuşadası to Samos at 8.30am. Tickets cost €30 for a single, €35 for a same-day return and €50 for an open return (this includes port tax).

If you stay the night you will be landed with a €10 tax for leaving Greece and another €10 tax for coming back into Turkey. If you ask ahead you can usually get a ticket that includes these fees – you can sometimes get these fees discounted or waived. You must be at the harbour 45 minutes before sailing time for immigration formalities. Check to make sure that you have a multi-entry Turkish visa in your passport, otherwise you might encounter some friction at the border when you try to get a new one.

The boats are operated by **Meander Travel** (www.meandertravel.com; Kıbrıs Caddesi 1; ☺9am-9pm), which has its office right by the dock and also offers a range of other domestic tours.

Bus

Kuşadası's otogar is at the southern end of Kahramanlar Caddesi on the bypass highway. Several companies have ticket offices on İsmet İnönü Bulvarı and offer *servis* (shuttle minibuses) to

EPHESUS, BODRUM & THE SOUTH AEGEAN KUŞADASI

WORTH A TRIP

KİRAZLİ

Set along a quiet back road connecting Kuşadası and Selçuk, the 'Place of Cherries' is a sleepy little spot known only to locals. While the tour buses careen up and down the main highway, Turkish roadtrippers make the special detour to have breakfast at **Köy Sofrası** (☏667 1003; www.koysofrasi.com; mains TL5-15; ☺breakfast, lunch & dinner). Set in a crooked thicket of gnarled orchard trees, this dusty bolthole offers bed-like booth seating and an excellent assortment of local nibbles. The venerable Emine and Nihat Firat run the place, and when they're not entertaining passers-by they're cooking up a storm for local weddings, circumcision celebrations and other religious festivities.

1

226

save you the trek out there. Note that dolmuşes leave from both the centrally located Adnan Menderes Bulvarı and the main otogar.

In summer, three afternoon buses run daily to Bodrum (TL20, 2½ hours, 151km); in winter, take a dolmuş to Söke (TL4, at least every 30 minutes all year). For Didyma, Priene and Miletus, see p229.

Dolmuşes run every 15 minutes to Selçuk (TL4, 30 minutes); ask the driver to let you off at Pamucak or Ephesus along the way.

ⓘ Getting Around

There are no direct links from Kuşadası to İzmir's Adnan Menderes airport. You can take a bus to İzmir otogar and switch to the local shuttle service, or a taxi. If you're feeling spend-y, a taxi from Kuşadası will cost around TL140. Ask your hotel about chartering a shared van if you're in a group.

Şehiriçi minibuses (TL1.25) run every few minutes in summer (every 15 to 20 in winter) from Kuşadası otogar to the town centre, and up and down the coast. Kadınlar Denizi minibuses speed along the coast road south to the beach.

Dilek Peninsula

About 26km south of Kuşadası, the Dilek Peninsula juts westwards into the Aegean, almost touching the Greek island of Samos. West of the village of Güzelçamlı is Dilek National Park (Dilek Milli Parkı; www.dilekyari madasi.com; admission per person/car TL4/10; ⊙7am-7.30pm Jun-Sep, 8am-5pm Oct-May), a peaceful, mountainous nature reserve with some fine walking trails, stunning viewpoints, and unspoilt coves for swimming.

Just outside the park entrance, look out for a brown sign for Zeus Mağarası, which indicates the location of a cave where you can swim in water that's icy cool in summer and warm in winter.

After the entry gate, you'll find four rounded bays with pebble beaches before the road tapers off at the entrance to a high-security military compound at the tip of the peninsula (thought to be a front for protecting a tract of land that's within swimming distance of Samos).

İçmeler Köyü, the first protected cove, is about 1km past the entrance. It's a steep walk down to the sandy beach, which is very popular locally (and inevitably rather cigarette butt-strewn). A paved road runs along the cliff tops, where purpose-built viewpoints offer perfect Kodak moments at any time of day.

About 3km beyond İçmeler Koyu an unpaved turn-off heads 1km downhill on the right to Aydınlık Beach, a quieter pebble-and-sand strand about 800m long with surf and backed by pines. Aydınlık is only slightly less busy than İçmeler; there's a lifeguard station here.

Less than 1km further along is a turn-off to a jandarma (police) station. Shortly afterwards a turn on the left is signposted kanyon. From here a walking path snakes deep into the forest, and after 15km you'll reach the charming hamlet of Doğanbey, where you can visit a small museum filled with stuffed animals. Non-permit holders can follow the first 6km of the walking path, after that, hikers are required to be accompanied by a guide.

The park's third bay is Kavaklı Burun, which has a sand-and-pebble surf beach as well. As at Aydınlık, there's a second entrance to the beach at the far end, another 1km along. The final beach, Karasu Köyü, is by far the quietest, and enjoys gorgeous views of mountainous Samos that juts skywards from the watery deep.

Camping is strictly forbidden within the park, and guests are gently advised to leave at closing time. All four of the beach-y bays have wood-slatted chairs that are free for use (though almost always occupied by early birds). A set of two plastic chairs is available for TL20 per day (umbrella included). Each of the four bays also has a restaurant shack (mains TL6-25) that serves a variety of items from steak to sea bass.

ⓘ Getting There & Away

Accessing the park is fairly simple and straightforward. Dolmuşes run from Kuşadası directly into the park (TL4.50, 40 minutes) every 15 minutes during the warmer months. The dolmuş only goes to the park's third bay (Kavaklı Burun), if you wish to access the fourth you'll have to pay an additional TL2 and notify the driver. Buses between Güzelçamlı and Kuşadası run until midnight. Expect to pay the park entrance fee while on the bus.

Priene (Güllübahçe)

☑ 0256

Priene is one of the most atmospheric of all of Turkey's ancient sites. Perched high on the craggy slopes of Mt Mykale near the village of Güllübahçe, it enjoys an isolated, windswept aesthetic and contrasts sharply with the crowds and commerce of Ephesus.

0 — 200 m
0 — 0.1 miles

Acropolis

⊙ Stone Bench

Byzantine
Buildings
◉

Temple of
Demeter

33 Houses

Temple of
Athena

Theatre

Roman
Gymnasium

Sanctuary of
Egyptian Gods

Ticket
Office
●
Ⓟ

Byzantine
Church

Sacred
Stoa

Prytaneion

Bouleuterion

Agora

Castle

Site
Entrance

Alexandrium

Sanctuary of Zeus

Sanctuary
of Cybele

Stadium

Ancient
Shoreline

Gymnasium

Though considered a prominent burg around 300 BC when the League of Ionian Cities held congresses and festivals here, Priene (☑547 1165; admission TL3; ⊙8.30am-7.30pm mid-May–mid-Sep, 8.30am-5.30pm mid-Sep–mid-May) was smaller and less important than nearby Miletus. As such, its Hellenistic buildings did not vanish beneath newer Roman ones.

Of the numerous buildings that remain, the most impressive are those of the Temple of Athena, which enjoys commanding views of the plain below. Designed by Pythius of Halicarnassus, it is regarded as the epitome of an Ionian temple. Five columns have been re-erected and the rest lie in sections, like giant stone wheels, all in seemingly good condition and arranged so neatly as to look like the careful preparations for something new, rather than the aftermath of something very old. Such a large number of column sections remain that the temple's former reality seems tantalisingly close.

Elsewhere, the theatre is one of the best-preserved examples from the Hellenistic period. It had a capacity to seat 6500 people; check out the finely carved front seats that were once reserved for VIPs. Also worth seeking out are the remains of the bouleuterion (council chamber), a Byzantine church, the gymnasium and the stadium.

✖ Eating

Attractively positioned in the shadow of a ruined Byzantine aqueduct, Selale Restaurant (mains TL10; ⊙breakfast, lunch & dinner) has a pool that's home to trout (which you can eat) and ducks (which you cannot). Next door is the Villa Sultan Café Bar Restaurant (mains TL6-10; ⊙breakfast, lunch & dinner) offering traditional fare in a converted kilim factory. The tables are set in a lovely courtyard with a fountain and orange trees.

ℹ Getting There & Away

Dolmuşes run every 15 minutes between Priene (Güllübahçe; TL3.25, 17km) and Söke; the last one back to Söke leaves Priene at 7pm. The dolmuş stops at the cluster of restaurants around 250m from the entrance to Priene.

Miletus (Milet)

📞 0256

The ancient town of **Miletus** (📞 875 5562; admission TL3; ⊙ 8.30am-7.30pm mid-May–mid-Sep, 8.30am-5.30pm mid-Sep–mid-May) lies 22km south of Priene, amid sweeping fields of wispy cotton groves. Its **Great Theatre**, rising up as you approach from the south, is the most significant (and impressive) reminder of a once-grand city, which was a commercial and governmental centre from about 700 BC to AD 700. When the harbour filled with silt, Miletus' commerce dwindled.

The 15,000-seat theatre was originally a Hellenistic building, but the Romans reconstructed it extensively during the 1st century AD. Though nearly 2000 years old, it's in good condition and has many features, including covered walkways around each tier of seating, still used in today's stadiums.

It's well worth climbing to the top of the theatre where the ramparts of a later Byzantine castle provide a viewing platform for several other groups of ruins. Look left and you'll see what remains of the harbour, called **Lion Bay** after the stone statues of lions that guarded it. Look right and you'll see the **stadium**; the northern, western and southern **agoras**; the vast **Baths of Faustina**, constructed for Emperor Marcus Aurelius' wife; and a **bouleuterion** between the northern and southern agoras.

South of the main ruins stands the fascinating **İlyas Bey Camii** (1404), dating from a period after the Seljuks but before the Ottomans, when the region was ruled by the Turkish emirs of Menteşe. The doorway and *mihrab* (niche indicating the direction

Miletus

ℕ 0 ———————— 200 m
   0 ———————— 0.1 miles

To Priene (22km);
Söke (28km)

Ancient
Shoreline

Lion Statue

Lion Bay

Hellenistic
Hero's Tomb

Great
Theatre

Harbour Monument

P

Ticket Office ℹ

Northern
Agora

Bouleuterion

Menekse
Bath

Snack Bars

Ionic
Stoa

Baths Stadium

Caravanserai

Southern
Agora

Baths of Faustina

Western Agora

İlyas Bey Camii

Ancient
Shoreline

Miletus Museum

Didyma Gate

To Akköy (5km);
Didyma (23km)

To Balat (2km);
Akköy (4.5km);
Didyma (20km)

'PMD' TOURS

Ephesus may be the *crème de la crème* of the Aegean archaeological sites, but south of Kuşadası lie the ruins of three ancient settlements that often fly under the radar. Priene occupies a dramatic position overlooking the plain of the Büyük Menderes (Meander) River; Miletus preserves a spectacular theatre; and Didyma wows visitors with the enormous remains of the Temple of Apollo. These three sites can be easily done in one whirlwind day.

The easiest way to visit all three ruins is to link up with a so-called 'PMD' tour. Most travel agents in Selçuk and Kuşadası (not Bodrum, however) can organise your visit in a jiff – though most outings require a quorum of four or more, so don't expect a tour on every day of the week. Figure around €35 for the day, which includes an hour at each site and lunch. Sadly a do-it-yourself PMD tour on public transportation is no longer possible, as dolmuşes do not run to Miletus. If you're only keen on visiting Priene and Didyma (which are, admittedly more interesting than Miletus) you can use the dolmuş service from Söke to reach both ruins, though you'll have to go all the way back to Söke to switch minibuses. Of course, the easiest way to tackle the three sites is to rent a car (easily accomplished at any agency in Selçuk, Kuşadası and Bodrum) – expect to drop around TL80 per day, and that doesn't include petrol (figure an extra TL55). Turn-offs to all three ruins are clearly marked with big brown signs along the highway.

of Mecca) are exquisite, and you'll probably have them to yourself. During prime nesting season you're almost always likely to see storks squatting on the roof.

Beyond the mosque on the Didyma road, you'll find the **Miletus Museum** (admission TL3; ⊙8.30am-4.30pm), which was being renovated at the time of research, but will soon display local archaeological finds.

Peckish? You'll find a row of (overpriced) food stalls and shacks lining the dusty road across from the Great Theatre.

❶ Getting There & Away

Miletus is often considered the least interesting of the three 'PMD' ruins, and public transportation has dwindled significantly over the last five years. These days it's virtually impossible to reach the site using dolmuşes. Your best bet is to join a tour or rent a private vehicle from either Bodrum or Kuşadası.

Didyma (Didim)

📞0256

Ah, what might have been. Just a few more columns and Didyma's **Temple of Apollo** (📞811 0035; admission TL3; ⊙9am-7.30pm mid-May–mid-Sep, 9am-5.30pm mid-Sep–mid-May) could've been one of the Seven Wonders of the Ancient World. But its 122 columns made it only the second-largest temple in the world, and with 127, the Temple of Arte-

mis (see p211) near Ephesus took the prize instead.

Didyma appropriately means 'twin' and was a very important site in its day, home to an oracle whose influence was second only to the one in Delphi (there's a bit of a pattern emerging here). But ancient Didyma was never a real town; only the priests who specialised in oracular temple management lived here. There's a town here now, all right, with the ruins of the temple crowded in on all sides by pensions, carpet stalls and restaurants.

It may be of little comfort now, but the ruins of the temple are much more impressive than those of Artemis. Significant sections of the thick, imposing walls remain standing and three columns have been reconstructed, showing their richly carved bases. Behind the temple porch is a great doorway where oracular poems were written and presented to petitioners. Covered ramps on both sides of the porch lead down to the *cella* (inner room), where the oracle sat and prophesied after drinking from the sacred spring. All around the ground are scattered fragments, including a photogenic head of Medusa (she of the snake hairdo). There used to be a road lined with statues that led to a small harbour, but after standing unmoved for 23 centuries the statues were taken to the British Museum in 1858.

230

Beyond Didyma lies **Altınkum Beach**, one of Turkey's busiest beaches, its swathe of 'golden sand' popular with the English package-holiday brigade for whom innumerable British-style cafes dish up the tastes of home. If you end your tour of the ruins at Didyma, you might want to take a quick dip in the sea at the beach before returning to base.

🛏 Sleeping & Eating

Of the three 'PMD' ruins, Didyma boasts the most formal (and best) lodging and dining options.

Medusa House   PENSION **€€**

(☏811 0063; www.medusahouse.com; d €60) Just around the corner from the temple on the Altınkum road is this restored 150-year-old stone house with five pleasantly decorated rooms set in a very attractive garden (complete with original Greek urns and shaded terraces).

Olio   INTERNATIONAL **€€**

(Apollon Temple Restaurant & Bar; mains TL12-36; ⊘lunch & dinner) Housed in a charming stone cottage with adorable and mismatched lodge-style furnishings, this German-run restaurant offers a wide selection of international dishes amid large paintings with ornate gilded frames. The wooden rooftop terrace has great views of Didyma's duo of sky-scraping columns. It's right across from the temple entrance.

Kamacı   AEGEAN **€€**

(☏811 0028; buffet TL10-15; ⊘lunch) Located at the back of the temple (and not to be confused with the like-named storefront near the entrance), Kamacı has an all-you-can-eat buffet that's wildly popular with tour groups. It's well worth stopping by even if you're travelling alone, as you can taste-test over 30 types of local mezes. Informative books on the region's ruins are available for purchase.

❶ Getting There & Away

Dolmuşes run frequently from Söke to Didim (TL7.50, one hour) and Altınkum (TL7.50, 1½ hours). There are also frequent dolmuşes from Didim to Akköy (TL3.25, 30 minutes).

Herakleia

☏0252

Once a gulf of blue Aegean waters, Bafa Gölü is now a landlocked lake after the shoreline receded many moons ago. Interestingly, the lake is 50% freshwater and 50% saltwater.

At the end of a twisting, rock-dominated road branching 10km off the main highway, you'll come to the ruins of **Herakleia** and Latmos around the village of **Kapıkırı**, which enjoys a dramatic lakeside setting.

Above the village looms dramatic **Beşparmak Dağı** (Five-Fingered Mountain; 1500m), the ancient Mt Latmos that features in Greek mythology as the place where the hunky shepherd boy Endymion happened to fall asleep. While he was napping, the moon goddess Selene glanced down and fell in love with him. Endymion had asked Zeus to grant him eternal youth in exchange for staying asleep for eternity. The unfortunate Selene could only gaze down at him night after night, as the moon is forever fated to look down on us mere mortals.

Bafa is an area where Christian hermits took refuge during the 8th-century Arab invasions (note the many ruined churches and monasteries in the vicinity). The monks reputedly considered Endymion a saint for his powers of self-denial.

Herakleia is a fascinating place where the urban and the rural co-exist in such proximity that it almost seems as if a village has been built in the middle of a farm. Fields dotted with beehives close in on all sides, chickens and donkeys stroll the roadsides and there are probably more cowsheds than houses. Remnants of ancient sites are strewn throughout the town, popping up here and there as you make your way around. In a way, the whole village is the attraction, which is why the ticket booth has been set up at its entrance (TL8 per vehicle if the attendant is around).

Tourism has brought much needed revenue to an otherwise impoverished community. However, there is still a good deal of poverty here, and you can pretty much guarantee that when you arrive, you will attract the attention of the town's women who all carry trays of purchasable goods – tablecloths, jewellery, lace etc – wrapped beneath a scarf on their backs.

◎ Sights & Activities

Herakleia's main draw is its glorious lake setting; the village enjoys wonderful views over the lake's silvery expanses. To get to its edge, head down the road past the **Temple**
EPHESUS, BODRUM & THE SOUTH AEGEAN

of Endymion, partly built into the rock, until you reach the ruins of a **Byzantine castle**, which looks down on the city's **necropolis** – a series of rectangular tombs cut directly into the rock.

At the lakeside, near the ruins of a **Byzantine church**, there's a small beach of white coarse sand. The island just offshore can sometimes be reached on foot as the lake's water level falls. Around its base can be seen the foundations of several ancient buildings.

Elsewhere, a path behind the Agora car park leads westwards to the large **Temple of Athena**, on a promontory overlooking the lake. Though only three walls remain, the large and beautifully cut building blocks (put together without cement) are impressive. Other signposted paths lead eastwards to the **agora**, the **bouleuterion** and, several hundred metres through stone-walled pastures and across a valley, to the unrestored and oddly sited **theatre**; its most interesting features are the rows of seats and flights of steps cut into the rock. Stretches of **city wall** dating from around 300 BC are also dotted about the village.

🛏 Sleeping & Eating

Herakleia is supremely popular with German tourists, so most pension owners speak very little English. Half-board accommodation is the norm, and almost all of the places to stay can hook you up with a two-hour boat tour (TL50 per boat) or take you for an afternoon hike to the Neolithic caves and ruins (TL90 for two people).

Karia Pansiyon & Restaurant   PENSION €€
(☑543 5490; www.kariapension.com; Kapıkırı Köyü; s/d incl half-board TL90/140, ✳) Duck through wreaths of shade-bearing ferns and leaves to reach Karia's lovely roof terrace and look out over serene Lake Bafa while listening to ambient rooster hoots and bird chirps. Rooms are upholstered with hanging pictures and intricately woven carpets. In the late afternoon you can join Cennet in the kitchen and watch her whip up the evening's local flavours.

Agora Pansiyon   PENSION €€
(☑543 5445; www.agora.pansiyon.de; s/d incl half-board from TL110/150; ✳@) Though the rooms are attractively decorated, the hotel's setting is its biggest asset, with flower-filled gardens and a peaceful outlook. There's also a hamam and shaded terrace with hammocks. A variety of accommodation options are on offer, including a cache of charming

wooden bungalows (with that lovely timber smell!); there are also a few homes in the village that are available for rent (TL210). In addition to hiking, the owner's son offers short bouldering and bird-watching trips.

Haus Yasemin Pension   PENSION €€
(☑543 5598; www.bafa-see.de; Kapıkırı Köyü; d incl half-board TL90) You'll inevitably clunk your head on one of the low-slung beams, but a bump on the noggin is about the only downside to this homely spot filled with the heirlooms and tools of a working family. Despite the clutter, chaos and cow patties the rooms are actually quite comfortable and good value considering the surrounding options have inflated price tags.

Selene's Pension   PENSION €€
(☑543 5221; www.bafalake.com; Kapıkırı Köyü; d incl half-board TL120-180; ✳✳) Founded in 1989 by a teacher and his family, Selene's was first pension in the area. Today there are nine rooms and a breezy restaurant split across three buildings.

Club Natura Oliv   HOTEL €€
(☑519 1072; www.clubnatura.com; Pıarcık Köyü; s/d with half-board €35/53; ✳@) If you don't fancy staying in the village, try Club Natura, 10km north of the Herakleia turn-off. This welcoming 30-room hotel is set in a charming olive plantation (it makes its own olive oil using a traditional stone mill) with awe-inspiring views over the water. A wide variety of guided nature walks are also on offer.

ℹ Getting There & Away

Herakleia is located 10 bumpy kilometres away from the main highway, which means that you'll usually have to find a second form of transport if you're dropped along the main road. Almost any long-distance bus passing the turn-off to Herakleia will be happy to let you off along the side of the motorway. A dolmuş service is extremely rare, but if you happen to catch one it costs TL3. Taxis will set you back TL15. At the time of research, a minibus departed the town at 8am and returned from the highway sometime between noon and 1pm. You can often wrangle free transportation (usually one-way only) from your accommodation of choice – make sure to call ahead and ask.

Milas & Around

☑0252 / POP 50,975

As Mylasa, Milas was capital of the Kingdom of Caria, except during the period when Mausolus ruled the kingdom from Halicarnassus (present-day Bodrum).

Today, it's a sleepy but sizeable agricultural town. On Tuesday there's an excellent local market, which has become an attraction in its own right, welcoming weekly tour parties in summer from Bodrum.

◉ Sights

Milas' most interesting sights orbit the town centre in a 20km radius. Roman ruins are sprinkled around the town itself, including Baltalı Kapı (Gate with an Axe), a well-preserved Roman gate. An eponymous double-headed axe is carved into the keystone on the northern side. Walk up a steep path sprouting off of Gümüşkesen Caddesi to find the Gümüşkesen ('That Which Cuts Silver' or 'Silver Purse'), a Roman tomb dating from the 2nd century AD and thought to have been modelled on the Mausoleum at Halicarnassus (albeit on a much smaller scale).

Euromos   RUINS
(admission TL8; ⊙8.30am-7pm May-Sep, to 5pm Oct-Apr) The ancient city of Euromos once stood on a site about 12km northwest of Milas and 1km from the village of Selimiye. Today, almost all that remains is the picturesque and partly restored Temple of Zeus, which has some unfluted columns that suggest it was never completed.

First settled in the 6th century BC, Euromos originally held a sanctuary to a local deity. With the coming of Greek (then Roman) culture, the local god's place was taken by Zeus. Euromos reached the height of its prosperity between 200 BC and AD 200. Emperor Hadrian, who built so many monuments in Anatolia, is thought to have also built the temple here.

To get here, take a Milas–Söke bus or dolmuş and ask to get off at the ruins, located 200m from the highway.

Iasos (Kıyıkışlacık)   RUINS
Postcard-pretty Iasos is a charming village (currently called Kıyıkışlacık) set on the sea where rustic sea shanties mingle with the majestic ruins of a forgotten empire. The walled acropolis-fortress (admission TL2; ⊙8.30am-5.30pm) sits on the olive-clad hill just across from the fishing docks. Excavations have also revealed the city's bouleuterion, agora, and a Roman temple of Artemis Astias (AD 190), among several other structures. Stop at Iasos Deniz Restaurant (fish from TL10; ⊙10am-midnight) to take in the serene views of the ruins as they tumble into the sea.

A dolmuş usually runs hourly between Iasos and Milas (TL4.25) during the summer months (and less frequent in winter). A winding, 20km-long road ends at the ruins; the turn-off to the village is clearly marked along the highway 10km northwest of Milas.

Labranda   RUINS
(admission TL8; ⊙8am-5pm) Set into a steep hillside in an area that once supplied the ancient city of Mylasa with its water, the site of ancient Labranda is surrounded by fragrant pine forests peopled by beekeepers. Late in the season (October) you can see their tents pitched in the groves as they go about their business of extracting the honey and rendering the wax from the honeycombs.

The ruin of Labranda was a holy place, where worship of a local god was going on by the 6th century BC and perhaps long before. Later it became a sanctuary to Zeus, controlled for a long time by Milas. The great Temple of Zeus honours the god's warlike aspect (Stratius, or Labrayndus means 'Axe-Bearing'). There may have been an oracle here; certainly festivals and Olympic games were also held at the site.

The junction for the road to Labranda is northwest of Milas on the road to Söke. It's 14km to the site, so a taxi is the most convenient option. Figure TL30 from Milas, including an hour of waiting (prices are negotiable).

Beçin Kalesi   RUINS
(Beçin Castle; admission TL3; ⊙8am-dusk) Just over 1km along the road from Milas to Ören (watch for the brown sign immediately after a corner), a road on the right leads to Beçin Kalesi, a Byzantine fortress on a rocky outcrop that was largely remodelled by the Turkish emirs of Menteşe, who used Beçin as their capital in the 14th century.

The castle walls are striking, perched on high, with a giant Turkish flag on the top flapping in the breeze, and offer great views of Milas down below. There's not a lot to see inside. Atop the adjacent hill, some 500m away, are other remnants of the 14th-century Menteşe settlement, including the Kızılhan (Red Caravanserai), the Ahmet Gazi tomb and, the highlight, a newly restored medrese (seminary).

❶ Getting There & Away

Milas' otogar is on the main Bodrum-Söke road, 1km from the centre, although dolmuşes from Bodrum (TL7, one hour) drop off in town as well.

A small **dolmuş station** (Köy Tabakhane Garaji) in the town centre offers timetabled minibus services to Iasos (TL4.25).

BODRUM PENINSULA

More than just a holiday destination, Bodrum is a namebrand synonymous with crystal seas, crowds of jetsetters and arid olive-clad cliffs. Everyone in Turkey knows the name Bodrum, and everyone yearns for their very own piece of it. Thousands of new summer homes sprout up each year, and wealthy İstanbullus arrive in droves – the women in flowing linen dresses, the men wearing Villebrequin swim trunks. Days are spent lazing next to the sea, while evenings start with fish and mezes, then roll on until dawn at one of the dozens of bumpin' nightclubs. Then it's lather-rinse-repeat until the holiday season ends in September.

ⓘ Getting There & Away

Air

The **Bodrum International Airport** (BJV), 60km from Bodrum town, is actually closer to the town of Milas than it is to the Bodrum Peninsula. Check the charter-flight brochures for bargains, especially at the start and end of the season, but prepare to be disappointed as there are fewer flights than you might expect. The office of **Turkish Airlines** (THY; www.thy.com; Kıbrıs Şehitler Caddesi) is in the Oasis Shopping Centre, about 2km out of town off the Gümbet road. To get here, take a dolmuş (TL1.25) from the otogar, asking for 'Oasis'. **AtlasJet** (www.atlasjet.com) also offers direct connections with İstanbul.

To get to the airport, you can take the Havaş bus (TL17), which runs in conjunction with Turkish Airlines, and leaves the Bodrum otogar (bus station) two hours before all Turkish Airlines departures. It also meets flights and drops passengers in central Bodrum. If you're not flying with Turkish Airlines, an expensive taxi (TL90 from the city centre; TL140 from the airport) is really your only option.

Boat

Bodrum has a brand new cruise port that welcomes large liners, and plans are underway to move most of the small ferry traffic here. Ferries for Datça and the Greek islands of Kos and Rhodes currently leave from the western bay. For information and tickets contact the **Bodrum Ferryboat Association** (www.bodrumferryboat.com; Kale Caddesi Cümrük Alanı 22; ⏰8am-8pm), on the dock past the western entrance to the castle. Check times, as they can change.

For Kos, ferries (one way or same-day return €28, open return €56) leave Bodrum daily throughout the year (weather permitting) at 9.30am, returning at 4.30pm from Kos. The trip takes about an hour. A hydrofoil service

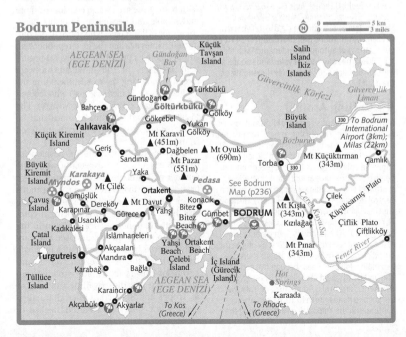

Bodrum Peninsula

operates from Monday to Saturday during July and August, departing at 9.30am and returning at 5pm. Note that this service was not running at the time of research, but may start up again in the near future.

For Rhodes, hydrofoils (one way and same-day return €60, open-day return €120, 2¼ hours) leave Bodrum from June to September at 8.30am on Monday and Saturday and return at 5pm the same day.

For Datça, ferries (single/return/car TL25/40/70, two hours) leave Bodrum at 9am every day from mid-June to September. In April, May, early June and October departures are at 9.30am on Tuesday, Thursday and Saturday only. Same-day returns are not possible. The ferry docks at Körmen on the peninsula's northern coast, and the onward bus journey to Datça (15 minutes) is included in your fare.

Ferries for Kalymnos depart daily from the marina in Turgutreis (€20, 45 minutes) between 25 May and 31 October.

Bus

Bodrum has bus services to more or less anywhere you could wish to go. The table lists some useful daily services. If you're interested in visiting a site or town along one of the main highways (like Didyma, for example) you can ask the driver to let you off along the side of the road.

Car & Motorcycle

Major car-rental agencies can be found on Neyzen Tevfik Caddesi. **Avis** (☑ 316 2333; www. avis.com; Neyzen Tevfik Caddesi 92/A) and **Neyzen Travel & Yachting** (☑ 316 7204; www. neyzen.com.tr; Kibris Sehitleri Caddesi 34) rent out a variety of automatic and manual vehicles for €30-45 per day. Motorcycles and scooters will set you back €10-30 per day depending on the brand.

Getting Around

Although the dolmuş service at Bodrum town's otogar may seem confusing at first, the peninsula actually has one of the most well-oiled public transportation systems in the entire country. Minibuses ply the roads to most places on the peninsula. They have an easy-to-remember system of colour coding: orange buses service central Bodrum town (TL2 to TL2.50), turquoise shuttles head all over the peninsula (TL2.50 to TL7), and the lime-green dolmuşes go to Gümbet (TL2.50). The terminus name is advertised in the windscreen or painted directly on the minibuses' hood. From Bodrum's otogar there are two main transport lines through the peninsula. The first heads west stopping in Gümbet, Bitez, Ortakent, Turgutreis, Gümüşlük and Yalıkavak; the second heads north to Torba and often continues in the Yalıkavak direction along the

northern coast visiting Türkbükü along the way. Turgutreis, Gümüşlük and Yalıkavak are also linked by a separate dolmuş line. Allow an hour to reach Bodrum from Yalıkavak, and 15 minutes to travel between bays. During high season it's possible to catch a dolmuş at any time around the clock; in the cooler months services run daily between 7am and 11pm. If you're looking to travel between, say, Bitez and Ortakent, you'll need to flag down a dolmuş along the main road and travel 'indi bindi' (TL2) to the next bay. Note that some of the bays, like Yalıkavak and Türkbükü, aren't connected by minibus service, so you'll have to head all the way into Bodrum town, then back out again on a different shuttle.

Bodrum

☑ 0252 / POP 39,320

The beating heart of the region and the namesake of the entire peninsula, the town of Bodrum has been a dot on the map for thousands of years. It first rose to fame on the back of the Mausoleum, the spectacular tomb of the Carian King Mausolus that Roman historian Pliny the Elder designated one of the Seven Wonders of the World. Today it's known throughout Turkey and beyond as a posh paradise where sun-kissed travellers dance the breezy summer nights away.

Long before Bodrum became synonymous with luxury, the area was a considered quite undesirable and became an informal penal colony for exiles. Those who spoke ill or committed crimes against the new republic were shipped here as punishment. Several prominent members of the intelligentsia were forced here during their exile, including the 'Fisherman of Halicarnassus', who coined the term *mavi yolculuk* (blue voyage). The Fisherman loved Bodrum so much that he chose to remain here even after being freed from exile.

Tourism really started to develop in the 1980s and '90s – especially when the founder of Atlantic Records (a major music brand in America) purchased a sumptuous beach manse directly in the heart of the city. Each summer he would bring a coterie of international celebrities down to the Aegean to indulge in the sand, sea and sun. This ushered in a new era that has slowly transformed the relative backwater and haven for misfits into a star-studded see-and-be-seen paradise rivalling the likes of St Tropez and St Barth. Other characters, like the late singer Zeki Müren, flocked to

DESTINATION	FARE (TL)	DURATION (HR)	DISTANCE (KM)	FREQUENCY (PER DAY)
Ankara	50-75	11	689	1 nightly
Antalya	35-38	7½	496	2 (9.30am, 10.30pm)
Denizli (Pamukkale)	25	4½	250	1
Fethiye	25	5	265	3 (9.30am, 12.30pm, 5.15pm)
İstanbul	60-81	12	851	10 nightly
İzmir	25	3½	286	hourly
Konya	45	12	626	6
Kuşadası	20	2½	151	4 (all after midday)
Marmaris	18	3	165	hourly
Milas	15	1	45	every 15 minutes
Muğla	13	2	149	hourly

Bodrum as well, putting the town on the map for gay travellers.

With strict laws restricting the height of the town's buildings, Bodrum has a nice architectural uniformity to it; the idyllic whitewashed houses with their signature bright-blue trim practically call out to tourists' cameras. Even when the clubs are bumpin' there's something rather refined about the town.

◉ Sights

Castle of St Peter MUSEUM
(📞316 2516; www.bodrum-museum.com; admission TL10; ⊙9am-noon & 1-7pm Tue-Sun summer, 8am-noon & 1-5pm winter) When Tamerlane invaded Anatolia in 1402, throwing the nascent Ottoman Empire temporarily off balance, the Knights Hospitaller based in Rhodes took the opportunity to capture Bodrum. By 1437 they had erected the Castle of St Peter, which they continued to augment with new defensive features – including moats, walls and water cisterns – over the ensuing decades. However, in 1522, when Süleyman the Magnificent captured the Knights' headquarters in Rhodes, the Bodrum contingent was forced to abandon the castle without having ever truly tested its fearsome defensive capabilities. The castle fell into decline during the succeeding centuries and suffered some shell damage during WWI. Reconstruction didn't begin in earnest until the 1960s, when it was used as an informal storage space for the booty collected during underwater archaeology missions, before becoming, in 1986, Bodrum's Museum of Underwater Archaeology.

It's an excellent museum and arguably the most important of its kind in the world, with imaginatively displayed, well-lit items, accompanied by plenty of information panels, maps, models, reconstructions, drawings, murals, dioramas and videos.

The views of the town from the battalions are spectacular and worth the entry price alone. As the museum is spread throughout the castle, you need two hours to do it justice. Arrows suggest routes around it (red for long; green for short), but guides are not available.

As you head up the stone ramp into the castle past a Crusader coats of arms carved in marble and mounted on the stone walls, keep an eye out for bits of marble filched from the ancient Mausoleum. The ramp leads to the castle's main court, centred on an ancient mulberry tree. To the left is a long display of amphorae – the castle owns one of the largest collections in the world – with examples from the 14th century BC to the present day, all recovered from the waters of southwest Turkey. The adjoining courtyard cafe, adorned with Greek and Roman statuary, provides a shady resting place, and there's a small glass-blowing workshop where you can watch glass bottles and jewellery being

Bodrum

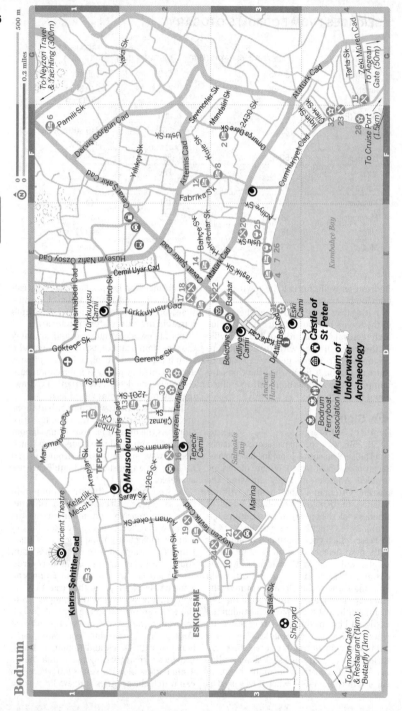

0 0.2 miles
0 500 m

created (similar to those recovered from coastal wrecks).

The chapel here contains both a one tenth-size complete model and a full-sized reconstruction of the stern of a late-Roman ship discovered off Yassıada. Visitors can walk the decks, stand at the helm, look below decks at the cargo of wine and peek into the galley.

Follow the path to the left of the chapel to ascend to the towers. Here you'll find the entrance to the **Glass Wreck Hall** (admission TL5; ⊙10-noon & 2-4pm Tue-Fri). As you enter, look for the castle-shaped dovecote on the castle wall. Discovered by a sponge diver in 1973 and excavated by the American Professor George Bass and a team of marine archaeologists, the 16m-long, 5m-wide ship sank in AD 1025 while carrying 3 tonnes of mainly broken glass between Fatimid Syria and the Black Sea.

Next up is a small **Glass Hall** where glass finds from the 15th century BC to the 14th century AD are displayed. The assorted Mycenean beads, Roman glass bottles and Islamic weights are kept in near darkness, with each piece backlit individually so as to better reveal its delicate structure. Next door is a small exhibition of coins, including numerous examples from ancient Caria.

Beyond, the **French Tower** has finds taken from the *Tektaş Burnu,* the only ancient Greek shipwreck (thought to date from around 480 BC to 400 BC) from the classical period to be fully excavated. Displays include numerous amphorae, talismanic marble discs, kitchen utensils, as well as photographs of the excavation itself, which took place off the coast of the Çeşme Peninsula in 2001.

Next door, the **Carian Princess Hall** (admission TL5; ⊙10am-noon & 2-4pm Tue-Sun) holds the remains and effects of a high-status woman, discovered by Turkish archaeologists in 1989. Though popularly said to belong to Queen Ada, the last Carian queen, who was brought back from exile and installed as monarch by Alexander the Great following his conquest of Halicarnassus in 334 BC, there is no concrete evidence for this. Buried with a gold crown, necklace, bracelets, rings and an exquisite wreath of gold myrtle leaves, her identity doesn't lessen the incredible value of the find.

Guarding the castle's southeast corner, the **English Tower** was built during the reign of King Henry IV of England (whose coat of arms is displayed above the entrance to the uppermost hall) and is now fitted out as a medieval refectory with a long central dining table surrounded by suits of armour, stag horns and the standards of the Grand Masters of the Knights Hospitaller and their Turkish adversaries. Piped medieval music plays in the background giving the place the feel of a Crusader Knights theme restaurant. Look out for the Latin graffiti carved into the stone window ledges by Crusaders.

Just to the north is the **Uluburun Wreck Hall** containing an extraordinary gallery of **Bronze Age shipwrecks**. Its principal exhibit is the 14th-century BC *Uluburun*, the oldest excavated shipwreck in the world. There are full-size replicas of the ship's interior and the wreck site on the seabed. The aptly named Treasure Room holds a wealth of finds, including Canaanite gold jewellery, bronze daggers, ivory cosmetic boxes, wooden writing boards and the gold scarab of Queen Nefertiti of Egypt.

Further north, descend the **Gatineau Tower** to the dungeons beneath. Over the inner gate is the inscription 'Inde Deus abest' (Where God does not exist). The **dungeon** was used as a place of confinement and torture by the Knights from 1513 to 1523. A sign warns that the exhibits of torture implements might not be suitable for children, but most video-game-hardened visitors will find the display dummies and the taped groans more laughable than disturbing.

Mausoleum   RUINS
(Turgutreis Caddesi; admission TL8; ☺8.30am-5.30pm Tue-Sun) Founded some time in the 11th century BC, the ancient kingdom of Caria (which encompassed modern-day Bodrum) became absorbed into the Persian Empire, although it continued to exercise a degree of autonomy until the arrival of Alexander two centuries later. During that time its most famous leader (satrap) was Mausolus (r 376–353 BC), an admirer of Greek culture, who moved the capital from Mylasa to Halicarnassus. After his death, his wife (and sister), Artemisia, undertook the construction of a monumental tomb, as planned by Mausolus himself and designed in a Hellenic-style by Pytheos, the man behind the Temple of Athena at Priene. The Mausoleum – an enormous white-marble tomb topped by a stepped pyramids – became one of the Seven Wonders of the Ancient World and stood relatively intact for almost 19 centuries, until it was broken up by the Crusaders in 1522 and the pieces were 'recycled' as building material for other structures. The most impressive remains, including friezes incorporated into the walls of the Castle of St Peter, and statues of Mausolus and Artemesia, were shipped off to the British Museum in London in the 19th century, where they remain.

Despite the almost utter obliteration the site is still worth visiting. It has pleasant gardens, with the excavations to the right and a covered arcade to the left. The arcade contains a copy of the famous frieze now in the British Museum. The four original fragments on display were discovered more recently. Models, drawings and documents give an idea of why this tomb made Pliny's list of Wonders. Other exhibits include a model of Halicarnassus at the time of King Mausolus, and a model of the Mausoleum and its precincts.

However, don't hold your breath in anticipation of the grandeur of the site. Of the remains, only a few things survive: the pre-Mausolean stairways and tomb chambers, the Mausolean drainage system, the entry to Mausolus' tomb chamber, a few bits of precinct wall and some large fluted marble column drums.

Myndos Kapısı   RUINS
(Turgutreis Caddesi) At the far western end of town are the restored remains of the Myndos Kapısı (Myndos Gate), the only surviving gate from the original 7km-long walls built by King Mausolus in the 4th century BC. In front of the twin-towered gate are the remains of a moat in which many of Alexander the Great's soldiers drowned in 334 BC.

Ancient Theatre   RUINS
(Kıbrıs Şehitler Caddesi) A restored ancient theatre, which could originally seat 13,000 people, is cut into the rock of the hillside behind the town, on the busy main road to Gümbet. These days, the beautiful theatre is used for frequent concerts.

Shipyard   RUINS
(Şafak Sokak; ☺9am-6pm) Just beyond the marina are the recently restored remains of the shipyard. In 1770 the entire Ottoman fleet was destroyed by the Russians at Çeşme and had to be rebuilt from scratch in boatyards like this. The shipyard was fortified as a defence against pirates in the 19th century. Its tower occasionally hosts art exhibitions, while the rest of the site is mainly

used as a children's playground and is principally memorable for the views from the top, where there are several old tombstones dating from the period when the Latin alphabet was replacing Arabic.

🏃 Activities

So-called **'Blue Cruises'** are the most popular daytime activity in Bodrum. Countless excursion boats are moored along Neyzen Tevfik Caddesi and depart each morning for a daytrip on the rolling blue. Itineraries vary greatly, but most boats don't go far (if you're trying to reach one of the other bays on the peninsula it's best to do it by dolmuş instead). One popular destination is Karaada (Black Island), where hot springs gush out of a cave and swimmers rub the orange mud on their skin (its curative powers remain to be seen).

Cruises can be booked at your hotel, or you can simply wander up to one of the docked boats and buy a ticket (it's best to do this at least one day before your excursion). Figure around €10 to €12 for a group tour.

Daytrips to some of the region's big-ticket sights, like Ephesus and Pamukkale, can be booked at any travel agency and at most hotels and pensions. A day at Ephesus, for example, will set you back around €30 (this includes lunch but not the entrance fee to the Terraced Houses).

If you're looking for a more upscale cruise try **Neyzen Travel & Yachting** (☑316 7204; www.neyzen.com.tr; Kibris Sehitleri Caddesi 34).

🛏 Sleeping

Bodrum's clutch of accommodation is merely a small piece of the greater peninsular puzzle, so don't shy away from checking out hotels on some of the other bays even if you plan on spending the bulk of your time in town. The city centre is dominated by cheap (and usually lacklustre) pension-style lodging, though in the last ten years, several great inns and upmarket sleeps have cropped up on the hills marking the city's edge.

Note that the closer you stay to the sea, the noisier it will be in the evenings. Action at the clubs rarely kicks off before midnight and usually goes on until well past 4am. During the height of summer, especially at weekends, Bodrum fills up quickly, so it's best to reserve well in advance.

Su Otel BOUTIQUE HOTEL €€€
(☑316 6906; www.suhotel.net; Turgutreis Caddesi, 1201 Sokak; s/d/ste €55/90/125; ✳@➰) Follow the blue mosaic snake down the alley to find this cheery number that epitomises Bodrum's idyllic white-and-bright-blue decor. Sun-filled bedrooms ring around the inviting azure pool and blue trellises frame the curves of the inn with radiant Aegean blooms. Relax with a book on a lounge chair under the sun or get cosy in the pillowed lounge amid trippy beats from the likes of Imogen Heap.

Mars Otel PENSION €
(☑316 6559; www.marsotel.com; Turgutreis Caddesi, İmbat Çikmazi 29; s/d €30/40; ✳@➰) Backpackers look no further – this is the best bang for your buck in the budget category. Located a good five-minute walk from the seaside, Mars strives for a mini resort feel with a welcoming pool, lounge chairs, small bar and a very friendly staff. The comfy rooms are smothered in excessive coats of green paint, but they're kept very clean. Murat, the owner, is keen to please and offers free bus station and port transfers.

Marmara Bodrum LUXURY HOTEL €€€
(☑313 8130; www.themarmarahotels.com; Suluhasan Caddesi; r/ste from €180/600; ✳@➰) Easily the most upmarket option in Bodrum town, the gorgeous Marmara Bodrum is perched high in the condo-clad bluffs, offering unparalleled views of the action below. The sprawling hotel boasts a batch of elegant rooms (though not all have sea views) and a cache of excellent amenities like tennis courts, a spa, and two swimming pools worthy of a magazine spread. Beachbums can hop on the complimentary shuttle that links to a private patch of sand in nearby Torba. Even if you're not staying at the hotel, it's a great place for a sundowner with friends.

Butterfly BOUTIQUE HOTEL €€€
(☑316 8358; www.thebutterflybodrum.com; Ünlü Caddesi, 1512 Sokak 24; d €165-275; ✳@➰) Perched high above the chaos on the headland separating Bodrum and Gümbet, the Butterfly is run by a friendly Bostonian who has turned his lovely villa into an intimate six-room B&B. The bay views from the infinity-edge pool are hard to beat.

Aegean Gate BOUTIQUE HOTEL €€
(☑316 7853; www.aegeangatehotel.com; Guvercin Sokak 2; s/d €70/100; ✳➰@) An untouchable favourite on a certain trip advising website (ahem), Aegean Gate is a friendly

spot that earns top marks for its eager-to-please staff and tranquil surrounds anchored around a turquoise pool. It's located two blocks back from Halıkarnas.

Marina Vista · RESORT €€€
(☎313 0356; www.majesty.com.tr; Neyzen Tevfik Caddesi 226; r from €160; ✳@🌊) Far nicer than its rather unmemorable facade, Marina Vista is a fairly large hotel tucked away in a courtyard just off the main coastal drag. Modern design details (think purple lighting and Cubist portraits) somehow fit right in with the glimmering Aegean whites. Tango, the attached Argentinean restaurant, is quite good.

Baç Pansiyon · PENSION €€
(☎316 1602; bacpansiyon@turk.net; Cumhuriyet Caddesi 16; r TL85-100; ✳) Baç rises above the crowds on Cumhuriyet Caddesi and provides some of the best sea views in Bodrum. A gem amid the market maelstrom, it sits right along the water and four of its 10 comfortable rooms have delightful balconies. Hallways are coated in dark marble and have great mood lighting; plasma TVs are an extra perk.

Kaya Pension · PENSION €€
(☎316 5745; www.kayapansiyon.com.tr; Cevat Şakir Caddesi, Eski Hükümet Sokak 14; r TL90; ✳@) Noticeably nicer than most of the other pensions in town (and slightly pricier too), Kaya wins the adorable courtyard award – breakfast is served in this cosy space amid fragrant bougainvillea and hibiscus blossoms. Upstairs, the rooms are perfectly prim, and sport basic wood-cut furniture.

Otel Atrium · RESORT €€
(☎316 3926; www.atriumbodrum.com; Fabrika Sokak 21; s/d incl halfboard from TL80/110; ✳@🌊) We did a double-take the first time we saw the price list – for only a small step up from pension prices Otel Atrium offers an informal half-board resort atmosphere complete with a sociable pool area and friendly staff. Luscious gardens curve around the property – the hotel's owner is an avid avian collector (there's even an egg incubator in the front office). Fills up quick.

El Vino Hotel · BOUTIQUE HOTEL €€€
(☎313 8770; www.elvinobodrum.com; Omurça Mahallesi Pamili Sokak; r from €120; ✳@🌊) The dark backstreet location doesn't look that promising, but behind the stone wall is one of the town's loveliest hotels. Rooms are large and well appointed with wooden

floors, large beds, TVs and writing desks. The best have views of the central pool, garden area (where breakfast is served) and the town. Even better vistas are available from the rooftop restaurant.

Anfora · PENSION €
(☎316 5530; www.anforapansiyon.com; Omurça Dere Sokak 23; s/d from TL30/60; ✳@) Although very little English is spoken, the pension-style rooms at Anfora are perfectly fine – in fact, they're a clear step up from similar accommodation in the penny-pinching category. Rooms are well-kept and sport prim white sheets and lots of floral print. Bar Street's only a few blocks away – but you're far enough from the action that a decent night's sleep is still on the cards.

The following lodging options are worth an honourable mention.

Antik Tiyatro Hotel · BOUTIQUE HOTEL €€€
(☎316 6053; www.antiquetheatrehotel.com; Kıbrıs Şehitler Caddesi 243; d €120-225; ✳🌊) Original artwork and antiques adorn stylish rooms. Stunning views over the castle and sea. Located up near the ancient theatre, as the name suggests.

Bahçeli Ağar Aile Pansiyonu · PENSION €€
(☎316 1648; 1402 Sokak 4; s/d €40/50) An endearing little pension with a vine-draped courtyard. Guests have use of the kitchen. Rooms are small but spotless; all have balconies.

Hotel Güleç · PENSION €
(☎316 5222; www.hotelgulec.com; Üçkuyular Caddesi 22; s/d from €25/37; ✳@) Ticks all the budget boxes with prim accommodation and friendly management.

Gözen Butik Hotel · PENSION €€
(☎316 2079; www.gozenbutikhotel.com; Cumhuriyet Caddesi 18/1; s/d from TL75/150; ✳@) A carbon copy of Baç Pansiyon just up the block.

Turunç Pansiyon · PENSION €
(☎316 5333; Atatürk Caddesi, 1023 Sokak 4/A; s/d from TL40/70; ✳@) Clean and simple does the trick for budget types.

Albatros Otel · PENSION €€
(☎316 7117; www.albatrosotel.net; Neyzen Tevfik Caddesi, Menekşe Sokak 6; s/d TL80/120; ✳@) Simple and well-maintained.

✗ Eating

Bodrum's dining scene is as changeable as its customers' tastes, with new restaurants emerging all the time to replace the ones that have suddenly gone out of fashion. Most upmarket eats can be found along the western bay; in the east you're more likely to find filler food after a wild night out at one of the adjacent bars or nightclubs.

All tastes have been accounted for in central Bodrum – you'll find everything from pizza to sushi, but the best places are the local joints serving scrumptious seasonal mezes and fresh-from-the-sea fish. Swing by the **fruit market** on Cevat Şakir Caddesi during the day for a colourful array of healthy snacks.

TOP CHOICE **Fish Market** SEAFOOD €€

(Cevat Şakir Caddesi; meze from TL4, fish TL20; ☉dinner Mon-Sat) Sometimes called *'manavlar'* for the bustling fruit stands that mark the entrance to this small network of back alleys, Bodrum's fish market is a lively spot that has gained a fair bit of attention in recent years. Every evening in summer, the cramped alleyways overflow with a chaotic scatter of tables, much like the side streets off of trendy İstiklal in İstanbul. Crowds of lively locals gather to gorge on mezes, savour fresh fish and shoot mouthfuls of rakı. To the uninitiated it can be confusing and complicated, so here's a quick how-to: first, grab a table at one of the handful of restaurants. Order your beverages and mezes, then head to one of the fishmongers to select your catch. Once you've chosen and paid for your fish or calamari (avoid the cheap farm fish), head back to your seats. The fishmonger will prep your selection and bring it over to your restaurant where it will be cooked to your specifications and served for an extra TL4. It's best to book in advance – swing by during the day or ring ahead. Our favourite restaurant is **Eray** (☏316 7944).

Orfoz AEGEAN €€€

(☏316 4285; www.orfoz.com/bodrum.htm; Cumhuriyet Caddesi 177/B; mains from TL20; ☉dinner) Sitting across a backstreet from the madness of Halıkarnas, Orfoz may not look like much to those who aren't in the know, but it's often lauded as Bodrum's best seafood restaurant. The decor is simple: white walls, painted tiles hung somewhat haphazardly and a generous smattering of evil eyes dangling from hand-carved knick-knacks. The homemade food is sensational, and served in small portions, which can quickly drive up the price – add wine and you're looking at about TL100 per person.

Döner Tepecik FAST FOOD €

(Neyzen Tevfik Caddesi; döner TL4; ☉breakfast, lunch & dinner) Hands down the best döner shop in Bodrum, this hole-in-the-wall spins scrumptious snacks to peckish passers-by all throughout the day. Grab a seat at one of the three wooden picnic-style tables out front and don't forget to request a jar of pickled green chillies to stuff inside your meat sandwich (ask for your döner on homemade toasted bread). There are no signs or banners – just look for the striped white-and-blue awning directly across from the mosque and listen for ambient 'yums'.

Küba INTERNATIONAL €€€

(www.kubabar.com; Neyzen Tevfik Caddesi 62; mains from TL20; ☉dinner) Although mostly known as the most happenin' club in central Bodrum, Küba is slowly earning a widespread reputation for its tasty assortment of dinner options. Prim white cloths stretch over welcoming outdoor tables as well-heeled diners select from a colourful assortment of mezes, fish and international mains (including attempts at Asian fusion). One by one, as each group finishes, their table evaporates and the dance floor grows. By 12.30am Küba has made its complete transformation into a full-on nightclub.

Gemibaşi AEGEAN €€€

(Neyzen Tevfik Caddesi; meze from TL5, mains TL15-25; ☉lunch & dinner) Gemibaşi's *Mamma Mia*-esque white-and-blue decor sets the tone for flavoursome tributes to the Aegean. Fresh meze and high-quality fish are served with a side of sea views and breezy shade.

Sünger PIZZA €

(Neyzen Tevfik Caddesi 218; mains TL8-30; ☉breakfast, lunch & dinner) Named after the owner's grandfather who was a *sünger* (sponge) diver, this bustling spot is hugely popular with locals. Most diners opt for the pizza (Sünger's known around town for having the best pies), but the fish soup is also very tasty and quite underrated.

La Pasión SPANISH €€

(Restaurante Español; www.lapasion-bodrum. com; cnr Atatürk Caddesi & Uslu Sokak; menu TL35; ☉lunch & dinner) Tucked away down one of the narrow side streets sprouting off of Cumhuriyet Caddesi, this inviting Spanish-themed restaurant fills an old flower-strewn courtyard and a charming stone house. Bossa nova moves through the air as Iberian-inspired platters are served to a contented mix of locals, expats and tourists.

Marina Yacht Club
ITALIAN €€

(☎316 1228; Neyzen Tevfik Caddesi 5; mains TL10-32; ⊗breakfast, lunch & dinner) Despite the rather grand entrance and chichi yachting surrounds, the food and prices are quite reasonable at this three-restaurant complex, and there's live music every night from 9pm to 1am. You'll have your choice of either Turkish or Italian cuisine.

Berk Balık Restaurant
SEAFOOD €€

(☎313 6878; Cumhuriyet Caddesi 167; meze from TL5, fish from TL12; ⊗lunch & dinner) Run by a group of friends, this restaurant specialises in fish and seafood, served on a terrific upstairs terrace that buzzes like a village tavern. It's absolutely packed with locals tossing down octopus in garlic and butter, or excellent fresh fish at pleasing prices.

Nazik Ana
LOCAL €

(Eski Hukumet Sokak 7; mains TL3-7; ⊗breakfast, lunch & dinner, closed Sun in winter) Hidden away down a narrow alley but definitely worth hunting out, this simple but atmospheric place is a huge hit locally, particularly with the police officers from next door. With its point-and-pick counter, it's great for sampling different Turkish dishes. Prices are kept so cheap that there's no buyer's remorse – if you don't like something just grab a new plate! It lies off Cevat Şakir Caddesi.

Limoon Cafe & Restaurant
LOCAL €

(www.limooncaferestaurant.com; Cafer Paşa Caddesi 10; mains TL8-16; ⊗breakfast, lunch & dinner) Tucked slightly away from the action in the far west corner of town, lazy Limoon occupies a lovely outdoor setting under the generous shade of large twisting trees. The 'village breakfast' is well worth the trek, as are the weekly Scrabble games organised by a small brigade of friendly expat ladies (usually on Wednesdays).

🍷 Drinking & Entertainment

As with accommodation and eating out, there's a simple rule of thumb: for cheap and cheerful head to the eastern bay, for expensive and classy, think west. Dr Alim Bey Caddesi and Cumhuriyet Caddesi function as Bodrum's 'Bar Street', offering a long line of loud and largely interchangeable waterfront bar-clubs. Expect happy hours, big-screen TVs showing major football matches, bartenders performing synchronised dance routines and a mostly (but not exclusively) foreign clientele. Clubs on the western bay tend to attract the Turkish jetset.

The castle and the antique theatre are often used for cultural events such as opera, ballet and rock performances. Check out www.biletix.com to see if anything is on while you're in town.

Halıkarnas
CLUB

(The Club; www.halikarnas.com.tr; Cumhuriyet Caddesi 178; admission weekday/weekend TL35/40; ⊗10pm-5am summer) Since 1979 the open-air Halıkarnas has been a clubbers' institution. With its kitschy Roman temple styling and top-notch sound-and-light equipment, it's an unforgettable experience, particularly when at capacity (5000 people). It doesn't get going much before 1am. Guests are asked to 'dress for the occasion' but it's unlikely you'll be refused entry.

Küba Bar
CLUB

(Neyzen Tevfik Caddesi 62; ⊗7pm-4am) The number-one spot for Bodrum's posh Turkish crowd to let loose on a night out on the town, Küba is bumpin' every night of the week in the height of summer. Swish countertops, eclectic DJed beats and plasmas showing pouting models – it all seems to get the partiers roaring. Earlier in the evening, Küba does smart international fare.

Helva
CLUB

(www.helvabodrum.com; Neyzen Tevfik Caddesi 54; ⊗2pm-3am) Quieter and a bit less superfashionable than Küba down the road, Helva is nonetheless aimed at the Turkish smart set. Despite its exhortations to 'express yourself in dance' this is more of a chilled out affair where dancing sporadically breaks out. It's stylish, lively and (inevitably) expensive.

Hadigari
CLUB

(www.hadigari.com.tr; 1025 Sokak 2; ⊗7pm-5am) Built in 1974, Hadigari officially takes the title as Bodrum's oldest bar. These days it's still going strong under the looming turrets of St Peter's Castle.

Körfez
BAR

(www.korfezbar.com; Uslu Sokak 2; ⊗9pm-5am summer) An old favourite (and not to be confused with the like-named restaurant along the western bay), Körfez is geared more towards rock beats and the dark-wood atmosphere is made to match. Sunday is '80s night.

Mavi Bar
LIVE MUSIC

(Cumhuriyet Caddesi 175; ⊗6pm-6am) Across from Halıkarnas, 'Blue' lures in great live acts five nights a week. It's an intimate spot with white stone walls and blue trim. Don't expect things to get rollin' until around 1am.

Moonlight   BAR
(www.moonlightbodrum.com; Cumhuriyet Caddesi 60/B) Nurse your Efes beer right along the rolling tide at Moonlight – one of the more chilled out and atmospheric spots on the otherwise hectic Cumhuriyet Caddesi. It's down a small side street that starts opposite Körfez.

Marine Club Catamaran   CLUB
(www.clubcatamaran.com; Dr Alim Bey Caddesi; admission weekday/weekend TL35/40; ◷10pm-4am mid-May–Sep) This floating nightclub sets sail at 1.30am for three hours of frenzied fun amid DJed beats and the occasional frolicking drag queen. Its transparent dance floor can pack in 1500 clubbers plus attendant DJs. A free shuttle operates every 15 minutes back to the eastern bay.

❶ Information

You can't swing an empty wallet without hitting an ATM along Cevat Şakir Caddesi or any of the harbour-front streets.

Post office (Cevat Şakir Caddesi; ◷8.30am-5pm, telephone exchange 8am-midnight)

Tourist office (Kale Meydanı; ◷8am-6pm Mon-Fri, daily in summer)

❶ Getting Around

It's easy to get around central Bodrum on foot – the intra-city dolmuş service costs TL1.25, though it can take an annoyingly long time to reach your destination by vehicle due to traffic and narrow, oft-blocked streets. If you're driving, note that most of Bodrum's roads follow a strict clockwise one-way system. Miss your turn and you'll probably have to go all the way out of town and do the whole thing again.

Gümbet

☑0252
Although the region's penchant for luxury has swept across the peninsula faster than wildfire, bustling Gümbet – just a quick 5km hop from Bodrum town – seems to have missed the memo. Rather than upmarket sleeps and champagne clinks, Gümbet is a relentless party machine fuelled by teenage adrenaline and cocktails named after sexual positions. Resorts operate on half-board schemes providing revellers factory-line fare to sop up an evening's worth of

punch and poison. Disco naps under the Aegean sun are commonplace and a daily all-night romp-fest goes without saying. Speaker volumes rumble at maximum capacity – the dancefloors too – as each club competes with their neighbour by blasting 'Top 40' remixes of Rihanna and the Black Eyed Peas. And thus, the peninsula's population of expats have affectionately dubbed the bay 'Scumbet'.

But all is not lost, however; the unceremonious blend of neon lights and eager youngsters can be a refreshing change from the see-and-be-seen catwalks of sand that flank the other bays. If you're keen on spending your vacation here, your best bet is Fuga (☑319 6500; www.fuga.com.tr; Adnan Menderes Cad; d incl full-board TL325; ✳@☒; ◷May-Oct), which has boutique-chic aspirations that starkly contrast the rather soulless array of surrounding lodging options.

If you're visiting Bodrum in the winter it's not worth stopping through – Gümbet off-season is a backwater filled with boarded-up hotels and stray dogs.

Bitez

☑0252
Framed by curling ripples of blue and orchards of gnarled orange groves, the lovely beachside village of Bitez feels miles away from the bumping discotheques of Bodrum, despite its relatively convenient location. Although the beachfront seems largely developed with a seamless string of chaise-studded sand, bitty Bitez is still trying to find its groove as it opens up to European travellers. In fact, it's not uncommon to find a gaggle of topless sunbathers relaxing under the shade of a looming minaret!

Archaeology buffs might be interested in the ruins of Pedasa, located on the main peninsular road near the turn-off down to Bitez. Erected by the ancient Lelegs (the predecessors of the Carians) more than 5000 years ago, this small site features the foundations of a defensive wall and the ruins of what is thought to be a temple.

🛏 Sleeping

Şah Hotel   BOUTIQUE HOTEL €€
(☑363 7721; www.sahhotel.com; Şah Caddesi; d TL120-220; ✳@☒) A small, unassuming doorway directly along the beach boardwalk opens into a charming courtyard filled with finely trimmed hedges, rustic

lawn-furniture and an inviting turquoise pool that draws in most of the focus. The rooms could benefit from a designer's touch – the standard accommodation is a tad cramped and the suite-style digs feel insufficiently furnished, but overall Şah wins out for its relaxed and friendly atmosphere.

Okaliptüs Otel PENSION €€€
(☑363 7957; www.okaliptus.com.tr; Bitez Yalısı; s/d incl half-board TL180/240; ✳@≋) Set behind the popular on-site restaurant with its signature spiderlike banyan tree, the accommodations at Okaliptüs are scattered around a series of alcoves and flower-filled trellises. Rooms are simply furnished and kept very clean – especially the marble bathrooms. There's a charming swimming pool, though most guests congregate along the adjacent pebble-strewn sand.

✗ Eating

Unlike some of the other bays, Bitez doesn't completely shut down during the winter months. In fact, many of the peninsula's locals flock here on weekends to savour a variety of brunch buffets served by the beachside restaurants.

TOP CHOICE Bağarası AEGEAN €€€
(☑358 7693; Pınarlı Caddesi 59; meze from TL4, fish TL20; ⊙lunch & dinner, closed Mon Nov-Apr) Tucked away in a residential garden, Bağarası is Bitez's best-kept secret and a perennial fave on the peninsula. Tables wobble under the weight of scrumptious mezes as the affable owner – a dead ringer for Shrek – dotes on his customers. His wife is in the kitchen whipping up an assortment of specials to accompany her classic fish dishes; don't miss the flavourful *kabak çiçeği* (stuffed zucchini flowers) and the tantalising *kıtır mantı* (crispy Turkish pasta with meat sauce and cream). Be sure to stay late enough to catch the owner's nightly joke heralded by the ceremonial blow of a whistle – it's in Turkish, of course, and usually involves a clever play on words, but it's still a great scene to witness even if you haven't mastered the language. Reservations are a must.

Bitez Mantıcı MANTICI €
(Atatürk Bulvarı 40; mains TL4-13; ⊙lunch & dinner) Short on atmosphere but big on taste, this veritable hole-in-the-wall serves up what most would consider the best *mantı* and *börek* on the peninsula. Shovel spoonfuls of Turkish pasta and devour savoury pastries on plastic-topped tables as floppy saucers of *gözleme* are arduously rolled out in the corner.

Black Cat LOCAL €€
(Mart Kedileri; www.martkedileri.com; mains TL7-20; ⊙breakfast, lunch & dinner) Set a block back from the beach near the Şah Hotel, Black Cat gets special mention for its traditional Turkish recipes – a pleasant departure from the usual fish-and-meze line-up.

Indian Salsa INDIAN €€
(Gözütok Sokak 4; menu TL32; ⊙lunch. dinner Jul-Aug) Spice things up at this newcomer, which offers an authentic taste of the subcontinent.

Ortakent
☑0252

Similar to Bitez next door, Ortakent is another up-and-comer with a generous 3km stretch of flaxen sand. Many locals consider Orakent to have the cleanest and coldest water on the peninsula due to the constant churning of the sea. Although a phalanx of lounge chairs has taken over most of the public beachfront, visitors can retreat to Scala Beach (www.scalabeach.net) for some quieter ray-catching at the east end of the bay.

🛏 Sleeping

Satsuma Suites APARTMENT €€€
(☑348 4249; www.satsumasuites.com; Eren Sokak 17; apt €145; ✳≋) This adults-only complex is a great option for vacationers seeking the amenities of an apartment and the service of a hotel. The inviting blue-tiled pool is framed with charming slats of sanded timber; comfortable rooms lie just beyond. The included breakfast earns top marks.

✗ Eating

Adasofra GOURMET €€€
(☑358 7414; www.adasofra.com; Mustafa Paşa Kulesi, Kule Sokak 29; mains TL16-38; ⊙dinner) Constructed as a watchtower by ancient marauders, Adasofra is now a chic dining venue that effortlessly embraces its surrounds while offering thoroughly modern cuisine. Enjoy a culinary tribute to the Med amid crumbling brick and snaking cacti; don't forget to pop your head into the ruined hamam.

Palavra AEGEAN €€€
(☑358 6290; www.palavrabalik.com; Yahşi Beldesi; meze TL5-15, fish TL20; ⊙8am-midnight) The 'Tall Tale' is perhaps named for the exagger-

ated chatter of the local fishermen who regularly claim to have caught a fish THIS BIG. Point to your meze of choice in the glass casing, choose a bottle of Kavaklıdere wine, then grab a seaside table and plunk your feet down in the sand. Evenings here are particularly charming when hanging fairy lights give the place a bit more atmosphere.

Gebora
AEGEAN €€

(☎348 3340; Yahşi Beldesi; meze TL5-15, fish TL20; ⊙9am-midnight) The owner of Gebora is a gruff fisherman who's been trolling the seas for over 35 years. His restaurant, on the main beachfront boardwalk near the Yalı Camii mosque, serves an excellent assortment of seafood staples and local mezes on prim white-cloth tables. Be sure to try the grilled calamari stuffed with shrimp; the local ferns are also a must.

Turgutreis

☑0252

Twenty years ago Turgutreis was a centre for the lucrative sponge diving industry, but today the area has transformed into a popular destination for holidaymakers who prefer villa and apartment rentals to resort vacations. The city – the second largest on the peninsula – is named after Admiral Turgut (reis means admiral), the Ottoman leader who took Bodrum from the Crusaders.

There's very little as far as must-see sights are concerned, but the area makes a pleasant daytrip for those looking to do a bit of shopping at the Saturday textile and food market. If you do swing through, consider checking out the modern marina and the statue of a pregnant woman sanding tall along the adjacent waterfront. She holds a conspicuous olive branch and is meant to represent the health, peacefulness and diversity of Anatolia.

Gümüşlük

☑0252

Of all the bays scalloping the rugged, olive grove–strewn peninsula, Gümüşlük is undoubtedly our favourite. Locals celebrate their fisherman roots with adorable shanty-like structures dotting the coastline, and ample seaside restaurants serve the freshest daily catch. The laid-back atmosphere has been attracting easygoing hippies for a couple of decades now; it's only recently

that the jetset crowd has caught on to the village's calm-inducing vibe.

Although the threat of development is evident (notice the white, Tetris-cube-like structures dotting the southern bluffs), local officials are keen to preserve the town's distinct 'fishing village' vibe, and thus new laws have been put in place to slow construction. In fact, road-paving is strictly forbidden; you'll only find dirt paths in Gümüşlük. Note that vehicles are banned from entering the village, but there is a municipal car park (TL3 per day) 300m from the waterfront.

It's hard to believe that this chilled-out village was once a sprawling city in the ancient world. Known as Myndos, the settlement was an important Carian stronghold and occupied an advantageous position with its deep harbour and calm seas. Mausolus, the city's founder, erected a three-metre-deep breaker in the middle of the bay to link the mainland and a small conical islet – known today as Rabbit Island – floating just offshore. Today you'll find an endless stream of tourists doing the veritable walk-on-water to reach the scrubby satellite.

🛏 Sleeping

These days, Gümüşlük's charm is undeniable and widely known, which means that prices are starting to soar and the crowd of visitors is slowly shifting away from hippie types. That said, it's still possible to score a spot in a family-run pension, just make sure to phone ahead. Villa rentals are also quite common.

Otel Gümüşlük
RESORT €€

(☎394 4828; www.otelgumusluk.com; Yalı Mevkii 28; d TL100-200; ❋@☒) The bay's best option sits slightly back from the seaside action on an acreage of flat, tree-lined gardens. Two-storey ranch-style hotel blocks sit around an inviting swimming pool, and inside the rooms sport savvy decorative features and clean lines that feel fashionable yet minimalist. Ask about the newly opened apartment accommodation further afield if you decide to extend your vacation.

Club Hotel Zemda
RESORT €€€

(☎394 3151; www.clubhotelzemda.com; d/ste €110/165; ❋@☒🐾) Run by a lovely French-Turkish couple, Zemda sits at the far south end of the bay and functions as the area's go-to spot for watersports enthusiasts. Daily windsurfing and paddling classes are the norm at this sprawling, sociable retreat. The rooms' mail-order furnishings are a bit ho-hum, but who really cares when days are spent lounging around the swimming pool. Evenings take place at the on-site bar or in the village centre just a stone's throw away.

Liman Motel   PENSION €€
(☎394 3747; www.limanmotelrestaurant.com; r TL100-160; ❄) Smack dab in the middle of the village, Liman is perched above the action behind a signature white-washed Aegean facade. The rooms are kept very simple and continue the all-white theme, but the sea views are unbeatable and worth the overpriced rack rate.

✖ Eating & Drinking

Excellent eating options are plentiful in Gümüşlük's fishing village. Do as the locals do and order a bottle of rakı with your sumptuous seafood meal – just don't schedule anything for the morning after! If you're interested in scoring some seafood to cook at your private apartment, head to the docks between 8am and 10am as the fishermen return to sell their catch to the local restaurants.

Mimoza   AEGEAN €€€
(☎394 3139; www.mimoza-bodrum.com; meze from TL20, mains from TL40; ☺lunch & dinner mid-Jun–Aug) With a noticeably more refined and trendy atmosphere than the other restaurants lining the curling tide, Mimoza – at the far north end of the bay – is the area's favourite dining destination and a must for vacationing İstanbullus. Well-heeled diners feast on expertly made mezes (the smoked aubergine is heaven) under a constellation of gourd-like lamps dangling in the trees overhead. Reservations are a must; and even if there's availability the owner will make an exaggerated ado about how his restaurant is just oh-so popular and busy.

Limon   AEGEAN €€
(☎394 4044; www.limongumusluk.com; meze TL14-28; ☺lunch & dinner mid-Jun–mid-Sep) Perched just above the fishing village on the old Myndos Rd to Yalıkavak, lovely Limon's menagerie of mismatched furniture (à la Alice in Wonderland) is splayed across the ruins of a crumbling Roman bath and Byzantine chapel. Savour tasty 'village breakfasts', mezes served tapas-style, or nurse a designer cocktail while enjoying one of the Aegean's signature sunsets.

Don't forget to check out the veritable car-boot sale of hipster trinkets lining Limon's entrance pathway.

Teldolap   LOCAL €€
(www.teldolaprestaurant.com; Sarıcayer Mevkii 2, Küme Evleri 85/2; mains TL12-28; ☺breakfast, lunch & dinner) High in the grove-clad hills flanking the scenic fishing village, the 'Wire Cupboard' sits in a stately stone villa adorned with Gaudí-esque mosaics. Delicious homemade breakfasts are the norm, as are the sweeping panoramic views of the bays and beyond. Teldolap is only accessible by private vehicle.

Ali Ruza'nin Yeri   AEGEAN €€€
(☎394 3097; www.balikcialirizaninyeri.com; meze TL8-20, mains from TL20; ☺lunch & dinner) One of the oldest restaurants in Gümüşlük's cluttered line-up of seaside fish huts, Ali Ruza'nin Yeri is run by a family of local fishermen who pride themselves on offering the freshest local catch – no farm fish here! It's worth ringing ahead to score one of the tables directly on the water's edge.

Soğan~Sarmısak   LOCAL €€€
(☎394 3087; mains from TL18; ☺lunch & dinner mid-Jun–Aug) Another one of Gümüşlük's *pied dans l'eau* gems, 'Onion and Garlic' is an informal clump of wire and wooden furniture amid potted plants. Homemade cuisine is the name of the game, and the owner/chef has made a bit of a name for herself on TV (so everything's overpriced, naturally). Come armed with plenty of conversation fodder – the food can take quite a while to prepare.

Gözleme Shack   STREET FOOD €
(gözleme TL4) Gözleme connoisseurs will be hard-pressed to find a better pancake than the ones crafted at this nameless, wall-less haunt near the junction of the beach road and the path to the car park. Plunk your feet in the dirt, select from the usual ingredients – spinach, cheese, mince and potatoes – and wash it down with a salty glass of homemade *ayran*. (yoghurt drink)

Mandarina   STREET FOOD €
(poğaça TL1; ☺6.30am-6.30pm) Just south of the road leading up to the car park, Mandarina's floor-to-ceiling stack of bright yellow preserves are as delicious as they are eye-catching. Come early in the morning to fill your belly with savoury homemade *poğaça* (puff pastry).

Yalıkavak

☎ 0252

It's hard to believe that sprawling Yalıkavak (which means 'tree by the sea') got its first volt of electricity a mere 30 years ago. Before tourism caught on, the town was a soporific settlement of sponge divers and fisherfolk. Windmills once generated most of the power, and several haunting ruins dot the rapidly developing landscape. As one of the furthest settlements from Bodrum town, Yalıkavak feels like a city unto itself, with a distinct central core and a cache of upmarket private beaches; **Xuma Beach Club** and **Dodo Beach Club** are the most popular.

Near the abandoned township of Yakaköy just outside of Yalıkavak, you'll find **Dibek Sofrası** (www.dibeklihan.com; Yakaköy Çilek Caddesi; ⊙May-Oct), a fascinating complex complete with a restaurant, art gallery, museum, boutique hotel (currently under construction) and a Provence-style vineyard. Dibek's *raison d'être* is the collection of jewelled daggers, antique fountain pens and ornate coffee cups that the owner has been slowly gathering from all over the former Ottoman Empire. They are neatly displayed in two small rooms off the main courtyard. It's worth stopping by on Wednesday evenings when classic Hollywood movies are projected on a white screen.

🛏 Sleeping

Hillview Gardens   APARTMENT €€

(☎363 8234; www.lotusholidayhomes.com; apt/villa from €42/70; ❄ ✸ @) Hillview represents the future of accommodation in Bodrum – and what a bright future it is! This brilliant holiday concept is a gated community of privately owned apartments and villas that are available for rent throughout the summer months. The accommodation winds around the crown of an arid hill offering stunning views out to sea. The properties are tastefully furnished and come fully equipped (breakfast is not included); many of the villas have private plunge pools. Guests have full access to a variety of onsite amenities like tennis courts, a spa, a restaurant (with surprisingly good food) and 10 communal pools. A frequent dolmuş service links Hillview to Yalıkavak and Gümüşlük.

Sandima 37 Suites   BOUTIQUE HOTEL €€€

(☎385 5337; www.sandima37suites.com; Atatürk Caddesi 37; ste TL240-400; ❄ ✸ @) A gorgeous addition to Bodrum's ever-growing clutch of boutique hotels, Sandima has seven stylish suites arranged around a lush garden. The most charming accommodation option is the gorgeously restored stone cottage that sits in the back near the pool.

4 Reasons Hotel   BOUTIQUE HOTEL €€€

(☎385 3212; www.4reasonshotel.com; Bakan Caddesi 2; d/ste from €149/239; ❄ @ ✸) 'Serenity, design, quality and attitude' are written in large letters at the entrance (just in case you thought there might be a typo in the hotel's name). Although the moniker may conjure up thoughts of a certain international hotel chain, 4 Reasons is an intimate hillside retreat run by a lovely Turkish couple who speak perfect English. Rooms have generous amounts of locally sourced marble accented by stylish wooden slatting. Wood-burning fireplaces and newly installed plasmas add an extra touch. Get the blood flowing with a game of bocce ball or a group yoga class (TL30). You needn't look far for a tasty meal – the on-site restaurant serves a delicious assortment of pan-Mediterranean cuisine that samples the local dishes of Morocco, France, Greece and, of course, Turkey.

Lavanta Hotel   HOTEL €€€

(☎385 2167; www.lavanta.com; Begonvil Sokak 17; s/d €105/130; ❄ ✸) Set on a rolling property of vine-draped gardens, Lavanta is situated high in the hillocks overlooking the sprawl of polished-white vacation homes. Delicate stone paths amble around the resort connecting each of the uniquely decorated rooms – most have a clutch of adorable antiques.

Adahan   HOTEL €€

(☎385 4759; www.adahanotel.com; Seyhulislan Ömer Lütfü Caddesi 55; d TL145; ⊙Apr-Oct; ❄ @ ✸) Designed to look like an old caravanserai with pointed arches and imposing wooden doors, the Adahan has spacious and comfortable rooms arranged around an arcaded courtyard containing a lovely pool. Crumbling Roman sculptures and Anatolian antiques furnish the corners, and from the kitchen comes scintillating smells – the charming owners also run a gourmet restaurant. It lies around 100m from the yacht harbour on the road to Gümüşlük.

Pink Life   APARTMENT €€€

(☎385 5838; www.pinklifehotel.com; Aratepe Mevkii; apt TL300; ⊙May-Oct; ❄ ✸) This complex of apartment blocks offers vacationers the chance to score a large seaside condo for a very reasonable price. The large two-bedroom apartments come with an equipped kitchen and simple tropical-style furnishings. Note that there's only air-conditioning in the living room of each unit, so it's best to leave your bedroom door open on humid evenings.

Eating

Yakıkavak has a long fishing tradition and the daily catch can be sampled in the Geriş Altı district at the west end of town towards Gümüşlük. On Thursdays it's worth stopping by Çinaraltı to check out the weekly bazaar – you'll find heaps of locally grown picnic fodder including fruit, veggies and goats cheese.

Kavaklı Köfteci
KÖFTECI **€**

(Merkez Çarşı İçı; köfte TL6-8; ⊙breakfast, lunch & dinner) Around 50m inland, this place is famous for its Yalıkavak *köfte* served up on simple wooden tables with garlic bread. Smoky-flavoured, slightly spiced and succulent, they're gorgeous! Fight for a table if you have to.

Deniz Kızı
SEAFOOD **€€€**

(The Mermaid; ☑385 2600; Gerişaltı; mains TL16-24; ⊙lunch & dinner) This choose-your-own-fish kinda place occupies a lovely setting directly along the sea. Scrumptious mezes fill the white-cloth tabletops along the breezy dock and charming indoor portion of the cottage-style restaurant.

Ali Baba
AEGEAN **€€€**

(İskele Meydanı 166; fish TL20; ⊙lunch & dinner) On the edge of the harbour with seafront seating, the Ali Baba does a fine line in fish and seafood, including grilled sea-bass, octopus casserole and pan-fried jumbo prawns, although, if you really want to get everyone's attention, order the amphora kebap, which your waiter will smash open at your table.

Gündoğan

☑0252

The bay of Gündoğan is noticeably more attractive than Yalıkavak, but lodging options are few and far between as most of the housing here is reserved for the private vacation homes of Istanbul's wealthy elite.

Sleeping

Hamak
BOUTIQUE HOTEL **€€€**

(☑387 9840; www.hamakhotel.com; Kızılburun Mevkii, Casa Costa Sitesi; d €130-290; ❄@) Gündoğan's best option in the hotel catego-

ry lives in a renovated apartment complex down by the sea. Colourful paintings cheer the rooms, most of which have fantastic views of the neighbouring hills and sea. The *piece de resistance,* however, is the gorgeous wood-slatted sundeck that stretches out into Aegean with its catwalk of crisp white chaise-lounges.

Eating

Reana
AEGEAN **€€**

(☑387 7117; Yalı Mevkii, Limaniçi; fish TL20; ⊙dinner) You'd never know it, but white-walled Reana is set in the shell of a former supermarket. Today the owners have done a wonderful job of livening up the space with flowing linens and candlelight. Fish is the specialty here – repeat local customers and crowds of returning İstanbullus confirm the deliciousness.

Türkbükü

☑0252

If the Bodrum Peninsula fancies itself the Côte d'Azur of Turkey, then Türkbükü is undoubtedly the St Tropez. Like any other playground of the rich and famous, the bay has achieved a veritable reputation that far outshines its actual virtues. In fact, the waters of Türkbükü are noticeably more turbid than those of the peninsula's southern beaches, so visitors prefer swank, slatted boardwalk lounging to the smattering of stone-strewn sand. Simple sarongs are replaced with diamond-studded frocks, beach babes wear stilettos instead of sandals, and prices are cranked up beyond reason to expedite the wallet-draining process. Think of the town as veritable celebrity safari – if you're well versed in Turkish pop-stardom then keep your eyes peeled for plastic divas and teen heart-throbs.

Sleeping

Sleeping in Türkbükü is a pricey venture no matter how you cut it. But if you're seeking a slice of jetset paradise, you'll find no better place in all of Turkey. Just be sure to bring your earplugs if you plan on fitting in a evening's worth of restful sleep – during the height of high season things get pretty rowdy on a nightly basis.

 Maçakızı
BOUTIQUE HOTEL **€€€**

(☑377 6272; www.macakizi.com; Kesire buğlu Mevkii; r from TL400; ❄@≋) Bodrum's flagship of jetsetterdom, the 'Queen of

Spades' honours the owner's bodacious mother who once ran a colourful and characterful pension nearby. Today, the hotel teems with celebs, moneyed foreigners, and a coterie of bikini-ed beach bunnies who have mastered the fine art of negotiating the pebble-laden sand in six-inch heels. Almost all of the action is focused around the capacious bar, sociable restaurant and stunning, wood-slatted boardwalk that stretches into the blue with its cache of comfy pillow-beds. The simply styled rooms are a bit lacklustre considering the hefty price tag, but the Acqua di Parma toiletries are a nice take-home souvenir.

Kuum   BOUTIQUE HOTEL €€€
(☑311 0060; www.kuumhotel.com; Atatürk Caddesi 150; r €185-555; ❄☀@) Kuum's unique 'industrial-chic' design scheme looks like the architect robbed a power plant, and although it may not appeal to every traveller you have to give the resort props for trying. Check out the Eames-inspired furnishings and giant magnetic block letters in the rooms. Don't miss the massive underground spa complex with scores of marble-laden hamams and dimly lit hallways resembling the decks of the starship *Enterprise*. An Aequalis signature spa treatment will set you back €105.

Kaktüs Çiçeği   PENSION €€€
(☑377 5254; www.kaktuscicegi.com.tr; Atatürk Caddesi 119; d TL160-240; ❄@☀) The area's only option in the 'pension' category is a wonderfully charming spot adorned with honey-tinged walls and brilliant bursts of bougainvillea. The Turkish-French owners have a special flair for unique decor – edgy graphics function as funky accent walls and antique doors have been transformed into tabletops down in the beachside restaurant. It's located just beyond the pedestrian bridge near the Divan Hotel.

YU   BOUTIQUE HOTEL €€€
(☑377 5275; www.yu-otel.com; Bağarası Caddesi 26; r €130-160; ❄@☀) A labyrinth of polished concrete and bleach-white walls, YU's unique complex feels like a Japanese video game. Although it's set 700m away from the beach, the hotel still embraces the area's penchant for boutique-chic styling, and perhaps goes a bit too far. Shaded curtains and glass panels function as room dividers and an inviting pool anchors the Escher-like stairwells. Inside you'll find

trippy triangular patterns and jacuzzis built directly into the bedding (you'll see).

Maki Hotel   HOTEL €€€
(☑377 6105; www.makihotel.com.tr; Keleşharımı Mevkii; d/ste from €150/240; ❄@☀) With a snazzy wooden deck and overstuffed body pillows like Maçakızı next door, this large resort complex scores high points if you're looking for Bodrum's trademark sea-sun-fun trio. Rooms come in a variety of shapes and sizes – most sport generous amounts of space-age steel and concrete. The common areas are filled with bikini-clad beachgoers relaxing under large umbrellas that sport the logos of famous brands.

5 Oda   BOUTIQUE HOTEL €€€
(Beş Oda; ☑377 6219; www.otel5oda.com; İnönü Caddesi 161; r €250; ☾May-Oct; ❄@) The name says it all – this hot new lodging option has five quaint rooms tucked behind a stately stone facade. Found objects from across the continents – like vases, pillows and beads – give the *odas* a certain extra *je ne sais quoi*. Each room looks out over the sea and the scatter of slatted boardwalks.

Divan Hotel   HOTEL €€€
(☑377 5601; Keleşharım Caddesi 6; d €125-260; ❄@☀) An old Türkbükü staple, the Divan (pronounced *diwan*) has a welcoming pool area that overflows with Turkish vacationers during the height of summer. Rooms come with predictable international furnishings that could use some serious sprucing. The on-site bar is popular and pricey.

Life Co   RESORT €€€
(☑377 6310; www.thelifeco.com; Bağ Arası Mahallesi, 136 Sokak 2; s/d €165/300; ❄@☀) An honest-to-goodness detox centre, Life Co just might be the perfect antidote to a week of liver-straining partying in Türkbükü. Yoga classes, diet seminars and exotic blended smoothies are the norm. You'll wanna stay forever.

🍴 Eating & Drinking
Posh sleeps beget posh eats – you'll find dozens of delectable options spread along the coast and inland as well. If you've got the dime, don't miss out on a meal at Maçakızı (p248), and – as always in the Bodrum Peninsula – make sure to book ahead!

Ship Ahoy   RESTAURANT-BAR €€€
(☑377 5070; Yalı Mevkii; ☾May-Aug) Next to the Divan Hotel, Ship Ahoy is a classic address that attracts tonnes of celebs with its

restaurant-cum-nightclub vibe. Tables along the sea are fashioned from used oil drums.

Fidèle
RESTAURANT-BAR €€€

(☎377 5081; www.fidelehotel.net; mains from TL20; ☺breakfast, lunch & dinner) A sea of white linen drapery covers the tables in the evening. Dine on seafood risotto or octopus carpaccio before Fidèle transforms into a nightclub, then sample the selection of house spirits – spicy vodka is the local fave.

Casita
MANTICI €€

(www.casita.com.tr; mains from TL15; ☺lunch & dinner) Istanbul's famous *mantı* (Turkish ravioli) house has opened its doors along the sands of Türkbükü. Daytime diners can recline on the restaurant's chaise lounges.

Gölköy
☎0252

While Türkbükü steals all the thunder and glory, Gölköy is often viewed as its ugly sister – a undeserved reputation that makes the bay wildly underrated and perfect for those seeking something slightly (only *slightly*) more low-key.

One of Gölköy's main draws is Bianca Beach (www.biancabeach.com; Akdeniz Caddesi 35; ☺10am-5am May-Oct) a bump-and-grind party venue directly on the sand that often attracts well-known live acts.

Sleeping

Villa Kılıç Hotel
BOUTIQUE HOTEL €€€

(☎357 8118; www.villakilic.com; Sahil Sokak 22; r/ste from TL350/550; ✹@☀) Villa Kılıç is a luxurious addition to Gölköy's small accommodation scene. There are 33 lavishly designed rooms with flat-screen TVs, hardwood floors and marble accents; the suites have private hot tubs. Take a dip in the large pool, grab a bite in the conservatory restaurant, or recline on the largest bathing platform in town (300 sq metres) where DJs play in summer.

Atami
RESORT €€€

(☎357 7416; www.atamihotel.com; Cennet Köyü; r/ste €135/450; ✹@☀) Although touted as a haven for relaxation, Atami feels like the set for the next instalment of *The Shining*. Barren hallways with dingy carpets twist through the quiet manse, and the mix of Japanese and Turkish design elements feels dusty and forgotten rather than stylish and unique. The only noticeable perk is the scenic positioning along one of Turkey's finest waterways – the well-hidden Paradise Cove (Cennet Köyü).

Torba
☎0252

Just a hop, skip and a short dolmuş ride from Bodrum town, little Torba, on the peninsula's northern coast, is a lovely place to call home during your Aegean foray. Framed by stout minarets and snaking rows of stone-cut houses, Torba is prime cottage country for İstanbullu escapists.

Sleeping

Casa Dell'Arte
LUXURY HOTEL €€€

(☎367 1848; www.casadellartebodrum; Kilise Mevkii Mutlu Sokak; ste €460-960; ✹@☀) If you happen to have an eccentric billionaire aunt who loves collecting art, then chances are high that her beach house looks something like Casa Dell'Arte. The 12 rooms here are named for the signs of the zodiac, and each one benefits from the owner's extensive collection of modern paintings, installations and *objets d'arts* flown in from every corner of the globe. Custom-made beds and a choose-your-own pillow service are the norm, as are organic breakfasts and regular artist workshops. (The hotel also has a dedicated wing for families that isn't particularly worth a second look.)

La Boutique Alkoçlar
BOUTIQUE HOTEL €€€

(☎367 1970; www.alkoclar.com.tr; Hoşgörü Sokak 1; r/ste incl full-board from TL250/330-700; ✹@☀) The popular Alkoçlar hotel chain's attempt at beachside sophistication is a promising property with plenty of boutique charm. Rooms are tastefully appointed with creamy colours and light wooden trim. The only design element that raises a few questions is the giant mirror with built-in disco lights that hangs above each bed...

Izer Hotel & Beach Club
RESORT €€€

(☎367 1910; www.izerhotel.com; Torba; d incl full-board €180; ☺May-Oct; ✹@☀⛵) Far from the all-inclusive madness in Gümbet, this family-friendly option has all the amenities of a cruise ship, not to mention a centrepiece of twisting waterslides that look like tangled shoelaces. While the common areas sport generous coats of cheery bright paint, the rooms incorporate a tasteful and calming colour scheme of beige, brown and light pastels.

Eating

Gonca Balık
AEGEAN €€

(fish TL20; ☺lunch & dinner) This simple affair with wooden tables strung along the ebbing waves is the go-to spot in Torba for a fish-and-meze meal. Psychedelic graffiti and generous coats of neon-orange paint cheer the makeshift furniture.

Da Vittorio
ITALIAN €€

(☑346 7002; Manastır Mevkii, Hoşgörü Sokak 5; mains TL10-20; ☺lunch & dinner) Housed on the Marmara Bodrum's private slice of sand (though very much open to the public), this trendy option embraces Bodrum's sleek wood-slat decor. Picky eaters will find several international staples, but make sure you don't miss dessert – the Italian-inspired confections are divine.

Eastern Peninsula

☑0252

The bays to Bodrum's east lack the name recognition of the peninsula's western beaches, but the area nonetheless offers some of the best accommodation around.

TOP CHOICE Kempinski Barbaros Bay
LUXURY HOTEL €€€

(☑311 0303; www.kempinski.com; Yalıçiftlik; r from €380; ❈@☎) The poshest and pretti-est address in all of Bodrum, the Kempinski occupies a privileged position on an arid sea-facing cliff. The luxurious collection of rooms and suites undulates across the entire resort, providing each guest with memorable panoramas of the snaking shoreline. The three excellent restaurants (including Italian and Asian) and an endless all-you-can-eat buffet breakfast make it quite difficult to work up the energy to leave the resort and explore other dining venues. The on-site spa is managed by noted wellness brand Six Senses – try a luxurious scrub down in one of the gorgeously appointed hamams whose skylights rise up through the hotel's massive amoeboid swimming pool (the largest pool in southern Turkey) – a haven for the visiting glitterati who lie in various states of undress.

Hapimag Sea Garden
RESORT €€€

(☑311 1280; www.hapimag-seagarden.com; Yal içiftlik; r per person incl full-board from €104; ❈@☎⋒) A city unto itself, Sea Garden is a sprawling campus of all-inclusive hotel-and-apartment units dedicated to family fun.

Western Anatolia

Includes »

Best Places to Stay

» Kitap Evi (p265)

» Babüssaade Konak (p273)

» Ali's Pension (p291)

Best Places to Eat

» Arap Şükrü (p266)

» Kebapçi İskender (p266)

» Mavi Boncuk (p269)

Why Go?

Often overlooked as the crossroads between many of Turkey's big-ticket items, western Anatolia has its own collection of surprisingly diverse attractions.

Once the beating heart of the thriving Ottoman Empire, the region features thousands of architectural emblems of world domination, many of which have been restored to their original glamour and are now charming boutique digs and eateries. Also dotting the landscape are sumptuous religious structures that showcase the area's trademark tile-work.

But long before mosques and minarets, western Anatolia featured prominently in the pages of classical history books. Rambling cities were established by a slew of vibrant ancient civilisations, from the mysterious Phrygians with their rock-hewn settlements, to the imperial Romans with their large-scale engineering and trademark colonnades.

Beyond the homages to the progress of man, the region boasts a memorable patchwork of natural wonders – crater lakes, rugged mountains and vast dusty plains – that seems to borrow from each of Turkey's other regions.

When to Go

Bursa

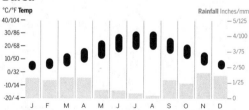

January & February	July & August	September
Swish down the slopes at Uludağ, Turkey's premier ski hill.	Escape the heat in breezy Eğirdir, set high in the Anatolian hills.	Enjoy Pamukkale's crystal travertines without the crowds.

Western Anatolia Highlights

1 Ogle the mammoth stadium at **Afrodisias** (p284), one of Turkey's most impressive archaeological sites

2 Tiptoe gingerly through the crystal travertines and bath amid tumbled columns at **Pamukkale** (p279)

3 Gorge on succulent kebaps and bargain for hand-woven silk in **Bursa** (p257), the original Ottoman capital

4 Fall asleep to the sound of lapping waves in **Eğirdir** (p289), then wander through the nearby ruins scattered along the St Paul Trail

5 Run your fingers under the ancient fountain at **Sagalassos** (p287) and snap your camera at the terraced Roman streets

6 Hike the haunting rock-hewn ruins of the **Phrygian Valley** (p270)

7 Marvel at modern **Eskişehir** (p272), a living allegory to Republic ideals

İznik

☎ 0224 / POP 23,200

The sleepy village of İznik, with its history as a tile-making town, may at first seem a rather inauspicious welcome mat to the western part of Anatolia. Today, teahouses dot the village centre – the haunts of local farmers, while a re-emerging interest in tile production lures handicraft-hunting İstanbullus and the odd foreign tourist.

History

İznik was founded around 1000 BC, and grew in significance under one of Alexander the Great's generals in 316 BC. A rival general, Lysimachus, captured it in 301 BC and named it after his wife, Nikaea. Nicaea became the capital city of the province of Bithynia, extending along the Sea of Marmara. By 74 BC the entire area was incorporated into the Roman Empire, but invasions by the Goths and the Persians ruined the flourishing city by AD 300.

Under Constantinople, Nicaea once again acquired importance. In AD 325 the first Ecumenical Council took place and produced the Nicene Creed, outlining the basic principles of Christianity. Four centuries later, the seventh Ecumenical Council was held in Nicaea's Aya Sofya (Hagia Sofia) church.

During the reign of Justinian I (AD 527–65), Nicaea was refurbished with buildings and defences that provided security when the Arabs invaded. Like Constantinople, Nicaea never fell to its Arab besiegers, but did eventually fall to the Crusaders.

In 1331 Sultan Orhan conquered İznik and established the first Ottoman theological school. In 1514 Sultan Selim I captured the Persian city of Tabriz and dispatched its artisans to İznik. The Persian craftsmen were skilled at making coloured tiles, and soon İznik's kilns were turning out *faience* (tin-glazed earthenware) unequalled even today.

Thanks to the excellent work of the İznik Foundation, tile-making is currently undergoing a revival in Iznik.

◉ Sights & Activities

Almost all of İznik's attractions sit protected within the town's fortifications.

Aya Sofya
RUINS

(Church of the Divine Wisdom; admission TL7; ⊙9am-7pm Tue-Sun) What was once the Aya Sofya is now a crumbling ruin slumbering in an attractively landscaped rose garden. The one building actually encompasses the ruins of three completely different structures. A mosaic floor and a mural of Jesus with Mary and John the Baptist survive from the

İznik

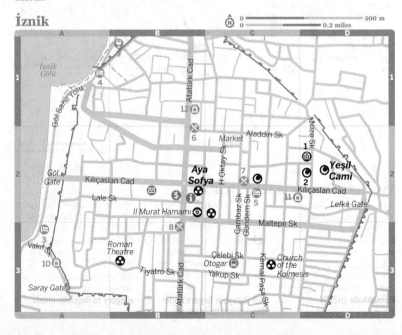

original church. Built during the reign of Justinian I and destroyed by an earthquake in 1065, it was later rebuilt with the mosaics set into the walls. After the Ottoman conquest the church became a mosque, but a fire in the 16th century again destroyed everything. Reconstruction was supervised by the great architect Mimar Sinan, who added İznik tiles to the decoration.

Yeşil Cami   MOSQUE
Built between 1378 and 1387 under Sultan Murat I, the Yeşil Cami (Green Mosque) has Seljuk Turkish proportions influenced more by Iran (the Seljuk homeland) than by İstanbul. The green- and-blue-glazed zigzag tiles of the minaret foreshadowed the famous industry that arose here a few decades later.

İznik Museum   MUSEUM
(İznik Müzesi; ☏757 1027; Müze Sokak; admission TL3; ☺9am-7pm Tue-Sun) Opposite the Yeşil Camii is the İznik Museum, housed in the old soup kitchen that Sultan Murat I had built for his mother, Nilüfer Hatun, in 1388. Born a Byzantine princess, Nilüfer married Sultan Orhan to cement a diplomatic alliance.

The museum's grounds are filled with marble statuary. Inside, the lofty whitewashed halls contain examples of original İznik tiles, with their milky bluish-white and rich 'İznik red' hues. Other displays include 8000-year-old finds from a nearby *tumulus* (burial mound) at Ilıpınar, believed to show links with Neolithic Balkan culture.

Across the road is the restored **Şeyh Kutbettin Camii** (1492).

City Walls & Gates   RUINS
With some imagination it's still possible to recreate İznik's imposing walls, which were first erected in Roman times, then rebuilt and strengthened under the Byzantines. Four main gates – İstanbul Kapısı, Yenişehir Kapısı, Lefke Kapısı and Göl Kapısı – still transect the walls, and the crumbling remains of another 12 minor gates and 114 towers are also evident. In places, the walls still rise to a height of 10m to 13m.

The **Lefke Gate** to the east actually comprises three gateways dating from Byzantine times. Climb to the top of the walls here for a good vantage point of the surrounding area.

The **İstanbul Gate** is similarly imposing, with huge stone carvings of heads facing outwards. However, little remains of the **Göl (Lake) Gate**. To the southwest are the remains of the more minor **Saray (Palace) Gate** – Sultan Orhan (r 1326–61) had a palace near here. Inside the walls nearby are the ruins of a 15,000-seat **Roman theatre**.

The walls between the **Yenişehir Gate** and the Lefke Gate still stand at a considerable height. Follow the footpath beside them for the best indication of the scale.

Diverting back inside the walls from the ruins of the minor **Horoz (Rooster) Gate** are the sparse ruins of the **Church of the Koimesis** (c AD 800), on the western side of Kaymakam S Taşkın Sokak. Only some foundations remain, but the church was the burial place of the Byzantine emperor Theodore I (Lascaris). When the Crusaders took Constantinople in 1204, Lascaris fled to Nicaea and established his court there. It was Lascaris who built Nicaea's outer walls, supported by over 100 towers and protected by a wide moat – no doubt he didn't trust the Crusaders, having already lost one city to them. In a bittersweet final twist, the church was dynamited after the War of Independence.

🛏 Sleeping

İznik's hotels are rarely full, in fact many of them have closed, leaving their rather unattractive carcasses behind. The town's best options are along the lake. It's also worth checking with the İznik Foundation (p257) – if they aren't busy with resident artists or visiting groups they usually rent out their eight cosy, granny-style rooms on the upper floors. Travellers looking for something a bit more off-the-beaten-track might consider heading to the village of Çamoluk, 10km from İznik. Here you'll find a cluster of homes with rooms for rent. Ask at the tourist information kiosk for details.

Cem Otel   HOTEL €€
(📞757 1687; www.cemotel.com; Göl Sahil Yolu 34; r TL90; ❈) Close to the lake and the city walls the Cem Otel is great value, with TV and plenty of space, especially in the family-friendly suites. If you can't land a lakefront room, score a seat downstairs in the terrace restaurant.

Çamlık Motel   HOTEL €€
(📞757 1632; www.iznik-camlikmotel.com; Göl Sahil Yolu; r TL100; ❈) At the southern end of the lakefront, this Western-style motel has spacious rooms and a restaurant with water views. Only a few of the suites face the lake, so Cem is a better option. Say hi to the friendly dogs playing in the garden.

Kaynarca Pansiyon   HOSTEL €
(📞757 1753; www.kaynarca.net; cnr Kılıcaslan Caddesi & Gündem Sokak 1; dm/s/d TL20/35/60) Quiet Kaynarca is a pious place where two travellers of the opposite gender will be turned away if they don't present a marriage certificate. Those who do make it through the door will find simple-but-clean digs at pinch-a-penny prices that don't include breakfast. Note that dorm rooms share a squat toilet – the private rooms have Western-standard latrines. The pension does not have an internet connection; you must use the shop next door (run by the same owner, of course).

🍴 Eating & Drinking

İznik is known for its lake fish as well as its local *köfte* (meatballs) recipe. At sunset, go for a table at one of the lakeside restaurants.

The low-cost **Bim supermarket** (Atatürk Caddesi; ⏰9.30am-9.30pm Mon-Sat, 9.30am-9pm Sun) offers a wide enough selection of food for a lunchtime picnicking along the water.

Köfteci Yusuf   KÖFTECI €
(Atatürk Caddesi 75; köfte by the plate/kilo TL6/30; ⏰lunch & dinner) Waiters in bright orange uniforms serve plates full of saucer-shaped meatballs with sides of thick-cut bread and hot green peppers. Hardcore *köfte* fans can purchase the mashed meat by the kilo.

Çamlık Restaurant   SEAFOOD €€
(Göl Sahil Yolu; meze from TL4; mains from TL8; ⏰lunch & dinner) Recommended by proud locals as İznik's best spot to enjoy fish, the Çamlık Restaurant is adjoined to the like-named motel. Enjoy simple meze and a cold beer in the lakeside garden.

Karadeniz   PIDECI €
(cnr Kılıçaslan Caddesi & Yeni Mahalle 130; mains from TL5; ⏰lunch & dinner) This busy main-drag eatery does a brisk trade in pide and *lahmacun* (Arabic-style meat pizza).

İZNİK TILES

Crafted from the 15th to 17th centuries, İznik tiles were an artistic high point of the Ottoman Empire. Following the end of the Ottoman era, the demand for significant public works evaporated and the tile makers' skills were buried in the mists of history. In 1993 the İznik Foundation was founded to revive this lost art. The foundation's journey has involved scouring 15th-century manuscripts, working with university laboratories and training craftspeople from across Turkey.

Made of 85% quartz from the hills surrounding İznik, the tiles' unique thermal properties keep buildings warm in winter and cool in summer. Reflected sound waves create perfect acoustic qualities; all reasons why İznik tiles were so popular for decorating the interiors of mosques in Ottoman times.

In a sunny atelier above the foundation's kilns, a team of designers meticulously detail floral designs onto pristine white tiles. True to tradition, only cross-sections of flowers are painted and, in a modern twist, all the designers are women. Apparently 'only women have the patience' to spend up to 70 days on one of the foundation's larger works; examples of which now grace structures as diverse as İstanbul's metro system and the World Bank in Ankara.

See p257 for information on arranging a visit to the studio.

Artı Bar BAR

(Göl Sahil Yolu) Shaded by weeping willows, this simple garden bar is not particularly arty (artı means 'plus'), but it's still a prime spot for a beer-and-sunset combo.

🛍 Shopping

If you're visiting İznik, make sure to check out the town's long-standing tradition of tile-making, visible in dozens of artisan shops. A visit to the **İznik Foundation** (☎757 6025; www.iznik.com; Vakıf Sokak 13) is a must. If you call in advance you can arrange a free tour of the compound and see the coterie of women hovered over their tiles with pin-thin paintbrushes in hand.

Additional shops line some of the smaller streets in the city centre, try the **Nilüfer Haltun** (🕔8.30am-8.30pm) behind the ministry of eduction on Kilicaslan Cad. Here you'll find young women selling charming earrings and pendants in an inviting cedar complex dotted with tea tables. North of the roundabout on Atatürk Caddesi, the **Sultan Hamamı** (🕔9am-9pm) is another restored building filled with craft shops and an art gallery.

ℹ Information

Internet cafe (per hr TL1; 🕔9am-11pm) Beside the Kaynarca Pansiyon

Tourist information kiosk (🕔9am-7pm mid-May–mid-Sep, 8am-5pm mid-Sep–mid-May) Friendly staff. At the Aya Sofya.

ℹ Getting There & Away

There are hourly buses to Bursa (TL7.50, 1½ hours) until around 7pm, plus frequent buses to Yalova (TL7.50, one hour).

Bursa

🔢0224 / POP 1.9 MILLION

The original flavour of Ottoman opulence, Bursa was the empire's first capital before forces controlled İstanbul. During the 14th century the city was a beacon of forward thinking and global aspirations. In fact, the world's first stock market was set up within the city's walls, and the word 'bourse' is believed to be a corruption of the city's name.

Today, Bursa is still known throughout Turkey for a variety of other claims. The city's football team, Bursaspor, won the coveted Süper Lig title for the 2009–10 season; giant green flags hang off civic buildings and ambient 'BURSA!' cheers can still be heard.

The city's culinary contributions are well known too: the recipe for İskender kebap was crafted here, and the meat dish has become so popular that the original creators have placed a patent over the name (everyone else has to call it 'Bursa kebap'). For dessert, try the signature *kestane şekeri* (scrumptious candied chestnuts plucked from the nearby valley).

Tourists will enjoy wandering through the parks of 'Green Bursa' that snake between a checkerboard of modern commercial buildings and elegant crumbling mosques. Although the city pales in comparison to jaw-dropping İstanbul just a couple of hours away, it offers an excellent insight into the Turkey beyond the flash of the tourist camera.

History

The settlement of Bursa dates back to at least 200 BC. According to legend, it was founded by Prusias, the King of Bithynia, but soon came under the sway of Eumenes II of Pergamum and thereafter under Roman rule.

Bursa rose in prominence in the early centuries of Christianity, when the thermal baths at Çekirge were developed. However, it was Justinian I who really put Bursa on the map.

With the decline of the Byzantine Empire, Bursa's location near Constantinople attracted the interest of would-be conquerors, including the Arabs and Seljuk Turks. Having rolled through much of Anatolia by 1075, the Seljuks took Bursa with ease. But 22 years later the First Crusade arrived, and the city entered a cycle of conquest and reconquest, changing hands periodically for the next 100 years.

With ongoing Turkish migrations into Anatolia during the 12th and 13th centuries, small principalities arose around individual Turkish warlords. The warlord Ertuğrul Gazi formed a small state near Bursa, and in 1317 the city was first besieged by his son Osman, who established the Ottoman line. He finally starved Bursa into submission in 1326 and made it his capital. Osman was succeeded by Orhan Gazi (r 1326–59), who expanded the fledgling Ottoman Empire to encircle the Byzantine capital at Constantinople.

Orhan took the title of sultan, struck the first Ottoman coinage and, near the end of his reign, was able to dictate to the Byzantine emperors, one of whom, John VI Cantacuzene, became his close ally and father-in-law.

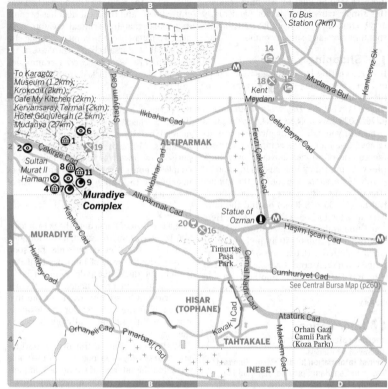

Although the Ottoman capital moved to Edirne in 1402, Bursa remained an important city. Both Osman and Orhan are buried here; their tombs are still important monuments.

With the founding of the Turkish Republic, Bursa developed as an industrial centre. The 1960s and '70s were a boom time as Fiat (Tofaş) and Renault established factories, and today it's still a major commercial centre.

◉ Sights & Activities

Sprawling Bursa can be roughly divided into three civic sections – Yıldırım, Osmangazi and Nilüfer (where the suburb of Çekirge lies).

YILDIRIM

East of Heykel, at Setbaşı, Namazgah Caddesi crosses the Gök Deresi (Gök Stream), which tumbles through a dramatic gorge.

Just after the stream, Yeşil Caddesi veers left to the Yeşil Camii and Yeşil Türbe, after which it changes names to become Emir Sultan Caddesi.

Yeşil Camii MOSQUE

(Green Mosque; Map p258) A few minutes' walk uphill from Setbaşı, the Yeşil Camii, built for Mehmet I between 1419 and 1424, is a beautiful building representing a turning point in Turkish architectural style. Before this, Turkish mosques echoed the Persian style of the Seljuks, but in the Yeşil Camii a purely Turkish style emerged, and its influence is visible in Ottoman architecture across the country. Note the harmonious facade and the beautiful carved marble work around the central doorway. Look closely and you'll see the calligraphy around the niches framing the main door is all different and in some cases unfinished, the legacy of construction petering out three years after the death of Mehmet I in 1421.

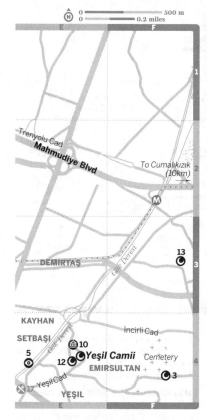

Bursa

◎ Top Sights

Muradiye Complex.............................A2
Yeşil Camii...E4

◎ Sights

1 Archaeology Museum.....................A2
2 Atatürk House................................A2
3 Emir Sultan Camii..........................F4
4 Hüsnü Züber Evi.............................A2
5 Irgandı Sanat Köprüsü...................E4
6 Kültür Parkı....................................A2
7 Muradiye Medresesi......................A2
8 Ottoman House Museum................A2
9 Sultan II Murat (Muradiye) Camii....A2
    Tombs.......................................(see 9)
10 Turkish & Islamic Arts Museum.......E4
11 Ulumay Museum of Ottoman
    Folk Costumes & Jewellery...........A2
12 Yeşil Türbe....................................E4
13 Yıldırım Beyazıt Camii....................F3

⏾ Sleeping

14 Black Cloud....................................C1
15 Tuğcu Hotel....................................C1

⊗ Eating

16 Arap Sükrü......................................C3
17 Mahfel Mado...................................E4
18 Uludağ Kebap.................................C1
19 Yusuf...A2

⊝ Drinking

20 Gren..B3

As you enter, you pass beneath the sultan's private apartments into a domed central hall with a 15m-high *mihrab* (niche indicating the direction of Mecca). The greenish-blue tiles on the interior walls gave the mosque its name, and there are also fragments of a few original frescoes. Inside the main entrance a narrow staircase leads to the sumptuously tiled *hünkar mahfili* (sultan's private box) above the main door. This was the sultan's living quarters when he chose to stay here, with his harem and household staff in less plush digs on either side.

FREE **Yeşil Türbe**　　　　　HISTORIC BUILDING
(Green Tomb; Map p258; ☺8am-noon & 1-5pm) In a small cypress-trimmed park surrounding the mosque is Yeşil Türbe, a mausoleum of Mehmed I (the fifth Ottoman sultan) constructed after his death in 1421. The structure is not actually green – the blue exterior tiles from Kütahya were added following the Bursa earthquake of 1855.

However, this relatively recent makeover doesn't distract from its sublime, simple beauty, and the original interior tiles still provide an authentic and poignant touch.

Walk round the outside to see the tiled calligraphy above several windows. Inside, the most prominent tomb is that of the Yeşil Cami's founder, Mehmet I (Çelebi), surrounded by those of his children. There's also an impressive tiled *mihrab*.

Yıldırım Beyazıt Camii　　　　　MOSQUE
(Mosque of Beyazıt the Thunderbolt; Map p258) Across the valley from the Emir Sultan Camii are the twin domes of the Yıldırım Beyazıt Camii, which was built earlier than the Yeşil Camii but forms part of the same architectural evolution.

Next to the mosque is its *medrese,* once a theological seminary, now a public health centre. Here you'll find the tombs of the mosque's founder, Sultan Beyazıt I, and his son İsa.

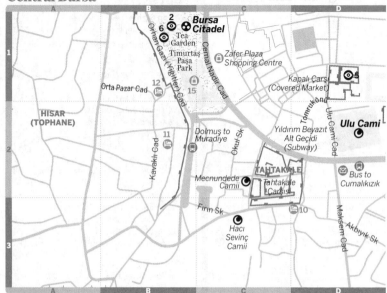

Emir Sultan Camii   MOSQUE

Rebuilt by Selim III in 1805 and restored in the early 1990s, the Emir Sultan Camii (Map p258) echoes the romantic decadence of Ottoman rococo style, rich in wood, curves and painted arches on the outside. The interior is surprisingly plain, but the setting, next to a tree-filled cemetery overlooking the valley, is very pleasant.

Take a dolmuş heading for Emirsultan or any bus with 'Emirsultan' in its name. Walking from Yeşil Camii and Yeşil Türbe, you'll pass a cemetery containing the **grave of İskender Usta**, the kebap maestro himself.

Turkish & Islamic Arts Museum   MUSEUM

(Map p258; admission TL3; ⊙8am-noon & 1-5pm) Nearby the Yeşil Camii is its *medrese* (seminary), which now houses the Turkish & Islamic Arts Museum. The collection includes pre-Ottoman İznik ceramics, the original door and *mihrab* curtains from the Yeşil Camii, jewellery, embroidery, calligraphy and dervish artefacts.

Irgandı Sanat Köprüsü   HISTORIC BUILDING

(Irgandı Bridge; Map p258) Crossing the river north of the Setbaşı road bridge, the Irgandı Sanat Köprüsü has been restored in Ottoman style as a charming arcade of tiny shops (think a mini Ponte Vecchio). Relaxed cafes and an array of artisans' workshops – with a definite emphasis on 'shops' – make it an interesting, if slightly touristy, spot to while away a lazy Bursa afternoon.

Tofaş Museum of Anatolian Carriages
MUSEUM

(☑329 3941; Kapıcı Caddesi, Yıldırım; ⊙10am-5pm Tue-Sun) A short uphill walk south from Setbaşı, along Sakaldöken Caddesi, brings you to a small museum exhibiting old cars and even older horse-drawn carts. If the kids are all mosqued-out, bring along a few picnic goodies to throw together in the lovely Ottoman gardens. The museum used to be a silk factory.

CENTRAL BURSA (OSMANGAZİ)

Bursa's main square is Cumhuriyet Alanı (Republic Sq), known as Heykel (statue) because of its large Atatürk monument. Atatürk Caddesi runs west from Heykel through the commercial centre to the Ulu Cami (Great Mosque). Further west stands the striking blue-glass pyramid of the Zafer Plaza shopping centre, a handy landmark as you approach the city centre.

Bursa City Museum   MUSEUM

(Bursa Kent Müzesi; Map p260; ☑220 2486; www.bursakentmuzesi.gov.tr; admission TL1.50;

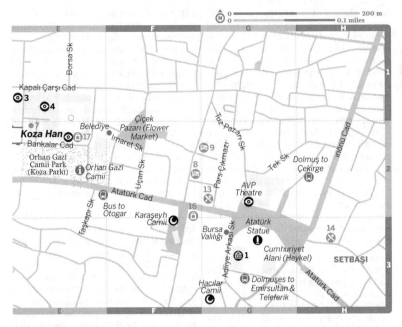

Central Bursa

⊘9.30am-5.30pm Tue-Sat) Bursa's modern City Museum is housed in the city's former courthouse. Ground-floor exhibits zip through the history of the city, with information on the various ruling sultans. Especially interesting is the display on the War of Independence. Most labels are in Turkish, so ask for the handy booklet with English translations. Upstairs the cultural and ethnographical collections need little explanation, and down in the basement are reconstructions of old shops with films showing old-fashioned artisans at work. Don't miss the multimedia touch screens that allow visitors to explore the gloriously retro music and acting careers of a few of Bursa's luminaries from last century.

Ulu Cami   MOSQUE
(Map p260) Prominently positioned on Atatürk Caddesi is the huge Ulu Cami, which is completely Seljuk in style and

easily the most imposing of Bursa's mosques. Yıldırım Beyazıt funded the monumental building in 1396. His original pledge – following victory over the Crusaders in the Battle of Nicopolis – was to build 20 new mosques. His grandiose plans eventually got watered down to one mosque with 20 small domes, but despite the design trade-off, Ulu Cami is still a bold architectural statement. A minaret of daunting girth augments the 20 domes of the exterior, while inside the 'bigger is better' theme continues with immense portals and a forest of square pillars. Notice the fine wooden carvings on the *mimber* (pulpit) and the preacher's chair, as well as the calligraphy on the walls. According to legend, the tradition of Karagöz shadow puppet theatre (see p264) began when the Ulu Cami was constructed.

Central Markets
MARKET

Behind the Ulu Cami, Bursa's sprawling **Kapalı Çarşı** (Covered Market; Map p260) is proudly local, especially if you find İstanbul's Grand Bazaar too touristy. At its centre the *bedesten* (covered market) was built in the late 14th century by Yıldırım Beyazıt, although it was reconstructed after an earthquake in 1855.

As you wander around the market, look for the **Eski Aynalı Çarşı** (Old Mirrored Market; Map p260), which was originally the Orhangazi Hamam (1335) – the bathhouse of the Orhan Camii Külliyesi – as indicated by the domed ceiling with its skylights. This is a good place to shop for Karagöz shadow puppets and other traditional items.

The Kapalı Çarşı tumbles out into the surrounding streets, but at some point you'll find the gateway into the **Koza Han** (Cocoon Caravanserai; Map p260), built in 1490. Unsurprisingly, the building is full of expensive *ipek* (silk) shops. In the courtyard is a small mosque constructed for Yıldırım Beyazıt in 1491.

Beside the Ulu Cami is the **Emir Han** (Map p260), used by many of Bursa's silk brokers. Camels from the silk caravans were corralled here and goods stored in the ground-floor rooms. Drovers and merchants slept and conducted business in the rooms above. It has a lovely fountain in its courtyard tea garden.

Bursa Citadel
CASTLE

Osman Gazi ve Orhan Gazi Türbeleri; Map p260; admission by donation, tombs & tower free) A steep cliff riddled with archaeological workings overlooks Cemal Nadir Caddesi. This oldest section of Bursa was once enclosed by stone ramparts and walls, parts of which still survive. From the Ulu Cami, walk west and up Orhan Gazi (Yiğitler) Caddesi, a ramplike street that leads to the section known as Hisar (Fortress) or Tophane.

In a park on the summit are the **Tombs of Sultans Osman and Orhan**, founders of the Ottoman Empire. The original structures were destroyed in the earthquake of 1855 and rebuilt in Ottoman baroque style by Sultan Abdül Aziz in 1868. Osman Gazi's tomb is the more richly decorated of the two. Remove your shoes before entering either tomb.

A six-storey **clock tower** is the last of four that originally doubled as fire alarms. Beside the clock tower is a delightful **tea garden** with fine views over the valley. Look for the bloke renting binoculars to give you a close-up view of the Bursa vista before you and the peak of Uludağ behind you. You won't need ocular assistance to spy the twin cooling towers on the horizon that have caused local *Simpsons* fans to dub Bursa 'Springfield'.

MURADİYE COMPLEX

Combining a shady park and a quiet cemetery, the **Sultan II Murat (Muradiye) Camii** (Map p258) is a peaceful oasis in busy Bursa. The mosque dates from 1426 and imitates the style of the Yeşil Cami, with painted decorations and a very intricate *mihrab*. Around the mosque the Ottoman houses lining the quiet backstreets of Muradiye are slowly being restored.

Beside the mosque are 12 **tombs** (Map p258; 8.30am–noon & 1-5pm) that date from the 15th and 16th centuries, including that of Sultan Murat II (r 1421–51) himself. Like other Islamic dynasties, the Ottoman one was not based on primogeniture, so any son of a sultan could claim the throne upon his father's death. As a result the designated heir (or strongest son) would often have his brothers put to death rather than risk civil war. Many of the occupants of the Muradiye tombs, including all the *şehzades* (imperial sons), were killed by close relatives.

The tombs are opened on a rotational basis and many are trimmed with beautiful İznik tiles. Other tombs are simple and stark with the final resting place of the ascetic, part-time dervish Murat II being unadorned and austere.

Across the park from the mosque is the **Ottoman House Museum** (Osmanlı Evi Müzesi; Map p258; admission TL2; ☺10am-noon & 1-5pm Tue-Sun), though you'll be lucky if anyone is around to open the doors. On the western side of the tombs is the 15th-century **Muradiye Medresesi**, a theological seminary restored in 1951 as a tuberculosis clinic.

Also nearby is the **Ulumay Museum of Ottoman Folk Costumes & Jewellery** (Osmanlı Halk Kıyafetleri ve Takıları Müzesi; Map p258; İkincimurat Caddesi; admission TL6; ☺9am-7pm), an impressive private collection opened in the restored 1475 Sair Ahmet Paşa *medrese* in 2004. The heritage building now houses around 70 costumes and more than 350 different pieces of jewellery.

On a short walk uphill behind the Sultan Murat II Hamam, follow the signs to the Ottoman **Hüsnü Züber Evi** (Map p258; Uzunyol Sokak 3; admission TL3; ☺10am-noon & 1-5pm Tue-Sun). Like the Ottoman House it's sporadically staffed, but worth a knock on the door if you're in the area. Nearby, winding alleys, local shops and crumbling Ottoman houses definitely reward map-free exploration.

KÜLTÜR PARKI

The Culture Park (Map p258) lies north of the Muradiye complex but some way down the hill. The whole park was relandscaped in 2006, and the lawns, trees and shrubs are now doing very well, thank you. If you've arrived in Bursa from dusty Anatolia, the grassy expanses will be a welcome change. Visit at dusk to share the twilight with scores of local families. As well as tea gardens, playgrounds and a couple of licensed restaurants, the park also houses the **Archaeology Museum** (Arkeoloji Müzesi; Map p258; admission TL5; ☺8.30am-12.30pm & 1.30-5pm Tue-Sun), a predominantly classical collection of finds from local sites with a frustrating lack of English signage.

FREE **Atatürk House**   NOTABLE BUILDING
(Atatürk Evi; Map p258; ☺8.30am-12.30pm & 1.30-5pm Tue-Sun) A few hundred metres west of the Archaeology Museum, across the busy road to Çekirge, Atatürk House is a swish 1895 chalet in a pretty garden framed by statuesque pine trees. The restored rooms are set up as they would have been during the Father of Turkey's occasional visits. We're not sure how authentic the stuffed dog is.

Reach the Kültür Parkı and Atatürk House from Heykel by any bus or dolmuş going to Altıparmak, Sigorta or Çekirge.

ÇEKİRGE

Heading northwest, Atatürk Caddesi becomes Cemal Nadir Caddesi, then Altıparmak Caddesi, and finally Çekirge Caddesi, which leads to the spa suburb of Çekirge, a 10-minute bus ride away. The warm mineral-rich waters that spring from the slopes of Uludağ have been famous for their curative powers since ancient times, and even today the ailing and infirm stay for several weeks to soak and recuperate. Most people stay in hotels with their own mineral baths, and there are also several independent *kaplıcalar* (thermal baths).

Çekirge's main street is I Murat Caddesi (Birinci Murat Caddesi). To get here, take a bus or dolmuş (both TL1.50) from Heykel or Atatürk Caddesi to Çekirge or SSK Hastanesi.

Yeni Kaplıca   HAMAM
(☎236 6955; Mudanya Caddesi 10; ☺6am-11pm) On the northwestern side of the Kültür Parkı, the Yeni (new) bath was renovated in 1522 by Sultan Süleyman the Magnificent's grand vizier, Rüstem Paşa, on the site of a much older bath built by Justinian I. Besides the Yen bath itself, you'll also find the Kaynarca (Boiling) baths, limited to women; and the Karamustafa baths, with facilities for family bathing. Last admission is at 10pm; the full massage costs TL25 per half-hour.

Eski Kaplıca   HAMAM
(☎233 9300; admission men/women TL55/50; ☺7am-10.30pm) Perhaps the most attractive bath is the beautifully restored Eski Kaplıca on Çekirge's eastern outskirts, managed by the Kervansaray Termal Hotel next door.

BURSA SILK

Raising silkworms is a local cottage industry, with a history almost as long as the city itself. Each April villagers buy silkworms from the cooperatives, take them home and feed them on mulberry leaves. Once the worms have spun their cocoons they're brought to the Koza Han to be sold. If you visit in June or September, you may see some of the 14,000 villagers who engage in the trade haggling over huge sacks of precious white cocoons.

The bath is done out in creamy marble and the hot rooms have plunge pools. The cost includes soap, shampoo, sauna and massage.

I Murat (Hüdavendigar) Camii   HAMAM

Çekirge's other main feature is the unusual I Murat Camii, behind the Ada Palas Oteli. Its basic design is the early-Ottoman inverted 'T' plan, which first appeared in the Nilüfer Hatun *imareti* (soup kitchen) in İznik. Here, however, the 'T' wings are barrel-vaulted rather than dome-topped. On the ground floor at the front are the rooms of a *zaviye* (dervish hostel). The 2nd-floor gallery on the facade, built as a *medrese,* is not evident from within except for the sultan's *loge* (box) in the middle at the back of the mosque. From the outside it almost looks like a Christian edifice.

Sarcophagus of Sultan Murat I
HISTORIC BUILDING

The huge sarcophagus of Sultan Murat I (r 1359–89), who died at Kosovo quelling a rebellion by his Albanian, Bosnian, Bulgarian, Hungarian and Serbian subjects, can be viewed in the tomb across the street from the mosque. Nearby is a tea garden with great city views that is popular with local families at the end of the day.

Tours

Karagöz Travel Agency   LOCAL TOURS

(Map p260; ☑221 8727; www.karagoztravel.com; cnr Kapalıçarşı & Eski Aynalı Çarşı 4) Offers interesting local tours, including city excursions and trips to Cumalıkızık.

★☆ Festivals & Events

The Uluslararası Bursa Festival (www.bursa festivali.org), Bursa's long-standing music and dance festival, runs for three weeks in June and July. Expect a diverse program featuring gems like Roma bands from Eastern Europe, *fado* music from Portugal, and the occasional dubious pleasure like Julio Iglesias. It's very affordable and tickets for the top acts are only around TL20. In July the **Golden Karagöz Dance Festival** draws international groups.

Every November the **Karagöz Festival** attracts Karagöz shadow puppeteers, Western puppeteers and marionette performers for five days of festivities and performances.

⌂ Sleeping

Sleeping in Bursa is very straightforward – you get what you pay for. The city does not fancy itself as a tourist town, so most accommodation options are of the business hotel ilk. Tighter budgets will be limited to two- and three-star options; if you're sensitive to smoke, make sure to check out a few rooms before throwing down your bags. Newer options are sprouting up near Kent Meydanı, just beyond the city centre. Travellers armed with a bit of Turkish can try knocking 10 or 20 liras off the asking price, but non-Turkish speakers won't have too much bargaining

---

SHADOW PUPPETS

In addition to kebap and silk, Bursa is also well-known as the birthplace of the Karagöz shadow puppet theatre, a Central Asian tradition brought to Bursa, from where it spread throughout the Ottoman lands. The puppets are cut from camel hide, treated with oil to make them translucent, and brought to life with coloured paint. Masters then manipulate the puppets behind a white cloth screen onto which their images are cast by backlighting.

Legend has it that one of the foremen working on Bursa's Ulu Camii was a hunchback called Karagöz. He and his straight man Hacivat indulged in such humorous antics that the other workers abandoned their tasks to watch. This infuriated the sultan, who had the two miscreants put to death. Their comic routines were immortalised, however, in the Karagöz shadow puppet shows. In 2006 the pair were brought to further prominence in Ezel Akay's film comedy *Hacıvat & Karagöz* (released as *Killing the Shadows* in English), starring Haluk Bilginer and Beyazit Öztürk.

In Bursa, Şinasi Çelikkol has worked hard to keep the tradition of Karagöz puppetry alive and was instrumental in the establishment of the Karagöz Museum (Karagöz Müzesi; ☑232 3360; www.karagozmuzesi.com; Çekirge Caddesi 59), opposite the Karagöz monument. It houses a small collection of puppetry with some magnificent examples from Uzbekistan. English-speaking apprentice puppeteers are often on hand to show visitors through the museum and provide introductions to Karagöz's quirky cast of characters.

power. If you're looking for some R&R, try one of the thermal hotels in the suburb of Çekirge (about 3km west of central Bursa).

TOP CHOICE **Kitap Evi** BOUTIQUE HOTEL €€€
(Bookshop Hotel; Map p260; ☑225 4160; www.kitapevi.com.tr; cnr Kavaklı Mahallesi & Burç Üstü 21; s/d/ste €90/120/220; ✲ @) In a city centre filled with unmemorable business hotels, Kitap Evi has shaken things up considerably with its cache of gorgeously appointed rooms set in a refurbished Ottoman manse. Once an old bookstore, Kitap Evi (which means 'bookhouse') had a faithful following of artistically inclined patrons, and much of this old-school panache has inspired the hotel's decor. Rows of bookshelves and empty leather suitcases welcome guests who then retreat to the inner cloister (now a lovely restaurant; p266), or curl up with a good read in their *karyola* bed upstairs. Try to score room 1 if you're intrigued by the idea of having a marble-lined hamam in your bathroom.

Hotel Gönlüferah LUXURY HOTEL €€€
(☑233 9210; www.gonluferah.com; Murat Caddesi, Çekirge; s/d €85/115; ✲ @ ✉) Dating from 1890, the hilltop Gönlüferah is a perfect blend of heritage charm and modern convenience. Rooms are undeniably slick, with their plush curls of carpeting, stylish padded headboards and thoroughly modern bathrooms. This is your best option if you're planning on staying amongst the thermal waters of Çekirge. The hotel offers day-use spa packages (TL20 per person) if you'd like to sweat it out Turkish-style, but aren't staying on the premises.

Black Cloud Hotel BUSINESS HOTEL €€
(Map p258; ☑253 7575; www.blackcloudhotel.com; Ulubatlı Hasan Bulvarı 33; s/d TL90/160; ✲ @) Okay, so it's not the best moniker for a hotel (it's a direct translation of the owner's name), but Black Cloud offers fresh-faced digs for the price of a well-worn room downtown. Expect plasma TVs, trendy bathroom fixtures and eyecatching stencil patterns on the walls in the breakfast nook.

Safran Otel PENSION €€
(Map p260; ☑224 7216; www.safranotel.com; Arka Sokak 4; s/d TL80/150; ✲) Near the Osman and Orhan tombs in a historic neighbourhood above the city, Safran sits in a restored mansion with golden tones and polished darkwood trim. The Ottoman trappings don't extend to the rooms (save a rug or two), but it's an inviting place nonetheless.

Otantik Club Hotel BOUTIQUE HOTEL €€€
(☑211 3280; www.otantikclubhotel.com; Soğanlı; s/d €75/110, ste €160-180; ✲ ✉ @) Tucked away in the botanic garden of Soğanlı (about 7km from Central Bursa) lurks this Disney-fied tribute to Ottoman sumptuousness. The sun-filled lobby welcomes guests amid colourful Turkish rugs and jagged stone walls covered in historic portraits. Upstairs, the generous suites are bathed in dark velvety tones; each one has a private hamam and antique fireplace. The standard rooms are still comfortable, but lack most of the old-school Bursa charm. Two great restaurants and a cosy bar provide the essential finishing touches.

Kervansaray Termal LUXURY HOTEL €€
(☑233 9300; www.kervansarayhotels.com; Çekirge; d from €87; ✲ ✉ @) Bursa's best attempt at luxury is a sprawling pleasure-plex that blends modern conventions with old Ottoman style. The resort's focus is the crumbling hamam where sourced thermal water is lavished over weary bodies. The standard rooms are a bit past their prime – upgrade to something a bit more stylish.

Tuğcu Hotel BUSINESS HOTEL €€€
(Map p258; ☑256 4500; www.tugcuhotel.com; Karşış Celal Bayar Caddesi 195; s/d €90/120; ✲ @) Tuğcu may take itself a bit too seriously, but swift and efficient service is of the utmost importance at this brand new option near Kent Meydanı. A strange touch-pad elevator (you'll see) brings guests up to the modern and prim rooms with catalogue-ordered furnishings. Sidenote: the staff is very proud of the make-your-own-omelette station at breakfast.

Hotel Efehan BUSINESS HOTEL €€
(Map p260; ☑225 2260; www.efehan.com.tr; Gümüşçeken Caddesi 34; s/d TL100/130; ✲ @) Though it's not winning beauty pageants, Efehan has the best price-value ratio in the heart of the centre. The staff is friendly and rooms come with familiar, standard-issue furnishings befitting an older international hotel. The big drawcard, however, is the top-floor breakfast hall with inspiring views of the rolling city through floor-to-ceiling windows. Try for a room near the elevator rather than a south-facing suite – the neighbouring mosque's call to prayer will wake even the soundest of sleepers.

Otel Güneş HOSTEL €
(Map p260; ☑222 1404; İnebey Caddesi 75; s/d TL28/48) One of the only options in Bursa catering to penny-pinchers, Güneş is a

WESTERN ANATOLIA BURSA

lively joint in the heart of the city that magically manages to cram in the owner's family and a gaggle of backpackers into a rather small space. Teeny rooms and shared toilets are the norm – there's a cute spot down the street where you can buy breakfast.

Hotel Çeşmeli   HOTEL €€
(Map p260; ☎224 1511; Gümüşçeken Caddesi 6; s/d TL60/100; ❄) In close proximity to Bursa's bustling market, Çeşmeli has slightly faded rooms, but a friendly all-female staff makes it an excellent choice for women travellers. You'll easily spot the place – it sits right behind a public waterspout that locals flock to with such strange alacrity it's as though they've been wandering the desert for forty years.

🍴 Eating & Drinking

Carnivores strap your bibs on! Bursa is known throughout Turkey for its İskender kebap and you'll find no shortage of places slinging gut-busting portions. Prices start around TL18 for *bir porsiyon* (one serving) or TL27 if you loosen your belt and order *bir buçuk porsiyon* (1½ portions). Also famous in Bursa are *kestane şekeri* (candied chestnuts; also called *maron glacé*), which will satisfy any sweet tooth after a meaty meal. If you happen to be in town over a weekend (on Sundays in particular), follow the crowd of locals out to Cumalıkızık for brunch.

TOP CHOICE   Arap Şükrü   AEGEAN €€
(Map p258; Sakarya Caddesi; meze TL4-20; ☺lunch & dinner) If you're wondering where all the locals went after dark (especially on weekends) then head to this wonderful cobblestone alley overflowing with a labyrinth of cloth-topped tables. Once the heart of Bursa's Jewish quarter, and technically known as Sakarya Caddesi – the street owes its current moniker to the eponymous Arap Şükrü, who returned home after the War of Independence and opened a seafood restaurant. It was so wildly successful that his descendants followed him into the business and the street now bustles with a dozen restaurants of the same name. As you wander down the street chatty managers will cajole you with offers of special tables – follow your hunch and grab a chair (really though, you can't go wrong). Then, savour scrumptious *karides güveç* (shrimp casserole), excellent octopus, and rakı with thick slices of melon while listening to the spirit strumming of the lively Roma musicians.

Arap Şükrü is about a 10-minute walk from the Ulu Cami.

Kebapçı İskender   KEBAPÇI €€
(Map p260; Ünlü Caddesi 7; iskender kebap TL18; ☺lunch & dinner) A legend throughout all of Turkey, this dimly lit kebap shop opened its doors in 1867 serving what would become one of the most popular meat platters in the nation. In fact, the recipe was such a wild success that the owners patented the name: İskender kebap. These days, pictures of good old Izzy himself line the walls of the faux-heritage building (think KFC's Colonel Sanders sans goatee.) There are roughly a dozen other branches around Bursa, though this one is the original. If you're visiting the botanic garden in Soğanlı be sure to check out the larger iteration, with satin-draped dining rooms and a 'museum' dedicated to the coveted shaved meat.

İskender   KEBAPÇI €€
(Map p260; Atatürk Caddesi 60; mains TL14.75; ☺lunch & dinner) This central spot also claims to be the original İskender maker. Leave the legal machinations to the lawyers and tuck into the slightly cheaper, but equally tasty, kebaps at this main-drag spot in a cosy wooden abode.

Cafe My Kitchen   INTERNATIONAL €€
(☎234 6200; www.cafemykitchen.com; Çekirge Caddesi 114; pizza TL11-18, mains TL17-24; ☺lunch & dinner; 🛜) The bark may be a bit bigger than its bite, but this snazzy new restaurant (formerly 'Sui') slings international fare in a slick atmosphere. Factory lamps and lipstick-red awnings dangle overhead as locals thumb through gossip mags on the couches and clink drinks at the wine bar. The imposing ivory manse in the back hides a modern interior set for upscale dining.

Mahfel Mado   RESTAURANT-BAR €
(Map p258; Namazgah Caddesi 2; mains TL5-10; ☺breakfast, lunch & dinner) If you lunched on kebap then you'll probably be too full for dinner (no joke), so drop by Bursa's oldest cafe for a late-night *dondurma* (ice cream) brought to you by one of Turkey's best-known brands. Mado is set along a gorgeous ravine; snag a table amid chatty 20-somethings and shady trees, or grab your cone to go.

Kitap Evi   INTERNATIONAL €€€
(Map p260; www.kitapevi.com.tr; cnr Kavaklı Mahallesi & Burç Üstü 21; mains TL15-30; ☺breakfast, lunch & dinner; 🛜) If you can't splurge on a night at this charming inn then at

least stop by for a smattering of international dishes. The hotel was once a bookstore, and the inner courtyard – with its high stone walls, trickling fountain and snaking olive grove – was used by the local literati who would gather here to discuss great works of literature and perhaps endeavour on some of their own. It's an inspiring place indeed – the perfect spot to update your blog. Keep your eyes peeled for the resident turtle!

Uludağ Kebap
KEBAPÇI €

(Map p258; Kent Meydanı; mains TL8-12; ⊘lunch & dinner; 🔊) If you don't have a mean case of the meat sweats after gobbling down platefuls of İskender kebab, then try 'Bursa kebap' (same thing; different name) at Uludağ. Like İskender, there are several branches of this savoury chain – our favourite location is the swankified spot on the ground level of Kent Meydanı, which seems to have borrowed a bit of its design aesthetic from the Starbucks next door.

Gren
BAR-CAFE €

(Map p258; ☑223 6064; www.grencafe.com; Sakarya Caddesi 46) If there were such a thing as a hipster hangout in Bursa, it would be Gren – the city's self-dubbed 'first photography cafe'. With an eclectic assortment of black-and-white snaps and antique cameras scattered about, it makes for a great place to relax with a glass of anything after a lively meal along Arap Şükrü just next door.

Krokodil
ITALIAN €€€

(Çekirge Meydanı, Zübeyde Hanım Caddesi; mains TL15-30; ⊘breakfast, lunch & dinner) This Bursa oldie, at the main roundabout in Çekirge, has been pleasing customers for over 25 years with its vast library of wine, cute cottage vibe and palate-pleasing Italian mains.

Yusuf
LOCAL €€

(Map p258; Kültür Parkı; meze TL4-14; ⊘lunch & dinner) While the local government continues to bring the Culture Park's tea houses and terrace restaurants up to code, 'Joe's Place' still feels like a relic from a bygone era, with tux-clad waiters and hearty locals shooting cloudy glasses of rakı.

Şifne
SEAFOOD €€€

(Soğanlı; meze TL3-15, mains TL15-25; ⊘dinner) Located in the Otantik Club Hotel, this restaurant – named for the fishing village near Çeşme – serves (unsurprisingly) seafood. Despite Bursa's inland location, Şifne has an excellent reputation locally,

and it's much more subdued than boisterous Arap Şükrü.

Oylum
BAR-RESTAURANT €€

(Ovlu Caddesi; mains TL13-22; ⊘lunch & dinner; 🔊) Oylum is a small complex with several restaurants and nightclubs located 1.5km down the hill from Çekirge. Big Momma's slings tasty pizzas (avoid the Tex-Mex) while Veni Vidi features live Turkish every night (if you're looking for Vici it's on the way to Mudanya). Despite the venue's international names, we'd bet good money that you won't find any foreigners here. Oylum is 200m from the Paşa Çiftliği metro station.

🛍 Shopping

Bursa is also famous for its silk, and the place for buying it is **Koza Han** (Cocoon Caravanserai; ⊘8.30am-8pm Mon-Sat, 10.30am-6pm Sun) in the city centre. Boutiques are arranged around the open-air square, each one selling similar silk items (mostly scarfs). You must always ask if you are buying synthetic fabric or the real thing – expect the store clerks to be honest. Additional crafts can be purchased at **Bali Bay Han** near Zafer Plaza.

For Bursa's famous *kestane şekeri* (candied chestnuts; also called *maron glacé*), look no further than **Kafkas** (www.kafkas.com; ⊘7am-11.30pm) – there's a branch of the chain directly across Atatürk Caddesi from İskender restaurant.

ℹ Information

There's a post office (with heaps of payphones) and numerous ATMs on Atatürk Caddesi, and plenty of exchange offices in the Covered Market.

Tourist office (Map p260; ⊘9am-5pm Mon-Fri, to 6pm Sat) Beneath Atatürk Caddesi, in the row of shops at the north entrance to Orhan Gazi Alt Geçidi. Expect a friendly welcome and fluctuating hours of operation.

Dangers & Annoyances

Heavy traffic and a lack of street lights make it difficult to cross Atatürk Caddesi, so use the *alt geçidi* (pedestrian underpasses). The Atatürk Alt Geçidi (the one nearest to Heykel) has a lift for disabled people; the nearby florist has the key to operate it.

ℹ Getting There & Away

Air

Direct flights link Bursa (Yenişehir) to Antalya, Erzurum and Trabzon, see **Turkish Airlines** (www.thy.com) for the latest details on flights to Bursa.

Bus

Bursa's otogar (bus station) is 10km north of the centre on the Yalova road. Information on some major bus routes and fares is provided in the table.

The fastest way to İstanbul is to take the metro-bus combo to Mudanya and then board the **İDO fast ferry** (☑444 4436; www.ido.com. tr). Ferries also link İstanbul to Yalova nearby.

Karayolu ile (by road) buses to İstanbul drag you all around the Bay of İzmit and take four to five hours. Those designated *feribot ile* (by ferry) take you to Topçular, east of Yalova, and then by ferry to Eskihisar, a much quicker and more pleasant way to go.

❶ Getting Around

To/From the Bus Station

City bus 38 crawls the 10km between the otogar and the city centre (TL2, 45 minutes). Returning to the otogar, it leaves from stop 4 on Atatürk Caddesi. Bus 96 from the otogar goes direct to Çekirge (TL2, 40 minutes).

A taxi from the otogar to the city centre costs around TL20 to TL25.

Bus

Bursa's city buses (BOİ; TL2) have their destinations and stops marked on the front and side. A major set of yellow bus stops is lined up opposite Koza Parkı on Atatürk Caddesi with clear signs marking the destinations and drop-offs. You can also pick up buses to the Botanik Parkı, bus station, and Cumalıkızık from here.

These days, all city buses run on a prepay system; you can buy tickets from kiosks or shops near most bus stops (keep an eye out for the BuKART sign). If you're staying for a few days there are various multitrip options available.

Dolmuş

In Bursa, cars and minibuses operate as dolmuşes. The destination is indicated by an illuminated sign on the roof. Dolmuşes are usually as cheap as buses and definitely faster and more frequent, especially linking central Bursa with Çekirge.

Dolmuşes go to Çekirge via the Kültür Parkı, Eski Kaplıca and I Murat Camii from a major dolmuş terminal immediately south of Heykel. Other dolmuşes wait in front of Koza Parkı. Figure TL1.5 from Heykel to Çekirge.

Metro

Metro tickets cost TL2 and are an effective way of reaching Mudanya if you're connecting to İstanbul by sea.

Taxi

Heykel to Muradiye is about TL5; TL10 to Çekirge.

Around Bursa

CUMALIKIZIK

☑0224 / POP 700

The early-Ottoman village of Cumalıkızık was an unknown entity – even to Bursans – until 2000 when it became the filming location for the popular series *Kınalı Kar* (Henna in the Snow). Then tourism started to pick up, and souvenir shops started to lure in starstruck visitors. A few years on, the village's star status is receding; these days the biggest game in town is the regular Sunday morning market. Cumalıkızık is a preferred destination of Bursa folk for a leisurely weekend brunch in an array of rustic garden restaurants, or as a spot to

SERVICES FROM BURSA'S OTOGAR

DESTINATION	FARE (TL)	DURATION (HR)	DISTANCE (KM)	FREQUENCY (PER DAY)
Afyon	30	5	290	8
Ankara	40	6	400	hourly
Bandırma	15	2	115	12
Çanakkale	30	5	310	12
Denizli	42	9	532	several
Eskişehir	15	2½	155	hourly
İstanbul	20	3	230	frequent
İzmir	25	5½	375	hourly
İznik	7.50	1½	82	hourly
Kütahya	20	3	190	several
Yalova	9	1¼	76	half-hourly

pick up fresh fruit, local honey and handicrafts. Come during the week though, and it could be just you and a few relaxed locals in the narrow uphill lanes. And although it's no longer a perfect authentic Anatolian village, Cumalıkızık does its darnedest to redefine the words 'quaint' and 'heritage'.

🍴 Sleeping & Eating

Most village houses along the main street offer breakfast and lunch. There are only two official places to sleep.

TOP CHOICE **Mavi Boncuk** PENSION €

(☏373 0955; www.cumalikizik-mavibon cuk.com; Saldede Sokak; r with breakfast per person TL65) The 'blue bead' (or, more commonly 'the evil eye') is set in an old village house guarded by hanging gardens. Cosy common spaces are covered in embroidered pillows and upstairs several snug rooms make the perfect place to get away from it all (room six is our favourite). The breakfast (TL20) is unbeatable and attracts a steady stream of Bursans who come for the platters of homemade jams, mouth-watering *menemen* (type of omlette), freshly baked bread toasted on an open fire, and muddy Turkish coffee. It's the kind of relaxed eatery you wish your hometown had.

Konak Pansiyon PENSION €

(☏372 3325; www.bulanlarkonak.com; d TL60) This beautifully restored guest house has eight rooms, with facilities ranging from Ottoman-style floor mattresses to *huge* double beds. The charming restaurant opposite offers standard kebaps, salads, mezes and *gözleme* amid large shady trees.

ℹ️ Getting There & Away

It's very simple to reach the village from Bursa. Marked dolmuşes (TL1.50) ply the route, as does bus 82 (TL2). There's roughly one departing every hour – the minivans usually leave when they have an acceptable quorum of passengers. Transport runs every 15 minutes on Sundays when Bursans head here for brunch. If you're arriving by private vehicle, there's a municipal car park at the entrance to the village (just off to the left at the blue building) – you'll be asked to pay a couple of liras to leave your car. Follow a side road behind the village if you are headed to Mavi Boncuk – it has its own parking lot.

MUDANYA

☏0224 / POP 35,120

The bustling seaside city of Mudanya is the perfect place for those who don't have time to make a run for the Aegean coast. With a rich Greek history, the site has been inhabited for thousands of years, namely due to its strategic position along the Marmara. In modern history, the city became famous for the Armistice of Moudania, which was an agreement signed by Italy, France, Britain and Turkey on 11 October 1922 (Greece reluctantly signed the pact three days later) recognising the lands west of Edirne, including Istanbul and the Dardanelles, under Turkish rule. The Treaty of Lausanne, a couple of months later, further ironed out the boundary details. A prominent white house in the west end of town commemorates the event with photographs.

🛏️ Sleeping

Montania LUXURY HOTEL €€

(☏554 6000; www.montaniahotel.com; İstasyon Caddesi; s/d/ste TL150/220/300; ✳️ @) Mudanya's most famous hotel sits in the old French customs house constructed in 1849. Today the Montania has expanded across several structures and includes a posh private swimming club. The rooms are nothing to write home about (though the 100s and 200s rooms are the best), but they do come with a few designer touches such as surprisingly quirky accent walls.

Golden Butik Hotel HOTEL €€

(☏554 6464; www.goldenbutikotel.com; Mustafa Kemalpaşa Caddesi 24; s/d TL70/120; ✳️ @) Just up the street from Eski Camii, this small hotel mixes old Ottoman flavours with trendy modern decor. Hallways have large black-and-white photos of old Turkish generals and in the back you'll find a vine-draped cloister where guests can relax over the included breakfasts.

Hotel Ferah HOTEL €€

(☏554 9956; mudanya@mudanyaferahhotel. com; Halitpaşa Caddesi 75; s/d TL60/120; ✳️ @) A preferred sleeping spot for Arab visitors, this simple place has a batch of sun-filled rooms sitting over a popular döner shop. Try to avoid the rooms painted neon orange. Ferah doesn't have as much style as Golden Butik, but there are unobstructed sea views here.

ℹ️ Getting There & Away

Take the metro from downtown Bursa (TL2) to the final terminus then switch to a public bus (TL3). For the return trip there are comfier dolmuş available. Mudanya has a ferry service to İstanbul (www.ido.com.tr), making the Bursa-to-İstanbul journey quite quick and painless.

With its proximity to İstanbul, Bursa and Ankara, Uludağ (Great Mountain; 2543m), on the outskirts of Bursa, is Turkey's most popular ski resort. A *teleferik* (cable car) runs up to Sarıalan, 7km from the town of Uludağ and the main hotel area (called 'Oteller', naturally). The cluster of accommodation and ski hires springs to life during the snow season from December to early April, and slumbers quietly in the off-season. Even if you don't plan to go skiing or do the three-hour hike to the summit, it's still a worthwhile trip year-round to take advantage of the view and the cool, clear air of Uludağ National Park.

At the cable-car terminus at Sarıalan there are a few snack and refreshment stands and a basic national park campground that's usually full. You're best to treat the 'Great Mountain' as a day trip in summer, or check out www.uludaghotels.com for accommodation options during the ski season – prominent Turkish chains, like Anemon, all have comfortable accommodation here.

❶ Getting There & Away

Take a Bursa city bus from stop 1 or a dolmuş marked 'Teleferik' (TL2) from behind the city museum to the lower terminus of the cable car, a 15-minute ride from Heykel. The cable cars (TL8 return, 30 minutes) depart every 40 minutes between 8am and 10pm in summer and between 10am and 5pm in winter, wind and weather permitting. At busy times they'll leave whenever there are 30 people on board.

The cable car stops first at Kadıyayla, then continues upwards to the terminus at Sarıalan (1635m). Stand at the rear of the car for the best views of Bursa as you go up.

Dolmuşes from central Bursa to Uludağ (TL7.50) and Sarıalan (TL10) run several times daily in summer and more frequently in winter.

At the 11km marker you must stop and pay an admission fee for the **national park** (per car TL5). The hotel zone is 11km up from the entrance.

The return ride can be difficult in summer, with little public transport on offer. In winter dolmuşes and taxis are usually eager to get at least some money for the trip downhill, so bargain hard.

Phrygian Valley

The rock-hewn monuments in the so-called Phrygian Valley (Frig Vadisi) are the most impressive relics to survive from Phrygian times. Even if you're not interested in the Phrygians, the valley is a beautiful part of Turkey, virtually untouched by tourism. Craggy escarpments dotted with fir trees conceal forgotten ruins and the spectacularly rugged scenery rivals that of Cappadocia.

The Phrygian Valley can be separated into three sections orbiting the area's three major cities; Eskişehir, Kütahya and Afyon. The ruins near Afyon are undoubtedly the best, followed by the sites near Eskişehir; the ruins at Kütahya are rather small and are of limited interest.

◉ Sights

Most sites are along dirt tracks and some can be very hard to find, even when you're right beside them. Navigation is slowly getting better as local municipalities are collecting money to pave a 'Tourist Route' through the region.

ESKİŞEHİR RUINS

Through Yazilikaya Valley, heading from Seyitgazi to Afyon, turn south after about 3km into a road marked with a brown sign pointing to Midas Şehri. Further along this rough road a sign leads right 2km to the Doğankale (Falcon Castle) and Deveboyukale (Camel-Height Castle), both of them plugs of rock riddled with formerly inhabited caves.

Further south another rough track to the right leads 1km to the Mezar Anıtı (Monumental Tomb), where a restored tomb is cut into the rock.

Continuing south is another temple-like tomb, called the Küçük Yazılıkaya (Little Inscribed Stone).

Midas Şehri is a few kilometres on from Küçük Yazılıkaya. Archaeologists call this important section Midas Şehri (Midas City) though it is actually the village of Yazılıkaya (Inscribed Rock), 32km south of Seyitgazi.

The sights at Yazılıkaya are clustered around a huge rock. Tickets (TL3) are sold at the library in front of the steps leading up to the site. The friendly local custodian will meet you and give you the excellent 'Highlands of Phrygia' brochure (he usually keeps them in the back of his car). A second 'Eskişehir' brochure has good maps of the entire Phrygian Valley, and an essential guide to exploring Yazılıkaya.

Carved into the soft tufa, the so-called Midas Tomb is a 17m-high relief covered in geometric patterns and resembling

Emigrants from Thrace to central Anatolia around 2000 BC, the Phrygians spoke an Indo-European language, used an alphabet similar to Greek, and established a kingdom with its capital at Gordion (p410), 106km west of Ankara. The empire flourished during the 8th and 7th centuries AD under a successive line of Midas and Gordias kings until it was overrun by the Cimmerians at the early 7th century. Although the Cimmerians sacked and burned Gordion and murdered many Phrygian leaders, the Phrygian culture continued to flourish under the new leaders and subsequent Lydian overtakers.

Considering they lived in rock dwellings, the Phrygians were a sophisticated people with a dedication to the arts. Phrygian culture was based on Greek culture, but with strong neo-Hittite and Urartian influences. They're credited with inventing the frieze, embroidery and numerous musical instruments, including the double clarinet, flute, lyre, syrinx (Pan pipes), triangle and cymbals. Not bad for cave dwellers – think of it as early 'rock' music.

Phrygian civilisation was at its most vigorous around 585 to 550 BC, when the rock-cut monuments at Midas Şehri – the most impressive Phrygian stonework still in existence – were carved. Phrygian relics can be seen in many Anatolian museums, providing fascinating insights into a culture that bridged the gap between 'primitive' and 'advanced' amid the scrub and rocks of central Turkey.

the facade of a temple. At the bottom is a niche where an effigy of Cybele would be displayed during festivals. Inscriptions in the Phrygian alphabet – one bearing Midas' name – circle the tomb. The Phrygians prayed here for centuries and lived in the flood plains below.

Behind the Midas Tomb a path leads down to a tunnel, then passes a second smaller tomb, unfinished and high up in the rock. The path continues upwards to the top of a high mound, which was an acropolis. Here you will find a stepped stone, labelled an altar, which may have been used for sacrifices, and traces of walls and roads. Even with a map following the paths can be confusing, but the main features are easy to spot. Note that it was here at the acropolis that the first evidence of water collecting was discovered – carved holes with slatted steps trapped rainwater for the dry season.

AFYON RUINS
The small village of Doğer boasts a *han* (caravanserai) dating back to 1434. It's usually kept locked so you must stop by the municipality building (across the street) and ask for the key. From here, dirt tracks go to lily-covered Emre Gölü (Lake Emre), a perfect picnic place overlooked by a small stone building once used by dervishes; and a rock formation with a rough staircase called the Kirkmerdiven Kayalıkları (Rocky Place with 40 Stairs). The dirt track

then continues on for 4km to Bayramaliler and Üçlerkayası with rock formations called *peribacalar* (fairy chimneys), just like Cappadocia.

After Bayramaliler is Göynüş Valley (Göynüş Vadisi), with fine Phrygian rock tombs decorated with lions *(aslantaş)*. This valley is a 2km walk from the main Eskişehir–Afyon road.

At Ayazini village there was once a rock settlement called Metropolis. Look out for a huge church with its apse and dome cut clear out of the rock face, and a series of rock-cut tombs with carvings of lions, suns and moons.

Around the village of Alanyurt are more caves at Selimiye and fairy chimneys at Kurtyurdu. Another concentration is around Karakaya, Seydiler and İscehisar, including the bunker-like rock Seydiler Castle (Seydiler Kalesi).

Tours
As the area grows in popularity, tour operators are beginning to design daytrips into the valley – most departing from Eskişehir. This is still very much in the works and you'll need to ask around to find a travel company to organise the trip (usually a four-person minimum is required).

In Afyon, there are currently two companies that are amenable to providing their services for a Phrygian Valley tour; Ceba (213 2715; A. Türkeş Bulvarı C/2 Erçelik Sitesi) and Aizanoi (213 1080; Ordu Bulvarı, Çamlı

62/31). In Eskişehir, head to the tourist office for information on organising a daytrip.

❶ Getting There & Around

If you really want to do justice to the Phrygian Valley (and you definitely should), you'll have to rent a private vehicle and explore. **Arhan** (☑213 1080; Ordu Bulvarı Çamii 62/31) and **Kaya** (☑212 5100; Dumlupinar Mh Süleyman Çaruş Caddesi Ozgün Sitesi C Blok Altı 27) are two reputable car rental companies in Afyon offering insured vehicle for TL85 to TL100. If you have your own insurance figure around TL60 per day.

Even with a private vehicle, it can sometimes be quite a challenge to find some of the ruins, as they easily blend into the landscape. Most are marked with large brown signposts, but scouting the sites can still be an exercise in patience. At the time of research, there were serious talks about completing a paved 'tourist road' linking many of the valley's most impressive sites.

If your funds are limited it's possible to visit a few of the Afyon sites by dolmuş. From central Afyon there are minibuses to Ayazini along the main Afyon–Eskişehir road. You'll be dropped at a church and have to walk 500m to reach Metropolis. From Ayazini, hop back on a dolmuş towards Afyon, but disembark at Gazlıgöl (about halfway back to Afyon) and switch to a dolmuş bound for Doğer. Buses plying the Afyon-Eskişehir route can drop you anywhere along the way, although it's pretty much impossible to hitch a ride once you're finished looking at the ruins as there is very little traffic in the area.

Eskişehir

☑0222 / POP 720,000

Eskişehir is one of the most delightful surprises in western Anatolia, and although its moniker means 'Old City', this vibrant burg is thoroughly modern.

The city's mayor – affectionately known as the *hoca,* or 'teacher' – is a former economics professor and seems to have a magical way with the municipal budget. In fact, he's deferred to with such reverence that he's become somewhat of a modern-day Atatürk within the city limits. Over the last ten years the city has transformed into a veritable civic work of art. Grand boulevards and pedestrian ways are perfectly manicured among a series of ornate bridges. Just up the hill is the historic Ottoman district with its cache of gorgeously refurnished manses, and further on are two sprawling university campuses, giving the city a wonderfully bright and forward-thinking attitude.

◉ Sights & Activities

Eskişehir is always changing, and new museums and sights are opening up each season. It's worth asking around to check in on the latest happenings – locals are fiercely proud of their vibrant burg. Plans are underway to open a new **archaeology museum** in 2011, which will feature over 2000 objects reflecting the 10,000 years of settlement in the region.

FREE **Ottoman Quarter**　　　HISTORIC AREA
The old Ottoman district, or *eski* Eskişehir, is a stunning community of elegant manses set slightly uphill overlooking the newer part of the city. Generous government funds have helped restore many of structures – you'll find a hotel, restaurant and several excellent museums scattered about. Be sure to check out the **Museum of Contemporary Glass Art** (◎10am-5pm Tue-Sun), which houses a truly admirable collection of international glass works. The tradition of melting and fusing glass dates back to the time of the Pharaohs, and a local Egyptologist (and professor at one of the city's universities) revived the art and opened a studio. Don't miss the gorgeous chandelier in the central courtyard, which looks like an amalgamation of fireworks and loose bedsprings. At the time of research curators were developing a wax museum in the basement.

Atlıhan Complex　　　NOTABLE BUILDING
(Pazaroğlu Sokak 8; ◎9am-10pm) Eskişehir is famous for its 'white gold', or *meerschaum* (*luletaşı* in Turkish) a light, porous white stone, which is mined in local villages and then shaped into pipes and other artefacts. The Atlıhan Complex features a handful of local artisans who sell their unique stone crafts. **Ak-Tas** (☑220 6652; Pazaroğlu Sokak 8; ◎9am-10pm), one of the shops, has a workshop in the back where you can watch the sculpting process and perhaps even try your hand at the art.

Kent Park　　　PARK
Beautiful 'City Park' (which kinda sounds like a greenspace somewhere in Britain) is a civic masterpiece sporting a variety of enticing sights and activities. The biggest draw is the man-made public beach, which lures crowds of locals during the summer months (sunbeds cost TL4). Also worth a mention is the horse stable offering lovely carriage rides through the city (TL10 per ride), and gondola rides along the

area's river (TL10 per boat; don't worry, the boatswains don't sing). Paths perfect for a romantic stroll are also part of the mayor's plan to turn the city into Turkey's 'Aşkşehir' (the 'City of Love').

Sazova Park
PARK

Just beyond the city centre in an area of cleared cane (*sazova* means 'cane field'), the city's newest park sits behind imposing green gates. A massive Japanese garden (apparently the biggest one outside of Japan) sprawls about, providing visitors with calm spaces to meditate and wander. Further on there's an Epcot-like complex arranged around a small lake. A giant castle befitting a fairytale looms high above, and just to the left is an enormous *Calyon* pirate ship – the ultimate playground for kids. A planetarium was under constuction when we visited. A taxi to Sazova from the city centre costs TL10.

🛏 Sleeping

TOP CHOICE **Babüssaade Konak**
HISTORIC HOTEL €€

(Babüssade Boutique Hotel; ☑233 7877; www.babussaade.com; Türkmenhoca Sokak 29; s/d/ste TL120/160/360; ❄️@) Babüssade's sumptuous, antique-clad rooms are set in a sprawling campus of beautifully restored Ottoman mansions. The exteriors boast an eye-pleasing palette of creamy reds, golds and blues, while elaborate kilims drape the expertly appointed interiors. The on-site **restaurant** (mains TL18-32; ◯breakfast, lunch & dinner) sits on two sumptuous floors that really don't hold back with their interpretation of over-the-top opulent decor.

Grand Namlı Otel
HOTEL €€

(☑322 1515; www.namliotel.com.tr; Üniversite Caddesi 14; s/d TL99/169; ❄️@) Checking off all the requirements for comfy digs – clean, spacious, fresh-faced, good service etc – this hotel in the city centre is one of the best values in town. The Namlı family made a name for themselves as high-end grocers, so don't miss the amazing buffet breakfasts. Discounts can be negotiated.

Ibis Hotel
HOTEL €

(☑211 7700; www.ibishotel.com; Siloönü Sokak 5; s/d TL100/180) Just up the street from the Namlı on the other side of the traintracks, Accor's contribution to Eskişehir's sleeping scene is a surprising break from the chain gang, built in a converted silo stack.

🍴 Eating & Drinking

The city has a surprisingly vast assortment of local and international eats that cater to a diverse community of locals, university students and expats. Evenings are best spent along the main pedestrian drag that features ornate bridges linking each side of the well-groomed riverbanks. Mahmut Kızılcıklı Caddesi also has a good showing of swank bars and cafes. There's a branch of Bursa's almighty **Kebapçı İskender** chain in Sazova Park.

Has Kırım Çibörekçisi
TATAR €

(Atalar Caddesi 20/A; mains TL4-8; ◯10.30am-9pm) Eskişehir has a large population of Tatars, and thus the city has a smattering of restaurants serving their traditional cuisine. One of the most popular options is this simple spot with light yellow walls and chintzy blue drapes. It specialises in *çiğ börek* (a puffed pastry pocket shaped like a bell and filled with small amounts of meat) from Crimea (Kırım). The restaurant is located at Mahmure tram station; there's a second branch in Kent Park.

Mezze
AEGEAN €€

(☑230 3009; Pehlivan Caddesi 15A Nazım Hikmet Sokak 2; mains from TL10; ◯lunch & dinner) So flavourful and fresh you'd swear that you were sitting at a *meyhane* (tavern) along the Bodrum coast, this excellent seafood restaurant is popular with Eskişehir's international crowd. Mezze's open-air seating is a great spot for people-watching along the city's main pedestrian drag.

Osmanlı Evi
LOCAL €€

(Yeşil Efendi Sokak 22; mains TL3.50-14, brunch TL12.50; ◯breakfast, lunch & dinner) The 'Ottoman House' has had an illustrious 200-year run – Atatürk even stayed during his campaign for independence. Today, the maids' quarters in the back have been transformed into a large kitchen and guests can grab a table in any of the main building's ornate rooms (check out the ceilings!) for fine local fare. Don't miss the great views of the city from the small dusty car park right across the street. It's up a side street behind the Kurşunlu Camii.

222 Park
INTERNATIONAL €€€

(www.222park.com; Pehlivan Caddesi 15A; mains from TL12; ◯lunch & dinner) The multi-venue complex known simply as 222 (that's 'two-two-two', not the less-appealing *iki-iki-iki*) is Eskişehir's attempt to out-swank Reina,

İstanbul's party palace. Enjoy a medley of swank restaurants befitting London or New York, or drop by for frequent bursts of live music. 222 is located across from the Espark shopping mall.

❶ Information

Eskişehir's **tourist office** (230 1752) is in the Valiliği (regional government) building on the southwest side of İki Eylül Caddesi.

Internet cafes and ATMs are at the southern end of Hamamyolu Caddesi.

❶ Getting There & Around

See **Turkish Airlines** (www.thy.com) for the latest details on flights to Bursa.

From the otogar there are regular buses to Afyon (three hours), Ankara (3¼ hours), Bursa (2½ hours), İstanbul (six hours), and Kütahya (1½ hours).

Eskişehir **train station** is an important railway terminus, and there are various services from İstanbul (four to six hours) and Ankara (2½ to four hours) day and night.

The train station is northwest of the centre; the otogar 3km east of the centre. Trams and buses run from the otogar to Köprübaşı, the central district just north of Hamamyolu Caddesi.

All official city transport runs on a prepay system – buy tickets (TL2) from a booth or kiosk. Trams, city buses and dolmuşes serve the vast otogar; look for signs saying 'Terminal' or 'Yeni Otogar'. A taxi from Köprübaşı costs around TL10.

Kütahya

0274 / POP 212,400

To call Kütahya charmless would be unfair, however this rather parochial burg rarely features on anyone's must-see list. Everyone in Turkey recognises the name Kütahya as a major producer of porcelain and tiles, much like İznik. However, while İnzik has resurrected its pedigree in the handmade and high-end sector, Kütahya prefers uninspired factory-line products. The city has several worthwhile museums showcasing its kilnfired past, and every July, history comes to life at the Dumlupınar handicrafts fair. Kütahya also has a local university, however the city remains far less diverse and forward thinking than vibrant Eskişehir.

History

Kütahya's earliest known inhabitants were Phrygians. In 546 BC it was captured by the Persians, and then had a succession of rulers including Alexander the Great, the kings of Bithynia, and the emperors of Rome and Byzantium, who called the town Cotiaeum.

The first Turks to arrive were the Seljuks in 1182. Ousted by the Crusaders, they returned to found the Emirate of Germiyan (1302–1428), with Kütahya as its capital. The emirs cooperated with the Ottomans in nearby Bursa, and when the last emir died his lands were incorporated in the growing Ottoman Empire. Tamerlane swept in at the beginning of the 15th century, made Kütahya his temporary headquarters and then returned to Central Asia.

After Selim I took Tabriz in 1514, he brought all of its ceramic artisans to Kütahya and İznik. Since then the two towns have rivalled one another in the quality of their tilework.

◉ Sights & Activities

A huge **vase-shaped fountain** marks Zafer (Belediye) Meydanı, the town's main square, which is overlooked by the *vilayet* (provincial government building) and *belediye* (town hall). The town's main commercial street is Cumhuriyet Caddesi, running southwest from the *vilayet* and on to the **Ulu Cami**, which has been lovingly restored several times since construction in 1410. Check out the use of local tiles on everything from shopfronts to street furniture.

Archaeology Museum   MUSEUM
(Arkeoloji Müzesi; ☑224 0785; admission TL3; ⊙9am-1pm & 2-5.45pm Tue-Sun) The Archaeology Museum is next door to the Ulu Cami in the Vacidiye Medresesi, which was built by Umur bin Savcı of the Germiyan family in 1314. The centrepiece of the collection is a Roman sarcophagus from Aizanoi's Temple of Zeus, carved with scenes of battling Amazons. There are also finds from the Phrygian Valley and interesting Roman votive stelae.

FREE **Tile Museum**   MUSEUM
(Çini Müzesi; ☑223 6990; ⊙9am-6.45pm Tue-Sun) The Tile Museum is housed in the İmaret Camii on the opposite side of the Ulu Cami, beneath a magnificent dome. Most of the collection is Kütahya pottery, including work by the master craftsman Hacı Hafiz Mehmet Emin Efendi, who worked on İstanbul's Haydarpaşa station. In deference to the town's main rival, there are also some wonderful İznik tiles and a lot of beautiful embroidery. To one side is the 14th-century, blue-tiled tomb of one Yakup Bey.

SEYİTGAZİ

Seyitgazi, 43km southeast of Eskişehir, is dominated by the hilltop 13th-century **Battalgazi mosque complex** (admission TL5). Combining Seljuk and Ottoman architecture, the complex also contains pieces of marble presumably taken from the ruins of the Romano-Byzantine town of Nacolea. The mosque commemorates Seyit/Seyyid Battal Gazi, a giant warrior who fought for the Arabs against the Byzantines and was killed in 740. His wildly elongated tomb sits in a side chamber off the main mosque.

Features of the *külliye* include an *aşevi* (kitchen) with eight skyline-piercing chimneys, a *semahane* (dance hall) where dervishes would have gathered, and a *medrese* containing several grim *çilehanes*, or 'places of suffering' – cells in which the devout lived (and died) like hermits with only their Qurans for company. Numerous calligraphic inscriptions singing the praises of Battal Gazi dot the walls.

Buses run from Eskişehir to Seyitgazi (TL5, 45 minutes). Some buses from Eskişehir to Afyon also pass through.

Dönenler Camii   MOSQUE

Nearby is the Dönenler Cami, which was built in the 14th century and later served as a *mevlevihane,* or home to a group of Mevlevi dervishes. Inside it has a wonderful, galleried *semahane* with paintings of tall Mevlevi hats on the columns.

FREE Kossuth House   HISTORIC BUILDING

(Kossuth Evi; ☑223 6214; ⊘9am-1pm & 2-5.45pm Tue-Sun) Follow the signs behind the Ulu Cami to Kossuth House, also called Macar Evi (Hungarian House) – the oldest house in Kütahya. Keep an eye out for plaques in Turkish and Hungarian.

Lajos Kossuth (1802–94) was a prominent member of the Hungarian parliament. In 1848, chafing at Hapsburg rule from Vienna, he and others rose in revolt, later declaring Hungary an independent republic in 1849. When Russian troops intervened on behalf of the Austrians he was forced to flee. The Ottomans offered him a refuge and he lived in Kütahya from 1850 to 1851.

A stately whitewashed exterior conceals various rooms that provide poignant insights into the life of upper-class Kütahyans in the mid-19th century. The 1st-floor veranda, overlooking a rose garden with a statue of Kossuth, offers lovely views of the encircling hills. A large map details Kossuth's international travels from 1849 to 1861. He certainly got around.

FREE Kütahya Fortress   CASTLE

Looming above the town, Kütahya fortress was built in two stages by the Byzantines, then restored and used by the Seljuks, the Germiyan emirs and the Ottomans. The latest building work seems to have taken place in the 15th century, the most recent restoration in the 1990s. One look at the remains of dozens of round towers makes it clear what a formidable obstacle this would have been to any army. It's a long walk up to the fortress so you might want to take a taxi (around TL10 to TL15). Afterwards you can descend along a steep, scree-covered path that ends near the Ulu Cami.

🛏 Sleeping

Kütahya has never been a tourist town, and thus, the array of accommodation is quite limited. There are a couple of lovely upmarket options, but travellers with tighter wallets will be hard-pressed to find an acceptable option in the budget category.

Ispartalılar Konağı   HISTORIC HOTEL €€

(☑216 1975; www.ispartalilarkonagi.com.tr; Germiyan Caddesi 58; s/d TL90/140; @) Owned by the local university, this 180-year-old house has been fully restored, revealing all of its Ottoman glory. Rooms come with darkwood antiques and handwoven rugs; slide a darkwood panel open to find the mini-WC (think Barbie's dream Ottoman toilet) tucked away in the cupboard. The on-site **restaurant** (mains TL5-18) has a good reputation for its international fare, and alcohol is served (a rarity in central Kütahya).

Hilton Garden Inn   BUSINESS HOTEL €€€

(☑229 5555; www.kutahya.hgi.com; Atatürk Bulvarı 21; s/d €113/140; ✱@) Miles beyond the rest of Kütahya's dreary business accommodation, the Hilton does exactly what the name promises: comfortable modern rooms with predictable furnishings and amenities.

Qtahya Otel HOTEL €€
(☑226 2010; www.q-tahya.com; Atatürk Bulvarı 56; s/d TL75/120; ❋ @) Convenient to the bus station, Qtahya is provincial Turkey's attempt at hip digs. Plasmas in the lobby and eager-to-please staff almost balance out the slightly musty rooms. There's a TL20 discount for double rooms occupied by members of the same gender...

✖ Eating & Drinking

Kütahya lacks the quality eats of Eskişehir and Afyon, but cheap grub can be easily scouted as the city has a large student population. Happy döner hunting along Atatürk Bulvarı.

Karavan Gözleme MUTFAK €
(www.karavangozleme.com; Atatürk Bulvarı 12/A; mains TL2-8) It may serve 15 types of *gözleme,* from *haşhaşlı* (poppy-seed) to chocolate, but the Karavan is more than just a pancake place, and also does great pide and *lahmacun.* Pop upstairs to find a small terrace with a mini-jungle and an inviting nargileh (water pipe) lounge. Check out **Hammamı Ziyafe** (Sevgi Yolu Tarihi Küçük Hamam; mains TL7-15), a swankier avatar of the same concept and owned by the same entrepreneurial folks.

Döner Restaurant LOCAL €€
(mains TL9-15; ☺lunch & dinner) Inside the ruins of the fortress, this popular spot is a strange throwback to the '70s with its dated decor – oh, and did we mention that it's a revolving restaurant? Yes, you read correctly – ask the owner to turn it on and you'll spin around the fortress at a decent clip. Come in the evening when the views are particularly magical.

Kütahya Konağı LOCAL €€
(mains TL6-16; ☺breakfast, lunch & dinner) If you ask the locals where to find the best traditional grub in town, you'll get a hundred fingers pointing to this local haunt. Try some homespun faves like the town's very own spin on kebap.

❶ Information

Tourist information kiosk (☑223 6213; Zafer Meydanı; ☺9am-6pm) Little English spoken but good maps.

❶ Getting There & Away

Kütahya is a provincial capital with regular services to Afyon (1½ hours), Ankara (five hours), Bursa (three hours), Denizli (five hours), Eskişehir (1½ hours), İstanbul (six hours) and İzmir (six hours).

Minibuses to Çavdarhisar, for Aizanoi (TL6, one hour), leave from the local bus stand next to the otogar.

Afyon (Afyonkarahisar)

☑0272 / POP 170,450

Modern Afyon is a provincial capital lounging in the shadow of its ancient and supremely spectacular castle. Once your neck has cramped from staring at the mighty citadel in the sky, you'll find a fine museum, magnificent mosques and some charming Ottoman houses.

History

Afyon's history started around 3000 years ago. After occupation by the Hittites, Phrygians, Lydians and Persians, it was settled by the Romans and the Byzantines. Following the Seljuk victory at Manzikert in 1071, Afyon fell under the Seljuk Turks. The important Seljuk vizier Sahip Ata took direct control of the town, and it was called Karahisar-i Sahip through Ottoman times (1428–1923).

During the War of Independence, Greek forces occupied the town on their push towards Ankara. During the Battle of Sakarya, in late August 1921, the republican armies under Mustafa Kemal (Atatürk) stopped the invading force within earshot of Ankara in one of history's longest pitched battles. The Greek forces retreated and dug in for the winter near Eskişehir and Afyon.

On 26 August 1922 the Turks began their counteroffensive along an 80km front, advancing rapidly on the Greek army. Within days Atatürk had set up his headquarters in Afyon's *belediye* building and had half the Greek army surrounded at Dumlupınar, 40km to the west. This decisive battle destroyed the Greek army as a fighting force and sent its survivors fleeing towards İzmir. Like Gallipoli, the battlefields are now protected, forming the Başkomutan National Historical Park.

In 2004 the town's official name changed from Afyon ('Opium') to Afyonkarahisar ('Black Fortress of Opium'), an attempt to reference the city's imposing citadel while taking a bit of the emphasis off of the town's reputation for growing opium.

◉ Sights & Activities

Afyon's main square, called Hükümet Meydanı, is marked by an imposing statue

WORTH A TRIP

AİZANOİ – TEMPLE OF ZEUS

The subdued farming village of Çavdarhisar, about 60km southwest of Kütahya, is home to Aizanoi, one of Anatolia's best-preserved Roman remains. The great Temple of Zeus (admission TL3; ☺8am-6.30pm) dates from the reign of Hadrian (r AD 117–138), and was dedicated to the worship of Zeus (Jupiter) and the Anatolian fertility goddess Cybele.

The temple stands deserted but proud in a quiet meadow, founded on a broad terrace created to serve as its precinct. Like the abandoned set of a Hollywood epic, the north and west faces of the temple have their double rows of Ionic and Corinthian columns intact, but the south and east rows have fallen into a picturesque jumble. The cella (inner room) walls are intact enough to give a good impression of the imposing whole. An enclosure beside the ticket office holds some of the best pieces of sculpture found here, and dotted around the site are good explanations in English.

If the ticket office is empty, the custodian will find you to sell you a ticket. Ask him to show you the cryptlike sanctuary of Cybele beneath the temple.

Çavdarhisar is on the Kütahya–Gediz road. From 11.30am to 7.20pm there are minibuses to Çavdarhisar from Kütahya otogar (TL6, one hour), dolmuşes run in the other direction from 8.30am to around 6pm. Buses bound for Gediz or Emet pass through Çavdarhisar – you can ask the driver to let you off on the way.

---

of a large muscular man beating another man who has fallen to the ground – it is meant to commemorate the Turkish victory over the Greek army in 1922. The statue sits northeast of the citadel at the intersection of Ordu Bulvarı and Milli Egemenlik (Bankalar) Caddesi.

FREE **Citadel**   CASTLE
Soaring from the plains, the craggy rock with the *kale* or *hisar* (citadel) hovers imposingly above the town. For a closer look find the lane across the street from the Ulu Cami and follow the green and brown signs. Around 570 steps lead to the summit, passing through a series of guard towers. It's a good workout and unfortunately there is no easier way up. Around the halfway mark, don't be surprised if you start questioning the wisdom of the people that managed, voluntarily, to build such a large fortress somewhere so inaccessible.

Blame the Hittite king Mursilis II for building the first castle here around 1350 BC. Every subsequent conqueror has added their own features. Despite its eventful history there's little to see inside, and contemporary restorations broke clumsily with the original *kara hisar* (black citadel) look by using white stones.

The views from the summit (226m) are spectacular, and it's worth coming up at prayer time for the surround sound of the muezzins from Afyon's many mosques. Note that the castle isn't lit at night, which can make it tricky if you're coming down after dusk.

For the best photos of the castle from below, head to the **Kültür ve Semt Evi** (Zaviye Türbe Caddesi), a restored hamam with unobstructed views from its raised terrace.

FREE **Archaeological Museum**   MUSEUM
(Arkeoloji Müzesi; ☺8.30am-5.30pm) Take a dolmuş along Kurtuluş Caddesi, the continuation of Bankalar Caddesi, to Afyon's Archaeological Museum, near the intersection with İsmet İnönü Caddesi. The collection features interesting Hittite, Phrygian, Lydian and Roman discoveries, including an impressive statue of Hercules in the museum's garden. There are lots of marble statues – the nearby quarries at Dokimeon (now İscehisar) were (and still are) an important source of the lustrous rock. At the time of research a new structure was under construction beyond the city centre (near the thermal hotels) to house an expanded collection of artefacts. Once the new museum is finished this site will close.

Mevlevihane Camii   MUSEUM
(Zaviye Caddesi) The Mevlevihane Camii was once a dervish meeting place and dates back to Seljuk times (13th century), when Sultan Veled, son of dervish founder Celaleddin Rumi, established Afyon as the empire's second-most important Mevlevi centre after Konya. The present mosque, with twin domes and twin pyramidal roofs

above its courtyard, dates from only 1908, when it was built for Sultan Abdül Hamit II. A new (and free!) museum explains the life and times of the mystical dervishes – ask for a pamphlet in English.

İmaret Camii
MOSQUE

Afyon's major mosque complex is just south of the traffic roundabout at the southern end of Bankalar Caddesi. Built for Gedik Ahmet Paşa in 1472, its design shows the transition from the Seljuk to the Ottoman style, with the spiral-fluted minaret decorated, Seljuk-style, with blue tiles. The entrance on the eastern side is like an *eyvan* (vaulted hall) and leads to a main sanctuary topped by two domes, front and back, a design also seen in the early Ottoman capitals of Bursa and Edirne. The shady park beside it provides a peaceful refuge from bustling Bankalar Caddesi.

Next door, the İmaret hamamı (⊙5am-midnight for men, 8am-8pm for women) is still well patronised and retains some of the precious old stone basins.

Ulu Cami
MOSQUE

Afyon's Ulu Cami (1273) is one of the most important surviving Seljuk mosques, so it's a shame that it's usually locked outside prayer times. If you do manage to get inside you'll find 40 soaring wooden columns with stalactite capitals and a flat-beamed roof. Note the green tiles on the minaret.

Ottoman Houses
HISTORIC AREA

The area around the Ulu Cami has many old Ottoman wooden houses. It's no Safranbolu, but Afyon showcases an interesting array of mansions, several of which have been turned into small restaurants.

Sleeping

If you're looking for a little spa action, check out the string of thermal hotels dotting the Afyon–Kütahya road several kilometres out of town.

Şehitoğlu Konaği
HISTORIC HOTEL €€€

(☎214 1313; www.sehitoglukonagi.com; Kuyulu Sokak 2-6; s/d TL110/180) Located within shouting distance of the Dervish Mosque, this beautifully restored manse is Afyon's worthy contribution to the current trend of turning old Ottoman houses into time-warped hotels. The in-house **restaurant** (mains TL10-20) gets a good report card for its hearty selection of local eats (namely *sucuk* – spicy sausage – and kebap). They even make their own wine in the basement.

Çakmak Marble Otel
HOTEL €€

(☎214 3300; www.cakmakmarblehotel.com; Süleyman Gonçer Caddesi 2; s/d TL87/140, ste TL240; ❈ ▨ @) One block east of Hükümet Meydanı, this older four-star stalwart is one of those rare instances where the rooms are actually nicer than the lobby. Service is excellent, guests have access to an indoor swimming pool and jacuzzi, and breakfast is served on the eighth floor with sweeping views over the city. The hotel's 'American Bar' has absolutely no atmosphere, however it's one of the only places in town to get a beer.

Hotel Soydan
HOTEL €€

(☎215 2323; Turan Emeksiz Caddesi 2; s/d TL40/80) This nominal two-star is well-priced without being too well-worn. The rooms are passable and most have balconies; you'll probably want to examine a few bathrooms before hanging your hat. There's a great fruit shop on the ground level.

Eating & Drinking

Scores of shops around town are draped with necklaces of locally made *sucuk* and padded out with pillows of cheese. Grab a loaf of crisp Turkish bread and that's lunch sorted.

Alcohol is not served at any restaurant in the city centre – visitors looking for a drink should head to one of the local hotels, such as the Çakmak Marble Otel.

Altınay
CONFECTIONER €€

(Millet Caddesi 5; ⊙6.30am-9pm) Of all the recipes for Turkish delight, Afyon's is by far the most famous due to the lip-licking local cream made from the protected opium plant. Altınay has perfected the recipe and is known throughout the region for its long strands of sticky heaven.

Mihrioğlu Konağı
LOCAL €

(mains TL5-12; ⊙breakfast, lunch & dinner) Set in an old Ottoman-style home and run by the family who owns it, Mihrioğlu clicks the culinary clock back a few centuries with its menu of traditional eats mixed with current local faves (Afyon kebap, *mantı* etc). Crinkled civic photos line the walls while antique tagines and sewing machines fill the corners. A rustic garden provides summer seating out back.

İkbal Lokantası
LOCAL €€

(Uzunçarşı Caddesi 21; mains TL6-15; ⊙lunch & dinner) Southwest of Hükümet Meydanı, İkbal is Afyon's oldest and most famous restaurant. Waiters in white uniforms deliver a hearty assortment of meaty mains to a regular crew of contented customers. In fact, İkbal is such a grand success that the owners opened a like-named thermal resort on the outskirts of the city.

❶ Information

Tourist office (☎213 5447; Hükümet Meydanı; ⏰8am-noon & 1.30-5.30pm Mon-Fri) Of debatable value to English-speaking travellers, but at least it offers a useful map.

❶ Getting There & Away

Afyon is on the inland routes connecting İstanbul with Antalya and Konya, and İzmir with Ankara and the east. There are regular buses to Ankara (four hours), Antalya (five hours), Denizli/Pamukkale (four hours), Eskişehir (three hours), Isparta (three hours), İstanbul (eight hours), İzmir (5½ hours), Konya (3¾ hours) and Kütahya (1½ hours).

Free dolmuşes access the city centre if you save your bus ticket (the same in the opposite direction once you purchase your ticket). A taxi out to the otogar costs around TL10.

Uşak

☑0276 / POP 173,000

History buffs should definitely consider stopping in Uşak to check out the excellent **Archaeology Museum** (Doğan Sokak; admission TL3; ⏰8.30am-1pm & 2-5.45pm Tue-Sun), just off the town's main square. The exhibition space features what has been dubbed the 'Lydian Hoard'; a treasure discovered in tumuli around the Gediz river valley that dates back to the second half of the 6th century BC. The museum made international headlines from 2006 to 2008 when it was discovered that many original artefacts had been stolen and replaced with fakes (by members of the museum's staff).

❶ Getting There & Away

Frequent minibuses connect Uşak with Afyon (TL10, 1½ hours), and there are periodic buses from İzmir (TL20 to TL25, 2½ hours). If you get dropped on the highway (Dörtyöl) follow the signs for the *şehir merkezi* (city centre); it's about 1.5km to the Otel Dülgeroğlu. From the otogar, a taxi should cost around TL10.

PAMUKKALE REGION

Pamukkale is undoubtedly the biggest tourist drawcard in western Anatolia, luring busloads of tourists who've seen the incredible photographs (quite possibly Photoshopped) of happy travellers frolicking in gleaming white travertines. At the top of the crystalline terraces lies Hierapolis – an ancient city and healing centre. But the most impressive ruins in the region are those at Afrodisias, which almost trump the columnar wonderland at Ephesus. Due to its faraway location, you'll likely have most of the site to yourself.

Denizli

☑0258 / POP 500,000

The prosperous town of Denizli is famous for its textiles, and lining the road to Pamukkale you'll see many outlet centres selling cheap but good quality towels and bed linen. For most travellers though, it's just a place to hop off a bus or train and onto a bus or dolmuş heading north to Pamukkale.

❶ Getting There & Away

Air

Turkish Airlines (www.thy.com) has daily flights to Denizli from İstanbul. From the airport a Turkish Airlines shuttle bus drops passengers at the Denizli otogar on request. A taxi from the airport to Denizli is around TL50 and around TL75 to Pamukkale.

Bus

Denizli is a key transport hub for all of Turkey. The local bus service to Pamukkale leaves from inside the otogar and runs every 15 minutes, with no waiting about for it to fill up.

Touts taking commissions from hotels may try to get you to take the dolmuşes that wait beside the otogar instead of the bus.

Buses and dolmuşes to Pamukkale cost TL2.50.

Pamukkale

☑0258 / POP 2500

Famed for its intricate series of calcite shelves and crowned by the elaborate ruins of a Roman spa city, the 'Cotton Castle' – a bleach-white mirage by day and alien ski slope by night – is one of the most unusual treasures in all of Turkey. Gingerly tiptoe through the crystal travertines and when you reach the top, reward yourself with a refreshing dunk in Hierapolis' ancient pool amid toppled columns and dramatic friezes.

Pamukkale was given the Unesco World Heritage label in 1988, and since then,

SERVICES FROM DENİZLİ'S OTOGAR

DESTINATION	FARE (TL)	DURATION (HR)	DISTANCE (KM)	FREQUENCY (PER DAY)
Afyon	22	4	240	8
Ankara	35	7	480	frequent
Antalya	25	5	300	several
Bodrum	25	4½	290	several
Bursa	42	9	532	several
Fethiye	25	5	280	several
Isparta	17	3	175	several
İstanbul	40 to 65	12	665	frequent
İzmir	21	4	250	frequent
Konya	35	6	440	several
Marmaris	23	3	185	several
Nevşehir	40	11	674	at least 1 nightly
Selçuk	20	3	195	several, or change at Aydın

extensive measures have been taken to protect the glistening bluffs. You won't be as free to roam around the travertines as tourists once were, but we are willing to guarantee that the photos still come out amazingly well.

◉ Sights & Activities

There are two main attractions in Pamukkale – the bleached-white travertines (also commonly referred to as 'terraces') and the crumbling ruins of Hierapolis. Both are located in one large complex (now protected as a national park) at the top of the whitewashed hill looming over the dusty little village.

There are three main entrances to the park – the south entrance is slightly over 2km from the village centre, the northern entrance is in the neighbouring village of Karahayıt (home to a number of luxury spa hotels), and the third entrance can be accessed from within the village. Tour operators and large buses use either the north or the south entrance. Pedestrians use the quieter third entrance marked by a small ticket kiosk just east of the Beyaz Cennet public park in town. The path up to the ticket kiosk starts along Mehmet Akif Ersoy Bulvarı just opposite the junction with Atatürk Caddesi. If you're staying the night in Pamukkale your best option is to get a lift out to the south entrance, wander through

Hieropolis, follow the travertines down to the pedestrian entry point and walk back to your accommodation.

One ticket (TL20) includes access to travertines and Hierapolis. Additional fees apply if you visit the archaeological museum and antique swimming pool. In the past, a ticket would grant tourists access to the park for a 24-hour period, but these days it's a one-shot deal. The park is open during daylight hours.

Travertines   NATURE RESERVE

The highlight of Pamukkale is the network of saucer-shaped travertines that wind down the powder-white mountain like a staircase built for a giant. To wander around you must take off your footwear – a security guard will furiously blow his whistle at you if you do not do so. Try wearing a pair of old socks if your soles are tender – some small stones are quite jagged. It's best to visit early in the morning or late in the afternoon to avoid the crowds and the shimmering sun that bounces off the bleached stone.

Hierapolis   RUINS

The ruins of Hierapolis brilliantly evoke life in the early centuries of the modern era. Here pagan, Roman, Jewish and early Christian elements evolved into a distinctly Anatolian whole.

Founded around 190 BC by Eumenes II, king of Pergamum, Hierapolis was a cure centre that prospered under the Romans and even more under the Byzantines, when it gained a large Jewish community and an early Christian congregation. Sadly, recurrent earthquakes regularly brought disaster and after a major tremor in 1334 the city was abandoned.

Start near the Hierapolis Archaeology Museum to find the ruined **Byzantine church** and the foundations of a **Temple of Apollo**. As at Didyma and Delphi, the temple had an oracle tended by eunuch priests. The source of inspiration was an adjoining spring called the Plutonium, dedicated to Pluto, god of the underworld. To confirm its direct line to Hades, the spring released toxic vapours, lethal to all but the priests, who would demonstrate its potent powers by tossing small animals and birds in to watch them die. To find the spring, walk up towards the Roman theatre, enter the first gate in the fence on the right, then follow the path down to the right. To the left, in front of the big, block-like temple, is a small subterranean entrance closed by a rusted grate and marked by a sign reading 'Tehlikelidir Zehirli Gaz' (Dangerous Poisonous Gas). Listen and you will hear the gas bubbling up from the waters below.

The spectacular **Roman theatre**, capable of seating more than 12,000 spectators, was built in two stages by the emperors Hadrian and Septimius Severus. Much of the stage survives, along with some of the decorative panels and the front-row 'box' seats for VIPs. It was restored by Italian stonecutters in the 1970s.

From the theatre, rough tracks lead uphill to the extraordinary octagonal **Martyrium of St Philip the Apostle**, built on the site where, as the name suggests, it is believed that St Philip was martyred. The arches of the eight individual chapels are all marked with crosses. The views are wonderful and few of the tours bring visitors this far.

Across the hillside in a westerly direction is the completely ruined **Hellenistic theatre**. Looking down you'll see the 2nd-century **agora**, one of the largest ever discovered. Marble porticoes with Ionic columns surrounded it on three sides, while a basilica closed off the fourth.

Walk down the hill and through the *agora,* and you'll re-emerge on the main road along the top of the ridge. Turn right towards the northern exit and you'll come to the marvellous colonnaded **Frontinus**

Pamukkale

Pamukkale

🛏 Sleeping
1	Artemis Yoruk Hotel	B2
2	Aspawa Pension	A3
3	Beyaz Kale Pension	A2
4	Hotel Dört Mevsim	A4
5	Hotel Hal-Tur	A1
6	Kervansaray Pension	A2
7	Melrose Hotel	B4
8	Ozbay	B2
9	Venüs Hotel	A4

🍴 Eating
10	Kayaş Restaurant & Bar	A2
11	Konak Sade Restaurant	B2
12	Mehmet's Heaven	B1
13	Mustafa's	B2

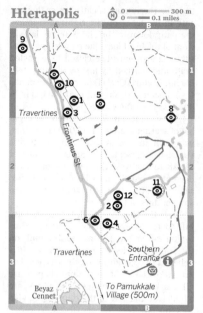

Hierapolis

⊙ Sights

1 Agora A1
2 Antique Pool B2
3 Arch of Domitian A1
4 Byzantine Church B3
5 Hellenistic Theatre A1
6 Hierapolis Archaeology Museum
  (Roman Baths) A3
7 Latrine A1
8 Martyrium of St Phillip the
  Apostle B1
9 Necropolis A1
10 Roman Baths A1
11 Roman Theatre B2
  Sacred Pool ....(see 2)
12 Temple of Apollo B2

Street, with some of its paving and columns still intact. Once the city's main north–south commercial axis, this street was bounded at both ends by monumental archways. The ruins of the **Arch of Domitian**, with its twin towers, are at the northern end, but just before them don't miss the surprisingly large **latrine** building, with two channels cut into its floor, one to carry away sewage, the other for fresh water.

Beyond the Arch of Domitian are the ruins of the **Roman baths**, then, the Appian Way of Hierapolis – an extraordinary **necropolis** (cemetery) – extends several kilometres to the north. Look out for a cluster of circular tombs, supposedly topped with phallic symbols in antiquity. In ancient times Hierapolis was a place where the sick came for a miracle cure, but the scale of the necropolis suggests the local healers had mixed results.

Antique Pool   RUINS
(admission TL25; ⊙9am-7pm) The focus of Hierapolis was its sacred pool, which is now the swimming pool in the courtyard of the Antique Pool spa. You can still bathe in it amid submerged sections of original fluted marble columns. The water temperature is a languid 36°C. In the peak season from around 11am to 4pm, the pool is a busy watery scrum of day trippers, but it generally empties out later in the afternoon.

Tighter budgets can indulge in a swim in the faux-travertines at the **public pool** (admission TL7.50; ⊙9am-8pm) down the hill on the edge of town.

Hierapolis Archaeology Museum
                                                    MUSEUM
(admission TL3; ⊙9am-12.30pm & 1.30-7pm Tue-Sun) Housed in what were once the Roman baths, this excellent museum has three separate sections, one housing spectacular sarcophagi, another small finds from Hierapolis and Afrodisias, and the third friezes and Roman-era statuary from the Afrodisias school. Those depicting Attis, lover of the goddess Cybele, and a priestess of the Egyptian goddess Isis, are especially fine.

🛏 Sleeping
Much like Selçuk near Ephesus (but on a noticeably smaller scale), the village of Pamukkale is riddled with pensions and inns catering to independent travellers (usually of the penny-pinching variety). Stiff competition ensures excellent value for money – expect internet access (computer terminals and wi-fi), swimming pools, filling repasts (only breakfast is included), and informal travel agencies. Prices tend to rise during the tourist swell in July and August (but not by much). If you know where you want to stay, we recommend calling ahead – you'll always find rooms in Pamukkale, but the best spots book up fast. Also, if you book ahead there's a good chance that you can arrange a complimentary pick-up

from the bus station in Denizli. Campers can usually pitch a tent on the grounds of a pension for a nominal fee – just ask around.

TOP CHOICE **Melrose Hotel** PENSION €
(272 2250; www.melrosehousehotel.com; Vali Vekfi Ertürk Caddesi 8; s/d TL50/60; ✳@≋) The lovely Mehmet & Ummu make every guest feel like a member of the family at this lovely pension near the entrance to town. Rooms are decorated with cheery pastels and a generous amount of gauzy drapery dangling over the windows. Refreshing dunks in the pool and hearty (and heart-warming) in-house dinner make this place an undeniable winner.

Venüs Hotel PENSION €
(272 2152; www.venushotel.net; Hasan Tahnsin Caddesi; s/d/tr €20/28/38; ✳@≋) Another excellent option, Venüs' rooms are beautifully decorated, not to mention immaculate. Excellent food is served in the poolside restaurant, and a wonderful kilim-lined den is the perfect spot for guests to get acquainted with the friendly and welcoming Durmuş family.

Hotel Hal-Tur HOTEL €€
(272 2723; www.haltur.net; Mehmet Akif Ersoy Bulvarı 71; s/d from €40/60; ✳@≋) With unencumbered views of the travertines and arguably Pamukkale's best swimming pool, the Hal-Tur is a step up from most other places around town. Enter through the faux-castle gate to enjoy all the mod-cons that come with an international hotel – the decor is a bit old-school though.

Artemis Yoruk Hotel HOSTEL €
(272 2073; www.artemisyorukhotel.com; Atatürk Caddesi; dm/s/d from TL15/30/50; ✳@≋) With a central location, this sprawling spot has a range of rooms, from backpacker dorms to single, double, triple and five-bed family rooms. It's a popular choice for small groups, so the bar offering 'bloody cold beer' can get pleasingly raucous.

Aspawa Pension PENSION €
(272 2094; www.aspawapension.com; Turgut Özal Caddesi 28; s/d €19/25; ✳@≋) Another centrally located pension, the Aspawa ticks all the requisite boxes for good value Pamukkale: pool, air-con, wi-fi and good food in a family atmosphere. A worthwhile backup.

Kervansaray Pension PENSION €
(272 2209; www.kervansaraypension.com; İnönü Caddesi; s/d TL40/60; ✳@≋) This honeysuckle-scented place has comfortable, clean rooms and a breezy terrace with excellent views of the travertines, especially when the spotlights are switched on after dark. Downstairs is a compact pool that's probably best enjoyed during daylight hours.

Beyaz Kale Pension PENSION €
(272 2064; www.beyazkalepension.com; Menderes Caddesi; s/d €20/25; ✳@≋) The 'White Castle' is handy to the centre of the village and has spotless air-con rooms arrayed around a pool. Welcoming family hostess Haçer is a whiz in the kitchen, especially when it comes to vegetarian food. Larger rooms sleeping up to six are also available.

Hotel Dört Mevsim PENSION €
(272 2009; www.hoteldortmevsim.com; Hasan Tahsin Caddesi 19; s/d TL30/50; ✳@≋) The 'Four Seasons' is quite different to its top-end namesakes, but has simple, family-run rooms in a quiet lane. Expect excellent home-cooked food, lots of bright decor and an even brighter welcome. Breakfast is an extra TL5.

Ozbay HOSTEL €
(272 2126; www.ozbayhotel.com; Mehmet Akif Ersoy Bulvarı 37; s/d TL40/50; ✳@) With more of a hostel vibe, Ozbay, along one of the main roads up to the travertines, has a buzzing international vibe and uberbasic rooms.

🍴 Eating & Drinking

Pensions and group travel dominate the Pamukkale market and conventional restaurants have struggled to hold their own. There are a couple worth trying, but the home-cooked food at your pension is your best bet, especially if you're only staying for one night.

Mehmet's Heaven LOCAL €
(Atatürk Caddesi 25; mains TL5-14; ⊘breakfast, lunch & dinner) Friendly Mehmet invites tourists to dine amongst a sea of overstuffed cushions. Thumb through giant tomes of autographs – basically everyone who has eaten here over the last 25 years – while enjoying the views of travertines out back.

Kayaş LOCAL €
(Atatürk Caddesi 3; mains TL5-14; ⊘lunch & dinner) As well as a diverse menu of pinch-a-penny eats, Kayaş offers plenty of scope for a fun night out, with cocktails, a nargileh corner and satellite-TV coverage of big football matches.

Konak Sade Restaurant LOCAL €€
(Atatürk Caddesi 23; mains TL8-14; ⊘breakfast, lunch & dinner) Free apple tea, giant lounge

chairs and use of the on-site swimming pool make this a good central choice for daytrippers.

Mustafa's LOCAL €€
(Atatürk Caddesi 22; mains TL8-13; ⊘breakfast, lunch & dinner) Scatter cushions and rustic tables overlooking the street are a top location for wood-fired pizzas and good-value falafel wraps.

Information

All pensions are well equipped to provide you with all the information you need about Pamukkale, in fact they're usually more helpful than the tourist offices. A **tourist office** (⊘8am-7pm Mon-Sat) sits on the plateau above the travertines.

ATMs can be found around town, and all pensions offer complimentary internet access. Major banks can be found in Denizli.

Getting There & Away

Bus

In summer Pamukkale has direct buses to a variety of tourist destinations like Selçuk (TL20) and Kuşadası. Though it's best to assume that for most destinations you'll have to change in Denizli. Check when you book your ticket.

Pamukkale has no proper otogar; buses drop off passengers in a few different places, including the ticket offices in Cumhuriyet Square.

Buses and dolmuşes (TL2.50) run between Denizli and Pamukkale with great frequency. The ride takes 30 minutes.

Taxi

You shouldn't have to take a taxi between Denizli and Pamukkale, as most accommodation will usually offer rides (either complimentary or heavily discounted). If you do need a taxi, it should cost around TL40 – though check to make sure that no dolmuşes are running.

Around Pamukkale

If you're sticking around Pamukkale for more than a day then consider checking out the following attractions, but make sure to start with the awesome archaeological ruins at Afrodisias located about 90km from town.

LAODICEA (LAODİKYA)

Once a prosperous commercial city at the junction of two major trade routes, Laodicea was famed for its black wool, banking and medicines. It had a large Jewish community and a prominent Christian congregation, and was one of the Seven Churches of Asia

mentioned in the New Testament Book of Revelation. Cicero lived here for a few years before being put to death at the behest of Mark Antony. Although the spread-out **ruins** (admission TL5; ⊘8.30am-5pm Tue-Sun) suggest a city of considerable size, there's not much of interest left The outline of the **stadium** is visible, although most of the stones were purloined to construct the railway. One of the two **theatres** is in better shape, with most of the upper tiers of seats remaining. More striking are the remains of the **agora**, with the ruins of the **basilica church** mentioned in the Bible right beside it.

❶ Getting There & Away

Heading from Pamukkale to Denizli by bus, a sign in the village of **Korucuk** leads to Laodicea. From the sign it's a 1km walk to the site. Alternatively, you might want to sign up for a tour from Pamukkale that also takes in other local sites (note that these tours don't run everyday). An infrequent dolmuş also plies the route (TL2.50).

KAKLIK MAĞARASI (KAKLIK CAVE) & AK HAN

Hidden away beneath a field, **Kaklık Mağarası** (admission TL2) is like an underground Pamukkale. Calcium-rich water flows from near the surface into a large sinkhole, creating a bright, white pyramid with warm travertine pools at the bottom. Guides claim that the deposits became white only after the local earthquake of the mid-1990s. Outside there is a pool for bathing. Surrounded by concrete it looks just like a pool at Sea World; cavort in the shallows for long enough and someone might throw you a fish.

En route to the cave, pause to inspect the **Ak Han** (White Caravanserai), a Seljuk *han* 1km past the Pamukkale turn-off on the main Denizli–Isparta highway. With a beautifully carved gateway, its excellent condition belies its construction in 1251.

❶ Getting There & Away

Getting to the cave by public transport is time-consuming and it's easiest to take a tour from Pamukkale. To visit independently, catch a bus or dolmuş (TL4) going west from Denizli to Afyon, Isparta or Burdur. In the village of Kaklık a huge sign points left (north) to the cave. Grab a ride on a farm vehicle, or walk 4km to the cave.

Afrodisias

If Afrodisias were closer to the sea or İstanbul it would clearly be one of Turkey's

You may be disappointed by the state of the travertines, especially if you've seen older photographs of Pamukkale. But since Unesco World Heritage protection was granted in 1988, significant steps have been taken to ensure the future of the site. Hotels on the plateau were demolished and the road that went through the heart of the travertines removed.

Despite the hearsay, it's not the pensions' swimming pools in the village below causing the pools to be bereft of water. A managed process authorised by Unesco actually drains and fills the pools of water on a rotating basis. The aim is to reduce pollution and algae in the pools and to allow the sun to bleach the pools a glistening white, only possible when the pools are empty of water.

most-visited attractions. Fortunately for you, its hard-to-reach location means that you could very likely have the site's exalted stadium and soaring colonnades all to yourself. The ruins are sprawling and well-preserved thanks to a heap of funding – it's not unusual to find small gangs of archaeologists lifting stones and tagging bumps in the earth. While there are finer individual ruins at Ephesus, Afrodisias is where the scale of an ancient city can be best appreciated – it's easy to conjure up the grandeur of this lost classical treasure.

History

Excavations have proved that the Afrodisias acropolis is a prehistoric mound built up by successive settlements from around 5000 BC. From the 6th century BC its famous temple was a popular pilgrimage site, but it wasn't until the 2nd or 1st century BC that the village grew into a town that steadily prospered. By the 3rd century AD Afrodisias was the capital of the Roman province of Caria, with a population of 15,000 at its peak. However, under the Byzantines the city changed substantially: the provocative Temple of Aphrodite was transformed into a chaste Christian church, and ancient buildings were pulled down to provide stone for defensive walls (c AD 350).

During the Middle Ages Afrodisias continued as a cathedral town, but it was abandoned in the 12th century. The village of Geyre sprang up on the site some time later. In 1956 an earthquake devastated the village, which was rebuilt in its present westerly location, allowing easier excavation of the site. The pleasant plaza in front of the museum was the main square of pre-1956 Geyre.

Afrodisias will always be associated with the work of Kenan T Erim, a Turkish professor from New York University, who directed work at the site from 1961 to 1990. His book *Afrodisias: City of Venus Aphrodite* (1986) tells its story. After his death, Professor Erim was buried at the site that he had done so much to reveal.

◉ Sights

Most ruins at **Afrodisias** (admission incl museum entry TL8; ⊙9am-7pm May-Sep, 9am-5pm Oct-Apr) date back to at least the 2nd century AD. The site is well laid out, with excellent signage in English and Turkish. Follow the anticlockwise route we outline to go against the flow of the occasional package-tour groups, which usually arrive around 11am. A train car (pulled by a tractor) transports visitors from the main highway 500m down the hill to the entrance. If you arrive by private car expect to pay an additional TL5 for the privilege of parking.

Turn right beside the museum and on the left you'll see the site of a grand **house** with Ionic and Corinthian pillars. Further along on the left is the magnificently elaborate **tetrapylon** (monumental gateway), which once greeted pilgrims as they approached the Temple of Aphrodite. It's been reconstructed using 85% of the original blocks. The tomb of Professor Erim is on the lawn nearby.

Follow the footpath until you come to a right turn that leads across a field of tall grass to the 270m-long **stadium**, one of the biggest and best preserved in the classical world. The stadium has a slightly ovoid shape to give spectators a better view of events. Most of its 30,000 seats are overgrown but still in usable condition, and you can easily imagine a big event taking place with thousands of cheering locals. Some seats were reserved for individuals or guilds. The eastern end of the stadium

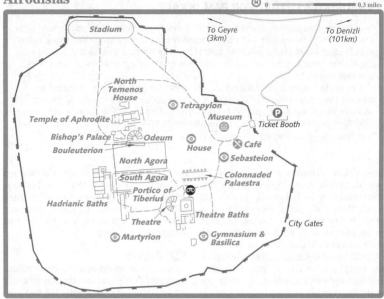

was converted into an arena for gladiatorial combats and you can still see the tunnels where the fighters made their menacing entrances.

Return to the main path and continue to the once-famous **Temple of Aphrodite**, completely rebuilt when it was converted into a basilica (c AD 500). Its cella was removed, its columns shifted to form a nave, and an apse was added at the eastern end, which makes it pretty hard to imagine how it must have been in the years when celebratory orgies were held here. Near the temple-church is the **Bishop's Palace**, a grand house that was thought to have accommodated the Roman governor long before any clergymen turned up.

Just after the Bishop's Palace, a path leads east to the beautiful marble **bouleuterion**, preserved almost undamaged for 1000 years in a bath of mud.

South of the odeum was the **north agora**, once enclosed by Ionic porticoes but now little more than a grassy field. The path then leads through the early 2nd-century AD **Hadrianic Baths** to the **south agora**, with a long, partially excavated pool, and the grand **Portico of Tiberius**.

Climb the stone stairs up the earthen mound (where a prehistoric settlement existed) to find the white marble **theatre**, a 7000-capacity auditorium complete with stage and individually labelled seats. Just south was the large **theatre baths** complex.

The path then wraps round and brings you onto the site of the **Sebasteion**, originally a temple to the deified Roman emperors. In its heyday it was a spectacular building, preceded by a three-storey-high double colonnade decorated with friezes of Greek myths and exploits of the emperors; 70 of the original 190 reliefs have been recovered, an excellent ratio for an excavation of this size. Many of the reliefs are displayed in the Afrodisias museum.

After touring the ruins, visit the **museum**. During Roman times, the area had a quarry of high-grade marble, and Afrodisias was home to a famous school for sculptors. The museum collection reflects the excellence of their work. Noteworthy sculptures include a 2nd-century cult statue of Aphrodite, shield portraits of great philosophers (deliberately vandalised by early Christians), and depictions of the mysterious Caius Julius Zoilos, a former slave of Octavian who not only won his freedom but also gained enough wealth to become one of Afrodisias' major benefactors.

ⓘ Getting There & Away

Afrodisias is 55km southeast of Nazilli and 101km by road from Denizli. If you are based in Pamukkale, ask your accommodation about booking a spot on a tour (TL60 per person). Daytrips leave with a minimum of four people, so they usually don't run every day – even in high season. You'll have around 2½ hours at the site. Your hotel can also help set you up with a car rental (TL80 per day) – figure an additional TL55 for petrol. A third option is a taxi, which isn't a bad option if you're travelling in a small group.

LAKE DISTRICT

Like an oasis amongst endlessly rolling hills, the region's lake district makes the perfect resting spot between long hauls across the forgotten recesses of inner Anatolia.

Overlooked by Davraz Dağı (Mt Davraz; 2635m), the town of Eğirdir has an enviable lakeside position and is increasingly important as a trekking and climbing base for travellers following the waymarked St Paul Trail (see p294). Classics enthusiasts should not miss the soaring ruins at Sagalassos, which promises to be the 'next Ephesus' when a few more years of excavations are complete.

The best time to visit this lush and verdant region is spring. In April the apple trees blossom, and from mid-May to mid-June the annual rose harvest takes place. Around a month later, the lakes become the favourite summer escape for Turkish families drawn to this relaxing 'coastline' many kilometres inland from the Aegean, Mediterranean or Black Seas.

Isparta

♪0246 / POP 190,100

Famous for its attar of roses, Isparta is an important junction west to Eğirdir. Turkey's ninth president (1993–2000), Süleyman Demirel, was a local boy, and there's a quirky statue of him in the town centre.

Like Denizli is to Pamukkale, Isparta largely functions as a transport junction for tourists, however there are a few sights of note including Ulu Cami (1417), the Firdevs Bey Camii (1561) with its neighbouring bedesten (covered market) and the huge Halı Saray (Carpet Palace; Mimar Sinan Caddesi).

ⓘ Getting There & Away

The most frequent services to Eğirdir leave from the Çarşı terminal (also called the köy garaj) in

the town centre, as do dolmuşes for Ağlasun (for Sagalassos). Coming north from Antalya you may find yourself dropped on the outskirts of Isparta and ferried to the otogar in a servis (minivan).

To get to Eğirdir (30 minutes) from the otogar, take any Konya-bound bus. Direct minibuses from the Çarşı terminal run every 30 minutes.

There are regular services from Isparta otogar to Afyon (three hours), Antalya (two hours), Burdur (45 minutes), Denizli (three hours), İzmir (six hours) and Konya (five hours).

To get to the Çarşı terminal catch a Çarşı city bus from in front of the otogar. Note that the hourly minibus service to Burdur leaves from the otogar, not from the Çarşı terminal.

Sagalassos

Dramatically sited on the terraced slopes of Ak Dağ (White Mountain), Sagalassos (admission TL5; ⊙7.30am-6pm) is a ruined ancient city backed by sheer rock. Since 1990 Belgian and British archaeologists have been excavating the city, one of the largest archaeological projects in the Mediterranean region. It's envisaged that Sagalassos may one day rival Ephesus or Pergamum in splendour. The researchers are reconstructing the civic buildings with original pieces; a process made possible because the city was never pillaged. Surrounded on three sides by mountains, the spectacular backdrop and valley views are unforgettable.

Sagalassos dates back to at least 1200 BC, when it was founded by a warlike tribe of 'Peoples from the Sea'. Later it became an important Pisidian city, second only to Antiocheia-in-Pisidia, near Yalvaç. The Pisidians built their cities high on easily defended mountains. Sagalassos's oldest ruins date from Hellenistic times, although most surviving structures are Roman. The Roman period was the city's most prosperous, but plague and earthquakes blighted its later history, and Sagalassos was largely abandoned after a massive 7th-century tremor.

As you enter the ruins you're faced with a decision: start from the top and work your way downhill (advised for feet that tire easily) or start from the bottom and work your way up – the way visitors would access the site in ancient times.

The stunning colonnaded street marks the southern entrance to the city from the valleys below. There are no traces of wheel indentations in the marble, which suggests that the access was solely pedestrian. The street functions as the spine and central axis of Sagalassos, stretching all the way up through the city. From the bottom, it appears as though the city's terraced fountains are actually one triple-tiered tower of water – a truly impressive optical illusion. After passing through the **Tiberian gate** you enter the **lower agora**, with the massive reconstructed complex of **Roman baths** to the right. At the back of the agora is the **Hadrianic nymphaeum** flanking the mountainside. The fountain is extremely well preserved – you can still make out the elaborate sculptures of mythic Nereids and Muses. A ruined **Odeon** sits just beyond.

The upper portion of the main civic area (and political core of the city) is anchored by the **Antonine nymphaeum**, which was located on the north side of the upper agora. The nymphaeum was a huge fountain complex that was ornately decorated with Medusa heads and fish motifs. The western edge of the agora was flanked by the **bouleuterion** – some of its seating remains intact. Rising up over the fountain in the northwest corner is a 14m-high **heroon** (hero's monument). It is believed that a statue of Alexander the Great once stood here – he captured the city in 333 BC. Now, look down over the southern edge of the agora to spot the **macellon** (food market), with its trademark Corinthian columns. Note the **tholos** in the middle – the deep fountain was used to sell live fish. The macellon was dedicated to emperor Marcus Aurelius.

Higher up in the hills you will find the late-Hellenistic **Doric fountainhouse** and the Roman **Neon library** with a fine mosaic floor. Both have been rebuilt, and the fountainhouse's piping has been reattached to the original source used over 2000 years ago. It's an exceptional structure, providing serene sanctuary from the unforgiving surroundings outside. Make sure to run your hands through the surprisingly cool water. The pavilion housing the Neon library is usually locked – ask for the key at the ticket booth.

Finally, at the very top of the hill is Sagalassos's biggest structure; a 9000-seat **Roman theatre**. Earthquakes have tumbled the rows of seats but otherwise it remains one of the most complete in all of Turkey. Scramble around the rear of the complex to see the tunnels where performers and contestants entered the arena.

A visit to Sagalassos should be teamed with a trip to Burdur's excellent museum.

ℹ Information

The best time to visit Sagalassos is between Monday and Thursday during the summer months, when archaeologists are busy digging and restoring ruins. They all speak English and offer informal tours of the site. Out of season you're likely to share the site with only a few hardy birds and even hardier lizards. The area is treeless and exposed, so aim for an early start to avoid the midday sun. The ticket office sells drinks. Walking the entire site via the 'scenic' route takes up to 3½ hours, or you can see the most significant structures near the ticket office in about two. Signage is excellent with detailed and colourful representations of how various structures looked in Sagalassos' halcyon days.

If you're coming with a guide you may be able to borrow a laminated map of the site – sometimes they have copies for tourists that are usually sold for a few liras.

ℹ Getting There & Away

Take a dolmuş south from Isparta's Çarşı terminal to Ağlasun (one hour, hourly from 6am to 5pm). The last dolmuş from Ağlasun to Isparta leaves at 8pm in summer.

From Ağlasun a signposted turn-off points 7km up the mountain. If you're fit, you could walk up, but it's probably easier to pay the dolmuş driver an extra TL20 to drive you there, wait for an hour and bring you back down again. To get the driver to wait longer you will probably have to agree on a higher fee.

The most straightforward alternative is to join an organised trip or arrange a shared taxi from Eğirdir for around TL30 to TL50.

WORTH A TRIP

BURDUR MUSEUM

After touring the ruins of Sagalassos, stop by the the **Burdur Museum** (Burdur Müzesi; admission TL5; ⊙9am-6pm Tue-Sun) in the town of Burdur. Hellenistic and Roman statues make up the majority of the collection, but there are also Neolithic finds from the nearby Hacılar and Kuruçay mounds; a 2nd-century bronze torso of an athlete; and several exquisitely carved 'man and wife' sarcophagi.

Hourly minibuses run to Burdur from the Isparta otogar (TL5, 45 minutes).

Eğirdir

♪ 0246 / POP 20,400

The Turkish military has a funny habit of establishing outposts and bases in some of the most beautiful places in the country, so it comes as no surprise that there's an enormous military installation just up the hill from this stunningly positioned town. Eğirdir sits along the quiet waters of Eğirdir Gölü (Lake Eğirdir), offering visitors a relaxing time warp amid hearty fishermen and roving donkeys. And just when you thought things couldn't get more charming, wander out to quiet Yesilada, a tiny island in the lake strapped to the shores by a thinly paved road.

Since Lydian times it's been a popular stopover spot, and the tradition continues today – the town sits along the roads connecting Central Anatolia (Konya and Cappadocia) to the Mediterranean (Antalya) and Aegean (Ephesus).

History

Founded by the Hittites, Eğirdir was taken by the Phrygians (c 1200 BC) and then the Lydians, captured by the Persians and conquered by Alexander the Great. Alexander was followed by the Romans, who called the town Prostanna. Contemporary documents suggest that it was large and prosperous, but no excavations have been done at the site, which lies within a large military enclave.

In Byzantine times, as Akrotiri (Steep Mountain), it was the seat of a bishopric. Later, it became a Seljuk city (c 1080–1280) and then the capital of a small principality ruled by the Hamidoğulları tribe. The Ottomans took control in 1417, but the population of Yeşilada remained mostly Greek Orthodox until the 1920s.

Under the Turks, Akrotiri became Eğridir, meaning 'crooked' or 'bent'. In the 1980s, this was changed to Eğirdir, which means 'she is spinning' – the new name was intended to remove the negative connotations of the old one (and stop the constant jokes), but is also supposedly a reference to an old folk tale about a queen who sat at home spinning, unaware that her son had just died.

⊙ Sights & Activities

Eğirdir's sights include the Hızır Bey Camii, built as a Seljuk warehouse in 1237, but turned into a mosque in 1308 by the Hamidoğulları emir Hızır Bey. The mosque

is quite simple, with a clerestory (row of windows) above the central hall and new tiles around the *mihrab*. Note the finely carved wooden doors and the blue tile trim on the minaret.

Opposite the mosque, the Dündar Bey Medresesi was built as a caravanserai by the Seljuk sultan Alaeddin Keykubat in 1218 but converted into a *medrese* in 1285 for the Hamidoğulları emir Felekeddin Dündar Bey. Now it's a bazaar filled with shops selling tacky stuff you didn't know you needed.

A few hundred metres towards Yeşilada stand the massive walls of the ruined castle. Its foundations were probably laid during the reign of Croesus, the 5th-century BC king of Lydia, but subsequent conquerors continually made additions to the now imposing structure.

Beaches

Although Yeşilada lacks an actual beach, there are several relaxing swimming spots around the lake with changing cabins and food stalls. Try the sandy Belediye Beach at Yazla, less than 1km from the centre on the Isparta road.

Pebbly Altınkum Beach is several kilometres beyond Belediye Beach. In summer, dolmuşes run here every 15 minutes (TL1) from in front of the otogar. A taxi is around TL10.

Further north, 11km down the road to Barla, Bedre Beach has 1.5km of pristine sand. Cycle here or catch a taxi (around TL12 each way).

☞ Tours

Tours can be organised by any of the pensions in town. The most popular option is a boat trip, which costs TL40 per person for the day. Trips only run during July and August. You'll be offered boat rental by cat-calling locals as you wander around the town on foot, especially along the shores of Yeşilada.

The local mountain club, Etudosd (♪311 6356), has its office on the road to Yeşilada and can advise on treks to Mt Davraz, the Barla massif and other good spots.

Other tours include trips to Sagalassos, Lake Kovada National Park or Yazılı Canyon Nature Park. Expect to pay around TL30 to TL40 per person, although this can be higher for smaller groups or couples. Pensions can also organise taxi shares to reduce the cost of transportation – these are

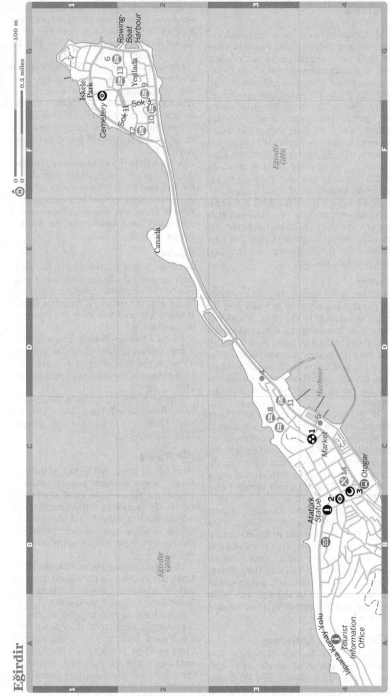

0 500 m
0 0.2 miles

Rowing-
Boat
Harbour

Yeşilada

İskele
Park

Cemetery

Sok 11

Sok 3

Eğirdir
Gölü

Canada

Harbour

Market

Atatürk
Statue

Otogar

Eğirdir
Gölü

Isparta Konağı Yolu

Tourist
Information
Office

Eğirdir

especially popular among travellers wanting to visit Sagalassos.

Eğirdir Outdoor Centre (☑311 6688; Ata Yolu Üzeri) can suggest itineraries and organise custom tours; it also hires out mountain bikes at TL5/20 per hour/full day. The office doubles as a cute place for a cup of tea.

🛏 Sleeping

Accommodation in Eğirdir is of the pension variety, with small family-run spots scattered around the castle ruins and out on Yeşilada – the tiny island tethered to the mainland by a narrow road. Unlike the rest of the region, most of the sleeping spots here do not have air-conditioning, as evenings are surprisingly cool and breezy, even in summer.

[TOP CHOICE] **Ali's Pension** PENSION €
(☑311 2547; www.alispension.com; Yeşilada; s/d TL40/60; @) It's not about the rooms here (but yes, they're simple and squeaky clean) – Ali's has made a name for itself amongst travellers for its genuine hospitality and awesome home-spun meals. Join the dear owners for a scrumptious morning repast loaded up with freshly baked pastries and delicious fruit. In the evenings, everyone gathers around once again to feast on tummy-pleasing lake fish – it's so good we guarantee you'll be back for seconds. Ali's is open year-round to cater

to ski and snowboard types heading for Mt Davraz.

Lale Pension PENSION €
(☑311 2406; www.lalehostel.com; Kale Mahallesi 5 Sokak 2; s/d without breakfast TL40/60; ✻ @) Up behind the castle, the Lale Pension has neat air-con rooms with private bathrooms and a quiet, family atmosphere. There are great lake views from a rooftop lounge that's also crammed with information on tours and treks. A second building, dubbed Lale Hostel, has additional comfy quarters. The entrepreneurial owners offer a wide variety of tours – they run the Eğirdir Outdoor Centre too.

Charly's Pension PENSION €
(☑311 4611; www.charlyspension.com; Kale Mahallesi; dm/s/d/tr TL18/35/55/65) Another building owned by the folks at Lale Pension, this heritage lakeside house (1890) has crazily sloping wooden floors and inviting chill-out areas looking onto a private beach. There's a funky backpacker vibe here; don't be surprised if you stay longer than originally planned. Breakfast is TL6.

Göl Pension PENSION €
(☑311 2370; ahmetdavras@hotmail.com; Yeşilada; r TL70-100; @) Run by the Davras siblings, little Göl has spacious and well-maintained rooms. Go for one of the rooms on the top floor – they have great lake views off a private terrace.

Mavigöl Hotel HOTEL €€
(☑311 6417; www.mavigolhotel.com; Yeşilada; s/d TL50/90; @ ✻) The Mavigöl is Eğirdir's only real attempt at hotel-style digs. The rooms are clean and well maintained, luring midrange types.

Şehsuvar Peace Pension PENSION €
(☑311 2433; www.peacepension.com; Yeşilada; s/d TL40/60) Spacious rooms and a quiet, shaded terrace trimmed with grapevines feature in this low-key family-run pension that's a few hundred metres inland near the island's sleepy *meydan* (main square). Rowboats and bicycles are available for rent, and the restaurant does a fine line in fish and lobster.

Choo Choo Pension PENSION €
(☑319 4926; huseyinp01@hotmail.com; Yeşilada; s/d TL40/60) The mock-castle exterior is a bit odd, but inside the spacious rooms are well kept and clean, and there's the convenient bonus of the Halikarnas lakefront restaurant a few metres away.

ROSE TOURS

Every May and June the fields around Isparta come into flower. Rose petals plucked carefully at daybreak are made into attar of roses, a valuable oil used in making perfume. The petals are placed in copper vats with steam passed over them. This steam is drawn off and condensed, leaving a thin layer of oil on the surface of the water to be skimmed off and bottled. A hundred kilos of petals produces just 25g of attar of roses, leaving a vast amount of rosewater to be sold locally.

To see the process in action, the pensions in Eğirdir can organise factory tours for TL40 per person, or you may be able to arrange something direct with a manufacturer. **Gülbirlik** (☎218 1288; www.gulbirlik.com) is the world's biggest source of rose oil, with four processing plants handling 320 tonnes of petals every day. Tours usually take place from mid-May to mid-June each year at the height of the rose season.

Çetin Pansiyon   PENSION €

(☎311 2154; Kale Mahallesi; s/d/tr TL40/60/70) On the quieter side of the castle, this family run spot has six bright rooms arranged up a teeny (and rather scary) staircase. Four of the rooms have excellent views across the lake to Mt Barla. Breakfast is an additional TL10 though you might be able to score it for free with a little bargaining.

✖ Eating

The best dining options are, without a doubt, the in-house restaurants at each of the pensions. In the evenings, visitors gather together at their accommodation to savour *istakoz* (crayfish) and the local lake fish. There are, of course, several restaurants peppered around town - you really can't go wrong with any of 'em. The Eğirdir Outdoor Centre is a good place for a spot of tea along the water. Try **Kemer Lokantasi** (Sahil Yolu 20; mains TL6-9; ☺lunch & dinner) near the mosques for tasty fare that's good value. A swarm of kebap stalls lurk nearby.

Eğirdir Market   MARKET

Eğirdir's normal weekly market takes place every Thursday under the shadow of the crumbling castle, but for the 10 Sundays between August and October the Yörük people from the mountain villages come to Eğirdir to sell their apples, goats and yoghurt, and to buy winter supplies. It's an opportunity for people from different villages to meet, and was traditionally the focus for inter-village dating.

ℹ Information

At the time of research the **tourist information office** (2 Sahilyolu 13) was closed, though it may open again in the future. It's located on the main road coming into town. A small kiosk at the otogar often informally hands out maps.

There is a huddle of ATMs near the Hotel Eğirdir.

ℹ Getting There & Around

Eğirdir has frequent connections to most major cities – İstanbul, Bursa, Antalya, Konya, Capaddocia and İzmir. If there's no bus leaving straightaway for your destination, hop on a minibus to Isparta (TL5, 30 minutes) and catch one from there.

Most of the town's best pensions are on Yeşilada or around the castle ruins. A taxi from the otogar to Yeşilada is around TL10 and a dolmuş makes the 1.5km journey (TL1) around 10 times daily.

Around Eğirdir

The following destinations are located within an 80km radius of sleepy Eğirdir – the perfect daytrip fodder after some lakeside R&R. Most spots feature prominently on the waymarked St Paul Trail (p294) and are organised in a south-to-north fashion; the way in which hikers from Perge would uncover them. If you're based in Eğirdir, your best bet is to ask your pension about tour options. Trips often run to Kovada Gölü, Çandır Kanyon and Zindan Cave (TL35 to TL40). A private taxi will set you back between TL50 and TL80 depending on the destination. During the warmer months it is possible to reach Sütçüler and Yalvaç by dolmuş (TL10 to TL12).

SÜTÇÜLER

Sütçüler is a fairly unremarkable town spread out along a winding mountain road. The views effortlessly whet the appetite for a good trek, however, and the location is convenient for hikers. Worth a look is the dramatic Roman road of Adada; remains of an agora and a temple of Trajan can be spotted as well.

Spend the night at Otel Karacan (📞351 2411; www.karacanotel.com; Atatürk Caddesi 53; half-board TL40-50; @), which has 25 spacious rooms, some without bathroom. A garden terrace and indoor restaurant look out to the green vistas below; a well-worn guitar and a row of nargilehs hint at fun nights after a long day's walking. Advance booking is recommended during prime walking months (July & August).

ZINDAN MAĞARASI (ZINDAN CAVE)
Roughly 30km southeast of Eğirdir, the kilometre-long Zından Cave has Byzantine ruins at its mouth, lots of stalactites and stalagmites, and a curious room dubbed the Hamam. You'll find the cave entrance about 1km north of Aksu marked by a fine Roman bridge. There's a pleasant walk along the river if caves aren't really your thing.

YAZILI CANYON NATURE PARK & ÇANDIR KANYON
About 73km south of Eğirdir, the Yazılı Canyon Nature Park (Yazılı Kanyon Tabiat Parkı; admission TL1, car TL2) protects a forested gorge deep in the mountains separating the Lake District (ancient Pisidia) and the Antalya region (Pamphylia). After paying the admission fee at the car park, follow a path 1km upstream through the glorious Çandır Kanyon to some shady bathing spots; the water is icy cold even in the warmer months. In July and August the canyon heaves with sunbathing Turkish families, but at other times you could be all alone.

KOVADA GÖLÜ NATIONAL PARK
Noted for its flora and fauna, Lake Kovada National Park (Kovada Gölü Milli Parkı) surrounds a small lake connected to Lake Eğirdir by a channel. It's a pleasant place for a hike and a picnic. Close by is the Kasnak Forest, visited by botanical enthusiasts for its butterflies and rare mountain flowers.

DAVRAZ DAĞI (MT DAVRAZ)
The skiing season on Mt Davraz (2635m) runs from mid-December to March. Both Nordic and downhill skiing are possible and there's one 1.2km-long chairlift. A day's skiing, with equipment hire and lift pass, costs around €40; summit treks and paragliding are also possible.

Accommodation is available at the main ski centre and the five-star Sirene Davraz Mountain Resort (www.sirene.com.tr/sirenedavras.asp), but it's really as easy (and cheaper) to stay in Isparta or Eğirdir.

ANTIOCHEIA-IN-PISIDIA
About 2km from Yalvaç lies the site of Antiocheia-in-Pisidia (admission TL3; ☺9am-6pm), an ancient city that was abandoned in the 8th century after Arab attacks.

From the gate, a Roman road leads uphill past the foundations of a triumphal archway, then turns right to the theatre. Further uphill, on a flat area surrounded by a semicircular wall of rock, is the city's main shrine. This was originally dedicated to the Anatolian mother goddess Cybele, then later to the moon god Men, but in Roman times it featured an imperial cult temple dedicated to Augustus. A path heads left to the nymphaeum, once a permanent spring but now dry.

WESTERN ANATOLIA AROUND EĞIRDIR

WORTH A TRIP

AKPINAR

High up on the steep slopes of Sivri Dağı ('Sharp Mountain'; 1749m) is the tiny village of Akpınar amid picturesque apple orchards. For a delicious snack and spectacular views of the lake and its precariously tethered islet, follow the main road up to the cliff's edge where you'll find a ramshackle collection of mismatched chairs, picnic tables and a large felt-folded tent. Savour freshly made *gözleme* (TL4) filled with an assortment of savoury and sweet ingredients and wash it down with homemade *ayran* (yoghurt drink).

It's about a 5km walk from Yeşilada – a taxi will set you back about TL15 to TL20 each way. Serious hikers can continue up into the hill, though make sure you stay away from the commando base, as chances are the boys in green won't appreciate your presence.

ST PAUL TRAIL

Follow in the footsteps of St Paul the apostle along this waymarked trail that winds through much of western Anatolia. The route starts in Perge, near Antalya, and carves a path north all the way to the small town of Yalvaç, near Eğirdir. You'll start at sea level and climb to 2200m, passing crumbling ancient ruins and photogenic vistas along the way. The trail's website (www.stpaultrail.com) offers basic information about the trek – we highly recommend purchasing the trail book, cleverly titled *St Paul Trail*, authored by Kate Clow (who also marked the more famous Lycian Way).

Several arches of the city's **aqueduct** are visible across the fields. Downhill from the nymphaeum are the ruins of the **Roman baths**. Several large chambers have been excavated and much of the original ceiling is intact. On the way back to the entrance you pass the foundations of **St Paul's Basilica**. The apostle's preaching provoked such a strong reaction that he and St Barnabas were expelled from the city.

After exploring the site drop into the **Yalvaç Museum** (Yalvaç Müzesi; admission TL3; ☉8.30am-5.30pm Tue-Sun), housed in a wonderfully restored heritage building. A plan of the ruins and a modest collection of unearthed artefacts will complete your visit.

Antalya & the Western Mediterranean

Why Go?

Turkey's Western Mediterranean coast is a region of endless azure sea lined with kilometres of sandy beaches and backed by mountains rising up to almost 3000m. It's a winning combination no matter how you look at it, but add to that an embarrassment of ancient ruins strewn through the aromatic scrub and pine forests and a sophisticated menu of sports and activities on offer and you've struck gold.

Indeed, the so-called Turquoise Coast's seamless mix of history and holiday inspires and excites from every direction. But by far the most dramatic way to see this stretch of coastline is by skimming through the crystal waters aboard a *gület* (traditional wooden yacht) or by following sections of the 500km-long Lycian Way on foot high above what the Turks call the Akdeniz (literally, 'White Sea').

Best Places to Stay

» Mehmet Ali Ağa Konağı (p305)
» Hoyran Wedre Country House (p344)
» Hotel Villa Mahal (p331)
» Turan Hill Lounge (p326)
» Happy Caretta (p312)

Best Places to Eat

» İkbal (p340)
» Korsan Fish Terrace (p333)
» Meğri Lokantasi (p319)
» Levissi Garden (p324)
» Çiftlik (p335)

When to Go

Antalya

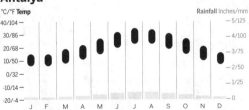

| **March & April** The hills are alive with technicolour spring bulb flowers (which actually originated in Turkey). | **July & August** It's peak season and everywhere is packed – as well as open and full of fun. | **December & January** Cool(er) but mostly bright and sunny days are perfect for walking in the hills. |

Antalya & the Western Mediterranean Highlights

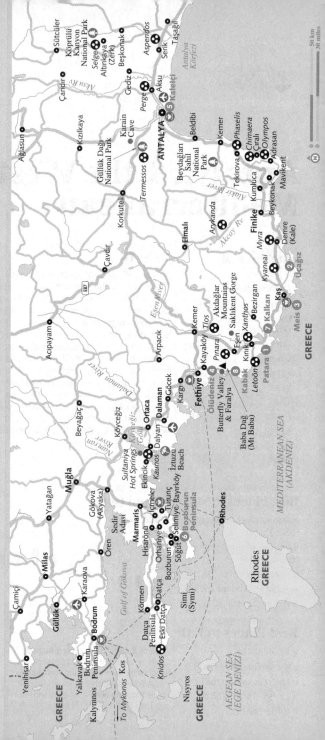

① Potter around the ruins of **Patara** (p329) before plunging into the sea on its 20km-long beach

② Kayak over the stunning sunken city of **Üçağız** (p342)

③ Experience 'instant Greece' on a 20-minute boat ride from Kaş to **Meis** (p295)

④ Sample a section of the

Lycian Way from the cliffs above **Ölüdeniz** (p322)

⑤ View the Ottoman splendour of **Kaleiçi** (p350) – the old quarter of Antalya –

and wander through a world-class museum

⑥ Explore the high roads and hidden coves of the **Bozburun Peninsula** (p303) by car or scooter

⑦ Dine in **Kalkan** (p333), an epi(curean)-centre of Mediterranean cooking

⑧ Chill and centre yourself while lux-camping at **Kabak** (p325)

Muğla

0252 / POP 56.600

Muğla (*moo*-lah) is a rarity for a Turkish provincial capital – compact and relaxed, with plane tree–lined boulevards and narrow streets that lead to a historic quarter. The whitewashed Ottoman houses are particularly well preserved and there's an array of chilled *çay bahçesi* (tea gardens) filled with friendly students from the nearby university. Muğla makes for a pleasant (and easy) re-introduction to Turkish urban life after a spell on the beach.

Sights & Activities

Old Town
HISTORIC AREA

From Cumhuriyet Meydanı, the traffic roundabout with the statue of Atatürk, walk north along Kurşunlu Caddesi to the **Kurşunlu Cami**, the blindingly white 'Lead-Covered Mosque' which was built in 1493 and had a minaret and courtyard added in 1900.

Continue walking north into the **bazaar**, its narrow lanes jammed with artisans' shops and restaurants. Proceed up the hill to see Muğla's 18th- and 19th-century **Ottoman houses** and the **Ulu Cami** (1344), which dates from the time of the Menteşe emirs though repairs made in the 19th century have rendered its pre-Ottoman design almost unrecognisable. Nearby is the Greek-built **clock tower** *(saatli kule)* dating from 1905 which sounds a church bell on the hour.

Muğla Museum
MUSEUM

(214 6948; Postane Sokak; admission TL3; 8am-noon & 1-5pm Tue-Sun) To the east, the Muğla Museum contains a small collection of Greek and Roman antiquities displayed in rooms around an open courtyard. Don't miss the new **Gladiator Room**, with mockups, weapons and stone carvings There's also a section containing traditional arts and crafts of the region. The museum faces the stunning **Konakaltı Kültür Merkezi** (Mustafa Muğlalı Caddesi 51), a traditional complex housing a cultural centre.

Vakıflar Hamamı
HAMAM

(Foundations Hamam; 214 2067; Mustafa Muğlalı Caddesi 1; bath & scrub TL20, with massage TL40; 7am-11pm) Built in the mid-14th century; facilities for men and women.

Sleeping

TOP CHOICE Mavi Konak
BOUTIQUE HOTEL €€

(214 7007; www.mavi-konak.eu; Kusular Çıkmazı 13; s €22.50-33, d €37-53; @) The 'Blue Mansion' is a 19th-century Greek residence in the historic centre with five delightful guestrooms filled with hand-crafted wooden furniture and centred around a leafy courtyard that has a modern kitchen/laundry for guests' use. Only one room has an en suite, but the shared bathroom – an ancient hamam – can accommodate a legion. The welcoming German owners, Claudia and Dieter, are fonts of local knowledge.

Petek Hotel
BUSINESS HOTEL €€

(214 1897; www.petekhotel.com, in Turkish; Marmaris Bulvarı 27; s/d/tr TL50/90/120; P ✳) Though the three-star, 64-room Petek is a bit characterless and faces a busy and rather noisy boulevard southeast of Cumhuriyet Meydanı, it is comfortable and professionally run.

Otel Saray
HOTEL €

(214 1594; www.muglasaray.com, in Turkish; Açık Pazar Yeri Sokak 11; s/d/tr TL35/60/90; P ✳) Hardly the 'Palace' it calls itself, this 51-room caravanserai has the advantage of being hard by the open-air market.

Eating & Drinking

Market day in Muğla is Thursday.

Konak Kuzine
RESTAURANT €€

(213 1000; Kurşunlu Caddesi 13; mains TL8.50-16; 10am-10pm) If you want to dine in style on pide (TL4.50 to TL9) and grills, head for this 19th-century Greek mansion opposite the Kurşunlu Cami.

Mavi Sofra
KÖFTECI, KABAPÇI €€

(212 5250; Kurşunlu Çıkmazı 4/2; mains TL8-15; 9am-11pm) Down a small alleyway opposite the Kurşunlu Cami, this hole-in-the-wall has become a favourite locally for its delicious kebaps and *köfte* (grilled meatballs).

Muğla Lokantası
LOKANTA €

(212 3121; İsmet İnönü Caddesi 53; mains TL3-6; 6.30am-10pm) With a great pick-and-point counter containing a delicious selection of traditional dishes at rock-bottom prices, this place is permanently packed.

Muğla Belediyesi Kültür Evi
CAFE

(Muğla Council Culture House; 212 8668; İsmet İnönü Caddesi 106; 8am-7.30pm) This 200-year-old house, with garden restored by the municipality in 2003, is a tranquil place to come for breakfast (TL5) or coffee.

Sobe
CAFE-BAR

(212 6271; Mustafa Muğlalı Caddesi 43; 8am-1am) This delightful place, with large grassy

courtyard and live music at the weekend, is popular with Muğla's university students.

ℹ Information

Tourist office (☑214 1261; www.mugla-turizm. gov.tr; Marmaris Bulvarı 22/A; ☺8am-5pm Mon-Fri) About 600m southeast of Cumhuriyet Meydanı and past the Petek Hotel; free useful maps of town centre and Muğla Province.

ℹ Getting There & Away

Muğla's otogar is about 750m southwest of the main square via Marmaris Bulvarı and then left on Zübeyde Hanım Caddesi. Buses leave every half-hour (hourly in low season) to Marmaris (TL8, one hour, 53km) and Bodrum (TL15, 2½ hours, 111km). If heading east along the coast, change in Marmaris.

Akyaka (Gökova)

☑0252 / POP 2500

A refreshing change from boisterous Bodrum to the west and maddening Marmaris to the south, the laid-back village of Akyaka is tucked between pine-clad mountains and a grey sand beach at the far end of the Gulf of Gökova. Confusingly, Akyaka is sometimes also called Gökova, which is an older township set inland, several hundred kilometres away.

The road from Muğla to the north goes through the Sakar Pass (Sakar Geçidi; 670m), so popular with paragliders, to reveal breathtaking views of the gulf and the sea.

Çınar Beach, 2km out of town, is the best spot to swim. To get there, turn right at the primary school as you head towards the marina, then take the high road veering right. The local sailing cooperative runs **boat tours** along the gulf for around TL40.

With its continuous (and safe) *maltemi* winds, Akyaka is an ideal spot for windsurfing and kite-boarding. **Rüzgar Sports Center** (☑243 4217, 0505 918 3600; www.go kovaruzgar.com; Sahil Sokak 2), by the beach, has equipment for hire as well as tuition and courses. It also rents out sea kayaks, canoes, sailing boats and mountain bikes.

Every Wednesday there is a busy **market** in the centre of Akyaka; Saturday is market day in Gökova.

🛏 Sleeping

Susam Hotel   HOTEL €€
(☑243 5863; www.susamhotel.com; Lütfiye Sakıcı Caddesi 30; s TL40-100, d TL50-120; ❋ ❄) On the main road down to the beach, the

Susam has 10 immaculate and themed (whirling dervish, evil eye, theatre) rooms – most with balconies – as well as a small garden with a pretty pool.

Yücelen Hotel   RESORT €€€
(☑243 5108; www.yucelen.com.tr; s/d TL95/190; ❋ ❄ ❄) The multi-faceted Yücelen group's 125-room hotel is large and well designed. Facilities include both indoor and outdoor pools, a fitness centre and a sauna. It's just up from the beach.

Okaliptüs Apart   APARTMENT €€
(☑243 4370; www.tomsanokaliptus.com; Volkan Sokak 2i; 2-bedroom apt €40-60, 3-bedroom €70-100; ❋ ❄) A good alternative, particularly if you plan to stay a few extra nights here, is to rent a holiday apartment. There are numerous options, including the 'Eucalyptus', which is a titch away from the action but still just 300m from the water.

Gökova Park Camping   CAMPGROUND €
(☑243 4055; www.yucelen.com.tr; per person/tent/car TL3/8/11, bungalow up to 6 people TL175) Next door to the Yücelen Hotel and part of the same group, this beachside site has bungalows, mobile homes and cottages as well as pitches.

🍴 Eating

The main beach is lined with restaurants, but our two favourites are the long-established **Şıkıdam** (☑243 5738; İncir Sokak 8; mains TL5-20; ☺8am-2am) at the eastern end next to the pier, which has a word-burning stove and specialises in fish; and **Spica** (☑243 4270; Sanat Sokak 4; mains TL11-19; ☺8am-midnight), a posher affair on the western side with a large breezy seafront terrace.

Golden Roof Restaurant   INTERNATIONAL €€
(☑243 5392; Karanfil Sokak 1; meze TL5, mains TL12-20; ☺8am-1am) On the best corner in town, this family-run institution does good pizza and pasta, as well as home-cooked Turkish dishes. The affable host is a good source of local information.

Tıkın House   KEBAPÇI €
(☑243 5444; Lütfiye Sakıcı Caddesi; dishes TL3.50-8.50; ☺8.30am-11pm) A cut above the usual kebap-and-pizza palace, the Tıkın also offers meze, grills, omelettes and salads. It's just opposite the Susam Hotel.

ℹ Getting There & Away

Minibuses run to Muğla (TL3, 30 minutes, 26km) every half-hour, and to Marmaris (TL4,

30 minutes, 31km) twice a day in high season only. Otherwise, minibuses from Marmaris will drop you at the highway junction 2.5km from the beach. You can either walk or wait for a minibus.

Marmaris

📞 0252 / POP 40,000

A popular resort town that swells to over 200,000 people during summer, Marmaris is loud, brash and in your face all over town all of the time. It's the closest thing Mediterranean Turkey has to Spain's Costa del Sol and one of the few places along the coast where you might leave feeling more stressed out than when you arrived.

On the other hand, if it's a last night out, a *gület* cruise along the coast, or a ferry to Greece you're after, then this tourist haven is pretty much the full Monty. Bar St offers unparalleled decadence, while from the promenade, charter-boat touts will happily whisk you eastward to Fethiye and beyond. And the place has even got some history. The stunning natural harbour is where Lord Nelson organised his fleet for the attack on the French at Abukir in northern Egypt in 1798.

👁 Sights & Activities

If you're in search of how Marmaris once looked before the drunken uncle arrived and stayed, stroll through the area behind İskele Meydanı where you'll find some of Marmaris' few remaining old buildings. Inland from İskele Meydanı is the *çarşı* (bazaar) district, much of it covered.

Marmaris Castle & Museum

FORTRESS, MUSEUM

(Marmaris Kalesi ve Müzesi; 📞 412 1459; admission TL3; ⏰ 8am-noon & 1-5pm Tue-Sun) The small castle on the hill south of the tourist office was built during the reign of Süleyman the Magnificent. In 1522 the sultan amassed 200,000 troops here for the attack and siege of Rhodes, which was defended by the Knights of St John. The fortress now contains the **Marmaris Museum**. Exhibits focus on the archaeology of the region, with remains from Knidos and Hisarönü, including amphorae, glassware and coins. Walk along the ancient walls for superb views over the marina.

Beaches

BEACH

Marmaris' beaches may be narrow and pebbly but you can actually swim in the city centre. Much nicer beaches, however, at **İçmeler** and **Turunç**, some 10km and

20km respectively to the southwest, can be reached by dolmuşes from outside the Tansaş Shopping Centre for TL2.50 and TL6. From May to October, water taxis also link the waterfront on either side of the Atatürk statue with İçmeler (TL7.50, 30 minutes, every 30 minutes) and Turunç (TL10, 45 minutes, every hour). The beach at **Günlücek Park**, a forest park reserve 3.5km southeast of Marmaris, is also accessible by dolmuş from outside Tansaş Shopping Centre.

Hamam

HAMAM

Supposedly the second-biggest in Turkey, the enormous **Armutalan Hamamı** (Pear Field Hamam; 📞 417 5374; 136 Sokak 1; bath & scrub TL20, with massage TL40; ⏰ 9am-10pm Apr-Oct) lies behind the government hospital just off Datça Caddesi, about 2km west from the town centre. Go after 6pm when the hamam is empty of tour groups. There's a frequent free shuttle service (Armutalan No 4) to and from the Tansaş Shopping Centre.

Boat Trips

CRUISE

An array of companies offer excellent day tours of Marmaris Bay, its islands and beaches. Expect to pay TL25 to TL30 in one of these 'dolmuş boats'.

If you want to get off the beaten current, consider hiring a boat with a group that will take you to quieter, less-known coves. It costs around €300 for up to seven people per boat, but you'll have to negotiate. One of the more reliable is **Zeus Boat** (📞 0532 247 4974; http://zeus-boat.netfirms.com), captained by Sadık Turgut.

Yachts sail roughly from May to October, departing between 9.30am and 10am and returning around 6pm to 6.30pm. Before signing up, check where the excursion goes, which boat you'll be on and what's on the lunch menu.

Overnight trips (around €350 for four people, including all meals and soft drinks) as well as two-day (€700) and three-day trips (€1050) often go to Dalyan and Kaunos. You can also charter longer, more serious boat trips to Datça and Knidos, west of Marmaris, or along the Bozburun Peninsula. There's also the ever-popular blue voyages (p319) to Fethiye and further adrift.

Diving

DIVING

Several centres at the water's edge along Yeni Kordon Caddesi offer scuba diving excursions and courses between April and

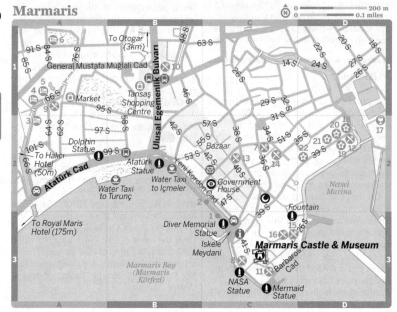

October. **Deep Blue Dive Center** (☎0541 374 5881, 0506 614 6408; www.sealung.com) charges €240 for a PADI open-water course over three days. Day excursions cost €29 including two dives, all equipment and lunch. **Professional Diving Centre** (☎0533-456 5888; www.prodivingcentre.com, in Turkish) charges €25 to €30 for the same deal.

🛏 Sleeping

Marmaris lives, eats and...well...sleeps for all-in package tour groups so good-value independent sleeping options are rather thin on the ground.

Royal Maris Hotel   HOTEL €€€
(☎412 8383; www.royalmarishotel.com; Atatürk Caddesi 34; s/d/tr TL110/170/200; P ❂ ❊) Two pools, a private beach, a hamam and fitness centre, spacious balconies with stunning views (try room 403!) and still remarkably affordable prices make this 67-room hotel a top choice in Marmaris. The roof terrace, shaped like a ship's deck with pool, is an oh-so-Marmaris feature.

Maltepe Pansiyon   PENSION €
(☎412 1629, 0532 346 4244; www.maltepepan-siyon.com; 66 Sokak 9; s/d TL30/60; ❊ @) The shady garden is just one of the attractions of this 22-room pension, a backpacker's fav-

ourite for a quarter-century. Rooms (15 of which have en suites) are small but spotless, there's free use of the kitchen, and the friendly manager Mehemt (Memo) goes out of his way to help. The house cat Nuriye is the fattest in Marmaris.

Özcan Pansiyon   PENSION €
(☎412 7761; ozcanpansitonmarmaris@hotmail. com; 66 Sokak 17; s/d TL35/60; ❊) What looks like an old apartment block from the outside is actually a good-value pension. A few of the 15 rooms have balconies (but not all have bathrooms) and there's a pleasant garden terrace.

Halıcı Hotel   HOTEL €€
(☎495 8201; www.halicihotel.com; Sokak 1; s/d TL70/140; P ❊ @ ❂ ❊) The 'Carpet Seller Hotel's' bread and butter is package tours so expect to find every possible facility – from pools and bars to a landscaped tropical garden – at this enormous, 174-room hotel. To find it, follow the canal up from the sea.

Barış Motel & Pansiyon   PENSION €
(☎413 0652; barismotel@hotmail.com; 66 Sokak 16; s/d TL40/60; ❊) This sleepy place with a dozen rooms is opposite the canal from the Maltepe and Özcan. Rooms are very basic and frayed though clean. Breakfast costs TL6 extra.

Marmaris

Uğur Pansiyon   PENSION €
(☑413 2120, 0507 286 2299; 91 Sokak 29; s/d/
tr 30/50/70; ⊛) If you can ignore the frayed
fitted carpet and student group romps, this
18-room pension a bit north of the action
could be an alternative in a pinch.

✕ Eating

Ney   RESTAURANT €€
(☑412 0217; 26 Sokak 24; meze TL5-6, mains
TL15-20) Tucked away up some steps from
the western end of the marina is this tiny
but delightful restaurant in a 250-year-old
Greek house. Decorated with seashells and
wind chimes, it offers delicious home cooking such as *tavuklu mantı böreği* (Turkish
ravioli with chicken; TL14).

Liman Restaurant   SEAFOOD €€
(☑412 6336; 40 Sokak 38; mains TL10-20;
⊙8am-1am) Something of an institution and
well known for its meze (TL6 to TL12) and

kavurma (a kind of lamb stir fry), this lively restaurant is in the heart of the covered
bazaar. The fish soup (TL9) is equally celebrated, as is the *balık buğlama* (fish stew;
TL40 for 500g).

Panorama Restaurant & Bar
                                         INTERNATIONAL €€
(☑413 4835; Hacı İmam Sokağı 40; mains TL10-
15; ⊙9am-1am) Just off 26 Sokak, this permanent fixture with its celebrated terrace
overlooking the marina has begun serving
food – simple things like pizza, pasta and
omelette prepared by affable owner Ali's
mother. So now you can enjoy the best views
in Marmaris while both wining and dining.

İdil Mantı Evi   LOCAL €€
(☑0534 296 4410; 39 Sokak 140; meze TL5-6,
mains TL8-20; ⊙4pm-5am) Conveniently located in Bar St, this is a great place to satisfy those wee-hour munchies. With simple
wooden tables and red leatherette seats
positioned around a traditional oven, it's
a delightful and atmospheric place. Veggie
dishes (TL8 to TL14) are available. The *gözleme* (filled filo pastry; TL6 to TL10) makes
a great snack.

Aquarium Restaurant   INTERNATIONAL €€€
(☑413 1522; Barboras Caddesi; mains TL15-30;
⊙9am-midnight) Run by a friendly Turkish-
Kiwi couple, this port-side restaurant
serves large grills and steaks to a jovial
crowd of Turks and visitors alike. It's expensive but you're paying for the location.

Meryemana   LOCAL €
(☑412 7855; 35 Sokak 5/B; mains TL5-6; ☏)
This simple place serves superb traditional
dishes. It has an excellent reputation locally
and is a good choice for vegetarians too (a
large mixed plate costs TL10 to TL15). Try
the *mantı* (Turkish ravioli; TL6).

Fellini   ITALIAN €€
(☑413 0826; Barboras Caddesi 71; mains TL15-25;
⊙9am-2am) Perennially popular with both
locals and visitors in the know, this film-
themed waterfront restaurant serves up
great thin-crust pizzas (TL18 to TL22) and
pasta (TL15 to TL24).

Alin's Cafe & Restaurant
                                      FAMILY RESTAURANT €€
(☑413 2525; www.alins.com.tr, in Turkish; 36
Sokak 23; mains TL5.90-14.90; ⊙8am-12.30am;
☏) It might be part of another stylish Turkish chain, but Alin's is always packed with
Turkish families feasting on healthy grills,
burgers and filled baked potatoes.

302

Doyum
KEBAPÇI **€€**

(☑413 4977; Ulusal Egemenlik Bulvarı 14; mains TL4-12; ☺24 hr) After a day and a night of round-the-clocktails on Bar St, this is a good place for an early breakfast (TL6), and there's an array of tasty veggie dishes (TL4 to TL5) too.

Cafe by Özel
KÖFTECI, KABAPÇI **€**

(☑413 32 84, 0536 810 6082; 62 Sokak 5; dishes TL3-8; ☺8am-2am) Chowdown Central caters to anyone and everyone ('Holland's kroket', anyone?).

Drinking & Entertainment

Marmaris is party town, capital P and T. If you're just looking for a quiet drink with a view, head for our favourite **Panorama Restaurant & Bar** (☑413 4835; Hacı İmam Sokağı 40; ☺9am-1am) or the **Keyif Bar** (☑412 1061; Netsel Marina Çarşısı; ☺8.30am-4am), a glassed-in lounge bar perched above the marina and over the footbridge.

Otherwise, the draw is aptly named Bar Street (actually 39 Sokak), which has a string of boozers and clubs that are wildly popular in summer. Unless stated otherwise, the following bars open from 7pm to 4am daily. Beers cost TL10, spirits TL15 and there are regular foam parties, as well as dance and laser shows.

Keeping up with the hottest clubs is hard work, but **Joy** (☑412 6572; 39 Sokak 99) rates tops for sheer loose behaviour. Next door the split personality **B52** (☑413 52 92; 39 Sokak 120) comes in two parts: a boisterous club on one side and a chilled cocktail bar with outside seating on the other. Another two venues worth a nudge on this end of the strip are the ever-popular **Back Street** (☑412 4048; 39 Sokak 123) and **Arena** (☑412 2906; 39 Sokak 125), with two bars on opposite sides of a large dance floor. If you still need a proper rinse out, try **Crazy Daisy** (☑412 4856; 39 Sokak 119) with its raised terraces.

❶ Information

Akasya Internet (☑413 6906; 2nd fl, Ulusal Egemenlik Bulvarı 6; per hr TL2; ☺9am-midnight) 40 computers above the main north–south thoroughfare.

Mavi Internet (☑413 4979; 26 Sokak 8; per hr TL2; ☺9am-11pm) In the old town near the Ney restaurant with 18 computers.

Tourist office (☑412 1035; İskele Meydanı 2; ☺8am-noon & 1-5pm Mon-Fri mid-Sep–May, daily Jun–mid-Sep) Right below the castle, it's arguably the least helpful tourist office in Turkey.

❶ Getting There & Away

Air

The region's principal airport is at Dalaman, 92km southeast of Marmaris. Turkish Airlines runs an airport bus (known as the Havaş bus; TL25) from Marmaris otogar, departing about three hours before each Turkish Airlines flight. Otherwise, take one of Marmaris Coop's buses to Dalaman (TL12) and then a short but quite expensive taxi ride (TL35) from there.

Boat

Catamarans sail daily to Rhodes in Greece (one-way/same-day return/open-return including port tax €43/45/63, 50 minutes) from the pier about a kilometre southeast of Marmaris. They run from mid-April to October, departing from Marmaris at 9am and returning from Rhodes at 4.30pm. Cars cost €95/120/175 for a one-way/same-day return/open-return ticket.

Greek catamarans also sail during the same period from Rhodes to Marmaris (one-way/same-day return/open-return €60/60/90) at 8am daily, returning from Marmaris at 4.30pm. Cars cost €110/135/190 for a one-way/same-day return/open-return.

Turkish cargo boats (carrying up to 78 passengers) also sail once a week in high season to Rhodes (same prices as the catamarans, two hours, departures usually at 11.30pm), and two to three times a week at 9am in low season, depending on the weather. They either return the same day or stay in Rhodes for a period of two or three days.

Note that catamarans do not operate from November to mid-April, and there are no Greek cargo boats then. Also note that the Sunday morning service runs only sporadically in June and July.

Tickets can be bought from any travel agency including **Yeşil Marmaris Travel & Yachting** (☑412 2290; www.yesilmarmaris.com; Barbados Caddesi 13; ☺7am-11.30pm Mon-Sat high season, 8.30am-6.30pm low season).

Book tickets at least one day in advance (more if you have a car) and bring your passport. You need to be at the ferry dock one hour before departure. Some agencies provide a free pick-up service from hotels in the town centre.

Bus

Marmaris' otogar lies 3km north of the centre of town. Dolmuşes run to and from the otogar along Ulusal Egemenlik Bulvarı every few minutes in high season. Bus companies have ticket offices around the Tansaş Shopping Centre.

Buses run to Bodrum (TL18, 3¼ hours, 175km) every hour in high season, and every two hours in low season. All year round, buses run to İstanbul (TL70, 13 hours, 810km) four times a day, to İzmir (TL30, 4¼ hours, 270km) every hour, to Göcek (TL14, 2¼ hours, 98km), to Dalaman (TL9, 1½ hours, 90km), to Fethiye (TL16, three hours, 138km) every half-hour and to Antalya (TL40, six hours, 365km) at least once a day. Closer to home, buses go every half-hour (hourly in low season) to Muğla (TL8, one hour, 53km).

For Datça (TL10, 1¾ hours, 71km) dolmuşes run every hour or so in high season and every two hours in low season. For Köyceğiz (TL8, 50 minutes, 63km), take the Fethiye bus. For Dalyan, take the Fethiye bus and change at Ortaca (TL10, 1½ hours, 84km) for the dolmuş. Domuşes depart five times a day for Selimiye and Bozburun (TL8, 55 minutes, 44km).

❶ Getting Around

Frequent dolmuşes run around the bay, beginning and ending at the Tansaş Shopping Centre on Ulusal Egemenlik Bulvarı. They have been colour-coded to denote different routes: green dolmuşes go to Uzunyalı (TL1.50, 3km) and Turban-Siteler (TL2, 6km), and orange ones to İçmeler (TL2.50, 10km).

Datça & Bozburun Peninsulas

If it is a less frenetic experience you're after, then head west or southwest for the rugged peninsulas that jut out from Marmaris and stretch for over 100km into the Aegean Sea. The western arm is called the Datça (or, rarely, Reşadiye) peninsula; its southern branch is known as the Bozburun (or Hisarönü) peninsula.

This is spectacular, raw Turkish coastline, seen from a bus, bike, boat or even scooter (p306). Aside from the joy of sailing near the peninsula's pine-clad coasts and anchoring in some of its hundreds of secluded coves, visitors come to explore fishing villages, mountain towns, wee hamlets and epic ruins such as Knidos at the tip of the Datça Peninsula.

DATÇA
📞 0252 / POP 14,800

The impossibly scenic highway – keep an eye open for traditional windmills along the way – running west from Marmaris through the Datça Peninsula dips down after 70km into the delightful harbour town of Datça (*dah*-cha). Despite being also accessible by a daily ferry from Bodrum in season and a weekly hydrofoil from Rhodes, Datça seems to have pulled anchor from the big resorts and floated to its isolated location.

Datça is an easy-going mix of locals, salty expats and trendy İstanbul holiday home-owners. For the short-term visitor, it's the closest town to the windswept ruins of Knidos, the picture postcard town of Eski Datça (Old Datça) a couple of kilometres north, and a series of remote coves. The town itself has three small beaches: **Kumluk Plajı** (Sandy Beach), tucked behind the shops on Atatürk Caddesi, the main street running downhill from the highway; **Hastanealtı** (literally 'Below the Hospital'), the bigger beach to the east; and **Taşlık Plajı** (Stony Beach), running west from the end of the harbour.

🛏 Sleeping

Before the small roundabout with a big tree and along Atatürk Caddesi are several small pensions. Further south, on the way to the harbour, you'll find another cluster of pensions on the left.

TOP CHOICE Villa Aşina
BOUTIQUE HOTEL €€€
(📞712 2444; www.villaasina.com.tr; Saklı Koyu Kargı Yolu; s/d TL120/190; ❄❆) The views of the endless sea and two beaches with direct access are just some of the treats at this new castle-like hotel rising above the road several kilometres west of the centre. The hotel counts 17 themed rooms, some with painstakingly carved wooden ceilings and round beds. The attention to detail is evident everywhere (there are even tiles on the stairway), the wall photos of Datça's flora are by the architect/owner, and complementary tea and sweets are served daily at 5pm. To get here, follow the road that branches to the right from Atatürk Caddesi at the mosque. Keep going for roughly 3km until you see a sign to the left.

Villa Tokur
BOUTIQUE HOTEL €€
(📞712 8728; www.hoteltokur.com; Koru Mevkii; d TL145, 1-bedroom ste for up to 4 people TL195; ❄❆) A lovely hilltop position above water, 15 quality rooms and furnishings, and a great swimming pool in a pretty garden make this an excellent choice. Owned and operated by a German-Turkish couple, it's a 10-minute walk uphill from Taşlık Plajı.

Tunç Pansiyon
PENSION €
(📞712 3036; www.tuncpansiyon.com; Buxerolles Caddesi; s/d TL30/60, apt for up to 5 people TL100; ❄@) Terrific in-town pension found down a street off the roundabout (look for the Ögür taxi stand). It's basic but spotless, featuring 22 sunny rooms with balconies

and a fabulous rooftop deck. The friendly owner also runs one-day car excursions to Knidos and surrounds, charging just for the petrol (TL30 to TL35 for up to three people).

Bora Hotel
HOTEL €€

(☎712 2040; www.borahotel.com.tr; Atatürk Caddesi; s/d TL60/120; ✲) This relatively new hostelry, perched at the top of the hill as it tumbles into the harbour, has 18 bright, airy rooms with balconies and views of the sea or the grassy courtyard. The lime green lobby decorated with African masks suggests a peripatetic owner.

Ilıca Camping
CAMPGROUND €

(☎712 3400; www.ilicakamping.com; Taşlik Plaji; tent & campervan per couple TL30, 2-bed bungalow with/without bathroom TL100/60, 3-bed bungalow TL150/120; ✲@) Meticulously run camping ground situated on the eastern shore of Taşlık Plajı since 1980. It's well shaded by eucalyptus trees and great for swimming in summer.

🍴 Eating

Datça's contribution to Turkish cuisine is *keşkek* (lamb mince and coarse wheat pounded), which is especially popular at weddings.

Zekeriya Sofrası
KÖFTECI, KABAPÇI €

(☎712 4303; Atatürk Caddesi 60; dishes TL7-9; ⊙8am-11pm) Run by its friendly namesake, Zekeriya Sofrası serves up the best home-cooked food in town. The servings are plentiful (including the vegetarian offerings), it's a good place for breakfast (TL7) and they do a mean *inegöl köfte* (mixed meat spicy meatballs) to Zekeriya's own secret recipe.

Papatya Restaurant & Bar
SEAFOOD €€

(☎712 2860; Kargı Yolu Caddesi 4; mains TL12-20; ⊙8.30am-5am) A breezy alternative to the marina haunts is this friendly restaurant in a pretty old stone house with a chic vine-covered terrace just as the main road branches to the west from the mosque. Try the *karides güveç şarapli fırında* (shrimps oven-baked in wine; TL20); simpler dishes like *köfte* and kebaps are available too.

Emek Restaurant
SEAFOOD €€

(☎712 3375; Yat Limanı; mains TL10-22) There are various operators side by side along the waterfront in the marina, but Emek is Datça's oldest and most reliable. The owner's son is a fisherman, which guarantees fresh fish at pleasing prices.

Fevzinın Yeri
SEAFOOD €€€

(☎712 9746; Atatürk Caddesi 33/4; mains TL25-30) The theme here is nautical and guests leave their comments – on the ceiling. It's on Kumluk Plajı, just down from the lone tree roundabout.

Culinarium
INTERNATIONAL €€€

(☎712 9770; www.culinarium-datca.com; Yat Limanı; mains TL20-35) Just next door to the Emek is the uber-refined Culinarium run by a German woman and her Turkish husband. The tantalising three-course set menu is excellent value at TL35 and the all-Turkish wine list is a cut above.

🍷 Drinking & Entertainment

Datça's nightlife centres around harbour bars, such as the following:

Bolero
BAR

(☎712 3862; Yat Limanı; beer TL5; ⊙8am-2am; ☎) Central and ever popular.

Mojo Bar
BAR

(☎712 4868; Yat Limani; beer TL5; ⊙7.30am-2am) At the start – or finish – of the relaxed bar strip, with high padded stools from which to toast the surf.

🛍 Shopping

Datça Köy Ürünleri
FOOD & DRINK

(☎712 8318; Atatürk Caddesi 51/A; ⊙9am-5pm, to 1am Jun-Sep) The peninsula is celebrated for three products – honey, almonds and olive oil – and 'Datça Village Products' has all three in infinite variety.

ℹ Getting There & Away

Dolmuşes run to Marmaris (TL10, 1¾ hours, 71km) from Cumhuriyet Meydanı, the main square, every hour in high season, and five times a day in low season. Change there for buses to other destinations.

Between May and September, hydrofoils usually sail to Rhodes (single/return TL90/180, 45 minutes) and Simi (single/return TL60/120, 15 minutes) on Saturday, normally at around 4pm, but double-check this information to be sure it is still current.

A *gület* sails two to three times a week from Datça to Simi (TL120, 70 minutes) at 9am. If there are fewer than eight people it doesn't go.

Knidos Yachting (☎712 9464; Yat Limanı 4/A), next to Emek Restaurant in the marina, sells tickets for the hydrofoils, ferries and *gülets*. For Rhodes and Simi, come at 11am on the Saturday of your departure with your passport; for the *gület*, you can reserve by telephone. Knidos also organises diving trips (TL70/110 for one/two dives).

From mid-June to mid-November regular ferries run daily between Bodrum and Körmen (the name of the harbour at Karaköy, about 5km northwest of Datça on the Gulf of Gökova). From June to mid-September, ferries leave daily for Bodrum (passenger single/return TL25/40, car and driver TL70, extra passengers TL10 each). In May they leave on Monday, Wednesday and Friday at 9.30am, and on Tuesday, Thursday, Saturday and Sunday at 5.30pm. In April and October they run on Monday, Wednesday and Friday and return the same day. The trip takes about two hours. From Bodrum they return on Tuesday, Thursday, Saturday and Sunday at 9.30am, and the rest of the week at 5.30pm. Tickets are sold in the **Bodrum Ferryboat Association** (✆712 2143; fax 712 4239; Turgut Özal Meydanı), next to the town mosque, and there's a free bus shuttle that takes you from Datça to Karaköy at 9am.

ESKİ DATÇA
✆0252 / POP 8000

'Old Datça' was once the capital of a district stretching all the way to Greece. Today it's a picturesque hamlet of cobbled streets and old stone houses, most of them lovingly restored.

🛏 Sleeping & Eating

TOP CHOICE Mehmet Ali Ağa Konağı

HISTORIC HOTEL €€€

(✆712 9257; www.kocaev.com; Stone House r €160-300, ste €350-405, Mansion r €375-425, ste €625-700; ✳@✳) This stunning boutique hotel, with 18 rooms in four buildings set amidst lush gardens in Reşadiye (formerly Elaki), just north of Eski Datça, is arguably the most beautiful place to stay in the region. Once home to the Tuhfezade family, who were politically influential in the area from the 17th century onwards, the mansion was largely derelict when renovations began in 2002. Today it is a veritable museum of Ottoman art, craftsmanship and comfort; you have to see the 'wheel of fortune' ceiling and wall engravings from 1831 in the main room to believe them. The attention to detail throughout is inspiring, from the revival of the family hamam as a spa and all the original prints to the unusual, Ottoman-inspired furnishing of the rooms in the three smaller stone houses. It's hard to imagine anything more romantic than a walk through the rose garden and citrus grove to the hotel's celebrated restaurant, **Elaki** (mains €25-40), with exquisite and original meze, fish and meat dishes that fuse the cuisines of the Turkish Aegean and Mediterranean regions.

Dede Garden Hotel HOTEL €€€

(✆712 3951; www.dedegardenhotel.com; Can Yücel Sokak; s/d TL160/200; ✳✳) A gorgeous walled garden, filled with unusual decorations created by the owner's wife, surrounds a 150-year-old stone house, pool and restful bar. The seven rooms have their own individual character, each with a little kitchen.

Yağhane Pansiyon PENSION €€

(✆712 2287; www.suryaturkey.com; Karaca Sokak 42; s/d TL70/130) This delightful seven-room pension at the heart of the Surya Yoga Centre is a blissful retreat where you can study yoga (hatha and iyengar) and take ayurvedic massage. The compact rooms, with nonallergenic wooden floors and cooled by fans, are inviting, though two share facilities.

Datça Sofrası LOKANTA €€

(✆712 4188; Hurma Sokak 16; mains TL6-10) With tables under a vine-clad pergola, Datça Sofrası is a picturesque place for lunch or dinner. It specialises in dishes based on aubergines (eggplants) though barbecued fish and meat is also available.

Antik Cafe CAFE €€

(✆712 9176; Can Yücel Sokak 1; dishes TL5-12; ⏰8.30am-1am Apr-Sep) A new, much simpler cafe that doubles as a craft and art centre.

🛍 Shopping

Olive Farm FOOD & DRINK, HOMEWARE

(✆712 8377; Güller Dağı Çiftliği 30; ⏰8am-7pm) About 600m before the Datça turn-off on the main highway, this place offers tours, tastings and a well-endowed shop selling anything and everything with an olive-tree provenance.

ℹ Getting There & Away
From Datça to Eski Datça (TL2), minibuses run every hour on the half-hour from May to October and on the hour from Eski Datça to Datça. In low season, they run every two hours.

KNİDOS

What remains of **Knidos** (admission TL8; ⏰8.30am-7pm May-Oct, 9am-6pm Nov-Apr), the once prosperous Dorian port city dating to 400 BC, lies scattered along 3km at the end of the Datça Peninsula. The setting is dramatic: steep hillsides terraced and planted with groves of olive, almond and fruit trees rise above two picture-perfect bays in which a handful of yachts can occasionally be seen at anchor.

BOZBURUN PENINSULA BY SCOOTER

The mountainous, deeply indented Bozburun (or Hisarönü) Peninsula is the perfect place to escape the madness of Marmaris.

It's a rugged place with remarkably varied landscapes; lush pine forests on a high plateau inland from Turunç give way to steep, bare, rocky hillsides as you approach Bozburun. You can go via the main road to Bozburun, but it's more fun to do a loop, heading down on village roads and coming back on the main one.

Setting off from Marmaris, head for **İçmeler** to the southwest via Atatürk Caddesi and the coastal road. In İçmeler the main road branches; take the road to the right, which leads around the back of the town and begins a steep, winding ascent towards Turunç. Follow the unpaved road to the right through the pine forest before you get there. The road narrows and gets steeper, slowly winding down to **Bayırköy**, an inland village with rustic houses. The village square is at the foot of an ancient plane tree and has pleasant restaurants with terraces overlooking the valley. After Bayırköy the landscape becomes much drier, and the hills drop away into inaccessible coves. From tiny **Söğüt** the road is relatively level on the way to **Bozburun**, which has several good places for lunch.

From Bozburun a good road leads back along the western side of the peninsula, past the idyllic bays of **Selimiye**, **Orhaniye** and **Hisarönü**, before rejoining the main Datça–Marmaris road. Between the first two, about 3km southeast of tiny Turgutköy, is a fabulous waterfall (follow the sign for '*şelale*') and pools where you can cool off in the frigid water after a dusty scooter trip.

The whole circuit of the peninsula is about 120km, and takes about six hours with rests, swims and photo stops. Many places in Marmaris rent scooters by the day, most for around TL40 in season. The roads are steep and winding, so speed is hardly an asset. Just bear in mind that Turkey has one of the highest road traffic accident rates in the world; it's necessary to wear a helmet, and appropriate clothing is advisable to protect against road rash if you come off.

The only petrol stations on this peninsula are at Bozburun and Turunç so it's best to fill up in Marmaris before setting out.

The winds change as one rounds the peninsula and ships in ancient times often had to wait at Knidos – or Cnidus (the 'k' and 'c' are pronounced) – for favourable winds, giving it a hefty business in ship repairs, hospitality and trading. The ship taking St Paul to Rome for trial in AD 50 or 60 was one of the many that had to take refuge at Knidos.

Few of the ancient buildings are easily recognisable, but the paths are well-laid. Don't miss the round **temple of Aphrodite**, which once contained the world's first freestanding statue of a woman; the Hellenistic **lower theatre** with 5000 seats; a 4th-century BC **sundial**; and the fine carvings in what was once a Byzantine church. There's a restaurant with great views here, but not much else.

❶ Getting There & Away

Knidos Taxi, near Cumhuriyet Meydanı in Datça, will take up to three people from Datça to Knidos and return, and wait up to two hours, for TL100.

Ask in Datça harbour about excursions to Knidos. Boats tend to leave around 9am or 9.30am and return in the early evening, and cost about TL25 per person.

SELİMİYE

☏ 0252 / POP 4900

The stark beauty of what remains, to some extent, a traditional boat-builders' village belies this town's proximity to mass tourism – Marmaris is just over an hour away to the southwest. Here on the Bozburun Peninsula you'll find real solitude by the seaside as quickly as drinking pals among a particularly laid-back yachting set. The town itself – a tiny stretch of promenade lined with restaurants, pensions and bars – lies on a calm bay beneath a few toppled ruins.

🛏 Sleeping

Jenny's House   HOTEL €€

(☏446 4289; www.turkey-vacation.co.uk; s/d TL75/120; ❄ ☀) Across the road from the harbour, this charming bed and breakfast subtitled *yolgeçen hanı*, or 'wayfarers' inn', has a dozen different types of room surrounding a lush garden. A couple of rooms give on to the pool in the centre but we prefer the two doubles on the 1st floor with the large shared balcony. The friendly eponymous owner cordially hosts many return visitors and tea at 5pm.

Nane Limon Pansiyon
PENSION €€

(✆446 4146; www.nanelimonpansiyon.com; s/d TL80/140; ❄️) Nejdet pops down from İstanbul for six months each year to oversee his blue-and-white guest house evocatively named 'Mint Lemon'. The 10 rooms in the large house set back from the water are bright, stylish and recently renovated; many have balconies. A garden path leads to a beachfront bar with swinging hammocks.

Begovina Motel
HOTEL €

(✆446 4292; www.begovinamotel.com; s/d TL60/80; ❄️@) Run by Hakan, an ex-football player, and his Finnish wife, this hotel at the northern end of town offers 30 good-sized rooms, some with leafy balconies and direct sea views. All have fridges and a few even have kitchenettes. It's just metres from a shingle beach.

Sardunya Bungalows
HOTEL €€

(✆446 4003; fax 446 4286; s/d with half-board TL120/150; ❄️@) This popular complex stands firm despite the arrival of much competition over the years. The nine stone bungalows circle a pretty garden just behind the beach; there are three additional rooms in the main house as well. Good for families.

Bahçe Apart Otel
HOTEL €€

(✆446 4235; bahceapart@hotmail.com; s/d/apt TL100/120/140; ❄️@) A fairly inconspicuous pension made up of three sparse, clean rooms literally 10 steps from the water's edge and four larger apartments. The three quiet Varol brothers do a fine job of running the place.

✖ Eating

Falcon Restaurant
FAMILY RESTAURANT €€

(✆446 4105; mains TL10-18) The owners of the Falcon have never stopped talking about the day in 1999 when a Greek boat disgorged HRHs William and Harry, who promptly sat down here and had a meal. And they have posted newspaper cuttings to prove it! There's a stone oven for pide and the *tandir* (clay oven) dishes are excellent.

Özcan Restaurant
SEAFOOD €€

(✆446 4233; mains TL10-14) A recent discovery, this simple fish restaurant has excellent (and cheap) meze (TL4), fresh seafood (es-

pecially recommended is the grilled squid, TL15) and friendly service.

Aurora Restaurant
SEAFOOD €€

(✆446 4097; mains TL10-15) The Aurora is attractively set in a 200-year-old stone house with a shaded terrace and tables right on the seafront. Fish is its speciality; the meze (TL2 to TL10) are mouth-watering too.

Cafe Ceri
CAFE €

(coffee TL3, frappés TL4.50; ⏱8.30am-11pm) Good drinks and delicious baked goods on the marina.

ℹ Getting There & Away

Dolmuşes run to and from Marmaris (TL7, 1¼ hours, 43km) every two hours. The bus from Marmaris to Bozburun stops on the main road at the northern end of Selimiye.

If you're driving, take the Bozburun road about 9km south of Orhaniye and follow the signs.

BOZBURUN
✆0252 / POP 2000

Lying 12km down the peninsula on Sömbeki Körfezi (Sömbeki Bay) is the charming village of Bozburun. Fishing and farming still engage many villagers, although the modest flow of tourists and yachties keeps some folk gainfully employed.

If you want to swim, walk around the harbour to the left as you face out to sea, where you can dip into the startlingly blue water from the rocks. This is also a good place to charter boats to explore the surrounding bays.

⏟ Sleeping

Pembe Yunus
PENSION €€

(Pink Dolphin; ✆456 2154; www.bozburunpembeyunus.com; Kargı Mahallesi 37; s/d with half-board TL80/160; ❄️) This delightful pension, 700m from the marina, feels more like a private house than a hotel, with lots of fluffy fabrics and mosquito netting crowning the beds. Rooms are decked out in rustic-style furniture, and some have stunning sea views and huge terraces. Fatma, the mother, cooks famously – three-course set dinners cost TL25.

Sabrinas Haus
LUXURY HOTEL €€€

(✆456 2045; www.sabrinashaus.com; d €260-300, ste €350-495) Reachable by boat (a liveried skipper picks up guests in a speedboat *Hawaii Five-O*-style) or a long half-hour walk along the bay's eastern shore, Sabrinas Haus is the ultimate pamperific, get-away-from-it-all place. There are

14 tastefully designed rooms (think lots of natural woods and shades of white) in three buildings hidden in a beautiful mature garden. The infinity pool and seafront deck and bar are super and the spa has massage and myriad treatments.

Dolphin Hotel   HOTEL **€€**
(☑456 2408; www.dolphinpension.com; Kargı Mahallesi 71; s/d with half-board TL90/180, ste per person TL150; ❋) Practically synonymous with Bozburun, the Dolphin has been resting on its laurels of late and we've had letters of complaint from readers about overcharging. Still, the 20 rooms are mostly well-proportioned and pleasantly decorated; some – like rooms 4 and 11 – have antique(ish) furnishings, balconies and sensational sea views.

Yilmaz Pansiyon   PENSION **€**
(☑456 2167; www.yilmazpansion.com; İskele Mahallesi 391; s/d TL40/75; ❋) Try to nab a balcony room in this friendly little pension with 10 simple, cheerful rooms and use of a great modern kitchen. The vine-covered terrace is metres from the sea where the hotel does a good breakfast spread. It's around 100m east of the marina.

✖ Eating & Drinking

Fisherman House   SEAFOOD **€€**
(☑456 2730; İskele Mahallesi 391; meze TL4, seafood meze TL12-15, fish per 500g TL20-30) Run by the same local fisherman who owns Yilmaz Pansiyon, this place offers fresh fish at the right prices. We love the waterfront seating.

Sabrinas Haus
    MODERN TURKISH, MEDITERRANEAN **€€€**
(☑456 2045; www.sabrinashaus.com; mains TL15-35) Serving inspired Turkish and Mediterranean cuisine in a lovely setting, this open-air seafront restaurant at the hotel of the same name has a fine reputation. Call to have a boat pick you up from the marina.

Kandil Restaurant   KEBAPÇI, SEAFOOD **€€**
(☑456 2227; İskele Mahallesi 3; mains TL10-12) Just off the main square, this local favourite serves excellent fresh fish and grilled dishes. Meze are a snip at TL4.

Marin Cafe Bar   CAFE-BAR
(☑456 2181; Atatürk Caddesi 56; beer TL5) Very chilled cafe-bar near the Dolphin with comfy sofas, backgammon and sleeping dog.

❶ Getting There & Away

Minibuses run to/from Marmaris (TL8, 1½ hours, 55km) six times a day via Selimiye.

Köyceğiz

☑0252 / POP 4000

A short distance off the main coastal highway, this scruffy little town lies on the northern side of Köyceğiz Gölü, the large and serene Lake Köyceğiz linked to the Mediterranean by the Dalyan River. As beautiful (and ecologically significant) as it is, a brackish lake is not major competition to the Med and this farming community attracts only modest tourism, depending still on citrus fruits, olives, honey and cotton for its livelihood. The region is also famous for its Oriental sweetgum trees (*Liquidambar orientalis*), the sap of which is used to produce frankincense.

◉ Sights & Activities

Köyceğiz (*keuy*-jay-iz) is a town for strolling, though watch out for broken pavements everywhere. Hit the lakeshore promenade (Kordon Boyu) and walk past the pleasant town park, shady tea gardens and waterfront restaurants. Most pensions have bicycles for guests, so take a ride out to the surrounding orchards and farmland. The road along the western shore of the lake to the Sultaniye mud pools offers superb views of the lake. It's 35km by road to the mud baths or you can take a boat excursion from the promenade.

Along the way take a brief detour to the village of **Hamitköy**, where you can see the last surviving example of a 'basket house', once common in the marshes. These unique woven dwellings, which could be picked up and moved, were the ideal type of housing in an area prone to flooding.

There's a small **waterfall** about 7km west of town, where locals go to swim. Take any minibus heading west towards Marmaris and Muğla and tell the driver you want to get off at the *şelale* (waterfall). It's about a 15-minute walk from the highway.

You can take **boat trips** across the lake south to Dalyan and the Kaunos ruins for TL15 to TL30 per person including lunch.

The surrounding **Köyceğiz-Dalyan Nature Reserve** has a growing reputation among outdoor types for its excellent hiking and cycling.

🛏 Sleeping

Most of the town's pensions and hotels are either on or just off Kordon Boyu along the lake.

Flora Hotel `TOP CHOICE` HOTEL €€
(☎262 4976; www.florahotel.info; Kordon Boyu 96; s/d/apt TL40/70/80; ❄ @) This backpacker favourite gets our vote as the best place in Köyceğiz, mostly because of its enthusiastic and very 'green' owner Alp, who can arrange walks into the nearby Gölgeli Mountains for bird-watching (148 species have been spotted) as well as fishing trips in the lake (catch and release) and on the sea. Some of the 16 rooms have balconies with views to the lake and the family rooms include a crib, pram and kitchenette. There are two kayaks and 10 bicycles for guests' use.

Hotel Alila HOTEL €€
(☎262 1150; www.hotelalila.com; Emeksiz Caddesi 13; s/d TL50/70; ❄ ≋) By far the most character-filled hotel in town, the bougainvillea-bedecked Alila has two dozen rooms, 16 of which have direct views of the lake. The friendly owner Ömer runs the place professionally and attends to every detail (right down to the swan-folded towels).

Tango Pension & Hostel HOSTEL, PENSION €
(☎262 2501; www.tangopension.com; Ali İhsan Kalmaz Caddesi 112; dm/s/d TL20/30/50; ❄ @) Managed by the local school sports teacher, this place is big on activities including boat trips (TL20), trekking (TL25) and rafting (TL60). Prices include lunch. The three-dozen rooms, including six dorms with a half-dozen beds each, are bright, cheerful and well maintained, and there's a pleasant garden. It's next door to Fulya Pension and away from the water. Bikes are free.

Fulya Pension PENSION €
(☎262 2301; fulyapension@mynet.com; Ali İhsan Kalmaz Caddesi 88; s/d TL20/40; ❄ @) This brilliant budget option, set back from the lake, has 16 spic-and-span rooms with balconies, and there's a large roof terrace with a bar and occasional live music. Bikes are available free of charge, and boat trips (TL20, including lunch) to the local attractions are a bargain.

Hotel Panorama Plaza HOTEL €€
(☎262 3773; www.panorama-plaza.net; Cengiz Topel Caddesi 69; s/d TL60/100; ❄ ≋ ≋) The last hotel on the promenade about a kilometre from the centre, the Panorama Plaza is in a stone-faced modern building with a lobby in need of an update. The 28 rooms are spiffy and well priced, while the garden swimming pool is five-star. There's free windsurfing for guests.

🍴 Eating

There are several predominantly fish restaurants bunched up along the lake and lots of cheap and cheerful eateries off the main square. You'll find several places along the lake selling *köyceğiz lokması*, a local speciality of round fried fritter drenched in syrup.

The local market is held every Monday near the police station opposite the tourist office at the southern end of Atatürk Bulvarı.

Colıba MODERN TURKISH €€
(☎262 2987; Cengiz Topel Caddesi 64; mains TL6-15; ⏰10am-1am) In this very stylish restaurant, cool-headed staff serve delicious *ordövr* (mixed meze platter; TL8) and *alabalık* (trout; TL15), though the grills (TL10) are more of a bargain. Whitewashed and wooden, the Colıba has a shaded terrace with views of the lake.

Pembe Restaurant SEAFOOD €€
(☎262 2983; Cengiz Topel Caddesi 70; mains TL8-14) Next door to the Colıba, the 'Pink' is housed in an unmissable house of that colour (with a bit of purple thrown in) and does relatively inexpensive seafood and meat dishes. Meze come in at between TL3 and TL4.

Thera Fish Restaurant SEAFOOD €€
(☎0541 833 6154; Cengiz Topel Caddesi; mains TL12-15; ⏰9am-midnight) On the other side of the Colıba you can pick your fish from a large tank on the waterfront terrace here. The red mullet fillets (TL15) are excellent, as is the sea bream (TL12). The excellent grilled prawns (TL25) are ideal for a special occasion.

Mutlu Kardeşler PIDECI, KEBAPÇI €
(☎262 2482; Fevzipaşa Caddesi; köfte & kebap TL6, pide TL3-5; ⏰7am-10pm) This simple place off the main square, much loved by locals, has tables on a little shaded terrace.

ℹ Information

Tourist office (☎262 4703; ⏰8.30am-5pm Mon-Fri) South of the main square and almost on the lake; stocks brochures and a simple hand-drawn map.

❶ Getting There & Away

The otogar serving Köyceğiz is just off the main highway, about 2.5km from the lake; dolmuşes (TL1) run every 15 minutes or so into town. Buses go to Dalaman (TL6, 30 minutes, 26km), Marmaris (TL8, 1¼ hours, 63km), Ortaca (TL5, 25 minutes, 22km) and Fethiye (TL10, 1½ hours, 65km) every half-hour.

Dalyan
📞 0252 / POP 3000

Once a sleepy farming community and now increasingly a package-tour destination, riverside Dalyan has somehow managed to retain its peaceful atmosphere. It makes an excellent base for exploring the surrounding fertile waterways, in particular Lake Köyceğiz and the turtle nesting grounds at İztuzu Beach. Dalyan's most famous feature is the impressive cliff-side ruins of ancient Kaunos, but you won't be alone when visiting; summer afternoons bring a virtual armada of excursion boats from Marmaris and Fethiye.

◉ Sights & Activities

Kaunos RUINS
(admission TL8; ⊙ 8.30am-7pm May-Oct, 8.30am-5.30pm Nov-Apr) Founded in the 9th century BC, Kaunos (or Caunus) was an important Carian city by 400 BC. Right on the border with Lycia, its culture reflected aspects of both empires. The famous **Kings' Tombs** in the cliffs, for instance, are largely Lycian style. If you don't take a boat excursion to the site, walk south from town along Maraş Caddesi to Kaunos Sokak to view the tombs across the Dalyan River.

When Mausolus of Halicarnassus ruled Caria, his influence reached the Kaunians, who eagerly adopted that Hellenistic culture. Kaunos suffered from endemic malaria; according to Herodotus, its people were famous for their yellowish skin and eyes. The Kaunians' prosperity was also threatened by the silting of their harbour. The Mediterranean, which once surrounded the hill on which the archaeological site stands, has now retreated 5km to the south, pushed back by silt from the river.

Apart from the tombs, the **theatre** is very well preserved; nearby there are parts of an **acropolis** and other structures, such as baths, fountains and defensive walls. The curious wooden structures in the river are

dalyanlar (fishing weirs), from where the town and river takes its name.

Two-hour guided boat trips cost around TL15. Alternatively, you might snag a rowboat (TL5) to the other side and walk for 25 minutes.

Boat Trips CRUISE
You can save yourself a lot of money and hassle by taking boats run by the **Dalyan Kooperatifi** (📞 284 2094), southwest of the main square. It's a fairly easy process, but if you need help, ask for Eddy (or call him on 📞 0541 505 0777).

Boats usually leave the quayside at 10am or 10.30am to cruise to the Sultaniye hot springs and mud baths, the ruins of Kaunos, and İztuzu Beach on the Mediterranean. These excellent tours, including lunch, cost around TL30 per person.

If you can drum up a team of like-minded folk, you can hire a passenger boat that holds from eight to 12 people. A two-hour tour just to Kaunos costs around TL50 for the boat; if you want to visit the Sultaniye hot springs as well, figure on three hours and TL100.

Dalyan

Boats belonging to the boat cooperative also operate a river dolmuş service between the town and İztuzu (or Turtle) Beach, charging TL8 for the return trip. In high summer boats head out every 20 minutes from 10am or 10.30am to 2pm and return between 1pm and 6pm. In high summer, minibuses make the 13km run to İztuzu (TL15) as well and will drop you at the less crowded end of the beach.

The boat cooperative also offers a two-hour early morning turtle-spotting tour, which leaves at 8am every day (TL25). Dolmuş boats also go to Kaunos three times a day (TL30 return), and to the mud baths (TL20) at 2pm.

Evening sunset cruises (TL35 per person including dinner) are also offered two or three times a week (usually Wednesday, Friday and/or Sunday) from June to September.

Other Activities
ACTIVITIES

Kaunos Tours (☎284 2816; www.kaunostours.com), on the main square opposite the landmark statue of the turtles, offers any number of organised activities both on and off the water, including sea kayaking and canoeing (each TL65), trekking (TL35), canyoning

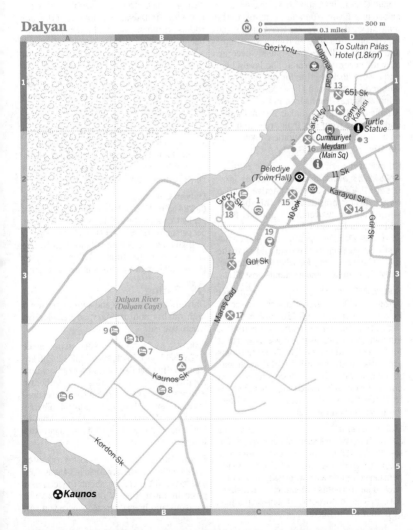

Dalyan

(TL65) and jeep safari (TL60). Prices include lunch. For diving, go to the **Dalyan Dive Centre** (📞284 2332; www.dalyandive.com; Yalı Sokak 5). A day-long excursion including two dives and lunch is TL100.

🛏 Sleeping

The preferred stretch of hotels and pensions is found along Maraş Caddesi, a 1km southbound road that ends at a sharp bend in the river and carries on as Kaunos Sokak.

TOP CHOICE / Happy Caretta   HOTEL €€
(📞284 2109; www.happycaretta.com; Kaunos Sokak 26; s/d TL100/150; 🌀@) National Geographic staff have stayed here and so might you after a few minutes in the magical garden of cypress trees, palms and caged songbirds. The 14 rooms are simple and on the small side, but stylishly decorated with natural materials. The lovely boat and leisure dock waiting for you to take the plunge is a plus, and the view of the illuminated King's Tombs by night is priceless. Affable owner İlknur makes her own plum and fig jams from her fruit trees and lays on a superb four-course home-cooked meal (TL40).

Kilim Hotel   HOTEL €€
(📞284 2253; www.kilimhotel.com; Kaunos Sokak 11; s/d/f TL40/80/100; 🌀🛜🌀) Active English owner Becky presides over this buzzing kilim- (pileless woven rug) and art-filled midrange hotel, which has just increased to 25 rooms with the opening of a somewhat rustic annexe across the road and near the river. There's a ramp for wheelchair access; daily yoga and aerobic workouts cost TL5.

Sultan Palas Hotel   HOTEL €€€
(📞284 2103; www.sultanpalasdalyan.co.uk; Horozlar Mevkii; s/d TL90/180; 🌀@🌀) Staying at this relaxed resort hotel a couple of kilometres upriver from Dalyan is worth it for the ferry ride alone. The 26 suite rooms are satisfyingly restrained and each has its own veranda. To get here, either catch one of the five scheduled daily boat shuttles from town or, outside hours, call the hotel for a ferry pick-up service.

Midas Pension   PENSION €€
(📞284 2195; www.midasdalyan.com; Kaunos Sokak 30; s & d TL80; 🌀) Selçuk and Saadet Nur are the welcoming hosts of this riverside pension complete with waterside deck-cum-dock. The 10 rooms are smartly furnished, with private bathrooms attached. It's just next door to the Likya.

Likya Pension   PENSION €€
(📞284 2233; www.likyapansion.com; Kaunos Sokak 32; s & d TL80; 🌀) The last property on a pension-rich street, the Likya is one of the oldest pensions in Dalyan and still one of the best. The smallish rooms have been freshened up a bit, the wood floors are cool and clean, and the flower-filled garden gives the place a genuine park vibe.

Çınar Sahil Otel   HOTEL €€
(📞284 2402; www.cinarsahilhotel.com; Yalı Sokak 14; s/d TL40/80; 🌀) Fronting the river and surrounded by plane trees, this simple but very central pension has 10 impeccably clean rooms and a terrace with possibly the best views in Dalyan. Ask for one of the four rooms with balconies and river views. Barbecues are organised in season and there's a boat accommodating up to four people for rent (TL60).

Dalyan Resort   RESORT €€€
(📞284 5499; www.dalyanresort.com; Kaunos Sokak 50; s/d €75/120, ste €150; 🌀🌀🌀) This elegant 58-room hotel is on its own little peninsula that juts into the river about 1.2km from the town centre. The service is discreet and there are full views of the Kaunos tombs from the classy pool. The health centre and spa are excellent.

Dalyan Camping   CAMPGROUND €
(📞284 5316, 0506 882 9173; Maraş Caddesi 144; per tent/caravan TL10/20, large/small bungalows per person TL20/25; 🕙Apr-Oct) This compact, well-shaded site is centrally located by the river opposite the tombs. The dozen or so pinewood bungalows are simple but clean.

🍴 Eating

Dalyan's restaurant scene swings between high quality and ordinary, so be selective where you eat.

Saki   FAMILY RESTAURANT €€
(📞284 5212; Geçit Sokak; mains TL12-22; 🕙10am-11pm) With a brilliant (and breezy) location right on the riverfront, this very authentic eatery serves some of the most wholesome Turkish food in Dalyan restaurant. There's no menu; choose from the glass cabinet of homemade meze (TL5 to TL8), meat and fish.

Beyaz Gül   MODERN TURKISH €€
(📞284 2304; www.beyazgul.info; off Maraş Caddesi; mains TL14-22) Just about the classiest place in town, the 'White Rose' boasts a gorgeous and breezy terrace where you can

dine while admiring the cliff-top tombs and listening to background jazz. And it caters to everyone: there's a play area for the kids, nargileh (water pipe) for the lads and ladettes, and stylish decor for the discerning.

Kordon — SEAFOOD €€€
(☎284 2261; Çarşı İçi 2; fish mains TL20-25) Considered by many to be Dalyan's best fish restaurant, the Kordon has a commanding position on the river. Ichtyphobes can choose from a large selection of steaks and grills and there are a half-dozen vegetarian choices on offer.

Atay Dostlar Sofrası — PIDECİ, LOKANTA €
(☎284 2156; Camı Karşısı 10; mains TL6-8; ☺6.30am-midnight) You'll find competent staff and unbeatable prices at this local workers' restaurant where visitors are greeted warmly. There's a point-and-pick counter and dishes are fresh daily. It's opposite the mosque and minibus stand.

Chinatown — CHINESE €€
(☎284 4478; Gülpınar Caddesi 16; mains TL9-20) OK, it ain't going to win any culinary awards but if you (like us) need the occasional fix of Asian-style rice and/or noodles (TL6 to TL13), this British-owned eatery can assist. There's a good choice of vegetarian dishes too.

Kösk — FAMILY RESTAURANT €€
(☎0537 352 4770, 284 2877; Maraş Caddesi; mains 10-14; ☺8am-11pm) This little place in the centre of Dalyan's high street is the busiest eatery in Dalyan, thanks to its home-style meze (TL4) and grilled dishes. There are tables in a little forecourt from where you can watch the evening parade.

Dalyan İz — CAFE €
(☎0542 451 5451; www.dalyaniz.com; sandwiches & salads TL6-12, cakes TL3-5; ☺9.30am-7pm) This excellent new addition to Dalyan's social scene is an art gallery and shop as much as a garden cafe. It's hugely popular with local expats and a great source of information.

Demet Pastanesi — CONFECTIONER, CAFE €
(☎284 4124; Maraş Caddesi 39; coffee TL2; ☺7.30am-midnight) With excellent pastries and tantalising Turkish puds (TL4.50), this is also a great place for breakfast and picnic supplies. The hazelnut and walnut tart (TL5) is to die for.

ℹ Information
Tourist office (☎284 4235; Cumhuriyet Medanı; ☺8am-noon & 1-5pm Mon-Fri) On the 1st floor of an office block on the south side of the main square.

Hadigari Internet Cafe (Karakol Sokak 25/A; per hr TL2; ☺10am-2am) East of Maraş Caddesi and just up from the Dalyan İz cafe.

ℹ Getting There & Away
Minibuses stop in Cumhuriyet Meydanı near the mosque. There are no direct minibuses from here to Dalaman. First take a minibus to Ortaca (TL3, every 25 minutes in high season, every hour in low season, 14km) and change there. At the Ortaca otogar, buses go to Köyceğiz (TL5, 25 minutes, 22km) and Dalaman (TL4, 15 minutes, 9km). A taxi to Dalaman airport from Dalyan costs TL75.

Around Dalyan

SULTANİYE HOT SPRINGS
For some good (and dirty) fun, head for the Sultaniye Hot Springs (Sultaniye Kaplıcaları; admission TL5), on the southeast shore of Köyceğiz Gölü (Lake Köyceğiz); accessible from both Köyceğiz and Dalyan. These bubbling hot mud pools (temperatures can reach 42°C) contain mildly radioactive mineral waters that are rich in chloride, sodium, hydrogen sulphide and bromide; drinking and bathing in the water is said to have a relaxing and beneficial effect on sufferers of rheumatism, skin disorders and bronchitis. At the smaller baths just before the Dalyan River joins the lake, pamper yourself with a restorative bodypack of mud in a steaming sulphur pool. To get here from Dalyan, take a dolmuş boat (TL8, 30 minutes), which leaves when full (every half-hour in summer, every hour otherwise) from the riverfront. From Köyceğiz the bus headed for Ekincik (TL4) at 9.30am will drop you off at the springs.

İZTUZU BEACH
An excellent swimming beach accessed from the Dalyan River, 4.5km-long İztuzu Beach has long been the target of greedy hotel developers. But as İztuzu is one of the Mediterranean nesting sites of the loggerhead turtle (see the boxed text, p373), special rules to protect it are enforced. Although the beach is still open to the public during the day, night-time visits are prohibited from May to September. A line of wooden stakes on the beach indicates the nest sites and visitors are asked to keep behind them to avoid disturbing the nests.

Minibuses (TL8, 15 minutes) run to the beach from Dalyan every half-hour in season.

Dalaman

☎0252 / POP 22,200

Little has changed for this agricultural town of poly-tunnels since the regional airport was built on the neighbouring river delta, with most arrivals moving on immediately.

It's just over 5km from the airport to the town and another 5km from the town to the D400 highway. Besides seasonal flights to many European cities, there are between four and seven daily flights from Dalaman to İstanbul year-round, costing TL80 oneway. In high season, several bus companies pick up passengers outside the airport. At other times you may need to get a taxi into Dalaman for an extortionate TL35.

From Dalaman's otogar, near the junction of Kenan Evren Bulvarı and Atatürk Caddesi, you can catch buses to Antalya (TL24, 6½ hours, 335km), Köyceğiz (TL6, 30 minutes, 26km) and Marmaris (TL9, 1½ hours, 90km). All routes north and east pass through either Muğla (TL10, two hours, 87km) or Fethiye (TL7, one hour, 46km).

Göcek

☎0252 / POP 4500

Göcek (*geuh*-jek) is the western Mediterranean's high-end yacht spot and the attractive bay makes a relaxing alternative to Fethiye despite all the building going on. For those desperate and/or boat-less, there's a fairly scrappy swimming beach at the western end of the quay.

🛏 Sleeping

Efe Hotel LUXURY HOTEL €€€
(☎645 2646; www.efehotelgocek.com; Yarpız Sokak; s/d €80/90, ste €100-110; ❀☀) Hidden in a lush garden about 200m from Skopea Marina, Göcek's most ambitious hotel has 19 large and bright rooms, a half-Olympic-sized pool and restful mountain views.

Tufan Pansiyon PENSION €
(☎645 1334, 0546 921 7460; Belediye Marina; s & d TL50-60; ❀) In the centre and just 25m from the sea, the family-run Tufan has eight small but spotless and rather sweet rooms, half of which have sea views from a shared balcony.

Villa Danlin HOTEL €€
(☎645 1521; www.villadanlin.com; Çarşı İçi; s/d TL100/120; ❀☀) This hotel, in a charming little building you'll pass on the main street,

only contains a lobby and three rooms; the other 10 are in a modern extension out in the back looking onto a generous-sized pool. Almost but not quite 'boutique', the Danlin is tantalisingly close to the sea but offers no views.

A&B Home Hotel HOTEL €€
(☎645 1820; www.abhomehotel.com; Turgut Özal Caddesi; s/d TL110/130; ❀☀) The 11 smallish rooms here have been given an update (wrought-iron bed stands, a preference for shades of yellow), but the real boon here is the medium-sized pool on the attractive front terrace. A good breakfast buffet is served.

Dim Hotel HOTEL €€
(☎645 1294; www.dimhotel.com; Sokak 14; s/d TL60/120; ❀☀) With 15 simple but well-furnished rooms and a pleasant terrace, medium-sized pool and a location 30m from the beach, this hotel to the west of the centre offers good value. All rooms have a fridge.

🍴 Eating & Drinking

Can Restaurant RESTAURANT €€
(☎645 1507; Skopea Marina; mains TL12-22; ⊙7am-midnight) Set back from the seafront but with a lovely terrace shaded by an old yucca tree, this local favourite serves a great selection of meze (TL6, seafood meze TL8 to TL18), some of them rather unusual. The local speciality – *tuzda balık* (fish baked in salt) – costs around TL240 and serves three people.

West Cafe & Bistro INTERNATIONAL €€
(☎645 2794; www.westcafegocek.com; Turgut Özal Caddesi; mains TL9-19; ⊙9am-midnight, to 12.30am high season; ☏) As the name suggests, it's Western in cuisine and feel, with bacon for breakfast (TL7 to TL13) and tarts for tea. If you're kebaped-out it makes a nice change. Comfortable *al fresco* seating too.

Kebab Hospital Antep Sofrası KEBAPÇI €€
(☎645 1873; Turgut Özal Caddesi; mains TL12-15; ⊙8am-midnight) Apparently this simple place backing on to the water is where everyone in Göcek comes for their kebaps (and pide and pizza and *lahmacun*), whether or not they're ailing. Service is friendly and efficient.

Dice Cafe CAFE-BAR
(☎620 8514; Safı Villalar Önü; ☏) Snappy little bar on the waterfront to the west has good mojitos (TL15) and free wireless connection.

Del Mar Cafe-Bar
CAFE-BAR

(☑620 2181; Skopea Marina) Trendy watering hole on the marina pier is popular with yachties and fashionistas.

🛍 Shopping

Muse Jewellery
JEWELLERY

(☑0533 361 6054; Turgut Özal Caddesi) You'll feel like a sultan while inspecting the antique Ottoman jewellery at this uber-posh bling shop. And with most of the baubles priced in euros with at least five digits, you'll need to be one too.

❶ Getting There & Away

Buses drop you at the petrol station on the main road, from where it's a 1km walk to the centre. Minibuses drive into the main square, with its requisite bust of Atatürk, a PTT and ATMs. Minibuses depart every half-hour for Fethiye (TL4, 45 minutes, 30km). For Dalyan, change at Ortaca (TL3, 25 minutes, 19km, hourly).

If you're driving from Marmaris, take the toll road (3TL) heading straight through the tunnel.

Fethiye

☑0252 / POP 74,000

In 1958 an earthquake levelled the harbour city of Fethiye (feh-*tee*-yeh), sparing only the remains of ancient Telmessos. More than half a century on and it is once again a prosperous, growing hub of the western Mediterranean. Fethiye is also incredibly low-key for its size, due mostly to the restrictions on high-rise buildings and the transitory nature of the *gület* gangs.

Fethiye's natural harbour is perhaps the region's finest, tucked away in the southern reaches of a broad bay scattered with pretty islands, in particular Şövalye Adası. About 15km south is Ölüdeniz, one of Turkey's seaside hot spots, and the surrounding countryside has many interesting sites to explore, including the ghost town of Kayaköy (or Karmylassos), waiting patiently and in silence just over the hill.

👁 Sights

Telmessos
RUINS

The **Tomb of Amyntas** (admission TL8; ⊙8am-7pm May-Oct, to 5pm Nov-Apr) is an Ionic temple facade carved into the sheer rock face in 350 BC. Located south of the centre, it is best visited at sunset. Other, smaller rock tombs lie about 500m to the east. In town you will notice curious Lycian stone sarcophagi dating from around 450 BC. There's one north of the *belediye* (city hall) and others in the middle of streets (eg on the way to Kayaköy). All were broken into by tomb robbers centuries ago.

On the hillside above (and south of) the town and along the road to Kayaköy, you can't miss the ruined tower of a **Crusader fortress** built by the Knights of St John at the start of the 15th century on earlier foundations.

Behind the harbour you'll see the partly excavated remains of a Roman **theatre** dating from the 2nd century BC.

Fethiye Museum
MUSEUM

(☑614 1150; 505 Sokak; admission TL5; ⊙8.30am-5pm) Reopened after a two-year refit and focusing on Lycian finds from Telmessos as well as the ancient settlements of Tlos and Kaunos, the museum exhibits pottery, jewellery, small statuary and votive stones (including the important Grave Stelae and the Stelae of Promise). Its most prized significant possession, however, is the so-called Trilingual Stele from Letoön, dating from 358 BC, which was used partly to decipher the Lycian language with the help of ancient Greek and Aramaic. The garden surrounding the museum contains an excellent lapidary of mostly Lycian sarcophagi and Roman tombstones, some of them portraying early Christian symbols and angels.

🏃 Activities

Next to the tourist office, the **Ocean Turizm & Travel Agency** (☑612 4807; www.oceantravelagency.com; İskele Meydanı 1; ⊙9am-9pm Apr-Oct) sells boat tickets and organises parasailing (TL125 for 45 minutes), day-long rafting trips (TL85) and half-day horse-riding excursions (TL50) along with lots of other water sports including so-called blue voyages (p319).

The very professional **Elite Diving Centre** (☑614 9614; www.elitedivingcentre.com; Uğur Mumcu Parkı Yanı), just up from the Fethiye Cultural Centre, organises diving trips (per person including two dives, all equipment and lunch TL110) and three-day PADI courses (TL760).

One of the best ways to see the Med up close is in a sea kayak. Kayaköy-based **Seven Capes** (☑0537 403 3779; www.sevencapes.com) has both daily tours (€30), including an excellent three-hour one between Ölüdeniz and Kabak via Butterfly Valley

316 **Fethiye**

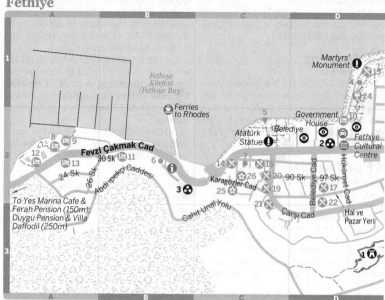

Fethiye

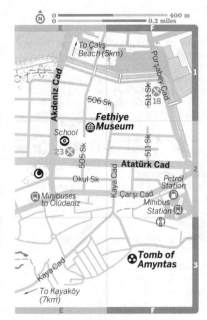

The normal tour visits **Yassıcalar** (Flat Island) for a stop and a swim, then **Tersane Adası** (Shipyard Island) for a dip and a visit to the ruins, followed by **Akvaryum** (Aquarium) for lunch, a swim and a snorkel. **Cennet Köyü** (Paradise Bay) is next for a dip, followed by **Kleopatra Hamamı** (Cleopatra's Bath) and finally **Kızılada** (Red Island) with its beach and mud baths.

If you have another day or so, excellent boat tours of the same length go to or include **Butterfly Valley** (per person TL25) via Ölüdeniz and allow you to walk, swim and visit ruins. There's also the **Saklıkent Gorge Tour** (per person TL40 to TL45), which includes the ruins at Tlos and a trout lunch; and the **Dalyan Tour** (per person TL40 to TL45; running 9am to 6.30pm), which includes a shuttle to Dalyan, a tour of Köyceğiz Gölü (Lake Köyceğiz), the Sultaniye mud baths, Kaunos ruins and İztuzu Beach.

🛏 Sleeping

The bulk of accommodation options are up the hill behind the marina in Karagözler or further west. Many pensions will organise transport from the otogar.

TOP CHOICE **Yildirim Guest House**

HOSTEL, PENSION €

(☎614 4627; www.yildirimguesthouse.com; Fevzi Çakmak Caddesi 37; dm/d/tr; dm/d/tr TL20/60/90; ❄ @) Our favourite budget option in Fethiye, this shipshape hostel-cum-pension just opposite the marina includes three dorms (two by gender and one mixed) with four to six beds and a half-dozen spotless rooms, some facing the harbour. Nothing is too difficult for well-travelled host Omer Yapis – from excursions and pick-ups to laundry and evening meals (TL10).

Ferah Pension   HOSTEL, PENSION €

(☎614 2816; www.ferahpension.com; Ordu Caddesi 23; dm/s/d TL20/30/50; ❄ @ ❄) Love, love, love what's also called Monica's Place with its leafy, glass-enclosed lobby terrace and little swimming pool, paintings by Monica and 'sexy dinners' (TL12) by same. The 10 sizeable, very tidy rooms include two dorms with three to six beds. One of the rooms at the top has windows on two sides and views to die for.

Villa Daffodil   PENSION €€

(☎614 9595; www.villadaffodil.com; Fevzi Çakmak Caddesi 139; s/d TL75/100; ❄ ❄) This large Ottoman-styled and flower-bedecked guest

(€50), and 'night paddling' (€35) under the stars from sunset to midnight.

About 5km northeast of the centre is **Çalış**, a narrow stretch of gravel beach lined with mass-produced hotels, pubs and chip shops and resident British expats. Dolmuşes depart for Çalış (TL1.50, 10 minutes) from the minibus station every five to 10 minutes throughout the day.

Low-key and small, the **Old Turkish Bath** (Tarihi Fethiye Hamamı; ☎614 9318; www.oldturkishbath.com; Hamam Sokak 2; bath & scrub TL30, with massage TL50; ❄7am-midnight) in Paspatur, the oldest section of Fethiye, dates to the 16th century.

🚶 Tours

Many travellers to Fethiye not joining longer cruises opt for the **12-Island Tour** (per person incl lunch TL20-25; ❄10.30am-6pm, mid-Apr–Oct), a boat trip around Fethiye Bay (Fethiye Körfezi). The boats usually stop at five or six islands and cruise by the rest, but either way it's idyllic (if a little crowded.) Travel agencies sell tickets or you can deal directly with the boat companies at the marina. One reliable company based along the promenade is **Kardeşler** (☎0612 4241, 0542 326 2314; muratmelez_kardesler@hotmail.com).

ON THE DEEP BLUE SEA

For many travellers a four-day, three-night cruise on a *gület* (traditional wooden sailing boat) along the Turquoise Coast – known locally as a blue voyage (*mavi yolculuk*) – is the highlight of their trip to Turkey. Usually advertised as a voyage between Fethiye and Olympos, the boats actually start or stop at Demre (Kale) and the trip to/from Olympos (1¼ hours) is by bus. From Fethiye, boats usually call in at Ölüdeniz and Butterfly Valley and stop at Kaş, Kalkan and Kekova, with the final night at Gökkaya Bay opposite the eastern end of Kekova. A less common (but some say prettier) route is between Marmaris and Fethiye.

Food and water (and sometimes soft drink) is usually included in the price, but you have to pay for alcohol. All boats are equipped with showers, toilets and smallish but comfortable double cabins (usually between six and eight of them). Most people sleep on mattresses on deck as the boats are not air-conditioned.

A blue voyage is not cheap – depending on the season, the price is between €135 and €185 – so it makes sense to shop around. Here are some suggestions to avoid getting fleeced:

» Ask for recommendations from other travellers.

» Avoid touts at the bus stations and go straight to agencies (especially those listed below).

» Bargain, but don't necessarily go for the cheapest option because the crew will skimp on food and services.

» Check out your boat (if you are in Fethiye or Marmaris) and ask to see the guest list.

» Ask whether your captain and crew speak English.

» Don't pay until the day you leave, just in case the weather turns foul.

house is one of the few older buildings to survive the earthquake and development. The 28 rooms have stylish furnishings and a homely feel; the best ones (such as room 205) have balconies and sea views. The breakfast terrace in front and decent-sized pool in the back are the centres of activity. Hussein, a retired colonel, is a genial manager.

Yacht Classic Hotel LUXURY HOTEL €€€
(☎612 5067; www.yachtclassichotel.com; Fevzi Çakmak Caddesi; s/d/ste TL150/250/350; P❄@♨) A massive facelift has 'boutiqued' this 36-room hostelry into a symphony in white with all the mod-cons, including just about the most stylish hotel hamam on the Med coast. The large pool terrace overlooking the harbour is a pleasing feature of this efficient and friendly large hotel, but we will fight (and die) for a room on the 3rd or 4th floors with huge terraces above the sea complete with jacuzzi.

Duygu Pension PENSION €
(☎614 3563; www.duygupension.com; Ordu Caddesi 54; s/d/tr TL40/60/90; ❄@♨) Another appealing budget option at the western end of the harbour, the salmon-coloured 'Feeling' has colourful stencils and carpets

brightening up its 10 spiffy rooms. It boasts a small pool and a roof-top terrace with blinding views of the harbour.

Ece Saray Marina & Resort RESORT €€€
(☎612 5005; www.ecesaray.net; 1 Karagözler Mevkii 1; s €90-165, d €100-195, ste €250-350; P❄@♨) Among Fethiye's top (or perhaps over the top) accommodation, the Ece boasts good facilities including 48 well-furnished rooms and suites (with jacuzzis), a large pool, landscaped gardens and a brilliant spa and wellness centre with hamam open to nonguests (TL50). There's also a fabulous sea-facing terrace restaurant.

Hotel Kemal HOTEL €€
(☎614 5010; www.hotelkemal.com; Kordon Gezi Yolu; s/d TL50/80; P❄@) It's four floors tall with no lift, the colour scheme is mud and chocolate, and the lobby – complete with dirty aquarium – feels more East European than western Mediterranean. But it's all about location (repeat, repeat) here and the Kemal is right on the seafront promenade in the centre of town with 21 balconied and very affordable rooms.

» Don't go for gimmicks such as free water sports; they often prove to be empty promises and boats rarely have insurance for them in case of accidents.

» Confirm whether the boat ever actually uses the sails (most don't) rather than relying on a diesel engine.

» Avoid buying your ticket in İstanbul, as pensions and commission agents there take a healthy cut.

» Book well ahead for a cruise in July and August.

We recommend the owner-operated outfits because they run a much tighter ship. Boats depart almost daily between late April and October (the Marmaris boats usually run twice a week from mid-May to the end of September).

Before Lunch Cruises (☎0535 636 0076, 0532 623 4359; www.beforelunch.com) Run out of Fethiye by an experienced Turkish-Australian couple who set their own itinerary; they're more expensive than most but apparently worth it!

Ocean Turizm & Travel Agency (☎0252-612 4807; www.oceantravelagency.com) Based at the marina in Fethiye.

Olympos Yachting (☎0242-892 1145; www.olymposyachting.com) Olympos-based outfit offers a four-day/three-night cruise direct from Olympos beach to Kaş.

V-Go Yachting & Travel Agency (☎0252-612 2113; www.bluecruisesturkey.com) Based in Fethiye with a branch in Olympos.

Yeşil Marmaris Travel & Yachting (☎0252-413 8914; www.yesilmarmaris.com) On the harbour in Marmaris.

Hotel Doruk HOTEL €€
(☎614 9860; www.hoteldoruk.com; Yat Limanı; s/d TL80/120; P❄@≋) Quieter and more private than many places to stay on this stretch, this hotel down a slip road to the marina offers a well-maintained medium-sized pool with a view and even a small cinema. At least half of the 36 rooms have balconies overlooking the bay. Avoid the mansard rooms on the top floor, which get claustrophobic.

Tan Pansiyon PENSION €
(☎614 1584; tanpansiyon@hotmail.com; 30 Sokak 41; s/d TL35/50; ❄) If the backpacker grind wears thin, try this somewhat frayed pension run by a charming family in Karagözler. The nine rooms are small (the bathrooms even smaller), but it's sparkling clean and quiet. It's good also for self-caterers; there's a kitchen on the stunning roof terrace.

✖ Eating

Fethiye's enormous market takes place on Tuesday along the canal between Atatürk Caddesi and Pürşabey Caddesi next to the stadium.

TOP CHOICE Meğri Lokantası LOKANTA €€€
(☎614 4047; www.megrirestaurant.com; Çarşı Caddesi 26; mains TL14-25; ☺8am-2am low season, 8am-4am high season) Looking for us at lunchtime in Fethiye? We're here. Packed with locals who spill onto the streets, the Meğri offers excellent and hearty home-style cooking at very palatable prices. Choose from the huge glass display window of meze and savoury mains or try one of their types of *güveç* (casserole; TL17 to TL20).

Deniz Restaurant SEAFOOD €€
(☎612 0212; Uğur Mumcu Parkı Yanı 10/1; mains TL12-25) Probably the best seafood restaurant in Fethiye away from the market, the 'Sea' exhibits everything alive and swimming in tanks (the grouper is best) and excels in making meze. Try the excellent *semizotu* (purslane) in yoghurt and the *ceviche* (fish preserved in lemon juice).

Paşa Kebab KEBAPÇI €
(☎614 9807; Çarşı Caddesi 42; meze TL4-5, pide TL4.50-8, kebabs TL8.50-10; ☺9am-1am) Considered locally to offer the best kebaps in town, this unpretentious place has a well-priced menu complete with useful

LOCAL KNOWLEDGE

CELAL COŞKUN: CARPET SELLER

Celal Coşkun learned to make carpets and weave kilims at his grandmother's knee in Malatya, before apprenticing himself as a carpet repairer in İstanbul and opening his shop in Fethiye. We asked this 30-year veteran of the trade his top tips on the buying and caring for carpets.

» Know the basics: a carpet is wool or silk pile with single (Persian) or double (Turkish) knots; a kilim is a flat weave and is reversible; a cicim is a kilim with one side embroidered.

» Establish in advance your price range and what you want in terms of size, pattern and colour.

» Deal only with a seller who you feel you can trust, be it through reputation, recommendation or instinct.

» Counting knots is only important on silk-on-silk carpets, though a double-knotted wool carpet will wear better than a single-knotted one.

» Most reputable carpet shops can negotiate discounts of between 5% and 10%, depending on how you may pay; anything higher than that and the price has been inflated.

» To extend the life of a carpet, always remove your shoes when walking over it, and never beat a carpet as this breaks the knots and warp (vertical) and weft (horizontal) threads.

» If professional cleaning is too expensive and the traditional method – washing it with mild soap and water and drying it on wood blocks to allow air to circulate beneath it – is too daunting, lay the carpet face (pattern) side down for a few minutes in fresh snow.

» Anything made by hand – including a carpet – can be repaired by hand.

little photos of dishes. Try the Paşa Special (TL12.50), a gigantic (and delicious) concoction of beef, tomato and cheese. There's also pizza (TL9.50 to TL13.50).

Recep's Place   SEAFOOD €€
(☑614 8297; Hal ve Pazar Yeri 51; mains TL10-20; ☺10am-midnight) One way to taste Fethiye's fabulous fish is to buy your own (per kilo TL18 to TL25) from the circle of fishmongers in the central covered market, then take it to one of the restaurants opposite to have them cook it the way you like it. Our favourite is Recep's, which charges TL5 for cooking the fish, a green salad, bread with garlic butter, a sauce to accompany the fish, fruit and coffee. They also do their own meze and meat dishes.

Pera Restaurant   OCAKBAŞI €€
(☑614 0395; Belediye Caddesi; mains TL10-22; ☺9am-1am) This stylish new kid on the block, with a large open terrace near the market and large outdoor oven, serves excellent meze (TL7 to TL15) as well as grills

and various types of *güveç* ('stews' cooked in an earthenware pot).

Duck Pond   RESTAURANT-BAR €€
(☑614 7429; Eski Cami Sokak 41; mains TL17-25) A lively place surrounded by a pond replete with fountain and a battalion of quacking feathered friends, the Duck Pond serves traditional Turkish food (such as Adana kebap; TL13) that is straightforward and wholesome.

Blue Cafe   CAFE €€
(☑614 4676; www.bluecafeturkey.com; 38 Sokak 4; breakfast TL7-12, dishes TL8-10; ☺8am-midnight; ☎) This bluer-than-blue hideaway with a *trompe l'œil* mural of the sea is famed for its smoothies, pancakes and Marmite toast. There are also good salads and sandwiches. Customers have free wireless access and there's a book exchange.

Nefis Pide   PIDECI €
(☑614 5504; Eski Cami Sokak 9; pide TL4.50-7; ☺9am-midnight) Stark and simple but sparkling clean, this popular place right next

to the mosque (no alcohol) offers delicious pide, pizza and döner.

Taş Fırın
PIDECI, KEBAPÇI €

(☑614 6683; Atatürk Caddesi 150; meals TL6-11; ☺9am-10pm) Opposite the centre's secondary school, the 'Stone Oven' is a hit with locals who chow down on cheap grills and kebaps.

🍸 Drinking & Entertainment

Most serious partygoers in these parts head for Hisarönü, an expat-choked suburb 12km to the southeast, after dark. The lion's share of Fethiye's bars and nightclubs stand cheek-by-jowl along Hamam Sokak, which runs north–south between Karagözler Caddesi and Cumhuriyet Sokak in the old town. Another happy hunting ground for bars is along Dispanser Caddesi, south of the Martyrs' Monument.

Yes Marina Cafe
BAR-CAFE

(☑614 2258; Fevzi Çakmak Caddesi; ☺9am-midnight) There are worse places than this fine cafe and bar with a large sea-facing terrace to while away a lazy sunny afternoon. It's in a small marina in the western harbour.

Val's Cocktail Bar
BAR

(☑612 2363; Uğur Mumcu Parkı Yanı; beer TL5; ☺9am-1am) Englishwoman Val has been keeping the local expat community well informed and happily quenched for a score of years now. Her cute little bar stocks a mean selection of poison and suitably strong coffee, has a free lending library going with more than 2000 books, and hosts a resident grey parrot.

Car Cemetery
CLUB

(☑612 7872; Haman Sokak 25; beer TL5; ☺10am-4am) British boozer–meets–club, this place with the whacko deco and live rock music at the weekend is particularly popular with locals.

Club Rain
CLUB

(☑612 0000; Hamam Sokak; beer TL5; ☺noon-4am) More stylish neighbour of the CC, this new kid in town is trying hard to win the hearts and minds of punters next door.

Club Bananas
CLUB

(☑612 8441; off Hamam Sokak; beer TL7; ☺10pm-5am) Any venue where staff set fire to the bar then dance on it is hard to overlook on a big night out. Bananas is Fethiye's premier party joint – expect foam parties and random remixes.

🛍 Shopping

Sister's Place
HERBALIST

(☑0536 614 3877; Hal ve Pazar Yeri; ☺7.30am-9.30pm, to 5pm in winter Mon-Sat) This tiny Aladdin's Cave of herbs, essential oils and – for real – magic potions is where everyone comes for a cure and a spell. You're in good hands with Nesrin and her brother Tarık – trust us.

Old Orient Carpet & Kilim Bazaar
HOMEWARE, TEXTILES

(☑0532 510 6108; c.c_since.1993@hotmail.com; Karagözler Caddesi 5) As solid as Gibraltar and reliable as rain, this shop is where the discerning buy their carpets and kilims following the sage advice of carpet seller Celal Coşkun.

Uniquecem
JEWELLERY, TEXTILES

(☑612 9515; uniquecem@gmail.com; 37 Sokak 19; ☺9am-8pm) The Unique emporium has two separate stores dedicated to silver, art, fashion and bric-a-brac as well as carpets, quilts and tapestries. Bargain hard.

ℹ Information

Land of Lights (www.landoflights.net) Sometimes useful local English-language freebie newspaper and website.

Millennium Internet Cafe (☑612 8125; 503 Sokak 2/A; per hr TL1.50; ☺8am-midnight) Three dozen computers southeast of the Martyrs' Monument.

Tourist office (☑614 1527; İskele Meydanı; ☺8.30am-7.30pm Mon-Fri, 10am-5pm Sat & Sun May-Sep, 8am-noon & 1-5pm Mon-Fri Oct-Apr) Helpful information centre for town and region opposite the marina.

ℹ Getting There & Away

Fethiye's busy otogar is 2.5km east of the town centre, with a separate station for minibuses 1km east of the centre near the petrol station.

Buses from the otogar go to Antalya (TL25, 7½ hours, 285km) head east along the coast at least every hour in high season, stopping at Kalkan (TL10, 1½ hours, 83km), Kaş (TL12, 2½ hours, 107km) and Olympos (TL22, five hours, 228km). The inland road to Antalya (TL18, four hours, 200km) is much quicker.

Minibuses destined for places in the immediate vicinity depart from the stops near the mosque. Destinations include Faralya (TL5), Göcek (TL4.50), Hisarönü (TL3), Faralya & Kabak (TL5), Kayaköy (TL3.50), Ovacık (TL3), Ölüdeniz (TL4), Saklıkent (TL7) and Tlos (TL5).

Catamarans sail daily to Rhodes in Greece (one-way/same-day return/open-return €58/65/85, 1½ hours) from the pier opposite

Ocean Turizm, where you can buy tickets. They run from mid-April to October, departing from Marmaris at 9am Monday, Tuesday, Thursday and Friday (and sometimes Sunday in high season), returning from Rhodes at 6.30pm.

❶ Getting Around

Minibuses (TL1.50) ply the one-way system along Atatürk Caddesi and up Çarşı Caddesi to the otogar as well as along Fevzi Çakmak Caddesi to the Karagözler pensions and hotels. A taxi from the otogar to the pensions west of the centre costs about TL15.

A couple of agencies along Atatürk Caddesi hire out scooters for between TL25 and TL40 per day.

Ölüdeniz

📞 0252 / POP 2000

With its sheltered (and protected) lagoon beside a lush national park, a long spit of sandy beach and Baba Dağ (Mt Baba) casting its shadow across the sea, Ölüdeniz (*eu*-leu-den-eez), some 15km south of Fethiye, is a tourist association's dream come true. Problem is, like most beautiful destinations, everyone wants to spend time here and a lot of people think package tourism has turned the motionless charms of the 'Dead Sea' into a Paradise Lost. But Ölüdeniz remains a good place to party before continuing on to the less-frenetic Butterfly Valley or Kabak. And it's a good starting point for the wonderful Lycian Way, which runs past some of the nicer hotels, high above the fun and frolic.

Note that the name of the lagoon – Ölüdeniz – is now synonymous with the town. Asking for Belcekız – its official name – might draw a blank, even from locals.

◉ Sights & Activities

Beach & Lagoon   BEACH
The beach is very much the centre of things here; it's at the bottom of the hill past the package-tour colonies of Ovacik and Hisarönü. Near the junction of the road with a *jandarma* post and opposite the PTT is the entrance to Ölüdeniz Tabiat Parkı (Ölüdeniz Nature Park; Ölüdeniz Caddesi; admission TL4; ☺8am-8pm) and its lagoon, still a lovely place to while away a few hours on the beach with mountains soaring above you. There are showers, toilets and cafes.

Boat Trips   CRUISE
Throughout the summer, boats set out to explore the coast, charging about TL20

for a day trip (including lunch). A typical cruise might take in Gemile Bay, the Blue Cave, Butterfly Valley and St Nicholas Island, with some time for swimming included.

Paragliding   PARAGLIDING
If ever you wanted to jump off a 1960m-high cliff, Ölüdeniz and the imposing Baba Dağ is the perfect place for it. The descent from the mountain can take up to 40 minutes, with amazing views over the Blue Lagoon, Butterfly Valley and, on a clear day, as far as Rhodes.

Various companies offer tandem paragliding flights, but prices can vary between TL100 and TL160. Just ensure the company has insurance and the pilot the appropriate qualifications. Parasailing (TL100) in the park is also possible.

🛏 Sleeping

Ölüdeniz's camping grounds are almost like budget resorts, with comfortable and stylish bungalows as well as pitches.

TOP CHOICE Sugar Beach Club
                    CAMPGROUND, RESORT €€
(📞617 0048; www.thesugarbeachclub.com; Ölüdeniz Caddesi 20; camp site per person/car/caravan TL10/10/10, bungalows per person TL50-140; ❄ @) About 500m north of the entrance to the park, this ultra-chilled Turkish-Australian venture is the pick of the crop in Ölüdeniz for backpackers. The design is first class – a strip of beach shaded by palms and lounging areas, with a waterfront bar and restaurant and backed by three dozen colourful bungalows with bathrooms and air-conditioning. Canoes and pedalos can be hired, there's a small shop on-site and special events like barbecues are a regular occurrence. If you're not staying here but want to hang out, it costs TL5 each to use the sun lounges, parasols and showers.

Oyster Residences   BOUTIQUE HOTEL €€€
(📞617 0765; www.oysterresidences.com; 1 Sokak; €110-150, tr €160-200; ❄ @ ≋) This delightful boutique hotel is a mere seven years old but looks a century older. It has 26 bright and airy rooms done up in vaguely neo-colonial style that will have most mortals swooning. The walk-in wardrobes are room-sized, the wooden basins are antique and the French doors open on to lush gardens that creep all the way up to the beach.

Paradise Garden
RESORT €€€

(☑617 0545; www.paradisegardenhotel.com; Ölüdeniz Yolu; s/d €90/130; 🏢 🏊) Situated up the hill to the right before you make the descent some 2km to the centre, this Eden-like place is well named. Set in a 6-hectare garden with three buildings, it boasts spectacular views, two pools (including a natural spring one in the mouth of a cave and one shaped like a heart), a menagerie with peacocks, and a cafe and gourmet restaurant. The 27 rooms are large and very tastefully furnished.

Blue Star Hotel
HOTEL €€

(☑617 0069; www.hotelbluestaroludeniz.com; Mimar Sinan Caddesi 8; s & d TL60-160; 🏢 @ 🏊) Quite attractively designed and well maintained, this place is 60m from the beach. Though they're not large, the 38 rooms shared by three buildings are light, bright and airy and have balconies overlooking the pool.

Sultan Motel
HOTEL €€

(☑616 6139; www.sultanmotel.com; s/d TL40/80; 🏢 🏊) Just off the main road on the left as you descend from Hisarönü (some 3km from Ölüdeniz), the Sultan is at a trailhead of the Lycian Way and is a favourite of walkers and trekkers. Its 16 rooms, eight of which have recently been renovated, are in stone chalets. Some have excellent views down to Ölüdeniz. Good home cooking available.

Seahorse Beach Club
CAMPGROUND, RESORT €€

(☑617 0123; www.seahorsebeachclub.com; Ölüdeniz Caddesi; camp site per person TL15-20, caravan d TL80-140; 🏢) Just next door to the Sugar Beach but light years away in terms of style and comfort, this camping ground has two dozen blue-and-white caravans with all the mod-cons, a restaurant and bar in a lofted wooden cabin and a beach a very short stroll away. The manager will consider discounts for longer stays.

✖ Eating & Drinking

Oba Motel Restaurant
FAMILY RESTAURANT €€

(☑617 0158; Mimar Sinan Caddesi; mains TL15-25; ⊗8am-midnight) Housed in a log cabin, the restaurant of the leafy Oba Motel has a great reputation for home-style food at palatable prices. It also does great Turkish/European breakfasts (TL10/12) including homemade muesli with mountain yoghurt and local pine honey. The menu offers everything from snacks to full-on mains, including six veggie dishes.

Buzz Beach Bar & Seafood Grill
INTERNATIONAL €€€

(☑617 0526; www.buzzbeachbar.com; 1 Sokak 1; mains TL17.50-28.50; ⊗restaurant 8am-midnight, bar noon-2am) With a commanding position on the waterfront, this two-level place offers a wide menu from pasta and kebaps to fillet steak and seafood. At lunch time you can watch the microlights plop down on the landing point outside.

Club Belcekız Beach
ASIAN €€

(☑617 0077; www.belcekiz.com; mains TL12-21; ⊗7-11pm) Set on a stunning terrace overlooking the sea, the flagship restaurant at this gigantic resort serves a potpourri of cuisines, including Indian and Thai, but by all accounts is more successful with the second. Multicourse set meals are TL47.

Help Lounge Bar
BAR

(☑617 0650; 1 Sokak; beer TL5; ⊗9am-4am) The most happening place in town, this funky joint has a large terrace with a bar right on the seafront with comfy cushioned benches, colourful murals on the walls and the front end of a Chevy coming through the wall. Happy hour (cocktails TL10) is from 5pm to 8pm and again from 10.30pm till midnight.

ℹ Information

Tourist office (☑617 0438; www.oludeniz.com.tr; Ölüdeniz Caddesi 32; ⊗8.30am-11pm Jun-Sep, to 5pm Oct-Apr) Helpful information booth and booking service on the road into town.

ℹ Getting There & Away

In high season, minibuses leave Fethiye (TL4, 25 minutes, 15km) for Ölüdeniz roughly every seven minutes during the day and every 10 minutes at night, passing through Ovacık and Hisarönü. In low season they go every 15 to 20 minutes by day and hourly at night. You can reach Faralya and Kabak on six minibuses a day in summer. A taxi to Kayaköy costs TL30. To Fethiye it's TL35 to TL40.

Kayaköy

☑0252 / POP 2000

About 14km south of Fethiye is Kayaköy (ancient Karmylassos), an eerie ghost town of 4000-odd abandoned stone houses and other structures that once made up the Greek town of Levissi and now form an open-air museum (admission TL8; ⊗8.30am-7pm May-Oct, 8am-6pm Nov-Apr) dedicated to Turkish-Greek peace and cooperation.

Levissi was deserted by its mostly Greek inhabitants in the general exchange of populations supervised by the League of Nations in 1923 after the Turkish War of Independence. Most Greek Muslims came from Greece to Turkey and most Ottoman Christians moved from coastal Turkey to Greece. The people of Levissi, who were Orthodox Christians, were moved to the outskirts of Athens where they established Nea Levissi (New Levissi). The abandoned town was the inspiration for Eskibahçe, the setting of Louis de Bernières' highly successful 2004 novel, *Birds Without Wings*.

As there were far more Ottoman Greeks than Greek Muslims, many Turkish towns were left unoccupied after the population exchange and Kayaköy, or Kaya as it is known locally, was badly damaged by earthquake in 1957.

With the tourism boom of the 1980s, a development company wanted to restore Kayaköy's stone houses and turn the town into a holiday village. Scenting money, the local inhabitants were delighted, but Turkish artists and architects were alarmed and saw to it that the Ministry of Culture declared Kayaköy a historic monument, safe from unregulated development. What remains is a timeless village set in a lush valley with some fine vineyards nearby. In the evening, when the stone houses are spotlit, Kayaköy is truly surreal.

There's not a whole lot to see but two **churches** are still prominent: the Kataponagia in the lower part of the town and the Taxiarkis further up the slope. Both retain some of their painted decoration and black-and-white pebble mosaic floors. There's an **ossuary** with the mouldering remains of the long-dead in the churchyard behind the former.

🛏 Sleeping & Eating

Villa Rhapsody   HOTEL **€€**
(📞618 0042; www.villarhapsody.com; s/d TL55/80; ❄❄) This welcoming place has 16 comfortable rooms with balconies overlooking a delightful walled garden and a swimming pool. Atilla and Jeanne, the Turkish-Dutch owners, can offer local advice and sketch maps for walking in the area as well as organise bike hire. Set meals are available on request (T25 to TL35).

Doğa Apartments   APARTMENT **€€**
(📞618 0373; www.dogaapartments.com; apt TL180; ❄❄) Just 200m from the entrance to the abandoned village, the six self-contained apartments at the 'Natural' are

housed in two old farm buildings, one of which dates back two and a half centuries. They're well equipped, with bedroom, living room with sofa bed and kitchen, and sleep up to four. The poolside bar is a delight, especially in the evening.

Selçuk Pension   PENSION **€**
(📞618 0075, 0535 275 6706; enginselcuk48@hotmail.com; s/d/apt TL30/50/80; ❄) Set amid flower and vegetable gardens, the Selçuk has a dozen rooms that are frayed but spotless, quite spacious and homely; four have lovely views of abandoned Kaya. Guests can use the swimming pool of the nearby İstanbul restaurant and the affable owner Engin is eager to please.

TOP / CHOICE **Levissi Garden**   MODERN TURKISH **€€**
(📞618 0108; www.levissigarden.com; Eski Köy Sokak; mains TL12-26) This 400-year-old stone building has been everything from a mayor's residence to a horse stables and now houses a stunning wine house and restaurant, with a cellar that stocks thousands of bottles of Turkey's finest drops. From its original stone oven, the Levissi produces a slow-cooked lamb stew (TL30) and mouthwatering *klevtiko* (leg of lamb cooked in red wine, garlic and herbs; TL30), and some of the meze (TL8) are unique.

Cin Bal   KEBAPÇI **€€**
(📞618 0066; www.cinbal.com; mains TL10-18; ⏰11am-midnight) Kayaköy's most celebrated grill restaurant specialises in lamb *tandır* (clay oven) dishes and kebaps, seats 300 people both inside and in its garden courtyard, and is always heaving. It's down the lane from the abandoned village just before the Doğa Apartments.

İstanbul Restaurant   FAMILY RESTAURANT **€€**
(📞618 0148; mains TL12-20; ⏰8am-midnight) Run by the same people who own the Selçuk Pension, this place serves up excellent homestyle grills and meze made from the produce of the surrounding vegetable patches and orchards. It's a delightful spot for dinner and the traditional Turkish dishes are delicious.

ℹ Getting There & Away

Minibuses run to Fethiye (TL3.50, 20 to 30 minutes, 14km) every half-hour or so from mid-June to September and every hour in low season. A taxi there costs TL30.

Two or three daily minibuses go to Hisarönü (TL3.50, 20 minutes, 6km) from where minibuses leave every 10 minutes for Ölüdeniz.

It's about a one-hour walk downhill through pine forest from Hisarönü to Kayaköy. You can also follow a very pretty trail to Ölüdeniz that takes two to 2½ hours (8km).

Butterfly Valley & Faralya

Tucked away on the Yedi Burun (Seven Capes) coast a dozen or so kilometres from Ölüdeniz is the village of Faralya (also called Uzunyurt) and below that the paradise-found of Butterfly Valley, where mellow young Turks lounge about in hammocks and curious day-trippers wish they'd packed an overnight bag. As well as being home to the unique Jersey tiger butterfly, from where it takes its name, the valley also has a fine beach, some lovely walks through a lush gorge and new yoga and dive centres.

There are two ways to reach Butterfly Valley: via boat from Ölüdeniz or on foot via a very steep path that wends its way down a cliff from Faralya. If you choose the latter, be sure to wear proper shoes and keep to the marked trail (indicated with painted red dots). It usually takes 30 to 45 minutes to descend and closer to an hour to come back up. There are fixed ropes along the path in the steepest or most dangerous parts. Faralya is on a stage of the Lycian Way (p29).

🛏 Sleeping

Accommodation in **Butterfly Valley** (Kelebekler Vadisi; ☑0555 632 0236; www.kelebekler vadisi.org; with half-board per person tent TL38, dormitory & bungalow TL48) itself is simple: tent pitches and stilted bungalows with thin mattresses on the floor. Be warned that these rooms bake during the summer. For those who prefer their creature comforts, the following places are all above the valley in Faralya.

George House   PENSION, CAMPGROUND €
(☑642 1102; www.georgehousefaralya.com; with half-board per person tent TL20, bungalow with/ without bathroom TL40/30; ✳ @ ☀) Now run by the eponymous George's enthusiastic son Hassan, this Faralya institution offers mattresses in the main house with facilities in basic bungalows and on tented platforms. The home cooking is delicious and ingredients come fresh from the family's garden. It has a spring water source and lovely pool and is right at the start of the path leading down to Butterfly Valley.

Melisa Pansiyon   PENSION €€
(☑642 1012; www.melisapension.com; s/d TL40/80; ✳) Offering as warm a welcome as you'll find anywhere along the coast, the Melisa has four well-maintained and cheerful rooms, a pretty garden and vine-bedecked terrace overlooking the valley. The owner, Mehmet, speaks English and is a good source of local information. Home-cooked vegetarian/meat-based meals (TL15/25) are offered.

Onur Motel   APARTMENT €€
(☑642 1162; www.onurmotelfaralya.com; half-board per person TL40-50; ✳ ☀) This new place above the road gets rave reviews from readers. Accommodation is in seven modern and very stylish bungalows on a hill at the end of town on the road to Kabak; the choicest ones are the three fronting the street. Excellent food, nice garden with pool.

Die Wassermühle   LUXURY HOTEL €€€
(The Watermill; ☑642 1245; www.natur-reisen.de; half-board per person €53-69; ☀) This unbearably tasteful resort property, owned by a German-Turkish couple, is hidden within a wooded slope to the left as you enter Faralya and is the coolest (in both senses) place around. The nine 'suites' contained within a 150-year-old mill and newer building are spacious, have kitchenettes and use all-natural materials; the views from the restaurant and pool terraces are commanding and the sound of rushing water hypnotic.

❶ Getting There & Away

You can take a tour of Butterfly Valley from Fethiye or Ölüdeniz, or take the shuttle boat (TL15 return), which departs from Ölüdeniz daily at 11am, 2pm and 6pm (with additional sailings at noon, 4pm and 7pm mid-June to mid-September). The boat is a good option if you want to spend the night. From Butterfly Valley back to Ölüdeniz, it leaves at 9.30am, 1pm and 5pm (and, in season, at 10.30am, 2.30pm and 6pm as well).

Six daily minibuses (TL5, 35 minutes, 26km) in summer (three in spring and two in winter) link Fethiye and Faralya via Ölüdeniz. If you should miss the bus, a taxi back to Fethiye should cost between TL35 and TL40.

Kabak

☑0252

The remote beach community of Kabak is slowly becoming the solitude-searchers' end point and many think it even more heavenly than Butterfly Valley. Regardless of how you make the steep trek downward to Kabak – by tractor (10 minutes) or on foot (20 minutes) – you'll be rewarded with a spectacular and empty beach flanked by two long cliffs. Eight kilometres south of Faralya – and worlds away from everywhere else – Kabak is for the camping and trekking enthusiast, yoga devotee or any fan of quiet, untapped beauty.

This area is on a section of the Lycian Way walk, described on p29.

🛏 Sleeping

Accommodation in Kabak consists of camping or tented platforms and bungalows. All include half-board in the price – there are no restaurants as such on Gemile Beach, only on the road to/from Faralya. Most camps open from May to October and will organise tractor transport (phone, email or text ahead).

Turan Hill Lounge CAMPGROUND €€
(☑642 1227; www.turancamping.com; with half-board d bungalow without bathroom TL80-110, with bathroom TL120-160, boutique TL160-240; @☒) The first accommodation to open in Kabak and still the trendsetter, this recently renamed place is seamlessly run by Ahmet and his dynamic wife Ece, who fell for the place on a holiday here. The Turan has 17 very different bungalows (including four beautiful decorated and furnished 'boutique' ones) as well as a half-dozen unusual tent platforms – one has a tree growing in the centre. It also has lovely views and lots of mellow lounging areas. Yoga courses are held regularly on the enormous platform in the valley below. Meals (mainly veg) are prepared with produce from the adjoining garden.

Reflections Camp CAMPGROUND €€
(☑642 1020; www.reflectionscamp.com; with half-board per person own tent/camp tent/bungalow TL35/40/55; @) Built from scratch and an 'ongoing project' for American Chris, this comfortable place with pitches and 11 bungalows (including two built of bamboo within the trees) gazes upon the surrounding forest. One toilet, with a 'living' roof planted with ferns and ginger plants, boasts one of the best 'seated' views in Turkey. No rooms have en suites.

Kabak Natural Life CAMPGROUND €€
(☑642 1185; www.kabaknaturallife.com; r per person TL35-70, with half-board TL50-100; @☒)

This long-time player has a mix of 20-odd bungalows (some stilted, some with bathrooms, others with lofts) spread over a large terraced area. There's a lovely pool fed with mountain spring water, platforms that have delightful little cushioned 'verandas' for chilling out, two kitchens and a popular bar.

Shambala CAMPGROUND €€
(☑642 1147; www.theshambala.com; with half-board per person Indian tent TL30-40, tree house TL50-85, bungalow TL60-180; @☒) Perhaps a titch too slick for some travellers, this vaguely Indian-themed place halfway down the valley has 17 bungalows in three categories, including some that are verging on the luxurious. Those on a stricter budget will opt for the spacious tree houses and breezy Indian tents with the ultimate sea view. There's also a swimming pool, bar, chilled-out hammocks for relaxing and a centre for 'shamanic healing' therapy.

🍴 Eating

Above Kabak, near the dolmuş stop and the end of the main road, are a couple of decent restaurants.

Olive Garden LOCAL €€
(☑642 1083; www.olivegardenkabak.com; meze TL6-10, mains TL13-16) Oozing with charm, the Olive Garden can be found down a side road 100m beyond Mamma's. With gorgeous views from the cosy hillside platforms, it's a wonderful place for a meal and is run by the affable Fatih, a former chef. Many of the ingredients come from his family's 15 hectares of fruit trees, olive groves and vegetable gardens. If you can't tear yourself away – it's on the Lycian Way and popular with trekkers – it has nine spic-and-span wooden cabins (TL50 per person with half-board).

Mamma's Restaurant FAMILY RESTAURANT €
(☑642 1071; mains TL7-10) Mamma's offers a couple of simple but hearty dishes as well as gözleme (TL3) and its own deliciously refreshing home-brewed ayran (yoghurt drink; TL2).

ℹ Getting There & Away

The twisting road from Faralya is as memorable for its views as for its knuckle-whitening corners. There are eight daily minibuses to/from Fethiye (TL5) between 8.30am and 8.30pm.

Tlos

📞 0252

On a rocky outcrop high above a pastoral plain, Tlos was one of the most important cities of ancient Lycia. Its prominence was matched only by its promontory; so effective was its elevated position that the well-guarded city remained inhabited until the early 19th century.

As you climb the winding road to the **ruins** (admission TL8; ⏱ 8.30am-8.30pm May-Oct, 8am-6pm Nov-Apr), look for the **acropolis** topped with an **Ottoman fortress** on the right. Beneath it, reached by narrow paths, are **rock tombs**, including that of the warrior Bellerophon. It has a temple-like facade carved into the rock face and to the left a fine bas-relief of our hero riding Pegasus, the winged horse.

The **theatre** is 100m further up the road from the ticket kiosk. It's in excellent condition, with most of its marble seating intact, although the stage wall is gone; look among the rubble of the stage building for blocks carved with an eagle and garlands. Off to the right of the theatre (as you sit in the centre rows) is an ancient **Lycian sarcophagus** in a farmer's field. Just across the road are ruins of the ancient **baths** (note the apothecary symbol carved on an outer wall).

Set in a pretty garden with a stream, a pool, lots of shade, seating areas and birdsong, **Mountain Lodge** (📞 638 2515; www.tlosmountainlodge.com; r per person €24-36; ❄ @ ☎) is a peaceful and attractive place with accommodation in four buildings designed to look like old stone houses. The eight themed rooms (think birds) are comfy and homely (rates vary according to size and position), each has a balcony or veranda and there is a pool set on a terrace with views. The charming Mel (short for Melahat) offers three-course home-cooked set menus (TL25) and makes her own oil, jams and bread.

From the theatre, it lies 2km back down the road to the right. If coming by minibus, get off at the village of Güneşli, and walk or hitch the 2km up the road to Yaka Köyü.

ℹ Getting There & Away

From Fethiye, minibuses travel to Saklıkent (TL7, 45 minutes) every 20 minutes via Güneşli, the jumping-off point for Tlos.

Saklıkent Gorge

📞 0252

This spectacular 18km-long gorge (adult/student high season TL4/2, low season free; ⏱ 8am-8pm) is literally a crack in the Akdağlar, the mountains towering to the northeast. Some 12km after the turn-off to Tlos heading south, the gorge is too narrow in places for even sunlight to squeeze through. Luckily you can, but prepare yourself for some very cold water year-round.

You approach the gorge along a wooden boardwalk towering above the river. On wooden platforms suspended above the water, you can relax, drink tea and eat fresh trout while watching other tourists slip and slide their way across the river, hanging onto a rope, and then drop into the gorge proper. Good footwear is essential, though plastic shoes can be rented (TL3). Guides can also be hired and it's a good place to try tubing (TL15).

Across the river from the car park is **Saklıkent Gorge Club** (📞 659 0074; www.gorgeclub.com; camp site TL20, dm on platform half-board TL25, tree house s/d TL35/60; @ ☎), a rustic backpacker-oriented camp with basic but actual tree houses (all have little fridges), a pool, bar and restaurant. All bathrooms are shared.

The club can organise various activities (which include transfer and drinks) such as rafting (TL30/60 for 45 minutes/three hours), canyoning (TL20/100/200 for trips of three hours/one day/two days and one night, minimum four people), fishing (TL10 including guide and equipment, two hours), and trekking (TL10, three hours). Also offered are jeep safaris (TL50 including lunch and guide) and tours of Tlos and Patara (TL20 each).

Along the road between Tlos and Saklıkent and near the village of Kadıköy is the **Saklıkent Carpet Weavers' Association** (📞 636 8790), with demonstrations of carpet weaving techniques, the harvesting of silk and the dying of threads.

ℹ Getting There & Away

Minibuses run every 20 minutes or so between Fethiye and Saklıkent (TL7, one hour).

Pınara

Some 46km southeast of Fethiye, before the village of Eşen, is a turn-off to the right for Pınara and its spectacular **ruins** (admission

The Lycian civilisation was based in the Teke peninsula, the bump of land jutting out into the sea and stretching from Dalyan in the west to Antalya in the east.

The Lycians date back to at least the 12th century BC, but they first appear in writing in the *Iliad* when Homer records their presence during an attack on Troy. It is thought they may have been descended from the Lukkans, a tribe allied with the ancient Hittites. A matrilineal people, they spoke their own unique language, which has still not been fully decoded.

By the 6th century BC the Lycians had come under the control of the Persian Empire. Thus began a changing of the guard that occurred as regularly as today's at Buckingham Palace. The Persians gave in to the Athenians who were defeated in turn by Alexander the Great, the Ptolemaic Kingdom in Egypt and then Rhodes.

Lycia was granted independence by Rome in 168 BC and it immediately established the Lycian League, a loose confederation of 23 fiercely independent city-states. Six of the largest city-states (Xanthos, Patara, Pınara, Tlos, Myra and Olympos) held three votes each, the others just one or two. The Lycian League is often cited as the first proto-democratic union in history.

Peace held for over a century but in 42 BC the league made the unwise decision not to pay tribute to Brutus, the murderer of Caesar, whom Lycia had supported during the Civil War. With his forces, Brutus besieged Xanthos and, determined not to surrender, the city-state's outnumbered population committed mass suicide.

Lycia recovered under the Roman Empire but in AD 43 all of Lycia was annexed to the neighbouring province of Pamphylia, a union that lasted until the 4th century when it became part of Byzantium.

Lycia left behind very little in the way of material culture or written documents. What it did bequeath to posterity, however, was some of the most stunning funerary monuments from ancient times. Cliff tombs, 'house' tombs, sepulchres and sarcophagi – the peninsula's mountains and valleys are littered with them and most are easily accessible on foot and by car.

TL8; ☉8.30am-8.30pm May-Oct, to 5pm Nov-Apr), which lie another 6km up in the mountains.

Pınara was one of the six most important cities in ancient Lycia, but although the site is vast the actual ruins are not the region's most impressive. Instead it's the sheer splendour and isolation that makes the site worth visiting.

Rising high above the site is a sheer column of rock honeycombed with **rock tombs**; archaeologists are still debating as to how and why they were cut here. Other tombs are within the ruined city itself. The one to the southeast called the **Royal Tomb** has particularly fine reliefs, including several showing walled Lycian cities. Pınara's **theatre** is in good condition, but its **odeion** and **temple** to Aphrodite (with heart-shaped columns) are badly ruined. Note the enormous phallus, a kind of early graffiti, carved on the steps of the latter.

The road winds through citrus orchards and across irrigation channels for 4km to just before the village of Minare, then takes a sharp left turn to climb the steep slope for another 2km.

Along the main road just opposite the turn-off to the ruins is Clos Pınara (☎637 1203; www.clospinara.com; ☉9am-5pm Mon-Sat), one of a handful of vineyards along the Turkish Mediterranean coast making a name for itself. It is open for tours and tastings.

Infrequent minibuses from Fethiye (TL4, one hour) drop you at the start of the Pınara road and you can walk to the site (take sufficient water) or try to hitch a ride. The village at Eşen, 3km southeast of the Pınara turn-off, has a few basic restaurants.

Letoön

Sharing a place with the Lycian capital Xanthos on Unesco's World Heritage List, Letoön is home to some of the finest ruins (admission TL5; ☉8.30am-8.30pm May-Oct, 9am-5.30pm Nov-Apr) on the Lycian Way. Located about 17km south of the Pınara turn-off, this former religious centre is often considered a double-site with Xanthos but Letoön has its own romantic charm.

Letoön takes its name and importance from a large shrine to Leto who, according to legend, was loved by Zeus and became the mother of Apollo and Artemis. Unimpressed, Zeus's wife Hera commanded that Leto spend an eternity wandering from country to country. According to local folklore she spent much of this time in Lycia and became the Lycian national deity; the federation of Lycian cities then built this very impressive religious sanctuary to worship her.

The site consists of three **temples** standing side by side and dedicated to Apollo (on the left), Artemis (in the middle) and Leto (on the right and now partially reconstructed). The Apollo temple has a fine mosaic showing a lyre, a bow and arrow and floral centre. The permanently saturated **nymphaeum** (ornamental fountain with statues), inhabited by frogs (said to be the shepherds who refused Leto a drink from the fountain), is appropriate as worship of Leto was associated with water. To the north is a large Hellenistic **theatre** in excellent condition.

❶ Getting There & Away

Minibuses run from Fethiye via Eşen to Kumluova (TL6.50, 60km, 65 minutes). Get out at the Letoön turn-off and walk with your thumb sticking out in hope.

If driving from Pınara, the turn-off is near the village of Kumluova. Turn right off the highway, go 4km and bear right at the signpost 'Letoön/Karadere'. After another 3.5km, turn left at the T-junction, then right after 100m (this turn is easy to miss) and proceed a kilometre to the site through fertile fields and orchards and hectares of poly-tunnels full of tomato plants.

Xanthos

At Kınık, 63km from Fethiye, the road crosses a river. Up on a rock outcrop is the ruined city of Xanthos (admission TL3; ☺9am-7.30pm May-Oct, 8am-5pm Nov-Apr), once the capital and grandest city of Lycia, with a fine **Roman theatre** and pillar **tombs**.

It's a short uphill walk to the site past the city gates and the plinth where the fabulous **Nereid Monument** (now in the British Museum in London) once stood. For all its grandeur, Xanthos had a che-

quered history of wars and destruction. Several times, when besieged by clearly superior enemy forces, the city was destroyed by its own inhabitants, who committed mass suicide.

You'll see the Roman theatre with the **agora** opposite the open car park but the **acropolis** is badly ruined. As many of the finest sculptures (eg the **Harpies Monument**) and inscriptions were carted off to London in 1842, most of the inscriptions and decorations you see today are copies of the originals.

Follow the path in front of the ticket office to the east along the colonnaded street to find the attractive **Dancers' Sarcophagus** and **Lion Sarcophagus** as well as some excellent **rock tombs**.

Minibuses run to Xanthos from Fethiye (TL7, one hour, 63km) and some long-distance buses may stop along the highway if you ask.

Patara

☎0242 / POP 945

Patara can claim Turkey's longest uninterrupted beach as well as some of Lycia's finest ruins; its village, laid-back little Gelemiş, is the perfect spot to mix ruin-rambling with some dedicated sand-shuffling. Once very much on the hippy trail, Gelemiş is almost never filled with travellers these days – a miracle given its obvious charms – and traditional village life still goes on.

Patara's lofty place in history is well documented. It was the birthplace of St Nicholas, the 4th-century Byzantine bishop of Myra who later passed into legend as Santa Claus. Before that, Patara was celebrated for its temple and oracle of Apollo, of which little remains. It was Lycia's major port – which explains the large storage granary still standing – and, according to Acts 21:1–2, Sts Paul and Luke changed boats here while on their third mission from Rhodes to Phoenicia.

◎ Sights & Activities

Ruins RUINS
From the highway turn-off, Gelemiş is 2km to the south and it's another 1.5km to the ruins (admission TL5; ☺9am-7.30pm May-Oct, 8am-5pm Nov-Apr), which includes admission to the beach and is valid for one week. You'll pass under a 2nd-century triple-arched **triumphal arch** at the entrance to the site with a necropolis containing a number of **Lycian**

tombs nearby. Next is a **baths complex** and the remains of a **Byzantine basilica**.

You can climb to the top of the **theatre** for a view of the site; note the stones at orchestra level carved with gladiator paraphernalia. On top of the hill to the south are the foundations of a Temple of Athena and an unusual circular **cistern**, cut into the rock with a pillar in the middle.

Just north of the theatre is the **bouleuterion**, ancient Patara's 'city hall' now slated for a TL6 million reconstruction, and the **colonnaded agora**. The latter leads to a dirt track and a **lighthouse**, only recently discovered and excavated. Across the ancient harbour (now a reedy wetland) is the enormous **Granary of Hadrian** and a Corinthian-style **temple-tomb**. The admission fee for the ruins allows you to enter for a week if you are staying in Gelemiş.

Beach
BEACH
Backed by large sand dunes, this splendid 18km-long sandy beach is unique for the region. You can get here by following the road for a kilometre past the ruins, or by turning right at the Golden Pension and following the track waymarked with blue arrows, which heads for the sand dunes along the western side of the archaeological zone. Between late May and October, local minibuses (TL1.50) trundle down to the beach from the village.

On the beach, which is never crowded (even in the height of the season), you can rent umbrellas (TL4) and sunbeds (TL3) and there is a refreshment stand providing shade and sustenance. Depending on the season, parts of the beach are off-limits as it is an important nesting ground for sea turtles. It always closes at dusk and camping is prohibited.

Activities
ACTIVITIES
Kirca Travel (☑843 5298; www.pataracanoeing.com), based at the Flower Pension, specialises in six-hour canoeing trips (TL40) on the Xanthos River but also offers three-hour horse-riding trips (TL70) through the Patara dunes, including lunch. If you'd like to tour the dunes, Xanthos and the Saklıkent Gorge at greater speed and on four wheels, talk to **Patara Jeep Safari** (☑843 5214; www.patarajeepsafari.com; tours TL50).

🛏 Sleeping
As you come into Gelemiş the hillside on your left contains various hotels and pensions. A turn to the right at the Golden Pen-

sion takes you to the village centre, across the valley and up the other side to more pensions.

Patara View Point Hotel
HOTEL €€
(☑843 5184; www.pataraviewpoint.com; s/d TL60/90; ❀@☒) Up the hill from the main road, the *très* stylish Patara View (owner Muzaffer was a French teacher) has a nice swimming pool, an Ottoman-style cushioned terrace, 27 rooms with balconies and, as its name suggests, killer views over the valley. You'll find old farm implements – heirlooms from Muzaffer's grandmother – both inside and out, including a 2000-year-old olive press. There's a tractor-shuttle to and from the beach daily at 10am and 3pm.

Flower Pension
PENSION €
(☑843 5164; www.pataraflowerpension.com; s/d TL20/40, 2-/3-person apt TL50/60; ❀@) On the road before the turn to the centre, the Flower has nine simple and airy rooms with balconies overlooking the garden as well as four kitchen-equipped studios and apartments accommodating four to six people. There's a free shuttle to the beach and owner Deputy Mayor Mustafa and son Bekir are fonts of local information.

Akay Pension
PENSION €
(☑843 5055; www.pataraakaypension.com; s/d/tr TL35/50/60; ❀@) Run by keen-to-please Kazım and his wife, Ayşe, the Akay has 13 very well-maintained rooms and comfortable beds with balconies overlooking citrus groves. Ayşe's cooking is legendary; sample at least one set meal (from TL15) while here.

Golden Pension
PENSION €
(☑843 5162; www.pataragoldenpension.com; s/d TL35/50; ❀@) With 15 homely rooms (all with balconies) and a friendly owner (Arif, the village mayor), Patara's original pension is peaceful despite its very central location on a crossroads. Day-long boat trips are available for TL40 and there's a popular restaurant with a pretty shaded terrace.

Zeybek 2 Pension
PENSION €
(☑843 5086; www.zeybek2pension.com; s/d TL30/50; ❀@) This family-run pension with a slightly rural feel has a dozen clean and sunny rooms with balconies and bedecked with traditional rugs. For the best view in town, climb up to the roof terrace that boasts 360-degree vistas of the hills and the ancient harbour. To reach the Zeybek, follow the road past the Lazy Frog restaurant and up the hill.

Hotel Sema
HOTEL €

(☏843 5114; hotelsema@hotmail.com; s/d TL30/40, apt TL80; 🅿 @) The Sema is not the most luxurious hotel around, but it's ideal for those who want to spend time with warm locals like Ali and Hanife, the proprietors. The large hotel sits in a garden 60 steep steps above the town where the dozen rooms and studios are basic but spotless, cool and mosquito-free.

✖ Eating & Drinking

Tlos Restaurant
FAMILY RESTAURANT €€

(☏843 5135; meze €5, mains €12-20; ⊗8am-midnight) Run by the moustached and smiling chef-owner Osman, the Tlos has an open kitchen by the centre and is shaded by a large plane tree. The *guveç* (TL12), Turkish goulash for lack of a better term, is recommended. It's BYO.

Lumiere
INTERNATIONAL €€

(☏843 5091; www.hotellumiere.com; mains TL18-25) This rather incongruous hotel restaurant on the main road into town has a French name and a yin-yang logo, and serves international and Turkish favourites cooked to order by owner Ferda. It's the most stylish place in Gelemiş.

Lazy Frog
LOCAL, INTERNATIONAL €€

(☏843 5160; mains TL15-25; ⊗8am-2am) With its very own kitchen garden, this central, popular place offers steaks as well as various vegetarian options and *gözleme* on its relaxing terrace.

Medusa Bar
BAR

(☏843 5193; beer TL5; ⊗9am-3am) Laid-back with cushioned benches and walls hung with old photos and posters, the Medusa plays music until the wee hours.

Gypsy Bar
BAR

(beer TL5; ⊗9am-3am) Tiny but traditional and much loved locally, the Gypsy has live Turkish music from 10pm every Monday, Wednesday and Saturday.

❶ Getting There & Away

Buses on the Fethiye–Kaş route drop you on the highway 4km from the village. From here dolmuşes run to the village every 45 minutes to an hour.

In season, minibuses depart from the beach via Gelemiş to Fethiye (TL10, 1½ hours, 73km), Kalkan (TL5, 20 minutes, 15km) and Kaş (TL8, 45 minutes, 40km). There's a daily departure to Saklıkent Gorge (TL10, one hour, 52km).

Kalkan
☏0242 / POP 3600

Kalkan is a well-heeled harbour town built largely on hills that look down on an almost perfect bay. It's as justly famous for its excellent restaurants as its small but central beach. Be warned that Kalkan is far more touristed, expat and expensive than most other places on the coast, including neighbouring Kaş.

Once the Greek fishing village of Kalamaki, Kalkan is now largely devoted to high-end tourism. Development continues up the hills, with scores of new villas appearing each season, but look for Kalkan's charms in the compact old town.

Most people use Kalkan as a base to visit the Lycian ruins or engage in the many activities in the surrounding area. But it's an excellent place for a day-long boat trip – a good choice is Ali Eğriboyun's **Anıl Boat** (⊗844 3030, 0533 351 7520; jacksonvictoria@ hotmail.com), which costs TL35 to TL40 per person (or TL350 for the boat), including an excellent lunch. Apart from the beach near the marina and **Kaputaş**, a perfect little sandy cove with a beach about 7km east of Kalkan on the road to Kaş, options for getting wet include **swimming platforms** at various hotels and pensions such as the Caretta Boutique Hotel and Hotel Villa Mahal, open to the public for a nominal fee.

🛏 Sleeping

With private villas the dominant form of accommodation here and many of the hotels block-booked by travel agencies and wholesalers, Kalkan doesn't offer the wide range of places to stay usually found in Turkish resort towns. The season here is May to October.

TOP CHOICE **Hotel Villa Mahal**
LUXURY HOTEL €€€

(☏844 3268; www.villamahal.com; d €180-290, ste €340; 🅿 ▨) One of the most elegant and stylish hotels in Turkey lies atop a cliff on the western side of Kalkan Bay, about 2km by road from town. The 13 rooms, all individually designed in whiter-than-white minimalist fashion with azure splashes here and there, have breathtaking views of the water and sunsets from the walls of windows that give on to private terraces. The sail-shaped infinity pool is spectacularly suspended on the edge of the void but a mere 180 steps will take you to the sea and a bathing platform. There's a free water

ANTALYA & THE WESTERN MEDITERRANEAN

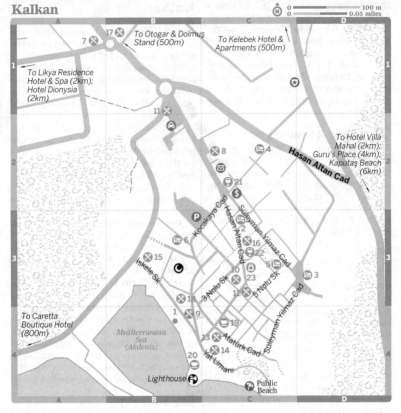

taxi into the centre; a normal taxi to/from Kalkan costs about TL15.

Caretta Boutique Hotel
HOTEL €€

(844 3435; www.carettaboutiquehotel.com; İskele Sokak 3; s TL80-100, d TL120-150; ❄ @) A perennial local favourite for its isolated swimming platforms and excellent home-style cooking, the Caretta has metamorphosed from pension caterpillar to boutique butterfly with 13 bright and sunny rooms, some with jacuzzi. For a total away-from-it-all experience, try to nab one of the two rooms away from the main house and down the steps along the cliff. There's free boat service from below the lighthouse in the marina, saving you from a long trek down a dirt road to this relatively isolated hotel.

White House Pension
PENSION €€

(844 3738; www.kalkanwhitehouse.co.uk; 5 Nolu Sokak; s TL50-60, d 100-120; ❄ @) Situated on a quiet corner at the top of the hill, this attentively run almost-boutique pension has 10 compact, breezy rooms – four with balconies – in a spotless family home. The real winner here, though, is the view from the terrace.

Türk Evi
PENSION €€

(844 3129; www.kalkanturkevi.com; Şehitler Caddesi 19; d TL70-100; ❄) An excellent mid-range choice, this attractive stone 'Turkish House', dating from the 1950s and surrounded by garden, houses nine large rooms individually decorated with period furniture and colourful carpets. Some of the rooms upstairs have wonderful sea views.

Likya Residence Hotel & Spa
RESORT HOTEL €€€

(844 1055; www.likyakalkan.com; Akdeniz Caddesi; s/d €130/145; ❄ @ ❄ ❄) This new favourite perched precariously on a steep cliff west of the centre is an all-in getaway with

27 stylish rooms and suites, three swimming pools, a more-than-comprehensive spa and the most romantic outdoor bar in Kalkan. There's direct access by footpath to the Yalı Beach Club with seaside swimming platforms.

Kelebek Hotel & Apartments

HOTEL, APARTMENT €

(☑844 3770; www.butterflyholidays.co.uk; Mantese Mah 4; s TL30-45, d TL50-65, 1-/2-bedroom apt TL60/115; 🖳@🐾) Though slightly away from the action in the 'highlands' to the north of the centre, the blue-and-white, family-run 'Butterfly' offers remarkably good value for Kalkan. Choose from among 22 rooms in the main building – with a pool table in the tiled lobby and fronted by a large swimming pool – and eight apartments with kitchens in a separate block.

Zinbad Butik Hotel

HOTEL €€

(☑844 3475; www.zinbadhotel.com; Mustafa Koca Kaya Caddesi 26; s/d TL50/100; 🖳) It's hard to see what's changed at this old stalwart to make it 'boutique' – its 21 rooms, some sponged Mediterranean blue and with balconies looking to the sea, are just as cheerful and comfortable as before. It's close to the waterfront and central.

Holiday Pansiyon

PENSION €

(☑844 3154; Süleyman Yılmaz Caddesi 2; d with/without breakfast TL40/60) Though the seven rooms are simple, they're spotless and charming; the three in the older Ottoman section are particularly atmospheric with

wooden beams, lacy curtains and delightful balconies with good views. It's run by the charming Ahmet and Şefika, who make delicious breakfast jams. Rooms are fan-cooled.

Hotel Dionysia

HOTEL €€

(☑844 3681; aldihotels@hotmail.com; Cumhuriyet Caddesi; s/d TL80/120; 🖳) It won't win any design awards but this new-build offers 23 rooms with balconies (most of them overlooking the bay) and fans. The pool is surrounded by olive trees and bougainvilleas and the hotel is a short stroll west of the centre.

Çelik Pansiyon

PENSION €

(☑844 2126; www.celikpansiyon.com; Süleyman Yılmaz Caddesi 9; s/d TL40/50; 🖳) One of Kalkan's very few cheap guest houses open year-round, the Çelik has eight rooms (with balconies) that are spartan but spotless and quite spacious. The two mansard rooms at the top look over the rooftops and marina, as does the roof terrace.

🍴 Eating

Kalkan's main market day is Thursday, though there is a much smaller one in the Akbel district to the northwest on Sunday.

TOP CHOICE **Korsan Fish Terrace**

SEAFOOD €€€

(☑844 3076; www.korsankalkan.com; Atatürk Caddesi; mains TL25-32; ☉10am-midnight) On the roof of Patara Stone House, this restaurant is arguably the finest seafood experience in Kalkan. Its homemade lemonade (TL3.50) is legendary and there's live jazz on Tuesday from 8.30pm. Other outlets in the mini Korsan empire, run by Turkish-British couple Uluç and Claire, include **Korsan Meze** (⌂844 3622; Yat Limanı; meze TL8-15, mains TL20-30; 🛜), opposite the town beach, one of the oldest (1979) and most consistent restaurants serving modern Turkish and international cuisine in Kalkan; and **Korsan Kebap** (⌂844 2116; Atatürk Caddesi; mains TL12-25; 🛜), a simpler place that's ideal for lunch on a terrace by the harbour with upscale kebaps and pide.

Maya　　　　　　FAMILY RESTAURANT €€€
(⌂844 1145; Hasan Altan Caddesi; mains €19-26; ☉7pm-midnight) A very homely eatery run by Sevilay, who keeps her menu small but perfectly chosen. There are just five tables, all on a roof terrace with great views.

Öz Adana　　　　　　KEBAPÇI €€
(⌂844 1140; Yalıboyu Mah; mains TL7-11) Just opposite the first roundabout and the turning to Kalamar, the 'Original Adana' is just that and serves the best kebaps, pide and *lahmacun* (Turkish 'pizza') in town.

Marina Restaurant　　　　OCAKBAŞI €€€
(⌂844 3384; İskele Sokak; mains TL18-27; ☉9am-1am) Just below the landmark Pirat Hotel, our favourite restaurant by the water does excellent (if pricey) grills and fish dishes but seems to excel at pide in all its infinite variety. Choose from 15 meze made daily.

Zeytinlik　　　　　MODERN TURKISH €€€
(⌂844 3408; Hasan Altan Caddesi; mains TL23-30) Another winning British-Turkish joint venture, the rooftop 'Olive Garden' serves some of the most adventurous Turkish food in town – try the fish *dolmas,* the samosa-like minced lamb in filo pastry triangles or any of the three vegetarian options. It's a popular place so make sure you book a front-row seat with a view.

Guru's Place　　　　　ANATOLIAN €€
(⌂844 3848; www.kalkanguru.com; Kaş, Yolu; meze plate TL15, mains TL7-27; ☉ 8am-11pm) Affable Hüseyin and his family, who have been in the area for four centuries, have been running this restaurant by the sea for 20 years. Food is authentic and fresh, coming from their own garden. The menu is often limited to daily specials. Its a bit out of town on the road to Kaş, so a free transfer service is provided.

Kalamaki　　MODERN TURKISH, INTERNATIONAL €€€
(⌂844 1555; Hasan Altan Caddesi 43; mains TL16-35; ☉noon-midnight) A modern venue

with a very stylish minimalist pub on the ground floor and restaurant above offers superb Turkish dishes with a European twist. Try the scrumptious lamb with plums (TL27) or the generous vegetarian casserole. Host Tayfun keeps it all hanging together.

Trio　　　　　　　　SEAFOOD €€€
(⌂844 3380; www.triokalkan.com; İskele Sokak; mains TL25-36; ☉7am-2am) Perennial favourite of expat Brits (just try to get in here on New Year's Eve), this waterfront restaurant and bar serves excellent fish dishes (eg grouper with samphire) but not exclusively. It's a great place for a mid-afternoon cocktail while sprawled on one of the comfy wicker lounges.

Belgin's Kitchen　　　　　MUTFAK €€
(⌂844 3614; 3 Nolu Sokak; mains TL16-26; ☉10am-midnight) A 150-year-old former olive oil–pressing workshop, Belgin's serves traditional Turkish food at very palatable prices. The speciality is *mantı* (TL16) and *çiğ börek* (börek stuffed with spicy ground beef and fried). Despite the preponderance of faux Ottoman artefacts, the roof terrace is very pleasant.

Foto's Pizza　　　　　　PIDECI €€
(⌂844 3464; www.fotospizza.com; İskele Sokak; medium pizza TL12-22.50) Listing a pizza joint in a town of such culinary repute seems sacrilege, but (a) Foto's has always been more pide than pizza for us and (b) the views from the terrace make it hard to overlook. It's just past the taxi rank on the way down the steep incline that locals call Heart Attack Hill.

Aubergine　MODERN TURKISH, INTERNATIONAL €€€
(⌂844 3332; www.kalkanaubergine.com; İskele Sokak; mains TL25-35; ☉8am-3am) With tables right on the marina, as well as cosy seats inside, this restaurant is a magnet for its location alone. But add to that specialities like its slow-roasted wild boar (TL32) and swordfish fillet served in a creamy vegetable sauce (TL31) and you have a winner.

Ali Baba　　　　　　　MUTFAK €
(⌂844 3627; Hasan Altan Caddesi; mains TL4-12.50; ☉5am-midnight low season, 24hr high season) With its generous opening hours and rock-bottom (for Kalkan) prices, this is everybody's favourite local cheapie. It's a great place for breakfast and also does some decent veggie dishes.

Merkez Cafe   CAFE, INTERNATIONAL €€
(☏844 2823; Hasan Altan Caddesi 17; ⊙8am-1am)
This modest-looking and very central (the
meaning of its name) cafe makes ethereal
pastries and cakes, including a gorgeous
chocolate baklava (TL6) and coconut and
almond macaroons. More substantial fare
includes pizzas (TL9 to TL15) and pasta.

Ada Patisserie   CAFE, CONFECTIONER €
(☏844 2536; Kalamar Yolu; cakes TL3-4; ⊛)
Charming little cafe/patisserie at the start
of the Kalamar road with shop-made delec-
tables and wi-fi.

🍷 Drinking

Kalkan now has a strip of trendy bars and
discos by the municipal parking lot oriented to a younger crowd, including Club Mo-
jito, Boaters Bar Code and Chocolate.

Fener Cafe   CAFE, TEA GARDEN
(☏844 3752; Yat Limanı; beer €5; ⊙8.30am-
2.30am) The closest thing Kalkan has to a
tea garden, the 'Lighthouse' (no prizes for
guessing its location) is as popular with locals as it is with expats and visitors.

Cafe Del Mar   CAFE
(☏844 1068; Hasan Altan Caddesi; ⊙9am-1am; ⊛)
Tiny but adorable place that claims to offer
over 70 varieties of coffee (TL4 to TL7) as well
as milkshakes and smoothies (from TL5).

Moonlight Bar   BAR
(☏844 3043; Süleyman Yılmaz Caddesi 17; beer
€5; ⊙9am-4am) Just down from the post
office, Kalkan's oldest bar is still its most
'happening', though a good percentage of
people sitting at the tables outside – or on
the small dance floor inside – are visitors.

Yalı Cafe Bar   CAFE-BAR
(☏844 1001; Hasan Altan Caddesi 19; beer TL4.50;
⊙1pm-midnight) Positioned as it is on a three-
road junction, this is a popular place for
meeting, greeting and drinking in public.

🛍 Shopping

Just Silver   JEWELLERY
(☏844 3136; Hasan Altan Caddesi 28) Just
about the most famous shop in Kalkan has
gals and dolls lining up for ear, nose, neck,
finger and toe baubles.

❶ Information

Internet cafe (☏844 3187; Hasan Altan Caddesi
1/f; per hr TL2; ⊙9am-5pm, until 9pm May-Oct)
Stationery shop opposite the taxi rank with four
computer terminals.

Kalkan Turkish Local News (KTLN; www.turk
ishlocalnews.com) Independent, comprehensive
and reliable website on all things Kalkan run by
British expat.

❶ Getting There & Away

Minibuses connect Kalkan with Fethiye (TL10,
1½ hours, 83km) and Kaş (TL5, 35 minutes,
29km) via the beach at Kaputaş (TL3, 15 minutes, 7km). Some eight minibuses also run daily
to Patara (TL5, 25 minutes, 15km).

Around Kalkan

BEZİRGAN

In an elevated valley some 17km northeast
of Kalkan sits the beautiful village of Bezirgan, a timeless example of Turkish rural
life. Towering some 725m above the fruit
orchards and fields of sticky sesame are the
ruins of the Lycian hilltop citadel of **Pirha**.

Accommodation is available at **Owlsland** (☏837 5214; www.owlsland.com; r per
person TL75, with half-board per person TL110),
a 150-year-old farmhouse idyllically surrounded by fruit trees and run by a charming Turkish-Scottish couple. Erol, a trained
chef, turns out traditional Turkish dishes
made with locally grown produce and Pauline makes her own jams and ginger cake.
The three rooms are simple but cosy, contain most of their original features and are
decorated with old farm implements; the
upstairs room with balcony is especially
nice. Walking tours (TL60 including lunch)
of the area are available.

❶ Getting There & Away

Owlsland can arrange pick-up from Kalkan for
TL15. Otherwise, hourly minibuses between
Kınık and Elmalı go via the Akbel section of Kal-
kan (TL3) and will drop you off in Bezirgan.

If you're under your own steam head north
from Kalkan, cross over the D400 linking Fethiye
and Kaş and follow the signs for Sütleğen and
Elmalı. The road climbs steadily, with stunning
views across the sea, and heads further up the
mountain. Once the road crests the pass, you
can see Bezirgan below. Ignore the first exit for
Bezirgan and take the second. The signposted
turning for Owlsland is just before the road begins climbing again to Sütleğen.

İSLAMLAR

A favourite destination is this alpine former Greek village in the mountains some
8km north of Kalkan. The draw here is as
much a temperature 5°C cooler than in
Kalkan in summer as the dozen or so trout

restaurants that make use of icy mountain streams to fill their tanks. In the village square, have a look at one of two working mills that still uses waterpower and a great millstone to turn local residents' grain into flour. Due south along a rough track is our favourite restaurant, **Çiftlik** (☑838 6055, 0537 421 6129), where fresh trout and a variety of meze, salads and chips won't cost much more than TL12 per person. The nearby **Değirmen** (☺838 6295, 0532 586 2734) is a posher but still authentic eatery that makes it own tahina from sesame picked from the fields and ground in the basement.

If you just can't tear yourself away there's a mini-paradise called **Grapevine Cottage** (☑838 6078, 0534 744 9255; verydeb@gmail. com; r TL75-100), set among citrus groves and vineyards just east of the Çiftlik restaurant. Run by Briton Deborah and her Turkish partner Ufuk, the place has two rooms, one in the main building decorated with Mexi-can tiles (Deborah has a house in Mexico) and Turkish carpets (Ufuk has a shop in the village) and an en suite one in a purpose-built cottage. The views down to the sea from the breakfast terrace are priceless, and Deborah makes her own bread, jams and wine. Transport to/from Akbel,a sub-urb to the northwest in Kalkan, can be arranged but getting here by public transport is not possible.

Kaş

☑0242 / POP 5925

A more workaday destination than Kalkan, Kaş – pronounced 'cash' – may not sport the finest beach culture in the region, but it's a yachties' haven and the atmosphere of the town is wonderfully mellow. The surrounding areas are ideal for day trips by sea or scooter, and a plethora of adventure sports are on offer, in particular some excellent wreck diving.

Kaş

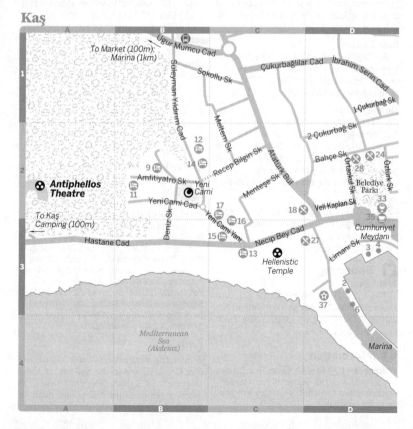

Extending to the west of the old town is the 6km-long Çukurbağ Peninsula. Here you'll find a well-preserved ancient theatre, about all that's left of ancient Antiphellos, the name of the original Lycian town here. Above the town several Lycian rock tombs in the mountain wall can be seen even at night when they are illuminated.

Lying just offshore is the geopolitical oddity of the Greek island of Meis (Kastellorizo).

◎ Sights & Activities

Antiphellos Ruins   RUINS
Walk up hilly Uzun Çarşı Sokak, what locals call Slippery Street, to the east of the main square to reach the **Lion Tomb**, a superb example of a Lycian sarcophagus, which is mounted on a high base and has lions' heads on the lid. Kaş was once littered with such sarcophagi but over the years most were broken apart for building materials.

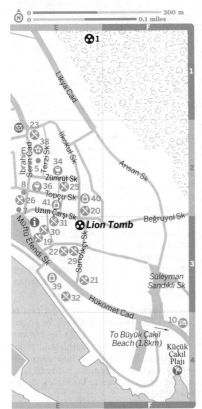

Antiphellos was a small settlement and the port for Phellos, the much larger Lycian town further north in the hills. The small Hellenistic **theatre**, 500m west of the main square, could seat some 4000 spectators and is in very good condition. You can walk to the **rock tombs** cut into the cliffs above town.

Beaches   BEACH
Büyük Çakıl (Big Pebble) is a relatively clean beach about 1.5km from the town centre and **Akçagerme Plajı** is a public beach opposite the exit to Gökseki along the main road west to Kalkan. But the best idea is to hop on one of the water taxis in the harbour and head for one of three beaches on the peninsula opposite at **Liman Ağzı** (TL10).

☞ Tours
Most companies offer more or less the same journeys, but you can always tailor your own for a negotiated price.

Among the stalwarts, the three-hour **bus and boat trip** (TL50) to Üçağız and Kekova is a fine day out, and includes time to see several interesting ruins as well as swim.

Other standard tours go to the Mavi Mağara (Blue Cave), Patara and Kalkan or to Longos and several small nearby islands. There are also overland excursions to Saklıkent Gorge.

A great idea is to charter a boat from the marina. A whole day spent around the islands of Kaş should cost about TL200 for the entire boat accommodating up to eight people.

There are several good tour companies:

Bougainville Travel   OUTDOOR ACTIVITIES
(☎836 3737; www.bougainville-turkey.com; İbrahim Serin Sokak 10) A long-established English-Turkish tour operator with a solid reputation and much experience in organising any number of activities lasting a full day (unless otherwise specified), including canoeing (TL70 on the Patara River, with individual rentals TL40/70 for a single/double); canyoning (TL100); mountain biking (TL72, with individual rentals TL44); paragliding (TL180 for flights lasting 20 to 30 minutes); scuba diving (TL56 per dive including all equipment); and sea kayaking (TL60).

Olympica Travel Agency   OUTDOOR ACTIVITIES
(☎836 2049; www.olympicatravel.com; Cumhuriyet Meydanı; ⊙8.30am-midnight) This

Kaş

place specialises in 'build your own activity packages' according to clients' time, interests and budget.

Xanthos Travel OUTDOOR ACTIVITIES
(☎836 3292; www.xanthostravel.com; İbrahim Serin Caddesi 5/A) An affable outfit that can organise any number of activities and excursions such as sea kayaking in Kekova (TL60, or TL90 including Aperlae).

Festivals & Events
The annual **Kaş Lycia Festival** runs for three days at the end of June. It features prominent folk-dancing troupes and musicians – and an international swimming race – and works to foster an improved relationship between Greece and Turkey.

Sleeping
Most – but not all – accommodation in Kaş is west and northwest of the centre along the waterfront and up the hill around the Yeni Cami (New Mosque).

Hideaway Hotel HOTEL €€
TOP CHOICE (☎836 1887; www.hotelhideaway.com; Amfitiyatro Sokak 7; s/d TL80/110; ❄@☀) The aptly named Hideaway is located at the far end of town and is quieter than most. Run by the unstoppable Ahmet, a font of local information, the Hideaway counts 19 comfortable rooms, all with balcony and a half-dozen facing the sea. Rooms are simple but in good order and all have a balcony. There's a smallish pool and a roof terrace with terminals, DVD player, honour-system bar and views over the water and amphitheatre. Meals as cheap as TL7 available.

White House Pension PENSION €€
(☎836 1513; www.orcholiday.com; Yeni Cami Caddesi 10; s/d TL65/100; ❄@) Decked out in wood, wrought iron, marble and terracotta paint, this is a stylish little gem with eight attractive rooms and a pretty terrace. Ask for the attic room to the back with the lovely balcony.

Gardenia Boutique Hotel
BOUTIQUE HOTEL €€€

(📞836 2368; www.gardeniahotel-kas.com; Hükümet Caddesi 41; s & d €80-110, ste €145; ❄) This stylishly restrained hostelry is southeast of the centre, on the way to the beaches and opposite the near identical waterfront restaurants with swimming platforms. The 11 rooms are styled with wicker, fringed lampshades and leather seating in reds and browns. Four have sea views; if yours doesn't, watch the sunset from the rooftop terrace.

Hadrian Boutique Hotel
RESORT €€€

(📞836 2856; www.hotel-hadrian.de; Doğan Kaşaroğlu Sokak 10; s/d/ste €80/115/160; ❄ ❄) The only accommodation we feel we can recommend on the building-site that is the Çukurbağ Peninsula, the German-owned Hadrian is a tropical oasis with 14 rooms and suites (though the faux classical statues add a touch of Teutonic kitsch). The large seawater pool and private swimming platform are excellent and we could spend most of the rest of our lives propped up at the terrace bar with wow-factor views. The Çukurbağ Peninsula starts just west of the town centre and extends for 6km into the sea.

Sonne Hotel
HOTEL €€

(📞836 1528; www.sonneotel.com; Yeni Cami Yanı 6; s/d TL90/120; ❄ @) The Sonne is a tightly run Turkish-German-owned beauty at the bottom of 'pension hill'. The 13 rooms are tasteful and quite spacious, all with LCD televisions and Ottoman-inspired mirrors; some have small balconies. The junior suite

(TL150) is worth the splurge. The breakfast terrace and bar offer stunning views.

Santosa Pansiyon
PENSION €

(📞836 1714; www.santosapension.com; Recep Bilgin Sokak 4; s/d TL45/70; ❄ @) Clean, quiet and cheap is how best to describe this backpacker hang-out. The 11 rooms are simple but attractively decorated with floral patterns, and are excellent for the price. The couple who run the show are cooks; try one of their barbecue (TL20) or vegetarian set meals (TL10).

Ateş Pension
PENSION €€

(📞836 1393; www.atespension.com; Amfitiyatro Sokak 3; dm/s/d TL25/50/80; ❄ @) Well run by Recep and Ayşe, this is a friendly place with 17 rooms including dorms with four beds and a pleasant roof terrace where barbecues (TL15) are sometimes held. Guests get to use the pool at the Hideaway Hotel.

Sardunya Otel
HOTEL €€

(📞836 3080; www.sardunyaotel.com; Hastane Caddesi 20; s/d 50/80; ❄) Set in a modern white building across from the coastal road, the Sardunya's dozen rooms are reasonably spacious and all have balconies, eight with direct sea views. Across the road is the hotel's restaurant where breakfast is served under mulberry and orange trees a few metres from the water. Just below, there's a sunbathing terrace and swimming platform.

Kaş Otel
HOTEL €€

(📞836 1271; www.myhotelkas.com; Hastane Caddesi 20; s/d 80/100; ❄) The rooms are simple here but you're paying for one of the best locations on the water. In fact, the sea is

---

MEIS EXPRESS

The **Meis Express** (📞836 1725; www.meisexpress.com; one-way or same-day return TL40) fast ferry sails throughout the year to the tiny Greek island of Meis (Kastellorizo) at 10am (10.30am in winter) and returns at 3pm or 3.30pm; the voyage takes just 20 minutes. Meis is a simple fishing village with a sprinkling of restaurants, a superb bakery, a duty-free shop selling Greek wine and pork, some excellent walks over the hill and a decent photo museum in the old church. It is also a relatively easy way to renew your Turkish visa (€15) should you need to. It's possible to spend the night in Meis, or continue onwards into Greece proper. There are regular ferries to Rhodes (€18, 4½ hours) three times a week and a high-speed catamaran (€32, 2½ hours) in summer. Meis even has a tiny landing strip from where you can fly to Rhodes (€26, 30 minutes) at 5.30pm Friday to Wednesday. On Meis your best source of information is **Papoutsis Travel** (📞+30 22460 49 286; www.greeklodgings.gr).

Tickets for Meis can be bought from any travel agency or directly from Mei Express in the harbour. Make sure you arrive a half-hour before sailing in order to complete immigration formalities.

so close you can hear it lapping from the pleasant terrace or the balconies of the 10 rooms – and there's a swimming platform. The rooms set back from the water are not as nice.

Hilal Pansiyon   PENSION €
(☑836 1207; www.korsan-kas.com; Süleyman Yıldırım Caddesi; s/d/tr TL45/70/90; ❄@) Run by the friendly Süleyman and family, the Hilal offers 16 unexceptional rooms and a leafy terrace that sometimes hosts barbecues (TL15). The travel agency below offers guests 10% discounts on activities including kayaking, diving and trips to Saklıkent.

Kaş Camping   CAMPGROUND €
(☑836 1050; www.kaskamping.com; Hastane Caddesi 3; camp site TL20, standard/deluxe bungalow TL55/140; ❄@) Located on an attractive rocky outcropping on the peninsula 800m west of town, this popular site is 100m from the sea and features a lively terrace bar. Deluxe bungalows have bathrooms and air conditioning.

✖ Eating

Kaş doesn't offer anything like the fine-dining scene that Kalkan does, though you'll find some excellent restaurants to the southeast of the main square, especially around Sandıkçı Sokak.

Every Friday there's a big outdoor market along the old road to Kalkan.

TOP CHOICE İkbal   MODERN TURKISH €€€
(☑836 3193; Sandıkçı Sokak 6; mains TL18-30; ❂9am-midnight) Kaş's best restaurant, run by Vecdi and his German wife Barbara, serves excellent prepared fish dishes and the house speciality, slow-cooked leg of lamb, from a small but well-chosen menu. We appreciate the good selection of Turkish wines from Mediterranean vineyards.

Bi Lokma   MUTFAK €€
(☑836 3942; Hükümet Caddesi 2; mains TL9.50-20; ❂9am-midnight) Also known as 'Mama's Kitchen', this place has tables meandering around a terraced garden overlooking the harbour. Sabo – the 'mama' in question – turns out great traditional dishes including her famous *mantı* (TL9.50) and *börek* (filled pastry; TL10.50).

Cafe Mola   CAFE €€
(☑836 1994; Emin Erdem Meydanı 3/B; dishes TL7-10; ❂9am-11pm) Our home away from home in Kaş, this convivial cafe is great for Turkish breakfast (TL10), sandwiches (TL7) or *mantı*.

It has an espresso machine and staff make fresh lemonade (TL4).

Blue House   MUTFAK €€
(☑836 1320; Sandıkçı Sokak 8; mains TL20-30) This restaurant, with its distinctive blue doorway and balcony, has a great atmosphere and lovely views. The meze are good and the main reason for coming. It's a family affair; the ladies work from the kitchen of their own house, which you have to pass through to get to the terrace.

Sultan Garden Restaurant   ANATOLIAN €€
(☑836 3762; www.sultangarden.co.uk; Hükümet Caddesi; mains TL15-30; ❂10am-11pm) This very leafy place, with a terrace overlooking the harbour and a functioning ancient cistern, is a perennial favourite offering excellent service and traditional and inventive Turkish dishes. Try the *hünkar beğendı* (spiced stewed lamb on aubergine puree; TL22).

Havana Balık Evi   SEAFOOD €
(☑836 4111; Öztürk Sokak 7; mains TL8-13; ❂9am-midnight) The Cuban reference is lost on us but we come to this place not for its more complex mains but for *balık ekmek* (TL4), the simple fish sandwich that is a staple in İstanbul. It's BYO.

2000 Restaurant   KEBAPÇI €
(☑836 3374; Atatürk Bulvarı 1; dishes TL3-4; ❂24hr) This hole in the wall across from the main mosque attracts for two reasons: its superb *dürüm* (kebap wrapped in pita) and its generous opening hours.

Natur-el   FAMILY RESTAURANT €€
(☑836 2834; Gürsöy Sokak 6; mains TL15-20) With its dishes cooked to traditional recipes passed down from generation to generation, Natur-el and the family who runs it provide a chance to sample Turkish cuisine at its best. If you haven't yet eaten *mantı*, then choose from the three varieties (TL12) here. They also served *aşure*, an everything-but-the-kitchen-sink pudding of dried fruit, nuts and beans.

Chez Evy   FRENCH €€€
(☑836 1253; Terzi Sokak 2; mains TL25-40; ❂7pm-midnight) This French restaurant, a Kaş institution run by the indefatigable Evy and tucked in the back streets above town, serves such classics as *gigot d'agneau* and *filet de boeuf sauce béarnaise* as well as a lot of salads. It's expensive for what it is but is an experience unique to Kaş, and has a pretty leafy forecourt.

Enişte'nin Yeri
LOCAL €

(📞836 4404; Necip Bey Caddesi; dishes TL2.50-10) Just opposite Yapı Kredi bank, 'Brother-in-Law's Place' has very good (and cheap) pide, grills, soups and salads, with a pretty courtyard and a lovely air-conditioned room for the hotter months.

Sempati
MEDITERRANEAN €€

(📞836 2418; www.sempatirestaurant.com; Gürsöy Sokak 11; meals TL11-20) The homestyle cooking at this place behind the blue door on the corner of Slippery Street attracts a loyal and regular following. Try the delicious aubergine fritters.

Alpler Restaurant
LOCAL €€

(📞836 3678; www.kasalperrestaurant.com; Cumhuriyet Meydanı 9; meze TL5, mains TL15-30; ⊘11.30am-11pm) Smack dab on the main harbour square, Alpler offers the perfect position for people-watching. The food (fish, grills, pide) is good and reasonably priced.

Bahçe Restaurant
LOCAL €€

(📞836 2370; Uzun Çarşı Sokak 31; mains TL14-30; ⊘10am-midnight) Behind the monumental Lion Tomb, this place has a pretty garden and serves excellent dishes at decent prices, including a terrific range of meze (TL6 to TL7). The fish in paper (TL22) gets good reviews.

Çınarlar
PIDECI €€

(📞836 2860; İbrahim Serin Sokak; pide TL7-11, pizza TL9-15; ⊘8am-1am) Perennially popular with Kaş' young bloods, who come for the affordable pide and pop music, Çınarlar has a pleasant courtyard tucked away off the street.

Cafe Corner
CAFE-BAR €€

(📞836 1409; İbrahim Serin Sokak; meze TL4, dishes TL9-15; ⊘8am-1am) This well-positioned cafe-bar has a nice relaxed atmosphere and well-priced drinks. It does decent snacks as well as light meals.

🍺 Drinking & Entertainment

Hideaway Cafe & Bar
BAR-CAFE

(📞836 3369; Cumhuriyet Caddesi 16/A; beer TL5; ⊘4pm-3am) Well named, this enchanting cafe-garden is accessible from the street via a secret doorway opposite Noel Baba Cafe. Turkish breakfast (TL17.50) and Sunday brunch is offered, as well as snacks and cakes.

Noel Baba Cafe
CAFE

(📞836 1225; Cumhuriyet Meydanı 1; beer TL5, tea TL1; ⊘8am-midnight) Occupying a shaded terrace on the main square and overlooking

the harbour, this is a favourite local meeting point.

Hi-Jazz Bar
BAR

(📞836 1165; Zümrüt Sokak 3; ⊘5pm-3am) This mellow little bar round the corner from Chez Evy has canned (and sometimes live) jazz. It's very friendly and cosy but with no outside space – not one for the height of summer.

Red Point Cafe Bar
BAR, CLUB

(📞836 1165; Topçu Sokak; ⊘5pm-3am) The Red Point doesn't really get going until after 10.30pm, with late-night drinking and a spot of dancing on the small dance floor.

Echo Cafe & Bar
BAR, CLUB

(📞836 2047; www.echocafebar.com; Limanı Sokak; ⊘8am-4am) Hip and stylish, this lounge near an ancient (5 BC, anyone?) cistern on the harbour has Kaş high society sipping fruit daiquiris to both live and canned jazz and acid jazz. The airy upstairs section hosts exhibitions and has nice little balconies overlooking the water. In winter, patrons snuggle up to the fireplace.

Moon River
BAR

(📞836 4423; İbrahim Serin Sokak 1/D; ⊘8am-3am; 📶) The erstwhile Harry's Bar has reinvented itself as a lounge with *türkü* (Turkish folk music) most nights. It has very good coffee and drinks are reasonably priced.

🛍 Shopping

Turqueria
ANTIQUES, HANDICRAFTS

(📞836 1631; Uzun Çarşı Sokak) Run by Orhan and Martina, a charming Turkish-German couple long resident in Kaş, Turqueria is an Aladdin's cave with everything from old prints and advertisements to Turkish puppets handcut from leather.

Merdiven Kıtabevi
BOOKSTORE

(📞836 3022; İlkokul Sokak 4/B; ⊘8.30am-10pm) Kaş' best bookshop is small but stocks a good collection of new and used books, including local titles.

Gallery Anatolia
CERAMICS

(📞836 1954; www.gallery-anatolia.com; Hükümet Caddesi 2; ⊘9am-11pm) This very upmarket gallery along the marina has locally designed ceramic pieces.

ℹ Information

Computer World (📞836 2700; Bahçe Sokak; per hr TL2; ⊘9am-11pm) Computer shop opposite the post office has 13 terminals.

ANTALYA & THE WESTERN MEDITERRANEAN KAŞ

MAKING SENSE & CENTS IN KEKOVA

Given the difficulty of getting here by public transport, most people end up taking a boat tour of the area from Kaş or even Kalkan, which starts with a bus ride to Üçağız where you board the boat for Kekova.

Along the northern shore of Kekova are ruins, partly submerged 6m below the sea and referred to as the Sunken City (Batık Şehir). The result of a series of terrible earthquakes in the 2nd century AD, most of what you can still see is a residential part of ancient Simena. Foundations of buildings, staircases and moorings are also visible. It is forbidden to anchor or swim around or near the Sunken City (though you can swim elsewhere around the island).

After the visit to Kekova you have lunch on the boat and then head on to Kaleköy, passing a couple of submerged (and very photo-worthy) Lycian tombs just offshore. There's usually about an hour to explore Kaleköy and climb up to the hilltop.

Tours from Kaş, which cost TL50 per person (TL80 including Aperlae), generally leave at 10am and return around 6pm. A similar tour organised locally in Üçağız will cost about TL35 per person; a boat for the day accommodating four/eight people costs from TL180/250. We like Mehmet Doğan's boat **Kumsal** (☎0532 685 2401; kumsal_boat.hotmail.com) or you could try Captain Turgay Poyraz at the **Onur Pension** (☎874 2071; www.onurpension.com).

The closest you'll get to the underwater ruins is on a sea-kayaking tour (TL60 per person, or TL90 with Aperlae, including transfers and lunch) run by one of the travel agencies in Kaş (p337) and suitable for all fitness levels.

Tourist office (☎836 1238; ☺8am-5.30pm daily May-Oct, 8am-noon & 1-5pm Mon-Fri Nov-Apr) Marginally helpful office on the main square has town plans.

❶ Getting There & Away

The otogar is along Atatürk Bulvarı 350m north of the centre. From here there are daily buses to İstanbul (TL65, 15 hours, 985km) at 6.30am. To reach Ankara (TL50, 11 hours, 740km) or İzmir (TL35, 8½ hours, 440km) you must change at Fethiye.

Closer to home there are dolmuşes every half-hour to Kalkan (TL5, 35 minutes, 29km), Olympos (TL15, 2½ hours, 109km) and Antalya (TL16, 3½ hours, 188km) and hourly to Fethiye (TL12, 2½ hours, 107km). Services to Patara (TL8, 45 minutes, 40km) run every half-hour in high season, and hourly at other times. You can also reach Saklıkent Gorge (TL10, one hour, 52km) from here.

Üçağız & Kekova

☑0242 / POP 450

Declared off-limits to development Üçağız (ooch-*eye*-iz) is a Turkish fishing and farming village in an absolutely idyllic setting on a bay amid islands and peninsulas. Little has changed here over the years aside from the steady trickle of visitors, most of whom leave by the end of the day. There's not a lot to do – the water isn't especially good for swimming – but it's a regular stop on the *gület* junket, and a final taste of the mainland before visiting the sunken city at Kekova or secluded Kaleköy, known locally as Kale.

A few words about where you are and what's what. The village you enter from the coastal highway is **Üçağız**, ancient Teimiussa, with its own Lycian necropolis. Across the water on the peninsula to the southeast is **Kaleköy** (Kale), a protected village on the site of the ancient city of Simena.

South of the villages and past the channel entrance is the long island of **Kekova** with its famous underwater ruins; local people generally use this name to refer to the whole area. To the west on the Sıcak Peninsula is **Aperlae**, an isolated and very evocative ancient Lycian city on the Lycian Way.

⌂ Sleeping & Eating

Üçağız's pensions all seem to have eight rooms and offer free boat service to the beaches on Kekova Island.

Onur Pension   PENSION **€€**
(☎874 2071; www.onurpension.com; s/d TL60/80; ❉@) With a picturesque setting right on the harbour, this well-run pension combines charm with attentive service. Locally born Onur can give great

trekking advice and act as a guide. Four of the rooms, kept shipshape by Onur's Dutch wife, Jacqueline, have full sea views (though the mansard ones at the top are a little claustrophobic).

Likya Pension   PENSION €
(☎874 2090; gokkaya07@mynet.com; s/d TL40/60; ✴@) Just up the steps from the harbour, gregarious carpet seller Mehmet runs this comfortable pension in an ancient stone complex hidden within lush gardens. Bargain hard for one of his kilims!

Kekova Pansiyon   PENSION €€
(☎874 2259; www.kekovapansiyon.com; d TL60-100; ✴@) Set in splendid isolation on the far end of the waterfront, this pension is in a handsome old stone building with a terrace dotted with flowerpots. Rooms are comfortable and share a lovely veranda with cushioned benches and views over the water.

Kordon Restaurant   SEAFOOD €€
(☎874 2067; meze TL4.50, grills & fish per 500g TL12-15; ⊙9am-midnight) With an attractive and cool terrace overlooking the marina and fresh fish – try the excellent grilled sea bass – the Kordon is considered the best restaurant in town.

Sevim Hanım   STREET FOOD €
(TL3; ⊙8am-8pm) Hard as we've looked, we've never found better *gözleme* than Madame Sevim's, cooked up fresh daily by the harbour steps.

❶ Getting There & Away

This is a very tricky place to reach. One dolmuş leaves Antalya for Üçağız daily at 2.30pm (TL16, 3½ hours) and returns at 8am. Dolmuşes also run every hour or so from Antalya to Demre (TL12, three hours), from where you can get a taxi (TL60) to Üçağız.

Taxi is the only option from Kaş (TL60). In summer, you might hitch a lift (one-way TL20, two hours) with one of the boat companies making daily tours to Üçağız.

From Kale (Demre), one dolmuş a day goes to Üçağız (TL4, 30 minutes) at 5pm. From Üçağız, dolmuşes leave at 8am.

Kaleköy (Kale)

☎0242 / POP 170

The watery paradise of Kaleköy is one of the western Mediterranean's truly delightful spots, home to the ruins of ancient **Simena** and an impressive Crusader **for-**

tress (TL8) perched above a hamlet facing out to sea. Within the fortress the ancient world's tiniest **theatre** is cut into the rock and nearby you'll find ruins of several temples and public baths; from the top you can look down upon a field of **Lycian tombs** and the old **city walls** are visible on the outskirts. The stately mansion, with the helipad overlooked by the castle, is owned by the Koç family, Turkey's richest, who have more or less paid the town off not to develop.

Be prepared for peace and quiet – Kaleköy is accessible only from Üçağız by motorboat (10 minutes) or on foot (45 minutes) along a rough track.

Kaleköy has a couple of pensions, but your first choice should be **Mehtap Pansiyon** (☎874 2146; www.mehtappansiyon.com; camp site TL20, s TL90-120, d TL110-140; ✴), with spectacular views over the harbour and submerged Lycian tombs below. Four rooms are in a 200-year-old stone house so quiet and tranquil you may start snoozing as you check in; another four are in a building dating back a millennium and there's one more in a purpose-built wood cottage. İrfan and his son Saffet are warm and knowledgeable hosts.

Down by the harbour, the eight homely rooms of the **Kale Pansiyon** (☎874 2111; www.kalepansiyon.com; s TL80-100, d TL140-160; ✴) all have balconies with direct views that are so close to the sea you can hear the water lapping. There's a nice swimming area too.

The family dynasty spreads to the similarly priced **Olive Grove** (☎874 2025), which is set back from the harbour. It's a gorgeous 150-year-old Greek stone house (look out for the lovely mosaic on the veranda). The four rooms of the house are simple but elegant and share a large veranda with sea views. Amid the cooing doves and ancient olive trees, it's a blissfully peaceful place.

You can either eat at your pension (three-course set meal about TL40) – Saffet's wife Nazike at the Mehtap grows her own vegetables and is an excellent cook – or there are some five restaurants along the seafront. **Likya** (☎874 2096; meze TL4, mains TL10-20), at the end of a long pier, is much favoured by yachties and their crews. And make sure you visit the **Ankh** (☎874 2171; www.ankhpansion.com; ice cream TL6), a cafe at the pension of that name with its own homemade peach, banana and hazelnut ice cream and million dollar views from its terrace.

Demre (Kale)

☎ 0242 / POP 15,600

Officially Kale but called by its old name Demre by just about everyone, this sprawling, dusty town was once the Lycian (and Roman) city of Myra and by the 4th century was important enough to have its own bishop – most notably St Nicholas, who went on to catch the Western world's imagination in his starring role as Santa Claus. In AD 60, St Paul put Myra on the liturgical map by changing boats at its port, Andriake, while on his way to Rome (or so Acts 27: 4-6 tell us).

Once situated by the sea, Demre moved further inland as precious alluvium flowed from the Demre stream. That silting is the foundation of the town's wealth and it remains a major centre for the growing and distribution of fruit and vegetables.

The street going west from the main square to the Church of St Nicholas is pedestrian Müze Caddesi and is lined with cafes and shops. Alakent Caddesi leads 2km north to the Lycian rock tombs of Myra while the street going south from the square passes the otogar (100m).

◉ Sights

Church of St Nicholas   CHURCH

(admission TL10; ⊙ 9am-7pm May-Oct, to 5.30pm Nov-Apr) Not vast like Aya Sofya or brilliant with mosaics like İstanbul's Chora Church (Kariye Museum), the **Church of St Nicholas** is nonetheless a star attraction for pilgrims and tourists alike. Nowadays almost all of them are Russian (Nicholas is the patron saint of Russia). The remains of the eponymous saint were laid here upon his death in AD 343.

The bare earthen church features some interesting Byzantine frescoes and mosaic floors. It was made a basilica when it was restored in 1043. Italian merchants smashed open the sarcophagus in 1087 and supposedly carted off St Nicholas' bones to Bari.

Restorations sponsored by Tsar Nicholas I of Russia in 1862 changed the church by building a vaulted ceiling and a belfry – something unheard of in early Byzantine architecture. More recent work by Turkish archaeologists is to protect it from deterioration.

There are a couple of statues of the saint – one of them the height of kitsch as Santa Claus – in the square in front of the church. St Nick's feast day (6 December) is a very big day here.

Myra   RUINS

(admission TL10; ⊙ 9am-7pm May-Oct, to 5.30pm Nov-Apr) If you only have time to see one striking honeycomb of **Lycian rock tombs**, then choose the memorable ruins of **Myra**. Located about 2km inland from Demre's main square, they are among the finest in Lycia. There's a well-preserved Roman **theatre** here, which includes several theatrical masks carved on stones lying in the nearby area. The so-called **Painted Tomb** near the river necropolis portrays a man and his family in relief both inside and out. A taxi ride from the square will cost about TL8.

Andriake   RUINS

About 5km southwest of the centre is the seafront settlement of Çayağzı, called Andriake by the Romans at a time when the port was an important entrepot for grain on the sea route between the eastern Mediterranean and Rome.

The ruins of the ancient town are strewn over a wide area to the north and south of the access road approaching Çayağzı, which is little more than a half-dozen boat-building yards and a few beachfront cafes. Much of the land is marshland, so the great **granary** built by Hadrian and completed in AD 139, to the south of the road, can be difficult to reach in wet weather. There's good bird-watching here.

Dolmuşes run sporadically out to Çayağzı; your best bet is probably a taxi (TL12).

🛏 Sleeping & Eating

Most visitors travel to Demre by day and sleeping options in the town centre are virtually nonexistent. If you're driving and get hungry, about 2km east of Demre, at the end of a long pebble beach, are several shacks serving freshly caught crab with chips and salad.

TOP CHOICE Hoyran Wedre Country House

BOUTIQUE HOTEL €€€

(☎ 875 1125; www.hoyran.com; Hoyran Köyu; s/d €60/80, ste €110; @ ⊠) A destination hotel if ever there was one, this complex of old and new stone buildings made to look old is a rural oasis 18km west of Demre. Some 500m up in the Taurus Mountains, with views of Kekova and minutes away from an important Lycian acropolis, Hoyran Wedre counts 16 rooms and suites done in traditional fashion (wattle-and-daub plastered walls) and decorated with antiques sourced in İstanbul. We love the pool shaped like a traditional cattle trough and the set meals (TL40) prepared entirely from locally grown produce (though some rooms have kitchens if you prefer to self-cater). It's 3km south of Davazlar off the D400.

Gaziantep Restaurant KEBAPÇI €€
(☑871 2812; Eynihal Caddesi; pide TL5-6, kebap TL9-12; ☉7am-midnight) Just opposite the square with the Church of St Nicholas and its accompanying faux icon shops, this simple but spotless place with outside seating is a local favourite.

Akdeniz Restaurant LOKANTA €
(☑871 5466; Müze Caddesi; pide TL3, köfte TL7, dishes TL5-7; ☉7am-11pm) On the main square west of the church, this welcoming eatery has a large array of tasty precooked dishes as well as pide and *köfte* (meatballs).

Sabancı Pastaneleri CAFE, CONFECTIONER €
(☑871 2188; Eynihal Caddesi; fresh orange juice TL3, pastries TL1.50-3; ☉6am-midnight) Down the road past the Gaziantep, this place is great for breakfast or a snack. It also serves ice cream (TL2 per scoop).

ℹ️ Getting There & Away

Buses and dolmuşes travel to/from Kaş (TL8, one hour, 45km) hourly and less frequently to/from Antalya (TL13, 2½ to three hours).

Olympos & Çıralı

☑0242
About 65km north of Demre, past Finike and Kumluca, a road leads southeast from the main highway – veer to the right then follow the signs – for 9km to Olympos. This is yet another ancient city bearing that name; this particular one was absorbed by Rome in AD 43, precisely the same year that Emperor Claudius and his forces occupied Britain. On the other side of the mountain and over the narrow Ulupınar Stream is Çıralı, a holiday hamlet with dozens of hotels and pensions that may look like it was born yesterday but contains that most

---

WORTH A TRIP

ARYKANDA

Some 26km east of Demre (Kale) is the unremarkable provincial centre of Finike, but there's also an exit off the D400 leading north for another 30km to the ancient city of Arykanda (admission TL10; ☉8am-7pm May-Oct, to 5pm Nov-Apr). Built on five terraces into a south-facing hillside, it is one of the best preserved – and dramatically situated – archaeological sites in Turkey.

One of the oldest sites on the peninsula, Arykanda was part of the Lycian League from its inception in the 2nd century BC but was never a member of the 'Big Six' group of cities that commanded three votes. This may have been due to its profligate and freewheeling ways as much as anything else; Arykanda was apparently the party town of Lycia and forever deeply in debt. Along with the rest of Lycia it was annexed by Rome in AD 43 and survived as a Byzantine settlement until the 9th century when it was abandoned.

Arykanda's most outstanding feature is its two-storey **baths** complex standing some 10m tall next to the gymnasium on the lowest terrace. Following a path northwards to the next terrace you'll come to a large **agora** colonnaded on three sides. Its northern arches lead into a small **odeion**; have a look at the relief of the Emperor Hadrian over the portal. Above that is a fine **theatre** dating from the 2nd century and a **stadium**. Other notable constructions on upper terraces to the northwest are another agora, a bouleterion and a large cistern (not all easy to reach).

Dolmuşes (TL5) headed for Elmalı from Demre (Kale) will drop you off at the foot of the hill leading to the site entrance or in the village of Ariif, about a kilometre to the north, from where a signposted path leads to the ruins. A taxi will cost about TL70 from Demre (Kale).

enigmatic of classical icons: the eternal flame of the Chimaera.

A few kilometres after the turnings for Olympos and Çıralı, the half-dozen or so trout restaurants in the tiny wooded hamlet of Ulupınar are a great place to stop for lunch.

OLYMPOS

An important Lycian city in the 2nd century BC, Olympos devoutly worshipped Hephaestus (Vulcan), the god of fire, which may have been inspired by the Chimaera, an eternal flame that still burns from the ground not far from the city. Along with the other Lycian coastal cities, Olympos went into a decline in the 1st century BC. With the arrival of the Romans here and at its larger neighbour, Phaselis, at the end of the 1st century AD, things improved, but in the 3rd century renewed pirate attacks brought decline. In the Middle Ages the Venetians and Genoese built fortresses along the coast but by the 15th century the site had been abandoned.

Set inside a deep shaded valley that runs directly to the sea, the ruins of Olympos (admission per day/week TL3/5; ☺9am-7.30pm May-Oct, 8am-6pm Nov-Apr) appear 'undiscovered' among the vines and flower trees. A rare treat is rambling along the trickling Ulupınar Stream that runs through a rocky gorge down to the beach with nary a tour bus in sight.

You can swim at the beach that fronts the site or engage in any of the numerous activities available from agencies and camps in Olympos. The Adventure Centre (☑8921316; ☺8.30am-10pm) at Kadır's Yörük Top Treehouse, for example, can organise the following (prices are per person): boat cruises (full-day trip TL40 with lunch); canyoning (full-day trip TL70, with lunch at trout farm); jeep safaris (full-day trip TL50 with lunch); mountain biking (four hours TL40); rock climbing (TL45 for two climbs on natural wall); diving (TL100 for two dives with equipment and lunch); sea kayaking (half-day trip TL45 with lunch); and trekking (six hours TL45 with lunch).

🛏 Sleeping & Eating

Staying in an Olympos 'tree house' at one of the dozen or so camps that line the track along the valley down to the ruins and beach has long been the stuff of travel legend. The former hippy-trail hot spot has gentrified considerably in past years and is today overcrowded and institutionalised; if you want to chill and commune with nature, head for Kabak. But, love it or hate it, Olympos still offers good value and an up-for-it party atmosphere in a lovely setting. Just remember that 'tree house' is a serious misnomer; few if any huts are actually up in the trees.

Unless specified otherwise, the prices for accommodation at the camps listed here is per person and includes half-board (ie breakfast and dinner); drinks are extra. Bathrooms are generally shared, though some bungalows have en-suite rooms and some even have air-conditioning. Not all tree houses have reliable locks, so store valuables at reception.

Be extra attentive to personal hygiene while staying at Olympos. In summer in particular the huge numbers of visitors can stretch the camps' capacity for proper waste disposal beyond its limit, so be vigilant in particular about where and what you eat. Every year some travellers wind up ill.

Şaban Tree Houses CAMPGROUND, PENSION € (☑892 1265; www.sabanpansion.com; dm/tree house TL25/35, bungalow with bathroom TL35-45; ❄ @) A personal favourite, this is the place to come if you want to snooze in a hammock in the shade of orange trees. In the words of the charming manager Meral, 'It's not a party place' and instead sells itself on tranquillity, space and great home cooking.

Kadır's Yörük Top Treehouse
CAMPGROUND, PENSION €
(☑892 1250; www.kadirstreehouses.com; dm TL15-25, bungalow with bathroom TL40-60; ❄ @) The place that started it all looks like a Wild West boom town that just kept a-growin' and not the Japanese POW camps that others resemble. There are pillows in wooden bungalows, cabins and dorm rooms for 350 heads, the Bull Bar is the liveliest in the valley and the Adventure Centre is on site.

Bayrams CAMPGROUND, PENSION € (☑892 1243; www.bayrams.com; dm TL25-30, tree house TL30-35, bungalow with/without air-con TL50/45; ❄ @) Here guests relax on cushioned benches playing backgammon or reading in the garden or puff away on a nargileh (water pipe) at the bar. Come here if you want to socialise but not necessarily party.

Doğa Pansiyon
CAMPGROUND, PENSION €

(☎892 1066; www.dogapansiyon.net; tree house TL30-35, bungalow with bathroom TL40-45) There's nothing artificial about the new place 'Nature', which is smaller and more subdued than most of the camps. The tree houses (ie elevated huts), with a lovely mountain backdrop, seem particularly well built.

Orange Pension
CAMPGROUND, PENSION €

(☎892 1307; www.olymposorangepension.com; r without/with bathroom TL40/45, bungalow TL45-60; ❄@) A bit edgier than most, this long-standing favourite is especially popular with young Koreans (ever since a popular writer used it as a setting). The Orange has morphed in size in recent years, but Yusuf and Apo still run a pretty good show. The wooden en-suite rooms upstairs feel like a Swiss Family Robinson future, while the concrete rooms downstairs are perhaps the future of Olympos. Deluxe bungalows even have TVs.

Varuna
LOCAL €€

(☎892 1347; www.olymposvaruna.com; mains TL10-15; ☺8am-midnight) Next to Bayrams, this popular restaurant serves a fair range of snacks and mains including pide (TL7-9), trout (TL8) and şiş kebaps (roast skewered meat; TL10 to TL12.50) in an attractive open dining room.

ÇIRALI

Çıralı (cher-*ah*-luh) is a relaxed, family-friendly hamlet of upscale pensions and hotels leading down to and along a beach. It makes an excellent alternative to the backpackers' 'paradise' down the beach at Olympos. And it's the closest thing to the magical and mystical Chimaera.

Some things are even better than you'd imagined – the Taj Mahal springs to mind – and the Chimaera (admission TL3.50, torch/flashlight rental TL3) is just that. Known in Turkish as Yanartaş or 'Burning Rock', it is a cluster of flames that blaze spontaneously from crevices on the rocky slopes of Mt Olympos. At night it looks like hell itself has come to pay a visit and it's not difficult to see why ancient peoples attributed these extraordinary flames to the breath of a monster – part lion, part goat and part snake.

In mythology, Chimaera was the son of Typhon, himself the fierce and monstrous son of Gaia, the earth goddess. Chimaera, who had terrorised Lycia, was killed by the hero Bellerophon on the orders of King Iobates of Lycia, who was testing his prospec-

tive son-in-law. Bellerophon killed the monster by aerial bombardment – mounting the winged horse Pegasus and pouring molten lead into Chimaera's mouth.

Today gas still seeps from the earth and bursts into flame upon contact with the air. The exact composition of the gas is unknown, though it is thought to contain methane. Although the flames can be extinguished by covering them, they will reignite close by into a new and separate flame. At night the 20 or 30 flames in the main area are clearly visible at sea.

The best time to visit is after dinner. From Çıralı, follow the road along the hillside marked for the Chimaera until you reach a valley and walk up to a car park. From there it's another 20- to 30-minute climb up a stepped path to the site; bring or rent a torch. It's a 7km walk from Olympos, but most pensions will run you there for TL5. Agencies organise three-hour 'Chimaera Flame Tours' for TL15, departing at 9pm.

🛏 Sleeping & Eating

Çıralı may look at first like just two dirt roads lined with pensions. But it's a delightful beach community for nature lovers and post-backpackers. Driving in, you cross a small bridge where a few taxis wait to run people back up to the main road. Continue across the bridge and you'll come to a junction in the road with innumerable signboards – there are about 60 pensions here. Go straight on for the pensions nearest to the path up to the Chimaera. Turn right for the pensions closest to the beach and the Olympos ruins.

Myland Nature
PENSION €€

(☎825 7044; www.mylandnature.com; s TL105-145, d TL152-195, tr TL194-250; ❄@) This is an artsy, holistic and very green place that is sure to rub you up the right way (massage, yoga and meditation workshops available). The 13 spotless bungalows are set around a pretty garden and the food (vegetarian set meal TL16.50) garners high praise. Bikes are available, there are daily boat trips and the slide shows of Turkey are inspired.

Hotel Canada
HOTEL €€

(☎825 7233; www.canadahotel.net; d €50-55, 4-person bungalow €75-80; ❄@🏊) This is a beautiful place to stay, offering pretty much the quintessential Çıralı experience: warmth, friendliness and house-made honey. The garden is filled with hammocks, citrus trees, a pool and eight bungalows (ideal for families), and the very comfortable main building has 26 rooms. Canadian Carrie and foodie husband Şaban are impeccable hosts; excellent set meals are TL20. The Canada is 750m from the beach; grab a free bike and pedal on down.

Arcadia Hotel HOTEL €€€
(☎825 7340; www.arcadiaholiday.com; s €70-100, d €90-125; ✿) Now double the size, with another five luxury bungalows at Arcadia 2 across the road, this verdant escape at the northern end of the beach is well laid out and managed, and the friendly owner Ahmet is keen to please. The food at the big circular restaurant with the central open hearth is of a high standard.

Sima Peace Pension PENSION €
(☎825 7245; www.simapeace.com; s TL40-60, d 60-100; ✿@) A comfortable throwback to the '60s (dig the peace sign logo), this nine-room gem has been hiding in a pretty garden down from the beach for decades. Aynur and her jewellery-making girlfriend are the consummate hosts and Koko the parrot adds a tropo feel to the place. Choose one of the rooms upstairs that feel like they were lifted from an old village house.

Olympos Lodge RESORT €€€
(☎825 7171; www.olymposlodge.com.tr; s €110-140, d €140-200; ✿@) Just about the poshest place in town, the Olympos Lodge is not only situated right on the beach but also boasts over 1.5 hectares of cool citrus orchards and verdant, manicured gardens. It's professionally managed and the 13 rooms in five separate villas are peaceful and very luxurious. The breakfasts here are legendary and there's a lovely winter garden open in the cooler months.

Orange Motel PENSION €€
(☎825 7327; www.orangemotel.info; s €30-45, d €40-55, 2-bedroom bungalow €70-85; ✿@) A smart and reasonably priced choice, the Orange is right on the beach. The garden is hung with hammocks and the wrought-iron circular stairs lead to 14 agreeable rooms and bungalows. The evening meal is a snip at TL20.

İpek Pastanesi CAFE, CONFECTIONER €
(☎825 7200; cakes TL5; ⏱8am-11pm) Should you require a sugar fix, you won't do any better than this excellent cafe and patisserie near the beach.

ℹ Getting There & Away

Virtually any bus taking the coastal road between Fethiye and Antalya will drop you off or pick you up at the stops near the Olympos and Çıralı junctions. Just make sure you specify which one you want. From there, minibuses (TL5 or TL6) leave for both destinations.

For Olympos (9km), minibuses depart every hour between 8am and 7pm from May to October. Returning, minibuses leave Olympos at 9am, then every hour until 8pm, picking up passengers along the road.

After October they will wait until enough passengers arrive, which can sometimes take quite a while. Assuming enough people show up, the dolmuş then passes all the camps until it reaches the one the driver is paid to stop at.

To Çıralı (7km) there are minibuses every two hours or so but they don't usually depart until there are at least four passengers. They usually do a loop along the beach road, then pass the turn-off to the Chimaera and head back along the edge of the hillside.

Most of the places to stay listed will pick you up from the highway if you ask them in advance.

Phaselis

About 6km north of the turn-offs for Olympos and Çıralı from the D400 is the incomparably romantic ancient Lycian city of Phaselis. Apparently founded by colonists from Rhodes as early as the 7th century BC on the border between Lycia and Pamphylia, its wealth came from its role as a port for the shipment of timber, rose oil and perfume, which it carried on doing until the early Middle Ages.

Shaded by pines, the **ruins of Phaselis** (admission TL8; ⏱8.30am-7pm May-Oct, 8am-5pm Nov-Apr) are arranged around three small, perfect bays, each with its own diminutive beach. The ruins are extensive and well-worth exploring but most date from Roman and Byzantine times. Look out for **Hadrian's Gate** – he visited in 129 AD – the **agora** at the South Harbour and the wonderful **colonnaded street** running down from the North Harbour.

The site entrance is about 1km from the D400, where there is a small building with soft drinks, snacks and souvenirs for sale. The ruins and the shore are another 1km further on.

If you're keen to sit on top of the world and look down on creation, a new cable car (teleferik) called **Tahtalı 2365** (☎814 3047; www.tahtali.com; adult/child 7-16yr TL50/25;

⏱9am-7pm May-Sep, 10am-6pm Oct-Apr) climbs almost to the top of **Tahtalı Dağ** (Wooded Mountain), the centrepiece of **Olympos Beydağları National Park** (Olimpos Beydağları Sahil Milli Parkı). The turn-off from the highway is about 3km before Phaselis. A well-paved but steep road then carries on for 7km to the cable car's lower station at 725m. The gondolas seat 80 people and depart every half-hour in summer and hourly in winter. The trip takes 12 minutes.

ℹ️ Getting There & Away

Frequent buses on the highway from Antalya (TL7.50, 45 minutes, 58km) and Kemer (TL4, 20 minutes, 15km) pass both the turn-offs for Phaselis and Tahtalı 2365. The cable car company also lays on a bus to/from Kemer (TL10), which you must book a day in advance.

Antalya

📞 0242 / POP 956,000

Once seen simply as the gateway to the Turkish Riviera, Antalya is today very much a destination in its own right. Situated directly on the Gulf of Antalya (Antalya Körfezi), the largest Turkish city on the western Mediterranean coast is both classically beautiful and stylishly modern. It boasts the wonderfully preserved antique quarter of Kaleiçi – literally 'within the castle' – a splendid Roman-era harbour and one of Turkey's finest museums. In the surrounding Bey Dağları (Bey Mountains) are some superb ruins.

Boutique hotels have sprung up in Antalya in recent years like mushrooms after rain and are of an international standard and good value. For partygoers, there are a number of excellent bars and clubs, while the opera and ballet season at the Aspendos amphitheatre continues to draw critical attention.

History

The city was named Attaleia after its 2nd-century founder Attalus II of Pergamum. Attaleia came under Roman rule in 133 BC and, when Emperor Hadrian visited three years later, he entered via a triumphal arch (now known as Hadrian's Gate) built in his honour.

The Byzantines took over from the Romans but in 1206 Seljuk Turks based in Konya snatched the city from them and gave Antalya both a new name and an icon: the Yivli Minare (Fluted Minaret). Antalya fell to the Ottomans in 1391.

After WWI the Allies divided up the Ottoman Empire and Antalya was ceded to Italy in 1918. In 1921 it was liberated

Antalya

◎ Top Sights

Antalya Museum...A2

✖ Eating

1 Can Can Pide ve Kebap Salonu...........D2
2 Club Arma..C2
3 Güneyliler...C1

Entertainment

    Club Arma......................................(see 2)

Antalya

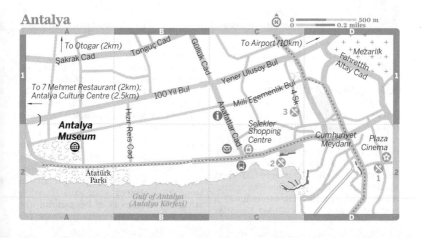

ANTALYA & THE WESTERN MEDITERRANEAN

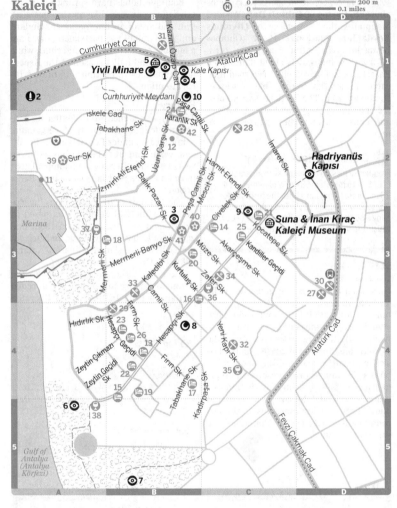

by Atatürk's army and made a provincial capital.

◉ Sights & Activities

Yivli Minare LANDMARK

Antalya's symbol is the Yivli Minare (Map p350), a handsome and distinctive 'fluted' minaret erected by the Seljuk sultan Aladdin Keykubad I in the early 13th century. The adjacent mosque is still in use. Within the complex is a heavily restored **Mevlevi tekke** (whirling dervish monastery; Map p350), which probably dates from the 13th century. It now houses **Güzel Sanatlar**

Galerisi (Fine Arts Gallery; Map p350; admission free; ⊙10am-7pm) with changing exhibits. Next door are two **türbe** (tombs; Map p350) from the late 14th century. The broad plaza to the west with the bombastic equestrian **statue of Atatürk** is Cumhuriyet Meydanı.

Kaleiçi HISTORIC AREA

Antalya's historical district begins at the main square called **Kale Kapısı** (Fortress Gate), which is marked by an old stone **clock tower** (saat kalesi) and a **statue of Attalus II of Pergamum**, the city's founder. To the northeast is the **İki**

Kapılar Hanı, a sprawling bazaar dating to the late 15th century.

Walk south along Uzun Çarşi Sokak, the street opposite the clock tower. On the left is the 18th-century **Tekeli Mehmet Paşa Camii** (Map p350), a mosque built by then Beylerbey (Governor of Governors) and repaired extensively in 1886 and 1926. Note the beautiful Arabic inscriptions in the coloured tiles above the windows.

Wander further into this protected zone; many of the gracious old **Ottoman houses** have been restored and converted into pensions, boutique hotels and shops. To the east and at the top of Hesapçi Sokak is the monumental **Hadriyanüs Kapısı** (Hadrian's Gate; Map p350), also known here as Üçkapılar or the 'Three Gates', erected during the Roman emperor's visit to Antalya in 130 BC.

The **Roman harbour** at the base of the slope was Antalya's lifeline from the 2nd century BC until late in the 20th century, when a new port was constructed about 12km west of the city, at the far end of Konyaaltı Plajı. The harbour was restored during the 1980s and is now a marina for yachts and excursion boats.

In the southern reaches of Kaleiçi is the **Kesik Minare** (Truncated Minaret; Map p350), a stump of a tower marking the ruins of a substantial building that played many roles over the century. Built originally as a 2nd-century Roman temple, it was converted into the Byzantine Church of the Virgin Mary in the 5th century and a mosque in 1361. Fire destroyed most of it in the 19th century but it is still possible to see bits of Roman and Byzantine marble from the outside.

At the southwestern edge of Kaleiçi, on the corner with **Karaalıoğlu Parkı**

(Map p350), a large, attractive, flower-filled park with good views, rises **Hıdırlık Kalesi** (Map p350), a 14m-high tower in the ancient walls from the 2nd century AD.

Suna & İnan Kiraç Kaleiçi Museum
MUSEUM

(Map p350; ☑243 4274; www.kaleicimuzesi.org; Kocatepe Sokak 25; admission TL3; ☺9am-noon & 1-6pm Thu-Tue) In the heart of Kaleiçi, just off Hesapçı Sokak, this small but well-formed ethnography museum is housed in a lovingly restored Antalya mansion. The 2nd floor contains a well-executed series of life-size dioramas depicting some of the most important rituals and customs of Ottoman Antalya. Much more impressive is the collection of Çanakkale and Kütahya ceramics found in the exhibition hall behind, the former Greek Orthodox church of Aya Yorgi (St George), which has been fully restored and is worth a look in itself.

Antalya Museum
MUSEUM

(Map p349; ☑236 5688; Konyaaltı Caddesi 1; admission TL15; ☺9am-7.30pm Tue-Sun Apr-Oct, 8am-5.30pm Tue-Sun Nov-Mar) On no account should you miss this comprehensive museum about 2km west of the centre and accessible on the *tramvay* (tram). The museum is large, with exhibitions in a dozen large halls that cover everything from the Stone and Bronze Ages to Byzantium, so allow sufficient time. Unmissable are the Hall of Regional Excavations, which exhibit finds from Lycian (eg Patara and Xanthos) and Pamphylian cities; the Marble Portraits Hall, with evocative busts bearing incredibly realistic expressions and emotions; and the sublime Hall of Gods.

Even those not especially interested in Greek mythology will be moved by this collection, which includes representations of some 15 Olympian gods, many of them in near-perfect condition. Most of the statues, including the sublime Three Graces, were found at Perge; viewing the gods, which are spotlighted as you approach, either before or after a visit is advised.

Upstairs are coins and other gold artefacts recovered from Aspendos, Side and some Byzantine sites. Taking pride of place is the so-called Elmalı Treasure of almost 2000 Lycian coins looted from Turkey in 1984, returned from the USA 15 years later and now on display for the first time.

Hamams
HAMAM

Kaleiçi is a great place to experience the joys of the traditional Turkish bath, most notably at the 700-year-old **Balık Pazarı Hamamı** (Map p350; ☑243 6175; Balık Pazarı Sokak; ☺8am-11pm) where a bath, a peeling, and a soap and oil massage costs TL35 (TL13 for a bath and scrub only). More of the same can be found at the atmospheric **Sefa Hamamı** (Map p350; ☑241 2321; www.sefahamam.com; Kocatepe Sokak 32; ☺9.30am-10pm), which retains much of its 13th-century Seljuk architecture. A bath here costs TL15; it's TL35 for the works. Both hamams have separate sections for men and women.

Boat & Rafting Trips
CRUISE

Excursion yachts tie up in the Roman harbour in Kaleiçi. Some trips go as far as Kemer, Phaselis, Olympos, Demre (Kale) and even Kaş. You can take one-/two-hour trips (TL20/35) or a six-hour voyage (TL60 with lunch) which visits Kemer and Phaselis, the Gulf of Antalya islands and some beaches for a swim.

Many travel agencies in town offer white-water rafting in the Köprülü Kanyon for around TL50.

★ Festivals & Events

Antalya's annual red-letter event is the **Golden Orange Film Festival** (Altın Portakal Film Festivalı; www.altinportakal.org.tr), held in early October. Another internationally recognised one is the **Antalya International Piano Festival** (Antalya Uluslararası Piyano Festivalı; www.antalyapianofestivali.com), held at the **Antalya Culture Centre** (Antalya Kültür Merkezi; ☑238 5444; 100 Yıl Bulvarı) west of the city centre.

🛏 Sleeping

The best place to stay in Antalya is the old town of Kaleiçi (Map p350), a virtually vehicle-free district that has everything you need, including some of the better guest houses in Turkey. Kaleiçi's winding streets can be confusing to navigate, although signs pointing the way to most pensions are posted on street corners.

⌂TOP⌂ **Tuvana Hotel** BOUTIQUE HOTEL €€€
CHOICE (Map p350; ☑247 6015; www.tuvanahotel.com; Karanlık Sokak 18; s & d €140-300; ❄@⛱) Among the most beautiful and intimate hotels on the Turkish Mediterranean coast, this discreet compound of six Ottoman houses has been converted into a refined city hotel with 46 rooms

and suites. The Tuvana's sophistication is personified by hosts Nermin and Aziz, who look after this 'Special Class' hotel (and dreamy breakfast table) with precision and grace. Rooms are suitably plush, with kilims, linen and light fittings as well as such mod-cons as DVD players. The swimming pool is a bonus in the warmer months and the main restaurant Seraser is world-class.

White Garden Pansiyon
PENSION €

(Map p350; ☎241 9115; www.whitegardenpansion.com; Hesapçı Geçidi 9; s/d TL35/45; ❄ @) The 15-room White Garden combines tidiness and class beyond its price level, with impeccable service from Metin and his staff. The building itself is a fine restoration; the courtyard is particularly charming. Guests get to use the pool at the Secret Palace (☎244 1060; www.secretpalacepansion.com; Fırın Sokak 10; s/d TL45/60; ❄ @), an Ottoman conversion in the same stable behind the White Garden with 11 rooms that have fridges.

Villa Perla
PENSION €€

(Map p350; ☎248 9793; Hesapçı Sokak 26; s/d TL100/160; ❄ ≋) We love this authentic Ottoman place hidden in a courtyard (with pool and tortoises) off Hesapçı Sokak. The 10 comfortable rooms are at the top of a staircase that starts with a 12th-century stone step, the wooden ceilings are the real deal and some rooms have four-post beds and folk-painted cupboards. Mama Perla makes all the meze at her in-house restaurant.

Mediterra Art Hotel
BOUTIQUE HOTEL €€

(Map p350; ☎244 8624; www.mediterraart.com; Zafer Sokak 5; s €52-84, d €69-126; ❄ @ ≋) This upscale masterpiece of wood and stone once housed a Greek tavern (see 19th-century frescoes and graffiti on the restaurant wall). The Mediterra offers sanctuary by a cutting-edge pool, a marvellous winter dining room and 20 small though modestly luxurious rooms. On the top floor via ancient stone steps is a small art gallery.

Sabah Pansiyon
PENSION €

(Map p350; ☎247 5345; www.sabahpansiyon.8m.com; Hesapçı Sokak 60; dm/s/d without shower TL20/30/40, s/d with shower TL35/45; ❄ @) Long one of the first ports of call for budget travellers to Antalya, the Sabah has 22 rooms that vary greatly so ask to see a couple. The Sabah brothers run the place with aplomb while Mama takes care of the kitch-

en. A real draw is the shaded courtyard, perfect for hooking up with other travellers.

Antalya Hostel
HOSTEL, PENSION €

(Map p350; ☎248 9723; www.antalyahostel.com; Hesapçı Sokak 54; dm/s/d/tr TL25/50/75/90; ❄ @) This attractive and attractively priced new kid on the block, just down from the Kesik Minare, has 14 rooms, including dormitory accommodation with four beds. Rooms are furnished simply but stylishly (love the gold-backed chairs and coloured lights in the stairwell) and some – rooms 205 and 206 – have sea views. Guests get to use the pool at the Hotel Blue Sea Garden.

Mavi & Anı Pansiyon
PENSION €

(Map p350; ☎247 0056; www.maviani.com; Tabakhane Sokak 26; s/d TL50/70; ❄ @) This lovingly restored Ottoman house has 15 rooms, some of which are loft-style, and the common areas are decorated in old Anatolian furniture and bric-a-brac. Try to bag a single or double room with attached terrace and sea view. There's a large family room (TL150) on the top floor.

Hotel Blue Sea Garden
HOTEL €€

(Map p350; ☎248 8213; www.hotelblueseagarden.com; Hesapçı Sokak 65; s/d TL60/90; ❄ @ ≋) The plus here is the swimming pool in a leafy courtyard – vital in the heat of summer. The rooms are nothing special (with small bathrooms), though the elevated ones are more peaceful and we hear good things about the in-house restaurant.

Kaleiçi Lodge
BOUTIQUE HOTEL €€€

(Map p350; ☎243 2270; www.kaleicilodge.com; Hesapçı Sokak 37; s/d TL120/180; ❄ @) This very central 14-room hotel is less-than-welcoming but stylish. The rather stark lobby gives on to a courtyard crammed with curiosities, and hallways lead to red-draped, sharp-lined rooms, with lots of wrought iron and old woods in attendance. The top-floor suite with two bedrooms is filled with antiques and has a jacuzzi.

La Paloma Hotel
HOTEL €€

(Map p350; ☎244 8497; www.lapalomapansion.com; Tabakhane Sokak 3; s/d TL70/100; ❄ @ ≋) Slightly away from the action and all the more attractive (and quiet) for that, La Paloma has 14 surprisingly large rooms for a single converted Ottoman building. The best of the lot face inwards to the figure-eight-shaped swimming pool. Some rooms have ceiling fans.

Atelya Art Hotel
HOTEL €€

(Map p350; ☑241 6416; www.atelyahotel.com; Civelek Sokak 21; s/d TL70/100; ✴@) Timelessness is hard to pin down, but the Atelya makes a bold effort in this eccentric art-inspired 30-room hotel contained in two old buildings and two newer ones. The owner displays his diverse portfolio on the walls, but it's the sultanic splendour of richly coloured fabrics and beautiful furniture cast in beams of sunlight that best capture the spirit of the Ottomans. It's an excellent midrange choice.

Otantik Butik Otel
BOUTIQUE HOTEL €€€

(Map p350; ☑244 8530; www.otantikbutikotel.com; Hesapçı Sokak 14; s/d TL160/200; ✴@) In a class of its own among Ottoman houses converted into boutique hotels, the Otantik is...well...'authentic' in that the 10 rooms are stylish but simple and on the small side. The restaurant has a particularly well-stocked wine cellar.

Marina Residence
LUXURY HOTEL €€€

(Map p350; ☑247 5490; www.marinaresidence.net; Mermerli Sokak 15; s/d €110/130; ✴☒) Located away from the hubbub, the Marina has been known as one of Antalya's signature top-end hotels for more than two decades. The 41 rooms have been freshened up and eight of them face the marina to the west. The Marina's oddest touch is its outdoor pool; a glass wall on one side allows cafe patrons a view of the underwater goings-on.

✖ Eating

A nearly endless assortment of cafes and eateries are tucked in and around the harbour area. For cheap eating, cross over Atatürk Caddesi into the commercial district.

Seraser
MEDITERRANEAN, MODERN TURKISH €€€

(Map p350; www.seraserrestaurant.com; Tuvana Hotel, Karanlık Sokak 18; mains TL28-45) The signature restaurant at the Tuvana Hotel and arguably the city's best, Seraser offers international dishes with a Mediterranean slant – try the grouper with rosemary and samphire or the quail with mustard honey glaze – in especially fine Ottoman surrounds. (We love the pasha-style chairs and the glass-bead chandelier.) The Turkish coffee *crème brûlée* is legendary.

Parlak Restaurant
ANATOLIAN €€

(Map p350; ☑241 6553; www.parlakrestaurant.com; Zincirli Han, Kazım Özlap Caddesi 7; mains TL8-20) Opposite the jewellery bazaar and just off the pedestrian Kazım Özlap Caddesi is this sprawling open-air patio restaurant in an old caravanserai favoured by locals and famous for its slow-roasted chicken (one-half TL8) and excellent meze.

Sim Restaurant
RESTAURANT €€

(Map p350; ☑248 0107; Kaledibi Sokak 7; mains TL12.50-20) A choice of seated areas makes this simple but charming restaurant a unique experience. When the weather's fine, dine underneath the canopy in the narrow passageway at the front wedged against ancient Byzantine walls. Inside, global graffiti gives it a youthful pulse, while upstairs, eclectic antiques complement *köfte*, white bean salads and glorious *cobra* (soups).

Hasanağa Restaurant
RESTAURANT-BAR €€

(Map p350; ☑247 1313; Mescit Sokak 15; mains TL15-20) Expect to find the garden dining area here packed on Friday and Saturday nights, when traditional Turkish musicians and folk dancers entertain from 8pm onwards. Dishes are predictable – *köfte*, mixed grills and the like – although the cooks do produce some veggie dishes (around TL15).

Vanilla
INTERNATIONAL €€

(Map p350; ☑247 6013; Zafer Sokak 13; mains TL20-30) Another indicator of Antalya's rising stock is this outstanding, ultra-modern restaurant led by British chef Wayne and his Turkish wife, Emel. Glass surfaces and creamy vanilla leather seating provide a warm, unfussy atmosphere and allow you to concentrate on the menu: French- and Italian-influenced international dishes.

Club Arma
SEAFOOD €€€

(Map p349; ☑244 9710; www.clubarma.com.tr; Yatlimanı 42; mains TL30-49) Current tenant of a former oil depot built right into the cliff-side above the harbour, this pricey fish restaurant specialises in meze (brought to you properly on a tray to choose from) and seafood in its infinite variety. As its name implies, the place moonlights as a club and is one of Antalya's sexiest venues to sip a gin and tonic. Just be careful not to fall off the fabulous open terrace or you'll literally end up in the drink.

Villa Perla
FAMILY RESTAURANT €€

(Map p350; ☑248 9793; Hesapçı Sokak 26; mains TL13-21) A small garden restaurant attached to a popular pension, this relaxing spot has a locally renowned meze plate (TL14) prepared by host Mama Perla and (among other things) a full nine rabbit dishes (around TL17) on offer.

7 Mehmet Restaurant   MODERN TURKISH €€€
(📞238 5200; www.7mehmet.com; Atatürk Kültür Parkı 333; meze TL5-9, mains TL12-30; ⏰noon-midnight) Antalya's most famous eatery is a couple of kilometres west of the centre, and its spacious indoor and outdoor dining areas occupy a hill overlooking Konyaaltı Plajı and the city. The menu of grilled mains, fish and meze is unsurprising but reliable; ask for a peek in the enormous kitchen.

Gül Restoran   RESTAURANT €€
(Map p350; 📞243 2284; Kocatepe Sokak 1; mains TL13-24) On the edge of Atatürk Caddesi is this intimate garden restaurant shaded by a grove of Antalya's famous orange trees and popular with visiting German couples. The meze (TL4) – there are seven different ones each day – are well known.

Can Can Pide ve Kebap Salonu   KEBAPÇI €
(Map p349; 📞243 2548; Arık Caddesi 4/A; pide TL3-4, dürüm TL5-6; ⏰9am-11pm Mon-Sat) Looking for something very cheap and cheerful? Fantastically prepared *çorba* (soup), pide and Adana *dürüm* (beef kebap rolled in pitta) are here at bargain prices. It's opposite the landmark Plaza Cinema.

Konukzade Konağı   LOCAL €€
(Map p350; 📞244 7456; Hıdırlık Sokak 20-22; mains TL13-21) This attractive home-style restaurant, with couches, art on display and a garden in front, is overseen by a friendly long-term expat Dutch woman. The busy kitchen makes reasonably priced Turkish dishes, plus a renowned *appeltaart* (apple pie; TL5).

Ottoman Garden   CAFE-BAR €€
(Map p350; 📞248 8890; Kocatepe Sokak 4-6; dishes TL10; ⏰9am-midnight) This delightful open-air cafe-bar serves drinks and nargileh as well as simple grilled dishes like *şiş* kebap.

Güneyliler   KEBAPÇI €€
(Map p349; 📞241 1117; 4 Sokak 12/A; meals TL9-12) With its cafeteria-style interior, this reasonably priced locals-only joint isn't much to look at. But the wood-fired *lahmacun* (Turkish-style pizza; TL6) and expertly grilled kebaps are served with so many complimentary extras, you'll want to return. If you get lost, ask for directions at the landmark Best Western Khan Hotel at Kazım Özlap Caddesi 55.

Paul's Place   CAFE €
(Map p350; 📞244 6894; www.stpaulcc-turkey.com; Yeni Kapı Sokak 24; latte TL4, cakes TL3.5; ⏰10am-6pm Mon-Fri; 🖥) The good word comes in coffee cups at this informal expat 'club' on the 2nd-floor of the St Paul Cultural Center. Regardless of your faith, enjoy the espresso or filter coffee and home-baked pastries on offer. There's a well-stocked lending library with 2500 books.

Hesapçı Lounge   CAFE, CONFECTIONER €
(Map p350; 📞247 6013; Zafer Sokak 13; ice cream TL3.50, cakes TL7.50; ⏰9am-1am; 🖥) Next door to the restaurant Vanilla and under the same management, this very slick cafe offers imported ice cream (it's Mövenpick) and a genuine Lavazza espresso machine for those weary of the Turkish coffee.

🍷 Drinking & Entertainment

Kaleiçi has a lot to offer after dark. There are buzzy beer gardens with million dollar views, live music venues with everything from rock to *türkü* (Turkish folk music) and raunchy clubs and discotheques where drinks are outrageously expensive and Russian prostitutes are in full force. Both Club Arma and the Hasanağa Restaurant don their party clothes after serving their last dessert.

Kale Bar   BAR
(Map p350; 📞248 6591; Mermerli Sokak 2; beer TL8; ⏰11am-2am) This patio bar attached to the CH Tükevi Hotel may very well command the most spectacular harbour and sea view in all of Antalya. Cocktails are priced accordingly (TL15 to TL22).

Terrace Bar   BAR-CAFE
(Map p350; Hıdırlık Sokak; beer TL5, coffee TL4; ⏰8am-midnight) High above the cliffs at the end of Hesapçı Sokak and opposite the Hıdırlık Kalesi, the Terrace offers drinks and end-of-the-world views.

Dem-Lik   BAR-CAFE
(Map p350; 📞247 1930; Hesapçı Sokak 16; beer TL4, coffee TL4; ⏰noon-midnight) Dem-Lik is located (mostly) in a large garden behind high stone walls, where Antalya's university crowd reshapes the world between ice-cold beers, while listening to (mostly) rock and blues.

Bar Nokta   BAR-CAFE
(Map p350; 📞247 4054; Yeni Kapı Sokak 9-11; beer TL4, coffee TL4; ⏰8am-midnight) Attached to a local culture centre on the top floor of a renovated Ottoman house, this is a low-key

SERVICES FROM ANTALYA'S OTOGAR

DESTINATION	FARE (TL)	DURATION (HR)	DISTANCE (KM)	FREQUENCY (PER DAY)
Adana	40	11	565	several buses
Alanya	15	3	135	every 20 min
Ankara	45	8	555	frequent
Çanakkale	65	12	770	several
Denizli (Pamukkale)	25	4	225	several
Eğirdir	25	3½	195	every hr
Fethiye (coastal)	25	7½	285	several
Fethiye (inland)	18	4	200	several
Göreme/Ürgüp	40	9	485	frequent
İstanbul	70	11½	785	frequent
İzmir	40	8	470	several
Kaş	16	3½	188	frequent
Kemer	7	1½	55	every 15 min
Konya	25	5	305	several
Marmaris	40	6	365	several
Olympos/Çıralı	13	1½	80	several minibuses & buses
Side/Manavgat	15	1½	65	every 20 min in high season

neighbourhood choice and a good place to start an evening out.

Kralın Bahçesi LIVE MUSIC
(Map p350; ☎248 4766; Paşa Camii Sokak 33; ◉7am-3am) A cafe (including amply supplied water pipes) by day and raging live-act rock and pop venue by night, the 'King's Garden' is a regal act any time you stop by.

Filika LIVE MUSIC
(Map p350; ☎244 8266; Mescit Sokak 46; ◉8pm-1am Sun-Thu, 9pm-2am Fri & Sat) This *türkü* (Turkish folk music) venue above Mescit Sokak in the centre of Kaleiçi attracts a way-cool young Turkish crowd.

Rock Bar CLUB, LIVE MUSIC
(Map p350; off Uzun Çarşı) Something of a throwback to the grunge era, this dark tavern features local guitar bands playing covers of alt-rock classics. Located down an alley directly across the street from Natta Travel Centre on Uzun Çarşı Sokak; look for the excavation site to the left.

Club Ally CLUB
(Map p350; ☎247 3824; Sur Sokak 4-8; admission TL20) A massive outdoor discotheque at the harbour complete with nine bars, laser lights, and an eardrum-shattering sound system featuring mostly Top 40 and hip-hop. Club Ally is best experienced late at night, when a sea of beautiful bodies can be found dramatically gyrating around the dance floor's circular bar.

ℹ Information
Bookshop
Owl Bookshop (Map p350; ☎0532 632 3275; owlbookshop@yahoo.com; Kocatepe Sokak 9; ◉10am-7pm Mon-Sat) Ever on the move, this second-hand bookshop south of Hadrian's Gate is pretty well stocked.

Internet Access
Rıhtım Cafe (Map p350; per hr TL1; ◉9am-midnight) A dozen computers in a nargileh cafe north of Cumhuriyet Meydanı.

Solemar Internet Cafe (Map p349; per hr TL1; ◉8am-11pm) Some 18 computers in a small space east of Hadrian's Gate.

Internet Resources

Antalya Guide (www.antalyaguide.org) A comprehensive site with info on everything from climate to TV channels.

Antalya Times (www.antalyatimes.com) Website of relatively useful monthly freebie available throughout town.

Tourist Information

Tourist office (Map p349; 241 1747; Anafatlar Caddesi 31; ☺8am-6pm Mon-Fri) Office with bankers' hours just north of the landmark Seleker Shopping Centre and tram stop.

Getting There & Away

Air

Antalya's busy airport is 10km east of the city centre on the D400 highway. There's a tourist information desk and a number of car-hire agencies have counters here as well. Turkish Airlines and its regional budget airline Anadolu have about a dozen daily nonstop flights year-round to/from İstanbul (TL60 to TL100 one-way) and four to/from Ankara (TL30 to TL165).

Bus

Antalya's otogar, about 4km north of the city centre on highway D650, consists of two large terminals fronted by a park. Looking at the otogar from the main highway or its parking lot, the Şehirlerarası Terminalı (Intercity Terminal), which serves long-distance destinations, is on the right. The İlçeler Terminali (Domestic Terminal), serving nearby destinations such as Side and Alanya, is on the left. Buses heading to Olympos and Kaş depart from a stop directly across the street from the Sheraton Voyager Antalya Hotel west of the centre.

Getting Around

Antalya's original 6km-long single-track *tramvay* (TL1.20) has 10 stops and provides the simplest way of crossing town. It runs every half-hour between 7am and 9pm. You pay as you board and exit through the rear door. Though there are plans to extend it, at present the tram runs from the Antalya Museum (the Müze stop is nearest to Konyaaltı Plajı) along Konyaaltı Caddesi, Cumhuriyet Caddesi, Atatürk Caddesi and Isıklar Caddesi.

A double-track tram line with 15 stations called AntRay, which opened in early 2009, links northern areas of the city to the south and the coast, and is for commuters not tourists (though it might help in getting to and from the otogar). The two tram lines are not linked at present though the İsmet Paşa stop on the AntRay is a short walk from the central Kale Kapısı stop on the tramway.

To/From the Airport

Havaş buses (TL10) depart from the Antalya airport every 30 minutes or so. Passengers are conveniently dropped off at the Sheraton Voyager Antalya Hotel or Kale Kapısı, just outside Kaleiçi. To return to the airport, catch the shuttle from along Cumhuriyet Caddesi (take the tramway to the Selekler stop).

To/From the Bus Station

The blue-and-white Terminal Otobusu 93 (TL1) heads for Atatürk Caddesi in the town centre every 20 minutes or so from the bus shelter near the taxi stand and takes about an hour. To get from Kaleiçi to the otogar, go out of Hadrian's Gate, turn right and wait at any of the bus stops along Atatürk Caddesi.

If you're in a hurry, the new AntRay has a stop called Otogar at the bus station that is eight stops from the central stop İsmet Paşa just outside Kaleiçi. Problem is, you have to cross a very busy highway to board it at present.

Too complicated? A taxi between the otogar and Kaleiçi should cost between TL18 and TL22.

Around Antalya

Antalya is an excellent base for excursions to the ancient sites of Phaselis, Termessos, Perge, Aspendos and Selge. If you're travelling strictly along the coast, however, substantial time can be saved by visiting Phaselis on your way to or from Olympos or Kaş. Likewise, visiting Perge and Aspendos is easiest when travelling to or from Side or Alanya.

There's a huge array of travel agencies in Antalya's Kaleiçi area offering tours, including smaller ones like **Yunaya Travel** (Map p350; ☺247 9971; www.yunayatour.com; Uzun Çarşı Sokak 15/B; ☺9am-9pm). A full-day tour to Termessos with a stop at the Düden Şelalesi (Düden Falls) costs TL60 including lunch. Ones to Perge and Aspendos with side-trips to Side and the Manavgat waterfall cost TL90. There are plenty of car-rental agencies here including **Gaye Rent a Car** (☺247 1000; www.gayerentacar.com; İmaret Sokak), hiring out cars for TL50 to TL70 (scooters TL30 to TL35) per day.

TERMESSOS

Hidden high in a rugged mountain valley, 34km northwest of Antalya, lies the ruined but still massive city of **Termessos** (admission TL10; ☺8am-7pm May-Oct, 8.30am-5pm Nov-Apr). Neither Greek nor Lycian, the inhabitants were Pisidian, fierce and prone to battling. They successfully fought off Alexander the Great in 333 BC, and the Romans (perhaps wisely) accepted Termessos' wishes to remain an independent ally in 70 BC.

Termessos is spread out and requires much scrambling over loose rocks and up steep though well-marked paths. Allow a minimum of two hours to explore; you need closer to four hours if you plan to see everything. And bring plenty of drinking water.

The first remains you'll come across at the end of the access road (King's Rd) are within the car park. The portal on the hillock to the west was once the entrance to the **Artemis-Hadrian Temple** and **Hadrian Propylaeum**. From here follow the steep path south; you'll see remains of the lower city walls on both sides and pass through the city gate before reaching, in about 20 minutes, the **lower gymnasium** and **baths** on your left. A short distance further on your right are the **upper city walls** and the **colonnaded street**. Next the **upper agora** and its five large **cisterns** is an ideal spot to explore slowly and to catch a bit of shade. Push on to the nearby **theatre**, which sits in an absolutely jaw-dropping locale atop a peak, surrounded by a mountain range that seems remarkably closer than it actually is; you can see Antalya on a clear day. Walk southwest from the theatre to view the cut-limestone **bouleuterion**, but use caution when scrambling across the crumbled **Temple of Artemis** and **Temple of Zeus** south of it.

The **southern necropolis** is at the very top of the valley, 3km – or one hour's walk – up from the car park. Viewed from afar, it's a rather disturbing scene of sarcophagi that seem to have been tossed indiscriminately from the mountainside by angry gods. In reality, earthquakes and grave robbers created the mess.

Termessos National Park (Termessos Milli Parkı), which surrounds the site, abounds in wildlife including mountain goats, speckled deer, golden eagles and 680 species of plant (80 of them endemic). At the entrance, the small **Flora and Fauna Museum** contains a bit of information about the ruined city, as well as about the botany and zoology of the immediate area.

❶ Getting There & Away

Taxi tours from Antalya cost around TL90, with excursions about TL60. An even cheaper option is to catch a bus from Antalya otogar bound for Korkuteli and alight at the entrance to the national park. Taxis waiting here in the warmer months will run you up the 9km-long King's Rd to the ruins and back for TL25.

KARAIN CAVE

The oldest settlement in Turkey, Karain Cave (Karain Mağarası), 12km northeast of Termessos, is believed by archaeologists (who first excavated the site between 1946 and 1973) to have been continuously occupied for 25,000 years. Much of what has been discovered, including stone hand axes and arrowheads, now resides in the Antalya Museum and in Ankara's Museum of Anatolian Civilisations, though an onsite **museum** (admission TL3; ☺9am-7.30pm Apr-Oct, 8am-5pm Nov-Mar) has a small but interesting collection of teeth and bones, including bone fragments of Neanderthal man and the skull of a child found in the cave. More recent excavations suggest the cave was used as a temple in the late Roman period.

The entrance to the cave is 250m (and 230 steps) up the hill behind the car park and museum to the cave.

❶ Getting There & Away

With your own car you can easily visit Termessos and Karain in the same day; a taxi tour combining the two costs around TL100. Descending from Termessos, take the Karain road just outside the national park then follow the signs. Coming from Antalya it's the next

Termessos

0 ———— 200 m
0 ———— 0.1 miles

To Antalya (34km)

Artemis-Hadrian Temple & Hadrian Propylaeum
Hadrian's Gate
Cistern
Lower City Walls
Rock Tomb
City Gate
Lower City Walls
Colonnaded Street
Gymnasium & Baths
Upper City Walls
Tomb of Alcetas
Termessian House
Unidentified Building
Attalos Stoa
Osbaras Stoa
Theatre
Corinthian Temple
Agora
Upper Agora
Heroon
Upper Gymnasium
To Southern Necropolis (2km)
Bouleuterion
Temple of Zeus
Temple of Artemis

left (heading toward Döşemealtı) after route E87/D350 to Korkuteli.

PERGE

Some 17km east of Antalya and 2km north of Aksu on highway D400, Perge (admission TL15; ☉9am-7pm Apr-Oct, 8.30am-5pm Nov-Mar) was one of the most important towns of ancient Pamphylia. It experienced two golden ages: during the Hellenistic period in the 2nd and 3rd centuries BC and under the Romans in the 2nd and 3rd centuries AD (from which most of the ruins here date). Turkish archaeologists first began excavations here in 1946 and a selection of the statues discovered – many in magnificent condition – can be seen at the Antalya Museum.

The **theatre** (capacity 14,000) and **stadium**, which sat 12,000, appear along the access road before you reach the site itself; both are closed at present. Inside the site, walk through the massive **Roman Gate** with its four arches; to the left is the **southern nymphaeum** and well-preserved **baths** and to the right the large square-shaped **agora**. Beyond the **Hellenistic Gate**, with its two huge towers, is the fine **colonnaded street**, where an impressive collection of columns still stands.

The water source for the narrow concave channel running down the centre of the colonnaded street was the **northern nymphaeum**, which dates to the 2nd century AD. From here it's possible to follow a path to the ridge of the hill with the **acropolis.** The ruins here date from the Byzantine era, when many of the city's inhabitants took refuge after attacks from invaders on the flat land below.

ℹ Getting There & Away

Dolmuşes leave for Aksu (TL2, 30 minutes, 15km) from Antalya otogar up to 15 times a day. You can easily walk the remaining 2km north to the ruins. An excursion to both Perge and Aspendos from Antalya should cost around TL90.

ASPENDOS

People come in droves to this ancient site near the modern-day village of Belkıs for one reason: to view the ancient city's awesome **theatre** (admission TL15, parking TL5; ☉9am-7pm Apr-Oct, 8am-5.30pm Nov-Mar), which is considered the best preserved Roman theatre of the ancient world.

The theatre was built by the Romans during the reign of Emperor Marcus Aure-

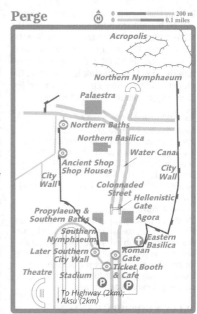

Perge

Acropolis

Northern Nymphaeum

Palaestra

Northern Baths

Northern Basilica

Water Canal

Ancient Shop
Shop Houses

City
Wall

City
Wall

Colonnaded
Street

Hellenistic
Gate

Propylaeum &
Southern Baths

Agora

Southern
Nymphaeum

Eastern
Basilica

Later Southern
City Wall

Roman
Gate

Theatre

Ticket Booth
& Cafe

Stadium

To Highway (2km);
Aksu (2km)

lius (AD 61–80), and used as a caravanserai by the Seljuks during the 13th century. But while Aspendos' golden age only stretched from the 2nd to 3rd centuries AD, the history of the city goes all the way back to as far as the Hittite Empire (800 BC).

After touring the area in the early 1930s, Atatürk declared Aspendos too fine an example of classical architecture to stay unused. Following a restoration that didn't please a lot of historians, the 15,000-seat theatre began to stage operas, concerts and other events and does so to this day. Seize the opportunity to attend should anything be on at the theatre during your visit; the acoustics are excellent and the atmosphere at night sublime.

The ruins of the ancient city are extensive and include a **stadium**, **agora** and 3rd-century **basilica**, but they offer little to look at. To reach them follow the trail to the right of the theatre exit. To the north are the remains of the city's **aqueduct**. To get here from the theatre, follow the trail on the left marked for 'Theatre Hill' and take the 'Aqueduct' fork.

✦ Festivals & Events

The internationally acclaimed Aspendos Opera & Ballet Festival (Aspendos Opera ve Bale Festivalı; www.aspendosfestival.gov.tr) is held in the Roman theatre in June. Tickets can be bought from the kiosk opposite the theatre and next to the museum in Side. Do not confuse this with the Fire of Anatolia (www.fireofanatolia.com), a rather hokey multimedia spectacle playing in season at the modern Gloria Aspendos Arena to the left as you approach the ancient theatre.

❶ Getting There & Away

Aspendos lies 47km east of Antalya. If you are driving, go as far as the Köprü Creek and have a look at the Seljuk humpback bridge with seven arches and dating from the 13th century (restored 1996–99). Turn left (north) along the western bank of the creek, following the signs to Aspendos.

From Antalya, minibuses (TL8) headed for Manavgat will drop you at the Aspendos turn-off, from where you can walk (45 minutes) or hitch the remaining 4km to the site. Taxis waiting at the highway junction will take you to the theatre for an outrageous TL20, or you can take a taxi tour or join an excursion from Antalya for TL90, stopping at Perge along the way.

SELGE & KÖPRÜLÜ KANYON

The ruins of ancient Selge (Zerk in Turkish) are strewn about the Taurus-top village of Altınkaya, 12km above spectacular Köprülü Kanyon and within a national park with peaks up to 2500m.

As you wander through the village and its ruins, consider that Selge once counted a population as large as 20,000. Because of the city's elevated position, its city walls and surrounding ravines, approaching undetected wasn't a simple task and the city was able to ward off most invaders. Nevertheless, the Romans eventually took hold of the territory, which survived into the Byzantine era.

About 350m of the wall still exists, but its most striking monument is its **theatre**. Close by is the **agora**.

At the foot of the ascent, you'll discover the dramatically arched **Oluk Bridge** spanning a deep canyon with the Köprü Irmağı (Bridge River) at its base. It has been in service since the Romans put it here.

✦ Activities

Around the bridge itself, you'll find villagers keen to guide you on hikes up from Köprülü Kanyon (Bridge Canyon) along the original Roman road, about two hours up (1½ hours down), for about TL50. An excellent qualified guide who knows the area inside and

out is Adem Bahar, who can be reached on ☏0535 762 8116 or via the Perge Pansiyon; he also organises rafting trips.

You can also arrange two-day mountain treks for groups to Mt Bozburun (2504m) and other points in the Kuyucak Dağları (Kuyucak Range) for about TL100. There is a three-day walk through the Köprülü Kanyon on the St Paul's Trail (p29).

There are more than two-dozen companies offering **rafting trips** in the canyon. One of the biggest is Medraft (☏312 6296; www.medraft.com), a large adventure company with young staff. A day on the excellent intermediate rapids is about TL50, which includes a lesson, a four-hour trip and lunch. The pensions listed here organise two-hour trips for TL30.

🛌 Sleeping

There are a couple of waterfront pensions with restaurants on the west side of the river about 4km past the modern Karabük Bridge. The first is the rather subdued Selge Pansiyon (☏765 3244, 0535 577 9475; s/d TL35/70), offering good value and perhaps best for families. Much more attractive and upbeat is Perge Pansiyon (☏765 3074, 0533 475 8108; s/d TL45/90), which has comfortable timber bungalows with good bathrooms and a decent restaurant right on the water's flowing edge. Camping is TL15 per person. For accommodation in Altınkaya just minutes on foot from the Selge ruins, contact Adem Bahar (☏0535 762 8116).

❶ Getting There & Away

Köprülü Kanyon Milli Parkı and Selge are included in tours from Antalya for about TL90 per person. Without your own wheels this is your only option.

If you do have your own vehicle, you can visit in half a day, though it deserves a lot more time. The turn-off to Selge and Köprülü Kanyon is about 5km east of the Aspendos road (51km east of Antalya) along highway D400. Another 30km up into the mountains the road divides, with the left fork marked for Karabük and the right for Beşkonak. If you take the Karabük road along the river's western bank, you'll pass rafting companies and the pensions. About 11km from the turn-off is the graceful old Oluk bridge. From here the paved road marked for Altınkaya (or Zerk) climbs some 13km to the village and the ruins through increasingly dramatic scenery.

If you follow the road through Beşkonak, it is 6.5km from that village to the canyon and the bridge.

Eastern Mediterranean

Why Go?

Turkey's eastern Mediterranean has long lived in the shadow of its more fashionable neighbour to the west. And why not? That's razzle-dazzle and this is 'real' Turkey, where enormous vegetable farms and fruit orchards work overtime between the mountains and stunning coastline, and timeless hillside villages peek down onto large industrial cities with nary a tourist in sight. Here you'll be rewarded with modern, secular and very friendly locals, as well as all the requisite fun things to see and do: ancient Hittite settlements, Crusade castles, trekking. To some visitors, though, it is the abundance of important Christian sites, places where the Apostles actually preached the Gospel and made converts to the new religion, that make this a chosen destination. Others will be fascinated by the peninsula that faces southward to Syria, an area offering one of Turkey's most fascinating mixes of cultures, religions, languages and foods.

Best Places to Stay

» Hotel Bosnalı (p383)
» Liwan Hotel (p391)
» Yaka Hotel (p378)
» Hotel Ünlüselek (p372)
» Beach House Hotel (p363)

Best Places to Eat

» Arsuz Otel (p389)
» Antakya Evi (p392)
» İskele Sofrası (p369)
» Side Paradise Restaurant (p364)
» Öz Asmaaltı (p384)

When to Go

Antakya

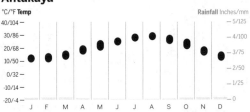

March & April
Spring, after the rain and before the crowds, is an ideal time to visit.

July & August
Steaming hot days, though offshore breezes help temper the furnace.

November to February Positively balmy along most of the coast, but often wet and the sea is chilly.

Eastern Mediterranean Highlights

1 Swim to the offshore **Maiden's Castle** (p377) at Kızkalesi, then hike to the isolated reliefs at **Adamkayalar** (p379)

2 View the finest mosaics in the world at the **Hatay Archaeology Museum** (p388), then climb to St Simeon's mountain-top **monastery** (p393)

3 Re-enact past glories in the Byzantine city of **Anemurium** (p371)

4 Descend into the massive **Chasm of Heaven** (p379) near Silifke, where Zeus is said to

have held the monster Typhon captive

5 Go way back in time at the Hittite ruins at **Karatepe** (p388), in the national park

6 Take a break from the ruins

at **Arsuz** (p389), down the coast from İskenderun

7 Enjoy the unbridled hedonism of the throbbing, laser-shooting nightclubs of **Alanya** (p367)

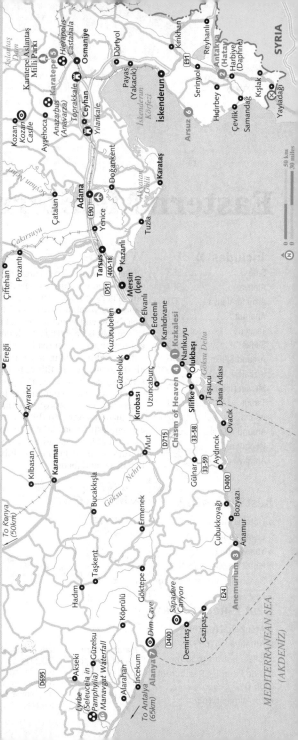

Side

♪ 0242 / POP 20,100

To some, the once docile fishing town of Side (*see*-day), 3km south of the coastal highway, is mass tourism at its worst, with endless rows of souvenir peddlers, sunbeds lined up along the beach and '*Gute Deutsche Küche*' (Good German Food) advertised everywhere.

But move a couple of streets over and you'll encounter a whole different side to Side. Entering the town through the monumental Vespasian Gate is like walking onto a film set: glorious Roman and Hellenistic ruins mark out the road, and a rebuilt agora could just as easily contain shoppers picking over togas as T-shirts. Adding to Side's appeal (and keeping its postcard industry in the black) is the Temple of Athena, a recreated colonnade marching towards the deep blue sea.

◎ Sights & Activities

Temples of Apollo & Athena   RUINS
Although small, these are among the most romantic sites you'll encounter on this Mediterranean coast. Dating from the 2nd century BC, they are at the southwestern tip of Side harbour. A half-dozen columns from the Temple of Athena have been placed upright in their original spots, and after dark a spotlight dramatically outlines their form.

Theatre   RUINS
(admission TL10; ⊙9am-7.30pm mid-Apr—mid-Oct, 8am-5.30pm mid-Oct—mid-Apr) Built in the 2nd century AD, the spectacular theatre rivals nearby Aspendos for sheer drama. In fact it's one of the largest in the region and could seat up to 20,000 spectators. Look to the wall of the *skene* (stage building) for reliefs of figures and faces, including those of Comedy and Tragedy.

East of the theatre and across the road from the museum are the remains of an agora, which once held a slave market. Nearby is the ruined circular-shaped **Temple of Tyche** dedicated to the goddess of fortune, and an arresting **latrine** with two-dozen marble seats.

Side Museum   MUSEUM
(admission TL10; ⊙9am-7.30pm Tue-Sun) Contained within a 5th-century bathhouse, the museum has an impressive (if small) collection of statues and sarcophagi.

Beaches   BEACHES
The main Western Beach is north of the centre; follow the main road out of town

(Side Caddesi) and turn left at Şarmaşık Sokak opposite the otogar (bus station). Closer is the smaller Eastern Beach off Barbaros Caddesi. On the way here you'll pass the large **State Agora**. There's a much longer beach further east.

✯✯ Festivals & Events

Tickets for the June **Aspendos Opera & Ballet Festival** can be purchased in season at the ticket kiosk (♪0532 548 6450; TL20-30, with transport TL65-80) next to the museum. It also sells tickets to the seasonal **Fire of Anatolia** multimedia spectacle at the Gloria Aspendos Arena, which cost TL80 including transportation. For more information, see www.fireofanatolia.com.

⏚ Sleeping

If you're driving and not staying here you must use the car park (per hour/day TL3/15), which is just beyond the theatre. Some pensions and hotels have parking spaces; call ahead to reserve a space.

TOP CHOICE Beach House Hotel   HOTEL €€
(♪753 1607; www.beachhouse-hotel.com; Barbaros Caddesi; s TL35-50, d TL75-85; P ❄ @) Run by Australian expatriate Penny and her Turkish husband, Ali, this is the most personable place to stay in town. Once the celebrated Pamphylia Hotel, a magnet for celebrities in the 1960s, the Beach House has a prime seafront location and the flow of regulars is steady; come three years in a row and you get your name engraved on the door. Most of the 22 rooms face the sea – room 206 is a gem – and all have spacious balconies. The roof terrace with jacuzzi is a delight and we love the ruins of a Byzantine villa (and the rabbits) in the garden.

Yalı Hotel   HOTEL €€
(♪753 1011; www.yalihotel.com; Barbaros Caddesi 50; s TL80-100, d TL100-130; P ❄ @ ≋) We've always wondered why this place, dramatically perched above the sea (literally for rooms 208, 209, 308 and 309), isn't constantly packed. It's true that the 25 rooms, though renovated, are fairly spartan. But staff are keen to please, the restaurant boasts killer views and the swimming pool is a welcome addition.

Onur Pansiyon   PENSION €
(♪753 2328; www.onur-pansiyon.com; Karanfil Sokak 3; s/d TL35/60; ❄ @) This excellent family-owned operation has regular guests year-round who return for its seven bright

Side

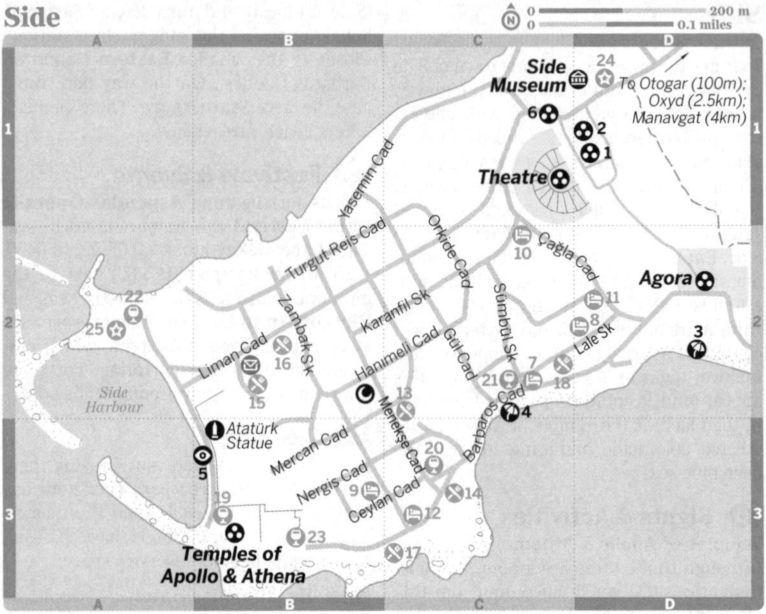

and cosy rooms – and (in cooler months) cocktails by the fireplace. The friendly manager is helpful with advice and local lore.

Hotel Lale Park HOTEL €€
(☎753 1131; www.hotellalepark.com; Lale Sokak 5; s TL70-90, d TL80-100; P ❄ ≋) One of Side's choicest small hotels for a quarter of a century, the 'Tulip Park' is surrounded by manicured lawns and flower beds with a pretty pool in the centre. Roman columns and stone walkways are scattered about and there's a garden bar. Some of the 22 rooms have Ottoman-style balconies giving onto the garden.

Side Doğa Pansiyon PENSION €€
(☎753 6246; www.sidedoga.net; Lale Sokak 8; s/d TL40/80; P ❄) A short distance from the theatre, this exceptionally laid-back nine-room pension is conveniently located across the street from a car park. Expect colourful and tidy rooms in an old stone house surrounded by an attractive courtyard garden.

Hotel Sevil HOTEL €
(☎753 2041; www.hotelsevil.com; Zambak Sokak 32; s TL40-55, d TL50-70; ❄) Set around a miniforest of mulberry trees and palms, this budget option features a smart little bar and a chilled vibe. The 15 rooms are heavy on wood panelling; those upstairs have balconies, some with sea views. It's just up from a strip of attractive waterfront restaurants and bars.

Eating

If you're staying out of town, most restaurants will arrange free transport.

TOP CHOICE **Side Paradise Restaurant** SEAFOOD €€€
(☎753 2080; www.sideparadise.com; Barbaros Caddesi 45; mains TL20-35; 👪) Our new favourite seafood place in Side, this family-first restaurant has a large play area for the wee ones, a substantial kids menu and very accommodating staff led by the affable Emrah. Adults, meanwhile, can enjoy fine sea views with their excellent meze and seafood.

Emir FAMILY RESTAURANT €€
(☎753 2224; Menekşe Caddesi; meze TL5-6, mains TL16-22; ⏰9am-midnight; 👪) The Emir almost leans on the ruins of the Roman baths where Cleopatra is said to have dallied. The open kitchen produces some excellent meze, grills and a generous array of vegetarian dishes (TL10 to TL13).

Moonlight Restaurant SEAFOOD €€€
(☎753 1400; Barbaros Caddesi 49; mains TL15-25; ⏰9am-2am) The waterfront Moonlight, in

situ since 1983, offers an extensive Turkish wine list and professional but unfussy service. The mostly seafood offerings are well presented and very fresh. The biggest drawcard, however, is the romantic back terrace, which is regularly filled with happy couples.

Ottoman Restaurant SEAFOOD €€€
(☑753 1434; mains TL20-30) Host Rasim and the terrace high above Side's main (and always busy) drag are the main reasons for dining at this excellent restaurant off Liman Caddesi, which serves a lot of fish.

Paşaköy Bar & Restaurant
RESTAURANT-BAR €€
(☑753 3622; Liman Caddesi 98; mains TL14-26) More theme park than restaurant, the infamous Paşaköy is well worth an evening of absurdist dining. It's hidden in a lush garden with hanging lamps, a bubbling brook and caged parrots fighting for space, the decor growing weirdly familiar with every drink. The food – a mix of standard Turkish and Italian – is reliable.

Soundwaves Restaurant INTERNATIONAL €€
(☑753 1059; Barbaros Caddesi; mains TL19-27) This ship-shaped institution with the Jolly Roger logo is in the same family as the Beach House Hotel, so the vibe is expectedly friendly and relaxed. But with 150 items on the menu we're not talking specialisation here, so best not to stray too far

from international favourites like pizza and standard Turkish.

🍷 **Drinking & Entertainment**

Apollonik BAR-CAFE
(☑753 1070; Liman Yolu; ☺9.30am-2.30am) Hidden within the ruins around the Temples of Apollo and Athena, the Apollonik is prima facie evidence that travel can be fun, romantic *and* full of surprises. It does food too, with mains (mostly grills) TL12 to TL20.

Royal Castle Pub LIVE MUSIC
(☑753 4373; Reis Caddesi) The most bizarre of the venues making up the nightlife zone area just up from the harbour, the always busy RCP takes the phrase 'theme bar' to new heights (or depths, depending on your view). Staff dressed like Robin Hood (or Elvis or Zorro or Vikings, depending on the night/mood) bounce quality cocktails (TL16 to TL18) to giggling tourists. Big screens show all manner of sports, and the faux-Britishness extends to a menu of pub grub. You've gotta love it.

Kiss Bar BAR
(☑753 3182; Barbaros Caddesi 64) This neon-lit open bar located just up from the water is a great spot for people-watching and a popular venue with Side expats and visitors.

Stones Rock Bar BAR

(☑512 1498, 0535 885 6179; Barbaros Caddesi 119) This dance bar with canned music and spectacular views is an excellent pre-club venue and perhaps all you need to reach the tiles.

Mehmet's Bar BAR

(Barbaros Caddesi; beer TL5) This ever-popular booze shack opposite the beach might be better suited to a tropical island than a Turkish promontory. It's decidedly laid-back and ideal for sipping a quiet drink while listening to the surf and reggae music.

Oxyd CLUB

(☑753 4040; Celal Bayar Bulvarı; admission TL20-30; ◷9pm-5am Wed, Fri & Sat) Resembling a sci-fi sandcastle (apparently) inspired by a church in Morocco, this super-duper club 3km north of town in Kumköy is among Turkey's best, and all about love-it-or-leave-it extravagance. Pack a swimming costume; there's a pool alongside. Best get there by taxi (TL15).

Light House CLUB

(☑753 3588; Liman Caddesi; ◷11.30am-5am) Italian and seafood restaurant by day, cheesy music factory by night, the Light House has the advantage of a makeshift marina where fishing boats dock alongside the outdoor patio. It's techno and Turkish pop mostly, with the odd (accent on) addition of pole dancers.

❶ Information

Cafe Keyif Internet Cafe (☑753 6675; 1st fl, Yasemin Sokak 5; per hr TL3; ◷24hr) Internet cafe that never sleeps.

Tourist office (☑753 1265; ◷8am-5pm May-Oct, closed Sat & Sun Nov-Apr) German- and Turkish-speaking office about 800m north of the centre.

❶ Getting There & Away

Side's otogar is east of the ancient city. To get to town on foot, follow signs for the main road, Side Caddesi, then turn left. In summer you can board the **Can Tren** (one way TL0.75; ◷10am-midnight), a 'toy' train that departs every 10 or 15 minutes.

Frequent minibuses connect Side otogar with the Manavgat otogar (TL2), 4km to the northeast, from where buses go to Antalya (TL8, 1½ hours, 75km), Alanya (TL8, 1½ hours, 60km) and Konya (TL25, four hours, 230km). Coming into Side, most buses either drop you at the Manavgat otogar or stop on the highway so you can transfer onto a free *servis* (shuttle bus) into Side. A taxi from Side to Manavgat otogar costs about TL15.

In summer Side has direct bus services once to three times a day to Ankara (TL30, 10 hours, 625km), İzmir (TL35, 8½ hours, 540km) and İstanbul (TL50, 13 hours, 850km).

Around Side

MANAVGAT WATERFALL

About 4km north of Manavgat on the Manavgat River, the course that carries more water than any other in Turkey is the appropriately named **Manavgat Waterfall** (Manavgat Şelalesi; admission TL2.50), a very popular attraction with locals and ringed by souvenir shops, snack bars and cafes, some of which sit metres from the horseshoe-shaped falls. Manavgat is well known for its trout.

❶ Getting There & Away

A dolmuş (minibus) from Manavgat centre to the falls costs TL1.60. In the town centre you'll also find boats willing to take you upriver here; an 80-minute round trip costs TL15 per person (minimum four people). From Side a full-day excursion to the falls including lunch is TL30. A taxi from Side otogar costs TL25; from Manavgat otogar it's TL17.

LYRBE (SELEUCIA IN PAMPHYLIA)

These ruins, about 15km north of the falls (23km northeast of Side), are appealing due to their location at the end of a rough road atop three vertical cliffs. Situated among an expanse of pine trees, the site can be cool even on hot summer days. Many of the buildings are difficult to identify, although you can clearly make out a surprisingly intact **city gate**, **bathhouse**, an **agora** with shops, a **colonnaded street** and a **necropolis**. A faded signposted map offers guidance.

For years, archaeologists believed this to be the site of Seleucia in Pamphylia, founded by Seleucus I Nicator, an egocentric officer of Alexander the Great who established a total of nine cities in his own honour. However, the discovery of an inscription here written in both Greek and the language of ancient Side has convinced researchers that this site is more likely the ruined city of Lyrbe, and Seleucia in Pamphylia is somewhere along the coast.

❶ Getting There & Away

The road to the ruins runs north from the waterfall. About a kilometre out you'll pass an ancient hump-backed bridge on the left and in another 2.5km or so the ruins of a Roman aqueduct; look for a sign on the left marked 'Lyrbe (Seleucia)'. Continue on through the village of Şıhlar, and take the road to the right opposite the minaret. This wends another 5.5km uphill on an unpaved road to the ruins.

If you don't have your own transport, taxi drivers across the bridge in Manavgat will run you to the ruins for TL60 return (TL70 with a stop at the waterfall).

Alanya

☎0242 / POP 86,800

In just a few short decades, Alanya has mushroomed from a sparsely populated highway town fronting a sandy beach to a densely populated tourist haven that at night can look like 'Vegas by the Sea'. Aside from taking a quick boat cruise or stroll along the waterfront, many visitors on 'all-in' visits here move only from the airport shuttle to the hotel pool, eat at the hotel and frequent the throbbing, laser-shooting nightclubs after dark.

But Alanya too has something up its ancient sleeve. Looming high above the promontory to the south of the modern centre is an impressive fortress complex, with the remains of a fine Seljuk castle, some atmospheric ruins and even something of a small traditional village. Sipping a beer in one of the many hillside cafes affords stunning views and a welcome break from the party below.

The closest thing this 20km-long city has to a main square is Hürriyet Meydanı, a nondescript traffic junction at the northern end of İskele Caddesi.

◉ Sights

Alanya Castle   FORTRESS
(Alanya Kalesı; admission TL10; ⊙9am-7pm Apr-Oct, 8am-5pm Nov-Mar) The sole 'must-see' site in Alanya is the awesome Seljuk-era castle, which overlooks the city, Pamphylian plain and Cilician mountains.

Before reaching the entrance to the castle, the road passes a turn-off for the village of **Ehmedek**, which was the Turkish quarter during Ottoman and Seljuk times. Today a number of old wooden houses still cluster around the fine 16th-century **Süleymaniye Mosque**, the oldest in Alanya. Also here is a former Ottoman **bedesten** (vaulted covered market) and the **Aksebe Türbesi**, a distinctive 13th-century mausoleum.

At the end of the road is the entrance to the **İç Kale** (Inner Fortress), where you'll find mostly poorly preserved ruins including a half-dozen **cisterns** and the shell of an 11th-century **Byzantine church**.

The winding road to the fortress – Kaleyolu Caddesi – is 3.5km long and uphill. If you don't want to walk, catch a bus from Hürriyet Meydanı (TL1.25, hourly from 9am to 7pm) or opposite the tourist office (15 minutes past the hour and, in summer, 15 minutes before the hour). Taxis at the bottom will take you up and down for around TL20.

Kızılkule   HISTORIC BUILDING
(Red Tower; admission TL3; ⊙9am-7pm Apr-Oct, 8am-5pm Nov-Mar) This five-storey octagonal defence tower, measuring nearly 30m in diameter and more than 30m high with a central cistern within for water storage, looms over the harbour at the lower end of İskele Caddesi. Constructed in 1226 by Seljuk Sultan Alaaddin Keykubad I (who also built the fortress), it was the first structure erected after the Armenian-controlled town surrendered to the sultan. There's a small **ethnographic museum** here and some 85 steps lead to a roof terrace with views of the harbour. To the south is the only Seljuk-built **tersane** (shipyard) remaining in Turkey.

Alanya Museum   MUSEUM
(İsmet Hilmi Balcı Caddesi; admission TL3; ⊙9am-7pm Tue-Sun Apr-Oct, 8am-5pm Tue-Sun Nov-Mar) Alanya's small museum is worth a visit for its artefacts, including tools, jugs and jewellery, collected from other Pamphylian sites in the area. Also on display is a life-sized mock-up of a traditional 19th-century Alanya home. The surrounding garden, a graveyard in Ottoman times, is delightful in summer.

Dripstone Cave   CAVE
(Damlataş Mağarası; admission TL4; ⊙10am-7pm) South of the tourist office and close to Cleopatra's Beach is the entrance to this cave with stalactites and a humidity of 95%. It is said to produce a certain kind of air that, if inhaled and exhaled for long enough periods, has the ability to relieve asthma sufferers.

✦ Activities

Cleopatra's Beach   BEACH
(Kleopatra Plajı) Sandy and quite secluded in low season, and with fine views of the fortress, Cleopatra's Beach is the city's best. Alanya's main beaches are also decent, although east of the centre they're fronted by a busy main road.

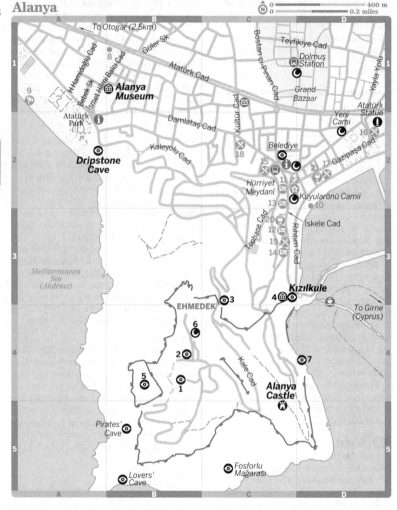

Alanya Aqua Centre   AMUSEMENT PARK
(☎512 5944; www.alanyaaquacenter.com; İsmet Hilmi Balcı Caddesi 62; adult/child TL20/15; ☺9am-6pm) Alanya boasts an impressive water park close to the centre.

☞ Tours

Many local operators organise tours to the ruins along the coast west of Alanya and to Anamur. A typical tour to Aspendos, Side and Manavgat will cost around TL65 per person, while a 4WD safari visiting villages in the Taurus Mountains will cost about TL50 per person.

Excursion Boats   BOAT TOURS
(per person incl lunch TL30) Every day at around 10.30am, boats leave from near Rıhtım Caddesi for a six-hour voyage around the promontory, visiting several caves as well as Cleopatra's Beach.

⌂ Sleeping

Alanya has hundreds of hotels and pensions, almost all of them designed for groups and those in search of *apart oteller* (self-catering flats). All of the independent places to stay recommended here can be found along İskele Caddesi.

Kaptan Hotel
HOTEL €€

(☏513 4900; www.kaptanhotels.com; İskele Caddesi 70; s/d TL100/170; ❋☒) This four-star hotel has a large and somewhat slick lobby with a nautical theme and a pleasant bar; the pool is off the mezzanine floor. The 56 perfectly clean and tidy rooms have all the mod cons and about half have balconies facing the sea. The Kaptan serves an excellent breakfast.

Seaport Hotel
BUSINESS HOTEL €€

(☏513 6487; www.hotelseaport.com; İskele Caddesi 82; s/d TL90/160; ❋) This business-style hotel, the last on the İskele hotel strip and just steps from the Red Tower, offers efficient service and brilliant sea views from half of its rooms. The 65 rooms are not huge but are very well appointed.

Temiz Otel
HOTEL €€

(☏513 1016; http://temizotel.com.tr; İskele Caddesi 12; s/d TL55/110; ❋) The refreshingly named 'Clean Hotel' is nothing short of that. Its 32 rooms on five floors are spacious, and the ones facing the sea with balconies offer a bird's-eye view of the thumping club and bar action down below.

Baba Otel
HOTEL €

(☏513 0095; İskele Caddesi 6; s/d TL25/50) Baba still offers the cheapest beds on İskele Caddesi, but you pay for what you get (which ain't much at this none-too-salubri-ous 30-room joint). The front entrance is located on the left side of a cement stairway just off the street.

🍴 Eating

Most of the restaurants listed here will pick you up from and bring you back to where you are staying.

İskele Sofrası
TOP CHOICE
SEAFOOD €€

(☏0532 782 4647; Tophane Caddesi 2b; mains TL18-30) For a truly authentic Turkish seafood meal, eschew the harbour restaurants and head for this intimate little place next to the Kaptan Hotel. Run by *père et fils* Öz, who count six-dozen meze in their repertoire, including *girit ezmesi,* an unforgettable mash of feta, walnuts, olive oil and other stuff, the 'Pier Table' serves only fresh fish and shellfish. The terrace with views to the harbour is a delight.

Ottoman House
MODERN TURKISH €€

(☏511 1421; www.ottomanhousealanya.com; mains TL18-24) Set inside a 100-year-old stone villa that once did time as a hotel, and surrounded by lush garden, the Ottoman House is the most atmospheric eatery in Alanya. The *beğendili taş kebabı* (TL24), a traditional Ottoman dish of sautéed lamb served on aubergine (eggplant) purée, is testament to the creativity of the kitchen staff. Likewise the grilled fish dishes (TL20 to TL22 per person), but come on Thursday or Sunday night for an all-you-can-eat fish barbecue (TL30). Live music is performed most evenings in summer.

Köfte D Köfte
KÖFTECI €€

(☑512 1270; Kaleyolu Caddesi; grills TL13-22; ⊙8am-3am) At the very bottom of castle hill, this is a good place for a bite before or after visiting the fortress, and open virtually round the clock. You can't miss it: a flashy yellow-and-red sign greets diners to this 'boutique' fast-food joint. Clean lines, attentive service and generous meat, rice and salad combinations are all part of the deal. Try one of the omelettes (TL6 to TL8).

Köyüm Gaziantep Başpınar
KEBAPÇI €€€

(☑513 5664; Hükümet Caddesi; meze TL8-13, mains TL17-28) For something more adventurous than the usual grills, this is one of central Alanya's best traditional (if somewhat pricey) Turkish options. Dishes from the eastern city of Gaziantep are on offer; try the *patlıcan kebabı* (aubergine kebaps; TL20) or the *beyti sarması* (spicy meatballs wrapped in flat bread; TL23).

Red Tower Brewery Restaurant
RESTAURANT-BAR €€€

(☑513 6664; www.redtowerbrewery.com; İskele Caddesi 80; sushi TL9-14, mains TL19-35) It's fusion confusion at this multistorey pleasure palace at the end of the hotel strip. The ground-floor brew pub serves its own decent lager, there's an international restaurant on the 1st floor, Turkish dishes on the 3rd floor, and sushi and live guitar music at the Sky Lounge on the 6th floor. You might never leave the building.

Mahperi Restaurant
INTERNATIONAL €€€

(☑512 5491; www.mahperi.com; Rıhtım Caddesi; mains TL25-30) Quite a feat in fly-by-night Alanya, this classy waterfront fish and steak restaurant has been in operation since 1947 and offers a good selection of international dishes. The welcome is always warm.

Drinking & Entertainment

Alanya features some of the most bawdy, bright and banging nightclubs in the land. It's all good fun – so long as you don't have to sleep within a kilometre of the blistering tech stompers.

James Dean Bar
BAR, CLUB

(☑512 3195; www.jamesdeanbaralanya.net; Gazipaşa Caddesi; ⊙9pm-3am) The embodiment of 'the most bawdy, bright and banging' club in the land, this homage to the

long-dead American film star is all about bubbles, boobs and, err, pulling. If you can't get a date here, go home.

Harem Cafe Bar
LIVE MUSIC

(☑511 9225; www.haremcafebar.com; İskele Caddesi 46; ⊙9am-3am) This great live Turkish music venue just up from the harbour is filled with local lads and lasses sipping beers (TL10) around small tables. The vibe is far more relaxed than any place down the hill. Music starts at 10pm.

Robin Hood Bar
BAR, CLUB

(☑511 2023; www.robinhoodalanya.com; Gazipaşa Caddesi 12; beer TL7-10; ⊙9pm-3am) Supposedly the biggest club in Alanya, the first two floors of this all-singin', all-dancin', all-flashin' monstrosity are decked out in (you guessed it) a Sherwood Forest theme.

Latin Club
BAR, CLUB

(www.latinoclubalanya.com) Above the Robin Hood Bar, the Latin Club is usually the one making all the noise.

ℹ Information

Alanya Guide (www.alanya.tv) Useful website for Alanya and surrounds.

Kisayol Internet Cafe (☑519 0549; İskele Caddesi; per hr TL1.50; ⊙9.30am-10pm) Internet cafe along 'hotel row'.

Murat Cafe (☑519 2306; per hr TL1.50; ⊙8am-midnight) Internet cafe with 20 computers in a backstreet off Müftüler Caddesi; to reach it, turn left at the Rafaello shop and take the first right.

Tourist office (☑513 1240; Damlataş Caddesi 1; ⊙8am-5pm May-Oct, closed Sat & Sun Nov-Apr) What might very well be the most helpful and informed tourist office in Turkey is opposite the Alanya Museum.

Tourist office branch (Damlataş Caddesi; ⊙9am-6pm Mon-Fri) A much smaller branch is at the eastern end of the same street between the *belediye* (town hall) and Kuyularönü Camii.

ℹ Getting There & Away
Boat

There are services to Girne (Kyrenia) in Northern Cyprus operated by **Fergün Denizcilik** (☑511 5565, 511 5358; www.fergun.net; İskele Caddesi 84). Boats leave Alanya at noon on Monday and Thursday, returning from Girne at 11am on Wednesday and Sunday.

You must buy a ticket and present your passport a day before departure for immigration formalities. Not included in the TL78/128 one-way/return ticket prices (students TL65/110) is a TL10 harbour tax from Alanya and a whopping TL32 one from Girne.

Bus

The otogar is on the coastal highway (Atatürk Caddesi), 3km west of the centre. It is served by buses to/from the city every half-hour (one way TL1.25). Most services are less frequent off-season, but buses generally leave hourly for Antalya (TL14, two hours, 115km) and eight times daily to Adana (TL35, 10 hours, 440km), stopping at a number of towns along the way. Buses to Konya (TL20, 6½ hours, 320km) take the Akseki–Beyşehir route.

ⓘ Getting Around

Dolmuşes to the otogar (one way TL1.50) can be picked up near the mosque behind the bazaar north of Atatürk Caddesi. From the otogar, you walk out towards the coast road and the dolmuş stand is on the right. A taxi to the otogar from the centre costs TL10.

Around Alanya

Some 14km west of Alanya is **Şarapsa Hanı**, a Seljuk *han* (caravanserai) built in the mid-13th century as a staging post between Alanya and Konya. It is now a restaurant. Another 16km west towards Side and just after Incekum beach is a turning for a road leading north for 9km to **Alarahan**, another 13th-century *han,* which can be explored with the help of a torch. At the head of the valley nearby are the ruins of **Alara Castle** (Alara Kalesi), dating from the same period.

Heading east from Alanya, the twisting road is cut into the cliffs. Every now and then it passes through the fertile delta of a stream, planted with bananas or crowded with greenhouses. It's a long drive until you get to Anamur, but the sea views and the cool pine forests are extremely beautiful.

This region was ancient Cilicia Tracheia (Rugged Cilicia), a somewhat forbidding part of the world because of the mountains and fearsome pirates who preyed on ships from the hidden coves. They were the same evil so-and-sos who double-crossed our hero Spartacus in the 1960 film of that name, after he'd hired them to transport his slave army to safety. Scoundrels.

There are several notable attractions on or just north of the D400 as you travel west from Alanya, including the seldom-visited ancient sites of **Laertes** and **Syedra**. A turn-off near the 11km marker leads northward for 6km to **Dim Cave** (Dim Mağarası;

adult/child TL8/4.50; ⊙low season 9am-5pm, high season to 8pm), with a 360m-long walkway leading past spectacular stalactite and stalagmite formations and a crystal-clear pool. Dolmuşes headed for Kestel from Alanya hourly in season will drop you off near the entrance to the cave. A return taxi will cost about TL60.

A turning at 27km and another road leading 18km northeast takes you to **Sapadere Canyon** (Sapadera Kanyonu; www.sapaderekanyonu.com; admission per person/car TL2/8; ⊙low season 9am-5pm, high season to 8pm), a place of incomparable natural beauty which opened to the public in 2007. It can be enjoyed from along a 750m-long path. A taxi will take you from Alanya to here and back for about TL80.

Anamur

📞 0324 / POP 35,800

As the closest town to the massive Byzantine city of Anemurium – and with a very pretty beach and waterfront of its own down at İskele – Anamur is a great place in which to put your feet up for a while. At the other end of town is the city's second magnet: the impressive Mamure Castle.

Even with those two treasures, easygoing Anamur has an agricultural industry that far outweighs its tourism. Anamur is the centre of the banana-growing industry in Turkey, and here the sweet yellow fruit reigns supreme. You'll see local *muzler* (bananas), which are shorter and sweeter than imported ones, on sale everywhere – in shops, at roadside stands, from the back of trucks.

◉ Sights

Anamur lies to the north of highway D400. About 2.5km southeast of the main roundabout (with its iconic statue of a girl bearing a large bunch of – you guessed it – bananas) is İskele, a popular waterfront district with most of the town's hotels and restaurants. Anemurium is 8.5km to the west while Mamure Castle is 7km east.

Anemurium   RUINS
(Anemurium Ancient City; admission TL3; ⊙8am-7pm Apr-Oct, 8am-5pm Nov-Mar) Approaching Anamur from the west or down from the Cilician mountains, a sign points south towards the ruins of Anemurium Antik Kenti. The road then bumps along for 2km to the *gişe* (ticket kiosk); it's another 500m to the car park.

EASTERN MEDITERRANEAN AROUND ALANYA

Although founded by the Phoenicians in the 4th century BC, most of the ruins visible at Anemurium today date from the late Roman period through to the Byzantine and medieval eras. The site is both sprawling and eerily quiet – a kind of Byzantine Kayaköy by the sea – with ruins stretching 500m to the pebble beach and massive city walls impossibly scaling the mountainside.

Historians and archaeologists are still out to lunch on how Anemurium fell. The city suffered a number of devastating setbacks throughout its active existence, including an attack in AD 52 by a vicious Cilician tribe. However, it was long believed that corsairs from Arabia plundered and pillaged themselves silly in the mid-7th century. More recently, however, archaeologists have uncovered evidence that a massive earthquake destroyed the city in about 580.

From the car park and sprawling **necropolis**, walk southeast past a 4th-century **basilica**; look behind it for a pathway of mosaic tiles leading to the sea. Above the church is one of two **aqueducts**. Opposite the **theatre** dating from the 2nd century AD is the more complete **odeion**, with 900 seats and a tile floor. The best-preserved structure in Anemurium is the **baths complex**; look for the coloured mosaic tiles that still decorate portions of the floor (but ignore some of the badly executed renovations).

Mamure Castle FORTRESS
(Mamure Kalesi; admission TL3; ⊙8am-7.30pm Apr-Oct, 8am-5pm Nov-Mar) This tremendous castle – with its crenellated walls, 39 towers and part of its original moat still intact – is by far the biggest and best-preserved fortification on the Turkish Mediterranean coast. The rear of the castle sits directly on the beach where sea turtles come in summer to lay their eggs (see p373), while its front end almost reaches the highway.

Mamure Castle dates from the 13th century; it was constructed by the rulers of the Armenian kingdom of Cilicia on the site of a Roman fortress dating from the 3rd century AD. Mamure was taken by Karamanoğlu Mehmet Bey and his troops in 1308 and alterations began, including the addition of a **mosque** in the eastern courtyard. Here you'll also see remnants of an **aqueduct** that brought water from the mountains 5km away, a **stable** that looks like a garage, and the holes in the walls that served as the **guards' barracks**. To the west is the **Ka-**

leiçi (castle interior), where the castle commander and other top brass lived.

Climbing the castle's **towers**, especially the one with a dungeon within, is something of an adventure, although some stairs are pretty crumbled so use extreme caution. If you're lucky the indefatigable Recep, the castle gardener, will be on hand to guide you. Your reward is an astounding view of the sea and the ruins of **Softa Castle** (Softa Kalesi), another fortress built by the Armenian rulers of Cilicia near Bozyazı some 18km to the east.

FREE **Anamur Museum** MUSEUM
(Anamur Müzesi; Adnan Menderes Caddesi 3; ⊙8.30am-5pm) This fine little museum in İskele is just the ticket after a visit to Anemurium. While the ethnographical section won't hold your interest for long, the archaeological finds from the ancient city will. These include frescoes from private houses, bathhouse mosaics painstakingly reassembled, an unusual clay sarcophagus and all manner of jewellery, oil lamps and early Christian religious objects. Look for the iron scales in the shape of a woman, her bulging eyes staring emptily into space.

🛏 Sleeping

The popular İskele (harbour) district is where most visitors to Anamur end up. Pensions and hotels run along Fevzi Çakmak Caddesi (or İskele Yolu) down to the harbour and around İnönü Caddesi, the main street running along the waterfront. Dolmuşes stop at the main intersection.

TOP Hotel Ünlüselek HOTEL €€
CHOICE (☎814 1973; www.unluselekhotel.com; Fahri Görgülü Caddesi; s TL40-55, d TL70-90, tr 100-120; ❄@❧) This sprawling, family-oriented hotel right on the beach is really a budget resort. Along with occasional live music at night, films are sometimes screened on a projector outside, where there's also a playground area for kids. The 35 rooms are spacious with sea views, balconies and – hurrah! – screens on the windows. We love the windmill-shaped shower, the coloured glass in the guestroom windows and the wi-fi on the beach. Helpful owner Halil loans his small boat to guests for a spot of rowing and fishing.

Hotel Luna Piena HOTEL €€
(☎814 9045; www.hotellunapiena.com; Süleyman Bal Sokak; s TL40-50, d TL80-100; ❄@) A comfortable hotel in a six-storey block just

paces from the beach, the 'Full Moon' offers 32 rooms with parquet floors, balconies with full sea views, proper showers and a preference for pink. Check out room 505 – on a clear day you'll see Cyprus.

Hotel Rolli   HOTEL €€
(☎814 4978; www.hotel-rolli.de; Yahevleri Mahallesi; half-board per person TL90; ✳@☎) This unique German-owned hotel is specifically designed to provide travellers with wheelchair access. Half of the 16 rooms are suites with an extra bedroom (and shower) for an accompanying care-giver. The polite staff are very well trained and helpful.

Hotel Dedehan   HOTEL €
(☎814 7522, 0532 267 4172; D400 Hwy, Otogar Yanı; s/d TL30/50; ✳) One of the very few hotels in central Anamur, this place is a good choice if you're stuck in town overnight between buses as it's right next to the otogar. The 20 rooms are a bit worn but clean and quite large. It's also a good base for excursions to Anemurium or Mamure Castle, as the friendly owner Ahmet allows guests free use of bicycles.

Şenay Hotel   HOTEL €
(☎814 9758, 0538 242 8819; Fevzi Çakmak Caddesi 173; s/d TL35/55; ✳@) A 21-room hotel on the road to the beach, the Şenay is tidy, its rooms tiled and with balconies, but lacks the character and convenience of some other hotels in İskele. Still it's a good budget choice and the owner will give discounts.

Hotel Tayfun   HOTEL €
(☎814 1161; www.tayfunotel.com; Fevzi Çakmak Caddesi 176; s/d/tr TL35/50/65; ✳@) This chaotically run newly built place some distance up from the beach has 28 rooms with views of the street to the front or polystyrene greenhouses to the back. Rooms are comfortable enough (and some even have multiple windows), but there's no lift and a blaring TV comes with breakfast.

✖ Eating

In the warmer months the İskele waterfront is filled with large open-air cafes serving kebaps, *gözleme* (savoury pancake) and other snacks.

Mare Vista Restaurant
                    INTERNATIONAL, ITALIAN €€
(☎814 2001; İnönü Caddesi 28; dishes TL8-12) Reasonably priced for its beachfront location, the 'Sea View' has international and some Italian-themed dishes (including the ubiquitous pizza), as well as salads and sandwiches.

Kap Restaurant   SEAFOOD €€
(☎814 2374; İskele Meydanı; mains TL7-23) On the main square in İskele just up from the pier, the family-run Kap – which may or may not be short for *kaptan* – is the fish

---

TURTLES AT RISK!

The beach at Anamur is one of a dozen nesting sites of the loggerhead turtle (*Caretta caretta*) along Turkey's Mediterranean coast.

The loggerhead (Turkish: *deniz kaplumbağası*) is a large, flat-headed turtle coloured reddish brown on top and yellow-orange below that spends most of its life in the water. An adult can weigh up to 200kg.

Between May and September, females come ashore at night to lay their eggs in the sand. Using their back flippers they scoop out a nest about 40cm deep, lay between 70 and 120 soft-shelled white eggs the size of ping-pong balls, then cover them over. If disturbed, the turtles may abandon the nests and return to the sea.

The eggs incubate in the sand for some 60 days and the temperature at which they do determines the gender of the hatchlings: below 30°C and all the young will be male, above 30°C they will be female. At a steady 30°C a mix is assured.

As soon as they're born (at night when it's cool and fewer predators are about), the young turtles make their way towards the sea, drawn by the reflected light. If hotels and restaurants are built too close to the beach (as is often the case in the western Mediterranean), their lights can confuse the youngsters, leading them to move up the beach towards danger – in Anamur's case the D400 highway.

The loggerhead turtle also nests on the beaches at Demirtaş and Gazipaşa, both southeast of Alanya, and in the Göksu Delta. In the western Mediterranean, important nesting grounds are at Dalyan, Fethiye, Patara, Demre (Kale), Kumluca and Tekirova (both northeast of Demre), and Belek (east of Antalya).

restaurant of choice in Anamur. The meze are also delicious (TL7 to TL10).

La Pizza
PIDECI €

(☎814 4929; Yasemin Sokak; mains TL3-7) Simple but clean, this popular place just up from the beach does delicious pide (Turkish-style pizza), pizza and döner kebap (spit-roasted lamb slices).

ℹ Information

Tourist office (☎814 5058; ⊙8am-noon & 1-5pm Mon-Fri) In the otogar complex behind the police station, with very little information.

ℹ Getting There & Away

There are several buses daily to Alanya (TL20, three hours, 130km), Taşucu/Silifke (TL28, three hours, 140km) and Adana (TL30, six hours, 305km).

ℹ Getting Around

Anamur's otogar is on the intersection of the D400 highway and 19 Mayıs Caddesi. Buses and dolmuşes to İskele depart from a small stand behind the otogar (TL1.50, every 30 minutes). A taxi between İskele and the otogar costs TL12.

Dolmuşes to Ören (TL2, half-hourly) also leave from next to the mosque, over the road from the otogar, and can drop you off at the Anemurium turn-off on the main highway, from where it's a 2.5km walk. Expect to pay TL50 for a taxi to Anemurium and back, with an hour's waiting time. Some of the hotels and pensions, including Hotel Dedehan, will run you there for TL20. Cycling is also an option.

Frequent dolmuşes headed for Bozyazı (TL2) will drop you off outside Mamure Castle.

Taşucu

☎0324 / POP 6750

The working port of nearby Silifke but a destination in its own right, Taşucu (tah-*shoo*-joo) is a low-key and quaint resort that has a decent city beach and friendly people. The town lives for the ferries and hydrofoils that carry foot passengers and cars to/from Girne in Northern Cyprus from the ferry pier just off the main square, which is just south of the D400 highway. The beach is fronted by Sahil Caddesi, which stretches east from the pier and has several good pensions.

🛏 Sleeping

Otel Olba
PENSION €

(☎741 4222, 0542 779 1442; Sahil Caddesi; s/d TL50/100; ❄) Cheek-by-jowl with Meltem Pansiyon and directly on the sea, the Olba is tidy and well run. The huge 2nd-floor terrace (where breakfast is served each morning) offers wonderful sea views. The 25 rooms are clad in cosy, kitsch wood panelling.

Meltem Pansiyon
PENSION €

(☎741 4391, 0533 360 0726; Sahil Caddesi 75; s TL30-50, d TL40-70; ❄ @) This family-run pension right on the beach is affordable and very friendly. Some eight of the 20 modest (though squeaky-clean) rooms face the sea, and breakfast is served on the delightful back patio. At last, a place that uses those plug-in electric mosquito repellers!

Lades Motel
HOTEL €

(☎741 4008; www.ladesmotel.com; İsmet İnönü Caddesi 45; s/d TL80/110; ❄ @ ☀) This hotel on the road into Taşucu is a favourite of birdwatchers who flock to the nearby Göksu Delta (p376). The two-dozen rooms, set around a large pool, are nothing to write home about, but there are wonderful harbour views from the balconies. The lobby and public spaces are well designed for comparing 'twitching' notes with fellow birders in residence.

Holmi Pansiyon
PENSION €

(☎741 5378; holmi.pansiyon.kafeterya@hotmail.com; Sahil Caddesi 23; s/d TL40/70; ❄ @) The covered front porch at this 11-room pension just around the corner from the beach is particularly nice for relaxing on a hot day. The rooms have small desks and balconies, and about half have sea views.

Hanımağa Motel
PENSION €

(☎741 3033, 0532 296 5846; Sahil Caddesi 5; s/d TL50/70; ❄) Just down from the Holmi and opposite the beach, this pension (err, motel) run by a nice young couple has 14 rooms with fridges and balconies; a few of them have decent sea views too. If yours doesn't, head for the spectacular roof-terrace restaurant.

🍴 Eating & Drinking

Denizkızı Restaurant
SEAFOOD €

(☎741 4194; İsmet İnönü Caddesi 62c; mains TL10-23) Opposite the Atatürk statue and ferry terminal, the rather upscale 'Mermaid' is good for meze, fish and grills, and as a much-needed cooling spot on the lovely roof terrace on a hot afternoon. From here you'll really see your boat come in.

Baba Restaurant
SEAFOOD €

(☑741 5991; İsmet İnönü Caddesi 43; mains TL10-20) Just down from the Lades Motel on the way to the harbour, Baba is regarded as the area's best eatery. The terrace is a beautiful place to sip a cold beer (or slurp imported Italian *gelato*; TL4 to TL5), but it's the food that brings the punters in and back, especially the tempting cart of meze (TL2.50 to TL3). And don't forget the selection of fresh fish on the chalkboard, which is updated daily.

Alo Dürüm
PIDECI €

(☑741 5657; İsmet İnönü Caddesi 17; dishes TL3-10) In the middle of the main drag along the seafront, this open-air döner and pide place is popular with locals and travellers alike. A 24-hour delivery service is available, should you get a hankering for a late *lahmacun* (Arabic-style pizza).

❶ Getting There & Away

Akgünler Denizcilik (☑741 2303; www.akgunler.com.tr; İsmet İnönü Caddesi) runs *feribotlar* (car ferries) and/or *ekspresler* (hydrofoils) between Taşucu and Girne in Northern Cyprus. It has a daily hydrofoil at 11.30am (one way/return TL69/114) and a car ferry (passenger one way/return TL59/99, car TL150/300) leaving at midnight from Sunday to Thursday. The hydrofoil leaves Girne at 9.30am daily while the car ferry leaves at noon Monday to Friday only.

Hydrofoils are faster (two hours) but the ride can be stomach-churning on choppy seas. Tickets cost less on the car ferry, but the trip can take anywhere from four to 10 hours, depending on the weather. Not included in the fares is the harbour tax: TL10 out of Taşucu and TL25 from Girne.

Dolmuşes drop you at the petrol station to the north of town – it's a five-minute walk to the beach. There are frequent dolmuşes between Taşucu and Silifke (TL1.50), where you can make long-distance connections.

Silifke

☑0324 / POP 53,000

Silifke is a riverside country town with a certain charm and long history. A striking castle towers above while a handsome park borders the mineral-rich blue-green Göksu River, which was called the Calycadnus in ancient times. In the vicinity are more sights of archaeological and natural importance, well deserving of a visit.

Seleucia ad Calycadnum, as Silifke was once known, was founded by Seleucus I

Nicator in the 3rd century BC. He was one of Alexander the Great's most able generals and founder of the Seleucid dynasty that ruled Syria after Alexander's death.

The town's other claim to fame is that Emperor Frederick Barbarossa (r 1152–90) drowned in the river near here while leading his troops on the Third Crusade. It was apparently the weight of his armour that brought him down.

◉ Sights

FREE Fortress
FORTRESS

The Byzantine hilltop fortress, with its two dozen towers, vaulted underground chambers and remains of a moat that can still be seen today, was once Silifke's command centre and is now a pleasant place with a wonderful cafe-restaurant.

Tekir Ambarı
HISTORIC BUILDING

From the fortress it's possible to see the Tekir Ambarı, an ancient cistern carved from rock that can be entered via a spiral staircase. To reach the cistern, first head to the junction of İnönü Caddesi and Menderes Caddesi, then walk up the steep road to the left of the Küçük Hacı Kaşaplar butcher shop. An alternative to a long and hot walk up the hill to the castle are the motorcycle drivers who wait at this corner. Expect to pay around TL15 per person.

Necropolis
RUINS

To the south of the cistern is ancient Silifke's necropolis. In the centre, the rather sad ruins of the Roman **Temple of Jupiter**, its columns used by storks as nesting posts, sits right along the side of very busy İnönü Caddesi. The temple dates from the 2nd century AD, but was turned into a Christian basilica sometime in the 5th century.

Silifke Museum
MUSEUM

(Taşucu Caddesi 29; admission TL3; ⊙8am-5pm Tue-Sun) To the east of the centre, Silifke's museum has a decent collection of Roman figures and busts on the ground floor and in the garden. There are three halls on the 1st floor, including one filled with ancient coins and jewellery (including ancient gold pieces placed on the eyelids of the dead), and an archaeological hall with amphora and other pottery, tools and weapons from the Roman and Hellenistic eras.

Merkez Camii
MOSQUE

(Central Mosque; Fevzi Çakmak Caddesi) Also called the Alaaddin Camisi, or Aladdin's Mosque, the Seljuk-era Merkez Camii dates from 1228, although it's seen many renovations over the centuries.

Reşadiye Camii
HISTORIC BUILDING
(İnönü Caddesi 138) Have a look at the Roman columns supporting the back and front porticoes.

Stone Bridge
BRIDGE
The stone bridge over the Göksu dates back to AD 78 and has been restored many times, including twice in the last century (1922 and 1972).

🛏 Sleeping

Göksu Otel
HOTEL €
(⌚712 1021; fax 712 1024; Atatürk Caddesi 20; s/d TL50/80; 🖳 @) The only real game in town, the Göksu has the midrange market pretty well cornered. It's a central place, facing the park on the northern bank of its namesake. Business in style and decor, its provincial sensibility gives it more warmth than expected and the 25 rooms are of a good size and standard. The ground-floor restaurant serves a decent breakfast for an extra TL8.

Otel Ayatekla
HOTEL €
(⌚715 1081; fax 715 1085; Otogar Civari; s/d TL35/70; 🖳) Really only an option if you are stuck between buses, this 24-room, two-star hotel is literally next door to the otogar and rather gloomy. Still, some rooms come with decent views of the city and mountains, and a suite with balcony is available.

🍴 Eating & Drinking

Try the local yoghurt (*Silifke yoğrdu*), which is famous throughout Turkey.

Gözde Restaurant
KEBAPÇI €€
(⌚714 2764; Balıkçılar Sokak 7; mains TL7-12) This döner kebap and *lahmacun* joint also serves up delicious soups, meze and grills in a shaded outdoor dining area down a small street. The English-speaking staff make it a fine and rather casual dining experience.

Lezzet Dünyası
RESTAURANT €€
(⌚714 5533; Fevzi Çakmak Caddesi; mains TL10-15) Near the otogar, this restaurant has unsurprising but well prepared fish, lamb and chicken dishes. And if you've got a bus to catch it can make a mean pide very fast.

Kale Restaurant
PIDECI, KEBAPÇI €
(⌚714 8292; mains TL3-12) With simple dishes at reasonable prices and the best place within kilometres for a sundowner, this eatery below the towers of the castle is not just a great place to stop on your way up or down but a destination in itself.

Göksu Pastanesi
TEA GARDEN, CONFECTIONER €
(pastries from TL1.50) A large and shaded terrace off Cavit Erdem Caddesi, perched atop the rumbling Göksu River and close to the stone bridge, this modest eatery sells çay and snacks.

ℹ Information

Tourist office (⌚714 1151; Veli Gürten Bozbey Caddesi 6; ⏰8am-5pm Mon-Fri) Just north of Atatürk Caddesi and the Göksu Otel.

ℹ Getting There & Away

Buses depart for Adana (TL15, 2½ hours, 165km, hourly) to the east throughout the day. Other services from Silifke include Mersin (TL8.50, two hours, 95km, three per hour), Alanya (TL30, six hours, 265km) and Antalya (TL35, nine hours, 395km, 10 per day).

Dolmuşes to Taşucu (TL1.50) depart every 20 minutes from opposite the Lezzet Dünyası restaurant and east of the otogar, or from a stand on the south bank of the Göksu. A taxi to Taşucu costs TL20.

Around Silifke

Just southeast of Silifke are the lush salt marshes, lakes and sand dunes of the **Göksu Delta**, an important wetland area and home to some 332 bird species. To the north and northeast, the slopes of the maquis-covered **Olba Plateau** stretch along the coast for about 60km before the Cilician plain opens into an ever-widening swath of fertile land. It is one of Turkey's richest areas for archaeological sites and includes many destinations more easily accessed from Kızkalesi.

CAVE CHURCH OF ST THECLA

This area is rich in early Christian pilgrimage sites, including this **church** (Ayatekla Yeraltı Kilisesi; admission TL3; ⏰8am-8pm Apr-Oct, to 5pm Wed-Sun Nov-Mar), a small rock shelter with a half-dozen columns, cells and altar hidden below the ruined apse of a 5th-century Byzantine church, still venerated by the faithful. St Thecla is thought to have been the first person to be converted to Christianity by St Paul and was persecuted. She spent her last few years in this grotto praying and fasting, and is the patron saint of teachers. Other structures scattered around the hill include a cistern, bath and necropolis.

ⓘ Getting There & Away

To get to the cave, which is 5km to the southwest of Silifke, take a Taşucu dolmuş (TL1.25) and ask to be dropped off at the Ayatekla junction, just over a kilometre from the site. A taxi there and back will cost TL20.

If travelling under your own steam, about 4km out of Silifke, look for the Alpet petrol station on your right. Next to it is signposted Ayatekla Sokak, which leads directly up a hill and to the site.

UZUNCABURÇ

The impressive ruins (admission TL3; ⊘8am-8pm Apr-Oct, to 5pm Nov-Mar) at Uzuncaburç, in the mountains some 30km northeast of Silifke, are well worth the trip. They sit within the ancient Roman city of Diocaesarea, originally a Hellenistic city known as Olba, home to a zealous cult that worshipped Zeus Olbius.

The **Temple of Zeus Olbius**, with some two dozen columns erect, is just inside the site to the left of a wonderful **colonnaded street**. But before you proceed, visit the Roman **theatre** half-sunken into the ground behind the car park. Some of the site's most important structures were built by the Romans, including a **nymphaeum** (AD 2nd or 3rd century) and arched **city gate** to the right, and the **Temple of Tyche** (AD 1st century) with five Corinthian columns at the end of the colonnaded street. Look around the Zeus temple for **sarcophagi** bearing reliefs (eg Medusa) and recumbent figures.

To view a Hellenistic structure built before the Romans sacked Olba, head north through the village where you'll pass a massive, five-storey **watch tower** with a **Roman road** behind it. Another 600m down into the valley leads to a long, roadside **necropolis** of **rock-cut tombs** and more **sarcophagi**.

On the road to Uzuncaburç some 8km out of Silifke at Demircili – ancient Imbriogon – you'll pass several superb examples of Roman **monumental tombs** that resemble houses.

ⓘ Getting There & Away

Minibuses to Uzuncaburç (TL5) leave from a side street near the Silifke tourist office at 10am, noon, 2pm, 4pm and 6pm. They usually depart Uzuncaburç in the morning before noon, though there is one at 4.30pm.

Hiring a taxi costs TL100 return, waiting time included, which would also allow you to inspect the tombs at Demircili along the way.

Kızkalesi

☑0324 / POP 1975

Wonderful Kızkalesi, bang up against the D400, is not your typical highway town. Not only does it front one of the region's loveliest sand beaches, but it boasts not one but two castles, one of which is offshore and seems to be floating at sea. It is also a springboard for the Olba Plateau, a virtual open-air museum of ruins set within the rocky hills.

Despite these strong magnets, Kızkalesi is kept down to earth by the relaxed vibe of its locals. For a visitor, the scene here is more inclusive and easygoing than you'd expect of a typical Turkish village of this size – perhaps thanks to the regularity of foreign archaeology buffs strolling the foreshore's fine promenade filled with holidaying Turks.

⊙ Sights

FREE **Kızkalesi Castle** FORTRESS

(Maiden's Castle) Lying 300m from the shore, Kızkalesi Castle is like a suspended dream. Although it is possible to swim to the castle, most people catch the boat (TL5) from the pier just in front of the Albatross restaurant. While here, have a look at the **mosaics** in the central courtyard and the vaulted **gallery**, and climb one of the four **towers** (the one at the southeast corner has the best views).

Corycus Castle FORTRESS

(Korykos Kalesi; admission TL3; ⊘8am-8pm Apr-Oct, to 5pm Nov-Mar) Very much on *terra firma* at the northern end of the beach, Corycus Castle is an antiquated fortress that was either built or rebuilt by the Byzantines, briefly occupied by the Armenian kingdom of Cilicia and once connected to Kızkalesi by causeway. The 'land castle' is a bit of a rough-and-ready site, but walk carefully to the east, where a ruined tower along the ramparts affords a fine view of the 'sea castle' and the Mediterranean.

Ruins RUINS

Across the highway from Corycus Castle is a **necropolis**, once the burial ground for tradespeople. There are tombs and rock carvings scattered about, including a 5th-century one with a relief of a warrior with a raised sword.

Some 4km northeast of Kızkalesi at Ayaş, and on either side of the D400, are the extensive but badly ruined remains of ancient **Elaiussa-Sebaste** (admission

EASTERN MEDITERRANEAN KIZKALESI

free), a city with foundations dating back to at least the early Roman period and perhaps even to the Hittite era. Important structures on the left (west) side include a 2300-seat hilltop **theatre**, the remains of a **Byzantine basilica**, a **Roman temple** with floor mosaics of fish and dolphins, and a total-immersion cruciform **baptistery**. The ruins on the eastern side are unstable and entry is forbidden.

Sleeping

Yaka Hotel
TOP CHOICE   HOTEL €€
(☑523 2444; www.yakahotel.com.tr; s TL50-70, d TL60-90; ❈@) Yakup Kahveci, the Yaka's multilingual and quick-witted owner, runs the smartest and most welcoming hostelry in Kızkalesi, and the 'Shore' should be your first port of call. The 17 rooms are impeccably tidy, breakfast (or specially ordered dinner) is eaten in the attractive garden, and local knowledge abounds; there's nothing in the area Yakup doesn't know and/or can't organise. The Yaka is also a great place to meet and join up with other travellers, especially those interested in archaeology.

Hotel Hantur   HOTEL €€
(☑523 2367; www.hotelhantur.com; s TL50-60, d TL60-80; ❈@) The Hantur has a front-row seat on the sea and guests need do little else but watch the tide roll in and out. The 20 peachy (literally) rooms are cool, comfortable and all have balconies, but try to grab one facing the sea (eg room 301). The breezy front garden is another bonus, as is the helpful and friendly management.

Rain Hotel   HOTEL €€
(☑523 2782; www.rainhotel.com; s TL40-70, d TL60-90; ❈@) With a youthful vibe set by manager Mehmet, the Rain is very much on the Med-travellers' circuit. Run by the same people as Cafe Rain and its attached travel agency, it's got a similar anything-is-possible ethos, including scuba diving trips. The 18 spotless and spacious rooms are sparingly decorated and, with fridges, conducive to long stays.

Baytan Otel   HOTEL €€
(☑523 2004; www.baytanotel.com; s TL40-70, d TL80-110; ❈@) It might be a titch faded, but the Baytan is right on the beach, its two dozen rooms are spacious, and the bar in the back garden offers live music from 8pm most nights in season. The rooftop terrace is great for a sundowner.

Korykos Hotel   HOTEL €€
(☑523 2212; www.korykoshotel.com; s TL35-70, d TL70-140; ❈@) This smart inland hotel near the Yaka is multistorey though there is a lift. Staff are attentive and professional, while the lobby space is particularly welcoming. The 25 rooms have TV and firm, big beds.

Eating & Drinking

Kızkalesi has yet to develop much of a dining scene, perhaps due to the fine kitchens of its pensions. Maybe consider the 10-minute bus ride (TL1.50) to Narlıkuyu to dine at one of the seafood restaurants there.

Cafe Rain   INTERNATIONAL €€
(☑523 2234; mains TL15-25) The rainbow decor here complements the cheery menu of tasty, good-value international favourites as well as what might be the finest *börek* (pastry filled with cheese or meat) on the eastern Mediterranean. In the evenings, travellers transform it into a companionable cocktail bar.

Villa Nur   FAMILY RESTAURANT €€
(☑523 2340; mains TL10-15) Readers have written raving letters about the meals served at this seafront pension next to the Baytan Otel, owned by a Turkish-German couple. The cakes are exceptional.

Paşa Restaurant   KEBAPÇI €
(☑523 2230; Plaj Yolu 5; mains TL6-10) This large open spot for grills, meze and light Turkish snacks just off central Cumhuriyet Meydanı has agreeable prices.

Albatross   BAR-RESTAURANT
(☑0536 676 3902) It's a restaurant too but we come here for sundowners at the open bar, with full views of the sea castle.

Titanic Bistro & Bar   BAR
(☑523 2669; Cetin Özvaran Caddesi) Not far from the Cafe Rain, this lounge bar has ample couches, pop posters, good indie music and a genuine gallivanting spirit.

Getting There & Away

Frequent buses link Kızkalesi with Silifke (TL3, 30 minutes, 24km) and Mersin (TL6, 1½ hours, 60km).

Around Kızkalesi

There are several places to the southwest and northeast of Kızkalesi that are of genuine historical interest and importance.

They include everything from an idyllic seaside village with an important mosaic to a descent into the very bowels of the earth.

NARLIKUYU

Tiny Narlıkuyu is more than just an attractive village on a cove 5km southwest of Kızkalesi. It's got a half-dozen popular fish restaurants, a mosaic of singular beauty and some other-worldly mountain caves nearby.

Inside the village's tiny **Mosaic Museum** (Mozaik Müzesi; admission TL3), which is contained in a pint-sized 4th-century Roman bath, you'll find a wonderful mosaic of the so-called Three Graces – Aglaia, Thalia and Euphrosyne – the daughters of Zeus.

Among the plethora of waterfront restaurants, with mains from TL15 to TL25, the **Kerim** (☑723 3295) is right on the water next to the museum, while the **Narlıkuyu** (☑723 3286) is above the opposite side of the cove.

Frequent dolmuşes run between Kızkalesi and Silifke via Narlıkuyu (TL1.50).

CAVES OF HEAVEN & HELL

After you return to the D400 from Narlıkuyu and wind your way north for 3km up the road, you'll reach several **caves** (admission TL3; ☺8am-8pm Apr-Oct, to 5pm Nov-Mar), which are sinkholes carved out by a subterranean river and places of great mythological significance.

For those expecting an easy ticket to ride to the hereafter, the **Chasm of Heaven** (Cennet Mağarası) – 200m long, 90m wide and 70m deep – is reached via 450-odd steps to the left of the car park. When you reach a landing not far from the cave mouth, check out the 5th-century Byzantine **Chapel of the Virgin Mary**, which for a short time in the 19th century was used as a mosque.

Continue along the path further into the cave, where you'll find the **Cave of Typhon** (Tayfun Mağarası), a damp, jagged-edged, devilish theatre; indeed, locals believe this cave to be a gateway to the eternal furnace and Strabo mentions it in his *Geography*. Should you hear a certain roaring sound, fear not: it's simply the sound of that underground river. Legend says that it connects with the River Styx.

About 100m up the hill from the steps to the Chasm of Heaven is the **Cave-Gorge of Hell** (Cehennem Mağarası), with its almost vertical walls; as close as you'll get is the heart-stopping viewing platform that extends out and over the 120m-deep pit. This charred hole is supposedly where Zeus imprisoned the 100-headed, fire-breathing monster Typhon after defeating him in battle.

Some 600m west of the caves is **Asthma Cave** (Astim Mağarası). Like Alanya's Dripstone Cave, it supposedly relieves sufferers of the affliction.

ADAMKAYALAR

Tricky to get to but well worth the effort is Adamkayalar (Men Rock Cliff), some 17 Roman-era reliefs carved on a cliff face about 8km north of Kızkalesi. They are part of a 1st century AD necropolis and immortalise warriors wielding axes, swords and lances, and citizens, sometimes accompanied by their wives and children. There are more ruins and tombs scattered around at the top of the cliff.

At the necropolis opposite Corycus Castle a sign points west to the site. Follow this road uphill for 5km and, at another sign, turn left; the car park is just under 3km down this road. Follow the painted blue arrows down a rather tricky incline into the glen for about 750m and don't go alone.

KANLIDiVANE

About 8.5km northeast of Kızkalesi at Kumkuyu is the road leading 4.5km to the frightening **ruins** (admission TL3; ☺8am-8pm Apr-Oct, to 5pm Nov-Mar) of Kanlıdivane, the ancient city of Kanytelis. The first structure to come into view upon entering the car park is a 17m **Hellenistic tower**, which was built by the son of a priest-king at Olba, today's Uzuncaburç, to honour Zeus.

Central to the ruins of Kanlıdivane, which means 'Bloody Place of Madness', is a 60m-deep chasm where criminals were tossed to ferocious wild animals. Various ruins ring the pit – notably four **Byzantine churches** in various states of decay and a **necropolis** along a Roman road to the northeast, with a stupendous 2nd-century **temple tomb**. Look to the cliff walls to see a relief of a six-member family (southwest) and a Roman soldier (northwest).

Mersin (İçel)

☑0324 / POP 825,000

Mersin was earmarked a half-century ago as the seaside outlet for Adana and its rich agricultural hinterland. Today it is the largest port on the Turkish Mediterranean and for the most part a sprawling, soulless place that most people leave quickly. But Mersin, whose official new name İçel (also the name of the province of which it is capital) is ignored by most everyone, does have its moments. Some of the streets around the harbour have almost a Marseilles feel to them, and signs of 'old Turkey' are on the streets everywhere: basket weavers, *çaycılar* (tea sellers) filling glasses with a hose attached to a bag on their backs, and professional 'writers' composing letters for the not-too-literate on old-fashioned typewriters.

◉ Sights & Activities

A stroll along the harbour is one way to get an idea of what Mersin is all about. Another is to wander through the crowded streets and lanes between Uray Caddesi and İstiklal Caddesi.

FREE **Atatürk Evi** MUSEUM
(Atatürk House; Atatürk Caddesi 36; ☺8am-7pm Mon-Sat Apr-Oct, 9am-noon & 1-4.30pm Mon-Sat Nov-Mar) Along the pedestrianised section of Atatürk Caddesi is a museum in a beautiful seven-room villa where Atatürk once stayed.

FREE **Archaeology & Ethnography Museum** MUSEUM
(Cumhuriyet Meydanı 62; ☺8am-noon & 1-7pm Apr-Oct, to 4pm Nov-Mar) A little further west, Mersin's archaeology museum has finds from nearby *höyükler* (tumuli) and sites (including Elaiussa-Sebaste near Kızkalesi), a great bronze of Dionysus and curious odds and ends like a Roman-era glass theatre 'token' on the ground floor. Upstairs are carpets, clothing and weapons.

Greek Orthodox Church CHURCH
(☺divine liturgy 9-11.15am Sun) Next to the museum, the walled church, built in 1852, is still in use and has a lovely *iconostasis*. To gain entry, go to the left side of the church facing 4302 Sokak and ring the bell.

There's also a functioning **Roman Catholic church** (Uray Caddesi 12; ☺mass 6pm Mon-Sat, 8am & 11am Sun) on the eastern side of town.

Roll House Bowling BOWLING
(☎325 9575; www.rollhouse.com; Adnan Menderes Bulvarı 13; games from TL5; ☺noon-midnight Sun-Thu, to 2am Fri & Sat) You probably didn't come to Mersin for it, but you can bowl a few strings next to the Mersin Hilton.

🛌 Sleeping

Nobel Oteli HOTEL €€
(☎237 2210; www.nobelotel.com; İstiklal Caddesi 73; s & d from TL75; P ✻) A very smart choice in the heart of the city, the Nobel has 74 big and comfortable rooms with some deft design touches and satellite TV. The foyer is a hive of business activity, and the adjoining restaurant is popular at lunch.

Hotel Savran HOTEL €
(☎232 4472; Soğuksu Caddesi 14; s/d TL35/55; ✻) This hotel has finally got the facelift it deserves and the upbeat decor now matches the can-do attitude of the staff. The 30 rooms are unexpectedly large, and it remains a popular budget choice for Mersin.

Hotel Gökhan HOTEL €
(☎232 4665; fax 237 4462; Soğuksu Caddesi 20; s/d TL40/60; P ✻) The decor of the public areas of this two-star hotel is vaguely art deco – though we don't know how the large aquarium fits in. The 28 airy rooms include satellite TV and minibar. Opt for one with a balcony.

Mersin Oteli HOTEL €€
(☎238 1040; www.mersinoteli.com.tr; İsmet İnönü Caddesi 62; s/d TL90/140; P ✻) This very large and relatively fancy four-star hotel in the centre offers 102 bland but nice-enough rooms, some with sea-view balconies. Weekend discounts are possible.

🍴 Eating & Drinking

Mersin's local speciality is *tantuni* kebap – chopped beef sautéed with onions, garlic and peppers, and wrapped in pittalike *lavaş ekmek;* it's not unlike a mild Mexican fajita. *Tantuni* is often accompanied by *şalgam suyu,* a crimson-coloured juice made by boiling turnips and adding vinegar (and very much an acquired taste). For something sweet, try *cezerye,* a semigelatinous confectionery made from carrots and packed with walnuts.

Deniz Yıldızı SEAFOOD €€
(☎237 7124; 4701 Sokak 10b; mains TL10-22) With tables out on a narrow lane, the 'Starfish' is the best of several fish restaurants on or just off Silifke Caddesi and within easy scaling distance of the fresh fish market.

Hacıbaba LOKANTA €€
(☎238 0023; İstiklal Caddesi 82; mains TL7-14) Opposite the Nobel, this is a delightful little restaurant with a bright neon sign and rolled out reddish carpets. The *zeytinyağli biber*

dolması (stuffed pepper; TL5.50) is excellent and there's döner, *lahmacun* and pide too.

Toscana
LOKANTA €€

(☑238 2228; Emlak Sokak 41; mains TL7-10) Confusingly named, this eatery up from Uray Caddesi and opposite the Taşhan Antik Galerya serves a range of stews and other Turkish dishes, and is relaxed and efficient.

Gündoğdu
LOKANTA €

(☑231 9677; Silifke Caddesi 22; dishes TL3-10) An especially toothsome fast-food joint that seems to be permanently heaving, this is the place to try *tantuni* (it does a chicken variety too).

Piknik
BAR-CAFE

(☑233 4848; 5218 Sokak; ⊗8am-2am) This bar-cum-cafe-cum-teahouse is one of a collection of humming little working-class drinking venues in the Taşhan Antik Galerya on a street between İsmet İnönü Caddesi and Uray Caddesi.

❶ Information

Bilgi Internet (1st fl, Soğuksu Caddesi 30; per hr TL2)

Tourist office (☑238 3271; İsmet İnönü Bulvarı; ⊗8am-noon & 1-5pm Mon-Fri) On the harbour.

❶ Getting There & Away

Bus

Mersin's otogar is on the city's eastern outskirts. To get to the centre, leave by the main exit, turn right and walk up to the main road (Gazi Mustafa Kemal Bulvarı). Cross to the far side and catch a bus travelling west (TL1.25). Buses from town to the otogar leave from outside the train station as well as from a stop opposite the Mersin Oteli.

From Mersin frequent buses run to Adana (TL10, 1½ hours, 75km), Silifke (TL10, two hours, 85km, three per hour) and Alanya (TL40, 8½ hours, 375km, eight per day). Other long-haul destinations include İstanbul (TL50, 12 hours, 935km) and Ankara (TL40, seven hours, 490km).

Train

There are rail services to Tarsus (TL2) and Adana (TL4) between 6am and 10.30pm.

Tarsus

☑0324 / POP 233,500

Should Tarsus' most famous son return to his hometown some two millennia after his birth, St Paul would hardly recognise the place through the sprawl of concrete apartment blocks. Indeed, though the beauty of Tarsus is largely historic, it is one of those towns that repays perseverance, and a stroll through the back lanes leading to both early Christian and even Old Testament sites can be reason enough to linger.

◎ Sights & Activities

Cleopatra's Gate
HISTORIC BUILDING

The Roman Kancık Kapısı, literally the 'Gate of the Bitch' but better known as Cleopatra's Gate, has nothing to do with the Egyptian queen, although she is thought to have had a rendezvous with Mark Antony here in 41 BC. Heavy-handed restoration has robbed it of any sense of antiquity.

St Paul's Well
RUINS

(St Paul Kuyusu; admission TL3; ⊗8am-8pm Apr-Oct, to 5pm Nov-Mar) Just over a kilometre north of Cleopatra's Gate (there are signs pointing the way) are the ruins of St Paul's house, his supposed birthplace, which can be viewed underneath sheets of plexiglass.

Old City
HISTORIC AREA

A couple of hundred metres south and southeast of St Paul's Well is the Old City (Antik Şehir), including a wonderful 60m-long stretch of **Roman road**, with heavy basalt paving slabs covering a lengthy drain, and some lovely examples of **historical Tarsus houses** (*tarihi Tarsus evleri*), one of which is now the boutique hotel Konak Efsus.

Southeast of the Old City are several historical mosques that have played other roles, including the **Eski Cami** (Old Mosque), a medieval structure that was originally a church dedicated to St Paul. Right beside it looms the barely recognisable brickwork of a huge old **Roman bath**. Across Atatürk Caddesi is the late-19th-century **Makam Camii** (Official Mosque); below it to the east is believed to be the **tomb of the Prophet Daniel**. To the west is the 16th-century **Ulu Cami** (Great Mosque), which sports a curious 19th-century minaret moonlighting as a clock tower. Next to that and from the same era is the **Kırkkaşık Bedesten** (Forty Spoons Market), which still functions as a covered bazaar.

Church of St Paul
CHURCH

(St Paul Kilisesi; admission TL3; ⊗8am-8pm) South of the market, parts of the Church of St Paul date from the 18th century.

A PLACE OF PILGRIMAGE

Jewish by birth, Paul (born Saul) was one of early Christianity's most zealous proselytisers and during his lifetime converted hundreds of pagans and Jews to the new religion throughout the ancient world. After his death in Rome about AD 67, the location of his birthplace became sacred to his followers. Today pilgrims still flock to the site of his ruined house in Tarsus to take a drink from the 30m-deep well on the grounds.

Tarsus Museum MUSEUM
(☑613 1865; Muvaffak Uygur Caddesi 75; admission TL3; ☺8am-7.30pm Apr-Oct, to 5pm Nov-Mar) About 750m southwest of the city centre, opposite the city stadium, the museum has a good collection of ancient statuary and coins, one of which dates back to the 6th century BC.

Waterfall WATERFALL
You can catch a dolmuş (TL1.25) from just in front of the Eski Cami to a cooling waterfall (şelale) on the Tarsus River (the Cydnus River in ancient times), some 3km to the north. There are tea gardens and restaurants nearby.

🛏 Sleeping & Eating

Konak Efsus BOUTIQUE HOTEL **€€**
(☑614 0807; www.konakefsus.com; Tarihi Evler Sokak 31-33; s & d TL160; 🞲@) This long-awaited addition to Tarsus' meagre accommodation listings is a delightful boutique hotel converted from a traditional Tarsus house in the centre of the Old City. The eight rooms, with stone walls, antique furniture and 21st-century plumbing, are all unique and bear different names. The Cleopatra Suite is especially fine, as is the lovely patio.

Cihan Palas Oteli HOTEL **€**
(☑624 1623; fax 624 7334; Mersin Caddesi 21; s/d TL30/50; 🞲) Acceptable only in a pinch (to be honest), this is a very basic hostelry just steps from the tourist information kiosk. It offers little in the way of creature comforts but the price is right.

Antik Cafe CAFE
(☑0538 866 6565; Tarihi Evler Sokak; 🛜) This pretty little cafe in a 200-year-old conversion opposite the Konak Efsus is just the ticket for a drink and a leg's up after a hot and dusty trawl through Tarsus.

ℹ Information

Tourist office (☑613 3888; Cumhuriyet Alanı; ☺8am-5pm Mon-Sat) Extremely helpful kiosk just in front of the Roman road.

ℹ Getting There & Away

Tarsus' otogar is 3km east of the centre. A taxi from there will cost TL10 or you can walk out the front exit and hop on a bus or dolmuş (TL1.25) on the same side of the street. There are plenty of buses and dolmuşes connecting Tarsus with Mersin (TL3.50, 29km) and Adana (TL4, 42km).

The train station, from where you can also reach Mersin (TL2) and Adana (TL3), is northwest of the tourist office at the end of Hilmi Seçkin Caddesi.

Adana

☑0322 / POP 1.52 MILLION

As hot as it can get here, entering this enormous city – Turkey's fourth largest – is like stepping into a cold shower after spending time on the beaches and in the ruins of the eastern Mediterranean. More or less cut in two by the D400, it's a thoroughly modern affair with some decent sights to detain you and good transportation links for a painless escape.

North of the city's main road, Turan Cemal Beriker Bulvarı, which runs west to east and over Kennedy Köprüsü (Kennedy Bridge), are leafy and well-heeled districts. South of the trendy high-rise apartments, the mood deepens and the houses start to sprawl. The Seyhan River delimits the city centre to the east.

◉ Sights & Activities

Mosques MOSQUES
The attractive 16th-century **Ulu Cami** (Great Mosque; Abidin Paşa Caddesi) is reminiscent of mosques found in northern Syria, with black-and-white banded marble and elaborate window surrounds. The tiles in the *mihrab* (prayer niche) came from Kütahya and İznik.

The central **Yeni Cami** (New Mosque; Özler Caddesi), dating from the early 18th century, follows the general square plan of the Ulu Cami, with 10 domes. The 16th-century **Yağ Camii** (Oil Mosque; Özler Caddesi), with its imposing portal to the southeast, started life as the church of St James.

Most imposing of all is the six-minaret **Sabancı Merkez Camii** (Sabancı Central Mosque; Turan Cemal Beriker Bulvarı), on the left bank of the river beside the Kennedy Bridge. The largest mosque between İstanbul and Saudi Arabia, it was built by the late industrial magnate Sakıp Sabancı (1933–2004) – philanthropist and founder of the second-richest family dynasty in Turkey after Koç – and is covered top to tail in marble and gold leaf. The mosque can accommodate an estimated 28,000 worshippers.

Adana Ethnography Museum   MUSEUM
(Ziyapaşa Bulvarı 143; admission TL3; ☉8am-5pm Tue-Sun) Just off İnönü Caddesi, this museum is housed in a nicely restored Crusader church, which later served as a mosque. These days it holds a display of carpets and kilims, weapons, manuscripts and funeral monuments.

Archaeology Museum   MUSEUM
(Fuzuli Caddesi 10; admission TL5; ☉8am-5pm Tue-Sun) Next door to the Sabancı mosque, the Archaeology Museum is rich in Roman statuary from the Cilician Gates, north of Tarsus. These 'gates' were the main passage through the Taurus Mountains and an important transit point as far back as Roman times. Note especially the 2nd-century Achilles sarcophagus, decorated with scenes from the *Iliad*. Hittite artefacts and Hellenistic monuments are also on display.

Stone Bridge   BRIDGE
Taşköprü, a Roman-era stone bridge over the Seyhan at the eastern end of Abidin Paşa Caddesi, was built under Hadrian (r 117–138) and repaired in the 6th century. The 300m-long span has 21 arches but you can only see 14 – the rest are underwater.

Great Clock Tower   HISTORIC BUILDING
(Büyük Saat Kulesi) Near Adana's sprawling **covered market** (*kapalı çarşı*), the Great Clock Tower dates back to 1881.

Hamams   HAMAMS
(per person TL9-15) There are two traditional hamams in the centre where you can go for a soak and a scrub: **Mestan Hamamı** (Merry Hamam; ☎351 5189; Pazarlar Caddesi 3; ☉5am-11pm), next to the Öz Asmaaltı restaurant, and the **Çarşı Hamamı** (Market Hamam; ☎351 8102; Ali Münif Caddesi 145; ☉men 5-9am & 4-10pm, women 9am-3.30pm) opposite the Great Clock Tower.

🛌 Sleeping

TOP CHOICE Hotel Bosnalı   BOUTIQUE HOTEL €€
(☎359 8000; www.hotelbosnali.com; Seyhan Caddesi 29; s/d €75/85, ste €130-160; ✳) We've fallen in love with this new riverfront boutique hotel, which has risen phoenix-like from a drop-dead gorgeous private mansion built in 1889. Stone-tile floors, original hand-carved wooden ceilings, antique Ottoman furnishings in the dozen rooms… The attention to detail is enviable and the views from the rooftop restaurant are breathtaking.

Erten Otel   BUSINESS HOTEL €€
(☎359 5398; www.adanaertenotel.com.tr; Özler Caddesi 53; s/d TL110/150; P✳@) Another great addition to Adana's four-star hotel choices, the Erten is right downtown and stars the city's friendliest reception. Most of the 67 very quiet rooms have sturdy desks, decent-sized sitting areas and showers with actual pressure.

Otel Mercan   HOTEL €
(☎351 2603; www.otelmercan.com; Küçüksaat Meydanı 5; s TL25-40, d TL40-70; ✳) Set among cheap fabric boltholes, the Mercan is a bona fide budget winner. It has 33 well-appointed (though smallish) rooms, a quaint breakfast area and a stylish lounge with unusual art.

Akdeniz Oteli   HOTEL €€
(☎/fax 363 1510; İnönü Caddesi 22; s/d TL50/80; ✳) This is a clean and smartly decorated two-star place with 30 rooms, all with glassed-in shower stalls. Don't miss the psychedelic mirrored staircase leading from the lobby to the 2nd-floor bar.

Hotel Mavi Sürmeli   BUSINESS HOTEL €€€
(☎363 3437; www.mavisurmeli.com.tr; İnönü Caddesi 109; s/d €150/200; P✳@) The slickest top-end hotel in Adana, the Mavi is centrally located and a truly luxurious choice for the business traveller. Its 117 rooms are spacious enough for contact sports and there's a cavalcade of outlets, including the Turunç Bar with live music at the weekend.

🍴 Eating & Drinking
This city is famous nationwide for its Adana kebap, which is minced beef or lamb mixed with powdered red pepper and grilled on a skewer. It is served with sliced onions dusted with the slightly acidic herb sumac and barbecued tomatoes.

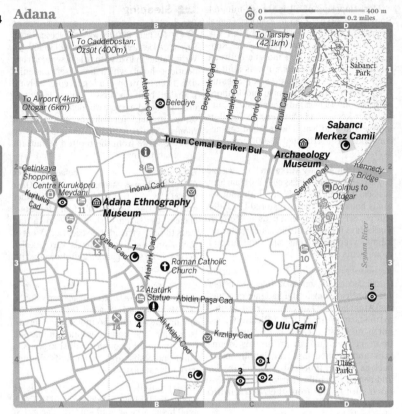

Öz Asmaaltı
RESTAURANT €€

(☑351 4028; Pazarlar Caddesi 9; mains TL12-25) Down from the Otel Mercan, this local favourite is just about the best restaurant of its class in Adana. It's a fairly spartan place, but the mains and meze are delightful. This is the place to try Adana kebap.

İmparator
KEBAPÇI €€

(☑352 3062; Özler Caddesi 43; mains TL10-25) There's a lot to like about this busy family-oriented restaurant covered in posters of Turkish folk heroes. The chunky Adana kebaps come with all manner of sides and the English-speaking manager knows everyone's name. Sometimes there's live music at the weekend.

Caddebostan
CAFE-BAR €€

(☑459 0957; Ziyapaşa Bulvarı 3; dishes TL15) Just south of the train station, the 'Street Market' is more cafe than restaurant, with fancy coffees and cakes and cold drinks.

But it does Italian- and French-inspired dishes, too, mostly pastas.

Özsüt
CONFECTIONER, CAFE €

(☑458 2424; Ziyapaşa Bulvarı 15c; cakes TL4.50-8; ◷8am-midnight) Cakes, puddings and a delightfully delicious assortment of ice creams are available at this branch of a popular chain at the end of the same block as the Caddebostan. There's a Starbuck's next door if you're desperate.

❶ Information

Tourist office (☑363 1448; Atatürk Caddesi 7; 8am-noon & 1-5pm Mon-Sat) One block north of İnönü Caddesi.

❶ Getting There & Away

Adana's airport (Şakirpaşa Havaalanı) is 4km west of the centre on the D400. The otogar is 2km further west on the north side of the D400. The train station is at the northern end of Ziyapaşa Bulvarı, 1.5km north of İnönü Caddesi.

Adana

Bus

Adana's large otogar has direct bus and/or dolmuş services to just about everywhere in Turkey. Note that dolmuşes to Kadirli (TL8, two hours, 108km) and Kozan (TL6, one hour, 72km) leave from the Yüreği otogar, on the right bank of the Seyhan River.

Train

Trains link the ornate *gar* (station) at the northern end of Ziyapaşa Bulvarı with İstanbul's Haydarpaşa Station (TL40, 19 hours) via Konya (TL16, seven hours). Departures are at 2.10pm daily. There are trains almost twice an hour between 6am and 11.15pm to Mersin (TL4) via Taurus (TL3).

ⓘ Getting Around

A taxi from the airport into town costs TL10 to TL15. A taxi from the city centre to the Yüreği otogar will cost TL7.50.

Around Adana

Inland from the Bay of İskenderun (İskenderun Körfezi) are the remains of castles and settlements connected with the Armenian kingdom of Cilicia, including its capital, Sis at Kozan. Some, like Anavarza, date back to Roman times or earlier.

KOZAN

This large market town and district seat 72km northeast of Adana via route No 815 was once Sis, the capital of the kingdom of Cilicia and the linchpin keystone of a cavalcade of castles overlooking the expansive (and hard-to-defend) Çukurova plain. Towering above the plain is stunning **Kozan Castle** (Kozan Kalesi; admission free), built by Leo II (r 1187–1219), stretching some 900m along a narrow ridge.

Walking (or driving) up the kilometre-long road to the castle, you pass a pair of crumbling towers before reaching the main gate. Along the way are the ruins of a church, locally called the *manastır* (monastery). From 1293 until 1921 this was the seat of the Katholikos (Patriarchate) of Sis, one of the two senior patriarchs of the Armenian Church.

Inside is a mess of ruined buildings, but if you continue upward you can see a many-towered keep on your right and on your left a massive tower, which once held the royal apartments. In all there are some 44 towers and lookouts as well as the remains of a *bedesten*.

The town of Kozan itself has some lovely old houses and makes a good day trip by minibus from Adana (TL6, one hour). If you decide to stay, one of the old houses dating from 1890 has been turned into a quirky inn. Called **Yaver'in Konaği** (Yaver's Mansion; 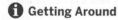515 0999; www.yaverinkonagi.com; Manastır Sokak 5; s/d TL50/75; ❄ @), it has 13 rather rustic but comfortable rooms in a traditional three-storey house and two newer outbuildings at the bottom of the ascent to the castle. There's a very good restaurant (last orders 9.30pm), serving superb *lahmacun* baked in an open-air stone oven.

YILANKALE

Yılankale (Snake Castle; admission free) was built in the mid-13th century when this area was part of the Armenian kingdom of Cilicia. It's said to have taken its name from a serpent that was once entwined in the coat of arms above the main entrance. It's 38km east of Adana and just over 2km south of the D400 highway. From the car park there's a well-laid path for 100m then a rough trail; reaching the castle's highest point requires a 20-minute steep climb over the rocks, past gatehouse, cisterns, vaulted chambers and even a dungeon. Standing high above the wheat and sunflower fields, though, you'll feel on top of the world.

EASTERN MEDITERRANEAN AROUND ADANA

DESTINATION	FARE (TL)	DURATION (HR)	DISTANCE (KM)	FREQUENCY (PER DAY)
Adıyaman (for Nemrut Dağı)	35	6	335	7 buses
Alanya	35	10	440	up to 8 buses
Ankara	35	7	475	hourly
Antakya	18	3½	190	hourly
Antalya	40	11	565	2 or 3 buses
Diyarbakır	35	8	535	several
Gaziantep	18	3	220	several
İstanbul	50	12	920	hourly
Kayseri	30	6	355	several
Konya	35	6	335	frequent
Şanlıurfa	25	6	360	several
Silifke	15	2½	165	14 buses
Van	60	15	910	at least 1 bus

EASTERN MEDITERRANEAN

ANAZARBUS (ANAVARZA)

When the Romans moved into this area in 19 BC, they built this fortress city on top of a hill dominating the fertile plain and called it Caesarea ad Anazarbus. Later, when Cilicia was divided in two, Tarsus remained the capital of the west and Anazarbus the main seat in the east. It changed hands at least 10 times over the centuries, falling to the Persians, Arabs, Byzantines, the Hamdanid princes of Aleppo, the Crusaders, a local Armenian king, the Byzantines again, the Turks and the Mamluks. When that last group finally swept away the Armenian kingdom of Cilicia in 1375, the city was abandoned.

Some 5km after leaving the highway, you reach a T-junction and a large **gateway** set in the city walls; beyond this was the ancient city, now just fields strewn with ancient stones. Turn right and you'll soon reach the house of the *bekçi* (watchman), the enthusiastic Yaşar Dilci, whose own property contains **Roman sarcophagi** (one with the face of the 3rd-century Emperor Septimius Severus) and pools with the most glorious **mosaics** of Titus as well as dolphins, fish and sea birds. Yaşar will guide you (be generous), pointing out the stadium, theatre, baths and, of course, the hilltop **castle** (which is quite a trek up 400 steps). Make sure you see the dedication stone of the ruined 6th-century **Church**

of the Apostles in the field, with a carved cross and the alpha and omega symbols; the very rare Roman **vaulted stables** south of the castle; and the **main aqueduct** with several arches still standing.

ℹ Getting There & Away

If driving from Yılankale, return to the D400 highway and take the exit to route 817 (Kozan/Kadirli) north for 27km to the village of Ayşehoca, where a road on the right is marked for Anavarza/Anazarbus, 5km to the east. If you're in a dolmuş or minibus you can get out here and hitch a ride. From Kozan follow route 817 south for 28km and turn left at Ayşehoca.

İskenderun

📞 0326 / POP 191.600

İskenderun (Alexandretta in ancient times) is a modern industrial town with a working port, and the gateway to the province of Hatay.

Strategically located, the town has more than once changed hands. Alexander the Great took charge in 333 BC, and it was occupied by the British in 1918. The following year the French took charge, administering it in some fashion or another until 1938. In 1939 the Republic of Hatay voted to join the nascent Turkish Republic.

İskenderun is a handy stopover between Adana and Antakya. It's got little of Hatay's energy but there are several places to stay and eat near the attractive waterfront, and it's a springboard for the beach town of Arsuz.

The main road along the waterfront is Atatürk Bulvarı. Şehir Pamir Caddesi is İskenderun's 'high street', running north from the waterfront and the massive monument to Atatürk and friends. Most hotels are within a few blocks of this monument.

Sleeping

Hataylı Oteli   BUSINESS HOTEL €€€
(☑614 1590; www.hataylioteli.com; Mete Aslan Bulvarı; s TL95-110, d TL145-180; ✳) This newish three-star hotel with all the mod cons is ideally located near the water at the eastern end of Atatürk Bulvarı. The excellent lobby bar has a mildly equine theme, and the 62 rooms are huge and handsome; some (eg room 415) have windows in two directions though the carpet is too busy for our eyes. The terrace restaurant offers a glorious breakfast vista.

Altındişler Otel   HOTEL €€
(☑617 1011; www.altindisler.com; Şehir Pamir Caddesi 11; s/d TL45/75; ✳) With the improbable name of 'Gold Teeth', this hotel with its colourful prints and large picture window in the 1st-floor lobby is a, well, toothsome operation. Its 30 rooms are spotless and ensure a good night's rest.

İmrenay Hotel   HOTEL €€
(☑613 2117; www.imrenayhotel.com; Şehir Pamir Caddesi 5; s/d TL75/120; ✳) This hotel is a titch gloomy, with its dark brown parquet

floors and 33 smallish rooms. Still the lobby, complete with a flat-screen TV, is sparkly enough and the management is welcoming.

Eating

Sirinyer   SEAFOOD €€
(☑641 3050; www.sirinyerrestaurant.com; Akdeniz Caddesi 113; mains TL15-25) Praised as far west as Kalkan for having some of the freshest fish on the Mediterranean, this upmarket destination restaurant with a lovely seafront terrace is a couple of kilometres southwest of the centre, on the road to Arsuz. Judging from the Arabic script everywhere, it's popular with visiting Syrians.

Hasan Kolcuoğlu   KEBAPÇI €€
(☑614 7333; Ziya Gökalp Caddesi 6; mains TL8-15) By far the busiest restaurant in town, the double-storey 'HK' has been pumping out delicious, wholesome kebaps for just over a century, so someone's doing something right. It's got an American diner feel – service is warm and casual – but a truly Turkish clientele.

Hasan Baba   PIDECI €
(☑617 6420; Ulucami Caddesi 35; mains TL3-12) This pide and *lahmacun* joint is sprawling and consistently packed with satisfied diners. Sit in the backyard and enjoy the fountain.

Petek   CONFECTIONER, CAFE €
(☑617 8888; Mareşal Çakmak Caddesi 16; cakes TL3.50-8) 'We can't forget a taste' says the

ARMENIAN KINGDOM OF CILICIA

During the early 11th century the Seljuk Turks swept westwards from Iran, wresting control of much of Anatolia from a weakened Byzantium and pushing into the Armenian highlands. Thousands of Armenians fled south, taking refuge in the rugged Taurus Mountains and along the Mediterranean coast, where in 1080 they founded the kingdom of Cilicia (or Lesser Armenia) under the young Prince Reuben.

While Greater Armenia struggled against foreign invaders and the subsequent loss of its statehood, the Cilician Armenians lived in wealth and prosperity. Geographically, they were in the ideal place for trade and they quickly embraced European ideas, including its feudal class structure. Cilicia became a country of barons, knights and serfs, the court at Sis (today's Kozan) even adopting Western-style clothing. Latin and French became the national languages. During the Crusades the Christian armies used the kingdom's castles as safe havens on their way to the Holy Land.

This period of Armenian history is regarded as the most exciting for science and culture, as schools and monasteries flourished, teaching theology, philosophy, medicine and mathematics. It was also the golden age of Armenian ecclesiastical manuscript painting, noted for its lavish decoration and Western influences.

The Cilician kingdom thrived for nearly 300 years before it fell to the Mamluks of Egypt. The last Armenian ruler, Leo V, spent his final years wandering Europe trying to raise support to recapture his kingdom, before dying in Paris in 1393.

WORTH A TRIP

KARATEPE

Archaeology buffs will want to make a beeline for the open-air **Karatepe-Aslantaş Open-Air Museum** (Karatepe-Aslantaş Acık Hava Müzesi; admission TL3; ☺8am-noon & 1-7pm Apr-Oct, to 5pm Nov-Mar) within the national park of that name. The ruins date from the 8th century BC, when this was a summer retreat for the neo-Hittite kings of Cilicia, the greatest of whom was named Azitawatas. The forested hilltop site overlooks Lake Ceyhan (Ceyhan Gölü), an artificial lake used for hydroelectric power and recreation.

Karatepe was defended by 1km-long walls, traces of which are still evident. A visit to the Hittite remains is in guided groups (you may have to wait) and begins at the southwest **Palace Gate**, which is protected by representations of lions and sphinxes and lined with fine reliefs, including one showing a relaxed feast at Azitawatas' court, complete with sacrificial bull, musicians and chariots. A circular path leads to the **Lower Gate** in the northeast with even better stone carvings, including reliefs of a galley with oarsmen, warriors doing battle with lions, a woman suckling a child under a tree and the Hittite sun god. There is an excellent **indoor museum** with items unearthed here and a scale model of the site, which helps put everything into perspective.

Karatepe is a tricky spot to reach without your own transport. If you're driving from Kozan, follow route 817 for 18km to Çukurköprü and then head east for another 18km to Kadirli, from where a secondary road leads for 22km to the site. It's easier to reach Karatepe along route 80-76 from Osmaniye, 30km to the southeast, which is served by dolmuşes from Adana (TL7, 1½ hours, 95km) and İskenderun (TL7, 1½ hours, 105km).

If carless, your best bet is to organise a taxi from Osmaniye, where you'll find a taxi rank beside the otogar. A return trip to Karatepe (two hours) with an hour's stop at the ruined Hellenistic city of Hierapolis-Castabala will cost TL75.

logo at this very stylish cake shop and cafe. In situ since 1942, the staff clearly have elephantine memories.

Getting There & Away

There are frequent minibus and dolmuş connections to Adana (TL10, 2½ hours, 135km), Antakya (TL5, one hour, 58km) and Osmaniye (TL8, one hour, 66km).

Regular dolmuşes scoot down the coast to Uluçınar (TL4, 30 minutes, 33km), better known as Arsuz.

Antakya (Hatay)

☏0326 / POP 212,700

Antakya, officially known as Hatay, is a prosperous and modern city near the Syrian border that doesn't have to dig deep for proof of its pedigree, built on the site of ancient Antiocheia ad Orontem. Under the Romans, Antioch's important Christian community developed out of the already large Jewish population that was at one time led by St Paul. Today Antakya is home to a mixture of faiths – Sunni, Alevi and Orthodox Christian – and has a palpable cosmopolitan and civilised air. Locals call their hometown Baris Şehri (City of Peace). That's just what it is.

The Arab influence permeates local life, food and language; indeed, the city only became part of Turkey in 1939 after centuries conjoined in some form or another to Syria. Most visitors come to Antakya for its museum and rightly so – the mosaics are unforgettable. But take time to stroll along the Orontes (Asi) River and through the bazaars and back lanes of a city that some people – including at least one of us – consider the jewel of the Turkish Mediterranean.

⊙ Sights

Hatay Archaeology Museum   MUSEUM
(Hatay Arkeoloji Müzesi; Gündüz Caddesi 1; admission TL8; ☺9am-6.30pm Tue-Sun Apr-Oct, 8.30am-noon & 12.30-4.30pm Nov-Mar) This museum contains one of the world's finest collections of Roman and Byzantine mosaics, covering a period from the 1st century AD to the 5th century. Many of them were recovered almost intact from Tarsus or Harbiye, what was Daphne in ancient times, 9km to the south.

Salons I to IV are large, naturally lit rooms with high ceilings, perfect for displaying mosaics of tiles so tiny that at first glance you may mistake them for paintings. Be sure to see the full-body mosaic of **Oceanus & Thetis** (2nd century; Salon 4) and the **Buffet Mosaic** (3rd century; Salon 2) with dishes of chicken, fish and eggs. As well as the standard scenes of hunting and fishing (eg **Thalassa & the Nude Fishermen**, with kids riding whales and dolphins, in Salon 4), there are stories from mythology, including the fabulous 3rd-century mosaics of **Narcissus** (Salon 2) and **Orpheus** (Salon 4). Other mosaics have quirkier subjects: don't miss (all in Salon 3) the happy hunchback with an oversized phallus, the black fisherman or the mysterious portrayal of a raven, a scorpion, a dog and a pitchfork attacking an 'evil eye'.

Other rooms contain artefacts recovered from various mounds and tumuli in the area, including a Hittite one near Dörtyol, 16km north of İskenderun. Taking pride of place in one room is the so-called **Antakya Sarcophagus** (Antakya Lahdı), an impossibly ornate tomb with an unfinished reclining figure on the lid.

Bazaar   BAZAAR

A sprawling market fills the back streets north of Ulus Alanı and Kemal Paşa Caddesi. The easier way to see it is to follow **Uzunçarşı Caddesi**, the main shopping street.

Around the 7th-century **Habib Neccar Camii** on Kurtuluş Caddesi you'll find most of Antakya's remaining **old houses**, with carved stone lintels or wooden overhangs, and courtyards within the compounds. The priests at the Catholic church believe St Peter would have lived in this area between AD 42 and 48, as it was then the Jewish neighbourhood.

Church of St Peter   CHURCH

(St Pierre Kilisesi; admission TL8; ☉9am-noon & 1-6pm Apr-Oct, 8am-noon & 1-5pm Nov-Mar) This early Christian church cut into the slopes of Mt Staurin (Mountain of the Cross) is thought to be the earliest place where the newly converted met and prayed secretly. Tradition has it that this cave was the property of St Luke the Evangelist, who was born in Antioch, and that he donated it to the burgeoning Christian congregation. Both Peter and Paul lived in Antioch for a few years; they almost certainly preached here. When the First Crusaders took Antioch in 1098, they constructed the wall at the front and the narthex, the narrow vestibule along the west side of the church.

To the right of the altar faint traces of an early fresco can be seen, and some of the simple mosaic floor survives. The water dripping in the corner is said to cure disease.

EASTERN MEDITERRANEAN ANTAKYA (HATAY)

WORTH A TRIP

ARSUZ

If you're up for a little R&R between exploring the remains of the Armenian Kingdom of Cilicia and making that pilgrimage to Antakya, you might head for Arsuz, a delightful fishing village officially called Uluçınar that sits on a bump of land jutting out into the sea 33km southwest of İskenderun. There's not a whole lot to do here but swim, gaze at the distant mountains and try your luck with the local lads at fishing in the nearby river, but that is the whole point, isn't it?

Accommodation of choice in these parts is at the **Arsuz Otel** (☏643 2444; www.arsuzotel.com; s/d from TL100/150), a rambling 'olde worlde' (though really only 50 years old) hotel fronting the sea with its own beach and 50 enormous and airy rooms. Splash out and take something over-the-top like room 28, a two-bedroom suite called Cennet (Paradise), with a balcony that goes on for a month of Sundays. The lobby, with its old-fashioned tiles and piano, has a vague belle époque South of France feel to it. And the restaurant is to die for, with grilled *mercan* (a locally caught fish called Red Sea bream in English) and Hatay meze like *oruk* (spicy beef croquette) and *sürk* (soft cheese flavoured with dried red pepper). You'll be back, trust us.

Dolmuşes link Arsuz and İskenderun (TL4, 30 minutes) throughout the day. Those with their own wheels and a sense of adventure might want to drive the 45km south to Čevlik, two thirds of which is along level but unsealed road, before carrying on to Antakya.

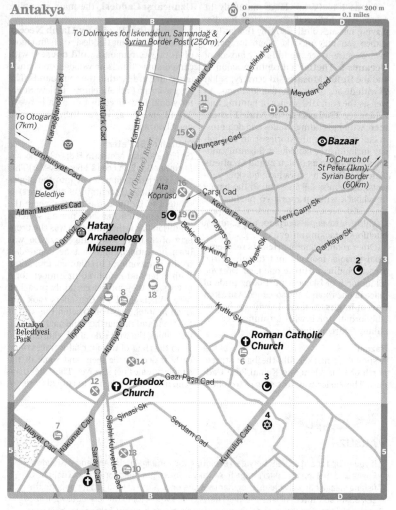

Just 2.5km northeast of town, the church is accessible on foot in about half an hour along Kurtuluş Caddesi.

Other Houses of Worship NOTABLE BUILDINGS
In the ecumenical city of Antakya you'll find at least five different religions and sects represented within a couple of blocks of one another. Most of the city's 1200-strong Christians worship at the fine **Orthodox church** (Hürriyet Caddesi 53; ◷divine liturgy 8.30am & 6pm). Rebuilt after a devastating earthquake in 1900 with Russian assistance, the church is fronted by a lovely courtyard up some steps from the street and contains some beautiful icons, an ancient stone lectern and valuable church plate.

The Italian-ministered **Roman Catholic church** (Kutlu Sokak 6; ◷10am-noon & 3-5pm, mass 8.30am daily & 6pm Sun) was built in 1852 and occupies two houses in the city's old quarter, with the chapel in the former living room of one house. Next door is the **Sermaye Camii** (Capital Mosque; Kurtuluş Caddesi 56), with a wonderfully ornate *şerefe* (balcony) on its minaret.

Just south is the underutilised **synagogue** (Kurtuluş Caddesi 56). And there's even the relatively new Korean-ministered Methodist **Antioch Protestant Church** (Saray Caddesi; ⊙9am-6pm), just south of the Antik Beyazıt Hotel.

🛏 Sleeping

TOP CHOICE **Liwan Hotel** BOUTIQUE HOTEL €€€
(☑215 7777; www.theliwanhotel.com; Silahlı Kuvvetler Caddesi 5; s/d TL140/180; ℙ❄) The newly opened Liwan is arguably the finest boutique hotel on the eastern Mediterranean coast. The Eclectic-style building, dating from the 1920s and once owned by the president of Syria, is a gem and contains two dozen very large, very tastefully furnished rooms over four floors (yes, there is a lift). The restaurant is in an open courtyard – once an internal garden with ogee arches – that becomes a covered courtyard with the flick of a switch. The atmospheric stone bar features some of the best live music in town at the weekend.

Antik Beyazıt Hotel BOUTIQUE HOTEL €€
(☑216 2900; www.antikbeyazitoteli.com; Hükümet Caddesi 4; s/d TL90/120; ℙ❄) Housed in a pretty French Levantine colonial house (1903) that once did time as a courthouse, Antakya's first boutique hotel is looking a bit frayed, though the antique furnishings, Oriental carpets and ornate chandelier in the lobby still evoke a more elegant past. The 27 rooms are fairly basic; the ones in the rear have loft-style bedrooms and access to a back studio.

Antakya Catholic Church Guesthouse
PENSION €
(☑215 6703; www.anadolukatolikkilisesi.org/anta kya; Kutlu Sokak 6; per person TL25) A positively delightful place to stay (if you can get in), this guesthouse run by the local Catholic church has eight tidy double rooms wrapped around a leafy (and suitably reflective) courtyard. Guests are invited (though not required) to attend daily mass in the church opposite.

Mozaik Otel HOTEL €€
(☑215 5020; www.mozaikotel.com; İstiklal Caddesi 18; s/d TL75/120) This 'almost boutique' hotel is an excellent midrange choice north of central Ulus Alanı and near the bazaar. The two dozen rooms are decorated with folksy bedspreads and mosaic repros, and the Sultan Sofrası restaurant is just next door.

Antik Grand Hotel HOTEL €€
(☑215 7575; www.antikgrand.com; Hürriyet Caddesi 18; s/d TL70/110; ℙ❄) This well-placed hotel offers 27 large and tasteful rooms in a beautiful faux-antique style. All rooms have TV and minibar. Long-stay discounts are available.

Hotel Saray HOTEL €
(☑214 9001; fax 214 9002; Hürriyet Caddesi 3; s/d TL40/60; ❄@) A bit rugged and definitely not what its name suggests, the 'Palace' has 35 rooms (TV included) that are large enough and some even have tiny balconies and mountain views.

GOOD EATING IN ANTAKYA

Arab – particularly Syrian – influences permeate Hatay's local cuisine, and Antakya is the best place to try these specialities. Handfuls of mint and wedges of lemon accompany kebaps. Hummus, rarely seen elsewhere in Turkey, is readily available here. And the unique *kekik salatasası* (fresh thyme salad made with spring onions and tomatoes) is a taste treat worthy of a sultan.

Special local dishes abound. Make sure to try *muhammara,* a meze dip of crushed walnuts, red pepper and olive oil (also called *cevizli biber,* or walnutty peppers); *oruk,* a torpedo-shaped croquette of spicy minced beef encased in bulgur wheat flour and fried that is not unlike Lebanese *kibbeh;* and a tangy soft cheese flavoured with dried red pepper called *sürk.*

For dessert, you can't miss *künefe,* a cake of fine shredded wheat laid over a dollop of fresh mild cheese, on a layer of sugar syrup topped with chopped walnuts. Several places near the Ulu Cami make a mean one for around TL3, including **Kral Künefe** (☎214 7517; Çarşı Caddesi 7).

✖ Eating & Drinking

There's a large choice of restaurants south of Ulus Alanı, either on or just off Hürriyet Caddesi. Good places to relax over a drink and a snack are the tea gardens in the riverside Antakya Belediyesi Parkı (Antakya City Council Park), on the left bank of the Orontes southwest of the museum.

Antakya Evi   LOCAL €
(☎214 1350; Silahlı Kuvvetler Caddesi 3; mains TL5-10; ⊙8am-midnight Mon-Sat) With a name like 'Antioch House' (their translation), it's little wonder that dining here feels much like eating at a friend's place. A personal favourite that we'll go back to, it's in an old villa tastefully decorated with photos and antique furniture, with very affordable local meze (TL4) and grills.

Anadolu Restaurant   RESTAURANT €€€
(☎215 3335; Hürriyet Caddesi 30a; mains TL8-35) Popular with families, the local glitterati and the expense-account brigade, Antakya's culinary hot spot serves a long list of fine meze (TL6 to TL8) on gold-cloth tablecloths in a splendid alfresco garden, where the palm trees push through the roof. Meat dishes include Anadolu kebap (TL15) and the special *kağıt,* or 'paper' kebap (TL12).

Hatay Sultan Sofrası   LOCAL €€
(☎213 8759; www.sultansofrasi.com; İstiklal Caddesi 20a; mains TL8-15; ⊙8am-midnight Mon-Sat) Antakya's premier spot for affordable local dishes, this place is spotless and turns out dishes at a rapid pace. The articulate manager loves to guide diners through the menu.

Antik Han Restaurant   KEBAPÇI €€
(☎214 6833; www.antikhan.org; Hürriyet Caddesi 17/1; mains TL8-15; ⊙8am-3am; ☻) The Han has been doing its thing for some time now, and the breezy terrace above the street and adjoining kids' play area still pull in the punters. The limited menu is satisfying enough – round it off with the wonderful *künefe* cake.

Vitamin Shop Center   CAFE
(☎216 3858; Hürriyet Caddesi 7) The juice bar to the stars, judging by the photo gallery, and a mecca for backpackers, this exceptionally friendly place is where to go for a classic 'atom shake' (TL5), a regional speciality of banana, pistachio, honey, apricot and milk that goes down a treat and will keep you full for half a day.

Shakespeare   CAFE
(☎216 8500; İnönü Caddesi 7a; ⊙8am-8pm; ☎) This cafe with the lovely modern decor attracts Antakya's young bloods with its free wi-fi and affordable pasta dishes (TL6.50 to TL10).

🔒 Shopping

Doğal Defne Dünyası   HOMEWARE, TEXTILES
(☎215 6030; Çarşı Caddesi 16) 'Natural Daphne World' sells high-quality soaps from ancient Daphne (now Harbiye to the south), as well as gorgeous silk scarves woven and block-printed by hand.

Kurşunluhan Bahartçısı   FOOD & DRINK
(☎0506 535 9744; Uzunçarşı Caddesi 73) Smack dab in the middle of the sprawling bazaar, visit Hüseyin's shop for all manner of jarred (including *sürk* cheese) and bottled (eg

pomegranate essence) goodies as well as local teas, coffees and every herb and spice ground on God's green earth.

ℹ Information

Tourist office (☑216 6098; Muammer Ürgen Alanı; ◑8am-noon & 1-5pm Mon-Fri) On a roundabout at the end of Atatürk Caddesi, a 10-minute walk from the centre.

ℹ Getting There & Around

Bus

TO & FROM SYRIA Turks and Syrians no longer need visas to cross each other's border but most everyone else does (see the boxed text p686).

The **Jet Bus Company** (☑444 0277; www. jetturizm.co.tr; cnr İstiklal Caddesi & Abdurrahman Melek Caddesi) at the old bus station has direct buses to Aleppo (TL10, three hours, 95km) and Damascus (TL15, seven hours, 320km) at noon daily, with an extra one to Aleppo at 9am as well. These buses follow the route that all cross-border buses and trucks take, the Reyhanlı–Bab al-Hawa border, so you'll need to brace yourself for waits, though we're told these have shortened since Turkey and Syria dropped their mutual visa requirements. To speed things up, try to cross the border before 8am or take a shared or private taxi, which will cost TL80 to Aleppo.

If you want to tackle the border in stages, local buses to Reyhanlı (TL5, 40 minutes) leave from near the petrol station on Yavuz Sultan Selim Caddesi at the top of İstiklal Caddesi. From Reyhanlı you can catch a dolmuş to the Turkish border and walk a couple of kilometres into Syria.

Alternatively, from the same spot catch a dolmuş south to Yayladağı, from where you pick up a taxi or hitch a few kilometres further to the border. Once across (and crossing takes all of 15 minutes here), you're just 2km from the Syrian mountain village of Kassab, from where regular microbuses make the 45-minute run to Lattakia.

WITHIN TURKEY Antakya's intercity otogar has moved 7km to the northwest of the centre and is at the end of Mehmet Kafadar Caddesi, the continuation of Cumhuriyet Caddesi. A taxi to/from the centre will cost TL12. Some bus companies still have offices in the old otogar.

Direct buses go to most western and northern points, including Ankara, Antalya, İstanbul, İzmir, Kayseri and Konya, usually travelling via Adana (TL15, 3½ hours, 190km). There are also frequent services to Gaziantep (TL20, four hours, 262km) and Şanlıurfa (TL30, seven hours, 400km), either direct or via Gaziantep. Minibuses and dolmuşes for İskenderun (TL5, one hour, 58km) and Samandağ (TL3, 40 min-

utes, 28km) leave from along Yavuz Sultan Selim Caddesi at the top of İstiklal Caddesi.

Around Antakya

MONASTERY OF ST SIMEON

The remains of the 6th-century **Monastery of St Simeon** (Aziz Simon Manastırı; admission free) sit atop a mountain some 18km southwest of Antakya on the road to Samandağ. The cross-shaped monastery contains the ruins of three churches. Bits of mosaics can be seen in the floor of the first (north) church, but the central one, the **Church of the Holy Trinity**, is the most beautiful, with rich carvings. The south church is more austere. The most interesting item here is the octagonal base of a **pillar**, atop which Saint Simeon Stylite the Younger (521–597), imitating a 5th-century Syrian predecessor deemed the 'Elder', would preach against the iniquities of Antioch. There are also the remains of a stepped structure next to the pillar that pilgrims would climb to address the saint.

ℹ Getting There & Away

The turn-off to the monastery is just past the village of Karaçay, reachable by a Samandağ dolmuş (TL2, 20 minutes) from Antakya. After travelling 5km through a massive (and horrid) wind turbine farm, the road branches; the monastery remains lie about 2km up the road leading to the right. A taxi from Antakya and back with an hour at the site will cost about TL80.

ÇEVLİK

The scant ruins of **Seleuceia in Pieria** at Çevlik, Antioch's port in ancient times some 5km northwest of Samandağ, are hardly impressive, but they include the **Titus & Vespasian Tunnel** (Titüs ve Vespasiyanüs Tüneli; admission TL3; ◑9am-7pm Apr-Oct, 8am-5pm Nov-Mar), an astonishing feat of Roman engineering. In its heyday, Seleucia lived under the constant threat of flooding from a stream that descended from the mountains and flowed through the town. To counter this threat, 1st-century Roman emperors Titus and Vespasian ordered that a 1.4km-long channel be cut through the solid rock to divert the stream.

A path from the car park leads to the *gişe* (ticket kiosk). From here follow the trail to the right of a metal arch along an irrigation canal and past some shelters cut into the rock, finally arriving at a humpback Roman bridge spanning the gorge. Here, steps lead down to the tunnel. Bring a torch, since the path is slippery. At the far end of the channel an inscription provides a date for the work carried out by sailors and prisoners from Judea. About 100m from the tunnel are a dozen Roman **rock tombs** with reliefs, including the excellent **Beşikli Mağarası** (Cave with a Crib).

ⓘ Getting There & Away

Dolmuşes run between Antakya and Samandağ (TL5, 40 minutes, 28km), where you can change for another bound for Çevlik (TL1.50, 15 minutes).

Ankara & Central Anatolia

Best Places to Stay

» Gül Evi (p414)

» Angora House Hotel (p404)

» Gordion Hotel (p405)

» Emin Efendi Konağı (p429)

» Cinci Hanı (p414)

Best Places to Eat

» Taşev (p416)

» Balıkçıköy (p405)

» Le Man Kültür (p406)

» Şehrazat (p432)

Why Go?

Somewhere between the cracks in the Hittite ruins, the fissures in the Phyrgian burial mounds and the scratches in the Seljuk caravanserais, the mythical, mighty Turks raced across this highland desert steppe with big ideas and bad-ass swords. Nearby, Alexander the Great cut the Gordion knot, King Midas displayed his deft golden touch and Julius Caesar came, saw and conquered. Atatürk forged his secular revolution along dusty Roman roads that all lead to Ankara, an underrated capital city and geo-political centre. Further north through the nation's fruitbowl, in Safranbolu and Amasya, 'Ottomania' is still in full swing. Here wealthy weekenders sip çay with time-rich locals who preside over dark timber mansions. Central Anatolia is the meeting point between the fabled past and the prosperous present – a sojourn here will enlighten and enchant.

When to Go

Ankara

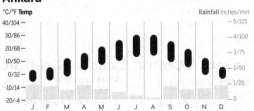

May/June Fruit harvest: cherries the size of a baby's fist, apricots sweeter than a baby's face...

June Summer storms light up the twin Ottoman towns of Safranbolu and Amasya.

December The Mevlâna Festival in Konya is a Sufi spectacular of extraordinary human spirit.

Ankara & Central Anatolia Highlights

❶ Join the sentimental summer tourists in Ottomanised **Safranbolu** (p411)

❷ Head to **Amasya** (p426) where Pontic tombs also poke out from craggy cliffs

❸ Try your hand at modern-day diplomacy in Ankara's trendy **Kızılay** (p406) and

Kavaklıdere (p406),then discover the real Turkish roots at the **Museum of Anatolian Civilisations** (p397)

❹ Hit the Hittite hills at **Hattuşa** (p422) and get your head around ancient Turkish history

❺ Pay homage to Rumi, the founder of Sufi Islam, at

Konya's **Mevlâna Museum** (p439) and whirl till your heart's content

❻ Dip your toes in eastern Turkey and the exfoliating fish at **Balıklı Kaplıca** (p437)

❼ Knock once at the divine doors at **Divriği** (p438)

Ankara

📞 0312 / POP 4.5 MILLION

The country's capital and second-largest city has made remarkable progress, from a dusty Anatolian stage to today's sophisticated arena for international affairs. Drawing comparisons with İstanbul is a pointless exercise – the flat, modest surrounds are hardly the stuff of national poetry – but the civic success of this dynamic and intellectual city is assured thanks to student panache and foreign-embassy intrigue.

The economic success of Turkey is reflected in the booming restaurant and bar scene around Kavaklıdere, and in the ripped-jean politik of Kızılay's sidewalk cafes and market stalls frequented by hip students, bums and businessmen alike. Meanwhile Ankara's unsentimental relationship with its physical past has at last been addressed, with old town Ulus and its citadel now destinations worthy of their historic significance. Ankara also boasts two monuments central to the Turkish story – the Anıt Kabir, an extraordinary tribute to life in death, and the beautifully conceived Museum of Anatolian Civilisations.

History

Although Hittite remains dating back to before 1200 BC have been found in Ankara, the town really prospered as a Phrygian settlement on the north–south and east–west trade routes. Later it was taken by Alexander the Great, claimed by the Seleucids and finally occupied by the Galatians around 250 BC. Augustus Caesar annexed it to Rome as Ankyra.

The Byzantines held the town for centuries, with intermittent raids by the Persians and Arabs. When the Seljuk Turks came to Anatolia, they grabbed the city but held it with difficulty. Later, the Ottoman sultan Yıldırım Beyazıt was captured near here by Tamerlane and subsequently died in captivity. Spurned as a jinxed endeavour, the city slowly slumped into a backwater, prized for nothing but its goats.

That all changed when Atatürk chose Angora, as the city was known until 1930, to be his base in the struggle for independence. When he set up his provisional government here in 1920, the city was just a small, dusty settlement of some 30,000 people. After his victory in the War of Independence, Atatürk declared it the new Turkish capital, and set

about developing it. European urban planners were consulted, resulting in long, wide boulevards, a forested park with an artificial lake, and numerous residential and diplomatic neighbourhoods. The city's position in the centre of Turkey made it more suitable than İstanbul as a capital for the new republic. From 1919 to 1927, Atatürk never set foot in İstanbul, preferring to work at making Ankara top dog.

⊙ Sights & Activities

Museum of Anatolian Civilisations

MUSEUM

(Anadolu Medeniyetleri Müzesi; Map p400; 📞 324 3160; Gözcü Sokak 2; admission TL15; ⊗ 8.30am–5pm) The superb Museum of Anatolian Civilisations is the perfect introduction to the complex weave of Turkey's ancient past, housing artefacts cherry-picked from just about every significant archaeological site in Anatolia.

The museum is housed in a beautifully restored 15th-century *bedesten* (covered market). The 10-domed central marketplace houses reliefs and statues, while the surrounding hall displays exhibits from the earlier Anatolian civilisations: Palaeolithic, neolithic, chalcolithic, Bronze Age, Assyrian, Hittite, Phrygian, Urartian and Lydian. The downstairs sections hold classical Greek and Roman artefacts and a display on Ankara's history. Get there early to avoid the flood of tour groups and school parties. If it's not too hot, you can climb the hill from Ulus to the museum (1km); from Ulus head east up Hisarparkı Caddesi and follow the road along the hillside, then turn left. A taxi from Ulus should cost about TL5.

Touring the Museum

The exhibits are chronologically arranged in a spiral: start at the Palaeolithic displays to the right of the entrance, then continue in an anticlockwise direction, visiting the central room last.

Çatalhöyük, southeast of Konya, is one of the most important neolithic sites in the world. Here you can see a mock-up of the inside of a dwelling typical of those uncovered at the site; the clay bull-head icons were a feature of the cult of the time.

Also on show are many finds from the Assyrian trading colony Kültepe, one of the world's oldest and wealthiest bazaars. These include baked-clay tablets found at the site, which dates to the beginning of the second millennium before Christ.

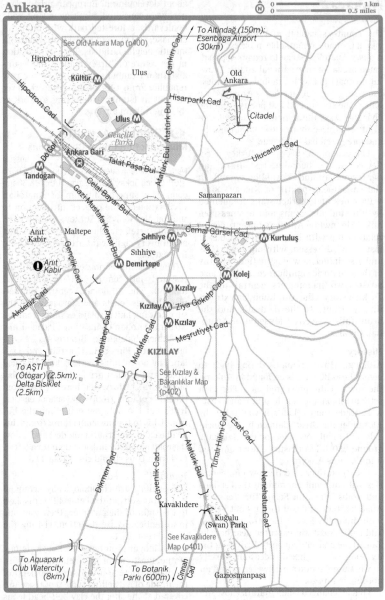

One of the striking Hittite figures of bulls and stags in the next room used to be the emblem of Ankara. The Hittites were known for their relief work, and some mighty slabs representing the best pieces found in the country, generally from around Hattuşa, are on display in the museum's central room.

Most of the finds from the Phrygian capital Gordion, including incredible inlaid wooden furniture, are on display in the museum's last rooms. The exhibits also include limestone blocks with a still-undecipherable inscription in text resembling the Greek alphabet, and lion- and ram-head ritual vessels, which show the high quality of Phrygian metalwork.

Spurred by rich metal deposits, the Urartians were Anatolia's foremost metalworkers, as the knives, horse-bit, votive plates and shields demonstrate. There are also terracotta figures of gods in human form, some revealing their divine powers by growing scorpion tails, and neo-Hittite artefacts.

Downstairs, the classical-period finds and regional history displays give the local picture. Excavations have unearthed a Roman road near the Column of Julian, and Ankara has its own 'missing link', the 9.8-million-year-old *Ankarapithecus* (a 30kg, fruit-eating primate).

Citadel   HISTORIC AREA

When you're done with the museum, make the most of its location by wandering to the imposing **hisar** (citadel; Ankara Kalesi; Map p400) just up the hill. The most interesting part of Ankara to poke about in, this well-preserved quarter of thick walls and intriguing winding streets took its present shape in the 9th century AD, when the Byzantine emperor Michael II constructed the outer ramparts. The inner walls, which the local authority is slowly rebuilding, date from the 7th century. To find it, head around the back of the museum up Gözcü Sokak, past the octagonal tower, to the **Parmak Kapısı** (Finger Gate), also called the Saatli Kapı (Clock Gate).

Opposite the gate, in the beautifully restored Çengelhan, the **Rahmi M Koç Industrial Museum** (Rahmi M Koç Müzesi; Map p400; [2]309 6800; www.rmk-museum.org.tr; Depo Sokak 1; adult/child TL3/1.50; ⊙10am-5pm Tue-Fri, 10am-7pm Sat & Sun) has three floors covering subjects as diverse as transport, science, music, computing, Atatürk and carpets, some with interactive features.

Walking straight ahead once you've entered Parmak Kapısı, through a gate on your left and past the And Evi cafe, you'll see Alaettin Camii on the left. The citadel mosque dates from the 12th century but has been extensively rebuilt. To your right a steep road leads to a flight of stairs taking you up to the Şark Kulesi (Eastern Tower), with panoramic city views. Although it's much harder to find, a tower to the north, Ak Kale (White Fort), also offers fine views. If you're coming up to the citadel along Hisarparkı Caddesi, look left about halfway up to see the remains of a Roman theatre from around 200 to 100 BC.

Inside the citadel local people still live as in a traditional Turkish village, and you'll see women beating and sorting skeins of wool. Broken column drums, bits of marble statuary and inscribed lintels are incorporated into the walls.

| FREE | Anıt Kabir | MONUMENT |

(Monumental Tomb; Map p398; ⊙9am-5pm mid-May–Oct, to 4pm Nov-Jan, to 4.30pm Feb–mid-May) The monumental mausoleum of Mustafa Kemal Atatürk (1881–1938), the founder of modern Turkey, is worth a visit to see how much sway he still holds over the Turkish people. Located high above the city, with an abundance of marble and an air of veneration, the **Anıt Kabir** is one of Ankara's more relaxing areas. As you approach the tomb, the **Hurriyet Kulesi** (Tower of Liberty) has interpretive panels and photos covering Atatürk's funeral, the construction of the tomb and the iconography of the site. Facing it, the **İstiklal Kulesi** (Tower of Independence) gives more detail, with models recreating scenes.

Continue along the **Lion Rd**, a 262m walkway lined with 24 lion statues – Hittite symbols of power used to represent the strength of the Turkish nation. The path leads to a massive courtyard, framed by colonnaded walkways, with steps leading up to the huge tomb on the left.

Entered to the right of the tomb, the extensive **museum** displays Atatürk memorabilia, personal effects, gifts from famous admirers, recreations of his childhood home and school, and his favourite dog, Fox (stuffed). Just as revealing as all the rich artefacts are his simple rowing machine and huge multilingual library, which includes tomes he wrote.

Downstairs, extensive exhibits about the War of Independence and the formation of the republic move from battlefield murals with sound effects to overdetailed explanations of post-1923 reforms. At the end, a gift shop sells Atatürk items of all shapes and sizes, including key rings, jigsaw puzzles, cufflinks, clocks, ties and even height charts.

As you approach the tomb itself, look left and right at the gilded inscriptions, which are quotations from Atatürk's speech celebrating the republic's 10th anniversary in 1932. Remove your hat as you enter, and bend your neck to view the ceiling of the

Old Ankara

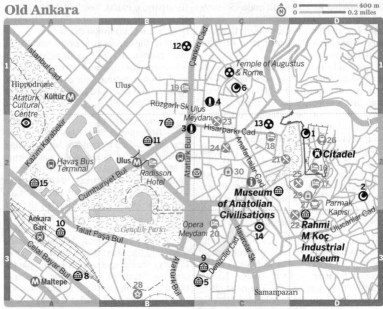

Old Ankara

lofty hall, lined in marble and sparingly decorated with 15th- and 16th-century Ottoman mosaics. At the northern end stands an immense marble **cenotaph**, cut from a single piece of stone weighing 40 tonnes. The actual tomb is in a chamber beneath it.

It should take around two hours to see the whole site. It is virtually a pilgrimage site, so arrive early to beat the crowds; school groups frequently drop by midweek, especially in May, June and September.

The memorial straddles a hill in a park about 2km west of Kızılay and 1.2km south of Tandoğan, the closest Ankaray station to the entrance. A free shuttle regularly zips up and down the hill; alternatively, it's a pleasant walk to the mausoleum (about 20 minutes) or you can take a taxi (TL5). Note that security checks, including a bag scan, are carried out on entry; taxi drivers should turn off the meter while the guards go through the formalities.

Ethnography Museum
MUSEUM

(Etnografya Müzesi; Map p400; Talat Paşa Bulvarı; admission TL3; ⊙8.30am-12.30pm & 1.30-5.30pm) The Ethnography Museum is housed inside a white marble post-Ottoman building (1927) that served as Atatürk's mausoleum until 1953. To get there, go to Ulus metro station and follow Talat Paşa Bulvarı until you see the 'Etnografya Müzesi' sign (not the 'Resim ve Heykel Müzesi' sign).

Past the equestrian statue out front, the mausoleum is preserved in the entrance hall. Around the walls are photographs of Atatürk's funeral. The collection is superb, with displays covering henna ceremonies, Anatolian jewellery, rug-making, Seljuk ceramics, early-15th-century doors and (opposite the anxious-looking mannequins in the circumcision display) coffee. Also of interest are the calligraphy and manuscript collections of Besim Atalay, who translated the Quran into Kurdish.

FREE Painting & Sculpture Museum
MUSEUM

(Resim ve Heykel Müzesi; Map p400; ⊙9am-noon & 1-5pm) Next door to the Ethnography Museum, the Painting & Sculpture Museum occupies an equally elaborate building. Ranging from angular war scenes to society portraits, the pieces demonstrate that 19th- and 20th-century artistic developments in Turkey paralleled those in Europe, with Atatürk appearing in increasingly abstract form.

Museum of the War of Independence & Republic Museum
MUSEUMS

(Kurtulus Savasi Müzesi; Map p400; Cumhuriyet Bulvarı; admission TL3; ⊙8.30am-5pm) The former has a collection of military photographs and documents, housed in Turkey's first parliament (the Republican grand national assembly held early sessions here).

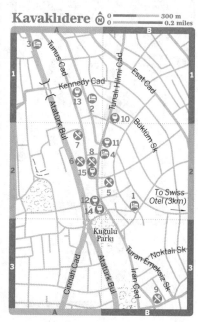

Kavaklıdere

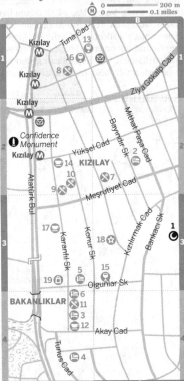

museum may relocate when fast trains to Konya become operational in 2011.

Turkish Aeronautical Association Museum (Türk Hava Kurumu Müzesi; Map p400; Hipodrom Caddesi 2) has a collection of old planes and some aviation displays in the shadow of its landmark parachute tower.

Atakule MONUMENT
(admission TL2.50; ⊙11am-3am) Ankara's landmark tower, the Atakule, has a revolving restaurant (mains TL16 to TL26) for 360-degree views; making a reservation exempts you from the admission fee. Shooting to the top in the glass lift is the hairiest part of the experience. There is a cinema in the mall at the bottom. Get here on Atakule- and Çankaya-bound buses down Atatürk Bulvarı.

Mosques MOSQUES
The huge outline of **Kocatepe Camii** (Map p402) in Kızılay is the symbol of Ankara. It is one of the world's largest mosques but is also very new (built between 1967 and 1987).

The latter was the assembly's second headquarters, and features exhibits on the republic's beginnings.

FREE **Transport Museums** MUSEUMS
Railway Museum & Art Gallery (Demiryolları Müzesi ve Sanat Galerisi; Map p400; ⊙9am-noon & 1-5pm) This is a small building on platform 1 at Ankara station that served as Atatürk's residence for 1½ years during the War of Independence. Right beside it is Atatürk's private 1930s rail coach. Take a look at them while waiting for a train.

The **Open-Air Steam Locomotive Museum** (Açık Hava Buharlı Lokomotif Müzesi; Map p400; Celal Bayar Bulvarı; admission TL1) is a collection of slowly rusting vintage engines. To find it, descend the underpass as though you're going to the train platforms, but keep walking straight on. Just before entering the Tandoğan Kapalı Çarşı shopping area, climb the steps to your left, then turn right and continue for around 800m. The

Ankara's most revered mosque is Hacı Bayram Camii (Map p400), near the Temple of Augustus and Rome. Hacı Bayram Veli was a Muslim 'saint' who founded the Bayramiye dervish order in about 1400. Ankara was the order's centre, and Hacı Bayram Veli is still revered by pious Muslims. The mosque was built in the 15th century, with tiling added in the 18th century. Surrounding shops sell religious paraphernalia (including wooden toothbrushes as used, supposedly, by the Prophet Mohammed).

If you turn left on leaving the *hisar* and walk downhill past the antique shops you'll come to the 13th-century Arslanhane Camii (Map p400), with pieces of Roman masonry in its walls.

Şengül Merkez Hamamı HAMAM
(Map p400; Acıçeşme Sokak 3; wash & massage TL10; ⊙5am-11pm for men, 7am-7pm for women) There are several hamams east of Opera Meydanı, including Şengül Merkez Hamamı, which has separate sections for men and women.

Parks PARKS
Walk south of Ulus Meydanı along Atatürk Bulvarı and you'll reach the entrance to Gençlik Parkı (Youth Park; Map p398), where Atatürk had a swamp converted into an artificial lake. The park gets going during summer, but at other times it appears to be returning to swampland. The Luna Park funfair overlooks the slow decay, and there are *çay bahçesi* (tea gardens) by the lake; single women should only go to those with *aile* (family) in their name. In fact, single women should avoid the park altogether.

Other oases in the city are Kuğulu Parkı (Swan Park; Map p398), at the southern end of Tunalı Hilmi Caddesi, and the Botanik Parkı (Botanical Park), spilling into a valley beneath the Atakule.

Further out of town in Gölbaşı, Aquapark Club Watercity (☑498 2100; www.ankaraaquapark.com, in Turkish; Haymana Yolu 6km, Gölbaşı; adult TL20-30, under 4yr/4-12yr free/TL15; ⊙10am-7pm) has outdoor, indoor and children's pools, water slides, sports facilities and restaurants. Dolmuşes (shared taxis; can be a minibus or sedan) run here from Opera Meydanı.

Roman Baths RUINS
(Roma Hamaları; Map p400; admission TL3; ⊙8.30am-12.30pm & 1.30-5.30pm) The sprawling ruins of these 3rd-century

baths are 400m north of Ulus Meydanı. The layout of the baths is clearly visible; look for the standard Roman *apoditerium* (dressing room), *frigidarium* (cold room), *tepidarium* (warm room) and *caldarium* (hot room). A Byzantine tomb and Phrygian remains have also been found here. More excavations are in the pipelines.

Column of Julian MONUMENT
(Jülyanus Sütunu; Map p400; off Ulus Meydani) Erected in honour of Roman Emperor Julian the Apostate's visit to Ankara. In a square ringed by government buildings, it is usually topped by a stork's nest.

🎆 Festivals & Events
Music and film fans are well catered for in the capital.

Ankara Film Festival FILM
(www.filmfestivalankara.com.tr) Kicks off each March.

Ankara Music Festival MUSIC
(www.ankarafestival.com) Three weeks of classical performances in April.

Flying Broom FILM
(www.ucansupurge.org) Women's film festival takes place in May.

Profestival Rock MUSIC
(www.theprofestival.com) A hardcore assault in late June.

FREE Büyük Ankara Festivali
MUSIC/FAMILY
Weeklong event in July that exists somewhere between summer concert series and carnival.

🛏 Sleeping
Book ahead, as many rooms are snapped up by businesspeople and bureaucrats. There are a number of budget and midrange hotels and restaurants around Ulus Meydanı, but the best cheap options are on the citadel hill. Most of the good midrange hotels are in Kızılay, while the top-end roosts are in Kavaklıdere.

ULUS
The older area around Ulus is currently undergoing a major revamp both inside and outside the citadel – a fancy Divan hotel opens here in 2011. However, given that most of the restaurants and nightlife are in Kızılay and Kavaklıdere, if you want to go out for the evening the added cost of public

transport or a taxi back to Ulus may mean that a room in Kızılay costs the same overall.

TOP CHOICE — Angora House Hotel
HISTORIC HOTEL €€

(Map p400; ☑309 8380; Kalekapısı Sokak 16-18; s/d TL60/120; ⊘Mar-Oct; ⊛) Despite what nearby rivals might claim, Angora House has not closed down. In fact, the new owners may appear a little overwhelmed but Angora House is the pick of the old town and one of the more authentic accommodation options in Ankara. The impressive walled courtyard shields the six tastefully decorated rooms from the citadel streets (avoid the noisy front room). The beds are super-comfy and the shared landing is all class.

And Butik Hotel
HISTORIC HOTEL €€

(Map p400; ☑310 2304; www.andbutikhotel. com; İstek Sokak 2; s/d/ste TL60/120/150) Immaculate new hotel around the corner from Angora House, boasting lemon-fresh rooms – some self-contained – with lovely stone floors and neat fittings. The owners are also involved in an interesting Turkish music restoration project.

Hotel Oğultürk
HOTEL €

(Map p400; ☑309 2900; www.ogulturk.com; Rüzgarlı Eşdost Sokak 6; s/d/tr TL50/60/70; ⊛) Just off Rüzgarlı Eşdost Sokak, the Oğultürk is one of central Ulus' smarter options, and on a par with many hotels in Kızılay. It's professionally managed and good for solo female travellers.

Otel Mithat
HOTEL €

(Map p400; ☑311 5410; www.otelmithat.com. tr; Tavus Sokak 2; s/d/tr €23/33/43) This 50-room hotel near Opera Meydanı is deceptively posh upon entering, but the rooms are miniscule with barely enough room to swing a punch. However the wi-fi is lightning, and the breakfast is super-sized.

Hitit Oteli
HOTEL €€

(Map p400; ☑310 8617; Hisarparkı Caddesi 12; s/d TL75/100) On the hill towards the citadel is this dated midrange hotel with a fish tank in the lobby and spotless, plain rooms with wooden flooring. The non-English-speaking staff are helpful, but there's an air of desperation in the empty hallways.

KIZILAY & BAKANLIKLAR
If you've just stepped off the steppe to find yourself craving some Anatolian urbania, the leafy streets of Kızılay and nearby Bakanlıklar are just the answer. Loads of students and inner-city folk stride the pedestrianised areas and good-value hotels abound – discounts are readily available.

Ankara Regency Hotel
HOTEL €€

(Map p402; ☑419 4868; www.ankararegencyho tel.com; Selanik Caddesi 37; s/d TL80/120; ⊛@) An absolute winner in three key categories: pimping lobby, cheesy smiles on the staff and proximity to bars. Opened in 2008, this friendly hotel is right in the thick of Kızılay. The big éclair-like rooms are cleverly laid out and blushed in forty shades of tan, with floral patterns galore and mini flat-screen TVs fixed to the wall. All in all, great value.

Hotel Gold
HOTEL €€

(Map p402; ☑419 4868; www.ankaragoldhotel. com; Güfte Sokak 4; s/d/tr TL80/120/140; ⊛@) With a lobby like the Turkish version of a gangster rap video, Hotel Gold sets the razzle-dazzle tone early with a pillared entrance, rock-and-roll lobby and marbled lifts. The rooms stare through the looking glass at candy-coloured bedspreads and suite rooms are yummier than Alice in Vegas.

Midas Hotel
HOTEL €€€

(Map p401; ☑424 0110; www.hotelmidas.com; Tunus Caddesi 20; s/d from €80/100, ste €130; ⊛@) This excellent midrange hotel of international standing has efficient staff (during the day) and an inviting spa and fitness centre. Rooms are elegant but contained, with enormous beds and pale interiors; the suites are more modern. The inclusive breakfast is extensive but head elsewhere for dinner.

Otel Elit
HOTEL €€

(Map p402; ☑417 5001; www.elitotel.com.tr; Olgunlar Sokak 10; s/d TL60/100) The so-bad-it's-good philosophy applies to this post-retro family operation of purple and gold leanings. The location is spot on and rooms are rigidly clean with a certain telemovie charm.

Hotel Eyüboğlu
HOTEL €€

(Map p402; ☑417 6400; www.eyubogluhotel.com; Karanfil Sokak 73; s/d TL70/120; ⊛@) A 1980s doozy complete with delegation-sized conference rooms and a whole snooker of billiard tables. The period rooms feature dark blinds with gold stars and white bedspreads with blue stars. The Amerikan Bar is orange.

Hotel Metropol
HOTEL €€

(Map p402; ☑417 3060; www.hotelmetropol. com.tr; Olgunlar Sokak 5; s/d TL70/100; ⊛) The three stars are just hanging in there at this longstanding midrange hotel on a popular Kızılay corner. The rooms are fading around the edges, but remain well-presented, with comfortable beds. The lobby is great for stretching out and the staff are forever courteous. The breakfast spread is excellent, but laundry rates are high.

KAVAKLIDERE

Gordion Hotel
HISTORIC HOTEL €€€

(Map p401; ☑427 8080; www.gordionhotel.com; Büklüm Sokak 59; d €80-140; ✿@❋) This independent hotel is a fabulously cultured inner-city residence that remains remarkably empty much of the year. In the middle of Kavaklıdere, guests will lap up the basement swimming pool, the Vakko textiles in the lobby, the centuries-old art engravings, conservatory restaurant, the beautiful beds and extensive DVD library. At night, the Gordion looks a picture.

Divan Hotel
HOTEL €€

(Map p401; ☑457 4000; www.divan.com.tr; Güniz Sokak 42; d €80; ❋) The award-winning Divan chain, known for its chic corporate vibe, has opened a sharp new place just off Tunalı Hilmi Caddesi with a bold glass and steel motif and modern, clean-lined furniture in the airy rooms. Wi-fi is fast and free, the service exemplary, and the creative-looking lobby restaurant – one of two – heaves with locals on weekends.

Tunalı Hotel
HOTEL €€

(Map p401; ☑467 4440; www.hoteltunali.com.tr; Tunalı Hilmi Caddesi 119; d from €70; ✿@) In the middle of Ankara's prime shopping strip, the Tunalı offers all the conveniences of a business hotel in excellent, Scandinavian-inspired rooms, plus a hearty breakfast. Good value for a hassle-free, anonymous stay.

Swiss Otel
HOTEL €€€

(☑455 0000; www.hilton.com; Yıldızevler Mah, Jose Marti Caddesi 21; s/d from €280/300, ste €445-820; ✿@❋) We love this five-star fit-out down in Çankaya, especially the basement health club that permeates wellness. Shame the location is so dull.

✗ Eating

ULUS

Most Ulus options are cheap and basic. If self-catering seems like a good option, Ulus Hali food market (Map p400) is the place to pick up provisions, from oversized chilli peppers to jars of honey. In and around

the citadel, a dozen old wood-and-stone houses have been converted into inviting, atmospheric licensed restaurants. Summer opening hours are from around noon to midnight; most places are better visited in the evening, when live music creates more atmosphere. The restaurants reduce their opening hours in winter.

Kubaşik Piknik
KEBAPÇI €

(Map p400; ☑309 7274; Hükümet Caddesi; kebaps TL2.50-4) This hole in the wall is actually part of a chain. *Köfte* (meatballs), döner kebaps and chicken alternatives are available to eat in or take away.

Kale Washington
INTERNATIONAL €€

(Map p400; ☑311 4344; www.washingtonrestaurant.com; Doyran Sokak 5-7; mains TL15-24; ☺noon-midnight) By far the most elegant eatery in the old town, the 'WR' serves international cuisine to visiting dignitaries (Hillary Clinton reportedly ate here) and some Turkish specialities including *halep işi kebap* and *su böreği*. The views from the white tablecloths are most palatable.

Çengelhan
ANATOLIAN €€€

(Map p400; ☑309 6800; Depo Sokak 1; mains TL16-25) Inside an old caravanserai, the Rahmi M Koç Industrial Museum restaurant nestles between vintage cars and a reconstructed Ottoman house. The outdoor terrace is delightful for a plate of pan-roasted sea bass (from many miles away!), aubergine (eggplant) kebap or an array of mezes.

Zenger Paşa Konağı
LOKANTA €€

(Map p400; ☑311 7070; www.zengerpasa.com; Doyran Sokak 13; mains TL12-17; ☺noon-12.30am; ❋) Crammed with Ottoman ephemera, the Zenger Paşa looks at first like a deserted ethnographic museum, but wealthy Ankaralıs love the pide, meze and grills, still cooked in the original Ottoman oven. The views of the city from the back porch are worth the visit alone; there's joyful live music most nights.

Boyacızâde Konağı
LOKANTA €€

(Map p400; ☑310 1515; Berrak Sokak 7/9; mains TL14-18; ☺from noon) Entered via a cluttered courtyard, this wonderfully converted mansion-restaurant offers great views, typical Ottoman-stalgic decor and good fish dishes. *Fasıl* (Turkish classical) music provides the entertainment.

Kınacızade Konağı
LOKANTA €€

(Map p400; ☑324 5714; www.kinacizadekonagi.com; Kale Kapısı Sokak 28; set menus TL12-20;

⊙noon-12.30am) Next door to And Butik hotel is this overcooked Ottoman house with period costumes hanging on sword edges. There's a divine courtyard to enjoy the tasty set menus.

KIZILAY

In the pedestrian zone north of Ziya Gökalp Caddesi, pavement eateries and stalls serve everything from döner to corn on the cob. Ogunlar Sokak is good for an alfresco sandwich.

TOP CHOICE Le Man Kültür INTERNATIONAL €

(Map p402; ☑310 8617; Konur Sokak 8a-b; mains TL6-11; ⊙10am-11pm) Named after a cult Turkish comic strip – and decorated accordingly – this is still the pre-party pick for a substantial feed and for spotting the beautiful young educated things. Among the multicultural fare on offer, we dig the Chinese egg rolls (TL10); of the few local dishes, the *köfteli sandviç* (TL8.50) is a tangy sure thing. Drinks are reasonably priced and the speakers crank everything from indie-electro to Türk pop.

Urfalı Kebap KEBAPÇI €

(Map p402; ☑418 9495; Karanfıl Sokak 69; mains TL5-10) One of the best kebap restaurants in the capital, Urfalı is fast and friendly and seats eighty-plus hungry diners, from merry students to a three-generation family. The *çiğer şiş* (TL8) and the *urfa kebap* (TL8) won't disappoint.

Cafe Sobe CAFE €

(Map p402; ☑425 1356; Konur Sokak 19A; mains TL5-10) Board games and cool tunes make this buzzing cafe-restaurant the pick of the Konur Sokak strip. The *tereyağında* (trout) and sautéed *biftek* are among the favourites.

Can Balık SEAFOOD €

(Map p402; ☑431 7870; Sakarya Caddesi 13; sandwiches TL4; ⊙10am-10pm) A popular alternative to pricey Piscean restaurants, Can Balık offers fried fish, served with salad or in a sandwich.

Diet Ev Yemekleri FAST FOOD €

(Map p402; ☑418 5683; Karanfıl Sokak; mains TL5) Chow down with the students on cheap, filling food including burgers, *köfte*, pizza, döner and İskender kebaps.

KAVAKLIDERE

The scene here is European and sophisticated, catering primarily to the embassy set.

Balıkçıköy SEAFOOD €

(Map p401; ☑466 0450; Abay Kunanbay Caddesi 4/1; mains TL21-37; ⊙noon-midnight) Up the hill from McDonalds is the third instalment of Ankara's favourite seafood restaurant. Take the waiter's recommendations for the cold meze (we loved the pickled whitebait, TL6), then take your own pick of the fried and grilled fish, all perfectly cooked and quick to the table. The skewered prawns (TL12) were the finest tastes on our travels. Book ahead to avoid disappointment.

Hayyami RESTAURANT-BAR €€

(Map p401; ☑466 1052; Bestekar Sokak 82B; mains TL12-25; ⊙noon-late) Named after the renowned Sufi philosopher, this thriving wine house/restaurant attracts a hobnobbing crowd to its lowered courtyard for *salçalı sosis* (barbecued sausage) and devilishly large cheese platters, among other less booze-worthy plates. The liquor and fortified wine list is very long.

Mezzaluna ITALIAN €€€

(Map p401; ☑467 5818; Turan Emeksiz Sokak 1; mains TL21-37; ⊙noon-11pm) The capital's classiest Italian restaurant is busy busy busy, with chefs slapping pizzas on the counter for apron-clad waiters. The choices include antipasti, risotto, wood-fire pizzas and seafood (a better bet than the steaks).

Italic ITALIAN €€

(Map p401; ☑426 3017; Bestekar Sokak 68; mains TL10-18; ⊙noon-late) It's less the standard Italian mains and more the powerful streetside cocktails, yummy antipasto platters (TL20) and eclectic furnishings that draw good-looking crowds to this new restaurant that morphs into nightclub ambience after dark.

Guangzhou Wuyang CHINESE €€

(Map p401; ☑427 6150; Bestekar Sokak 88/B; mains TL12-24; ⊙noon-late) Sometimes all you need is a half-decent Chinese meal and a half-dozen beers. Luckily this busy place is more than half decent, with delicious seafood and vegetarian options available.

🍷 Drinking

Kızılay is Ankara's cafe central, with terraces lining virtually every inch of space south of Ziya Gökalp Caddesi.

Aylak Madam CAFE

(Map p402; ☑419 7412; Karanfıl Sokak 2, Kızılay) A super cool French bistro/cafe with a mean weekend brunch (from 10am to 2.30pm), plus sandwiches and headkicking cappuccinos to a kickback jazz-fusion soundtrack. Postgraduates and artists swing open laptops and tap pens against half-finished manuscripts; other customers cuddle.

The Edge
BAR

(Map p401; ☑426 0516; Remzi Oğuz Mah, Kavaklıdere) Generous happy-hour drink specials, good indie music and a mixed crowd make this corner spot popular throughout the week.

Random Bar
PUB

(Map p401; ☑468 3420; Tunalı Hilmi Caddesi 114; mains TL14-21; ☺8.30am-11pm) Next to Kuğulu Park, this popular watering hole with a cool patio draws everyone from post-work suits to pre-club charlatans. Catchy singalong Turkish music kicks in on weekends.

Locus Solus
BAR

(Map p401; ☑468 6788; Bestekar Sokak 60) A change in owners has led to a change in clientele at this big space beside a petrol station. It's no longer high on the agenda for the alternative clique (who mostly hide in Kızılay), but still serving plenty of drinks to loose-limbed locals circling the dancefloor.

Dolphin Cafe Bar
BAR

(Map p401; ☑427 6468; Tunalı Hilmi Caddesi 99d) For the past decade little Dolphin Bar, tucked off Tunalı Caddesı, has provided quality blues music to a discerning crowd.

Sade Cafe
TEA HOUSE

(Map p400; ☑428 0035; İçkale Kapısı) This newly opened, accomplished, contemporary teahouse makes its own unique blends. The service, stylish mod-Ottoman decor and the numerous coffee options are equally impressive.

And Evi
CAFE

(Map p400; ☑312 7978; İçkale Kapısı) Sit on the citadel walls and enjoy fabulous views at this Ottoman-style cafe near Angora House Hotel. The carrot cake (TL6) is deliciously moist.

Qube Bar
BAR

(Map p402; ☑432 3079; Bayındır Sokak 16b) Slightly more sophisticated than the neighbouring pubs, Qube has a removable glass roof. Food is available.

Café des Cafés
CAFE

(Map p401; ☑428 0176; Tunalı Hilmi Caddesi 83; mains TL14-21; ☺8.30am-11pm) Trust the moniker and stick to the hot drinks and sweet crepes, then sit on the red-and-white sofa and sharpen up your people-watching skills.

TUĞÇE ÇELIK: STUDENT

Whoever comes to Ankara says 'what a serious city!', but after a weekend here they always reverse their opinion.

Best places to go clubbing?

Tunalı Hilmi Caddesi, **Yedinci Sokak**, **Arjantin Sokak** and **Park Sokak**. But as you'll see, a weekend isn't enough for Ankara!

Fidan Café
CAFE

(Map p402; ☑425 8326; Karanfıl Sokak 15) This smoky 1st-floor cafe is run by an amicable couple, with paintings by their grandchildren on the wall.

Simit Bahane
CAFE

(Map p402; Karanfıl Sokak 36a) An antidote to Kızılay's smoother establishments, with backgammon, newspapers and nargilehs (traditional water pipes) providing the entertainment.

Papillon
BAR

(Map p402; ☑419 7303; Olgunlar Sokak 9) This neighbourhood bar has rock on the stereo and brick walls decorated with number plates and Hollywood posters.

☆ Entertainment

Some of Ankara's cinemas occasionally show Western films in the original language; check the *Hürriyet Daily News* or www.askfest.org. Screens include **Metropol Sineması** (Map p402; ☑425 7478; Selanik Caddesi 76, Kızılay; adult/student TL10/9), which costs TL6 on Thursdays. Ankara has a spectrum of clubs and live music venues, from student dives to recherché nightspots. Consult fellow drinkers, bar staff, flyers or local listings to get the latest tips. For a night out with Ankara's student population, head to Kızılay – particularly Bayındır Sokak between Sakarya and Tuna Caddesis. The tall, thin buildings pack in up to five floors of bars, cafes and *gazinos* (nightclubs). Many of the clubs offer live Turkish pop music, and women travellers should feel OK in most.

IF Performance Hall
LIVE MUSIC

(☑418 9506; www.ifperformance.com; Tuna Caddesi 14a Kavaklıdere) This grand basement venue stages big acts, both international and Turkish, with a distinctive '90s rock flavour.

Cer Modern GALLERY
(Map p400; ☎310 0000; www.cermodern.org; Altunsoy Caddesi 3, Sıhhiye; ☺10am-6pm Tue-Sun)
This huge new artist park and gallery located in an old train depot exhibits modern art from across Europe, plus there's a really cool cafe and shop.

Ankara State Opera CONCERT HALL
(www.dobgm.gov.tr) This new organisation is drawing solid crowds for a variety of performaces, including classical music, most notably on Fridays. Folk dances can be seen at venues including the Atatürk Cultural Centre and the Painting and Sculpture Museum; ask at the tourist office for more details.

🛍 Shopping

It's cheapest to shop in downtown Ulus or in **Altındağ** and **Samanpazarı**, where a string of small galleries, antique and craft shops have opened near the citadel. To see what fashionable Turkey spends its money on, head south along Tunalı Hilmi Caddesi.

Müni (Map p400; ☎310 2850; Atpazari Sokak 22; www.munioart.net) is a ceramics gallery

BAHAR TEGIN: SHOP OWNER, SAMANPAZARI

How should a traveller spend a morning in the citadel?

Start with a local coffee served the Ottoman way, with syrup and *lokum* (Turkish delight). It's good fuel for the Museum of Anatolian Civilisation.

Best lunch?

Definitely Çengelhan, then visit Rahmi m Koç Industrial Museum while you're there.

What next?

Drop by the nearby art galleries to buy paintings, sculpture and designer jewellery.

Best place for a drink?

The American Bar at the Divan Hotel.

Time to go home?

Not before you see the copperware and kilim (rug) shops in the small streets around Samanpazarı. Pick up a bag of nuts and spices for the walk and end your day on a high.

that also runs pottery **courses** (TL45 per person; Wed, Fri & Sat ☺1-5pm).

Nearby lots of local stores stand alongside more-familiar names such as the British department store **Marks & Spencer**. Just below the Sheraton Hotel is **Karum** (Map p398; İran Caddesi), a glass-and-marble mall with European chain stores. On Konya Caddesi, behind the Ulus Hali food market, is the **Vakıf Suluhan Çarşısı** (Map p400) a restored *han* (caravanserai) with clothes shops, a leafy cafe, toilets and a small free-standing mosque in its courtyard. The area around the Parmak Kapısı entrance to the citadel was traditionally a centre for trading in angora wool. Walking downhill towards Arslanhane Cami from the dried-fruit stalls in front of the gate, there are some carpet and antique shops. You'll come across copper-beaters and other assorted craftsworkers carrying on their age-old trades.

On tree- and cafe-lined Olgunlar Sokak is a row of **secondhand bookstalls**. **Dost Kitabevi** (Map p402; ☎418 8327; Konur Sokak 4, Kızılay) stocks some foreign-language novels and local-interest titles. **Turhan Kitabevi** (Map p402; ☎418 8259; Yüksel Caddesi 8/32, Kızılay) stocks coffee-table books, guidebooks, English novels, Turkish dictionaries and phrasebooks, and periodicals.

ℹ Information

Internet Access

There are many internet cafes in Ulus and Kızılay, particularly around Ulus Meydanı and Karanfıl Sokak, but they are scarcer in Kavaklıdere. Wi-fi is widely available in hotels, cafes and bars.

Medical Services

Pharmacists take it in turns to open around the clock; look out for the *nobetçi* (open 24 hours) sign.

Bayındır Hospital (☎428 0808; Atatürk Bulvarı 201, Kavaklıdere) An up-to-date private hospital.

City Hospital (☎466 3838; Büklüm Sokak 72, Kavaklıdere) Near Tunalı Hilmi Caddesi, with a Women's Health Centre (Kadın Sağlığı Merkezi).

Hospital Information Hotline (☎444 0911)

Money

There are lots of banks with ATMs in Ulus, Kızılay and Kavaklıdere. To change money, *döviz bürosu* (currency-exchange offices) generally offer the best rates, often without commission.

Post & Telephone

There are PTT branches in the train station, at the AŞTİ otogar and on Atatürk Bulvarı in Ulus. All have phone booths nearby.

Tourist Information

The Guide, available at the Rahmi M Koç Industrial Museum and some bookshops, has listings for Ankara.

Tourist office (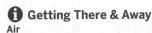310 8789, 231 5572; Gazi Mustafa Kemal Bulvarı; ⊙9am-5pm Mon-Fri, 10am-5pm Sat) Located opposite the train station, staff are reasonably helpful and have lots of brochures available.

Travel Agencies

Raytur (☑417 0021; www.raytur.com.tr; Karanfil Sokak 12/12, Kızılay) Operated by Turkish Railways. Sells train and air tickets, jeep safaris, domestic and outbound tours.

Saltur (☑425 1333; www.saltur.com.tr; Atatürk Bulvarı 175/4, Kavaklıdere) Airline and international tour agent.

❶ Getting There & Away

Air

Ankara's **Esenboğa airport**, 33km north of the city centre, is the hub for Turkish Airlines' domestic-flight network. Although many domestic and international budget carriers serve Ankara, İstanbul's airports offer more choice. Even flying domestically, it may save you time and money to travel via İstanbul.

Turkish Airlines and Atlasjet offer direct flights between Ankara and destinations including Adana, Antalya, Bodrum, Cyprus, Diyarbakır, Erzurum, Gaziantep, İstanbul, İzmir, Kars, Malatya, Trabzon and Van.

International airlines offer both direct services to/from Ankara and flights with connections in İstanbul.

Bus

Every Turkish city or town of any size has direct buses to Ankara. The gigantic otogar, also referred to as **AŞTİ** (Ankara Şehirlerarası Terminali İşletmesi) is at the western end of the Ankaray underground train line, 4.5km west of Kızılay.

Ankara is a major hub for buses throughout central Turkey. Buses to/from İstanbul (TL30, six hours), Antalya (TL40, eight hours), İzmir (TL45, eight hours) and other major destinations leave numerous times daily. Buses to Cappadocia often terminate in Nevşehir. Be sure your ticket states your *final* destination (eg Göreme, Ürgüp).

Because there are so many buses to many parts of the country, you can often turn up, buy a ticket and be on your way in less than an hour. Don't try this during public holidays, though.

RIGHTEOUS ANGORA

Can you tell the difference between a goat and a rabbit? It's not as easy as you think – or at least not if all you have to go on is the wool. One of the most popular misconceptions about Ankara's famous angora wool is that it comes from angora goats, a hardy breed believed to be descended from wild Himalayan goats. Not so: the soft, fluffy yarn produced from these goats is correctly known as mohair. Angora wool in the strictest sense comes from angora rabbits, also local but much cuter critters whose fur, weight for weight, was once worth as much as gold.

The *emanet* (left-luggage room) on the lower level charges TL4 per item stored; you'll need to show your passport.

Train

Ankara Garı, near the terminus for the Havaş airport buses, is just over 1km southwest of Ulus Meydanı, along Cumhuriyet Bulvarı. Train services between İstanbul and Ankara are the best in the country, and an even faster rail link should be open in 2011.

Ankara services lines to many cities and towns, including İstanbul (seat/sleeper TL23/80, eight hours), Diyarbakır (via Kayseri, TL23/61, 35 hours), Adana (TL20/65, 12 hours) and İzmir (TL26/80, 14 hours).

❶ Getting Around

To/From the Airport

Esenboğa airport is 33km north of the city. **Havaş** (☑444 0487; Kazım Karabekir Caddesi) airport buses depart from Gate B at 19 May Stadium every half-hour between 4.30am and midnight daily (TL10, 45 minutes). They may leave sooner if they fill up, so get there early to claim your seat.

The same buses link the airport and the AŞTİ otogar (TL10 to TL12.50, 60 minutes), leaving the station every half-hour between 4.30am and 11.30pm from in front of the passenger arrival lounge.

Buses from the airport are scheduled according to flight arrivals. Don't pay more than TL60 for a taxi between the airport and the city.

To/From the Bus Station

The easiest way to get into town is on the Ankaray metro line, which has a station at the AŞTİ otogar. Go to Maltepe metro station for the train station (a 10-minute walk), or to Kızılay for midrange hotels. Change at Kızılay (to the Metro line) for Ulus and cheaper hotels.

A taxi costs about TL20 to the city centre.

To/From the Train Station

Ankara Garı is about 1km southwest of Ulus Meydanı and 2km northwest of Kızılay. Many dolmuşes head northeast along Cumhuriyet Bulvarı to Ulus, and east on Talat Paşa Bulvarı to Kızılay.

It's just over 1km from the station to Opera Meydanı; any bus heading east along Talat Paşa Bulvarı will drop you within a few hundred metres if you ask for Gazi Lisesi.

Bus

Ankara has a good bus, dolmuş and minibus network. Signs on the front and side of the vehicles are better guides than route numbers. Buses marked 'Ulus' and 'Çankaya' run the length of Atatürk Bulvarı. Those marked 'Gar' go to the train station, those marked 'AŞTİ' to the otogar.

Standard TL3 tokens, available at subway stations and major bus stops or anywhere displaying an EGO Bilet sign, are valid for 45 minutes on multiple journeys. They work on most buses as well as the subway, and a 10-token pass costs TL12.

These tokens are not valid on express buses, which are the longer buses with ticket counters halfway down the vehicle.

Car

Driving within Ankara is chaotic and signs are inadequate; it's easier to ditch your car and use public transport.

If you plan to hire a car to drive out of Ankara, there are many small local companies alongside the major international firms; most have offices in Kavaklıdere along Tunus Caddesi, and/or at Esenboğa airport.

Metro

Ankara's underground train network currently has two lines: the Ankaray line running between AŞTİ otogar in the west through Maltepe and Kızılay to Dikimevi in the east; and the Metro line running from Kızılay northwest via Sıhhiye and Ulus to Batıkent. The two lines interconnect at Kızılay. Trains run from 6.15am to 11.45pm daily.

A one-way fare costs TL1. Standard tokens cost TL3 and a 10-token pass is TL12. Note that there are separate barriers for adult and child/student tokens at some subway stations, so if your token doesn't seem to work, check that you're using the right lane.

Taxi

Taxis are everywhere and they all have meters, with a TL1.70 base rate. It costs about TL8 to cross the centre; charges rise at night and the

same trip will cost well over TL10. In Kızılay, beware the one-way roads, as the taxi may have to backtrack (without switching off the meter) to access a road going in the right direction.

AROUND ANKARA

You don't have to go far from Ankara to hit some major pieces of Anatolian history, but if it's a leisurely day trip you're after rather than an overnighter, consider the Phrygian archaeological site at Gordion or the small Ottoman town of Beypazarı.

Gordion

The capital of ancient Phrygia, with some 3000 years of settlement behind it, Gordion lies 106km west of Ankara in the village of Yassıhöyük.

Gordion was occupied by the Phrygians as early as the 9th century BC, and soon afterwards became their capital. Although destroyed during the Cimmerian invasion, it was rebuilt before being conquered by the Lydians and then the Persians. Alexander the Great came through here and famously cut the Gordian knot in 333 BC, but by 278 BC the Galatian occupation had effectively destroyed the city.

The moonscape-like terrain around Yassıhöyük is dotted with tumuli (burial mounds) that mark the graves of the Phrygian kings. Of some 90 identified tumuli, 35 have been excavated; you can enter the largest tomb, and also view the site of the Gordion acropolis, where digs revealed five main levels of civilisation, from the Bronze Age to Galatian times.

Midas Tumulus & Gordion Museum RUINS (admission incl museum TL3; ⊙8.30am-5.30pm) In 1957 the Austrian archaeologist Alfred Koerte discovered Gordion, and with it the intact tomb of a Phrygian king, probably buried some time between 740 and 718 BC. The tomb is actually a gabled 'cottage' of cedar surrounded by juniper logs, buried inside a tumulus 53m high and 300m in diameter. It's the oldest wooden structure ever found in Anatolia, and perhaps even in the world. The tunnel leading into the depths of the tumulus is a modern addition, allowing you to glimpse some of the interior of the fenced-off tomb.

Inside the tomb archaeologists found the body of a man between 61 and 65 years of age, 1.59m tall, surrounded by burial objects, including tables, bronze *situlas* (containers) and bowls said to be part of the funerary burial feast. The occupant's name remains unknown (although Gordius and Midas were popular names for Phrygian kings).

In the museum opposite, Macedonian and Babylonian coins show Gordion's position at the centre of Anatolian trade, communications and military activities, as do the bronze figurines and glass-bead jewellery from the Syro-Levantine region of Mesopotamia.

Acropolis   RUINS
Excavations at the 8th-century-BC acropolis yielded a wealth of data on Gordion's many civilisations.

The lofty main gate on the city's western side was approached by a 6m-wide ramp. Within the fortified enclosure were four *megara* (square halls) from which the king and his priests and ministers ruled the empire. The mosaics found in one of these halls, the so-called Citadel of Midas, are on display outside the museum.

❶ Getting There & Away

Baysal Turizm buses connect Ankara's otogar (ticket counter 28) with Polatlı every half-hour (TL5, one hour). Once in Polatlı, you can travel the last 18km to Yassıhöyük in a minibus (TL3), but this involves a 1.5km walk across town to the minibus stand, and services depart sporadically. A taxi will charge about TL50 to drive you to the main sites and back to Polatlı otogar.

Beypazarı
📞0312 / POP 34,500
A considered approach from a proactive town mayor has turned this picturesque Ottoman town set high above the İnönü Vadisi into the weekend destination *du jour* for Ankara's escapees. More than 3000 Ottoman houses line the narrow streets in the hilltop old quarter, where 500-plus buildings and some 30 streets have been restored. Coppersmiths and carpenters beaver away, shopkeepers flog model Ottoman houses in little bags to Ankaralı day trippers, and the 200-year-old market recalls Beypazarı's position on the Silk Road.

Occupying a sizeable Ottoman mansion, the museum (Beypazarı Tarih ve Kültür Evi; admission TL1.50; ⊙10am-6pm Tue-Sun) is good for nosing around to a classical music soundtrack. Exhibits range from Roman

and Byzantine pillars to an Ottoman depiction of an elephant, and the characteristic cupboard-bathrooms are still intact.

On the first weekend in June, the Havuc Guvec (Traditional Dish Festival) celebrates the humble carrot (the area grows more than half of the carrots consumed in Turkey). Additional attractions, if any are needed, include craftwork markets and Ottoman house tours.

While you're here try the local delicacies, which include *havuç lokum* (carrot-flavoured Turkish delight), clumpy *cevizli sucuğu* (walnuts coated in grape jelly) and Beypazarı mineral water, bottled here and swigged throughout the country.

Me'vaların Konağı (📞762 3698; Köstyolu Sokak Müzeyanı 31; r with/without bathroom TL80/70), one of a few Ottoman house hotels on the square near the museum, has beautiful bedcovers and cupboard-bathrooms.

Occupying one of the town's most noted Ottoman piles, Tarihi Taş Mektep (📞762 7606; Alaaddin Sokak 4; mains TL7-10; ⊙8am-10pm) is popular for dishes such as the surprisingly spicy salad, *yaprak sarma* (stuffed vine leaves) and grilled trout.

❶ Getting There & Away

From Ankara, take a Metro train to Akköprü and cross the motorway, heading away from the Ankamall. Walk to your left, away from the flyover, until you reach the area between the M Oil garage and the pedestrian bridge, where you can hail passing Beytaş Turizm minibuses to Beypazarı (TL6, 1½ hours). In the Beytaş Turizm office across the road from the town centre bus stop (decorated with the Ottoman mural), you can check the time of the last bus back to Ankara.

Safranbolu
📞0370 / POP 38,300
Driving past the Karabük steel smelter and into the unremarkable Greek quarter of 'upper' Safranbolu might have you cursing both your guidebook and your bus driver for bringing you to this isolated source of a precious spice. But veer downhill and you'll soon stumble over Turkey's most thoroughly preserved Ottoman town, a leisurely period piece with a Çarşı (old town) full of candy stores and cobblers and bathrooms hidden in cupboards. The hotels are brilliant, and a day at the old hamam or browsing through junk shops is about as strenuous as it gets here. If the weekend influx of domestic

tourists makes your gums bleed, and history feels a bit like old news, then hiking in the wondrous Yenice Forest, remapped and rediscovered, should give you cause to reconsider exactly why Unesco stamped this region in 1994.

History

During the 17th century, the main Ottoman trade route between Gerede and the Black Sea coast passed through Safranbolu, bringing commerce, prominence and money to the town. During the 18th and 19th centuries, Safranbolu's wealthy inhabitants built mansions of sun-dried mudbricks, wood and stucco, while the larger population of prosperous artisans built less impressive but similarly sturdy homes. Safranbolu owes its fame to the large numbers of these dwellings that have survived.

The most prosperous Safranbolulus maintained two households. In winter they occupied town houses in the Çarşı (market) district, which is situated at the meeting point of three valleys and so protected from the winter winds. During the warm months they moved to summer houses in the garden suburb of Bağlar (vineyards). When the iron- and steelworks at Karabük were established in 1938, modern factory houses started to encroach on Bağlar, but Çarşı has remained virtually untouched.

During the 19th century about 20% of Safranbolu's inhabitants were Ottoman Greeks, but most of their descendants moved to Greece during the population exchange after WWI. Their principal church, dedicated to St Stephen, was converted into Kıranköy's Ulu Cami (Great Mosque).

⊙ Sights

FREE **Ottoman Houses** ARCHITECTURE
Just walking through Çarşı is a feast for the eyes. Virtually every house in the district is an original, and what little modern development there is has been held in check. Many of the finest historic houses have been restored, and as time goes on, more and more are being saved from deterioration and turned into hotels, shops or museums.

Kaymakamlar Müze Evi, the most interesting of three old houses that have been turned into museums, has all the typical features of Ottoman homes. It was owned by a lieutenant colonel and still feels like an address of note as you climb the stairs towards the wooden ceiling decoration.

OTTOMAN STYLE

Looking at the concrete cityscapes synonymous with Turkish modernity, it's hard to imagine being back in the 19th century, when fine wooden houses were the rule. Luckily, growing tourism has encouraged an Ottoman revival, and restoration has become a boom trade. Excellent examples can be found in Afyon, Amasya and Tokat, but Safranbolu is universally acknowledged to contain the country's single finest collection of pre-independence domestic architecture.

Ottoman wooden houses generally had two or three storeys, the upper storeys jutting out over the lower ones on carved corbels (brackets). Their timber frames were filled with adobe and then plastered with a mixture of mud and straw. Sometimes the houses were left unsealed, but in towns they were usually given a finish of plaster or whitewash, with decorative flourishes in plaster or wood. The wealthier the owner, the fancier the decoration.

Inside, the larger houses had 10 to 12 rooms, divided into *selamlık* (men's quarters) and *haremlik* (women's quarters). Rooms were often decorated with built-in niches and cupboards, and had fine plaster fireplaces with *yaşmaks* (conical hoods). Sometimes the ceilings were very elaborate; that of the Paşa Odası of Tokat's Latifoğlu Konağı, for example, is thought to emulate a chandelier in wood.

Details to look out for inside the Safranbolu houses include their *hayats* (courtyard areas where the animals lived and tools were stored); ingenious *dönme dolaplar* (revolving cupboards that made it possible to prepare food in one room and pass it to another without being seen); bathrooms hidden inside cupboards; and central heating systems that relied on huge fireplaces. *Sedirs* (bench seating that ran round the walls) doubled up as beds, with the bedding being stored in the bathrooms, which converted neatly into cupboards during the day. Space-efficient, certainly, but sometimes you wonder how anyone ever found anything!

Tableaux recreate everyday scenes such as bathing in the cupboard, and the wedding feast, when the women served the men using the *dönme dolaplar* (revolving cupboard).

Kileciler Evi (1884) also has 1950s period pieces among the family heirlooms in its cupboards. However, the whitewashed interior has been attractively renovated, with exhibits including family photos, carpets and mannequins clad in traditional clothes. As the information sheet explains, the 99 cupboards symbolise the 99 names of God.

The exhibition rooms in the houses are generally open daily from 9am to 7pm and charge TL2 to TL2.50 for adult admission (TL1 for children). Tea is served in their gardens and the properties open more sporadically during winter.

Some of the largest houses had indoor pools, which, although big enough for swimming, were used instead to cool the rooms with running water, which also provided pleasing background noise. The best and most accessible example in Çarşı is the **Havuzlu Asmazlar Konağı** (Mansion with Pool; Çelik Gülersoy Caddesi 18, Çarşı), now run as a hotel.

Kent Tarihi Müzesi   MUSEUM
(☑712 1314; Çeşme Mahallesi Hükümet Sokak; admission TL3; ⊙9am-7pm Apr-Oct, 9am-5pm Nov-Mar) Safranbolu's hilltop castle was demolished early in the last century to make way for the yellow Eski Hükümet Konağı (old government building), which was restored following a fire in 1976. English interpretive panels are scarce in the museum inside, but the exhibits are a decent introduction to local life. The reconstructions of old shops in the marble-floored basement include a chemist's store with the inevitable saffron teinture among the elixirs.

The ticket to the museum also covers the neighbouring **clock tower** (1797), built by grand vizier (prime minister) İzzet Mehmet Paşa. Climb the tower on the hour to see its clockwork hammer strike and hear the chimes ring around the surrounding hills.

Cinci Hamam   HAMAM
One of the best bathhouses in all of Turkey, with separate baths for men and women – but steeply priced at TL40 for the works.

Cinci Hanı   CARAVANSERAI
(Eski Çarşı Çeşme Mahalessi; adult/student TL2/1) Çarşı's most famous and imposing structure, a brooding 17th-century caravanserai that's

now an upmarket hotel. On Saturdays a market takes place in the square behind it.

Köprülü Mehmet Paşa Camii   MOSQUE
This beefy, helmet-roofed building beside the *arasta* (row of shops beside a mosque) dates to 1661. The metal sundial in the courtyard was added in the mid-19th century.

İzzet Paşa Camii   MOSQUE
One of the largest mosques built during the Ottoman Empire, built by the grand vizier in 1796 and restored in 1903, and showing European architectural influence.

Hıdırlık Parkı   PARK
(admission TL3) Uphill past the Kaymakamlar Müze Evi, enjoy panoramic views from here.

Tours

A couple of tours allow you to look around Safranbolu and the surrounding sights in a day. **Batuta Turizm** (☑725 4533; www.batuta. com.tr; Çeşme Mahallesi Hükümet Sokak) offers buggy tours, with circuits lasting from 40 minutes to three hours (TL8.50 to TL22.50). The short tour is a reasonable introduction to Safranbolu, but spending any longer in the company of the cheesy voiceover (available in English and Japanese) may be detrimental to your mental health.

More recommended is its excellent half-day tour of Bağlar (p417). The tour leaves at 1.30pm and costs TL50 including entrance fees. **Çarşı Taksi** (☑725 2595; Hilmi Bayramgil Caddesi) offers a longer tour of these sights and two others for TL70.

Festivals & Events

Geleneksel Sezzetler Şenliği   FOOD
A popular May food festival run by the Association of Anatolian Cuisine.

Golden Saffron Documentary Film Festival   FILM
(www.altinsafranbolu.com) Prestigious documentary film festival held in September.

FREE **Safranbolu Architectural Treasures & Folklore Week**
                    TRADITIONAL CULTURE
Also in September with exhibitions and performances across town.

Sleeping

Safranbolu is very popular with Turkish tourists at weekends and holidays. Prices may rise at particularly busy times, and it can be worth booking ahead. Splashing out a bit is virtually an obligation, as you may

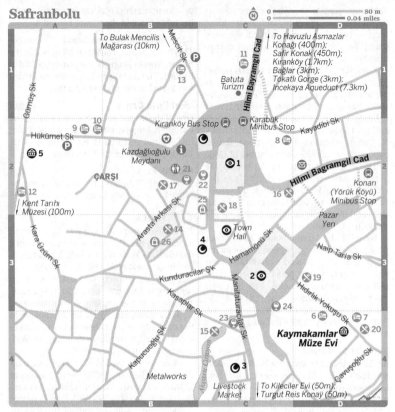

0   80 m
0   0.04 miles

To Bulak Mencilis
Mağarası (10km)

Mescit Sk

To Havuzlu Asmazlar
Konağı (400m);
Safir Konak (450m);
Kıranköy (1.7km);
Bağlar (3km);
Tokatlı Gorge (3km);
Incekaya Aqueduct (7.3km)

Batuta
Turizm

Hilmi Bayramgil Cad

Kıranköy Bus Stop
Karabük
Minibus Stop

Kayadıbı Sk

Gümüş Sk

Hükümet Sk

Kazdağlıoğulu
Meydanı

ÇARŞI

Hilmi Bagramgil Cad

Konarı
(Yörük Köyü)
Minibus Stop

Pazar
Yeri

Kent Tarihi
Müzesi (100m)

Kara Üzüm Sk

Arasta Arkası Sk

Town
Hall

Hamamönü Sk

Naip Tarla Sk

Kunduracılar Sk

Kasaplar Sk

Manifaturacılar Sk

Hıdırlık Yokuşu Sk

Kaymakamlar
Müze Evi

Çavuşoğlu Sk

Kapucuoğlu Sk

Akçasu Çayın

Metalworks

Livestock
Market

To Kileciler Evi (50m);
Turgut Reis Konaÿ (50m)

never get another chance to sleep anywhere so authentically restored. If you'd rather stay in a family home than a hotel, the tourist office has a list of 25 basic pensions (the *Safranbolu'daki Ev Pansiyonları Listesi*). They are cheaper than hotels, though often of lower quality, and generally cost TL25 to TL30 per person.

TOP CHOICE Gül Evi   HISTORIC HOTEL €€€
(725 4645; www.booking.com; Hükümet Sokak 46; s €60-83, d €80-110, ste €165-330) An eminent architect-designer couple from Ankara is wholly responsible for Safranbolu's most striking reinterpretation of the Ottoman aesthetic. 'Rose House' is an affordable masterpiece, with each room individually styled in soft colours – the bathrooms and beds are reminiscent of an urban spa retreat – but the real drawcard is the shaded, grassy garden, a rare refuge from the town's cobblestone streets. A second house contains the stunning 65-sq-

metre suite, occupying the former *selamlık*. The restaurant, which features a small banquet area for larger groups, serves exquisite breakfasts at 9am daily. A lunch or dinner feast using the pick of local produce is available at weekends on request.

Cinci Hanı   HISTORIC HOTEL €€
(712 0680; www.cincihan.com; Eski Çarşı Çeşme Mahalessi; s/d/tr from TL90/140/190) It's worth taking the chance to sleep in this Silk Road caravanserai at the centre of the Çarşı, if only for the stony sense of history. Rooms are smallish and could do with a regular sweep, but the cave-like acoustics are a bit of kick and it's a short stumble from the local bars. The huge Han Ağası Odası suite is a gem, with kitchen, sitting room and a bathroom with an old stone hamam basin.

Imren Lokum Konak   HISTORIC HOTEL €€
(725 2688; www.imrenkonak.com; Kayyim Ali Sokak; s/d TL70/140;) This lovely new

mansion concealed from the main square attracts a sociable crowd to its large open courtyard and spacious, good value Ottoman rooms. It's a little underfurnished in parts, such as the oddly bare sitting room, but the friendly, laid-back service ensures a holiday vibe.

Safir Konak HISTORIC HOTEL €€
(✆712 7060; www.safirkonak.com; Koyici Meydanı Arslanlar Caddesi; s/d TL60/120; ◉) A small, professional hotel with nine restored rooms furnished by a learned couple who have an eye for design and an ear for their guests' needs. The Gelin Odası (bridal room) is as humble as a good marriage and the beautiful garden is a little bit English village.

Bastoncu Pansiyon PENSION €
(✆712 3411; www.bastoncupension.com; Hıdırlık Yokuşu Sokak; dm/s/d/tr TL25/45/70/80; ◉) In a 300-year-old building, Bastoncu is an institution for both backpackers and folks who choose it over more-expensive options for its unrivalled sense of history. The rooms and three-bed dorms have all their original wood panelling, tiled bathrooms, jars of dried flowers, and some closet toilets. It's run by a friendly Turkish couple who speak English and Japanese and appreciate travellers' needs, offering a laundry service, lifts from the otogar, tours and traditional, two-course dinners (TL10).

Turgut Reis Konağı HISTORIC HOTEL €€
(✆725 1301; www.turgutreiskonak.com, in Turkish; Akpınar Sokak 27; s/d/tr TL30/70/100) Boasting a quiet position and some of Safranbolu's best views, this friendly hotel is one of the best deals around. The 200-year-old building has been sensitively restored, with stylish furnishings and touches such as steps leading to the beds in room 106.

Selvili Köşk HISTORIC HOTEL €€
(✆712 8646; fax 725 2294; Mescit Sokak 23; s/d/tr TL90/140/160) From the engraved banisters to the carved ceilings, this decidedly blue hotel is the pick of another Ottoman cluster. The pretty garden is a welcome retreat while the salon is plenty big and grand enough for some legs-akimbo Turkish dancing.

Efe Backpackers Pension HOSTEL €
(✆725 2688; www.backpackerspension.com; Kayadibi Sokak; dm/s/d/tr TL15/25/45/55; ◉) Named after the polyglot matriarch's energetic little son, the Efe is a fabulous little backpacker pension with eight rooms containing up to four beds each and a shared bathroom on each of the three floors. There are good views from the terrace and it offers the same services as its older sibling, the classier Bastoncu.

Havuzlu Asmazlar Konağı
HISTORIC HOUSE €€€
(✆725 2883; www.safranbolukonak.com; Çelik Gülersoy Caddesi 18, Çarşı; r week/weekend from

TL150/200) The tiny bathing pool in the lobby is the first of many audacious quirks in this beautiful house set in a garden filled with trees, flowers and summer bees. The rooms are beautifully furnished with brass beds, *sedirs* and kilims. An unusual and undeniably beautiful hotel, but as the HAK is a destination in its own right, a stay can lack privacy.

Ebrulu Konağı HISTORIC HOUSE €€
(☏712 0714; www.ebrulukonak.com; Hıdırlık Yokuşu Sokak 13; s/d/tr TL75/145/180) Modern fittings don't dispel the sense of history – instilled by low ceilings and broad stone windowsills – in this hillside mansion. There are great views of Safranbolu and a pleasant courtyard restaurant.

Paşa Konağı HISTORIC HOUSE €€
(☏725 3572; www.safranbolupasa.com; Kalealtı Sokak 1-7; s/d TL80/120) Two hundred years after Izzet Mehmet Paşa occupied his mansion, the spacious rooms and secluded garden foster a romantic nostalgia. Certain bathrooms are inside cupboards with high steps, which might be tricky for some guests.

Otel Asmalı Konak HISTORIC HOUSE €€
(☏712 7474; www.otelasmalikonak.com; Asmazlar Caddesi 13; s/d TL45/80, half-board TL60/90) This neat refurb popular with Turkish families is in a handy spot on the way into town. The decor is cookie-cutter Ottoman with dark timber panelling, white walls and rich floral fabrics, but the open outdoor seating area is great for self-caterers and large groups with kids.

✗ Eating

Safranbolu's dining scene is gradually on the up, but many visitors still stick to their hotel restaurants. Aside from the ubiquitous sweet shops, be sure to try all flavours of the locally produced soft drink, Bağlar Gazozu, an institution since 1936 – locals can be sensitive about the C-word.

Taşev MODERN TURKISH €€
(☏712 0680; www.tasevsanatvesarapevi.com; Baba Sultan Mahallesi, Hıdırlık Yokuşu Sokak 14) Visitors to Safranbolu now have a bonafide contemporary dining option that delivers on thick steaks and creamy pasta dishes. Service is more aloof than elsewhere in town, but the alluring wall art, multi-purpose exhibition space and extensive wine menu make this a long overdue change from Ottoman-inspired dining.

Kadıoğlu Şehzade Sofrası PIDECI €
(☏712 5657; Arasta Sokak 8; mains TL6-12; ⊙11.30am-10.30pm) Tucked behind a pretty courtyard and sought after by savvy locals, this mansion restaurant has a lowdown Ottoman seating plan. We recommend any of the huge, steaming hot pide, *çorba* (soup), grills and *zerde* (saffron dessert). The rooms are tacky but pretty large.

Cinci Hanı ANATOLIAN €€
(☏712 0680; Eski Çarşı Çeşme Mahallesi; mains TL10-15) There's enough room for two Turkish weddings in this beautiful caravanserai restaurant, so it can feel a little lonely at times. Still, it's worth dining here if you're not staying the night. The menu features healthy selections of pide, grills and Western favourites. There is also a cafe-bar.

Bizim Cafe LOKANTA €
(Çeşme Mahallesi, Kasaplar Sokak 17; mains TL5-8) Deep in the old shopping district is this welcoming little family-run restaurant that serves whatever's on the stove, which luckily is always pretty good, including *dolmades* rolled on the street and deliciously spicy soups. Locals love it.

Safranbolu Sofrası LOKANTA €
(☏712 1451; Hıdırlık Yokuşu Sokak 28a; mains TL5-7; ⊙9am-9pm) This friendly cafe offers an authentic local experience – in the sense that Turkish soap operas and music videos accompany dining. The delicious dishes include *dolma* with yoghurt and tomato sauce and *cevizli yayım* (macaroni topped with walnuts). If you like the saffron tea, buy a jar of the yellow powder.

Çevrikköprü 3 ANATOLIAN €€
(☏725 2586; Hamamönü Sokak 1; mains TL8-18; ⊙11am-11pm) Down the hill towards the old town is the third branch of this one-town chain (number 2 is next door). Despite it being a chain restaurant, it's inviting and serves huge plates of traditional food at cheeky prices. The service is keen and the menu the length of a novella.

Merkez Lokantası TURKISH €
(☏725 1478; Yukarı Çarşı 1; mains TL4-5; ⊙10am-10pm) This quaint, clean and friendly place still uses a wood fire to cook its tasty basic staples.

🍷 Drinking & Entertainment

Sade Kahve COFFEE HOUSE
(Manifaturacılar Caddesi 17; coffee TL2, desserts TL2-6) Opposite a slew of tinkerers and

metalbenders, this is a fabulous little find run by coffee fanatics who make a mean brew, Turkish or otherwise, and the most delicious waffles in town. From the curvy cup handles to the complimentary chocolate, Sade is smooth.

Türkü Cafe
BAR
(Musalla Mahallesi Han Arkası Sokak 16) On Safranbolu's equivalent of a bar strip, this friendly place is run by a cool mother and daughter team who pour ice cold Efes in the shadow of Cinci Hanı. Türkü also hosts regular live music in the form of locals belting out pop tunes.

Meydan
CAFE
(Arasta Arkası Sokak; snacks TL2.50-6) This central hang-out is popular with young guys who sit outside playing backgammon. The menu features *gözleme* (savoury pancake), *çeşitlerli* (Turkish pancake) and *çorba*. The menu has English translations.

Arasta Lonca Kahvesi
CAFE
(Boncuk Café; Yemeniciler Arastası) This is one of the town's most congenial places for a coffee, but it's in the thick of the *arasta* action, so you pay for the atmosphere (çay TL2.50); head to the backstreets for a quieter, cheaper cuppa.

Arasna Pension
LIVE MUSIC
(☎712 4170; Arasta Arkası Sokak 5, Çarşı) This pension below the main mosque and tourist office has a bar with regular live music. Its atmospheric stone walls are illuminated by electric candles.

🔒 Shopping
Safranbolu is a great place to pick up handicrafts – especially textiles, metalwork, shoes and wooden artefacts – whether locally made or shipped in from elsewhere to supply coach tourists. The restored **Yemeniciler Arastası** (Peasant Shoemakers' Bazaar) is the best place to start looking, although the makers of the light, flat-heeled shoes have long since moved out. The further you go from the *arasta* the more likely you are to come across shops occupied by authentic saddle-makers, felt-makers and other artisans.

The town is so packed with sweet shops that you half expect the houses to be made out of gingerbread. One regional speciality is *yaprak helvası,* delicious chewy layers of white *helva* (halva) spotted with ground walnuts. Pick it up at the sweet shops on the north side of Çarşı's main square and at **Safrantat**, which has five stores around

town. You can also visit the Safrantat factory behind the petrol station in Kıranköy to see how *lokum* is made. **417**

ℹ Information
Tourist office (☎712 3863; www.safranbolu. gov.tr; ⊗9am-12.30pm & 1.30-6pm) Off the main square; gives out a helpful *rehberi* (map).

ℹ Getting There & Away
There are several bus company offices along Sadrı Artunç Caddesi and just off Adnan Menderes Caddesi in Kıranköy, where you can buy tickets to destinations including Ankara (TL25, three hours), İstanbul (TL40, seven hours) and Kastamonu (TL11, two hours). You will probably be taken by *servis* bus to meet the coach at Karabük otogar.

From İstanbul, Ulusoy and İzmir Turizm have a couple of daily services to Safranbolu.

Metro Doğuş (☎712 1966) and **Şavaş Turizm** (☎712 7480) each have five daily services to Bartın (TL10, 1½ hours), where you change for Amasra; start early in the day to make the onward connection. During summer, Şavaş Turizm has three direct daily services to Amasra (TL14, two hours).

If your ticket only takes you to Karabük, you can catch a minibus straight to Çarşı (TL1.40), Safranbolu's old town, 10km away.

Driving, exit the Ankara–İstanbul highway at Gerede and head north, following the signs for Karabük/Safranbolu.

There is a direct train from Karabük to Ankara, but the bus is a much easier option.

ℹ Getting Around
Every 30 minutes or so until 10pm, local buses (TL1) ply the route from Çarşı's main square over the hills past the main roundabout at Kıranköy and up to the Köyiçi stop in Bağlar. A taxi from Çarşı to Kıranköy will cost you TL9.

Around Safranbolu
YÖRÜK KÖYÜ
Along the Kastamonu road, 15km east of Safranbolu, Yörük Köyü (Nomad Village) is a beautiful settlement of crumbling old houses once inhabited by the dervish Bektaşi sect (see p470). The government forced the nomads to settle here so it could tax them, and the villagers grew rich from their baking prowess.

Sipahioğlu Konağı Gezi Evi (admission TL4; ⊗8.30am-sunset) is one of the village's enormous Ottoman houses. The builder's

WORTH A TRIP

YENICE FOREST

Yenice is an adorable district 35km west of Karabük and surrounded by the breathtaking **Yenice Forest**. With roughly 85% of Yenice composed of wild forest, Governor Nurullah Çekır (elected in 2009) pressed his love of nature upon locals in a bid to provide an alternative to the logging industry. His results are impressive, as the forest can now claim 396km of walking trails through sublime, lush countryside, an impeccable hiking guide available in Safranbolu and Karabük, and a loghouse built on approach to Şeker Canyon. Three national parks converge in one of Turkey's most accessible wilderness areas fed by cool springs and containing an array of flora and fauna. The Zonguldak-bound slow train to Yenice (one-way/return TL2/4, 1¼ hours, four daily) passes through 16 tunnels and a deep valley where the Filyos River flows deep.

warring sons divided the mansion in two, and you tour the *selamlık* and *haremlik* separately. Look for the incredible early central heating system that used the fire to heat running water and behind-the-wall heating; painted clocks showing the time the painters finished their job; and the top-floor gazebo with its stand for the owner's fez.

Nearby in Cemil İpekçi Sokağı is the 300-year-old *çamaşırhane* (laundry), with arched hearths where the water was heated in cauldrons. Ask at Sipahioğlu Konağı Gezi Evi for the key.

🛏 Sleeping & Eating

There's a **kahvehane** (coffee house) near the mosque.

Tarihi Yörük Pansiyon   PENSION **€**
(📞737 2153; s/d without bathroom TL30/60) A lovely old wood-and-stone house with an inviting garden. Accommodation is simple but comfortable, although there is just one squat toilet between the four rooms. In one room you sleep on the *sedir,* Ottoman-style.

Yörük Sofrası   ANATOLIAN
Serves traditional Anatolian dishes, *ayran* (yoghurt drink), baklava and *gözleme* at indoor and outdoor tables.

❶ Getting There & Away

There is no direct bus service from Safranbolu to Yörük Köyü, but there are a few dolmuşes a day to the nearby village of Konarı. If you ask the driver he may drop you at Yörük Köyü (TL1.50). Getting back, you'll have to walk the 1km to the main road. It's much less hassle to go there from Safranbolu on a tour (see p413) or by taxi, which costs TL30 return.

BULAK MENCİLİS MAĞARASI

Deep in the Gürleyik hills 10km northwest of Safranbolu, this impressive cave network opened to the public a decade ago, although troglodytes may have lived here many millennia before that. You can walk through 400m of the 6km-long network, enough to reveal a fine array of stalactites and stalagmites with inevitable anthropomorphic nicknames. There are steps up to the **cave** (adult/child TL4/2; ⏱9am-7.30pm) and you should wear sturdy shoes as the metal walkway inside can be slippery and wet. A taxi from Safranbolu costs TL30 return.

İNCEKAYA AQUEDUCT

Just over 7km north of Safranbolu you can visit this **aqueduct** (Su Kemeri), which was originally built in Byzantine times but restored in the 1790s by İzzet Mehmet Paşa. Its name means 'thin rock' and the walk across it, high above the beautiful **Tokatlı Gorge**, would not suit sufferers of vertigo. A taxi from Safranbolu costs TL20 return, but the walk there is recommended, following the steep gorge through lovely, unspoilt countryside.

Kastamonu
📞0366 / POP 80,600

A town where the shops are full of chainsaws and milking machines doesn't seem immediately promising, but Kastamonu makes a reasonable stopover between central Anatolia and the Black Sea. Potential distractions include two museums, a castle, some old mosques, Ottoman houses and, further afield, Kasaba's wooden mosque and Pınarbaşı's 37,000-hectare national park.

History

Kastamonu's history has been as chequered as that of most central-Turkish towns. Archaeological evidence suggests there was a settlement here as far back as 2000 BC, but the Hittites, Persians, Macedonians and Pontic (Black Sea) kings all left their mark.

In the 11th century the Seljuks descended, then the Danışmends. The 13th-century Byzantine emperor John Comnenus tried to hold out here, but the Mongols soon swept in, followed by the Ottomans.

Bizarrely, Kastamonu's modern history is inextricably linked to headgear: Atatürk launched his hat reforms here in 1925, banning the fez due to its religious connotations and insisting on the adoption of European-style titfers.

◎ Sights

Archaeology Museum   MUSEUM
(🏛214 1070; Cumhuriyet Caddesi; admission TL3; ☺8.30am-noon & 1-5pm Tue-Sun) About 50m south of Cumhuriyet Meydanı, this museum has introductions to Atatürk's sartorial revolution and Anatolian archaeology, with predominantly Hellenic and Roman finds from the area.

Ethnography Museum   MUSEUM
(🏛214 0149; off Cumhuriyet Caddesi; admission TL3; ☺9am-5pm Tue-Sun) Heading south of Nasrullah Meydanı on the main street, turn right at the Akbank ATM to reach this excellent museum. Occupying the restored 1870 Liva Paşa Konağı, it's fully furnished as it would have been in Ottoman times.

FREE Kale   CASTLE
(☺9am-5pm) Kastamonu's castle, built on a tall rock behind the town, is a steep 1km climb through the streets of the old town. Parts of the building date from Byzantine times, but most belong to Seljuk and Ottoman reconstructions. Follow the walls round and admire the views before descending the spiral stairs to the portcullis (you have to jump the last metre).

Nasrullah Meydanı   SQUARE
Centres on the Ottoman **Nasrullah Camii** (1506) and the double fountain where men wash their feet. Poet Mehmet Akif Ersoy delivered speeches in this mosque during the War of Independence. The former **Munire Medresesi** (seminary) at the rear houses some craft shops. The area immediately west of the square is filled with old market buildings, including the **Aşirefendi Hanı** and the 15th-century **İsmail Bey Hanı**.

🛏 Sleeping

Most of the new hotels are clustered around Nasrullah Bridge. The bus companies' offices and an internet cafe are in the same area.

Uğurlu Konakları   HISTORIC HOTEL €€
(🏛212 8202; www.ugurlukonagi.com; Şeyh Şaban Veli Caddesi 47-51; s/d TL70/140) Uğurlu Konakları is an impressive accommodation option for such a small, unassuming town. A short walk from the castle, these two houses have been faithfully restored with Indian carpets, red-brown trimmings and a booming stone and grass courtyard. The firm beds are fresh from the plastic.

Osmanlı Sarayı   HISTORIC HOTEL €€
(Ottoman Palace; 🏛214 8408; www.osmanlisarayi.tr.cx; Belediye Caddesi 81; s/d TL60/80) Atatürk once visited this former town hall, built between 1898 and 1915. The beautifully restored rooms have wooden ceilings and authentic but newly fitted cupboard-bathrooms. There is a basic restaurant in the basement.

Toprakçılar Konakları   HISTORIC HOTEL €€
(🏛212 1812; www.toprakcilar.com; Alemdar Sokak 2; s/d/ste TL70/120/220) More restored Ottoman splendour, this time in two townhouses across the road from İsfendiyarbey Parkı. The rooms have been faithfully restored and the courtyard restaurant (mains TL6 to TL10) sometimes hosts live music, when you'd be better off in the second building.

Otel Mütevelli   HOTEL €
(🏛212 2018; www.mutevelli.com.tr; Cumhuriyet Caddesi 10; s/d TL50/75) Kastamonu's best business hotel, near Cumhuriyet Meydanı, has drab but well-serviced rooms beyond its gaudy reception.

🍴 Eating & Drinking

The winding streets to the west of Nasrullah Meydanı are great for a wander and a çay.

Eflanili Konağı   OTTOMAN €
(🏛214 1118; Gazipaşa İlköğr Yanı; mains TL5-8) This restaurant in a restored Ottoman house has beautiful upstairs dining rooms and tables among fountains in the courtyard. Staff will happily recommend local specialities.

Ismail Bey Konağı   ANATOLIAN €€
(🏛214 8788; www.ismailbeykonak.com; Beyçelebi Mahallesi, Atatürk Caddesi 133; mains TL6-16) Perfect for an afternoon *ayran* or something more solid in the tiled courtyard with a small fountain and tableclothed picnic tables. The six-page menu includes döner, fish, mezes and a long list of salads.

Canoğlu   PATISSERIE €
(🏛213 9090; Cumhuriyet Caddesi; ☺6am-8pm) Near Nasrullah Bridge, this patisserie with

floor-to-ceiling windows on its second level is Kastamonu's premier catch-up spot. Goodies such as pizzas and burgers are also available.

🔒 Shopping

Kaveldo Kastamonu El Dokumaları
TEXTILES

(📞212 4207; Sanat Okulu Caddesi; ⊙8.30am-noon & 1-5pm) A textile workshop where visitors can purchase garments and tableclothes straight from the loom.

ℹ️ Getting There & Away

Kastamonu's otogar offers regular departures for Ankara (TL25, 4½ hours), İstanbul (TL45, nine hours) and Samsun (TL25, six hours). There are direct services to Sinop (TL20, three hours), but it may be quicker to change in Boyabat (TL10, two hours). There are hourly departures for Karabük (TL10, two hours), with some buses continuing to Safranbolu.

Minibuses for İnebolu (TL10, two hours) also leave from the otogar.

Around Kastamonu

KASABA

The tiny village of Kasaba, 17km northwest of Kastamonu, is a pretty but unlikely place to find one of Turkey's finest surviving wooden mosques. The minaret of Mahmud Bey Camii (1366) stands out from miles away. Its restored interior has four painted wooden columns, a wooden gallery and fine-painted ceiling rafters. You can climb some rough ladders to the third storey of the gallery and look at the ornate beam-ends and interlocking motifs topping the pillars.

A return taxi from Kastamonu, with waiting time, costs TL35, and the driver should know where the imam lives if the mosque is locked. A cheaper option is to take the Pınarbaşı bus and jump off at the Kasaba turn-off, but it is a 4km walk to the village from there and you will have to ask around for the imam if Mahmud Bey Camii is shut.

PINARBAŞI

Pınarbaşı, a little hill town 97km northwest of Kastamonu, is the main access point for the 37,000-hectare Küre Dağları National Park (Küre Dağları Milli Parkı; 📞0366-771 2465; www.ked.org.tr/empty.html), which was gazetted in 2000. Despite some marketing efforts made by the local government, the Küre Mountains are still largely undiscovered by tourists and you will likely have the park to yourself. Spots worth seeking out include the Ilgarini 'Inn' and Ilıca 'Hamam' caves, Ilıca waterfall and Horma Canyon.

You can stay at a basic ecolodge in the park, near the Ilıca waterfall. The dinky five-person cabins and smarter four-person cabin at Park Ilıca Turizm Tesisi (📞0366-771 2046; www.parkilica.com; per person TL45) have single beds on two floors. With thermal springs nearby, the cabins make a great base for looking around the park.

There are a couple of minibuses a day from Kastamonu to Pınarbaşı, but you really need your own transport to move around the park. For TL150, a taxi will take you there and spend the afternoon touring the park before returning to Kastamonu.

Boğazkale, Hattuşa & Yazılıkaya

Out in the centre of the Anatolian plains, two Unesco World Heritage sites evoke a vital historical moment at the height of Hittite civilisation. Hattuşa was the Hittite capital, while Yazılıkaya was a religious sanctuary with fine rock carvings.

The best base for visiting the sites around here is Boğazkale, a farming village 200km east of Ankara. Boğazkale has simple traveller services; if you want or need something fancier you'll need to stay in Çorum (p425) or, if you get going early enough in the morning, Ankara.

BOĞAZKALE
📞0364 / POP 1600

The village of Boğazkale has ducks, cows and wheelbarrow-racing children wandering its cobbled streets, farmyards with Hittite and Byzantine gates, and a constant sense that a once-great city is just over the brow. Most visitors come solely to visit Hattuşa and Yazılıkaya, which can be accessed on foot if it's not too hot, but there is more to explore. Hattuşa is surrounded by valleys with Hittite caves, eagles' nests, butterflies and a neolithic fort. Head 4km east of Yazılıkaya and climb the Yıldız Dağı (Star Mountains), as they are known locally, to watch the sun set on the sites.

Late in the day, the silence in Boğazkale is broken only by the occasional car kicking up dust on the main street, and the rural soli-

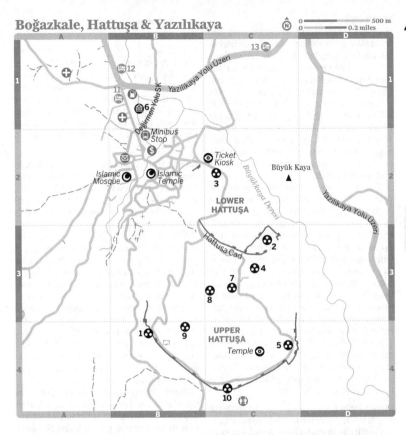

Boğazkale, Hattuşa & Yazılıkaya

⊙ Sights

1 Aslanlı Kapı	B4
2 Büyük Kale	C3
3 Büyük Mabet	C2
4 Güney Kale	C3
Hieroglyphics Chamber	(see 4)
5 Kral Kapı	C4
6 Boğazkale Museum	B1
7 Nişantaş	C3
8 Sari Kale	C3
9 Yenice Kale	B4
10 Yer Kapı	C4

🛏 Sleeping

11 Aşıkoğlu Hotel	B1
12 Hittite Houses	B1
13 Kale Hotel	C1

tude may tempt you to stay an extra night. Apart from the accommodation options, the village's only facilities are some small shops, a post office and bank with an ATM.

Unsurprisingly, Hittite artefacts dominate the small **Boğazkale Museum** (admission TL3; ⊙8am-5pm, closed Mon afternoon). Its disappointing collection includes examples of cuneiform tablets (including a state treaty between kings), signature seals, whimsically shaped vessels, arrow and axe heads, and a series of weathered black-and-white photographic displays. If you look closely at the Turkish/German labels you'll find that some items are copies, the originals having been taken to Ankara.

Hattuşa (adult/student TL4.50/free, also valid for Yazılıkaya; ⊙9am-5pm) was the capital of an ancient kingdom that stretched from Syria to Europe, and squared up to the Egyptian, Babylonian and Assyrian empires. The mountainous, isolated site was a busy and impressive city, with 50,000 inhabitants, a 100-step pyramid and seven ponds that each stored enough water for 10,000 people. Its defences included stone walls over 6km in length, some of the thickest in the ancient world, with watchtowers and secret tunnels.

The best way to tour the atmospheric ruins is to get up early and walk the 5km circuit, before the 21st century intrudes in the form of coaches and souvenir sellers (better-quality serpentine statues are available at the Yazılıkaya stands). As you climb out of the village to the site, an evocative reconstruction of a section of city wall comes into view. Imagine the sense of purpose that drove the Hittites to haul stone to this remote spot, far from oceans and trade routes, and build an engineering masterpiece that launched a mighty empire.

A word of warning: some nasty touts and carpet sellers have begun posing as 'compulsory guides' around the Hattuşa site and outside the entrance to Yazılıkaya. Remain firm, as this is clearly a con.

Büyük Mabet   HITTITE TEMPLE

The first site you come to is the vast complex of the **Büyük Mabet** (Great Temple), dating from the 14th century BC and destroyed around 1200 BC. It is the best preserved of the Hittite temples, but you'll need plenty of imagination.

Enter uphill from the ticket kiosk, opposite the remains of a house on the slope. As you walk down the wide processional street, the administrative quarters of the temple are to your left. The well-worn cube of green rock, supposedly one of only two in the world, was a present from Ramses II after signing the Kadesh peace treaty.

The main temple, to your right, was surrounded by storerooms, thought to be several storeys high. In the early 20th century, huge clay storage jars and thousands of cuneiform tablets were found in these rooms. Look for the threshold stones at the base of some of the doorways to see the hole for the hinge-post and the arc worn by the door's movement. The temple is believed to have been a ritual altar for Teshub and Hepatu;

the large stone base of one of their statues remains.

Sarı Kale   HITTITE CASTLE

About 250m south of the Büyük Mabet, the road forks; take the right fork and follow the winding road up the hillside. On your left in the midst of the old city you can see several ruined structures fenced off from the road, including the **Sarı Kale** (Yellow Castle), which may be a Phrygian fort on Hittite foundations.

Castle Walls & Gates   HITTITE RUINS

From the fork in the road it's about 750m uphill to the **Aslanlı Kapı** (Lion Gate), where two stone lions (one badly defaced) protect the city from evil spirits. This is one of at least six gates in the city's defensive walls, though it may never have been completed. You can see the best-preserved parts of the fortifications from here, stretching up the ridge southeast to Yer Kapı and from there to Kral Kapı. These 4000-year-old walls illustrate the Hittites' engineering ingenuity, which enabled them to either build in sympathy with the terrain or transform the landscape, depending on what was required. Natural outcrops were appropriated as part of the walls, and massive ramparts were built to create artificial fortresses.

Head 600m downhill to the **Yer Kapı** (Sfenksli Kapı; Earth or Sphinx Gate), once defended by four great sphinxes, which are now in museums in İstanbul and Berlin. It is the most impressive gate, with an artificial mound pierced by a 70m-long **tunnel**. The Hittites built the tunnel using a corbelled arch (two flat faces of stones leaning towards one another), as the 'true' arch was not invented until later. Primitive or not, the arch has done its job for millennia, and you can still pass down the stony tunnel as Hittite soldiers did, emerging from the **postern**. Afterwards, re-enter the city via one of the **monumental stairways** up the wide stone glacis, and enjoy the wonderful views over the site and its surroundings.

Head northeast down the slope from the Yer Kapı, past some of the upper city's 28 **temples** on the left, and you'll reach the **Kral Kapı** (King's Gate), named after the regal-looking figure in the relief carving. The kingly character, a Hittite warrior god protecting the city, is a copy; the original was removed to Ankara for safekeeping.

While the name may evoke images of skin-clad barbarians, the Hittites were a sophisticated people who commanded a vast Middle Eastern empire, conquered Babylon and challenged the Egyptian pharaohs more than 3000 years ago. Apart from a few written references in the Bible and Babylonian tablets, there were few clues to their existence until 1834 when a French traveller, Charles Texier, stumbled on the ruins of the Hittite capital of Hattuşa.

In 1905 excavations turned up notable works of art, most of them now in Ankara's Museum of Anatolian Civilisations. Also brought to light were the Hittite state archives, written in cuneiform on thousands of clay tablets. From these tablets, historians and archaeologists were able to construct a history of the Hittite empire.

The original Indo-European Hittites swept into Anatolia around 2000 BC, conquering the local Hatti, from whom they borrowed their culture and name. They established themselves at Hattuşa, the Hatti capital, and in the course of a millennium enlarged and beautified the city. From about 1375 to 1200 BC Hattuşa was the capital of a Hittite empire that, at its height, shared Syria with Egypt and extended as far as Europe.

The Hittites worshipped over a thousand different deities; the most important were Teshub, the storm or weather god, and Hepatu, the sun goddess. The cuneiform tablets revealed a well-ordered society with more than 200 laws. The death sentence was prescribed for bestiality, while thieves got off more lightly provided they paid their victims compensation.

Although it defeated Egypt in 1298 BC, the empire declined in the following centuries, undone by internal squabbles and new threats such as the Greek 'sea peoples'. Hattuşa was torched and its inhabitants dispersed. Only the city states of Syria survived until they, too, were swallowed by the Assyrians.

Nişantaş & Güney Kale   HITTITE FORTRESS

Heading downhill again you'll come to the Nişantaş, a rock with a Hittite inscription cut into it. The lengthy inscription dates to the time of Suppiluliuma II (1215–1200 BC), the final Hittite king, and narrates his deeds.

Immediately opposite, a path leads up to the excavated Güney Kale (Southern Fortress) and to what may have been a royal tomb, with a fine (fenced-off) hieroglyphics chamber with human figure reliefs. About 200m downhill are the ruins of Büyük Kale (Great Fortress). Although most of the site has been excavated, many of the older layers of development have been re-covered to protect them, so what you see today can be hard to decipher. This fortress held the royal palace and the Hittite state archives.

YAZILIKAYA

Yazılıkaya means 'Inscribed Rock', and that's exactly what you'll find in these outdoor rock galleries, just under 3km from Hattuşa. There are two galleries: the larger one, to the left, was the Hittite empire's holiest religious sanctuary; the narrower one, to the right, has the best-preserved carvings. Together they form the largest known Hittite rock sanctuary, sufficiently preserved to make you wish you could have seen the carvings when they were new.

In the larger gallery, Chamber A, the fast-fading reliefs show numerous goddesses and pointy-hatted gods marching in procession. Heads and feet are shown in profile but the torso is shown front on, a common feature of Hittite relief art. The lines of men and women lead to some large reliefs depicting a godly meeting. Teshub stands on two deified mountains (depicted as men) alongside his Hepatu, who is standing on the back of a panther. Behind her, their son and (possibly) two daughters are respectively carried by a smaller panther and a double-headed eagle. The largest relief, on the opposite wall, depicts the complex's bearded founder, King Tudhaliya IV, standing on two mountains. The rock ledges were probably used for offerings or sacrifices and the basins for libations.

On the way into Chamber B, you should supposedly ask permission of the winged, lion-headed guard depicted by the entrance before entering. The narrow gallery is thought to be a memorial chapel for Tudhaliya IV, dedicated by his son Suppiluliuma II.

The large limestone block could have been the base of a statue of the king. Buried until a century ago and better protected from the elements, the carvings include a procession of 12 scimitar-wielding underworld gods. On the opposite wall, the detailed relief of Nergal depicts the underworld deity as a sword; the four lion heads on the handle (two pointing towards the blade, one to the left and the other to the right) double as the deity's knees and shoulders.

🛏 Sleeping & Eating

The following generally offer camping for about TL5 to TL8 per site.

Hittite Houses   FAMILY HOTEL €
(☑452 2004; www.hattusas.com; Sungurlu Asfalt Caddesi; d TL80) The recent addition of this apartment hotel by the knowledgeable owners of Aşıkoğlu Hotel is proving a hit with summer groups and families. Each self-contained room smells of fresh paint and varnish.

Aşıkoğlu Hotel   HOTEL €
(☑452 2004; www.hattusas.com; Sungurlu Asfalt Caddesi; s/d/tr TL40/80/100) Just walking around the Aşıkoğlu is educational: the modern rooms, which have bright bedspreads and all amenities, are named after Hittite figures. There is a restaurant (mains TL10) with a terrace, patio and cinevision screen for documentaries, and an Ottoman-style cafe with a fireplace. In summer, the hotel often fills up with tour groups.

Kale Hotel   HOTEL €
(☑452 3126; www.bogazkoyhattusa.com; Yazılıkaya Yolu Üzeri; s/d/tr TL30/45/60; ☺Apr-Oct) Kale's light, good-value rooms have cheery floral linen and bathrooms; the top ones at the front have good views and some have balconies. The restaurant, with its adjoining terrace, mostly caters to groups.

ℹ Getting There & Away

To get to Boğazkale by public transport, you'll need to go via Sungurlu. Many of the buses from Ankara to Sungurlu (TL12, three hours, hourly) are run by Mis Amasya (counter 23 at Ankara's

otogar). From Sungurlu, make your way to the Boğazkale dolmuş stand, 1km from the otogar near the soccer stadium; buses may drop you there if you ask. There are more dolmuşes (TL3) in the morning, but they run until about 5.30pm. Taking a taxi may be your only resort at the weekend; don't pay more than TL30. Travellers coming from Cappadocia should note that dolmuşes between Boğazkale and Yozgat, 41km southeast, are thin on the ground. You're probably better off going via Kırıkkale and Sungurlu.

ℹ Getting Around

To get around Hattuşa and Yazılıkaya without your own transport you'll need to walk or hire a taxi. It's 1km from the Aşıkoğlu Hotel to the Hattuşa ticket kiosk. From there the road looping around the site from the ticket kiosk (not including Yazılıkaya) is another 5km. The walk itself takes at least an hour, plus time spent exploring the ruins, so figure on spending a good three hours here. There is no shop on the site so take a bottle of water, and start early in the day before the sun is too hot, as there's little shade.

As Alacahöyük is closer to the main highway, another option is to tour Hattuşa on foot and catch a taxi to the highway (where you can pick up dolmuşes in either direction) via Yazılıkaya and Alacahöyük; this can be accomplished in a day and costs about TL90. In all cases, negotiating a price should be cheaper than using the meter.

Alacahöyük

The tiny farming hamlet of Alacahöyük is 36km north of Boğazkale and 52km south of Çorum. It's a very old site, settled from about 4000 BC, but so little remains that it's really only worth the effort if you've got your own transport and have some time spare after Hattuşa. As at the other Hittite sites, movable monuments have been taken to the museum in Ankara, although there is a small museum and a few worn sphinxes at the entrance to the complex.

The **museum** (admission TL4; ☺8am-noon & 1.30-5.30pm) is right by the ruins, displaying artists' impressions of the site at various points in its history, as well as finds dating back to the chalcolithic and Old Bronze ages. A glass case shows the 15 layers of Alacahöyük's buried history, from 5500 to 600 BC.

At the ruins, the monumental gate has two eyeless sphinxes guarding the door. The detailed reliefs (copies, of course) show musicians, a sword swallower, animals for sacrifice and the Hittite king and queen – all part of festivities and ceremonies dedicated to Teshub, shown here as a bull. The extensive site also includes the foundations of a granary, up the wooden planks on the right, and of a temple, where some rocks have holes for sacrificial offerings. On the far left is an underground tunnel. Walk through it and look down at the fields to see how the site was built up over the millennia.

There's a small cafe at the museum entrance.

ⓘ Getting There & Away

There's no public transport between Alacahöyük and Boğazkale. If you're really keen, you could take a bus or dolmuş from Çorum to Alaca and another from Alaca to Alacahöyük (one or two services per day, none at weekends). Taxis can take you from Boğazkale to Alacahöyük, wait for an hour and then run you to Alaca or the busy Sungurlu–Çorum highway.

Çorum

📞 0364 / POP 178.500

Set on an alluvial plain on a branch of the Çorum River, Çorum is an unremarkable provincial capital, resting on its modest fame as the chickpea capital of Turkey. The town is full of *leblebiciler* (chickpea roasters) and sacks upon sacks of the chalky little pulses, all sorted according to fine distinctions obvious only to a chickpea dealer.

If you're travelling north or east from Boğazkale you may have to change buses in Çorum. Its museum is excellent preparation for Hattuşa and the other Hittite sites to the southeast, and the town can be a handy base for visiting them. It is a friendly place and offers some glimpses of provincial Turkish life.

◉ Sights

Çorum Museum   MUSEUM
(admission TL3; ⊙8am-noon & 1-7pm Tue-Sun) On the far side of Anitta Otel from the otogar, this excellent museum is well worth a visit before heading to Hattuşa et al. Major improvements were underway when we visited, but the exhibits on display traced Anatolian history from the Bronze Age to the Roman

period. The centrepiece is a reconstruction of the royal tomb at Alacahöyük, with bull skulls and a crumpled skeleton clad in a crown, and there are some incredible artefacts such as a Hittite ceremonial jug with water-spouting bulls around its rim.

🛏 Sleeping & Eating

Anitta Otel   LUXURY HOTEL €€
(📞213 8515; www.anittahotel.com, in Turkish; İnönü Caddesi 80; s/d/tr TL70/120/160; ❉ ⚍) Çorum might be the place to splurge on a good hotel, as the city's grandest digs are good value for money, with prices including access to the swimming pool and hamam. Rooms have glass-fronted minibars, plasma TVs and profuse mirrors.

Real Residence Hotel   HOTEL €€
(📞225 7331; www.realresidencehotel.com; İnönü Caddesi 62; s/d TL50/80, ste TL120) A dazzling new business hotel that symbolises Çorum's status as an emerging commercial region. A hundred metres from the Çorum Museum, this professional establishment has apartment-style rooms with ample space for mapping your next business venture.

Grand Park Hotel   HOTEL €€
(📞212 3044; www.grandpark.com.tr; İnönü Caddesi 60; s/d TL55/90) Next door to Real Residence is another fine business hotel with 60-plus huge rooms, plush carpets and a spacious, dark brown lobby. There's a cool playroom for the little ones.

Atak Hotel   HOTEL €
(📞225 6500; hotelatak@hotmail.com; İnönü Caddesi 38; s/d/tr TL30/45/60) Between the otogar and the clock tower, Atak's rooms have bathrooms and are a reasonable choice for one night.

Katipler Konağı   OTTOMAN €€
(📞224 9651; Karakeçili Mahallesi, 2 Sokak 20; mains TL6-11; ⊙11am-9pm) This restaurant is spread across two floors of a restored Ottoman house. Highlights include the mulberry juice and filling local starters (TL3 to TL7) such as *çatal aşı* (lentil and wheat soup) and *keşkek* (roasted wheat, chicken, red pepper and butter). To find it from Hotel Sarıgül turn left, cross the road and turn right; turn right on to the side street behind the mosque, turn left and it's on the right.

ⓘ Getting There & Away

Being on the main Ankara–Samsun highway, Çorum has good bus connections. Regular buses go to Alaca (TL4, 45 minutes), Amasya (TL7, two hours), Ankara (TL15, four hours), Kayseri (TL20, 4¾ hours), Samsun (TL15, three hours) and Sungurlu (TL5, 1¼ hours).

Amasya

☏ 0358 / POP 74,400

Amasya is a tale of two shores. On the north of Yeşilırmak River, rows of half-timbered Ottoman houses sit squeezed together like chocolate cakes in a patisserie window. To the south, the newer, more modern Turkey tries to get on with things in an outward-looking ode to the succession of empires that reigned in this narrow, rocky valley. Towering above the minarets and the *medreses* are pockmarks of Pontic tombs, etched into the highrise bluff and guarded by a lofty citadel. Amasya's setting may evoke high drama, but life here unfolds as slowly as the train runs apples out of town via a mountain tunnel. In local folklore, these tunnels were dug by Ferhat, a star-crossed lover who was tragically in love with Sirin, the sister of a sultan queen.

History

Called Hakmış by the Hittites, the Amasya area has been inhabited continuously since around 5500 BC. Alexander the Great conquered Amasya in the 4th century BC, then it became the capital of a successor kingdom ruled by a family of Persian satraps (provincial governors). By the time of King Mithridates II (281 BC), the Kingdom of Pontus entered a golden age and dominated a large part of Anatolia from its HQ in Amasya.

During the latter part of Pontus' flowering, Amasya was the birthplace of Strabo (c 63 BC to AD 25), the world's first geographer. Having travelled in Europe, west Asia and North Africa, Strabo wrote 47 history and 17 geography books. Though most of his history books have been lost, we know something of their content because many other classical writers quoted him. He left an account of Amasya under Roman rule, which began here in 70 BC.

Amasya's golden age continued under the Romans, who named it a 'first city' and used it as an administrative centre for rulers such as Pompey. It was Julius Caesar's conquest of a local town that prompted his immortal words *'Veni, vidi, vici'* – 'I came, I saw, I conquered'.

After Rome came the Byzantines, the Danişmend Turks, the Seljuks, the Mongols and the national republic of Abazhistan. In Ottoman times, Amasya was an important military base and testing ground for the

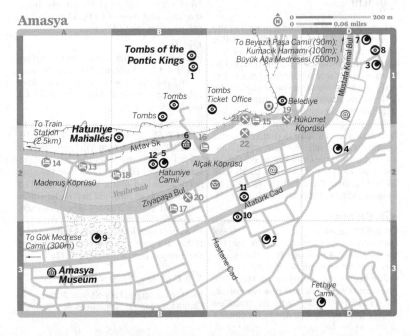

sultans' heirs; it also became a centre of Islamic study, with as many as 18 *medreses* and 2000 theological students by the 19th century.

After WWI, Atatürk met his supporters here and hammered out the basic principles of the Turkish struggle for independence, which were published in the Amasya Circular. The monument in the main square commemorates the meeting and depicts the unhappy state of Anatolian Turks before the revolution. Each year, Amasyalıs mark the revolutionary rendezvous with a week-long art and culture festival.

⊙ Sights & Activities

Pontic Tombs   TOMBS
(Kral Kaya Mezarları; admission TL3; ⊙9am-noon & 1-6.30pm) Looming above the northern bank of the river is a sheer rock face with the conspicuous rock-cut **Tombs of the Pontic Kings**. The tombs, cut deep into the limestone as early as the 4th century BC, were used for cult worship of the deified rulers. There are more than 20 (empty) tombs in the valley (nicknamed Kings' Valley).

Climb the steps from the souvenir stalls to the ticket office. Just past the office the path divides: turn left to find the **Baths of the Maidens Palace**, built in the 14th century and used until the 19th century, and, through a rock-hewn tunnel, a couple of tombs. Turn right to find more tombs and the remnants of the **Palace of the Maidens** (Kızlar Sarayı). In the cliff behind the terrace are several more tombs.

Mirror Cave   TOMB
Another Pontic tomb, the Mirror Cave (Aynalı Mağara), sits apart from the others, northeast of Amasya. One of the finest tombs, its name derives from the glaring effect produced by the sun on its pale facade. Although built during Pontic times, it's likely the cave was later used as a chapel by the Byzantines, who painted the fast-fading frescoes. With a Greek inscription high on the facade, this is one of the few tombs with any type of adornment.

The cave is 4km from the main square (TL10 return in a taxi). Follow the Yeşilırmak north and cross it on Künç Köprüsü, then look for the signpost on your right after a few hundred metres; Mirror Cave is 3km before Ziyaret.

Citadel   CITADEL
Above the tombs is the *kale* (citadel), also referred to as Harşena castle, perched precariously atop rocky Mt Harşena and offering magnificent views down the valley. The remnants of the walls date from Pontic times, perhaps around King Mithridates' reign, but a fort stood here from the early Bronze Age. The castle was destroyed and repaired by several empires, including the Danışmend Turks. It had eight defensive layers, descending 300m to the Yeşilırmak, and a tunnel with 150 steps cut into the mountain. On a ledge just below the citadel is an old Russian cannon, fired during Ramazan to mark the end of the daily fast.

The castle is being renovated and is popular for family days out, but travellers of

ANKARA & CENTRAL ANATOLIA AMASYA

Amasya

either sex are advised not to go up unaccompanied later in the day. To reach the citadel, cross Künç Köprüsü and follow the Samsun road for about 1km to a street on the left marked 'Kale'. It's 1.7km up the mountainside to a small car park, then another steep 15-minute climb to the summit, marked by a flagpole.

Amasya Museum
MUSEUM

(☑218 4513; Atatürk Caddesi; admission TL3; ⊙8.15am-noon & 1-4.45pm Tue-Sun) Amasya's museum packs in Ottoman artefacts including vibrant banners, unwieldy manuscripts, and an armoury of flintlock guns, gunpowder flasks and inscribed daggers. Displays cover crafts such as rope-making, and wooden doors from Amasya's Gök Medrese Camii show the progression between Seljuk and Ottoman carving. The extensive collection also covers earlier periods; look out for the famous Statuette of Amasya, a bronze figure of the Hittite storm god Teshub, with conical hat and almond-shaped eyes.

Outside, a tiled Seljuk tomb in the garden contains a unique collection of mummies dating from the 14th-century İlkhan period. The bodies, mummified without removing the organs, were discovered beneath the Burmalı Minare Camii. None of it's for squeamish or young eyes, although, touchingly, one ruler is accompanied by his son, daughter and concubine.

Hatuniye Mahallesi
HISTORIC NEIGHBOURHOOD

Immediately north of the river, the Hatuniye Mahallesi is Amasya's wonderful neighbourhood of restored Ottoman houses, interspersed with good modern reproductions to make a harmonious whole.

Just past the steps up to the Pontic Tombs is the Hazeranlar Konağı (admission TL3; ⊙8.15am-noon & 1-4.45pm Tue-Sun), constructed in 1865 and restored in 1979. Hasan Talat, the accountant of governor-poet Ziya Paşa, built the mansion for his sister, Hazeran Hanım. The restored rooms are beautifully furnished in period style, with a refined feel to their chandeliers and carved wood, and have models to illustrate their use. The Directorate of Fine Arts gallery in the basement has changing exhibitions.

Hamams
HAMAMS

Amasya has several venerable hamams that are still in operation. Attached to Hatuniye Camii, the Yıldız Hamamı (Star Hamam; wash & massage TL13) was built by a Seljuk commander in the 13th century and restored in

the 16th century. On the northern side of the Darüşşifa is the 1436 Ottoman Mustafa Bey Hamamı (wash & massage TL6), while not far away is the 1495 Kumacık Hamamı (wash & massage TL13). All are open from about 6am to 10am and 4pm to 11pm for men; from 10am to 4pm for women.

SOUTH OF THE RIVER

You could spend a very pleasant couple of hours exploring Amasya's minor sights on both banks of the river. The advantage of the south bank is that you can see the scenic north bank from it, especially at night, when the castle and rock tombs are artily lit in neon. The bulk of Amasya's old religious buildings are also on this side of the river. At the northeastern end of the south bank, near Künç Köprüsü, is the Beyazıt Paşa Camii (1419). The early-Ottoman mosque follows a twin-domed plan that was a forebear in style to Bursa's famous Yeşil Camii.

Follow the river southwest and you'll come to the pretty Mehmet Paşa Camii, built in 1486 by Lala Mehmet Paşa, one of Sultan Beyazıt II's viziers. Don't miss the embroidered marble *mimber* (pulpit). The complex originally included the builder's tomb, an *imaret* (soup kitchen), *tabhane* (hospital), hamam and *handan* (inn).

Continue along the river, and on the left you'll see the Darüşşifa (1309), or Bimarhane, on Mustafa Kemal Bulvarı. With its intricately carved portal, it was built as a mental hospital by Ilduş Hatun, wife of the İlhanid Sultan Olcaytu, and may have been the first place to try to treat mental disorders with music. The İlkhans were the successors to Genghis Khan's Mongols, who had defeated the Anatolian Seljuks. Their architecture reflects motifs borrowed from many conquered peoples, and the building is based on the plan of a Seljuk *medrese*. Today the building is often used for exhibitions, concerts and events.

A bit further along the river is Amasya's main square with its imposing memorial to the War of Independence. Perched on a rise to the east of the square, the boxy mosque with a wooden dome is the Gümüşlü Cami (Silvery Mosque; 1326). The town's earliest Ottoman mosque, it was rebuilt in 1491 after an earthquake, in 1612 after a fire, and again in 1688, then added to in 1903 and restored yet again in 1988.

If you keep walking west and head inland from the river you'll come to the 15th-century Vakıf Bedesten Kapalı Çarşı

(Covered Market), still in use today. Keep heading west along Atatürk Caddesi and on the left you'll see the partly ruined **Taş Han** (1758), an Ottoman caravanserai. Behind it is the Seljuk **Burmalı Minare Camii** (Spiral Minaret Mosque). It was rebuilt in 1590 after an earthquake, and following a fire in 1602, when its wooden minaret was superseded by the current stone structure with elegant spiral carving.

Keep walking west and you'll come to the graceful **Sultan Beyazıt II Camii** (1486), Amasya's largest *külliye* (mosque complex), with a *medrese*, fountain, *imaret* and *muvakkithane* (astronomer's house). The mosque's main door, *mihrab* (niche indicating the direction of Mecca) and pulpit are made of white marble and its windows feature *kündekari* (interlocking wooden carving).

Finally, you'll reach the 13th-century **Gök Medrese Camii** (Mosque of the Sky-Blue Seminary), built for Seljuk governor Seyfettin Torumtay. The *eyvan* (vaulted hall) serving as its main portal is unique in Anatolia, while the *kümbet* (domed tomb) was once covered in *gök* (sky-blue) tiles.

NORTH OF THE RIVER

Across Künç Köprüsü is the impressive **Büyük Ağa Medresesi** (1488). With an octagonal layout, rarely seen in Ottoman *medrese* architecture, it was built by Sultan Beyazıt II's chief white eunuch Hüseyin Ağa, also known as Grandagha. It still serves as a seminary for boys who are training to be *hafız* (theologians who have memorised the entire Quran) and is not open to the public.

🛏 Sleeping

Like Safranbolu, Amasya is one of those places where it's worth paying a bit more to stay in a real Ottoman house.

TOP CHOICE **Emin Efendi Konağı** HISTORIC HOTEL €€
(📞212 6622; Ziyapaşa Bulvarı 2c; s/d TL80/140; ❄@) Brought to life by one of Amasya's oldest families, the Emin Efendi is the hot new hotel for northern Turkey's weekend elite. The entrance and spiral staircase have a rather grandfatherly elegance, while the flash daggy rooms – ceiling-high black bedheads, fallen roses and white leather chairs – are just plain grand. Every evening the courtyard restaurant (mains TL9 to TL19) is the place for fine dining and dealing.

Şükrübey Konağı HISTORIC HOTEL €€
(📞212 6285; www.sukrubeykonagi.com.tr; Hazeranlar Sokak 55; s/d/tr TL55/100/150) An excellent choice with an established record and colourful, spacious rooms, with bathrooms and TVs perched on wooden stands or tables. The real highlight is the balconies with wooden stools and views of the tombs or the river below. The restaurant also has views across the Yeşilırmak.

Ezgi Pansiyon PENSION €
(📞213 0477; Hatuniye Mahallesi, Yali Boyu Sokak 28; s/d TL45/80) The enclosed tree-lined courtyard is the selling point of this cute pension in a line of many Ottoman houses with heavy beams and dark wood furniture. The rooms are simple yet sympathetic and the on-site restaurant makes excellent savoury *katmer* (pastry).

Harşena Otel HISTORIC HOTEL €€
(📞218 3979; info@harsenaotel.com; Hatuniye Mahallesi; s/d/tr TL75/120/150; ❄) Regularly booked out on weekends, the Harşena offers a choice between the old and the new. On one side of the road is the old house hanging out by the river and courted by a fine bar and restaurant; on the other side is the more modern Harşena, air-brushed and at your service. Perhaps spend a night in each?

Konfor Palas Hotel HOTEL €
(📞218 1260; www.konforpalas.com, in Turkish; Ziyapaşa Bulvarı 2c; s/d/tr TL40/65/85) This enthusiastically titled hotel's rooms are comfortable enough if you overlook the stained carpets and minor design flaws. It has a central location right next to the cafes; choose a back or side room to avoid ambient noise.

Grand Pasha Hotel HISTORIC HOTEL €€
(📞212 4158; www.grandpashahotel.com; Tevfik Hafız Çıkmazı 5) While the new young owners bypass customer service and cleanliness in favour of good live music and keen young fans, it's still one of the more authentic and quirky Ottoman-style places to stay. New rooms were being added at the time of research.

🍴 Eating & Drinking

As well as the hotels listed above, there are a few reasonable cafes and restaurants in Hatuniye Mahallesi and a smattering of more basic options around town. Amasya is famed for its apples, which give autumn visitors one more thing to sink their teeth into.

Strabon Restaurant   MODERN ANATOLIAN €€
(☑212 4012; Tevfık Hazız; mains TL7-16) Next to Grand Pasha Hotel is this beautiful new restaurant with our favourite riverside deck in Amasya. The hot or cold mezes (TL5 to TL9) are tasty and fresh; the meat grills and grilled *balik* (fish) are low on oil and literally fall off big serving plates. If you're not hungry, Strabon doubles nicely as a fun venue for drinking booze. If it's raining, ascend to the groovy indoor seating.

Bahçeli Ocakbaşı   LOKANTA €
(☑218 5692; Ziyapaşa Bulvarı; mains TL4-5) You can gaze up at the tombs from this cafe, one of half a dozen *lokantas* competing amiably for business in a lively, crowded courtyard.

Amasya Şehir Kulübü   LOKANTA €€
(☑218 1013; mains TL10; ◷11am-11pm) Downstairs from the smarter Amasya Şehir Derneği, this restaurant is popular for its food and balconies, which overlook the river next to the Hükümet Köprüsü. The menu includes meze, pizza, pide, Tokat kebap and the onion-laden Izgara *köfte,* which is recommended unless you are a Ferhat trying to woo his Şirin (or vice versa).

Other recommendations:

Ali Kaya Restaurant   LOKANTA €€
(☑218 1505; Çakallar Mevkii; mains TL12; ◷noon-11pm) The best time to visit this simple licensed restaurant above Amasya is at sunset, when you can recharge after the steep climb with meze while taking in views of town and the tombs. Taxis will ferry you up for TL8.

Subaşı Çay Bahçesi   TEA GARDEN
(Tevfık Hafız Çıkmazı) On the riverbank, opposite the Grand Pasha Hotel, is a popular tea garden. Several pleasant tea gardens also line the Yeşilırmak around Belediye Parkı and Sultan Beyazıt II Camii.

ℹ Information

Tourist Office (Hazeranlar Konağı; ◷9am-5pm)

ℹ Getting There & Away

A number of companies have daily services to locations including Ankara (TL30, five hours), Çorum (TL10, two hours), İstanbul (TL40, 10 hours), Kayseri (TL35, eight hours), Malatya (TL35, eight hours), Nevşehir (TL50, nine hours), Samsun (TL10, two hours), Sivas (TL25, 3½ hours) and Tokat (TL10, two hours).

To get to Safranbolu, the cheapest option is to take an early-morning minibus to Gerede, alight at the Karabük junction and flag down a bus to

Safranbolu, probably via Karabük. It's a long day; travelling via Ankara is easier.

Amasya **train station** (☑218 1239; ◷4am-10pm) is served by daily trains between Samsun (4.53am and 2.09pm, three hours, TL6) and Sivas (11.27am, 5½ hours, TL11).

Tokat

☑0356 / POP 128,000

Locals claim you can hear the steps of civilisations creeping up behind you in Tokat, where history buffs gorge themselves on the mosques, mansions, hamams and *hans* in this ancient town at the heart of Anatolia. Others come more for the immediacy of a famed Tokat kebap – a delectable mess of lamb and vegetables – then wash their greasy hands in the river that splits the town in two.

Physically on the rise due to seven centuries of sodden silt, Tokat's booming antique trade and architectural treats such as Gök Medrese guarantee the town won't sink into obscurity any century soon. As in Amasya, the rocky promontories rise high on all sides here, providing natual protection from foreign invaders and tourist hordes.

You can easily spend a day rummaging through the *yazma* (headscarf) and copperware stalls in the glorious Taş Han, or getting knuckled by Tokat's notorious masseurs.

History

Tokat's history features an inevitable rollcall of Anatolian conquerors. The Hittites and Phrygians, the Medes and the Persians, the empire of Alexander the Great, the Kingdom of Pontus, the Romans, the Byzantines, the Danışmend Turks, the Seljuks and the Mongol İlkhanids all marched through here.

By the time of the Seljuk Sultanate of Rum, Tokat was Anatolia's sixth-largest city and on important trade routes; the approach roads are littered with Seljuk bridges and caravanserais. However, the Mongols and their subordinates the İlkhanids reversed the trend around the mid-13th century, leaving the city disinherited.

Only in 1402, under the Ottomans, did Tokat resume its role as an important trading entrepôt, agricultural town and copper-mining centre. Gazi Osman Paşa even rose from a poor Tokat background to become one of the empire's greatest generals, and the main street here bears his name.

Significant non-Muslim populations (Armenian, Greek, Jewish) were in charge of Tokat's commerce until the cataclysm of WWI, and there's still a small but active Jewish community.

◉ Sights & Activities

Gök Medrese   HISTORIC BUILDING
(Blue Seminary; GOP Bulvarı; admission TL3; ☺8am-noon & 1-5pm Tue-Sun) Constructed after the fall of the Seljuks and the coming of the Mongols by Pervane Muhinedin Süleyman, a local potentate, the 13th-century Gök Medrese has also served as a hospital, a school and, today, Tokat's museum.

Very few of the building's *gök* (sky-blue) tiles are left on the facade, but there are enough on the interior courtyard walls to give an idea of what it must have looked like in its glory days.

Although the courtyard is the highlight of the museum, the collection packs in Roman tombs, Seljuk carpets, Hellenic jewellery and local folkloric dresses, with informative signs in English. Look out for Bronze Age and Hittite artefacts, icons and relics from Tokat's churches (including a Greek Orthodox representation of John the Baptist with his head on a platter) and dervish ceremonial tools and weapons (fancy a 'mystic awl' or 'stones of submission'?). An ethnographic section on costume and textiles explains the local art of *yazma*-making.

The seminary contains the **Tomb of 40 Maidens** (Kırkkızlar Türbesi; 1275), actually an assembly of 20 tombs, possibly of the seminary's founders, though another theory has it that they are the tombs of 40 nurses who worked here.

FREE Taş Han & Around   CARAVANSERAI
(GOP Bulvarı; ☺8am-8pm) Virtually next door to the Gök Medrese is the 17th-century **Taş Han**, an Ottoman caravanserai and workshop with a cafe in the courtyard. Two floors of shops sell a mixture of local garb and copperware, and paintings of sailboats and doe-eyed puppies.

Behind the Taş Han are streets lined with old half-timbered **Ottoman houses**. There are more shops in this area; some of the designs you see on *yazmas*, kilims and carpets were assimilated from Afghan refugees who settled here during the Soviet invasion of Afghanistan in the 1980s.

In the fruit and vegetable market, across GOP Bulvarı from the Taş Han, stand the **Hatuniye Camii** and ruined *medrese*, dating from 1485 and the reign of Sultan Beyazıt II.

A few hundred metres north of the Taş Han, behind some plastic sandal stands on the same side of the street, look out for **Sümbül Baba Türbesi** (1291), an octagonal Seljuk tomb. Beside it a road leads up around 1km to the **citadel**, built in the 5th century and restored during the Seljuk and Ottoman eras. Little remains but the fine view, and women travellers should not go up alone.

Ali Paşa Hamam   HAMAM
(GOP Bulvarı; ☺5am-11pm for men, 9am-5pm for women) Ask around the steam rooms of Turkey's thousands of hamams, and you'll probably find that one of Tokat's biggest exports is its expert masseurs. Assuming there are actually any left in town, it seems like the perfect excuse to go for a scrub n rub at the wonderful Ali Paşa Hamam. These baths, under domes studded with glass bulbs to admit natural light, were built in 1572 for Ali Paşa, one of the sons of Süleyman the Magnificent. They have separate bathing areas for men and women, and the full works should cost around TL15.

FREE Latifoğlu Konağı   NOTABLE BUILDING
(GOP Bulvarı) South of Cumhuriyet Meydanı, the splendid 19th-century house **Latifoğlu Konağı** is a fine example of Baroque architecture in the Ottoman style.

AUBERGINE DREAM

The Tokat kebap is made up of skewers of lamb and sliced aubergine (eggplant) hung vertically, then baked in a wood-fired oven. Tomatoes and peppers, which take less time to cook, are baked on separate skewers. As the lamb cooks, it releases juices that baste the aubergine. All these goodies are then served together with a huge fist of roasted garlic, adding an extra punch to the mix.

It's almost worth coming to Tokat just to sample the dish, and in fact you might have to; it's inexplicably failed to catch on in menus much further afield than Sivas or Amasya, and Tokat's chefs do it best anyway. Standard aubergine döners that crop up are a far cry from the glorious blowout of the original.

The two-storey dwelling has been recently restored and converted into a small museum and is well worth a visit.

FREE Sulusokak Caddesi
HISTORIC NEIGHBOURHOOD

Many of Tokat's old buildings still survive, though in ruins, along Sulusokak Caddesi, which was the main thoroughfare before the perpendicular Samsun–Sivas road was improved in the 1960s.

Sulusokak Caddesi runs west from the north side of Cumhuriyet Meydanı, past Ali Paşa Camii, which was built at the same time as the nearby hamam and has classical Ottoman features on its grand central dome. Continue along the road and on the right you'll see the tiny Ali Tusi Türbesi (631–1233), a brick Seljuk work that incorporates some fine blue tiles. Next up, also on the right, is a crumbling wooden caravanserai, Katırcılar Han, with some vast pots lying in its courtyard.

Further on, on the same side of the road, the brick-and-wood Sulu Han is painted turquoise and white. The 17th-century Ottoman caravanserai provided accommodation for merchants visiting the *bedesten*, the remains of which are next door. Nearby, the 16th-century Takyeciler Camii, displaying the nine-domed style of great Ottoman mosques, is at one end of a line of structures currently being restored.

On the other side of Sulusokak Caddesi, past the 14th-century Kadı Hasan Camii, is the Ottoman Paşa Hamamı (1434). Also on this side of the street is the 16th-century Ottoman Deveciler Hanı, one of Tokat's finest caravanserais. The two-storey structure had a covered barn and a residential section with a porch and a courtyard.

Clock Tower
NOTABLE BUILDING

To the south of the centre, don't miss this 19th-century clock tower with the numerals on its faces still in Arabic, and a watch-repair shop (what else?) at the bottom.

FREE Mevlevihane
MUSEUM

(Bey Sokağı; ⊙9am-6pm) Just across the canal, among Ottoman houses and cobbled lanes, is this 19th-century building built as a dervish lodge and dancing hall, before serving as a women's prison in the 20th century. The exhibits include carpets and prayer rugs, Ottoman perfume bottles and candlesticks, and Qurans from down the centuries.

🛏 Sleeping

Yücel Hotel
HOTEL €€

(☑212 5235; Çekenli Caddesi 20; s/d/tr TL35/70/105; @⊠) Cheap, but with some major plusses – the 5th-floor restaurant and the hamam (included in the price). Rooms have minibars, TVs and cheap furniture, and there's a digital TV and internet area in the lobby. Prices can be haggled down.

Çavuşoğlu Otel
HOTEL €

(☑213 0908; GOP Bulvarı 168; s/d/tr TL45/65/80) This smart, central bargain has pistachio-coloured bathrooms, TVs, hairdryers and a breakfast buffet.

Otel Yeni Çınar
HOTEL €€

(☑214 0066; GOP Bulvarı 167; s/d/tr TL45/80/90) A good range of blue-framed rooms with nice bathrooms and vistas over the hills from the back. The receptionist is super cool, though the glass lobby is a bit stinky. The 1st-floor restaurant does a good line in grills, including one of the better Tokat kebaps in town (TL12.50).

Grand Gümüş Otel
HOTEL €€

(☑214 1331; GOP Bulvarı; s/d/tr TL45/70/115; ❀) Virtually opposite the Taş Han, this good-value option offers comfortable rooms with stripy duvets and excellent facilities, including minibars and TVs. The bar-restaurant has violet tablecloths and a series of meal deals (TL5 to TL10).

🍴 Eating & Drinking

You can tuck into a famed Tokat kebap at any number of restaurants here. Another delicious local dish is *zile pekmezi*, a fermented white grape spread.

Kebaps and *köfte* are the usual fare here, with eateries clustered around the fruit and vegetable market near the Hatuniye Camii. More upmarket restaurants and *pastanes* are found around Cumhuriyet Meydanı.

Şehrazat
ANATOLIAN €

(☑444 1406; Tokat-Sivas Karayolu; mains TL7-20; ⊙11am-11pm) On the side of the highway from Sivas (on the left about 1km before Tokat) is this totally twisted universe where leftover theme-park bits reassembled themselves into giant plastic love hearts around stagnant ponds covered in pagodas and mini bridges leading nowhere. Shockingly, it's always packed, and even more shockingly, the food is really good. Guess what? We recommend the Tokat kebap (TL13) – locals consider it one of the best.

Hacivat Köftole
FAST FOOD €

(🖉212 9418; GOP Bulvarı 275; set menus TL4-5; ☺9am-11pm) Opposite the Metro bus office, Hacivat is popular with a young crowd. Magazine cuttings and photos decorate the stone walls, allowing you to swot up on modern Turkish culture as you wait for one of the top-value daily set menus.

Yeşil Köşe Et Lokantası
FAST FOOD €

(GOP Bulvarı 1; mains TL5-6; ☺6.30am-10pm) This takeaway joint and cafe, popular at lunchtime for kebaps, moussaka and çorba, is another one of the best places in town to try a Tokat kebap (TL12). There is quieter seating upstairs.

Konak Café
CAFE €

(🖉214 4146; GOP Bulvarı; ☺9am-11pm) At the rear of a restored Ottoman building, this friendly cafe has multilevel outdoor seating available.

🔒 Shopping

At one time Tokat had a monopoly on the right to make *yazmas,* the richly colourful block-printed headscarves traditionally worn by many Turkish women, and it's still a good place to buy souvenir scarves or printed tablecloths. For years the Gazioğlu Han (block-printers' *han*) near the Gök Medrese was the centre of the trade. However, these days the materials are prepared in a modern **factory** (Yazmacılar Sitesi; Rodi Halısaha), opposite the Küçük Sanayi Sitesi 4km northwest of the town centre; you can visit to see the cloths being made.

🛈 Information

Tourist office (🖉211 8252; Taş Han, GOP Bulvarı 138/I; ☺8am-5pm) An informative Tokat brochure is available and an English-speaking Fenerbahçe fan may be on hand to help out.

🛈 Getting There & Away

Tokat's small otogar is about 1.7km northeast of the main square. Bus companies should provide a *servis* to ferry you to/from town; otherwise, if you don't want to wait for a dolmuş, a taxi will cost about TL10. A ride across town in one of the dolmuşes that regularly trundle along GOP Bulvarı costs about TL0.70.

Several bus companies have ticket offices around Cumhuriyet Meydanı.

There are regular buses to Amasya (TL10, two hours), Ankara (TL30, 6½ hours), Erzurum (TL40, 8½ hours), İstanbul (TL50, 12 hours), Samsun (TL20, four hours) and Sivas (TL12, 1¾ hours).

Local minibuses leave from the separate İlçe ve Köy terminal.

Around Tokat

Ballıca Cave
CAVE

(Ballıca Mağarası; 🖉0356-261 4236; adult/child TL4/2; ☺daylight hr) The Ballıca Cave, 26km west of Tokat, is one of Turkey's most famous caves. The limestone labyrinth, 3.4 million years old and 8km long (680m is open to the public), bristles with rock formations such as onion-shaped stalactites and mushroom-like stalagmites. Smugglers used to live here and the squeaks of the current residents, dwarf bats, add to the atmosphere created by dripping water.

Unfortunately, the ambience is quickly lost if you share the metal walkways with many others. With its copious lighting and signposts, the cave can feel like an underground theme park; exploring Safranbolu's less-visited Bulak Mencilis Mağarası (p418) is more rewarding.

There are a lot of steps both inside and outside the cave, although many schoolchildren manage it without snapping their pencils. The views from the cafe at the entrance are stunning, but its toilets are not the cleanest in Anatolia.

Returning, pause in Pazar to inspect the beautiful remains of a Seljuk *han* on the way out of town on the Tokat road. You can wait outside it for minibuses to Tokat.

🛈 Getting There & Away

To get to Ballıca, take a minibus from Tokat's İlçe ve Köy minibus terminal to Pazar (TL2.50, 40 minutes), where a taxi will be waiting to run you up the winding country road to the cave (8km). Drivers exploit their captive audience and you may have to pay as much as TL20 return (including an hour's waiting time). If you are driving from Amasya, Pazar is signposted 14km south of the main road to Tokat.

Sivas

🖉0346 / POP 294,000

With a colourful, sometimes tragic history and some of the finest Seljuk buildings ever erected, Sivas is a good stopover en route to the wild east and the best base for visiting the diverse attractions to the southeast. The city lies at the heart of

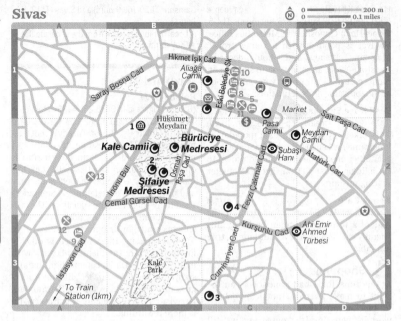

Turkey politically as well as geographically, thanks to its role in the run-up to the War of Independence. The Congress building resounded with plans, strategies and principles as Atatürk and his adherents discussed their great goal of liberation. The Turkish hero commented: 'Here is where we laid the foundations of our republic'. At night, as the red flags on the *meydanı* compete for attention with the spotlit minarets nearby, İnönü Bulvarı might be central Anatolia's slickest thoroughfare outside Ankara. The occasional horse and cart gallops down the boulevard, past the plasma screens and neon lights, like a ghost of Anatolia past.

History

The tumulus at nearby Maltepe shows evidence of settlement as early as 2600 BC, but Sivas itself was probably founded by the Hittite king Hattushilish I in around 1500 BC. It was ruled in turn by the Assyrians, Medes and Persians, before coming under the sway of the kings of Cappadocia and Pontus. Eventually the city fell to the Romans, who called it Megalopolis; this was later changed to Sebastea, then shortened to Sivas by the Turks.

Byzantine rule lasted from AD 395 to 1075, when the city was seized by the Danışmend emirs. The Seljuks and the Danışmends slogged it out for supremacy between 1152 and 1175 until the Seljuks finally prevailed, only to be dispossessed by the Mongol invasion of 1243. The İlkhanids succeeded the Mongols, and the city was then grabbed by the Ottomans (1398), Tamerlane (1400) and the Ottomans again (1408).

More recently Sivas was the location for the famous Sivas Congress in September 1919. Seeking to consolidate Turkish resistance to the Allied occupation and partition of his country, Atatürk arrived here from Samsun and Amasya, and gathered delegates to confirm decisions made at the Erzurum Congress. The two congresses heralded the War of Independence.

◉ Sights

Kale Camii & Bürüciye Medresesi

HISTORIC BUILDINGS

Most of Sivas' Seljuk buildings are in the park just south of Hükümet Meydanı. Here you'll find the **Kale Camii** (1580), a squat Ottoman work constructed by Sultan Murat III's grand vizier Mahmut Paşa.

Just east of the Kale Camii, reached through a monumental Seljuk gateway, is the **Bürüciye Medresesi**, built to teach

Sivas

◉ Top Sights

◉ Sights

🛏 Sleeping

🍴 Eating

'positive sciences' in 1271 by the Iranian businessman Muzaffer Bürücerdi, whose tiled tomb is inside. The tea garden in the courtyard, where exhibitions are held, is good for a çay in the evening, when spotlights illuminate the building.

Şifaiye Medresesi   HISTORIC MEDRESE
Across the park from the Bürüciye Medresesi is one of the city's oldest buildings, the Şifaiye Medresesi (1218). It was one of the most important medical schools built by the Seljuks and was once Anatolia's foremost hospital.

Look to the right as you enter the courtyard to see the porch that was walled up as a tomb for Sultan İzzettin Keykavus I, who commissioned the building before he died of tuberculosis.

The decoration features stylised sun/lion and moon/bull motifs, beautiful blue Azeri tile work and a poem in Arabic, composed by the sultan. The main courtyard has four *eyvans,* with sun and moon symbols on either side of the eastern one.

Çifte Minare Medrese   HISTORIC MEDRESE
Commissioned by the Mongol-İlkhanid vizier Şemsettin Güveyni after defeating the Seljuks at the battle of Kösedağ, the Çifte

435

Minare Medrese (Seminary of the Twin Minarets; 1271) has a *çifte* (pair) of mighty minarets. In fact, that's about all that is left, along with the elaborate portal and facade. Stand on the path between the Çifte and Şifaiye *medreses* to see the difference made by half a century and a shift in power.

Ulu Cami   MOSQUE
The town's other sights are southeast of Hükümet Meydanı along Cemal Gürsel and Cumhuriyet Caddesi; walk just past the southern end of the park and turn left onto Cemal Gürsel Caddesi.

The Ulu Cami (Great Mosque; 1197) is Sivas' oldest significant building, and one of Anatolia's oldest mosques. Built by the Danışmends, it's a large, low room with a forest of 50 columns. The super-fat leaning brick minaret was added in 1213. Inside, 11 handmade stone bands surround the main praying area and the ornate *mihrab* was discovered during renovations in 1955. It has a certain old-Anatolian charm, slightly marred by modern additions.

Gök Medrese   HISTORIC MEDRESE
From the Ulu Cami, turn right (south) on Cumhuriyet Caddesi and you will soon see the twin minarets of the glorious Gök Medrese (Sky-Blue Seminary). This was built in 1271 at the behest of Sahib-i Ata, the grand vizier of Sultan Gıyasettin Keyhüsrev III, who funded Konya's Sahib-i Ata mosque complex. The facade is exuberantly decorated with tiles, brickwork designs and carving, covering not just the usual inlaid portal but the walls as well. The blue tile work on the minarets gave the school its name.

Atatürk Congress & Ethnography
Museum   MUSEUM
(Atatürk Kongre ve Etnografya Müzesi; İnönü Bulvarı; admission TL3; ⏰8.30am-noon & 1.30-5pm Tue-Sun) Opposite the Kale Camii is the imposing Ottoman school building that hosted the Sivas Congress in 1919. Today it's a museum (enter via the rear).

The extensive Ottoman ethnographical collection, displayed on the ground floor, features a fine selection of kilims and carpets, including some impressive examples showing local weaving style; a demonstration of pillowcase-making (another local craft); a 12th-century wooden *mimber* from Divriği's Ulu Cami (see p439); and dervish ceremonial beads, weapons and mystics' caps.

🛏 Sleeping

Most hotels are within a few minutes' walk of the junction of Atatürk Caddesi and Eski Belediye Sokak.

Eray Pansiyon PENSION €
(✆223 1647; www.eraypansiyon.com; Eski Belediye Sokak 12; dm per person TL20) One of few communal dorm rooms in Central Anatolia, the Eray is very good value. Smart marble stairs and sturdy brown doors lead to clean six-bed dorms, which are often unoccupied. The friendly owner speaks German.

4 Eylül Otel HOTEL €€
(✆222 3799; www.dorteylulotel.com; Atatürk Caddesi 15; s/d/tr TL70/120/150; 🖳) The discreet entrance next to the Akbank ATM sets the tone for this low-key hotel, where rooms have dark wood, minibars concealed in tables and paintings of Ottoman mansions. There is a rooftop restaurant and the popular hotel offers a similar experience to the Sultan but for less money. Breakfast is TL17.50.

Otel Madımak HOTEL €
(✆221 8027; Eski Belediye Sokak 2; s/d/tr TL60/90/115) This rebuilt 1st-floor hotel has comfortable digs with a burgundy theme, right down to the chairs and tiled bathrooms. Be aware, however, that the name has sad resonances.

Sultan Otel HOTEL €€
(✆221 2986; www.sultanotel.com.tr; Eski Belediye Sokak 18; s/d/tr TL90/140/170) The perfect mix of quality and price, with ample extras including a roof bar-restaurant with live music, safes built into the TV cabinets, extensive breakfast buffets and free hot drinks. Oh, and the bathrooms are virtually as big as the rooms themselves. Popular with business travellers midweek.

Sivas Büyük Otel LUXURY HOTEL €€€
(✆225 4763; www.sivasbuyukotel.com; İstasyon Caddesi; s/d/tr TL120/190/225; 🖳) Plain corridors and stately rooms characterise the city's original luxury hotel, a chunky seven-storey block laced with marble and mosaics. Refreshingly, one thing it's not short on is space. Breakfast is TL15.

Otel Köşk HOTEL €€
(✆225 1724; www.koskotel.com; Atatürk Caddesi 7; s/d/tr TL130/180/220; 🖳) You can't get much more modern than this towering glass block. From the fire-engine-red

seats in reception to the laminate floors, glass washbasins and curvy showers in the rooms, slick design rules. Even the views of the dive bar across Atatürk Caddesi manage to be cool thanks to the neon Efes sign.

🍴 Eating

On summer evenings everyone promenades along İnönü Bulvarı and Atatürk Caddesi, where stalls sell everything from *gözleme* to corn on the cob. There is a fruit and vegetable market around Subaşı Hanı.

TOP CHOICE **Sema Hanımın Yeri** ANATOLIAN €
(✆223 9496; İstasyon Caddesi Öncü Market; mains TL3.50-6; ◷8am-midnight) In this rustic, wood-panelled restaurant, the welcoming Madame Sema serves home-cooked food such as *içli köfte* (meatballs stuffed with spices and nuts). Watch *gözleme* being made while trying three dishes for TL4.

Büyük Merkez Lokantası LOKANTA €
(✆223 2354; Oyakbank Bitişiği Sultan Yanı; mains TL7; ◷4am-midnight) This *lokanta* is popular at lunchtime, when you may find yourself sharing a table with an office clerk. The menu includes döners and the house speciality *sebzeli Sivas kebapı* (TL14.50), a local take on the Tokat kebap.

Perde Café CAFE €
(✆223 2321; İstasyon Caddesi; snacks TL3-7; ◷10am-11pm) This two-storey hangout for teenagers and university students feels like a fun secret that everybody's keeping. Milkshakes, boardgames, burgers and waffles are the favourites; it's behind the Sivas Büyük Otel.

Edessa Lahmacun LAHMACUN €
(✆222 2638; Selçuklu Sokak; lahmacun TL4-8; ◷9am-11pm) The pick of the *lahmacun* joints is conveniently near the hotels and the friendly manager speaks serviceable English.

ℹ Information

Hemi (✆0506-273 4662; Tekel Sokak) This local sports association, which has English-speaking members, can give advice about skiing, scuba diving, rafting, canoeing, climbing and paragliding; the latter is popular on the hills above the city's university.

Sanem Internet Café (Tekel Sokak; per hr TL1; ◷8.30am-midnight)

Tourist office (✆222 2252; ◷9am-5pm Mon-Fri) In the European Union office on the first floor of the *valilik;* the helpful representatives give out brochures.

The original Otel Madımak was the site of one of modern Turkey's worst hate crimes, on 2 July 1993, when 37 Alevi intellectuals and artists were burned alive in a mob arson attack. The victims, who had come for a cultural festival, included Aziz Nesin, the Turkish publisher of Salman Rushdie's *Satanic Verses*. A crowd of 1000 extreme Islamist demonstrators gathered outside the hotel after Friday prayers to protest about the book's publication, and in the ensuing chaos the hotel was set alight and burned to the ground. The Madımak has since reopened (with a kebap shop in the foyer!).

Some groups are calling for it to be turned into a memorial, others want to see the trial of the Madımak suspects reopened, believing they were let off too lightly. Thirty-one death sentences, upheld in a 2001 appeal, were commuted to life in prison when Turkey abolished the death sentence the following year.

The scars from the tragedy show no signs of fading, and Sivas' name has become synonymous with the incident. Demonstrations and vigils take place in Sivas on the anniversary of the attack; in 2010, State Minister Faruk Çelik became the first Turkish politician to attend the annual memorial service, soon after announcing plans to expropriate the hotel for an official memorial site.

ℹ Getting There & Away

Bus

Bus services from Sivas aren't all that frequent. From the otogar (TL8 from the city centre by taxi) there are fairly regular services to Amasya (TL20, 3½ hours), Ankara (TL30, six hours), Diyarbakır (TL35, eight hours), Erzurum (TL30, seven hours), İstanbul (TL50, 13 hours), Kayseri (TL16, three hours), Malatya (TL20, four hours), Samsun (TL30, six hours) and Tokat (TL12, 1½ hours).

Yenişehir-Terminal dolmuşes (TL0.70) pass the otogar and end their run just uphill from the Paşa Camii, a five-minute walk from the hotels on Atatürk Caddesi and Eski Belediye Sokak.

Train

Sivas **station** (☎221 7000) is a major rail junction for both east–west and north–south lines. The main daily east–west express services, the *Doğu Ekspresi* and the *Erzurum Ekspresi*, go through Sivas to Erzurum and Kars (16 hours) or back to Ankara and İstanbul (22 hours); the *Güney Ekspresi* (from İstanbul to Kurtalan) runs four times a week in either direction and the *Vangölü Ekspresi* (between İstanbul and Tatvan) runs twice in either direction. There are also local services to Kangal, Divriği and Amasya (five hours).

'İstasyon' dolmuşes run from the station to Hükümet Meydanı and the Paşa Camii.

Around Sivas

Balıklı Kaplıca   SPA
(Hot Spring with Fish; ☎469 1151; www.balikli.org, in Turkish; visitor/patient TL5/30; ⊙8am-noon & 2-6pm) Visiting (and bathing) at the health spa at Balıklı Kaplıca is a satisfyingly unusual experience from the moment you enter Kangal, 12km southwest of the resort. The tiny service town gave its name to the black-faced, pale-bodied Kangal dogs seen throughout Turkey and a statue of a spiky-collared mutt guards the approach from Sivas.

A shepherd boy is said to have discovered the healing qualities of the local mineral water, which is high in the dermatologically curative element selenium. Amazingly, the warm water is inhabited by 'doctor fish', which not only live at a higher temperature than most fish can survive at, but nibble fingers, toes and any other body part you offer them. The fish supposedly favour psoriasis-inflicted skin and the spa attracts patients from all over the world, but the swarming school happily gets stuck into any patch of flesh. It is wonderfully therapeutic to dangle your feet in the water and feel nature giving you a thorough pedicure, with the nippers tickling and then soothing like tiny vacuum cleaners.

The spa complex has six sex-segregated pools set amid trees, and a hotel (r & ste TL80-125; @) with a buffet restaurant, a cafe above the mineral water, a weighing machine and some massage chairs. Rates depend on whether you define yourself as 'normal' or 'ill'; the recommended course for genuine patients is eight hours a day in the pool for three weeks! If you are staying overnight, full board costs TL35 extra; half-board TL20.

ℹ Getting There & Away

Minibuses from the terminal beside Sivas' otogar run to Kangal (TL5, one hour), from where you can take a taxi to the resort (TL20). Balıklı Kaplıca offers group transfers from Sivas.

Kangal train station is served by three daily services to/from Sivas (TL2.50, 4¼ hours) and the daily *Doğu Ekspresi* and *Erzurum Ekspresi* to/from Erzurum (TL10, 11 hours).

Divriği

📞 0346 / POP 14,500

Arriving in Divriği from the west, the village has an aged feel, perhaps because it lies on the edge of Anatolia's distinct eastern region. It is also a dead end, in a valley between 2000m-plus mountains, and you must detour 100km to the northwest to continue into eastern Anatolia by car or bus. But there are three good reasons to come here: a trio of 780-year-old stone doorways, which are so intricately carved that some say their craftsmanship proves the existence of god. The doors belong to one of Turkey's finest old religious structures, Divriği's mosque-*medrese* complex, which is remarkably undervisited despite its inclusion on the Unesco World Heritage list.

Divriği village occupies a fertile valley and still has an agricultural economy. Its population is mostly made up of Alevis. The narrow streets conceal a busy market, post office, internet cafe, some simple restaurants and a couple of banks with ATMs; there are petrol stations on the main road.

◉ Sights

FREE **Ulu Cami & Darüşşifa**   MOSQUE
(Grand Mosque & Mental Hospital; ⊗8am–5pm) Uphill from the town centre stands the beautifully restored Ulu Cami and Darüşşifa, adjoining institutions founded in 1228 by the local *emir* Ahmet Şah and his wife, the lady Fatma Turan Melik.

It's the ornamental gateways overlooking the village that put Divriği on the map (and the World Heritage list). The entrances to both the Ulu Cami and the Darüşşifa are truly stupendous, their reliefs densely carved with a wealth of geometric patterns, stars, medallions, textured effects and intricate Arabic inscriptions, all rendered in such minute detail that it's hard to imagine the stone ever started out flat. It's the tasteful Ottoman equivalent of having a cinema

in your house, the sort of thing only a provincial *emir* with more money than sense could have dreamt of building.

Inside the hospital, built on an asymmetrical floor plan, the stone walls and uneven columns are completely unadorned. The octagonal pool in the court has a spiral run-off, similar to the one in Konya's Tile Museum (see p442), which allowed the tinkle of running water to break the silence of the room and soothe patients' nerves. A platform raised above the main floor may have been for musicians who likewise soothed the patients. The building was used as a *medrese* from the 18th century.

The mosque is also very simple inside, with 16 columns, carpets, some fresco fragments and a plain *mihrab*. The valley views from the terrace outside are equally impressive, as is the entrance facing the clifftop castle, with more detailed stonework.

The complex is generally open during the listed hours, but if you find it locked, ask around and someone will probably find the key.

ℹ Getting There & Away

Minibuses from Sivas to Divriği (TL12, three hours), 176km southeast, depart from the minibus terminal. Services are infrequent and you may speed up your journey by changing in Kangal. It is possible to get there and back in a day from Sivas, but if you do not start early, you may have to stay the night at Balıklı Kaplıca (p437).

A return taxi ride from Sivas, stopping in Balıklı Kaplıca and Divriği, costs about TL190. Take some ID as there is sometimes a police checkpoint between Kangal and Divriği.

The train station is about 1.5km north of the Ulu Cami, served by trains including the daily Doğu Ekspresi and Erzurum Ekspresi between Sivas (TL6, 4¼ hours) and Erzurum (TL12, 7½ hours).

Drivers should note that there's no through road to Erzincan from Divriği, forcing you to head northwest to Zara and the highway before you can start driving east.

Konya

📞 0332 / POP 762,000

Turkey's equivalent of the 'Bible Belt', Konya treads a delicate path between its historical significance as the home town of the whirling dervish orders and a bastion of Seljuk culture on the one hand, and its modern importance as an economic boom town on the other. The city derives considerable charm from this juxtaposition of old and new. Ancient mosques and the mazey market district rub up against contemporary Konya around Alaaddin Tepesi, where hip-looking university students talk religion and politics in the tea gardens. If you are passing through this region, say from the coast to Cappadocia, bear in mind that the wonderful shrine of the Mevlâna is one of Turkey's finest and most characteristic sights.

History

Almost 4000 years ago the Hittites called this city 'Kuwanna'. It was Kowania to the Phrygians, Iconium to the Romans and then Konya to the Turks. Iconium was an important provincial town visited several times by Sts Paul and Barnabas. There are few remains of its early Christian community, but Sille (p447) has several ruined churches.

From about 1150 to 1300 Konya was capital of the Seljuk Sultanate of Rum, which encompassed most of Anatolia. The Seljuk sultans endowed Konya with dozens of fine buildings in an architectural style that was decidedly Turkish, but had its roots in Persia and Byzantium. Traditionally Konya lay at the heart of Turkey's rich farming 'bread basket', but these days light industry and pilgrimage tourism are at least as important.

◉ Sights

Mevlâna Museum   MUSEUM
(☑351 1215; admission TL2; ⊙9am-6.30pm Tue-Sun, 10am-6pm Mon) For Muslims and non-Muslims alike, the main reason to come to Konya is to visit the Mevlâna Museum, the former lodge of the whirling dervishes. On religious holidays the museum (really a shrine) may keep longer hours.

Celaleddin Rumi, the Seljuk Sultanate of Rum, produced one of the world's great mystic philosophers. His poetry and religious writings, mostly in Persian, the literary language of the day, are among the most beloved and respected in the Islamic world. Rumi later became known as Mevlâna (Our Guide) to his followers.

Rumi was born in 1207 in Balkh (Afghanistan). His family fled the impending Mongol invasion by moving to Mecca and then to the Sultanate of Rum, reaching Konya by 1228. His father, Bahaeddin Veled, was a noted preacher, known as the Sultan of Scholars, and Rumi became a brilliant student of Islamic theology. After his father's death in 1231, he studied in Aleppo and Damascus, returning to live in Konya by 1240.

In 1244 he met Mehmet Şemseddin Tebrizi (Şemsi Tebrizi or Şems of Tabriz), one of his father's Sufi (Muslim mystic) disciples. Tebrizi had a profound influence on Rumi but, jealous of his overwhelming influence on their master, an angry crowd of Rumi's disciples put Tebrizi to death in 1247. Stunned by the loss, Rumi withdrew from the world to meditate, and wrote his greatest poetic work, the 25,000-verse *Mathnawi* (*Mesnevi* in Turkish). He also wrote many aphorisms, *ruba'i* and *ghazal* poems, collected into his 'Great Opus', the *Divan-i Kebir*.

Tolerance is central to Mevlâna's teachings, as in this famous verse:

Come, whoever you may be,
Even if you may be
An infidel, a pagan, or a fire-worshipper, come.
Ours is not a brotherhood of despair.
Even if you have broken
Your vows of repentance a hundred times, come.

Rumi died on 17 December 1273, the date now known as his 'wedding night' with Allah. His son, Sultan Veled, organised his followers into the brotherhood called the Mevlevi, or whirling dervishes.

In the centuries following Mevlâna's death, over 100 dervish lodges were founded throughout the Ottoman domains. Dervish orders exerted considerable conservative influence on the country's political, social and economic life, and numerous Ottoman sultans were Mevlevi Sufis (mystics). Atatürk saw the dervishes as an obstacle to advancement for the Turkish people and banned them in 1925, but several orders survived on a technicality as religious fraternities. The Konya lodge was revived in 1957 as a 'cultural association' intended to preserve a historical tradition.

For Muslims, this is a very holy place, and more than 1.5 million people visit it a year, most of them Turkish. You will see many people praying for Rumi's help. When entering, women should cover their heads and shoulders, and no one should wear shorts.

A guide is not essential, but if you want to hire one, recruit a professional through the tourist office rather than engaging one of the carpet salesmen at the entrance.

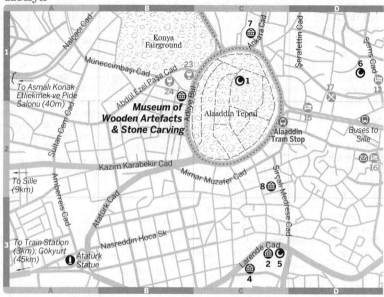

Konya

Visiting the Museum

The lodge is visible from some distance, its fluted dome of turquoise tiles one of Turkey's most distinctive sights. After walking through a pretty courtyard with an ablutions fountain and pictures narrating the Mevlâna story, you remove your shoes and pass into the Tilavet (Quran reading) room, also known as the calligraphy room due to its calligraphic displays.

turbans) and 10 to lodge leaders (with white turbans).

Mevlâna's tomb dates from Seljuk times. The mosque and *semahane,* where whirling ceremonies were held, were added later by Ottoman sultans (Mehmet the Conqueror was a Mevlevi adherent and Süleyman the Magnificent made charitable donations to the order). Selim I, conqueror of Egypt, donated the Mamluk crystal lamps.

The small mosque and *semahane* to the left of the sepulchral chamber contain exhibits such as musical instruments, the original copy of the *Mathnawi,* Mevlâna's prayer rug, and a 9th-century gazelle-skin Christian manuscript. There is a casket containing strands of Mohammed's beard, with holes in the display case to smell the hair's scent of roses, and a copy of the Quran so tiny that its author went blind writing it. This was actually a mark of honour in the Ottoman Empire, which prized miniature art; grains of rice inscribed with prayers are also on display. Look to the left of the *mihrab* for a *seccade* (prayer carpet) bearing a picture of the Kaaba at Mecca. Made in Iran of silk and wool, it's extremely fine, with some three million knots (144 per square centimetre).

The rooms surrounding the courtyard were once the dervishes' offices and quarters – one near the entrance is decorated as it would have been in Mevlâna's day, with mannequins dressed as dervishes. Look out for the wooden practice board, used by novice dervishes to learn to whirl. Across from the museum entrance is the **Selimiye Camii**, built between 1566 and 1574 when Sultan Selim II was the governor of Konya.

Museum of Wooden Artefacts & Stone Carving
MUSEUM

(Tas ve Ahsap Eserler Müzesi; ☑351 3204; Adliye Bulvarı; admission TL3; ☺9am-noon & 1.30-5.30pm) On the western side of Alaaddin Tepesi is the İnce Minare Medresesi (Seminary of the Slender Minaret), now the Museum of Wooden Artefacts & Stone Carving. It was built in 1264 for Seljuk vizier Sahip Ata, who may have been trying to outdo the patron of the contemporaneous Karatay Medresesi.

The extraordinarily elaborate doorway, with bands of Arabic inscription, is more impressive than the small building behind it. The octagonal minaret in turquoise relief is over 600 years old and gave the seminary

At the entrance to the mausoleum, the Ottoman silver door bears the inscription, 'Those who enter here incomplete will come out perfect'. Entering the mausoleum, look out for the big bronze *Nisan tası* (April bowl) on the left. April rainwater, vital to the farmers of this region, is still considered sacred and was collected in this 13th-century bowl. The tip of Mevlâna's turban was dipped in the water and offered to those in need of healing. Also on the left are six sarcophagi belonging to Bahaeddin Veled's supporters who followed him from Afghanistan.

Continue through to the part of the room directly under the fluted dome. Here you can see **Mevlâna's Tomb** (the largest), flanked by that of his son Sultan Veled and those of other eminent dervishes. They are all covered in velvet shrouds heavy with gold embroidery, but those of Mevlâna and Veled bear huge turbans, symbols of spiritual authority; the number of wraps denotes the level of spiritual importance. Bahaeddin Veled's wooden tomb stands on one end, leading devotees to say Mevlâna was so holy that even his father stands to show respect. There are some 65 sarcophagi on the platform, not all visible; 55 belong to Mevlâna's family (with green

its popular name. If it looks short, this is because the top was sliced off by lightning. Inside, many of the carvings feature motifs similar to those used in tiles and ceramics. The Seljuks didn't heed Islam's traditional prohibition of human and animal images: there are images of birds (the Seljuk double-headed eagle, for example), humans, lions and leopards. The *eyvan* in particular contains two delightful carvings of Seljuk angels. The Ahşap Eserler Bölümü (Carved Wood Section) contains some intricately worked wooden doors.

FREE **Tombstone Museum**   MUSEUM
(Mezar Anıtlar Müzesi; 353 4031; Sırçalı Medresi Caddesi; 8.30am-5.30pm) Several other Seljuk monuments lurk in the narrow warren of streets to the south of Alaaddin Tepesi. Look for the pint-sized **Kadı Mürsel Camii**, then turn down the side of it, opposite the brown school building with the blue sign. After a few minutes you'll come to another Seljuk seminary, the **Sırçalı Medrese** (Glass Seminary), named after its tiled exterior. Sponsored by the Seljuk vizier Bedreddin Muhlis, the 13th-century building houses a small Tombstone Museum, with a collection of tombstones featuring finely carved inscriptions. The *eyvan* on the western side of the courtyard was used for classes; it is decorated with blue tiles and its arch has a band of particularly fine calligraphic tile work.

Archaeological & Ethnographic Museums   MUSEUMS
Beside the Sahib-i Ata Külliyesi, the **Archaeological Museum** (351 3207; Larende Caddesi; admission TL3; 9am-12.30pm & 1.30-5pm Tue-Sun) is like a continuation of the museum at Çatalhöyük, with neolithic finds including the skeleton of a baby girl, clutching jewellery made of stone and bone. Artefacts range across the millennia, from chalcolithic terracotta jars to Hittite hieroglyphs, an Assyrian oil lamp shaped like a bunch of grapes, and bronze and stone Roman sarcophagi, one narrating the labours of Hercules in high-relief carvings. Nearby, the dusty **Ethnographic Museum** (Larende Caddesi; admission TL3; 8.30am-noon & 1.30-5.30pm Tue-Sun) has a good collection of Ottoman craftwork, including some keys the size of 21st-century doors.

FREE **Koyunoğlu Museum**   MUSEUM
(Kerimler Caddesi 25; 8.30am-5.30pm Tue-Sun) This little-visited museum contains the legacy of Izzet Koyunoğlu. The railway inspector built up his esoteric collection of rare, er, collectables on his travels through Turkey. Our heart goes out to the tired-looking stuffed pelican, but there is a wonderful variety of exhibits, encompassing prehistoric bones, rhinoceros-horn rosaries, boxwood spoons bearing words of wisdom about food, 19th-century carriage clocks, and old photos of Konya and whirling dervishes. Ask the guards to unlock the recreated **Koyunoğlu Konya Evi**, which shows how a well-heeled Konyalı family lived a century ago. Izzet lived in the original building with US$3 million of art around him. The quickest way to the museum lies alongside the **Üçler Cemetery**. Carry straight on at the roundabout at the end of the cemetery, taking the road just to the left of the garage. If you decide to walk through the graveyard, only do so during the day when other people are about; women are advised not to walk through alone.

Tile Museum   MUSEUM
(Karatay Müzesi; 351 1914; Alaaddin Meydanı; admission TL3; 9am-noon & 1.30-5.30pm) Housed in a former Seljuk theological school, this museum was closed for restoration when we visited. The building was constructed in 1251–52 by Emir Celaleddin Karatay, a Seljuk general, vizier and statesman who is buried in one of the corner rooms. The museum is well worth a look if it reopens before your visit; the outstanding collection of ceramics includes interesting octagonal Seljuk tiles.

Alaaddin Camii   MOSQUE
(8.30am-5.30pm) Konya's most important religious building after the Mevlâna shrine, this Seljuk mosque bestrides Alaaddin Tepesi. You may be able to wander in outside the listed opening hours. Built for Alaeddin Keykubad I, Sultan of Rum from 1219 to 1231, the rambling 13th-century building was designed by a Damascene architect in Arab style. Over the centuries it was embellished, refurbished, ruined and restored. Today, the mosque is entered from the east. The grand original entrance on the northern side incorporates decoration from earlier Byzantine and Roman buildings. The courtyard here features two huge Seljuk *türbes* (tombs), the left of which is the most impressive part of the complex, containing the blue-tiled tombs of 12th- and 13th-century notables. The mosque's exterior is otherwise plain, but the interior

has old marble columns surmounted with recycled Roman and Byzantine capitals. There's also a fine wooden *mimber* and an old marble *mihrab* framed by modern Seljuk-style blue-and-black calligraphy.

Sahib-i Ata Külliyesi   MOSQUE
(Sahib-i Ata Mosque Complex; ⊘9am-noon & 1-5pm) A few blocks south of the Tombstone Museum, along Sırçalı Medrese Caddesi, is this mosque complex. Behind its requisite grand entrance with built-in minaret is the Sahib-i Ata Camii, originally constructed during the reign of Alaaddin Keykavus. Destroyed by fire in 1871, it was rebuilt in 13th-century style. The *mihrab* is a fine example of blue Seljuk tile work. Alongside the mosque another grand gateway once led to a dervish lodge.

Dotted about town are other interesting mosques.

Şemsi Tebrizi Camii   MOSQUE
Contains the elegant 14th-century tomb of Rumi's spiritual mentor, in a park just northwest of Hükümet Meydanı.

Aziziye Camii   MOSQUE
Originally built in the 1670s and destroyed in a fire, this was rebuilt in 1875 in late-Ottoman, baroque and rococo styles. Located in the bazaar, it has twin minarets with sheltered balconies, and a sign pointing out its interesting features.

✸ Festivals & Events
The annual **Mevlâna Festival** (☎353 4020) runs for a fortnight, culminating on 17 December, the anniversary of Mevlâna's 'wedding night' with Allah. Tickets (and accommodation) should be booked well in advance; contact the tourist office or Selene Tourism for assistance. If you can't get a ticket, other venues around town host dancers during the festival, although they are not of the same quality. At other times of year, **semas** (Aslanı Kişla; ⊘8pm Sat) take place behind the Mevlâna Museum. Tickets to the one-hour performances are free and can be organised through travel agencies, hotels or the tourist office.

🛏 Sleeping
There's certainly no shortage of hotels in Konya, but the steady flow of pilgrims can lead to high prices.

TOP CHOICE ⟩ Ulusan Otel   HOTEL €
(☎351 5004; Çarşi PTT Arkasi 4; s/d from TL40/70) Behind the post office is this bril-

liant little hotel with spotless rooms, graceful management and hearty breakfasts. The shared bathrooms are palatial and immaculately kept, which puts some private bathrooms in Konya to shame. The pick of the town.

Mevlâna Sema Otel   HOTEL €
(☎350 4623; www.semaotel.com; Mevlâna Caddesi 67; s/d/tr TL50/75/100; ✸) With a great position, some swanky decor and comfortable, beige rooms, the Mevlâna Sema has a lot going for it. Ask for a room at the rear, away from noisy Mevlâna Caddesi.

Hotel Rumi   HOTEL €€
(☎353 1121; www.rumihotel.com; Durakfakih Sokak 5; s/d/tr/ste TL100/150/200/250; ✸@) Boasting a killer position near the Mevlâna Museum, the stylish Rumi's rooms and suites have an abundance of curvy chairs, slender lamps and mirrors. The palatial breakfast room with views of the museum, the friendly staff and the hamam make this an oasis of calm in central Konya.

Otel Mevlâna   HOTEL €
(☎352 0029; Cengaver Sokak 2; s/d/tr from TL40/60/85) Across Mevlâna Caddesi from Otel Bera Mevlâna, this friendly central option is a good choice for backpackers of both sexes. Rooms have firm beds, fridges, bathrooms and kitschy paintings.

Selçuk Otel   HOTEL €€€
(☎353 2525; www.otelselcuk.com.tr; Babalık Sokak 4; s/d/tr €60/100/125; ✸) Both comfort and character are on offer at the Selçuk, where fish tanks part a sea of beige seats in the lobby. Prices are high, but the facilities, decor and professional service are worth it.

Konya Deluxe Otel   HOTEL €€
(☎351 1546; Ayanbey Sokak 22; s/d TL80/150; ✸) This new hotel down the road from Rumi is clean and friendly with smallish rooms and spiffy bathrooms. It's a good option for solo travellers who prefer to remain solo.

Otel Derya   HOTEL €€
(☎352 0154; Ayanbey Sokak 18; s/d/tr TL50/80/100; ✸) Quiet and spotless, the Derya is a good choice for families and female travellers. Rooms are slightly bland, with pink bathrooms, TVs and minibars, but the management is friendly and efficient and overall it's recommended.

Otel Anı & Şems   HOTEL €€
(☎353 8080; www.hotelani.com; Şems Caddesi 6; s/d/tr €30/45/60; ✸) The mosque-side locale

DANCING WITH DERVISHES

The Mevlevi worship ceremony, or sema, is a ritual dance representing union with God; it's what gives the dervishes their famous whirl, and appears on Unesco's third Proclamation of Masterpieces of the Oral and Intangible Heritage of Humanity. Watching a sema can be an evocative, romantic, unforgettable experience. There are many dervish orders worldwide that perform similar rituals, but the original Turkish version is the smoothest and purest, more of an elegant, trancelike dance than the raw energy seen elsewhere.

The dervishes dress in long white robes with full skirts that represent their shrouds. Their voluminous black cloaks symbolise their worldly tombs, their conical felt hats their tombstones.

The ceremony begins when the hafız, a scholar who has committed the entire Quran to memory, intones a prayer for Mevlâna and a verse from the Quran. A kettledrum booms out, followed by the plaintive sound of the ney (reed flute). Then the şeyh (master) bows and leads the dervishes in a circle around the hall. After three circuits, the dervishes drop their black cloaks to symbolise their deliverance from worldly attachments. Then one by one, arms folded on their breasts, they spin out onto the floor as they relinquish the earthly life to be reborn in mystical union with God.

By holding their right arms up, they receive the blessings of heaven, which are communicated to earth by holding their left arms turned down. As they whirl, they form a 'constellation' of revolving bodies, which itself slowly rotates. The şeyh walks among them to check that each dervish is performing the ritual properly.

The dance is repeated over and over again. Finally, the hafız again chants passages from the Quran, thus sealing the mystical union with God.

may not look promising, but the interiors have a distinct charm. The rooms are worn but serviceable, with minibars and TVs, and there's an in-house travel agent.

✗ Eating

Konya's speciality is fırın kebap, slices of (hopefully) tender, fairly greasy oven-roasted mutton served on puffy bread. The city bakers also make excellent fresh pide topped with minced lamb, cheese or eggs, but in Konya pide is called etli ekmek (bread with meat). Be careful what you eat; if you ask a local to recommend a restaurant, they may mumble darkly about food poisoning. Some restaurants around the Mevlâna Museum and tourist office have great views, but their food is not recommended. The fast-food restaurants on Adilye Bulvarı, competing with the golden arches, are lively places for a snack, but check that the swift grub is thoroughly cooked.

Köşk Konya Mutfağı
CONTEMPORARY ANATOLIAN €
(☑352 8547; Mengüç Caddesi 66; mains TL8; ☺11am-10pm) Southeast of the centre, this excellent traditional restaurant is run by the well-known food writer Nevin Halıcı, who puts her personal twist on Turkish

classics. The service is excellent and the outside tables rub shoulders with vine-draped pillars and a fragrant rose garden. The menu features some unusual dishes like the mouth-clogging dessert höşmerim.

Gülbahçesı Konya Mutfağı
LOKANTA €
(☑351 0768; Gülbahçe Sokak 3; mains TL4-8; ☺8am-10pm) One of Konya's best restaurants, mostly because of its upstairs terrace with views of the Mevlâna Museum. Dishes include yaprak sarma, Adana kebap and etli ekmek. There are occasional sema performances.

Asmalı Konak Etliekmek ve Pide Salonu
PIDECI €
(☑322 7175; Babalık Mahallesi, Yahya Çavuş Caddesi 11/B; mains TL3-6; ☺8am-10pm) This tiny backstreet eatery rightfully claims the mantle of best köfte in Konya. The pides and salads aren't far behind either.

Aydın Et Lokantası
LOKANTA €
(☑351 9183; Şeyh Ziya Sokak 5e; mains TL4.50-7) This lokanta's decor centres on a fake green oak tree with an ailing goldfish in the pool at its base, but the open kitchen is reassuring. You can try etli ekmek here and the menu has English translations.

ANKARA & CENTRAL ANATOLIA AROUND ANKARA

Şifa Lokantası
KEBAPÇI €

(☑352 0519; Mevlâna Caddesi 29; mains TL5-8)
Tandır kebap tops Şifa's bill of standards.
Service can be pretty rushed when it's busy,
but at least there's a good view of the main
drag.

Bazaar
SELF-CATERING €

For self-caterers, the bazaar is the most
exciting place to buy produce.

Makromarket
SELF-CATERING €

(Mevlâna Caddesi) Supermarket.

Sürüm
SWEETS €

(İstanbul Caddesi) Sugar addicts can satisfy
their cravings at this chocolate shop,
established in 1926.

Drinking

In summer few things could be more pleasurable than relaxing in one of the innumerable tea gardens dotting the slopes of
Alaaddin Tepesi. As Konya is among Turkey's more devout Islamic cities, alcohol is
notably absent from all venues.

Osmanlı Çarşısı
CAFE

(☑353 3257; İnce Minare Sokak) Looking like
an apple-smoke-spewing pirate ship, this
early-20th-century house has terraces and
seats on the street, where students talk politics or just inhale a lungful.

Café Zeugma
CAFE

(☑350 9474; Adliye Bulvarı 33; cover charge
weekend TL3) With its backlit carvings and
strobes, this cavernous cultural centre is
quite popular with students for its live
music.

Shopping

Bazaar
BAZAAR

Konya's bazaar sprawls back from the modern PTT building virtually all the way to
the Mevlâna Museum, cramming the narrow streets with stalls, roving vendors and
the occasional horse-drawn cart. There's
a concentration of shops selling religious
paraphernalia and tacky souvenirs at the
Mevlâna Museum end.

Ikonium
FELT MAKER

(☑350 2895; www.thefeltmaker.net; Bostan
Çelebi Sokak 12a) Konya was traditionally a
felt-making centre but the art is fast dying out in Turkey. Passionate *keçeki* (felt-
maker) Mehmet and his Argentinean wife
Silvia offer treats including op-art-style
patterns and what might be the world's
largest hand-decorated piece of felt.

Information

Elma Net (Çinili Sokak 14; per hr TL1; ⊘10am-
11pm) Internet cafe.

Selene Tourism (☑353 6745; www.selene.
com.tr; Ayanbey Sokak 22b) Organises tours
and, during summer, dervish performances for
groups.

Tourist office (☑353 4020; Mevlâna Caddesi
21; ⊘8.30am-5.30pm Mon-Sat) Gives out a
city map and a leaflet covering the Mevlâna
Museum; can also organise guides for the
museum.

Dangers & Annoyances

Konya has a long-standing reputation for religious conservatism; you'll see more women in
religious headscarves here than in many other
towns, and you'll find Friday observed as a day
of rest in a way it rarely is elsewhere. None of
this should inconvenience you, but take special
care not to upset the pious and make sure
you're not an annoyance! If you visit during
Ramazan (see p15) don't eat or drink in public
during the day, as a courtesy to those who are
fasting.

Non-Muslim women seem to encounter more
hassle in this bastion of propriety than in many
other Turkish cities, and dressing conservatively
will help you avoid problems. Men can wander
around in shorts without encountering any tension, but may prefer to wear something longer to
fit in with local customs.

If you want a guide for the Mevlâna Museum,
try to arrange it through the tourist office rather
than hiring one of the carpet salesmen who loiter
at the museum entrance.

Male travellers have reported being proposi-
tioned in the Tarihi Mahkeme Hamamı.

Getting There & Away

Air

There are three flights every day to and from
İstanbul with **Turkish Airlines** (☑321 2100;
Ferit Paşa Caddesi; ⊘8.30am-5.30pm Mon-Fri,
8.30am-1.30pm Sat).

The airport is about 13km northeast of the
city centre; TL40 by taxi. Havaş was setting up
a shuttle-bus service at the time of research;
enquire at the tourist office.

Bus

Konya's **otogar** is about 7km north of Alaaddin
Tepesi, accessible by tram from town. Regular
buses serve all major destinations, including
Afyon (TL25, 3¾ hours), Ankara (TL20, four
hours), İstanbul (TL45, 11½ hours), Kayseri
(TL25, four hours) and Sivas (TL30, seven
hours). There are lots of ticket offices on Mevlâna Caddesi and around Alaaddin Tepesi.

The **Eski Garaj** (Old Bus Terminal or Karatay Terminal), 1km southwest of the Mevlâna Museum, has services to local villages.

Train

The **train station** (☎332 3670) is about 3km southwest of the centre. You can get to Konya by train from İstanbul Haydarpaşa (13½ hours) on the Meram Ekspresi, the Toros Ekspresi (İstanbul to Gaziantep) or the İç Anadolu Mavi (İstanbul to Adana), all via Afyon. A new direct, high-speed train link between Konya and Ankara, scheduled to open in 2010, will trim the journey time from 10½ hours to 1¼ hours.

ⓘ Getting Around

As most of the city-centre sights are easily reached on foot, you only need public transport to get to the otogar or train station. To get to the city centre from the otogar take any tram from the east side of the station to Alaaddin Tepesi (30 minutes); tickets, which cover two people, cost TL2.20. Trams run 24 hours, with one per hour after midnight. A taxi costs around TL25.

There are half-hourly minibuses from the train station to the centre (TL1.25). A taxi from the station to Hükümet Meydanı costs about TL15.

Innumerable minibuses ply Mevlâna Caddesi if you're heading to the far end (TL1).

Cars can be rented from **Decar** (☎247 2343; Özalan Mahallesi, Selçuklu), based at the Dedeman Konya Hotel.

Around Konya

ÇATALHÖYÜK

No, this isn't a hallucination brought on by the parched Konya plain. Rising 20m above the flatlands, the East Mound at Çatalhöyük (admission TL3; ☺8am-5pm) is left over from one of the largest neolithic settlements on earth. About 9000 years ago, up to 8000 people lived here, and the mound comprises 13 levels of buildings, each containing around 1000 structures.

Little remains of the ancient centre other than five excavation areas, which draw archaeologists from all over the world. If you visit between June and September, when the digs mostly take place, you might find an expert to chat to. At other times, the museum does a good job of explaining the site and the excavations, which began in 1961 under British archaeologist James Mellaart and have continued with the involvement of the local community. The museum's eight-minute video is worth watching before looking at the exhibits, which are mostly reproductions of finds now in Ankara's Museum of Anatolian Civilisations, including some of Anatolia's oldest pottery vessels, the world's oldest ceramic shaker and manmade mirror, and a representation of the mother goddess. Mellaart's controversial theories about mother-goddess worship here caused the Turkish government to close the site for 30 years.

Near the museum entrance stands the experimental house, a reconstructed mud-brick hut used to test various theories about neolithic culture. People at Çatalhöyük lived in tightly packed dwellings that were connected by ladders between the roofs instead of streets, and were filled in and built over when they started to wear out. Skeletons were found buried under the floors and most of the houses may have doubled as shrines. The settlement was highly organised, but there are no obvious signs of any central government system.

The site's guardian will happily show you the marquee-covered south area; a tip would probably be appreciated. With 21m of archaeological deposits, many of the site's most famous discoveries were made here. The lowest level of excavation, begun by Mellaart, is the deepest at Çatalhöyük and holds deposits left more than 9000 years ago. If you come during summer, you may be able to visit other excavation areas.

ⓘ Getting There & Away

To get here by public transport from Konya, 33km northwest, get the Karkın minibus, which leaves the Eski Garaj at 9am, noon and 3pm. Get off at Kük Koy (TL2.50, 45 minutes) and walk 1km to the site, or you may be able to persuade the driver to take you the whole way. Going back, minibuses leave Kük Koy at noon, 3pm and 5pm.

Alternatively, take a minibus from Eski Garaj to Çumra (TL3, 45 minutes) and then hire a taxi from beside the otogar for the last 11km (TL35 return).

You should get going early on both routes to give yourself time to tour Çatalhöyük and catch the last minibus back to Konya. A taxi from Konya to the site and back will cost about TL80.

GÖKYURT (KİLİSTRA, LYSTRA)

A little piece of Cappadocia to the south-west of Konya, the landscape at Gökyurt is reminiscent of what you'll see in Güzelyurt or the Ihlara Valley: a gorge with dwellings and medieval churches cut into the rock face, but without the crowds.

St Paul is thought to have stayed here on his three Anatolian expeditions and the area has long been a Christian pilgrimage site; especially for 12 months from June 2008, declared by Pope Benedict XVI as 'the year of St Paul' to celebrate the 2000th anniversary of the saint's birth.

There's one particularly fine church cut completely out of the rock, but no frescoes. A trip out here makes a lovely half-day excursion, and the surrounding landscape is simply stunning.

ⓘ Getting There & Away

The easiest way to get here from Konya, 45km away, is by car or taxi; the latter will charge TL120 return (including waiting time). There are several daily buses from Konya's Eski Garaj to Hatunsaray, 18km from Gökyurt, but taxis there are actually more expensive than from Konya as the drivers make the most of their captive audience. If enough Gökyurt villagers want to visit Konya, a minibus will travel to the city, and you can jump on the bus on its return journey.

Driving, you should take the Antalya road, then follow signs to Akören. After about 34km, and a few kilometres before Hatunsaray, look for a tiny brown-and-white sign on the right (marked 'Kilistra-Gökyurt, 16km'). Cyclists need to watch out for sheepdogs roaming about.

SİLLE
☎0332 / POP 2000

If you're looking for an excursion from Konya, head past the 'turtle crossing' road signs to the pretty village of Sille, a patch of green surrounded by sharp rocky hills. A rock face full of cave dwellings and chapels overlooks bendy-beamed village houses in several states of decay and a few bridges across the dry river.

The domed Byzantine **St Helen's Church** (Ayaelena Kilisesi), near the last bus stop, was reputedly founded by Empress Helena, mother of Constantine the Great. It was completely restored in 1833; the vandalised and fast-fading frescoes date from 1880. Despite its later use as a WWI military depot and a clinic where a German doctor attached artificial limbs, the church retains some of its old woodwork, including a broken pulpit and an iconostasis stripped of its icons. If you find it closed, ask at Sille Konak restaurant for the key.

On the hill to the north stands a small ruined chapel, the **Küçük Kilese**; it's worth the scramble up for the views over the village.

At **Sille Konak** (☎244 9260; mains TL5-9), a restored Greek house lovingly decorated by the family who run it, a team of headscarf-clad cooks rustles up home-cooked food. The owner will happily recommend dishes such as Konak kebap and *düğün* (soup with yoghurt, mint and rice, often served at weddings); order a selection, as portions are small.

There are a couple of cafes and a family restaurant at the entrance to the village, overlooking the glass-studded hamam.

ⓘ Getting There & Away

Bus 64 from Mevlâna Caddesi (near the post office) in Konya leaves every half-hour or so (less often on Sunday) for Sille (TL1.10, 25 minutes).

Karaman
☎0338 / POP 252,400

After the fall of the Seljuk Empire, central Anatolia was split into several different provinces with different governments, and for some time Karaman served as a regional capital. Although little visited these days, it boasts a selection of fine 13th- and 14th-century buildings and makes a base for excursions to Binbirkilise (p448).

The **Hacıbeyler Camii** (1358) has a magnificent squared-off entrance, with decoration that looks like a baroque variant on Seljuk art. The **Mader-i Mevlâna (Aktepe) Cami** (1370) is the burial place of the great

---

HAN SWEET HAN

The Seljuks built a string of *hans* (caravanserais) along the route of the 13th-century Silk Road through Anatolia. These camel-caravan staging posts were built roughly a day's travel apart (about 15km to 30km), to facilitate trade. Expenses for construction and maintenance of the *hans* were borne by the sultan, and paid for by the taxes levied on the rich trade in goods.

As well as the Sultanhanı, fine specimens include the Sarıhan (p469), 6km east of Avanos, and the Karatay Han, 48km east of Kayseri. Many other *hans* dot the Anatolian landscape, including the Ağzıkara Hanı (p489), 16km northeast of Aksaray on the Nevşehir highway, and the Sultan Han (p494), 45km northeast of Kayseri off the Sivas highway.

Mevlâna's mother and has a dervish-style felt hat carved above its entrance. The adjacent hamam is still in use.

The tomb of the great Turkish poet Yunus Emre is beside the Yunus Emre Camii (1349). Extracts from his verses are carved into the walls of a poetry garden to the rear of the mosque.

The slightly disorganised Karaman Museum (Turgut Özal Bulvarı; admission TL3; ☺8am-noon & 1-5pm Tue-Sun) contains cave finds from nearby Taşkale and Canhasan and has a fine ethnography section. Next door, the magnificent Hatuniye Medresesi (1382), whose ornate portal is one of the finest examples of Karaman art, now houses a restaurant.

If you get caught in Karaman overnight, the two-star Nas Hotel (☎214 4848; İsmetpaşa Caddesi 30; r TL50) is low on luxury but comfortable, welcoming to travellers of both sexes and close to the sights.

ℹ Getting There & Away

Regular buses link Karaman with Konya (TL20, two hours) and Ereğli (TL20, two hours). Getting to Karaman from Nevşehir (Cappadocia) is more time-consuming, as you must change in Niğde and Ereğli. The Toros Ekspresi and İç Anadolu Mavi trains (see p446) stop here between Konya and Adana.

Binbirkilise

Just before WWI, the great British traveller Gertrude Bell travelled 42km northwest of Karaman and recorded the existence of a cluster of Byzantine churches set high on a lonely hillside and rather generously known as Binbirkilise (1001 Churches). Later Irfan Orga came here in search of the last remaining nomads, a journey recorded in his book *The Caravan Moves On*. You won't see any nomads around these days, or indeed much to mark the ruins out as churches, but half a dozen families live around the ruins (and in them, in the case of some of their animals) and the site is a rural alternative to busier attractions.

It's easiest to reach the churches with your own transport. Drive out of Karaman on the Karapınar road and follow the yellow signs. The first sizeable ruin pops up in the village of Madenşehir, 36km north, after which the road becomes increasingly rough. There are fantastic views all along the road, which is just as well, as you'll have to come back the same way.

A taxi from Karaman's otogar should cost around TL100 for the return trip; the drivers know where the churches are.

Sultanhanı

0382

The highway between Konya and Aksaray crosses quintessential Anatolian steppe: flat grasslands as far as the eye can see, with only the occasional tumbleweed and a fist of mountains in the distance breaking the monotony. Along the way, 110km from Konya and 42km from Aksaray, is the dreary village of Sultanhanı, its only redeeming feature being one of several Seljuk *han* bearing that name. This stunning Sultanhanı (admission TL3; ☺7am-7pm), 200m from the highway, is the largest in Anatolia.

The site is a popular stop for tour groups, and you may field invitations to visit the nearby carpet-repair workshop. If you resist such offers, you could easily explore Sultanhanı in half an hour.

The building was constructed in 1229, during the reign of the Seljuk sultan Alaaddin Keykubad I and restored in 1278 after a fire (when it became Turkey's largest *han*). Through the wonderful carved entrance in the 50m-long east wall, there is a raised *mescit* (prayer room) in the middle of the open courtyard, which is ringed with rooms used for sleeping, dining and cooking. A small, simple doorway leads to the atmospheric *ahır* (stable), with arches, domes and pillars in the pigeon-soundtracked gloom.

ℹ Getting There & Away

Regular buses run from Aksaray's otogar Monday to Friday (TL5, 45 minutes); there are fewer services at weekends. Leaving Sultanhanı, flag down a bus or village minibus heading to Aksaray or Konya on the main highway. If you start out early you can hop off the bus, see the *han* and be on your way again an hour or so later.

Cappadocia

Best Places to Stay

» Esbelli Evi (p473)
» Serinn House (p473)
» Kelebek Hotel & Cave Pension (p456)
» Koza Cave Hotel (p457)
» Gamirasu Hotel (p478)
» Flintstones Cave Hotel (p459)

Best Places to Eat

» Ziggy's (p476)
» Seten Restaurant (p461)
» Aravan Evi Restaurant (p478)
» Elai (p465)

Why Go?

When Erciyes Daği erupted many millennia ago, no one could've guessed the aftermath would look so dandy. This 'land of wild horses' is eerie, beautiful and geologically unique. Where lava once ran valleys now undulate to the horizon's dusty hilt. The human history here is equally remarkable, most notably that of the Byzantines, whose underground world features frescoes and intimate, cavernous rock-cut churches. Travellers descend on the prehistoric moonscape from hot-air balloons and low-cost carriers, as the poster child of Anatolian tourism continues to define its unselfconscious style. Göreme is the village-turned-'buzz town', where outdoor enthusiasts are rivalled by the cultured set enjoying fine local wine and deluxe cave suites. Meanwhile, Ürgüp and Uçhisar provide a more upscale, down-tempo prehistoric escape; former Greek settlements offer peace and quiet; and, outside, colourful valleys twist and turn, shot through with wildflowers, snow or giant phallic boulders. Cappadocia is an ultimate trip.

When to Go

Kayseri

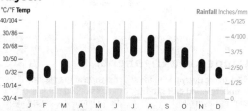

June Brilliant roses shock the stark desert moonscape in Rose Valley and beyond.

July to September Listen to classical music concerts in natural outdoor rock venues.

November to March Disperse the snow bunnies atop Erciyes Daği, a rugged Turkski spot.

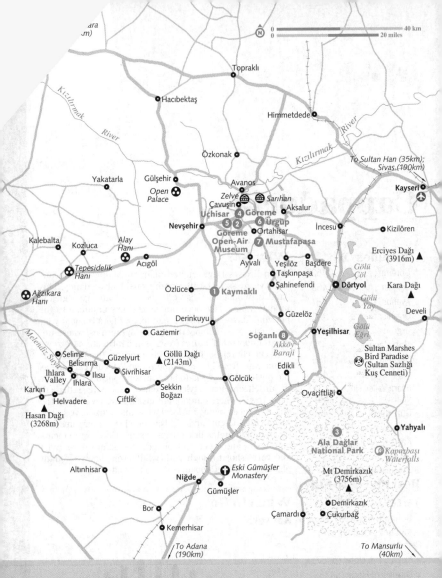

Cappadocia Highlights

1 Explore Byzantine tunnels of **underground cities** (p481), such as Kaymaklı

2 Examine fresco-covered churches in the **Göreme Open-Air Museum** (p452)

3 Tackle nature in the waterfalls and trails of **Ala Dağlar National Park** (p481)

4 Gaze at the pigeon houses riddling cliffs and fairy chimneys (thin spires of rock) in Göreme's labyrinthine **valleys** (p457)

5 Gasp at the outcrop doubling as a castle in **Uçhisar** (p463)

6 Drink in the views over multiple mezes in chic **Ürgüp** (p472)

7 Part the vines and peer into a tumbledown Greek mansion in **Mustafapaşa** (p478)

8 Trek through a secluded monastic settlement in **Soğanlı** (p480)

History

The Hittites settled Cappadocia (Kapadokya) from 1800 BC to 1200 BC, after which smaller kingdoms held power. Then came the Persians, followed by the Romans, who established the capital of Caesarea (today's Kayseri). During the Roman and Byzantine periods, Cappadocia became a refuge for early Christians and, from the 4th to the 11th century, Christianity flourished here; most churches, monasteries and underground cities date from this period. Later, under Seljuk and Ottoman rule, Christians were treated with tolerance.

Cappadocia progressively lost its importance in Anatolia. Its rich past was all but forgotten until a French priest rediscovered the rock-hewn churches in 1907. The tourist boom in the 1980s kick-started a new era, and now Cappadocia is one of Turkey's most famous and popular destinations.

Dangers & Annoyances

If travelling to Cappadocia by bus, make absolutely sure that your ticket clearly states that it is for Göreme; having it state 'Cappadocia' is not enough. With this proof, you will be able to insist on a free shuttle transfer if your driver attempts to set you off in nearby Nevşehir (even if it means refusing to get off the bus!). If you find yourself in trouble, phone your hotel to arrange onward transport or call a taxi.

For more information about transport from Nevşehir's otogar (bus station), see p469 and p470.

Walking in central Cappadocia's valleys is a wonderful experience and should not be missed, but lone travellers, particularly women, should take care there. Solo travellers who do not want to hire a guide are advised to avoid the areas away from Göreme et al in the evening.

Tours

Travel agents abound in Cappadocia. Prices are usually determined by all operators at the beginning of each season. Make your decision based on the quality of the guide and the extent of the itinerary.

Most tour companies offer either full-day tours, guided day hikes or an Ihlara Valley trip.

Similarly priced, **full-day tours** often take in one of the underground cities, a stretch of the Ihlara Valley and one of the caravanserais, but others go to Soğanlı and Mustafapaşa.

Guided day hikes are usually in the Rose, Sun, Red or Pigeon Valleys. Costs vary according to the destination, degree of difficulty and length, but should not exceed those of the full-day tours as less motor transport and petrol are involved.

A full day, the **Ihlara Valley trip** includes a guided hike and lunch; most operators charge TL60 to TL70, but prices go up to TL90.

Most itineraries finish at a carpet shop, onyx factory or pottery workshop, but it is still worth taking a tour. It is interesting to see a traditional Cappadocian craftsman at work, but make it clear before the trip begins if you are not interested. Most of the pensions either operate their own tours or work with one of the travel agencies.

We strongly advise you to avoid booking an expensive tour package upon arrival in İstanbul. If your time is limited and you want to take a tour in Cappadocia, you're better off booking a tour directly from an agent in Cappadocia itself.

For listings of tour agencies, see p455 (for Göreme), p466 (Çavuşin), p467 (Avanos) and p472 (Ürgüp).

Getting There & Away

AIR Two airports serve central Cappadocia: Kayseri and Nevşehir. Operators include Turkish Airlines (www.thy.com), Onur Air (www.onurair.com) and Sun Express (www.sunexpress.com).

BUS Buses from İstanbul to Cappadocia travel overnight (in high summer there may also be day buses) and bring you to Nevşehir, where there should be a *servis* to take you to Uçhisar, Göreme, Avanos or Ürgüp. From Ankara you can travel more comfortably during the day.

TRAIN The nearest train stations are at Niğde and Kayseri. See p483 and p492 for information about services.

Getting Around

TO/FROM THE AIRPORT The easiest solution is to request your hotel or pension in Cappadocia to pick you up, though transfer buses operate between Kayseri airport and accommodation in central Cappadocia. The buses pick up from and drop off to hotels and pensions in Ürgüp, Göreme, Uçhisar, Avanos and Nevşehir, and cost TL15 (for Ürgüp) to TL20 (for the other destinations). If you want to use the service you *must* pre-book by phone or email with Argeus Tours (p472) in Ürgüp if you fly Turkish Airlines; or through Peerless Travel Services (p472), also in Ürgüp, if you fly Onur Air or Sun Express.

OLD GÖREME RESTORATION FUND (OGRF) *PAT YALE*

Once upon a time Old Göreme was full of lovely honey-coloured cave-houses that blended gently into the background so that they looked almost as if they had sprung straight out of it. Today the village is a conservation area but over the decades a lot of incidental ugliness has developed as people used breeze blocks and other cheap materials to carry out repairs and extensions. The Old Göreme Restoration Fund (www.goremecharity.com) was set up in 2007 to pay for small improvements to the visual environment, in particular to replace some of the concrete with natural stone. With funding from Intrepid Travel in Australia and other generous individuals it has refaced some breeze block walls, cleaned up old fountains and reopened viewpoints that had been blocked. To raise money it holds twice-yearly 'Open House' events, when visitors are able to see some of the privately owned homes. It's a rare chance to see how carefully the old houses were designed to suit a lifestyle in which almost all foodstuffs were laboriously homemade.

Until the 1970s most Göreme residents made their living from farming and kept pigeons so that their droppings could be used for manure. The arrival of chemical fertilisers put an end to the pigeons and the coming of tourism saw most people abandoning their fields too. The OGRF has now cleaned out some of the old pigeon houses, and invested in a new generation of pigeons. The hope is to restart some farming here and then perhaps sell produce such as organic apricot jam to the hotels. Ultimately this might make it possible to provide some work other than in tourism for the village.

Pat Yale works for OGRF and is a resident of Göreme.

CAR & MOTORCYCLE Cappadocia is great for self-drive visits. Roads are often empty and their condition is reasonable. There is ample parking space but pulling up outside some cave hotels might be tricky.

PUBLIC TRANSPORT Belediye Bus Corp dolmuşes (TL1.85 to TL2.10 depending on where you get on and off) travel between Ürgüp and Avanos via Ortahisar, the Göreme Open-Air Museum, Göreme village, Çavuşin and (on request) Paşabağı and Zelve. The services leave Ürgüp every two hours between 8am and 4pm (6pm in summer) and Avanos between 9am and 5pm (7pm in summer). You can hop on and off anywhere around the loop.

There's also an hourly *belediye* (municipal council) bus running from Avanos to Nevşehir (TL4) via Çavuşin (10 minutes), Göreme (15 minutes) and Uçhisar (30 minutes). It leaves Avanos from 7am to 6pm.

The Ihlara Valley in southwest Cappadocia can be visited on a tour from Göreme; it is difficult to visit in a day by bus, as you must change in Nevşehir and Aksaray.

TAXI Taxis are a good option for moving from town to town. Meters operate but a negotiated price is also welcome.

Göreme

📞 0384 / POP 6350

Göreme is a remarkable honey-coloured village that continues to send travellers giddy. There are enough unexplored trails nearby

to keep your horse happily unbridled for days. The sun sets pink in Rose Valley and almost always on a honeymoon terrace. An amble around rock-cut churches or a picnic at the feet of Roman pigeon houses high atop caramel cliffs is both stirring and strange. The Open-Air Museum is an all-in-one testament to Byzantine life. Yet with only a handful of local families still living the dream – and another new pension at every turn – the village can feel on the cusp of theme-park status. Fortunately, serious efforts are being made to preserve a modicum of village life, and, for now, there's still nowhere in the world like Göreme.

⦿ Sights & Activities

Göreme Open-Air Museum MUSEUM
(📞271 2167; Göreme Açık Hava Müzesi; admission TL15; ⊗8am-5pm) One of Turkey's World Heritage sites, the Göreme Open-Air Museum is an essential stop on any Cappadocian itinerary and deserves a two-hour visit. First an important Byzantine monastic settlement that housed some 20 monks, then a pilgrimage site from the 17th century, the cluster of rock-cut churches, chapels and monasteries is 1km uphill from the centre of the village.

Follow the cobbled path until you reach **Aziz Basil Şapeli**, the chapel dedicated to Kayseri-born St Basil, one of Cappadocia's most important saints. The grate-covered holes in the floor were the graves of the chapel's architects and financiers; the small boxes contained less-affluent folks' bones. In the main room, St Basil is pictured on the left; a Maltese cross is on the right, along with St George and St Theodore slaying a (faded) dragon, symbolising paganism. On the right of the apse, Mary holds baby Jesus, with a cross in his halo.

Above Aziz Basil Şapeli, bow down to enter the 12th-century **Elmalı Kilise** (Apple Church), overlooking a valley of poplars. Relatively well preserved, it contains both simple, red-ochre daubs and professionally painted frescoes of biblical scenes. The Ascension is pictured above the door. The church's name is thought to derive from an apple tree that grew nearby or from a misinterpretation of the globe held by the Archangel Gabriel, in the third dome.

Byzantine soldiers carved the **Azize Barbara Şapeli** (Chapel of St Barbara), dedicated to their patron saint, who is depicted on the left as you enter. They also painted the mysterious scenes on the roof – the middle one could represent the Ascension; above the St George representation on the far wall, the strange creature could be a dragon, and the two crosses, the beast's usual slayers. The decoration is typical of the iconoclastic period, when images were outlawed – red ochre was painted on the stone without any images of people or animals.

Uphill, in the **Yılanlı Kilise** (Snake Church or Church of St Onuphrius), the dragon is still having a bad day. To add insult to its fatal injuries, it was mistaken for a snake when the church was named. The hermetic hermaphrodite St Onuphrius is pictured on the right, holding a genitalia-covering palm leaf. Straight ahead, the small figure next to Jesus is one of the church's financiers.

The museum's most famous church, the stunning, fresco-filled **Karanlık Kilise** (Dark Church; admission TL8), is definitely worth the extra outlay. The supplementary fee is due to its costly renovation, and an attempt to keep numbers down and preserve the frescoes. One of Turkey's finest surviving churches, it took its name from the fact that it originally had very few windows.

Just past the Karanlık Kilise, the small **Azize Katarina Şapeli** (Chapel of St Catherine) has frescoes of St George, St Catherine and the Deesis.

The 13th-century **Çarıklı Kilise** (Sandal Church) is named for the footprints marked in the floor, representing the last imprints left by Jesus before he ascended to heaven. The four gospel writers are depicted below the central dome; in the arch over the door to the left is the Betrayal by Judas.

Downhill, the cordoned-off **Rahibeler Manastırı** (Nun's Convent) was originally several storeys high; all that remains are a large plain dining hall and, up some steps, a small chapel with unremarkable frescoes.

When you exit the museum, don't forget to cross the road and visit the **Tokalı Kilise** (Buckle Church), 50m down the hill towards Göreme. Covered by the same ticket, it is one of Göreme's biggest and finest churches, with an underground chapel and fabulous frescoes painted in a narrative (rather than liturgical) cycle. Entry is via the 10th-century 'old' Tokalı Kilise, through the barrel-vaulted chamber with frescoes portraying the life of Christ. Upstairs, the 'new' church, built less than a hundred years later, is also alive with frescoes on a similar theme. The holes in the floor once contained tombs, taken by departing Christians during the population exchange (p634).

El Nazar Kilise   CHURCH
(Church of the Evil Eye; admission TL8; ⊘8am-5pm) On the road between Göreme and the Open-Air Museum, a sign points to the 10th-century El Nazar Kilise. Carved from a ubiquitous cone-like rock formation, the church has been restored and is considerably quieter than the Open-Air Museum, although its frescoes are in worse condition. It's a pretty 10-minute walk from the main road.

ⓘ VISITING THE MUSEUM

» Arrive early in the morning, at midday, or near closing to bypass tour groups.

» Avoid weekends if possible.

» Don't scrounge on the church – it's worth the extra TL8.

» Your ticket is valid all day if you want to leave and come back.

» The museum is an easy 1km walk from town.

» Beware the sun – this is an 'open-air' museum.

Göreme

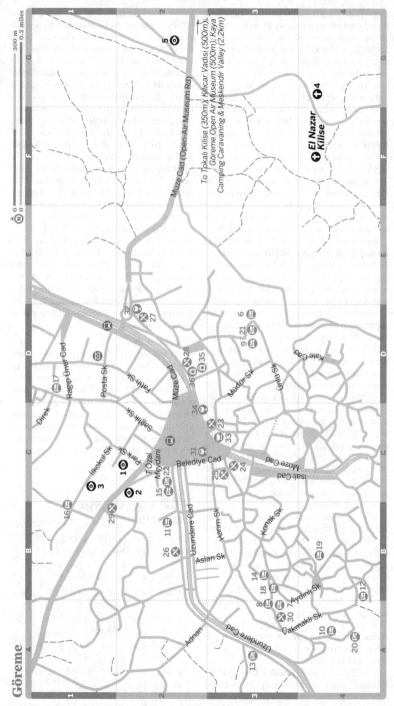

300 m
0.2 miles

To Tokalı Kilise (350m); Kılıçcar Vadisi (500m);
Göreme Open-Air Museum (500m); Kaya
Camping Caravaning & Meskendir Valley (2.2km)

Müze Cad (Open-Air Museum Rd)

El Nazar Kilise

Ragıp Üner Cad

Posta Sk

Fatih Sk

Sağlık Sk

Direk

İlkokul Sk

Park Sk

T Özal
Meydanı

Müze Cad

Belediye Cad

Müdür Sk

Ünlü Sk

Kale Cad

İsali Cad

Müze Cad

Uzundere Cad

Harım Sk

Aslan Sk

Konak Sk

Aydınlı Sk

Çakmaklı Sk

Adnan

Uzundere Cad

Saklı Kilise   CHURCH
Back towards the Open-Air Museum, a yellow sign points to the Saklı Kilise (Hidden Church). When you reach the top of the hill, follow the track to the left and look out for steps leading downhill to the right.

UFO Museum   MUSEUM
(admission TL3; ⊙9am-7pm) ET says *hoş geldiniz* (welcome) at this UFO Museum that is as unassuming as a midnight visitor. Mostly consisting of magazine cuttings displayed haphazardly on cave walls, the exhibition ends with video footage of a possible seven-UFO sighting in Göreme.

Elis Kapadokya Hamam   HAMAM
(☑271 2974; Adnan Menderes Caddesi; admission TL35, massage TL10; ⊙10am-midnight) Unwind after the chimney-spotting and treat yourself to a thorough massage at the beautiful Elis Kapadokya Hamam, which has mixed and women-only areas.

☞ Tours

The following tour businesses have been recommended by Lonely Planet readers or can be vouched for by us. However, the list is by no means exhaustive.

Yama Tours   GUIDED TOUR
(☑271 2508; www.yamatours.com; Müze Caddesi 2) Offers three-day trips to Nemrut Dağı (€150), leaving on Monday and Thursday. An excellent choice of tour with an incredibly friendly owner/guide, Mehmet.

Middle Earth Travel   TREKKING
(☑271 2559; www.middleearthtravel.com; Cevizler Sokak 20) The adventure-travel specialist offers climbing and treks ranging from local, one-day expeditions (€30 to €40) to one-week missions along the Lycian Way or St Paul's Trail, through the Kaçkar Mountains or up Mt Ararat.

Heritage Travel   GUIDED TOUR
(☑271 2687; www.turkishheritagetravel.com; Yavuz Sokak 31) Local tours with the knowledgeable Mustafa are highly recommended (TL60 for four people minimum and €100 for a private tour). It's based at the Kelebek Hotel & Cave Pension. The company also offers traditional Turkish weddings and longer packages such as two-week cuisine tours (€2800).

EKREM ILHAN

When Persia ruled Turkey (see p624), Katpatuka (Cappadocia) was famous throughout the empire for its beautiful horses. In Iran's Persepolis palace, among the reliefs depicting delegates from Persia's subject states, visitors from Katpatuka are pictured with equine offerings.

It seems appropriate, then, that present-day Göreme has a horse whisperer. Ekrem Ilhan brings wild horses to Göreme from Erciyes Dağı (Mt Erciyes), where a tribe of 400 has grown as local farmers have replaced them with machinery.

'They are in shock when they arrive here, but when their eyes open they see me, talking and giving them sweet things,' he says. 'People teach animals to bite and kick, because they are angry with them. But when you're friends, and you talk to them and give them some carrot and cucumber, you don't have any problems.'

Looking like a Cappadocian Clint Eastwood in a hat brought from America by a carpet-dealing friend, Ilhan tells a story about two pregnant mares he returned to Mt Erciyes to give birth. 'One year later, I went into the mountains, among the 400 horses, and called their names and they came directly to me.'

Ilhan treats the 11 horses in his cave stable using homemade remedies, such as grape water to extract parasites, and olive oil, mint and egg for indigestion. He has started a trekking company, called **Dalton Brothers** (☑0532 275 6869; 2hr TL50), at the suggestion of a Canadian traveller and *Lucky Luke* fan. 'People like wild horses because it's difficult riding in the mountains, it's rocky, and the horses are used to it,' he says.

Göreme-born Ekrem Ilhan and Dalton Brothers are based at the stables behind the Anatolian Balloons office in Göreme.

New Goreme Tours GUIDED TOUR
(☑271 2166; www.newgoreme.com; El Sanatlari Carsis 24) Fun and friendly private tours.

Nomad Travel GUIDED TOUR
(☑271 2767; www.nomadtravel.com.tr; Müze Caddesi 35) Offers an excellent Soğanlı tour.

Neşe Tour NEMRUT DAĞI TOUR
(☑271 2525; www.nesetour.com; Avanos Yolu 54) Offers trips to Nemrut Dağı (Mt Dağı) lasting between two and four days.

Alpino Tours GUIDED TOUR
(☑271 2727; www.alpino.com.tr; Müze Caddesi 5) A well-established company offering good local and national expeditions.

⚡ Festivals & Events

Klasik Keyifler CHAMBER MUSIC
(☑0532 614 4955; www.klasikkeyifler.org) Klasik Keyifler is an innovative organisation run by an American musician that holds chamber music concerts by Turkey's brightest stars in intimate natural settings. The summer series hits Cappadocia in July and August, when you can hear the sounds of Schumann bouncing off the Hidden Valley walls. Workshops run in conjunction with the performance.

🛏 Sleeping

If you're visiting between October and May, pack warm clothes as it gets very cold at night and pension owners may delay putting the heating on. Ring ahead, too, to check that your choice is open. There is a cluster of rock-cut retreats on Aydınlı Hill (around Orta Mahallesi Camii), gazing across the fairy-chimney-punctured village.

TOP CHOICE **Kelebek Hotel & Cave Pension**
CAVE HOTEL €€
(☑271 2531; www.kelebekhotel.com; Yavuz Sokak 31; fairy chimney s/d €28/35, deluxe s €35, d €45-70, ste €70-180; @☒) It's reassuring to know the oldie is still the goodie and the 'Butterfly' is still alight in the heart of Göreme. Local guru Ali Yavuz leads a charming team at the village's original boutique hotel that has seen a travel industry virtually spring from beneath its stunning terrace. The pension proper is spread over two gorgeous stone houses with each fairy chimney protruding skyward, everything skilfully restored and Anatolian-ised. On the lowest level are 10 larger suites facing an incredible summer garden and private dining area where smitten guests (and guests of guests!) recover from the most luxurious hamam experience in Cappado-

cia. Next door is the newly opened Sultan Cave Suites, overseen by friendly Mehmet, which offers quieter cave retreats, slightly removed from the gentle hubbub of the bustling Kelebek breakfast scene.

TOP CHOICE **Koza Cave Hotel** CAVE HOTEL €€
(☎271 2466; www.kozacavehotel.com; Aydınlı Mahallesi, Cakmaklı Sokak 49; s/d €70/90, deluxe r €120; @) Beautiful new 'Cocoon' is the inspiration of Dervish, who recently returned after decades spent living in Holland. The same Dutch eco-sensibility has given Cappadocia's hoteliers a valuable lesson in sustainable tourism. Luckily for guests Dervish doesn't sacrifice style and comfort in the pursuit of sustainable living, as each stunning room is either hand-crafted or uses recycled materials. Highly recommended.

Köse Pension HOSTEL €
(☎271 2294; www.kosepension.com; Ragıp Üner Caddesi; dm TL15, s without bathroom TL25, tw hut TL50, d & tw with bathroom TL80, tr with/without bathroom TL90/75; ☎) A complete refurbishment in early 2009 and the tireless efforts of Scottish owner Dawn and her Turkish husband Mehmet help to ensure Köse will remain a travellers' favourite for years to come. A range of spotless rooms suited to all budgets feature brilliant bathrooms, bright linens and comfortable beds. The three-course Turkish feast for TL15 is up there with the best value in Cappadocia and the swimming pool and gardens are lovingly attended. Köse is a real winner for families and independent folk alike. It's set in a small residential area close to the otogar.

WALKS AROUND GÖREME

Göreme village is surrounded by the magnificent Göreme National Park. A handful of valleys are easily explored on foot; each needs about one to three hours. Most are interconnected, so you could easily combine several in a day, especially with the help of the area's many dolmuşes (minibuses).

For example, you can walk to the Göreme Open-Air Museum and have a look around, then catch a Belediye Bus Corp *otobus* to Ürgüp, which stops outside the museum at 10 minutes past every even hour, to Zelve (TL2). Ask the driver to stop there or he may head straight to Avanos on the main road. It may be possible to get off further on at Aktepe (for Devrent Valley). Walk back to Göreme from Zelve via Paşabağı, Çavuşin and Meskendir Valley, Rose Valley and Red Valley. Don't forget a bottle of water and sunscreen!

Some of the most interesting and accessible valleys:

Bağlıdere (White Valley) From Uçhisar to Çavuşin.

Güllüdere (Rose Valley) Connecting Çavuşin and Kızılçukur viewpoint.

Güvercinlik (Pigeon Valley) Connecting Göreme and Uçhisar; colourful dovecotes.

İçeridere (Long Valley) Running south from Rock Valley Pension.

Kılıçlar Vadısı (Swords Valley) Running off the Göreme Open-Air Museum road.

Kızılçukur Vadısı (Red Valley) Superb dovecotes and churches with frescoes.

Meskendir Valley Trail head next to Kaya Camping; tunnels and dovecotes.

Zemi Valley (Love Valley) West of the Göreme Open-Air Museum, with some particularly spectacular rock formations.

A word of warning: most of the valleys have signposts directing you to them, but nothing to keep you on the straight and narrow once you get there. Nor are they all particularly easy to walk, and there's no detailed map available – you'll have to rely on basic printouts. If you are exploring the Meskendir Valley area, it is easier to get lost if you climb out of the valleys.

Mehmet Güngör (☎0532 382 2069) is one local guide with an encyclopedic knowledge of Göreme's highways and byways. Most pension owners will also happily guide you for a minimal fee (it may even be complimentary).

CAPPADOCIA FROM ABOVE

If you've never taken a flight in a hot-air balloon, Cappadocia is one of the best places in the world to try it. Flight conditions are especially favourable here, with balloons operating most mornings from the beginning of April to the end of November. It's a truly magical experience and many travellers judge it to be the highlight of their trip.

Flights take place at dawn. The reputable companies have an unwritten agreement that they will only offer one early flight per day due to the fact that the winds can become unreliable and potentially dangerous later in the morning. Transport between your hotel and the balloon launch site is included in the hefty price, as is a champagne toast.

You'll quickly realise that there's a fair amount of hot air between the operators about who is and isn't inexperienced, ill-equipped, underinsured and unlicensed. Be aware that hot-air ballooning can be dangerous. It's your responsibility to check the credentials of your chosen tour operator carefully and make sure that your pilot is experienced and savvy – even if it means asking to see their licences and logbooks. And don't pick the cheapest operator if it means they might be taking short cuts with safety (eg operating two flights per day).

It's important to note that the balloons travel with the wind, and that the companies can't ensure a particular flight path on a particular day. All companies try to fly over the fairy chimneys, but sometimes – albeit rarely – the wind doesn't allow this. Occasionally, unfavourable weather conditions mean that the pilot will cancel the flight for the day for safety reasons; if this happens you'll be offered a flight on the next day or will have your payment refunded. All passengers should take a warm jumper or jacket and women should wear flat shoes and trousers. Children under seven and adults over 70 will not be taken up by most companies.

The following agencies have good credentials:

Ez-Air Balloons (☑0384-341 7096; www.ezairballoons.com; Kavaklionu Mahallesi 8a, Ürgüp) Running since 1991, and offering the services of veteran pilot Hasan Ezel, Ez-Air charges €160 for a one-hour-minimum flight. Its two balloons have capacities of eight and 20 passengers.

Butterfly Balloons (☑0384-271 3010; www.butterflyballoons.com; Uzundere Caddesi 29, Göreme) The new wing of Heritage Travel is a seamless operation, with superlative pilots Mustafa, the first Turkish citizen to gain a US pilot's licence, and Englishman Mike, who has vast international experience and is a fellowship member of the Royal Meteorological Society. Flights costs around €175 a pop.

Kapadokya Balloons (☑0384-271 2442; www.kapadokyaballoons.com; Adnan Menderes Caddesi, Göreme) The premium balloon airline, partly because it is the only operator to change its launch site based on wind direction, ensuring the most scenic flight path. Run by Kaili and Lars, who kicked off Göreme's ballooning industry 20 years ago, and their team of four multilingual pilots, the company offers an exclusive deluxe flight (adult €250, child aged six to 12 €125, at least 1½ hours, 10 passengers) and a sponsored flight (€175, one hour, up to 20 passengers).

Sultan Balloons (☑0384-353 5249; www.sultanballoons.com; Kaktus Sokak 21, Mustafapaşa Kasabası, Ürgüp) Established in 2005 by long-time chief pilot Ismail Keremoglu, the company offers a standard flight (€160, one hour) in its 12- and 20-passenger balloons. It is the only operator to offer VIP flights for two passengers in a small balloon (€600 for two, 1¼ hours).

Fairy Chimney Inn CAVE HOUSE €€
(☑271 2655; www.fairychimney.com; Güvercinlik Sokak 5-7; s/d/tr from €33/55/66, students €22; @) At the high point of Göreme is this highbrow retreat run by Dr Andus Emge and his lovely wife, who offer academic asides to their wonderful hospitality. The views from the garden and various peepholes are magnificent, while the rooms temper the senses with simple furniture, traditional textiles and an understated Byzantine class. Communal meals in the tranquil garden area will invariably induce happiness.

Travellers' Cave Hotel
CAVE HOTEL €€

(✆271 2780; www.travellerscave.com; Görçeli Sokak 7; s/d/tr €45/55/75, deluxe €65-75, ste €105-120; @) Friendly Bekir presides over an excellent newish midrange hideaway at the top of Aydınlı Hill. Removed from the village hubbub, the Travellers has a variety of rooms sprawled between, at, in, under and around stone staircases. Our pick is room 17, delightfully tucked away with its own private courtyard. The hotel's communal terrace is huge and magnificent and the food reassuringly Turkish. The attentive staff speak good English and can swiftly arrange all sorts of rocky, rolling tours. Bekir also runs a recommended pension, with slightly cheaper digs, on the other side of the village.

Flintstones Cave Hotel
HOSTEL €

(✆271 2555; www.theflintstonescavehotel.com; Uzundere Caddesi, Karşıbucak Sokak 3; dm incl/excl breakfast TL20/15, s/d TL20/40, with jacuzzi TL40/60; @☎) The premium budget joint in Göreme has outlived its party reputation to outshine many budget rivals. An expansion includes 11 slick jacuzzi rooms in a spacious new wing, while dorm raiders should seek out the five-bedder with communal areas and private bathroom. The large swimming pool is the best in town and the slate surface and numerous reclining chairs make it a sunbathing paradise. The huge bar replete with pool table and giant noticeboard is a bundle of potential activity. The kitchen also makes use of an organic vegetable patch. Owners Fatih and Mehmet are fun and professional.

Aydınlı Cave House
CAVE HOTEL €€

(✆271 2263; www.thecavehotel.com; Aydınlı Sokak 12; tw €60, ste €70-110; @) Lovely little Aydınlı gets it right on every level. Proprietor Mustafa has masterfully converted his family home into a six-room haven for honeymooners and those requiring a little rock-cut style with their solitude. Guests rave about the warm service and immaculate, spacious cave rooms, formerly used for drying fruits, storing wheat and making wine. If children are in tow, take the family suite, which includes an active tandoor oven and antique kitchen utensils. Couples should nab room 3, with the rock balcony and slick Turkish hamam taps.

Canyon View Hotel
CAVE HOTEL €€

(✆271 2333; www.canyonviewhotel.com; Yavuz Sokak; s/d/tr TL50/65/75, with jacuzzi TL60/85/100; @) If you're tired of prehistoric living then this understated and classy conversion of a 9th-century church and Byzantine house offers a choice of winery, pigeon house and stable. Owners Seyit and Hasan proudly furnish the rooms with ceramic aplomb and host satisfied guests with arms open to what we reckon is the best terrace view in town.

Kaya Camping Caravaning
CAMPGROUND €

(✆343 3100; kayacamping@www.com; Göreme Yolu; camp sites per adult/child TL15/10; @☎) This impressive camping ground is 2.5km from the centre of Göreme town, uphill from the Göreme Open-Air Museum. Set among fields of vines and a good sprinkling of trees, it has magnificent views and top-notch facilities such as clean bathrooms, plentiful hot water, a restaurant, supermarket, communal kitchen and washing machines. It's an excellent place for a family holiday, particularly as it has a large swimming pool complete with kiddie pool and sun lounges.

Shoestring Cave Pension
CAVE PENSION €

(✆271 2450; www.shoestringcave.com; Aydınlı Mahallesi; dm TL15, r per person with/without bathroom TL35/25; @☎) This rocky remnant of old-school backpacker paradise was one of the first and remains one of the best budget options in town. The unimpressive entrance gives way to an impressive rock wall fitted with musty dorm and cave rooms. The courtyard restaurant and adjacent travel office are packed with travellers jousting over the merits of their respective itineraries. The management can be overly keen to book guests in for tours but you can find respite in the semi-swank double rooms and cool rooftop swimming pool.

Walnut House
HOTEL €

(✆271 2235; www.cevizliev.com; Karşıbucak Caddesi; s/d/tr TL25/45/65; @) Located right by the otogar, the Walnut is a chestnut for wizened solo travellers who value convenience over hilly ascents and remember when Göreme was just a blip on the guidebook landscape. The newer rooms are superior for their shiny bathrooms and forgiving beds. The lush rose garden and liberal spread of kilims (woven rugs) give the old Ottoman mansion an authentic saving grace.

Divan Cave House
CAVE PENSION €€

(✆271 2189; www.divancavehotel.com; Aydınlı Mahallesi; s/d TL40/80; @) This charming newcomer located in a peaceful hilltop neighbourhood offers a stylish abode at better-than-budget value. The brand spanking new rooms are tastefully prepared by Osman and

DR ANDUS EMGE: ANTHROPOLOGIST

Tell us what you do in Göreme.

Ten years after my ethnologic research in Cappadocia I came back and bought an old ramshackle cave dwelling, which now functions as the base for the Cappadocia Academy and its 'Fairy Chimney' guesthouse. I am involved in several pilot projects related to Cappadocia and continue with my academic work on the region.

How can travellers get involved?

Travellers should take advantage of the unique characteristics of the region by choosing traditional cave dwellings as accommodation and asking their hosts to serve local products from Cappadocia to support a regional sustainable agriculture.

What aspects of traditional cave life should we try to retain?

The local cave dwellings are not only good for storing things, but they are also ideal for living. They are cool in summer and warm in winter. Instead of building new houses with air-conditioning one could take advantage of typical regional characteristics for future building.

What hopes do you have for the future of Göreme?

I hope that subregional building characteristics don't get totally lost and that the Unesco World Heritage Site of Göreme-Cappadocia will present itself in a modern individual way, avoiding total 'Disneyfication' of the tourism sector.

Describe your dream cave house.

After restoring an old cave house, I am now thinking about realising a modern, functional, low-energy cave dwelling, which would combine current architectural design forms with the location-specific advantages.

his courteous staff who also serve simple breakfasts in a flower-filled, spacious courtyard. With a quiet locale and open surrounds, this could be the start of a good thing.

Cappadocia Cave Suites   CAVE HOTEL €€€
(☏271 2800; www.cappadociacavesuites.com; Ünlü Sokak 19; d/ste from TL210/340; @) A forerunner in luxury cave living, this open, inviting premises still maintains an edge on many top-end rivals due to its uncomplicated service, spacious, modern-meets-megalithic suite rooms and cool, converted stables. Fairy Chimney 1 (US$280) is our pick for its cosy living room ideal for balloon viewing. The restaurant also comes highly recommended. Avoid the double rooms if possible.

Vezir Cave Suites   CAVE HOTEL €€
(☏271 2069; www.vezircavesuites.com; Gaferli Mahallesi Ünlü Sokak 24; d/ste €70/95; @) Newcomer Vezir offers a classic cave hotel experience reminiscent of more expensive top-end hotels. The eight rooms are spotless and stylish, cut deep into the rockface. Each contains countless alcoves that bounce

soft light against spare, quality furniture. The modern showers, private balconies and friendly staff make this a smart choice.

Kismet Cave House   CAVE HOTEL €€
(☏271 2416; www.kismetcavehouse.com; Kağnı Yolu 9; d TL120-160) Kismet's fate is assured as guests consistently hail the intimate experience created by the unobtrusive Faruk and his family at this honest-to-impending-greatness Anatolian cave house. The eight rooms – all attentively drawn with local antiques and colourful rugs – include en suite bathrooms with jacuzzis and mostly stunning views. The smaller downstairs rooms can be a bit noisy at times – try to book an arched one upstairs. Day trips are available throughout Cappadocia and come highly recommended.

Elysee Pension   PENSION €€
(☏271 2244; www.elyseegoreme.com; Orta Mahallesi, Mizraz Sokak 18; s/d/tr TL50/70/90, deluxe TL130-150, ste TL200-240; @) Highly recommended by readers is this cute little pension in a restored farmhouse with colourful touches throughout. The charismatic manag-

er, Cengiz, arranges excellent hiking trips to surrounding valleys. The rose garden is shaded by pear trees and naturally enough, given the name, French and English are spoken.

Anatolian Houses · CAVE HOTEL €€€
(☑271 2463; www.anatolianhouses.com.tr; Gaferli Mahallesi, Ünlü Sokak; ste €250-800; @ 🕿) This bastion of underground opulence in Cappadocia hits and misses. If you nail room 302 or 402, you'll have a five-star experience with your own terrace and rooms decorated with stylish pottery and gorgeous wooden antiques. Elsewhere though rooms can be gloomy and compact for the price. The onsite wellness centre, including hamam and indoor/outdoor swimming pool, is suitably decadent, though guests have complained about poor service.

Kemal's Guest House · CAVE PENSION €
(☑271 2234; www.kemalsguesthouse.com; Karşıbucak Caddesi; dm incl breakfast TL20, s/d/tr/q TL50/75/105/120) The large Ottoman and cave rooms at evergreen Kemal's may not always meet the squeaky-clean standards of Göreme's boutique lodging scene but Kemal is a terrific cook and his Dutch wife Barbara knows her way around the region's hiking trails like perhaps no other hotelier. Pull up a comfy sofa in reception, grab a dog-eared book off the shelf and thumb your nose at your 'boutique' friends.

✗ Eating

There is a strip of good eateries on the quiet side of the dry canal, away from the busy Bilal Eroğlu Caddesi.

TOP CHOICE · Seten Restaurant · ANATOLIAN €€
(☑271 3025; www.setenrestaurant.com; Aydınlı Mah; mains TL15-25; ⊗11am-11pm) This brand-new project for the enterprising Kelebek crew is the centrepiece of a proposed cultural centre dedicated to preserving the historical flavour of Göreme. Fortunately, the food matches the glorious setting. Named after the old millstones used to grind bulgur wheat, this restaurant is an education for newcomers to Anatolian cuisine and a treat for well-travelled tongues. Signature chefs and attentive service complement classic dishes done right and a dazzling array of mezes done differently enough to keep you coming back.

Orient Restaurant · MODERN TURKISH €€
(☑271 2346; Adnan Menderes Caddesi; mezes TL8, mains TL12-40, 3-course set menus TL20) Göreme's most atmospheric restaurant

swoons under the weight of its own reputation as coupled-up diners nestle behind an extensive wine list. Juicy steaks, tender veal clay pots and a stack of flavoursome pasta dishes head the impressive, meaty menu. It's easy to order poorly though, as the cold mezes are oily, and the fish is dry. A safe bet is the decent three-course set menu (TL20). Service is delightful.

Nazar Börek · BÖREKÇİSİ €
(☑271 2441; Müze Caddesi; mains TL7) This expat and industry hangout joint on the canal serves simple yet delicious meals, and the atmosphere is eternally fun and friendly. Fresh plates of *börek* (filled pastries), *gözleme* (savoury pancakes) and *sosyete böregi* (stuffed spiral pastries served with yoghurt and tomato sauce) are presented by jovial men with can-do attitudes. The canal-side chill-out area is where you'll get the skinny on local people and places.

Dibek · ANATOLIAN €
(☑271 2209; Hakkı Paşa Meydanı 1; mains TL10-12; ⊗9am-11pm) An ancient agricultural theme pervades this warm family restaurant set inside a 475-year-old building, still churning out strong, homemade wine. Diners sprawl on cushions in low-lit alcoves and feast on dishes such as *saç tava* (cubed lamb with tomatoes, peppers and garlic; TL13) and *kurufasulye* (white beans with tomato sauce and optional sun-dried lamb; TL6). Many groups book ahead (at least three hours) for the slow-cooked *testi kebap* ('pottery kebap', with meat or mushrooms and vegetables cooked in a sealed terracotta pot, which is broken at the table; TL18).

Fırın Express · PIDECI €
(☑271 2266; Eski Belediye Yanı Sokak; pide & pizza TL4-8, mains TL8-13; ⊗11am-11pm) Simply the best *lahmacun* (very thin Turkish pizza) and pide in town are found in this local haunt that also does take away *(paket)* by the boxload. The cavernous wood oven fires up meat and vegetarian options and anything doused with egg. Traditional stews are also available but we suggest an *ayran* (yoghurt drink) and a *çoban salatası* (sheperd's salad) for a delicious bargain feed.

Local Restaurant · MODERN TURKISH €
(☑271 2629; Müze Caddesi 38; mains TL11-20) This reliable upper-echelon eatery stands on its own en route to the Open-Air Museum, and stands out for its wholesome continental meat dishes including stews, steaks, lamb shanks and *tavuklu mantarli krep* (chicken

RUDE BOYS

The *peribacalar* (fairy chimneys) that have made Cappadocia so famous were formed when erosion wiped out the lava covering the tuff (consolidated volcanic ash), leaving behind isolated pinnacles. They can reach a height of up to 40m, have conical shapes and are topped by caps of harder rock resting on pillars of softer rock. Depending on your perspective, they look like giant phalluses or outsized mushrooms. The villagers call them simply *kalelar* (castles).

and mushroom pancake). The white tablecloths and stone-walled terrace provide some consolation for indifferent service.

Meeting Point Café   INTERNATIONAL €
(Müze Caddesi; mains TL10) Missing your favourite comfort foods? Cenap and Anniesa, a Turkish–South African couple, dish up curries, burgers, fruit smoothies, filter coffee and home-baked cakes. Sit on the balcony above the canal or in the cabin-like restaurant. Also sells a good selection of secondhand English-language books.

Hanim Sofrası   LOCAL €
(🖉 271 2932; Uzundere Caddesi 46; mains TL8)
On the road to Flintstones Cave, this newly opened, gigantic concrete restaurant also doubles as a function centre for local weddings. The home-cooked local dishes are cheap, fresh and tasty, including *balmya* (okra), *menemen* (scrambled eggs and vegetables) and various *şiş*. It's a relaxing escape from the main drag.

Cappadocia Kebap Center   KEBAPÇI €
(🖉 271 2682; Müze Caddesi; mains TL3.50) This tiny, friendly joint is a great place for a fast feed. You can enjoy a chicken döner kebap sandwich for a mere TL3 or *acılı ezme* (spicy tomato and onion paste) kebap sandwich for TL4, accompanied by chips (TL3.50) and a beer (TL3.50) or fresh orange juice (TL3).

🍺 Drinking

Fat Boys   PUB
(🖉 0535 386 4484; Belediye Caddesi; mains TL7; 🕙24hr) The premier party joint in the village is akin to an office break room, but is surprisingly cool, with suitably loud poprock tunes, two large pool tables, classic bar

food (think burger, fries and, er, Vegemite), all overseen by an Australian-Turkish couple with a penchant for the waterpipe and for long, generous pours.

Red Red Wine House   BAR
(🖉 271 2183; Müze Caddesi) *Stay close to me-e-e!* In a former stable with arched ceilings, this seductive local feels like an ancient bootlegger's secret mixing den decorated by lovers of adult contemporary. A steady chain of guests smoke fruity pipes and sip increasingly palatable Cappadocian wines; hot, cold or shimmering at room temperature. It's open year round to honour the memory of former visitor Carlos Santana, whose spirit continues through live music most nights.

Mydonos Cafe & Bistro   CAFE
(Müze Caddesi 18) Recently opened, this cute little upstairs coffee shop and cakery plays cruisy jazz tunes to a young Turkish crowd jostling for seats with knowledgeable locals. We loved the honey cake as much as the plate it sat on.

Flintstones Cave Bar   BAR
(Müze Caddesi) Retaining 'it' club status with the closure of some other after-hours joints, Flintstones is more than just another licensed hole-in-the-rock. It's a favourite among young foreign single somethings who like to clench their fists, reach for the stars and roast their cold beers by the fireplace.

🛍 Shopping

Argos   MODERN CERAMICS
(🖉 271 2750; Cevizler Sokak 22; 🕙10am-8pm)
A classy selection of handmade ceramics, both modern and Asian-inspired, as well as unusual stone pieces.

Tribal Connections   CARPETS
(🖉 271 2400; Müze Yolu 24; 🕙10am-8pm) Both an unofficial welcome service thanks to gregarious Kiwi partner Ruth Lockwood and home to some mighty fine rugs.

ℹ Information
Internet Access

Get an hour free for donating a tome to the book swap at **Flintstones Internet Centre** (Belediye Caddesi; per hr TL2; 🕙10am-midnight). **Mor-tel Telekom Call Shop/Internet Café** (Roma Kalesi Arkası; per hr TL2; 🕙9am-midnight) also offers cheap international calls.

Money

There are four ATMs in booths at the otogar (Vakif Bank, Türkiye Bankası, HSBC and Garanti

Bankası). The one at Deniz Bank on Müze Caddesi dispenses lira, euros and US dollars. Some of the town's travel agencies will exchange money, although you're probably better off going to the PTT.

Post

Post office (off Bilal Eroğlu Caddesi) has phone, fax and money-changing services.

Tourist Information

There's an information booth at the otogar that is open when most long-distance buses arrive, but it's run by the **Göreme Turizmciler Derneği** (Göreme Tourism Society; ☑271 2558; www.goreme.org). This coalition of hotel and restaurant owners is solely aimed at directing travellers to accommodation in the village and staff can't supply any meaningful information. They give out free maps and sell one for TL5.

🛈 Getting There & Away

There are daily long-distance buses to all sorts of places from Göreme's otogar, although normally you're ferried to Nevşehir's otogar to pick up the main service (which can add nearly an hour to your travelling time).

Note that the morning bus to İstanbul goes via Ankara, so takes one hour longer than the evening bus. For Aksaray, change in Nevşehir.

🛈 Getting Around

There are several places to hire mountain bikes, scooters, cars and the objectionable quads, including **Hitchhiker** (☑271 2169; www.cappadociahitchhiker.com; T Özal Meydanı), **Oz Cappadocia** (☑271 2159; www.ozcappadocia.com; T Özal Meydanı) and **Motodocia** (☑271 2517;

Uzundere Caddesi), all located near the otogar. It pays to shop around, as prices vary dramatically.

As a rule, mountain bikes cost between TL10 and TL15 for a day; TL4 to TL6 for an hour. Mopeds and scooters go for TL30 to TL45 for a day; TL25 to TL30 for half a day. A small Renault or Fiat car costs TL40 to TL100 for a day, with features such as air-con, automatic gears and a diesel engine available.

Since there are no petrol stations in Göreme and the rental companies will hike petrol prices, refill your tank in Nevşehir, Avanos or Ürgüp, or at one of the garages on the main road near Ortahisar and İbrahimpaşa.

Uçhisar

🎵0384 / POP 6350

Pretty little Uçhisar has undergone rapid development since the heady Club Med days. The French love affair with the cliff-top village continues each summer as busloads of Gallic tourists unpack their *joie de vivre* in trendy hotels at the foot of Uçhisar Castle. The royal rectangular crag visible from nearby Göreme is the dramatic centrepiece of a stylish Cappadocian aesthetic, albeit at times a touch manufactured. If you need respite from the many shades of sun-kissed rock, divert your gaze to the white peaks of Erciyes Dağı (Mt Erciyes; 3916m), which is a wild world away from your shaded terrace. Uçhisar remains a quieter alternative to Göreme as a base for exploring the region.

There are Vakif Bank and Garanti Bankası ATMs on the main square, and

SERVICES FROM GÖREME'S OTOGAR

DESTINATION	FARE (TL)	DURATION (HR)	FREQUENCY (PER DAY)
Adana	30	5	3
Ankara	25	4½	6
Antalya	35	9	2 evening
Çanakkale	60	16	1 evening
Denizli (for Pamukkale)	35	11	2 evening
Fethiye	55	14	1 evening
İstanbul	40	11-12	1 morning & 2 evening
İzmir	40	11½	1 evening
Kayseri	10	1½	hourly morning, afternoon & evening
Konya	20	3	2 morning
Marmaris/Bodrum	55	13	2 evening
Selçuk	50	11½	1 evening

an **internet cafe** (per hr TL1; ⊗9am-midnight) and a PTT nearby.

Watching the sun set over the Rose and Pigeon Valleys from the wonderful vantage point of **Uçhisar Castle** (Uçhisar Kalesi; admission TL3; ⊗8am-8.15pm) is a popular activity. A tall volcanic-rock outcrop riddled with tunnels and windows, the castle is visible for miles around. Now a tourist attraction complete with terrace cafes at its entrance, it provides panoramic views of the Cappadocian countryside. Unfortunately, many of the bus groups that visit leave rubbish, which diminishes the experience. The lack of barriers means you should be very careful – one photographer died when he fell over the edge after stepping back to get a good shot.

There are some excellent **hiking** possibilities around Uçhisar; see the boxed text, p457, for more information.

🛏 Sleeping

Kilim Pension
PENSION €

(☎219 2774; www.sisik.com; Tekelli Mahallesi; s/d/tr TL60/80/100) The pride of fun-loving, multilingual 'Sisik', Kilim Pension is a spacious and unpretentious small hotel at the top of the village and hospitable to the very last nargileh (water pipe). The nine hip rooms are sparingly decorated with ample space for morning floor routines, though the upstairs ones are brighter and take full advantage of the all-important views. The food is first-class and best accompanied by some pulsating *darbouka* (Turkish drum) beats. The chaperoned hikes into the valleys below are highly recommended.

Kale Konak
HISTORIC HOTEL €€

(☎219 3133; www.kalekonak.com; Kale Sokak 9; r TL150; @) A stay at Kale Konak, a wonderful new hotel set away from the main drag and in the shadow of Uçhisar Castle, feels akin to a stately retreat. An afternoon unwinding on the Roman arched terrace and an evening in the marble hamam will have you primed for your luxurious brass bed. Underground passageways and secret doors only add to the magic of this surprisingly affordable hotel experience.

Taka Ev
BOUTIQUE HOTEL €€

(☎0532 740 4177; www.takaev.net; Kayabasi Sokak 43; s/d TL50/100; @) An impressive and cost-friendly addition to the high-end side of the hill, Taka Ev is an unassuming hotel with plenty of positives. Aside from the ubiquitous gorgeous views, the smallish rooms are brand new, spotless and feature

swanky bathrooms with powerful showers. Friendly Murat offers free guided hikes to guests. Dining options are limited.

Les Maisons de Cappadoce
APARTMENT €€€

(☎219 2813; www.cappadoce.com; Belediye Meydanı 28; studios €130-180, villas €240-980) If only all real-estate barons could use French architect Jacques Avizou's tasteful expansion policy then maybe we could all live in places like Les Maisons de Cappadoce in the old quarters of ancient towns with little breakfast baskets hanging on our door every morning. Located above Pigeon Valley, these intelligently designed serviced villas range from studios to sublime family fun houses. Reception is in a first-floor office in the main square.

Anatolia Pension
PENSION €

(☎219 2339; Hacialibey Caddesi; d €30-35; @) The best budget option on the main street, Anatolia has 15 bright, spotless rooms inside a sturdy stone house. Manager Ahmet is a charming host who provides discerning travel advice and services. Traditional Turkish meals are available.

Karlık Evi
HISTORIC HOTEL €€€

(☎219 2995; www.karlikevi.com; Karlık Mahallesi; s/d from €120/140; ✻) The poor patients at this former hospital checked out too early and missed the fabulous conversion to a rustic hotel. The 20-odd rooms are individually decorated using plush tones and ornate wooden furniture. Painting workshops are run annually; budding artists can take inspiration from a nightly hamam and massage, or wet their easel in the garden or roof terrace.

Şira Hotel
BOUTIQUE HOTEL €€

(☎219 3037; www.hotelsira.com; Göreme Caddesi 87; d TL100-150; @) This new hotel run by former Japanese-speaking guides is an assured addition to the Uçhisar landscape. The 12 beautiful rooms have been chiselled smooth and feature wooden floorboards, quality light fixtures and a palpable sense of calm. Some are a bit dark so check out a few before you pick one. The real bonus is management's appreciation for wine, food and nature, all on show in the organic restaurant that explodes with nightly feasts. Grape-harvesting tours and culinary workshops are available on request.

Argos
LUXURY HOTEL €€€

(☎219 3130; www.argosincappadocia.com; r €200-250, ste €400-600) This is a new level of style from the Istanbul advertising firm with its very fancy feet now in the hotel game. A series of stairs on the site of an old monastery lead to some of the finest rooms in Cappadocia, some with indoor swimming pools and all sporting renowned architect Turgur Cansever's sympathetic restorative edge. Take refuge in the subterranean tunnels and old cellars then rise to the manicured lawns. On-site is Bezirhane, a former linseed press and now an acoustic hall staging regular music performances and private parties. With designer luxury throughout and magazine-style photos at every turn, a double room is well worth the splash.

Lale Saray APARTMENT HOTEL €€
(📞219 2333; www.lalesaray.com; Göreme Caddesi; s €45-80, d €50-85, tr €60-95; @🕸) Lale Saray offers the comfort of French apartment living in the Cappadocian countryside, with fragrant cave rooms decked in oranges and pinks, therapeutic showers and rejuvenating minibars. The private terrace allows you to contemplate your next move.

✗ Eating

Center Café & Restaurant LOCAL €
(📞219 3117; Belediye Meydanı; mains TL10-15) A former top-notch Club Med chef now presides over this humble town-square cafe-restaurant. The verdant garden setting hums with satiated locals and young glamour pusses coo over *dondurma* (ice cream) and crispy, half-wasted salads. We almost wish this place was still secret.

Elai MODERN TURKISH €€€
(📞219 3181; www.elairestaurant.com; Eski Göreme Yolu; mains TL24-45; 🕙10.30am-2.30pm & 6.30-11pm) This prime example of an emerging Cappadocian style is as far removed from the desert communities it once served as the Turkish fusion menu is from original Anatolian cuisine. In a converted cafe, where the gossiping old men have been replaced by a sharp dining room with velvety curtains and exposed beams, guests can kick off with a drink on the terrace, with its magnificent view, before moving inside to sample dishes ranging from duck confit to grilled jumbo shrimp. Dishes travel around the world but really shine when they are Turkish in inspiration.

Le Mouton Rouge FRENCH €€
(📞219 3000; Belediye Meydanı; mains TL10) When a group of old friends reunite in a small French bistro in the centre of Turkey, the laconic owner can't tear himself from an afternoon hammock romance and the sleepy waiter ploughs a stranded couple with ice cold beer and large, fresh sandwiches, and hilarity ensues. The Red Sheep is the heartbeat of Uçhisar, with a cool jewellery store inside.

Kandil House CAFE €
(📞219 3191; Göreme Caddesi; snacks TL4) With its spot-on views of Rose Valley, randomly painted furniture and backgammon board, the cafe under the arches makes a pleasant hideout on a hot day.

🛍 Shopping

Göreme Onyx JEWELLERY
(Güvercinlik Vadisi Karşısı) The full gamut of precious stones is on offer in this large shop on the outskirts of Uçhisar.

ℹ Getting There & Away

Dolmuşes and minibuses leave from outside the *belediye* for Göreme, Çavuşin and Avanos (TL1.80 to TL2.80, every hour from 7am to 7.30pm, to 6pm in winter). Similarly priced and timed buses to Ortahisar and Ürgüp depart from near Chez Kemal on the main square. Both services stop at Nevşehir after Uçhisar on their return journeys.

A taxi to Göreme costs TL15 and to Ürgüp TL30.

Çavuşin
📞0384

Midway between Göreme and Avanos is sleepy little Çavuşin, where the main activity is at the souvenir stands beneath the cliff houses. It has some sterling accommodation options and offers an authentic village experience.

On the highway you'll find the **Çavuşin Church** (Big Pigeon House Church; admission TL8; 🕗8am-5pm, last admission 4.30pm), accessed from the pottery shop via a steep and rickety iron stairway. Cappadocia's first post-iconoclastic church, it served as a pigeon house for many years and is home to some fine frescoes.

Walk up the hill through the new part of the village and continue past the main square to find the old part of Çavuşin. Here you can explore a steep and labyrinthine complex of abandoned houses cut into a rock face, as well as one of the oldest churches in Cappadocia, the **Church of John the Baptist**, which is located towards the top of the cliff.

Çavuşin is the starting point for scenic **hikes** to the southeast, through Güllüdere (Rose Valley), Kızılçukur Vadısı (Red Valley) and Meskendir Valley. You can even go as far as the Zindanönü viewpoint (6.5km), then walk out to the Ürgüp–Ortahisar road and catch a dolmuş back to your base.

The village has no bank or ATM. There are three internet cafes, including **MustiNet** (per hr TL1; ⊙4pm-midnight) near İn Pension.

☞ Tours

Mephisto Voyage   OUTDOOR TOURS
(✆532 7070; www.mephistovoyage.com) Based at the İn Pension, this group has a very good reputation. It's been operating for over a decade and offers trekking and camping packages ranging from a two-day local wander to a 14-day trip around Cappadocia and the Taurus Mountains (€500). It also rents out bicycles and offers tours by bike, horse cart and, for mobility-impaired people, the Joëlette system.

🛏 Sleeping & Eating

Village Cave Hotel   BOUTIQUE HOTEL €€
(✆532 7197; www.thevillagecave.com; r TL150-200) The most interesting lodging in the village is this newly restored 18th-century stone house with six bedrooms carved on two floors in view of gorgeous St John's church. Bathrooms are a little tight. The friendly host Halim is the third generation to manage the property.

Green Motel   MOTEL €
(✆532 7050; www.motelgreen.com; camp sites TL7, r TL50-80; @) In the shadow of Red Valley, Çavuşin's version of country splendour is this trusted, large motel on leafy grounds where horses once brayed. It's a bit tired in parts but rooms 213 and 305 are worth requesting for their balconies alone. The onsite Yesil Restaurant is decent for Turkish pizza and a chat with the friendly locals.

Turbel Hotel   HOTEL €€
(✆532 7084; www.turbelhotel.com; s/d TL40/80, cave TL125/150) A good choice, Turbel has commanding views from its restaurant and rooms, which have basic private bathrooms and rugs, folkloric dolls and kitschy paintings for decor. Owner Mustafa, who spent 15 years in Strasbourg and resembles the French actor Roger Hanin, attracts many French travellers. A new underground cave section has five rooms with jacuzzis and a disco-bar.

İn Pension   PENSION €
(✆532 7070; www.pensionincappadocia.com; s/d/tr TL35/70/80, s/d without bathroom TL15/30; @) This basic cheap option by the main square comes with built-in travel advice courtesy of owner Mephisto Voyage. Rooms have been spruced up with new linen and white paints, though beds and bathrooms are pretty small. The rooftop cafe holds promise for an evening come-down.

Camping Cappadocia   CAMPGROUND €
(✆532 7070; 2 people incl tent & breakfast €10, sleeping bag €2) This camp site was recently opened by the Mephisto Voyage team to help break up its excellent treks through places such as Red Valley.

Ayse & Mustafa's Place   TURKISH €
(✆0535 947 8649; snacks TL3-4; ⊙9am-5pm) Sitting under the plum trees, sample Ayse's home-cooked *gözleme, menemen* and bigger meals on reservation. Fresh fruit juice, beer and nargilehs are also available.

❶ Getting There & Away

See p465 for information about the bus services that connect Çavuşin with nearby villages.

Zelve

The road between Çavuşin and Avanos passes a turn-off to the **Zelve Open-Air Museum** (admission incl Paşabağı TL8, parking TL2; ⊙8am-5pm, last admission 4.15pm), where three valleys of abandoned homes and churches converge. Zelve was a monastic retreat from the 9th to the 13th century. It doesn't have as many impressive painted churches as the Göreme Open-Air Museum, but its sinewy valley walls with rock antennae could have been made for poking around. The valleys were inhabited until 1952, when they were deemed too dangerous to live in and the villagers were resettled a few kilometres away in Aktepe, also known as Yeni Zelve (New Zelve). Remnants of village life include the small, unadorned, rock-cut **mosque** in Valley Three and the old *değirmen* (mill), with a grindstone and graffitied wooden beam, in Valley One.

Beyond the mill, the **Balıklı Kilise** (Fish Church) has fish figuring in one of the primitive paintings. Adjoining it is the more impressive **Üzümlü Kilise** (Grape Church), with obvious bunches of grapes.

Unfortunately, erosion continues to eat into the valley structures and parts may be closed because of the danger of collapse, while others require scrambling and ladders. If Valley Two is open, what's left of the **Geyikli Kilise** (Church with Deer) is worth seeing.

There are cafes and *çay bahçesis* (tea gardens) in the car park outside.

Paşabağı, a valley halfway along the turn-off road to Zelve near a fairy-chimney *jandarma* (police station), has a three-headed formation and some of Cappadocia's best examples of mushroom-shaped fairy chimneys. Monks inhabited the valley and you can climb up inside one chimney to a monk's quarters, decorated with Hellenic crosses. Wooden steps lead to a chapel where three iconoclastic paintings escaped the Islamic vandals; the central one depicts the Virgin holding baby Jesus.

ⓘ Getting There & Away

The hourly buses running between Ürgüp, Göreme, Çavuşin and Avanos (see p465) will stop at Paşabağı and Zelve on request. If you're coming from Ürgüp, Göreme or Çavuşin and tell the driver that you want to go to Paşabağı or Zelve, the bus will turn off the highway past Çavuşin, let you off and then go up to Aktepe and on to Avanos. If no one wants Paşabağı or Zelve, the bus will not make this detour. Getting a bus from Zelve is more difficult; you may have to walk the 3.5km from the site to the main highway, from where you can flag down a bus going towards either Göreme or Avanos.

Devrent Valley

Look, it's a camel! Stunning Devrent Valley's volcanic cones are some of the best-formed and most thickly clustered in Cappadocia, and looking at their fantastic shapes is like gazing at the clouds as a child. See if you can spot the dolphin, seals, Napoleon's hat, kissing birds, Virgin Mary and various reptilian forms.

Most of the rosy rock cones are topped by flattish, darker stones of harder rock that sheltered the cones from the rain until all the surrounding rock was eaten away, a process known as differential erosion.

To get to Devrent Valley (also known as Imagination Valley) from Zelve, go about 200m back down the access road to where the road forks and take the right road, marked for Ürgüp. After about 2km you'll come to the village of Aktepe (Yeni Zelve). Bear right and follow the Ürgüp road uphill for less than 2km.

Avanos

📞0384 / POP 11,800 / ELEV 910M

The Kızılırmak (Red River) is the slow-paced pulse of this provincial town and the unusual source of its livelihood, the distinctive red clay that, mixed with a white, mountain mud variety, is spun to produce the region's famed pottery. Typically painted in turquoise or the earthy browns and yellows favoured by the Hittites, the beautiful pieces are traditionally thrown by men and painted by women. Aside from the regulation tour groups, Avanos is relatively devoid of foreign visitors, leaving you alone to ponder the Zelve sunset or your umpteenth riverside çay.

⊙ Sights & Activities

Tour groups are shuffled into the pottery warehouses outside of town. Others should patronise one of the smaller **pottery workshops** in the centre, most of which will happily show you how to throw a pot or two. These are located in the small streets around the main square and in the group of shops opposite the PTT. Our favourite is **Le Palais du Urdu**, a unique drum-making and pottery studio that caused a minor stir in ceramic circles with a recent TV appearance. Also worth a visit is **Chez Galip** (📞511 5758; Firin Sokak 24), an extensive pottery gallery with the infamous 'Hair Museum', a creepy collection of 16,000 samples of women's hair.

If you fancy going horse-riding, **Akhal-Teke** (📞511 5171; www.akhal-tekehorsecenter. com; Camikebir Mahallesi, Kadı Sokak 1) and **Kirkit Voyage** (📞511 3148; www.kirkit.com; Atatürk Caddesi 50) organise guided treks in the area. Prices range from TL80 for two hours to TL160 for a full day; it's worth shopping around.

⊊ Tours

Kirkit Voyage has an excellent reputation. As well as the usual guided tours, it can arrange walking, biking, canoeing, horse-riding and snowshoe trips. It's an agency for Onur Air, Pegasus Airlines, Turkish Airlines and Atlasjet, and runs a shuttle between Avanos and Kayseri airport (TL50, reservation essential).

🛏 Sleeping

Kirkit Pension
PENSION **€€**

(☑511 3148; www.kirkitpension.com; Atatürk Caddesi; s/d/tr €30/40/55; @) This Avanos institution just off the main thoroughfare consists of two old stone houses with a lovingly restored courtyard in between and makes a low-key base for trips around Cappadocia. Kilims, black-and-white photographs, and *suzani* (Uzbek bedspreads) spark up the smallish rooms. Guests can enjoy a home-cooked local meal (TL15 for dinner) in the highly recommended vaulted restaurant or pleasant courtyard.

Sofa Hotel
HOTEL **€€**

(☑511 5186; www.sofa-hotel.com; Orta Mahallesi, Baklacı Sokak 13; s/d TL60/100) Resident artist Hoja has spent a fair chunk of his life purchasing and redesigning this collection of Ottoman houses that now welcomes guests to live among the beautiful madness. Featuring staircases that lead to bridges that wind through corridors and merge in terraced gardens, the Sofa is a wonderland for lost children and adults struck by wanderlust. Rooms are traditionally decorated with idiosyncrasies at every turn, and incongruously modern bathrooms. Breakfast is a hit.

Tokmak Konuk Evi
HISTORIC HOTEL **€€**

(☑511 4587; www.tokmakkonukevi.com; Yukarı Mah, Cami Sokak 11; d TL70) This popular restored home in the heart of the old town looks like a full-sized Turkish doll's house. It's run by a friendly team and the well-presented rooms are dotted with locally sourced antiques, deep bathtubs and coffee-making facilities; rooms 118 and 119 have more space and colour. The stone courtyard fills with French tour groups in summer. Tokmak is next to an excellent carpet store, Galerie Yoruk.

Ada Camping
CAMPGROUND **€**

(☑511 2429; www.adacampingavanos.com; Jan Zakari Caddesi 20; camp sites per person incl electricity TL10; ➽) Take the Nevşehir road and bear right to reach this large, family-run camping ground, in a superb setting near the river. The toilet block could be cleaner but there's lots of shade and grass, a restaurant and a cold but inviting swimming pool.

🍴 Eating

Dayının Yeri
OCAKBAŞI **€**

(☑511 6840; mains TL10) In a new location near the bridge, this shiny, modern *ocakbaşı* (grill restaurant) is one of Cappadocia's best. The kebaps are sensational and the pide is just as good. Don't even think of leaving without sampling the freshly prepared *künefe* (strands of cooked batter over a creamy sweet cheese base baked in syrup; TL4), cooked on little hobs near the tables. No alcohol is served.

Bizim Ev
INTERNATIONAL **€€**

(☑511 5525; Orta Mahallesi, Baklacı Sokak 1; mezes TL6, mains TL11-15) 'Our House', next to Sofa Hotel, is the best choice for lovers of the white tablecloth. The wine and dining is divided into four sections: cave cellar, terrace, cave entrance and stone room. We prefer the open spaces upstairs, but wherever you sit, a clay pot of local trout (TL11) or the surprisingly pleasant catfish skewers (TL12) are among the more interesting selections.

Seçkin Kebap
FAST FOOD **€**

(Ataturk Çaddesi; mains TL4-7) A kebab's throw from Kirkit Pension is this breezy gourmet fast food shop with pumping tunes and lively young owners. Welcome to the new generation of meat-on-a-stick.

Adana Kebap
FAST FOOD **€**

(Atatürk Caddesi; mains TL4-7) This old-school equivalent of fast-food dining, with sticky floors and greasy tables, churns out huge kebaps stuffed to the marrow with chilli and garlic to locals and regional gourmands.

Sofra Restaurant
ANATOLIAN **€**

(☑511 4324; Hükümet Konağı Karşısı; mains TL7-8) In a line of restaurants catering to the tour groups visiting the nearby pottery shops, Sofra has a wide-ranging meze menu, pottery dishes and a small terrace.

ℹ Information

The **tourist office** (☑511 4360; Atatürk Caddesi; ⊙8.30am-5pm), which doesn't always stick to its opening hours, is on the main square. Several ATMs are on or around the main square.

To check your email or surf the net, head to the **Hemi Internet Café** (Uğur Mumcu Caddesi; per hr TL1; ⊙9am-midnight).

ℹ Getting There & Around

There are two bus routes from Avanos to Nevşehir: one leaves every 30 minutes and goes direct and the other leaves every hour and travels via Çavuşin and Göreme. Both services operate from 7am to 7pm and charge TL2.50 per ticket. There's also an hourly *belediye* bus running from Avanos to Nevşehir via Çavuşin (10 minutes), Göreme (15 minutes) and Uçhisar (30 minutes). It departs from Avanos from 7am to

6pm and costs between TL1.50 and TL3 depending on where you get on and off.

Dolmuşes to Ürgüp (TL2) pass through town at 9am, 11am, 1pm, 3pm and 5pm.

Kirkit Voyage hires out mountain bikes for TL25 per day or TL15 for half a day.

Around Avanos

SARIHAN

Built in 1249, the Sarıhan (Yellow Caravanserai; admission TL3; ☺9am-midnight) has an elaborate gateway with a small mosque above it. Having been restored in the late 1980s, it's one of the best remaining Seljuk caravanserais. Gunning down the highway towards it makes you feel like a 13th-century trader, ready to rest his camels and catch up with his fellow dealers.

Inside, you also have to use your imagination in the bare stone courtyard. Visitors are allowed on the roof, but the main reason to come here is the 45-minute whirling dervish ceremony (☎511 3795; admission €25; ☺9.30pm Apr-Oct, 9pm Nov-Mar). You must book ahead – most pensions in Göreme, Ürgüp, Avanos and Uçhisar will arrange it for you. The price may vary according to how much commission your tour agent or pension is skimming off the top.

Though the setting is extremely atmospheric, the *sema* (ceremony) is nowhere near as impressive as those staged at the Mevlevi Monastery in İstanbul's Beyoğlu (see p80). If you've seen one of those you should probably give this a miss.

❶ Getting There & Away

Getting to the Sarıhan, 6km east of Avanos, without your own transport is difficult, as there are no dolmuşes and few vehicles with which to hitch a ride. An Avanos taxi driver will probably want around TL30 to take you there and back, including waiting time.

ÖZKONAK UNDERGROUND CITY

About 15km north of Avanos, the village of Özkonak hosts a smaller version of the underground cities of Kaymaklı and Derinkuyu (see boxed text, p480), with the same wine reservoirs, rolling stone doors etc. Özkonak underground city (admission TL8; ☺8.30am-5.30pm) is neither as dramatic nor as impressive as the larger ones, but is much less crowded.

The easiest way to get there is by dolmuş from Avanos (TL1.50, 30 minutes), but there are few services on weekends. Ask to be let

off for the *yeraltı şehri* (underground city); the bus stops at the petrol station, a 500m stroll from the entrance.

Nevşehir

♪0384 / POP 81,700 / ELEV 1260M

According to local lore, if you set eyes on the beautiful view from Nevşehir's hilltop castle, you will be compelled to stay here for seven years. The legend must be very old, because the provincial capital is an ugly modern town that offers travellers little incentive to linger.

Dangers & Annoyances

We suggest that you avoid any dealings with the tour agents here and follow the advice outlined on p451 to ensure that your bus ticket includes a shuttle-bus transfer to your final destination from Nevşehir. Unfortunately, malpractice is so institutionalised at the otogar that even people at the bus companies' counters may take you to the travel agents. If you do find yourself in need of a *servis* or a taxi and you have booked a hotel, it is worth phoning it for assistance; Nevşehir's otogar has long been problematic for travellers and the tourist industry in the rest of Cappadocia is well aware of it.

◎ Sights

Nevşehir Museum (☎213 1447; Türbe Sokak 1; admission TL3; ☺8am-5pm Tue-Sun) is housed in an ugly building 1km from the centre and 400m east of the tourist office. The collection includes an archaeological room with Phrygian, Hittite and Bronze Age pots and implements, as well as Roman, Byzantine and Ottoman articles. Upstairs, the dusty ethnographic section is less interesting.

The statue in the small park in front of the cultural centre is of Nevşehir'li Damat İbrahim Paşa (1662–1730), the Ottoman grand vizier after whom the town is named. The local luminary endowed the town's grand mosque complex, which is clearly visible on the hill to the south of Atatürk Caddesi and still has a functioning mosque, a *medrese* (seminary – now a library), a hamam and a tea house.

⌷ Sleeping & Eating

Aside from the Safir, Nevşehir's accommodation is pretty bleak for travellers. Even if you arrive here in the middle of the night, we recommend that you make your way to nearby Göreme, where the accommodation is cheaper and infinitely superior.

Hotel Safir
HOTEL €€

(⌂214 3545; www.otelsafir.com; Yeni Mah, Paşa Bulvarı 27; s/d TL70/110; ✳@) Finally, a half-decent hotel in Nevşehir with large, tiled, spotless rooms, a swanky lift and keen-enough staff.

Nevşehir Konaği
ANATOLIAN €

(⌂213 6183; Aksaray Caddesi 46; mezes TL2.50, mains TL7; ⊙9am-9.30pm) There is one good reason to visit Nevşehir. This municipal restaurant, set up to serve local cuisine, serves Cappadocian specialities such as *bamya çorba* (okra soup) and *dolma mantı* (ravioli). The location – an Ottoman-style building with Greek-style pillars in the park at the Kültür Merkezi (City Cultural Centre), 1.5km southwest of the centre – is the perfect place to tuck into scrumptious dishes such as *yoğurtlu beyti* (Adana kebap with yoghurt).

 Information

Nevşehir's **tourist office** (⌂214 4062; Atatürk Bulvarı; ⊙8am-5pm) is in a large government building on the town's main road. Staff here can supply a basic map of Nevşehir, but not much else. There are also a number of banks with ATMs along here.

 Getting There & Away

Turkish Airlines (www.thy.com) has a returning flight from İstanbul to Nevşehir on Wednesday, Friday, Saturday and Sunday (TL69 to TL199 one way).

Nevşehir is the main regional transport hub. There are bus services to surrounding towns and villages from the otogar and other stops. These go to Göreme (TL1.75, every 30 minutes from 8am to 6pm Monday to Friday, every hour on weekends); Uçhisar (TL1, every 30 minutes from 7.30am to 6pm Monday to Friday, every hour on weekends); Niğde (TL7, every two hours from 7.30am to 6pm) via Kaymaklı and Derinkuyu; and Ürgüp (TL3.50, every 15 minutes from 7.30am to 10pm). Some Ürgüp buses go via Ortahisar and all can drop you at the turn-off on the main highway, a 1km walk from the town centre. There are two services to Avanos: one leaves every hour and goes direct and the other leaves every 30 minutes and travels via Göreme and Çavuşin. Both operate from 7am to 7pm and charge TL2 per ticket. The otogar is 2.5km southwest of the city.

A taxi to Göreme should cost around TL35.

Around Nevşehir

If you're heading for Ankara, consider stopping off to see Gülşehir and especially Hacıbektaş along the way. While this is easily done if you have your own vehicle, it's not too hard by public transport either.

GÜLŞEHİR
⌂0384 / POP 9800

This small town 19km north of Nevşehir has two rocky attractions on its outskirts that are worth visiting if you're passing through.

Four kilometres before Gülşehir's town centre you'll find the **Open Palace** (Açık Saray; admission free; ⊙8am-5pm), a fine rock-cut monastery dating from the 6th and 7th centuries. It includes churches, refectories, dormitories and a kitchen, all of which are cut into fairy chimneys.

Two kilometres closer to town, just before the turning to the centre, is the rock-cut **Church of St John** (admission TL8; ⊙8am-5pm). A five-minute walk down a

---

HACI BEKTAŞ VELİ & THE BEKTAŞI SECT

Born in Nishapur in Iran in the 13th century, Hacı Bektaş Veli inspired a religious and political following that blended aspects of Islam (both Sunni and Shi'ite) with Orthodox Christianity. During his life he is known to have travelled around Anatolia and to have lived in Kayseri, Sivas and Kırşehir, but eventually he settled in the hamlet that is now the small town of Hacıbektaş.

Although not much is known about Hacı Bektaş himself, the book he wrote, the *Makalât*, describes a mystical philosophy less austere than mainstream Islam. In it he laid out a four-stage path to enlightenment (the Four Doors). Though often scorned by mainstream Islamic clerics, Bektaşi dervishes attained considerable political and religious influence in Ottoman times. Along with all the other dervishes, they were outlawed by Atatürk in 1925.

The annual pilgrimage of Bektaşi dervishes is an extremely important event for the modern Alevi community. Politicians tend to hijack the first day's proceedings, but days two and three are given over to music and dance.

signed road on the left of the highway, it's signposted 'Church of St Jean/Karşı Kilise'. The 13th-century church on two levels has marvellous frescoes, including scenes depicting the Annunciation, the Descent from the Cross, the Last Supper, the Betrayal by Judas, and the Last Judgment (rarely depicted in Cappadocian churches). The frescoes are particularly well preserved due to the fact that until restoration in 1995 they were covered in a layer of black soot.

Buses and dolmuşes to Gülşehir (TL1.50, 15 minutes) depart from the dolmuş and bus stop in the centre of Nevşehir. Ask to be let off at the Açık Saray or Karşı Kilise to save a walk back from town. Returning, just flag the bus down from the side of the highway. Onward buses to Hacıbektaş leave from Gülşehir's small otogar opposite the Kurşunlu Camii (TL2, 30 minutes).

HACIBEKTAŞ

Not to be confused with the town's normally closed Ethnographic Museum, the **Hacıbektaş Museum** (Hacıbektaş Müze; admission TL3; ⊙8am-noon & 1-5pm Tue-Sun) contains the tombs of Hacı Bektaş Veli and his followers. Pilgrims carry out superstitious activities such as hugging a pillar, kissing door frames and tying ribbons around a mulberry bush known as *dilek ağacı* (wish tree). Several rooms are arranged as they might have been when the Bektaşi order lived here, with exhibits such as photos of the dervishes and earrings worn by celibate members of the sect.

Hacıbektaş has limited hotel options. The unremarkable **Evrim Hotel** (☑441 2900; s/d TL30/60) or the slightly more popular **Hünkar Otel** (☑441 3344; s/d TL35/60), on the *meydanı* (town square) between the shrine and the otogar, offer basic rooms with blue and yellow furniture and reasonable bathrooms. Prices should be negotiable except in August, when it's booked solid. Eating options are limited to the basic *lokantas* (eateries serving ready-made food), *pastanes* (patisseries) and *kebapçıs* (kebab eateries) on the main street.

Buses from the centre of Nevşehir to Hacıbektaş (TL3, 45 minutes, 11 daily between 7.30am and 6.15pm on weekdays, fewer services on weekends) depart from the 'Has Hacıbektaş' bus office, just down from the Alibey Camii on the road to Gülşehir. The last bus from Hacıbektaş' otogar to Nevşehir leaves at 5pm (4.45pm on weekends).

Ortahisar

☑0384 / POP 4800

When Cappadocia's cartographers first got together, the farming village of Ortahisar must have been left off the tourist map. Known for its jagged castle that gives the town its name, Ortahisar is the epitome of the sleepy town where craggy-faced men lean listlessly against craggy houses and work storing citrus fruit in underground caves. The cobbled streets in the gorge are silenced by the surrounding canyons and emptied by sunset. The Culture Folk Museum is excellent and draws a steady number of tour groups.

Staff at the small **tourist office** (☑343 3071; Tepebaşı Meydanı; ⊙8am-5pm) near the castle are friendly, but don't speak English. They will probably take you to 'Crazy Ali', who runs the neighbouring antique shop and speaks some English, French and German. The loquacious poet, who says he was given his nickname when he drove an ox cart to the moon, offers guided walks to spots such as Pancarlık Valley.

You can check emails at **Antiknet** (Huseyin Galif Efendi Caddesi; per hr TL1; ⊙8am-midnight), downhill from the PTT.

◉ Sights

There are no monuments in the village other than the **castle** (kale; TL3; ⊙9am-6pm), an 18m-high rock used as a fortress in Byzantine times.

On the main square near the castle, the **Culture Folk Museum** (Kültür Müzesi; Cumhuriyet Meydanı 15; admission TL5; ⊙9am-7pm) gets bombarded with tour groups but is a good place to get to grips with the basics of local culture. In the dioramas, with their multilingual interpretive panels, mannequins in headscarves and old men's *şapkas* (hats) make *yufka* (thinly rolled, unleavened bread), *pekmez* (syrup made from grape juice) and kilims.

On the road to the AlkaBris hotel, the municipal park **Manzara ve Kültür Parkı** is slightly dishevelled but its grassed areas are good picnic spots. Near some holes in the cliff big enough to accommodate Volvo-driving pigeons, the cafe has views down the gorge to the castle.

🛏 Sleeping & Eating

AlkaBris   BOUTIQUE HOTEL €€€

(☑343 3433; www.alkabris.com; Cedid Mahallesi, Ali Reis Sokak 23; r TL200-250, ste TL280; ◎) Hosts Sait and Kamer have carved out a special Cappadocian retreat at the top of the town, featuring two vintage cave suites, two cave rooms and one stand-alone room sporting views of both the castle and Erciyes Dağı. All are named after figures from Hittite history – we couldn't split Gilgamış and Pankuş – but the mosaic tiles and soft colours are consistent throughout. Bathrooms are ultra cool, the breakfast spread is plentiful and lovingly prepared, and the terraces rock. The restaurant (dinner TL50) is pricey but good.

Hisar Evi   CAVE HOTEL €

(☑343 3555; www.hisarevi.com; Esentepe Mah, Tahirbey Sokak; r €65-80, ste €100; @) Over in Esentepe Mah is 'Castle House', popular with booking agencies thanks to busy host Ismail who also plays a mean game of backgammon. Hisar Evi has a relaxing terrace and clean, cool cave rooms, some far larger than others. The suites have enclaves suitable for small children.

Park Restaurant   GARDEN RESTAURANT €

(☑343 3361; Tepebaşı Meydanı; pides TL6-9, mains TL9-15) Overlooking the main square, with the castle as a backdrop, this attractive garden is a perfect spot to recharge with a meat pide and green salad, accompanied by a beer (TL5) or glass of 'energy drink' (fresh orange juice, TL3).

Cultural Museum Restaurant   TURKISH €

(☑343 3344; set menus TL20; ⊘lunch & dinner) The museum's attractive upstairs restaurant mainly caters to groups, but it is possible for individuals to dine here, particularly if you phone ahead. Dishes on offer include meatballs and *testi kebap* (pottery kebap). The English-speaking manager Cenk, a good source of local information, has proudly served Fenerbahçe players, Hungarian politicians and the Queen of Spain.

ⓘ Getting There & Away

Hotel shuttle buses run between Ortahisar and Kayseri (65km, 45 minutes).

Dolmuşes make the 5km run between Ortahisar and Ürgüp every 30 minutes from 8am to 5pm Monday to Saturday (TL1.50). See p451 for details of the Belediye Bus Corp dolmuşes between Ortahisar and Avanos via Göreme and Çavuşin. All services stop next to the museum. There are buses to Nevşehir, but it may be quicker to walk 1km to the Ortahisar turn-off on the main highway, as passing buses pick up passengers there.

Bus companies including Metro, Kent and Nevşehir have offices in the village.

Ürgüp
☑0384 / POP 15,500

When the Greek settlement was evicted from Ürgüp in 1923, there must have been buckets of tears shed at the borders. Nearly 90 years later and tourists from all over the world are pained to disperse from their temporary boutique residences. Ürgüp is elegant without even trying, like your favourite Turkish aunt who visits once a year. Better still, there's not a lot to do, no obligatory sights to see, just a few fine restaurants, a fabulous hamam, an up-and-coming winery and valley views that taste like honey on a stick. Perhaps Turkey's hippest rural retreat, Ürgüp is the connoisseurs' base for exploring the geographical heart of Cappadocia.

◉ Sights & Activities

Northwest of the main square is the oldest part of town, or old village, with many fine old houses, reached through a stone arch. It's well worth a stroll, after which you can head up Ahmet Refik Caddesi and turn right to Temenni Wishing Hill (⊘9am-11pm), home to a saint's tomb, a cafe and 360-degree views over the town. It doesn't always stick to its opening hours.

Right by the main square is the Tarihi Şehir Hamamı (admission TL15; ⊘7am-11pm), the hamam. Partly housed in what was once a small church, it offers mixed but respectable bathing.

The museum (admission TL3; ⊘8am-noon & 1-5pm Tue-Sun) features some 10-million-year-old teeth from a forerunner of the elephant, unearthed at Mustafapaşa, but the overall collection is uninspiring.

The abundant sunshine and fertile volcanic soil of Cappadocia produce delicious sweet grapes, and several wineries carry on the Ottoman Greek winemaking tradition. You can sample some of the local produce at Turasan Winery (☑341 4961; Çimenli Mevkii; ⊘7.30am-8pm).

ⓒ Tours

Several Ürgüp-based travel agents run tours around Cappadocia. Argeus Tours (☑341 4688; www.argeus.com.tr, www.cappadociaexclusive.com; İstiklal Caddesi 7) offers three- to nine-day packages, including an eight-day mountain-biking option, as well as day tours and flights, and is Ürgüp's Turkish Airlines representative. Peerless Travel Services (☑341 6970; www.peerlessexcursions.

com; İstiklal Caddesi 59a) is also Ürgüp's representative for Onur Air, Sun Express, Atlasjet and Pegasus Airlines.

Horseriding Kapadokya (☑299 8131, 342 7171; www.horseriding-kapadokya.com) is a highly recommended horse-riding company operating between Ürgüp and Ortahisar that leads excursions for all levels lasting from one day to one week.

🛏 Sleeping

Ürgüp has a glut of boutique hotels, mostly on Esbelli hill, and a couple more-central budget and midrange options worth considering. Many close down between November and March, when Ürgüp's weather keeps locals indoors and travellers elsewhere.

Esbelli Evi ⎡TOP CHOICE⎦ BOUTIQUE HOTEL €€
(☑341 3395; www.esbelli.com; Esbelli Mahallesi Sokak 8; s/d/ste €90/120/200; ❄@) Jazz in the bathroom, whiskey by the tub, secret tunnels to secret gardens lifted from photo shoots, privacy and company at alternate turns, this is the pick of accommodation in Cappadocia. A lawyer who never practiced, Süha Ersöz instead (thank God) purchased the nine surrounding properties over two decades and created a highly cultured, yet decidedly unpretentious hotel that stands out on exclusive Esbelli hill. The 15 detailed rooms feel more like first-class holiday apartments for visiting dignitaries, from the state-of-the-art family room with fully decked kids' room to the raised beds and provincial kitchens in the enormous cave suites. The breakfast spread is organic and delicious, while an enchanting evening on the terrace is an education in local history, humility and grace.

Serinn House ⎡TOP CHOICE⎦ BOUTIQUE HOTEL €€
(☑341 6076; www.serinnhouse.com; Esbelli Mahallesi Sokak 36; d €100-140; @) Jetsetter hostess Eren Serpen has truly set a new standard for hotel design in Cappadocia with this contemporary effort that seamlessly merges İstanbul's European aesthetic with Turkish provincial life. The five minimally furnished rooms employ dashes of colour, and feature Archimedes lamps, signature chairs, hip floor rugs and tables too cool for coffee. The toiletries are top shelf, the restaurant ruled by a trained gourmet chef, and the achingly beautiful open courtyard leaves guests in no doubt that their kind has evolved from that staid old prehistoric cave life.

Hotel Elvan BUDGET HOTEL €
(☑341 4191; www.hotelelvan.com; Barbaros Hayrettin Sokak 11; s/d/tr TL45/70/90; @) The best budget guesthouse in Ürgüp is thankfully still a well-kept family secret. The 20 neat rooms feature satellite TVs and minibars, and a congenial atmosphere runs through the shared lounges and leafy rooftop garden. The small restaurant is rated highly by locals who have the bellies to prove it.

Hotel Kilim HOTEL €€
(☑341 3131; www.hotelkilim.com; Dumlupinar Caddesi 50; s/d/tr from TL40/80/100; ❄@) A renovation in 2008 fluffed up the carpet and stripped back the paint to reveal bright rooms with private balconies and calming interiors prepared by orderly, professional staff. One of Ürgüp's better cheap places, it's in the town centre.

Yunak Evleri LUXURY HOTEL €€
(☑341 6920; www.yunak.com; Yunak Mahallesi; d €100-115, ste €145; @) Warranting its own postcode (and interior decorating company!), Yunak is a labyrinth of good taste that tumbles down the cliffside. This regal hotel, its structure in some parts dating back to the 5th century, unfurls itself in a string of Arabic lights that guide guests to its marble-walled chambers. Rooms are suitably lavish, with discreet entrances and sectioned landings. From the bronze desk lamps to the wireless entertainment systems and handcrafted wooden furniture, this is a hotel for connoisseurs of exceptional travel.

Melekler Evi BOUTIQUE HOTEL €€
(☑341 7131; www.meleklerevi.com.tr; Dereler Mahallesi Dere Sokak 59; d €90-145) The 'House of Angels' at the top of the old town contains seven flawless rooms a short flight from the pigeon houses across the way. Each room is an individual piece of interior design heaven – tackling the big issues such as *huzur* (peace), *sevgi* (love) and *sonsukluk* (eternity) – courtesy of a gracious architectural duo from İstanbul. The sandstone bathrooms contrast hi-tech shower systems with wooden scaffolding and hi-fi music heaven with smatterings of winged sculpture. Delectable meals are prepared each day on request in a former stable, as enchanted residents come and go with a handmade map in one hand and a glass of local *şarap* (wine) in the other.

Elkep Evi Pansiyon PENSION €€
(☑341 6000; www.elkepevi.com.tr; Esbelli Mahallesi Sokak; s/d €50/70, with jacuzzi from

Ürgüp

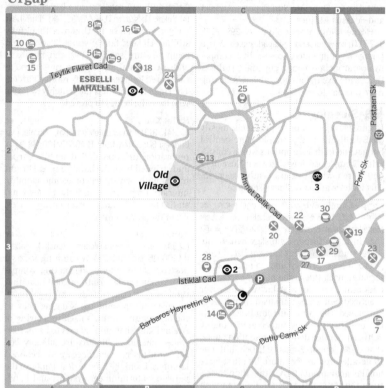

Ürgüp

N 0 ——— 200 m
0 ——— 0.1 miles

Six-Gated Tomb
(Altıkapılı Türbe)

Şehit Turan Cad

Kayseri Cad

1

Kayseri Cad

Belediye
(Town Hall)

Güllüce Cad

Mustafapaşa
Otogar

21

12

Dumlupınar Cad

Fabrika Cad

26

Cappadocia Palace
BOUTIQUE HOTEL €

(341 2510; www.hotel-cappadocia.com; Duayeri Mahallesi Mektep Sokak 2; s/d/tr TL35/70/85, cave TL60/120/140; @) If prolonged cave dwelling doesn't appeal, this converted Greek house makes a very reasonable hotel stay. Bekir and Aden are conspicuous hosts who happily oblige guest requests in the shadows of Cumhuriyet Meydanı. The 13 motel-style rooms have satellite TV and small bathrooms. The newer suites are more troglodytic and there's also a lovely arched restaurant-lounge. Book ahead.

Ayvansaray Butik Hotel
HOTEL €€

(3414406; www.ayvansarayboutiquehotel.com; Eski Kayseri Caddesi 62; d from TL100; ❄ @) Shades of Central Asia reign in this recently opened stone house conversion on the Kayseri road. The three self-contained rooms – Ukbek, Seluklu and Turkmen – are studies in red fabrics and dark woods. Street noise can be a concern, but the rooms are immaculate, with quality fittings and comfortable beds. The cheery owner's attached cafe is run by his erstwhile wife who fixes a mean meal.

Sacred House
LUXURY HOTEL €€€

(341 7102; www.sacred-house.com; Dutlu Cami Mahallesi, Barbaros Hayrettin Sokak 25; d €115-190; @) Yezim and her all-female team have raided Ottoman jumble sales and dusted off a hundred objet d'art stores in search of the right piece to fill the 12 spacious rooms at this haute-couture hotel that employs a maximum design philosophy. Luckily the service lacks pretension, while the ostentatious colour tones will have you contemplating what our Greek ancestors would've made of modern man.

Hotel Assiana
HOTEL €€

(341 4960; www.assianahouse.com; Esbelli Mahallesi Dolay Sokak 1; s/d/ste €65/85/100; @) The small hotel on Esbelli hill has three cave rooms and two arched stone rooms. The interiors are simple but tasteful, with maroon bedding, rugs on the varnished wooden floors, the occasional pot on a clutter-free shelf and a tree carving in one wall. The stone rooms upstairs are our favourites – the suite has a living room with a small fireplace and a vintage radio.

✗ Eating

The range of restaurants in Ürgüp is more limited than in Göreme, but the overall standard is much higher. If you're passing

€80/100, with Turkish bath from €100/120; @) Since fleeting with fame in the hit TV series *Asmali Konak,* these four cave houses hugging the cliff atop Esbelli Mahallesi have been targeted by midrange hotel harriers in search of dark-hued, spacious rooms. Each has its own private al fresco area – ask for one with a hamam – but the more sociable can retreat to the obligatory rooftop terrace or the pillared garden that is yet to make a nationwide televised cameo.

Antik Cave House
CAVE HOTEL €€

(341 4428; www.antikcavehouse.com; Dolay Sokak 14; s/d TL60/120, ste TL140; @) A youthful vibe permeates this happening new hotel on Esbelli hill. The seven rooms – three suites and four doubles – are small by comparison elsewhere in Ürgüp and feature a hodge-podge of styles including cave, *konak* (mansion), chimney and arched.

through the otogar, there are plenty of *pastanes* and cafes right outside.

TOP CHOICE Ziggy's MODERN TURKISH €€
(☑341 7107; Yunak Mahallesi, Teyfik Fikret Caddesi 24; mezes TL6-12, set menus TL35, mains TL15-18) This tribute to the adored pet dog (and a camp David Bowie) of charismatic hosts Selim and Nuray, who is often decked in her beautiful handmade jewellery available downstairs, is a luscious success. With the finest meze menu in Cappadocia, and a two-tiered terrace that fills day and night with humming tunes, strong cocktails and a hip clientele, Ziggy's backs up its glowing reputation with professional service and an innovative, award-worthy menu.

Han Çirağan Restaurant MODERN TURKISH €€
(☑341 2566; Cumhuriyet Meydanı; mains TL10-18) The Han is a hugely improved restaurant that has undergone a terrific renovation under new management. The terrace dining area is lovely (though lacks breeze) and the food is high quality. The lamb chops (TL14) and trout (TL13) are highly recommended. After dinner, retire to the cool new bar downstairs that has a city atmosphere and an excellent wine list.

Dimrit MODERN TURKISH €€
(☑341 8585; Yunak Mahallesi, Teyfik Fikret Caddesi 40; mains TL10-21) One of the top choices in Ürgüp for that oft-elusive ambience, Dimrit's menu is long, familiar, but not particularly illustrious for the price. The location on a hillside terrace more than compensates, however, and the presentation is divine. The rakı (aniseed brandy) comes in a number of distillations and the service is attentive.

Ürgüp Pide Salonu PIDECI €
(☑341 8242; Terminal İçi, Onur İşhanı, pides TL5-12) Beside the otogar but worthy of more than hungry commuters, this Turkish pizza joint is one of the best in the region. Better still, it will deliver to your hotel room free of charge.

Teras Cafe CAFE-RESTAURANT €
(☑341 2442; Cumhuriyet Meydanı 42; mains TL5-10) New owners and a decent renovation have given this pleasant indoor/outdoor cafe the physical profile its prime position at the foot of the hill deserves. The kerbside outdoor area includes a big-screen TV and comfy couches under giant, colourful umbrellas. The small restaurant inside and upstairs dishes up dirt-cheap Turkish staples, including kebaps and spicy soups. There's

free wi-fi for customers with laptops; some terminals are available on the 3rd floor (TL1 per hr).

Ehlikeyf ANATOLIAN €€
(☑341 6110; Cumhuriyet Meydanı; mains TL12-25) Competing with nearby Şömine in the sophistication stakes, and suffering from the same flaws, Ehlikeyf occupies a sleek dining room with a wavy ceiling. Dishes such as the fabulous Ehlikeyf kebap (steak served on slivered fried potatoes, garlic yoghurt and a demi-glace sauce; TL19) arrive on glass plates; a gloved waiter wielding a carving knife accompanies the *testi kebap*. The large, well-spaced tables with leather chairs are comfortable for spending an evening, but the bill at the end of it will be as ambitious as the presentation.

Micro Café & Restaurant MODERN TURKISH €€
(☑5341 5110; Cumhuriyet Meydanı; mains TL11) It's not the plaza's most popular restaurant, but Micro's diverse menu, ranging across Ottoman chicken, spinach crepes and peppered T-bone steak, attracts some tourists and locals. Its outside seating has unlimited people-watching potential. The semolina with chocolate sauce and ice cream is recommended, but the spoon salad is not.

Ailanpa Wine House LOCAL €
(☑341 6972; mains TL5-10, wine TL10) This wine house halfway up the hill features delicious homemade food care of warm-hearted Emine, the mother of the family business that produces plonk of varying quality, hot or cold.

Ocakbaşı OCAKBAŞI €€
(☑341 3277; Güllüce Caddesi 44; mains TL8-13) Above the otogar is this massive restaurant bordering on an institution that serves delectably oily mezes and huge plates of grilled meat and rice to grinning locals who slosh down beer and fresh *ayran*, often in the same gulp.

Drinking
The main square is the best place to grab an alcoholic or caffeinated beverage at an outside table and watch Cappadocia cruise by. *Pastanes* and cafes such as Şükrüoğlu and Café Naturel vie for attention with sweet eats and shiny window displays.

Bookended by carpet shops, the pedestrian walkway running northeast from Ehlikeyf restaurant is full of cafes, bars and old men playing backgammon.

Mahzen Sarap Evi
WINE HOUSE

(☑341 6110; İstanbul Caddesi; ☺11am-late) Often the traditional Turkish wine houses are musty affairs filled with shamefaced drinkers sitting on piles of sour grapes. This trendy number happily breaks the mould, thanks to the sprightly female owner who palms coffee, booze and sandwiches from late afternoon to late at night to shared booths from her little kitchenette facing the street. The beauty shop crowd across the road sets the tone after dark, swaying at tables to Turkish indie and downbeat Kurdish electronica.

Barfiks
LIVE MUSIC

(☑341 8442; Cumhuriyet Meydanı; mezes TL5, salads TL5-7, mains TL9-15) Even modest Turkish towns should have a restaurant like Barfiks where modesty makes fleeting appearances amid soulful, traditional tunes to accompany traditional Turkish food prepared by a stellar chef. The downstairs cave bar has a history of bringing people together.

Angel Café Bistro
BAR

(☑341 6894; Cumhuriyet Meydanı; TL6-14) Straight from the big city comes this incongruously cool rock bar with bright red beanbags out the front and tasty pizza (TL8) on the menu. It comes into its own after dark.

❶ Information

There are several banks with ATMs on or around the main square. The post office is northeast of Cumhuriyet Meydanı.

The helpful **tourist office** (☑0341 4059; Kayseri Caddesi 37; ☺8am-5pm Mon-Fri Oct-Apr, 8am-5.30pm Mon-Fri May-Sep) gives out a colour walking map and has a list of Ürgüp's hotels.

There is wi-fi at the arcade next to Kardeşler Restaurant and Vodafone, and at **Eftelya** (Refik Basaran Heykeli; per hr TL1.50; ☺9.30am-11pm).

❶ Getting There & Away

Dolmuşes travel to Nevşehir every 15 minutes from 6.55am to 11.30pm (TL2.50). A service runs between Ürgüp and Avanos (TL2) via Ortahisar, the Göreme Open-Air Museum, Göreme village and Çavuşin every two hours between 8am and 6pm.

Seven buses per day (fewer on Sunday) travel between Ürgüp and Mustafapaşa between 8.15am and 5.30pm (TL1). They leave from the Mustafapaşa otogar, next to the main otogar.

❶ Getting Around

The steep walk from the centre of town up to Esbelli Mahallesi is an absolute killer – many people instead opt to catch a taxi (TL5) from the rank next to Micro Café & Restaurant on the main square.

Ürgüp is a good base for hiring a car, with most agencies located on the main square or İstiklal Caddesi. Rates hover around TL70 to TL75 per day for a small manual sedan such as a Fiat Palio and climb to TL90 to TL120 for a larger automatic. **Decar** (☑341 6760) is more expensive but provides the best service; you can also try **Astral** (☑341 3344), **National** (☑341 6541) and **Avis** (☑341 2177). If you plan to drop the car off

SERVICES FROM ÜRGÜP'S OTOGAR

DESTINATION	FARE (TL)	DURATION (HR)	FREQUENCY (PER DAY)
Adana (via Nevşehir)	25	5	3 morning & afternoon
Aksaray	7	1½	hourly
Ankara	25	4½	7
Antalya	40	10	1 night (& 1 morning in summer)
Çanakkale	60	16	1 afternoon
İstanbul	40	11	1 morning, 2 evening
İzmir & Selçuk	40-50	11½	1 evening
Kayseri	6	1¼	hourly 7am to 7.30pm (to 5.30pm in winter)
Konya	20	4	5
Marmaris/Bodrum/Pamukkale	55	11-15	1 evening

in another part of Turkey, your best bet is Decar. If you book ahead, it does not charge the prohibitively large relocation fees (eg TL200 to drop off in Ankara) that other companies levy.

Several outlets rent mopeds and motorcycles from TL50 a day, and bicycles from TL25. Try Astral, **Safari** (☏341 6480) or **Alpin** (☏341 7522).

Ayvalı

☏0384 / POP 500

This lovely little village in a valley south of Ürgüp could still be late-Ottoman Greece if it weren't for the kids in Barcelona soccer shirts kicking balls beneath shiny NTT signage. Vegetables and dried flowers line the cobbled streets and tourists are virtually unsighted...for now.

🛏 Sleeping & Eating

Gamırasu Hotel   BOUTIQUE HOTEL €€€
(☏341 5825; www.gamirasu.com; d €90-140, ste €200-400) Occupying a 1000-year-old Byzantine monastery, Gamırasu offers top-end comfort and style in a secluded gorge where the only noise at night is the frogs. It has an on-site restaurant reached by a bridge, a church with frescoes, and an ancient winery on the premises. A walking trail leads down the valley and horse-riding and cycling can be organised.

Ovku Evi   CAVE HOTEL €€
(☏354 5852; www.ovkuevi.net; Ayse Gaffaroglu; d €90-140) A lovely new cave hotel overlooking a patch of wilderness, featuring colourcoded rooms – red or blue are the pick. The hard-working matron is good fun and her son speaks serviceable English.

Aravan Evi Restaurant   TRADITIONAL €
(☏341 5838; www.aravan.com; mains TL7-15; ⊙lunch) One of the best restaurants in Cappadocia. Simple flavours, quality produce and popular with in-the-know Turks, this restrained, brilliant restaurant on a gorgeous white terrace whips up favourites like *dolmades* and *çorbasi* with delicate surety. You should phone ahead before arriving and crash in the family guesthouse if the exquisite desserts make you woozy.

Mustafapaşa

☏0384 / POP 1600

Another beautiful Cappadocian village shifting slowly from yesteryear but remaining well beneath the tourist radar is Mustafapaşa. Still known widely by its pre-WWI Greek name of Sinasos, the stone-carved architecture here is a reminder of its prosperous Hellenic past. The minor rock-cut churches may satisfy your cultural craving, while the gentle pace is appropriate given the remarkable natural scenery. Wise travellers are choosing to stay here as an alternative to the more obvious destinations nearby.

You enter Mustafapaşa at an enlarged intersection, the Sinasos Meydanı, where a signboard indicating the whereabouts of the local rock-cut churches is located. Follow the road downhill and you'll come to Cumhuriyet Meydanı, the centre of the village, which sports the ubiquitous bust of Atatürk and several tea houses.

There's no tourist office in town, and no ATMs; internet access is available on the main square and at **Monastery Hotel** (per hr TL1.50; ⊙8.30am-midnight).

👁 Sights

Ayios Vasilios Kilise   CHURCH
(St Basil Church; admission TL5; ⊙9am-6pm) A sign pointing off Sinasos Meydanı leads 1km to the 12th-century Ayios Vasilios Kilise, perched near the top of a ravine. Its interior features unimpressive 20th-century frescoes. There should be someone there with a key; if not, enquire at the *belediye*.

Ayios Kostantinos-Eleni Kilise   CHURCH
(Church of SS Constantine & Helena; admission TL5; ⊙8.30am-noon & 1-5.30pm) Cumhuriyet Meydanı is home to the imposing Ayios Kostantinos-Eleni Kilise, erected in 1729 and restored in 1850. A fine stone grapevine runs around the door but the ruined interior with faded 19th-century frescoes is not worth the admission charge. If you are keen to see it, a uniformed council worker should be posted outside; if not, ask for the key at the nearby *belediye*.

There are also churches in **Monastery Valley**, but they're disappointing compared with others in Cappadocia. Nonetheless, it's a lovely walk. Also to the west of Mustafapaşa, there are 4km to 8km walks in **Gomeda Valley**, where there is a ruined 11th-century Greek town. Local guide Niyazi, who charges €25 for individuals and groups, can be contacted through Old Greek House.

Between Sinasos Meydanı and Cumhuriyet Meydanı is a 19th-century **medrese** with a fine carved portal. The stone columns on either side of the doorway are supposed to swivel when there's movement in the foundations, thus warning of earthquake damage.

🛏 Sleeping & Eating

Many of Mustafapaşa's accommodation options are closed from November to March.

Most of the hotels and pensions offer meals and this is fortunate, as the town's other eateries are dreadful. For lunch or dinner, we recommend Old Greek House and Hotel Pacha; set menu €8).

Perimasali Cave Hotel   CAVE HOTEL €€
(☑353 5090; www.perimasalihotel.com; Davatlu Mahallesi, Sehit; s/d €60/120) The 'Fairytale' comes alive in this dreamy renovation by owner Salih Birbilen, who turned the rooms of an old Greek house on a quiet hill into an opulent Cappadocian cave hideaway. The attention to detail befits a five-star hotel, with beautiful linens, stunning en suite bathrooms and deep, lush reds and blues. This is underground chic with killer above-ground views.

Hotel Pacha   PENSION €
(☑353 5331; www.pachahotel.com; Sinasos Meydanı; s/d TL50/80) Popular with discerning fans of the old-fashioned homestay, this revamped Ottoman-Greek number is the playground of matriarchal Demra, who wows guests with a dozen spotless rooms of various ilks and a famed upstairs restaurant. Entering among the lifted vines provides a tickle of serendipity.

Old Greek House   HISTORIC HOTEL €€
(☑353 5306; www.oldgreekhouse.com; Şahin Caddesi; s TL60, d TL80-120) If it's good enough for the ex-mayor to sleep here, it's good enough for us. These days, the mansion is best known for its Ottoman-flavoured set menus (TL20 to TL30) starring good versions of the usual suspects: *mantı*, *köfte* (meatballs), lima beans, crispy salads and baklava. If the Turkish coffee hasn't kicked in, grab a large room with polished floorboards and a genuine *antik* vibe.

Ukabeyn Pansiyon   BOUTIQUE HOTEL €€
(☑353 5533; www.ukabeyn.com; d/tr TL110/150; ❄) The double-headed eagle of Hittite mythology sitting above the hotel entrance lends regality and a name to this well-presented, modern cave venture that backs onto Hidden Valley and the St Basil rock church. The swimming pool on the lower terrace is a big tick, as are the views from the two levels above. The fully equipped

WORTH A TRIP

SOĞANLI ROAD TRIP

If you only rent a car once on your trip, the day you visit Soğanlı could be the time to do it. Not only are the valleys tricky to reach by public transport but the drive there is beautiful. The open countryside makes a change from central Cappadocia's canyons and you can stop in sleepy country villages that give an idea of what Göreme was like 30 years ago.

Signposted from the main road, some 10km south of Mustafapaşa, the rock-cut Byzantine complex at **Keşlik Monastery** includes vandalised frescoes and 16 houses where hundreds of monks lived. Inside the dwellings, you can see chimneys, fireplaces, bookshelves and grey nicks left on the rock by metal chisels. The kitchen features a hatch for passing meals to the refectory, which has seats at the far end for the teachers.

Some 7km further south, tractors bounce along hilly, cobbled streets in **Taşkınpaşa**, which is named after its 600-year-old Seljuk **mosque**. Photos near the entrance to the mosque show its original, 14th-century pulpit, now in Ankara's Museum of Anatolian Civilisations (p397). Outside, Taşkın Paşa himself is buried in one of the two Seljuk tombs; traders stayed under the arches during the caravanserai days. On the way back to the main road you will see a *medrese* with an ornate door frame.

At the ancient city of **Sobesos** (admission free; ☉8.30am-5.30pm), signposted from Şahinefendi, the various sections of the Roman baths can easily be distinguished. There are also some fine Roman mosaics, a mummy and a Byzantine church, built during renovations of the Roman city in the late 4th century.

Some day tours also stop at these sights.

GOING UNDERGROUND

During the 6th and 7th centuries, when Persian and Arabic armies set off to vanquish the Christians, beacons were lit and the warning could travel from Jerusalem to Constantinople in hours. When the message reached Cappadocia, the Byzantine Christians would escape into secret tunnels leading to vast underground cities.

Some 37 cities have already been opened, and there are at least 100 more. Excavations have not proceeded further because they have uncovered little more than graves and pottery pieces, as the cities' inhabitants took their possessions with them when they returned to the surface.

Some 10,000 people lived at **Derinkuyu** and 3000 at **Kaymaklı**, spending months at a time down there. They cunningly disguised the air shafts as wells. The Persian horsemen might throw some poison into the 'wells', thinking they were contaminating the water supply. They wouldn't notice any smoke from the fires burning beneath their feet, as the soft tuff rock absorbed most of it and the remaining fumes dispersed in the shafts.

The shafts, which descend almost 100m in some of the cities, also served a construction purpose. As rooms were made, debris would be excavated into the shaft, which would then be cleared and deepened so work could begin on the next floor.

Touring the underground cities, mentioned by the ancient Greek historian Xenophon in his *Anabasis*, is like tackling an assault course for history buffs. Narrow walkways lead you into the depths of the earth, through stables with handles used to tether animals, churches with altars and baptism pools, walls with air circulation holes, granaries with grindstones, and blackened kitchens with ovens.

Visiting the cities is fascinating, but be prepared for unpleasantly crowded and sometimes claustrophobic passages. Avoid visiting on weekends, when busloads of domestic tourists descend. Even if you don't normally like having a guide, it's worth having one

---

apartment (€75 to €95) could keep you in town long term.

ⓘ Getting There & Away

Nine buses a day (three on Sunday) travel the 5km between Ürgüp and Mustafapaşa (TL1, 10 minutes). The first leaves Mustafapaşa at 7.45am and the last leaves Ürgüp at 7pm. A taxi costs TL20.

Soğanlı

♩ 0352 / POP 400

Let's get one thing straight: despite the science fiction setting, no scene in *Star Wars* was ever filmed near Soğanlı, or anywhere else in Turkey! But don't despair, Chewbacca fans, there's still ample reason to travel to this tiny village 36km south of Mustafapaşa, namely a reverential series of rock-cut churches hidden in two dramatic, secluded valleys. An afternoon exploring at the foot of these sheer faces may inspire you to rewrite your own script.

To reach Soğanlı turn off the main road from Mustafapaşa to Yeşilhisar and proceed 4km to the village. Buy your ticket for the **churches** (adult/child TL2/free; ⊗8am-8.30pm, to 5pm in winter) near the Kapadokya Restaurant. In the village square, local women sell the dolls for which Soğanlı is supposedly famous.

⊙ Sights

The valleys of **Aşağı Soğanlı** and **Yukarı Soğanlı** were first used by the Romans as necropolises and later by the Byzantines for monastic purposes (similar to Göreme and Zelve), with ancient **rock-cut churches**.

Most of the interesting churches are in the right-hand valley (to the north), easily circuited on foot in about two hours. All are signposted, but be careful as many are in a state of disrepair.

Coming from the main road, about 800m before the ticket office, signs point to the **Tokalı Kilise** (Buckle Church), on the right, reached by a steep flight of worn steps; and the **Gök Kilise** (Sky Church), to the left across the valley floor. The Gök has twin naves separated by columns and ending in apses. The double frieze of saints is badly worn.

The first church on the right after the ticket booth, the **Karabaş** (Black Hat), is one of the most interesting. It is covered in

when you tour an underground city, since they can conjure up the details of life below ground better than you can on your own.

Kaymaklı underground city (yeraltı şehri; admission TL15; ◔8am-5pm, last admission 4.30pm) features a maze of tunnels and rooms carved eight levels deep into the earth (only four are open). As this is the most convenient and popular of the underground cities, you should get here early in July and August to beat the tour groups, or from about 12.30pm to 1.30pm when they break for lunch.

To reach **Özlüce underground city** (admission free), turn right as you enter Kaymaklı from the north and you'll be heading for the small village of Özlüce, 7km further away. More modest than Kaymaklı or Derinkuyu, this underground city is also less developed and less crowded.

Derinkuyu underground city (Deep Well; admission TL15; ◔8am-5pm, last admission 4.30pm), 10km south of Kaymaklı, has larger rooms arrayed on seven levels. When you get all the way down, look up the ventilation shaft to see just how far down you are – claustrophobics beware!

There are also underground cities at Güzelyurt (p487) and Özkonak (p469), near Avanos.

Getting There & Away

Although you can visit one of the cities on a day tour from Göreme, Avanos or Ürgüp, it's also easy to see them on your own. The half-hourly Nevşehir–Niğde bus stops in both Kaymaklı (TL2, 30 minutes) and Derinkuyu (TL3, 40 minutes). You could easily visit Kaymaklı and Derinkuyu and then continue onto Niğde the same day using the local buses.

You'll need a taxi to take you to Özlüce from Kaymaklı.

paintings showing the life of Christ, with Gabriel and various saints. A pigeon in the fresco reflects the importance of pigeons to the monks, who wooed them with dovecotes cut into the rock.

Furthest up the right-hand valley is the **Yılanlı Kilise** (Church of St George or Snake Church), its frescoes deliberately painted over with black paint, probably to protect them. The hole in the roof of one chamber, surrounded by blackened rock, shows fires were lit there.

Turn left at the Yılanlı Kilise, cross the valley floor and climb the far hillside to find the **Kubbeli** and **Saklı Kilisesi** (Domed and Hidden Churches). The Kubbeli is unusual because of its Eastern-style cupola cut clean out of the rock. Nestling in the hillside, the Hidden Church is indeed hidden from view – until you get close.

In the left-hand valley, accessed from the village, you'll first come across the **Geyikli Kilise** (Deer Church), where the monks' refectory is still clearly visible. The **Tahtalı Kilise** (Church of Santa Barbara), 200m further on, has well-preserved Byzantine and Seljuk decorative patterns.

🍴 Sleeping & Eating

Kapadokya Restaurant INTERNATIONAL €
(☎653 1045; set menus TL8; ◔lunch) Kapadokya boasts tables set under shady trees and serves stodgy but acceptable omelettes, casseroles and çorba. The camp site (TL5) is a patch of grass with a decrepit toilet block. Modest **Soğanlı Restaurant** (☎653 1016; ◔lunch only) has a shady garden for sipping çay. Nearby, the village's only pension, the family-run **Emek** (☎/fax 653 1029; dm with half-board TL40) has simple, clean cave dorms. Meals are cooked by the owner's wife and served on a pleasant upstairs terrace.

ℹ Getting There & Away

It's basically impossible to get to Soğanlı by public transport. Best bet: go to Yeşilhisar from Kayseri (TL2.50, every 30 minutes from 7am to 9pm) then negotiate for a taxi to take you there. Or, you can rent a car (see boxed text, p479) or sign up for a day tour in Ürgüp or Göreme.

Ala Dağlar National Park

The Ala Dağlar National Park (Ala Dağlar Milli Parkı) protects the rugged middle range of the Taurus Mountains between Kayseri, Niğde and Adana. It's famous throughout the country for its extraordinary trekking routes, which make their way through craggy limestone ranges dotted with waterfalls. It's best to trek between mid-June and late September; at other times weather conditions can be particularly hazardous, especially since there are few villages and little support other than some mountaineers' huts. Bring warm gear and prepare for extreme conditions.

The most popular walks start at the small villages of **Çukurbağ** and **Demirkazık**, which lie beneath Demirkazık Dağı (Mt Demirkazık, 3756m), 40km east of Niğde.

You can also reach the mountains via Yahyalı, 70km due south of Kayseri, a short drive away from the impressive **Kapuzbaşı Waterfalls** on the Zamantı River.

Although there are a variety of walks in the mountains, many people opt for the two-day minimum walk to the beautiful **Yedigöller** (Seven Lakes, 3500m), which starts and finishes at Demirkazık. An easier three- to four-day walk begins at Çukurbağ and leads through the forested Emli Valley, before finishing at Demirkazık.

Although solo trekkers do sometimes venture into the mountains, unless you're experienced and prepared you should consider paying for a guide or joining a tour. A guide should cost around TL100 per day; a horse, which can carry up to four people's luggage, about TL60. If you want to do a full trek in the range (about TL400 for a week, all inclusive), Middle Earth Travel (p455) is a good first port of call in Göreme. The agency offers a five-day program for TL550 per person, for a minimum of six people. **Osman Üçer** (☎0536 813 6032) and **Ahmet Üçer** (☎0536 712 0728) are two guides based in the park, and there are agencies in Niğde: **Demavend Travel** (☎0388-232 7363; www. demavendtravel.com; 5th fl, Esenbey Mahallesi Bahadir Is Merkezi 15, Niğde) and **Sobek Travel** (☎0388-232 1507; www.trekkinginturkeys.com; Avanoğlu Apt 70/17, Bor Caddesi, Niğde).

🛏 Sleeping & Eating

Ala Dağlar Camping   CAMPGROUND €
(☎0388-724 7033; www.aladaglarcamping. com; Çukurbağ; camp sites per person TL10, d per person with/without bathroom TL25/16; @) The pick of the camping ground is this newcomer with real mountain log cabins, a cute chalet and ample camping area.

Shared amenities are excellent. Guides cost roughly T200 per day, as do transfers from Adana airport.

Şafak Pension & Camping
         PENSION & CAMPGROUND €
(☎0388-724 7039; www.safaktravel.com; Çukurbağ; camp sites per person TL20, d per person with half-board TL50; @) This is run by the friendly, English-speaking walking and climbing guide Hassan. Rooms are simple but clean, with plentiful hot water, heating and comfortable beds. Camp sites have electricity and their own bathroom facilities. The terrace and garden command magnificent views of Mt Demirkazık.

On the other side of the road, the same family has another, similar pension, **Öz Şafak**, which charges the same rates. You'll find both pensions near the main road, about 1.5km from the bridge and the signpost marked 'Demirkazık 4, Pinarbaşı 8'.

Çukurbağ has basic shops for supplies.

❶ Getting There & Away

From Niğde, take a Çamardı-bound minibus (TL5, 90 minutes, every hour between 7am and 5.30pm) and ask to be let off at the Şafak Pension (it's 5km before Çamardı).

Niğde

☎0388 / POP 331,677
Backed by the snowcapped Ala Dağlar range, Niğde, 85km south of Nevşehir, was founded by the Seljuks. It's an agricultural centre with a clutch of historic buildings. You won't want to stay, but may have to if you want to visit the fabulous Eski Gümüşler Monastery, 10km to the northeast. You may also pass through en route to the base-camp villages for trekking in the Ala Dağlar National Park.

French is spoken in the helpful **tourist office** (☎232 3393; Belediye Sarayı 38/39; ☺8am-noon & 1-5pm Mon-Fri), located on the 1st floor of the ugly Kültür Merkezi (City Cultural Centre) on Bor Caddesi. There are plenty of internet cafes on the main street, including **Cafe In** (Bor Caddesi; per hr TL1; ☺9am-midnight), opposite the tourist office. ATMs are dotted along Bankalar/İstiklal/Bor Caddesi.

◉ Sights

Niğde Museum   MUSEUM
(Niğde Müzesi; ☎232 3397; admission TL3; ☺8am-noon & 1-5pm Tue-Sun) Niğde Museum houses a well-presented selection of finds

SULTAN MARSHES

An afternoon ploughing the Sultan Marshes in your gumboots might not sound like your cup of birdseed, but there's something undeniably comforting about observing a flock of flamingos at a waterhole, or an eagle swooping to snap the neck of a curious baby squirrel. The giant patch of wetland in between Soğanlı and Ala Dağlar is world-famous among the twitching fraternity who descend here year-round to spot the 300-odd different species on stopover from Africa, Russia and continental Europe. Despite a local myth that bushfires have killed all the ornithology, birdlife here is thriving and even a short detour to the flat, open fields can be richly rewarding.

If you decide to stay, the **Sultan Pansiyon** (☎658 5549; www.sultanbirding.com; s/d/tr/q TL30/45/70/80; ✲ @) is pretty much your only option. Luckily it's very comfortable and backs onto the marshes themselves. The affable owners and resident bird freaks can whip you around in their car and help you tick off your newly discovered hitlist. It's free and easy to drive yourself, as long as it's not too wet.

from the Assyrian city of Acemhöyük near Aksaray, through the Hittite and Phrygian ages to sculptures from Tyana (now Kemerhisar), the former Roman centre and Hittite capital 19km southwest of Niğde. Several mummies are exhibited too, including the 11th-century mummy of a blonde nun discovered in the 1960s in the Ihlara Valley.

The Seljuk **Alaeddin Camii** (1223), on the hill crowned with the fortress, is the town's grandest mosque, but the **Süngür Bey Camii**, on a terrace at the end of the marketplace, is more interesting. Built by the Seljuks and restored by the Mongols in 1335, it is a curious blend of architectural styles. The attractive **Ak Medrese** (1409) houses a cultural centre that may – or may not – be open. Also in the centre are the **Hüdavend Hatun Türbesi** (1312), a fine Seljuk tomb, and the Ottoman mosque, **Dış Cami**.

🛏 Sleeping & Eating

Niğde has several drab concrete hotels and numerous cheap and cheerful *lokantas* and *pastanes* on its thoroughfares.

Hotel Nahita   HOTEL €
(☎232 3536; Emin Erişingil Caddesi 19; s/d/tr TL45/60/70) On the main road into town and close to the otogar, this three-star block lacks character but is clean and comfortable and has a large green-and-orange restaurant.

Saruhan   TRADITIONAL €
(☎232 2172; Bor Caddesi 13; mains TL6-10) Occupying a restored *han* (caravanserai) dating from 1357, Saruhan is heavy on atmosphere and no lightweight when it comes to its food. It serves delicious kebaps as well as rustic dishes such as *işkembe çorba* (tripe

soup). We enjoyed the Adana kebap and were blown away by how cheap everything was. No alcohol is served.

Arısoylar Restaurant   ANATOLIAN €
(☎232 5035; Bor Caddesi 8; mains TL7-9) This sleek modern eatery offers classics such as İskender kebap, *çiğ köfte* (patties of raw spiced lamb) and *beyti sarma* (wrapped lamb with garlic, TL9). Its air-conditioned dining room with pink and white tablecloths is a perfect place to escape the heat and noise of Niğde.

❶ Getting There & Away

Niğde has a brand-new otogar. There are buses to Adana (TL15, 3½ hours, five daily), Aksaray (TL10, 1½ hours, hourly between 7am and 9pm), Ankara (TL25, five hours, five daily), İstanbul (TL50, 11 hours, five daily), Kayseri (TL10, 1½ hours, hourly between 7am and 9pm), Konya (TL20, 3½ hours, 10 daily) and Nevşehir (TL10, one hour, hourly from 7am to 6pm).

Niğde is on the Ankara–Adana train line. A daily service leaves for Adana at 6am (TL15, four hours) and for Ankara at 11.30pm (TL25, 9¼ hours).

Around Niğde
ESKİ GÜMÜŞLER MONASTERY

The ancient rock-hewn **Eski Gümüşler Monastery** (admission TL3; ⊙8.30am-noon & 1-5pm), sprawling along the base of a cliff about 10km northeast of Niğde, has some of Cappadocia's best-preserved frescoes.

The monastery was only rediscovered in 1963. You enter via a rock-cut passage, which opens onto a large courtyard with reservoirs for wine and oil, and rock-cut dwellings, crypts, a kitchen and a refectory.

A small hole in the ground acts as a vent for a 9m-deep shaft leading to two levels of subterranean rooms. You can descend through the chambers or climb to an upstairs bedroom.

Even the pillars in the lofty main church are decorated with colourful Byzantine frescoes, painted between the 7th and 11th centuries. The charming Nativity looks as if it is set in a rock-caved structure like this one, and the striking Virgin and Child to the left of the apse has the elongated Mary giving a *Mona Lisa* smile – it's said to be the only smiling Mary in existence.

ℹ️ Getting There & Away

Gümüşler Belediyesi minibuses (TL1, 15 minutes) depart every hour from the minibus terminal beside Niğde's otogar. As you enter Gümüşler, don't worry when the bus passes a couple of signs pointing to the monastery – it eventually passes right by it. To catch a bus back to Niğde, walk to the roundabout 500m from the monastery entrance and flag down a minibus heading to the left.

Ihlara Valley (Ihlara Vadisi)

☏ 0382

Southeast of Aksaray, Ihlara Valley scythes through the stubbly fields. Once called Peristrema, the valley was a favourite retreat of Byzantine monks, who cut churches into the base of its towering cliffs. Following the river (Melendiz Suyu), which snakes between painted churches, piles of boulders and a sea of greenery ringing with birdsong, is an unforgettable experience. In the words of one Slovakian traveller, Radovan: 'The deep canyon with lots of churches and trees opens up as you approach Selime. After that you're in a sleepy valley with the river flowing, big mountains typical of Cappadocia in the distance, and a gorgeous monastery in Selime.'

Good times to visit are midweek in May or September when fewer people are about. Midway along the valley, at Belisırma, a swath of riverside restaurants means you needn't come weighed down with provisions.

There are no ATMs in Ihlara village, Selime or Belisırma. Internet access is available at **Kappadokya Café** (per hr TL1; ⏱9am-midnight), near Akar Pansion in Ihlara village, and at **Derren Net** (per hr TL1.50; ⏱8am-10pm), next to the supermarket and the PTT in Selime.

◉ Sights & Activities

Walking Ihlara Valley

There are four entrances along the **Ihlara Valley** (admission TL5, parking TL2; ⏱8am-6.30pm). If, like most people, you only want to walk the short stretch with most of the churches, then enter via the 360 knee-jarring steps leading down from the Ihlara Vadisi Turistik Tesisleri (Ihlara Valley Tourist Facility), perched on the rim of the gorge 2km from Ihlara village. Alternatively there are entrances near the derelict Star Otel in Ihlara village (follow the path uphill to the left), at Belisırma and at Selime. It takes about 2½ to three hours to walk from the Ihlara Vadisi Turistik Tesisleri to Belisırma, and about three hours to walk from Belisırma to Selime. You'll need seven to eight hours if you want to walk all the way from Ihlara village to Selime, stopping in Belisırma for lunch along the way. If you're planning to walk all the way, it's best to start early in the day, particularly in summer, when you'll need to take shelter from the fierce sun. The ticket for the valley should also cover Selime Monastery and Güzelyurt's Monastery Valley & Antique City (p487). Along the valley floor, signs mark the different churches. Although they're all worth visiting if you have the time, the following list includes the real must-sees:

Kokar (Fragrant) Kilise   CHURCH
This church has some fabulous frescoes – the Nativity and the Crucifixion for starters – and tombs buried in the floors.

Sümbüllü (Hyacinth) Kilise   CHURCH
Some frescoes remain, but the church is mostly noteworthy for its well-preserved, simple but elegant facade.

Yılanlı (Serpent) Kilise   CHURCH
Many of the frescoes are damaged, but it's possible to make out the one outlining the punishments for sinners; especially the three-headed snake with a sinner in each mouth and the nipple-clamped women (ouch!) who didn't breastfeed their young.

Kırk Dam Altı (St George) Kilise   CHURCH
It's a scramble to get to, but the views of the valley make all the puffing worthwhile. The frescoes are badly graffitied, but above the entrance you can see St George on a white horse, slaying a three-headed snake.

Bahattın'ın Samanlığı (Bahattin's Granary) Kilise   CHURCH
With some of the valley's best-preserved frescoes, the church is named after a

local who used to store grain here. Frescoes show scenes from the life of Christ, including the Crucifixion, Massacre of the Innocents and Baptism scenes.

Direkli (Columned) Kilise CHURCH
This cross-shaped church has six columns, hence the name. The large adjoining chamber originally had two storeys, as you can see from what's left of the steps and the holes in the walls from the supporting beams. There are burial chambers in the floor.

Selime Monastery MONASTERY
(☉dawn-dusk) The monastery at Selime is an astonishing rock-cut structure incorporating a vast kitchen with soaring chimney, a church with a gallery around it, stables with rock-carved feed troughs and other evidence of the troglodyte lifestyle. The admission price is included in the Ihlara Valley ticket. The entrance is just opposite the Ali Paşa Tomb (1317).

👉 Tours
Travel agencies in Göreme (p455), Avanos (p467) and Ürgüp (p472) offer full-day tours to Ihlara for TL50 to TL60 per day, including lunch.

🛏 Sleeping & Eating
If you want to walk all the way along the gorge there are modest pensions handily placed at both ends (in Ihlara village and Selime). You can also break your journey into two parts with an overnight stay in Belisırma's camping grounds or pension. Note that all accommodation is closed out of season (December to March).

IHLARA VILLAGE
Akar Pansion & Restaurant PENSION €
(☑453 7018; www.ihlara-akarmotel.com; s/d/tr TL20/40/55; ⊛) One of the only places in town, Akar's 18 motel-style rooms are simple but clean with private bathrooms. The restaurant (mains from TL6 to TL7) serves *saç tava*, grilled local trout, fried chicken and omelettes, and a small shop sells picnic ingredients. Owner Cengiz shuttles people to Selime (TL20), Belisırma (TL15) and the Ihlara Vadisi Turistik Tesisleri (free). There's a small tea house next door, cheap laundry on-site (TL6 per load) and complimentary wi-fi.

BELİSIRMA
Midway along the gorge, below Belisırma village, four low-key licensed restaurants

To Aksaray (45km)
● Selime
Melendiz Suyu
Selime Monastery
Piri Pension
Çatlak Restaurant
Yaprakhisar ●   Ticket Office
Kayabaşı Motel
Anatolia Valley Restaurant & Camping; Tandırcı Restaurant & Camping
To Güzelyurt (9km); Aksaray (48km)
Direkli (Columned) Kilise   **Belisırma** ●   Vadi Pansiyon
Ticket Office
Kırk Dam Altı (St George) Kilise   *Yılanlı (Serpent) Kilise*
Ihlara Vadisi Turistik Tesisleri   *Sümbüllü (Hyacinth) Kilise*
Bahattın'ın Samanlığı (Bahattın's Granary) Kilise
Ticket Office ●
Kokar (Fragrant) Kilise
Star Otel
Akar Pansion & Restaurant   **Ihlara Village** ●
To Ilısu (2km); Güzelyurt (13km)

feed the hungry hikers. They are not worth a special trip, but benefit from their position right by the river. Two have wonderful tables on platforms above the water – the hottest property on the strip. All serve basic meals of grilled trout, *saç tava*, kebaps, salads and soups, and charge about the same: TL10 for a main and TL5 per site in their camp sites, which have basic ablution blocks.

Anatolia Valley Restaurant & Camping CAMPGROUND, RESTAURANT €
(☑457 3040; lunch TL10, camp site TL5) This good site has a couple of vine-covered pergolas for shade, although the toilet block isn't

BIG HASAN

If a stroll through Ihlara Valley gets you salivating for more walking, the area around Cappadocia's second-highest mountain, Hasan Dağı (Mt Hasan), is good for trekking. The closest village to the 3268m inactive volcano is **Helvadere**, about 10km southwest of Ihlara village and 20km east of Taşpınar. Helvadere is the site of the ancient city of Nora, the architecturally unique remains of which can be seen 1km east of the village. From the mountain hut, 8km southwest of Helvadere, it takes eight hours to hike to and from the summit, where the basement of what was once Turkey's highest church remains. There are views of the Ala Dağlar and Bolkar ranges and Tuz Gölü, the country's second-largest salt lake. The challenging trek requires some mountaineering experience during the winter. You can get more information in Göreme at Middle Earth Travel (p455), which offers a two-day trip incorporating Kaymaklı and Ihlara Valley from €150.

too clean. The owner will drive hikers back to Ihlara car park for TL15 if they are tired.

Belisırma Restaurant

CAMPGROUND, RESTAURANT €

(☑457 3057; lunch TL10, camp site TL5) On the opposite bank of the river, Belisırma's balconies are popular with groups. The camp site at the rear makes up for its lack of shade with respectable toilets and some hammocks.

Tandırcı Restaurant & Camping

CAMPGROUND, RESTAURANT €

(☑457 3110; lunch TL15, camp site free) Camp sites are dotted among vegetable gardens and a small orchard. Groups often bypass the restaurant, leaving a mellow, shady spot and a chance of scoring a river platform. There's a pension in the scruffy village on the hill, across the bridge from the restaurants. The spartan **Vadi Pansiyon** (☑457 3067; d TL50) has rooms with small private bathrooms, and a terrace cafe with views.

SELİME

The cheapest and most pleasant accommodation option at the northern end of the gorge is the worn but clean **Piri Pension** (☑454 5114; s/d TL20/40), a tranquil, friendly place overlooking some fairy chimneys. Owner Mustafa guides around the valley and the nearby monastery (TL15). In an olive-green block 2km outside the village on the road to Belisırma, the bare, clean rooms at **Kayabaşi Motel** (☑454 5565; s/d TL25/50) are chiefly notable for their views of the yawning mouth of the gorge. There is a ramshackle eatery, **Çatlak Restaurant**, on a muddy riverbank a few steps from the start of the walk.

❶ Getting There & Away

Ten dolmuşes a day travel down the valley from Aksaray, stopping in Selime, Belisırma, Ihlara

village and Ilısu en route to Güzelyurt (p489). In Belisırma, dolmuşes stop in the new part of the village, up on the plateau, and you have to hike a few hundred metres down into the valley. To travel in the opposite direction, you have to catch a taxi. A taxi between Ihlara village and Selime should cost about TL35; from Selime to Aksaray, about TL55. See p488 for taxi fares from Güzelyurt.

Güzelyurt

☑0382 / POP 3735 / ELEV 1485M

According to signposts on the deserted roads east of Ihlara Valley, 'a trip without Güzelyurt is not a Cappadocia trip'. It may seem an optimistic slogan, but Güzelyurt both ticks all the important Cappadocian sightseeing boxes and receives a refreshing lack of visitors. A scree slope with Hollywood-style letters spelling out the town's old name, Gelveri, overlooks underground cities, rock-cut churches, stone houses and a lakeside monastery.

In Ottoman times Karballa (Gelveri) was inhabited by 1000 Ottoman Greek families and 50 Turkish Muslim families. In the population exchanges between Turkey and Greece in 1924, the Greeks of Gelveri went to Nea Karvali in Greece, while Turkish families from Kozan and Kastoria in Greece moved here. The relationship between the two countries is now celebrated in an annual **Turks & Greeks Friendship Festival** held in July.

Güzelyurt has a PTT, a branch of the TC Ziraat Bankası (but no ATM) and several shops. English-speaking staff at the helpful **tourist office** (☑451 2498; ◷8.30am-7pm) in the main street can supply information about both the town and the Ihlara Valley. The poorly signed **Arikan Internet Café** (per hr TL1; ◷8am-11pm) is on the 1st floor of a *pastane* in a small square behind the bank.

◎ Sights

Monastery Valley & Antique City RUINS
Walk downhill from the main square following the signs to the Monastery Valley and Antique City. About 300m from the square, a sign points left to a small, uninteresting satellite of the underground city (yeraltı şehri; admission TL5; ⊙8am-6.30pm). Next stop is the ticket booth; admission should be free with an Ihlara Valley ticket. The restored complex ranges across several levels and includes one hair-raising section where you descend through a hole in the floor.

The valley is also home to several churches, most impressive of which is the Aşağı or Büyük Kilise Camii (Lower or Big Mosque). Built as the Church of St Gregory of Nazianzus in AD 385, it was restored in 1835 and turned into a mosque following the population exchange in 1924. St Gregory (330–90) grew up locally and became a theologian, patriarch and one of the four Fathers of the Greek Church. Check out the wooden sermon desk that was reputedly a gift from a Russian tsar. There are plans to uncover the whitewashed frescoes. Further on are the Koç (Ram) church and the neighbouring Cafarlar (Rivulets), with its interesting frescoes.

Afterwards you can continue through the 4.5km Monastery Valley, a sort of Ihlara in miniature. Panoramic viewpoints abound and just walking through it is pleasant, but there are more rock-cut churches and dwellings to explore. Some 2km after the previous group, the Kalburlu Kilisesi (Church with a Screen) has a superb entrance. The almost-adjoining Kömürlü Kilisesi (Coal Church) has carvings including an elaborate lintel above the entrance and some Maltese crosses.

Yüksek Kilise & Manastır RUINS
Perched high on a rock overlooking Güzelyurt lake is the Yüksek Kilise and Manastır (High Church and Monastery), some 2km south of a signposted turn-off on the Ihlara road 1km west of Güzelyurt. The road there creeps between huge boulders balancing on other rocks like outsized sculptures in a gallery. The walled compound containing the plain church and monastery is graffitied inside and looks more impressive from afar, but has sweeping views of the lake and mountains.

Gaziemir UNDERGROUND CITY
(admission TL3; ⊙8am-6pm) Some 18km east of Güzelyurt, just off the road to Derinkuyu,

Gaziemir's underground city opened in 2007. Churches, a winery with wine barrels, food depots, hamams and tandoor fireplaces can be seen. Camel bones and loopholes in the rock for tethering animals suggest that it also served as a subterranean caravanserai.

🛏 Sleeping & Eating

Halil Pension PENSION €€
(☑451 2707; www.halilpension.com; Yukarı Mahallesi Amaç Sokak; s/d/tr with half-board TL80/120 /150; @) This family home makes a great base for those intending to explore the area for a few days. The meals, packed with goodies from the garden and served at a table fashioned from an antique door, could be the culinary highlight of your trip. In a modern extension to the original 140-year-old Greek house, the rooms have loads of natural light, small but spotlessly clean bathrooms and cheerful modern decor. The roof terrace has magnificent views of Yüksek Kilise and one room has a private balcony. As you enter town from the west, it's signposted off to the right, a short walk downhill from the centre.

Aslani Pansiyon PENSION €
(☑451 2726; pensionlion@hotmail.com; Yeni Camii Yani; s/d TL30/50) Hidden behind a large door with a lion for a knocker, this is an authentic homestay opposite a busy mosque. The little old Turkish lady of the house presents two double rooms filled with flowers and fresh linen. Breakfast is a tablecloth of spreads and breads. Highly recommended.

Hotel Karballa HISTORIC HOTEL €€
(☑451 2103; www.karballahotel.com; standard s/d/tr/q €40/55/75/100, deluxe €50/65/85/110; ❄❀) We bet the monks enjoyed living in this 19th-century Greek monastery above the town centre. The hotel has retained a contemplative atmosphere and you feel like a father breaking his fast in the arched former refectory, now the restaurant (dinner €10). The rooms, named after the holy one-time inhabitants, have cross-shaped windows, bright Uzbeki bedspreads and mezzanines. Some of the standard rooms, reached by spiral staircases, snuggle into their vaulted ceilings. There is even a pensive atmosphere in the pool, which overlooks the town's Gelveri sign.

Kadir's Houses OTTOMAN HOUSE €€
(☑451 2166; www.kadirshouses.com; s/d/tr/q TL60/100/120/140) An overpriced budget version of Hotel Karballa, Kadir's occupies a 120-year-old Ottoman house entered

through an antique carved wooden door. The three rooms have modern bathrooms, subtle lighting, mezzanines and beds with natural, woollen duvets. Homemade wine is served in the small outdoor bar and dinner costs TL15. The owner is low-key.

There are three similar *lokantas* on and around the main square, serving cheap beer and rakı and dishes such as kebaps and pide.

ℹ️ Getting There & Away

Returning buses travel from Güzelyurt to Aksaray (TL5, one hour) every two hours between 6.30am and 5.30pm. On Sundays there are fewer buses.

You'll have to catch a taxi to get to Selime (TL25), Ihlara village (TL35) and Hasan Dağı (Mt Hasan; TL60). A taxi to Aksaray costs TL60.

Aksaray

📞0382 / POP 152,000

Aksaray is symptomatic of Turkey's economic rise; quietly prospering with high consumer confidence. The canals here are pretty and the vibe is youthful. In parts it's an ugly modern town that only snares travellers en route to the Ihlara Valley, but an afternoon among the throng in the attractive town square in the shadow of gaudy government buildings is an unequivocally Anatolian experience.

⊙ Sights

The **Ulu Cami** (Great Mosque; Bankalar Caddesi) has decoration characteristic of the post-Seljuk Beylik period. A little of the original yellow stone remains in the grand doorway.

The **Aksaray Museum** (Aksaray Müzesi; admission TL3; ⊙8.30am-noon & 1-5pm), in a new building en route from the otogar to the centre, covers ethnography and archaeology. Exhibits include neolithic beads, a Hellenic child's sarcophagus, Roman perfume bottles, carpets from the Ulu Cami and, in the hall of mummies, a mummified cat.

The older part of town, along Nevşehir Caddesi, has the curious **Eğri Minare** (Crooked Minaret), built in 1236 and leaning at an angle of 27 degrees. Inevitably, the locals know it as the 'Turkish Tower of Pisa'.

🛏️ Sleeping & Eating

All of the following are on, or within walking distance of, the main square.

Otel Yuvam HOTEL €

(📞212 0024; Eski Sanayi Caddesi Kavşağı; s/d/tr TL25/40/60) It's rock and roll retro at this friendly budget option located on the main

square next to the Kurşunlu Cami. Rooms sport lino floor coverings and solid wooden furniture. Bathrooms are spotless and beds are hard but have crisp, clean linen. The small lounge with satellite TV is a good retreat – until the call to prayer sounds.

Otel Erdem HOTEL €

(📞214 1500; Bankalar Caddesi 19A; s/d TL35/50) A young manager oversees this great budget hotel with small, spotless rooms. All the town planning can be seen from your balcony. It's next to Harman.

Otel Vadim HOTEL €

(📞212 8200; 818 Vadi Sokak 13; s/d/tr TL30/50/60; @) It is certainly worth paying a few extra lira to upgrade from Otel Yuvam to this excellent midrange choice. Located in a quiet side street off Büyük Kergi Caddesi, the southern extension of Bankalar Caddesi, it has a green-tiled facade and large, comfortable rooms with wi-fi.

Harman MODERN OCAKBAŞI €

(📞212 3311; Bankalar Caddesi 16a; mains TL7) Aksaray's best restaurant, a few doors from Yeni Merkez Lokantası, is adorned with photos of visiting celebrities posing with the star-struck waiters. It offers a great selection of *izgara* (grills, TL6.50), döner kebaps (TL7), pide and soups (TL2). Those who enjoy a sweet at the end of the meal will be impressed by the excellent homemade baklava and *künefe* (syrup-soaked dough and sweet cheese sprinkled with pistachios, TL4).

Yeni Merkez Lokantası LOKANTA €

(📞213 1076; Bankalar Caddesi, Valilik Karsısı 8d; mains TL4-7) A local favourite, this friendly place facing the *vilayet* has an array of daily specials on display in the bains-marie, or you can order specialities such as the İskender kebaps. Takeaway döner sandwiches are available here and at the street vendors nearby.

Melisa Pastanesi PATISSERIE €

(📞212 3134; Eski Sanayi Caddesi 11; cakes TL2-10) This patisserie near Otel Yuvam serves the usual range of sweet treats and the friendly staff speak some English; particularly Tariq, who worked in a kebap shop in Stoke-on-Trent, England.

ℹ️ Information

French is spoken in the helpful **tourist office** (📞213 2474; Taşpazar Mahallesi; ⊙8.30am-noon & 1.30-5pm Mon-Fri). To find it, walk along Ankara Caddesi (which runs west off Bankalar Caddesi near the *vilayet*), walk past the Zafer Okulu (school) and take the first left. You can check your emails near Harman at **VIP Net** (Hükümet Sokak 10; per hr TL1; ☺9am-10pm), where fish tanks glow alongside six flat screens.

❶ Getting There & Away

From Aksaray, direct buses go to Ankara (TL18, 3½ hours, 230km), Konya (TL14, two hours, 140km) via Sultanhanı (TL5, 45 minutes, 50km), Nevşehir (TL10, one hour, 65km) and Niğde (TL10, 1½ hours, 115km).

Dolmuşes run between the old otogar and Güzelyurt (TL5, one hour, 45km, six daily) every two hours between 7.30am and 6pm, stopping in Selime, Belisırma, Ihlara village and Ilısu. Between 9am and 2pm, there are also four dolmuşes for Ihlara Valley alone. Sultanhanı (TL5, 45 minutes, 50km, 10 daily) is also served; there are few Sunday services.

Around Aksaray

The road between Aksaray and Nevşehir follows one of the oldest trade routes in the world, the Uzun Yol (Long Rd). The route linked Konya, the Seljuk capital, with its other great cities (Kayseri, Sivas and Erzurum) and ultimately with Persia (Iran).

The Long Rd was formerly dotted with *hans* where the traders would stop for accommodation and business. The remains of three caravanserais can be visited from Aksaray, the best preserved being the impressive **Ağzıkara Hanı** (admission TL3; ☺7.30am-8pm), 16km northeast of Aksaray, which was built between 1231 and 1239. From Aksaray a taxi will charge about TL50 for the run there and back. If you'd prefer to go by bus, catch one heading to Nevşehir and jump off at the Ağzıkara Hanı. Day tours from Göreme and Ürgüp also call in on the caravanserai.

Further towards Nevşehir you'll pass the scant remains of the 13th-century **Tepesidelik Hanı**, 23km northeast of Aksaray, and the 12th-century **Alay Hanı**, another 10km on.

Kayseri

🕿0352 / POP 1.2 MILLION / ELEV 1067M

Mixing Seljuk tombs, mosques and modern developments, Kayseri is both Turkey's most Islamic city after Konya and one of the economic powerhouses nicknamed the 'Anatolian tigers'. Colourful silk headscarfs are piled in the bazaar, one of the country's biggest, and businesses shut down at noon on Friday, but Kayseri's religious leanings are less prominent than its manufacturing prowess. The city's residents, overlooked and inspired by Erciyes Dağı, are confident of its future and proud of its past. With no need to rely on the tourism game for their income, Kayseri's people are often less approachable than folk in Göreme et al, and this can be frustrating and jarring if you arrive fresh from the fairy chimneys. However, if you are passing through this transport hub, it's worth taking a look at a Turkish boom town with a strong sense of its own history.

History

Under the Roman emperor Tiberius (r AD 14–37), Eusebia (as the settlement at Kayseri was known) was renamed Caesarea. The Arabs renamed it Kaisariyah and the Seljuks gave it its current name.

Kayseri became famous as the birthplace of St Basil the Great, who organised the monastic life of Cappadocia. Its early Christian history was interrupted by Arab invasions from the 7th century. The Seljuks took over in 1084 and held the city until the Mongols' arrival in 1243, except for a brief period when the Crusaders captured it on their way to the Holy Land.

When Kayseri had been part of the Mongol empire for almost 100 years, its governor set up his own emirate (1335). This lasted just 45 years and was succeeded by another emirate, before being conquered by the Ottomans, captured by the Mamluks, and finally retaken by the Ottomans in 1515 – all in just over a century.

◉ Sights

Now acting as an overflow valve for the nearby bazaar, the monumental, black volcanic-stone walls of the **citadel** (*hisar* or *kale*) were constructed in the early 13th century, during the Seljuk sultan Alaattin Keykubat's reign. Kayseri saw its first castle in the 3rd century, under the Roman emperor Gordian III, and the Byzantine emperor Justinian made alterations 300 years later. The present building has been restored over the years – twice in the 15th century.

Among Kayseri's distinctive features are several important building complexes that were founded by Seljuk queens and princesses, including the austere-looking **Mahperi Hunat Hatun Complex** (Seyyid Burhaneddin (Talas) Caddesi), east of the citadel. It comprises the Mahperi Hunat Hatun Camii (1238), built by the wife of Alaattin Keykubat; the Hunat Hatun Medresesi (1237); and a hamam, which is still in use.

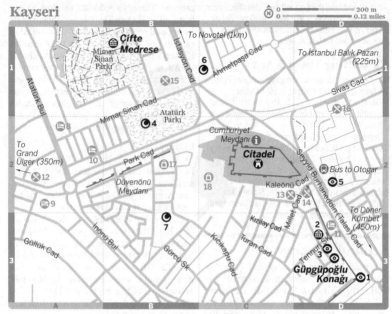

Kayseri

Another striking monument is the **Çifte Medrese** (Twin Seminaries). These adjoining religious schools, set in Mimar Sinan Parkı north of Park Caddesi, were founded at the bequest of the Seljuk sultan Gıyasettin I Keyhüsrev and his sister Gevher Nesibe Sultan (1165–1204). The **Museum of Medical History** (TL1.50; ⊘8am-noon & 1-5pm) inside is located in the former theatre of one of the world's first medical training schools.

Back towards the citadel is the Ottoman-style **Kurşunlu Cami** (Lead-Domed Mosque; Atatürk Parkı). Also called the Ahmet Paşa Camii after its founder, it was built in the late 16th century, possibly following plans drawn up by the great Sinan (who was born in a nearby village). North of Cumhuriyet Meydanı, be sure to have a look at the **Sahabiye Medresesi** (from 1267; Ahmetpaşa

Caddesi), an Islamic theological school that now functions as a book bazaar.

Another notable mosque is Kayseri's **Ulu Cami** (Great Mosque), begun in the mid-12th century by the Danışmend Turkish emirs and finished by the Seljuks in 1205. It features some good examples of early Seljuk style, such as the brick minaret, one of the first built in Anatolia.

Kayseri is dotted with conical **Seljuk tombs**, the most famous of which is the so-called **Döner Kümbet** (Revolving Tomb; Talas Caddesi) at Kartal Junction. On the way to the Archaeological Museum, you'll pass a cluster of Seljuk monuments, including the **Alaca Kümbet** (Alaca Tomb; Seyyid Burhaneddin (Talas) Caddesi), with a typical quadratic design and pyramidal roof.

The 19th-century **Surup Krikor Lusavoriç Kilise** (Church of St Gregory the Illuminator; off Nazım Bey Bulvarı) is one of Anatolia's few remaining Armenian churches. *Asiatic Review* described it as 'tawdry' back in 1937, and the seldom-used building is certainly dilapidated. However, the domed interior is worth a look, mostly for the three gilded altars, containing paintings that replaced the originals last century. The painting on the left, with four fiery columns topped by flaming crosses, depicts the vision of St Gregory, who grew up in Kayseri. Located in a bad part of town, the church is tricky to find, so take a taxi (TL15 return from the tourist office, including waiting time). Ring the bell on the west side of the building to gain entry and leave a tip for the caretaker at the end of your visit.

Museums

Just southeast of the citadel is the 18th-century **Güpgüpoğlu Konağı** (off Tennuri Sokak), a stone Ottoman mansion with beautiful wooden balconies and doorways. Inside, the **Ethnography Museum** (admission TL3; ⊙8am-5pm Tue-Sun) is split between an exhibition of Ottoman craft and a mannequin-inhabited section, evoking how life was lived under the multicoloured beams.

Nearby is the stylish **Atatürk Evi** (Tennuri Sokak; admission free; ⊙8am-5pm Mon-Fri), a small, originally furnished Ottoman-era house where Atatürk stayed when he visited.

If you have half an hour to spare, wander through the park to the small **Archaeological Museum** (Kışla Caddesi 2; admission TL3; ⊙8am-5pm Tue-Sun), a minor magpie's nest featuring finds from nearby Kültepe (ancient Kaniş, the chief city of the Hatti people and the first Hittite capital). The largest city mound discovered in Anatolia, Kültepe yielded the area's oldest written documents. Many relate to commerce, such as the Assyrian clay tablets and envelopes from 1920 BC to 1840 BC. Other exhibits include a stunning sarcophagus illustrating Hercules' chores, a Bronze Age mother goddess idol, child mummies, Roman and Hellenistic jewellery, hieroglyphic inscriptions relating to King Tuthalia IV and a decapitated but imposing statue of the Hittite monarch.

🛏 Sleeping

Due to Kayseri's cult status among chain-smoking Turkish businessmen, you should book accommodation in advance. Once installed in a room, ensure you reserve it for the duration of your stay or the management may give it to the next claimant.

Hotel Almer   HOTEL €€
(☑320 7970; www.almer.com.tr; Osman Kavuncu Caddesi 15; s/d/tr TL80/100/150; ✳ @)

WORTH A TRIP

SKI ERCİYES DAĞI

If you pluck up the resolve to confront the rugged and handsome Erciyes Dağı, please dispel any notion that you've bagged a Swiss alpine beauty. This is ski season Turkish style, where getting knocked down by an errant snowmobile or devouring a mouthful of yellow snow is considered part of the adventure. For most ski lovers though, this amounts to just a pain in the arse. Luckily it's beautiful as hell up here and the hardcore will still find plenty of empty pistes and not a red flag in site. Remember when you see a rock, turn!

The popular Erciyes Dağı Ski Resort is on the northeast side of the mountain, which is also the best area for mountaineering. In summer, you can camp at sites around Cobaini. The best hotel is **Grand Ergas Erciyes** (☑342 2128; Erciyes Dağı; s/d TL100/200; @ ≋), which is new and a bit fancy.

TRAINS FROM KAYSERİ

Trains depart daily unless otherwise stated.

DESTINATION	FARE (TL)	DURATION (HR)	DEPARTURES
Adana	14	6	2.15am & 7.40am
Ankara	13	8	midnight, 12.55am, 2.51am (not Sun), 4am & 4.19am
İstanbul	22	18	2.51am (not Sun) & 4am
Kars	26	20½	1.30am & 10.17pm
Kurtalan	21	20	11.50am (Mon, Wed, Fri & Sat)
Malatya	15	9	2.52am & 11.50am (not Thu)
Tatvan	22	24	11.50am (Tue & Sun)

Kayseri's top sub-Hilton establishment is smoothly professional from the moment you reel through the revolving door. The relaxing reception has a backlit bar and little alcoves for working your way through the magazine rack. Mirrored pillars glint between pink tablecloths in the restaurant, and the wi-fi-enabled rooms are surprisingly quiet despite the busy road.

Hotel Çapari   HOTEL €€
(☎222 5278; Gevher Nesibe Mahallesi, Donanma Caddesi 12; s/d/tr/ste TL60/90/110/120; ❄) With thick red carpets and friendly staff, this three-star hotel on a quiet street off Atatürk Bulvarı is one of the best deals in town. The well-equipped rooms have satellite TV, wi-fi and massive minibars.

Hotel Sur   HOTEL €
(☎222 4367; Talas Caddesi 12; s/d/tr TL40/60/75) Beyond the dark reception and institutional corridors, the Sur's rooms are bright and comfortable. The management is friendly and the hotel's withered international flags can almost lean on the ancient city walls for support.

Novotel   HOTEL €€
(☎207 3000; www.novotel.com; Kocasinan Bulvarı; s €120-135, d €140-155; ❄ @) This is a very good version of the dependable international chain, featuring clean lines, bright colours and five-star service.

Grand Ülger   HOTEL €€
(☎323 8303; www.grandulgerhotel.com; Osman Kavuncu Caddesi 55; s/d TL50/90; ❄ @) Upon entering the city from Göreme you'll come across this flashy business hotel, which is a good choice for its leather-and-marble

lobby. The comfortable rooms and decent restaurant are further bonuses.

Bent Hotel   HOTEL €€
(☎221 2400; www.benthotel.com; Atatürk Bulvarı 40; s/d/tr TL75/100/120) Its name may not inspire confidence, but the Bent is a good midrange choice overlooking the pedal boats in Mimar Sinan Parkı. The small but comfortable rooms are brown and smoky but all have TVs, Efes-stocked minibars and 24-hour room service.

✖ Eating

Kayseri boasts a few special dishes, among them *pastırma* (salted, sun-dried veal coated with *çemen,* a spicy concoction of garlic, red peppers, parsley and water), the original pastrami.

Few restaurants serve alcohol – if you want a tipple with your tucker, try Hotel Almer (mains TL12, open 7pm to 11.30pm) or **Kale Rooftop Restaurant** (☎207 5000; Cumhuriyet Meydanı, İstasyon Caddesi 1; mains TL20-40; ☺noon-2am) at the Hilton.

The western end of Sivas Caddesi has a strip of fast-food joints that still seem to be pumping when everything else in town is quiet.

Elmacıoğlu İskender et Lokantası
                                          LOKANTA €
(☎222 6965; 1st & 2nd fl, Millet Caddesi 5; mains TL8-10; ☺9am-10.30pm) Ascend in a lift to Kayseri's best restaurant, with waiters sporting bow ties and big windows overlooking the citadel. İskender kebaps are the house speciality, available with *köfte* or in 'double' form (TL13), and other dishes include *pastırma* pide (TL8.50). Recommended.

İstanbul Balık Pazarı   SEAFOOD €
(☑231 8973; Sivas Caddesi; mains TL3; ☺8am-11pm) Choose between the fish frying at the door, then head past the glistening catches in the fishmongers to the small dining room, with its mishmash of nautical and historical paintings.

Tuana   ANATOLIAN €
(☑222 0565; 2nd fl, Sivas Caddesi; mains TL7) Entered from the lane leading from the PTT to Sivas Caddesi, the smart Tuana offers a roll-call of classics such as kebaps and Kayseri *mantı*. When it's quiet, the ocean of red tables and chairs adorned with golden ribbons have the air of an out-of-season seaside resort, but it's easy to distract yourself with the views of the citadel and Erciyes Dağı.

Divan Pastanesi   PATISSERIE €
(☑222 3974; Millet Caddesi; TL2-9) Across Millet Caddesi from the Elmacioğlu İskender et Lokantası, this modern pastry shop is a favourite among Kayseri's sweet tooths.

Anadolu Et Lokantası   LOKANTA €
(☑320 5209; Osman Kavuncu Caddesi 10; mains TL5-10) Meaty goodness is the order of the day at this happening lunch-time hangout.

🔒 Shopping

Set at the intersection of age-old trade routes, Kayseri has been an important commercial centre for millennia and its *kapalı çarşı* (vaulted bazaar) was one of the largest built by the Ottomans. Restored in the 1870s and again in the 1980s, it remains the heart of the city and is well worth a wander. The adjoining *bedesten* (covered market), built in 1497, was first dedicated to the sale of textiles and is still a good place to pick up carpets and kilims. An antique carpet auction takes place here on Monday and Thursday.

ℹ️ Information

English and German are spoken at the helpful **tourist office** (☑222 3903; Cumhuriyet Meydanı; ☺8am-5pm Mon-Fri), which gives out maps and brochures.

You'll find numerous banks with ATMs in the centre. To collect your email, head to **Soner Internet Café** (Düvenönü Meydanı; per hr TL1.50; ☺8am-midnight).

ℹ️ Getting There & Away

Air

Turkish Airlines (☑222 3858; Tekin Sokak Hukuk Plaza 6c) has three daily flights to and from İstanbul (TL69 to TL169 one way, 1½ hours) and one Sun Express flight to and from İzmir (TL74 one way, 1½ hours) on Wednesday and Saturday mornings.

Onur Air (☑231 5551; Ahmetpaşa Caddesi 7) has a daily flight to and from İstanbul (TL54 to TL174 one way).

A taxi between the city centre and the *havaalanı* (airport) costs TL15 and a dolmuş is TL1.25. There are shuttle buses between the airport and hotels in central Cappadocia (see p451).

Bus

On an important north–south and east–west crossroads, Kayseri has plenty of bus services.

The otogar has an internet cafe, luggage storage (TL6 for 24 hours), a barber, car rental and a cafe with an *ayran* fountain. If there's no *servis*

SERVICES FROM KAYSERİ'S OTOGAR

DESTINATION	FARE (TL)	DURATION (HR)	FREQUENCY (PER DAY)
Adana	22	5	frequent
Ankara	25	5	hourly
Erzurum	40	10	frequent
Gaziantep	25	6	6 a day
Göreme	10	1½	hourly
Kahramanmaraş	20	4	hourly
Malatya	25	5	frequent
Nevşehir via Ürgüp	12/6	1½/1¼	hourly
Sivas	18	3	frequent
Van	50	13	frequent

from there to the *merkezi* (centre), grab a taxi (TL15) or catch a local bus (TL1.25).

Dolmuşes run to Ürgüp (TL5, 1¾ hours) from the west garage.

Train

Kayseri is served by the *Vangölü Ekspresi* (between İstanbul and Tatvan), the *Güney Ekspresi* (between İstanbul and Kurtalan), the *Doğu Ekspresi* (between İstanbul and Kars), the *Erzurum Ekspresi* (between Ankara and Kars), the *Çukurova Mavi* (between Ankara and Adana) and the *4 Eylül Mavi Train* (between Ankara and Malatya). The RAJA Passenger Trains İstanbul–Tehran service (see p686) stops in Kayseri en route to Iran.

To reach the centre from the train station, walk out of the station, cross the big avenue (Çevre Yol) and board any bus heading down Atatürk Bulvarı to Düvenönü Meydanı. Alternatively you could walk along Altan Caddesi, which isn't as busy as Atatürk Bulvarı.

Tram

A state-of-the-art tram system is now running in Kayseri from 6am to 2am daily. It's a very efficient way of getting around and single tickets cost TL1.

Around Kayseri

SULTAN HAN

Built in the 1230s, the Sultan Han (admission TL3; ⊙dawn-dusk) is a striking old Seljuk caravanserai on the old Kayseri–Sivas highway, 45km northeast of Kayseri. It is a fine, restored example of a Seljuk royal caravan lodging – the largest in Anatolia after the Sultanhanı, near Aksaray.

Locals should unlock the door and issue tickets, but visitors have reported frustrated attempts to gain access. If you are coming from Kayseri, enquire at Kayseri's Archaeological Museum (p491).

Sultan Han is southeast of the Kayseri–Sivas road, near Tuzhisar. To get there from Kayseri, take a Sivas-bound bus (TL5), or a dolmuş (TL2.50) heading to Sarioğlan or Akkişla from the *doğu* (east) garage.

Black Sea Coast & the Kaçkar Mountains

Best Places to Stay

» Zinos Country Hotel (p501)
» Sebile Hanim Konaği (p505)
» Otel Ural (p511)
» Fora Pansiyon (p523)
» Otel Doğa (p523

Best Places to Eat

» Saray Restaurant (p502)
» Çakırtepe (p505)
» Mıdı (p506)
» Trabzon Mangal Dünyasi (p513)
» Evvel Zaman (p518)

Why Go?

Quick. Turn around. There's an entire travel experience that you probably haven't even considered. While you've been planning your Turkish sojourn south to the Med or west to the Aegean, to the north and east the Black Sea (Karadeniz) is equally deserving.

The craggy and spectacular coastline is scattered with the legacy of civilisations and empires that have ebbed and flowed in this historic region. Castles, churches and monasteries recall the days of the kings of Pontus, the Genoese and the Ottomans. Even earlier times are marked by myths of Amazon warriors and Jason and his Argonauts. The very existence of modern Turkey owes a massive debt to the passionate local support thrown behind Atatürk's republican revolution. After Sinop's Mediterranean-style vibe, or Trabzon's modern Turkey buzz, explore the isolated mountain villages and alpine lakes and valleys of the Kaçkar Mountains. It's often quite surprising what's hidden behind you, isn't it?

When to Go

Trabzon

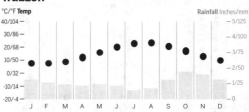

| **May** Celebrate the coming of spring at the four-day International Giresun Aksu Festival. | **June to August** Trek in the beautiful alpine valleys of the Kaçkar Mountains. | **April & September** Be one of the few travellers enjoying the lazy-day charm of Amasra and Sinop . |

Black Sea Coast & the Kaçkar Mountains Highlights

❶ Absorb the beauty of centuries-old Byzantine frescoes in the improbable cliff-face setting of the **Sumela Monastery** (p516)

❷ Walk off tasty home-cooked food amidst the stunning lakes, valleys and peaks of the **Kaçkar Mountains** (p520)

❸ Count the glorious, vertigo-inducing curves on the drop-dead scenic coastal road from **Amasra to Sinop** (p499)

❹ Slow down and imbibe the easygoing Mediterranean-style ambience of the fishing harbour at **Sinop** (p500)

❺ Explore the winding labyrinth of alleys and lanes in **Amasra's castle** (p497)

❻ Fulfil your cosmopolitan urges in the busy streets and bustling big smoke of **Trabzon** (p509)

❼ Take to the back roads to discover Perşembe and Çaka beach on the old coast road from **Bolaman to Ordu** (p507)

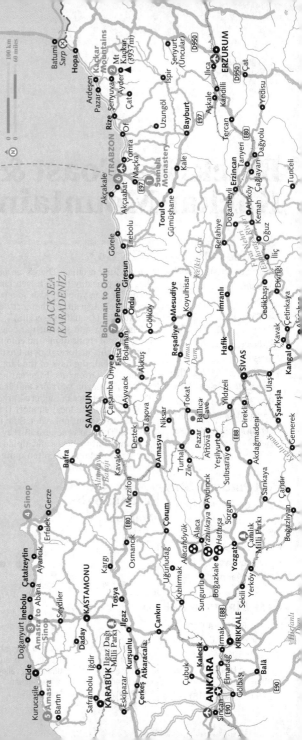

BLACK SEA COAST

Amasra

☑ 0378 / POP 7000

From İstanbul to Amasra is a six-hour journey, but when you first glimpse Amasra from the hills above you'll see the trip was worthwhile. The first substantial town along the Black Sea coast, Amasra effortlessly assumes the mantle of the region's prettiest port.

It's a popular tourist centre, but is low-key in contrast to the resorts of the Aegean coast. International visitors are still relatively uncommon, and the welcome from locals and Turkish visitors will be warm and unaffected. Summer weekends are busy, but visitors are guaranteed sleepy streets and coves during the week.

The Byzantines held Amasra as part of the Pontic kingdom, but rented the port to the Genoese as a trading station from 1270 until 1460, when Mehmet the Conqueror waltzed in without a fight. Under Ottoman rule, Amasra lost its commercial importance to other Black Sea ports, and today it's a laid-back spot to relax, dine on excellent seafood, and plan your impending journey along the Black Sea coast.

Entering Amasra, on your left is the museum in an old stone building. Most buses stop at an intersection near the post office (PTT). Follow the sign to 'Şehir Merkezi' (north) for the Küçük Liman (Small Harbour) with restaurants and pensions. Walk straight (east) to hit the sandy strip of the Büyük Liman (Large Harbour). The entrance to the citadel lurks around souvenir shops in the Küçük Liman.

If you're driving from Amasra to Sinop, fill up on fuel across the hill in Bartın.

⊙ Sights & Activities

North of the two harbours, three massive gateways lead to Amasra's **kale** (citadel). It encompasses the promontory fortified by the Byzantines when the port was known as Sesamos Amastris.

The inside of the citadel is now mainly a residential area. The original walls and some relics survive, including the 15th-century **Eski Chapel** (Old Chapel). The excellent **Amasra Museum** (Amasra Müzesi; Dereoğlu Sokak 4; admission TL4; ⊙9am-5.30pm Tue-Sun), overlooking Küçük Liman, contains Roman, Byzantine and Hellenistic finds, showcasing Amasra's many-mastered history.

Amasra's location is best admired from the sea. Operators in Büyük Liman offer **boat trips** around the harbour and along the coastline. Expect to pay about TL7 for a short tour (45 minutes) and TL35 for a longer tour (six hours), including swimming stops and lunch on a nearby island. Boats are more likely to run on weekends in summer.

🛏 Sleeping

Rates in Amasra can rise by 10% to 40% on busy summer weekends from mid-June to mid-September. Many places will charge solo travellers the cost of a double room across this period. Prices quoted here are for midweek, and assume a discount for solo travellers. You'll definitely need to negotiate.

Amasra is a good spot for *ev pansiyonu* (pensions in private homes). Look for 'Pansiyon' notices on the seafront and in the *kale*.

All *pansiyons* close from November to April, and most hotels will only be open on weekends during these months.

Hotel Türkili   HOTEL €€

(☑315 3750; turkiliotel@ttnet.net.tr; Özdemirhan Sokak 6; s/d TL70/100; ❀) The wrought-iron balconies and pink facade add a European tinge to this Amasra favourite. Wi-fi, satellite TV and good English skills at reception add up to one of Amasra's best. Türkili's 5th-floor restaurant offers views over both harbours.

Timur Otel   HOTEL €€

(☑315 2589; www.timurotel.com; Çekiciler Caddesi 27; s/d/tr TL50/80/110; ❀) Good English is spoken at this central option with spotless, pretty-in-pink rooms overlooking a quiet square. Double-glazing on the windows ensures a good night's kip.

Çarşı Butik Otel   PENSION €€

(☑315 1146; www.carsibutikotel.com; Zeki Çakan Caddesi 23; s/d TL80/100; ❀) In the market near the castle entrance, this place offers private patios decorated with comfy cushions. The wood-trimmed rooms somehow manage to be modern and rustic at the same time. We wouldn't go as far as calling it a 'Butik Otel', though.

Kuşna Pansiyon   PENSION €

(☑315 1033; kusnapansiyon@mynet.com; Kurşuna Sokak 36; s/d TL40/80; @) Bright and modern rooms overlooking a verdant (read: 'pleasantly overgrown') garden feature at this castle *ev pansiyonu* looking out onto a rocky cove. It's a fair walk through the castle with your bags, but the reward is a lovely private location.

Büyük Liman Otel HOTEL €€
(☏315 3900; Turgut Işık Caddesi; s/d TL70/110; ☀) In need of a lick of paint but in an excellent location on the harbour road, look forward to spacious rooms, some with beachfront balconies.

Pansiyon Evi PENSION €
(☏661 6337; Küçük Liman 33a; s/d TL35/70; ☀) Just inside the castle gates, this rambling three-storey wooden house has tidy rooms and breakfast on a breezy terrace overlooking Küçük Liman. Amasra's postage-stamp sized pub district is nearby.

Şahil Otel HOTEL €
(☏315 2211; Turgut Işık Caddesi 82; s/d TL40/80; ☀) Opposite the sailing club on the Büyük Liman, this compact but modern option has sea-facing balconies. Good waterfront eating and drinking is just a stroll away.

Balkaya Pansion PENSION €
(☏315 1434; İskele Caddesi 35; s/d TL35/70) The cheapest formal pension in town, offering small, basic rooms on a side street between the harbours.

✕ Eating

Amasra has licensed seafront restaurants serving *canlı balık* (fresh fish) by the portion. Or grab takeaway and take your pick of two harbours.

Çeşmi Cihan Restaurant SEAFOOD €€
(Büyük Liman; mains TL8-22; ☉11am-11pm) This is the locals' pick for a splurge, with harbour views, cold beers and three floors of seafood-loving diners. *Levrek* (bass) and *istavrit* (mackerel) are regulars on the menu, and the excellent salads will convert the staunchest of carnivores. Pricey, but worth it.

Mustafa Amca'nın Yeri SEAFOOD €€
(Küçük Liman Caddesi 8; mains TL12-24; ☉11am-11pm) This sea shell–clad fish restaurant is popular both with tour groups and locals. Go early to grab a waterfront table for a chilled sunset beer.

Hamam Cafe TEA GARDEN €
(Tarihi Sağır Osmanlar Hamamı; mains TL3-10) In an old hamam, this reader-recommended spot has an easygoing ambience perfect for sipping tea and challenging the locals to a game of backgammon. The *gözleme* (savoury pancakes) are particularly moreish.

Amasra Sofrası LOKANTA €
(Mithat Ceylan Caddesi; mains TL4-12) On a quiet square midway between the two harbours,

this is Amasra's prime grill house, with plenty of chicken dishes and a pretty garden. Grab a *paket servis* (takeaway) kebap and choose from two alfresco harbour locations.

Karadeniz Aile Pide Salonu PIDECI €
(Mustafa Cengiz Caddesi 9; mains TL7-10) This streetside spot just off Küçük Liman does great pide (Turkish-style pizza). Try the Amasra Special (TL7) with a dash of zingy chilli.

Lotti's SEAFOOD €€
(Büyük Liman; mains TL8-16; ☉11am-11pm) The standout in a row of cheaper seafood restaurants lining the edge of Büyük Liman. Sea views are limited, but prices are lower than other flasher places around town.

🍷 Drinking

Ağlayan Ağaç Çay Bahçesi TEA GARDEN
(Nöbethane Sokak; ☉8am-8pm) Head up through the *kale* to this cliff-top kiosk with views of squawking seagulls a few hundred metres offshore. Signs point the way. Bring a book because it's the kind of place you can easily spend a few leisurely hours.

Hayalperest Café & Bistro BAR-CAFE
(Küçük Liman Caddesi 3) Crisply chilled draught beer and a wide range of cocktail-ready spirits make the classy Hayalperest the best spot in town for an Amasra sunset. Live music kicks off most nights at 9pm. Between songs and drinks, make time for tasty bar snacks and tapas (TL5 to TL8).

Lutfiye CAFE
(Küçük Liman Caddesi 20a; ☉11am-6pm) The brick-lined Lutfiye doubles as a classy retail alternative to Amasra's overly kitsch market – buy Lutfiye's delicious *lokum* (Turkish delight) studded with nuts – and is a relaxed cafe with an impressive array of teas and coffees from around the globe.

Han Bar BAR
(Küçük Liman Caddesi 17) The most popular of Amasra's small cluster of pubs, Han Bar is sandwiched between houses opposite the castle walls. There's usually *canlı musik* (live music) at night.

Han Kir Çay Bahçesi TEA GARDEN
(Küçük Liman; ☉8am-10pm) Sip away and see how many different plant species you can spy in this leafy tea garden.

Na Bar BAR
(Büyük Liman 50b) Tucked between beachfront apartments on Büyük Liman, this

friendly pub with rustic decor is less rowdy than Amasra's other bars.

❶ Information

INTERNET ACCESS Can Internet Café (Atatürk Kültür Parkı; per hr TL1.50; ⊗9am-10pm) Near the statue of Atatürk.

TOURIST INFORMATION A tourist office opens in a small booth beside the Hamam Cafe from June to September. Opening hours are often restricted to weekends.

❶ Getting There & Away

If you're travelling east from Amasra, get an early start. Dolmuşes (minibuses) become increasingly scarce later in the day.

Intercity bus companies don't travel to Amasra. Instead, minibuses to Bartın (TL3, 30 minutes) leave every 40 minutes from near the PTT. From Bartın there are buses to Safranbolu (TL14, two hours), Ankara (TL32, five hours) and İstanbul (TL45, seven hours).

Amasra to Sinop

Winding sinuously around rugged hills hugging the Black Sea, the road from Amasra east to Sinop (312km) is wonderfully scenic, and has echoes of California's Hwy 1 or New Zealand's west coast. Expect minimal traffic and stunning views at every turn. There are narrow roads and it is slow going though (average speed is 40km/h to 50km/h, taking seven or eight hours to Sinop), with the road surface often broken and the occasional *heyelan* (landslide). By public transport, you'll need to use local services between the settlements along the way. Get an early start, and if you're lucky you might nab one of the daily bus services from İstanbul.

A few villages have camping grounds, and with your own wheels you can stop where and when the vista is most appealing. From west to east, have a swim at Bozköy beach, west of Çakraz, or visit the boat-builders in Kurucaşile, 45km east of Amasra. Both towns have modest hotels and pensions.

Consider also the picturesque two-beach village of Kapısuyu, or the tiny harbour at Gideros, the perfectly idyllic cove of your dreams. There are a couple of restaurants where you can feast on local seafood and watch the sunset.

About 63km east of Amasra, the road descends to a sand-and-pebble beach stretching several kilometres to the aptly named Kumluca (Sandy). The beach continues 8km eastward to Cide, a small town where

BLACK SEA HISTORY 101

The thin, meandering coastal strip of the Black Sea has been a hotspot of civilisation, war and conquest for more than a thousand years.

The coast was colonised in the 8th century BC by Milesians and Arcadians, who founded the towns at Sinop, Samsun and Trabzon. Later it became the Kingdom of Pontus. The Pontic king, Mithridates VI Eupator, waged war against the Romans from 88 to 84 BC. He conquered Cappadocia and other Anatolian kingdoms, but had to settle for for peace based on prewar borders.

From 74 to 64 BC he was at it again, this time encouraging his son-in-law, Tigranes I of Armenia, to seize Cappadocia from the Romans. The Roman response was to conquer Pontus, forcing Mithridates to flee. He later committed suicide. The Romans left a small kingdom of Pontus based in Trebizond (Trabzon).

The coast was subsequently ruled by Byzantium. Alexius Comnenus, son of Emperor Manuel I, proclaimed himself emperor of Pontus when the Crusaders sacked Constantinople in AD 1204. His descendants ruled until 1461, when Pontus was captured by the Ottomans under Mehmet the Conqueror.

While Alexius remained in Trabzon, Samsun was under Seljuk rule and the Genoese had trading privileges. But when the Ottomans came, the Genoese burned Samsun to the ground and sailed away.

After WWI the region's Ottoman Greek citizens attempted to form a new Pontic state with Allied support. Disarmed by the Allied occupation authorities, Turkish inhabitants were persecuted by ethnic Greek guerrillas who still had weapons. Under these circumstances, local Turks proved responsive to calls for revolution. Mustafa Kemal (later named Atatürk) escaped the sultan's control in İstanbul and landed at Samsun on 19 May 1919. He soon moved inland to Amasya to organise Turkey's battle for independence.

many dolmuş services terminate. Pensions huddle near the seafront at the western end of town, around 2km from the central otogar (bus station). Ask to be let off at the **Sahil Pansiyon**.

Leaving Cide, there's a panoramic viewpoint by the flagpole above town. Around 12km on is **Kuscu Köyü**, a small village with access to the **Aydos Canyon**, a steep river ravine.

Doğanyurt, 31km before İnebolu, is yet another pleasant harbour town, while further east from İnebolu, **Abana** has a decent beach.

Over halfway to Sinop, **İnebolu** is a handy stopping point, especially as onward transport by late afternoon may be hard to find. The Yakamoz Tatıl Köyü (☑0366-811 3100; inebolu@yakamoztatilkoyu.com; İsmetpaşa Caddesi; bungalow s/d TL60/90, s/d/tr TL60/90/110; ✳☀) is a beachside resort 800m west of the centre with a restaurant (mains TL8 to TL16), bar and cafe. In the town centre are old Ottoman houses, and a restored mansion where Atatürk stayed in 1925.

About 41km east of İnebolu, near **Çatalzeytin**, is a long pebble beach surrounded by beautiful scenery. At **Ayancık** the road divides, with the left (northern) fork offering the more scenic route to Sinop, about 2½ hours from İnebolu.

Sinop
☑0368 / POP 120,000

Wrapped around a rocky promontory, Sinop is the only southern facing town along the Black Sea. Maybe that's why the town feels more Akdeniz (Mediterranean) than Karadeniz (Black Sea). Colonised from Miletus in the 8th century BC, Sinop's trade grew, and successive rulers – including the Pontic kings (who made it their capital), Romans and Byzantines – turned it into a busy trading centre.

The Seljuks used Sinop as a port after taking it in 1214, but the Ottomans preferred to develop Samsun, which had better land communications. On 30 November 1853, a Russian armada attacked Sinop without any warning, overwhelming the local garrison and inflicting great loss of life. The battle hastened the beginning of the Crimean War, in which the Ottomans allied with the British and French to fight Russian ambitions in the Near East.

With a history as a trading port for over a thousand years, Sinop still retains a bustling, cosmopolitan air. The town's heritage is also reflected in the many shops selling model ships.

In 2006 this region was earmarked as the site of one of Turkey's first nuclear power plants. Resistance in normally reticent

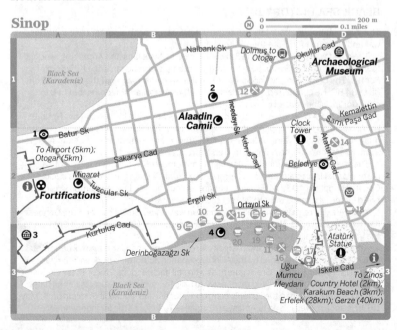

Sinop

Turkey has been well organised and robust (see www.sinopbizim.org), but in May 2010 the Turkish government announced a partnership with a South Korean company to further explore the viability of the project. In the interim, look forward to seeing protest flags fluttering proudly on fishing boats in Sinop's compact harbour.

⊙ Sights & Activities

Fortifications FORTRESS

Open to attack from the sea, Sinop has been fortified since 2000 BC, but the existing walls are developments of those originally erected in 72 BC by Pontic king, Mithridates VI. At one time the walls, some 3m thick, were more than 2km long, with seven gates, and towers 25m high. Walk along the ramparts for sea views. On the northern side is an ancient bastion called

the **Kumkapı** (Sand Gate). On the southern side is the **Tarihi Cezaevi** (Old Jail; admission TL3; ⊙9am-6pm), a hulking former prison. Inside is a modest selection of craft shops.

Archaeological Museum MUSEUM
(Okullar Caddesi; admission TL3; ⊙8am-5pm Tue-Sun) Sinop's best museum has an excellent collection of poignant Roman stele, Byzantine icons, and an Ottoman tomb in the cool and shady garden.

Alaadin Camii MOSQUE
Also called the Ulu Cami, this mosque (1267) on Sakarya Caddesi is set in an expansive walled courtyard. It was constructed for Muinettin Süleyman Pervane, a powerful Seljuk grand vizier. The mosque has been repaired many times; its marble *mihrab* (the niche indicating the direction of Mecca) and *mimber* (pulpit) were added by the local Candaroğlu emir. Diligent restoration was completed in 2010, and the mosque's austere interior and spacious courtyard are essential havens from Sinop's energetic buzz.

Pervane Medresesi MOSQUE
Built by Süleyman Pervane in 1262 to commemorate the second conquest of Sinop, the Pervane Seminary is now full of shops selling local crafts, including excellent woven linen. Enquire at the booth advertising 'Tourist Information' for a good map of Sinop and a smattering of English-language guidance and conversation.

Tersane Hacı Ömer Camii MONUMENT
Secreted away near the harbour, the poignant Şehitler Çeşmesi (Martyrs' Fountain) was built in 1903 in memory of the Turkish soldiers who died in the surprise Russian attack of 1853. It was built using money recovered from the soldiers' pockets.

☞ Tours

Sinope Tours LOCAL TOURS
(☏261 7900; www.sinopetours.com; Atatürk Caddesi 26) Runs daily city and local tours.

🛏 Sleeping

Zinos Country Hotel
[TOP CHOICE] BOUTIQUE HOTEL €€
(☏260 5600; www.zinoshotel.net; Enver Bahadır Yolu 75; s/d TL90/150; ❄ @) Around 2km from town en route to Karakum beach, the Zinos is hardly in the country. But despite the geographical confusion, this is a splurge-worthy spot with romantic Ottoman-styled rooms, rug-trimmed wooden floors and sea views.

Across the road, there's a hilltop bar, and a trail leads to a private swimming platform.

Otel Mola
HOTEL €€

(☑261 1814; www.sinopmolaotel.com.tr; Derinboğazağzı Sokak 34; s/d/tr TL50/80/100; ❄@) A lovely garden and sea views give this spot near the harbour high marks. Rooms are very comfortable, and the breakfast offering is a definite cut above with delicious *menemen* (type of omelette).

Denizci Otel
HOTEL €€

(☑260 5934; www.denizciotel.com; Kurtuluş Caddesi 13; s/d/tr TL60/80/110; ❄@) The flashest spot in town, with a maritime-themed restaurant, spacious rooms and heritage decor. The friendly staff summon up all of the English they know for English-speaking guests.

Otel 57
HOTEL €

(☑261 5462; www.otel57.com; Kurtuluş Caddesi 29; s/d TL40/60; ❄@) Spic-and-span leather chairs in reception give way to comfortable rooms with bright duvets and crisp wooden floors. It's very popular with business travellers so try and book ahead.

Otel Sarı Kadır
HOTEL €

(☑260 1544; Derinboğazağzı Sokak 22; s/d TL40/60; ❄) Plain but spacious rooms with TV, sofa and fridge make this waterfront establishment a good-value choice. There are sea views from the balconies, and a tea garden right opposite.

Yılmaz Aile Pansiyonu
PENSION €

(☑261 5752; Tersane Çarşısı 11; s/d/tr TL30/40/60) Great value, these plain but neat rooms have TV and individual gas showers. Try and score room 47 for excellent sea views. The friendly old chap at reception comes complete with a cute dog.

Mavi Ev
PENSION €

(☑260 3500; İskele Caddesi; s/d/tr TL25/40/60; ❄) Simple rooms hover just metres from the harbour at this good value pension. That means you've got more to spend in the positively gleaming restaurant downstairs. Try the rich and creamy *mantı* (Turkish ravioli).

✗ Eating

Sinop's waterfront is lined with licensed open-air restaurants.

Saray Restaurant
SEAFOOD €€

(İskele Caddesi 18; fish mains TL10-18; ⊙11am-11pm) Excellent salads and continuously sipped rakı (aniseed brandy) make this the preferred spot for local fans of caught-this-morning seafood. Grab a spot on the floating pontoon and begin your meal with Saray's excellent mezes.

Gaziantep Sofrası
LOKANTA €

(Atatürk Caddesi; mains TL5-10) Families and dating couples crowd the upstairs salon for foot-long aubergine (eggplant) kebaps and excellent *lahmacun* (pizza). It's a welcoming place that's good for female travellers.

Sahil Ocakbaşi
OCAKBAŞI €

(Ortayol Sokak; mains TL3-6) A tiny GYO – 'Grill Your Own' – spot sandwiched between fish and seafood stalls in a busy lane. Choose from *köfte* (meatballs), *tavuk* (chicken), and fresh aubergine and peppers. Solo female travellers may not feel 100% comfortable amidst the blokey ambience.

Dolunay Pastanesi
PATISSERIE €

(Kurtuluş Caddesi 14; desserts from TL2) This modern take on the pastry shop serves up ice cream and baklava. Both are perfect for a stroll along the nearby harbour.

Diyarbakır
KEPABÇI €

(Nalbank Sokak 1; mains TL4-6) Diyarbakır may be slightly rough and ready, but this popular spot provides top-notch versions of kebaps from Adana to Bursa. The *paket servis* option is good for bus journeys.

Mangal
OCAKBAŞI €

(Kurtuluş Caddesi 15; grills TL3-7) Delicious *gözleme* and grilled meat and vegetables are served up in this cosy, shimmering brass grill. The *mantı* is also very good.

☕ Drinking

Zeyden Mutfak
CAFE

(Derinboğazağzı Sokak 9; coffee TL3-5; ⊙7am-midnight; ⊛) This coolly minimalist cafe has a wide range of tea and coffee. There are muffins and cookies galore.

Yalı Kahvesi
TEA GARDEN

(Derinboğazağzı Sokak 14; ⊙8am-10pm) Harbourside tables and shady umbrellas combine at this popular tea garden.

Konak Şira Evi
CAFE

(cnr Atatürk Caddesi & Konak Sokak; ⊙noon-10pm) The Konak Juice House definitely lives up to its name with a tropical forest full of freshly squeezed treats. There's a handy internet cafe right next door.

Burç Café
BAR

(Sinop Kalesi, Tersane Caddesi) In the fortified tower, this atmospheric spot attracts a young crowd for live music, ocean views and cold beer. Bring something warm to wear as it can get chilly.

Liman TEA GARDEN
(İskele Caddesi 20; ⊘noon-10pm) Bring your backgammon A-game to this harbourside bar. Or, if you're a novice, perhaps just settle for a sunset beer.

Pub PUB
(İskele Caddesi 19; ⊘noon-10pm) How about a cold 0.7L beer outside beside colourful fishing boats?

ℹ Information

INTERNET ACCESS Wi-fi is available at the Zeyden Mutfak cafe or at **Konak Internet** (cnr Atatürk Caddesi & Konak Sokak; ⊘noon-10pm), which is adjacent to the Konak Şira Evi juice bar.

TOURIST INFORMATION Tourist office (✆261 5298; Gazi Caddesi; ⊘8.30am-5pm mid-Jun–mid-Sep) Helpful with English-speaking staff. There is another booth at the entrance to the Tarihi Cezaevi.

ℹ Getting There & Away

AIR Turkish Airlines (www.turkishairlines.com) Has daily flights from İstanbul's Atatürk airport.

BUS For Amasra take a direct minibus or change at İnebolu or Cide. Sinop's otogar is 5km northwest of town on the main road to Kastamonu.

ℹ Getting Around

Dolmuşes (TL1.50) to the Sinop otogar depart 100m west of the Archaeological Museum. You can get a taxi to the airport (TL20), which is 5km west of the centre.

Around Sinop

Consult Sinop's tourist booths or Sinope Tours for suggestions for local tours. The most common excursions are to **Erfelek**, famed for its 28 waterfalls, the historic fishing town of **Gerze**, and the area around **Ayancık**. Walking and canoeing are popular pastimes for the more energetic visitor.

The black-sand **Karakum beach** (admission TL1) with a restaurant and camping, is 3km east of Sinop harbour.

Samsun

✆0362 / POP 504,000
Sprawling Samsun is the Black Sea's biggest port. Few travellers stop for more than a change of bus. Even the enterprising Genoese only paused long enough to burn the city to the ground in the 15th century. With accommodation and eateries handily crammed around the centre, it's a convenient stop on your journey east or west. Samsun also marks the beginning of the four- to six-lane Black Sea Coastal Hwy. The city centre is Cumhuriyet Meydanı (Republic Sq), inland, and just west of Atatürk Park, which lies on the coastal highway. The Samsun *valiliği* (provincial government headquarters) is slightly to the north. Cumhuriyet Caddesi runs along the south side of the park.

⦿ Sights

Archaeology & Ethnography Museum MUSEUM
(Arkeoloji ve Etnoğrafya Müzesi; Fuar Caddesi; admission TL3; ⊘8.30am-noon & 1-7pm Tue-Sun) With an hour to spare it's worth visiting this museum, west of the big pink Samsun *valiliği* building. Most striking is a huge Romano-Byzantine mosaic depicting Thetis, Achilles and the Four Seasons, found nearby at Karasamsun (Amissos). Other highlights include the elegant gold jewellery

SERVICES FROM SİNOP'S OTOGAR

DESTINATION	FARE (TL)	DURATION (HR)	DISTANCE (KM)	FREQUENCY (PER DAY)
Ankara	40	8	443	3
İnebolu	20	3	156	1 at 8am
İstanbul	50	11	700	5
Karabük (for Safranbolu)	35	5	340	5
Samsun	20	3	168	hourly
Trabzon	50	10	533	1 at 8pm

thought to date from around 120 to 130 BC, which was the time of the legendary Mithridates (VI Eupator), and a scary display on ancient skull surgery.

Atatürk Museum   MUSEUM
(Atatürk Müzesi; Fuar Caddesi; admission TL3; ⏱8.30am-1pm & 2-5pm) Adjacent to the Archaeology & Ethnography Museum, this museum commemorates the start of the War of Independence here on 19 May 1919.

🛏 Sleeping & Eating

Explore the clothing bazaar (Bedesten) area, near Hotel Necmi, if you are looking for budget accommodation.

Hotel Necmi   HOTEL €
(☑432 7164; Bedestan Sokak 6; s/d/tr without bathroom TL45/50/70) Downstairs is a pot plant–filled lounge, while the rooms upstairs are compact with mushroom-coloured carpet and shared bathrooms.

Samsun Park Otel   HOTEL €
(☑435 0095; www.samsunparkotel.com; Cumhuriyet Caddesi 38; s/d/tr TL60/70/100; ❄@) A lift covered in hieroglyphics whisks you to compact but comfortable rooms at this hotel, 200m east of Cumhuriyet Meydanı. Reception is open to negotiating room prices.

Vidinli Oteli   HOTEL €€
(☑431 6050; Kazımpaşa Caddesi 4; s/d TL75/150; ❄@) The Vidinli plays the business traveller card a little strongly, with the comfortable rooms veering towards blandness. Plus points are the tiled bathrooms and an expense account–friendly bar-restaurant.

Gaziantep Kebap Salonu   PIDECI €
(Osmaniye Caddesi 7; mains TL4-8) Superb chilli-studded *lahmacun* and freshly made *ayran* (yoghurt drink) feature at this slice of southeast Turkey relocated on the Black Sea. Walk 100m east from Cumhuriyet Meydanı on Cumhuriyet Caddesi and turn right after the Hotel Amisos.

Samsun Balık Restaurant   SEAFOOD €€
(Kazımpaşa Caddesi 20; mains TL10-16; ⏱11am-10pm) Samsun's number-one fish eatery is in a quaint brick house. A glistening array of piscine beauties awaits your choice, and upstairs is a flower-trimmed dining room.

Gül Köfteci   KÖFTECI €
(Osmaniye Caddesi 8; mains TL4-10) Just opposite Gaziantep Kebap Salonu, this snazzy corner location turns out robust *güveç* (Turkish casserole) and a full range of kebabs.

ℹ Information

INTERNET ACCESS Internet cafes huddle around Cumhuriyet Meydanı.

TOURIST INFORMATION At the time of writing, Samsun's tourist office was between addresses, and a new location was yet to be confirmed. Ask at the Samsun Park Hotel for an update.

ℹ Getting There & Away

AIR Turkish Airlines (www.turkishairlines.com) Flies direct from İstanbul to Havaalani Samsun (Samsun Airport) up to five times daily. There are also direct flights to Ankara, Antalya and İzmir.

Onur Air (www.onurair.com) Daily flights to İstanbul.

Pegasus Airlines (www.flypgs.com) Flies to İzmir three times a week.

BUS Samsun's otogar is 3km inland. Most major bus companies have offices at the Cumhuriyet Meydanı end of Cumhuriyet Caddesi. Bus companies run *servis* (shuttle buses) from Cumhuriyet Meydanı to the otogar. There are also frequent dolmuşes (TL2) from the otogar to Cumhuriyet Meydanı, and left-luggage facilities at the otogar.

CAR & MOTORCYCLE Samsun has car-rental agencies around Lise Caddesi including **Avis** (☑231 6750; Ümraniye Sokak 2) and **Eleni** (☑230 0091; Ümraniye Sokak 6). Head southeast for 700m from Atatürk Park along Cumhuriyet Caddesi to Lise Caddesi. After 150m veer right into Ümraniye Sokak.

TRAIN Daily trains run from Samsun **station** (☑233 5002) to Sivas (TL19.50, 8½ hours) at 8.20am and 5.04pm, and to Amasya (TL7.50, three hours) at 6pm and 9.08pm. The train station is 500m southeast of Cumhuriyet Meydanı on the main coastal road.

ℹ Getting Around

Frequent dolmuşes (TL1.50) run from the otogar to Cumhuriyet Meydanı. **Havas** (www.havas.net) run regular shuttle buses from the airport to central Samsun.

Ünye

☑0452 / POP 72,800

Today's Ünye is popular with holidaying Turks, but this bustling spot 95km east of Samsun also has one of the longest settlement histories in Anatolia. There is evidence of civilisation during the Palaeolithic period, and Ünye was an important port at the junction of the Silk Road and the coastal highway during the Ottoman period. Former residents include the 14th-century Turkish

DESTINATION	FARE (TL)	DURATION (HR)	DISTANCE (KM)	FREQUENCY (PER DAY)
Amasya	10	2½	130	frequent
Ankara	49	7	420	frequent
Artvin	40	8	577	4
Giresun	20	3½	220	5
İstanbul	79	11	750	several
Kayseri	45	9	530	a few
Sinop	20	3	168	several
Trabzon	30	6	355	several
Ünye	8	1½	95	half-hourly

BLACK SEA COAST & THE KAÇKAR MOUNTAINS ÜNYE

mystical poet Yunus Emre, and St Nicholas, before his life morphed into the legend of Santa Claus. Today it's a modern city combining a coastal promenade and a labyrinth of well-kept winding streets and lanes.

⊙ Sights & Activities

About 7km inland stands **Ünye Castle**, a ruined fortress founded by the Pontics and rebuilt by the Byzantines, with an ancient tomb cut into the rock face below. Catch a minibus heading to Kaleköy or Akkuş (TL1) from the Niksar road, and ask to be dropped off at the road to the castle. It's a further half-hour trek to the top.

Another excursion is the **Tozkoparan Kay Mezarı** (Tozkoparan Rock Tomb), off the Trabzon road, 5km from the centre. Any eastbound minibus can drop you by the cement factory at the turn for the cave.

Back in town, just east of the square is the **Ali-Namık Soysal Eski Hamam**. It was once a church, but now it's open for bathing to men from early morning to noon and all day Sunday, and for women from noon until 4pm Monday to Saturday.

🛏 Sleeping

As well as the accommodation listed here, camping grounds and a handful of beach pensions are spread out along the Samsun road west of town.

TOP CHOICE Sebile Hanim Konaği

BOUTIQUE HOTEL €€

(☎323 7474; www.sebilehanimkonagi.com; Çamurlu Mahallesi Paşabahçe Arif, Çubukçu Sokak; s/d TL70/120; ❋) Boutique hotel style comes to Ünye at this gloriously restored

and romantic hilltop property in the former Armenian district. Each cosy wood-lined room is equipped with a personal hamam, and the atmospheric downstairs restaurant (mains TL10 to TL16) is open to outside guests and specialises in Black Sea cuisine. Booking ahead for both restaurant and hotel is recommended. Follow the signs up the steps from the western edge of the old city walls.

Otel Çınar HOTEL €

(☎323 1148; Hükümet Caddesi 18; s/d TL25/40) This central budget option has shared bathrooms and no breakfast is provided. From the main square turn left and head one block inland.

Otel Lider HOTEL €

(☎324 9250; Hükümet Caddesi 36; s/d TL25/45) Centrally located, the Lider has a rooftop terrace. No breakfast is served but there's a good kebap place nearby that can rustle up *kahvaltı* (breakfast).

Cafe Gülen Plaj Camping CAMPGROUND €

(☎324 7368; Devlet Sahil Yolu; camp sites per 2 people TL25, bungalows TL60) This has an excellent setting and cute wooden bungalows.

✖ Eating & Drinking

Çakırtepe LOKANTA €

(Çakırtepe; mains TL5-10; ⊙11am-10pm) Atop the hill west of town, this picnic site and cafe is a local favourite for long summer lunches. Tuck into excellent pide or *güveç*. Minibuses leave from the southwest side of Cumhuriyet Meydanı and pass close to the restaurant.

Iskele
RESTAURANT €€

(Devlet Sahil Yolu 32; meals TL10-16) The most common answer to 'So, what's the best restaurant in Ünye?', Iskele enjoys a water's edge location and a region-wide reputation for seafood and grilled meats. Ignore the unnecessary diversions into Italian and Mexican flavours, and stay firmly local with red mullet or sea bass. The elegant dining room also features interesting black and white snapshots of Ünye's past.

Trip Café
CAFE €

(Cumhuriyet Meydanı 25; snacks TL3-6) This hip, retro themed cafe overlooks the eastern edge of Cumhuriyet Meydanı and is frequented by young locals enjoying nargileh (water pipes) and the best views in town. It's not licensed, but crisp and crunchy salads and savoury flat breads are essential culinary diversions.

Café Vanilya
CAFE €

(Cumhuriyet Meydanı 3; snacks TL2-5; ⊙24hr; 🕿) Set in a restored villa-style townhouse on the southwest edge of the main square, the Vanilya is a chic but unpretentious terrace cafe serving Ünye's bright young things. Backgammon and Turkish pop videos provide a mix of old and new.

Yunus Emre Çay Bahçesi
TEA GARDEN €

(Yunus Emre Parkı; mains TL4-8) This well-frequented tea garden beside the pier serves substantial pides and stews as well as the usual drinks.

🛈 Getting There & Away
Bus companies have offices on the coastal road. Minibuses and midibuses travel to Samsun (TL10, 1½ hours) and Ordu (TL10, 1¾ hours).

Ordu
☑ 0452 / POP 124,000

Ordu is 60km east of Ünye, with a well-kept centre around a palm tree–lined seafront boulevard. The city sprawls in both directions, but winding narrow lanes give central Ordu a villagelike ambience.

⊙ Sights
Pasha's Palace & Ethnography Museum
MUSEUM

(Paşaoğlu Konağı ve Etnoğrafya Müzesi; Taşocak Caddesi; admission TL3; ⊙9am-noon & 1.30-5pm Tue-Sun) This interesting museum occupies a late-19th-century house 500m uphill from Cumhuriyet Meydanı. Signs reading

'Müze – Museum' direct you here past a handicrafts bazaar. The re-created rooms on the 1st floor are telling reminders that upper-class Ottomans enjoyed a sophisticated and cosmopolitan life. There's also a chair where Atatürk supposedly had a rest in 1924. We hope he also enjoyed pide from the wood-fired oven in the peaceful garden.

Tasbaşı Cultural Centre
HISTORIC BUILDING

Now a cultural centre, this former Greek church (1853) offers magnificent coastal views from its location atop a rocky bluff around 800m west from the main square. For more breathtaking views and good restaurants, catch a dolmuş west to **Boztepe Picnic Place** from the main square (TL4, 6.5km).

🛏 Sleeping & Eating
Ordu's accommodation and eating scene features a couple of good-value splurges.

Taşbaşı Butik Otel
BOUTIQUE HOTEL €€

(☑225 3530; www.tasbasibutikotel.com; Kazım Evi Sokak 1; s/d TL65/110; 🕸) The decor occasionally strays into chintzy territory, but the Black Sea views are terrific at this newly restored hilltop mansion in Taşbaşı, Ordu's former Greek neighbourhood. Reception is adept at booking coastal boat trips, and slightly more rugged journeys into the *yayla* (mountain valleys) inland from Ordu.

Karlıbel Atlıhan Hotel
HOTEL €€

(☑225 0565; www.karlibelhotel.com.tr; Kazım Karabekir Caddesi 7; s/d/tr TL70/95/120; 🕸) A professional establishment with spacious rooms in subdued colours and a horsey predilection for equine art. It's one block back from the seafront behind the *belediye* (town hall). The same company also runs two nearby boutique hotels, the seafront Atherina, and the hilltop İkizevler.

Otel Kervansaray
HOTEL €

(☑212 2815; Şarkiye Mahallesi; s/d/tr TL35/60/80; mains TL4-8; 🕸) Tucked in behind Ordu's tourist office, the Kervansaray team provides the essential travellers' combination of clean and comfortable rooms, and an always-busy, always-good restaurant downstairs. Lunchtime is particularly recommended, with an ever-changing array of prepared dishes. The salad bar (TL5) is a good value way to eat your daily greens.

Mıdı Restaurant
SEAFOOD €€

(İskele Üstü 55; mains TL8-15; ⊙11am-11pm) Ordu's best eating combines with Ordu's best

Around 25km east of Ünye just after the town of Bolaman, the Black Sea Coastal Hwy veers inland and doesn't touch the coast again until just before Ordu. It's a spectacular stretch, traversing Turkey's longest road tunnel (3.28km), and the diversion inland has created a lovely alternative route on the old coast road.

A winding few kilometres east from Bolaman is rugged **Cape Yason**, where a tiny chapel marks the spot where sailors used to pray at a temple dedicated to Jason and his Argonauts. To the east is the surprising **Çaka beach**, a 400m strip of white sand regarded as the Black Sea's best beach. A grill restaurant and beer garden makes it easy to enjoy.

Further on, 15km west of Ordu, **Perşembe** is a fishing port framed by two lighthouses. The rooms at the two-star **Dede Evi** (☑0452-517 3802; Atatürk Bulvarı; s/d TL40/80; ✱@) have parquet floors and sea views. Later at night locals fish from the slender pier and fish restaurants prepare the day's catch.

This meandering detour is best achieved with your own transport, but there are also relatively frequent dolmuşes to Perşembe from Fatsa to the west, and Ordu to the east.

---

seafront ambience at this long and classy pontoon restaurant that's good for equally long and classy lunches. The local seafood is the culinary highlight, beer and wine are available, and black-and-white pictures of old Ordu turn the heritage charm up to 11.

Jazz Café CAFE €
(Sımpasa Caddesi 28; snacks TL3-6) A sleek and cosmopolitan spot on Ordu's pedestrian shopping drag, offering sweet treats, including hot chocolate and waffles. Savoury palates shouldn't miss the excellent *sigara böreği* (feta cheese and pastry snacks).

Ayışığı RESTAURANT-CAFE €
(Atatürk Bulvarı; mains TL5-10; ☺from 11am) Occupying a whitewashed concrete structure on the beach, the 'Moonlight' weirdly combines a terrace cafe, restaurant and *meyhane* (tavern) to good effect. Next door is a pleasant Mondrian-styled tea garden.

ℹ Information

INTERNET ACCESS Dream Net (Fidangör Sokak 1; per hr TL1.25; ☺10am-midnight) Turn right 200m east of Jazz Café.

TOURIST INFORMATION Tourist office (☑223 1444; www.ordu.gov.tr; Şarkiye Mahallesi 1; ☺8am-6pm daily May-Sep & 8am-5pm Mon-Fri Oct-Apr) Excellent English is spoken at this well-resourced office in the provincial government building. Recommendations include a trip inland to visit the Black Sea *yayla*.

ℹ Getting There & Around

Ordu's otogar is 5km east on the coastal road. Buses depart regularly to Giresun (TL5, one

hour) and Ünye (TL10, 1¾ hours). You can also usually flag down buses along the coastal road.

Local dolmuşes regularly loop through the city centre. Line 2 goes from the centre of town uphill past the Tasbaşı Cultural Centre in one direction, and near the otogar in the other.

Giresun

☑0454 / POP 84,000

The historic town of Giresun, 46km east of Ordu, was founded around 3000 years ago. The city is credited with introducing cherries to Italy, and from there to the rest of the world. The name Giresun comes from the Greek for cherry.

Now the humble hazelnut (*fındık*) drives Giresun's economy, and the area has Turkey's finest plantations. Enjoy the edible treats and fabulous views from the hillside park near the centre.

Giresun's centre is Atapark on the coastal road. The town hall is just inland from the park. The main commercial street is Gazi Caddesi, climbing uphill from the town hall.

◉ Sights & Activities

City Museum MUSEUM
(Şehir Müzesi; Atatürk Bulvarı 62; admission TL2; ☺8am-5pm) This museum occupies the 18th-century Gogora church, 1.5km around the promontory east of Atapark on the coastal road. The well-preserved building's collection outshines the usual archaeological and ethnographic exhibits. Catch any 'Hastanesi' dolmuş heading east (TL1.25) and ask to be let off at *'muze'*.

Kalepark
PARK

Perched on the steep hillside above the town, this shady park with the remains of a castle has panoramic views, beer gardens and barbecues. Weekends are very busy. No public transport serves the park, so you'll need to walk (about 2km) inland and uphill from Atapark on Gazi Caddesi and turn left onto Bekirpaşa Caddesi. It's a good way to burn off the calories from your consumption of cherries and hazelnuts. Alternatively, a taxi from town costs around TL4.

Alpine Plateaus
ALPINE PLATEAUS

If you've got time, head to these plateaus, which are about 40km inland and offer opportunities for walking and winter sports.

✯✯ Festivals & Events

The four-day **International Giresun Aksu Festival**, starting annually on May 20, hails fecundity and the new growing season with concerts, traditional dance performances and other open-air events. The boat trips out to compact Giresun Island are a highlight.

🛏 Sleeping & Eating

Er-Tur Oteli
HOTEL €

(☑216 1026; otelertur@mynet.com; Çapulacılar Sokak 8; s/d TL30/50; ❄) International flags hint at something flasher, but the two-star standards are entirely acceptable at this welcoming spot on a side street east of Atapark. Colourful bed linen and a young English-speaking crew on reception make this a top place to break your journey east to Trabzon and beyond.

Otel Çarıkçı
HOTEL €€

(☑216 1026; Osmanağa Caddesi 6; s/d TL65/100; ❄) More excellent value in this price range with laminate floors and tiled bathrooms. It's down the first street east off Gazi Caddesi. Look for the sign featuring a curly-toed shoe.

Otel Başar
HOTEL €€

(☑212 9920; www.hotelbasar.com.tr; Atatürk Bulvarı; s/d/tr TL80/130/150; ❄) Scratch the surface of this eight-storey blue and yellow eyesore overlooking the coastal road, and you'll find a surprisingly comfortable hotel with English-speaking staff, a cosy brick-lined bar, and a rooftop restaurant.

Orta Kahve
CAFE €

(Topal Sokak 1; snacks TL4-10; ⊙8am-8pm) This cosy hangout for Giresun's more cosmopolitan, younger crowd makes a welcome change from the fluoro-illuminated pide and *lokanta* (eatery serving ready-made food) places elsewhere along the coast. Old typewriters and brand new travel and design magazines provide the background for different teas and coffees. Healthy snacks include salads (TL5.50 to TL7) and crepes (TL5 to TL7). Turn left 50 metres uphill on Gazi Caddesi after Café Piccolo.

Deniz Lokantası
LOKANTA €

(Alpaslan Caddesi 3; mains TL4-10; ⊙10am-10pm) Next to the town hall, this modernised cafeteria has been churning out good-value meals since 1953. Expect a short wait at lunchtime, but it's worth it.

Ellez
PIDECI €

(Fatih Caddesi 9; pide TL5-12; ⊙10am-11pm) One block north of Atapark, this compact pide-and-pizza joint attracts a younger crowd with top food and Turkish flags protruding from a tiny balcony.

ⓘ Information

At the time of writing, the local tourist information centre was closed. Ask at the Otel Başar for a good map and brochure. Internet cafes are a few hundred metres uphill from the town hall.

ⓘ Getting There & Away

The bus station is 4km west of the centre, but buses usually drop people at Atapark, too. Minibuses shuttle from Giresun to Trabzon (TL10, two hours) and to Ordu (TL5, one hour). Trabzon services leave from the bus offices near Atapark. Buses to Ordu stop across the road outside the sprawling car park.

Giresun to Trabzon

From Giresun it's another 150km to Trabzon, but the Black Sea Coastal Hwy has tarnished the coastal vistas. The road passes through several small towns, including the attractive town of **Tirebolu**, with a compact harbour and two castles (St Jean Kalesi and Bedrama Kalesi). The Çaykur tea-processing plant signals your arrival in Turkey's tea country.

Heading east, the town after Tirebolu is **Görele**, famous for big, round loaves of bread. Next is **Akçakale** with the ruins of a 13th-century Byzantine castle on a little peninsula. Shortly before reaching Trabzon is **Akçaabat**, famous for its *köfte* restaurants: the Korfez and Cemilusta are two worth trying.

Trabzon

Trabzon

☎ 0462 / POP 770,000

Trabzon's one of those 'love it or hate it'
kind of places. Some are polarised by its
slightly seedy, port-town character, while
others appreciate the city's cosmopolitan
buzz. Arguably the Black Sea coast's most
sophisticated city – sorry Samsun – Trabzon is too caught up in its own whirl of activity to worry about what's happening in
far-off İstanbul or Ankara.

The Black Sea's past is displayed nearby
in the gracious, medieval church of Aya
Sofya, and in the Byzantine monastery at
Sumela, but in Atatürk Alanı, Trabzon's
crazily busy main square, the modern world
shines through. Beeping dolmuş traffic
hurtles around like a modern chariot race,
while local students team headscarves with
Converse All Stars beneath a giant screen
showcasing the city's beloved Trabzonspor

Trabzon

◎ Top Sights

Bazaar District C2
Sekiz Direkli Hamamı A1
Trabzon Museum D3

◎ Sights

1 Çarşı Camii C2
2 Taş Han C2

✕ Eating

3 Bordo Mavi D3
4 İstanbul Kır Pidesi D3
5 Kalendar D3
6 Kılıçoğlu D3

◻ Drinking

Cingil Bar .... (see 9)
7 Stress Cafe C3

✦ Entertainment

8 Luna Park B1
9 Sinema Lara D3

football team. The idolised local team is one of two teams outside İstanbul to have ever won the Turkish national league. In 2010, Bursaspor spoilt Trabzonspor's record as the country's only non-İstanbul champions.

Trabzon is the eastern Black Sea's busiest port, handling and dispatching goods for Georgia, Armenia, Azerbaijan and Iran. The city makes an impression, and it's as quintessential a Black Sea experience as Amasra's laid-back castle ambience, or the Kaçkars' lakes and mountains. The buzz is infectious after take-it-easy times in the Black Sea's smaller centres.

Trabzon's heart is the Atatürk Alanı district, also known as Meydan Parkı. The port is east of Atatürk Alanı, down a steep hill. There are cafes and restaurants west of Atatürk Alanı along Uzun Sokak (Long Lane) and Kahramanmaraş Caddesi (Maraş Caddesi for short). West of the centre, past the bazaar, is Ortahisar, a picturesque old neighbourhood straddling a ravine.

History

Trabzon's recorded history begins around 746 BC, when Miletus colonists came from Sinop and founded a settlement, Trapezus, with an acropolis on the *trápeza* (table) of land above the harbour.

The busy port town did reasonably well for 2000 years, until the Christian soldiers of the Fourth Crusade seized and sacked Constantinople in 1204, forcing its noble families to seek refuge in Anatolia. The Comnenus imperial family established an empire along the Black Sea coast in 1204, with Alexius Comnenus I reigning as the emperor of Trebizond.

The Trapezuntine rulers skilfully balanced alliances with the Seljuks, the Mongols and the Genoese. Prospering through trade with eastern Anatolia and Persia, the empire peaked during the reign of Alexius II (1297–1330), before declining in factional disputes. The empire of Trebizond survived until the Ottoman conquest in 1461, eight years longer than Constantinople.

When the Ottoman Empire was defeated after WWI, Trabzon's Greek residents sought to establish a Republic of Trebizond, echoing the old Comneni Empire. The Turks were ultimately victorious, and Atatürk declared Trabzon 'one of the richest, strongest and most sensitive sources of trust for the Turkish Republic'.

◉ Sights & Activities

Trabzon Museum   MUSEUM

(Trabzon Müzesi; Map p509; Zeytinlik Caddesi 10; admission TL3; ⊙9am-noon & 1-6pm Tue-Sun). Just south of Uzun Sokak, this Italian-designed mansion was originally built for a Russian merchant in 1912 and inhabited briefly by Atatürk. The fantastic interiors and original furnishings put most Ottoman re-creations to shame, with a series of impressive high-ceilinged rooms displaying ethnographic and Islamic artefacts, mostly

AYA SOFYA MUSEUM

Originally called Hagia Sophia (Church of the Divine Wisdom), the Aya Sofya Museum (Aya Sofya Müzesi; admission TL3; ⊙9am-6pm Tue-Sun Apr-Oct, 9am-5pm Tue-Sun Nov-Mar) is located 4km west of Trabzon's centre on a terrace that once held a pagan temple. Built in the late Byzantine period, between 1238 and 1263, the church has clearly been influenced by Georgian and Seljuk design, although the wall paintings and mosaic floors follow the prevailing Constantinople style of the time. It was converted to a mosque after the Ottoman conquest in 1461, and later used as an ammunition storage depot and hospital by the Russians, before being fully restored in the 1960s.

Enter the Aya Sofya through the western entrance into the vaulted narthex to view the best-preserved frescoes of various biblical themes. The church has a cross-in-square plan, topped by a single dome, showing Georgian influence. Look for a fresco in the southern portico that depicts Adam and Eve's expulsion, and for a relief of an eagle, the symbol of the church's founders, the Comnenus family. Unfortunately most of the frescoes within arm's reach have been heavily defaced. Flash photography is prohibited to preserve the remaining painted fragments.

Beside the museum is a square bell tower, a reconstructed farmhouse, and a *serander* (granary) from Of county, set on tall posts to combat vermin.

The site is above the coastal highway, reachable by dolmuş (TL1.50) from the southeastern side of Atatürk Alanı.

labelled in English. The basement archaeological section also has significant pieces, including a flattened bronze statue of Hermes from local excavations at Tabakhane and Byzantine finds from near Sumela.

Atatürk Villa HISTORIC BUILDING
(Atatürk Köşkü; ☑231 0028; admission TL3; ⊙8am-7pm May-Sep, 8am-5pm Oct-Apr) Escape busy Trabzon at the Atatürk Villa, 5km southwest of Atatürk Alanı. Set above Trabzon in a forested neighbourhood, it has fine views and lovely gardens. The three-storey white villa, designed in a Black Sea–style popular in the Crimea, was built between 1890 and 1903 for a wealthy Trabzon banking family, and given to Atatürk when he visited in 1924. It's now a museum of Atatürk memorabilia. Don't miss the simple table in the study with a map of the WWI Dardanelles campaign scratched into the wood.

City buses labelled 'Köşk', leave from the bus park (Map p509) opposite the old coast road (Devlet Sahil Yolu Caddesi) and drop you outside the villa (TL1.50). Don't get out at the stop that says 'Atatürk Köşk 200m'. The actual stop is a steep 1km trek further up the hill.

Bazaar District MARKET
(Map p509) Trabzon's bazaar is west of Atatürk Alanı in the Çarşı (Market) quarter, accessible by the pedestrianised Kunduracılar Caddesi from Atatürk Alanı. After the touristy vibe of İstanbul's Grand Bazaar, it's down to earth and proudly local. Close to the restored **Çarşı Camii** is the **Taş Han** (or Vakıf Han), a single-domed *han* (caravanserai) constructed around 1647, and the oldest marketplace in Trabzon. It's now full of workshops and stores.

Gülbahar Hatun Camii MOSQUE
West of the centre, Gülbahar Hatun Camii (Mosque of the Ottomans) is another interesting mosque. It was built in 1514 by Selim the Grim, the great Ottoman conqueror of Syria and Egypt, in honour of his mother, Gülbahar Hatun. Next to it, there is a tea garden and a reconstructed wooden *serander*. Heading west on Zağnos Cadessi in the neighbourhood of Ortahisar, turn left into Şenol Güneş Caddesi.

Boztepe Picnic Place HISTORIC AREA
On the hillside 2km southeast of Atatürk Alanı, is the Boztepe Picnic Place (Boztepe Piknik Alanı), with fine views of the city and the sea, tea gardens and restaurants. In ancient times, Boztepe harboured temples to the Persian sun god Mithra. Later, the Byzantines built churches and monasteries here. Now it's a top place for a sunset beer.

From Atatürk Alanı, take a frequent Boztepe dolmuş (TL1.50) from near the southeastern end of Atatürk Alanı. The route goes uphill 2.2km to Boztepe park.

Sekiz Direkli Hamamı HAMAM
(Direkli Hamami Sokak; sauna & massage TL25; ⊙men 7am-5pm Fri-Wed, women 8am-5pm Thu) Six hundred metres west of the Çarşı Camii, this is Trabzon's best Turkish bath. The rough-hewn pillars – 'Sekiz Direkli' translates to 'Eight Columns' – date from Seljuk times, although the rest of the building has been modernised. A few of the creaking old-timers who work here appear to be only slightly younger. They're damn strong though. Expect a very robust massage.

Meydan Hamam HAMAM
(Map p512; Kahramanmaraş Caddesi; sauna TL15; ⊙men 6am-11pm, women 9am-6pm) The Meydan Hamam in central Trabzon is clean and efficiently run, but not as atmospheric as the Sekiz Direkli. The women's entrance is around the corner.

⟱ Tours

Eyce Tours (Map p512; ☑326 7174; www.eycetours.com, in Turkish; Taksim İşhanı Sokak 11) offers day trips to Sumela (TL20, departing 10am daily), Uzungöl (TL30, departing 10am daily) and Ayder (TL50, minimum six people).

Bus companies **Ulusoy** and **Metro** (Map p512) also run day trips in summer to Sumela (TL20) and Uzungöl (TL25), leaving from outside their offices at the southern end of Atatürk Alanı.

🛏 Sleeping

Some of the cheapies off the northeastern corner of Atatürk Alanı and along the coastal road double as brothels. At the time of writing, the following places had the tourist office tick of approval. Most places are open to negotiation on posted rates.

Otel Ural HOTEL €€
(Map p512; ☑326 8281; Güzelhisar Caddesi 3; s/d 50/80; ❄) The newest opening along Trabzon's hotel alley raises the bar considerably with spotless and spacious rooms with warm chocolate-brown decor, flat screen TVs, and perhaps the flashest bathrooms this far east of İstanbul. It's popular with business travellers, so definitely ask for a discount at weekends.

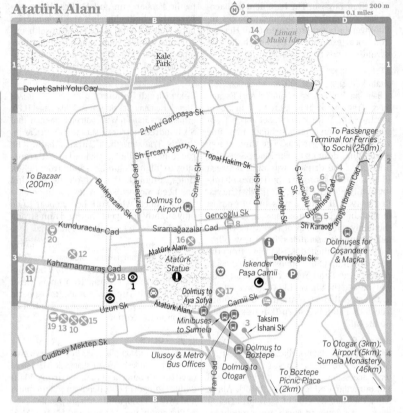

Novotel
HOTEL €€

(✆455 9000; www.novotel.com; Cumhuriyet Mahallesi, Yomra; r TL150; ※@☀) Around 9km east of Trabzon in the town of Yomra, at the Novotel you're trading off a central location for seafront vistas, and hands-down the most comfortable and amenities-laden hotel rooms for many a kilometre. There's plenty of passing dolmuş traffic just outside to whizz you into Trabzon's big smoke. Check the website for good-value deals. Rates do not include breakfast.

Hotel Nazar
HOTEL €€

(Map p512; ✆323 0081; www.nazarhotel.com.tr; Güzelhisar Caddesi 5; s/d TL70/100; ※) Look beyond the flagrant photoshopping in the brochure (flower gardens in central Trabzon? Yeah right) and the Nazar is a smart business-class option. There's usually someone on board who speaks English.

Hotel Anıl
HOTEL €

(Map p512; ✆326 7282; Güzelhisar Caddesi 12; s/d TL40/70; ※) A promisingly flash reception lures travellers in, and the rooms in pink and yellow are actually good value, especially with super-clean bathrooms, wi-fi and aircon. It's built into the side of a hill, so even the downstairs rooms have views.

Hotel Nur
HOTEL €

(Map p512; ✆323 0445; Camii Sokak 15; s/d 40/60; ※) A long-standing, but often over-popular travellers' favourite, with amiable, English-speaking staff and small, brightly painted rooms. Downstairs is a lounge that's good for getting the latest travellers' low-down on Georgia. The nearby mosque doesn't skimp on the 5am call to prayer.

Otel Horon
HOTEL €€

(Map p512; ✆326 6455; www.hotelhoron.com; Sıramağazalar Caddesi 125; s/d TL90/125; ※)

Atatürk Alanı

The aubergine-coloured exterior conceals unflashy rooms amidst 1970s decor. Wi-fi, well-stocked minibars and city views from the rooftop bar-restaurant overcome any shortcomings in design.

Hotel Can HOTEL €
(Map p512; ☏326 8281; Güzelhisar Caddesi 2; s/d 30/60; ⊛) Simple, but clean rooms; a good-value, central choice if you're conserving your travel funds for onward travel to Georgia.

✕ Eating

Trabzon is not the Black Sea's gastronomic high point, but scores of good eateries line Atatürk Alanı and the two streets to the west.

Trabzon Mangal Dünyasi OCAKBAŞI €€
(Map p512; Atatürk Alanı; mains TL8-12) Grilled perfection awaits at this classier version of a traditional Turkish *ocakbaşi* (grill restaurant) three floors up above Atatürk Alanı. Grab a spot at the shared tables arrayed around the *mangal* (barbecue) grills and tuck into superlative kebaps, fluffy flatbreads and chargrilled veggies. If you're a really hungry carnivore, you can even order specialist cuts of *kuzu* (lamb) by the kilo.

Kalendar CAFE €
(Map p509; Zeytinlik Caddesi 10; mains TL5) Low tables and mood lighting give this place near the Trabzon Museum a cosmopolitan vibe. It's perfect for a post-museum coffee or brunch of *menemen* and toast if you're getting tired of cucumbers, tomatoes and cheese.

Bordo Mavi CAFE €€
(Map p509; Halkevi Caddesi 12; meals TL7-12; ⊙11am-10pm) This cosmopolitan garden-cafe adjoins the clubhouse of Trabzonspor, the local football team. It's not at all boozy and noisy, though. The strongest drink you'll get is a Coke, and the excellent pizzas and pasta have an authentic tinge of Italy. Next door is a shop selling Trabzonspor merchandise. Blue and red is such a fetching combination, don't you think?

Reis'in Yeri RESTAURANT-BAR €€
(Map p512; Liman Mukli İdare; meals TL8-14; ⊙11am-11pm) Surrounded by traffic around Atatürk Alanı, it's easy to forget Trabzon is a coastal city. Head down the hill and across the pedestrian overbridge to this sprawling fish/chicken/*köfte* grill place that also doubles as a beer garden. It's guaranteed dolmuş-free, and you can even hire rowboats to steer around the tiny cove.

Seyidoğlu STREET FOOD €
(Map p512; Uzun Sokak 15a; dishes TL1.50-2.50) This compact snack stop has been serving up succulent, thin-crusted *lahmacun* and kebaps for four decades. Roll up a few *lahmacun* with fresh salad and you can't go wrong.

İstanbul Kır Pidesi PİDECİ €
(Map p509; Uzun Sokak 48; mains TL4-7) Three floors of wood-fired goodness for the pide and *börek* (filled pastries) aficionado within. C'mon, pide is *almost* good for you.

Üstad LOKANTA €
(Map p512; Atatürk Alanı 18b; meals TL5-8) Locals squeeze into this compact *lokanta* right on Trabzon's main square. We can thoroughly recommend the *biber dolması* (stuffed peppers) that come with a surprisingly robust pinch of chilli, reinforcing how far east you've travelled.

Fevzi Hoca Balık-Köfte   SEAFOOD €€

(Map p512; İpekyolu İş Merkezi, Kahramanmaraş Caddesi; meals TL12-25; ☺noon-9.30pm) There are no menus at this fish restaurant. Just choose your glistening beastie and it comes in a meal deal with salads, pickles and dessert. The hushed ambience makes it resemble somewhere you'd go with your parents for a birthday dinner. Cheaper *köfte* meals (TL7) are available if you're a bargain-seeking fish phobic. It's on the 1st floor of a shopping arcade.

Also recommended, especially for those with a sweet tooth:

Kılıcoğlu   PATISSERIE €

(Map p509; Uzun Sokak 42; desserts from TL3) An irresistible array of ice cream and pastries.

Mevlana Kuruyemiş   CONFECTIONER €

(Map p512; Uzun Sokak 31) Trabzon's renowned *kuruyemiş* (dried fruit) vendor also sells *lokum* (Turkish delight), *helva* (a traditional sweet made from sesame seeds), *pestil* (sheets of dried fruit) and excellent *kestane balı* (chestnut honey).

Beton Helva   CONFECTIONER €

(Map p512; Uzun Sokak 15b) Sweet slabs of *helva* that look like loaves of bread.

Cirav Fındık   CONFECTIONER €

(Map p512; Ticaret Mektep Sokak 8c) Off Kahramanmaraş Caddesi, this tiny shop has served Trabzon folk hazelnuts and confectionery since 1940.

🍷 Drinking & Entertainment

Trabzon has a small drinking scene, but most places close by midnight.

Koza Caffe   BAR-CAFE

(Map p512; cnr Kunduracılar Caddesi & Sanat Sokak 1; ☺10am-11pm) Ignore the incongruous medieval decor and settle in for coffee and snacks with a soundtrack of bouncy Turkish pop. Get lucky and grab a seat at the tiny outdoor balcony. They'll even outsource a beer or a glass of wine if you ask them nicely.

Stress Cafe   CAFE

(Map p509; Uzun Sokak; ☺10am-11pm) Stress? You must be joking. One of Trabzon's best live music and nargileh spots, the Stress Cafe is so laid-back it's almost horizontal. The Ottomans-R-Us decor is a bit naff, but this is a relaxing haven. Look for the backgammon-playing mannequins out front.

Live music kicks off at 8pm most Friday and Saturday nights.

Cingil Bar   BAR

(Map p509; 1st fl Gazipaşa Mahallesi Saray Çarşisi, Kasımoğlu Sokak) Hidden in a shopping arcade, this cosy music bar with a collage of your favourite musos (c 1975) is a good spot for a quiet drink away from the blokey beer halls. There's occasional live music at weekends. From Sinema Lara, head upstairs to the opposite end of the arcade.

Efes Pub   PUB

(Map p512; Kahramanmaraş Caddesi 5; ☺noon-11pm) Two floors of smokey, blokey ambience with good bar snacks and draught Efes in 0.7L glasses and 2L 'beer towers' – perfect for sharing with the Russian sailors on the adjacent table. Female travellers may prefer Cingil Bar.

Keyif Coffee & Tea Store   CAFE

(Map p512; Canbakkal İş Merkezi, Uzun Sokak 37; ☺8am-10pm) Trabzon's studenty types gather amidst Anglophile vintage sporting gear and leather armchairs to enjoy more than 200 varieties of hot beverage.

Sinema Lara   CINEMA

(Map p509; Gazipaşa Mahallesi Saray Çarşisi 5, Kasımoğlu Sokak; admission TL10) Hollywood blockbusters show just days after their international release. How's that for globalisation?

Luna Park   FAIRGROUND

Head to this park (Map p509) between the old and new coastal roads for Black Sea fairground action.

🛍 Shopping

Thanks to the influx of cheap goods from former Soviet territories, Trabzon is a good place for cheap clothes, especially from the stalls along Karaoğlanoğlu Caddesi. If you're lucky you might even find a few correctly spelt Western logos on the T-shirts, sweatshirts and sports shoes.

Leather shops along Sıramağazalar Caddesi sell jackets, bags and other garments, with alterations and made-to-measure fittings available. Expect to pay around half as much as in İstanbul's Grand Bazaar.

❶ Information

Banks, ATMs, exchange offices and the PTT are along or around Maraş Caddesi.

 EMERGENCY Tourist Police (☎326 3077; Atatürk Alanı)

INTERNET ACCESS **Çağri Internet** (Atatürk Alanı; ☺10am-11pm)

VIP Internet (Gazıpaşa Caddesi 6; per hr TL1.50; ☺9am-midnight)

TOURIST INFORMATION **Tourist office** (☎326 4760; Camii Sokak; ☺8am-5.30pm Jun-Sep, 8am-5pm Mon-Fri Oct-May) This helpful place is used to travellers' needs and English is usually spoken.

TRAVEL AGENCIES **Ustatour** (☎326 9545; İskenderpaşa Mahallesi 3) Domestic airline agent in the Usta Park Hotel.

❶ Getting There & Away

Air

Turkish Airlines (www.thy.com) Daily flights to Ankara, İstanbul (both airports) and İzmir. There are also flights to Bursa (Wednesday and Saturday) and Antalya (Thursday and Sunday).

Pegasus Airlines (☎444 0737; www.flypgs. com) Two daily direct flights to İstanbul (Sabiha Gökçen airport) and one to Ankara.

Onur Air (☎444 6687; www.onurair.com. tr) Three daily direct flights to İstanbul Atatürk.

SunExpress (☎444 0797; www.sunexpress. com.tr) Flies to İstanbul five times a week, Sivas and Bursa twice a week, and Adana and Antalya once a week.

Boat

Timetables for ferries to Sochi, Russia change with alarming regularity, so you'll need to check the latest situation at the following shipping offices.

Apollonia II (İskele Caddesi)

Princess Victoria Lines (İskele Caddesi 53a)

Both offices are down the hill from Atatürk Alanı on İskele Caddesi. The ferry trip takes around 12 hours; be prepared to spend a few nights in Trabzon waiting for departure. One-way tickets cost around US$80.

When you book your ticket ask when you'll need to report to the port police, as it's usually several hours before the departure time. For visa information, see p687.

Bus

Bus company offices serving all destinations, including Georgia and Azerbaijan are scattered around Atatürk Alanı.

There are no direct buses to Ayder and the Kaçkar Mountains. Catch a bus heading to Hopa and change at Pazar or Ardeşen. If you miss the daily bus to Kars, head to either Erzurum or Artvin for more services.

Car

Car rental agencies include **Avis** (☎322 3740; Gazıpaşa Caddesi 20) and **Eko Rent A Car** (☎322 2575; Gazıpaşa Caddesi 3/53).

BLACK SEA COAST & THE KAÇKAR MOUNTAINS TRABZON

SEVICES FROM TRABZON'S OTOGAR

DESTINATION	FARE	DURATION (HR)	DISTANCE (KM)	FREQUENCY (PER DAY)
Ankara	TL40	12	780	several
Artvin	TL25	4½	255	frequent
Baku, Azerbaijan	US$70	30		1
Erzurum	TL25	4	325	several
Hopa	TL18	3½	165	half-hourly
İstanbul	TL50	18	1110	several
Kars	TL40	10	525	1
Kayseri	TL50	12	686	several
Rize	TL7	1	75	half-hourly
Samsun	TL30	6	355	frequent
Sinop	TL340	9	533	1 at 8pm
Tbilisi, Georgia	TL40	20		several
Yerevan, Armenia	US$80	25		8am Thu & Sun

ⓘ Getting Around

To/From the Airport

The *havaalanı* (airport) is 5.5km east of Atatürk Alanı. Dolmuşes to the airport (TL2) leave from a side street on the northern side of Atatürk Alanı, but drop you on the opposite side of the coastal road, 500m from the terminal entrance.

A taxi costs about TL25. Buses bearing 'Park' or 'Meydan' go to Atatürk Alanı from the airport. Havas (www.havas.net) operate a shuttle bus between the airport and central Trabzon.

Bus & Dolmuş

Trabzon's otogar is 3km east of the port, on the landward side of the coastal road. To reach Atatürk Alanı from the otogar, cross the shore road in front of the terminal, turn left, walk to the bus stop and catch any bus with 'Park' or 'Meydan' in its name. The dolmuş for Atatürk Alanı is marked 'Garajlar-Meydan'. A taxi between the otogar and Atatürk Alanı costs around TL12.

To get to Trabzon's otogar catch a dolmuş marked 'Garajlar' or 'KTÜ' from the northeastern side of Atatürk Alanı.

Dolmuşes mainly leave from Atatürk Alanı, although you can flag them down along their routes. Whatever your destination, the fare should be TL1.50.

Taxi

Trabzon's main taxi stand is on Atatürk Alanı.

Sumela Monastery

The Greek Orthodox Monastery of the Virgin Mary (admission TL8; ☉9am-6pm) at Sumela, 46km south of Trabzon, is undeniably a highlight of the Black Sea coast. The monastery was founded in Byzantine times and abandoned in 1923 after the creation of the Turkish Republic quashed local Greek aspirations for a new state.

Sumela clings improbably to a sheer rock wall, high above evergreen forests and a rushing mountain stream. It's a mysterious place, especially when mists swirl in the tree-lined valley below and the call of a hidden mosque drifts ethereally through the forest.

To get to Sumela, take the Erzurum road and turn left at Maçka, 29km south of Trabzon. It's also signposted as Meryemana (Virgin Mary), to whom the monastery was dedicated. The road then winds into dense evergreen forests, following the course of a rushing mountain stream, punctuated by commercial trout pools and fish restaurants.

At the entrance to the **Altındere Vadısı Milli Parkı** (Altındere Valley National Park) there's a TL10 charge for private vehicles. If you're visiting by public transport, try to catch a dolmuş from Trabzon at around 8am to avoid the mid-morning flow of tour groups.

At the end of the road from the entrance you'll find a shady riverside park with picnic tables, a post office, restaurant and several bungalows for rent (no camping is allowed).

The main trail to the monastery begins by the restaurant and is steep but easy to follow. From the restaurant to the monastery, you'll ascend 250m in about 30 to 45 minutes, and the air gets noticeably cooler as you climb through forests and alpine meadows. A second trail begins further up the valley. Follow the concreted road 1km uphill and across two bridges until you come to a wooden footbridge over the stream on the right. This trail cuts straight up through the trees, past the shell of the Ayavarvara chapel. It's usually much quieter than the main route and takes the same amount of time.

If you drive further up the road from the restaurant, you'll reach a small car park, from which it's only a 10-minute walk to the monastery. A few kilometres before the car park is a lookout point, from where you can see the monastery suspended on a cliff face high above the forest.

After the ticket office, a steep flight of stairs leads to the monastery complex, sheltered underneath a hefty outcrop. The main chapel, cut into the rock, is the indisputable highlight, covered both inside and outside with colourful frescoes. The earliest examples date from the 9th century, but most of them are actually 19th-century work. Sadly, bored shepherd boys used the paintings as targets for their catapults, and later heedless visitors – from Russian tourists to US Air Force grunts (1965 vintage) – scratched their names into them. Even in a new century, some visitors sadly feel the need to commemorate their visit with the scrawl of a marker pen.

In recent years the monastery has been substantially restored to showcase the various chapels and rooms used by pious types in earlier centuries. Restoration continues, but in no way detracts from this essential Black Sea experience.

🛏 Sleeping & Eating

Most travellers visit Sumela as a day trip from Trabzon, but the following is a good base for exploring the surrounding area.

Coşandere Tesisleri Restaurant & Pansiyon PENSION €

(☑0462-531 1190; www.cosandere.com, in Turkish; Sümela Yolu; r from TL40) Located in Coşandere, a sleepy stream-fed village 5km south of Maçka, this place has three converted, pine-clad *seranders* (granaries) sleeping up to six, and a huge motel-like building favoured by tour groups. The owners organise various tours, treks and day trips. Anyone for a *yayla* safari or a 4WD truck trip? It's a handy way to get out and about in the mountains if you don't have your own transport.

ℹ Getting There & Away

From May to the end of August, Ulusoy and Metro run buses (TL20 return) from Trabzon to Sumela, departing at 10am and returning at 3pm.

Dolmuşes for Maçka and Coşandere village depart Trabzon all day from the minibus ranks down the hill from Atatürk Alanı on Karaoğlanoğlu Caddesi. It'll cost you around TL15 return to Sumela, but you may have to wait until the driver decides enough people are coming. For an extra TL5 you'll know exactly when you're leaving with Ulusoy or Metro.

Trabzon to Erzurum

Heading south into the mountains, you're in for a long (325km) but scenic ride. Along the highway travelling south from Trabzon, **Maçka** is 29km inland. About 1.5km north of Maçka, look out for basaltic rock columns resembling California's Devil's Postpile or Northern Ireland's Giant's Causeway. From Maçka, the mountain road ascends through active landslide zones towards the **Zigana Geçidi** (Zigana Pass; 2030m).

The dense, humid air of the coast disappears as you rise and becomes light and dry as you reach the southern side of the eastern Black Sea mountains. Snow can be seen in all months except perhaps July, August and September.

Gümüşhane, about 145km south of Trabzon, is a small town in a mountain valley with a few simple travel services.

At the provincial capital of **Bayburt**, 195km from Trabzon, you reach the rolling steppe and low mountains of the high Anatolian plateau. A dry, desolate place, Bayburt has a big medieval fortress.

The road from Bayburt passes through rolling green farm country with poplar trees and flocks of brown-fleeced sheep. In early summer wild flowers dominate.

Exactly 33km past Bayburt is the **Kop Geçidi** (Kop Pass; 2370m), with excellent views. From Kop Geçidi, the open road to Erzurum offers fast, easy travelling.

Uzungöl

☑0462 / POP 2800

With its lakeside mosque and Swiss-style forested mountains, Uzungöl is another Turkish scene that's on display in tourist offices around the country. The idyllic setting still exists, but be prepared for the overlay of a few tacky hotels and a growing number of visitors from the Gulf States. You'll even see a few menus in Arabic dotted around town. Uzungöl is a worthwhile day trip or overnight stop, and a good base for day hikes in the Soğanlı Mountains to the lakes around Demirkapı (Holdizen). Note that summer weekends get very busy, so try and visit during the week.

Ensar Otel (☑656 6321; www.ensarotel. com; Fatih Caddesi 18; r TL150-200) is an attractive resort with comfortable bungalows. Everything is wood panelled except the roof, and there's traditional decoration throughout. The bungalows sleep up to four, and the restaurant has live music on summer weekends. It's at the opposite end of the lake to the mosque, amidst a clutch of wood-trimmed *pansiyons* (around TL45/90 for a single/double). Nearby you can rent mountain bikes (per hr TL2) to circumnavigate the lake.

On the main road into Uzungöl are cheaper and simpler *pansiyons* (around TL30/60 for a single/double).

A couple of **minibuses** travel daily between Trabzon and Uzungöl. Ulusoy and Metro have a daily service at 9am in summer (TL25). Alternatively, take a Rize-bound dolmuş to Of (TL5) and then wait for another heading inland.

Rize

☑0464 / POP 78,000

Around 75km east of Trabzon, in the heart of Turkey's tea-plantation area, Rize is a modern city centred on a bustling main

GOOD-TASTING CABBAGE? SURELY NOT!

The eastern Black Sea has a unique culture, and chances are you'll first experience the region's uncommon character via your stomach. The local cuisine provides a few taste sensations that you won't find anywhere else.

The people of the Black Sea have a reverence for cabbage only surpassed by certain Eastern Europeans, and no trip would be complete without sampling *labana sarması* (stuffed cabbage rolls) or *labana lobia* (cabbage and beans). Even if you're not a cabbage fan, you'll find that these fibre-rich dishes are both healthy and tasty.

Also very popular are *muhlama* (or *mıhlama*) and *kuymak,* both types of thick molten cheese served in a metal dish, much like a fondue or raclette, but without the fiddly carrot and celery sticks. Scooped up with bread for breakfast, it can sit heavily in your stomach, especially if it's followed by a long bus ride. Try it instead in the mountain villages of the Kaçkars, where it's cooked with egg for a lighter effect. It will set you up for a long day's trekking.

If your taste buds aren't reacting to these savoury treats, consider *laz böreği,* a delicious flaky pastry layered with custard. Like most Turkish desserts, a few bites can easily become a daily addiction. And when you consider that many of Turkey's pastry chefs are from the Black Sea, you just know it's going to be good.

A good place to try Black Sea cuisine is the Evvel Zaman in Rize.

square. The hillsides above town are thickly planted with tea, which is dried, blended, and shipped throughout Turkey. There are a couple of excellent eating options, and Rize is a good spot for a refreshing cuppa as you break your journey east or west.

The main square, Atatürk Anıtı with a beautifully reconstructed PTT and the Şeyh Camii, is 200m inland from the coastal road, Menderes Bulvarı. The hotels are east of the main square along or just off Cumhuriyet Caddesi, one block inland and parallel to Menderes Bulvarı.

◉ Sights

Up the hill behind the tourist office you'll find the Rize museum (☎214 0235; Ulubatlı Sokak; admission TL3; ◷9am-noon & 1-4pm Tue-Sun), a fine reconstructed Ottoman house with a lovely *serander.* The rooms upstairs have been decorated in traditional style, with artefacts and an old radio to remind you that the later Ottomans were part of the modern age. Mannequins model traditional Laz costumes from central Rize and Hemşin costumes from the Ayder region.

Don't miss Rize's fragrant and floral **tea garden**, 900m above town via the steep road behind the Şeyh Camii (it's signposted in English 'Çaykur Tea and Botany Garden'). Enjoy the superb views with a fresh brew of the local leaves (TL2) – a typical Rizeli experience. A taxi from outside the mosque is around TL7.

Rize's ancient **castle** was built by the Genoese on the steep hill at the back of town. Signs point the way up Kale Sokak from Atatürk Caddesi.

🛌 Sleeping

Hotel Milano   HOTEL €
(☎213 0028; www.hotelmilanorize.com, in Turkish; Cumhuriyet Caddesi 169; s/d/tr TL40/60/110; ❄@) Decked out in yellow tones and with Ezy-Kleen tile floors, this friendly spot has perhaps the best shower pressure in all of Rize.

Otel Kaçkar   HOTEL €€
(☎213 1490; www.otelkackar.com, in Turkish; Cumhuriyet Caddesi 101; s/d/tr TL60/90/120; ❄@) Just off the main square, look out for the Kaçkar's mosaic facade, which conceals the neat and simple rooms.

✕ Eating & Drinking

TOP CHOICE **Evvel Zaman**   MUTFAK €€
(Eminettin Mahallesi; mains TL8-11) This lovingly restored Ottoman house – the interior is like a joyously jumbled museum – is a wonderful place to try traditional Laz food, such as *muhlama* (a fonduelike dish) and *labana sarması* (stuffed cabbage rolls). There's no written menu, so you may need to trust the judgement of the friendly restaurant staff. Evvel Zaman is at the southeastern (uphill) edge of the main square.

Deragh Pastaneleri PATISSERIE €
(Deniz Caddesi 19; mains TL4-7; ⏱7am-10pm; 📶) This gleaming modern *pastane* (patisserie) has been luring fans of sweet and savoury flavours since 1985. There's also wi-fi access, so come early for breakfast and check your email.

Bekiroğlu LOKANTA €
(Cumhuriyet Caddesi 161; mains TL6-10) A cut above most Turkish *lokantas,* Bekiroğlu has a modern interior, and the busy, bustling waiters summon up all of the English they know to treat you like a regular. Inside the huge display cases are 1001 variations on salads and kebaps, but there's also top-notch pide on offer.

❶ Information

INTERNET ACCESS **Sahra Internet Café** (Atatürk Caddesi; per hr TL1; ⏱10am-11pm) One block back from the main square.

TOURIST INFORMATION **Tourist office** (📞213 0408; ⏱9am-5pm Mon-Fri mid-May–mid-Sep) On the main square next to the PTT.

❶ Getting There & Away

From Rize's otogar, frequent minibuses run to Hopa (TL8, 1½ hours) and Trabzon (TL7, 1½ hours). For Ayder, take an eastbound minibus either to Pazar (TL7) or Ardeşen (TL6) and change for Ayder. Departures to Ayder are more frequent from Pazar. A few local minibuses also travel to Hopa and Trabzon from a mini-otogar 150m northeast of Rize's main square on the old coastal road.

Rize's main otogar is along Cumhuriyet Caddesi, 1km northwest of the main square.

Hopa
📞0466 / POP 24,000

Hopa is the archetypal border town, with cheap hotels, traders markets and a depressingly functional vibe. Just 30km southwest of the Georgian border and 165km east of Trabzon, it's best appreciated on a grey day with a bad rakı hangover. It'll probably feel like that anyway. Stay here only if you're heading to, or arriving from, Georgia and have arrived too late to move on. There's a PTT, a couple of banks with ATMs and internet cafes.

🛏 Sleeping

Otel İmren HOTEL €
(📞351 4069; Cumhuriyet Caddesi; s/d TL20/30) Here's one for the budget-conscious Georgia-bound traveller. With spearmint decor and relatively clean rooms, these are cheap digs for before or after the border crossing. Downstairs, cards are played in a smoky and very masculine atmosphere. It's on the main drag, in the centre of town.

Otel Huzur HOTEL €
(📞351 4095; Cumhuriyet Caddesi 25; s/d TL40/60; ❄) Newish rooms, some with sea views, feature at this friendly spot used by travellers doing the Black Sea shuffle to Georgia. It's on the main road opposite the truck park.

🍴 Eating & Drinking

Green Kebap PIDECI €
(Cumhuriyet Caddesi; mains TL3-7) This spot does exactly what it says on the tin, with two terraces and a brick dining room dishing up pide and kebaps in a shady park. There's a

---

ONE OF THE LAZ

Rize is the last major centre of the Laz people (see p658), a loose community of around 250,000 people, 150,000 of whom still speak the Caucasian-based Lazuri language. Known for their colourful traditional costumes and *lazeburi* folk music, you can see Laz cultural performances at any major local festival in the Rize region.

However, calling someone Laz is not straightforward. The Turkish Laz strenuously dispute any kind of categorisation that would lump them in with their Georgian counterparts. Local non-Laz folk distinguish themselves as 'Karadenizli' (from the Black Sea) but, despite this, many Turks use Laz as a lazy (or should that be Lazy?) catch-all term for anyone living east of Samsun.

The majority population in towns such as Pazar and Ardeşen, the Laz are just as keen to distance themselves from other coastal citizens, and dismiss the stereotype of the simple anchovy-munching 'Laz fisherman' that is the butt of countless Turkish jokes.

The Laz are actually having the last laugh because many of Turkey's shipping lines are owned by wealthy Laz families. They routinely resource their boats with Laz sailors, so don't be surprised if a few retired maritime types regale you (in pretty good English) with their memories of San Francisco, Sri Lanka or Singapore.

nearby *tekel bayii* (off-licence kiosk) to score a cold beer after a dusty bus journey.

ℹ Getting There & Away

Hopa's otogar is on the old coast road around 1km west of town. Direct buses from Hopa to Erzurum (TL30, six hours) leave at 9am, 4pm and 7pm. There are also regular buses or minibuses to Artvin (TL12, 1½ hours), Rize (TL8, 1½ hours) and Trabzon (TL18, 3½ hours). For Kars (TL20, seven hours), there's one direct bus per day.

For Georgia, up to 10 buses depart to Batumi (TL10, one hour) and two to Tbilisi (TL35, eight hours), but you'll most likely catch a through departure from Trabzon or Rize.

KAÇKAR MOUNTAINS

The Kaçkar Mountains (Kaçkar Dağları) form a rugged range bordered by the Black Sea coast to the north and the Çoruh River to the south. The range stretches for about 30km, from south of Rize almost to Artvin at its northeastern end. Dense forest covers the lower valleys, but above 2100m grasslands carpet the passes and plateaus, and the jagged ranges are studded with lakes and alpine summer *yayla*.

The Kaçkars are renowned for their trekking opportunities. Popular locations include the highest point, **Mt Kaçkar** (Kaçkar Dağı; 3937m), with a glacier on its northern face, and the northeastern ranges around the peak of **Altıparmak** (3310m). Visiting the Kaçkars on a day trip is possible, but a longer stay of at least three days will uncover the best of this beautiful region.

🏃 Activities

Trekking

The Kaçkars' trekking season is very short, and you can only trek the higher mountain routes between mid-July and mid-August, when the snowline is highest. From mid-

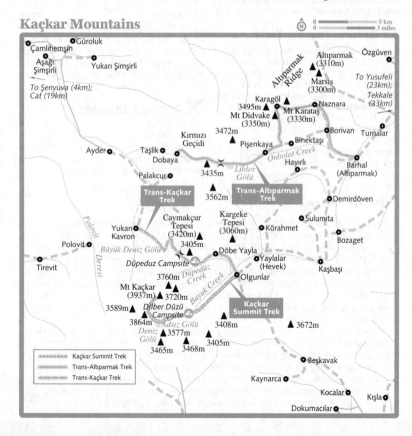

Kaçkar Mountains

May to mid-September there are plenty of walks on the lower slopes.

One of the most popular multiday trips is the **Trans-Kaçkar Trek**. The trek to the **Kaçkar Summit** by its southern face takes an easy three days, but may require specialist snow equipment. The three- to four-day **Trans-Altıparmak** route is similar to the Trans-Kaçkar, except that it crosses the Altıparmak range and doesn't climb the summit. If you stay in **Barhal (Altıparmak)** you could trek for four to five sweaty hours up to **Karagöl**, camp overnight, and return the next day.

Most people base themselves in Ayder or Çamlıhemşin, or start treks from the eastern flanks of the range at Barhal, Yaylalar (Hevek) or Olgunlar. **Day walks** around the slopes and lakes are possible from Yukarı Kavron, Caymakçur and Avusor, all served by limited dolmuş traffic from Ayder.

See the excellent website, www.trekkinginturkey.com for more information, or to purchase *The Kaçkar – Trekking in Turkey's Black Sea Mountains*. The book details 30 different Kaçkar routes.

For details online see www.kackarlar.org, which includes downloadable maps and summaries of the main trekking routes and trails.

TREKKING GUIDES

In the Kaçkars it's a good idea to hire a local who knows the tracks. The walks are mostly unsigned, and misty weather conditions can make orientation difficult. It can be difficult to arrange a guide upon arrival in the region – especially outside of the main trekking season – and it's recommended that you make contact and book a guide beforehand.

A good tent, stove and sleeping bag is necessary, but you could get away with walking boots and warm clothes if you're trekking with an all-inclusive operator.

For fully guided tours for two people, including guide fee, tents and bedding, but excluding transport and food, expect to pay around US$150 per day from Ayder.

Reliable English-speaking guides include Mehmet Demirci (☑0464-651 7787, 0533-341 3430; www.turkutour.com), a friendly local entrepreneur offering day walks, longer treks, 4WD safaris, biking trips and rafting. During the trekking season you'll find him at the Fora Pansiyon (p523) in Ayder. Many guides in Ayder work through

his company Turku Tourism (www.turkutour.com). See the website for details of multiday excursions, including horse-riding, mountain biking, trekking and photography.

Another recommended trekking contact is Egemen Cakir (☑0532-606 4096; egemen_cakir@yahoo.com). He's based across the mountains near Erzurum, but can arrange trekking guides (per day around TL150) from the Ayder and Çamlıhemşin area. See www.kackarlar.org for contact details of other local guides.

There are also mountain guides in Yusufeli, Tekkale and Barhal, on the southern side of the range (see p542). Or you could join a tour led by Middle Earth Travel (www.middleearthtravel.com; 1-week Kaçkars trek €570).

If you don't wish to arrange a guide beforehand, another option is to catch a dolmuş from Ayder to the mountain village of Yukarı Kavron where there are simple pensions where guides can sometimes be arranged.

White-Water Rafting

White-water rafting is possible in July and August on the rapids west of Çamlıhemşin. Ask at the hotels or at Dağraft (☑0464-752 4070; www.dagraft.com.tr; per person TL50-70). You'll find them 9km from the coast on the Ayder to Çamlıhemşin road. Their 'Amateur Course' is a 9km Grade 1 to 2 scenic spin, but Dağraft's 'Professional Course' is an 18km Grade 3 to 4 journey all the way from Çamlıhemşin.

The rapids around Çamlıhemşin are smaller compared to the more exciting waters near Yusufeli (p542), but the Black Sea region has arguably the more impressive scenery.

Winter Sports

Some **winter sports**, such as cross-country skiing are also possible in the region, but as there are few people around outside the trekking season this is best organised in advance. Contact Mehmet Demirci (☑0464-651 7787, 0533-341 3430; www.turkutour.com) for more information.

Çamlıhemşin & Around

☑0464 / POP 2400

At an altitude of 300m, 20km off the coastal road, Çamlıhemşin is definitely a climatic transition point. Mist and drizzle will flag you've left the coastal zone, and once you start heading up the valleys towards Ayder,

LOCAL KNOWLEDGE

MEHMET DEMIRCI – TREKKING GUIDE

Best Place to Stay

Ekodanitinap (p523) has got treehouses and cottages, and is in a quiet spot near the village in Çamlıhemşin. There's solar power and an organic farm. When we're not in Ayder during the trekking season, I stay there with my family. There are no people and I just love looking up at the solar system.

Favourite Kaçkar Mountains Trek

My favourite is a week-long trek beginning in Çamlıhemşin and going up the Fırtına Valley to Çat. It carries on to an altitude of 2650m, and then we descend slightly to spend three nights using the Kotençur Mountain House at 2300m as a base. After that, we travel back down to the hot springs at Ayder before returning to Çamlıhemşin.

expect a stronger alpine influence in the climate, terrain and vegetation.

Travelling from Çamlıhemşin to Ayder, you'll pass several ancient **humpback bridges** across the Fırtına Çayı (Storm Stream), which were restored for the 75th anniversary of the Turkish Republic in 1998. There are a couple of camping spots and Dağraft's rafting base between here and the coast.

Just beyond Çamlıhemşin the road forks. Straight ahead (signposted 'Zil Kale & Çat') follows the river to Şenyuva, and left (signposted 'Ayder Kaplıcaları') heads uphill to Ayder (17km).

Çamlıhemşin is a functional village with the only ATM in the Kaçkars. Stock up on provisions or refuel in the cheap eateries.

Accommodation-wise you're best to push on to Ayder, except for one hidden gem. Ekodanitap (☑651 7230; www.turkutour.com; half-board per person Hemşin house/treehouse US$60/45) is a combination of traditional Hemşin houses and treehouses concealed up a steep hill on the main road coming into Çamlıhemşin from the coast. With an organic garden and solar power, sustainability is a priority, but there are also modern features, such as fridges and solar showers. Meals are served in a shared pavilion overlooking a river valley.

There is no direct dolmuş from Trabzon or Rize – you'll need to go from Çamlıhemşin or Ayder (from Pazar or Ardeşen).

The town offers basic cafes, as well as Yeşilvadi (☑651 7282; İnönü Caddesi; meals TL10-14), by the Ayder bridge. It serves excellent trout dinners and mezes in the conservatory. Situated 1km along the road from Çamlıhemşin to Ayder, Dağdibinde (meals TL6-10) has alfresco eating beside the graceful arch of a centuries-old stone bridge.

Frequent dolmuş traffic runs from Pazar or Ardeşen to Çamlıhemşin.

Şenyuva
☑0464

Şenyuva is beautiful and atmospheric, and with Ayder becoming more busy it's a wonderful place to experience a very traditional atmosphere. The locals are so keen to retain its special ambience that in 2010 they banned TV from the valley.

Even getting to Şenyuva is special, negotiating verdant valleys crisscrossed with winch wires for hoisting goods up to the remote mountain houses. Look for the hilltop mansions built in the early 20th century when locals returned flush with cash after working as chefs and bakers in pre-Revolutionary Russia.

A few hundred metres north of Fırtına Pansiyon is the graceful arch of the **Şenyuva Köprüsü** (Şenyuva Bridge, 1696). From here, the road continues for 9km to the spectacularly situated ruins of **Zil Castle** (Zil Kale), a round stone tower on a stark rock base, surrounded by lush rhododendron forests. It's a superb walk, but tough-going for cars. Another 15km will lead you to **Çat** (1250m), a mountain hamlet used as a trekking base, where you'll find a shop, a couple of seasonal pensions and the start of the even rougher roads into the heart of the mountains.

🛏 Sleeping

Note that accommodation in Şenyuva is limited and booking ahead is highly recommended. Pension owners can organise hikes in the surrounding area.

 Otel Doğa PENSION €
(☎651 7455; www.hoteldogafirtina.com; half-board per person TL45) This friendly base about 4km from Çamlıhemşin is nestled in a gentle bend of the Fırtına river. The well-travelled owner, İdris Duman, speaks French and English, and is a passionate champion of his home region. Most rooms have private bathrooms and balconies, and the home-cooked food is the ideal pick-me-up after a long day of walking. The hotel is popular, so booking ahead is recommended. During summer, dolmuşes pass by the front door heading for the villages in the Kaçkars' high meadows.

Fırtına Pansiyon PENSION €
(☎653 3111; www.firtinavadisi.com; half-board per person TL65; ☺Apr-Sep) Around 2km further up the river valley, this friendly spot features cute bungalows near the river and cheerful rooms in former school buildings. A recent makeover has added new rooms lined in warm pine and decked out with colourful bed linen. The shared lounge area – with an open fire, musical instruments and lots of books – could just be Turkey's cosiest spot. All accommodation has shared bathrooms.

❶ Getting There & Away

Only one minibus a day runs between Şenyuva and Çamlıhemşin, so you may have to walk (6km) or take a taxi for about TL20 each way.

Ayder

☎0464
Ayder is the hub of tourism in the Kaçkars. This high-pasture village revels amidst a valley perched at 1300m, with snow-capped mountains and waterfalls cascading to the river below. Earlier, un-regulated development saw ugly concrete buildings encroach on the glorious setting, but now charming alpine-chalet structures dominate, and new buildings must be in 'traditional style' (ie sheathed in wood).

Ayder is firmly on the agenda for Turk-ish tourists, and is becoming increasingly popular with walking groups from West-ern countries, Israel especially. As a result, Ayder's budget-travel ethos is creeping up-market, resulting in a better standard of accommodation but also slightly higher prices.

It's still really only busy during the trek-king season (mid-May to mid-September) and at other times there may only be a few local families living here. But if you come in the second week of June for the annual **Çamlıhemşin Ayder Festival** (see boxed text p524), or during weekends in July and August, Turkish tourists fill most accom-modation by mid-afternoon.

The nominal centre of the village has a few restaurants, a supermarket, an internet cafe, the minibus office and bus stop, and several gift shops. Other accommodation, restaurants and souvenir shops are scat-tered for about 1km along the road uphill either side of the centre. There is nowhere to change money and the nearest ATM is in Çamlıhemşin.

About 4.5km below, Ayder is the gate marking the entrance to the Kaçkar Dağları Milli Parkı (Kaçkar Mountains National Park), with an admission fee of TL8 per vehicle.

🏃 Activities

Most people use Ayder as a base for **trek-king** in the mountains, but even if you don't have time to do that it's still worth popping up for an overnight stay to experience the glorious scenery.

Post-trek muscle relief can be had at the spotless kaplıca (hot springs; admission TL8, private cabin TL25; ☺8am-8pm), where the wa-ter reaches temperatures of 56°C.

🛏 Sleeping

Much of Ayder's accommodation is set half-way up the hill next to the road, reached by narrow, slanting paths. Getting up to them can be tricky when the mist rolls in. Usu-ally your bags will be dragged up the hill on nifty winch arrangements.

Fora Pansiyon PENSION €
(☎657 2153; www.turkutour.com; half-board per person without bathroom US$40) One of Ay-der's hillside pensions provides a cosy sit-ting room, pine-clad bedrooms with shared bathrooms, balconies and a laundry. The Demirci family are very welcoming, and dinner on the view-laden terrace with the kids shouldn't be missed. Just don't blame us if you get homesick all of a sudden.

Zirve Ahşap Pansiyon PENSION €
(☎657 2162; s/d without bathroom TL30/60) One for the budget crowd, this hillside house is pretty rustic, but there's a kitch-

If you visit Ayder over a summer weekend you may get the chance to witness some of the last surviving Hemşin culture (see p658). In the meadows of the village, groups of Hemşin holidaymakers often gather to dance the *horon,* a cross between the conga and the hokey-cokey set to the distinctive whining skirl of the *tulum,* a type of goatskin bagpipe. Even if you don't run into one of these parties, you'll see women all around the mountains wearing splendid headdresses, often incongruously matched with cardigans, long skirts and running shoes or woollen boots. In the second week of June many Hemşin émigrés return from overseas for the annual Çamlıhemşin Ayder Festival. Accommodation can be almost impossible to secure at this time.

en for guests, it's friendly and English is spoken.

Yeşil Vadi Otel   HOTEL **€€**
(☑657 2050; www.ayderyesilvadi.com, in Turkish; s/d TL70/140) Clad in more pine than a Swedish sauna, this is a good central option by the main road with rustic timber rooms, heavy duvets and impeccable bathrooms. Many rooms boast valley views, and the restaurant out the front does a great *menemen* if you want something different for breakfast.

Kuşpuni Pansiyon   PENSION **€€**
(☑657 2052; www.ayderkuspuniotel.com; s/d TL60/120) Another very appealing family-run chalet-pension, Kuşpuni revels in a stove-heated lounge with decent views and hearty meals, including a mean *muhlama.* In fact, visitors rave about the food, often served on the pleasant terrace overlooking the valley. Adjacent is a pleasingly rustic *serander.*

Otel Ayder Haşimoğlu   HOTEL **€€**
(☑657 2037; www.hasimogluotel.com; s/d/tr TL80/105/140) Run by Ayder Turizm, which also operates the hot springs and the Ayder Sofrası restaurant up the hill, this flash pine-clad place is riverside and 100m downhill from the centre (follow the path by the town mosque). With facilities including a fitness centre and spa, you're losing the personal, family touch available at other smaller places around town, but these are Ayder's most-comfortable digs.

✖ Eating & Drinking
Most people go for the half-board option at their pensions, but there are other options.

Nazlı Çiçek   RESTAURANT **€**
(mains TL6-10) Right in the centre of the village, this charming old house specialises in freshly caught trout, but also whips up a limited range of standards and Black Sea specialities such as *muhlama.*

Yilmaz Cafeterya   LOKANTA **€**
(mains TL4-8) Welcoming and cosy, the Yilmaz is a top spot for traditional Black Sea food. The *muhlama* and *labana sarması* are both great, and we found the *menemen* studded with spicy green peppers the perfect brunch on a cool Kaçkars morning. The Yilmaz is near the top of the hill on the left – a brisk walk, but well worth it.

Zümrut Café   CAFE **€**
Ayder's best selection of sweet treats and coffee comes complete with waterfall views straight from an advertisement for mineral water. Try the creamy custard and pastry treat called *laz böreği* in these parts.

ℹ Getting There & Away
From mid-June to mid-September frequent dolmuşes run between Pazar on the coast to Ayder (TL8, one hour) via Ardeşen and Çamlıhemşin. On summer Sundays the trickle of minibuses up to Ayder turns into a flood. Otherwise, passengers are mostly shoppers from the villages, so dolmuşes descend from Ayder in the morning and return from Pazar in the early afternoon.

In season, morning dolmuşes also run from Ayder to other mountain villages, including Galer Düzü, Avusor, Yukarı Kavron and Caymakçur. Check with locals for exact schedules.

Even in the low season there are still four minibus services daily between Pazar and Çamlıhemşin.

Uçhisar, Cappadocia (p463)
Hot-air ballooning is the ideal way to witness the many shades of sun-kissed rock across the dramatic Cappadocian landscape

1. Black Sea cuisine
Sample a traditional Black Sea meal of fish, meze and rakı (aniseed brandy)

2. Sheep grazing, Van region
Sheep are reared and grazed on fertile pastures

3. Taking tea at the market, Milas (p232)
The town of Milas may be sleepy but its weekly market is a popular attraction

4. İshak Paşa Palace, Doğubayazıt (p557)
This romantic palace perches on a plateau abutting stark cliffs overlooking a plain, framed by Mt Ararat

GREG ELMS

1. Baklava
Gaziantep (p563) is reckoned to produce the best *fıstıklı* (pistachio) baklava in Turkey

2. Lake Van (p609)
This vast expanse of water surrounded by snowcapped mountains adorns a scenic and virtually untouched landscape

3. Tea for sale
Drinking çay (tea) is the national pastime; grab a cup from a tea seller at the local market

4. Mevlâna Museum, Konya (p439)
This holy place houses the tomb of Rumi (Mevlâna to his followers), one of world's great mystic philosophers and poets

5. Kaçkar Mountains (p520)
Renowned for trekking, this region features forested valleys, grassy plateaus and jagged ranges studded with lakes

GREG ELMS

3

1. Amasra (p497)
Located along the Black Sea coast, Amasra effortlessly assumes the mantle of the region's prettiest port

2. Hittite rock carvings (p420)
Uncover ancient Hittite rock carvings at the Unesco World Heritage sites of Hattuşa and Yazılıkaya

3. Kaymaklı, Cappadocia (p480)

Vast underground cities once housed thousands during times of attack in the 6th and 7th centuries

4. Mt Ararat (p560)

Towering at 5137m and 3895m a piece, the twin peaks of this mountain have figured in legends since time began

5. Meze (p643)

These small tasting dishes derive thier name from the Persian word for pleasant, enjoyable taste

PETER PTSCHELINZEW

Halilur Rahman Camii, Şanlıurfa (p576)
This much-photographed mosque, fronted by a pool of sacred carp, marks the site where Abraham fell to the ground

Northeastern Anatolia

Best Places to Stay

» Karahan Pension (p544)
» Ski Lodge Dedeman (p539)
» Grand Ani Hotel (p550)
» Greenpeace Camping (p542)
» İhtiyaroğlu (p543)

Best Places to Eat

» Ocakbaşı Restoran (p550)
» Erzurum Evleri (p537)
» Ani Ocakbaşı (p550)
» Güzelyurt Restorant (p537)
» Yöresel Yemek Evi (p559)

Why Go?

If you've got a soft spot for far-flung outposts, why not push at Turkey's back door? Despite its wealth of attractions, northeastern Anatolia remains a secretive world (even for the Turks) and is refreshingly crowd and coach-party free. Your biggest surprise: the startling variety of landscapes, from precipitous gorges and unending steppes to muscular mountains and highland pastures. No wonder it's prime territory for trekking (make a beeline for Mt Ararat and the Kaçkars), white-water rafting and skiing.

Other key experiences here lie in the culture. On top of the standout highlights, the ruins of Ani and the Işhak Paşa Palace, there are numerous hidden treasures, including a bonanza of palaces, castles, Georgian churches and Armenian monuments in splendid isolation, all testifying to Turkey's once-flourishing ancient civilisations. If you need to catch urban vibes, Erzurum and Kars will deliver.

Turkey at its best? You be the judge.

When to Go

Erzurum

May The steppe is in full blossom, the scents are memorable and the vivid hues unforgettable.

July to September Don your walking shoes and explore the Kaçkar mountains or scale Mt Ararat.

December to April Cut the fresh powdery snow at the Palandöken or Sarıkamış ski resorts.

Northeastern Anatolia Highlights

1 Lose yourself in the former glories of **Ani** (p552), once a thriving Armenian capital

2 Rip up some powder at the **Palandöken** (p539) ski resort

3 Test your mettle on a white-water run through the **Çoruh Gorge** (p542)

4 Leap off the map into the **Karagöl Sahara National Park** (p547) and wander around its quaint villages and gorgeous alpine forests

5 Measure how far your jaw drops in front of the **İshak Paşa Palace** (p557) in Doğubayazıt

6 Let time pass you by in the oh-so-serene hamlets of **Barhal** (p544) and **Olgunlar** (p545)

7 Hit the summit of iconic **Mt Ararat** (p560), Turkey's highest mountain.

Erzurum

✆ 0442 / POP 402,000 / ELEV 1853M

Lovers of architecture will be in paradise in Erzurum, the architectural capital of eastern Anatolia. They'll absolutely devour the city's fantastic Seljuk monuments and wonderful *medreses* (seminaries) and mosques that line the main drag. They'll also rave about the fantastic panorama from the citadel, with the steppe forming a heavenly backdrop.

But this is not a city resting on its considerable laurels of historical significance – the vibrant life coursing through its streets lined with flashy shopping centres has earned it a reputation as a dynamic cultural hub and modern metropolis. Although it's said to be a pious, conservative city (like Konya), the hip-looking university students add a liberal and relaxed buzz to the air. And come winter, the nearby high-octane Palandöken ski resort has a thriving nightlife.

History

Being in a strategic position at the confluence of roads to Constantinople, Russia and Persia, Erzurum was conquered and lost by armies of Armenians, Persians, Romans, Byzantines, Arabs, Saltuk Turks, Seljuk Turks, Mongols and Russians. As for the Ottomans, it was Selim the Grim who conquered the city in 1515. It was captured by Russian troops in 1882 and again in 1916.

In July 1919 Atatürk came to Erzurum to attend the congress that provided the rallying cry for the Turkish independence struggle. The Erzurum Congress is most famous for determining the boundaries of what became known as the territories of the National Pact, the lands that became part of the Turkish Republic.

⊙ Sights

Çifte Minareli Medrese MEDRESE
(Twin Minaret Seminary; Cumhuriyet Caddesi) Lying east of the centre, the single most definitive image of Erzurum dates from the 1200s when Erzurum was a wealthy Seljuk city, before it suffered attack and devastation by the Mongols in 1242. The facade is an example of the way the Seljuks liked to try out variation even while aiming for symmetry: the panels on either side of the entrance are identical in size and position but different in motif. The panel to the right bears the Seljuk eagle; to the left the motif is unfinished.

The twin brick **minarets** are decorated with eye-catching small blue tiles. Don't look for the tops of the minarets – they are gone, having succumbed to the vagaries of Erzurum's violent history even before the Ottomans claimed the town.

The main courtyard has four large niches and a double colonnade on the eastern and western sides. At the far end of the courtyard is the grand, 12-sided domed hall that served as the Hatuniye Türbesi, or Tomb of Huand Hatun, the founder of the *medrese*.

Ulu Cami MOSQUE
(Great Mosque; Cumhuriyet Caddesi) Unlike the elaborately decorated Çifte Minareli, the Ulu Cami, built in 1179 by the Saltuk Turkish emir of Erzurum, is restrained but elegant, with seven aisles running north to south and six running east to west, resulting in a forest of columns. You enter from the north along the central aisle. Above the third east–west aisle, a striking stalactite dome opens to the heavens. At the southern end of the central aisle are a curious wooden dome and a pair of bull's-eye windows.

A short hop from the Ulu Cami, you'll notice the small Ottoman **Caferiye Camii** (Caferiye Mosque; Cumhuriyet Caddesi).

Üç Kümbetler MAUSOLEUMS
(Three Tombs) Walk south between the Çifte Minareli and the Ulu Cami until you come to a T-junction. Turn left then immediately right and walk a short block up the hill to these three mausoleums that lie in a fenced enclosure. Note the near-conical roofs and the elaborately decorated side panels.

Yakutiye Medrese MEDRESE
(Yakutiye Seminary; Cumhuriyet Caddesi) Rising over a square slap bang in the centre, the imposing Yakutiye Medrese is a Mongol theological seminary dating from 1310. The Mongol governors borrowed the basics of Seljuk architecture and developed their own variations, as is evident in the entrance to the *medrese*. Of the two original minarets, only the base of one and the lower part of the other have survived; the one sporting superb mosaic tile work wouldn't be out of place in Central Asia. The *medrese* now serves as Erzurum's **Turkish-Islamic Arts & Ethnography Museum** (Türk-İslam Eserleri ve Etnoğrafya Müzesi; admission TL3; ⊙8am-noon & 1-5pm Tue & Thu-Sun). Inside, the striking central dome is lined with faceted stalactite work that catches light from the central opening to make a delightful pattern.

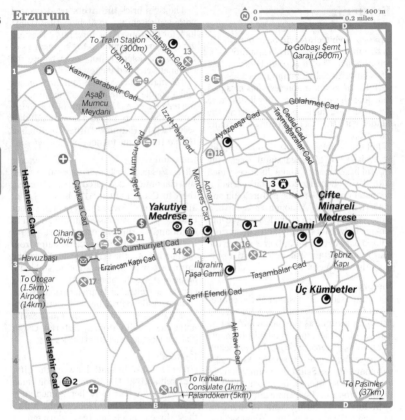

The appealing building you see right next to the Yakutiye Medrese is the classical **Lala Mustafa Paşa Camii**, dating from 1562.

Kale
FORTRESS

(admission TL3; ⊗8am-5pm) Anyone unafraid of a bit of sweat should head up to Erzurum's best views, at the citadel, perched on the hilltop to the north of the Çifte Minareli. It was erected by the emperor Theodosius around the 5th century.

Erzurum Museum
MUSEUM

(Erzurum Müzesi; Yenişehir Caddesi; admission TL3; ⊗8am-5pm Tue-Sun) Archaeology buffs will make a beeline for this museum, which houses finds from nearby digs. It lies several long blocks southwest of the Yakutiye Seminary.

🛏 Sleeping

Erzurum has a couple of dependable budget and midrange options, but if you want full-on luxury you'll need to stay at the Palandöken ski resort, 5km southwest of Erzurum.

Yeni Çınar Oteli
HOTEL €

(☑213 6690; Ayazpaşa Caddesi; s/d TL30/40) This place may not look like much, but it's clean, safe, quiet and within walking distance of everything you might need. Avoid the rooms at the rear, which have obstructed views. Breakfast is not included. Hungry? There's a *lokanta* (eatery serving ready-made food) next door. It's in the market, a short bag-haul from İstasyon Caddesi. The only flaw is the deserted, dimly lit street at night.

Grand Hotel Hitit
HOTEL €€

(☑233 5001; www.grandhitithotel.com; Kazım Karabekir Caddesi; s/d TL80/120) Enjoying a trendy makeover since we last visited, the Hitit offers well-appointed rooms with TV, dark wood furnishings, prim bathrooms and well-sprung mattresses. It's professionally managed and a good choice for lone

Erzurum

women. Top marks go to the bright top-floor breakfast area – the perfect spot to eye up the city. It's within walking distance of everything.

Esadaş Otel　　　　　　　　　　HOTEL €
(☏233 5425; www.erzurumesadas.com.tr; Cumhuriyet Caddesi; s/d TL60/90) Pros: right on the main thoroughfare, close to everything, including the magnetic Kılıçoğlu pastry shop. Cons: right on the main thoroughfare, dangerously close to Kılıçoğlu, and a bit noisy (traffic ceases around 11pm). Well maintained and efficiently run. Excellent breakfast, too. Bargain down the prices a bit if it's slack.

Hotel Dilaver　　　　　　　　　HOTEL €
(☏235 0068; www.dilaverhotel.com.tr; Aşağı Mumcu Caddesi; s/d TL60/120; ❇) This char-

acterless monolith is a bit overpriced, but it's within spitting distance of the main sights, in a tranquil street and sports serviceable rooms with good bathrooms. Enjoy a copious breakfast while savouring stupendous views of the entire city spread out below you.

Yeni Ornek　　　　　　　　　　HOTEL €
(☏233 0053; Kazım Karabekir Caddesi; s/d TL40/65) The Yeni Ornek is as no-frills as it gets but the rooms are well kept and the staff pleasing, making it a reliable lower-midrange option. After a long day's turf pounding, sink into the comfy leather armchairs in the lobby while marvelling at the ancient switchboard.

✗ Eating & Drinking

TOP CHOICE **Erzurum Evleri**　　　　CAFE €
(Cumhuriyet Caddesi, Yüzbaşı Sokak; mains TL7-13) A stunner set in an old wooden house near the main drag. It feels like half the paraphernalia from six centuries of the Ottoman Empire has ended up here, with an onslaught of kilims (pileless woven rugs), pictures, weapons, farming tools and other collectibles from floor to ceiling. Surrender to the languor of the private alcoves with cushions and low tables and treat yourself to a soup, a *börek* (filled pastry) or a *tandır* kebap (stew). The nearby Daşhane, which has the same management, features live music on Friday and Saturday evenings. If only it was licensed!

Güzelyurt Restorant　　　　RESTAURANT €€
(Cumhuriyet Caddesi; mains TL8-15) This iconic restaurant, in business since 1928, is so adorable because it feels so anachronistic, with shrouded windows, old-fashioned charm and thick carpets. It's also a great place to spill money on a great meal. The mezes are a headliner, with about 20 different specialities, but the menu also features a smattering of mains, including 'Bof Straganof' (no typo), all served by old-school, bow-tied waiters. It's licensed as well.

Kılıçoğlu　　　　　　　　　PATISSERIE €
(Cumhuriyet Caddesi; snacks & pastries from TL2) It's difficult for even the staunchest dieter to pass by the tantalising display of treats – they're presented almost as beautifully as a jewellery store – offered by this slick pastry shop and ice-cream parlour. If you can resist the squishy *fıstıklı* (pistachio) baklavas, you're just not human.

NORTHEASTERN ANATOLIA ERZURUM

Küçükbey Konağı CAFE €
(Cumhuriyet Caddesi, Erzurum Düğün Salonu Karşısı; mains TL4-9) Set in a rambling old mansion-turned-cafe, this welcoming oasis is popular with students of both sexes, here to gossip, flirt and puff a nargileh (traditional water pipe). Food-wise, it features simple dishes and some nibbles, but it's the atmosphere that most come to ingest. It's tucked away in a side street off the main drag.

Arzen ICE CREAM €
(Cumhuriyet Caddesi; ice creams & snacks from TL2) Hands down the best ice-cream parlour in town, Arzen is a hip place that draws baklava-holics like bees to a honey pot. One lick of the *fıstıklı* ice cream and you'll be hooked. It also serves snacks, sandwiches and cakes.

Gel-Gör Cağ Kebabı KEBAPÇI €
(İstasyon Caddesi; mains TL5-10) This charismatic Erzurum eatery specialises in *cağ* kebap (mutton grilled on a horizontal spit) served with small plates of salad, onions and yoghurt. It's a concept that's been a cult since 1975, so dedicated carnivores can't go wrong here.

TWI RESTAURANT-BAR €€
(İsmetpaşa Caddesi; mains TL7-15) A sassy newcomer. This multifunction venue – bar, restaurant and disco – serves up a broad variety of Turkish staples in fairly classy surroundings. The bar is popular with well-heeled students of both sexes.

Aspava KEBAPÇI €
(Cumhuriyet Caddesi; mains TL7-12) Brisk, buzzing, filling and good value, this popular eatery on the main street doles out well-executed pide (Turkish-style pizza) and satisfying kebaps in rosy surrounds. The food is fresh and hygienically prepared.

Shopping

Erzurum is known for the manufacture of jewellery and other items from *oltutaşı*, the local black amber. You'll find these at the atmospheric **Rüstem Paşa Çarşısı** (Adnan Menderes Caddesi), which was built between 1540 and 1550 by Süleyman the Magnificent's grand vizier.

Information

CONSULATE The **Iranian consulate** (☏316 2285; fax 316 1182; Atatürk Bulvarı; ☉8.30am-noon & 2.30-4.30pm Mon-Thu & Sat) is about 2km south of the centre, towards the Palandöken ski resort (for visa information, see p687).

INTERNET ACCESS Internet cafes are plentiful in the centre.

MONEY Most banks have branches with ATMs on or around Cumhuriyet Caddesi. There are also a few moneychangers, including **Cihan Döviz** (☏234 9488; Çaykara Caddesi; ☉8am-7pm Mon-Fri, 10am-5pm Sat & Sun), which keeps longer hours.

TOURIST INFORMATION The **tourist office** (☏235 0925; Cemal Gürsel Caddesi; ☉8am-5pm Mon-Fri) has some brochures and, if you're lucky, a city map.

Getting There & Away
Air

Durmazpınar Turizm (☏233 3690; Cumhuriyet Caddesi; ☉8am-8pm) sells tickets on behalf of Sun Express, Turkish Airlines and Onur Air. Sun Express has five weekly flights to İstanbul's Sabiha Gökçen International Airport (from TL110) and five weekly flights to İzmir (from TL80, two hours). Onur Air has five weekly flights to İstanbul (from TL118, two hours). Turkish

SERVICES FROM ERZURUM'S OTOGAR

DESTINATION	FARE (TL)	DURATION (HR)	DISTANCE (KM)	FREQUENCY (PER DAY)
Ankara	50	13	925	about 10 buses
Diyarbakır	35	8	485	5 buses
Doğubayazıt	20	4½	285	5 buses
İstanbul	65	19	1275	7 buses
Kars	15	3	205	frequent
Kayseri	45	10	628	several
Trabzon	25	6	325	several
Van	30	6½	410	about 3 buses

Airlines has daily flights to İstanbul (from TL108) and Ankara (from TL64, 90 minutes).

Bus

The otogar (bus station), 2km from the centre along the airport road, handles most of Erzurum's intercity traffic.

For Iran (if you already have your visa), take a bus to Doğubayazıt, from where you can catch a minibus to the Iranian frontier.

The Gölbaşı Semt Garajı, about 1km northeast of Adnan Menderes Caddesi through the back streets (take a cab to get there), handles minibuses to towns to the north and east of Erzurum, including Artvin, Hopa, Rize and Yusufeli. Minibuses to Yusufeli leave at *approximately* 9am, 1.30pm and 4pm daily (TL20, three hours, 129km); minibuses to Artvin (TL20, four hours, 215km), Hopa and Rize leave around 7.30am, 11.30am, 2pm, 4.30pm and 6pm.

Train

The train station is about 1km north of Cumhuriyet Caddesi. The *Doğu Ekspresi* leaves daily at noon for İstanbul via Sivas, Kayseri and Ankara (TL40); for Kars, it departs at 5.20pm (TL12). The *Erzurum Ekspresi* leaves for Ankara, via Sivas and Kayseri, daily at 1.30pm (TL40, 24 hours); for Kars, it departs at 11am (TL10, 4½ hours).

❶ Getting Around

A taxi to/from the airport, about 14km from town, costs around TL40.

Minibuses and city buses pass the otogar and will take you into town for TL1; a taxi costs about TL10.

Car rental is available through **Avis** (☎233 8088; www.avis.com.tr; Terminal Caddesi, Mavi Site 1 Blok 5; ⏰8am-7pm).

Around Erzurum

PALANDÖKEN SKI RESORT
☎0442

It usually comes as a surprise to many travellers to discover that the best ski resort in the country is a mere 5km south of Erzurum, at Palandöken. Excellent ski runs for all levels and top-notch infrastructure, including ski lifts, cable cars, snowboard parks and even impressive jumping hills, are the calling cards of Palandöken, which gained international recognition in January 2011 when the Universiade (the World University Winter Games) were held here.

At weekends from December to April, be prepared to jostle with other snow-lovers for a spot on the slopes and a place in the

ski-lift queues. There's also an excellent après-ski scene.

🛏 Sleeping & Eating

With the exception of the Dedeman, the following places to stay are open all year. All hotels have their own restaurants, bars and discos. The prices quoted here are high-season winter rates (expect discounts of up to 30% in low season). They're usually negotiable.

Ski Lodge Dedeman   HOTEL €€€
(☎317 0500; www.dedeman.com; s/d with half-board TL380/400; P ✳) The most stylish and intimate of the lot.

Dedeman   HOTEL €€
(☎316 2414; www.dedeman.com; s/d with half-board TL280/430; P ✳) Right at the foot of the ski runs, at 2450m.

Palan Otel   HOTEL €€
(☎317 0707; www.palanotel.com; s/d with half-board TL200/280; P ✳ ✳) Unexciting but has comprehensive amenities.

Polat Renaissance   HOTEL €€
(☎232 0010; www.polatrenaissance.com; s/d with half-board TL250/350; P ✳ ✳) The pyramid-shaped Polat feels like a mini-city.

❶ Getting There & Away

From central Erzurum, a taxi will set you back about TL17.

Georgian Valleys

In addition to being spectacular, the mountainous country north of Erzurum towards Artvin is also one of northeastern Anatolia's most culturally peculiar areas. It was once part of the medieval kingdom of Georgia, and has numerous churches and castles to show for it. They mix characteristics of Armenian, Seljuk and Persian styles, and are seldom visited. If you happen to be passing in mid-June, the orchards of cherries and apricots should be in bloom – a special treat.

For a vivid account of this little corner of Turkey, look no further than Tony Anderson's *Bread and Ashes: A Walk Through the Mountains of Georgia,* which includes a chapter about the Georgian Valleys.

History

The Persians and Byzantines squabbled over this region from the 4th century AD. Then it was conquered by the Arabs in the 7th century, recovered by the Byzantines,

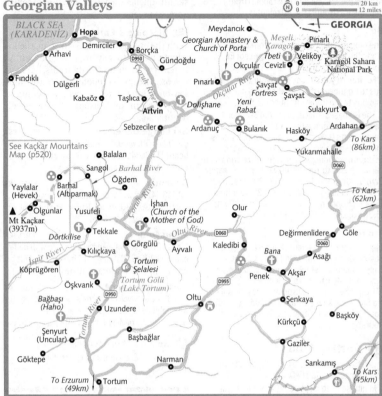

lost again and so on. It was part of the medieval Georgian kingdom in the 10th century, governed by the Bagratids, from the same lineage as the Armenian Bagratids ruling over the Kars region. A mixture of isolation brought about by the rugged terrain, piety and the support of Byzantium all fostered a flourishing culture that produced the churches you see today.

However, it was the ambitious King Bagrat III who looked outside the sheltered valleys and unified Georgia's warring kingdoms in 1008. Bagrat III shifted the focus of the newly formed kingdom by moving the capital from Tbilisi, nominally under the control of the Arabs, to Kutaisi, and by gradually disengaging from the southwest valleys that had been under the sway of the Byzantines since 1001.

The southwest provinces had been coexisting relatively harmoniously between the Byzantines and Georgians, but the arrival of the Seljuk Turks in 1064 dashed hopes of real stability. King David IV ('The Builder'; 1089–1125) defeated the Seljuks in 1122, and took up where King Bagrat III had left off by reunifying Georgia with Tbilisi and the southwest provinces. So began the 'golden age' for Georgian culture, which reached its peak during the rule of Queen Tamar (1184–1213).

Following the arrival of the Mongol conqueror Tamerlane in 1386, the kingdom was dealt its most savage blow by the Ottoman capture of Constantinople in 1453 and the ending of the protection the Georgians had enjoyed under quasi-Byzantine rule. The kingdom went into decline, the Ottomans annexed the Georgian Valleys and, later, imperial Russia took care of the rest.

Today many locals have Georgian heritage, but most converted to Islam or left after the troubles in the early 20th century.

❶ Getting There & Away

The small mountain villages in the valleys are a delight to explore, but public transport to and from most of them consists of one minibus that heads between Erzurum and Artvin early in the morning, returning in the afternoon. Buses run between Erzurum and Yusufeli, though these allow little opportunity for exploration. It's best to hire a car in Erzurum or a taxi in Yusufeli (about TL250 for a day).

The following itinerary starts from Yusufeli.

İŞHAN

From Yusufeli, drive to the petrol station along the Artvin–Erzurum road (9km) and go another 8km until you reach the junction with the D060. Take the road on the left marked for Olur and Ardahan. You'll reach İşhan after 6km. Turn left at a junction marked by a sign reading 'İşhan Kilisesi'. The upper village is spectacularly situated, 6km up a steep, narrow road carved out of the mountainside. At the time of research, this road was pretty deteriorated; it shouldn't be braved in wet weather.

Located past the modern white mosque, the wonderful Church of the Mother of God was built in the 8th century and enlarged in the 11th. There are traces of blue frescoes in the near-conical dome (vanishing fast – 25 years ago whole walls were covered in them), and a superb arcade of horseshoe-shaped arches in the apse, all with different capitals. The four pillars are impressive, as in Öşkvank. Unfortunately, a huge dividing wall was built in the nave – half of this church functioned as a mosque until the replacement mosque was built in 1984.

The most detailed of the many fine reliefs – above the portal of the small chapel next door – ascribes the founding of the church to King Bagrat III. Also worth admiring are the inscriptions above the bricked-up portal of the main building and an elaborate fretwork around the windows. The drum also sports some fine blind arcades and elegantly carved colonnades.

TORTUM GÖLÜ & TORTUM ŞELALESİ

Back at the junction with the D060, take Hwy 950 in the Erzurum direction (south). You'll reach the impressive Tortum Şelalesi (Tortum Waterfalls) after about 16km, signposted 700m off the main road.

Continuing south, Hwy 950 skirts the western shore of Tortum Gölü (Lake Tortum), which was formed by landslides about

three centuries ago. You can break your journey at the İskele Et & Balık Lokantası (fish dishes TL6-10), about 4km south of the waterfalls, and enjoy well-prepared fish dishes right by the lake. The setting is awesome and boats are available for rent (TL20). Camping is also possible here (TL10).

ÖŞKVANK

Continuing 8km south on Hwy 950, you'll reach the turn-off to Öşkvank, which is 7km off the highway. Keep on the main road winding up the valley to the village, where you can't miss the impressive cathedral, built in the late 10th century. It's the grandest of the Georgian cathedrals in this region, with a three-aisled basilica topped off by a dome. Keep an eye out for the blind arcades and the reliefs of the archangels.

The central nave has two walled-off aisles on either side. The southwest aisle, like the triple-arched narthex, is still in relatively good shape – notice the intricate carvings on the capitals, with elaborate geometric designs, typical of Georgian church decoration. There are other fine relief carvings, both on the massive capitals that supported the equally majestic dome and on the exterior walls. Look for the fine relief of the Three Wise Men, to the right (northeast) of the main entrance; the relief of Mary and Joseph has been destroyed.

Much of the roof has fallen in, but there are still well-preserved fragments of frescoes; look in the half-dome on the inside of the main porched portal.

BAĞBAŞI (HAHO)

About 15km south of the turn-off to Öşkvank is another turn-off on the right (west), over a humpbacked bridge, to the village called Haho by the Georgians. Look out for the sign 'Pehlivanlı Bağbaşı Serdarlı'. Go about 5km up the asphalted road through orchards and fields to the village, then bear right at a sign marked 'Taş Camii Meriem Ani Kilisesi' and after 3km the monastery complex comes into view. It dates from the late 10th century. Don't miss the conical-topped dome, with its multicoloured tiles, or the fine reliefs, including a stone eagle grasping a doe in its claws. The use of alternating light and dark stones adds to the elegance of the building.

The church is used as a mosque, so some restoration work has taken place here.

OLTU

Continue south along Hwy 950 until you reach the turn-off to Narman. Drive past Narman. When the road meets the D955, turn left (north). Along the D955, the peaceful town of Oltu is huddled beneath a startling kalesi (citadel), painstakingly restored in 2002. Little is known about its history, but it is supposed to have been built by Urartus in 1000 BC. The castle was probably used by Genoese colonies and was of some importance during the Roman and Byzantine periods, before being occupied by the Seljuks and then by the Ottomans in the 16th century.

BANA & PENEK

Continuing a further 18km north along the D955 brings you to the junction with the D060. Turn left and drive for about 4km and you'll see a castle on a mound. It's an eerie sight, in keeping with the surreal landscape, where craggy gorges alternate with reddish bluffs. About 400m further on you'll see a second crumbling castle on the left, built on a rocky outcrop and overlooking a river lined with poplars. Backtrack to the junction with Highway 955. From the junction, turn left onto the D060 towards Kars. A further 14.2km will lead you past a bridge crossing the Penek Çayı (it's signposted). About 100m past the bridge, take the side track on the left. It goes uphill for 2km to the village of Penek. Continue through the village and the awesome Armenian church of Bana soon comes into view, standing on a hill with the mountains forming a fantastic backdrop. Its most distinctive architectural feature is its rotunda shape. You can approach the church by following a dirt road that branches off to the left about 600m after leaving the village (don't brave it in wet weather with an ordinary car).

Yusufeli

☎0466 / POP 6400 / ELEV 560M

This may be the last time this book has a section about Yusufeli. Indeed, the town and part of the nearby valley is slated to vanish underwater. The Yusufeli dam project, which is part of Turkey's national plan to expand its use of hydropower and move towards greater energy independence, is under way in spite of local and international resistance. That said, nobody knows exactly when the flooding is going to happen, which makes matters even more painful for residents, who are waiting for the axe to fall. They will be relocated higher in the mountains, and Turkish officials have guaranteed that no church will be submerged.

Before this happens there's a lot to see and do here. The Çoruh River and its tributaries offer magical white-water experiences for both first-time runners and seasoned enthusiasts. The town's also an excellent base for hikers and culture vultures alike. And the Georgian Valleys are only a short drive away.

Activities
White-Water Rafting

The Çoruh River is one of the world's best rafting rivers, with superb rapids and brilliant play holes around Yusufeli. The river and its tributaries offer a wide range of rafting options for all skill levels, from II to V depending on the stretches and the levels of water. Beginners will tackle more forgiving sections on the nearby İspir River (usually from Tekkale to Yusufeli) or the Barhal River (from Sarıgöl to Yusufeli). Rafting is best in May, June and July; in August the volume of water is usually insufficient.

Various local operators run day trips out of Yusufeli for about TL60 per person (minimum two to three people) for around three hours of rafting; reputable guides include Necmettin Coşkun (☎0505 541 2522; www.coruhriver.com), who's in town in July and speaks good English; Sıralı Aydin (☎0533 453 3179, 0542 405 3658; www.coruhoutdoor.com, www.coruhrafting.com); and Oktay Alkan (☎811 3620; www.birolrafting.com), who's a former kayak champion (Oktay can be found at Greenpeace Camping, which is run by his father).

Trekking

From Yusufeli, guides can lead you on customised treks up into the Kaçkar Mountains (Kaçkar Dağları); one recommended guide is Cumhur Bayrak (☎0537 562 4713; cumhur bayrak@hotmail.com). Guides also organise day walks in the nearby valleys.

Sleeping

Unfortunately, Yusufeli doesn't have a lot of good accommodation, and it's no wonder – the dam project has blighted tourism development.

YUSUFELİ
Greenpeace Camping   GUESTHOUSE €
(☎811 3620; birol_alkan@hotmail.com; camping per person TL10, tree house TL30, s/d TL25/45;

P @) Greenpeace boasts an excellent setting and has various types of accommodation. For budget travellers, the ultrabasic tree houses hiding in the leaves of an orchard can do the trick, or you can pitch your tent in the grassy grounds. The newish rooms in two buildings in the orchard represent good value. There's a pleasant restaurant by the riverside (dinner is about TL15) and, yes, it's licensed. Add another TL10 for breakfast. Rafting and trekking trips can be organised here. Cross the bouncing suspension footbridge beside the Hotel Baraka and follow the signs to find this place about 700m from the bridge.

Otel Barcelona   HOTEL €€
(☑811 2627; www.hotelbarcelona.com.tr; Arikli Mahallesi; s/d €55/75; P ✳ ✥) Under Turkish-Spanish (well, Catalan) management, this upmarket abode provides a restful retreat and flaunts bright, colourful rooms with scrupulously clean bathrooms, a big pool and a bar (with cold Efes, we promise). The owners are very well clued up and can organise various trips in the area. Oh, and staff speak good English. If you can secure a good discount, it is a worthwhile splurge.

Hotel Baraka   HOTEL €
(☑0538 604 1775; Enver Paşa Caddesi; s/d TL25/40) Formerly known as the Barhal Hotel, the Baraka is the most obvious choice for budget-minded travellers. Sure, the stained carpets and cramped bathrooms are nothing to write home about, but it gets by on its handy location, smack dab in the centre and right by the suspension bridge. Some rooms open onto the river, and there's an on-site restaurant. If it's full, there's an annexe across the street. Breakfast is extra.

BETWEEN YUSUFELİ & BARHAL
The following ventures are on the road to Barhal, right by the Barhal River, and easily accessible by minibus from Yusufeli (TL5).

Hotel River   GUESTHOUSE €€
(☑824 4345; Bostancı; s/d with half-board TL65/90; ✳ @) This family-run pension is about 12km from Yusufeli. Rooms are neat and cosy, with pine cladding, TV, well-sprung mattresses, private bathrooms and air-con (hence the rather steep prices). Rooms 106 to 109 get the best views. Meals are served on a breezy terrace; treat yourself to fresh trout while ogling at the gushing river below.

İhtiyaroğlu   GUESTHOUSE €€
(☑824 4086; www.apartagara.com; Sarıgöl Yolu; camping per person TL10, s/d with half-board TL40/80, mains TL5-10) A place of easy bliss, 1.5km further on from Hotel River. The verdant property is soothingly positioned right by the riverside and invites relaxation. The three chalet-like buildings shelter 19 small but impeccable rooms. You can also pitch your tent in a grassy area. Meals get appreciative reviews and can be enjoyed under gazebos overlooking the river.

✗ Eating
Both Hotel Baraka and İhtiyaroğlu have a restaurant that's open to nonguests.

Hacıoğlu Cağ Döner   RESTAURANT €
(İnönü Caddesi; mains TL5-9) Close to the tourist office, with energy-boosting servings of meat (including *cağ* döner at lunchtime) and fish dishes, as well as *sulu yemekler* (ready-made meals). Avoid the latter – too much gravy – and go for the fresh trout, best enjoyed on the terrace overlooking the river.

Köşk Cafe & Restaurant   RESTAURANT €
(İnönü Caddesi; mains TL5-9) Clad in more pine than a Swedish sauna, this jolly good venture above the tourist office is a good place to fill your belly after completing a rafting outing. It serves all the usual suspects, including fish dishes.

Çoruh Pide ve Lahmacun Salonu   PIDECİ €
(Ersis Caddesi; mains TL4-7) You wouldn't guess it from the humble surrounds, but this place does excellent Turkish and Arabic pizzas, served freshly baked from the oven.

ℹ Information
INTERNET ACCESS You'll find a couple of internet cafes on or off the main drag.

MONEY Banks with ATMs are available on the main street.

TOURIST INFORMATION The **tourist office** (İnönü Caddesi; ☺8am-6pm Mon-Sat) is near the otogar, on the main drag. In principle, it's staffed by English-speaking students.

ℹ Getting There & Away
The otogar is in the centre, near the tourist office. From Yusufeli there are at least three buses in the morning for Erzurum (TL20, three hours), a 9am service to Trabzon (TL40) and several minibuses to Artvin (TL15; last departure around 1.30pm). For Kars, you'll have to take a taxi out to the petrol station (TL25) along the Artvin–Erzurum road and catch the bus from there, at

NORTHEASTERN ANATOLIA YUSUFELİ

LOCAL KNOWLEDGE

NECMETTIN COŞKUN: RAFTING EXPERT

A rafting guide based in Yusufeli, Necmettin Coşkun regularly takes travellers on rafting trips on the Çoruh River.

Best Season

The rafting season begins in June. For beginners, it's best to come in July or August, because the level of water is lower and the rapids less challenging.

Why it's Special Here

The Çoruh and its tributaries are long rivers; you can paddle for hours, even several days if you want. And for serious action, the Çoruh is simply world class, with thrilling sections complete with rapids, pools and big rocks – they're not called 'King Kong' and 'High Tension' for nothing. The scenery adds to the appeal, with deep gorges, castles and picturesque villages.

Beginners' Corner

We begin with a practice session and a briefing on a calm section of the river, usually on the Ispir River, before tackling more thrilling sections, though there's no obligation to overdo it. There's always a guide on the boat, who gives the instructions to the team, and a minibus follows along the road and picks us up at the end of the ride.

What if the Dam Project...

I think we still have a few more years before the dam becomes reality. Anyway, once it's completed, we'll find other sections on the Çoruh, the Ispir or the Barhal Rivers. There are alternatives.

---

about 1pm (TL27); any Artvin-bound minibus can also drop you at the petrol station (TL4).

Around Yusufeli

BARHAL (ALTIPARMAK)

☎0466 / POP 1000 / ELEV 1300M

About 27km northwest of Yusufeli, Barhal is a place of easy bliss. Imagine a *köy* (village) nestled in a verdant valley, a rippling stream running through its heart, a lovely mountainscape and a handful of cosy pensions. Another pull is the well-preserved, 10th-century Georgian church that stands beside Karahan Pension. You can also take the walk up to the small ruined chapel in a meadowed ridge above the town – it's worth the 45-minutes pant for the bird's-eye views over the town and the jagged peaks beyond. The (unsigned) walk starts over a plank footbridge near Karahan Pension.

Opportunities for hiking abound. Pension owners arrange two- to four-day treks across the mountains to Ayder with horses (or donkeys) to carry your baggage. One horse, costing TL100, can porter for two trekkers. Add another TL100 per day for a guide (flat fee). Other costs are negotiable.

🛌 Sleeping & Eating

Once you arrive in Barhal you won't want to leave, especially since the handful of pensions here are far more inviting than those in Yusufeli.

Karahan Pension GUESTHOUSE €
(☎0538 351 5023, 826 2071; www.karahanpension.com; half-board per person TL60) Run by Mehmet Karahan and his son Ebubekir, this pension is as cosy as a bird's nest and boasts an adorable setting on a hillside on the outskirts of the village. The main house is full of nooks and crannies, and harbours 20 smallish rooms. Tip: angle for a room with a bathroom and a view over the valley (rooms 107, 108, 114 and 115 are hot favourites). Food here is a definite plus; let the breeze tickle your skin while you eat authentic cuisine alfresco on the covered terrace. And Barhal's Georgian church is almost on your doorstep.

Barhal Pansiyon GUESTHOUSE €
(☎0535 264 6765; half-board per person TL75) The first place you'll pass on the road into town, this pension prides itself on its 15 recent rooms with private facilities (but no views to speak of) in two separate build-

ings; there's a fresh feel in this modernish abode but some rooms get more natural light than others. The copious dinner includes six çeşit (dishes).

Marsis Village House
GUESTHOUSE €

(☑826 2002; www.marsisotel.com; half-board per person TL50) Almost next door to Barhal Pansiyon, just back from the river. It feels like a cosy doll's house, with 16 rooms, an agreeable terrace and amiable staff. Three rooms come with private bathrooms. If you're travelling solo, aim for rooms 106 and 107, which feature river views. The wholesome dinners are warmly praised.

🛈 Getting There & Away

A couple of minibuses make the run from Yusufeli (TL12, two hours), usually around 2pm and 4pm or 5pm. If you have your own vehicle, note that only the first 18km (until Sarıgöl) are surfaced. From Sarıgöl to Barhal (9km), only 6km of road are surfaced. If it's dry, the winding, narrow road can be braved by confident drivers in an ordinary car, but it's wise to seek local advice before setting off.

YAYLALAR (HEVEK)
☑0466 / POP 500

It's a darn tiring ride on a bumpy road to get to Yaylalar, about 22km further from Barhal, but you'll be rewarded with an uberbucolic setting – expect plenty of traditional farmhouses and scenic *yaylalar* (highland pastures) all around.

Yaylalar's only place to stay is **Çamyuva Pension** (☑832 2001; www.kackar3937.com; half-board per person TL50-65), with a variety of sleeping options. You can bunk down either in the plain rooms with shared bathrooms in the first building or, if you seek more privacy, in one of the four adjoining cabins, which are called, with some exaggeration, bungalows (up to four persons). A second building resembling a big Swiss chalet features spotless rooms with bathrooms. Your hosts, İsmail and Naim, also run a well-stocked food shop and a bakery, and can arrange hiking trips. İsmail is the minibus driver to Yusufeli.

Minibuses to Barhal usually travel a further 22km to the end of the line at Yaylalar (TL20 from Yusufeli).

OLGUNLAR
☑0466 / POP 30

This is a sweet, bucolic spot. About 3km further up from Yaylalar, accessed by a scenic white-knuckle road, the quiet hamlet of Olgunlar really feels like the end of the line. Standing in splendid isolation, it

has bags of natural panache, with soaring peaks, soul-stirring vistas, babbling brooks and the purest air you'll ever breathe in Turkey.

Olgunlar is a terrific place to kick off your shoes for a few days, but if you've got itchy feet there's plenty to keep you occupied too, with fabulous hiking options in the area. Olgunlar is the starting point for the Trans-Kaçkar Trek (p520) and the mind-boggling hike to **Mt Kaçkar** (3937m). It takes about two to three days to reach Ayder, through the Çaymakçur Pass (approximately 3100m); the return trip to Mt Kaçkar is usually done in two days.

It's a good idea to hire a local guide who knows the tracks, for walks are mostly unsigned. Cumhur Bayrak (☑0537 562 4713; cumhurbayrak@hotmail.com), based in Yusufeli, has good credentials, is knowledgeable about flora and fauna, and can get by in English. Pension owners in Barhal and Olgunlar also arrange guided treks. They can provide mules, horses, a guide and camping equipment. Without a guide, you can tackle the ascent to Dilber Düzü camp site (the path is well defined); allow seven to eight hours to complete this out-and-back walk.

🛏 Sleeping & Eating

You'll find a couple of decent pensions in Olgunlar, by the stream.

Kaçkar Pansion
PENSION €

(☑824 4011, 0538 306 4564; www.kackar.net; half-board per person TL75) A top choice for walkers, this haven of peace complete with pine cladding features super-clean rooms with private facilities, a kitchen for guests' use, a comfy sitting area and delectable meals. Be sure to bag a room overlooking the stream. Some English is spoken by Ismail, the friendly owner. And yes, there's wi-fi!

Denizgölü Pansion
PENSION €

(☑832 2105; half-board per person TL65) Next door to Kaçkar Pansion, this guesthouse is a bit more basic but pleasant nonetheless.

Olgunlar Cafe
CAFE €

Joy of joys, there's also a family-run tea shop at the end of the hamlet, where the walking trail starts. It also sells basic foodstuffs. You'll also find basic supplies at Kaçkar Pansion, next door to Denizgölü Pansion.

🛈 Getting There & Away

Minibuses to Yaylalar can drop you in Olgunlar, about 3km from Yaylalar, for a few more liras.

TEKKALE & DÖRTKİLİSE

📞0466 / POP 2000

Peaceful Tekkale lies 7km southwest of Yusufeli. It's an ideal jumping-off point for exploring **Dörtkilise** (Four Churches), a ruined 10th-century Georgian church and monastery lying about 6km further upstream on a hillside (there's no sign). The building is domeless, with a gabled roof and very few frescoes. It's similar to, but older and larger than, the one at Barhal. It's a perfect picturesque ruin, with weeds and vines springing from mossy stones.

On the way to Tekkale you'll pass the ruins of a **castle** almost hanging above the road.

The term 'cheap and cheerful' could have been written for **Cemil's Pension** (📞811 2908, 0536 988 5829; cemil_pansion@hotmail. com; Tekkale; half-board per person TL50). This budget stalwart has lots of nooks and crannies as well as a convivial terrace right beside the river and a tank full of trout. Aim for a room in the new building, which won't cost you any more and is much friendlier on the eyes. Note that bathrooms are shared. Evening meals are available by arrangement. Cemil Albayrak, the chirpy owner, can arrange treks into the surrounding countryside, as well as rafting trips. He may also play *saz* (guitar) for his guests in the evening.

ℹ️ Getting There & Away

To get to Tekkale, take a minibus from the south side of the bridge (along Mustafa Kemal Paşa Caddesi) in Yusufeli towards Kılıçkaya or Köprügören; there are about three services per day (TL3). A taxi costs about TL25.

From Tekkale you can hike to Dörtkilise (6km), bearing in mind that there is no sign for the church, which is high up amid the vegetation on the left-hand side of the road. If you have a car, the road is partly surfaced but pretty rough from Tekkale and shouldn't be braved if it's wet. From Yusufeli, a taxi costs about TL50.

Artvin

📞0466 / POP 21,000 / ELEV 600M

Artvin's main claim to fame is its spectacular mountain setting – it's precariously perched on a steep hill above the road linking Hopa (on the Black Sea coast) and Kars. Sadly, in the last few years this has turned into a spectacularly scarred setting, thanks to kilometres of dam and road works. Apart from a couple of ancient houses, the city itself does not have much to captivate you, but it's the best launching pad for exploring the mystifying *yaylalar*. And if you plan a visit in summer, try to make it coincide with the Kafkasör Kültür ve Sanat Festivalı (Caucasus Culture & Arts Festival), held on the last weekend of June and featuring bloodless bull-wrestling matches.

Up the main drag is a roundabout overlooked by the **tourist office** (📞212 3071; artvin@ttmail.com; İnönü Caddesi; ⏱8am-5pm Mon-Fri), where you can pick up a couple of brochures and a useful map of the area.

🛏 Sleeping & Eating

Most hotels are within a block of the *valiliği* (provincial government building). Many hotels double as brothels, but you should do fine if you stick to the tourist-friendly **Karahan Otel** (📞212 1800; www. artvinkarahan.com; İnönü Caddesi; s/d TL60/80; ❄), which is a good deal if you can ignore the grotty entrance on the main drag (the second entrance at the back is much more appealing).

For cheap fare, stroll along İnönü Caddesi and size up the small eateries and pastry shops. **Bakıroğlu Kebap** (İnönü Caddesi; mains TL4-7) has a great reputation for expertly cooked kebaps at a palatable price.

ℹ️ Getting There & Away

The otogar lies further down the valley, about 500m from the town centre, off a hairpin bend. There's one morning bus a day to Kars (TL30, five hours, 270km) and regular buses to Trabzon (TL25, 4½ hours, 255km). For Erzurum there are three daily buses and minibuses (TL25, five hours, 215km). Some buses coming from Erzurum or Ardahan and heading on to Hopa don't go into the otogar but drop you by the roadside at the bottom of the hill.

There are also frequent minibuses to Hopa (TL12, 1½ hours, 70km), about two minibuses to Ardahan (TL25, 2½ hours, 115km) and at least seven minibuses to Yusufeli (TL15, 2¼ hours, 75km). There are also regular services to Ardanuç (TL12, one hour, 30km) and to Şavşat (TL15, 1½ hours, 60km).

Kars

📞0474 / POP 78,500 / ELEV 1768M

With its stately, pastel-coloured stone buildings dating from the Russian occupation and its well-organised grid plan, Kars looks like a slice of Russia teleported to northeastern Anatolia. And the mix of influences – Azeri, Turkmen, Kurdish, Turkish and Russian – adds to the feeling of surprise. No wonder it provided the setting for Orhan Pamuk's prize-winning novel *Kar (Snow)*.

Kars is usually regarded as a base for excursions to Ani, but it would be a shame not to take time exploring its excellent sights and soaking up the eclectic vibe. And don't leave Kars without sampling

A MAGICAL TRIP IN THE BACKCOUNTRY

In summer, the area that extends to the northeast of Artvin is simply stunning. There's a tapestry of bucolic ambience, with lakes, rivers, canyons, mountains, forests, *yaylalar* (high-altitude pastures), traditional wooden houses and villages...with the added appeal of a distinctly Caucasian flavour, courtesy of the proximity of Georgia. Amid this lovely setting stand the ruins of several churches and castles, as well as off-the-beaten-track towns that are definitely worth a look. This territory lends itself perfectly to a DIY approach, preferably with your own wheels as public transport is infrequent. All you need is a map (the *Artvin İli Şehir Planı ve İl Haritası*, which is available at the tourist office in Artvin, but any good touring map of the country should suffice); it's also wise to seek local advice before setting off, as some secondary roads may be in bad shape.

About 17km east of Artvin, on the road to Kars and Ardanuç, a signposted turn-off ('Dolişhane Kilisesi 3km') leads to the beautiful 10th-century **church of Dolişhane**, blessed with a few reliefs. The road to Ardanuç is blissfully scenic. Coming from Artvin, you'll first drive past the **Ferhatlı castle** (look up on your right, it's perched on a rocky outcrop) and, another 8.5km further east, the **Gevernik castle** (signed 'Adakale') before entering **Ardanuç**, set in a dramatic canyon guarded by an impregnable fortress. Feeling adventurous? Head to the harder-to-reach **church of Yeni Rabat**, about 17km past Ardanuç, near the village of Bulanık. Seek local advice at Ardanuç before driving any further, as some sections of the road might be deteriorated.

The 10th-century **Georgian Monastery and Church of Porta** is accessed by a rough road branching off the Artvin–Şavşat road, about 10km before the turn-off to Meydancık. At the time of research, the last 3km couldn't be tackled by car due to rockslides. If you're after the quintessential *yaylalar* settlement, make a beeline for **Meydancık**, near the Georgian border; follow the tarred road that branches off the Artvin–Şavşat road (in good shape at the time of writing).

The old Georgian town of **Şavşat** is worth a peek for its fairy-tale **castle** standing sentinel on the western outskirts of town. From Şavşat, a road leads up to the **Karagöl Sahara National Park**, an area blessed with spectacular mountain scenery and a lovely lake called Meşeli Karagöl, reached after 23km on a tarred road. On the way to the park, you can make a small detour to the **church of Tbeti** (in the village of Ciritdüzü, look for the sign marked 'Tibet' and after about 4km you'll reach the church). This 10th-century church is in ruins but in a beautiful setting. Look for the elaborately carved windows.

Back in Şavşat, a wonderfully scenic road leaves the lush, wooded valleys behind and snakes steeply around numerous twists and turns to the Çam Pass (2540m) before reaching **Ardahan**, a typical steppe town with a citadel and an old bridge.

Sleeping & Eating

Should you fall under the spell of this lovely area, you can bunk down at the **Laşet Tesisleri** (☑0535 734 6711; Şavşat Ardahan Karayolu; s/d TL50/100, mains TL5-10), an adorable little hotel on the Şavşat–Ardahan road, about 8km east of Şavşat. There's an excellent on-site restaurant. Ask for Koray, who speaks good English.

Other commendable options include the **Saray Motel & Restaurant** (☑0466-517 2947; Köprüyaka Köyü, Şavşat; r TL70, meals TL5-9), about 4km west of Şavşat, on the main road, and **Karagöl Pansiyon** (☑0536 259 5783; Meşeli Karagöl; r TL80-100, mains TL5-10), just by the shore of the Meşeli Lake; be sure to bag a room with a lake view. The restaurant turns out toothsome fish dishes.

Kars

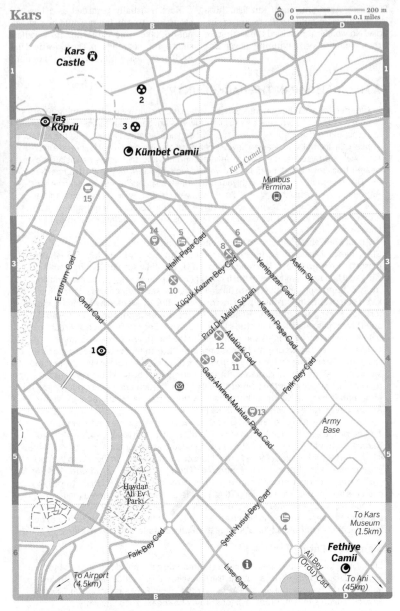

Kars Castle

2

Taş Köprü

3

Kümbet Camii

Kars Canal

Minibus Terminal

15

14   5

8   6

Halit Paşa Cad

Yenipazar Cad

Aşkin Sk

7

10

Küçük Kazım Bey Cad

Erzurum Cad

Ordu Cad

Prof Dr Metin Sözen

Kazım Paşa Cad

12   Atatürk Cad

1

9   11

Gazi Ahmet Muhtar Paşa Cad

Faik Bey Cad

13

Army Base

Haydar Ali Ev Parkı

Faik Bey Cad

Şehit Yusuf Bey Cad

4

To Kars Museum (1.5km)

Fethiye Camii

Lise Cad

Ali Bey (Ordu) Cad

To Airport (4.5km)

To Ani (45km)

0   200 m
0   0.1 miles

the delicious local *bal* (honey) and *peynir* (cheese).

The border with nearby Armenia was still closed at the time of writing, but when it's reopened it should foster a thriving business between Kars and Erevan – not to mention an exhilarating overland route to the Caucasus.

History

Dominated by a stark medieval fortress, Kars was once an Armenian stronghold,

Kars

capital of the Armenian Bagratid kingdom (before Ani) and later a pawn in the imperial land-grabbing tussle played out by Turkey and Russia during the 19th century. The Russians captured Kars in 1878, installed a garrison and held it until 1920 and the Turkish War of Independence, when the republican forces retook it. Many of the sturdier stone buildings along the main streets date back to the Russian occupation.

The locals are said to be descended from the Karsaks, a Turkic tribe that came from the Caucasus in the 2nd century BC and gave their name to the town.

◎ Sights

FREE **Kars Castle** FORTRESS
(Kars Kalesi; ⊙8am-5pm) North of the river in the older part of the city, this is worth the knee-jarring climb, if only for the smashing views over the town and the steppe in fine weather. Records show that Saltuk Turks built a fortress here in 1153. It was torn down by the Mongol conqueror Tamerlane in 1386 and rebuilt several times in the following centuries. The castle was the scene of bitter fighting during and after

WWI. When the Russian armies withdrew in 1920, control of Kars was left in the hands of the Armenian forces, until the republican armies took the *kalesi*.

Kümbet Camii MOSQUE
On the way to the castle, along the riverbanks huddle assorted crumbling reminders of Kars' ancient past, including this former church. Built between 932 and 937 for the Bagratid King Abas, it was turned into a mosque in 1579 when the Ottomans rebuilt much of the city; the Russians added the porches in the 19th century. The 12 relief carvings on the drum are of the apostles.

Near the mosque you'll see the ruins of the **Ulu Cami** and the **Beylerbeyi Sarayı** (Beylerbeyi Palace) nestling beneath the castle.

Taş Köprü BRIDGE
One of the more attractive – and intact – structures in the older part of the city is this 15th-century stone bridge, ruined by an earthquake and rebuilt in 1725.

Kars Museum MUSEUM
(Kars Müzesi; Cumhuriyet Caddesi; admission TL3; ⊙8am-5pm Tue-Sun) On the eastern fringes of the town, the Kars Museum has exhibits from the Old Bronze Age, the Urartian, Roman and Greek periods, and the Seljuk and Ottoman eras. Photographs show excavations at Ani and the ruins of some of the Armenian churches in Kars province.

Russian Monuments HISTORIC BUILDINGS
As you walk around the town, you will see a gobsmacking collection of Russian belle époque mansions and other buildings sprinkled around the city centre. Many of them have been restored and turned into administrative offices. The best place to start exploring is the **Fethiye Camii**, a converted 19th-century Russian Orthodox church, which stands majestically south of the centre.

🛏 Sleeping

Güngören Hotel HOTEL €
(☑212 6767; fax 212 5630; Millet Sokak; s/d TL40/70) As far as physical beauty goes, this is a real plain Jane, but it's a secure spot to hang your rucksack, the rates are good, breakfast is copious and it's set in a quiet street, a kebap's throw from Barış Cafe Pub. Rooms are spacious, bathrooms are well scrubbed and it's a safe bet for female travellers too. One grumble: there's no lift.

GETTING INTO GEORGIA

Getting into Georgia from northeastern Anatolia is pretty straightforward. From Kars, you can take a minibus to Posof (TL25), then ask the driver to continue to the border at Türkgözü, a further 16km ride (TL25). Cross the border (no hassles), then take a taxi to Akhaltsikhe, the nearest substantial town. From here, there are buses to Borjomi, where you can find accommodation. A more direct option would be to take a minibus to Ardahan (TL12 from Kars), where you can hop on the daily bus proceeding from İstanbul and heading to Tbilisi, which leaves from Ardahan at around 9.30am (TL50). It stops in front of the office of the **Özlem Ardahan** (☎0478-211 3568; Kongre Caddesi) bus company, in the centre, and also uses the Türkgözü border crossing. From Ardahan to Türkgözü, it takes about 2½ hours; from the border, it shouldn't take more than six hours to Tbilisi. If you're stuck in Ardahan, the **Büyük Ardahan Oteli** (☎0478-211 6498; Kars Caddesi; r TL50), on the outskirts of town (in the direction of Kars), is OK for a night's kip.

Grand Ani Hotel   HOTEL €€€
(☎223 7500; Ordu Caddesi; www.grandani.com; s/d/ste €70/90/120; [P] [❄] [≋]) No-one could accuse the newly opened Grand Ani of a lack of ambition – the list of facilities is prolific, with a pool, a sauna, a hamam, a fitness centre and a top-notch restaurant. It pulls in foreign groups and Turkish businessmen interested in comfortable rooms with shiny-clean bathrooms, flat-screen TVs, huge beds and professional service.

Kar's Otel   BOUTIQUE HOTEL €€€
(☎212 1616; www.karsotel.com; Halit Paşa Caddesi; s/d TL200/280; [❄]) With just eight rooms, this boutique hotel – a rarity in northeastern Anatolia – housed in an old Russian mansion feels like a luxurious cocoon. The rooms are suitably comfortable, though some might find the white colour scheme a bit too clinical and the furniture slightly dated. There's an on-site restaurant.

Hotel Temel   HOTEL €
(☎223 1376; fax 223 1323; Yenipazar Caddesi; s/d TL35/60) The Güngören's main competitor offers neat rooms with immaculate sheets and a soothing blue and yellow colour scheme, but it feels less congenial and breakfast isn't as satisfying. Unlike the Güngören, there's a lift. There's an annex across the street, the Temel 2, with cheaper but more basic rooms.

✖ Eating

Kars is noted for its excellent honey. It's on sale in several shops along Kazım Paşa Caddesi, which also sell the local *kaşar peyniri* (a mild yellow cheese), *kuruyemiş* (dried fruits) and other sweet treats – the perfect ingredients for a picnic in the steppe.

If you want to splurge, make a beeline for Kar's Otel and Grand Ani Hotel; both harbour excellent restaurants, with menus translated in English. With its contemporary furnishings and mood lighting, Kar's Otel is ideal for romantic meals, and its original menu brings a much needed diversity to a kebap-jaded palate. Grand Ani Hotel specialises in Turkish classics prepared to perfection; the *kuzu sarma* (stuffed lamb) melts in the mouth. Both are licensed.

TOP CHOICE Ocakbaşı Restoran   RESTAURANT €€
(Atatürk Caddesi; mains TL6-12) Resisting the passage of time, this well-established restaurant remains at the pinnacle of Kars' eating scene. The *ali nazık* (aubergine purée with yoghurt and meat) or the Anteplim pide (sesame bread stuffed with meat, cheese, parsley, nuts and eggs), its two signature dishes, should win awards. The pictorial menu, with fairly accurate English translations, is of great help. It has two adjoining rooms, including a mock troglodytic one (wow!), but it's not licensed (boo!).

Ani Ocakbaşı   RESTAURANT €€
(Kazım Paşa Caddesi; mains TL7-11) This busy restaurant is held in high esteem by locals, offering a wide menu from salads and soups to kebaps and stews. Save room for the exquisite *sütlaç* (rice pudding). Clean, friendly and always open, it's also a good place for an early breakfast (TL14). The walls are embellished with photos of old Kars.

Döneristan Et Lokantası   LOKANTA €
(Atatürk Caddesi; mains TL6-10) There's a lot to like about this bright venue. Munch on

ultra-fresh *sulu yemekler*, salads, mezes and döner kebaps at puny prices. The menu changes daily according to seasonal produce and whim.

Doğuş Pastanaleri   PATISSERIE €
(Gazi Ahmet Muhtar Paşa Caddesi; mains TL2-10) Cakes, puddings and a delightfully delicious assortment of ice creams and other goodies are on offer at this Kars standby. Don't have a sweet tooth? Come anyway, as it also features the usual suspects.

Semazen   LOKANTA €
(Atatürk Caddesi; mains TL6-10) This buzzy joint cranks out above-average kebaps and pide, as well as tasty ready-made meals. The B&W pictures of old Kars hung on the walls are a nice touch, too.

🍷 Drinking

Barış Cafe Pub   PUB
(Atatürk Caddesi; ☉8am-late) Housed in a historic mansion, this atmosphere-laden cafe-bar-disco has a happening buzz and is a magnet for students of both sexes who come here to gossip, puff a nargileh and listen to live bands (three times a week). If hunger beckons, snacks are available. The disco in the basement is something to behold – headscarved women tear it up on the dance floor!

Antik Cafe & Pastane   CAFE
(Gazi Ahmet Muhtar Paşa Caddesi; pastries & mains from TL4; ☉8am-late) Brimming with good cheer, this trendy, relaxed cafe is a good place to recharge the batteries after a walking tour in the centre. Chow down on snacks and cakes, or linger over a cuppa.

İstihkam Çay Bahçesi   TEA GARDEN
(Atatürk Caddesi; ☉8am-9pm) This leafy spot by the canal is the perfect salve after trudging up to the castle. Sip a glass of tea in the shade.

ℹ Information

CONSULATE The **Azerbaijani consulate** (☎223 6475, 223 1361; Ordu Caddesi; ☉9.30am-12.30pm Mon-Fri) is northwest of the centre. Convenient if you plan to go to Nakhichevan (p557).

INTERNET ACCESS There's no shortage of internet cafes in the centre.

MONEY Banks with ATMs are plentiful in Kars.

TOURIST INFORMATION Limited tourist information is available at the **tourist office** (☎212 6817; Lise Caddesi; ☉8am-noon & 1-5pm Mon-Fri), west of the centre. To organise transport to Ani (and other sites in the area), a good bet is to contact **Celil Ersoğlu** (☎0532 226 3966; celil-ani@hotmail.com), who acts as a private driver (guiding is extra) and speaks good English. He'll probably meet you at your hotel's reception.

ℹ Getting There & Around

Air
A *servis* (shuttle bus; TL4) runs from the agencies to the airport, 6km from town. **Turkish Airlines – Sun Express** (☎212 3438; Faik Bey Caddesi; ☉8am-8pm) sells tickets on behalf of the two airlines. Turkish Airlines has one or two daily flights to/from Ankara (from TL70, 1¾ hours) and to/from İstanbul (from TL158, two hours). Sun Express has two weekly flights to İzmir (from TL110).

Bus
Kars' otogar, for long-distance services, is 2km southeast of the centre, although *servises* ferry people to/from the town centre. The major local bus companies, **Doğu Kars** (Faik Bey Caddesi), **Serhat Kars** (Faik Bey Caddesi) and **Kafkas Kars** (Faik Bey Caddesi), have a ticket office in

SERVICES FROM KARS' OTOGAR

DESTINATION	FARE (TL)	DURATION (HR)	DISTANCE (KM)	FREQUENCY (PER DAY)
Ankara	50	16	1100	a few
Ardahan	12	1½	80	frequent minibuses
Artvin	30	6	270	1 in the morning
Erzurum	15	3	205	frequent minibuses
Iğdır	15	3	132	several
Posof	25	2	142	1 in the morning and afternoon
Trabzon	35	9-10	525	2 direct, or change at Erzurum or Artvin
Van	35	6	370	1 in the morning

the centre. **Turgutreis** (cnr Faik Bey & Atatürk Caddesis), a few doors away from Doğu Kars, has a daily bus to Van.

Minibuses to local towns (including Iğdır, Erzurum, Sarıkamış, Ardahan and Posof) leave from the **minibus terminal** (Küçük Kazım Bey Caddesi). If you're heading for Doğubayazıt, be warned that there are no direct services. The usual way to get there is to take a minibus to Iğdır, then another to Doğubayazıt.

For Georgia, take a minibus to Posof or take the first minibus to Ardahan at 8am to hop on the bus to Tbilisi at around 10am. For Yusufeli, take a bus to Artvin and ask to be dropped at the nearest junction (about 10km to Yusufeli) along the Artvin–Erzurum road, from where you'll have to hitch a ride to Yusufeli. For information on hitching in Turkey, see p694. For details of transport to Ani, see p555.

Car

Steer clear of the car-selling companies in the centre – they claim they can rent cars but we're told that they don't provide proper insurance.

Train

The *Doğu Ekspresi* leaves for İstanbul (TL45), via Erzurum, Kayseri and Ankara, at 7.10am daily. The *Erzurum Ekspresi* (TL40) leaves for Ankara, via Erzurum and Kayseri, at 9am daily. It's worth considering these trains for the relatively short hop to Erzurum (TL12, about four hours).

Ani

The ruins of Ani, 45km east of Kars, are an absolute must-see, even if you're not an architecture buff. Your first view of Ani is stunning: wrecks of great stone buildings adrift on a sea of undulating grass, landmarks in a ghost city that was once the stately Armenian capital and home to nearly 100,000 people, rivalling Constantinople in power and glory. The poignant ruins, the windswept plateau overlooking the Turkish–Armenian border and the total lack of crowds make for an eerie ambience that is unforgettable. Come here to ponder what

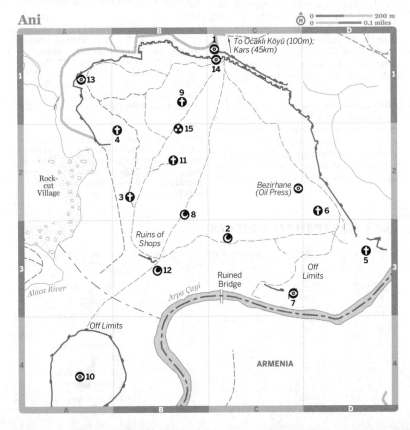

Ani

went before: the thriving kingdom; the solemn ceremony of the Armenian liturgy; and the travellers, merchants and nobles bustling about their business in this Silk Road entrepôt.

Given the proximity of the border, the area is still under military control, but it's hassle-free and no permit is required.

History

On an important east–west trade route and well served by its natural defences, Ani was selected by the Bagratid king Ashot III (r 952–77) as the site of his new capital in 961, when he moved here from Kars. His successors Smbat II (r 977–89) and Gagik I (r 990–1020) presided over Ani's continued prosperity, but after Gagik, internecine feuds and Byzantine encroachment weakened the Armenian state.

The Byzantines took over the city in 1045, then in 1064 came the Great Seljuks from Persia, then the Kingdom of Georgia and, for a time, local Kurdish emirs. The struggle for the city went on until the Mongols arrived in 1239 and cleared everybody else out. The nomadic Mongols had no use for city life, so they cared little when the great earthquake of 1319 toppled much of Ani. The depredations of Tamerlane soon afterwards were the last blow: trade routes shifted, Ani lost what revenues it had managed to retain, and the city died. The earthquake-damaged hulks of its great buildings have been slowly crumbling away ever since.

◉ Sights

The only entrance to the **ruins** (admission TL5; ⊙8.30am-5pm) is through the gate called Arslan Kapısı. Follow the path to the left and tour the churches in clockwise order. Not all the site is open to visitors; some parts are still off limits. Allow at least 2½ hours at the site. Bring food and water as there are no facilities.

Arslan Kapısı   GATE
The sturdy Arslan Kapısı (also called Aslan Kapısı) gate was supposedly named after Alp Arslan, the Seljuk sultan who conquered Ani in 1064, but probably also suggested by the *aslan* (lion) in relief on the inner wall.

Church of the Redeemer   CHURCH
Just past the remains of an **oil press**, the Church of the Redeemer (Church of St Prkitch) soon comes into view. It's a startling vision – only half of the ruined structure remains, the other half having been destroyed by lightning in 1957. This church dates from 1034–36 and was supposedly built to house a portion of the True Cross brought here from Constantinople; Armenian inscriptions on the facade relay the history. The facade also sports a superb *khatchkar* (cross stone) designed on an elaborate rectangular background, about 3m above ground. The architecture is typical of the circular-planned, multi-apsed Armenian churches built in this era.

Church of St Gregory (Tigran Honentz)   CHURCH
Beyond the Church of the Redeemer, down by the walls separating Ani from the gorge of the Arpa Çayı and easy to miss, is the Church of St Gregory the Illuminator (in Turkish, Resimli Kilise – Church with Pictures). Named after the apostle to the Armenians, it was built by a pious nobleman named Tigran Honentz in 1215, and although exposure and vandalism have done great damage to the interior, it is still in better condition than most other buildings here. Look for the long Armenian inscription carved on the exterior walls, as well as the colourful and lively frescoes depicting scenes from the Bible and Armenian church history. It also features well-preserved relief work, as well as a small sundial.

CULTURAL FESTIVALS

If you happen to visit northeastern Anatolia in summer, try to make your trip coincide with the **Kafkasör Kültür ve Sanat Festivalı** (Caucasus Culture & Arts Festival), which takes place over the last weekend of June in the Kafkasör Yaylası, a pasture 7km southwest of Artvin, with *boğa güreşleri* (bloodless bull-wrestling matches) as the main attraction. In Doğubayazıt, don't miss the **Kültür ve Turizm Festival** (Culture and Arts Festival), which is held in June or July; call a local travel agency for exact dates. This is a great occasion to immerse yourself in Kurdish culture, with singing, dancing and theatre.

Convent of the Virgins (Kusanatz)
CHURCH

Dramatically perched on the edge of the Arpa Çayı gorge, the Convent of the Virgins is off limits but is clearly visible from the Menüçer Camii. Its distinctive, serrated-domed chapel is enclosed by a defensive wall. Scant ruins of a **bridge** (under restoration) across the river lie to the west in an area that is also off limits.

Cathedral
CHURCH

Up on the plateau again, the cathedral, renamed the Fethiye Camii (Victory Mosque) by the Seljuk conquerors, is the largest and most impressive of the buildings. Ani cathedral was begun by King Smbat II in 987 and finished under Gagik I in 1010.

Ani was once the seat of the Armenian Orthodox Patriarchate; the three doorways served as separate entrances for the patriarch, the king and the people. As the grandest religious edifice in the city, it was transformed into a mosque whenever Muslims held Ani, but reverted to a church when the Christians took it back again. Unfortunately, the spacious dome, once supported by four massive columns, fell down centuries ago.

Seen from a distance, the building looks quite featureless, but a closer inspection reveals eye-catching decorative elements, including several porthole windows, slender windows surrounded by elegant fretwork, several triangular niches, inscriptions in Armenian near the main entrance and a blind arcade with slim columns running around the structure.

Walking towards the Menüçer Camii to the west, you'll go past an excavated area, supposed to be a former street lined with shops. Further north, the ruins of a toppled minaret, which is supposed to have belonged to the **Ebul Muhammeran Camii**, have been exposed.

Menüçer Camii
MOSQUE

The rectangular building with the tall octagonal, truncated minaret, the Menüçer Camii is said to have been the first mosque built by the Seljuk Turks in Anatolia (1072). Six vaults remain, each of them different, as was the Seljuk style. This odd but interesting blend of Armenian and Seljuk design probably resulted from the Seljuks employing Armenian architects, engineers and stonemasons. The alternating red-and-black stonework is a distinctive feature. Look also for the polychrome stone inlays that adorn the ceilings. The structure next to the mosque may have been a Seljuk *medrese* or palace.

The minaret sports an inscription in Arabic, which is *bismillah* ('in the name of Allah'). Climbing up the minaret is forbidden – the spiral staircase is steep and narrow, and there's no parapet at the top.

Nearby is a recently excavated area, which contains remains of houses, with ovens, a granary and bathrooms.

İç Kale
FORTRESS

Across the rolling grass, southwest of the mosque, rises the monumental İç Kale (the Keep), which holds within its extensive ruins half a ruined church. Beyond İç Kale on a pinnacle of rock in a bend of the Arpa Çayı is the small church called the **Kız Kalesi** (Maiden's Castle). You'll have to look from a distance – both these sites are out of bounds.

Church of St Gregory (Abughamrentz)
CHURCH

On the western side of the city, this rotunda-shaped church topped by a conical roof dates from the late 900s. It was built for the wealthy Pahlavuni family by the same architect of the Church of the Redeemer. On the 12-sided exterior you'll see a series of deep niches topped by scallop-shell carvings. Then look up to see the windows of the drum, framed by a double set of blind arcades.

From the church you can savour the view of a rock-cut village beyond the river escarpment, on the Armenian side.

Kervansaray (Church of the Holy Apostles)
CHURCH

The Church of the Holy Apostles (Arak Elots Kilisesi) dates from 1031, but after their conquest of the city in 1064 the Seljuks added a gateway with a fine dome and used the building as a caravanserai, hence its name.

It's fairly well preserved and features decorative carvings, porthole windows, diagonally intersecting arches in the nave, and ceilings sporting geometric patterns made of polychromatic stone inlays; also worthy of note are the various Armenian inscriptions and a *khatchkar* carved on a rectangular background.

Church of St Gregory (Gagik I)
CHURCH

Northwest from the Kervansaray, the gigantic Church of St Gregory was begun in 998 to plans by the same architect as Ani's cathedral. Its ambitious dome collapsed shortly after being finished, and the rest of the building is now also badly ruined. You can still see the outer walls and a jumble of columns.

Zoroastrian Temple (Fire Temple)
TEMPLE

North of the Church of the Holy Apostles are the remains of a Zoroastrian temple, thought to have been built between the early 1st century and the first half of the 4th century AD. It might have been converted into a Christian chapel afterwards. The only remains consist of four circular columns, not exceeding 1.5m in height – it's not easy to spot them in the undulating steppe. They lie between the Church of the Holy Apostles and the Georgian Church – proceed about 100m due north from the Church of the Holy Apostles and you should come across the temple.

Georgian Church (Ürcü Kilisesi)
CHURCH

You can't miss the only surviving wall of the Georgian Church, north of the Zoroastrian temple, which was probably erected in the 11th century. It used to be a large building, but most of the south wall collapsed around 1840. Of the three arcades left, two sport bas-reliefs, one representing the Annunciation, the other the Visitation.

Seljuk Palace
PALACE

To the northwest of the Church of St Gregory (Gagik I) is a Seljuk palace built into the city's defensive walls and painstakingly over-restored so that it looks quite out of place.

❶ Getting There & Away

Transport to Ani has always been a problem. Most people opt for the taxi minibuses to the site organised by Kars' tourist office or **Celil Ersoğlu** (☑0532 226 3966; celilani@hotmail.com), for about TL35 per person, provided there's a minimum of six persons. If there are no other tourists around, you'll have to pay the full fare of TL140 return plus waiting time; the drive takes around 50 minutes. You can also hire a taxi (from TL90). Make sure that your driver understands that you want a minimum of 2½ hours and preferably three hours at the site.

North of Kars

Very few tourists even suspect **Çıldır Gölü's** existence. Far less talismanic than Lake Van, this loch-like expanse of water about 60km north of Kars is worth the detour nonetheless, if only for the complete peace and quiet. It's also an important breeding ground for various species of birds, best observed at Akçekale Island. **Doğruyol**, the only significant town on the eastern shore, has an eye-catching hilltop church.

From the town of Çıldır, on the northern shore, continue 3.5km until you reach the village of Yıldırımtepe. From there, a path snakes into a gorge and leads up to **Şeytan Kalesi** (Devil's Castle). Standing sentinel on a rocky bluff over a bend of the river, it boasts a sensational setting.

You'll need your own transport to reach these places.

South of Kars

The Kurdish village of **Çengilli** is home to a superb 13th-century Georgian monastery, which jabs the skyline. It's similar in many respects to the Armenian churches near Ani, but the views over the Aras mountains are unforgettable. Çengilli is about 20km off the D965-04 (the road that connects Kars with Kağızman). The road that leads up from the D965-04 to Çengilli is not tarred, and some sections are very steep.

Further north (towards Kars), at Ortaköy village, a secondary road leads to the

DON'T MISS

ARMENIAN CHURCHES AROUND ANİ

So you loved Ani and want more? No problem, there are other impressive Armenian churches and castles in the vicinity. These sites usually boast awesome settings, in the middle of the steppe. It's also a great way to see a slice of rural Anatolia.

To get to these (unsigned) sites, the most convenient and hassle-free way is to contact Celil Ersoğlu (☑0532 226 3966; celilani@hotmail.com), who'll drive you around, with a chance to take tea with villagers. Expect to pay around TL150. There are no tourist facilities, so stock up on food and water.

About 40km from Kars, the monumental 10th-century Oğuzlu church rises up from the steppe and dominates the surrounding houses. It's in a bad state of preservation. An earthquake in 1936 caused the dome and other structures to collapse.

In Yağkesen, a further 6km from Oğuzlu, you'll be overwhelmed by the eerie sight of the Kızıl Kilise (Karmir Vank) church standing on a small mound. It's the sole towering element in an otherwise flat, treeless grassland. If you're lucky, you'll see Mt Ararat in the distance. Outstanding features include a conical roof, V-shaped niches on the exterior and slender windows, an inscription in Armenian above the portal and some handsome carvings.

Closer to Ani, at the Kurdish village of Kozluca, you can admire two Armenian monuments, which are known as Bagnair Monastery. The larger church, thought to have been constructed in the 11th century, is badly damaged, whereas the minor one, 200m across a small ravine, is still in good shape, with a nice 12-sided dome-drum adorned with blind arcades. Both are used as cattle pens.

Magazagh Fortress lies near the village of Üçölük. Unfortunately, this pearl of an Armeno-Byzantine fortress standing atop a rock spur and overlooking a bend in the Arpa Çayı River, right on the border with Armenia, was off limits to foreigners at the time of writing.

village of Keçivan, which boasts superb ruins of a castle, precariously perched on a ridge – another dazzling sight.

Still not enough for you? Make a bee-line for Beşkilise (Five Churches), which must rank as one of Turkey's most dramatically situated religious buildings. This Armenian church is about 35km south of Kars, off the road to Digor and Iğdır, in the Digor River gorge. Access is hard to find; coming from Kars, it's about 4km before Digor and 600m before a dirt track leading to a white-pumice quarry, on the right. From the main road, you'll have to walk across pastures to find the entrance of the gorge, then follow the valley upstream staying on a vague path on the hillside, midway between the valley floor and cliff top above. After about 30 minutes, the church appears like a mirage, perched on a ledge overlooking the valley floor. There were initially five churches (hence the name) here. The one you see, dating from the 11th century, is the only survivor. Despite some names scratched into the walls, it's still in good shape, with

an intact dome and elaborate Armenian inscriptions.

These sights are difficult to reach without your own transport. Your best bet is to hire a taxi and a cooperative driver for a day in Kars. Celil Ersoğlu (☑0532 226 3966; cel ilani@hotmail.com) in Kars can also drive you to these sights.

Sarıkamış

The town and ski resort of Sarıkamış, 55km southwest of Kars, has deep, dry powder combined with terrain that pleases both skiers and snowboarders. There's also interesting cross-country options. The vibe is more down-to-earth and family-oriented than at Palandöken (p539) and the area much less windy. The slopes are also more scenic, with vast expanses of Scotch pines. The ski season generally lasts from December to April, but Sarıkamış can also be enjoyed in summer, with a good network of hiking trails.

The infrastructure is surprisingly state-of-the-art, with two computerised *telesiej* (chair lifts) and nine ski runs (three beginner runs, three intermediate and three advanced), at an altitude ranging from 2200m to 2634m. Rental equipment is available at the hotels (about TL30 per day).

The ski resort proper is 3km away from the town centre. The welcoming Çamkar Hotel (✆0474-413 5259; www.camkar.com; s/d with full board winter TL200/270, summer TL70/130; @🖳) and the massive Toprak Hotel (✆0474-413 4111; www.sarikamisto prakhotels.com; s/d with full board winter from TL300/400, summer TL160/200; @🖳) are just at the foot of the ski runs and offer excellent amenities, including a kids' club, sauna, bar, disco, shops and licensed restaurants. Prices include ski passes.

Regular minibuses ply the route between Kars and Sarıkamış (TL7, 45 minutes). From Sarıkamış, take a taxi to the resort (TL10).

Kars to Doğubayazıt

To reach Doğubayazıt and Mt Ararat, head south from Kars via Digor, Tuzluca and Iğdır, a distance of 240km. From Tuzluca the road follows the Armenian frontier.

You can break your journey in Iğdır, which has a good choice of accommodation, though most establishments double as brothels. Try the Hotel Dedemin (✆0476-227 3920; Bağlar Mahallesi Gençler Sokak; s/d TL40/60), not far from the belediye (local council). On the same street, you can also check out the Yıldırım Otel, which was under construction at the time of research.

Minibuses for Kars (TL15, three hours, about seven daily services; last departure around 5pm) leave from the main thoroughfare; look for the 'Serhat Iğdır Turizm' shop, about 300m before the Grand Otel Derya (coming from Kars).

If you come from Kars and want to go to Doğubayazıt (TL5, 45 minutes, every hour), the minibus 'terminal' is tucked one block away from the main thoroughfare, near a mosque; from the Kars minibus stop, cross the main drag and ask for directions (it's a five-minute walk or so).

Doğubayazıt

📞0472 / POP 36,000 / ELEV 1950M

The setting is superb. On one side, the talismanic Mt Ararat (Ağrı Dağı, 5137m), Turkey's highest mountain, hovers majestically over the horizon. On the other side, İshak Paşa Palace, a breathtakingly beautiful fortress-palace-mosque complex deploys itself 6km southeast of town. The town itself doesn't have much to detain you, but it's an obvious base to climb Mt Ararat and explore the area. Doğubayazıt is also the main kicking-off point for the overland trail through Iran (the border is a mere 35km away).

Coming from Kars, you'll quickly realise that the atmosphere is noticeably different here. A predominantly Kurdish town, Doğubayazıt it prides itself on its strong Kurdish heritage, which it celebrates each year during the Kültür ve Turizm Festival.

⊙ Sights

İshak Paşa Palace   PALACE
(İshak Paşa Sarayı; admission TL3; ⊙9am-5.30pm Apr-Oct, 9am-5pm Nov-Mar) Located 6km uphill southeast of town, this is the epitome of the Thousand and One Nights castle. Part of its magic derives from its setting – it's perched on a small plateau abutting stark cliffs and overlooking a plain, framed by Mt Ararat.

The palace was begun in 1685 by Çolak Abdi Paşa and completed in 1784 by his son, a Kurdish chieftain named İshak (Isaac). The architecture is a superb amalgam of Seljuk, Ottoman, Georgian, Persian and Armenian styles.

The palace's elaborate main entrance leads into the first courtyard, which would have been opened to merchants and guests.

Only family and special guests would have been allowed into the second courtyard. Here you can see the entrance to the haremlik,

---

GETTING INTO NAKHICHEVAN & AZERBAIJAN

From Iğdır, the bus company Iğdır Turizm has direct services east to the Azerbaijani enclave of Nakhichevan (TL10, 3½ hours, at least eight daily buses; last departure around 5.30pm). The bus company has an office opposite the belediye, right in the centre. Note that you need a visa (there's an Azerbaijani consulate in Kars). This enclave is cut off from the rest of Azerbaijan by Armenia, and you'll have to take one of the few daily flights to get to Baku. For visa information, see p687.

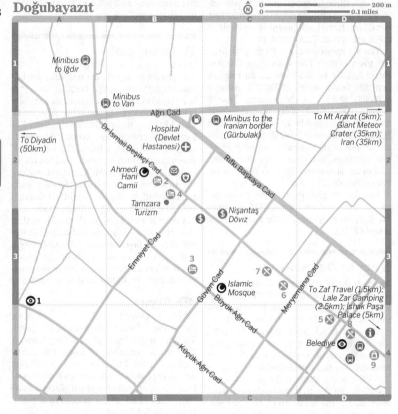

selamlık, guards' lodgings and granaries to the south, and the tomb in the northwest corner. The tomb is richly decorated with a mix of Seljuk carvings and Persian relief styles. Steps lead down to the sarcophagi.

From the second court you can pass through the marvellously decorated portal of the haremlik into the living quarters of the palace. The harem's highlight is undoubtedly the beautiful dining room, a melange of styles with walls topped by Seljuk triangular stonework, Armenian floral-relief decoration and ornate column capitals betraying Georgian influence. It also contains a kitchen and a colonnaded dining hall.

You'll have to return to the second courtyard to enter the selamlık from the northern side. Entry is via the stately hall where guests would have been greeted before being entertained in the ceremonial hall-courtyard to the right. The selamlık also has a library and a lovely mosque, which

has kept much of its original relief decoration (note the life tree) and ceiling frescoes.

Across the valley from the palace are the ruined foundations of **Eski Beyazıt** (Old Beyazıt), which was probably founded in Urartian times c 800 BC. Modern Doğubayazıt is a relative newcomer, the villagers having moved from the hills to the plain only in 1937. You can also spot a well-worn mosque, a tomb and the ruins of a fortress, which may date from Urartian times (13th to 7th centuries BC).

Minibuses (TL2) rattle between the otogar and the palace, but there's no fixed schedule – they leave when they are full; otherwise a taxi driver will want about TL20 for a return trip, waiting time included.

🛏 Sleeping

There's no shortage of hotels in the centre but good, reliable accommodation options were hard to find at the time of writing.

Doğubayazıt

Hotel Tahran HOTEL €

(☏312 0195; www.hoteltahran.com; Büyük Ağrı Caddesi 124; s/d TL25/40; @) The perfect soft landing into Doğubayazıt, the well-managed Tahran exudes mellow vibes. Although on the small side, the rooms come equipped with crisp sheets and the views of Mt Ararat might provide some diversion. Same verdict for the private bathrooms: tiny but salubrious, with hygienic red floor tiles. Precious perks include a rooftop terrace, with an internet terminal (free access), a kitchen for guests' use, and laundry service. Going to Iran? Bilal, the affable manager, is well clued up on the subject. A safe bet for solo women travellers, too.

Hotel Grand Derya HOTEL €€

(☏312 7531; fax 312 7833; Dr İsmail Beşikçi Caddesi; s TL60-70, d TL100-120; ❄) An ideal retreat after a few days' clambering in knee breeches and hiking boots. This well-run venue offers comfortable rooms with all mod cons. The dearer rooms boast smashing Ararat views – well worth the price hike. Bring earplugs or the call to prayer at 5am emanating from the nearby mosque will be etched forever on your mind.

Hotel Urartu HOTEL €

(☏312 7295; fax 312 2450; Dr İsmail Beşikçi Caddesi; s/d TL30/60) Reliable and central, the Urartu is not a bad place to start your Ararat adventure but it has one problem: it's fully booked by öğretmen (teachers) and other civil servants during the school year.

From mid-June to September, though, it welcomes travellers. No breakfast is served.

Lale Zar Camping CAMPGROUND €

(☏0544 269 1960; lalezarcamping@hotmail.com; İshakpaşa Yolu Üzeri; camp site per person incl tent TL10) Over the years this campground, run by two friends, Bertil and Mecit (one Dutch, one Kurd), has morphed into a picnic site popular with local families, but it remains an option if you don't mind music until midnight at weekends (weddings). It's set in a well-tended property dotted with a few grassy areas, on the outskirts of town, on the road to the İshak Paşa Palace. There's an on-site food store and restaurant.

There are also two camping grounds-cum-pensions, Paraşüt and Murat Camping, in the vicinity of İshak Paşa Palace. You'll feel a bit lonely here, but the views are superb. Both are OK for unfussy (male) backpackers; women travellers should stick to the Hotel Tahran or Hotel Grand Derya.

Eating & Drinking

Yöresel Yemek Evi RESTAURANT €

(Dr İsmail Beşikçi Caddesi; mains TL5-7) This establishment is run by an association of Kurdish women whose husbands are imprisoned. They prepare lip-smacking yöresel (traditional) meals at bargain-basement prices. Servers speak minimal English but do their best to explain the contents of their stainless-steel trays to the clueless. The döner kebap is also worth every bite.

Ehli Kebap KEBAPÇI €

(Dr İsmail Beşikçi Caddesi; mains TL6-10) One word describes this downtown hot spot: yum. The eclectic food – kebaps, pide and soups – is well presented and of high quality, with service and bright surrounds to match. One grumble: the two dining rooms feel a bit cramped.

Saray Restaurant KEBAPÇI €

(Dr İsmail Beşikçi Caddesi; mains TL4-8) Locals rate this place, and it's easy to see why. The service is attentive, ingredients are fresh and prices are very reasonable for the scrumptious kebaps, pide and ready-made meals.

Doğuş Restaurant RESTAURANT €€

(cnr Dr İsmail Beşikçi & Belediye Sarayı Caddesis; mains TL6-11) A bit touristy and slightly overpriced, but it's the only restaurant in town that boasts views of Mt Ararat from its upstairs terrace – invaluable.

NORTHEASTERN ANATOLIA DOĞUBAYAZIT

YENİ HAMAM

If you've climbed Mt Ararat you may feel the need to rejuvenate tired and sore muscles after all that exertion. The **Yeni Hamam** (Şehit Mehmet Özer Caddesi; ☺6am-midnight), southwest of the centre, comes recommended by trekking guides and locals alike. It's very well run and as clean as a whistle. Go for a private massage (TL15) – you've earned it.

Türkü Cafe BAR-CAFE **€**
(Dr İsmail Beşikçi Caddesi; snacks TL3-6) The closest thing the town has to a 'smart' cafe, with a chilled-out vibe. Though it's not licensed, it may serve beer to foreigners, or you may bring your own. Snacks are available. There's live music in the evening.

Shopping

Local Crafts CARPET SHOP
(İshak Paşa Caddesi; www.kurdishcrafts.com; ☺8am-9pm) If you're after Kurdish carpets, rugs or saddlebags, make a beeline for this shop near the otogar. The affable owner, Osman Akkuş, speaks some English and won't push you into buying. Most items come from the neighbouring villages.

❶ Information

INTERNET ACCESS There are several outlets on the main drag where you can check your emails.

MONEY Most banks in the centre have ATMs. There are also several money changers, including **Nişantaş Döviz** (Dr İsmail Beşikçi Caddesi; ☺7am-7pm Mon-Sat, 7am-noon Sun), which keeps longer hours and happily changes cash.

TOURIST INFORMATION Various travel agencies will be able to help with queries and help arrange permits to climb Mt Ararat. Try **Zaf Travel** (☎0531 822 9282; www.trekkinginararat.com; Dr İsmail Beşikçi Caddesi; ☺8am-8pm), run by knowledgeable Zafer Onay; **Tamzara Turizm** (☎0544 555 3582; www.letsgotomtararat. com; Emniyet Caddesi; ☺8am-8pm) in the Hotel Urartu; and **Murat Camping** (☎0542 437 3699, 0543 635 0494), which has an office opposite the otogar. Staff speak English.

❶ Getting There & Away

Minibuses (TL5) to the Iranian border (Gürbulak) leave from near the junction of Ağrı and Rıfkı Başkaya Caddesis, just past the *petrol ofisi* (petrol station), approximately every hour. The last one departs around 5pm. For visa information, see p687.

There are no buses to Van, only minibuses that leave at *approximately* 6.30am, 8am, 9am, noon, 2pm and 3.30pm daily (TL15, three hours, 185km). Getting to Kars, you'll have to catch a minibus to Iğdır (TL5, 45 minutes, 51km, every hour) and change there. From Iğdır to Kars should cost TL15.

Go to the main otogar for services to other long-distance destinations; often you'll have to travel via Erzurum (TL20, four hours, 285km).

Around Doğubayazıt

The travel agencies and most hotels in Doğubayazıt can help you organise a daily excursion to sights around the town. Half-day tours (about TL60 per person) take in the İshak Paşa Palace, 'Noah's Ark' (an elongated oval shape in stone that is supposed to be Noah's boat), the overrated 'Meteor Crater' (most probably a geological aberration) at the Iranian border and a village at the base of Mt Ararat. Full-day tours cover the same sites plus a visit to the Diyadin Hot Springs, 51km west of Doğubayazıt.

Mt Ararat (Ağrı Dağı)

A highlight of any trip to eastern Turkey, the twin peaks of Mt Ararat have figured in legends since time began, most notably as the supposed resting place of Noah's Ark. The left-hand peak, called Büyük Ağrı (Great Ararat), is 5137m high, while Küçük Ağrı (Little Ararat) rises to about 3895m.

Climbing Mt Ararat

For many years permission to climb Ararat was routinely refused because of security concerns, but this fantastic summit is now back on the trekking map, albeit with restrictions. A permit and a guide are mandatory. At the time of research you needed to apply at least 30 days in advance; your application had to be endorsed by a Turkish travel agency and you had to include a passport photocopy and a letter requesting permission and stating the dates you wish to climb. You can apply through any reputable agency in Turkey, including Zaf Travel, Tamzara Turizm and Murat Camping in Doğubayazıt. That said, at the time of writing there were talks of easing these restrictions; by the time you read this, the permit might be issued directly in Doğubayazıt in just a few days – contact one of the aforementioned travel agencies for up-to-date information.

If unofficial guides, hotel staff and touts in Doğubayazıt tell you they can get the permit in a couple of days, *don't* believe them. There's probably some bribery involved or, even worse, a scam, whereby they take your passport and let you think they've obtained the permit but in reality will be taking you up Ararat unofficially. Follow the official procedure, even if you have to endure the slow-turning wheels of bureaucracy.

And now, the costs. Whatever agency you use, expect to cough up about €450 per person for the trek (three days, including guides, camping and food) from Doğubayazıt (a bit less if you're a group). Most reputable agencies recommend four-day treks in order to facilitate acclimatisation before tackling the summit.

Despite the extortionate fare, climbing Ararat is a fantastic experience. Expect stupendous views and stunning landscapes. The best months for climbing are July, August and September. You'll need to be comfortable with snow-climbing techniques using crampons past 4800m, even in the height of summer.

The usual route is the southern one, starting from Eliköyü, an abandoned village in the foothills, at about 2500m. There's another route starting from the village of Çevirme, but it's seldom used. The first camp site is at 3200m, and the second one at 4200m.

You can also do daily treks around the mountain. Provided you stay under 2500m you won't have to go through so much official hoo-ha – it's best to go with a local agent. Expect to pay around TL300 per person.

Southeastern Anatolia

Includes »

Best Places to Stay

» Asude Konak (p568)

» Yuvacali Village
Homestay (p582)

» Aslan Konuk Evi (p577)

» Kasr-ı Nehroz (p605)

» Hacı Abdullah Bey
Konaği (p605)

Best Places to Eat

» Yörem Mutfağı (p569)

» İmam Çağdaş (p570)

» Beyaz Köşk (p578)

» Kamer Vakif (p602)

» Sütçü Fevzi & Sütçü
Kenan (p614)

Why Go?

Southeastern Anatolia is a unique part of Turkey, and apart from small Arabic and Christian pockets, this expansive region is predominantly Kurdish. Choose from a menu of historical cities, including Mardin, on a hill dominating Mesopotamia; Şanlıurfa, swathed in historical mystique; the old city of Diyarbakır, ensnared in mighty basalt walls; and the endangered honey-coloured riverside town of Hasankeyf. Move on to Nemrut Dağı, topped with colossal ancient statues, or shimmering Lake Van, edged with snowcapped mountains. Wonderfully isolated spots include Darende and the perfect hilltop village of Savur, and Gaziantep is a must-visit destination for passionate and well-travelled foodies. A few places could be off limits to foreigners when you visit – mainly near the border with Iraq – but most of southeastern Anatolia is safe and accessible to independent travellers. What will linger longest in your memory is an incredibly warm-hearted welcome from some of Turkey's friendliest people.

When to Go

Gaziantep

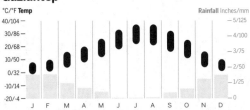

May & September Avoid the most extreme of the southeastern Anatolian heat.

June The International Kahta Kommagene Festival near Nemrut Dağı.

As soon as possible Before the rivers of the Tigris submerge beautiful Hasankeyf.

Kahramanmaraş (Maraş)

📞 0344 / POP 543,900

If you're heading to this neck of the woods from Cappadocia or the Mediterranean coast, a stop in Kahramanmaraş is mandatory for all ice-cream lovers. This town produces an insanely good *dövme dondurma* (beaten ice cream), which is justly revered throughout Turkey. If you find that's not reason enough to stop here, there are a handful of cultural treasures that will keep you busy for at least a day, including the **Ulu Cami** (Atatürk Bulvarı), built in Syrian style in 1502, the hilltop **kale** (fortress) and the lively **bazaar**.

The **Hotel Belli** (📞223 4900; www.otelbelli.com; Trabzon Caddesi; s/d TL45/80; ❄) features spruce rooms, prim bathrooms and the appeal of an end-of-day drink in the hotel's bar.

From the otogar (bus station) there are hourly minibuses to Gaziantep (TL14, two hours, 80km), while five daily buses ply the stunning route to Kayseri (TL22, 5½ hours, 291km).

Gaziantep (Antep)

📞 0342 / POP 1.8 MILLION

There's one Turkish word you should learn before visiting Gaziantep: *fıstık* (pistachio). This fast-paced and epicurean city is reckoned to harbour more than 180 pastry shops producing the world's best pistachio baklava. Other culinary treats are also on offer to adventurous foodie travellers.

Antep is a greatly underrated city that proclaims a modern, laissez-faire attitude while thumbing its nose at Şanlıurfa's piety. One of the most desirable places to live in southeastern Anatolia, it's high on ambitions, and not only in the gastronomic domain. With the biggest city park this side of the Euphrates and a buzzing cafe culture, Antep has lots of panache and thinks the time has come to share it with the outside world. And it also has one attraction that alone makes the trip across Turkey worth the fare: the Gaziantep Museum. Even if you've never had any enthusiasm for Roman mosaics you'll be a convert the minute you cast your eyes upon the *Gypsy Girl*.

The city is being reinvigorated, and the fortress, bazaars, caravanserai and smattering of old stone houses have been lovingly restored. One of southeastern Anatolia's gateways, Gaziantep has rarely been as full of confidence and hope for the future as it is today.

The city's centre is the intersection of Atatürk Bulvarı and Suburcu, Hürriyet and İstasyon Caddesis, marked by a large equestrian statue of Atatürk and still called *hükümet konağı* (government house) square.

History

Before the Arabs conquered the town in 638, the Persians, Alexander the Great, the Romans and the Byzantines had all left their imprints on the region. Proceeding from the east, the Seljuk Turks strolled into the picture around 1070.

Aintab (the former name of Gaziantep) remained a city of Seljuk culture, ruled by petty Turkish lords until the coming of the Ottomans under Selim the Grim in 1516.

During the Ottoman period, Aintab had a sizeable Christian population, especially Armenians. You'll see Armenian churches, community buildings and mansions scattered throughout the city's historical core.

In 1920, as the victorious Allies sought to carve up the Ottoman territories, Aintab was besieged by French forces intent on adding Turkish lands to their holdings in Syria and Lebanon. Aintab's fierce nationalist defenders surrendered on 8 February 1921. The epithet 'Gazi' (War Hero) was added to Antep in 1973 to pay homage to their tenacious defence.

◉ Sights

Ask at the tourist office for the *Gaziantep Tarih ve Kültür Yolu* (Gaziantep History & Culture Road) brochure, a handy map detailing 40 sights dotted around the city. Fans of restored caravanserais and mosques will be in seventh heaven.

Gaziantep Museum & Zeugma Kültür ve Müze Merkezi
MUSEUM

(İstasyon Caddesi; admission TL2; ⏰8.30am-noon & 1-5pm Tue-Sun) Even if the idea of an archaeology museum would usually send you to sleep, the Gaziantep Museum will amaze you with its collection of the many mosaics unearthed at the rich Roman site of Belkıs-Zeugma, just before the new Birecik Dam flooded some of the site forever. It's impossible not to fall in love with the *Gypsy Girl*, from the 2nd century AD, the museum's highlight. Also make a beeline for the famous *Scene of Achilles being sent to the Trojan War*.

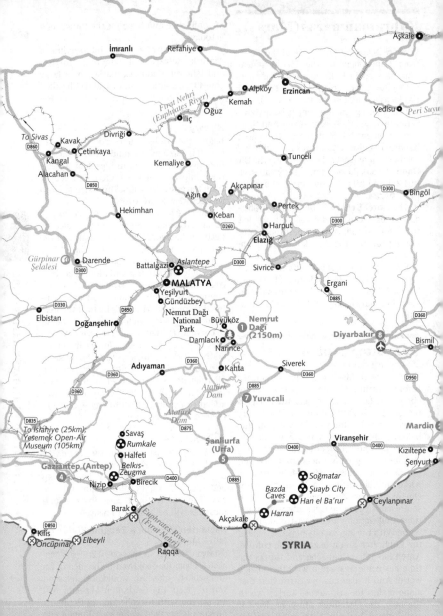

Southeastern Anatolia Highlights

1 Feel elation while watching the sun set (or rise) from **Nemrut Dağı** (p583), the 'thrones of gods'

2 Go heritage-hunting among the historic buildings

and honey-coloured stone houses of pretty **Mardin** (p600)

3 Bliss out by a gushing river in the perfect valley-village seclusion of **Savur** (p604)

4 Fall in love with the *Gypsy Girl* and feast on culinary delights in **Gaziantep** (p563)

5 Nourish your soul in the great pilgrimage city of **Şanlıurfa** (Urfa; p573)

ERZURUM

Mt Ararat
(Ağrı Dağı)
(5165m)

Ağrı

Doğubayazıt

Bāzargān

Tutak

D965

D975

Patnos

Çaldıran

Malazgirt

Erciş

Muradiye

Süphan Dağı
(Mt Süphan)
(4053m)

D959

D965

Özalp

IRAN

Nemrut Dağı
(Mt Nemrut)
(3050m)

Ahlat

Adilcevaz

D300

Erçek

Muş

Lake Van
(Van Gölü)

Van

Hoşap

D300

Reşadiye

Akdamar
Island

Güzelsu

D300

Tatvan

Altınsaç
Kilisesi

Gevaş

Gürpınar

Çavuştepe

D975

Bitlis

Bahçesaray

Başkale

D360

Siirt

Botan Çayı

To Orumiyeh
(40km)

D360

Esendere

Batman

Dicle Nehri
(Tigris River)

D370

Ortasu Çayı

Hakkari

Yüksekova

Hasankeyf

Cilo Dağı
(Mt Cilo)
(4168m)

Tür Abdin
Plateau

Şırnak

Uludere

Çığlı

Kıllıt

Midyat

Dargeçit

Morgabriel

D400

Savur

Cizre

Silopi

Yeşilli

Deyrul
Zafaran

Dara

D380

Habur

Nusaybin

D400

Zakho

IRAQ

Qamishle

SYRIA

0   70 km
0   40 miles

Mosul

---

6 Marvel at the Armenian
architecture of **Akdamar
Kilisesi** (p609) on a boat trip
out to Akdamar Island

7 Immerse yourself in
Kurdish family life in the

sleepy village of **Yuvacali**
(p582)

8 Explore **Diyarbakır's**
(p593) compelling labyrinth
of markets, winding alleys,

restored Armenian houses and
ancient, hushed churches

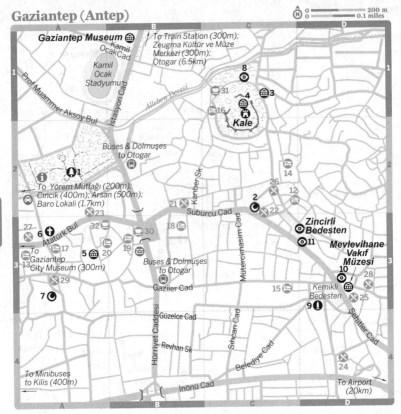

All the mosaics are due to be transferred to a new museum called **Zeugma Kültür ve Müze Merkezi**, which should have opened behind the railway station by the time you read this. The current museum will then focus on archaeology.

FREE Kale   FORTRESS
(Citadel; ⊙dawn-dusk) Get your bearings of the urban sprawl you're going to embrace by climbing up the unmissable castle. The citadel is thought to have been constructed by the Romans. It was restored by Emperor Justinian in the 6th century AD, and rebuilt extensively by the Seljuks in the 12th and 13th centuries. The interior of the castle contains the grandiosly named Gaziantep Defence and Heroism Panoramic Museum (admission TL1; ⊙9am-6pm Mon-Fri, 9am-7pm Sat & Sun), a tribute to the men and women who bravely defended the city in 1920. Life-size statues of generals, soldiers and ordinary people bring alive the city's tenacious struggle against the French. Comprehensive information panels are in English.

The quarter at the foot of the citadel has been entirely revamped over the last few years. Old shops and workshops have been smartened up, losing some of their character in the process.

Bakırcılar Çarşısi   BAZAAR
South of the kale is Gaziantep's rambling and labyrinthine bazaar area, which includes the Zincirli Bedesten (Coppersmiths' Market), now fully restored and full of tap-tap-tap metalworkers and makers of handmade shoes. It's touristy – though definitely with a small 't' – so keep exploring (and getting lost occasionally) to find excellent food markets with mini-mountains of multicoloured spices and graceful garlands of dried chillies. South of the Zincirli Bedesten, in the **Elmacı Pazarı** area, you'll find the original **Güllüoğlu** baklava shop. Get

Gaziantep (Antep)

there around 8am when the famous pastries are still warm.

For a coffee break, seek out **Tahmis Kahvesi** (Buğdaypazarı Sokak), possibly the most atmospheric *kahvehane* (coffeehouse) in Gaziantep, set in a restored caravanserai right in the heart of the bazaar, on a par with the more institutionalised **Tütün Hanı** (Eski Saray Caddesi Yanı).

Gaziantep City Museum   MUSEUM
(Gaziantep Kent Müzesi; Atatürk Bulvarı; admission TL1; ◎9am-6pm Mon-Fri, 9am-7pm Sat & Sun) Gaziantep's excellent new city museum is housed in the wonderfully restored Bayazhan – where traders and their camels used to stay the night. Lots of interactive displays and foreign-language audioguides steer visitors through everything from the story of baklava to Gaziantep's history of shoemaking. After some mental sustenance, relax with a tea or coffee in the Bayazhan's courtyard cafe.

FREE **Mevlevihane Vakıf Müzesi**   MUSEUM
(Tekke Camii Yanı; ◎9am-5pm Tue-Sun) This interesting museum focuses on the Mevlevi Sufis (a dervish order), with various artworks, kilims (pileless woven rugs), manuscripts, clothing worn by the Mevlevi

and other dervish paraphernalia. Panels are in English.

Emine Göğüş Culinary Museum   MUSEUM
(Köprübaşı Sokak; admission TL1; ◎9am-6pm Mon-Fri, 9am-7pm Sat & Sun) Concealed in a narrow lane under the citadel, this newly opened museum provides both information and inspiration before you begin exploring Gaziantep's terrific eateries. Excellent English-language translations and the occasional local treat cooked up by the on-site chef are key ingredients in the museum's successful recipe.

Hasan Süzer Ethnography Museum
    MUSEUM
(Hanefioğlu Sokak; admission TL3; ◎8am-noon & 1-5pm Tue-Sun) Occupying a restored 200-year-old Gaziantep stone house tucked away in a side street off Atatürk Bulvarı, this museum is well worth a visit. A central *hayat* (courtyard) patterned with light and dark stone provides access to the rooms. Those on the ground floor were for service; those on the 1st floor made up the *selamlık* (quarters for male family members and their visitors); and those on the 2nd floor made up the *haremlik* (for female family members and their visitors).

Naib Hamamı · HAMAM
(Kale Arası; spa & massage TL25; ⊙men 5.30am-9.30am, 5.30pm-midnight, women 9.30am-5.30pm) Recently restored, this elegant hamam is immediately north of the citadel and provides spa and massage sessions.

Şıra Hanı · HISTORIC BUILDING
On the southwestern edge of the bazaar, the beautifully restored Şıra Hanı is the location for the stylish Sahan restaurant.

100 Yil Atatürk Kültür Parkı · PARK
If you're all market-ed and museum-ed out, this park is within spitting distance of Gaziantep's traffic-snarled main thoroughfares. It's a lovely space in the middle of the city and provides a green haven for nature lovers, families and courting 20-somethings. There are also a couple of good places for a relaxed sunset beer.

Kurtuluş Camii · MOSQUE
Kurtuluş Camii is the most impressive of Gaziantep's many mosques, and is built on a small hill off the main thoroughfare. Initially constructed as a cathedral in 1892, it features alternating black-and-white stone banding.

Another mosque worth admiring is the Alaüddevle Camii, near the Coppersmiths' Market. Many other Gaziantep mosques have been recently restored, and are detailed on the *Gaziantep History & Culture Road* map available from the tourist office.

Kendirli Kilisesi · CHURCH
(Atatürk Bulvarı) Wedged between modern buildings smack in the centre, this church is a startling vision. It was constructed by French priests with the help of Napoleon III in 1860. Seen from a distance, the building looks quite featureless, but a closer inspection reveals a number of eye-catching decorative elements, including black-and-white medallions.

🛏 Sleeping
Gaziantep is rolling in accommodation, much of it on or near Atatürk Bulvarı and Suburcu, Hürriyet and İstasyon Caddesis. Hotel prices are high in comparison to other eastern Turkish cities, but the city has some excellent boutique hotels.

Asude Konak · BOUTIQUE HOTEL €€
TOP CHOICE (☑231 2044, 0535 381 3798; www.asudekonak.com; Arkası Millet Sokak 20; s €40-50, d €50-70; ❋@) With just five rooms decked out in a rustic combo of antiques, refurbished timber and traditional fabrics, this lovingly restored courtyard house is more like staying with friends or family. Meals are prepared by host Jale Özaslan, and are a superb introduction to Gaziantep's culinary firepower. Highlights include gossamer-light *katmer* (flatbread layered with nuts and clotted cream) for breakfast, and the local speciality of *yuvarlama* (soup made with rice, meat, chickpeas and yoghurt) for dinner. Evening meals are often lingering alfresco occasions where conversation comes very naturally after a tipple of rakı (aniseed brandy), beer or wine.

Anadolu Evleri · BOUTIQUE HOTEL €€€
(☑220 9525, 0533 558 7996; www.anadoluevleri.com; Köroğlu Sokak; s/d €70/90, 1-/2-person ste €90/105; ❋@) This tastefully restored old stone house provides the perfect soft landing into Gaziantep. Local tradition is celebrated with a beguiling courtyard, beamed or painted ceilings, mosaic floors, secret passageways, and antique furniture and artefacts. It's within spitting distance of the bustling bazaar, yet feels quiet and restful. No two rooms are identical. Rooms 1 and 2 on the ground floor are wonderfully cosy, and the other 11 rooms, including three gleaming suites, bathe in oodles of natural light. Host Timur Schindel rules his kingdom with relaxed bonhomie, and will give you the low-down in perfect English on all that's worth seeing in the city.

Zeynep Hanim Konaklari · BOUTIQUE HOTEL €€
(☑221 0207; www.zeynephanimkonaklari.com; Eski Sinema Sokak; s/d TL80/150; ❋) Comfortable and spacious rooms look out onto a central courtyard in Gaziantep's newest boutique hotel. Look forward to sparkling bathrooms and supercomfy beds after a tasting session in the subterranean wine cellar. The surrounding Mahalessi neighbourhood is Antep's hippest area for new cafes and restaurants.

Kale Evi · BOUTIQUE HOTEL €€
(☑231 4142; www.kaleevi.com, in Turkish; Köprübaşı Sokak; s/d €40/60; ❋) This eight-room hotel aims to offer a boutique stay for less, but gets sidetracked by a few tacky touches – such as huge air-conditioners and cheesy bedspreads in the rooms and a mock fresco of the *Gypsy Girl* in the restaurant. Tucked under the citadel, it's got a terrific location though, and the alfresco restaurant is exceptionally pleasant.

SELIN ROZANES – CULINARY TRAVEL GUIDE

Although she is based in İstanbul, Selin Rozanes regularly leads groups of travellers to explore the culinary heritage of Gaziantep and southeastern Anatolia. Back in İstanbul, she introduces visitors to the flavours of Anatolia at cookery classes in her apartment with **Turkish Flavours** (www.turkishflavours.com); see p85.

Local Antep Specialities

Don't miss trying an *ali nazik* kebap with a base of smoky aubergine (eggplant) mashed with yoghurt. Gaziantep's odd breakfast habit is *beyran*. Very garlicky and delicious, it's a soup, tandoori meat and rice all in one.

Something Sweeter

Try *katmer* (flatbread layered with nuts and clotted cream) and have a box of *kahke*, a wafer-thin biscuit. My favourite is *köylü kahkesi*, peasant-style, made with grape molasses and flavoured with spices and studded with flax seeds and nigella. Not so sweet and really tasty.

Must Try

A good place to try local dishes is **Yörem Mutfağı**. For baklava the **Güllüoğulu** shop in Elmacı Pazarı is better than their other branches, and you should have coffee in the nearby **Tahmis Kahvesi**.

Yesemek Otel
HOTEL €€
(☎220 8888; www.yesemekotel.com; İsmail Sokak; s/d TL50/80; ❄) Come across the modern exterior and imposing lobby and you could easily mistake the Yesemek for a bank. Bang in the thick of things, this well-regarded pile offers great service and facilities including a restaurant and a private *otopark* (car park) just next door.

Nil Hotel
HOTEL €€
(☎220 9452; www.nilhotel.net; Atatürk Bulvarı 53; s/d TL60/90; ❄) There's nothing overly adventurous in this small 'high-rise' hotel, but what do you want from a middle-of-the-road establishment? At least the bathrooms are spotless and it's high on facilities, with satellite TV, air-con and a central location.

Yunus Hotel
HOTEL €
(☎221 1722; hotelyunus@hotel.com; Kayacık Sokak; s/d TL35/60; ❄) As far as physical beauty goes, this is a real plain Jane, but it's a secure spot to hang your rucksack, the rates are good and it's handily set in the centre of town. It features anodyne rooms with well-scrubbed bathrooms.

Güzel Otel
HOTEL €
(☎221 3216; Gaziler Caddesi 7; s/d TL25/40; ❄) A convenient marketside location and clean, spacious rooms add up to one of Gaziantep's best-value hotels. Caution: must like rose-coloured walls.

Anit Hotel
HOTEL €
(☎220 9656; anithotel@yahoo.com; Atatürk Bulvarı 81; s/d TL40/70; ❄) Solid budget to midrange offering with spacious and sunny rooms in a quiet, leafy street. There's a bar on the 1st floor, and Antep's best cafes are just a short stroll away.

✗ Eating

Gaziantep is a nirvana for gastronomads, with a prodigious selection of eateries and pastry shops to suit all palates and budgets. Get a copy of the excellent *Gaziantep Mutfaui* (Gaziantep Cuisine) book from the tourist office, listing the city's best restaurants and describing its iconic dishes.

TOP CHOICE Yörem Mutfağı
MUTFAK €€
(İncilipınar Mahallesi 3, Sokak 15; mains TL8-10) What began as a simple *lokanta* (eatery serving ready-made food) feeding nearby office workers has morphed into an elegant spot serving some of Gaziantep's best homestyle food. Good-value lunches are a pick-and-point affair – the dishes change daily – and dinner is more formal with a wider range. The country cottage decor belies the actual sophistication of some of the city's best food. To find Yörem Mutfağı, look for the AK Parti sign on the street skirting the northen edge of the Atatürk Kültür Parkı, and turn right.

For any baklava devotee, Gaziantep is a Shangri-la. The city is reckoned to produce the best *fıstıklı* (pistachio) baklavas in Turkey, if not in the world. When they are served ultrafresh, they're impossible to beat. With more than 180 pastry shops scattered around the city, it's hard to determine which is the best, but some baklava shops have reached cult status, such as **Güllüoğlu** (Elmacı Pazarı), **Çavuşoğlu** (Eski Saray Caddesi), **Baklava Ünlüler** (Suburcu Caddesi) and the talismanic **İmam Çağdaş** (Kale Civarı Uzun Çarşı).

We asked Burhan Çağdaş the owner of the eponymous İmam Çağdaş, which has been tormenting carb-lovers since 1887, what the qualities of a perfectly crafted baklava are. 'I carefully choose the freshest ingredients imaginable. Everything is organic. I know the best oil and pistachio producers in the Gaziantep area. The nature of the soil here gives a special aroma to pistachios. And we don't go into mass production.'

How can one judge whether a baklava is fresh? 'It's simple: when it's in your mouth, it should make like a *kshhhh* sound,' says Burhan Çağdaş.

He's right. You'll never forget the typical *kshhhh* that characterises a fresh baklava when it titillates your taste buds.

İmam Çağdaş   RESTAURANT €€

(Kale Civarı Uzun Çarşı; mains TL10-16) This talismanic pastry shop and restaurant is run by the Çağdaş family, and their wicked pistachio baklava is delivered daily to customers throughout Turkey. If there were a kebap Oscar, this place would be a serious contender. The secret? Fresh, carefully chosen ingredients and the inimitable 'Çağdaş touch'. Our pick? The creamy, chargrilled aubergine flavours of the *ali nazik* kebap.

Çınarlı   MUTFAK €

(Çınarlı Sokak; mains TL6-12) Resisting the passage of time, the Çınarlı still enjoys a great reputation for its *yöresel yemeks* (traditional dishes), a perfect excuse to experiment with lesser-known dishes such as *ekşili ufak köfte* (small sour meatballs), *yuvarlama* (chickpea, meat and yoghurt soup) or *kuruluk dolma* (spicy stuffed aubergine). The decor works a treat, with three small rooms decorated with rugs, weapons and other collectibles, as well as a bigger dining room upstairs where you can enjoy live music in the afternoon. It's a pistachio's toss from the war memorial (walk down the stairs).

Çulcuoğlu Et Lokantası   LOKANTA €

(Kalender Sokak; mains TL5-10; ⊙11.30am-10pm Mon-Sat) Surrender helplessly to your inner carnivore at this Gaziantep institution. The yummy kebaps are the way to go, but grilled chicken also puts in menu appearances. Don't be fooled by the unremarkable entrance; there's a vast, neat dining area at the back. It's tucked away down a narrow side street across the *otopark* near the Şıra Hanı, about 20m from a little mosque called Nur Ali.

Metanet Lokantası   LOKANTA €

(Kozluca Camii Yanı; mains TL6-9; ⊙11am-3pm) Left, right, left again. That's it, over there. The sort of place you only find if you go looking for it. Tucked away in a side street near Kozluca Camii, the Metanet has always been part of the local knowledge. The moustached waiters, who seem to have been a fixture here for decades, conscientiously mince the meat around noon in front of a big grill. *Ayran* (yoghurt drink) is served in a tin bowl, and the atmosphere is convivial. Much less institutionalised than İmam Çağdaş.

Baro Lokali   RESTAURANT-BAR €€

(Yıl Atatürk Kültür Parkı; mains TL8-12; ⊙11am-11pm) It's the setting that's the pull here, an enchanting leaf-dappled outdoor terrace at the western end of the 100 Yıl Atatürk Kültür Parkı (about TL8 by taxi) – perfect for escaping sticky Gaziantep on a hot summer day. Good choice of mezes and meat dishes. You can order beer, rakı or wine with your meal.

Sahan   RESTAURANT €€

(Şıra Hanı; mains TL12-16; ⊙noon-11pm) Located in the restored Şıra Hanı, Sahan dishes up excellent versions of local specialities. It's licensed, so at the very least pop in for a beer, wine and a few meze in the elegant and spacious courtyard.

Çavuşoğlu   PATISSERIE €

(Eski Saray Caddesi; mains TL4-9) Partly *baklavacı*, partly *kebapçı*, this sprightly outfit rustles up dishes that will fill your tummy without emptying your wallet. Portions are copious, the meat is perfectly slivered and the salads are fresh.

Mado Café
CAFE €€
(Atatürk Bulvarı; mains TL8-10) The super-slick Mado is *the* place to meet Gaziantep's movers and shakers. You can nosh on snacks and sip fruity cocktails, but the pastries and ice creams are what make the place tick.

Önder Lahmacun Salonu
PIDECI €
(Eyüboğlu Caddesi; pide from TL5) Turkish pizzas never tasted so good in this modern eatery situated a short bag-haul from Kurtuluş Camii.

Drinking

TOP CHOICE Papirüs Cafeteria
CAFE
(Noter Sokak; ☺10am-10pm) A student crowd (male *and* female, we promise) gathers here to take advantage of the delightfully authentic setting – it's housed in a historic mansion off Atatürk Bulvarı – and swap numbers in the leafy courtyard. Don't miss the ancient frescoes in the upstairs rooms.

Adana Şalgamacısı – Gürbüz Usta
CAFE
(Hürriyet Caddesi; juices from TL2; ☺8.30am-8pm) See the heaps of grapefruit, banana and orange on the counter at this buzzing hole-in-the-wall? They're just waiting to be squeezed. Try the delicious *atom* (an explosive mixture of milk, honey, banana, hazelnuts and pistachio).

Cıncık
BAR-RESTAURANT
(Atatürk Kültür Parkı; ☺noon-11pm) The grills and salads at Cıncık are perfectly fine, but we really like it for its leafy and relaxed garden bar filled with Antep folk lounging on bean bags, and kicking back with a relaxed combo of draught Efes beer and the occasional nargileh (water pipe). It's a short stroll through Atatürk Kültür Parkı from the city centre. Mind the canoodling locals after dark.

Tütün Hanı
TEA GARDEN
(Eski Saray Caddesi Yanı; ☺8.30am-8pm) Set in the picturesque courtyard of the carefully restored Tütün Hanı, this teahouse is a great place to enjoy a cheap tea and nargileh. It has bags of character, featuring rugs, low wooden tables and cushions.

Kir Kahvesi
COFFEE HOUSE
(Köprübaşı Sokak; Turkish coffee TL4; ☺8.30am-6pm) This cafe in an over-restored historic building at the foot of the citadel lacks the patina and atmosphere of the Papirüs, but it's still a good place to recuperate after visiting the area.

Information

The post office and ATMs are on or around the main square, while internet cafes line up in a lane parallel to Atatürk Bulvarı.

Arsan (☎220 6464; www.arsan.com.tr; Nolu Sokak; ☺8am-7pm) Reputable travel agency that can arrange various tours (from TL90 per person), including the 'Magical Triangle' (Birecik, Halfeti/Rumkale, Belkıs-Zeugma), Yesemek and even Aleppo (Syria).

Tourist office (☎230 5969; 100 Yıl Atatürk Kültür Parkı İçi; ☺8am-noon & 1-5pm Mon-Fri) In a black and grey building in the city park. The well-informed staff speak English and German.

Getting There & Away

Air

Gaziantep's Oğuzeli airport is 20km from the centre. Ask at a travel agency about the Havas bus to the airport. A taxi is around TL30.

Onur Air (www.onurair.com.tr, in Turkish) Daily flight to/from İstanbul (from TL66).

Pegasus (www.flypgs.com) Daily flights to/from İstanbul (from TL66).

Turkish Airlines (www.thy.com) Daily flights to/from İstanbul (from TL51), to/from Ankara (from TL51), and two flights weekly to/from Antalya (from TL51).

Bus

The otogar is 6.5km from the town centre. Catch a bus (TL2) or minibus in Hürriyet Caddesi, north of Gaziler Caddesi, or in İstasyon Caddesi, about 400m further north. A taxi costs about TL15.

There's no direct bus to Syria; you'll have to go to Kilis first, then take a taxi to the border or to Aleppo. Minibuses to Kilis (TL8, 65km) leave every 20 minutes or so from a separate *garaj* (minibus terminal) on İnönü Caddesi.

Private taxis to Aleppo leave from around the Syrian consulate near the tourist office. Expect to pay around US$60 for up to four people.

Note that because Turkish citizens no longer need visas for Syria, the border can be very busy.

Car

To see surrounding sights, especially the Yesemek Open-Air Museum, Arsan can arrange car rental at no extra cost. Plan on TL90 a day.

Train

At the time of writing, trains to Gaziantep from other parts of Turkey had been suspended due to long-term line maintenance. A train to Aleppo in Syria leaves Gaziantep at 8.30pm on Tuesday

SERVICES FROM GAZİANTEP'S OTOGAR

DESTINATION	FARE (TL)	DURATION (HR)	DISTANCE (KM)	FREQUENCY (PER DAY)
Adana	18	4	220	frequent buses
Adıyaman	14	3	162	frequent minibuses
Ankara	45	10	705	frequent buses
Antakya	15	4	200	frequent minibuses
Diyarbakır	25	5	330	frequent buses
İstanbul	60	15	1136	several buses
Kahramanmaraş	10	1½	80	frequent buses & minibuses
Mardin	30	6	330	several buses
Şanlıurfa	10	2½	145	frequent buses
Van	50	12	740	several buses

and Friday. A train to Mosul in Iraq began running in February 2010, but was suspended in April 2010 due to security issues. Check the Turkish Railways website (www.tcdd.gov.tr) for the latest.

The train station is 800m north of the city centre and is connected to central Gaziantep by a newly built light rail service.

Around Gaziantep

KİLİS

☑0348 / POP 70.700

Kilis bristles with lovely ancient buildings scattered around the city centre, including mausoleums, caravanserais, hamams, mosques, fountains and *konaks* (mansions). Many have been recently restored. On or around the main square, look for the superb **Adliye**, the **Mevlevi Hane**, the **Tekye Camii**, the **Paşa Hamamı** and the **Kadı Camii**. The Cuneyne Camii and Çalik Camii are a bit more difficult to find (ask around).

Take a minibus from Gaziantep and allow a day in this surprising city. For an overnight stay, the **Mer-Tur Otel** (☑814 0834; mer-turotel@hotmail.com; Zekerya Korkmaz Bulvarı; s/d TL60/90; ❀) is an OK choice.

There are frequent minibus services to Gaziantep (TL8, 65km, one hour). For Aleppo in Syria, take a taxi to Öncüpınar at the border (TL12, 7km). From the Syrian side of the border, you can pick up a taxi for Aleppo.

YESEMEK OPEN-AIR MUSEUM

The Yesemek Open-Air Museum (Yesemek Açık Hava Müzesi; admission TL2; ☉dawn-dusk) is a vast hillside studded with some 300 Hittite stones and statues with a picturesque setting.

The use of the site is intriguing. From around 1375 BC this hillside was a Hittite quarry and sculpture workshop. For over 600 years it churned out basalt blocks, weighing anywhere from 1.5 to 8 tonnes, that were carved into lions, sphinxes and other designs. Today, the pieces are left in various states of completion, abandoned at the end of the Hittite era. Recent landscaping has added a gentle stream, and an outdoor studio has been added for contemporary sculptors to showcase their 21st-century creations.

Yesemek is a long 113km haul from Gaziantep. Getting there by public transport is a chore, because there's no direct service. It's easier to hire a car in Gaziantep. You could do a scenic loop, taking in Kilis, Yesemek and İslahiye. From Kilis, follow the D410 to Hassa/Antakya, then bear right onto the gravel road marked for Yesemek.

BELKIS-ZEUGMA

Once an important city, Belkıs-Zeugma was founded by one of Alexander the Great's generals around 300 BC. It had its golden age with the Romans, and later became a major trading station along the Silk Road. Unfortunately, it has lost much of its appeal since most of the site disappeared under the waters of the Birecik Dam. Most interesting mosaics and finds have been transferred to Gaziantep Museum, where some are on display. All that is left of the city's former grandeur is a pile of rubble and a couple of dilapidated pillars.

Nor are there any explanatory signs. There are plans for an open-air museum to give the site a bit more lustre – stay tuned.

The site is about 50km from Gaziantep and 10km from Nizip, off the main road to Şanlıurfa (it's signposted from Nizip), but there's no minibus service. If you don't have your own vehicle, you may think it's too much effort getting there for too little reward.

HALFETİ & RUMKALE

If you need a break in a more secluded place, **Halfeti** is for you. This peaceful village lies about 40km north of Birecik, on the bank of the Euphrates. It's the perfect spot to unwind before tackling the busy cities of Şanlıurfa to the east or Gaziantep to the west. The setting couldn't be more appealing, with attractive houses that trickle down the hillside above the river. Sadly, construction of the Birecik Dam meant that half of the city, including several archaeological sites, was inundated and part of the population had to be resettled.

There are several places to soak up the atmosphere along the river. The leafy **Siyah Gül Restaurant** (📞0414-751 5235; mains TL7-10), overlooking the river, is a sound option and alcohol is served. The licensed **Duba Restaurant** (📞0414-751 5704; mains TL7-10), at the end of the village (just go along the road that follows the river), is also worth considering, with a purpose-built pontoon on the water and a teensy *bahçe* (garden). Other eateries have recently opened up but their locations are not too great. Should you decide

to stay overnight, the welcoming **Şelaleli Konak** (📞0414-751 5500; d per person TL30) fits the bill, but there are only three rooms (one with private bathroom). Ask at the police station next door if no-one is around.

From Halfeti, boats to **Rumkale** can be organised (about TL50 for the whole boat) – a must-do. The boat putt-putts along for about 20 minutes until it reaches the base of the rocky bluff on top of which sits this ruined **fortress**. Accessible by a short but steep path (be careful if with children), the fortress features a mosque, church, monastery, well and other remains, all in a relatively good state of preservation. Back at your boat, ask the driver to continue until **Savaş**, another partly inundated village, a mere 10 minutes' boat ride from Rumkale. There's limited infrastructure in Savaş, but nothing beats a cup of çay in one of the tea gardens by the river.

Halfeti is relatively easily accessible by public transport on weekdays. Hourly minibuses ply the route between Birecik and Halfeti (TL4), leaving from near Birecik's Hotel Acar. Regular dolmuş departures leave from Gaziantep's otogar to Birecik (TL8).

Şanlıurfa (Urfa)

📞0414 / POP 650,000 / ELEV 518M

After the secular foodie pleasures of Gaziantep, it's time to exercise your soul in mystical and pious Şanlıurfa (the Prophets' City; also known as Urfa), a spiritual centre par excellence and great pilgrimage town. This

---

GAP – THE SOUTHEAST ANATOLIA PROJECT

The character of the landscape in southeastern Anatolia is changing as the Southeast Anatolia Project (Güneydoğu Anadolu Projesi), better known as GAP or Güneydoğu, comes online, bringing irrigation waters to large arid regions and generating enormous amounts of hydroelectricity for industry. Parched valleys have become fish-filled lakes, and dusty villages are now booming market towns and factory cities.

The scale of the project is awe-inspiring, affecting nine provinces and two huge rivers (the Tigris and the Euphrates). By 2008, 17 dams (out of a planned total of 22) had been completed. In around 2012, when the project is completed, 19 power generating plants will provide 22% of Turkey's total electricity needs, and more than 1.7 million hectares of land will have been brought under irrigation.

Such a huge, hope-generating project can also generate sizeable problems, especially ecological and sanitary ones, due to the change from dry to wet agriculture. According to data from the Malaria Division of the Turkish Health Ministry, the reported cases of malaria rose from 8680 in 1990 to 18,676 in 1992.

The project has also generated political problems, as Syria and Iraq, the countries downriver for whom the waters of the Tigris and Euphrates are also vital, complain bitterly that Turkey is using or keeping a larger share of the water than it should. Innumerable archaeological sites have also disappeared under dam water, or are slated to do so.

is where the prophets Job and Abraham left their marks. Just like centuries of visiting pilgrims before you, your first sight of the Dergah complex of mosques and the holy Gölbaşı area will be a magical moment – especially with the call to prayer as an essential soundtrack.

It's also in Urfa that you begin to feel you've reached the Middle East, courtesy of its proximity to Syria. Women cloaked in black chadors elbow their way through the odorous crush of the bazaar streets; moustached gents in *şalvar* (traditional baggy Arabic pants) swill tea and click-clack

Şanlıurfa (Urfa)

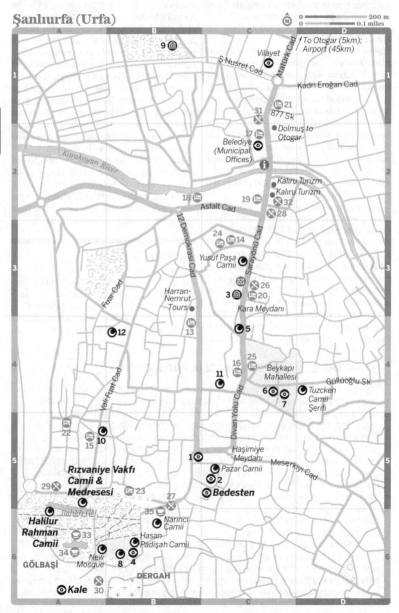

0 _____ 200 m
0 _____ 0.1 miles

To Otogar (5km);
Airport (45km)

Vilayet

Ş Nusret Cad

Atatürk Cad

Kadri Eroğan Cad

877 Sk

31

21

17

Dolmuş to Otogar

Belediye (Municipal Offices)

Kırakoyun River

Kalıru Turizm

Kalıru Turizm

18

19

32

Asfalt Cad

28

12 Demokrasi Cad

Sarayönü Cad

24

14

Yusuf Paşa Camii

Harran-Nemrut Tours

3

26

20

Kara Meydanı

13

12

5

Fuar Cad

16

25

Beykapı Mahallesi

11

Güllüoğlu Sk

6

7

Tuzcken Camii Şerifi

Divan Yolu Cad

22

15

10

Vali Fuat Cad

1

Haşimiye Meydanı

Meserkıyı Cad

Pazar Camii

2

Rızvaniye Vakfı Camii & Medresesi

29

23

Bedesten

27

35

Narıncı Camii

Bahlûl Göl

Halilur Rahman Camii

33

Hasan Padişah Camii

34

New Mosque

8

4

GÖLBAŞI

DERGAH

Kale

30

backgammon pieces in shady courtyards; pilgrims feed sacred carp in the shadows of a medieval fortress.

But fuelled by investment in the nearby Southeast Anatolia Project, a surprisingly cosmopolitan sheen is now being added to Urfa's centuries-old heritage. A sparkling new airport and otogar make getting there painless, and the city's streets hum with an energetic buzz.

The area surrounding the modern town remains a utilitarian collection of apartment blocks and concrete eyesores, but Urfa still deserves a couple of days to see all the sights and soak up the irresistible atmosphere of the back streets.

History

The Hittites imposed their rule over the area around 1370 BC. After a period of Assyrian rule, Alexander the Great hit Urfa. He and his Macedonian mates named the town Edessa, after a former capital of Macedonia, and it remained the capital of a Seleucid province until 132 BC, when the local Aramaean population set up an independent kingdom and renamed the town Orhai, which turned out to be only temporary. Orhai finally succumbed to the Romans, as did everywhere hereabouts.

Edessa pursued its contrary history by speedily adopting Christianity (c 200) before it became the official religion of the conquerors.

Astride the fault line between the Persian and Roman empires, control of Edessa was batted back and forth from one to the other. In 533 the two empires signed a Treaty of Endless Peace – that lasted seven years. The Romans and Persians kept at it until the Arabs swept in and cleared them all out in 637. Edessa enjoyed three centuries of peace under the Arabs, after which everything went to blazes again.

Turks, Arabs, Armenians and Byzantines battled for the city from 944 until 1098, when the First Crusade under Count Baldwin of Boulogne arrived to set up the Latin County of Edessa. This odd European feudal state lasted until 1144, when it was conquered by a Seljuk Turkish *emir* (tribal leader).

Şanlıurfa (Urfa)

SOUTHEASTERN ANATOLIA ŞANLIURFA (URFA)

The Seljuk Turkish *emir* was succeeded by Saladin, then by the Mamluks. The Ottomans, under Selim the Grim, conquered most of this region in the early 16th century, but Edessa did not become Urfa until 1637, when the Ottomans finally took over.

Urfa became Şanlıurfa (Glorious Urfa) in 1984. Since 1973, when Heroic Antep (Gaziantep) was given its special name, the citizens of Urfa had been chafing under a relative loss of dignity. Now that their city is 'Glorious', the inhabitants can look the citizens of 'Heroic' Antep straight in the eye.

⊙ Sights

Gölbaşı   HISTORIC AREA

Legend had it that Abraham (İbrahim), who is a great Islamic prophet, was in old Urfa destroying pagan gods one day when Nimrod, the local Assyrian king, took offence at this rash behaviour. Nimrod had Abraham immolated on a funeral pyre, but God turned the fire into water and the burning coals into fish. Abraham himself was hurled into the air from the hill where the fortress stands, but landed safely in a bed of roses.

The picturesque Gölbaşı area of Urfa is a symbolic re-creation of this story. Two rectangular pools of water (**Balıklı Göl** and **Ayn-i Zeliha**) are filled with supposedly sacred carp, while the area west of the Hasan Padişah Camii is a gorgeous rose garden. Local legend has it that anyone catching the carp will go blind. Consequently, these appear to be the most pampered, portly fish in Turkey.

On the northern side of Balıklı Göl is the elegant **Rızvaniye Vakfı Camii & Medresesi**, with a much-photographed arcaded wall, while at the western end is the **Halilur Rahman Camii**. This 13th-century building, replacing an earlier Byzantine church, marks the site where Abraham fell to the ground. The two pools are fed by a spring at the base of Damlacık hill, on which the castle is built.

Bazaar   MARKET

(⊙Mon-Sat) Spreading east of the Narıncı Camii, Urfa's bazaar is a jumble of streets, some covered, some open, selling everything from sheepskins and pigeons to jeans and handmade shoes. It was largely built by Süleyman the Magnificent in the mid-16th century. The best idea is just to dive in and inevitably get lost. Women should be on guard for lustful hands.

One of the most interesting areas is the **bedesten** (covered market), an ancient caravanserai where silk goods were sold. Today you'll still find silk scarves here, as well as gaudy modern carpets and the lovely blue and red scarves worn by local women. Right by the *bedesten* is the **Gümrük Hanı** (customs depot), with a delightful courtyard that is always full of tea- or coffee-swilling moustached gents playing backgammon, providing an authentic ambience.

Buried in the lanes of the bazaar are several ancient and very cheap hamams, including **Arasa Hamamı**.

Kale   FORTRESS

(Citadel; admission TL3; ⊙8am-8pm) With astounding views, the fortress on Damlacık hill, from which Abraham was supposedly tossed, is an absolute must-see. Multiple conflicting histories claim it was either (a) built in Hellenistic times, (b) built by the Byzantines, (c) built during the Crusades or (d) built by the Turks. In any case, it's vast, looks magnificent when floodlit, and can be reached via a flight of stairs or a tunnel cut through the rock. On the top, the most interesting things are the pair of columns that local legend has dubbed the Throne of Nemrut after the supposed founder of Urfa, the biblical King Nimrod.

Dergah   PARK

Southeast of Gölbaşı is the Dergah complex of mosques and parks surrounding the colonnaded courtyard of the **Hazreti İbrahim Halilullah** (Prophet Abraham's Birth Cave; admission TL1), built and rebuilt over the centuries as a place of pilgrimage. Its western side is marked by the **Mevlid-i Halil Camii**, a large Ottoman-style mosque. At its southern side is the entrance to the cave where Abraham was reputedly born. He lived here in hiding for his first seven years – King Nimrod, responding to a prophecy he'd received in a dream, feared that a newborn would eventually steal his crown, so he had all babies killed. This is still a place of pilgrimage and prayer, with separate entrances for men and women.

To visit these important places of worship you should be modestly dressed.

Mosques   MOSQUES

Urfa's Syrian-style **Ulu Cami** dates from the 1170–75 period. Its 13 *eyvans* (vaulted halls) open onto a spacious forecourt with a tall tower topped by a clock with Ottoman numerals.

At Kara Meydanı, the square midway between the *belediye* (town hall) and Dergah, is the **Hüseyin Paşa Camii**, a late-Ottoman work built in 1849.

On Vali Fuat Caddesi, which leads up from behind Gölbaşı to the Cevahir Konuk Evi guesthouse and restaurant, is the enormous, beautifully restored **Selahattin Eyubi Camii**. It was once St John's Church, evidenced by the altar. Further north is the restored **Yeni Fırfırlı Camii**, once the Armenian Church of the Twelve Apostles.

Şanlıurfa Museum MUSEUM

(Şanlıurfa Müzesi; admission TL3; ⊗8am-noon & 1.30-5pm Tue-Sun) Up the hill off Atatürk Caddesi, the Şanlıurfa Museum showcases eastern Turkey's archaeological evolution.

The gardens contain various sculptures, and near the entrance are several mosaics, the most interesting showing assorted wild animals. Inside are Neolithic implements, Assyrian, Babylonian and Hittite relief stones, and other objects from Byzantine, Seljuk and Ottoman times.

Old Houses HISTORIC BUILDINGS

Delve into Urfa's back streets to discover the city's distinctive limestone houses with protruding bays supported on stone corbels. Although many are falling into decay (and are too large for modern families), a few have been restored. Most notable is the house of Hacı Hafızlar, near the PTT. Now an art gallery, the **Güzel Sanatlar Galerisi** (⊗8am-5.30pm Mon-Fri, noon-4pm Sat), its courtyards feature finely carved stonework.

The **Şurkav** (Balıklı Göl Mevkii), a local government building, has a courtyard is draped with greenery.

North of the market area, in the neighbourhood called Beykapı Mahallesi (take 1001 Sokak), try to find the **İl Özel İdaresi Kültür ve Sanat Merkezi**, another splendid house restored in 2002. It was once a church. Nearby, a stately building now houses a school, the **İlköğretim Okulu**.

🛏 Sleeping

TOP CHOICE Aslan Konuk Evi PENSION €

(☎215 1575, 0542 761 3065; www.aslankonukevi.com; Demokrasi Caddesi 12; s/d TL50/75, per person with shared bathroom TL25-30; ❈ @) Simple but spacious high-ceilinged rooms are arranged around a shared central courtyard in a heritage Urfa building. Efficiently run by local English teacher Özcan Aslan, with excellent food (and cold beer!) available in the rooftop terrace restaurant. Outside guests are welcome for dinner, but you'll need to make a booking in the morning. Aslan is a good choice for female budget travellers, and Özcan will also pick you up from the Urfa otogar for free. His new private rooms are excellent value.

Manici Hotel HISTORIC HOTEL €€€

(☎215 9911; www.manici.com.tr; Balıklı Göl Mevkii; s/d TL110/180; ❈) Formerly two adjacent hotels, the recently opened Manici has a spread of beautifully restored rooms that will effortlessly fulfil your expectations of a romantic getaway. The luxe furnishings stop just short of being OTT, and there's more of a contemporary vibe than other heritage accommodation around town. The shared public areas are relaxed and calm-inducing.

Otel Urhay HISTORIC HOTEL €

(☎216 2222, 0544 215 7201; otelurhay@hotmail.com; Sarayönü Caddesi, Beyaz Sokak; s/d TL30/50; ❈) Here's your chance to enjoy heritage ambience at a reasonable rate. A cool kilim-decorated lounge/restaurant combines with simple whitewashed rooms that feature both air-con – essential during an Urfa summer – and private bathrooms. The quiet inner courtyard is perfect for a combo of drinking tea and getting your travel diary up-to-date. Note that weddings and parties are sometimes hosted on weekends.

Hotel Arte BOUTIQUE HOTEL €€

(☎314 7060; www.otel-arte.com; Köprübaşı Caddesi; s/d TL60/100; ❈) Style and sleekness in Urfa? Yes, it's possible at the Arte. The design-led interior, with Barbie-esque plastic chairs in the lobby, laminated floors and contemporary furniture in the rooms, is appealing, and the floor-to-ceiling windows afford superb views of the main drag. A touch-up of paint here and there would be nice though.

Kilim Otel HOTEL €€

(☎313 9090; cnr Atatürk Caddesi & 877 Sokak; s/d TL70/100; ❈) Located down a quiet lane just off the main drag, the Kilim's modern business stylings are equally appealing to midrange travellers. Rooms are spacious with spotless bathrooms and views across Urfa's expansive sprawl. Breakfast is one of Urfa's best, especially the tasty *menemen* (Turkish omelette).

Hotel Rabis BUSINESS HOTEL €€

(☎216 9595; www.hotelrabis.com, in Turkish; Sarayönü Caddesi; s/d TL70/120; ❈) One of Urfa's newest hotels provides shiny midrange quality, and is popular with visiting business types. The decor is light brown and beige, with thick carpets, flat-screen TVs and double-glazing. Good views from the rooftop terrace, too. One of the better deals in town.

Lizbon Guest House PENSION €
(0535 373 8926; lizbonguesthouse@hotmail.com; Balıklı Göl, Yeni Mahallesi, Sokak 1286; half-board per person TL35; @) In a local neighbourhood near the Balıklı Göl, the Lizbon is run by a Kurdish couple who speak pretty good English. Rooms are very simple with a shared bathroom. Look forward to tasty traditional food, but we've had reports that host Izzet can be a little too eager to upsell guests to trips around the surrounding area.

Hotel Güven HOTEL €€
(215 1700; www.hotelguven.com; Sarayönü Caddesi; s/d TL60/90; ❄) The Güven's whiff of hospital-strength disinfectant is testament to the place's spotlessness. The neon-lit corridors are equally institutional, but it is super central, and the rooms are well insulated from the hubbub of the main drag.

Hotel Bakay HOTEL €
(215 8975; Asfalt Caddesi; s/d TL40/60; ❄ @) The Bakay is a safe bet that won't hurt the hip pocket, and is remarkably clean, but be prepared to trip over your backpack in the tiny rooms. Some are brighter than others, so check out a few before settling in.

✕ Eating

Urfa's culinary specialities include Urfa kebap (skewered chunks of lamb served with tomatoes, sliced onions and hot peppers); *çiğ köfte* (minced uncooked mutton), *içli köfte* (deep-fried, mutton-filled meatballs covered with bulgur); and *şıllık* (crepe filled with walnuts and syrup). Urfa folk like their food spicy, and many dishes come with a hearty addition of *ızot* (dried flaked peppers). You'll see – and smell – mini-mountains of *ızot* in Urfa's market area. Look out also for bottles of pomegranate dressing – used to add a sweet but zingy touch to most salads around town.

It pays to be a bit careful what you eat in Urfa, especially in summer, because the heat makes food poisoning more likely. Alcohol is not usually served, but an exception is the restaurant at the Aslan Konuk Evi guesthouse.

Beyaz Köşk KEBAPÇI €
TOP CHOICE (Akarbaşı Göl Cadessi 20; mains TL4-7) Turkey's best *lahmacun* (Arabic-style pizza) restaurants reputedly huddle in the labyrinth of lanes in the Gölbaşı area, and the 'White House' is a great place to try plate-covering pizza studded with spicy *ızot*. Also served is *ciğer* kebap (grilled skewered liver), a popular breakfast. Grab an upstairs table on the breezy terrace and observe Urfa's gentle mayhem down below as you dig in.

Gülhan Restaurant RESTAURANT €€
(Atatürk Caddesi; mains TL6-12) Razor-sharp waiters (wearing ties); well-presented food that impresses rather than threatens; the right mood; slick and salubrious surrounds; a pictorial menu with English translations to help you choose – all good ingredients. For dessert, don't miss the *şıllık*.

Çift Mağara RESTAURANT €€
(Çift Kubbe Altı Balıklıgöl; mains TL7-12) The dining room is directly carved into the rocky bluff that overlooks the Gölbaşı, but the lovely terrace for dining alfresco beats the cavernous interior (views!). It's famed for its delicious *içli köfte*.

Zahter Kahvaltı & Kebap Salonu LOKANTA €
(Köprübaşı Caddesi; mains TL4-7) Skip your hotel's breakfast and instead wolf down gooey honey, *pekmez* (grape syrup), jam and cream on flat bread at this cute little place on the main drag. Wash it all down with a large glass of çay or *ayran* – all for around TL6.

Baklavacı Badıllı Dedeoğlu PATISSERIE €
(Sarayönü Caddesi; pastries TL2) Death by pistachio baklavas and pistachio *sarması* ('vine leaves'). Pick your sweet poison and thicken your arteries.

Büyükfırat RESTAURANT €
(Sarayönü Caddesi; mains TL5-10) With a fountain and breezy outdoor seating, this restaurant-cafe-fast-food place dishes up burgers, pizzas, stews and kebaps, and freshly squeezed orange juice.

🍷 Drinking

For a cup of tea in leafy surrounds, head for the various *çay bahçesis* (tea gardens) in the Gölbaşı park. For a cold beer, book in for dinner at the Aslan Konuk Evi.

Gümrük Hanı COFFEE HOUSE
(Urfa bazaar; coffee TL2; ⊙7am-5pm) Here's the ideal spot for the first coffee of the day – a

Urfa is famed for its atmospheric *konuk evi* – charming 19th-century stone mansions that have been converted into restaurants and, to a lesser extent, hotels. They usually feature a courtyard around which are arranged several comfy *şark odası* (Ottoman-style lounges), as well as a few rooms upstairs. They are smart places to rest your head and get a typical Urfa experience but can be noisy at weekends when they host *sıra geceleri* (live music evenings) or weddings. Also note that not all rooms have private facilities, and you're definitely paying a premium for the heritage ambience.

Both the Otel Urhay and the Aslan Konuk Evi offer a similar experience for less.

Beyzade Konak (216 3535; www.beyzadekonak.com, in Turkish; Sarayönü Caddesi, Beyaz Sokak; s/d TL40/80, mains TL6-12;) Good food and comfy lounges but the rooms don't quite live up to the atmospheric surrounds.

Çardaklı Köşk (Vali Fuat Caddesi, Tünel Çıkışı; mains TL8-15) This old house has been so restored it feels almost new. Food is only so-so – the real wow is the view over Gölbaşı from the upstairs terrace. No accommodation.

Cevahir Konuk Evi (215 4678; www.cevahirkonukevi.com, in Turkish; Yeni Mahalle Sokak; s/d TL150/180, mains TL8-12;) Excellent *tebbule* (tabouleh) and faultlessly cooked *tavuk şiş* (roast chicken kebap) is served on the expansive terrace. Accommodation-wise, the rooms are disappointing, with kitsch paintings of Ye Olde Ottoman times and mismatched antique furniture.

Gülizar Konukevi (215 0505; www.gulizarkonukevi.net, in Turkish; Divan Yolu Caddesi 23; s/d TL50/80, mains TL8-15;) Recently relocated on Urfa's main street, the Gülizar Konukevi features six rooms in a restored mansion. It serves good food and is a popular wedding venue so book ahead and be prepared for party times on weekends.

Yıldız Sarayı Konukevi (215 9494; www.yildizsarayikonukevi.com, in Turkish; Yıldız Meydanı, 944 Sokak; s/d TL50/80, mains TL8-12;) This magnificent courtyard residence has a wide array of rooms – sleep on mattresses on the floor or in more traditional bedrooms. There's also an on-site hamam, trimmed with gorgeous turquoise tiles from İznik.

wonderfully restored caravanserai crowded with locals enjoying a caffeine hit. Ask for *kahve mirra*, the super-strong and bitter local variation. You're not at Starbucks now...

Şampiyon Vitamin CAFE
(Akarbaşi Göl Cadessi; juices from TL2; 7am-10pm) Recharge and replenish your inner traveller at this terrific fresh juice bar on the edge on the Urfa bazaar. It's all good, but we found the zingy *greyfurt suyu* (grapefruit juice) especially refreshing. If you're after something more substantial, the *atom* is a delicious smoothie combining yoghurt, banana and chopped pistachios – almost a mini-meal in itself.

☆ Entertainment

Urfa is an equivocal city: pious during the day, wild in the evening. What makes the city tick is the *sıra geceleri* that are held in the *konuk evi* usually at weekends. Guests sit, eat, sing and dance in *şark odası* (Ottoman-style lounges) and, after the meal, a live band plays old favourites that keep revellers rocking and dancing. Foreigners are welcome to join the party and showcase their dance repertoire. BYO earplugs if you're sleeping upstairs.

Information

The post office, internet cafes and ATMs are on Urfa's main drag.

Harran-Nemrut Tours (215 1575, 0542 761 3065; www.aslankonukevi.com; Demokrasi Caddesi 12) A small travel agency efficiently run by Özcan Aslan, a local teacher who speaks very good English and is a mine of local information. He organises tours to nearby sites, including Harran, Şuayb City, Soğmatar, Mardin and Nemrut Dağı; he can also arrange car rental (per day TL80). You'll find him at the Aslan Konuk Evi guesthouse.

Tourist kiosk (0535 334 7482; serdaravic 78@hotmail.com; Sarayönü Caddesi) Local tourist guide Serdar Avci can supply maps and English-language information.

DESTINATION	FARE (TL)	DURATION (HR)	DISTANCE (KM)	FREQUENCY (PER DAY)
Adana	30	6	365	frequent buses
Ankara	55	13	850	5-6 buses
Diyarbakır	15	3	190	frequent buses
Erzurum	50	12	665	1 bus
Gaziantep	15	2½	145	frequent buses
İstanbul	70	20	1290	a few buses
Kayseri	35	9	515	2 buses
Malatya	25	7	395	1 bus
Mardin	20	3	175	a few buses
Van	40	9	585	2 buses

❶ Getting There & Away

Air

The airport is 45km from Urfa on the road to Diyarbakır. Ask about the Havas bus at **Kalıru Turizm** (☑215 3344; fax 216 3245; Sarayönü Caddesi; ⊗8.30am-6.30pm). **Turkish Airlines** (www.thy.com) has daily flights to/from Ankara (from TL29) and İstanbul (TL59).

Bus

Urfa's new otogar is 5km north of town off the road to Diyarbakır. Note: some buses will drop passengers at a roundabout around 300m from the otogar. Buses to the otogar can be caught on Atatürk Caddesi (TL2). Taxis usually ask TL15. Minibuses to Akçakale (TL4), Harran (TL4), Kahta (TL12.50) and Adıyaman (TL10, two hours) leave from the regional minibus terminal underneath the otogar. If you're travelling to Syria, catch a minibus to Akçakale, then catch a taxi over the border to Talabiyya. Note that because Turkish citizens no longer need visas for Syria, the border can be very busy, especially at weekends.

Car

For car hire (around TL80 per day) try **Kalıru Turizm** (☑215 3344; fax 216 3245; Sarayönü Caddesi; ⊗8.30am-6.30pm) or **Harran-Nemrut Tours** (☑215 1575, 0542 761 3065; www.aslankonukevi.com; Demokrasi Caddesi 12).

Harran

☑0414 / POP 6900

Harran is reputedly one of the oldest continuously inhabited spots on earth. The Book of Genesis mentions Harran and its most famous resident, Abraham, who stayed here for a few years way back in 1900 BC.

Its ruined walls and Ulu Cami, crumbling fortress and beehive houses are powerful, evocative sights that give the town a feeling of deep antiquity. Traditionally, locals lived by farming and smuggling, but the coming of the Atatürk Dam now sees cotton fields sprouting over what was once arid desert.

On arrival in Harran you are officially expected to buy a ticket (TL3), but there may not be anyone in the booth to collect the money. If anyone in the castle tries to charge you, insist on being given the official ticket. Harran is an easy day trip by public minibus from Şanlıurfa. Good luck dealing with the cheeky local kids who can be slightly annoying.

History

Besides being the place of Abraham's sojourn, Harran is famous as a centre of worship of Sin, god of the moon. Worship of the sun, moon and planets was popular in Harran, and at neighbouring Soğmatar, from about 800 BC until AD 830, although Harran's temple to the moon god was destroyed by the Byzantine emperor Theodosius in AD 382. Battles between Arabs and Byzantines occupied the townsfolk until the Crusaders came. The fortress, which some say was built on the ruins of the moon god's temple, was restored when the Crusaders approached. The Crusaders won and maintained it for a while before they, too, moved on.

◉ Sights

Beehive Houses   HISTORIC AREA

Harran is famous for its beehive houses, the design of which may date back to the 3rd century BC, although the present examples were mostly constructed within the last 200 years. It's thought that the design evolved partly in response to a lack of wood for roofs and partly because the ruins provided a source of reusable bricks. Although the Harran houses are unique in Turkey, similar buildings can be found in northern Syria.

The **Harran Kültür Evi**, within walking distance of the castle, is set up to allow visitors to see inside one of the houses and then sip cold drinks in the walled courtyard afterwards. The **Harran Evi** is similar.

Kale
FORTRESS

On the far (east) side of the hill, the crumbling *kale* stands right by some beehive houses. A castle probably already existed here from Hittite times, but the current construction dates mainly from after 1059 when the Fatimids took over and restored it. Originally, there were four multi-angular corner towers, but only two remain. There were also 150 rooms here, but many of these have caved in or are slowly filling up with silt.

City Walls
RUINS

The crumbling stone city walls were once 4km long and studded with 187 towers and four gates. Of these, only the overly restored **Aleppo Gate**, near the new part of town, remains.

Ulu Cami
MOSQUE

Of the ruins inside the village other than the *kale*, the Ulu Cami, built in the 8th century by Marwan II, last of the Umayyad caliphs, is most prominent. You'll recognise it by its tall, square and very un-Turkish minaret. It's said to be the oldest mosque in Anatolia. Near here stood the first Islamic university, and on the hillside above it you'll see the low-level ruins of ancient Harran dating back some 5000 years.

❶ Getting There & Away

Minibuses (TL4, one hour) leave from Urfa's otogar approximately every hour and will drop you at the new part of Harran near the *belediye* and PTT – it's a 10-minute walk to the old part. Minibus traffic back to Urfa diminishes from midafternoon so it's best to ask for details at the Urfa bus station before you leave in the morning.

Around Harran

Although the sites beyond Harran are missable if you're pushed for time, it would be a shame not to see the astonishing transformation wrought on the local scenery by the GAP project – field upon field of cotton and barley where once there was just desert.

To get around the sites without your own transport is virtually impossible unless you have limitless time. The roads have been upgraded over the last few years but signage is insufficient, so the tours offered by **Harran-Nemrut Tours** (☏0414-215 1575, 0542 761 3065; www.aslankonukevi.com; Demokrasi Caddesi 12) in Şanlıurfa are certainly worth considering. Costing TL25 per person for three or more people, you visit Harran, Han el Ba'rur, Şuayb City and Soğmatar, with a chance to take tea with villagers. Expect a simple taxi service with often limited English-language guidance. You may need to take a picnic lunch, or you might have a village lunch stop. It's useful to have a pocketful of change for the tips you'll be expected to give.

Another option for an organised tour is **Nomad Tours Turkey** (☏0533 747 1850; www.nomadtoursturkey.com).

Bazda Caves
RUINS

About 20km east of Harran you can visit the impressive Bazda Caves (signed 'Bazda Mağaları'), which are supposed to have been used to build the walls of Harran.

Han el Ba'rur
RUINS

A further 6km east are the remains of the Seljuk Han el Ba'rur, a caravanserai built in 1128 to service the local trade caravans. Minor restoration work has been done here.

Şuayb City
RUINS

Another 12km northeast of Han el Ba'rur are the extensive remains of Şuayb City, where hefty stone walls and lintels survive above a network of subterranean rooms. One of these contains a mosque on the site of the supposed home of the prophet Jethro. Once again, don't expect to find any services, and it's a good idea to bring a torch (flashlight) and to wear sturdy shoes.

Soğmatar
RUINS

About 18km north of Şuayb, the isolated village of Soğmatar is a very atmospheric, eerie place, surrounded by a barren landscape with bare rocks and ledges. On one of the ledges there was once an open-air temple, where sacrifices were made to the sun and moon gods, whose effigies can be seen carved into the side of the ledge. Like Harran, Soğmatar was a centre for the cult worship of Sin, the moon god, from about AD 150 to AD 200. This open-air altar was the central, main temple. In a cave near the

Around one hour north of Şanlıurfa, the sleepy Kurdish village of Yuvacali hosts one of the only homestay programs in eastern Turkey. Accommodation is in a simple, but spotless, village house with basic, shared facilities and the attention of a friendly Kurdish family. During summer the best sleeping option is on the roof, under the stars, waking up to the early-morning sounds of the host family's fat-tailed sheep. They're the same sheep that provide milk for the homemade cheese and yoghurt – a perfect accompaniment to freshly made and still-warm flatbread for breakfast. Dinner is also a shared affair, with grilled chicken, bulghur wheat and fresh salads.

The Yuvacali homestay program supports the local kindergarten and school, and is a friendly and relaxed option to break up the usual southeastern Anatolian routine of cheap pensions and hotels. See **Nomad Tours Turkey** (☑0533 747 1850; www.nomad toursturkey.com; per person TL25, with full board TL60) for more details. Transfers from Hilvan – on the main highway from Diyarbakır to Şanlıurfa – to Yuvacali are TL5.

Run by knowledgeable expat (and Yuvacali resident), Alison Tanik, Nomad also runs full-day tours to Harran (€50), Şanlıurfa (€40), Nemrut Dağı (€100) and Diyarbakır (€60). Longer multiday tours incorporate Mardin, Midyat and Hasankeyf, and trips to Syria and Iraqi Kurdistan are also possible. See the website for full details.

centre of the village you'll find 12 carved statues as well as Assyrian inscriptions.

Standing on the summit of the structure, you can see remains of other temples on the surrounding hills. There were apparently seven in all.

Once again there are no services at Soğmatar, although villagers will no doubt be happy to point out the sites.

Kahta

☑0416 / POP 60,700

Dusty Kahta doesn't exactly scream 'Holiday', but it's well set up for visits to Nemrut Dağı with tours and hotels on tap. Accommodation actually on the mountain, such as the Karadut Pension, Çeşme Pansion and Hotel Euphrat, is more inspiring and scenic.

Around 25 June, the three-day **International Kahta Kommagene Festival** has music and folk dancing. It's essential to book accommodation ahead at this time.

🛏 Sleeping

Hotel Kommagene & Camping PENSION €
(☑725 5385, 0532 200 3856; kommagenem@ hotmail.com; Mustafa Kemal Caddesi 1; camp sites per person TL8, caravans TL18, per person with-out/with bathroom TL18/25; ❊) The most obvious choice for budget-minded travellers, not so much because of its inherent merits but because of the lack of competitors in this price bracket. Rooms are clean and secure, some with comfy new beds. Campers

can pitch their tent on the parking lot, and the ablutions block is shipshape. Add TL7 for breakfast. Expect some insistent selling of tours to Nemrut and beyond at some point. An all-inclusive deal incorporating one night's accommodation and a Nemrut trip is TL95 per person – it can use alternative hotels in the area. Other multiday tours around eastern Turkey are available through **Mezopotamya Tours & Travel** (☑0532 200 3856; www.nemruttours.info).

Zeus Hotel HOTEL €€
(☑725 5694; www.zeushotel.com.tr; Mustafa Kemal Caddesi; camp sites per person TL20, s/d €60/80; ❊❊) This solid three-star option gets an A+ for its swimming pool in the manicured garden – blissful after a long day's travelling by bus. Angle for the renovated rooms, which feature top-notch bathrooms and flat-screen TVs. Campers can pitch tents on the parking lot, and have their own ablutions block.

🍴 Eating

All accommodation options have restaurants. For something different take a taxi (about TL10) to the vast lake formed by the Atatürk Dam, about 4km east of Kahta. The lure is the licensed restaurants serving fresh fish, with lovely views over the lake.

Papatya Restaurant LOKANTA €
(Mustafa Kemal Caddesi; mains TL5-8) This snappy place opposite the Zeus Hotel whips up all the usual suspects. There's no menu – just point at what you want.

Kahta Sofrası LOKANTA €
(Mustafa Kemal Caddesi; mains TL5-8) Just off the main intersection, this simple spot dishes up tasty kebaps and melt-in-your-mouth pide.

Akropalian RESTAURANT-BAR €€
(Baraj Yolu; mains TL7-11) Perched on a hillside, about 1km from the lakeshore. Bag a seat in the verdant *bahçe* and drink in the views.

Neşetin Yeri RESTAURANT-BAR €€
(Baraj Yolu; mains TL7-11) The leafy garden is soothingly positioned right by the lakeside (avoid the hospital-like dining room). Tuck into a faultless grilled *alabalık* (trout), served in a *kiremit* (clay pot).

❶ Getting There & Away

Kahta's small otogar is in the town centre, with the minibus and taxi stands right beside it. There are regular buses to Adıyaman (TL2, 30 minutes, 32km), Ankara (TL45, 12 hours, 807km), İstanbul (TL70, 20 hours, 1352km), Kayseri (TL40, seven hours, 487km), Malatya (TL15, 3½ hours, 225km) and Şanlıurfa (TL12, 2½ hours, 106km).

There are minibuses every couple of hours to Karadut (TL7). They return from Karadut between 7.30am and 8.30am the next day.

The road east to Diyarbakır was flooded by the lake formed behind the Atatürk Dam, and buses from Kahta now travel to Diyarbakır north of the lake (TL22, five hours, 174km). A more interesting way to travel is via minibus to Siverek, timed to meet the ferries across the lake. In Siverek you may have to wait half an hour or so for a connection to Diyarbakır, but some departures do go all the way through to Diyarbakır.

Nemrut Dağı National Park

Mt Nemrut National Park (Nemrut Dağı Milli Parkı) is probably the star attraction of eastern Turkey. The enigmatic statues sitting atop the summit have become a symbol of the country. The stunning scenery and historical sights, and the undeniable sense of mystique and folly that emanates from the site, make a visit here essential.

The spellbinding peak of **Nemrut Dağı** (*nehm*-root dah-uh) rises to a height of 2150m in the Anti-Taurus Range between the provincial capital of Malatya to the north and Kahta in Adıyaman province to the south.

Nobody knew anything about Nemrut Dağı until 1881, when a German engineer,

employed by the Ottomans to assess transport routes, was astounded to come across the statues covering this remote mountaintop. Archaeological work didn't begin until 1953, when the American School of Oriental Research undertook the project.

The summit was created when a megalomaniac pre-Roman local king cut two ledges in the rock, filled them with colossal statues of himself and the gods (his relatives – or so he thought), then ordered an artificial mountain peak of crushed rock 50m high to be piled between them. The king's tomb and those of three female relatives may well lie beneath those tonnes of rock. Nobody knows for sure.

Earthquakes have toppled the heads from most of the statues, and now many of the colossal bodies sit silently in rows with the 2m-high heads watching from the ground.

Although it's relatively easy to get to the summit with your own vehicle, most people take tours, organised in either Kahta or Malatya or, increasingly, as a day trip from Şanlıurfa or Cappadocia.

Plan to visit Nemrut between late May and mid-October, and preferably in July or August; the road to the summit becomes impassable with snow at other times. Even in high summer it will be chilly and windy on top of the mountain. This is especially true at sunrise, the coldest time of the day. Take warm clothing on your trek to the top no matter when you go.

There are various accommodation options on the mountain. Stunning views and the peaceful setting make up for any lack of mod cons. Check that adequate blankets are provided.

There are three ways of approaching the summit. From the southern side, you pass through **Karadut**, a village some 12km from the top, before embarking upon the last few kilometres to the car park. From the southwestern side, you travel via a secondary road that goes past **Eski Kale** (Arsameia) and climbs steeply for about 10km until it merges with the Karadut road, some 6km before the car park at the summit. From the northern side, you can start from Malatya – it's a long 98km haul, but it's a very scenic drive and the road is (largely) asphalted until the Güneş Hotel, near the summit. Note that it is not possible to cross the summit by car from the northern side to the southern side.

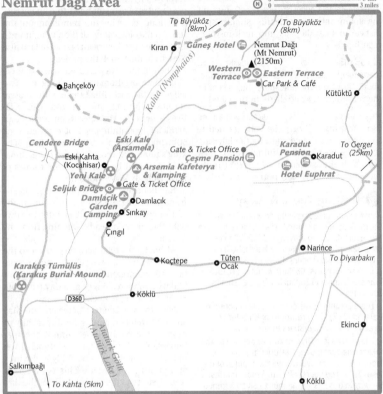

It costs TL6.50 to enter Mt Nemrut National Park. Coming from the southwest, the entrance gate is at the turn-off to Eski Kale; from the south, the gate is just past Çeşme Pansion; from the north, the gate is at the Güneş Hotel.

History

From 250 BC onwards, this region straddled the border between the Seleucid Empire (which followed the empire of Alexander the Great in Anatolia) and the Parthian Empire to the east, also occupying a part of Alexander's lands. A small but strategic area, rich, fertile and covered in forests, it had a history of independent thinking ever since the time of King Samos (c 163 BC).

Under the Seleucid Empire, the governor of Commagene declared his kingdom's independence. In 80 BC, with the Seleucids in disarray and Roman power spreading into Anatolia, a Roman ally named Mithridates I Callinicus proclaimed himself king and set up his capital at Arsameia, near the modern village of Eski Kahta. Mithridates prided himself on his royal ancestry, tracing his forebears back to Seleucus I Nicator, founder of the Seleucid Empire to the west, and to Darius the Great, king of ancient Persia to the east.

Mithridates died in 64 BC and was succeeded by his son Antiochus I Epiphanes (r 64–38 BC), who consolidated his kingdom's security by immediately signing a nonaggression treaty with Rome, turning his kingdom into a Roman buffer against attack from the Parthians. His good relations with both sides allowed him to grow rich and revel in delusions of grandeur, seeing himself as equal to the great god-kings of the past. It was Antiochus who ordered the building of the fabulous temples and funerary mound on top of Nemrut.

In the 3rd decade of his reign, Antiochus sided with the Parthians in a squabble with

Rome, and in 38 BC the Romans deposed him. From then on, Commagene was alternately ruled directly from Rome or by puppet kings until AD 72, when Emperor Vespasian incorporated it into Roman Asia. The great days of Commagene were thus limited to the 26-year reign of Antiochus.

⊙ Sights & Activities

Karakuş Tümülüs   LANDMARK
Highway D360, marked for Nemrut Dağı Milli Parkı (9km), starts in Kahta next to the Hotel Kommagene. After a few kilometres, you'll reach a fork; the road to the left takes you 1.5km to Karakuş Tümülüs. Like the Nemrut mound, the Karakuş burial mound, built in 36 BC, is artificial. A handful of columns ring the mound – there were more but the limestone blocks were used by the Romans to build the Cendere Bridge. An eagle tops a column at the car park, a lion tops another around the mound, and a third has an inscribed slab explaining that the burial mound holds female relatives of King Mithridates II.

Cendere Bridge   BRIDGE
Some 10km from the Karakuş Tümülüs, the road crosses a modern bridge over the Cendere River. On the left-hand side, you'll see a magnificent humpback Roman bridge built in the 2nd century AD. The surviving Latin stelae state that the bridge was built in honour of Emperor Septimius Severus and his wife and sons (long after Commagene had become part of Roman Asia). Of the four original Corinthian columns (two at either end), three are still standing.

Eski Kahta (Kocahisar) & Yeni Kale RUINS
About 5km from the bridge is a 1km detour off the main road to **Eski Kahta** (Kocahisar). There was once a palace here, built at the same time as the Commagene capital of Arsameia. What you now see are the ruins of a 13th-century Mamluk castle, **Yeni Kale** (New Fortress). The castle was being renovated at the time of writing and due to reopen in 2011.

At the base of the path up to the castle is the **Kocahisar Halı Kursu** (Kocahisar Carpet Course), a rudimentary workshop where local women learn carpet-weaving techniques to keep the tradition alive. They don't sell the carpets here, but it's OK to have a look around.

After Yeni Kale, cross the Kahta (Nymphaios) River to see the old road and the graceful **Seljuk Bridge**.

Eski Kale (Arsameia)   RUINS
About 1.5km further along the main road, a road to the left takes you 2km to Eski Kale, the ancient Commagene capital of Arsameia. Just after the turn-off is the park entrance for payment for the Arsameia site and summit access (TL6.50).

At Eski Kale there is a large **stele** depicting Mithras (or Apollo), the sun god, wearing a cap with sunrays radiating from it. Further along are two more stelae. Only the bases have survived, but they were thought to depict Mithridates I Callinicus, with Antiochus I, the taller stele, holding a sceptre. Behind them is a cave entrance leading to an underground room thought to have been built for Mithras-worshipping rites.

Further uphill is a virtually undamaged **stone relief** portraying Mithridates I shaking hands with the god Heracles. Just adjacent another cave temple descends 158m through the rock. The steps into the temple are dangerous. The long Greek inscription above the cave describes the founding of Arsameia; the water trough beside it may have been used for religious ablutions.

On the hilltop above are the ruined foundations of Mithridates' capital city.

Arsameia to the Summit
From Arsameia you can take the 16km partly surfaced short cut to the summit or backtrack to the main road, which is a longer route but less steep and fully surfaced. The short cut leaves from beside the entrance to Arsameia and slogs up the mountain for about 8km to join the main route about 6km before the summit car park. It's passable only during daytime and in dry weather. The last 2km is unsealed and the road has precipitous hairpin bends.

Most tours combine the two routes, thus making a loop. Sunrise tours take the longer route (via Narince and Karadut) on the way up and take the short cut to descend back to Kahta. Sunset tours take the short cut on the way up and the longer route to get back to Kahta.

If you take the longer route from Arsameia, return to the main road and turn left. About 3km further is the sleepy village of Damlacık. At Narince, a turn-off to the left is marked for Nemrut. North of Karadut, the last half-hour's travel (12km) is very steep.

Hiking
Travellers staying in Karadut can walk the 12km to the summit. It's a clearly marked road with a steady gradient.

ORGANISED TOURS TO NEMRUT DAĞI (MT NEMRUT)

The main tour centres are Kahta and Malatya, but there are also tours from Karadut, Şanlıurfa and Cappadocia.

From Karadut

Several pensions in Karadut offer return trips to the summit, with one hour at the top, for about TL50 per vehicle (Karadut Pension) or TL75 (Hotels Euphrat or Kervansaray).

From Kahta

Kahta has always had a reputation as a rip-off town so you will need to be wary of what's on offer. Always check exactly what you will be seeing during the tour, in addition to the heads themselves, and how long you'll be away for. The hotels and guesthouses in Kahta run most of the tours to Nemrut Dağı.

The majority of tours are timed to capture a dramatic sunrise or sunset. If you opt for the 'sunrise tours', you'll leave Kahta at about 2am via Narince and Karadut, arriving at Nemrut Dağı for sunrise. After an hour or so, you'll go down again following the upgraded direct road to Arsameia. Then you'll stop at Eski Kahta, Yeni Kale, Cendere Bridge and Karakuş Tümülüs. Expect to be back in Kahta at about 10am. If you sign up for the 'sunset tour', you'll do the same loop but in the reverse direction – in other words, you'll leave at 1.30pm and start with the sights around Arsameia, then go up to the summit, before descending via Karadut and Narince. You'll be back in Kahta by 9.30pm.

A third option is the 'small tour', which lasts about three hours. It zips you from Kahta to the summit and back again, allowing about an hour for sightseeing. It's less expensive, but much less interesting. Mezopotamya Tours & Travel at the Hotel Kommagene runs guaranteed daily departures from April to October (per person short/long tour TL60/65).

If you're in a group you may be able to hire a taxi from Kahta for around TL100. We've had occasional reports of some Kahta tour operators putting pressure on local taxi drivers, so good luck negotiating.

Although Kahta hotels and guesthouses advertise these services as 'tours', you'll quickly catch on that they're only taxi services when your driver proffers comments like, 'That's an old bridge.' If you want an informative English-speaking guide, go with **Mehmet Akbaba** (☎0535 295 4445; akbabamehmet@hotmail.com) or **Nemrut Tours** (☎0416-725 6881; Mustafa Kemal Caddesi), based in the Hotel Nemrut. Expect to pay an additional TL150 per group for an English-speaking guide.

The Summit

The **park entrance** (admission TL6.50; ⊙dawn-dusk) is 200m up from Çeşme Pansion and 2.5km before the junction with the short cut to Arsameia.

Beyond the building, hike 600m (about 20 minutes) over the broken rock of the stone pyramid to the **western terrace**. Antiochus I Epiphanes ordered the construction of a combined tomb and temple here. The site was to be approached by a ceremonial road and was to incorporate what Antiochus termed 'the thrones of the gods', which would be based 'on a foundation that will never be demolished'.

The first thing you see is the western temple with the conical funerary mound of fist-sized stones behind it. Antiochus and his fellow gods sit in state, although their bodies have partly tumbled down, along with their heads.

From the western terrace it's five minutes' walk to the **eastern terrace**. Here the bodies are largely intact except for the fallen heads, which seem more badly weathered than the western heads. On the backs of the eastern statues are inscriptions in Greek.

Both terraces have similar plans, with the syncretistic gods, the 'ancestors' of Antiochus, seated. From left to right they are Apollo, the sun god (Mithra to the Persians; Helios or Hermes to the Greeks); Fortuna, or Tyche; in the centre Zeus-Ahura Mazda; then King Antiochus; and on the far right Heracles, also known as Ares or Artagnes.

From Malatya

Malatya offers an alternative way to approach Nemrut Dağı. However, visiting Nemrut from this northern side means you miss out on the other fascinating sights on the southern flanks (reached via Kahta). You can get the best of both worlds by traversing the top by foot and hitching a ride to Kahta; if you're travelling by car you'll have to take the long route via Adıyaman.

The Malatya tourist office organises hassle-free minibus tours to Nemrut Dağı from early May to the end of September, or to mid-October if the weather is still warm. Tours leave at noon from near the tourist information booth in the tea garden behind the *valiliği* (provincial government offices). Ask for Kemal at one of the tea shops.

The three-hour ride through dramatic scenery to the summit is asphalted all the way up. After enjoying the sunset for two hours, you overnight at the Güneş Hotel before heading back up to the summit for sunrise. After breakfast at the Güneş, you return to Malatya at around 10am.

The per-person cost of TL100 (minimum two people) includes transport, dinner, bed and breakfast, but excludes admission to the national park and the site. In theory, there are daily tours, but solo travellers may have to pay more if no-one else wants to join you.

From Şanlıurfa

Tours (TL100 per person, minimum two) to Nemrut are available from **Harran-Nemrut Tours** (www.aslankonukevi.com) in Şanlıurfa. Unlike other tours, they arrrive at Nemrut around 10am. You're missing out on sunset or sunrise, but the upside is far less people at the summit when you visit. The cost per person reduces to TL75 for groups of four or more.

Nomad Tours Turkey (www.nomadtoursturkey.com), based in the Kurdish village of Yuvacali, also runs full-day tours (€100 per person).

From Cappadocia

Many companies in Cappadocia (p455) offer minibus tours to Nemrut from mid-April to mid-November, despite the distance of over 500km each way. Two-day tours cost about TL280 and involve many hours of breakneck driving. If you have enough time, it's better to opt for a three-day tour, which allows the journey to be broken into more manageable chunks. Three-day tours usually also include Harran and Şanlıurfa. Ask for details on night stops and driving times before committing.

Low walls at the sides of each temple once held carved reliefs showing processions of ancient Persian and Greek royalty, Antiochus' 'predecessors'. Statues of eagles represent Zeus.

🛏 Sleeping & Eating

There are several places to stay along the roads to the summit. The village of Karadut has a few small eateries. Places are listed in order of appearance, starting from the southwestern side (Eski Kale) up to the summit.

Damlacık Garden Camping CAMPGROUND €
(☎0416-741 2027; tavsi_camping@hotmail.com; camp sites per person TL8; @) At Damlacık, about 2km from the junction for the entrance gate, this simple camping ground has a welcoming host family and grassed camping areas. There's also a secure parking lot for campervans, equipped with electricity. Meals are available (TL10). Transport to Nemrut is TL100 per vehicle.

Arsemia Kafeterya & Kamping
CAMPGROUND €
(☎0416-741 2224, 0533 682 1242; kal_bin_sasi@hotmail.com; camp sites per person TL6) Pitch your tent or park your campervan on a well laid-out ridge (no grass or shade) and enjoy valley views. Simple meals are available (TL10). Transport to Nemrut costs TL80 per vehicle. It's in Eski Kale, about 1km past the entrance gate. The easygoing owners can arrange trekking and fishing excursions in the surrounding valleys.

Karadut Pension
PENSION €

(☑0416-737 2169, 0532 566 2857; www.karadut pansiyon.net; camp sites per person TL5, d per person TL25; ❄ @) This pension-cum-hostel at the northern end of Karadut has 14 neat, if compact, rooms (some with air-con), cleanish bathrooms and a shared kitchen. Meals are available (TL10) along with a tipple (wine, beer or rakı) in the alfresco terrace bar. Campers can pitch their tent in a partially shaded plot at the back, with good views over the mountains and a super-clean ablutions block. It's regularly used by overland tour groups, so booking ahead is recommended.

Çeşme Pension
PENSION €

(☑0416-737 2032; www.cesmepansion.com; camp sites per person TL5, per person half-board TL40) The closest shut-eye option to the summit (only 6km; the owners will drive you there for TL40). The rooms (all with private bathrooms) are basic but clean, and campers will enjoy a shaded garden setting.

Hotel Euphrat
HOTEL €€

(☑0416-737 2175; www.hoteleuphratnemrut.com, in Turkish; s/d with half-board TL80/160; ❄ ☀) The low-rise Euphrat is popular with tour groups in peak season. Recent renovations have made the rooms larger and more comfortable, and the views from the restaurant terrace and new pool are spectacular. The food is very good, including freshly baked bread every morning.

Güneş Hotel
HOTEL €

(☑0535 760 5080, 0542 2720 0130; nemruttour malatya@yahoo.com; half-board per person TL50) Standing in Gothic isolation about 2.5km from the eastern terrace, and in the valley below, this hotel is of use mostly to those coming up from Malatya. The setting is dramatic (bordering on spooky on a cloudy day), amid rocky boulders, the hush is enjoyable and the rooms are ordinary yet clean.

❶ Getting There & Away

Car

To ascend the southern slopes of Nemrut from Kahta, drive along the D360 via Narince, or take a longer but more scenic route that includes Karakuş, Cendere, Eski Kahta and Arsameia, then the 15km short cut to the summit. Make sure you have fuel for at least 250km of normal driving. Though the trip to the summit and back is at most 160km, you have to drive some of that in low gear, which uses more fuel. Be prepared for the rough, steep last 3km up to the summit.

You can also approach the summit from Malatya (98km one way) and drive up to the Güneş Hotel. The road is mainly surfaced, but be prepared for lots of roadworks along the very scenic route. From there, a rough road leads to the eastern terrace, a further 2.5km. It's OK with a normal car in dry weather, but definitely only for confident drivers.

Note there is no road at the summit linking the southern and the northern sides, but a (very!) rough road does skirt the base of the mountain linking the Kahta (southern) side to the Malatya (northern) side. From Kocahisar, a road goes 21km to the village of Büyüköz. The first 7km, up to the village of Kıran, are surfaced. The next 6km, on to the hamlet of Taşkale, deteriorate markedly and gradually become gravel; the last 8km, up to Büyüköz, are unsurfaced and the road is narrow and very steep (expect nerve-racking twists and turns). The distance is shorter than backtracking via Adıyaman, but the road is very poor and only for confident drivers. Look forward to losing a few hubcaps as well. Don't brave it in wet weather and seek local advice at Kocahisar (if you're coming from Kahta and going to Malatya) or at Büyüköz (if you're doing Malatya–Kahta) before setting off.

Taxi & Minibus

During the summer season there are minibuses (TL10) around every two hours between Kahta and the Çeşme Pension, about 6km from the summit. They stop at Karadut village (TL7) on the way. Pension owners can also pick you up at Kahta's otogar (but set the price beforehand). Don't believe anyone in Kahta who tells you there are no minibuses to the Çeşme Pension and Karadut village from Kahta.

All pensions and hotels can run you up to the summit and back, but don't expect anything in the way of guidance. The closer to the summit, the cheaper it will be. Hotels in Kahta charge about TL150 for a whole minibus (up to eight people), while Çeşme Pension charges only TL40.

Malatya

☑0422 / POP 600,000 / ELEV 964M

What percentage of *yabancı* (foreigners) traversing central Anatolia en route to eastern Turkey actually stop in Malatya? Definitely not enough.

The architecture wins no prizes and sights are sparse, but the city soon grows on you. Malatya's rewards include verdant parks, tree-lined boulevards, chaotic bazaars and the smug feeling that you're the only tourist for miles around. For cultural sustenance, there's the nearby historic site of Battalgazi.

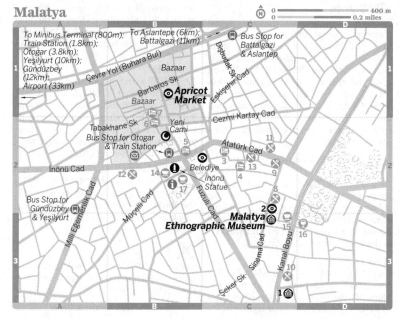

Malatya is also Turkey's *kayısı* (apricot) capital, and after the late-June harvest, thousands of tonnes of the luscious fruit are shipped internationally.

Malatya stretches along İnönü/Atatürk Caddesi, but travellers' needs are clustered near the main square with its massive statue of İsmet İnönü, Turkey's second president after Atatürk.

Malatya also offers tours to Nemrut Dağı.

History

The Assyrians and Persians alternately conquered the city, and later the kings of Cappadocia and Pontus did the same. In 66 BC Pompey defeated Mithridates and took the town, then known as Melita. The Byzantines, Sassanids, Arabs and Danışmend *emirs* held it until the Seljuks arrived in 1105. Then came the Ottomans (1399), the armies of Tamerlane (1401), Mamluks, Dülkadır *emirs* and the Ottomans again (1515).

When the forces of Egypt's Mohammed Ali invaded Anatolia in 1839, the Ottoman forces garrisoned Malatya, leaving much of it in ruins on their departure. Later the residents returned and established a new city on the present site. You can visit the remains of old Malatya (Eski Malatya), now called Battalgazi, nearby.

⦿ Sights

Bazaar MARKET

Malatya's vibrant market sprawls north from PTT Caddesi and the Malatya Büyük Otel. Especially fascinating is the lively metalworking area. Brush up your Turkish and wind your way to the **Apricot Market** *(kayisi pazarı* or *şire pazarı).* You won't leave Malatya without filling your bags with the fruit. It's a major crime if you skip town without trying the sensational chocolate-covered apricots.

FREE **Malatya Ethnographic Museum**

MUSEUM

(Sinema Caddesi; ⊗8am-5pm) Great English-language information brings alive this showcase of jewellery, weaving and a fearsome collection of old weapons. It's all housed in one of five restored **old Malatyan houses** along Sinema Caddesi.

Museum MUSEUM

(Fuzuli Caddesi; admission TL3; ⊗8am-5pm Tue-Sun) About 750m from the town centre, Malatya's museum has interesting finds from the excavations at Aslantepe.

⎙ Sleeping

Malatya has good-value options, conveniently located in the bazaar and the centre. They are suitable for female travellers.

Grand W Aksaç Hotel HOTEL €€

(☑324 6565; www.aksachotel.com, in Turkish; Saray Mahallesi, Ömer Efendi Sokak 19; s/d TL80/120; ▣) The newly opened Grand W Aksaç celebrates a quiet central location with flash services including a hamam, and shiny and spacious bathrooms. Flat-screen TVs, huge beds and chocolate-covered apricots for sale in reception sound like a winning combination if you've been travelling just a little too quickly.

Grand Sinan Otel HOTEL €€

(☑321 2907; www.grandsinanotel.com; Atatürk Caddesi; s/d TL70/100; ▣) Enjoying a trendy makeover since we last visited, the Grand Sinan has relatively compact rooms decked out in designer colours and equipped with new bathrooms. The main-drag location is convenient, and double-glazing masks most traffic noise. The hip young crew at reception speaks excellent English.

Malatya Büyük Otel HOTEL €€

(☑325 2828; fax 323 2828; Halep Caddesi, Yeni Cami Karşısı; s/d TL50/80; ▣) This characterless monolith behind the Yeni Cami sports serviceable (if smallish) rooms with good bathrooms and dashing views of the huge mosque across the street. The location is very handy – the bazaar is just one block behind.

Yeni Hotel HOTEL €

(☑323 1423; yenihotel@turk.net; Yeni Cami Karşısı Zafer İşhanı; s/d TL45/70; ▣) This well-run establishment enlivens its rooms with pastel hues, electric blue bedspreads and spotless laminated floors. Keen shoppers should relish the location, right on the edge of the market area.

Hotel Pehlivan HOTEL €

(☑321 2609; Cumhuriyet Caddesi; s/d TL35/45) Offering good-value digs on the edge of the market, the Pehlivan has clean and spacious rooms decked out in a variety of colours.

✕ Eating

Atatürk Caddesi is awash with inexpensive eateries, and Kanal Boyu's tree-lined boulevard features hip cafes.

Sarı Kurdela Restaurant & Cafe

RESTAURANT €

(İnönü Caddesi; mains TL6-10) This super-trendy joint ticks all the boxes, with contemporary decor, efficient wait staff and an eclectic menu, including excellent ready-made meals, vegetarian dishes and a wide choice of sweets. Prices are cheaper in the downstairs cafeteria – and the food is just as good.

Beşkonaklar Malatya Mutfaği MUTFAK €€

(Sinema Caddesi; mains TL10-15; ⊗noon-10pm) Housed in the same restored row of houses as the Ethnographic Museum, Beşkonaklar Malatya Mutfaği showcases traditional local food. The interior is crammed with antiques, and if the weather is warm, adjourn to the spacious garden to enjoy interesting dishes like *anali kizli* (soup with marble-sized meatballs and chickpeas).

Mangal Vadisi OCAKBAŞI €€

(Kışla Caddesi; mains TL6-12; ⊗noon-10pm) Vegetarians, don't even bother reading this review: the huge *mangals* (barbecues) that take centre stage on the ground floor set the tone. This well-regarded restaurant has a wide choice of grilled meat, and is in a little street off Atatürk Caddesi.

Sevinç PATISSERIE €

(Atatürk Caddesi; pastries from TL2) This pastry shop features a sleek, modern interior and a batch of mouth-watering desserts, including baklava and cakes. There's a welcoming *aile salonu* (family dining room) upstairs.

Mado CAFE €
(Kanal Boyu; ice creams from TL3) The best outfit for enjoying an ice cream, coffee or pastry in civilised surrounds.

Hacıbey Lahmacun PIDECI €
(Kışla Caddesi; mains TL6-10) Hands down the best joint for a hearty pide or *lahmacun* pizza with a thin, crispy base topped with chopped lamb, onion and tomato, washed down with a refreshing *ayran*.

🍷 Drinking

Nostalji CAFE
TOP CHOICE (Müçelli Caddesi; coffee TL2, snacks TL4-7; ⊙11am-10pm) As soon as you step inside this squeaky-boarded, old Malatya mansion packed with memorabilia, stress quickly evaporates. Soak up the cool karma in the light-filled main lounge while listening to mellow music and sipping Turkish coffee. Simple dishes are also available, and it's a good place to meet students of both sexes.

Vilayet Çay Bahçesi – VIP Cafe TEA GARDEN
(Vilayet Tea Garden; İnönü Caddesi; tea TL1, snacks TL4-8; ⊙8am-9pm) Nab a table at VIP Cafe and chow down on burgers or *gözleme* (thin savoury crepes cooked with cheese, spinach or potato), or linger over a cuppa. No doubt you'll be approached by the friendly Kemal, who runs the Nemrut Dağı information booth nearby.

Semerkant CAFE
(Kanal Boyu; coffee TL2, mains TL3-7; ⊙10am-11pm) We can still smell the sweet aroma of nargileh wafting from the door. This relaxed cafe with a few amusing rustic touches (think fake stone walls and small wooden chairs) is a good place to imbibe the atmosphere of Kanal Boyu.

Taşkent CAFE
(Kanal Boyu; coffee TL2, mains TL3-7; ⊙10am-11pm) Just across the road, the Taşkent cafe offers a similarly laid-back atmosphere with excellent *manti* (Turkish ravioli). Enjoy your Central Asian journey from Samarkand to Tashkent.

ℹ Information

ATMs and internet cafes are plentiful in the centre.

Information booth (⌨0535 760 5080; Atatürk Caddesi; ⊙8am-7pm May-Sep) In the tea garden behind the tourist office – ask for Kemal –

and managed by the Güneş Hotel at Nemrut Dağı. Good English is spoken.

Tourist office (⌨323 2942; Atatürk Caddesi; ⊙9am-5pm Mon-Fri) On the ground floor of the *valiliği* (provincial government headquarters) in the heart of town, with good town maps and useful brochures.

ℹ Getting There & Away

Air
The airport is 35km northwest of the centre. Ask at one of the travel agencies on Atatürk Caddesi about the Havas bus.

Onur Air (www.onurair.com.tr) One daily flight to/from İstanbul (from TL64).

Turkish Airlines (www.thy.com) Two daily flights to/from İstanbul (from TL89), and a daily flight to/from Ankara (from TL89).

Bus
Malatya's enormous otogar, MAŞTİ, is around 4km out on the western outskirts. Most bus companies operate *servises* (shuttle minibuses) there from the town centre. If not, minibuses from the otogar travel along Turgut Özal Bulvarı/ Buhara Bulvarı (aka Çevre Yol). However, they aren't allowed into the town centre. Ask to be let off at the corner of Turan Temelli and Buhara Caddesis, and walk from there. City buses to the otogar leave from near the *vilayet*. A taxi to the otogar costs about TL20.

Car
Meydan Rent a Car (⌨325 3434; www.meydan oto.com.tr, in Turkish; İnönü Caddesi, Sıtmapınarı Ziraat Bankası Bitişiği; ⊙8am-7pm) is a reliable outlet. Other companies dot the city centre.

Train
Right in the middle of Turkey, Malatya is a major railway hub and is well connected by train to the east of the country (Elazığ, Tatvan, Diyarbakır), the west (İstanbul, Ankara, Sivas, Kayseri) and the south (Adana). A train via here can be a good alternative to tiring bus trips.

The *Vangölü Ekspresi* leaves for İstanbul via Sivas, Kayseri and Ankara on Tuesday and Sunday (TL30.75); for Elazığ and Tatvan (TL12.25) it leaves on Wednesday and Sunday.

The *Güney Ekspresi* leaves for İstanbul via Sivas, Kayseri and Ankara on Monday, Wednesday, Friday and Sunday (TL30.75); for Elazığ and Diyarbakır (TL7.50), it departs on Tuesday, Thursday, Saturday and Sunday.

The *4 Eylül Ekspresi* leaves daily for Ankara via Sivas and Kayseri (TL19.75).

The *Firat Ekspresi* leaves daily for Adana (TL15) and for Elazığ (TL5.75).

Check at the train station for exact departure times of all trains.

SERVICES FROM MALATYA'S OTOGAR

DESTINATION	FARE (TL)	DURATION (HR)	DISTANCE (KM)	FREQUENCY (PER DAY)
Adana	25	8	425	a few buses
Adıyaman	12	2½	144	frequent buses
Ankara	30	11	685	frequent buses
Diyarbakır	23	4	260	a few buses
Elazığ	8	1¾	101	hourly buses
Gaziantep	18	4	250	a few buses
İstanbul	50	18	1130	a few buses
Kayseri	20	4	354	several buses
Sivas	25	5	235	several buses

Malatya's train station can be reached by minibus (TL1) or by 'İstasyon' city buses from near the *valiliği*. City buses and minibuses marked 'Vilayet' operate between the station and the centre.

Around Malatya

ASLANTEPE

The scant finds of this archaeological site (⊘8am-5pm), about 6km from Malatya, are not exactly gripping, but if you have an interest in Anatolian archaeology you'll enjoy Aslantepe and its pretty village setting.

When the Phrygians invaded the Hittite kingdom at Boğazkale, around 1200 BC, many Hittites fled southeast over the Taurus Mountains to resettle and build walled cities. The city of Milidia, now known as Aslantepe, was one of these neo-Hittite city-states. On-off excavations since the 1930s have so far uncovered seven layers of remains.

To get to Aslantepe from Malatya, catch a bus marked 'Orduzu' (TL1.50, 15 minutes) from the southern side of Buhara Bulvarı near the junction with Akpınar Caddesi. Buy an extra ticket for the return trip, and tell the driver where you want to get off; the site is a pleasant 500m stroll from the bus stop.

BATTALGAZİ (OLD MALATYA)

You don't need to be an archaeology buff to be captivated by the remains of old Malatya, the walled city settled alongside Aslantepe, about 11km north of Malatya at Battalgazi.

As you come into the village you'll see the ruins of the old **city walls** with their 95 towers, built during Roman times and completed in the 6th century. They've lost all their facing stone to other building projects, and apricot orchards now fill what were once city blocks. The village of Battalgazi has grown in and around the ruins.

The bus from Malatya terminates in the main square. Just off here, beside the mosque boasting the smooth-topped minaret, is the **Silahtar Mustafa Paşa Hanı,** an Ottoman caravanserai dating from the 17th century. At the time of writing it was being restored, and it promises to be a quite majestic structure.

From the caravanserai, turn right and follow Osman Ateş Caddesi for about 600m until you see the broken brick minaret of the finely restored 13th-century **Ulu Cami** on the left. This stunning, if fast-fading, Seljuk building dates from the reign of Alaettin Keykubad I. Note the remaining Seljuk tiles lining the dome over the *mimber* (pulpit) and worked into Arabic inscriptions on the *eyvan* and *medrese* (seminary) walls. Also worthy of interest is the **Ak Minare Camii** (White Minaret Mosque), about 50m from the Ulu Cami. This also dates from the 13th century.

Close by is the 13th-century **Halfetih Minaret,** made completely of bricks, and the **Nezir Gazi Tomb.**

Buses to Battalgazi (TL1.50, 15 minutes) leave every 15 minutes or so from the same bus stop in Malatya as those for Aslantepe. After your archaeological meanderings, grab a bite to eat in Battalgazi's pleasant main square – a sleepy alternative to the busy streets of Malatya.

YEŞİLYURT & GÜNDÜZBEY

In summer, it's a true pleasure to enjoy the refreshingly peaceful atmosphere of Yeşilyurt and Gündüzbey, respectively 10km and 12km from Malatya. Old houses, lots of greenery, pleasing tea gardens, picnic areas...so cool! Take a minibus from Milli Eğemenlik Caddesi in Malatya (TL1.50, 20 minutes) and enjoy the hush.

Diyarbakır

🕿 0412 / POP 665,400 / ELEV 660M

Filled with heart, soul and character, Diyar is finally tapping into its fantastic potential as a destination for travellers. While it's proud of remaining the symbol of Kurdish identity and tenacity, thanks to increasing promotion and restoration programs, Turkish and foreign tourists are streaming back. Behind the grim basalt walls, the old city's twisting alleyways are crammed full of historical buildings and Arab-style mosques.

Speak to Turks from western Turkey and they will recoil in fear if you mention Diyarbakır because, since the 1980s, this animated city has been the centre of the Kurdish resistance movement, and violent street demonstrations still occur from time to time. And yes, nowhere else in eastern Turkey will you hear people priding themselves so much on being Kurdish.

Banned until a few years ago, the Nevruz festival takes place on 21 March and is a great occasion to immerse yourself in Kurdish culture.

Apart from a few slightly annoying street kids, Diyarbakır is as safe as any other city in the region.

History

Mesopotamia, the land between the Tigris and Euphrates Valleys, saw the dawn of the world's first great empires. Diyarbakır's history begins with the Hurrian kingdom of Mitanni around 1500 BC and proceeds through domination by the civilisations of Urartu (900 BC), Assyria (1356–612 BC), Persia (600–330 BC) and Alexander the Great and his successors, the Seleucids.

SOUTHEASTERN ANATOLIA DİYARBAKIR

DARENDE – THE FORGOTTEN OASIS

Who knows if the utterly mellow town of Darende, about 110km west of Malatya, will be able to handle all this publicity, but it can't go without mention because it's a terrific place to kick off your shoes for a day or two in a fabulous setting. Darende itself won't knock your socks off but it has a splendid canyon right on its doorstep as well as a smattering of well-preserved architectural treasures, including the **Somuncu Baba Camii ve Külliyesi** (with a museum), the **Kudret Havuzu**, a purpose-built rock pool set in the **Tohma Canyon** near the Somuncu Baba Camii, and the **Zengibar Kalesi**, perched on a rocky outcrop.

Few things could be more pleasurable than tucking into a fresh trout in one of the few restaurants that have been set up along the riverbank in the canyon. Hasbahçe (🕿 0422-615 2215; Somuncu Baba Camii Civarı; mains TL6-12) is a firm favourite. Or you could picnic in one of the numerous sheltered *köşk* (picnic areas). In summer, you can dunk yourself in the Kudret Havuzu – just blissful. Action seekers, rejoice: rafting (🕿 0422-615 3513, 0555 565 4935; www.tohmarafting.com) is also available in the Tohma Canyon in summer. Don't expect massive thrills, but look forward to transiting through stunning canyons against the background of a stark cobalt sky.

The brilliant-value Tiryandafil Otel (🕿 0422-615 3095; s/d/tr TL60/90/110; ✻ @) is conveniently located on the outskirts of Darende, about 1km before the canyon and monuments. It has impeccable and very spacious rooms with the requisite mod cons. The on-site restaurant is a winner, with excellent local specialities – try the *şelale sızdırma* (meat with melted cheese, mushrooms and butter) – but it's not licensed. Ask for Hassan or Tahla – both speak good English and can help with any queries.

With your own wheels, you can easily reach the **Gürpinar Şelalesi** (waterfalls), about 7km from Darende (from the hotel, follow the road to Ankara for 6km; then it's signposted). Don't expect Niagara-like falls, but it's an excellent picnic spot.

Regular buses (TL12) and minibuses (TL8) ply the route between Malatya and Darende. In Malatya, they depart from the minibus terminal (also known as 'Eski Otogar') on Çevre Yol.

Diyarbakır

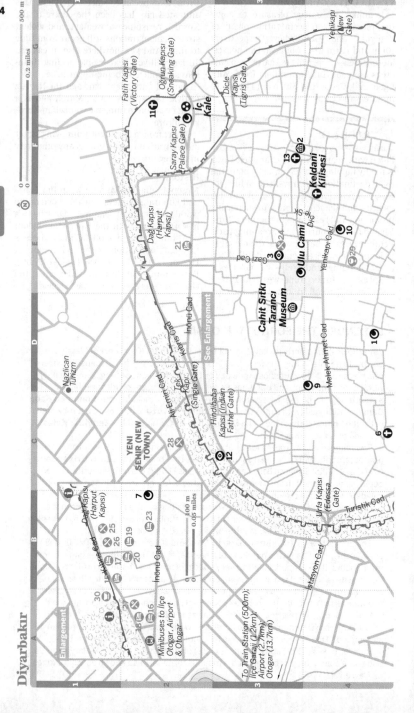

500 m
0.2 miles

Yenikapı (New Gate)

Fatih Kapısı (Victory Gate)

Oğrun Kapısı (Sneaking Gate)

11

Dicle Kapısı (Tigris Gate)

4

İç Kale

Saray Kapısı (Palace Gate)

13

2

Keldani Kilisesi

Dağ Kapısı (Harput Kapısı)

21

İnönü Cad

See Enlargement

İlçe Sk

Dıç

24

Gazi Cad

3

Ulu Cami

10

29

Yenikapı Cad

Cahit Sıtkı Tarancı Museum

Kıbrıs Cad

Tek Kapı (Single Gate)

Ali Emri Cad

Melek Ahmet Cad

9

1

Nazlıcan Turizm

YENİ ŞEHİR (NEW TOWN)

28

Hindibaba Kapısı (Indian Father Gate)

12

6

Urfa Kapısı (Edessa Gate)

Turistik Cad

İstasyon Cad

To Train Station (500m);
İlçe Garajı (1.2km);
Airport (2.7km);
Otogar (13.7km)

100 m
0.05 miles

Enlargement

Dağ Kapısı (Harput Kapısı)

Kıbrıs Cad

7

30

25

26

17

20

19

23

18

16

İnönü Cad

Minibuses to İlçe Otogar, Airport & Otogar

0.05 miles

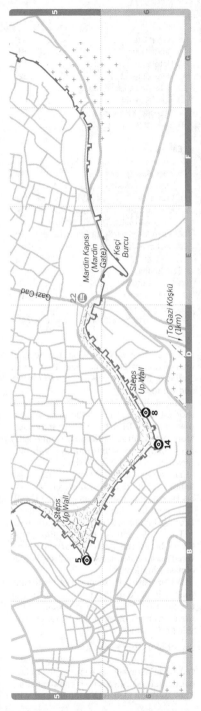

The Romans took over in AD 115, but because of its strategic position the city changed hands numerous times until it was conquered by the Arabs in 639. The Arab tribe of Beni Bakr that settled here named their new home Diyar Bakr, which means the Realm of Bakr.

For the next few centuries the city was occupied by various tribes, until 1497 when the Safavid dynasty founded by Shah İsmail took over Iran, putting an end to more than a century of Turkoman rule in this area. The Ottomans came and conquered in 1515, but even then, Diyarbakır was not to know lasting peace. Because it stood right in the way of invading armies originating from Anatolia, Persia and Syria, it suffered many more tribulations.

◉ Sights

City Walls & Gates   FORTRESS

Diyarbakır's single most conspicuous feature is its great circuit of basalt walls, probably dating from Roman times, although the present walls date from early Byzantine times (AD 330–500). At almost 6km in length, these walls are said to be second in extent only to the Great Wall of China.

Numerous bastions and towers stand sentinel over the massive black walls. There were originally four main gates: **Harput Kapısı** (north), **Mardin Kapısı** (south), **Yenikapı** (east) and **Urfa Kapısı** (west).

Fortunately, the most easily accessible stretch of walls is also the most interesting in terms of inscriptions and decoration. Start near the Mardin Kapısı close to the Deliller Han, a stone caravanserai now home to the Otel Büyük Kervansaray. Don't miss **Nur Burcu** (Tower Nur), the **Yedi Kardeş Burcu** (Tower of Seven Brothers), with two Seljuk lion bas-reliefs – only visible from outside the walls – and the bas-reliefs of the **Malikşah Burcu** (Tower of Malik Şah).

Ascend the walls of the **İç Kale** (keep) for fine views of the Tigris. The İç Kale has been undergoing restoration for several years, and includes the beautifully resurrected **St George Church**. Dating from the 3rd century AD, the spacious and airy building is now used as an exhibition space. The entrance to İç Kale hosts an excellent local market every Sunday.

At various spots inside the walls are brightly painted, open-air **Sufi sarcophagi**, notable for their turbans – their size is

Diyarbakır

Top Sights
Cahit Sıtkı Tarancı Museum ... D3
İç Kale ... F2
Keldani Kilisesi ... F4
Ulu Cami ... E3

Sights
1 Behram Paşa Camii ... D4
2 Esma Ocak Evi ... F3
3 Hasan Paşa Hanı ... E3
4 Hazreti Süleyman Camii ... F2
5 Malikşah Burcu ... B5
6 Meryem Ana Kilisesi ... C4
7 Nebi Camii ... B2
8 Nur Burcu ... C6
9 Safa Camii ... D4
10 Şeyh Mutahhar Camii ... E4
11 St George Church ... F2
12 Sufi Sarcophagi ... C3
13 Surpağab Kilisesi ... F3
14 Yedi Kardeş Burcu ... C6

Sleeping
15 Aslan Palas ... B1
16 Balkar Otel ... A2
17 Grand Güler Hotel ... B1
18 Hotel Evin ... A2
19 Hotel Güler ... B2
20 Hotel Kaplan ... B2
21 Hotel Surkent ... E2
22 Otel Büyük Kervansaray ... E5
23 SV Business Hotel ... B2

Eating
24 Kebapçı Hacı Halid ... E3
25 Küçe Başı Et Lokantası ... B1
Meşhur Kahvaltıcı ... (see 3)
26 Ocakbaşl ... B1
Otel Büyük Kervansaray ... (see 22)
27 Şafak Kahvaltı & Yemek Salonu ... A2
28 Şelim Amca'nın Sofra Salonu ... C2
Şeyhmus Tatlıcısı ... (see 16)

Drinking
29 Class Hotel ... E4
30 Doğal Vitamin ... A1
Hasan Paşa Hanı ... (see 3)
Otel Büyük Kervansaray ... (see 22)

a symbol of spiritual authority. There's a cluster a few hundred metres northeast of the Urfa Kapısı.

Be prudent when walking on and along the walls as there have been reports of attempted robberies. Try to go in a group.

Mosques MOSQUES

Diyarbakır's most impressive is the **Ulu Cami**, built in 1091 by Malik Şah, an early Seljuk sultan. Incorporating elements from an earlier Byzantine church on the site, it was extensively restored in 1155 after a fire. It's rectangular in plan – Arab style, rather than Ottoman. The entrance portal, adorned with two medallions figuring a lion and a bull, leads to a huge courtyard. This is the most elegant section of the building, with two-storey arcades, two cone-shaped *şadırvans* (ritual ablutions fountains), elaborate pillars, and friezes featuring fruits and vegetables.

Across Gazi Caddesi is the **Hasan Paşa Hanı**, a 16th-century caravanserai occupied by carpet shops and souvenir sellers. It was extensively restored in 2006 and has some top spots for a leisurely breakfast. Live music is also regularly advertised.

Black-and-white stone banding that alternates is a characteristic of Diyarbakır's mosques. The **Nebi Camii** (1530) at the main intersection of Gazi and İzzet Paşa/İnönü Caddesis, has a detached minaret in black-and-white stone.

The **Behram Paşa Camii** (1572), in a residential area deep in the maze of narrow streets, is Diyarbakır's largest mosque. More Persian in style, the **Safa Camii** (1532) has a highly decorated minaret with blue tiles incorporated in its design.

The **Şeyh Mutahhar Camii** (1512) is also famous for its detached minaret, but also because its tower stands on four slender pillars about 2m high – earning it the name Dört Ayaklı Minare (Four-Legged Minaret).

The 12th-century **Hazreti Süleyman Camii**, beside the İç Kale, is particularly revered because it houses the tombs of heroes of past Islamic wars.

When visiting these mosques, try to time your visit for 20 to 25 minutes after the call to prayer (when the prayers should be finished), as most of them will be locked outside prayer times.

Diyarbakır House Museums NOTABLE BUILDINGS

Old Diyarbakır houses were made of black basalt and decorated with stone stencilling. They were divided into summer and winter quarters, and the centre of the summer part was always the *eyvan,* a vaulted room opening onto the courtyard with a fountain in the centre. In summer, the family moved high wooden platforms called *tahts* into the courtyard for sleeping, making it possible to catch any breeze.

To see inside these old houses, visit one of the museums inside the city walls. The poet Cahit Sıtkı Tarancı (1910–56) was born in a two-storey black basalt house built in 1820, in a side street about 50m north of the Ulu Cami. It now houses the Cahit Sıtkı Tarancı Museum (Ziya Gökalp Sokak; admission free; ☺8am-5pm Tue-Sun).

The beautiful grey-and-white-striped Esma Ocak Evi was built in 1899 by the Armenian Şakarer family and restored in 1996 by a female writer, Esma Ocak. A live-in caretaker – and her twin daughters – will show you the gracefully furnished living rooms. Admission is by donation (TL3 is expected).

Churches
CHURCHES

The population of Diyarbakır once included many Christians, mainly Armenians and Chaldeans, but most of them were pushed out or perished during the troubles in the early 20th century or, more recently, with the Hezbollah.

The Keldani Kilisesi (Chaldean Church), off Yenikapı Caddesi, is a plain, brightly lit church, still used by Christian families of the Syrian rite (in communion with the Roman Catholic Church). The chaplain from the Meryem Ana Kilisesi holds a service here on the second Sunday of the month. Walk past the detached minaret of the Şeyh Mutahhar Camii, take the first left (Dicle Sokak) then the first right (Şeftali Sokak). The caretaker usually sits outside the Nebi Camii.

The Armenian Surpağab Kilisesi, also just off Yenikapı Caddesi, was closed for restoration at the time of writing. It's across the lane from the Esma Ocak Evi.

The wonderful Meryem Ana Kilisesi (Church of the Virgin Mary) is still used by Orthodox Syrian Christians. The church is beautifully maintained, although only about seven families still attend services. Local kids will show you the way.

An old church near the Şeyh Mutahhar Camii is now a post office.

Gazi Köşkü
HISTORIC BUILDING

(admission TL1) About 1km south of the Mardin Kapısı, the Gazi Köşkü is a fine example of the sort of Diyarbakır house to which its wealthier citizens would retire in high summer. The house dates from the time of the 15th-century Akkoyunlu Turkoman dynasty and stands in a well-tended park. The caretaker will expect a tip for showing you around.

To get there, it's a pleasant, if rather isolated, downhill walk. Taxis charge TL12. Look forward to unimpeded views of Diyarbakır's dramatic walls.

About 2km further south is the 11th-century **On Gözlu Köprüsü** (Ten-Eyed Bridge).

Archaeology Museum
MUSEUM

(Arkeoloji Müzesi) Diyarbakır's Archaeology Museum was closed at the time of writing for refurbishment, but scheduled to reopen in 2012. Ask at the Diyarbakır tourist office for an update.

Before renovation, the well-presented collection included finds from the Neolithic site of Çayönü (7500–6500 BC), 65km north of Diyarbakır. Also showcased was a decent Urartian collection and relics from the Karakoyunlu and Akkoyunlu, powerful tribal dynasties that ruled much of eastern Anatolia and Iran between 1378 and 1502.

🛏 Sleeping

Most accommodation options are conveniently located on Kıbrıs Caddesi and nearby İnönü Caddesi. Kıbrıs Caddesi does suffer from traffic noise, so try and secure a room at the back. In summer it's scorching hot in Diyarbakır, another thing to consider when choosing a room. The best accommodation choices for solo female travellers are the Balkar Otel, the Hotel Evin and the more-expensive options.

Hotel Evin
HOTEL €€

(☎228 6306; fax 224 9093; Kıbrıs Caddesi 38; s/d TL60/80; ❄) Newly opened in 2009, the Evin is a sparkling addition to the Kıbrıs Caddesi hotel scene. Rooms are spacious and sunny, and the views from the rooftop breakfast salon will have you lingering for another glass of tea. Get in quick before the familiar aroma of cigarette smoke takes hold.

SV Business Hotel
BUSINESS HOTEL €€€

(☎228 1295; www.svbusinessotel.com; İnönü Caddesi 4; s/d €60/100; ❄) Diyar's first stab at a modern boutique/business hotel mixes up cool, pastel colours, almost too-trendy furniture, and a relaxed, but professional, English-speaking vibe at reception. Rooms are moderately sized, but showing no sartorial 1980s hangover from this address' former incarnation as the Büyük Hotel. A compact sauna and fitness centre provides assistance if the city's cuisine is proving too irresistible.

Hotel Surkent
HOTEL **€**

(☎228 1014; fax 228 4833; İzzet Paşa Caddesi; s/d TL25/40; ✳) Tangerine frames and aluminium plates on the facade, flamingo-pink walls, technicolour bed linen and flashy orange curtains: the owners of the Surkent certainly like your life to be colourful. The top-floor rooms boast good views (for singles, rooms 501, 502 and 503 are the best). It's in a peaceful street, close to everything. One downside: there's no lift – good to know if your backpack weighs a tonne. Breakfast is an additional TL5.

Otel Büyük Kervansaray
HISTORIC HOTEL **€€**

(☎228 9606; fax 228 9606; Gazi Caddesi; s/d TL100/200; ✳ ▨) This is your chance to sleep in the 16th-century Deliller Han, a converted caravanserai. It is not the height of luxury, but it scores high on amenities, with a restaurant, bar, hamam and nifty pool in which to cool off. The standard rooms are itty-bitty, but how much time are you going to spend in your room when the inner courtyard is so agreeable? At the very least, pop around for a relaxed tea or a cooling beer.

Aslan Palas
HOTEL **€**

(☎228 9224; fax 223 9880; Kıbrıs Caddesi; s/d TL30/60; ✳) A worthwhile back-up for cash-strapped (male) travellers, but ageing plumbing is about the worst surprise you'll get. Air-con is in all the rooms. Prices don't include breakfast, but you'll find several *kahvaltı salonu* (eateries specialising in full Turkish breakfasts) on the street. There's also no lift and bathrooms are shared.

Grand Güler Hotel
HOTEL **€€**

(☎229 2221; www.grandgulerotel.com; Kıbrıs Caddesi 13; s/d TL60/110) The billet of choice for tour groups, the Güler is not *that* grand but its blue mosaic facade brings a touch of chintzy glamour to an otherwise dull street. The front rooms have double-glazing so you're (almost) insulated from traffic noise along Kıbrıs Caddesi.

Balkar Otel
HOTEL **€€**

(☎228 6306; fax 224 6936; Kıbrıs Caddesi 38; s/d TL60/90; ✳) This typical middling three-star boasts well-appointed rooms with TV and minibar, but very compact bathrooms.

Bonuses include a hearty breakfast and a rooftop terrace with sterling views.

Hotel Güler
HOTEL **€**

(☎/fax 224 0294; Yoğurtçu Sokak; s/d TL40/70; ✳) Tucked away in an alleyway off Kıbrıs Caddesi, this two-star outfit has impersonal yet well-looked-after rooms, good mattresses and prim, if pint-sized, bathrooms.

Hotel Kaplan
HOTEL **€**

(☎229 3300; Kıbrıs Caddesi, Yoğurtçu Sokak; s/d TL30/50; ✳) Centrally located with restaurants literally on your doorstep, the Kaplan's a good choice for long-term travellers really watching their budget.

✕ Eating

Kıbrıs Caddesi has plenty of good-value, informal eateries. For expertly grilled meat, join the blokey throngs at the various *ocakbaşı* places lining the narrow lanes adjoining Kıbrıs Caddesi.

TOP CHOICE Selim Amca'nın Sofra Salonu
RESTAURANT **€€**

(Ali Emiri Caddesi; mains TL8-15, set menu TL23) This bright eatery outside the city walls is famous for its *kaburga dolması* (lamb stuffed with rice and almonds). Round it off with a devilish *İrmik helvası* (a gooey dessert). The *saç kavurma* (braised lamb) is also excellent.

Meşhur Kahvaltıcı
CAFE **€€**

(Hasan Paşa Hanı; breakfast TL15) More expensive than the *kahvaltı* spots along Kıbrıs Caddesi, but worth it for the glorious ambience of the restored Hasan Paşa Hanı. Enjoy a leisurely breakfast on the balcony and feel pleased with yourself for adding Diyarbakır to your Turkish itinerary.

Şafak Kahvaltı & Yemek Salonu
LOKANTA **€**

(Kıbrıs Caddesi; mains TL6-10) Nosh on freshly prepared meat dishes and hearty casseroles and stuffed vegetables in this brisk Diyarbakır institution. It's also a good place to partake in a restorative morning breakfast with still-warm flatbread, luscious *kaymak* (clotted cream) and gooey honey. It also does superb crisp wood-fired pide.

Otel Büyük Kervansaray
RESTAURANT-BAR **€€**

(Gazi Caddesi; mains TL8-12; ⊙11am-10pm) Even if you're not staying in this historic hotel it's worth popping in for a meal in the restaurant, which is a converted camel stable. There's live music here most nights and, joy of joys, it's licensed.

Küçe Başı Et Lokantası
LOKANTA €

(Kıbrıs Caddesi; mains TL6-12) This outfit has a wide-ranging menu and original setting (the room at the back is designed like a rustic barn). Try innovative dishes like *tavuk tava* (deep-fried chicken meat in a flat-bottomed pan).

Kebapçı Hacı Halid
KEBAPÇI €

(Borsahan Sokak; mains TL5-10) Tasty kebaps and ready-made meals served in bright surroundings. Look for the black-and-white pictures of old Diyarbakır on the 1st floor. It's in a small pedestrianised side street off Gazi Caddesi.

Şeyhmus Tatlıcısı
PATISSERIE €

(Kıbrıs Caddesi; ⊙7am-8pm) Keep up your strength with a delectable baklava or a sticky *kadayıf* (dough soaked in syrup).

🍷 Drinking & Entertainment

Otel Büyük Kervansaray
TEA GARDEN

(Gazi Caddesi; ⊙11am-10pm) The expansive courtyard is a great place to unwind over a cup of tea and take in the atmosphere. It's also licensed if you feel like a cold beer.

Class Hotel
HOTEL BAR

(Gazi Caddesi; ⊙10am-10pm) The draw here is the restored **Çizmeci Köşkü** (a carved wooden pavilion) in the gardens. It's a lovely spot for a tea, coffee or something stronger.

Hasan Paşa Hanı
COFFEE HOUSE

(Gazi Caddesi; ⊙8am-10pm) This restored caravanserai is slightly touristy, but it still has some great cafes and teahouses. Keep an eye out for flyers advertising *canlı müzik* (live music).

Doğal Vitamin
CAFE

(Kıbrıs Caddesi) Fresh juices from a caravan.

❶ Information

Old Diyarbakır is encircled by walls pierced by several main gates. Within the walls the city is a maze of narrow, twisting, mostly unmarked alleys. Most services useful to travellers are in Old Diyarbakır, on or around Gazi Caddesi, including the post office, internet cafes, travel agencies and ATMs.

Municipal information bureau (⊙9am-noon & 1-6pm Tue-Sat) Municipal office, off Kıbrıs Caddesi.

Tourist office (☑228 1706; Kapısı; ⊙8am-5pm Mon-Fri) Provincial office housed in a tower of the wall.

❶ Getting There & Away

Air

Minibuses A1, A2 and A3 run to the airport (TL1.50) from near Dağ Kapısı. A taxi will cost about TL10.

Onur Air (www.onurair.com.tr) Two daily flights to/from İstanbul (from TL94) and one daily flight to/from İzmir (from TL84).

Pegasus Airlines (www.flypgs.com) A daily flight to/from İstanbul (from TL76), and daily flights to/from Adana (from TL42).

Turkish Airlines (www.thy.com) Five daily flights to/from İstanbul (from TL59), four daily flights to/from Ankara (from TL59), four flights a week to/from Antalya (from TL53) and two daily flights to/from İzmir (TL83).

Bus

Many bus companies have ticket offices on İnönü Caddesi or along Gazi Caddesi near the Dağ Kapısı. The otogar is about 14km from the centre, on the road to Urfa (about TL15 by taxi).

There's a separate minibus terminal (İlçe Garajı) about 1.5km southwest of the city walls, with services to Batman (TL5, 1½ hours), Elazığ (TL10,

SERVICES FROM DİYARBAKIR'S OTOGAR

DESTINATION	FARE (TL)	DURATION (HR)	DISTANCE (KM)	FREQUENCY (PER DAY)
Adana	40	8	550	several buses
Ankara	60	13	945	several buses
Erzurum	35	8	485	several buses
Malatya	20	5	260	frequent buses
Mardin	10	1½	95	hourly buses
Şanlıurfa	15	3	190	frequent buses
Sivas	40	10	500	several buses
Tatvan	20	4	264	several buses
Van	35	7	410	several buses

two hours), Mardin (TL10, 1¼ hours), Malatya (TL20, five hours), Midyat (TL12) and Siverek (to get to Kahta without going right round the lake via Adıyaman). For Hasankeyf, change in Batman (TL5). To get to the minibus terminal, take a bus from near the Balkar Otel, across the street, and ask for 'İlçe Garajı' (TL2), or take a taxi (TL6).

For Iraq, take a bus to Cizre (TL20, four hours) or Silopi (TL22, five hours) from the main otogar. There are about four services per day. For more information, see the boxed text on p603.

Car

Avis (📞236 1324, 229 0275; www.avis.com.tr; Elazığ Caddesi; ⏰8am-7pm) Opposite the *belediye* and at the airport.

Train

The train station is about 1.5km from the centre, at the western end of İstasyon Caddesi. The *Güney Ekspresi* leaves for İstanbul (TL44) via Malatya (TL7.50) and Sivas (TL23) at 8.42am on Monday, Wednesday, Friday and Sunday. Check times at the train station.

Mardin

📞0482 / POP 55,000 / ELEV 1325M

Filled with heart, pretty-as-a-picture Mardin is a highly addictive and unmissable spot. With its minarets poking out of a baked brown labyrinth of lanes, its old castle dominating the old city, and the honey-coloured stone houses that cling to the hillside, Mardin emerges like a phoenix from the sun-roasted Mesopotamian plains. As a melting pot of Kurdish, Yezidi, Christian and Syrian cultures, it also has a fascinating cultural mix.

Don't expect to have the whole place to yourself, though. With regular flights from İstanbul and lots of positive coverage in the Turkish media, you'll see lots of local visitors in summer. If you really want something extra special, take a little detour to Dara or, better still, to Savur.

Coming from Diyarbakır, you first pass through the new part of Mardin. Continue up the hill to the roundabout where the road forks. Go uphill to the main drag, Cumhuriyet Caddesi (still called by its former name, Birinci Caddesi), to find the hotels and the main square, Cumhuriyet Meydanı, with the statue of Atatürk. The right-hand road from the roundabout, Yeni Yol, curves round the hillside on a lower level to rejoin Cumhuriyet Caddesi, just north of the İlçe Otogar.

History

As with Diyarbakır, Mardin's history is one of disputes between rival armies over millennia, though in recent years the only dis-

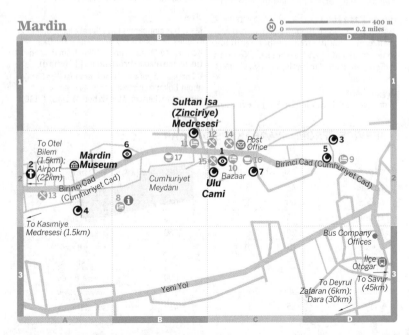

Mardin

pute that anyone has really cared about is the one between the PKK (Kurdistan Workers Party) and the government. A castle has stood on this hill from time immemorial, and the Turkish army still finds the site useful to assert authority.

Assyrian Christians settled here during the 5th century, and the Arabs occupied Mardin between 640 and 1104. After that, it had a succession of Seljuk Turkish, Kurdish, Mongol and Persian overlords, until the Ottomans under Sultan Selim the Grim took it in 1517. In the early 20th century many of the Assyrian Christians were pushed out or perished during the troubles, and in the last few decades many have emigrated. An estimated 600 Christians remain, with 11 churches still in use on a rotational basis.

◉ Sights

Bazaar MARKET
Mardin's rambling commercial hub parallels Cumhuriyet Caddesi one block down the hill. Here charmingly decorated donkeys

are still the main form of transport. Look out also for saddle repairers who can seemingly resurrect even the shabbiest examples.

Keep your eyes open for the secluded **Ulu Cami**, a 12th-century Iraqi Seljuk structure that suffered badly during the Kurdish rebellion of 1832. Inside it's fairly plain, but the delicate reliefs adorning the minaret make a visit worthwhile.

Mardin Museum MUSEUM
(Mardin Müzesi; Cumhuriyet Caddesi; admission TL3; ⊙8am-5pm Tue-Sun) This superbly restored late-19th-century mansion sports carved pillars and elegant arcades on the upper floor. Inside, it has a small but well-displayed collection including a finely detailed 7th-century-BC Assyrian vase and finds from Girnavaz, a Bronze Age site 4km north of Nusaybin.

Afterwards, head east along Cumhuriyet Caddesi, keeping your eye out for a fabulous example of the town's domestic architecture on your left – the three-arched facade of an ornately carved **old Mardin house**.

Sultan İsa (Zinciriye) Medresesi HISTORIC BUILDING
(Cumhuriyet Caddesi) Dating from 1385, the complex's highlight is the imposing recessed doorway, but make sure you wander through the pretty courtyards, lovingly tended by the caretaker, and onto the roof to enjoy the cityscape.

Post Office HISTORIC BUILDING
(Cumhuriyet Caddesi) Turkey's most impressive post office is housed in a 17th-century caravanserai with carvings, including those around the windows and teardrops in stone dripping down the walls.

Emir Hamamı HISTORIC BUILDING
(Cumhuriyet Caddesi; treatments from T15; ⊙men 6.30am-noon & 6.30-10pm, women noon-5.30pm) This hamam's history goes back to Roman times and it is one of the most atmospheric in Turkey. After a sauna and massage combo, take in the great views of the Mesopotamian plains from the hamam's terrace.

Şehidiye Camii MOSQUE
(Cumhuriyet Caddesi) Across the street from the post office rises the elegant, slender minaret of this 14th-century mosque. It's superbly carved, with colonnades all around, and three small bulbs superimposed at the summit. The base of the minaret sports a series of pillars.

Also worth visiting is the 14th-century **Latifiye Camii**, behind the Akbank, where a shady courtyard has a *şadırvan* in the middle.

Nearby, in the vicinity of the Artuklu Kervansarayı, the eye-catching **Hatuniye** and **Melik Mahmut Camii** have been restored.

Forty Martyrs Church — CHURCH
(Kırklar Kilisesi; Sağlık Sokak) To the west of town and dating from the 15th century, the church has an entrance decorated with martyrs. Knock on the door to alert the caretaker. Services are held here each Sunday.

Kasımiye Medresesi — HISTORIC BUILDING
Built in 1469, two domes stand over the tombs of Kasım Paşa and his sister, but the highlights are the sublime courtyard walled with arched colonnades and the magnificent carved doorway. Upstairs, you can see the students' quarters, before ascending the stairs to the rooftop for another great Mardin panorama. It's 800m south of Yeni Yol.

🛌 Sleeping

Mardin's popularity as a destination for Turkish tourists means that accommodation is expensive. Mardin's increasing number of boutique hotels are undeniably atmospheric, but too often rooms are on the small side and lacking natural light. Make sure to ask the right questions when you're booking. Summer weekends are particularly busy, and you might find it easier to visit Mardin as a day trip from Midyat or Diyarbakır.

Antik Tatlıede Butik Hotel
BOUTIQUE HOTEL €€
(✆213 2720; www.tatlidede.com.tr, in Turkish; Medrese Mahallesi; s/d TL100/150; ❄) In a quiet location near Mardin's bazaar, a labyrinthine heritage mansion is filled with rooms of varying sizes. Most are fairly spacious, and all are filled with a rustic mix of old kilims and antique furniture. The expansive lobby flows effortlessly to huge terraces with views across the plains of Mesopotamia.

Artuklu Kervansarayı — BOUTIQUE HOTEL €€€
(✆213 7353; www.artuklu.com; Cumhuriyet Caddesi; s/d TL150/200; ❄) With dark floorboards and furniture, stone walls and sturdy wooden doors, this place feels like a castle. We're not quite sure how to take the Artuklu, but at least it broke the mould when it conceived the 'medieval' interior of this venture. It

sports a wide range of amenities but there are no views to speak of.

Zinciriye Butik Hotel — BOUTIQUE HOTEL €€
(✆212 4866; www.zinciriye.com; Sok 243, Medrese Mahallesi; s/d TL90/140; ❄) Tucked away just off the main drag, the Zinciriye features small but quaintly decorated rooms with centuries-old stone walls. Some downstairs rooms lack windows, so try and head upstairs, with the added attraction of a shared terrace with superb views.

Erdoba Konakları — BOUTIQUE HOTEL €€€
(✆212 7677; www.erdoba.com.tr; Cumhuriyet Caddesi; s/d TL150/200; ❄) Such serenity after the clamour of the main drag. Right in the heart of the old town, this boutique hotel – the first of its kind in Mardin – comprises four finely restored mansions, with lots of period charm. The downside: only five rooms come with a view (although a few terraces at the back look onto the Mesopotamia plain).

Mardin Homestays — PENSION €
(Nomad Tours Turkey; ✆0533 747 1850; www.nomadtoursturkey.com; per person TL25, with full board TL60) Basic accommodation in family homestays in the old town can be booked through Nomad Tours Turkey. Guests are met at the Mardin otogar by their hosts.

Otel Bilem — HOTEL €€
(✆213 0315; fax 212 2575; Yenişehir; s/d TL60/100; ❄) The Bilem is a safe but unsexy choice in the new part of Mardin (Yenişehir), 2km northwest of Cumhuriyet Meydanı. Its boxy concrete frame boasts comfortable modern facilities but little personality. From the İlçe Otogar, catch any blue dolmuş going to 'Yenişehir'. Regular dolmuş traffic links the new town to the old town.

Otel Başak — HOTEL €
(✆212 6246; Cumhuriyet Caddesi; s/d TL25/40) The only budget hotel in town combines clean rooms with so-so shared bathrooms. Rooms face onto the main drag, so it can be noisy.

🍴 Eating & Drinking

TOP CHOICE Kamer Vakif — MUTFAK €€
(Cumhuriyet Caddesi; mains TL10-15) Operated by the Kamer Vakif ('Moon Foundation'), a support organisation for women who are victims of domestic violence, this terrific restaurant serves some of the best local cuisine in Mardin. Up

to 10 different women cook on a rotating basis, dishing up authentic and tasty versions of Kurdish bulgur wheat pilav and *içli köfte*. Welcome to one of the best eateries in eastern Turkey.

Cercis Murat Konağı

GOURMET RESTAURANT €€€

(☑213 6841; Cumhuriyet Caddesi; mains TL20-25; ⊙noon-11pm) The Cercis occupies a traditional Syrian Christian home with two finely decorated rooms and a terrace with stunning views. Treat yourself to a series of dainty dishes featuring recipes from the days of yore and a creative twist (not a kebap in sight). *Mekbuss* (aubergine pickles with walnut), *kitel raha* (Syrian-style meatballs) and *dobo* (lamb with garlic, spices and black pepper) rank among the highlights. Dive into the meze platter (TL30) for a taste of everything that's good. Try and book a couple of days ahead, or drop by at lunchtime and book for dinner. Wine and beer are also served. Service can be a tad stuffy, so dig out your cleanest dirty shirt.

Antik Sur

RESTAURANT €€

(Cumhuriyet Caddesi; mains TL10-15) Ignore the incongruous Ronald McDonald statue out the front and disappear into the shaded surrounds of this wonderfully restored caravanserai. Turkish tourists love the authentic local flavours and the opportunity to try Assyrian wine. Live music kicks off around 8pm most weekends, and laid-back teahouses fill the upper level if you're ready to bring out your backgammon A-game.

Vitamin

CAFE €

(Cumhuriyet Caddesi; juices from TL2) With its dramatic bright orange walls adorned with musical instruments, this pea-sized joint on the main drag has to be Mardin's kookiest spot. Freshly squeezed juices are served in glasses filled to the brim.

Çay Bahçesi

TEA GARDEN €

(Cumhuriyet Caddesi) The perfect place to scribble a few postcards: 'The views over old Mardin and Mesopotamia are phenomenal...'

Kepapçı Pide

PIDECI €

(Cumhuriyet Caddesi 219; mains TL6-8) Cheap and cheerful wood-fired gems, perfect for the cash-strapped overland traveller.

İpek Yemek Salonu

LOKANTA €

(Cumhuriyet Caddesi 217; mains TL4-7) Pop in here for tasty and filling prepared dishes and soups.

ℹ Information

The post office, ATMs and internet cafes are all along Cumhuriyet Caddesi, old Mardin's one-way street.

Tourist office (☑212 3776; iktm47@kultur turizm.gov.tr; Valilik Binası 2nd fl; ⊙8.30am-5.30pm) Opposite the Antik Tatlıede Butik Hotel and just below the bazaar. Some English is spoken and good maps and brochures are available, including a comprehensive guide to Mardin's architectural heritage.

GETTING TO KURDISH IRAQ

Crossing to Kurdish Iraq is a relatively straightforward exercise at the Turkish–Iraqi border at Habur, 15km southeast of Silopi (reached by bus from Mardin or Diyarbakır via Cizre). Once you're at Silopi, you're in the increasingly entrepreneurial hands of the local taxi mafia. They'll handle all the formalities up to the Iraqi border post, and will be looking for anything up to US$70 (or the equivalent in Turkish lira or euros) per taxi for the privilege. We've heard of other travellers getting the same result for around US$50 per taxi, so it's definitely time for your negotiation A-game.

At the Iraqi border you may be asked where you are staying in Iraq – just mention any hotel in Zakho or Dohuk. Queues and waiting time going from Turkey into Iraq are relatively short – around 90 minutes or so – but can be much longer entering Turkey from Iraq. That's because all cars are searched thoroughly for smuggled good, including petrol and cigarettes.

Once you're through Iraqi immigration, your Turkish taxi driver will deliver you to the border transport hub of Zakho, where there are a few cheap hotels, or you can continue your journey on to Dohuk or Erbil.

For more about travelling in Kurdish Iraq, see Lonely Planet's *Middle East* or check out the 'Travel to Kurdistan' Fact Sheet at www.krg.org, the website of the Kurdistan Regional Government.

ⓘ Getting There & Away

Air

Mardin airport is around 20km south of Mardin. There's no airport shuttle, but any minibus to Kızıltepe can drop you at the entrance (TL2).

Turkish Airlines (www.thy.com) Up to two daily flights to/from İstanbul (from TL79) and one daily flight to/from Ankara (from TL59).

Bus

Most buses leave from the İlçe Otogar east of the centre. For long-distance destinations, buses stop in front of the bus company offices in the old town and in new Mardin. From around 4pm services start to dry up so it's best to make an early start.

Minibuses depart every hour or so for Diyarbakır (TL8, 1¼ hours), Midyat (TL6, 1¼ hours) and the Syrian border at Nusaybin (TL6, one hour). There are also up to 10 minibuses to Savur (TL8, one hour). Other useful regular services for travellers include Şanlıurfa (TL20, three hours), Cizre (TL15, 2½ hours) and Silopi (TL20, three hours), for travel to northern Iraq.

Around Mardin

DEYRUL ZAFARAN

The magnificent Deyrul Zafaran (monastery of Mar Hanania; adult/concession TL3/2; ⊙8.30am-noon & 1-5pm) stands about 6km along a good but narrow road in the rocky hills east of Mardin. The monastery was once the seat of the Syrian Orthodox patriarchate but this has now moved to Damascus.

In 495 the first monastery was built on a site previously dedicated to the worship of the sun. Destroyed by the Persians in 607, it was rebuilt, only to be looted by Tamerlane six centuries later.

Shortly after you enter the walled enclosure via a portal bearing a Syriac (a dialect of Aramaic) inscription, you'll see the original **sanctuary**, an eerie underground chamber with a ceiling of huge, closely fitted stones held up as if by magic, without the aid of mortar. This room was allegedly used by sun worshippers, who viewed their god rising through a window at the eastern end. A niche on the southern wall is said to have been for sacrifices.

A guide will then lead you through a pair of 300-year-old doors to the **tombs** of the patriarchs and metropolitans who have served here.

In the chapel, the **patriarch's throne** to the left of the altar bears the names of all the patriarchs who have served the monastery since it was refounded in 792. To the right of the altar is the **throne of the metropolitan**. The present **stone altar** replaces a wooden one that burnt down about half a century ago. The walls are adorned with wonderful paintings and wall hangings. Services in Aramaic are held here.

In the next rooms you'll see litters used to transport the church dignitaries, and a baptismal font. In a small side room is a 300-year-old **wooden throne**. The floor **mosaic** is about 1500 years old.

A flight of stairs leads to very simple guest rooms for those coming for worship. The patriarch's small, simple bedroom and parlour are also up here.

There's no public transport here so you must take a taxi or walk around 90 minutes from Mardin. Hopeful drivers wait outside the bus company offices in Mardin and will ask TL30 to run you there and back.

Try and visit on a weekday or the monastic hush could be disturbed by busloads of Turkish tourists.

DARA

About 30km southeast of Mardin is a magnificent ancient Roman city forgotten in time. Dating back to the 6th century, Dara is where Mesopotamia's first dam and irrigation canals were built. Ongoing excavation promises to reveal one of southeastern Anatolia's forgotten gems. The highlight is walking down ancient stairways into the towers of Dara's underground aqueducts and cisterns. Natural light ebbs and flows into the expanse to create a remarkable cathedral-like ambience.

Bar a couple of teahouses, there are no facilities in Dara. From Mardin, there are three daily services (TL4).

SAVUR

This diamond of a town appears like a mirage in the countryside, just an hour's minibus ride (60km) from Mardin. Savur is a miniature Mardin, without the crowds. The atmosphere is wonderfully laid-back and the setting enchanting, with a weighty citadel surrounded by a honey-coloured crinoline of old houses, lots of greenery and a gushing river running in the valley.

With your own wheels, you can drive to **Dereiçi**, also known as Kıllıt, about 7km east of Savur. This Syrian Orthodox village has two restored churches.

🛏 Sleeping & Eating

TOP CHOICE **Hacı Abdullah Bey Konağı**

PENSION €

(📞 0535 275 2569; savurkonagi@hotmail.com; r per person half-board TL80) The moment you step through the door into this sturdy *konak* perched on the hilltop, you know you're in for something special. The seven cocoonlike rooms are cosily outfitted with kilims, comfortable furnishings, brass beds, antiques and old fabrics. Bathrooms are shared, but that's a minor inconvenience when you factor in all the positives. Another pull is the friendly welcome of the Öztürk family. They don't speak much English, but they create a convivial atmosphere and serve traditional meals prepared from simple fresh ingredients. The rooftop terrace view will keep you intrigued for hours.

Uğur Alabalık Tesisleri & Perili Bahçe

RESTAURANT €

(📞 0482-571 2832; Gazi Mahallesi; mains TL6-10; ⏰ 8am-9pm) For a leisurely alfresco meal, head to this shady garden by the gushing river. Relish fresh trout, salads from local organic veggies, and *içli köfte,* and sluice it all down with a glass of *kıllıt* (local wine) or rakı. The welcome from both the owner – a retired teacher – and his dogs is genuine and heartfelt.

ℹ Getting There & Away

From Mardin there are up to 10 daily minibus services to Savur (TL8, one hour) during summer. In winter, services are more restricted.

Midyat

📞 0482 / POP 61,600

About 65km east of Mardin lies sprawling Midyat, with a drab new section, Estel, linked by 3km of potholed Hükümet Caddesi to the inviting old town. Midyat has lots of potential but is not as touristy as Mardin, mostly because it lacks Mardin's hillside setting.

The centrepiece of the old part of town is merely a traffic roundabout. Close by, **honey-coloured houses** are tucked away behind a row of jewellery shops. Here, the alleyways are lined with houses whose demure doorways open onto huge courtyards surrounded by intricately carved walls, windows and recesses.

As at Mardin, Midyat's Christian population suffered in the early 20th century and during the last few decades, and much of

the community has emigrated. There are nine Syrian Orthodox **churches** in the town, though not all regularly hold services. Although you can see the steeples, it's hard to find the churches in the maze of streets so the best option is to accept the help of one of the local pint-sized guides.

🛏 Sleeping & Eating

Kasr-ı Nehroz

BOUTIQUE HOTEL €€€

(📞 464 2525; www.hotelnehroz.com; Işıklar Mahallesi Caddesi, Sokak 219; r from €120; ❄ @) In the old part of town, this restored courtyard mansion is one of the loveliest places to stay in all of eastern Turkey. Luxury bathrooms combine with pristine stone walls and colourful kilims, while the spacious inner courtyard demands exploration with staircases and turrets leading to views of Midyat's centuries-old rooftops. Standard rooms are a tad compact, but the glorious shared spaces – including a library and reading room – are where you'll feel right at home.

A short stroll through sleepy Midyat leads to the hotel's licensed restaurant (mains TL12 to TL20) curved around an elegant courtyard pool. Prepare to linger for longer than normal at the hotel's superb buffet breakfast that's stacked with local specialities. The restaurant is also open to outside guests.

Hotel Demirdağ

HOTEL €

(📞 462 2000; www.hoteldemirdag.com, in Turkish; Mardin Caddesi; s/d TL40/60; ❄ @) Across in new Midyat, the Demirdağ has well-equipped rooms, colourful as a box of Smarties (but avoid rooms 107 and 109, which are windowless). Its location is handy – the otogar is just one block behind.

Saray Lokantası

LOKANTA €

(Mardin Caddesi; mains TL7-9) On the same street as the Hotel Demirdağ, this local haunt delivers good-value kebaps and pide.

ℹ Getting There & Away

Minibuses regularly ply the bumpy route from outside the Saray Lokantası to old Midyat to save you the charmless walk. Midyat has two otogars, one in new Midyat (one block behind the Hotel Demirdağ) and one in old Midyat, some 200m south of the roundabout along the road to Cizre. There are frequent services for Hasankeyf (TL5, 45 minutes), Batman (TL7, 1½ hours, 82km) and Mardin (TL6, 1¼ hours) from the new Midyat otogar. Minibuses for Cizre (TL9, 1½ hours) and Silopi (TL10, two hours), for Iraq, leave from the otogar in old Midyat.

Culture vultures and independent travellers: provided you have your own wheels or you're OK with arranging a taxi for a day in Midyat (as there's no public transport), we've got something for you: the plateau of Tür Abdin, a traditional homeland of the Syrian Orthodox Church, just east of Midyat (towards Dargeçit). Dotted around the plateau are historic village churches and monasteries, some recently restored. Not-to-be-missed places include **Mor Yakup**, near Barıştepe; **Mor Izozoal**, perched on a knoll in Altıntaş; **Mor Kyriakos** in Bağlarbaşı; **Mor Dimet** in İzbarak; **Meryemana** in Anıtlı; and **Mor Eliyo** in Alagöz (about 3km from Anıtlı).

Roads are asphalted, villages are signposted and villagers will be happy to point you in the right direction. From Midyat, take the road to Hasankeyf (due north). After about 7km you'll reach the turn-off to Mor Yakup, on your right. *İyi yolculuklar* (have a good trip)!

Minibuses from Mardin will pass through the new town, then drop you off at the roundabout in the old town. You could easily base yourself in Midyat and make a day trip to Mardin or Hasankeyf.

Around Midyat

MORGABRIEL

About 18km east of Midyat, Morgabriel (Deyrul Umur) Monastery (☉9-11.30am & 1-4.30pm) rises like a mirage from its desert-like surroundings. Though much restored, the monastery dates back to 397. St Gabriel, the namesake of the monastery, is buried here – the sand beside his tomb is said to cure illness. You'll see various frescoes and the immense ancient dome built by Theodora, wife of Byzantine emperor Justinian, and a more recent bell tower.

Morgabriel is home to the archbishop of Tür Abdin (Mountain of the Servants of God), the surrounding plateau. These days he presides over a much-diminished flock of around 70 people, the majority students. Many students have returned from living overseas in Europe and North America, so you may be lucky in getting an English-speaking guide.

At the time of writing, the monastery's land was being threatened by up to six legal claims from nearby villages – despite the monastery having been established for more than 1600 years. See the website of the Syriac Universal Alliance (www.sua-ngo. org) for more information.

Ask about visiting some of the other churches in the region, such as the **Meryem Ana Kilisesi** at Anıttepe.

To get to the monastery from Midyat, take a Cizre minibus (TL6) to the signpost-ed road junction and walk 2.5km uphill to the gate. Start early in the morning as minibuses become less frequent later in the day. A taxi is about TL50 return, including waiting time.

HASANKEYF
☏0488 / POP 5500

Hasankeyf is a heartbreaker. This gorgeous honey-coloured village clinging to the rocks of a gorge above the Tigris River is a sort of Cappadocia in miniature and a definite must-see, but it's slated to vanish underwater. Nobody knows exactly when this will happen because the Turkish authorities keep silent on the issue. Meanwhile, don't miss Hasankeyf, which has become a popular tourist destination, especially on weekends with local visitors.

◉ Sights

On the main road towards Batman, on the right-hand side of the road, is the conical **Zeynel Bey Türbesi**, isolated in a field near the river. This turquoise-tiled tomb was built in the mid-15th century for Zeynel, son of the Akkoyunlu governor, and it's a rare survivor from this period. Recent work has restored much of its former glory.

A modern bridge now spans the Tigris, but to the right are the broken arches and pylons of the **Eski Köprüsü** (Old Bridge). Their size reinforces the importance of Hasankeyf in the period immediately before the arrival of the Ottomans.

Across the bridge a sign to the right points to the kale and mağaras (caves). The **El-Rizk Cami** (1409) sports a beautiful, slender minaret similar to those in Mardin and is topped with a stork's nest. Just past the mosque, the road forks. The right fork leads down to the banks of the river with a great wall of rock soaring up on the left. The left fork cuts through a rocky defile, the rock faces pitted with caves. Take the slippery stone steps leading up on the right to the kale (admission TL2). This strategic site has been occupied since Byzantine times, but most of the relics you see today were built during the reign of the 14th-century Ayyubids. Beyond the gate are caves, which youthful guides will describe as shops and houses. At the top of the rock are the ruins of the 14th-century **Küçük Saray** (Small Palace), with pots built into the ceiling and walls for sound insulation.

Nearby is a small **mosque**, once a Byzantine church, and the **Büyük Saray** (Big Palace), with a creepy jail underneath. Adjacent is a former watchtower teetering on the edge of the cliff. The 14th-century **Ulu Cami** was built on the site of a church.

Sleeping & Eating

There is only one (very mediocre) accommodation option in Hasankeyf, so it's worth considering visiting from Midyat or Diyarbakır (via Batman) as a day trip.

Another option is to kip in one of the *çardaks* (leafy-roofed shelters) that have been set up along the riverbank. You'll be expected to eat at an adjoining restaurant (around TL10), but come nightfall you can bed down amidst cushions and kilims. Female travellers may wish to err on the side of caution and book a more secure room at the motel.

Hasankeyf Motel HOTEL €
(☑381 2005; Dicle Sokak; s/d TL20/40) This modest 'motel' has a good location, right by the Tigris bridge, but rooms are definitely no-frills, carpets are battered and the grim bathrooms are shared (Turkish toilets). Aim for one of the rooms at the back, with a balcony that overlooks the river. Hot water and towels are available on request.

Yolgeçen Hanı RESTAURANT €€
(Dicle Kıyısı; mains TL7-11) A three-storey labyrinth of riverside rock-hewn dining rooms provide the ultimate cooling escape from the southern heat. Sit on lumpy cushions and tuck into a kebap or a grilled fish.

Naman's Place CAFE €
(Dicle Kıyısı; mains TL5-8) An absolute riverside location and simple grills, flatbreads and salads add up to a lazy afternoon beside the Tigris. Ask if the friendly Idris is around – he can give you an update of the local situation – all in perfect English.

You'll find Naman's directly opposite the rocky entrance to the Yolgeçen Hanı restaurant, and it's one of the *çardaks* where you can bed down for the night.

❶ Getting There & Away

Frequent minibuses run from Batman to Midyat, transiting Hasankeyf (TL3, 40 minutes, 37km). Another option is to visit from Diyarbakır, changing buses in Batman.

Bitlis

☑0434 / POP 44,000

Underrated Bitlis has one of the highest concentrations of restored historic buildings in eastern Anatolia – many of them EU-sponsored projects. A smorgasbord of monuments testifies to rich ancient origins, in striking contrast with neighbouring Tatvan. While modern Tatvan boasts an orderly street plan, Bitlis is chaotically squeezed into the narrow valley of a stream.

A **castle** dominates the town, and two ancient bridges span the stream. Make a beeline for the **Ulu Cami** (1126), while the **Şerefiye Camii** dates from the 16th century. Other must-sees include the splendid **İhlasiye Medrese** (Quranic school), the most significant building in Bitlis, and the **Gökmeydan Camii**.

The **İl Kültür Merkez** (Cumhuriyet Caddesi; ⊗8am-5pm Mon-Fri) has good maps of the city and brochures covering the area. It's housed inside the İhlasiye Medrese.

Around 2km before Bitlis on the road from Tatvan is the recently restored **El-Aman Kervansaray**. Constructed by Hüsrev Paşa in the 16th century, it now incorporates shops, a hamam and a mosque.

The **Dideban Hotel** (☑226 2821; didebanotel@hotmail.com; Nur Caddesi; s/d TL45/70) features spruce rooms and is near local restaurants. It's conveniently located about 100m from the minibus stand for Tatvan and near most monuments. Some double rooms are rather compact. Regular minibuses travel from Tatvan to Bitlis (TL4, 30 minutes).

Finally, don't leave town without trying the excellent local *bal* (honey).

Tatvan

☑0434 / POP 54,000

Tatvan is ideally positioned to visit spectacular Nemrut Dağı (not to be confused with the higher-profile Nemrut Dağı south of Malatya), Ahlat and Bitlis. Several

HASANKEYF UNDER THREAT

Hasankeyf is a gem of a place, but the cloud of a giant engineering project hangs over it. Despite its beauty and history, the town is destined to vanish beneath the waters of the İlisu Dam, part of the GAP project, and scheduled for construction from 2012. The proposed dam will flood a region from Batman to Midyat, drowning this historic site and several other archaeological treasures, and displacing over 37 villages. In 2008 investment partners from Germany, Switzerland and Austria suspended their support for the project, citing concern over its cultural and environmental impact, and in 2010 a proposal was put forward to conserve Hasankeyf by building five smaller dams rather than one large dam.

Opposition continues to mount, supported by the work of the Doğa ('Nature') Foundation (www.dogadernegi.org). Stop by its booth in Hasankeyf to sign its petition to save Hasankeyf, or show your support online at http://hasankeyf.dogadernegi.org/English.aspx.

At the time of writing, the saga of Hasankeyf had two new chapters – Chinese investors were being courted to replace the desertion by European investors in 2008, and the local provincial government was offering to build actual-size replicas of the historical buildings and structures scheduled to be submerged by the waters of the dam. Thanks but no thanks...

kilometres long and just a few blocks wide, Tatvan is not much to look at, but its setting on the shores of Lake Van (backed by bare mountains streaked with snow) is magnificent. It is also the western port for Lake Van steamers.

Sleeping & Eating

Tatvan Kardelen HOTEL €€
(825 9500; Belediye Yanı; s/d TL60/90) This tour group–friendly high-rise enjoys a quiet location next to the *belediye*. It sports spacious and well-equipped rooms, but the furnishings are dated and the neon-lit corridors as sexy as a hospital's.

Hotel Dilek HOTEL €
(827 1516; Yeni Çarşı; s/d TL40/70) The Dilek gets good marks for colourful rooms with tiled bathrooms. Singles are tiny, so angle for rooms 201, 202, 301 or 302, which are more spacious and get more natural light. It's in a street running parallel to the main drag.

Eyvan Pide Lahmacun ve Melemen Salonu PIDECI €
(1 Sokak; mains TL4-7) This compact joint is the best place in town for thin-crust pide or a *lahmacun*. After a flavoursome *kaşarli pide* (cheese pide), faultlessly cooked in the *fırın* (wood-fired oven) on the ground floor, we reckon it's one of the best pide spots in eastern Turkey. The homemade *ayran* is pretty special, too.

Kaşı Beyaz İzgara Salonu OCAKBAŞI €
(PTT Yanı; mains TL6-10) Locals flood here for super tasty kebaps, cooked to perfection on a big *ocak* (grill) on the ground floor. Choose your victim from the display case then snap up a table upstairs. Excellent pide, too. On the same street as Hotel Dilek.

Gökte Ada RESTAURANT €
(Cumhuriyet Caddesi; mains TL6-11) This snazzy spot atop Tatvan's new cinema and shopping complex combines tasty renditions of pide and kebaps with expansive views of Lake Van. It's at the western edge of the town centre.

Getting There & Away

If you're heading to Van, you can take the ferry that crosses the lake twice a day (TL8 per person, about four hours). It doesn't have a fixed schedule. Buses to Van run around the southern shore of the lake (TL10, 2½ to three hours, 156km).

Minibuses to Ahlat (TL3, 30 minutes) leave every hour or so from PTT Caddesi, beside Türk Telekom and the PTT. The minibus stand for Bitlis (TL3, 30 minutes) is a bit further up the street. Direct minibuses to Adilcevaz are infrequent; you'll have to change in Ahlat.

Around Tatvan

NEMRUT DAĞI (MT NEMRUT)

Nemrut Dağı (3050m), rising to the north of Tatvan, is an inactive volcano with several crater lakes – not to be confused with the more famous Nemrut Dağı near Malatya that's topped with the giant heads.

A trip up this Nemrut Dağı is also an unforgettable experience. On the crater rim (13km from the main road), there are sensational views over Lake Van and Tatvan, and over the nearby water-filled craters. From the crater rim, you can hike to the summit, reached after 30 to 45 minutes – just follow the lip of the crater (the last stretch is a bit of a scramble). Midweek, the only company you're likely to have is the shepherds with their flocks (and dogs) and the hoopoes, nuthatches, skylarks and other birds. Follow the dirt road leading down to the lake from the crater rim and find your own picnic area.

Visiting is only possible from around mid-May to the end of October. At other times the summit is under snow.

❶ Getting There & Away

It's not easy to get to Nemrut, as there are no regular services from Tatvan. In high season, you could try to hitch a ride. A taxi from Tatvan is around TL120 return.

With your own transport, leave Tatvan by the road around the lake and then turn left towards Bitlis. About 300m further, turn right following a sign saying 'Nemrut 13km'. The road is rough but passable in an ordinary car except in wet weather. You'll reach the crater rim, from which a dirt road winds down into the crater and connects with other dirt roads that snake around the crater.

Around Lake Van (Van Gölü)

📞 0432

After the rigours of central Anatolia, this vast expanse of water surrounded by snow-capped mountains sounds deceptively promising for beaches and water sports. Lake Van has great potential for activities, but nothing has been really developed yet and infrastructure is lacking. However, this means it's very scenic and virtually untouched.

The most conspicuous feature on the map of southeastern Turkey, this 3750-sq-km lake was formed when a volcano (Nemrut Dağı) north of Tatvan blocked its natural outflow.

SOUTH SHORE

Travelling south around the lake between Van and Tatvan, the scenery is beautiful but there's little reason to stop except at a point 5km west of Gevaş, where the 10th-century Church of the Holy Cross on Akdamar Island is a glorious must-see.

GEVAŞ

Like Ahlat on the north shore, Gevaş has a cemetery full of tombstones dating from the 14th to 17th centuries. Notable is the polygonal **Halime Hatun Türbesi**, built in 1358 for a female member of the Karakoyunlu dynasty.

AKDAMAR

One of the marvels of Armenian architecture is the carefully restored Akdamar Kilisesi (Church of the Holy Cross; admission TL3). It's perched on an island 3km out in the lake, and motorboats ferry sightseers back and forth.

In 921 Gagik Artzruni, King of Vaspurkan, built a palace, church and monastery on the island. Little remains of the palace and monastery, but the church walls are in superb condition and the wonderful relief carvings are among the masterworks of Armenian art. If you're familiar with biblical stories, you'll immediately recognise Adam and Eve, Jonah and the whale (with the head of a dog), David and Goliath, Abraham about to sacrifice Isaac, Daniel in the lions' den, Samson etc. There are some frescoes inside the church.

ALTINSAÇ KİLİSESİ

Another relatively well-preserved Armenian church, Altınsaç Kilisesi is perched on a mound overlooking the lake. If you have your own wheels, be sure to squeeze it into your itinerary.

From Akdamar, drive 12km towards Tatvan until you reach a junction. Turn right onto the road marked for Altınsaç. After 3km the asphalt road ends and becomes a gravel road. The road skirts the shore of the lake for another 14km, until you reach the village of Altınsaç. On a clear day this is a wonderfully scenic drive. From the village it's another 2km to the church, which is visible from some distance.

🛏 Sleeping & Eating

Akdamar Camping ve Restaurant

CAMPGROUND

(📞216 1505; camp sites free; ☺Apr-Sep) This basic camp site – just a grassy expanse and no showers – is immediately opposite the ferry departure point for Akdamar Island. The restaurant (mains TL10 to TL15) has a terrace with lake views, and while the fish is fresh, you're paying a premium for the lakeside location. Another speciality is the *kürt tavası* (meat, tomato and peppers cooked in a clay pot). It's licensed so grab a beer while you're waiting for a boat to Akdamar to fill up. If you're camping, you'll be expected to eat in the restaurant.

ⓘ Getting There & Away

Minibuses run the 44km from Van to Akdamar harbour for TL5 during high season. At other times, there's an hourly minibus to Gevaş (TL5). Most drivers will arrange for you to be transferred to another minibus from Gevaş to Akdamar harbour. Alternatively, catch a minibus heading to Tatvan and ask to be let off at Akdamar harbour. Make sure you're out on the highway flagging a bus back to Van by 4pm, as soon afterwards the traffic dries up and buses may be full.

Boats to Akdamar Island (TL5) run as and when traffic warrants it (minimum 15 people). During summer, boats fill up on a regular basis so waiting time is usually minimal.

NORTH SHORE

The journey around the north shore of Lake Van from Tatvan to Van is even more beautiful than going around the south shore.

The major bus companies take the shortest route around the south of the lake from Tatvan to Van. To travel around the north shore take a minibus to Ahlat from Tatvan, then hop on another minibus to Adilcevaz, where you can overnight. The next morning catch another bus to Van.

AHLAT

A further 42km along the lakeshore from Tatvan is the small town of Ahlat, famous for its splendid Seljuk Turkish tombs and graveyard. Don't overlook this largely underrated site.

Founded during the reign of Caliph Omar (AD 581–644), Ahlat became a Seljuk stronghold in the 1060s. When the Seljuk sultan Alp Arslan rode out to meet the Byzantine emperor Romanus Diogenes in battle on the field of Manzikert, Ahlat was his base. Later, Ahlat had an extraordinarily eventful history even for Anatolia, with *emir* defeating prince and king driving out *emir*.

Just west of Ahlat is an overgrown polygonal 13th-century tomb, **Usta Şağirt Kümbeti** (Ulu Kümbeti), 300m off the highway. It's the largest Seljuk tomb in the area.

Further along the highway on the left is a museum, and behind it a vast **Selçuk Mezarlığı** (Seljuk cemetery), with stele-like headstones of lichen-covered grey or red volcanic tuff with intricate web patterns and bands of Kufic lettering.

Over the centuries earthquakes, wind and water have set the stones at all angles, a striking sight with spectacular Nemrut Dağı as a backdrop. Most stones have a crow as sentinel, and tortoises cruise the ruins.

On the northeastern side of the graveyard is the unusual **Bayındır Kümbeti ve Camii** (Bayındır Tomb and Mosque; 1477), with a colonnaded porch and its own *mihrab* (niche indicating the direction of Mecca).

The small museum (⊙8am-noon & 1-5pm Mon-Sat) has a reasonable collection that includes Urartian bronze belts and needles as well as some Byzantine glass-bead necklaces.

Other sites in Ahlat include the **Çifte Kümbet** (Twin Tombs), about 2km from the museum towards the town centre, and the **Ahlat Sahil Kalesi** (Ahlat Lakeside Fortress), south of the Çifte Kümbet, which was built during the reign of Süleyman the Magnificent.

From Tatvan, minibuses leave for Ahlat (TL4, 30 minutes) from beside Türk Telekom and the PTT. Get let off at the museum on the western outskirts of Ahlat, or you'll have to walk back from the town centre. From Ahlat, there are regular minibuses to Adilcevaz (TL3, 20 minutes).

ADİLCEVAZ

About 25km east of Ahlat is the town of Adilcevaz, once a Urartian town but now dominated by a great Seljuk Turkish **fortress** (1571).

Snowmelt from the year-round snowfields on Süphan Dağı flows down to Adilcevaz, making its surroundings lush and fertile. On the western edge of town is the **Ulu Camii**, built in the 13th century, and still used for daily prayer.

From the centre of town, take a taxi to the **Kef Kalesi**, another Urartian citadel perched higher up in the valley (about TL25 return).

The best accommodation in town is the newly opened Cevizlibağ Otel (☎0434-311 3152; www.cevizlibagotel.com; Recep Tayyip Erdoğan Bulvarı 31/1; s/d TL35/70; ❄), handily located midway between the otogar and the town centre. The spacious rooms are trimmed in shiny marble with wooden floors and spotless bathrooms. Downstairs is a good restaurant.

From Adilcevaz, there are five direct buses to Van (TL15, 2½ hours), but the last one departs around 2pm – make sure you start out early in the day.

SÜPHAN DAĞI (MT SÜPHAN)

The Kilimanjaro-esque bulk framing the horizon is **Süphan Dağı** (4053m), Turkey's second-highest mountain after Mt Ararat (Ağrı Dağı). It offers excellent hiking options and is a good way to prepare for the more challenging climb of Mt Ararat. Contact one of the travel agencies in Doğubayazıt.

Van

0432 / POP 391.000 / ELEV 1727M

Frontier towns never looked so liberal. Young couples walking hand in hand on the main drag, students flirting in the pastry shops, live bands knocking out Kurdish tunes in pubs (nightlife, at last!), and unscarved girls sampling an ice cream on a terrace and daring eye contact with foreigners. More urban, more casual and less rigorous, Van is very different in spirit from the rest of southeastern Anatolia.

Good news: Van boasts a brilliant location, near the eponymous lake. Bad news: forget about water sports and beaches. Instead, focus on the striking monuments, including Van Kalesi (Van Castle or the Rock of Van), spend a few days journeying around the lake, and explore the nearby historic sites of Çavuştepe, Hoşap and Yedi Kilise. To really escape, take the daily minibus to the remote mountain village of Bahçesaray.

Hotels, restaurants, internet cafes, ATMs, the post office and bus company offices all lie on or around Cumhuriyet Caddesi.

History

The kingdom of Urartu, the biblical Ararat, flourished from the 13th to the 7th centuries BC. Its capital was on the outskirts of present-day Van. The Urartians borrowed much of their culture (including cuneiform writing) from the neighbouring Assyrians, with whom they were more or less permanently at war. The powerful Assyrians never subdued the Urartians, but when several waves of Cimmerians, Scythians and Medes swept into Urartu and joined in the battle, the kingdom met its downfall.

Later the region was resettled by a people whom the Persians called Armenians. By the 6th century BC the area was governed by Persian and Median satraps (provincial governors).

In the 8th century AD, Arab armies flooded through from the south, forcing the Armenian prince to take refuge on Akdamar Island. Unable to fend off the Arabs, he agreed to pay tribute to the caliph. When the Arabs retreated, the Byzantines and Persians took their place, and overlordship of Armenia seesawed between them as one or the other gained military advantage.

After defeating the Byzantines in 1071 at Manzikert, north of Lake Van, the Seljuk Turks marched on, with a flood of Turkoman nomads in tow, to found the sultanate of Rum, based in Konya. The domination of eastern Anatolia by Turkish *emirs* followed and continued until the coming of the Ottomans in 1468.

During WWI, Armenian guerrilla bands intent on founding an independent Armenian state collaborated with the Russians to defeat the Ottoman armies in Turkey's east. From then on the Armenians, formerly loyal subjects of the sultan, were viewed by the Turks as traitors. Bitter fighting between Turkish and Kurdish forces on the one side and Armenian and Russian forces on the other brought devastation to the entire region and to Van. For more, see p635.

The Ottomans destroyed the old city of Van (near Van Castle) before the Russians occupied it in 1915. Ottoman forces counterattacked but were unable to drive the invaders out, and Van remained under Russian occupation until the armistice of 1917. After the founding of the Turkish Republic, a new planned city of Van was built 4km east of the old site.

⊙ Sights

Van Castle (Van Kalesi) & Eski Van RUINS

Nothing is quite so impressive in Van as Van Castle (Rock of Van; admission TL3; ☺9am-dusk), which dominates the view of the city, about 4km west of the centre. Try to visit at sunset for great views across the lake.

The site is fairly spread out, something to bear in mind when it's scorching hot. The bus will drop you at the northwestern corner of the rock, where there's the ticket office and a tea garden.

Just past the ticket office is an old **stone bridge** and some willows. To the left, a stairway leads up the rock. On your way up is a ruined **mosque** with a minaret, as well

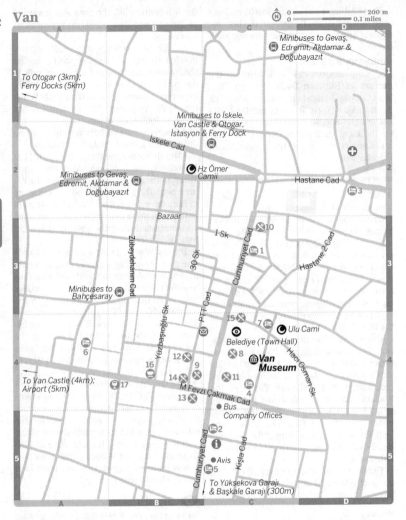

as an arched-roof building, which used to be a Quranic school.

From the summit the foundations of **Eski Van** (the old city) reveal themselves on the southern side of the rock. The flat space punctuated by the grass-covered foundations of numerous buildings was the site of the old city, destroyed during the upheavals of WWI. A few buildings have survived and are clearly visible from the top: the **Hüsrev Paşa Külliyesi**, dating back to 1567, which has been restored and has a *kümbet* (tomb) attached; the nearby **Kaya Çelebi Camii** (1662), with a similarly striped minaret; the brick minaret of the Seljuk **Ulu Cami**; and the **Kızıl Camii** (Red Mosque).

At the ticket office ask the custodian (he'll expect a tip) to show you the huge cuneiform inscriptions (ask for the *tabela*) as well as the numerous *khachkars* (Armenian crosses) that are carved into the southern side of the rock. Look out also for the water reservoir, an ancient hamam and a ruined palace (not visible from the top of the rock). The Kızıl Cami and Ulu Cami can also easily be approached, further south. Taking some distance from the rock to get a wider perspective, the custodian may point

Van

out various rock-cut **funeral chambers** (not visible from the base of the rock), including that of King Argishti.

On the way back to the ticket office, ask the custodian to show you the **Sardur Burcu** (Sardur Tower; 840–830 BC), in the little willow forest (as there's no sign, it's not easy to find). It's a large black stone rectangle sporting cuneiform inscriptions in Assyrian praising the Urartian King Sardur I.

To get to Van Kalesi take a 'Kale' minibus (TL2) from İskele Caddesi opposite the Hz Ömer Camii.

Van Museum   MUSEUM
The small **Van Museum** (Van Müzesi; Kışla Caddesi; admission TL3; ⊙8am-noon & 1-5pm Tue-Sun) boasts an outstanding collection of Urartian exhibits. The Urartian gold jewellery is the highlight, but the bronze belts, helmets, horse armour and terracotta figures are also well worth seeing.

The ethnographic exhibits upstairs include local Kurdish and Turkoman kilims and a carpeted sitting area, such as is found in village houses. The Genocide Section is

a piece of one-sided propaganda displaying the contents of graves left from the massacres of Turks and Kurds by Armenians at Çavuşoğlu and Zeve.

The museum has a good bookshop with plenty of foreign-language titles about the region.

🛏 Sleeping

Van has a decent range of accommodation, but it is more expensive than elsewhere in eastern Turkey.

Hotel Bayram   HOTEL €€
(☑216 1136; www.hotelbayram.com; Cumhuriyet Caddesi 1a; s/d TL70/120; ❋) Centrally located just off Van's main drag, this sparkling new opening has spacious rooms decked out in warm, chocolate brown tones. Bathroom fittings still gleam and feature lots of natural wood, and good restaurants and bars are all within a 50m stroll.

Hotel Tamara   BUSINESS HOTEL €€€
(☑214 3295; Yüzbaşıoğlu Sokak; s/d TL155/185; ❋) Classic comfort and a convenient location combine to showcase cosy rooms with all mod cons, a hamam, unflappable staff and the impressive hotel restaurant's *mangal* grills. It caters mainly for businesspeople, and there's also a pretty decent stab at an English pub. On weekends, definitely line up a sharp discount.

Otel Bahar   HOTEL €
(☑215 5748, 0539 729 6838; Ordu Caddesi 20; s/d TL25/50) One of the best cheapies in town, the Bahar features simple rooms with clean bathrooms and compact balconies. When the nearby mosque wakes you early in the morning, take in the laneway views with lots of teashops and barbers. Reception is friendly but may be slightly offended when you forgo the OK hotel breakfast for the wonders of Van's *kahvaltı* options just around the corner.

Hotel Kahraman   HOTEL €
(☑216 1525; ercan_216646@mynet.com; Cumhuriyet Caddesi 111; s/d TL25/50; ❋) It's location plus at the Kahraman, with (mostly) spacious rooms overlooking Van's main thoroughfare. Pastel tones and colourful bed linen brighten the budget ambience. Most rooms share bathroom facilities, but they're kept clean and are fine for a low-cost stay.

Büyük Asur Oteli   HOTEL €€
(☑216 8792; www.buyukasur.com; Cumhuriyet Caddesi, Turizm Sokak; s/d TL60/90; ❋) Even if

BREAKFASTS OF CHAMPIONS

Van is famed for its tasty *kahvaltı* (breakfast). Skip your usually bland hotel breakfast and head straight to Eski Sümerbank Sokak, also called 'Kahvaltı Sokak' (Breakfast St), a pedestrianised side street running parallel to Cumhuriyet Caddesi. Here you'll find a row of eateries specialising in complete Turkish breakfasts, including the buzzing **Sütçü Fevzi** (☎216 6618; Eski Sümerbank Sokak; ☺7am-noon) and **Sütçü Kenan** (☎216 8499; Eski Sümerbank Sokak; ☺7am-noon), which have tables set up outside. The other restaurants on the street are equally good.

On summer mornings the street literally heaves with punters sampling *otlu peynir* (cheese mixed with a tangy herb, Van's speciality), *beyaz peynir* (a mild yellow cheese), honey from the highlands (mmm!), olives, *kaymak* (clotted cream), butter, tomatoes, cucumbers and *sucuklu yumurta* (omelette with sausage). Whet your appetite by checking out the pictures on www.vandakahvalti.com (in Turkish). A full breakfast will set you back around TL12 to TL15. An essential Van experience.

you're on a tight budget, consider spending a little more to enjoy the comforts of this reliable midrange venture. The rooms are colourful and come complete with fresh linen, TV and well-scrubbed bathrooms. English is spoken and the hotel can organise tours to Akdamar Island, Hoşap Castle and other local attractions.

Büyük Urartu Oteli　　HOTEL €€
(☎212 0660; www.buyukurartuotel.com; Hastane 2 Caddesi; s/d TL90/130; ❄❄) This reassuring choice gives off a serious hotel vibe, with professional staff and an impressive lobby. The motel-like rooms are nothing to write home about but the full array of amenities, including a sauna, pool and rooftop restaurant, offer ample compensation.

Ada Palas　　HOTEL €€
(☎216 2716; www.vanadapalas.tr.gg; Cumhuriyet Caddesi; s/d TL80/120; ❄) The 2nd floor is *yeşil* (green), the 3rd floor canary yellow and the 4th floor electric *mavi* (blue). The owners of the centrally located and well-organised Ada Palas certainly like to add colour to life.

✖ Eating

Tamara Ocakbaşı　　OCAKBAŞI €€
(Yüzbaşıoğlu Sokak; mains TL10-15; ☺5pm-late) A meal here is dizzying, especially for carnivores. In the Hotel Tamara, the dining room eatery features 40 *ocak* – each table has its own grill. Mood lighting adds a touch of atmosphere in the evening. High-quality meat and fish dishes feature prominently, but the list of meze is equally impressive. The attached North Shield pub

is a slice of ersatz Tyneside in southeastern Turkey.

Kebabistan　　KEBAPÇI €€
(Sinemalar Sokak; mains TL6-10) You're within safe boundaries here: the kitchen turns out expertly cooked kebaps (go for the *kuşbaşı*, with little morsels of beef). A second branch, across the street, specialises in pide. Getting there is half the fun: it's in a side street where men can be seen sitting on low chairs, playing backgammon and drinking tea. And yes, it may just have the planet's best name for a kebap eatery.

Saçi Beyaz Et Lokantası　　RESTAURANT €€
(Kazım Karabekir Caddesi; mains TL5-12) With an appetising selection of pastries and other delicacies, carb lovers should make this pastry shop their first port of call. The vast, vivacious terrace is usually packed to bursting with Van's movers and shakers in the late afternoon. Snacks, pasta and grills available are routinely devoured in the upstairs restaurant section.

Halil İbrahim Sofrası　　LOKANTA €€
(Cumhuriyet Caddesi; mains TL7-12) One word describes this downtown hot spot: yum. The eclectic food is well presented and of high quality, with service to match, served in sleek surrounds. Try the rich and tender İskender kebap. Pide buffs should target the generous 'pide special', with a bit of everything.

Safa 3, Çorba 1 Paça Salonu　　LOKANTA €
(Kazım Karabekir Caddesi; soups TL3; ☺24hr) If you're an adventurous foodie, head to this quirky little restaurant. Regulars swear by the *kelle* (mutton's head) – the spicy lentil soup is more approachable.

Ayça Pastaneleri PATISSERIE €
(Kazım Karabekir Caddesi; snacks TL2-5) With its see-and-be-seen glass front on the 1st floor and modern furnishings, this place lures in students in search of a pleasant spot to flirt and relax over toothsome baklavas and decent snacks.

Akdeniz Tantuni STREET FOOD €
(Cumhuriyet Caddesi; sandwiches TL4) This delightful little den on the main drag prepares devilish chicken sandwiches at paupers' prices and in the *tantuni* style from the Akdeniz (Mediterranean) city of Mersin.

Çavuşoğlu PATISSERIE €
(Cumhuriyet Caddesi; pastries from TL2) Luscious ice creams and dangerously good baklavas.

🍷 Drinking & Entertainment

Halay Türkü Bar BAR-RESTAURANT
(Kazım Karabekir Caddesi) Multiple floors add up to multiple ways to enjoy Van's low-key nightlife scene. Kick off with tasty meze and grilled meat before graduating to draught beer, generously poured local spirits and regular live music.

North Shield PUB
(Hotel Tamara, Yüzbaşıoğlu Sokak) Go on – wanting a cold pint in a dusty Kurdish city is not a hanging offence. Head to the North Shield in the Hotel Tamara for a familiar English pub-type ambience. After a couple of beers make a beeline for the excellent *mangal* restaurant upstairs.

Durum X CAFE
(Kazım Karabekir Caddesi; fresh juices from TL2; ⊙8am-10pm) Apple, orange, kiwi, grapefruit – the list goes on at this handy hole-in-the-wall juice bar. Also on offer are cheap grilled sandwiches. Grab a quick lunch and keep exploring.

🛈 Information

ATMs and internet cafes are easily found on Cumhuriyet Caddesi.

Tourist office (☑216 2530; Cumhuriyet Caddesi; ⊙8.30am-noon & 1-5.30pm Mon-Fri) English is spoken and there are good maps and brochures.

🛈 Getting There & Away

Air
A taxi to the airport costs about TL20.

Pegasus Airlines (www.flypgs.com) Has six weekly flights to/from Ankara (from TL90) and daily flights to/from İstanbul (from TL80).

Turkish Airlines (www.thy.com) Has one to two daily flights to/from İstanbul (from TL90) and one daily flight to/from Ankara (from TL90).

Boat
A ferry crosses Lake Van between Tatvan and Van twice daily. There's no fixed schedule. The trip costs TL8 per passenger and takes about four hours. 'İskele' dolmuşes ply İskele Caddesi to the harbour (TL2).

Bus
Many bus companies have ticket offices at the intersection of Cumhuriyet and Kazım Karabekir Caddesis. They provide *servises* to shuttle

SERVICES FROM VAN'S OTOGAR

DESTINATION	FARE (TL)	DURATION (HR)	DISTANCE (KM)	FREQUENCY (PER DAY)
Ağrı	20	3	213	frequent buses
Ankara	70	22	1250	frequent buses
Diyarbakır	35	7	410	frequent buses
Erciş	10	1¼	95	several buses
Erzurum	35	6	410	several buses
Hakkari	15	4	205	a few buses
Malatya	50	9-10	500	frequent buses
Şanlıurfa	40	9	585	a few buses
Tatvan	10	2½	156	frequent buses
Trabzon	60	12	733	a few direct buses, most via Erzurum

passengers to and from the otogar on the north-western outskirts.

Minibuses to Bahçesaray (TL18, three hours, one morning service) leave from near a teahouse called Bahçesaray Çay Evi, south of the bazaar. For Hoşap and Çavuştepe (TL5, 45 minutes), you can take a minibus that leaves from the Yüksekova Garajı or the Başkale Garajı, both on Cumhuriyet Caddesi, a few hundred metres south of the Büyük Asur Oteli.

Minibuses to Gevaş and Akdamar (TL3, about 45 minutes) depart from a dusty car park down a side street on the right of the northern extension of Cumhuriyet Caddesi. Transport to Doğubayazıt also leaves from here, an 185km run that's worth taking for the magnificent pastoral scenery along the way, especially if you can pause at the spectacular Muradiye Waterfalls.

To get to Iran, there are direct buses to Orumi-yeh (in Iran).

Car

Consider renting a car to journey around Lake Van. **Avis** (☎214 6375; www.avis.com.tr; Cumhuriyet Caddesi), near the tourist office, rents cars for about TL100 per day. Other rental agencies line Cumhuriyet Caddesi.

Train

The twice-weekly *Vangölü Ekspresi* from İstanbul and Ankara terminates at Tatvan; from Tatvan, the ferry will bring you to the dock at Van. The weekly *Trans Asya Ekspresi* connects İstanbul

to Tehran and stops at Van. It leaves for Tehran (TL48) on Tuesday and Friday any time between 9pm and midnight; for İstanbul (TL65), it also leaves on Tuesday and Friday. A train also departs Van for Tabriz (TL20, nine hours) in Iran around 9.30pm on a Thursday. Confirm exact times at the train station.

The main train station is northwest of the centre near the otogar, with another station, İskele İstasyonu, several kilometres to the northwest on the lakeshore. Catch 'İstasyon' minibuses from İskele Caddesi.

❶ Getting Around

For Van Kalesi and the *iskele* (ferry dock), catch a minibus from İskele Caddesi.

Around Van
YEDİ KİLİSE

The poignant, crumbling **Yedi Kilise** (Seven Churches; admission by donation) is about 9km southeast of Van, in a typical Kurdish village. It used to be a large monastery. The arched portal sports elaborate stone carvings with various Armenian inscriptions above it. Inside there are well-preserved frescoes. Women selling knitted gloves and socks usually wait near the building.

There's no reliable public transport to Yedi Kilise. The most practical way to get there is by taxi (about TL35 including waiting time).

VISITING TURKEY'S DEEP SOUTHEAST

The remote southeastern corner of Turkey (east of Siirt and Midyat) still carries a fearsome reputation among travellers and among Turks from western Anatolia. The southeast was at the epicentre of the Kurdish rebellion during the 1980s and '90s and for a long time was off limits to travellers.

During research for this book, conflict between the Turkish army and the PKK (Kurdistan Workers Party, or PKK/Kongra-Gel) was at its lowest level for many years, and we were able to travel without problems to southeastern towns with just the minor inconvenience of a few army checkpoints and passport controls.

Soon after, however, the PKK called off its 14-month ceasefire and renewed attacks on the Turkish military. Conflict was focused on Hakkari and the border areas with Iraq, but activity also reached close to larger cities including Van.

The remote southeast's appeal to travellers is undeniable, with jagged mountains and sweeping canyons and gorges. In less troubled times, the area around Hakkari should be a rugged hub for trekking in the Cilo Dağı mountains. Kurdish hospitality also reaches a peak in this area.

By the time you read this, the security situation may have improved again, so undertake some solid homework before you leave by monitoring up-to-date information sources like Lonely Planet's Thorn Tree forum. Expect a significant military presence and keep your passport handy for army checkpoints.

From Van to Hakkari, there are regular bus services (TL17, four hours). There are also several daily minibuses to Yüksekova (TL8, 78km), from where you can cross the border at Esendere–Serö and journey on to Iran.

BAHÇESARAY

From Van, the 110km ride to reach this town in the middle of nowhere, set deep in the mountains, is exhilarating. Bahçesaray's main claim to fame is its isolation. Because of snow it's cut off from the outside world at least six months of the year. 'Half the year we belong to God,' say the locals.

From Van, the highly scenic road crosses the steppe before gradually ascending to the Karabel Geçiti, at 2985m, dizzying. On your way look for *zoma* (encampments), with Kurdish shepherds, their flocks and their huge dogs. The scenery is captivating on a clear day. The air is intoxicatingly crisp and the surrounding mountains make a perfect backdrop.

Bahçesaray is a place to get away from it all, but there are also a few nearby monuments that are worth a visit, including a couple of Armenian churches and an ancient bridge. Take on the locals at chess – they're reputedly the best players in eastern Anatolia – and don't leave without sampling the delicious local honey *(bal)*.

At the time of writing, Bahçesaray had no formal accommodation facilities on offer, but visitors are usually offered the chance to kip down at the local high school. Ask for the *oğretmenevi* (teacher's house).

In summer, you could reach Bahçesaray with a normal vehicle, but the road is sealed only up to Yukarı Narlıca and deteriorates markedly near the pass – a 4WD or a high-clearance vehicle would be more appropriate. If it's wet, this part of the road is impassable with a normal vehicle. This ride is definitely not for the faint-hearted – expect lots of twists and turns, steep gradients and precipitous ravines.

One or two minibuses leave daily except Sunday from a small minibus stand in Van (ask for Bahçesaray Çay Evi, off Zübeydehanım Caddesi). The bumpy ride takes about three hours and costs TL15. You'll definitely need to stay the night before returning to Van.

HOŞAP & ÇAVUŞTEPE

A day excursion southeast of Van along the road to Başkale and Hakkari takes you to the Urartian site at Çavuştepe (25km from Van) and the spectacular Kurdish castle at Hoşap, 33km further along. Both sites amply reward the effort of visiting them.

Hoşap Castle (admission TL3) perches photogenically on top of a rocky outcrop alongside Güzelsu, a hicksville truck-stop village. Cross one of the two bridges (the one with alternate dark and light stones dates from the 17th century) and follow the signs around the far side of the hill to reach the castle entrance, above which are superb lion reliefs. Looking east there is a row of mud defensive walls that once encircled the village. Built in 1643 by a local Kurdish chieftain, Mahmudi Süleyman, the castle has a very impressive entrance gateway in a round tower. Significant restoration work on the castle was completed in 2010.

The narrow hill on the left side of the highway at **Çavuştepe** was once crowned by the fortress-palace **Sarduri-Hinili**, home of the kings of Urartu and built between 764 and 735 BC by King Sardur II, son of Argishti. These are the best-preserved foundations of any Urartian palace.

From the car park, the **yukarı kale** (upper fortress) is up to the left, and the vast **aşağı kale** (lower fortress) to the right.

Climb the rocky hill to the lower fortress temple ruins (Mabet), marked by a gate of black basalt blocks polished to a gloss; a few blocks on the left-hand side are inscribed in cuneiform. Note other illustrations of Urartian engineering ingenuity, including the cisterns under the pathways, the storage vessels, the kitchen and palace. Down on the plains to the south are canals also created by the Urartians.

To get to the Hoşap and Çavuştepe sites, catch a minibus from Van heading to Başkale or Yüksekova and get out at Hoşap (TL6). After seeing the castle, flag down a bus back to Çavuştepe, 500m off the highway, and then catch a third bus back to Van. Frequent minibuses and buses ply the route.

Understand Turkey

population per sq km

TURKEY   USA   UK

≈ 30 people

Turkey Today

The very heart of the world during the Ottoman and Byzantine empires, Turkey remains pivotal on the global stage. Its position at the meeting of Europe and Asia informs its political bent: the secular country has a moderate Islamic government and good relations with the West, for which Turkey is a key ally in the Middle East.

You will notice all the nibbles placed in the street for dogs and cats by animal-loving Turks. What's more, a global Reuters poll found Turks were most likely, at 49%, to spend Valentine's Day with their pet rather than their spouse or partner.

A few events have troubled Turkey's international relations recently. In May 2010, Israeli troops stormed the *Mavi Marmara,* a Turkish vessel in a Gaza-bound aid flotilla, and the activists suffered nine deaths. Ankara recalled its ambassador from Israel and cancelled joint military exercises, and a UN report characterised the killings as 'extra-legal, arbitrary and summary executions'. Meanwhile, efforts to normalise Turkish-Armenian relations faltered and the countries' border remains closed. Turkey also voted against a fresh round of UN sanctions against Iran over its nuclear program, instead brokering a nuclear fuel swap with its neighbour.

To the west, Turkey's bid to join the European Union (EU) continues; accession talks started in 2005 and discussions relating to 13 of the 35 policy chapters have opened. Key obstacles are Turkey's refusal to recognise EU member Cyprus; the marginalisation of its Kurdish minority in eastern Anatolia; freedom of speech (YouTube, for example, was banned for carrying anti-Atatürk content); and EU discomfort about embracing a 99% Muslim country, despite the deployment of Turkish troops against the Taliban and Al Qaeda in Afghanistan.

Domestically, the most pressing problem is Turkey's own 'war on terror' – the Kurdish issue. After decades of clashes between the military and the Kurdistan Workers Party (PKK), classed internationally as a terrorist group, the situation simmered down, following government moves such as allowing Kurdish broadcasts. The PKK then ended its

Top Books

See p650 for more on books and films.

» **The Snake Stone** (Jason Goodwin)

» **Portrait of a Turkish Family** (Irfan Orga)

» **Birds Without Wings** (Louis de Bernières)

» **Snow** (Orhan Pamuk)

» **The Bastard of İstanbul** (Elif Şafak)

» **Magic Bus: On the Hippie Trail from Istanbul to India** (Rory MacLean)

» **Turkey: Bright Sun, Strong Tea** (Tom Brosnahan)

Body Language

» 'Yes' is a slight downward nod.

» 'No' is a slight upward nod while making the 'tsk' sound.

» Never point the sole of your foot at anyone.

» The 'OK' sign indicates homosexuality.

ethnic groups
(% of population)

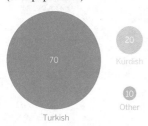

70
Turkish

20
Kurdish

10
Other

if Turkey were 100 people

80 would be Muslims
19 would be Alevi Muslims
1 other religions

14-month ceasefire in 2010, with its chief promising to take the fight out of the mountains of southeastern Anatolia and Kurdish Iraq – to western Turkey. However, weapons were again laid down at Ramazan. The main contact most travellers will have with the Kurdish problem is military roadblocks in the southeast.

Taking a democratic approach to the Kurdish troubles has been one of the progressive moves by Prime Minister Erdoğan's Justice and Development (AKP) government. Another was the referendum on constitutional reform, in which Turkey voted for change; the military's powers are set to be lessened in what will hopefully be a move towards greater democracy. Such is the enduring loyalty to the secular republic founded by Atatürk, whose picture still crowns every *kebapçı* (kebap eatery), that a coup plot and a legal case have (unsuccessfully) targeted the AKP's 'non-secular activities'. The former İstanbul mayor and his party have served two terms, and look likely to win the July 2011 elections.

Certainly, Islam is a strengthening force here, but it's unwise to make firm electoral predictions in a country where military coups used to be a regular fixture. The gregarious people embrace this uncertainty, with conversation filled with claim, counter claim and conspiracy theory. Intrigue has been a local speciality since the decadent days of the Ottoman sultans. However, most people agree that the economy is bullish, having avoided the worst problems experienced by Europe; exports are increasing and unemployment has dropped to 11%. In the tourism sector, a Deloitte survey found that İstanbul's hotels lost just 3.5% of revenue in crisis-hit 2009 – compared with the European average of 16.7% – so don't expect to receive extra discounts from Turkey's famously sharp business people.

Demonstrating the business acumen of Turks, soon after Paul the psychic German octopus famously pre-dicted the results of soccer World Cup matches in 2010, a Turkish ad offered what it claimed to be Paul's distant cousin – Polat.

Top Films

» **Vizontele** Black comedy about the first family to get a TV in a small town.

» **Filler ve Çimen** Tells the stories of desperate characters.

» **Edge of Heaven** Follows a political dissident.

» **Babam Ve Oglum** Portrays the generation gap in an Aegean village.

» **Üç Maymun** Follows a poor İstanbul family's struggles.

» **Veda** Good summary of Atatürk's life.

» **Hamam** Turkish expat inherits a hamam; addresses gay issues.

Etiquette

» **Punctuality** Take it seriously.

» **Restaurants** If you are invited, your host pays; if you invite someone, you pay.

» **Meals** Leave nothing on your plate when at someone's house.

» **Wine** Check if your host drinks before taking it as a gift.

History

Fate has put Turkey at the junction of two continents. A land bridge, meeting point and battleground, it has seen peoples moving between Europe and Asia throughout history.

Cultures began arising in Anatolia (the land mass of Turkey within Asia) a very long time ago, with the history's first recognised 'city' being established at Çatalhöyük over 8000 years ago. Later the Hittites created the first Anatolian empire – they ruled over various other peoples while also fending off arrivals from Greece intent on colonising the coastal regions. One of the most recognisable of these colonies was Troy (of Homer and the *Iliad* fame); meanwhile a litany of ancient peoples – Lycians, Lydians, Phrygians amongst others – flitted across the historical stage.

The Persians arrived from the east, prompting Alexander the Great to chase them back again. Alexander's empire didn't last but it sped the Hellenisation of Anatolia with great wealth being created through Greek trade networks. The canny Romans arrived in 190 BC to exploit trade and resources, then stuck around to see – and harass – the first Christian communities. Christianity quietly spread until, in the 4th century, the Roman emperor Constantine himself converted and established Constantinople (modern İstanbul). This was to become the capital of the Byzantine Empire, a Greek-speaking, Christian remnant of Rome which persisted for over 1000 years.

Byzantine control of Anatolia was challenged by the Seljuk Turks, who arrived out of Central Asia in the 11th century. The Seljuks were succeeded by the Ottoman Turks, who swallowed up Anatolia and finished the Byzantines off in the 15th century. From then on the Ottomans expanded into southeastern Europe, reaching the very walls of Vienna before being relentlessly pushed back. By 1912 Greek and Serbian armies were advancing on İstanbul, and during and after WWI the European powers sought to dismember Turkey entirely. It was only

Until the rediscovery of the ruins at Boğazkale in the 19th century, the Hittites were known only through several obscure references in the Old Testament.

Archaeologist Ian Hodder's *Catalhoyuk: The Leopard's Tale* is an account of the excavation of the site, which vividly portrays life as it was during the city's heyday.

TIMELINE

c 6500 BC
Founding of Çatalhöyük, the world's first city. Over time 13 layers of houses were built, beehive style, interconnected and linked with ladders. At its peak the city housed around 8000.

c 4000–3000 BC
Hattian culture develops at Alacahöyük during the early Bronze Age, though settlement has been continuous since the chalcolithic age. The Hatti develop distinctive jewellery and metalwork and weapons.

c 2000 BC
The Hittites, an Indo-European people, arrive in Anatolia and conquer the Hatti, claiming their capital at Hattuşa. The Hittites go on to create a kingdom extending to Babylon and Egypt.

the inspired leadership of Mustafa Kemal Atatürk that saved the day. In the struggle for independence, Atatürk and his armies ejected the foreign interlopers, then established the Turkish Republic in 1923. Turkey has since undergone an extensive process of modernisation, all the while building a viable democracy and re-establishing itself on the international stage.

It's been a long story, but one full of remarkable and intriguing events, cultures and individuals – enough for many a history book.

Early Cultures, Cities & Clashes

Archaeological finds indicate that Anatolia was first inhabited by hunter-gatherers during the Palaeolithic era. By around the 7th millennium BC some folk formed settlements. Çatalhöyük, which arose around 6500 BC, may be the first-ever city. It was certainly a centre of innovation, locals developing crop irrigation, domesticating pigs and sheep, and creating distinctive pottery. Relics from this settlement can be seen at Ankara's Museum of Anatolian Civilisations (p397).

The chalcolithic age saw the rise of Hacılar, in Central Anatolia, and communities in the southeast that absorbed Mesopotamian influences, including the use of metal tools. Across Anatolia more and larger communities sprung up and interacted – not always happily: settlements were often fortified.

By 3000 BC advances in metallurgy allowed canny individuals to concentrate power in their own hands, leading to the creation of various Anatolian kingdoms. One such was at Alacahöyük, in the heart of Anatolia, yet even this place showed Caucasian influence, evidence of trade well beyond the Anatolian plateau.

Trade was increasing on the western coast too, with Troy trading with the Aegean islands and mainland Greece. Around 2000 BC the Hatti people established a capital at Kanesh (Kültepe, near Kayseri), ruling over a web of trading communities. Here for the first time Anatolian history materialises from the realm of archaeological conjecture and becomes 'real': clay tablets provide written records of dates, events and names.

No singular Anatolian civilisation had yet emerged, but the tone was set for millennia to come: cultural interaction, trade and war would be the recurring themes of Anatolian history.

Ages of Bronze: The Hittites

The Hatti were a temporary presence. As they declined, the Hittites assumed their territory. From Alacahöyük, the Hittites shifted their capital to Hattuşa (near present-day Boğazkale) around 1800 BC.

The Hittites' legacy consisted of their great capital, as well as their state archives (cuneiform clay tablets) and distinctive artistic styles. By

LYCIANS

For further discussion of the highs and lows of life in ancient Lycia and detailed information on the sites of Turkey's Lycian coast, visit www.lycianturkey.com.

BAH/IMAGEBROKER

» The ruins of Troy were lost until the 19th century

c 1200 BC

The destruction of Troy, later immortalised in Homer's *Iliad*. For 10 years the Mycenaeans had besieged the city strategically placed above the Dardanelles and the key to Black Sea trade.

c 1100 BC

After the fall of the Hittites several neo-Hittite kingdoms arose, while the Assyrians and various Georgian groups encroached on southern Anatolia. The Phoenicians brought the alphabet to Anatolia around this time.

HOMER

1450 BC the kingdom, having endured internal ructions, was reborn as an empire. In creating the first Anatolian empire, the Hittites were warlike but displayed other imperial trappings – they ruled over myriad vassal states and princelings while also displaying a sense of ethics and an occasional penchant for diplomacy. This didn't prevent them from overrunning Ramses II of Egypt in 1298 BC, but did allow them to patch things up with the crestfallen Ramses by marrying him to a Hittite princess.

The Hittite empire was harassed in later years by subject principalities, including Troy. The final straw was the invasion of the iron-smelting Greeks, generally known as the 'sea peoples'. The Hittites were landlocked – hence disadvantaged during an era of burgeoning sea trade – and lacked the latest technology: iron.

Meanwhile a new dynasty at Troy was establishing itself as a regional power. The Trojans in turn were harried by the Greeks, which led to the Trojan War in 1250 BC. This allowed the Hittites breathing space but later arrivals sped their demise. Some pockets of Hittite culture persisted in the Taurus Mountains, but the great empire was dead. Later city states created a neo-Hittite culture, which attracted Greek merchants and became the conduit for Mesopotamian religion and art forms to reach Greece.

Classical Empires: Greece & Persia

Post-Hittite Anatolia was a patchwork of peoples, indigenous Anatolians and recent interlopers. In the east the Urartians, descendants of Anatolian Hurrians, forged a kingdom near Lake Van (Van Gölü). By the 8th century BC the Phrygians arrived in western Anatolia. Under King Gordius, of Gordian knot fame, the Phrygians created a capital at Gordion, their power peaking later under King Midas. In 725 BC Gordion was put to the sword by horse-borne Cimmerians, a fate that even King Midas' golden touch couldn't avert.

On the southwest coast, the Lycians established a confederation of independent city states extending from modern-day Fethiye to Antalya. Inland the Lydians dominated western Anatolia from their capital at Sardis and are credited with creating the first-ever coinage.

Meanwhile, Greek colonies spread along the Mediterranean coast and Greek cultural influence infiltrated Anatolia. Most of the peoples of the Anatolian patchwork were influenced by the Greeks: Phrygia's King Midas had a Greek wife; the Lycians borrowed the legend of the Chimera; and Lydian art was an amalgam of Greek and Persian art forms. It seems that at times admiration was mutual: the Lycians were the only Anatolian people the Greeks didn't deride as 'barbarians', and

547 BC	333 BC	205 BC	133 BC
Cyrus of Persia overruns Anatolia, setting the scene for a long Greco-Persian rivalry. Later Darius I and Xerxes further Persian influence in Anatolia and forestall the expansion of Greek colonies.	Alexander the Great rolls the Persians and conquers most of Anatolia. Persian Emperor Darius abandons his wife, children and mother, who is so appalled she disowns him and 'adopts' Alexander.	Lycian League is formed by a group of city-states along the Mediterranean coast including Xanthos, Patara and Olympos. Later Phaselis joined. The leagues persisted after the imposition of Roman rule.	On his deathbed Pergamene king Attalus III leaves his state to Rome. The Romans swiftly establish a capital at Ephesus, an already buzzing port, and capitalise on vigorous sea trade.

the Greeks were so impressed by the wealth of the Lydian king Croesus they coined the expression 'as rich as Croesus'.

Increasing manifestations of Hellenic influence didn't go unnoticed. Cyrus, the emperor of Persia, would not countenance such temerity in his backyard. He invaded in 547 BC, initially putting paid to the Lydians, then barrelled on to extend control to the Aegean. Over a period of years under emperors Darius I and Xerxes, the Persians checked the expansion of coastal Greek trading colonies. They also subdued the interior, ending the era of home-grown Anatolian kingdoms.

Ruling Anatolia through local *satraps* (provincial governors), the Persians didn't have it all their own way. They contended with periodic resistance from feisty Anatolians, such as the revolt of the Ionian city of Miletus in 494 BC. Allegedly fomented from Athens, the revolt was abruptly put down. The Persians used the connivance of Athens as a pretext to invade mainland Greece, but were routed at Marathon.

Alexander & After

Persian control of Anatolia continued until 334 BC, when a new force stormed across Anatolia. Alexander and his Macedonian adventurers crossed the Dardanelles intent on relieving Anatolia of the Persian yoke. Sweeping down the coast, they rolled the Persians near Troy then pushed down to Sardis, which willingly surrendered. After later successfully besieging Halicarnassus (modern-day Bodrum), Alexander ricocheted ever-eastwards, disposing of another Persian force on the Cilician plain.

Alexander was more disposed to conquest than to nation-building. When he died in Babylon in 323 BC, leaving no successor, his empire was divided in a flurry of civil wars. However, if Alexander's intention was to remove Persian influence and bring Anatolia within the Hellenic sphere, he was monumentally successful. In the wake of Alexander's armies, steady Hellenisation occurred, a culmination of the process begun centuries earlier that had annoyed Cyrus. A formidable network of municipal communities – the lifeblood of which

> According to legend, Alexander's mother dreamed that a lightning strike had struck her womb, while his father dreamed that his wife's womb had been sealed by a lion. A seer told them this meant their child would have the character of a lion.

ALEXANDER & THE GORDIAN KNOT

In 333 BC in the former Phrygian capital of Gordion, Alexander encountered the Gordian knot. Tradition stated that whoever untied it would come to rule Asia. Frustrated in his attempts to untie it, an impatient Alexander dispatched it with a blow of his sword. As he resumed his eastward advance, Asia lay before him; he and his men thundered all the way across Persia to the Indus until all the known world was his dominion. However, the enormous empire Alexander created was to prove short-lived – perhaps he should have been more patient unravelling that pesky twine...

AD 45–60	330	395	412
St Paul, originally from Antioch (modern Antakya), undertakes his long proselytising treks across Anatolia. St John and the Virgin Mary are thought to have ended up in Ephesus.	Constantine declares his 'New Rome', later Constantinople, as the capital of the eastern Roman Empire (Byzantium). He had earlier converted to Christianity and in 325 hosted the Council of Nicaea.	Under Theodosius the Roman Empire becomes Christian, with paganism forbidden and Greek influence pervasive. Upon his death the empire is split along the line Diocletian had set a century earlier.	Theodosius II builds the land walls of Constantinople to protect the riches of his capital. They prove effective, withstanding multiple sieges, and are only to be breached once: by Mehmet in 1453.

was trade – spread across Anatolia. The most notable of these was Pergamum (now Bergama). The Pergamene kings were great warriors and enthusiastic patrons of the arts. Greatest of the Pergamene kings was Eumenes, who was responsible for much of what remains of Pergamum's acropolis. As notable as the building of Hellenic temples and aqueducts in Anatolia was the gradual spread of the Greek language, which eventually extinguished native Anatolian languages.

The cauldron of Anatolian cultures continued to bubble, throwing up various flavour-of-the-month kingdoms. In 279 BC the Celts romped in, establishing the kingdom of Galatia centred on Ancyra (Ankara). To the northeast Mithridates had carved out the kingdom of Pontus, centred on Amasya, and the Armenians (long established in the Lake Van region) reasserted themselves, having been granted autonomy under Alexander.

Meanwhile, across the Aegean, the increasingly powerful Romans were casting covetous eyes on Anatolia's rich trade networks.

Roman Rule

The Roman legions had defeated the Seleucid king at Magnesia (Manisa) in 190 BC, but Pergamum, the greatest of the post-Alexandrian cities, became the beachhead for the Roman embrace of Anatolia when King Attalus III died in 133 BC, bequeathing the city to Rome. In 129 BC Ephesus was nominated capital of the Roman province of Asia and within 60 years the Romans had overcome spirited resistance from Mithridates of Pontus and extended their reach to Armenia, on the Persian border.

Over time, the might of the Roman Empire gradually waned. In the late 3rd century Diocletian tried to steady the empire by splitting it into eastern and western administrative units, simultaneously attempting to wipe out Christianity. Both endeavours failed. Diocletian's reforms resulted in a civil war from which Constantine emerged victorious. An earlier convert to Christianity, Constantine was said to have been guided by angels in choosing to build a 'New Rome' on the ancient Greek town of Byzantium. The city came to be known as Constantinople (now İstanbul). On his deathbed Constantine was baptised and by the end of the century Christianity had become the official religion of the empire.

Rome Falls, Byzantium Arises

Even with a new capital at Constantinople, the Roman Empire proved no less unwieldy. Once the steadying hand of Theodosius (379–95) was gone, the empire split. The western – Roman – half of the empire eventually succumbed to decadence and sundry 'barbarians'; the eastern half – Byzantium – prospered, gradually adopting the Greek language and with Christianity its defining feature.

527–65	+600s	654–76	867
During the reign of Justinian, Byzantium enjoys a golden age. His military conquests include much of North Africa and Spain. He also pursues reform within the empire and embarks on building programs.	The Sassanid Persians, age-old rivals of the Greeks, invade, sweeping across Anatolia and into Byzantine territory in Egypt. This brings about an economic collapse and weakens the Byzantine Empire.	Muslim Arab armies capture Ankara and besiege Constantinople. Arab incursions in the west are temporary but the eastern and southern fringes (Syria and Egypt) of the Byzantine domain are lost forever.	Basil I helps to restore Byzantium's fortunes, catalysing a resurgence in military power and a flourishing of the arts. He was known as the 'Macedonian' but was actually an Armenian from Thrace.

Under Justinian (527–65), Byzantium took up the mantle of imperialism that had once been Rome's. Historians note Justinian as responsible for the Aya Sofya (p45) and codifying Roman law, but he also pushed the boundaries of the empire to envelop southern Spain, North Africa and Italy. It was at this stage that Byzantium came to be an entity distinct from Rome, although sentimental attachment to the idea of Rome remained: the Greek-speaking Byzantines still referred to themselves as Romans, and in subsequent centuries the Turks would refer to them as 'Rum'. However, Justinian's exuberance and ambition overstretched the empire. Plague and encroaching Avars and Slavic tribes north of the Danube curtailed further expansion.

Later a drawn-out struggle with their age-old rivals the Persians further weakened the Byzantines, leaving the eastern provinces of Anatolia easy prey for the Arab armies exploding out of Arabia. The Arabs took Ankara in 654 and by 669 had besieged Constantinople. Here were a new people, bringing a new language, a new civilisation and, most crucially, a new religion: Islam.

On the western front, Goths and Lombards impinged as well, so that by the 8th century Byzantium was pushed back into the Balkans and Anatolia. The empire hunkered down until the emergence of the Macedonian emperors. Basil assumed the throne in 867 and the empire's fortunes were on the up, as Basil chalked up victories against Islamic Egypt, the Bulgars and Russia. Basil II (976–1025) earned the moniker the 'Bulgar Slayer' after allegedly putting out the eyes of 14,000 Bulgarian prisoners of war. When Basil died, the empire lacked anyone of his calibre – or ferocity, perhaps – and the era of Byzantine expansion was comprehensively over.

European observers referred to Anatolia as 'Turchia' as early as the 12th century. The Turks themselves didn't do this until the 1920s.

The First Turkic Empire: The Seljuks

During centuries of Byzantine waxing and waning, a nomadic people, the Turks, had moved ever-westward out of Central Asia. En route the Turks encountered the Persians and converted to Islam. Vigorous and

FLEDGLING CHRISTIANITY

The reign of Emperor Augustus, which ended in AD 14, was a period of relative peace and prosperity for Anatolia. In this milieu the fledgling religion of Christianity began to spread, albeit clandestinely and subject to intermittently rigorous persecution. Tradition states that St John retired to Ephesus to write the fourth Gospel, bringing Mary with him. John was buried on top of a hill in what is now Selçuk; the great Basilica of St John (p213) marks the site. Mary is said to be buried at Meryemana (p210) nearby. The indefatigable St Paul capitalised on the Roman road system, his sprightly step taking him across Anatolia spreading the word.

976–1014	1071	1080	1204
Under Basil II (the Bulgar Slayer), Byzantium reaches its high-tide mark. He overcomes internal crises, pushes the frontiers to Armenia in the east, retakes Italy and defeats the Bulgarians.	New arrivals, the Seljuk Turks take on and defeat a large Byzantine force at Manzikert. The Seljuks don't immediately follow on their success but it is a body blow for the Byzantines.	The Armenians, fleeing the Seljuks in Anatolia, establish the kingdom of Cilicia on the Mediterranean coast. The kingdom raises Armenian culture to new heights and lasts almost 300 years.	The rabble of the Fourth Crusade sack Constantinople, an indication of the contempt with which the Western Christians regard the Eastern Orthodox church.

BYZANTIUM: THE UNDERRATED EUROPEAN EMPIRE

Byzantium is often relegated to being merely an afterthought in European history. As the Byzantines never accepted the authority of the popes in Rome they were regarded as being outside Latin Christendom, hence barely a part of Europe. Nonetheless Byzantium acted as a bulwark for Europe, protecting it for centuries against the expanding armies of Islam. Left on the periphery of Europe, with its combination of Greek learning and language and Orthodox Christianity, Byzantium forged a magnificent cultural and artistic legacy for 11 centuries, yet it is generally – somewhat dismissively – remembered merely for the complexity and intrigue of its politics.

After the fall of Constantinople in 1453, Europe largely forgot the Greeks. Only in the 19th century did Greece again became flavour of the month; Romantics, such as Lord Byron and other Hellenophiles, rallied to the cause of Greek liberation, but it was the glories of classical Greece that they aspired to, the Greece of Plato, Aristotle and Sappho, rather than Byzantium that they idealised.

martial by nature, the Turks assumed control of parts of the moribund Abbasid empire, and built an empire of their own centred on Persia. Tuğrul, of the Turkish Seljuk clan, took the title of sultan in Baghdad, and from there the Seljuks began raiding Byzantine territory. In 1071 Tuğrul's son Alp Arslan faced down the might of the Byzantine army at Manzikert north of Lake Van. Although vastly outnumbered, the nimble Turkish cavalry prevailed, laying all Anatolia open to wandering Turkic bands and beginning the final demise of the Byzantine Empire.

Roxelana, the wife of Súleyman, has inspired many artistic works, including paintings, Joseph Haydn's Symphony No 63 and novels in Ukrainian, English and French.

Not everything went the Seljuks' way, however. Both the 12th and 13th centuries saw incursions by Crusaders, who established short-lived statelets at Antioch (modern-day Antakya) and Edessa (now Şanlıurfa). In a sideshow to the Seljuk saga, an unruly army of Crusaders sacked the city of Constantinople, the capital of the Christian Byzantines, ostensibly the allies of the Crusaders. Meanwhile the Seljuks were riven by power struggles in their ranks and their vast empire fragmented.

The Seljuk legacy persisted in Anatolia in the Sultanate of Rum, centred on Konya. Although ethnically Turkish, the Seljuks were purveyors of Persian culture and art. They introduced knotted woollen rugs to Anatolia and endowed the countryside with remarkable architecture – still visible at Erzurum, Divriği, Amasya and Sivas. These buildings were the first truly Islamic art forms in Anatolia, and were to become the prototypes on which Ottoman art would later be modelled. Celaleddin Rumi (p439), the Sufi mystic who founded the Mevlevi, or whirl-

JEAN-PIERRE LESCOURRET

» Whirling dervishes

1207–70	1243	1300
The lifetime of Celaleddin Rumi, known as Mevlâna, founder of the Mevlevi Sufi order of whirling dervishes. A great mystic poet and philosopher, Rumi lived in Konya after fleeing the Mongols.	The Mongols rumble out of Central Asia, taking Erzurum and defeating the Seljuks at Köse Dağ. The Seljuk empire limps on and the Mongols depart, leaving only some minor states.	Near Eskişehir on the marches between the moribund Byzantines and the shell-shocked Seljuks, Osman comes to prominence. He takes on the Byzantine army, slowly attracting followers and gaining momentum.

ing dervish, order, was an exemplar of the cultural and artistic heights reached in Konya.

In the meantime, the Mongol descendants of Genghis Khan rumbled through Anatolia defeating a Seljuk army at Köse Dağ in 1243. At the Mongol onslaught, Anatolia fractured into a mosaic of Turkish *beyliks* (principalities) and Mongol fiefdoms. But by 1300 a single Turkish *bey* (tribal leader), Osman, established the Ottoman dynasty that would eventually end the Byzantine line.

The Fledgling Ottoman State

Osman's bands flitted with impunity around the borderlands between Byzantine and formerly Seljuk territory, but once galvanised they moved with zeal. In an era marked by destruction and dissolution, they provided an ideal that attracted legions of followers and quickly established an administrative and military model that allowed them to expand. From the outset they embraced all the cultures of Anatolia – as many Anatolian civilisations before them had done – and their traditions became an amalgam of Greek and Turkish, Islamic and Christian elements, particularly in the janissary corps, which were drawn from the Christian populations of their territories.

Vigorous and seemingly invincible, the Ottomans forged westward, establishing a first capital at Bursa, then crossing into Europe and taking Adrianople (now Edirne) in 1362. By 1371 they had reached the Adriatic and in 1389 they met and vanquished the Serbs at Kosovo Polje, effectively taking control of the Balkans.

In the Balkans the Ottomans encountered a resolute Christian community, yet they absorbed them neatly into the state with the creation of the *millet* system, by which minority communities were officially recognised and allowed to govern their own affairs. However, neither Christian insolence nor military bravado were countenanced: Sultan Beyazıt trounced the armies of the last Crusade at Nicopolis in Bulgaria in 1396. Beyazıt perhaps took military victories for granted thereafter, himself being insolent and taunting the Tatar warlord Tamerlane. Beyazıt was captured, his army defeated and the burgeoning Ottoman Empire abruptly halted as Tamerlane lurched through Anatolia and out again.

The Ottomans Ascendant: Constantinople & Beyond

It took a decade for the dust to settle after Tamerlane departed, dragging a no-doubt chastened Beyazıt with him. Beyazıt's sons wrestled for control until finally a worthy sultan emerged. With Mehmet I at the helm the Ottomans got back to the job at hand: expansion. With a

Concise, yet covering the vast sweep of Ottoman history, *Osman's Dream* by Caroline Finkel is rich in telling detail and investigates the goings on of the sultans over six centuries.

Cemal Kafadar's scholarly *Between Two Worlds* takes an intriguing look at the motivations of the early Ottomans and their interactions with the Byzantines.

1324	1349	1396	1402
Osman dies while campaigning against the Byzantines at Bursa; he installs his son Orhan as his successor. Bursa becomes the first Ottoman capital, ruling over a rapidly expanding realm.	As allies of the Byzantines, the Ottomans, under Orhan, make their first military foray into Europe. Orhan had earlier consolidated Islam as the religion of the Ottomans.	The Crusade of Nicopolis, a group of Eastern and Western European forces, aims to forestall the Turks marching into Europe with impunity. Ottoman forces abruptly defeat them; Europe is left unguarded.	Beyazıt, victor over the Crusade of Nicopolis, turns his focus to the ultimate prize, Constantinople. Ever cocky, he takes on the forces of Tatar warlord Tamerlane. His army is crushed and he is enslaved.

Byzantium: The Surprising Life of a Medieval Empire by Judith Herrin takes a thematic approach to life in the Byzantine realm and in doing so reveals the secrets of the little-understood empire.

Wild Europe: The Balkans in the Gaze of Western Travellers by Bozidar Jezernik is a fascinating record of travellers' observations of the Balkans under Ottoman rule.

Anatolia is so named for the Greek word *anatolē* meaning 'rising of the sun'. The Turkish *Anadolu* translates, very roughly, as 'mother lode'.

momentum born of reprieve they scooped up the rest of Anatolia, rolled through Greece, made a first attempt at Constantinople and beat the Serbs for a second time in 1448.

The Ottomans had regained their momentum when Mehmet II became sultan in 1451. Constantinople, the last redoubt of the beleaguered Byzantines, was encircled by Ottoman territory. Mehmet, as an untested sultan, had no choice but to claim it. He built a fortress on the Bosphorus, imposed a naval blockade and amassed his army. The Byzantines appealed forlornly to Europe for help. After seven weeks of siege the city fell on 29 May 1453. Christendom shuddered at the seemingly unstoppable Ottomans and fawning diplomats likened Mehmet to Alexander the Great, declaring him a worthy successor to great Roman and Byzantine emperors.

The Ottoman war machine rolled on, alternating campaigns between eastern and western borders of the empire. The janissary system, by which subject Christian youths were converted and trained for the military, meant that the Ottomans had the only standing army in Europe. They were agile, highly organised and motivated. Successive sultans expanded the realm, Selim the Grim capturing the Hejaz in 1517, and with it Mecca and Medina, thus claiming for the Ottomans' status as the guardians of Islam's holiest places. It wasn't all mindless militarism, however: Sultan Beyazıt II demonstrated the multicultural nature of the empire when he invited the Jews expelled by the Spanish Inquisition to İstanbul in 1492.

The Ottoman golden age came during the reign of Sultan Süleyman (1520–66). A remarkable figure, Süleyman was noted as much for codifying Ottoman law as for his military prowess. Under Süleyman, the Ottomans enjoyed victories over the Hungarians and absorbed the Mediterranean coast of Algeria and Tunisia; Süleyman's legal code was a visionary amalgam of secular and Islamic law, and his patronage of the arts saw the Ottomans reach their cultural zenith.

Süleyman was also notable as the first Ottoman sultan to marry. Where previously sultans had enjoyed the comforts of concubines, Süleyman fell in love and married Roxelana. Sadly, monogamy did not make for domestic bliss: palace intrigues brought about the death of his first two sons. A wearied Süleyman died campaigning on the Danube in 1566.

The Ottoman Juggernaut Falters

Determining exactly when or why the Ottoman rot set in is tricky, but some historians pinpoint the death of Süleyman. His failure to take Malta in 1565 was a harbinger of what was to come. With hindsight it is easy to say that the remarkable line of Ottoman sovereigns – from Osman to Süleyman, inspirational leaders and mighty generals all – could

1421–51	1453	1480–1	1512–16
Murat II restores Ottoman fortunes after the Tamerlane setback. He takes Greece and retires to his palace in Manisa twice, but both times is forced to reassume the throne.	Mehmet II lays siege to Constantinople, coinciding with a lunar eclipse. The defending Byzantines interpret this as a fatal omen, presaging the doom of Christendom. Sure enough, the Turks are soon victorious.	Mehmet II endeavours to establish himself as a true heir to Roman glory by invading Italy. He succeeds in capturing Otranto in Puglia, but he dies before he can march on Rome.	Selim the Grim defeats the Persians at Çaldiran. He proceeds to take Syria and Egypt, assuming the mantle of Caliph, then captures the holy cities of Mecca and Medina.

not continue indefinitely. The Ottoman family tree was bound to throw up some duds eventually. And so it did.

The sultans following Süleyman were not up to the task. Süleyman's son by Roxelana, Selim, known disparagingly as 'the Sot', lasted only briefly as sultan, overseeing the naval catastrophe at Lepanto, which spelled the end of Ottoman naval supremacy. The intrigues and power broking that occurred during the 'sultanate of women' contributed to the general befuddlement of later sultans, but other vested interests, putting personal advancement ahead of that of the empire, also played a role.

Furthermore, Süleyman was the last sultan to lead his army into the field. Those who came after him were coddled and sequestered in the fineries of the palace, having minimal experience of everyday life and little inclination to administer the empire. This, coupled with the inertia that was inevitable after 250 years of unfettered expansion, meant that the Ottoman military might, once famously referred to by Martin Luther as irresistible, was declining.

Miguel Cervantes was wounded fighting against the Ottomans at the battle of Lepanto. It is said that his experiences served as inspiration for some scenes in *Don Quixote*.

The Sick Man of Europe

The siege of Vienna in 1683 was effectively the Ottomans' last tilt at expanding further into Europe. It failed. Thereafter it was a downward spiral. The empire was still vast and powerful, but it had lost its momentum

THE SULTANATE OF WOMEN

The Ottoman Empire may have been the mightiest Islamic empire, but for a time women commanded great influence in the machinations of the realm. More than ever before or after, from the reign of Süleyman the Magnificent until the mid-17th century, some women of the Ottoman court assumed and wielded considerable political clout.

This period, sometimes referred to as the 'sultanate of women', began with Lady Hürrem, known to the West as Roxelana. A concubine in the harem of Süleyman, she quickly became his favourite consort, and when his mother died Roxelana became the most powerful woman in the harem. She then proceeded to shore up her own position, persuading Süleyman to marry her – something no concubine had done before.

A master of palace intrigue, she manoeuvred the sultan into doing away with Mustafa, his son from an earlier coupling, and İbrahim, his grand vizier. This left the way open for Roxelana's son, Selim, to succeed Süleyman as sultan.

Such conniving had a lasting legacy on the fortunes of the empire. Selim proved to be an inept and inebriated leader, and some claim that the precedent of behind-the-scenes manipulation, set by Roxelana, contributed to the increasing incompetence and eventual downfall of the Ottoman aristocracy.

1520–66

The reign of Süleyman the Magnificent, the zenith of the Ottoman Empire. Süleyman leads his forces to take Budapest, Belgrade and Rhodes, doubling the size of the empire.

1553

Mustafa, Süleyman's first-born, is strangled upon his father's orders. Allegedly, Roxelana, who Süleyman had married earlier, conspired to have Mustafa killed so her own son could succeed to the throne.

IZZET KERIBAR

» The ornate tomb of Süleyman the Magnificent

and was rapidly falling behind the West socially, militarily and scientifically. Napoleon's swashbuckling 1799 Egypt campaign indicated that an emboldened Europe was willing to take the battle up to the Ottomans, and was the first example of industrialised Europe meddling in Middle Eastern affairs.

It wasn't just Napoleon who was hovering. The Habsburgs in central Europe and the Russians were increasingly assertive, while Western Europe had grown rich after centuries of colonising and exploiting the 'New World'. Meanwhile, the Ottomans remained moribund, inward looking and unaware of the advances happening in Europe. An earlier clear indication of this was the Ottoman clergy's refusal to allow the use of the printing press until the 18th century – a century and a half after it had been introduced into Europe.

But it was another idea imported from the West that was to speed the dissolution of the empire: nationalism. For centuries manifold ethnic groups had coexisted relatively harmoniously in the Ottoman Empire, but the creation of nation states in Western Europe sparked a desire in the empire's subject peoples to throw off the Ottoman 'yoke' and determine their own destinies. So it was that pieces of the Ottoman jigsaw wriggled free: Greece attained its freedom in 1830. In 1878 Romania, Montenegro, Serbia and Bosnia went their own ways, while at the same time Russia was encroaching on Kars.

As the Ottoman Empire shrunk there were various attempts at reform, but it was too little, too late. In 1829 Mahmut II abolished the janissaries and succeeded in modernising the armed forces. In 1876 Abdülhamid allowed the creation of an Ottoman constitution and the first ever Ottoman parliament. But he used the events of 1878 as an excuse for doing away with the constitution. His reign henceforth grew increasingly authoritarian.

But it wasn't just subject peoples who were restless: educated Turks, too, looked for ways to improve their lot. In Macedonia the Committee for Union and Progress (CUP) was created. Reform minded and Western looking, the CUP, who came to be known as the 'Young Turks', forced Abdülhamid in 1908 to abdicate and reinstate the constitution. Any rejoicing proved short-lived. The First Balkan War saw Bulgaria and Macedonia removed from the Ottoman map, with Bulgarian, Greek and Serbian troops advancing rapidly on İstanbul.

The Ottoman regime, once feared and respected, was now deemed the 'sick man of Europe'. European diplomats bombastically pondered the 'eastern question' and plotted how to cherry-pick the empire's choicest parts.

A Peace to End All Peace: Creating the Modern Middle East, 1914–1922 by David Fromkin is an intriguing account of how the map of the modern Middle East was arbitrarily drawn by European colonial governments.

1571	1595–1603	1638	1683
The Ottoman navy is destroyed at Lepanto by resurgent European powers who are in control of Atlantic and Indian Ocean trades, and who are experiencing the advances of the Renaissance.	Stay-at-home sultan, Mehmet, has his 19 brothers strangled to protect his throne. His successor institutes 'the Cage' to keep potential claimants to the throne distracted with concubines and confections.	The Ottomans sign the Treaty of Zohrab with Persia, finally bringing peace between the two Islamic states after nearly 150 years of intermittent war on the eastern fringe of Anatolia.	Sultan Mehmet IV besieges Vienna, ending in the rout of his army. By century's end, the Ottomans have sued for peace for the first time and have lost the Peloponnese, Hungary and Transylvania.

Engaged on multiple fronts during WWI, the Ottomans held their own only at Gallipoli. This was due partially to the inept British high command but also to the brilliance of Turkish commander Mustafa Kemal. Iron-willed, he inspired his men to hold their lines, while also inflicting shocking casualties on the invading British and Anzac (Australian and New Zealand Army Corps) forces, who had invaded on 25 April 1915.

Difficult territory, exposure to the elements on the windswept peninsula and the nature of hand-to-hand trench warfare meant that the campaign was a bloody stalemate; however, there are reports of remarkable civility between invading and defensive forces. The allies withdrew after eight months.

Unbeknown to anyone at the time, two enduring legends of nationhood were born on the blood-spattered sands of Gallipoli: Australians see that brutal campaign as the birth of their independence, while the Turks regard the successful campaign to defend the Gallipoli shore as the birth of their national consciousness.

WWI & Its Aftermath

The military crisis saw a triumvirate of ambitious, nationalistic and brutish CUP *paşas* (generals) stage a coup and take de facto control of the ever-shrinking empire. They managed to push back the unlikely alliance of Balkan armies and save İstanbul and Edirne, but their next move was to choose the wrong side in the looming world war. As a consequence the Ottomans had to fend off the Western powers on multiple fronts during WWI: Greece in Thrace, Russia in northeast Anatolia, Britain in Arabia and a multinational force at Gallipoli. It was during this time of turmoil that the Armenian scenario unfolded.

The end of WWI saw the Turks largely in disarray. The French occupied southeast Anatolia; the Italians controlled the western Mediterranean; the Greeks occupied İzmir; and Armenians, with Russian support, controlled parts of northeast Anatolia. The Treaty of Sèvres in 1920 ensured the dismembering of the empire, with only a sliver of steppe left to the Turks. European haughtiness did not count on a Turkish backlash, but backlash there was. A slowly building Turkish nationalist movement developed, motivated by the humiliation of Sèvres. At the head was Mustafa Kemal, the victorious leader at Gallipoli. He secured the support of the Bektaşi dervishes, began organising Turkish resistance and established a national assembly in Ankara, far from opposing armies and meddling diplomats.

In the meantime, a Greek expeditionary force pushed out from İzmir. The Greeks (who, since attaining independence in 1830, had dreamed of re-creating the Byzantine Empire) saw this opportunity to realise

1720	1760–90s	1826	1839
Ahmet III is an extravagant sultan, spending vast amounts on follies on the Bosphorus. His rule is marked by nepotism and corruption. The Austrian Habsburgs and Russia emerge as major rivals.	Despite attempts to modernise and military training from France, the Ottomans lose ground to the Russians under Catherine the Great, who anoints herself protector of the Ottomans' Orthodox subjects.	Major attempts at reform under Mahmut II. He centralises the administration and modernises the army, resulting in the 'Auspicious Event' where the unruly janissaries are put to the sword.	Reform continues with the Tanzimat, a charter of legal and political rights, the underlying principle of which was the equality of the empire's Muslim and non-Muslim subjects.

their *megali idea* (great idea). Capitalising on Turkish disorder, the Greeks took Bursa and Edirne and pushed towards Ankara. This was just the provocation that Mustafa Kemal needed to galvanise Turkish support. After an initial skirmish at İnönü, the Greeks pressed on for Ankara seeking to crush the Turks. But stubborn Turkish resistance stalled them at the Battle of Sakarya. The two armies faced off again at Dumlupınar. Here the Turks savaged the Greeks, sending them in panicked retreat towards İzmir, where they were expelled from Anatolia amid stricken Greek refugees, pillage and looting.

Mustafa Kemal emerged as the hero of the Turkish people. Macedonian-born himself, he had realised the dream of the 'Young Turks' of years past: to create a modern Turkish nation state. The Treaty of Lausanne in 1923 undid the humiliations of Sèvres and saw foreign powers leave Turkey. The borders of the modern Turkish state were set and the Ottoman Empire was no more, although its legacy lives on from Albania to Yemen.

Bruce Clark's *Twice a Stranger* is an investigation of the Greek–Turkish population exchanges of the 1920s. Analysing background events and interviewing those who were transported, Clark shines new light on the two countries' fraught relationship.

Atatürk: Reform & the Republic

The Turks consolidated Ankara as their capital and abolished the sultanate. Mustafa Kemal assumed the newly created presidency of the secular republic. Later he would take on the name Atatürk (literally 'Father Turk'). Thereupon the Turks set to work. Mustafa Kemal's energy was apparently limitless; his vision was to see Turkey take its place among the modern, developed countries of Europe.

At the time, the country was devastated after years of war, so a firm hand was needed. The Atatürk era was one of enlightened despotism. Atatürk set up the institutions of democracy while never allowing any opposition to impede him. He brooked little dissent and indulged an occasional authoritarian streak, yet his ultimate motivation was the betterment of his people. One aspect of his vision, however, was to have ongoing consequences for the country: his insistence that the state be solely Turkish. Encouraging national unity made sense, considering the nationalist separatist movements that had bedevilled the Ottoman Empire, but in doing so a cultural existence was denied the Kurds, many of whom had fought valiantly during the independence struggle. Sure enough, within a few years a Kurdish revolt erupted in southeast Anatolia, the first of several to recur throughout the 20th century (see p657).

The desire to create unified nation states on the Aegean also prompted population exchanges between Greece and Turkey: Greek-speaking communities from Anatolia were shipped to Greece, while Muslim residents of Greece were transferred to Turkey. These exchanges brought great disruption and the creation of ghost villages, vacated but never reoccupied, such as Kayaköy (p323). It was a pragmatic move aimed at

1876	1908	1912–13	1915–18
Abdülhamid II takes the throne. The National Assembly meets for the first time and a constitution is created but Serbia and Montenegro, emboldened by the pan-Slavic movement, fight for independence.	The Young Turks of the Committee for Union and Progress (CUP), based in Salonika, demand the reintroduction of the constitution. In the ensuing elections the CUP wins a convincing majority.	The First and Second Balkan Wars. An alliance of Serbian, Greek and Bulgarian forces take Salonika, previously the second city of the Ottoman Empire, and Edirne. The alliance later turns on itself.	Turks fight in WWI on the side of the Central Powers. Encroached upon on four fronts, the Turks repel invaders only at Gallipoli. At war's end, a British fleet is positioned off the coast of İstanbul.

forestalling ethnic violence, but it was a melancholy episode and, importantly, hobbled the development of the new state. Turkey found itself without much of its Ottoman-educated classes, many of whom had not been Turkish-speakers; in their stead, Turkey accepted impoverished Muslim peasants from the Balkans.

Atatürk's zeal for modernisation was unwavering, giving the Turkish state a makeover on micro and macro levels. Everything from headgear

THE FATE OF ANATOLIA'S ARMENIANS?

The final years of the Ottoman Empire saw human misery on an epic scale, but nothing has proved as enduringly melancholy and controversial as the fate of Anatolia's Armenians. The tale begins with eyewitness accounts, in spring 1915, of Ottoman army units marching Armenian populations towards the Syrian desert. It ends with an Anatolian hinterland virtually devoid of Armenians. What happened in between remains mired in conjecture, obfuscation and outright propaganda.

Armenians maintain that they were subject to the 20th century's first orchestrated 'genocide', that 1.5 million Armenians were summarily executed or killed on death marches and that Ottoman authorities issued a deportation order intending to remove the Armenian presence from Anatolia. To this day, Armenians demand an acknowledgment of this 'genocide'.

Turkey, though, refutes that any such 'genocide' occurred. It admits that thousands of Armenians died but claim the order had been to 'relocate' Armenians without intending to eradicate them. The deaths, according to Turkish officials, were due to disease and starvation, direct consequences of the chaos during a time of war. A few even claim that it was the Turks who were subjected to 'genocide', at the hand of Armenian guerrillas.

Almost a century after the events the issue is unresolved, but it would seem slow progress is being made. The murder of outspoken Turkish-Armenian journalist Hrant Dink in early 2007 at the hand of Turkish ultranationalists appeared to confirm that rapprochement is impossible. But what happened? Thousands of Turks marched in protest and in solidarity with the slain journalist bearing placards saying 'We are all Armenians'.

The 'football diplomacy' of 2009, when Turkish and Armenian presidents visited each other's countries to watch football matches, saw the re-establishment of diplomatic contact. Political obstacles remain, but there is increasing contact between Turkish and Armenian artists, academics and civil-society groups. Meanwhile, brisk Turkish–Armenian trade continues, despite their mutual border being closed. Turkish manufacturers send goods to Armenia on a circuitous route through neighbouring Georgia, surely proof that Turks and Armenians have much to gain if they bury their mutual distrust.

Is the problem solvable? We hope so.

1919–20	1922	1923
The Turkish War of Independence begins. The Treaty of Sèvres (1920) reduces Turkey to a strip of Anatolian territory but the Turks, led by Mustafa Kemal, rise to defend their homeland.	The Turks push back the Greek expeditionary force, who had advanced into Anatolia, and eject them from Smyrna (İzmir). Turkey reasserts its independence and the European powers accede.	The Treaty of Lausanne, signed by the steadfast İsmet İnönü, undoes the wrongs of Sèvres. The Republic of Turkey is unanimously supported by the members of the National Assembly.

IZZET KERIBAR

» Turkish memorial, Gallipoli

to spoken language was scrutinised and where necessary reformed. Throughout the 1920s and '30s Turkey adopted the Gregorian calendar (bringing it in line with the West), reformed its alphabet (adopting the Roman script), standardised the Turkish language, outlawed the fez, instituted universal suffrage and decreed that Turks should take surnames, something they had previously got by without. By the time of his death in November 1938, Atatürk had, to a large degree, lived up to his name, having been the pre-eminent figure in the creation of the nation state and dragging it into the modern era.

Democratisation & the Coups

Though reform proceeded apace, Turkey remained economically and militarily weak and Atatürk's successor, İsmet İnönü, stepped carefully to avoid involvement in WWII. The war over, Turkey found itself allied to the USA. A bulwark against the Soviets (the Armenian border then marked the edge of the Soviet bloc), Turkey was of great strategic importance and received significant US aid. The new friendship was cemented when Turkish troops fought in Korea, and Turkey became a member of NATO.

Meanwhile, the democratic process gained momentum. In 1950 the Democratic Party swept to power. Ruling for a decade, the Democrats, however, failed to live up to their name and became increasingly autocratic; the army stepped in during 1960 and removed them. Army rule lasted only briefly, and resulted in the liberalisation of the constitution, but it set the tone for years to come. The military considered themselves the guardians of Atatürk's vision – pro-Western and secular – and felt obliged and empowered to step in when necessary to ensure the republic maintained the right trajectory.

The 1960s and '70s saw the creation of political parties of all stripes, but the profusion did not make for a more vibrant democracy. The late 1960s were characterised by left-wing activism and political violence that prompted a move to the right by centrist parties. The army stepped in again in 1971 before handing power back in 1973. Several months later the military was ordered into Cyprus by President Bulent Ecevit to protect the Turkish minority, in response to a Cypriot Greek extremist organisation that had seized power and was espousing union with Greece. The invasion divided the island into two political entities – one of which is only recognised by Turkey – a situation that persists.

Political and economic chaos reigned for the rest of the '70s so the military seized power again to re-establish order in 1980. This they did through the creation of the highly feared National Security Council, but they allowed elections in 1983. Here, for the first time in decades, was a happy result for Turkey. Turgut Özal, leader of the Motherland Party

Former BBC Turkey correspondent Chris Morris ponders the rhythms and cadences of modern Turkish life in *The New Turkey: The Quiet Revolution on the Edge of Europe.*

MODERN TURKEY

1938	1945–50	1950–53	1971
Atatürk dies, at the age of 57, in the Dolmabahçe Palace in İstanbul on 10 November – all the clocks in the palace are stopped at the time that he died: 9.05am.	After WWII, which the Turks avoided, the Truman Doctrine brings aid to Turkey on the condition of democratisation. Democratic elections are held (1950) and the Democratic Party emerges victorious.	Turkey sends three battalions to serve alongside the US in the Korean War; Turkish soldiers serve with distinction and Turkey becomes a key Cold War ally of the US.	Increasing political strife prompts the military to step in again to restore order. The military chief handed the prime minister a written ultimatum, thus this was known as a 'coup by memorandum'.

(ANAP), won a majority and, unhindered by unruly coalition partners, was able to set Turkey back on course. An astute economist and pro-Islamic, Özal made vital economic and legal reforms that brought Turkey in line with the international community and sowed the seeds of its current vitality.

The late 1980s, however, were notable for two aspects – corruption and Kurdish separatism – that were to have an impact long beyond Özal's tenure.

The 1990s: Modernisation & Separatism

The first Gulf War kick-started the 1990s with a bang. Turkey played a supporting role in the allied invasion of Iraq, with Özal supporting sanctions and allowing air strikes from bases in southern Anatolia. In

FATHER OF THE MOTHERLAND

To Westerners unused to venerating figures of authority, the Turks' devotion to Atatürk may seem unusual. In response the Turks simply remark that the Turkish state is a result of his energy and vision; that without him there would be no Turkey. From an era that threw up Stalin, Hitler and Mussolini, Atatürk stands as a beacon of statesmanship and proves that radical reform, deftly handled, can be hugely successful.

The Turks' gratitude to Atatürk manifests itself throughout the country. He appears on stamps, banknotes, statues – often in martial pose astride a horse – and in town squares across the country. His name is affixed to innumerable bridges, airports and highways. And seemingly every house where he spent a night from the southern Aegean to the Black Sea is now a museum.

Turkish schoolchildren are well versed in Atatürk's life and achievements – they learn them by rote and can dutifully recite them. But it may be that the history-book image of Atatürk is more simplistic than the reality. An avowed champion of Turkish culture, he preferred opera to Turkish music. Though calling himself 'Father Turk', he had no offspring and a single short and troubled marriage.

Atatürk died relatively young (aged 57) in 1938. No doubt years as a military man, reformer and public figure took their toll. His friend and successor as president, İsmet İnönü, ensured that he was to be lauded by his countrymen. The praise continues to this day. Indeed, any perceived insult to Atatürk is considered not only highly offensive but is also illegal. Cynicism about politicians may be well and good at home, but it is a no-no in Turkey as regards Atatürk.

There are two outstanding Atatürk biographies. Patrick Kinross' *Ataturk: Rebirth of a Nation* is engagingly written and sticks closely to the official Turkish view, while Andrew Mango's *Atatürk* is a detached, objective and highly detailed look at a remarkable life.

1980	1983	1985–99	1997
The third of Turkey's military coups, this time as the military moves to stop widespread street violence between left- and right-wing groups. The National Security Council is formed.	In elections after the 1980 coup, the Özal era begins. A populist and pragmatic leader, Özal embarks on economic reform, encouraging foreign investment. Turkey opens to the West and the tourism industry takes off.	Abdullah Öcalan establishes the Kurdistan Workers Party (PKK), a terror group calling for a Kurdish state. There is a long, low-intensity war in southeast Anatolia until Öcalan's capture in 1999.	The coalition government headed by Necmettin Erbakan's Islamically inspired Refah (Welfare) Party is disbanded, apparently under military pressure, in what has been called a 'post-modern coup'.

so doing, Turkey, after decades in the wilderness, affirmed its place in the international community, while also becoming a more important US ally. At the end of the Gulf War millions of Iraqi Kurds, fearing reprisals from Saddam, fled north into southeastern Anatolia. The exodus caught the attention of the international media, bringing the Kurdish issue into the spotlight, and resulted in the establishment of a Kurdish safe haven in northern Iraq. This in turn emboldened the Kurdistan Workers' Party (PKK), who stepped up their campaign, thus provoking more drastic and iron-fisted responses from the Turkish military, such that the southeast effectively endured a civil war.

Meanwhile, Turgut Özal died suddenly in 1993, creating a power vacuum. Various weak coalition governments followed throughout the 1990s, with a cast of figures flitting across the political stage. Tansu Çiller served briefly as Turkey's first female prime minister, but her much-vaunted feminine touch and economic expertise did not find a solution to the Kurdish issue or cure the ailing economy.

In December 1995 the religious Refah (Welfare) Party managed to form a government led by veteran politician Necmettin Erbakan. Heady with power, Refah politicians made Islamist statements that raised the ire of the military. In 1997 the National Security Council declared that Refah had flouted the constitutional ban on religion in politics. Faced with what some dubbed a 'postmodern coup', the government resigned and Refah was disbanded.

The capture of PKK leader Abdullah Öcalan in early 1999 may have seemed like a good omen after the torrid '90s. His capture offered an opportunity – still largely unrealised – to settle the Kurdish question. Later that year the disastrous earthquakes centred on İzmit put paid to any premillennial optimism. The government's handling of the crisis was inadequate; however, the global outpouring of aid and sympathy – not least from traditional foes, the Greeks – did much to reassure Turks they were valued members of the world community.

2001	2002	2005	2008
The economy collapses, and the Turkish lira plummets. With an unwieldy coalition in political deadlock, massive foreign debt and human rights violations, Turkey is at a low ebb.	Recep Tayyip Erdoğan's Justice and Development Party (AKP) wins a landslide election victory, a reflection of the Turkish public's disgruntlement with the established parties. The economy recovers.	EU-accession talks begin, and economic and legal reforms begin to be implemented. Resistance to Turkish membership by some EU states leads to a decrease in approval by some Turks.	After a resounding election victory in mid-2007 the AKP is threatened with closure on the grounds it is undermining the secular nature of the Turkish nation.

Architecture

Settled over millenia by countless civilisations, Turkey boasts a dizzying array of architectural styles and remnants that display their creators cultural influences, technical prowess and engineering techniques.

Ancient

The earliest Anatolian architectural remnants, dated at around 7000 years old, are those of Çatalhöyük, revealing mud brick constructions which were accessed through their roofs. Dating from 4000 BC, Alacahöyük was characterised by more complex buildings. By the time that Troy was established classical temple design was beginning to develop, meanwhile the Hittite remains at Hattuşa, including hefty gates, stone walls and earthen ramparts, reveal increasing sophistication in working with the landscape.

In the treeless southeast distinctive 'beehive' construction techniques developed; these can still be seen at Harran.

Greek & Roman

The architects of ancient Greece displayed a heightened sense of city planning and increasing sophistication in design and construction, incorporating vaults and arches into their buildings. The later-arriving Romans built upon the developments of the Greeks. Elements of classical design such as the amphitheatre, agora and forum can be seen at Side, while Letoön features fine examples of temple-building that characterise the Greco-Roman architecture.

The Romans were also accomplished road builders, establishing a comprehensive network linking trading communities and military outposts – portions of Roman road are still visible at Tarsus.

Byzantine

Ecclesiastical construction distinguishes Byzantine architecture from that of the earlier pagan Greeks. The Byzantines developed church and basilica design while working in new media, such as brick and plaster,

For a scholarly investigation of the challenges facing Byzantine architects see *The Master Builders of Byzantium* by Robert Ousterhout.

THE CAPITAL OF ROMAN ASIA

Ephesus is the pre-eminent example of Roman city construction in Turkey; its flagstoned streets, gymnasium, sewerage system, mosaics, frescoes and theatre form a neat set piece of Roman design and architecture.

As a prosperous trading city, Ephesus was endowed with significant buildings. The Temple of Artemis, boasting a forest of mighty columns, was one of the Wonders of the Ancient World, but was later destroyed under orders from a Byzantine archbishop. The Great Theatre, one of the biggest in the Roman world, is evidence of the Roman expertise in theatre design and acoustics, while the nearby Library of Celsus, is ingeniously designed to appear larger than it actually is.

THE IMPERIAL MOSQUES

The rippling domes and piercing minarets of mosques are the quintessential image of Turkey for many travellers. The most impressive mosques, in size and grandness, are the imperial mosques commissioned by members of the royal households.

Each imperial mosque had a *külliye,* or collection of charitable institutions, clustered around it. These might include a hospital, asylum, orphanage, *imaret* (soup kitchen), hospice for travellers, *medrese* (seminary), library, baths and a cemetery in which the mosque's imperial patron, his or her family and other notables could be buried. Over time, many of these buildings were demolished or altered, but İstanbul's Süleymaniye mosque complex still has much of its *külliye* intact.

The design, perfected by the Ottoman's most revered architect Mimar Sinan (see boxed text, p78) during the reign of Süleyman the Magnificent, proved so durable that it is still being used, with variations, for modern mosques all over Turkey.

and displaying a genius for dome construction, such as that in the Aya Sofya.

Mosaics were a principle Byzantine design feature; fine examples can be seen in the Antakya Archaeology Museum or in situ at the nearby the Church of St Peter. Examples of the burgeoning skill of Byzantine engineers include the Basilica Cistern and the Aqueduct of Valens in İstanbul, while the Chora Church is often described as the pinnacle of Byzantine fresco painting.

In the east, skilled Armenian stonemasons, developed their own distinctive architectural style. The 10th-century church at Akdamar is a stunning example, while the site of Ani includes some fascinating ruins and remnants.

Ottoman architectural styles spread beyond the boundaries of modern Turkey. There are still Ottoman constructions – mosques, fortresses, streetscapes, bridges – throughout the Balkans.

Seljuk

The architecture of the Seljuks reveals significant Persian influences, both in design and in its decorative flourishes, including Kufic lettering and intricate stonework. The first Islamic power in Turkey, the Seljuks created a legacy of magnificent mosques and *medreses* (seminaries), distinguished by their elaborate entrances; you can see the best of them in Konya, Sivas and Divriği. As patrons and beneficiaries of the Silk Road, the Seljuks also built a string of caravanserais through Anatolia, such as at Sultanhanı and in Cappadocia.

In the southeast, the Artuklu Turks created the cityscapes of Mardin and Hasankeyf, featuring distinctive honey-toned stonework and apricot-coloured brick tombs.

Godfrey Goodwin's *A History of Ottoman Architecture* is an accessible and readable history, with some black-and-white photos.

Ottoman

From the 14th century, as the Ottomans expanded across Anatolia, they became increasingly influenced by Byzantine styles, especially ecclesiastical architecture. This is particularly clear from the Ottoman's use of domes as a design feature. Ottoman architects absorbed these Byzantine influences and incorporated them into their existing Persian architectural repertoire to develop a completely new style: the T-shape plan. The Üç Şerefeli Cami in Edirne became the model for other mosques, not only because it was one of the first forays into this T-plan, but because it was the first Ottoman mosque to have a wide dome and a forecourt with ablutions fountain.

Aside from mosques, the Ottomans also developed a distinctive style of domestic architecture, consisting of multistorey houses with a stone ground floor topped and protruding upper floors balanced on carved brackets (see p412). Cities including Amasya, Safranbolu, Muğla and neighbourhoods of İstanbul still feature houses of this design.

In later centuries in İstanbul, architects developed the *yalı*, expansively grand seaside mansions generally constructed solely of wood, to which notable families would escape at the height of summer. Prime examples are still visible on the Bosphorus.

Turkish Baroque & Neoclassical

From the mid-18th century, rococo and baroque influences hit Turkey, resulting in a pastiche of hammed-up curves, frills, scrolls, murals and fruity excesses, sometimes described as 'Turkish baroque'. The period's archetype is the extravagant Dolmabahçe Palace. Although building mosques was passé, the later Ottomans still adored pavilions where they could enjoy the outdoors; the Küçüksu Kasrı in İstanbul is a good example.

In the 19th and early 20th centuries, foreign or foreign-trained architects began to unfold a neoclassical blend: European architecture mixed in with Turkish baroque and some concessions to classic Ottoman style. Vedat Tek, a Turkish architect educated in Paris, built the capital's central post office, a melange of Ottoman elements and European symmetry. Sirkeci Train Station, by the German architect Jachmund, is another example of this eclectic neoclassicism.

Modern Architecture

There's little worth mentioning as far as modern architecture goes. The most interesting development in recent decades is that Turks have begun to reclaim their architectural heritage, especially those parts of it that can be turned into dollars via the tourism industry. These days, restorations and new buildings built in Sultanahmet and other parts of İstanbul – and even Göreme, in Cappadocia – are most likely to be in classic Ottoman style.

The visually stunning *Constantinople: Istanbul's Historical Heritage,* by Stephane Yerasimos, provides history and context to many of the city's magnificent buildings.

The Turkish Table

Mention Turkish cuisine and many people conjure up images of greasy, pre-hangover döner kebaps and an array of supermarket-purchased dips. Oily and bland stuffed vine leaves may leap to mind, along with chewy shish kebaps incinerated on backyard barbecues. Fortunately, the reality on the ground couldn't be more different.

Here, kebaps are swooningly succulent, *yaprak dolması* (stuffed vine leaves) are filled with subtly spiced rice, and meze dishes such as dips are made daily with the best seasonal ingredients. Freshly caught fish is expertly cooked over coals and served unadorned, accompanied by field-fresh salads and Turkey's famous aniseed-flavoured drink, rakı. Strong çay served in delicate glasses accompanies honey-drenched baklava studded with plump pistachios from Gaziantep.

Food here is not merely belly fuel – it's a celebration of community and life. Meals are joyful, boisterous and almost always communal. Food is used to celebrate milestones, cement friendships and add cohesion to family life. For Turks, the idea of eating in front of a TV or from a freezer is absolute anathema – theirs is a cuisine that is social, slow and seasonal.

The basics of Turkish cooking may have evolved on the steppes of Central Asia, but as the Ottoman Empire grew it swallowed up the ingredients of Greece, Persia, Arabia and the Balkans, creating a deliciously diverse cuisine. Each region has specialities and signature ingredients, meaning that travelling here will truly tantalise your taste buds.

Eating Through the Day

Breakfast

The Turks say 'Afiyet olsun' ('May it be good for your health') before starting to eat. After the meal, they say 'Elinize sağlık' ('Health to your hands') to compliment the host or hostess on their cooking.

The common Turkish *kahvaltı* (breakfast) consists of fresh-from-the-oven white *ekmek* (bread), jam or honey, black olives, slices of cucumber and juicy tomatoes, a hard-boiled egg, a block of *beyaz peynir* (salty white cheese made from ewe's or goat's milk) and innumerable glasses of sweetened black çay. Expect this feast at every hotel. Other breakfast dishes to look out for are *menemen* (eggs scrambled with tomatoes, onions, peppers and white cheese), and bread served with floral-scented honey and rich *kaymak* (clotted cream).

Lunch

Many locals eat *öğle yemeği* (lunch) in a *lokanta*. These cheap and cheerful spots serve *hazır yemek* (ready-made food) kept warm in bains-marie. The etiquette is to check out what's in the bain-marie and tell the waiter or cook behind the counter what you would like to eat. You can order one portion (*bir porsiyon*), a *yarım* (half) *porsiyon* or a plate with a few different choices – you'll be charged by the *porsiyon*.

Dishes to choose from will usually include *çorba* (soup) – the most common are *mercimek* (lentil), *ezo gelin* (red lentil and rice) and *domates* (tomato) – plus a wide range of meat and vegetable dishes, *pilavs* (rice dishes) and *dolmas* (vegetables stuffed with rice or meat).

Dinner

There are plenty of dining options when it comes to *akşam yemeği* (dinner). In a *meyhane* (Turkish tavern) customers usually start with a selection of mezes and then enjoy fish for the main course. A *kebapçı* (kebap restaurant) is where you should go if you're keen on sampling kebaps and a *köfteci* is the equivalent for *köfte* (meatballs) – both usually serve mezes to start the meal. The *ocakbaşı* (fireside) versions of the *kebapçı* are the most fun, with patrons sitting around the sides of a grill and watching their meat being prepared and cooked. Most *restorans* (restaurants) serve mezes, a mixture of kebap and *köfte* dishes, and fish.

What's on the Menu?

Turkey is one of the few countries that can feed itself from its own produce and have leftovers. This means that produce makes its way from

sidebar
The Ottomans were masters of the evocative culinary description, inventing such delights as 'Ladies' Thighs', 'The Sultan's Delight', 'Harem Navel' and 'Nightingale Nests'.

THE TURKISH TABLE WHAT'S ON THE MENU?

MARVELLOUS MEZES

Mezes aren't just a type of dish, they're a whole eating experience. If you eat in a local household, your host may put out a few lovingly prepared dishes for guests to nibble on before the main course is served. In *meyhanes*, waiter heave around enormous trays full of cold meze dishes that customers can choose from – hot meze dishes are usually ordered from the menu.

Turks credit Süleyman the Magnificent with introducing mezes into the country. During one of his Persian campaigns, Süleyman learned from the cunning Persian rulers that food tasters were a particularly good idea for every sultan who wanted to ensure his safety. Once home, Süleyman decreed that *çeşni* (taste) slaves be given small portions of his meals before he sat down to the table. These portions became known as meze, the Persian word for pleasant, enjoyable taste.

Mezes are usually vegetable-based, though seafood dishes can also feature. You will probably encounter the following dishes while eating your way around the country:

Acılı ezme Spicy tomato and onion paste.
Ançüez Pickled anchovy.
Barbunya pilaki Red-bean salad.
Beyaz peynir White ewe's- or goat's-milk cheese.
Cacık Yoghurt with cucumber and mint.
Çerkez tavuğu Circassian chicken, made with chicken, bread, walnuts, salt and garlic.
Enginar Cooked artichoke.
Fasulye pilaki White beans cooked with tomato paste and garlic.
Fava salatası Mashed broad-bean paste.
Haydari Yoghurt with roasted aubergine (eggplant) and garlic.
Kalamar tava Fried calamari, usually served with a *tarator* (breadcrumb, walnut and garlic) sauce.
Lakerda Strongly flavoured salted kingfish.
Muhammara Dip of walnuts, bread, tahini and lemon juice; also known as *acuka* or *civizli biber*.
Patlıcan kızartması Salad of fried aubergine with tomato.
Patlıcan salatası Fried aubergine with tomatoes.
Piyaz White-bean salad.
Semizotu salatası Green purslane with yoghurt and garlic.
Sigara böreği Deep-fried cigar-shaped pastries, often stuffed with *peynir* (cheese).
Yaprak sarma/yaprak dolması Vine leaves stuffed with rice, herbs and pine nuts.
Yeşil fasulye Green beans.

ground to table quickly, ensuring freshness and flavour. Here, being a locavore is taken for granted.

Meat – the Turkish Way

Overall, the Turks are huge meat eaters, which can be a bit of a problem if you're a vegetarian (p647). Beef, lamb, mutton, liver and chicken are prepared in a number of ways. The most famous of these is the kebap – *şiş* and döner – but *köfte, saç kavurma* (stir-fried cubed meat dishes) and *güveç* (meat and vegetable stews cooked in a terracotta pot) are just as common. In Cappadocia, many restaurants serve *testi kebabı*, kebap in a mushroom and onion sauce that is slow cooked (ideally over coals) in a sealed terracotta pot that is then theatrically broken open at the table. The most popular sausage in Turkey is the spicy beef *sucuk*, and garlicky *pastırma* (pressed beef preserved in spices) is regularly used as an accompaniment to egg dishes; it's occasionally served with warm hummus as a meze.

When travelling through central Anatolia, you will often encounter *mantı* (Turkish ravioli stuffed with beef mince and topped with yoghurt, garlic tomato and butter). It's perfect in winter but can be overly rich and heavy in hot weather.

Favourites from the Sea

Fish is wonderful here, but can be pricey. In a *balık restoran* (fish restaurant) you should always try to do as the locals do and choose your own fish from the display. This is important, as the occasional dodgy restaurant may try to serve you old fish. The eyes should be clear and the flesh under the gill slits near the eyes should be bright red, not burgundy. After your fish has been given the all-clear, ask the approximate price. The fish will be weighed, and the price computed at the day's per-kilogram rate.

Popular species include *hamsi* (anchovy), *lüfer* (bluefish), *kalkan* (turbot), *levrek* (sea bass), *lahos* (white grouper), *mezgit* (whiting), *çipura* (gilthead bream) and *palamut* (bonito). See p645 to find out their seasons.

Try to avoid eating *lüfer* when the fish are small (under 24cm in length) – a recent campaign by Slow Food Turkey's İstanbul convivium (http://fikirsahibidamaklar.blogspot.com, in Turkish) has highlighted the fact that overfishing is endangering the future of this much-loved local species.

Soul Foods – Vegetables & Salads

Turks love vegetables, eating them fresh in summer and pickling them for winter (pickled vegetables are called *turşu*). There are two particularly Turkish ways of preparing vegetables: the first is known as *zeytinyağlı* (sautéed in olive oil) and the second *dolma* (stuffed with rice or meat). *Patlıcan* (aubergine) is the sultan of all vegetables, cooked in every conceivable manner and loved by Turks with a passion.

Simplicity is the key to Turkish *salata* (salads), with crunchy fresh ingredients being caressed by a shake of oil and vinegar at the table and eaten with gusto as a meze or as an accompaniment to a meat or fish main course. The most popular summer salad is *çoban salatası* (shepherd's salad), a colourful mix of chopped tomatoes, cucumber, onion and pepper. It's sometimes served as a meze.

Sugar, Spice & Everything Nice

Turks don't usually finish their meal with a dessert, preferring to serve fruit as a finale. Most of them love a mid-afternoon sugar hit, though, and will often pop into a *muhallebici* (milk pudding shop), *pastane* (cake shop) or *baklavacı* (baklava shop) for a piece of syrup-drenched baklava, a plate of chocolate-crowned profiteroles or a *fırın sütlaç* (rice pudding) tasting of milk, sugar and just a hint of exotic spices. Turkish sweet specialities worth sampling are *fırın sütlaç; dondurma* (the local

Look out for the symbolic *perde pilavı*, often served at weddings and sometimes in restaurants. It's made from chicken and rooster meat (symbolising the bride and groom) cooked with rice (for blessing) and almonds (for children) and encased in pastry sheets (symbolising the home).

In society Ottoman-era houses chefs made baklava with over one hundred layers of filo pastry per tray. The master of the house would test the thickness with a gold coin: if it fell to the bottom of the tray the chef kept the coin.

BAKLAVA

In Turkey, as everywhere, it's always best to sample produce when it's in season. Here's a handy guide:

MONTH	FISH	VEGETABLE, NUT & FRUIT
January	anchovy, bonito, horse mackerel, bluefish	chestnut, radish, apple, pomegranate, orange
February	turbot, white grouper, sea bass, fresh anchovies, bonito, horse mackerel, whiting	chestnut, radish, apple, pomegranate, orange
March	turbot, sea bass, white grouper, whiting	radish, lemon
April	turbot, sea bass, whiting, shrimp, crab	artichoke, broad bean, lemon
May	sea bass, whiting, shrimp, crab, eel, scorpionfish	artichoke, broad bean, cucumber, green plum, strawberry
June	crab, eel, swordfish, scorpionfish, tuna, lobster	artichoke, broad bean, cucumber, bell pepper, green bean, tomato, green plum, strawberry, cherry
July	crab, scorpionfish, swordfish, tuna, lobster, gilthead bream, sardine	cucumber, bell pepper, green bean, corn, tomato, cherry, watermelon
August	gilthead bream, swordfish, lobster, sardine	walnut, cucumber, bell pepper, green bean, corn, tomato, watermelon, fig
September	bonito, sardine, gilthead bream	walnut, cucumber, bell pepper, green bean, corn, tomato, watermelon, fig
October	bonito, gilthead bream, bluefish	chestnut, cucumber, green bean, tomato, pomegranate, fig
November	anchovy, bonito, horse mackerel, bluefish, gilthead bream	chestnut, tomato, pomegranate, orange
December	anchovy, bonito, horse mackerel, bluefish	chestnut, apple, pomegranate, orange

ice cream); *kadayıf* (dough soaked in syrup and topped with a layer of *kaymak*); and *künefe* (layers of *kadayıf* cemented together with sweet cheese, doused in syrup and served hot with a sprinkling of pistachio).

These days, the best baklava is made in Gaziantep (p570).

Fast Food Nation

The nation's favourite fast food is undoubtedly döner kebap – lamb slow-cooked on an upright revolving skewer and then shaved off before being stuffed into bread or pide. Soggy cold French fries and green chillies are sometimes included, at other times garlicky yoghurt, salad and a sprinkling of slightly sour sumac are the accompaniments.

Coming a close second in the popularity stakes is pide, the Turkish version of pizza. It has a canoe-shaped base topped with *peynir* (cheese), *yumurta* (egg) or *kıymalı* (minced meat). A *karaşık* pide has a mixture of toppings. You can sit down to eat these in a *pideci* (Turkish pizza parlour) or ask for your pide *paket* (wrapped to go). *Lahmacun* (Arabic-style pizza) has a thinner crust than pide and is usually topped with chopped lamb, onion and tomato.

Börek (filled pastries) are distinguished by their filling, cooking method and shape, and are sold at small take-away outfits called *börekçi*, usually in the morning only. They come in square, cigar or snail shapes and are filled with *peynir*, *ispanak* (spinach), *patates* (potatoes) or *kıymalı*.

Forget the Golden Arches – Turkey's favourite fast-food chain is Simit Sarayı, which sells the country's much-loved *simit* (sesame-encrusted bread ring) to tens of thousands of happy customers every day, usually around breakfast time.

The kebap (meat grilled on a skewer) is undoubtedly the national dish, closely followed by *köfte* (meatballs). These meat dishes come in many forms, and are often named after their place of origin. The most popular are the following:

Adana kebap Spicy *köfte* wrapped around a flat skewer and barbecued, then served with onions, sumac, parsley, barbecued tomatoes and pide (bread).

Alinazik Aubergine purée with yoghurt and ground *köfte*.

Beyti sarma Spicy ground meat baked in a thin layer of bread.

Çiğ köfte Raw ground lamb mixed with pounded bulgur, onion, clove, cinnamon, salt and hot black pepper.

Döner kebap Compressed meat (usually lamb) cooked on a revolving upright skewer over coals, then thinly sliced.

Fıstıklı kebap Minced lamb studded with pistachios.

İçli köfte Ground lamb and onion with a bulgur coating, often served as a hot meze.

İskender (Bursa) kebap Döner lamb served on a bed of crumbled pide and yoghurt, then topped with tomato and burnt butter sauces.

Izgara köfte Grilled meatballs.

Karışık İzgara Mixed grilled lamb.

Patlıcan kebap Cubed or minced meat grilled with aubergine.

Pirzola Lamb cutlet.

Şiş kebap Small pieces of lamb grilled on a skewer and usually served with a side of bulgur and char-grilled peppers. *Çöp şiş* is served rolled in a thin pide with onions and parsley.

Şiş köfte Wrapped around a flat skewer and barbecued.

Tavuk şiş Chicken pieces grilled on a skewer.

Tekirdağ köftesi Served with rice and peppers.

Tokat kebap Lamb cubes grilled with potato, tomato, aubergine and garlic.

Urfa kebap A mild version of the Adana kebap served with lots of onion and black pepper.

Bun-shaped *poğaca* are glazed with sugar or stuffed with cheese and olives. *Su böreği*, a melt-in-the-mouth lasagne-like layered pastry laced with white cheese and parsley, is the most popular of all *börek* styles – you're sure to be instantly infatuated.

Gözleme (thin savoury crepes cooked with cheese, spinach or potato) are also great quick snacks.

Celebrating with Food

In Turkey, every celebration has an associated sweet. Some say this can be attributed to the Quranic verse 'To enjoy sweets is a sign of faith'. The good news is that even though these sweets are a focus during celebrations and festivities, many of them can also be enjoyed year-round.

Baklava is traditionally reserved for festive occasions such as Şeker Bayramı (Sweets Holiday; p676), the three-day holiday at the end of Ramazan, but is also popular for engagements and weddings, proving sugary stamina for the rollicking hours of party-making ahead as the couple's wedding night (wink, wink). Other sweets such as *helva* (sweet prepared with sesame oil, cereals and honey or syrup) and *lokum* (Turkish delight; p106) are commonly part of more reflective occasions such as deaths and *kandil* days (the five holy evenings in the Muslim calendar). A bereaved family will make *irmik helvası* (semolina *helva*) for visiting friends and relatives, and *helva* is shared with guests at circumcision feasts.

Aşure (Noah's Ark pudding) is a sacred pudding traditionally made with 40 different dried fruits, nuts and pulses, supposedly first baked from the leftovers on Noah's Ark when food provisions ran low. These days *aşure* is traditionally made after the 10th day of Muharram (the first month of the Islamic calendar), and distributed to neighbours and friends.

In 2010, the town of Seferihisar on the North Aegean coast near Sığacık was named Turkey's first official Slow Food City by the international Slow Food Foundation for Biodiversity (www.slowfood-foundation.com). The town is known for its delicious tangerines and satsumas.

Savoury dishes are integral to celebrations in Turkey, too. *Kavurma* is a simple lamb dish cooked with the sacrificial lamb or mutton of the Kurban Bayramı (Feast of Sacrifice; p676). The meat is cubed, fried with onions and baked. During Ramazan a special round flat pide is baked in the afternoon and collected in time for *iftar* (the break-of-fast feast).

Vegetarians & Vegans

Though it's normal for Turks to eat a vegetarian (*vejeteryen*) meal, the concept of vegetarianism is quite foreign. Say you're a vegan and Turks will either look mystified or assume that you're 'fessing up to some strain of socially aberrant behaviour.

The meze spread is usually dominated by vegetable dishes, and meat-free salads, soups, pastas, omelettes, pides and *böreks,* as well as hearty vegetable dishes, are all readily available. Ask *'etsiz yemek var mı?'* ('is there something to eat that has no meat?') to see what's on offer.

The main source of inadvertent meat eating is *et suyu* (meat stock), which is often used to make otherwise vegetarian *pilav* (a rice dish), soup and vegetable dishes. Your hosts may not even consider *et suyu* to be meat, so they will reassure you that the dish is vegetarian; ask *'et suyu var mı?'* ('is there meat stock in it?') to check.

Eating Etiquette

In rural Turkey locals usually eat two meals a day, the first at around 11am and the second in the early evening. In the cities three meals a day is the norm. In urban areas people sit down to meals at tables and chairs, but in villages it is still usual to sit on the floor around a *tepsi* (low round table or tray) with a cloth spread over one's knees to catch the crumbs. These days people mostly eat from individual plates, although sometimes there will be communal dishes. Most Turks eat with a spoon (*kaşık*) and fork (*çatal*), rarely with a knife (*bıçak*).

In restaurants, it's not considered very important that everyone eats the same courses at the same pace, so the kitchen will deliver dishes as they are ready: it's quite normal for all the chicken dishes to arrive and then, five minutes later, all the lamb. You don't have to wait for everyone's food to arrive to begin eating.

Turkish waiters have a habit of snatching plates away before the diner has finished. Saying *'kalsın'* ('let it stay') may slow them down. When you have finished, put your knife and fork together to indicate that the waiter can take the plate. If this has no effect (or you don't have a knife), say *'biti, alabilirsin'* ('finished, you can take it') to the waiter.

Toothpicking should be done behind your hands, but you don't need to be particularly discreet. Try to avoid blowing your nose in public; sniff or excuse yourself if you need to do this.

Cooking Courses & Tours

Turkey has a growing number of operators offering foreign-language cookery courses and culinary tours, with several highly regarded cooking schools in İstanbul (p84), as well as a residential cooking course at Ula, 135km from Bodrum, run by well-known Turkish cooking writer and broadcaster Engin Akin (www.enginakin.com). Selin Rozanes of Turkish Flavours runs culinary tours in İstanbul and around the country that are perfect for serious foodies, as does the Istanbul Culinary Institute.

The Local Tipples

Alcoholic Drinks

In tourist-heavy destinations along the coast virtually every restaurant serves alcohol. The same applies to more expensive restaurants in the

Turkish Cookbooks

» *Classical Turkish Cooking* (Ayla Esen Algar)

» *Cooking New Istanbul Style* (Refika Birgül)

» *Turquoise: A Chef's Travels in Turkey* (Greg and Lucy Malouf)

The most famous *patlican* (aubergine) dish is *imam bayıldı* (the imam fainted), simply aubergines slow-cooked in olive oil with tomatoes, onion and garlic. According to legend, an imam fainted with pleasure on first sampling it – and after tasting it you may understand why.

THE TURKISH TABLE THE LOCAL TIPPLES

big cities. In smaller towns, there's usually at least one restaurant where alcohol is served, although in religiously conservative places such as Konya you may have to hunt hard to find one. Be warned that although Turks have a fairly relaxed attitude towards alcohol, public drunkenness is frowned upon.

Turkey's most beloved tipple is rakı, a grape spirit infused with aniseed. Similar to Greek ouzo, it's served in long thin glasses and is drunk neat or with water, which turns the clear liquid chalky white; if you want to add ice (*buz*), do so after adding water, as dropping ice straight into rakı kills its flavour.

Bira (beer) is also popular. The local drop, Efes, is a perky pilsener that comes in bottles, cans and on tap.

Turkey grows and bottles its own *şarap* (wine), which has greatly improved in quality over the past decade but is quite expensive due to high government taxes. Head to Ürgüp (p472) in Cappadocia or to the idyllic Aegean island of Bozcaada (p163) to taste-test. If you want red wine ask for *kırmızı şarap;* for white ask for *beyaz şarap*. Labels to look out for include Sarafin (chardonnay, fumé blanc, sauvignon blanc, cabernet sauvignon, shiraz and merlot); Karma (cabernet sauvignon, shiraz and merlot); Kav Tuğra (narince, kalecik karası and öküzgözü) and DLC (most grape varieties). All are produced by the Doluca company (www.doluca.com). Its major competitor, Kavaklidere (www.kavaklidere.com), is known for the wines it puts out under the Pendore, Ancyra and Prestige labels (the Pendore boğuazkere is particularly good), as well as its eminently quaffable Çankaya white blend.

Together, Doluca and Kavaklidere dominate the market, but local boutique wineries are starting to build a reputation for themselves. One such winery is Vinkara (www.vinkara.com, in Turkish) – look out for its Doruk narince.

Nonalcoholic Drinks

Drinking çay is the national pastime, and the country's cup of choice is made with leaves from the Black Sea region. Sugar cubes are the only accompaniment and you'll find these are needed to counter the effects of long brewing, although you can always try asking for it *açık* (weaker). In hotels and Western-style cafes it's acceptable to ask for milk (*süt*), but don't bother trying elsewhere.

The wholly chemical *elma çay* (apple tea) is caffeine-free and only for tourists – locals wouldn't be seen dead drinking the stuff.

Grumbly tummy? Ask for an *ihlamur* çay (linden tea). Turks always have it on hand for upset stomachs.

Don't drink the grounds when you try *Türk kahve* (Turkish coffee). Instead, go to the 'Turkish Coffee'/'Fortune Telling' section of www.mehmetefendi.com, Turkey's most famous coffee purveyor, for a guide to reading your fortune in them.

TURKISH GRAPE VARIETIES

As well as producing vintages of well-known grape varieties such as chardonnay, fumé blanc, sauvignon blanc, cabernet sauvignon, shiraz and merlot, Turkish winemakers also use local varietals including the following:

Boğuazkere Strong-bodied red wine with distinctive dried-fruits taste and aroma. Black Sea region, eastern Anatolia and southeastern Anatolia.

Çalkarası Sweetish red wine with strong fruit flavours. Western Anatolia.

Emir Light and floral white wine with pleasant acidic finish. Central Anatolia.

Kalecik Karası Elegant red wine with aroma of vanilla and cocoa. Aegean coast and central Anatolia.

Narince Fruity yet dry white wine with distinctive golden colour. Black Sea region and eastern Anatolia.

Öküzgözü (Ox Eye) Dry red wine with fruity flavours. Black Sea region, eastern Anatolia and southeastern Anatolia.

Sultaniye Dry white wine. Aegean coast.

Like most countries, Turkey has some dishes that only a local could love. Top of the confrontational stakes for most visitors is *kokoreç*, seasoned lamb or mutton intestines wrapped around a skewer and grilled over charcoal.

İşkembe (tripe) soup reputedly wards off a hangover; it's even more popular than *kelle paça* (sheep's trotter) soup.

Locals in need of extra reserves of sexual stamina swear by spicy *koç yumurtası* (ram's 'eggs'). When these don't do the trick they often resort to *boza*, a mucous-coloured beverage made from water, sugar and fermented grain.

Surprisingly, *Türk kahve* (Turkish coffee) isn't widely consumed. A thick and powerful brew, it's drunk in a couple of short sips. If you order a cup, you will be asked how sweet you like it – *çok şekerli* means 'very sweet', *orta şekerli* 'middling', *az şekerli* 'slightly sweet' and *sade* 'not at all'. Your coffee will be accompanied by a glass of water, which is to clear the palate before you sample the delights of the coffee.

Freshly squeezed juice is popular and cheap. *Taze portakal suyu* (fresh orange juice) is everywhere, and delicious *nar suyu* (pomegranate juice) can be ordered in season.

Ayran is a refreshing drink made by whipping yoghurt with water and salt; it's the traditional accompaniment to kebaps.

Sahlep is a hot milky drink that takes off the winter chill. Made from wild orchid bulbs, it's reputed to be an aphrodisiac. You might also want to try *şalgam suyu* – the first gulp is a revolting salty shock, but persevere and you may find yourself developing a fondness for this turnip concoction.

Arts

Turkey's artistic traditions are rich and diverse, displaying influences of the many cultures and civilisations that have waxed and waned in Anatolia over the centuries. Here, we offer an introduction to some of them.

Carpets

The art form that travellers are most likely to associate with Turkey is the carpet – certainly, there are few who do not encounter a carpet tout somewhere on their travels.

The carpets that travellers know and love are the culmination of a textile-making tradition that has developed over centuries. Long ago Turkic nomads wove goat-hair tents and woollen saddle bags and established carpet-making techniques on the steppes of Central Asia. The oldest-known carpet woven in the Turkish double-knotted Gördes style dates from between the 4th and 1st centuries BC.

As in so many aspects of their culture, the Turks adopted and adapted from other traditions. As well as robust floor coverings they later began making elegant Islamic prayer rugs while incorporating Persian design motifs like palmettes and rosettes and Chinese cloud patterns. Moving ever westward the Turks eventually brought hand-woven carpets to Anatolia in the 12th century.

Within Anatolia, distinctive regional designs evolved. Uşak carpets, with their star and medallion motifs, were the first to attract attention in Europe: Renaissance artists Holbein and Lotto included detailed copies of them in their paintings. Thereafter, carpet-making gradually shifted from being the preserve of women to become big business. During the Ottoman era, textile production and trade contributed significantly to the economy.

Village women still weave carpets but usually work to fixed contracts for specific shops. Generally they work to a pattern and are paid for their final effort rather than for each hour of work. A carpet made to a fixed contract may still be of great value to its purchaser. However, the selling price should be lower than for a one-off piece.

Other carpets are the product of a division of labour, with different individuals responsible for dyeing and weaving. What such pieces lose in individuality is more than made up for in quality control. Most silk Hereke carpets are mass-produced but to standards that make them some of the most sought-after of all Turkish carpets.

Fearing the loss of the old carpet-making methods, the Ministry of Culture has sponsored several projects to revive traditional weaving and dyeing methods in western Turkey. One such scheme is the Natural Dye Research and Development Project (Doğal Boya Arıştırma ve Geliştirme Projesi; see p168). Some shops keep stocks of these 'project carpets', which are usually of high quality.

Jon Thompson's beautifully illustrated *Carpets: From the Tents, Cottages and Workshops of Asia* is an excellent introduction that may well tempt you into investing in a carpet.

Literature

Historically, Turkish literature was all about poetry. The Turkish literary tradition consisted of warrior epics passed down orally, Sufi mystical verses, including those of Rumi (founder of the Mevlevi order of whirling dervishes; see p439), and the legends, lullabies and elegies of wandering *aşık* (minstrels). During the Ottoman era, highly ritualised and formal divan poetry grew popular. It is only in the last century that Turkey has developed a tradition of novel writing, but there is a treasure trove of writing by Turks and about Turkey that can give you insight into the destination and will make fine holiday reading.

Yaşar Kemal was the first Turkish novelist to gain an international audience, attracting acclaim for his retelling of Anatolian legends and his gritty novels of village life. His *Memed, My Hawk,* a gut-wrenching insight into the desperate lives of villagers on the Çukurova Plain, won him nomination for the Nobel Prize for Literature on several occasions.

For some time, the Turkish-American writer Elif Şafak has been attracting an international audience. Her first novel, *The Flea Palace,* is a dense and wordy story of an elegant İstanbul apartment building fallen on hard times. The follow-up, *The Bastard of Istanbul,* is a coming-of-age saga bristling with eccentric family members. Şafak's latest, *The Forty Rules of Love,* delves into Sufi mysticism as a lovelorn American woman encounters the poetry of Rumi and then sees her life follow unexpected turns.

Buket Uzuner is another well-regarded female author. Her prize-winning *Mediterranean Waltz* is an unrequited love story, while her *Long White Cloud, Gallipoli* describes the fallout after a New Zealand woman claims a soldier revered as a war hero in Turkey is actually her great-grandfather. Another recommended read is *Dear Shameless Death* by Latife Tekin – a heady whirl of Anatolian folklore and magic realism.

Irfan Orga's autobiographical *Portrait of a Turkish Family,* set during the late Ottoman/early Republican era, describes the collapse of his well-to-do İstanbullu family and its struggle to rebuild (beautifully mirroring the times). In *The Caravan Moves On* Orfa offers a glimpse of rural life in the 1950s as he travels with Yörük nomads while witnessing sword dances and traditional weddings and hearing folk tales of the Taurus Mountains.

ARTS LITERATURE

Evoking an earlier era is a lyrical novel by Ahmet Hamdi Tanpınar, *A Mind at Peace,* sometimes called the Turkish equivalent to *Ulysses.* Orhan Pamuk describes this as the best novel ever written about İstanbul.

A magnificent collection of images collected over decades, *Nomads in Anatolia* by Harald Böhmer and Josephine Powell looks at the lost traditions of textile making in Anatolia. Difficult to find but hugely rewarding.

ORHAN PAMUK: NOBEL LAUREATE

Effortlessly assuming the mantle of the scion of Turkish literature is internationally acclaimed author Orhan Pamuk. Long-feted in Turkey, Pamuk has steadily built an international audience since first being translated in the early 1990s. Pamuk is an inventive prose stylist, sometimes compared to Calvino and Borges, creating elaborate plots and finely sketched characters while dealing with the weighty issues confronting contemporary Turkey.

His *Black Book* is an İstanbul existential whodunit told through a series of florid newspaper columns; while *My Name is Red,* set in 16th century İstanbul, is a murder mystery that also delves into Eastern and Western concepts of art. In his nonfiction *İstanbul: Memories and the City,* Pamuk ruminates on his complex relationship with the beguiling city. *The Museum of Innocence,* his latest novel, wrestles with issues of desire, memory and loss. This tale, detailing a love affair between wealthy urbanite Kemal and shop girl Füsun, is illustrative of Pamuk's uncanny ability to evoke the sights, moods and ambience of modern Turkey.

Pamuk was awarded the Nobel Prize for Literature in 2006. He is the only Turk to have won a Nobel Prize.

Jewish-Turkish writer Moris Farhi's *Young Turk* clearly draws on events from his own life, and includes moments of pathos and comedy, as well as sensual encounters.

Istanbul: Poetry of Place, edited by Ateş Orga, is a collection of star-struck poets, from Sultan Süleyman to WB Yeats, painting portraits of the great city.

Music

Even in the era of MTV and pervasive Western cultural influences, Turkish musical traditions and styles have remained strong. The Turkish music industry continues to produce new stars and attract growing international audiences.

Pop, Rock, Experimental

Home-grown Turkish pop continues to thrive. When Sertab Erener won the Eurovision Song Contest in 2003 with her hit song 'Every Way that I Can' Turkish pop finally won worldwide recognition.

Sezen Aksu is widely regarded as the queen of Turkish pop music, releasing a string of albums in diverse styles over three decades, however, it is Tarkan, the pretty-boy pop star, who has achieved most international recognition. His '94 album, *A-acayıpsın,* sold over two million copies in Turkey and almost a million in Europe, establishing him as Turkey's biggest-selling pop sensation. 'Şımarık', released in 1999, and since covered by Holly Valance (as 'Kiss Kiss'), became his first European number one. His English-language album *Come Closer* flopped, but Tarkan's metrosexual hip-swivelling ensures he remains a household name in Turkey.

The Turkish Coast Through Writers' Eyes, edited by Rupert Scott, collects a diverse range of musings on the landscape, archaeology and way of life of this beguiling stretch where the land plunges into the blue sea.

If you are a fan of guitar-based rock look out for Duman, Replikas, and Yakup who all offer versions of East-meets-West oriental-indie-grunge rock.

Burhan Öçal (www.burhanocal.com) is one of the country's finest percussionists. His seminal *New Dream* is a funky take on classical Turkish music, yet he has garnered critical acclaim experimenting in diverse styles. His 2006 Trakya All-Stars album is a Roma-Balkan investigation of the music of his native Thrace.

Mercan Dede has released a string of albums incorporating traditional instruments with electronic beats and world-music elements. In a similar vein, albeit more given to performance 'events', Baba Zula create a fusion of dub, *saz* (Turkish lute), electronic and pop – all accompanied by live belly dancing!

Folk

Turkish folk music consists of various subgenres that may not be distinguishable to Western ears. Ensembles consist of *saz* accompanied by various drums and flutes. Arrangements tend to include plaintive vocals and swelling choruses. Names to look out for include female Kurd-

FOREIGN SCRIBES & TURKEY TALES

There is a growing trend for foreign writers – expat or otherwise – to set their tales in Turkey.

Louis de Bernières' *Birds Without Wings* is a lyrical epic backgrounded by the events of early-20th century Turkey. Barbara Nadel writes gripping whodunits featuring the chain-smoking, unshaven İstanbul habitué, Inspector Çetin İkmen. *Belshazzar's Daughter,* her first, is one of the best. *River of Death* sees Nadel taking the action to Mardin and the dusty towns of the southeast, while in *Death by Design* İkmen goes undercover in the Turkish community of north London. And long-term Turkophile, Jason Goodwin has penned murder mysteries, *The Janissary Tree, The Snake Stone* and *The Bellini Card,* which feature one of modern literature's more unlikely heroes, an Ottoman eunuch named Yashim.

A BEGINNERS' GUIDE TO TURKISH MUSIC

ARTS MUSIC

These are our top picks to start your collection:

» *Turkish Groove* (compilation). Must-have introduction to Turkish music with every-one from Sezen Aksu to Burhan Öçal.

» *Crossing the Bridge: the Sound of İstanbul* (compilation). Soundtrack to Fatih Akın's documentary about İstanbul's music scene.

» *Işık Doğdan Yükselir* – Sezen Aksu (contemporary folk). Stunning collection draw-ing on regional Turkish folk styles.

» *Nefes* – Mercan Dede (Sufi-electronic-techno fusion). Highly danceable synthesis of beats and Sufi mysticism.

» *Keçe Kurdan* – Aynur (Kurdish folk). Aynur's impassioned debut album, sung entirely in Kurdish.

» *Duble Oryantal* – Baba Zula (fusion). Baba Zula's classic, 'Belly Double', is mixed by the British dub master Mad Professor.

» *Gipsy Rum* – Burhan Öçal and İstanbul Oriental Ensemble (gypsy). A thigh-slapping introduction to Turkey's gypsy music.

» *Avaz* – Replikas (Turkish rock). Guitar-based rock influenced by Sonic Youth.

ish singers Aynur Doğan and the ululating Rojin, whose hit 'Hejaye' has an addictive, sing-along chorus.

Fasıl is a lightweight version of Ottoman classical. This is the music you hear at *meyhanes* (taverns), usually played by gypsies. This skittish music is played with clarinet, *kanun* (zither), *darbuka* (a drum shaped like an hourglass) and often an *ud* (a six-stringed Arabic lute), *keman* (violin) and a *cumbus* (similar to a banjo). It's usually hard to distin-guish between *fasıl* and gypsy music.

If you're lucky you may spot wandering minstrels playing the *zurna* (pipe) and boom-slapping *davul* (drum). They perform at wedding and circumcision parties, and also congregate in bus stations on call-up day to ensure that the latest band of cadet conscripts get a rousing farewell as they leave for the compulsory national service.

Tarkan has been called many things, from the 'prince of Turkish pop' to the 'Orhan Pamuk of Turkish music'; he has also had an MP3 player named after him and has marketed his own line of perfume.

Arabesk

A favourite of taxi drivers across Turkey is arabesk, an Arabic-influenced blend of crooning backed by string choruses and rippling traditional percussion.

The two biggest names in arabesk are the hugely successful Kurd-ish singer İbrahim Tatlıses, a burly, moustachioed, former construction worker from Şanlıurfa, and Orhan Gencebay, a prolific artist and also an actor.

Classical & Religious

Traditional Ottoman classical and religious (particularly Mevlevi) mu-sic may sound ponderous and lugubrious to the uninitiated. These mu-sical forms use a system of *makams,* an exotic-sounding series of tones similar in function to Western scales. In addition to the familiar West-ern whole- and half-tone intervals, Turkish music often uses quarter-tones, unfamiliar to Western ears and perceived as 'flat' until the ear becomes accustomed to them.

After the banning of the Mevlevi at the beginning of the Republic, it wasn't until the early '90s that a group called Mevlana Kültür ve Sanat Vakfı Sanatçıları was set up to promote the Sufi musical tradition.

For hard-to-find Turkish music, books and paraphernalia you can't go past US-based online Turkish shopping emporium, Tu-lumba.com (www.tulumba.com), shipping right to your door; and you can hear music samples online.

Cinema

The first screening of a foreign film in Turkey took place at the Yıldız Palace in İstanbul in 1896. In the early years of the Republic, a nascent film industry began producing documentaries and patriotic feature films. Comedies and documentaries followed, and within a decade Turkish films were winning international competitions. During the 1960s and '70s films with a political edge were being made alongside innumerable lightweight Bollywood-style movies, usually lumped together and labelled *Yeşilçam* movies. During the 1980s the film industry went into decline as TV siphoned off its audiences, but the 1990s saw a resurgence in Turkish cinema, with films being critically acclaimed both in Turkey and abroad.

Following in the footsteps of Güney, many Turkish directors continue to make political films. *Güneşe Yolculuk* (Journey to the Sun), by Yeşim Ustaoğlu, is about a Turk who migrates to İstanbul and is mistaken for a Kurd and treated appallingly. Nuri Bilge Ceylan's excellent *Uzak* (Distant) is also a bleak meditation on the lives of migrants in Turkey – it won the Jury Prize at Cannes. Ceylan's next, *İklimler* (Climates), which he also starred in, looks at relationships between men and women in Turkey. His latest, *Üç Maymun* (Three Monkeys), won him the gong for best director at Cannes in 2008.

It's not all politics, though. Yılmaz Erdoğan's *Vizontele* is a wry look at the arrival of the first TV in Hakkari, a remote town in the southeast. Ferzan Özpetek received international acclaim for *Hamam* (Turkish Bath), which skilfully explores cultural nuances and follows a Turk living in Italy who reluctantly travels to İstanbul after he inherits a hamam. It's also noteworthy for addressing the hitherto hidden issue of homosexuality in Turkish society. His *Harem Suare* (Soireé in the Harem) was set in the Ottoman harem, while his more recent offering, *Karşı Pencere* (The Window Opposite), ponders issues of homosexuality and marriage.

Fatih Akın captured the spotlight winning the Golden Bear award at the 2004 Berlin Film Festival with *Duvara Karsi* (Head On), a gripping and often violent spotlight on Turkish immigrants' life in Germany. He followed this with *Edge of Heaven,* again pondering the Turkish experience in Germany, and the third part of the trilogy is coming soon. In 2010 Semih Kaplanoğlu won the Golden Bear award with *Bal* (Honey), a meditative account of a boy growing up in the Black Sea region; while Reha Erdem has won acclaim as an up-and-coming director.

A peep inside the Turkish film industry, *Turkish Cinema: Identity, Distance and Belonging* by Gönül Dönmez-Colin, sheds lights on movements and identities for an English-speaking audience.

Reha Erdem's *Kosmos,* a heady, allegorical tale set in snowy eastern Anatolia, has won acclaim at international movie festivals.

Visual Arts

The Islamic proscription of the visual representation of living creatures means that Turkey does not have a long tradition of painting or portraiture. Instead Turks channelled their artistic urges into textile- and

TURKEY'S TRAGIC CINEMATIC REBEL

Several Turkish directors have won worldwide recognition, most notably the late Yılmaz Güney. Joint winner of the best film award at Cannes in 1982, his *Yol* explored the dilemmas of a group of men on weekend-release from prison, a tale that manages to be gripping and tragic at the same time, and which Turks were forbidden to watch until 2000. Previously a hugely successful actor, through film Güney sought to address issues affecting the dispossessed in Turkey. In the charged political atmosphere of the '70s this lead to confrontations with authorities and several stints in prison. His last film, *Duvar* (The Wall), was made in France before his untimely death from cancer at only 46.

carpet-making, as well as *ebru* (paper marbling), calligraphy and ceramics. İznik became a centre for tile production from the 16th century. The exuberant tiles that adorn the interior of İstanbul's Blue Mosque and many other Ottoman-era mosques hail from İznik. You'll find examples of *ebru,* calligraphy and ceramics in bazaars across Turkey.

By the late 19th century, educated Ottomans were influenced by European-style painting. In the Republican era, Atatürk encouraged this artistic expression, and the government opened official painting and sculpture academies, promoting this 'modern' secular art in place of the religious art of the past. Various artistic 'schools' developed thereafter. Fikret Mualla is one of Turkey's most famous contemporary artists; he lived most of his life in Paris. Once again, İstanbul is the best place to see what modern artists are up to. İstanbul Modern and Santralİstanbul are the country's best modern art galleries, but the small private art galleries along İstiklal Caddesi are worth seeing as well.

Ara Güler is one of Turkey's most respected photographers. For over 50 years he has documented countless facets of Turkish life; his *Ara Güler's İstanbul* is a poignant photographic record of the great city.

Dance

If you thought that Turks, being Muslims, would be staid on the dance floor, then think again. Turkey boasts a range of folk dances, ranging from the frenetic to the ponderous and hypnotic, and Turks tend to be enthusiastic and unselfconscious dancers, swivelling their hips and shaking their shoulders in ways that are entirely different from Western dance styles.

Folk dance can be divided into several broad categories. Although originally a dance of central, southern and southeastern Anatolia, the *halay,* led by a dancer waving a handkerchief, can be seen all over the country, especially at weddings and in *meyhanes* in İstanbul when everyone has downed their fill of rakı (aniseed-flavoured brandy). But it may well be the *horon,* from the Black Sea region, that you most remember, since it involves the men getting down and indulging in all manner of dramatic kicking, Cossack-style.

The *sema* (dervish ceremony) of the whirling dervishes is not unique to Turkey, but it's here that you are most likely to see it performed; see the boxed text, p80.

Belly dancing may not have originated in Turkey, but Turkish women have mastered the art, reputedly dancing with the least inhibition and most revealing costumes. Although belly dancers are frequently seen at weddings and, incredibly, at many end-of-year company parties, your best chance of seeing a decent belly dancer is at a folk show in İstanbul.

ARTS DANCE

PHOTOGRAPHY

Panoramic Photographs of Turkey, by noted film director Nuri Bilge Ceylan, is a cloth-bound, limited-edition album of stunningly beautiful images of Turkish landscapes and cityscapes.

Osman Hamdi (1842–1910), whose orientalist paintings are in vogue, was also the man responsible for establishing the İstanbul Archaeology Museums.

People

Turkey has a population of approximately 77 million, the great majority of whom are Muslim and Turkish. Kurds form the largest minority, but there is an assortment of other groups – both Muslim and non-Muslim – so that some say Turkey is comprised of 40 nations.

Since the 1950s there has been a steady movement of people away from the countryside and into urban areas, so that today some 70% of the population live in cities. This process has been a result of people seeking economic opportunity, but also fleeing the disruption that plagued the southeast during the 1990s. As a consequence, cities such as İstanbul have turned into pervasive sprawls, their historic hearts encircled by rings of largely unplanned new neighbourhoods inhabited by economic emigrants from across the country.

Nonetheless, whether urban or rural, Muslim or Christian, Turkish, Kurdish or otherwise, all the peoples of Turkey tend to be family focused, easy going, hospitable, gregarious and welcoming of visitors. Many travellers return from a holiday in Turkey remarking on the friendliness of the locals. Chances are that the strongest impression of your time in Turkey will be of the hospitality and welcome that you received.

Turkey has the youngest population in Europe; some 22 million (27% of the population) are under 14 years old.

Turks

The first definitive mentions of the Turks appear in Medieval Chinese sources, which record them as the Tujue in 6th-century Mongolia and Siberia. The modern Turks are the descendants of a string of Central Asian tribal groupings that began moving westward through Eurasia

IN THE FAMILY WAY

Perhaps exhibiting vestiges of their nomadic, tribal origins, the Turks retain a strong sense of family within their community. Indeed, one of the more endearing Turkish habits is to use familial titles to embrace friends, acquaintances and even strangers into the extended family. A teacher may refer to his student as '*çocuğum*' (my child); a passer-by will address an old man on a street corner as '*dede*' (literally, 'grandfather'); and the old woman on the bus would not bat an eyelid if a stranger called her '*teyze*' (auntie).

It is also common for children to refer to family friends as '*amca*' (uncle) and for males of all ages to address slightly older men as '*ağabey*' (pronounced 'abi', and roughly analogous to English men saying 'guv'nor'). You will also hear small children referring to their teenage sisters as '*abla*', equivalent to 'big sister', which may sound obvious but which is rather charming in its simplicity.

These terms are a sign of deference and respect but also of affection and inclusiveness. And perhaps this intimacy explains how the sense of community found in rural villages persists amid the tower blocks of sprawling cities, where the majority of Turks now live.

over 1000 years ago. As such the Turks retain cultural and linguistic links with various peoples through southern Russia, Azerbaijan, Iran, the nations of Central Asia and the western corner of China, Xinjiang.

As they moved westward the predecessors of the modern Turks encountered the Persians and converted to Islam. The Seljuks established the Middle East's first Turkic empire (see p627). The Seljuks' defeat of the Byzantines in battle in 1071 opened up Anatolia to wandering Turkish groups, thus speeding up the westward drift the Turks had been pursuing for hundreds of years. Over the following centuries, Anatolia became the heartland of the Ottoman Empire and the core of the modern Turkish Republic. During the Ottoman centuries, Turkish rule extended into the Balkans and around the Black Sea so that today there are people of Turkish ancestry in Cyprus, Iraq, Macedonia, Greece and Bulgaria, parts of the Caucasus mountains and the Crimean peninsula in Ukraine.

The ancestry that Turks share with peoples in Central Asia and the Balkans means that Turks can merrily chat to locals all the way from Novi Pazar in Serbia to Kashgar in China. This is because Turkish is one of the Turkic languages, a family of – largely mutually intelligible – languages spoken by over 150 million people across Eurasia.

Kurds

Turkey has a significant Kurdish minority estimated at 15 million. The sparsely populated eastern and southeastern regions are home to perhaps eight million Kurds, while seven million more live elsewhere in the country, more or less integrated into mainstream Turkish society. Kurds have lived for millennia in the mountains and plateaus where the modern borders of Turkey, Iran, Iraq and Syria meet – Xenophon identified them as wilful and untameable horsemen in the 4th century BC.

Despite having lived side by side with Turks for centuries, the Kurds retain a distinct culture and folklore and speak a language related to Persian (and, more distantly, to the Indo-European tongues of Europe). The majority of Turkish Kurds are Sunni Muslims, although small numbers profess Judaism or Christianity. The Kurds have their own foundation myth which is associated with Nevruz, the Persian New Year (celebrated on 21 March), although some Kurds claim descent from the Medes of ancient Persian history.

The struggle between Kurds and Turks has been very well documented. Kurds and Turks fought together during the battle for independence in the 1920s, but unlike the Greeks, Jews and Armenians, the Kurds were not guaranteed rights as a minority group under the 1923 Treaty of Lausanne. The Turkish state was decreed to be unitary, or inhabited solely by Turks, hence the Kurds were denied a cultural existence. After the fragmentation along ethnic lines of the former domains of the Ottoman Empire, such an approach may have seemed prudent, but as the Kurds were so numerous problems swiftly arose. As early as 1925 the Kurds rebelled against restrictions placed on their identity.

Until relatively recently the Turkish government refused to recognise the existence of the Kurds, insisting they were 'Mountain Turks'. Even today the census form does not allow anyone to identify as Kurdish, nor can they be identified as Kurdish on their identity cards. This is in spite of the fact that many people in the east, particularly women, speak the Kurmancı dialect of Kurdish as their first language and may have a limited grasp of Turkish. However, this lack of recognition has now largely been overcome, with vigorous debate ensuing on how a Kurdish identity can be accommodated in Turkey.

Various (not exactly academically rigorous) theories state that the Turks are descendants of Japheth, the grandson of Noah. The Ottomans themselves claimed that Osman could trace his genealogy back through 52 generations to Noah.

PEOPLE KURDS

The Turkic Speaking Peoples, edited by Ergün Çağatay and Doğan Kuban, is a monumental doorstop of a volume investigating, in full colour, the traditions and cultures of Turkic groups across Eurasia.

The Kurds: A People in Search of Their Homeland by Kevin McKiernan recounts travels among the Kurds of Turkey, Iran and Iraq and discusses their current plight in light of their history and the geopolitics of the region.

For many travellers, Turkey is their first experience of Islam. While it may seem 'foreign', Islam in fact has much in common with Christianity and Judaism. Like Christians, Muslims believe that Allah (God) created the world and everything in it, pretty much according to the biblical account. They also revere Adam, Noah, Abraham, Moses and Jesus as prophets, although they don't believe that Jesus was divine. Muslims call Jews and Christians 'People of the Book', meaning those with a revealed religion (in the Torah and Bible) that preceded Islam.

Where Islam differs from Christianity and Judaism is in the belief that Islam is the 'perfection' of these earlier traditions. Although Moses and Jesus were prophets, Mohammed was the greatest and last to whom Allah communicated his final revelation.

Islam has diversified into many 'versions' since the time of Mohammed, however, the five basic 'pillars' of Islam – the profession of faith, daily prayers, alms giving, the fasting month of Ramazan, pilgrimage to Mecca – are shared by the entire Muslim community (or *umma*).

Islam is the most widely held belief in Turkey, however many Turks take a fairly relaxed approach to religious duties and practices. Fasting during Ramazan is widespread and Islam's holy days and festivals are treated with due respect, but for many, the holy day (Friday) and Islamic holidays are the only times they'll visit a mosque. You can also tell by the many bars and *meyhanes* (taverns) that Turks like a drink or two. Turkish Muslims have also absorbed and adapted other traditions over the years, so it's not uncommon to see Muslims praying at Greek Orthodox shrines or monasteries, while the Alevis, a heterodox Muslim minority, have developed a tradition combining elements of Anatolian folklore and Shia Islam, from Iran.

If you've travelled in other Muslim countries where Islamic rulings are strictly observed, you'll find the practice of Islam in Turkey quite different.

Muslim Minorities

Turkey is home to a range of other Muslim minorities, both indigenous and more recent arrivals, most of whom are regarded as Turks, but who nonetheless retain aspects of their culture and their native tongue.

Small numbers of Turkish Kurds profess the Yazidi faith, a complex mix of indigenous beliefs and Sufi tradition, in which *Tavus Melek* – a peacock angel – is seen as an earthly guardian appointed by God.

Laz & Hemşin

The Black Sea region is home to the Laz and the Hemşin peoples, two of the largest Muslim minorities after the Kurds.

The Laz mainly inhabit the valleys between Trabzon and Rize. East of Trabzon you can hardly miss the women in their vivid red- and maroon-striped shawls. Laz men are less conspicuous, although they were once among the most feared of Turkish warriors: for years black-clad Laz warriors were Atatürk's personal bodyguards.

Once Christian but now Muslim, the Laz are a Caucasian people who speak a language related to Georgian. The Laz are renowned for their sense of humour and business acumen, with many involved in the Turkish shipping industry and construction.

Speaking a language related to Armenian, the Hemşin, like the Laz, were originally Christian. They mainly come from the far eastern end of the Black Sea coast, although perhaps no more than 15,000 of them still live there; most have long since migrated to the cities where they earn a tasty living as bread and pastry cooks. In and around Ayder, Hemşin women are easily identified by their leopard-print scarves (even more eye-catching than those worn by Laz women) coiled into elaborate headdresses.

Others

The last link to the wandering Turkic groups who arrived in Anatolia in the 11th century, the Yörük maintain a nomadic lifestyle in and around the Taurus Mountains. Named from the verb *yürük* (to walk), the Yörük move herds of sheep between summer and winter pastures.

In Turkey's far southeast, particularly around the Syrian border, there are various communities of Arabic speakers.

There are also various Muslim groups who arrived from the Caucasus and the Balkans during the latter years of the Ottoman Empire. These include Circassians, Abkhazians, Crimean Tatars, Bosnians and Albanians.

Non-Muslim Groups

The Ottoman Empire was notable for its large Christian and Jewish populations. These have diminished considerably in the modern republic, nonetheless some remain.

There has been a Jewish presence in Anatolia for over 2000 years. A large influx of Jews arrived in the 16th century fleeing the Spanish Inquisition. Today most of Turkey's Jews live in İstanbul, and some still speak Ladino, a Judaeo-Spanish language that was spoken in Muslim Spain.

Originally from the Caucasian highlands, Armenians have lived in Anatolia for a very long time. Some say they are descended from the Urartians, but a distinct Armenian people existed by at least the 4th century, at which point they became the first nation to convert wholly to Christianity. The Armenians created their own alphabet and a highly literate culture, and went on to establish various kingdoms, usually in the borderlands between larger empires: Byzantine and Abbasid, Persian and Ottoman. Until 1915 there were significant communities throughout Anatolia. The controversy surrounding the Armenians in those final years of the Ottoman Empire ensures that

Christopher de Bellaigue's *Rebel Land* is an account of life in the rugged Varto district of eastern Anatolia, where Turks, Kurds, Alevis and Armenians have long interacted and battled for the upper hand.

PEOPLE NON-MUSLIM GROUPS

SEPARATISM OR THE 'BROTHERHOOD' OF PEOPLES?

In 1984 Abdullah Öcalan formed the Kurdistan Workers Party (PKK), which became the most enduring – and violent – Kurdish organisation that Turkey had seen. The PKK remains an outlawed organisation. Many Kurds, while not necessarily supporting the demands of the PKK for a separate Kurdish state, wanted to be able to read newspapers in their own language, have their children taught in their own language and watch Kurdish TV. The Turkish government reacted to the PKK's violent tactics and territorial demands by branding calls for Kurdish rights as 'separatism'. Strife escalated until much of southeastern Anatolia was in a permanent state of emergency. After 15 years of fighting, forced relocations, suffering and the deaths of over 30,000 people, Öcalan was captured in Kenya in 1999.

There has since been some progress made in solving the 'Kurdish question', but a definitive solution remains elusive. Following the arrest of Öcalan, an increasingly pragmatic and reasoned approach on the part of both the military and government bore some fruit. In 2002 the Turkish government approved broadcasts in Kurdish and gave the go-ahead for Kurdish to be taught in language schools and emergency rule was lifted in the southeast. The government's 2009 'Kurdish opening' was an attempt to address the problem in its social and political dimensions. The creation of TRT6, a government-funded Kurdish-language TV channel, was hailed as a positive initiative. However, there is concern at the extent to which the PKK, and Öcalan, remain influential within Kurdish political parties. Nonetheless, it appears that in not solely relying on military solutions, more recent initiatives will be more likely to resolve the Kurdish issue.

NAZAR BONCUK

Throughout Turkey, the blue glass *nazar boncuk* is an amulet said to protect against the 'evil eye', a tradition dating back centuries. You will see them displayed on buildings, vehicles and even babies' blankets.

relations between Turks and Armenians in Turkey and abroad remain predominantly sour (see boxed text, p635). About 70,000 Armenians still live in Turkey, mainly in İstanbul, and in isolated pockets in Anatolia. Turkish-Armenian relations are tense, but happily there are signs of rapprochement. In 2007 the Armenian church on Akdamar Island was refurbished by the Turkish Culture Ministry and reopened amid hopes that relations would improve. In September 2010 a service was held in the church – the first in nearly a century – attracting worshippers from across the border.

Turkey's other significant Christian minority is the Greeks. Large Greek populations once lived throughout the Ottoman realm, but after the population exchanges of the early Republican era and acrimonious events in the 1950s, the Greeks were reduced to a small community in İstanbul and a few Pontic Greeks in remote eastern Black Sea valleys. Recent years, however, have seen a warming of relations between Greece and Turkey and the return of some Greek young professionals and students to İstanbul.

Rugged southeastern Anatolia is also home to ancient Christian communities. These include adherents of the Syriac Orthodox Church, who speak Aramaic, centred on Midyat and who maintain the monastery of Deyrul Zafran. There's also the Chaldean Catholic Church, some of whom remain in Diyarbakır.

Turkey's Environment

The Land

Turkey has one foot in Europe and another in Asia, its two parts separated by İstanbul's famous Bosphorus, the Sea of Marmara and the infamous Dardanelles. Eastern Thrace (European Turkey) makes up a mere 3% of Turkey's 779,452 sq km land area. The remaining 97% is Anatolia (Asian Turkey).

Boasting 8300km of coastline, snowcapped mountains, rolling steppes, vast lakes and broad rivers, the country is stupendously geographically diverse.

Geographical Regions

The Aegean coast is lined with coves and beaches, and the Aegean islands (most belonging to Greece) are never more than a few kilometres offshore. Inland, western Anatolia has two vast lake districts, and Uludağ (Great Mountain, 2543m), which is one of Turkey's highest mountains and is popular with ski buffs.

The Mediterranean coast is backed by the jagged Taurus Mountains. East of Antalya, however, it opens up into a fertile plain as far as Alanya, before the mountains close in again.

Central Anatolia consists of a vast high plateau of rolling steppe broken by mountain ranges and Cappadocia's fantastical landscape. The action of wind and water on *tuff* (rock composed of volcanic ash), thrown for miles around by volcanic eruptions in prehistory, created Cappadocia's famous fairy chimneys.

Like the Mediterranean, the Black Sea is often hemmed in by mountains, and at the eastern end they drop right down into the sea. At the far eastern end, the 3937m Mt Kaçkar (Kaçkar Dağı) is the highest point of the popular Kaçkar trekking and mountaineering area, where *yaylas* (mountain valleys) come ringed with peaks and glaciers.

Mountainous and somewhat forbidding, northeastern Anatolia is also wildly beautiful, especially around Yusufeli and in the Doğubayazıt area, where snowcapped Mt Ararat (Ağrı Dağı; 5137m) dominates the landscape for miles around. Southeastern Anatolia offers windswept rolling steppe, jagged outcrops of rock, and Lake Van (Van Gölü), an extraordinary alkaline lake.

Earthquake Danger

Turkey lies on at least three active earthquake fault lines: the North Anatolian, the East Anatolian and the Aegean. Most of Turkey lies south of the North Anatolian fault line, which runs roughly parallel with the Black Sea coast. As the Arabian and African plates to the south push

As traditional agricultural practices die out, the pigeon houses (which once served to harvest the birds' droppings for use as fertiliser) dotting Cappadocia's fairy chimneys and valleys are becoming increasingly disused.

Dolphins live in İstanbul's Bosphorus strait – marine biologists have likened them to street children for the hardy lives they lead.

TAKE ONLY PHOTOS, LEAVE ONLY FOOTPRINTS

Tourism is not the only thing that has had a damaging impact on the Turkish environment, but it is certainly one of them. So what can you do to help?

» Never drop litter anywhere (although, to be fair, tourists are not the worst offenders when it comes to abandoned rubbish).

» Don't buy coral or seashells, no matter how lovely they look in a necklace.

» Avoid using plastic bags, although in Turkey these are occasionally made from recycled material.

» Complain to the captain if you think your excursion boat is discharging sewage into the sea or if it's dropping its anchor in an environmentally sensitive area. Even better, complain to **Greenpeace Mediterranean** (☎0212-292 7619; www.greenpeace.org/mediterranean).

» Consider staying in pensions and hotels that have been designed with some thought for their surroundings.

» Refrain from purchasing water in plastic bottles wherever possible. Water in glass bottles is served in many Turkish restaurants, and you can buy water filtration systems from home before your departure. At the very least, buy the 5L bottles of water, which you can keep in your hotel room and use to fill up a reusable smaller bottle for carrying with you during the day.

northward, the Anatolian plate is shoved into the Eurasian plate and squeezed west towards Greece.

More than 25 major earthquakes, measuring up to 7.8 on the Richter scale, have been recorded since 1939. A 7.6-magnitude quake in August 1999 hit İzmit (Kocaeli) and Adapazarı (Sakarya) in northwestern Anatolia, killing more than 18,000. If a major earthquake hit İstanbul, much of the city would be devastated, due to unlicensed, jerry-built construction. Locals are mostly fatalistic – no one doubts it's coming.

Wildlife
Animals

When a 4.4 magnitude quake shook İstanbul in October 2010, no deaths or damage were caused but it highlighted how ill-prepared the city was, with locals hitting the phone and social networking sites rather than evacuating their houses.

In theory, you could see bears, deer, jackals, caracal, wild boars and wolves in Turkey, although you're unlikely to spot any wild animals unless you're trekking.

Instead, look out for Kangal dogs, which are named after a small town near Sivas. Kangals were originally bred to protect flocks of sheep from wolves and bears on mountain pastures. People wandering off the beaten track, especially in eastern Turkey, are often alarmed at the sight of these huge, yellow-coated, black-headed animals, especially as they often wear ferocious spiked collars to protect them against wolves. Their mongrel descendants live on Turkey's streets.

An excellent animal-related holiday read is Jeremy James' *The Byerley Turk: The True Story of the First Thoroughbred,* a fictionalised biography of the Ottoman horse, whose descendants are the world's finest racing horses today.

Birds

Some 400 species of bird are found in Turkey, with about 250 of these passing through on migration from Africa to Europe. Spring and autumn are particularly good times to see the feathered commuters. It's particularly easy to spot eagles, storks, (beige) hoopoes, (blue) rollers and (green) bee-eaters. There are several bird sanctuaries (*kuş cennetleri;* bird paradises) dotted about the country, although unfortunately they are often popular with noisy, picnicking locals who frighten the birds away.

Enthusiastic birdwatchers should head east to Birecik, between Gaziantep and Şanlıurfa, one of the last-known nesting places in the world of the *Geronticus eremita* (eastern bald ibis). Also well off the beaten track is Çıldır Gölü (Çıldır Lake; p555), north of Kars in northeastern Anatolia. It's an important breeding ground for various species of birds. More readily accessible is the Göksu Delta (p376), near Silifke, where 332 species have been recorded, including the rare purple gallinule; and Pamucak (see p220), home to flamingos during February and March.

Walking and Birdwatching in South West Turkey, by Paul Hope, is an introduction to some of the country's best birdwatching spots.

Endangered Species

Anatolia's lions, beavers and Caspian tigers are now extinct, and its lynx, striped hyena and Anatolian leopard have all but disappeared. The last possible sighting of the distinctive leopard was in 1974, when one was shot for mauling a village woman outside Beypazarı.

Rare loggerhead turtles still nest on various beaches in Turkey, including Anamur Beach, İztuzu Beach at Dalyan, the Göksu Delta and Patara Beach (see boxed text, p373). A few rare Mediterranean monk seals live around Foça (p183), but you would be very lucky to see them.

Greenpeace has criticised Turkey for not following international fishing quotas relating to Mediterranean bluefin tuna, which is facing extinction.

Happily, the Anatolian wild sheep, unique to the Konya region, is making a comeback.

Plants

Turkey is one of the world's most biodiverse temperate-zone countries. Not only does its fertile soil produce an incredible range of fruit and vegetables, it is also blessed with an exceptionally rich flora: over 9000 species, 1200 of them endemic, with a new species of flora reportedly discovered here every week (on average). Common trees and plants you will see as you travel the country are pine, cypress, myrtle, laurel, rosemary, lavender and thyme.

Turkey is one of the last remaining sources of *Liquidambar orientalis* (frankincense trees), which grow along the southwest coast of the Mediterranean, especially around Köyceğiz. The Egyptians used the trees' resin during the embalming process; today, it is exported for use in perfume and incense. Also on this coast, on the Reşadiye peninsula and around Bodrum and Kumluca, is the endemic *Phoenix theophrastii* (Datça palm). The last remaining populations of these trees in the world are found here and on Crete.

Other notable plants include purple bougainvillea on the coast, introduced from South America. Olive trees, synonymous with the Mediterranean, originated in the Turkish part of the region and spread west during the Roman era. Turkey also introduced cherries to Italy, and from there to the world, via Giresun on the Black Sea coast.

The Most Beautiful Wild Flowers of Turkey, by Erdoğan Tekin, is the best field guide on the market, with detailed charts on each flower and more than 700 photos.

National Parks & Reserves

In the last few years, thanks to EU aspirations, Turkey has stepped up its environmental protection practices. It has 13 Ramsar sites (wetlands of international importance) and is a member of Cites, which covers

---

Regarded as harbingers of spring, storks migrate to Turkey around March. Their lofty nests can be seen along the west coast and in cities such as İstanbul, Konya and Ankara (often atop the Column of Julian). Some communities repair the nests to encourage the birds to return.

The beautiful, pure-white Van cat, often with one blue and one amber eye, has become endangered in its native Turkey. They are said to be able to swim in Lake Van – not that their owners would let these valuable pets do so.

TURKEY'S ENVIRONMENT ENVIRONMENTAL ISSUES

Tulips are commonly associated with the Netherlands, but the flower originated in Turkey and grew popular during the Ottoman Empire, when it was exported to Europe. Sultan Ahmet III's peaceful 18th-century reign (r 1703–1730) is known as the 'Tulip Era'.

international trade of endangered species. The growing number of protected areas includes 33 *milli parkıs* (national parks), 16 nature parks and 35 nature reserves. It also includes 58 'nature monuments' – mostly protected trees, including a 2000-year-old cedar in Finike, southwest of Antalya. In the parks and reserves the environment is supposedly protected, and hunting is controlled. Sometimes the regulations are carefully enforced, but at other times problems such as litter-dropping picnickers persist.

Tourism to national parks is not well developed in Turkey, and they are rarely well set up with facilities. It is not the norm for footpaths to be clearly marked, and camping spots are rarely available. Most of the well-frequented national parks are as popular for their historic monuments as they are for the surrounding natural environment.

Popular Parks

The following national parks are among the most popular with foreign visitors to Turkey. Visit the Turkish Ministry of Culture and Tourism (www.turizm.gov.tr) for more information.

Gallipoli National Historic Park (p131) Historic battlefield sites on a gloriously unspoilt peninsula surrounded by coves.

Göreme National Park (p457) An extraordinary landscape of gorges and fairy chimneys spread over a wide area.

Kaçkar Dağları National Park (Kaçkar Mountain National Park; p520) Stunning high mountain ranges popular with trekkers.

Köprülü Kanyon National Park (Bridge Canyon National Park; p360) Dramatic canyon with spectacular scenery and facilities for white-water rafting.

Nemrut Dağı National Park (Mt Nemrut National Park; p583) Pre-Roman stone heads surmounting a man-made mound with wonderful views.

Saklıkent National Park (p327) Famous for its 18km-long gorge.

Environmental Issues

Turkey faces the unenviable challenge of balancing environmental management with rapid economic growth and urbanisation, and to date it's done a sloppy job. Inadequate enforcement of environmental

NUCLEAR TURKEY

One of the biggest challenges facing Turkey's environmentalists is the current government's plan to build three nuclear power plants. One plant is slated to be built at Akkuyu, on the eastern Mediterranean coast, a controversial site located 25km from a seismic fault line. Previous plans to build a plant there were scrapped in 2000. Another proposed location is the Black Sea town of Sinop, with a vocal opponent in the community-run Sinop is Ours (www.sinopbizim.org).

The government says the three plants will have a total capacity of about 5000 megawatts, eliminating the possibility of an energy shortage and reducing dependency on supplies from other countries. Turkey currently imports over 90% of its oil and natural gas, and Russian gas cuts, including the Europe-wide cut in January 2009, have put internal energy security firmly on the agenda.

Experts also claim that sharing a border with Iran (which has a nuclear program) has pushed Turkey to develop some nuclear capacity. In 2010 Turkey and Brazil tried to help Iran avoid further international sanctions by negotiating a deal in which Iran would outsource its uranium enrichment to Turkey.

Privatisation of the Turkish energy sector picked up pace in 2008 following legislation to encourage investment. It is hoped that this will lead to improvements in the country's current infrastructure before implementation of nuclear energy is looked at. The country's seismic vulnerabilities increase the risk posed by nuclear reactors.

Turkey's intended accession to the EU is thankfully forcing it to lift its environmental standards. The country has started to overhaul environmental practices and laws, and even signed the Kyoto Protocol in 2009.

The government aims to harmonise all environmental legislation with the EU, an ambitious project that could cost some €70 billion, although the European Commission believes Turkey will eventually recoup €120 billion from the investment. In 2009, Turkey received the first-ever loan given by the World Bank's Clean Technology Fund, amounting to US$250 million.

Although Prime Minister Erdoğan has displayed an ambivalent attitude towards environmentalists, we imagine that his Environment and Forestry Ministry would be having many meetings to work out which challenge to start with. Priorities include waste-water disposal and the building of water treatment facilities. Food safety has been a major stumbling block, although EU accession talks covering this area began in 2010, following the opening of the environment chapter the previous year. Currently items including meat and meat products cannot be exported from Turkey to the EU.

laws, lack of finances and poor education have placed the environment a long way down on the country's list of priorities. But there are some glimmers of improvement, largely due to the country's desire to join the EU.

The Bosphorus

One of the biggest environmental challenges facing Turkey is the threat from maritime traffic along the Bosphorus. The 1936 Montreux Convention decreed that, although Turkey has sovereignty over the strait, it must permit the free passage of shipping through it. At that time, perhaps a few thousand ships a year passed through, but this has risen to over 45,000 vessels annually; around 10% are tankers, which carry over 100 million tons of hazardous substances through the strait every year.

There have already been serious accidents, such as the 1979 *Independenta* collision with another vessel, which killed 43 people and spilt and burnt some 95,000 tonnes of oil (around 2½ times the amount spilt by the famous *Exxon Valdez*). Following the Gulf of Mexico disaster, the Turkish government renewed its efforts to find alternative routes for oil transportation, which currently include a pipeline between Azerbaijan and the Turkish eastern Mediterranean port of Ceyhan. Pipelines between Samsun and Ceyhan, and between Bulgaria and Greece, are on the drawing board.

Construction & Dams

Building development is taking a terrible toll on the environment, especially along the Aegean and Mediterranean coasts. Spots such as Kuşadası and Marmaris, once pleasant fishing villages, have been near swamped by urban spread and are in danger of losing all appeal. Worse still, much of the development is only used during the warmer months, placing intensive strains on the infrastructure. The number of secluded bays glimpsed on the blue voyage (p319) cruises has plummeted, and the development continues to spread: a new yacht marina appeared in Sığacık, in the north Aegean, in 2010.

Short of water and electricity, Turkey is one of the world's main builders of dams. There are more than 650 dams in the Black Sea region alone, and controversy surrounds proposed developments. The gigantic Southeast Anatolia Project (p573), known as GAP, is one of Turkey's

The oil pipeline running from Baku, Azerbaijan to Ceyhan, Turkey via Tbilisi, Georgia is one of the world's longest; it takes oil a month to travel from one end of the 1800km pipe to the other.

TURKEY'S ENVIRONMENT ENVIRONMENTAL ISSUES

OIL PIPELINE

major construction efforts. Harnessing the headwaters of the Tigris and Euphrates Rivers, it's creating a potential political time bomb, causing friction with the countries downstream that also depend on this water.

In 2008, Hasankeyf (p608) featured on the World Monuments Watch list of the planet's 100 most endangered sites, thanks to the İlisu Dam Project's plans to drown the historic southeastern town. The İlisu consortium has offered to recreate the town, which was historically a Silk Road commercial centre on the border of Anatolia and Mesopotamia, but the actual ruins would be lost, along with their atmospheric setting on the Tigris River. Despite European backers pulling out on two occasions, and European export credit agencies withdrawing due to social and environmental concerns, the project is expected to be completed by 2013, potentially displacing 50,000-plus people.

Near Bergama, the Yortanlı Dam poses a similar threat. Already built, the dam will bring water to an arid region but flood the ruins of a 1st-century Roman spa at Allianoi.

Other Issues

Blue recycling bins are an increasingly common sight on the streets of İstanbul, but the government still has a long way to go in terms of educating its citizens and businesses. The head of a parliamentary environmental commission said in 2010 that Turkish municipalities were improperly disposing of more than 60% of urban waste. The country is adopting the EU's 'polluters' pay' policy.

Key issues for the country are soil erosion, deforestation, degradation of biodiversity and water pollution. Environment and Forestry Minister Veysel Eroğlu recently addressed two of those issues, saying Turkey had reforested nearly one million hectares of land and ensured clean potable water across its 81 provinces.

However, despite moves to curb Turkey's carbon emissions, air pollution in the major cities remains a problem, and many feel the government often shuts the gate after the horse has bolted. In early 2006, fines for dumping toxic waste increased from a maximum of €4500 to €1.5 million – legislative changes that were announced only after barrels of toxic waste were discovered in empty lots around İstanbul. One of the worst-hit places was Dilovası, with deaths from cancer nearly three times the world average, and a report saying it should be evacuated and labelled a medical disaster area. Neither happened, and the over-industrialised area on the Sea of Marmara remains a reminder of the country's environmental shortcomings.

To end on a happy note, Turkey is doing well when it comes to beach cleanliness, with 313 beaches and 14 marinas qualifying for Blue Flag status; go to www.blueflag.org for the complete list.

The Isparta area is one of the world's leading producers of attar of roses, a valuable oil extracted from rose petals and used in perfumes and cosmetics. See p292 to find out how you can see the harvest in late spring.

ROSES

Survival Guide

Directory A-Z

Accommodation

Turkey has accommodation options to suit all budgets, with concentrations of good, value-for-money hotels, pensions and hostels in places most visited by independent travellers, such as İstanbul and Cappadocia.

The rates quoted in this book are for high season (May to September) and include tax (KDV) and, unless otherwise mentioned, breakfast. Listings are ordered by preference, and prices ranges are based on the cost of a double room with en suite bathroom:

　€ Up to TL75
　€€ TL75 to TL175
　€€€ TL175 to hundreds of euros

Prices in İstanbul are at the high ends of these brackets. Out east, prices are lower than elsewhere in the country.

Rooms are discounted by about 20% during the low season (October to April), but not during the Christmas period and major Islamic holidays (see p676). Places within easy reach of İstanbul and Ankara may hike their prices during summer weekends.

If you plan to stay a week or more in a coastal resort, check the prices in package-holiday brochures before booking. British, French and German tour companies in particular often offer money-saving flight-and-accommodation packages to the South Aegean and Mediterranean.

Accommodation options in more-Westernised spots such as İstanbul often quote tariffs in euros as well as (or instead of) lira. Accommodation in less-touristy locations generally quote in lira. Most places happily accept lira or euro (or even US dollars in İstanbul). We've used the currency quoted by the business being reviewed.

Sleeping options generally have a website, where reservations can be made.

Many pensions operate in informal chains, referring travellers from one to another. If you've enjoyed staying in a place, you will probably enjoy its owner's recommendations, but stay firm and try not to sign up to anything sight unseen.

Apartments

» Apartments offer good value for money, especially for families and small groups.

» Outside İstanbul and a few Aegean and Mediterranean locations, apartments for holiday rentals are often thin on the ground.

» In addition to our listings, www.ownersdirect.co.uk and www.holidaylettings.co.uk feature Turkish apartments. Or see www.turkeyrenting.com, www.vrbo.com or www.perfectplaces.com.

» In coastal spots such as Kaş, Antalya and the Bodrum Peninsula, *emlakci* (real-estate agents) hold lists of available holiday rentals, and are used to dealing with foreigners. See p234 for further details on Bodrum.

Camping

» Most camping facilities are along the coasts and are usually privately run.

» Inland, camping facilities are fairly rare, with the exception of Cappadocia and a few places in eastern Anatolia, notably Nemrut Dağı National Park.

» The best facilities inland are often on Orman Dinlenme Yeri (Forestry Department land); you usually need your own transport to reach these.

» Pensions and hostels will often let you camp in their grounds and use their facilities for a fee.

BOOK YOUR STAY ONLINE

For more reviews by Lonely Planet authors, check out hotels.lonelyplanet.com. You'll find independent reviews, as well as recommendations on the best places to stay. Best of all, you can book online.

DIRECTORY A–Z ACCOMMODATION

» Camping outside official sites is often more hassle than it's worth, because:

- The police may drop by to check you out and possibly move you on.
- Out east, there are wolves living in the wild; be wary, and don't leave food and rubbish lying outside your tent.
- Also look out for Kangal dogs (p662).
- We recommend female travellers stick to official sites and camp where there are plenty of people, especially out east.

Hostels

» There are plenty of hostels with dormitories in popular destinations, where dorm beds usually cost about TL15 to TL20 per night.

» Turkey has no official hostel network, but there are Hostelling International members in İstanbul, Cappadocia and the Aegean and Western Mediterranean areas.

TREE HOUSES

Olympos, on the Mediterranean coast, is famous for its 'tree houses' (p346): rough-and-ready shelters in forested settings near the beach. The success of these backpacker hangouts has spawned imitators elsewhere in the Western Mediterranean, for example in nearby Çıralı and Saklıkent Gorge.

Hotels
BUDGET

» In most cities and resort towns, good, inexpensive beds are readily available.

» The most difficult places to find good cheap rooms are İstanbul, Ankara, İzmir and package-holiday resort towns such as Alanya and Çeşme.

» The cheapest hotels charge around TL25 for a single room.

» The cheapest hotels are mostly used by working-

class Turkish men and are not suitable for solo women.

MIDRANGE

» One- and two-star hotels cost around TL70 to TL120 for a double room with shower.

» One- and two-star hotels are less oppressively masculine in atmosphere, even when the clientele is mainly male.

» Three-star hotels are generally used to catering for female travellers.

» Hotels in more-traditional towns normally offer only Turkish TV, Turkish breakfast and none of the 'extras' that are commonplace in pensions.

» Prices should be displayed in reception.

» You should never pay more than the prices on display, and you will often be charged less.

» Often you will be able to haggle.

» Unmarried foreign couples don't usually have problems sharing rooms.

» Out east, couples are often given a twin room even if they ask for a double.

» Some establishments still refuse to accept an unmarried couple when one of the parties is Turkish.

» The cheaper the hotel, and the more remote the location, the more conservative its management tends to be.

BOUTIQUE HOTELS

Increasingly, old Ottoman mansions, caravanserais and other historic buildings are being refurbished, or completely rebuilt, as hotels

equipped with all mod cons and bags of character. Most of these options are in the midrange and top-end price brackets. Some are reviewed in this guide; many more are in The Little Hotel Book (www.smallhotels.com.tr), available in bookshops in İstanbul.

Pensions

In all of the destinations popular with travellers you'll be able to find pansiyons (pensions): simple, family-run guest houses, where you can get a good, clean single or double for around TL40 or TL70. Many pensions also have triple and quadruple rooms. Be sure to remove your shoes when you enter.

In touristy areas in particular, the advantages of staying in a pension, as opposed to a cheap hotel, include:

» A choice of simple meals

» Book exchange

» Laundry service

» International TV channels

» Staff who speak at least one foreign language

EV PANSIYONU

In a few places, old-fashioned ev pansiyonu (pensions in a private home) survive. These are simply rooms in a family house that are let to visitors at busy times of the year. They do not normally advertise their existence in a formal way: ask locals where to find them and look out for kıralık oda (room for rent) signs. English is rarely spoken by the proprietors, so some knowledge of Turkish would be helpful.

PRACTICALITIES

» Turkey uses the metric system for weights and measures.

» Electrical current is 230V AC, 50Hz.

» You can buy plug adaptors at most electrical shops.

» Take a surge protector.

» A universal AC adaptor is also a good investment.

» *Today's Zaman* (www.todayszaman.com) is an English newspaper. *Hürriyet Daily News* (www.hurriyetdailynews.com) and *Sabah* (www.sabahenglish. com) have English editions.

» *Cornucopia* (www.cornucopia.net) is a glossy magazine in English about Turkey.

» Turkish Airlines' in-flight monthly, *Skylife* (www.thy.com), is also worth a read.

» *Turkey Post* (http://wn.com/s/turkeypost/index.html) collates international press reports about Turkey.

» The APA Group's guides to İstanbul, Ankara and Bodrum feature listings and articles.

» TRT broadcasts news daily, in languages including English, on radio and at www. trt.net.tr.

» Digiturk offers numerous Turkish and international TV channels.

Touts

In smaller tourist towns such as Selçuk, touts may approach you as you step from a bus and offer you accommodation. Some may string you a line about the pension you're looking for, in the hope of reeling you in and getting a commission from another pension. Taxi drivers sometimes play this game, too.

It's generally best to politely decline these offers, but if you're on a budget, touts sometimes work for newly opened establishments offering cheap rates. Before they take you to the pension, make it known you're only looking and are under no obligation to stay.

Business Hours

In the areas covered by the following table, reviews in destination chapters only specify opening hours if they differ from those listed below. Reviews of sights always list opening hours.

Most museums close on Monday and, from April to October, close 1½ to two hours later. The following also experience seasonal varia-

tion; a bar is likely to open later in the summer than in the winter, and tourist offices in popular locations open longer hours and at weekends during the summer.

The working day gets shortened during the holy month of Ramazan, which currently falls during the summer (see p676). More Islamic cities such as Konya and Kayseri virtually shut down during noon prayers on Friday (the Muslim sabbath); apart from that, Friday is a normal working day.

Banks, post offices 8.30am-noon & 1.30-5pm Mon-Fri

Restaurants breakfast 8am-11am, lunch noon-4pm, dinner 6-10pm

Bars 4pm-late

Nightclubs & entertainment venues 9pm-late

Shops 9am-6pm Mon-Fri (longer in tourist areas and big cities – including weekend opening)

Children

Check out Lonely Planet's *Travel with Children*, which has lots of practical informa-

tion and advice on how to make travel with children as stress-free as possible.

Attitudes

» *Çocuklar* (children) are the beloved centrepiece of family life and your children will be welcomed wherever they go.

» Your child's journey will be peppered with *Maşallah* (glory be to God) and they will be clutched into the adoring arms of strangers.

» Perhaps learn your child's age and sex in Turkish – *ay* (month), *yıl* (year), *erkek* (boy) and *kız* (girl).

» To make polite inquiries about the other person's children: *kaç tane çocuklarınız varmı?* (How many children do you have?).

» Most Turkish women breastfeed their babies (discreetly) in public; no one is likely to mind you doing the same.

Practicalities

» Children are not very well catered for in Turkey.

» Most hotels can arrange some sort of babysitting service, but kids' clubs and agencies are rare.

» If you are looking for childcare, **Child Wise** (www.childwise.net) offers general advice.

» Hotels and restaurants will often prepare special dishes for children.

» High chairs in restaurants are uncommon.

» Most hotels do not have cots, but will organise one with advance notice.

» Public baby-changing facilities are rare, but found in branches of the *kebapçı* (kebap restaurant) chain, Kırçiçeği.

» Seaside towns and cities often have playgrounds, but check the equipment for safety.

» Buses often do not have functioning toilets, although they normally stop every few hours.

» Most car-rental companies provide child-safety seats for a small extra charge.

» Dangerous drivers and uneven surfaces make using strollers an extreme sport.

» A 'baby backpack' is useful for walking around sights.

» See p681 for info about restaurants and tea gardens that are suitable for families.

Products

» Double-check the suitability of prescriptions your children are given while in Turkey (see also p700).

» Pasteurised UHT milk is sold in cartons everywhere, but fresh milk is harder to find.

» Consider bringing a supply of baby food: what little you find here, your baby will understandably find inedible; or it will just be mashed banana.

» Migros supermarkets have the best range of baby food.

» Most supermarkets stock formula, although it is very expensive, and vitamin-fortified rice cereal.

» Disposable *bebek bezi* (nappies or diapers) are readily available.

» The best nappies are Prima and Huggies, sold in pharmacies and supermarkets; don't bother with cheaper local brands.

Safety

» Safety consciousness in Turkey rarely meets Western norms.

» In hotels and other buildings, look out for open power points.

» On the street, watch for:

• Turkey's notorious drivers, particularly those on pavement-mounting mopeds.

• Crudely covered electric mains.

• Open stairwells.

• Serious potholes.

• Open drains.

• Carelessly secured building sites.

Sights & Activities

Beaches are an obvious draw, but Turkey doesn't have many attractions designed with children in mind. A few museums in İstanbul and Ankara have fun interactive features; see p85.

Activities are a better bet, depending on the child's age. Boating, ballooning, horse riding, snorkelling and white-water rafting are all great options. Apart from the coasts, the area most likely to appeal to older children is Cappadocia, with its underground cities, cave dwellings and kooky landscapes. Ferries in cities such as İstanbul and İzmir are popular, as are the antique tram and funicular railways in the former.

Customs Regulations

Imports

Items valued over US$15,000 should be declared, to ensure you can take them out of the country when you leave. Goods including the following can be imported duty-free:

» 200 cigarettes

» 50 cigars

» 200g of tobacco

» 1.5kg of coffee

» 1kg of chocolate or confectionery

» One 100cl or two 75cl bottles of wine or spirits

» Five 120ml bottles of different types of perfume

» One camera with five films

» One video camera with five tapes

» Unlimited currency

Exports

» It's illegal to export genuine antiquities.

» Carpet shops should be able to provide a form certifying that your purchase is not antique.

» Ask for advice from vendors you buy items from and keep receipts and paperwork.

Discount Cards

The following are available in Turkey but easier to get in your home country.

International Student Identity Card (ISIC; www.isic.org) Discounts on accommodation – typically 25% – and eating, entertainment, shopping and transport. To get it, you need documents including a matriculation card or letter from your college or university stating that you are a student.

These cards offer similar benefits to ISIC, but far fewer businesses accept them:

International Youth Travel Card (IYTC; http://tinyurl.com/25tlbv7) To get one, you need a passport or something similar showing you are aged under 26.

International Teacher Identity Card (ITIC; http://tinyurl.com/25tlbv7) Applicants need documents including a letter from an educational establishment stating that they are working there for a minimum of 18 hours per week and one academic year.

Embassies & Consulates

» Most embassies and consulates in Turkey open from 8am or 9am to noon Monday to Friday, then after lunch until 5pm or 6pm for people to pick up visas.

» The embassies of some Muslim countries may open Sunday to Thursday.

» To ask the way to an embassy, say: '[Country] *başkonsolosluğu nerede?*'

» For details on getting visas to neighbouring countries, see p687.

» Visit http://tinyurl.com/6ywt8 for details of other countries' missions.

» The embassies in Ankara are listed in the table, and there are consulates in other Turkish cities (check the websites listed under 'Contact Details' in the table for their locations).

EMBASSIES IN TURKEY

EMBASSY	CONTACT DETAILS	ADDRESS
Armenia	Contact Russian embassy; www.armeniaforeignministry.com	
Australia	☎0312-459 9500; www.embaustralia.org.tr	7th fl, MNG Building, Uğur Mumcu Caddesi 88, Gaziosmanpaşa, Ankara
Azerbaijan	☎0312-491 1681; www.mfa.gov.az/eng	Diplomatik Site, Baku Sokak 1, Oran, Ankara
Bulgaria	☎0312-467 2071; www.bulgaria.bg/en/	Atatürk Bulvarı 124, Kavaklıdere, Ankara
Canada	☎0312-409 2700; www.canadainternational.gc.ca	Cinnah Caddesi 58, Çankaya, Ankara
France	☎0312-455 4545; www.ambafrance-tr.org	Paris Caddesi 70, Kavaklıdere, Ankara
Georgia	☎0312-491 8030; www.turkey.mfa.gov.ge	Diplomatik Site, Kılıç Ali Sokak 12, Oran, Ankara
Germany	☎0312-455 5100; www.ankara.diplo.de	Atatürk Bulvarı 114, Kavaklıdere, Ankara
Greece	☎0312-448 0647; www.mfa.gr/ankara	Zia Ur Rahman Caddesi 9-11, Gaziosmanpaşa, Ankara
Iran	☎0312-468 2820; www.mfa.gov.ir	Tehran Caddesi 10, Kavaklıdere, Ankara
Iraq	☎0312-468 7421; http://iraqmissions.hostinguk.com	Turan Emeksiz Sokak 11, Gaziosmanpaşa, Ankara
Ireland	☎0312-459 1000; www.embassyofireland.org.tr	3rd fl, MNG Building, Uğur Mumcu Caddesi 88, Gaziosmanpaşa
Netherlands	☎0312-409 1800; http://turkije.nlambassade.org	Hollanda Caddesi 5, Yıldız, Ankara
New Zealand	☎0312-467 9054; www.nzembassy.com/turkey	4th fl, Iran Caddesi 13, Kavaklıdere, Ankara
Russia	☎0312-439 2122; www.turkey.mid.ru	Karyağdı Sokak 5, Çankaya, Ankara
Syria	☎0312-440 9657; http://tinyurl.com/6ywt8a	Sedat Simavi Sokak 40, Çankaya, Ankara
UK	☎0312-455 3344; http://ukinturkey.fco.gov.uk	Şehit Ersan Caddesi 46a, Çankaya, Ankara
USA	☎0312-455 5555; http://turkey.usembassy.gov	Atatürk Bulvarı 110, Kavaklıdere, Ankara

Electricity

230V/50Hz

230V/50Hz

Food

Listings in this book are ordered by preference, and prices are based on the cost of a main course:

€ Up to TL9
€€ TL9 to TL17.50
€€€ More than TL17.50

Prices in İstanbul are at the high ends of these brackets. For more information about eating and drinking in Turkey, see p642.

Gay & Lesbian Travellers

Homosexuality is legal in Turkey and attitudes are changing, but prejudice remains strong and there are sporadic reports of violence towards gays – the message is discretion.

İstanbul has a flourishing gay scene, as does Ankara. In other cities there may be a gay bar or two.

Club Mancha (www.gay shareresorts.com) Resort in Bodrum for gay men.

Kaos GL (www.kaosgl. com) Based in Ankara, it publishes a quarterly gay-and-lesbian magazine (in Turkish).

Lambda İstanbul (www. lambdaistanbul.org, in Turkish) LGBT support group.

Pride Travel Agency (www. turkey-gay-travel.com) Gay-friendly travel agent, with useful links on the website.

Insurance

» A travel insurance policy covering theft, loss and medical expenses is a good idea.

» A huge variety of policies is available, so check the small print.

» Some policies exclude 'dangerous activities', which can include scuba diving, motorcycling and even trekking.

» Some policies may not cover you if you travel to regions of the country where your government warns against travel (see p679).

» If you decide to cancel your trip on the advice of an official warning against travel, your insurer may not cover you.

» For information on health insurance, see p698.

» For information on motor insurance, see p693.

» Worldwide travel insurance is available at www. lonelyplanet.com/bookings/ insurance.do. You can buy, extend and claim online anytime – even if you're already on the road.

Internet Access

» Throughout the country, the majority of accommodation options of all standards offer wi-fi.

» We have used the internet icon (@) where the option provides a computer with internet access for guest use.

» In Eating and Drinking reviews, we have used the wi-fi icon (📶) where the business has a network.

» Wi-fi networks are found at locations from travel agencies and carpet shops to otogars (bus stations) and ferry terminals.

» See www.ttnet.com.tr for wi-fi hot spots.

Internet Cafes

Internet cafes are widespread. They are typically open roughly from 9am until midnight, and charge around TL2 an hour. Connection speeds vary, but are generally fast, although viruses are rife.

The best internet cafes have English keyboards. Some cafes have Turkish ones, on which 'ı' occupies the position occupied by 'i' on English keyboards. On a Turkish keyboard, create the '@' symbol by holding down the 'q' and ALT keys at the same time.

Language Courses

İstanbul is the most popular place to learn Turkish, though there are also courses in Ankara, İzmir and a few other spots around the country. Try to sit in on a class before you commit, as the quality of your experience definitely depends on the teacher and your classmates.

Private tuition is more expensive, but tutors often advertise at http://istanbul.craigslist.com.tr and in the 'yellow pages' section of the expat website www.mymerhaba.com.

Teach Yourself Turkish by David and Asuman Çelen Pollard is the best of the many books available.

Schools include the following. Tömer and Dilmer are the most popular, but both have their detractors as well as fans.

Dilmer (www1.dilmer.com) Located near İstanbul's Taksim Square, it offers four- and eight-week courses, covering seven levels (€288 to €384).

EFINST Turkish Centre (www.turkishlesson.com) The school in Levent, İstanbul offers options including part-time 10-week courses

(€578) and private lessons (from €42).

Spoken Turkish (www.spokenenglishtr.com) Conveniently located on İstanbul's İstiklal Caddesi (as well as other parts of the city), but relatively untested, it offers part-time intensive courses.

Tömer (www.tomer.com.tr) Affiliated with Ankara University, and with branches throughout the country, Tömer offers four- and eight-week courses (€290 and €350).

Legal Matters

Technically, you should carry your passport at all times. There have been cases of police stopping foreigners and holding them until someone brings their passport. In practice, you may prefer to carry a photocopy.

There are laws against lese-majesty (p677), antiquities smuggling (p671) and illegal drugs. Turkish jails are not places where you want to spend any time.

The age of consent in Turkey is 18 – as is the legal age for voting, driving and drinking.

See p691 for more advice about driving.

Maps

Maps are widely available at tourist offices and bookshops, although quality maps are hard to find. In İstanbul, look in the bookshops we've listed on p107, plus others on and around İstiklal Caddesi; online, check Tulumba.com and Amazon.com.

Mep Medya's city and regional maps are recommended, as is its touring maps including the following:

Türkiye Karayolları Haritası (1:1,200,000) A sheet map of the whole country.

Adım Adım Türkiye Yol Atlası (Step by Step Turkey Road Atlas; 1:400,000)

Money

Turkey's currency is the Türk Lirası (Turkish lira; TL). The lira comes in notes of five, 10, 20, 50, 100 and 200, and coins of one, five, 10, 25 and 50 kuruş and one lira.

Prices in this book are quoted in lira or euros (€), depending on which currency is used by the business being reviewed.

After decades of rampant inflation, the lira is now stable. The Yeni Türk Lirası (new Turkish lira; YTL) was used between 2005 and 2008 as an anti-inflationary measure; watch out for people dumping their old-currency kuruş coins on you. Yeni Türk Lirası is no longer valid, but if you have some notes and coins left over from a previous visit to Turkey, branches of Ziraat bank will exchange your 'new' lira for the same value of today's lira.

Because hyperinflation led to Turkish lira having strings of zeros (six noughts were dropped from the notes in the transition to new lira in 2005), many people, confusingly, still work in thousands and millions. Don't be alarmed if you're buying items worth, say, TL6 and

TIPPING IN TURKEY

SERVICE	TIP
Budget restaurant	A few coins
Midrange or top-end restaurant	10% to 15% of the bill
Hotel porter	3% of the room price
Budget hotel	Not expected
Metered taxi fare	Round up to the nearest 50 kuruş (eg TL4.70 to TL5)
Dolmuş	Not expected
Hamam	10% to 20% to the masseur
Special tour (eg by a custodian)	From a few lira

THE ART OF BARGAINING

Traditionally, when customers enter a Turkish shop to make a significant purchase, they're offered a comfortable seat and a drink (çay tea, coffee or a soft drink). There is some general chitchat, then discussion of the shop's goods in general, then of the customer's tastes, preferences and requirements. Finally, a number of items in the shop are displayed for the customer's inspection.

The customer asks the price; the shop owner gives it; the customer looks doubtful and makes a counteroffer 25% to 50% lower. This procedure goes back and forth several times before a price acceptable to both parties is arrived at. It's considered very bad form to haggle over a price, come to an agreement, and then change your mind.

If you can't agree on a price it's perfectly OK to say goodbye and walk out of the shop. In fact, walking out is one of the best ways to test the authenticity of the last offer. If shopkeepers know you can find the item elsewhere for less, they'll probably call after you and drop their price. Even if they don't stop you, there's nothing to prevent you from returning later and buying the item for what they quoted.

To bargain effectively you must be prepared to take your time, and you must know something about the items in question, not to mention their market price. The best way to do this is to look at similar goods in several shops, asking prices but not making counteroffers. Always stay good-humoured and polite when you are bargaining – if you do this the shopkeeper will too. When bargaining you can often get a discount by offering to buy several items at once, by paying in a strong major currency, or by paying cash.

If you don't have sufficient time to shop around, follow the age-old rule: find something you like at a price you're willing to pay, buy it, enjoy it, and don't worry about whether or not you received the world's lowest price.

In general, you shouldn't bargain in food shops or over transport costs. Outside tourist areas, hotels may expect to 'negotiate' the room price with you. In tourist areas pension owners are usually fairly clear about their prices, although if you're travelling in winter or staying a long time it's worth asking about *indirim* (discounts).

the shopkeeper asks you for TL6,000,000.

Lack of change is a constant problem; try to keep a supply of coins and small notes for minor payments. Post offices have Western Union counters.

ATMs

ATMs dispense Turkish lira, and occasionally euros and US dollars, to Visa, Master-Card, Cirrus and Maestro card holders. Look for these logos on machines, which are found in most towns. Machines generally offer instructions in foreign languages including English.

It's possible to get around Turkey using only ATMs, if you draw out money in the towns to tide you through the villages that don't have them. Also keep some cash in reserve for the inevitable day when the machine

throws a wobbly. If your card is swallowed by a stand-alone ATM booth, it may be tricky getting it back. The booths are often run by franchisees rather than by the banks themselves.

Credit Cards

Visa and MasterCard/Euro Card are widely accepted by hotels, shops and restaurants, although often not by pensions and local restaurants outside main tourist areas. You can also get cash advances on these cards. Amex is more commonly accepted in top-end establishments. Inform your credit card provider of your travel plans, as credit-card fraud does happen in Turkey.

Foreign Currencies

Euros and US dollars are the most readily accepted foreign currencies. Foreign

currencies are accepted in shops, hotels and restaurants in many tourist areas, and taxi drivers will take them for big journeys.

Moneychangers

The Turkish lira is weak against Western currencies, and you will probably get a better exchange rate in Turkey than elsewhere. The lira is virtually worthless outside Turkey, so make sure you spend it all before leaving.

US dollars and euros are the easiest currencies to change, although many exchange offices and banks will change other major currencies such as UK pounds and Japanese yen.

You'll get better rates at exchange offices, which often don't charge commission, than at banks. Exchange offices operate in tourist areas and market

MAJOR ISLAMIC HOLIDAYS

ISLAMIC YEAR	NEW YEAR	PROPHET'S BIRTHDAY	RAMAZAN	ŞEKER BAYRAMI	KURBAN BAYRAMI
1432	7 Dec 2010	15 Feb 2011	1 Aug 2011	30 Aug 2011	6 Nov 2011
1433	26 Nov 2011	4 Feb 2012	20 July 2012	18 Aug 2012	25 Oct 2012
1434	15 Nov 2012	24 Jan 2013	9 July 2013	8 Aug 2013	15 Oct 2013

areas, with better rates often found in the latter. Exchange offices are also found at some post offices (PTTs), shops and hotels.

Banks are more likely to change minor currencies, although they tend to make heavy weather of it. Turkey has no black market.

Tipping

Turkey is fairly European in its approach to tipping and you won't be pestered with demands for baksheesh as elsewhere in the Middle East.

Some more-expensive restaurants automatically add the *servis ücreti* (service charge) to your bill, although there's no guarantee this goes to the staff.

Travellers Cheques

Banks, shops and hotels usually see it as a burden to change travellers cheques, and will either try to persuade you to go elsewhere or charge you a premium for the service. If you do have to change them, try one of the major banks.

Photography

People in Turkey are generally receptive to having their photo taken. The major exception is when they are praying in the mosque or performing other religious activities. As in most countries, do not take photos of military sites, airfields, police stations and so on, as it could arouse the authorities' suspicions. For inspiration and tips, pick up Lonely Planet's *Travel Photography* book.

Post

Turkish *postanes* (post offices) are indicated by black-on-yellow 'PTT' signs. Most post offices follow the hours we've listed on p670, but a few offices in major cities have extended opening hours.

Letters take between one and several weeks to get to/ from Turkey. Postcards sent abroad cost TL0.80; letters cost from TL0.85.

When posting letters, the *yurtdışı* slot is for mail to foreign countries, *yurtiçi* for mail to other Turkish cities, and *şehiriçi* for local mail. Visit www.ptt.gov.tr for more information.

Parcels

If you are shipping something from Turkey, don't close your parcel before it has been inspected by a customs official. Take packing and wrapping materials with you to the post office.

Parcels take months to arrive.

International couriers including DHL also operate in Turkey.

Public Holidays

New Year's Day (Yılbaşı; 1 January)

National Sovereignty & Children's Day (Ulusal Egemenlik ve Çocuk Günü; 23 April) Commemorates the first meeting of the Turkish Grand National Assembly in 1920.

Youth & Sports Day (Gençlik ve Spor Günü; 19 May) Dedicated to Atatürk and the youth of the republic.

Victory Day (Zafer Bayramı; 30 August) Commemorates the republican army's victory over the invading Greek army at Dumlupınar during the War of Independence.

Şeker Bayramı (Sweets Holiday; 30 August to 1 September 2011, 18 to 20 August 2012) Also known as Ramazan Bayramı, it celebrates the end of Ramazan.

Republic Day (Cumhuriyet Bayramı; 28 to 29 October) Commemorates the proclamation of the republic by Atatürk in 1923.

Kurban Bayramı (Festival of the Sacrifice; 6 to 10 November 2011, 25 to 29 October 2012) The most important holiday of the year, it marks İbrahim's near-sacrifice of İsmael on Mt Moriah (Quran, Sura 37; Genesis 22).

Safe Travel

Although Turkey is by no means a dangerous country to visit, it's always wise to be a little cautious, especially if you're travelling alone.

Turkey is not a safety-conscious country: holes in pavements go unmended; precipitous drops go unguarded; safety belts are not always worn; lifeguards on beaches are rare; dolmuş (minibus) drivers negotiate bends while counting out change.

The two areas to be most cautious are İstanbul, where various scams operate, and southeastern Anatolia, where the PKK (Kurdistan Workers Party) stepped up its terrorist activities in 2010.

The Kurdish issue occasionally also leads to violence in western Turkey; in 2010, the PKK's commander vowed to attack cities and resorts in the west of the country, and the group bombed a military bus on the outskirts of İstanbul.

Flies & Mosquitoes

In high summer, mosquitoes are troublesome even in İstanbul; they can make a stay along the coast a nightmare. Some hotel rooms come equipped with nets and/or plug-in bugbusters, but it's a good idea to bring some insect repellent and mosquito coils.

Lese-Majesty

The laws against insulting, defaming or making light of Atatürk, the Turkish flag, the Turkish people, the Turkish Republic and so on are taken very seriously. Even if derogatory remarks were never made, Turks have been known to claim they were in the heat of a quarrel, which is enough to get the foreigner carted off to jail.

Scams & Druggings

In Sultanahmet, İstanbul, if a shoe cleaner walking in front of you drops his brush, don't pick it up. He will insist on giving you a 'free' clean in return, before demanding an extortionate fee.

In another İstanbul scam, normally targeted at single men, a pleasant local guy befriends you in the street and takes you to a bar. After a few drinks, and possibly the attention of some ladies, who you offer drinks, the bill arrives. The prices are astronomical and the proprietors can produce a menu showing the same prices. If you don't have enough cash, you'll be frogmarched to the nearest ATM. If this happens to you, report it to the tourist police; some travellers have taken the police back to the bar and received a refund.

A less-common variation on this trick involves the traveller having their drink spiked and waking up in an unexpected place with their belongings, right down to their shoes, missing – or worse.

Single men should not accept invitations from unknown folk in large cities without sizing the situation up carefully. You could invite your new-found friends to a bar of *your* choice; if they're not keen to go, chances are they are shady characters.

Do not buy coins or other artefacts offered to you by touts at ancient sites such as Ephesus and Perge. It is a serious crime here, punishable by long prison terms, and the touts are likely in cahoots with the local policemen.

Smoking

Turks love smoking and there's even a joke about the country's propensity for puffing: Who smokes more than a Turk? Two Turks.

Note that smoking in enclosed public spaces is banned, and punishable by a fine. Hotels, restaurants and bars are generally smoke-free, although bars sometimes relax the rules as the evening wears on. Public transport is meant to be smoke-free, although taxi drivers and bus drivers sometimes smoke at the wheel.

Traffic

As a pedestrian, note that Turks are aggressive, dangerous drivers; 'right of way' doesn't compute with many motorists, despite the little green man on traffic lights. Give way to vehicles in all situations, even if you have to jump out of the way.

See p691 for advice about driving.

Telephone

Türk Telekom (www. turktelekom.com.tr) has a monopoly on phone services, and service is efficient if costly. Within Turkey, numbers starting with 444 don't require area codes and, wherever you call from, are charged at the local rate.

Country code ☑90
International access code ☑00

Kontörlü Telefon

If you only want to make one quick call, it's easiest to look for a booth with a sign saying *kontörlü telefon* (metered telephone). You make your call and the owner reads the meter and charges you accordingly. In touristy areas you can get rates as low as TL0.50 per minute to Europe, the UK, the US and Australia.

Mobile Phones

» Turks adore mobile (*cep*, pocket) phones, and reception

PTT AIR MAIL TARIFFS

DESTINATION	FIRST KG	EACH KG THEREAFTER
Australia	TL42.90	TL20.40
France	TL36.80	TL4.10
Germany	TL43	TL4.40
UK	TL42.10	TL7.90
USA	TL29.10	TL9.30

TIME DIFFERENCES IN SUMMER

COUNTRY	CAPITAL CITY	DIFFERENCE FROM TURKEY
Australia	Canberra	+7 hours
Canada	Ottawa	-7 hours
France	Paris	-1 hour
Germany	Berlin	-1 hour
Japan	Tokyo	+6 hours
Netherlands	Amsterdam	-1 hour
New Zealand	Wellington	+9 hours
UK	London	-2 hours
USA	Washington DC	-7 hours

is excellent throughout nearly all of the country.

» Mobile phone numbers start with a four-figure number beginning with 🖥️05.

» The major networks are **Turkcell** (www.turkcell.com. tr), which is the most comprehensive, **Vodafone** (www. vodafone.com.tr) and **Avea** (www.avea.com.tr).

» A pay-as-you-go Turkcell SIM card costs TL25 (including TL5 credit) or TL35 (with TL20 credit).

» You need to show your passport and ensure the seller phones your details through to Turkcell to activate your account.

» SIM cards and *kontör* (credit) are widely available – at streetside booths and shops as well as mobile phone outlets.

» If you buy a local SIM card and use it in your mobile from home, the network detects and bars foreign phones within a month.

» To avoid barring, register your phone by going to a certified cell phone shop with your passport and filling out a short form declaring your phone in Turkey. The process costs TL5. You can only declare one phone.

» You can pick up a basic mobile phone for about TL50.

» Turkcell credit comes in cards with units of TL5, TL10, TL15, TL20 (*standart*), TL30 (*avantaj*), TL50 (*süper*), TL95 (*süper plus*) and TL180 (*mega*).

» The bigger the card, the better the rates you receive.

Payphones & Phonecards

» Türk Telekom payphones are found in most major public buildings and facilities, public squares and transport terminals.

» International calls can be made from payphones.

» All payphones require cards that can be bought at telephone centres or, for a small mark-up, at some shops. Some payphones accept credit cards.

» Two types of card are in use: floppy cards with a magnetic strip, and Smart cards, which are embedded with a chip. The cards come in units of 50, 100, 200 (TL15) and 350 (TL19).

» Both types of card cost about TL3.75 for 50 units, sufficient for local calls and short intercity calls, and TL7.50 for 100 units, suitable for intercity or short international conversations.

INTERNATIONAL PHONECARDS

» Phonecards are the cheapest way to make international calls.

» Cards can be used on landlines, payphones and mobiles.

» As in other countries, you call the access number, key in the PIN number on the card and dial away.

» Stick to reputable phonecards such as IPC.

» With a TL20 IPC card you can speak for 240 minutes to Australia, Germany and the UK, and 200 minutes to Japan.

» Cards are widely available in the tourist areas of major cities, but can be difficult to find elsewhere.

Time

» Standard Turkish time is two hours ahead of GMT/ UTC.

» During daylight saving (summer time), the clocks go forward one hour, and Turkey is three hours ahead of GMT/UTC.

» Daylight saving runs from the last Sunday in March until the last Sunday in October.

» Turkish bus timetables and so on use the 24-hour clock, but Turks rarely use it when speaking.

» Visit www.timeanddate. com for more on time differences.

Toilets

Most hotels have sit-down toilets, but hole-in-the-ground models – which have a conventional flush, or a tap and jug – are common in Turkey. Toilet paper is often unavailable, so keep some on you. In most bathrooms you can flush paper down the toilet, but in some places doing this may flood the premises. If you're not sure, play it safe and put it in the bin provided.

Public toilets can usually be found at major attractions and transport hubs; most require a payment of around 50 kuruş. In an emergency it's worth remembering that mosques have basic toilets (for both men and women).

Tourist Information

Every Turkish town of any size has an official tourist office, run by the **Ministry of Culture and Tourism** (www.goturkey.com). Staff are often enthusiastic and helpful, particularly when it comes to supplying brochures, but may have sketchy knowledge of the area, and English speakers are rare. Tour operators, pension owners and so on are often better sources of information.

Turkish tourist offices overseas include:

Berlin and Frankfurt (www.goturkey.com)
London (www.gototurkey.co.uk)
New York, Los Angeles and Washington DC (www.tourismturkey.org)
Paris (www.infosturquie.com)
The Hague (www.welkomin turkije.nl)
Tokyo (www.tourismturkey.jp)

Travellers with Disabilities

Turkey is a challenging destination for disabled (*engelli* or *özürlü*) travellers. Ramps, wide doorways and properly equipped toilets are rare, as are Braille and audio information at sights. Crossing most streets is particularly challenging, as everyone does so at their peril.

Airlines and the top hotels and resorts have some provision for wheelchair access, and ramps are beginning to appear elsewhere. Dropped kerb edges are being introduced to cities, especially in western Turkey – in places such as Edirne, Bursa and İzmir they seem to have been sensibly designed. Selçuk, Bodrum and Fethiye have been identified as relatively user-friendly towns for people with mobility problems because their pavements and roads are fairly level. In İstanbul, the tram and the metro are the most wheelchair-accessible forms of public transport.

Turkish Airlines offers 25% discounts to travellers with minimum 40% disability and their companions. Disabled travellers get a 20% discount on Turkish State Railways.

Organisations

Businesses and resources serving travellers with disabilities include the following:

Access-Able (www.access-able.com) Includes a small list of tour and transport operators in Turkey.
Apparleyzed (www.apparelyzed.com) Features a report on facilities in İstanbul.
Hotel Rolli (see p373) Specially designed for wheelchair users.
Mephisto Voyage (see p466) Special tours for mobility-impaired people, utilising the Joëlette system.
Physically Disabled Support Association (www.bedd.org.tr) Based in İstanbul.
SATH (www.sath.org) Society for Accessible Travel and Hospitality.

Visas

» Nationals of countries including Denmark, Finland, France, Germany, Israel, Italy, Japan, New Zealand, Sweden and Switzerland

679

DIRECTORY A-Z TOILETS

GOVERNMENT TRAVEL ADVICE

For the latest travel information log on to the following websites:
www.auswaertiges-amt.de German Federal Foreign Office
www.fco.gov.uk/travel UK Foreign & Commonwealth Office
www.minbuza.nl Dutch Ministry of Foreign Affairs
www.mofa.go.jp Japanese Ministry of Foreign Affairs
www.safetravel.govt.nz New Zealand Ministry of Foreign Affairs and Trade
www.smartraveller.gov.au Australian Government's travel advice and consular information
www.travel.state.gov US Department of State's Bureau of Consular Affairs
www.voyage.gc.ca Canadian Consular Services Bureau

don't need a visa to visit Turkey for up to 90 days.

» Nationals of countries including Australia, Austria, Belgium, Canada, Ireland, the Netherlands, Norway, Portugal, Spain, the UK and the USA need a visa, but it is just a sticker bought on arrival at the airport or border post (see p683). You will be given a 90-day multiple-entry visa.

» Nationals of countries including Slovakia and South Africa are given a one-month multiple-entry visa.

» Check the **Ministry of Foreign Affairs** (www.mfa.gov.tr) for the latest information.

» The cost of the visa varies. At the time of writing, Australians and Americans paid US$20 (or €15), Canadians US$60 (or €45) and British citizens UK£10 (or €15 or US$20).

» You *must* pay in hard-currency cash. The customs officers expect to be paid in one of the above currencies, and don't give change.

» No photos are required.

» For details on getting visas to neighbouring countries, see p687.

Residency Permits

» There are various types of *ikamet tezkeresi* (residence permit), which you must apply for within 30 days of arrival.

» Plug http://yabancilar.iem.gov.tr (the foreign department of İstanbul's *emniyet müdürlüğü* – security police) into Google Translate for more information.

» If you don't have a Turkish employer or spouse to support your application, you can get a permit for touristic purposes.

» Touristic permits are theoretically available for anything from one month (TL78) to five years (TL3186), with administrative charges amounting to a few hundred lira. In practice,

different lengths are available to residents of different countries.

» You have to show evidence of accommodation, such as a hotel booking or rental contract.

» You also have to show you have US$1000 to support yourself for every month of your intended stay.

» This evidence can be in the form of a currency exchange slip showing you changed the relevant amount into lira, or a statement from a Turkish bank account.

» To open a Turkish bank account, you need a rental contract or similar showing your Turkish address and a Turkish tax number. Go to a big branch; small branches will say you need a residence permit to open an account.

» A Turkish tax number is relatively easy to get; take your passport and some photocopies to the *belediye* (town hall).

» To apply for a residence permit in İstanbul, make an appointment with the *emniyet müdürlüğü* in Fatih; visit http://tinyurl.com/28ck5vo. The process is demoralising and the bureaucrats are unhelpful; those behind the desks in cities such as İzmir (www.izmirpolis.gov.tr) are reputedly far more helpful.

» Little English is spoken, so take a Turkish-speaking friend with you if possible.

» If your application is successful, you will be given a 'blue book', which is like a mini-passport.

» There are more details in Pat Yale's *A Handbook for Living in Turkey*, a comprehensive source of information for people planning to settle in Turkey.

» The websites mentioned under Work (p681) are also sources of (anecdotal) information and advice.

Working Visas

» Visit www.e-konsolosluk.net for information on obtaining a *çalışma izni* (work permit).

» Your Turkish employer should help you get the visa. If it's an employer such as a school or international company, they should be well versed in the process and can handle the majority of the paperwork.

» The visa can be obtained in Turkey, or from a Turkish embassy or consulate.

Volunteering

There is a slowly growing number of volunteering opportunities in Turkey, offering everything from teaching to working on an organic farm.

Alternative Camp (www.alternativecamp.org) A volunteer-based organisation running camps for disabled people around the country.

Gençlik Servisleri Merkezi (www.gsm-youth.org) GSM runs voluntary work camps in Turkey.

Gençtur (www.genctur.com) A portal for various volunteering schemes throughout the country, and a good first port of call to see what's on offer.

Ta Tu Ta (www.bugday.org/tatuta) Organises work on dozens of organic farms around the country, where you can stay for free or for a small donation to cover costs.

Volunteer Abroad (www.volunteerabroad.com) A UK-based company listing volunteering opportunities through international organisations in Turkey.

Women Travellers

Travelling in Turkey is straightforward for women, provided you follow some simple guidelines.

Clothing

Tailor your behaviour and your clothing to your surrounds. Look at what local women are wearing. On the streets of Beyoğlu in İstanbul you'll see skimpy tops and tight jeans, but cleavage and short skirts without leggings are a no-no everywhere except nightclubs in İstanbul and heavily touristed destinations along the coast.

Bring a shawl to cover your head when visiting mosques.

On the street, you don't need to don a headscarf, but in eastern Anatolia long sleeves and baggy long pants should attract the least attention.

Regional Differences

Having a banter with men in restaurants and shops in western Turkey can be fun, and many men won't necessarily think anything of it.

Particularly out east, however, passing through some towns you can count the number of women you see on one hand, and those you do see will be headscarved and wearing long coats. Life here for women is largely restricted to the home. Eastern Anatolia is not the place to practise your Turkish (or Kurdish) and expect men not to get the wrong idea; even just smiling at a man or catching his eye is considered an invitation. Keep your dealings with men formal and polite, not friendly.

Holiday Romances

It is not unheard of, particularly in romantic spots such as Cappadocia, for women to have holiday romances with local men. As well as fuelling the common Middle Eastern misconception that Western women are more 'available', this has led to occasional cases of men exploiting such relationships. Some men, for example, develop close friendships with visiting women, then invent sob stories, such as their mother has fallen ill, and ask them to help out financially.

Transport

When travelling by taxi and dolmuş avoid getting into the seat beside the driver.

On the bus, lone women are often assigned seats at the front near the driver. There have been cases of male passengers or conductors on night buses harassing female travellers. If this happens to you, complain loudly, making sure that others on the bus hear, and repeat your complaint on arrival at your destination; you have a right to be treated with respect.

See p690 for more advice on travelling by bus for women and unmarried couples.

Accommodation

The cheapest hotels, as well as often being fleapits, are generally not suitable for lone women. Stick with family-oriented midrange hotels.

If conversation in the lobby grinds to a halt as you enter, the hotel is not likely to be a great place for a woman.

If there is a knock on your hotel door late at night, don't open it; in the morning, complain to the manager.

We recommend female travellers stick to official camp sites and camp where there are plenty of people around – especially out east. If you do otherwise, you will be taking a risk.

Eating & Drinking

Restaurants and tea gardens that aim to attract women and children usually set aside a special room (or part of one) for families. Look for the term *aile salonu* (family dining room), or just *aile*.

Work

Outside professional fields such as academia and the corporate sector, bagging a job in Turkey is tough. Most people teach English or nanny.

Many employers, notably language schools, are happy to employ foreigners on an informal basis, but unwilling to organise work permits due to the time and money involved in the bureaucratic process. This necessitates working illegally on a tourist visa, and doing a 'visa run' every three months to pick up a new visa.

Following the worldwide economic crash, locals also occasionally report illegal workers, and there have even been cases of English teachers being deported.

Job hunters may have luck with http://istanbul.craigslist.org, www.sahibinden.com/en and the expat websites www.mymerhaba.com, www.expatinturkey.com and www.sublimeportal.com.

Nannying

One of the most lucrative non-specialist jobs open to foreigners is nannying for the wealthy city elite, or looking after their teenage children and helping them develop their language skills.

There are opportunities for English, French and German speakers, and a few openings for young men as well as women.

You must be prepared for long hours, demanding employers and spoilt children.

Accommodation is normally included, and the digs will likely be luxurious. However, living with the family means you are always on call, and you may be based in the suburbs.

With representatives in Turkey, the UK and France, **Anglo Nannies** (www.anglonannies.com) is the main agency dealing with placements.

Teaching English

You can earn a decent living, mostly in İstanbul and the other major cities, as an

English teacher at a university or a school. Good jobs require a university degree and TEFL certificate or similar.

As well as the job-hunting resources listed in the introduction to this section, log onto www.eslcafe.com, which has a Turkey forum, and www.tefl.com.

If you want to proactively contact potential employers, Wikipedia has lists of schools in İstanbul and Turkish universities.

DERSHANE

There are lots of jobs at *dershane* (private schools), which pay good wages and offer attractions, such as accommodation (although it may be on or near the school campus in the suburbs) and work permits. Some even pay for your flight to Turkey and/or flights home.

Jobs are available at all levels, from kindergarten to high school. Teachers who can't speak Turkish often find very young children challenging; many are spoilt anyway and misbehave around foreign teachers. The best preschools pair a foreign teacher with a Turkish colleague.

You will often be required to commit to an unpaid trial period, lasting a week or two.

Unless a teacher has dropped out before the end of their contract, these jobs are mostly advertised in May and June, when employers are recruiting in preparation for the beginning of the academic year in September. Teachers are contracted until the end of the academic year in June.

The typical monthly salary is TL2000 to TL3500.

LANGUAGE SCHOOLS

Teaching at a language school is not recommended. The majority are exploitative institutions untroubled by professional ethics; for example making false promises in job interviews. Schools with a bad reputation are often 'blacklisted' on Craigslist.

At some you teach in a central classroom, but at business English schools you often have to schlep around the city between the clients' workplaces.

Schools often promise you a certain number of hours a week, but classes are then cancelled, normally at the last minute, making this a frustrating and difficult way to make a living in Turkey.

The typical hourly rate is TL19 to TL25, rising to TL35 at business English schools where you travel to clients' offices and give one-to-one tuition.

PRIVATE TUITION

The advantage of this is you don't need a TEFL certificate or even a university degree. You can advertise your services on http://istanbul.craigslist.org and www.sahibinden.com/en.

The disadvantage is that, unless you are willing to travel to clients' offices and homes (which is time-consuming, and potentially risky for women), they tend to cancel when they get busy and learning English suddenly becomes a low priority. As with business English schools, most teaching takes place on weekends and evenings, when the students have spare time.

Hourly rates range from TL35 to TL60.

UNIVERSITIES

University jobs command the best wages, with work permits and, often, flights thrown in. Universities also generally operate more professionally than many establishments in the above sectors.

The teacher's job is often to prepare freshman students for courses that will largely be taught in English.

As with *dershane,* jobs are advertised around May and June, and run roughly from September until June.

Tourism

Travellers sometimes work illegally for room and board in pensions, bars and other businesses in tourist areas. These jobs are generally badly paid and only last a few weeks, but they are a fun way to stay in a place and get to know the locals.

Given that you will be in direct competition with unskilled locals for such employment, and working in the public eye, there is a danger of being 'shopped' and deported.

Transport

GETTING THERE & AWAY

Flights, tours and rail tickets can be booked online at lonelyplanet.com/bookings.

Entering the Country

The main idiosyncrasy to be aware of is that most visitors need a 'visa' – really just a sticker in their passport, issued at the point of entry (see p679 for more information). You must buy the visa before joining the queue for immigration. Rarely do customs officers stop you to check your bags at airports (see p671 for customs regulations).

At many land border crossings there are no ATMs or money-changing facilities; make sure you bring enough of the appropriate currency to pay for your visa.

Security on borders with countries to the east and southeast (Georgia, Azerbaijan, Iran, Iraq and Syria) is generally tight, and customs officers may want to see what you are bringing in. If you're travelling by train or bus, expect to be held up at the border for two to three hours – or even longer if your fellow passengers don't have their paperwork in order.

See p687 for information on getting visas for Turkey's neighbouring countries.

Passport

683

Make sure your passport will still have at least six months' life in it after you enter Turkey.

Air

Airports & Airlines

Turkish Airlines (www.thy.com) is the national carrier, with budget subsidiaries **Sun Express** (www.sunexpress.com) and **Anadolu Jet** (www.anadolujet.com). Turkish Airlines has had nine crashes since 1974; most recently, nine people died when one of its planes crashed at Amsterdam's Schiphol airport in 2009.

The main international airports are in western Turkey:

İstanbul Atatürk (www.ataturkairport.com) Turkey's principal international airport, with flights from Europe, North America, the Middle East, North Africa and Asia.

İstanbul Sabiha Gökçen (www.sgairport.com) Mostly flights from Europe with budget carriers such as EasyJet, plus a few flights from the Middle East.

Antalya (www.aytport.com) Flights from Europe.

İzmir (www.adnanmenderesairport.com) Flights from Europe and the Middle East.

Bodrum (www.bodrum-airport.com) Flights from Europe and a few other cities in the region.

CLIMATE CHANGE & TRAVEL

Every form of transport that relies on carbon-based fuel generates CO_2, the main cause of human-induced climate change. Modern travel is dependent on aeroplanes, which might use less fuel per person than most cars but travel much greater distances. The altitude at which aircraft emit gases (including CO_2) and particles also contributes to their climate change impact. Many websites offer 'carbon calculators' that allow people to estimate the carbon emissions generated by their journey and, for those who wish to do so, to offset the impact of the greenhouse gases emitted with contributions to portfolios of climate-friendly initiatives throughout the world. Lonely Planet offsets the carbon footprint of all staff and author travel.

Dalaman (www.atmairport.
aero) Flights from Europe,
especially the UK, and a few
other cities in the region.

Ankara (www.esenboga
airport.com) Flights from
Europe and the Middle East.

Tickets

It's a good idea to book at
least two months in advance
for flights to Turkey if you
plan to arrive in the country
any time from April until late
August. If you plan to visit
a resort, check with your
local travel agents for flight
and accommodation deals.
Sometimes you can also
find cheap flights by using
less-usual airlines such as
Azerbaijan Airlines.

Flights quoted in this
chapter are for peak season
and include airport taxes.

AUSTRALIA & NEW ZEALAND

You can fly from the main cities in Australia and New Zealand to İstanbul with airlines
including the following; fares
start at around A$2000
return from Sydney.

Emirates Airlines (via
Dubai, and via Australia
from Auckland and
Christchurch)

Malaysia Airlines (via Kuala
Lumpur)

Singapore Airlines (via
Singapore and Dubai)

You can often get cheaper
flights with European airlines, but you'll have to take
an indirect route with a
change in Europe (eg in Germany with Lufthansa).

CONTINENTAL EUROPE

With the exception of Germany, there's not much
variation in fares from one
European airport to another.
Most European national carriers fly direct to İstanbul for
around €200 return. Cheaper return flights can be found
for around €150 but usually
involve changing planes en
route, so if you travelled
from Amsterdam to İstanbul

with Lufthansa, you'd fly via
Frankfurt or Munich. Having
the biggest Turkish com-
munity outside Turkey has
enabled some great deals
from Germany.

Charter airlines Fly between
several German cities and
the Turkish airports listed
above; try Condor, German
Wings or Corendon Airlines.

EasyJet Flies between
France's Basel-Mulhouse-
Freiburg airport and
İstanbul.

Lufthansa Flies from
Munich, Frankfurt and
Cologne/Bonn to İstanbul,
İzmir, Antalya and Ankara
from about €150 return.

Pegasus Airlines Flies from
a range of European cities
including Paris and Berlin.

Sun Express Flies from a
range of European cities
including Amsterdam and
Zurich.

MIDDLE EAST & ASIA

From Central Asia and the
Middle East, you can usually
pick up a flight with Turkish Airlines or the country's
national carrier.

Armenia Armavia Airlines
has four flights a week between İstanbul and Yerevan.

Azerbaijan Turkish Airlines
flies Baku–İstanbul, and
Azerbaijan Airlines, generally a cheap option, also flies
to Ankara.

Georgia Turkish Airlines
flies İstanbul–Tbilisi.

Iran Turkish Airlines flies
İstanbul–Tabriz, and from
İstanbul or Ankara to Te-
hran; Pegasus Airlines flies
Van–Tehran.

Iraq Atlasjet flies from
İstanbul and İzmir to Erbil in
northern Iraq.

Syria Turkish Airlines flies
from İstanbul to Damascus
and Aleppo.

One of the cheapest ways to
fly to northeast or southeast
Asia from İstanbul is via
Dubai.

Emirates Airlines Flies via
Dubai to cities throughout

India and Pakistan, and
further afield to Bangkok
and China.

Singapore Airlines Flies
to cities throughout Asia,
including Hong Kong and
Tokyo, via Dubai and
Singapore.

UK & IRELAND

Atlasjet Flies Manchester–
Antalya, and from Stansted
to Antalya and Ankara.

British Airways Flies
Heathrow–İstanbul Atatürk,
Gatwick–İzmir and Gatwick–
Antalya.

Charter flights Usually
cheaper at the beginning
and end of the season; try
the online charter flight
agents **Just the Flight**
(www.justtheflight.co.uk) and
Thomsonfly.com (www.
thomsonfly.com).

EasyJet Links Gatwick,
Luton, Stansted, Bristol,
Manchester and Liver-
pool with İstanbul Sabiha
Gökçen, Antalya, Bodrum
and Dalaman.

Pegasus Airlines Flies from
Birmingham to Antalya; Gat-
wick to Antalya, Dalaman
and İstanbul Sabiha Gökçen;
Manchester to Antalya,
Dalaman and Lekfoşa (Nico-
sia) in Northern Cyprus; and
Stansted to locations across
Turkey.

Turkish Airlines Flies
to İstanbul Atatürk from
Heathrow, Birmingham,
Manchester and Dublin.

USA & CANADA

Most flights connect with
İstanbul-bound flights in the
UK or continental Europe, so
it's worth looking at carriers
such as Lufthansa, KLM and
British Airways in addition to
the North American airlines.

Air Canada Indirect
flights in partnership with
Lufthansa.

American Airlines Flies via
London in partnership with
British Airways.

Delta Airlines Com-
petitive prices direct or via
Amsterdam.

Turkish Airlines Flies from 11 cities, with direct flights from Toronto, Chicago and Los Angeles.

Land

Crossing borders by bus and train is fairly straightforward, but expect delays of between one and three hours. You'll usually have to get off the bus or train and endure a paperwork and baggage check of all travellers – on both sides of the border. The process is elongated by a trainload of passengers or the long lines of trucks and cars that build up at some borders.

Turkey's relationships with most of its neighbours tend to be tense, which can affect the availability of visas and when and where you can cross. Check with the Turkish embassy in your country for the most up-to-date information before leaving home.

Crossing the border into Turkey with your own vehicle should be fairly straightforward. No special documents are required to import a car for up to six months, but be sure to take it out again before the six months is up. If you overstay your permit, you may have to pay customs duty equal to the full retail value of the car. If you want to leave your car in Turkey and return to collect it later, the vehicle must be put under a customs seal, which is a tedious process.

Armenia

At the time of writing, the Turkey–Armenia border was closed to travellers.

BUS

Several daily buses depart from Trabzon to Tbilisi (Georgia), with connections to Armenia.

Azerbaijan

The remote **Borualan–Sadarak** crossing, east of Iğdır (Turkey), leads to the Azerbaijani enclave of Nakh-ichevan, from where you need to fly across Armenian-occupied Nagorno-Karabakh to reach Baku and the rest of Azerbaijan.

BUS

Several daily buses depart from Trabzon to Tbilisi (Georgia), with connections to Baku, and one daily bus runs directly to the Azerbaijani capital.

Bulgaria & Eastern Europe

Bulgarian border guards only occasionally allow pedestrians to cross the frontier; take a bus or hitch a lift with a cooperative motorist. There are three border crossings:

Kapitan Andreevo–Kapıkule This busy, 24-hour post is the main crossing, located 18km northwest of Edirne on the E80 and 9km from Svilengrad in Bulgaria.

Lesovo–Hamzabeyli Some 25km northeast of Edirne, this is favoured by big trucks and lorries and should be avoided.

Malko Tărnovo–Aziziye Some 70km northeast of Edirne via Kırklareli and 92km south of Burgas (Bulgaria), this is only useful for those heading to Bulgaria's Black Sea resorts.

BUS

There are several daily departures to Sofia, Varna and Burgas (Bulgaria) from İstanbul; at least six companies offer services. There are also daily departures to Skopje, Tetovo and Gostivar (Macedonia), and to Constanța and Bucharest (Romania).

Drina Trans (www.drinatrans.com) Daily departures for Skopje (€30, 14 hours).

Metro Turizm (www.metroturizm.com.tr) Daily departures for locations including Sofia (TL50, 10 hours), Varna (TL55, nine hours) and Burgas (TL55, seven hours).

Öz Batu (☏0212-658 0255) Serves cities including Ljublana (Slovenia) and Sofia.

Varan Turizm (www.varan.com.tr) One of the best Turkish companies, with coaches to Sofia and Tervel (Bulgaria).

TRAIN

The daily **Bosfor Ekspresi** runs from İstanbul to Bucharest (Romania), with connections including Budapest (Hungary). Change in Dimitrovgrad (Bulgaria) for Sofia (Bulgaria) and Belgrade (Serbia). At the time of writing, a rail replacement bus was operating on a short, 100km section of the route between İstanbul and Çerkezköy in Marmara.

You'll need to take your own food and drinks as there are no restaurant cars on these trains. Note also that the Turkey–Bulgaria border crossing is in the early hours of the morning and you need to leave the train to get your passport stamped. We've heard stories of harassment, especially of women, at the border, so lone women may be best taking an alternative route. Travelling in the sleeper cars is the safest and most comfortable option. For more information, see **Turkish State Railways** (www.tcdd.gov.tr/tcdding/avrupa_ing.htm).

Georgia

On the Black Sea coast between Hopa (Turkey) and Batumi (Georgia), **Sarp** is the main, 24-hour crossing.

Türkgözü Near Posof (Turkey), north of Kars and southwest of Akhaltsikhe (Georgia). It should open from 8am to 8pm, but in winter you might want to double-check it's open at all.

BUS

Several daily buses depart from Trabzon to Tbilisi. The boxed text on p550 suggests routes from northeastern Anatolia to Tbilisi.

Mahmudoğlu (www.mah
mudoglu.com) Runs direct
buses between İstanbul and
Tbilisi (€47, 30 hours).

Greece & Western Europe

Greek and Turkish border
guards allow you to cross the
frontier on foot. The following are open 24 hours.

Kastanies–Pazarkule 9km
southwest of Edirne.

Kipi–İpsala 29km northeast of Alexandroupolis
(Greece) and 35km west of
Keşan (Turkey), which has
major transport links.

BUS

Germany, Austria and
Greece have most direct
buses to İstanbul, so if you're
travelling from other European countries, you'll likely
have to catch a connecting
bus.

Gürel Metro (⏹0284-714
1051) Four daily minibuses
from Keşan to Greek destinations including Thessaloniki and Athens.

Öz Batu (0212-658 0255)
Serves cities including
Prague and Zurich.

Varan Turizm (www.varan.
com.tr) Serves cities including Berlin (€140, 36 hours).

CAR & MOTORCYCLE

The E80 highway makes its
way through the Balkans to
Edirne and İstanbul, then
on to Ankara. Using the car-
ferries from Italy and Greece
can shorten driving time
from Western Europe, but at
a price (see p687).

From Alexandroupolis,
the main road leads to Kipi-
İpsala, then to Keşan and
east to İstanbul or south to
Gallipoli, Çanakkale and the
Aegean.

TRAIN

From Western Europe (apart
from Greece) you will come
via Eastern Europe. A suggested route from **London
to İstanbul** is the three-
night journey via Paris, Munich, Budapest and Bucha-

rest; see www.seat61.com/
Turkey.htm for more information and other routes.

The best option for travelling between Greece and
Turkey is the **Dostluk–Filia
Express**, the overnight train
between İstanbul and Thessaloniki (13 hours, first/
second class from €26/39),
where you can connect to
Athens. Accommodation is in
comfy, air-conditioned sleeper cars. You can buy tickets
at the train stations but not
online. At the time of writing,
a rail replacement bus was
operating on a short, 100km
section of the route between
İstanbul and Çerkezköy in
Marmara.

**Hellenic Railways Organi-
sation** (www.ose.gr)

Turkish State Railways
(www.tcdd.gov.tr/tcdding/
avrupa_ing.htm)

Iran

The busier **Gürbulak–
Bazargan** post, 35km
southeast of Doğubayazıt
(Turkey), is open 24 hours.

Esendere–Sero Southeast
of Van. This crossing should
be open from 8am until
midnight, but double-check
in winter. Travellers are increasingly using this crossing, which takes you through
the breathtaking scenery of
far southeastern Anatolia.

BUS

There are regular buses
from İstanbul and Ankara to
Tabriz and Tehran; and services from Van to Orumiyeh
(Iran) via Esendere-Sero.

Dolmuş from Doğubayazıt
You can go to Gürbulak,
then walk across the border.
The crossing might take up
to an hour. From Bazargan
there are onward buses to
Tabriz.

Dolmuş from Van There
are several daily to Yüksekova, west of Esendere-Sero.

Thor Travel Agency (www.
thortourism.com) Nightly
buses from İstanbul and
three a week from Ankara to
Tabriz and Tehran.

TRAIN

For more information on the
following, visit **RAJA Passenger Trains Co** (www.raja.
ir/default.aspx?Culture=en
-US&page=home) or, better,
Turkish State Railways
(www.tcdd.gov.tr/tcdding/
ortadogu_ing.htm).

Malatya–Tehran (€27, 42
hours) The weekly service
from Damascus (Syria)
passes through the Turkish
cities of Malatya and Van,
with a ferry across Lake Van.

Trans-Asya Ekspresi
Leaves İstanbul every
Wednesday and arrives in
Tehran (€40) on Saturday,
travelling via Ankara, Kayseri and Van before crossing
the border at Kapikoi/Razi
and stopping in Salmas,
Tabriz and Zanjan. The
journey involves a five-hour
ferry crossing of Lake Van.

Van–Tabriz (€10, nine hours)
Leaves Thursday night.

Iraq

Between Silopi (Turkey) and
Zahko (Iraq), there's no town
or village at the **Habur–
Ibrahim al-Khalil** crossing
and you can't walk across it.

TAXI

A taxi from Silopi to Zahko
costs between US$50 and
US$70. Your driver will ma-
noeuvre through a maze of
checkpoints and handle the
paperwork. On the return
journey, watch out for taxi
drivers slipping contraband
into your bag. See the boxed
text on p603.

TRAIN

The weekly **Gaziantep–
Mosul** (€25, 17 hours) train
had been suspended at
the time of writing; check
www.tcdd.gov.tr/tcdding/
ortadogu_ing.htm for updates.

Syria

Turks currently don't require
visas to enter Syria, and
many of the eight Turkey–
Syria border posts can get
very busy, especially at
weekends.

Reyhanlı–Bab al-Hawa
The most convenient, and busiest.

Yayladağı Also close to Antakya (Hatay).

Öncüpınar Outside Kilis, 65km south of Gaziantep; another busy crossing.

Akçakale 54km south of Şanlıurfa, open 11am to 3pm Saturday to Thursday; also busy.

Nusaybin–Qamishle 75km southeast of Mardin.

BUS

It's possible to buy tickets direct from İstanbul to the Syrian cities of Aleppo (Halab) and Damascus (Şam).

Hatay Pan Turizm (www.ozpanturizm.com) İstanbul to Damascus via Antakya (TL65).

From southeastern Anatolia:

From Antakya Daily buses run to Aleppo (TL10, three hours) and Damascus (TL15, seven hours). See p393 for information on local buses to Reyhanlı-Bab al-Hawa, dolmuşes to Yayladağı, and taxis.

From Gaziantep Minibuses leave every 20 minutes for Kilis (TL8), from where you'll have to take a taxi to Öncüpınar or Aleppo. A taxi straight to Aleppo is another option.

From Şanlıurfa Minibus to Akçakale, then a taxi over the border to Tabiyya.

From Mardin Minibuses depart roughly every hour for Nusaybin (TL6, one hour).

TRAIN

The **Toros Ekspresi** between İstanbul and Aleppo had been indefinitely suspended at the time of writing. See **Turkish State Railways** (www.tcdd.gov.tr/tcdding/ortadogu_ing.htm) for updates on all these trains.

Gaziantep–Aleppo (€13, 5 hours) Twice-weekly night train.

Mersin–Aleppo (€14, 10 hours) Weekly night train via Adana.

Van–Damascus (€25, 40 hours) The weekly service beginning in Tehran (Iran) passes through the Turkish cities of Van and Malatya, with a ferry across Lake Van.

Sea

Departure times change between seasons, with fewer ferries generally running in the winter. For more information see the websites listed below or the relevant destination chapters. A good starting point for information is **Ferrylines** (www.ferrylines.com).

Daytrips on ferries to Greece are popular in the Bodrum area. Remember to take your passport, and ensure you have a multiple-entry Turkish visa so you can get back into the country at the end of the day.

Tours

The following international tour companies' trips to Turkey generally receive good reports:

Backroads (www.backroads.com) US-based company offering combined bike and sailing tours on the Mediterranean.

Cultural Folk Tours of Turkey (www.boraozkok.com) US-based company offering group and private cultural and history tours.

Exodus (www.exodus.co.uk) UK-based adventure company offering a range of tours covering walking, biking, rafting and history.

Imaginative Traveller (www.imaginative-traveller.com) UK-based company offering a variety of overland adventures through Turkey.

Intrepid Travel (www.intrepidtravel.com.au) Australia-based company with a variety of small-group tours for travellers who like the

philosophy of independent travel but prefer to travel with others.

Pacha Tours (www.pachatours.com) US-based Turkey specialist offering general tours as well as special-interest packages.

Visas for Neighbouring Countries

Visa regulations do change, particularly for some of the Middle Eastern and Central Asian countries listed below, so it's worth checking the websites we've listed.

Armenia

Most nationalities can get 21/120-day visitor visas online or on arrival at the border (including the airport) for €6/30; or a three-day transit visa for €20. Note that Armenia's border with Turkey is closed (see p685). See www.armeniaforeignministry.com for more information.

Azerbaijan

The visa conditions for Azerbaijan can be a little tricky to pin down; the information on the Ministry of Foreign Affairs website (www.mfa.gov.az/eng) is somewhat opaque.

According to other sources, most nationalities require a visitor visa, which can be obtained at Armenian embassies and consulates; you need a letter of support or hotel booking and three passport photos.

Residents of regions including the EU and USA can obtain visas at Baku's Heydar Aliyer International Airport, although there has been discussion about phasing this service out, and visas are generally not available on land borders. The consulate in Kars issues visitor visas, which cost €50 and take about three days to process.

FERRIES FROM TURKEY

ROUTE	FREQUENCY	DURATION	FARE (ONE WAY/ RETURN)	COMPANY
Ayvalık–Lesvos, Greece	Mon-Sat May-Sep; 3 weekly Oct-Apr	1½hr	€40/50, car €60/70	Jale Tour (www.jaletour.com)
Alanya–Girne (Kyrenia), Northern Cyprus	2 weekly	3½hr	TL78/128	Fergün Denizcilik (www.fergun.net)
Bodrum–Kos, Greece	daily	1hr	€28/56	Bodrum Ferryboat Association (www.bodrum ferryboat.com)
Bodrum–Rhodes, Greece	2 weekly Jun-Sep	2¼hr	€60/120	Bodrum Ferryboat Association (www.bodrum ferryboat.com)
Çeşme–Chios, Greece	daily mid-May–mid-Sep; 2 weekly mid-Sep–mid-May	1½hr	€25/40, car €70/120	Ertürk (www.erturk.com.tr)
Çeşme–Ancona, Italy	weekly May-Sep	60hr	one way €215 to €505, car €260	Marmara Lines (www.marmaralines.com)
Datça–Rhodes, Greece	Sat May-Sep	45min	TL90/180	Knidos Yachting (www.knidosyachting.com)
Datça–Simi, Greece	hydrofoil Sat May-Sep, gület on demand	hydrofoil 15min, gület 70min	hydrofoil TLL60/120, gület one way TL120	Knidos Yachting (www.knidosyachting.com)
İstanbul–Sevastapol, Ukraine	weekly	32hr	return from €185	Sudostroyenie
Kaş–Meis (Kastellorizo), Greece	daily	20min	single or same-day return TL40	Meis Express (www.meisexpress.com)
Kuşadası–Samos, Greece	daily Apr-Oct	1¼hr	€30/50	Meander Travel (www.meandertravel.com)
Marmaris–Rhodes, Greece	2 daily Apr-Oct, twice weekly Nov-Mar	50min to 2hr	from €43/45, car from €95/120	Yeşil Marmaris Travel & Yachting (www.yesilmarmaris.com)
Taşucu–Girne (Kyrenia), Northern Cyprus	daily	2hr	TL69/114	Akgünler Denizcilik (www.akgunler.com.tr)
Trabzon–Sochi, Russia	weekly	12hr	one way €65	Apollonia II & Princess Victoria Lines
Turgutreis–Kalymnos, Greece	2 weekly	1¼hr	€43/86	Bodrum Ferryboat Association (www.bodrum ferryboat.com)
Turgutreis–Kos, Greece	5 weekly	45min	€28/56	Bodrum Ferryboat Association (www.bodrum ferryboat.com)

Bulgaria

Citizens of nations including Australia, Canada, Israel, Japan, New Zealand, the US and most EU countries can enter Bulgaria for up to 90 days without a visa. See www.mfa.bg.

Georgia

Most people (including from Canada, Israel, Japan, Switzerland, EU countries, the US, Australia and New Zealand) can enter Georgia for up to 360 days without a visa. See www.mfa.gov.ge.

Greece

Nationals of Australia, Canada, all EU countries, New Zealand and the USA can enter Greece for up to three months without a visa. See www.mfa.gr.

Iran

Most visitors to Iran need to get a visa in advance, apart from New Zealanders, who can obtain a one-week tourist visa at the airport. There is an embassy in Ankara and consulates in Erzurum, İstanbul and Trabzon. Some people wait a week to hear whether their application has been granted, others over a month.

American, British, Canadian and Danish applicants aren't too popular, and Israelis (and anyone with an Israeli stamp in their passport) are not allowed entry. You can apply in Turkey (the consulate in Trabzon is reportedly quicker than its counterpart in Erzurum), but it's safer to arrange it in advance, although you must enter Iran within 90 days of the visa's issue date.

You need a letter from an Iranian sponsor, which can be a travel or visa agency; see the list under 'Practical Information' at www.lonely planet.com/iran. Women are advised to cover their head in their application photos, and when picking up their passport from an Iranian mission. There is an electronic visa

service and some information at www.mfa.gov.ir.

Iraq

According to the Ministry of Foreign Affairs (www. mofa.gov.iq), 15-day tourist visas are available for US$15 and extendable one-month visitor visas are available from US$40. Although Iraqi foreign missions are generally reluctant to issue visas to regular travellers, those in Turkey are authorised to issue visas.

The Kurdish Regional Government issues its own tourist visa, which is good for travelling within Kurdish Iraq only. Citizens of most countries, including Australia, New Zealand and the USA as well as the European Union, are automatically issued a free, 10-day tourist visa at the point of entry. Extensions can be obtained at the Directorate of Residency in Erbil (Arbil).

You may be searched and interviewed by guards at both borders. Be honest. It helps to have the name and phone number of an Iraqi Kurdish contact. As the Kurdish issue is a sensitive topic in Turkey, never refer to your destination as 'Kurdistan', and don't carry patriotic Kurdish items.

Northern Cyprus

Visas for the Turkish Republic of Northern Cyprus (TRNC) are available on arrival, on similar conditions to those for Turkey. If you're planning to visit Greece as well, remember that relations between the Greek Cypriot-administered Republic of Cyprus (in the south) and Northern Cyprus remain chilly. If you enter the TRNC and have your passport stamped you may later be denied entry to Greece. The Greeks will only reject a stamp from the TRNC, *not* a stamp from Turkey proper. Instead of your passport, Cypriot border officials should stamp the visa paper you are asked to fill in; a procedure

with which they are familiar. See www.mfa.gov.cy and www.mfa.gov.tr.

Syria

Almost all foreigners need a visa to enter Syria, which has an embassy in Ankara and consulates in İstanbul and Gaziantep. Costs of the 15-day, single- or multiple-entry visa are based on a reciprocal system, and range from about US$35 to US$100. You need two passport photos and you can generally pick up the visa on the same day as you lodge your application. Apply at home if possible, as Syria's missions in Turkey request a letter from your country's embassy in Ankara. Do not leave it until the border, as travellers have been knocked back – even if there's no Syrian representation in their home nation.

GETTING AROUND

Air

Airlines in Turkey

Turkey is well connected by air throughout the country, although many flights go via the hubs of İstanbul or Ankara. Internal flights are a good option in such a large country, and competition between the following Turkish airlines keeps tickets affordable.

Anadolu Jet (☑444 2538; www.anadolujet.com) The Turkish Airlines subsidiary serves some 30 airports in its parent company's network.

Atlasjet (☑444 3387; www. atlasjet.com) A limited network including Adana, Ankara, Antalya, Bodrum, Dalaman, İstanbul, İzmir, and Lefkoşa (Nicosia) in Northern Cyprus.

Onur Air (☑444 6687; www.onurair.com.tr) Flies from İstanbul to Adana, Antalya, Bodrum, Dalaman,

Diyarbakır, Erzurum, Gaziantep, İzmir, Malatya, Samsun and Trabzon.

Pegasus Airlines (☏444 0737; www.pegasusairlines. com) A useful network of some 20 airports, including most of the locations mentioned in the above listings plus less-usual spots such as Kayseri and Van.

Sun Express Airlines (☏444 0797; www.sunexpress. com.tr) The Turkish Airlines subsidiary has an extensive network, particularly from Antalya, İstanbul and İzmir.

Turkish Airlines (☏0212-252 1106; www.thy.com) State-owned Turkish Airlines provides the main domestic network, covering airports from Çanakkale to Kars.

Bicycle

Turkish cycling highlights include the spectacular scenery, easy access to archaeological sites, which you may have all to yourself in some obscure corners, and the curiosity and hospitality of locals, especially out east.

Bikes and parts Good-quality spare parts are generally only available in İstanbul and Ankara. Bisan is the main bike manufacturer in Turkey, but you can buy international brands in shops such as **Delta Bisiklet** (www.deltabisiklet.com), which has six branches in İstanbul and Ankara. Delta services bikes and can send parts throughout the country.

Hazards These include Turkey's notorious road-hog drivers, rotten road edges and, out east, stone-throwing children, wolves and ferocious Kangal dogs. Avoid main roads between cities – take secondary roads, which are safer and more scenic.

Hire You can hire bikes for short periods in tourist

towns along the coast and in Cappadocia.

Maps The best map for touring by bike is the *Köy Köy Türkiye Yol Atlası*, available in bookshops in İstanbul.

Transport You can often transport your bike by bus, train or ferry free of charge, although mini- and midi-buses will charge for the space it takes up.

Boat

İstanbul Deniz Otobüsleri (p109; İstanbul Fast Ferries; www.ido.com.tr) operates passenger and car ferries across the **Sea of Marmara**, with routes including:
» İstanbul Kabataş–Bursa and the Princes' Islands.
» İstanbul Yenıkapı–Bandırma, Bursa and Yalova.

Bus

Turkey's intercity bus system is as good as any you'll find, with modern, comfortable coaches crossing the country at all hours and for very reasonable prices. Virtually every first-time visitor to the country comments on the excellence of its bus system. On the journey, you'll be treated to hot drinks and snacks, plus liberal sprinklings of the Turks' beloved *kolonya* (lemon cologne).

Bus Companies

These are some of the best companies, with extensive route networks:

Kamil Koç (☏444 0562; www.kamilkoc.com.tr, in Turkish) A good network in western Turkey.

Metro Turizm (☏444 3455; www.metroturizm.com.tr) An extensive nationwide network.

Ulusoy (☏444 1888; www. ulusoy.com.tr) Excellent coaches and a nationwide network.

Varan Turizm (☏444 8999; www.varan.com.tr) Covers western Turkey extensively, with a few buses going east to Samsun and Gaziantep. Its 'bistro coach' between İstanbul and Ankara features a restaurant.

Costs

Bus fares are subject to fierce competition between companies, and bargains such as student discounts may be offered. Prices reflect what the market will bear, so the fare from a big city to a village is likely to be different to the fare in the opposite direction.

ISIC Some companies are nominally part of the scheme (see p671), but it doesn't guarantee you a saving.

Tickets

Although you can usually walk into an otogar (bus station) and buy a ticket for the next bus, it's wise to plan ahead on public holidays, at weekends and during the school holidays from mid-June to early September. You can reserve seats online with some of the companies listed above.

» **At the otogar** When you enter bigger otogars prepare for a few touts offering buses to the destination of your choice. It's usually a good idea to stick to the reputable big-name companies. You may pay a bit more, but you can be more confident the bus is well maintained, will run on time, and will have a relief driver on really long hauls. For shorter trips, other companies have big localised networks.

» **Men and women** Unmarried men and women are not supposed to sit together, but the bus companies rarely enforce this in the case of foreigners. You may be asked if you are married, without having to produce any proof of your wedlock, or both travellers may find their tickets marked with *bay* (man).

FEZ BUS

A hop-on, hop-off bus service, the Fez Bus (☑0212-516 9024; www.feztravel.com) links the main tourist resorts of the Aegean and the Mediterranean with İstanbul and Cappadocia. The big bonuses of using the Fez Bus are convenience (you won't have to organise journeys on ordinary Turkish buses), flexibility (the passes are valid from July to October and you can start anywhere on the circuit) and atmosphere (it's fun and energetic, with a strong party vibe). The downsides? You spend most of your time with other travellers rather than with locals, which can start to grate once you've had your fill of the backpacker fraternity. And it doesn't work out to be cheaper than doing it yourself with point-to-point buses.

A Turkish Delight bus pass (adult/student €225/210) allows you to circle from İstanbul via Çanakkale, Ephesus, Köyceğiz, Fethiye, Olympos, Antalya, Konya, Cappadocia and Ankara.

» **Refunds** Getting a refund can be difficult; exchanging it for another ticket with the same company is easier.

» **Seats** All seats can be reserved, and your ticket will bear a specific seat number. The ticket agent will have a chart of the seats with those already sold crossed off. They will often assign you a seat, but if you ask to look at the chart and choose a place, you can avoid sitting in the following blackspots:

* **At the front** On night buses you may want to avoid the front row of seats behind the driver, which have little legroom, plus you may have to inhale his cigarette smoke and listen to him chatting to his conductor into the early hours.

* **Above the wheels** Can get bumpy.

* **In front of the middle door** Seats don't recline.

* **Behind the middle door** The seats have little legroom.

* **At the back** Can get stuffy, and may have 'back of the cinema' connotations if you are a lone woman.

Otogar

Most Turkish cities and towns have a bus station, called the otogar, *garaj* or *terminal*, generally located on the outskirts. Besides intercity buses, the otogar often handles dolmuşes (minibuses that follow prescribed routes) to outlying districts or villages. Most bus stations have an *emanetçi* (left luggage) room, which you can use for a nominal fee.

Particularly in eastern Anatolia, don't believe taxi drivers at otogars who tell you there is no bus or dolmuş to your destination; they may be trying to trick you into taking their taxi. Check with the bus and dolmuş operators.

Servis

Because most bus stations are some distance from the town or city centre, the bus companies provide free *servis* shuttle minibuses. These take you to the bus company's office or another central location, possibly with stops en route to drop off other passengers. Ask '*Servis var mı?*' ('Is there a *servis*?'). Rare cities without such a service include Ankara and Konya.

Leaving town Ask about the *servis* when you buy your ticket at the bus company's central office; they will likely instruct you to arrive at the office an hour before the official departure time.

Drawbacks This service saves you a taxi or local bus fare to the otogar, but involves a lot of hanging around. If you only have limited time in a location, a taxi fare may be a good investment.

Scams Pension owners may try to convince you the private minibus to their pension is a bus company *servis*.

Car & Motorcycle

Driving around Turkey gives you unparalleled freedom to enjoy the marvellous countryside and coastline. You can stop at roadside stalls selling local specialities, explore back roads leading to hidden villages and obscure ruins, and picnic at every opportunity, just like the locals.

Bear in mind that Turkey is a huge country and spending time in the car travelling long distances will eat up your time. Consider planes, trains and buses for covering long journeys, and cars for localised travel.

Public transport is a much easier and less stressful way of getting around the traffic-clogged cities.

Automobile Associations

Turkey's main motoring organisation is the **Türkiye Turing ve Otomobil Kurumu** (Turkish Touring & Automobile Association; ☑0212-282 8285; www.turing.org.tr).

Motorcyclists may want to check out **One More Mile Riders Turkey** (www.omm riders.com), a community resource for riding in Turkey, and the Turkey-related information on **Horizons Unlimited** (www.horizonsunlimited.com/country/turkey), which has some useful contacts.

Bring Your Own Vehicle

You can bring your vehicle into Turkey for six months without charge. However, the fact that you brought one in with you will be marked in your passport to ensure you take it back out again. Don't plan on selling it here, and be prepared to be charged a hefty fine for any time over the six months. Ensure you have your car's registration papers, tax number and insurance policy on you.

Checkpoints

In southeastern Anatolia, you may encounter roadblocks, part of military operations against the PKK (Kurdistan Workers Party). They will likely check your ID and vehicle papers before waving you on, although roads in the region are sometimes closed completely if there is trouble ahead.

Driving Licences

Drivers must have a valid driving licence. Your own national licence should be sufficient, but an international driving permit (IDP) may be useful if your licence is from a country likely to seem obscure to a Turkish police officer.

Fines

You may be stopped by blue-uniformed *trafik polis*, who can fine you on the spot for speeding. If you know you have done nothing wrong and the police appear to be asking for money, play dumb. You'll probably have to pay up if they persist, but insisting on proof of payment may dissuade them from extracting a fine destined only for their top pocket. If the police don't ask for on-the-spot payment, contact your car-rental company (or mention the incident when you return the vehicle), as it can pay the fine and take the money from your card. Do the same in the case of fines for other offences, such as leaving a motorway via the wrong exit and not paying the toll. Note that you get a discount for early payment.

Fuel & Spare Parts

Turkey has some of the world's most expensive fuel prices. Petrol and diesel both cost over TL3 per litre. There are petrol stations everywhere, at least in western Turkey, and many are mega enterprises. In the vast empty spaces of central and eastern Anatolia, it's a good idea to have a full tank when you start out in the morning.

Yedek parçaları (spare parts) are readily available in the big cities, especially for European models such as Renaults, Fiats and Mercedes-Benz. Ingenious Turkish mechanics can also contrive to keep some US models in service. The *sanayi bölgesi* (industrial zone) on the outskirts of every town generally has a repair shop, usually closed on Sunday, and repairs are usually quick and cheap. Roadside repair shops can often provide excellent, virtually immediate service, although they (or you) may have to go somewhere else to get the parts. It's always wise to get an estimate of the repair cost in advance. For tyre repairs find an *oto lastikçi* (tyre repairer).

Spare motorcycle parts may be hard to come by everywhere except the big cities, so bring what you might need, or rely on the boundless ingenuity of Turkish mechanics to find, adapt or make you a part. If you do get stuck for a part you could also ring an İstanbul or Ankara repair centre and get it delivered.

Hire

You need to be at least 21 years old, with a year's driving experience, to be able to hire a car in Turkey. Most car hire companies require a credit card. Most hire cars have standard (manual) transmission; you'll pay more for automatic. The majority of the big-name companies charge a hefty drop-off fee starting at around TL150 (eg pick up in İstanbul and drop off in İzmir).

The big international companies – including Avis, Budget, Europcar, Hertz, National and Sixt – operate in the main cities, towns and most airports. Particularly in eastern Anatolia, stick to the major companies, as the local agencies often do not have insurance. Even some of the major operations are actually franchises in the east, so you should always check the contract carefully; particularly the section relating to insurance. Ask for a copy in English.

If your car incurs any accident damage, or if you cause any, do not move the car before finding a police officer and obtaining a *kaza raporu* (accident report). The officer may ask you to take an alcohol breath-test. Contact your car-rental company as soon as possible. In the case of an accident, your hire-car insurance may be void if it can be shown you were operating under the influence of alcohol or drugs, were speeding, or if you did not submit the required accident report within 48 hours to the rental company.

Because of high local fuel prices, some budget and local agencies deliver cars with virtually no fuel.

» **Economy Car Rentals** (www.economycarrentals.com) Gets excellent rates with other companies, including Budget; recommended.

» **Car Rental Turkey** (www. carrentalturkey.info) İstanbul-based.

» **Green Car** (www.green autorent.com) One of the largest operators in the Aegean region.

» **CarHireExpress.co.uk** (http://turkey.carhireexpress. co.uk) A booking engine.

Insurance

You must have international insurance, covering third-party damage, if you are bringing your own car into the country (further information is available from the Turkish Touring & Automobile Association, www.turing. org.tr/eng/green_card.asp). Buying it at the border is a straightforward process (one month €80).

As in most countries, if you hire a car you will be offered a higher level of insurance for an extra fee. The basic, mandatory insurance package should cover damage to the vehicle and theft protection – with an excess, which you can waive for an extra payment. You may be offered personal accident insurance; your travel insurance should cover any personal accident costs in the case of a crash.

Parking

Parking is easy to find in most towns and smaller settlements, but space is at a premium in cities and some towns. In these places, there are normally plenty of car parks where you can park cheaply for an hour or so, or safely leave your car overnight. As you can generally park next to accommodation options and sights outside Turkey's main centres, we have only used the parking icon (**P**) in this book in cities.

Accommodation Top-end and a handful of midrange hotels offer undercover parking for guests, and most midrange and budget options have a roadside

parking place or two that is nominally theirs to use. If they don't, parking will be close by in an empty block overseen by a caretaker, or on the road; in both cases you have to pay a fee. Your best bet is to set it up in advance when you book your room.

Clamping This is a fact of life in Turkey. Park in the wrong place and you risk having your car towed away, with the ensuing costs and hassle.

Road Conditions

Road surfaces and signage are generally good – on the main roads, at least. The most popular route with travellers, along the Aegean and Mediterranean coasts, offers excellent driving conditions. There are good *otoyols* (motorways) from the Bulgarian border near Edirne to İstanbul and Ankara, and from İzmir all the way around the coast to Antalya.

Elsewhere, roads are being steadily upgraded, although they still tend to be worst in the east, where severe winters play havoc with the surfaces. In northeastern Anatolia, road conditions change from one year to another; seek local advice before setting off on secondary roads. There are frequent road works in the northeast; even on main roads traffic can crawl along at 30km/hour. The new dams near Artvin and Yusufeli will flood some roads.

In winter, be careful of icy roads. In bad winters, you will need chains on your wheels almost everywhere except along the Aegean and Mediterranean coast. The police may stop you in more-remote areas to check you're properly prepared for emergencies. Between İstanbul and Ankara, be aware of the fog belt around Bolu that can seriously reduce visibility, even in summer.

Road Rules

In theory, Turks drive on the right and yield to traffic approaching from the right. In practice, they often drive in the middle and yield to no one. Maximum speed limits, unless otherwise posted, are 50km/h in towns, 90km/h on highways and 120km/h on *otoyols*.

Safety

Turkey has one of the world's highest motor-vehicle accident rates. Turkish drivers are impatient and incautious; rarely use their indicators and pay little attention to anyone else's; drive too fast both on the open road and through towns; and have an irrepressible urge to overtake – including on blind corners.

To survive on Turkey's roads:

» Drive cautiously and defensively.

» Do not expect your fellow motorists to obey road signs or behave in the manner you would generally expect in Western countries, especially during Ramazan, when people are irritable and their alertness is affected by fasting.

» *Never* let emotions affect you, as you can be sure other drivers will make that mistake.

» As there are only a few divided highways and many two-lane roads are serpentine, reconcile yourself to spending hours crawling along behind slow, overladen trucks.

» Avoid driving at night, when you won't be able to see potholes, animals, or even vehicles driving without lights, with lights missing, or stopped in the middle of the road. Drivers sometimes flash their lights just to announce their approach.

» Rather than trying to tackle secondary, gravel roads when visiting remote sights such as northeastern

Anatolia's churches, hire a taxi for the day. It's an extra expense, but the driver should know the terrain and peace of mind is invaluable. The US embassy in Ankara has a page of safety tips at http://turkey.usembassy. gov/driver_safety_briefing. html.

Dolmuşes & Midibuses

As well as providing transport within cities and towns, dolmuşes (minibuses) run between places; you'll usually use them to travel between small towns and villages. Ask, '[Your destination] dolmuş var mı?' (Is there a dolmuş to [your destination]?). Some dolmuşes depart at set times, but they often wait until every seat is taken before leaving. To let the driver know that you want to hop out, say 'inecek var' (someone wants to get out).

Midibuses generally operate on routes that are too long for dolmuşes, but not popular enough for full-size buses. They usually have narrow seats with rigid upright backs, not at all comfortable on long stretches.

Hitching

Although we don't recommend it, if you must otostop (hitch), offer to pay something towards the petrol, although most drivers pick up foreign hitchers for their curiosity value. You could be in for a long wait on some roads in central and eastern Anatolia; ask locals about the viability of your intended hitch before setting out. As the country is large and vehicles scarce in some areas, short hitches are quite normal. If you need to get from the highway to an archaeological site, hitch a ride with whatever comes along, be it a tractor, lorry or private car.

Instead of sticking out your thumb for a lift, you should face the traffic, hold your arm out towards the road, and wave it up and down as if bouncing a basketball.

Local Transport

Bus

For most city buses you must buy your bilet (ticket) in advance at a special ticket kiosk. Kiosks are found at major bus terminals and transfer points, and sometimes attached to shops near bus stops. The fare is normally around TL1.50.

Private buses sometimes operate on the same routes as municipal buses; they are usually older, and accept either cash or tickets.

Local Dolmuş

Dolmuşes are minibuses or, occasionally, taksi dolmuşes (shared taxis) that operate on set routes within a city. They're usually faster, more comfortable and only slightly more expensive than the bus. In larger cities, dolmuş stops are marked by signs; look for a 'D' and text reading 'Dolmuş İndirme Bindirme Yeri' (Dolmuş Boarding and Alighting Place). Stops are usually conveniently located near major squares, terminals or intersections.

Metro

Several cities now have underground or partially underground metros, including İstanbul, İzmir, Bursa and Ankara. These are usually quick and simple to use, although you may have to go through the ticket barriers to find a route map. Most metros require you to buy a jeton (transport token; around TL1.50) and insert it into the ticket barrier.

Taxi

Turkish taxis are fitted with digital meters. If your driver doesn't start his meter, mention it right away by saying 'saatiniz' (your meter). Check your driver is running the right rate, which varies from city to city. The gece (night) rate is 50% more than the gündüz (daytime) rate, but some places, including İstanbul, do not have a night rate.

Some taxi drivers – particularly in İstanbul – try to demand a flat payment from foreigners. In this situation, drivers sometimes offer a decent fare; for example to take you to an airport, where they can pick up a good fare on the return journey. It is more often the case that they demand an exorbitant amount, give you grief, and refuse to run the meter. If this happens find another cab and, if convenient, complain to the police. Generally, only when you are using a taxi for a private tour involving waiting time (eg to an archaeological site) should you agree on a set fare, which should work out cheaper than using the meter. Taxi companies normally have set fees for longer journeys written in a ledger at the rank – they can be haggled down a little. Always confirm such fares in advance to avoid argument later.

Tram

Several cities have tramvays (trams), which are a quick and efficient way of getting around, and normally cost around TL1.50 to use.

Tours

Every year we receive complaints from travellers who feel they have been fleeced by local travel agents, especially some of those operating in Sultanahmet, İstanbul. However, there are plenty of good agents alongside the sharks. Figure out a ballpark figure for doing the same trip yourself using the prices in this book, and shop around before committing.

MAN IN SEAT 61 *MARK SMITH*

According to an old Turkish joke, the Germans were paid by the kilometre to build most of Turkey's railways, and they never used a straight line where a dozen curves would do! You'll certainly come to believe this as your train snakes its way across Turkey, round deep valleys and arid mountains, with occasional glimpses of forts on distant hilltops. Turkish train travel is incredibly cheap, but the best trains are air-conditioned and as good as many in Western Europe. The scenery is often better! Chilling out over a meal and a beer in the restaurant car of an İstanbul-Ankara express is a great way to recover from trekking round the sights of İstanbul, and the night trains from İstanbul to Denizli (for Pamukkale) or Konya are a most romantic and time-effective way to go. Other trains are slower and older, but just put your feet up, open a bottle of wine, and let the scenery come to you!

Mark Smith, aka the Man in Seat 61, is a global rail travel authority and founder of the website www.seat61.com. If you're interested in travelling by train, check it out.

Tour Operators

In addition to the agents we have listed in destination chapters, the following are some Turkish tour operators we believe offer a reliable service:

Amber Travel (www.ambertravel.com) British-run adventure travel company specialising in hiking, biking and sea kayaking.

Bougainville Travel (www.bt-turkey.com) Kaş-based adventure travel specialist offering trekking, biking, canyoning, paragliding, sea kayaking and diving.

Fez Travel (www.feztravel.com) Backpacker tours around Turkey, including Gallipoli tours. Also operates the Fez Bus (p691).

Hassle Free Travel Agency (www.hasslefreetour.com) Headquartered in Çanakkale, and offering tours of western Turkey.

Kirkit Voyage (www.kirkit.com) Cappadocia specialists offering customised tours around Turkey, including İstanbul and Ephesus. French spoken too.

Trooper Tours (www.troopertours.com) Gallipoli specialist, offering one- to nine-day tours of western Turkey starting and finishing in İstanbul or Kuşadası.

Train

Train travel through Turkey is becoming increasingly popular as improvements are made. A growing number of fans appreciate no-rush travel experiences such as the stunning scenery rolling by and immersion with fellow passengers (see p695).

The occasional unannounced hold-up and public toilets gone feral by the end of the long journey are all part of the adventure. And if you're on a budget, an overnight train journey is a great way to save accommodation costs.

Network

The railway network, run by **Turkish State Railways** (☑ 444 8233; www.tcdd.gov.tr), covers the country fairly well, with the notable exception of the coastlines. For the Aegean and Mediterranean coasts you can travel by train to either İzmir or Konya, and take the bus from there.

Useful routes include:

» İstanbul–Ankara
» İstanbul–İzmir (including ferry)
» İzmir–Ankara
» İzmir–Selcuk
» Konya–Ankara (set to open in 2011)

Long-Haul Trips

Long-distance, overnight trips include:

» İstanbul–Adana
» İstanbul–Kars
» İstanbul–Konya
» İstanbul–Tatvan (Lake Van)

Classes

Turkish trains typically have several seating and sleeping options. Most have comfortable reclining Pullman seat carriages. Some have 1st- and 2nd-class compartments, with six and eight seats respectively; sometimes bookable, sometimes 'first come, best seated'.

A *küşet* (couchette) wagon has shared four- or sometimes six-person compartments with seats that fold down into shelf-like beds. Bedding is not provided unless it's an *örtülü küşetli* ('covered' couchette). A *yataklı* wagon has one- and two-bed compartments, with washbasin and bedding provided; the best option for women travelling alone on overnight trips.

Costs

Train tickets are usually about half the price of bus tickets. A return ticket is 20% cheaper than two singles. Students (though you may need a Turkish student card), seniors (60 years plus; proof of age required) and disabled travellers (disability card required) get a 20% discount. Children under eight travel free, and those aged between eight and 11 travel half-price.

InterRail and Balkan Flexipass passes are valid on the Turkish railway network, but Eurail passes aren't. Train Tour Cards allow unlimited travel on Turkish trains for a month.

Reservations

Most seats and all sleepers on the best trains must be reserved. For the *yataklı* wagons, reserve as far in advance as possible, especially if a religious or public holiday is looming. Weekend trains tend to be busiest. You can reserve tickets at www.tcdd.gov.tr.

Timetables

You can double-check train departure times, which do change, at www.tcdd.gov.tr.

Timetables usually indicate stations rather than cities; most refer to Haydarpaşa and Sirkeci rather than İstanbul, and to Basmane and Alsancak in İzmir.

Health

BEFORE YOU GO

Recommended Vaccinations

Vaccinations for the following are recommended as routine for all travellers, regardless of the region they are visiting. The consequences of these diseases can be severe, and outbreaks do occur in the Middle East.

» tetanus
» diphtheria
» pertussis (whooping cough)
» varicella (chicken pox)
» measles
» mumps
» rubella
» polio

The vaccinations for the following are also recommended for travellers to Turkey:

» typhoid
» hepatitis A and B

Rabies is endemic in Turkey, so if you will be travelling off the beaten track consider an antirabies vaccination.

Malaria is found in a few areas on the Syrian border.

Many vaccines don't ensure immunity until two weeks after they are given, so visit a doctor four to eight weeks before departure.

Ask your doctor for an International Certificate of Vaccination or Prophylaxis (otherwise known as ICVP or 'the yellow card'), listing all the vaccinations you've received.

Medical Checklist

Here is a list of items you should consider packing in your medical kit:

» acetaminophen/paracetamol (Tylenol) or aspirin
» adhesive or paper tape
» antibacterial ointment (eg Bactroban) for cuts and abrasions
» antibiotics (if travelling off the beaten track)
» antidiarrhoeal drugs (eg loperamide)
» antihistamines (for hay fever and allergic reactions)
» anti-inflammatory drugs (eg ibuprofen)
» bandages, gauze and gauze rolls
» insect repellent for the skin that contains DEET

» insect spray for clothing, tents and bed nets
» iodine tablets (for water purification)
» oral rehydration salts (eg Dioralyte)
» pocket knife
» scissors, safety pins and tweezers
» steroid cream or cortisone (for allergic rashes)
» sun block (it's very expensive in Turkey)
» syringes and sterile needles (if travelling to remote areas)
» thermometer

Websites

It's a good idea to consult your government's travel health website before departure, if one is available.

Australia (www.smartraveller.gov.au)

Canada (www.phac-aspc.gc.ca)

International Association for Medical Assistance to Travellers (IAMAT; www.iamat.org)

Lonely Planet (www.lonelyplanet.com)

MD Travel Health (www.mdtravelhealth.com)

UK (http://tinyurl.com/6jx4yw)

US (www.cdc.gov/travel)

World Health Organization (www.who.int)

Further Reading

The following are recommended references:

» *Travellers' Health* by Dr Richard Dawood
» *International Travel Health Guide* by Stuart R Rose MD
» *The Travellers' Good Health Guide* by Ted Lankester (useful for volunteers and long-term expats)
» *Travel With Children* published by Lonely Planet

IN TURKEY

Prevention is the key to staying healthy while travelling in Turkey. Infectious

INSURANCE

Find out in advance if your insurance plan will make payments directly to providers or reimburse you later for overseas health expenditures (Turkish doctors generally expect payment in cash). If you are required to pay upfront, make sure you keep all documentation. Some policies ask you to call a centre in your home country (reverse charges) for an immediate assessment of your problem. It's also worth ensuring your travel insurance will cover ambulances or transport, either home or to better medical facilities elsewhere. Not all insurance covers emergency medical evacuation home by plane or to a hospital in a major city, which may be the only way to get medical attention in a serious emergency.

diseases can and do occur here, but they are usually associated with poor living conditions and poverty, and can be avoided with a few precautions. Most injuries to travellers occur because of car accidents.

Availability & Cost of Health Care

Getting Treated

If you need basic care for problems such as cuts, bruises and jabs, you could ask for the local *sağulık ocağuı* (health centre) but don't expect anyone to speak anything but Turkish.

The travel assistance provided by your insurance may be able to locate the nearest source of medical help – otherwise, ask at your hotel. In an emergency, contact your embassy or consulate.

Standards

The standard of Turkey's health care varies. Although the best private hospitals in İstanbul and Ankara offer world-class service, they are expensive. Elsewhere, even private hospitals don't always have high standards of care and their state-run equivalents even less so.

Hospitals & clinics Medicine, and even sterile dressings or intravenous fluids, may need to be bought from a local pharmacy. Nursing care is often limited or rudimentary, the as-

sumption being that family and friends will look after the patient.

Dentists Standards vary and there is a risk of hepatitis B and HIV transmission via poorly sterilised equipment, so watch the tools in use carefully. Your travel insurance will not usually cover you for anything other than emergency dental treatment.

Pharmacists For minor illnesses, such as diarrhoea, pharmacists can often provide advice and sell over-the-counter medication, including drugs that would require a prescription in your home country. They can also advise when more-specialised help is needed.

Infectious Diseases

Diphtheria

Spread through Close respiratory contact.

Symptoms & effects A high temperature and severe sore throat. Sometimes a membrane forms across the throat requiring a tracheotomy to prevent suffocation.

Prevention The vaccine is given as an injection alone, or with tetanus, and is recommended for those likely to be in close contact with the local population in infected areas.

Hepatitis A

Spread through Contaminated food (particularly shellfish) and water.

Symptoms & effects Jaundice, dark urine, a yellow colour to the whites of the eyes, fever and abdominal pain. Although rarely fatal, it can cause prolonged lethargy and delayed recovery.

Prevention Vaccine (Avaxim, VAQTA, Havrix) is given as an injection, with a booster extending the protection offered. Hepatitis A and typhoid vaccines can also be given as a combined single-dose vaccine (hepatyrix or viatim).

Hepatitis B

Spread through Infected blood, contaminated needles and sexual intercourse.

Symptoms & effects Jaundice and liver problems (occasionally failure).

Prevention Travellers should make this a routine vaccination, especially as the disease is endemic in Turkey. Many countries give hepatitis B vaccination as part of routine childhood vaccination. It is given singly, or at the same time as hepatitis A.

HIV

Spread through Infected blood and blood products; sexual intercourse with an infected partner; 'blood to blood' contact, such as contaminated instruments during medical, dental, acupuncture and other body-piercing procedures, or sharing used intravenous needles.

Leishmaniasis

Spread through The bite of an infected sandfly or dog.

Symptoms & effects A slowly growing skin lump or ulcer. It may develop into a serious, life-threatening fever, usually accompanied by anaemia and weight loss.

Leptospirosis

Spread through The excreta of infected rodents, especially rats. It is unusual for travellers to be affected unless living in poor sanitary conditions.

Symptoms & effects Fever, jaundice, and hepatitis and renal failure that may be fatal.

Malaria

Spread through Mosquito bites. You stand the greatest chance of contracting malaria if you travel in southeastern Turkey. The risk is minimal in most cities, but check with your doctor if you are considering travelling to rural areas.

Symptoms & effects Malaria almost always starts with marked shivering, fever and sweating. Muscle pain, headache and vomiting are common. Symptoms may occur anywhere from a few days to three weeks after a bite by an infected mosquito. The illness can start while you are taking preventative tablets if they are not fully effective, or after you have finished taking your tablets.

Prevention Taking antimalarial tablets is inconvenient, but malaria can kill. You must take them if the risk is significant.

Poliomyelitis

Spread through Contaminated food and water.

Symptoms & effects May be carried asymptomatically, although it can cause a transient fever and, in rare cases, potentially permanent muscle weakness or paralysis.

Prevention Polio is one of the vaccines given in childhood, and should be boosted later on.

Rabies

Spread through Bites or licks on broken skin from an infected animal.

Symptoms & effects Initially, pain or tingling at the site of the bite with fever, loss of appetite and headache. With 'furious' rabies, there is a growing sense of anxiety, jumpiness, disorientation, neck stiffness, sometimes seizures or convulsions, and hydrophobia (fear of water). 'Dumb' rabies (less common) affects the spinal cord, causing muscle paralysis then heart and lung failure. If untreated, both forms are fatal.

Prevention People travelling to remote areas, where a reliable source of postbite vaccine is not available within 24 hours, should be vaccinated. If you have not been vaccinated and you get bitten, you will need a course of injections starting as soon as possible after the injury.

Tuberculosis

Spread through Close respiratory contact and, occasionally, infected milk or milk products.

Symptoms & effects Can be asymptomatic, although symptoms can include a cough, weight loss or fever months or even years after exposure. An X-ray is the best way to confirm if you have tuberculosis.

Prevention BCG vaccine is recommended for those likely to be mixing closely with the local population – visiting family, planning a long stay, or working as a teacher or health-care worker. As it's a live vaccine it should not be given to pregnant women or immunocompromised individuals.

Typhoid

Spread through Food or water that has been

TRAVELLER'S DIARRHOEA

To prevent diarrhoea, avoid tap water unless it has been boiled, filtered or chemically disinfected (with iodine tablets). Eat fresh fruits or vegetables only if they're cooked or if you have peeled them yourself, and avoid dairy products that might contain unpasteurised milk. Buffet meals are risky since food may not be kept hot enough; meals freshly cooked in front of you in a busy restaurant are more likely to be safe.

If you develop diarrhoea, be sure to drink plenty of fluids, preferably an oral rehydration solution containing lots of salt and sugar. A few loose stools don't require treatment, but if you start having more than four or five motions a day, you should start taking an antidiarrhoeal agent (such as loperamide) – or if that's not available, an antibiotic (usually a quinolone drug). If diarrhoea is bloody, persists for more than 72 hours or is accompanied by fever, shaking chills or severe abdominal pain, you should seek medical attention.

TAP WATER

» It's not wise to drink tap water if you're only in Turkey on a short visit. Stick to bottled water, boil tap water for 10 minutes or use water-purification tablets or a filter.

» Do not drink water from rivers or lakes, since it may contain bacteria or viruses that can cause diarrhoea or vomiting.

contaminated by infected human faeces.

Symptoms & effects Initially, usually fever or a pink rash on the abdomen. Septicaemia (blood poisoning) may also occur.

Prevention Typhim V or, typherix vaccine. In some countries, the oral vaccine Vivotif is also available.

Yellow Fever

Yellow fever vaccination is not required for Turkey, but travellers arriving from a yellow fever infected country (and people who have been in such a country recently) need to show proof of vaccination before entry.

Environmental Hazards

Heat Illness

Causes Sweating heavily, fluid loss and inadequate replacement of fluids and salt. Particularly common when you exercise outside in a hot climate.

Symptoms & effects Headache, dizziness and tiredness.

Prevention Drink sufficient water (you should produce pale, diluted urine). By the time you are thirsty you are already dehydrated.

Treatment Replace fluids by drinking water, fruit juice,

or both, and cool down with cold water and fans. Treat salt loss by consuming salty fluids, such as soup or broth, and adding a little more table salt to foods.

Heatstroke

Causes Extreme heat; high humidity; dehydration; drug or alcohol use or physical exertion in the sun. Occurs when the body's heat-regulating mechanism breaks down.

Symptoms & effects An excessive rise in body temperature, sweating stops, irrational and hyperactive behaviour, and eventually loss of consciousness and death.

Treatment Rapidly cool down by spraying the body with water and using a fan. Emergency fluids and replacing electrolytes by intravenous drip is usually also required.

Insect Bites & Stings

Causes Mosquitoes, sandflies (located around the Mediterranean beaches), scorpions (frequently found in arid or dry climates), bees and wasps (in the Aegean and Mediterranean coastal areas, particularly around Marmaris).

Symptoms & effects Even if mosquitoes do not carry malaria, they can cause irritation and infected bites. Mosquitoes also spread dengue fever. Sandflies have a nasty, itchy bite, and can carry the rare skin disorder leishmaniasis. Turkey's small white scorpions can give a painful bite that will bother you for up to 24 hours.

Prevention DEET-based insect repellents. If you have a severe allergy (anaphylaxis) to bee or wasp stings, carry an adrenalin injection or similar.

Snake Bites

Prevention Do not walk barefoot or stick your hands into holes or cracks.

Treatment If bitten, do not panic. Half of those bitten by venomous snakes are not actually injected with poison (envenomed). Immobilise the bitten limb with a splint (eg a stick) and bandage the site with firm pressure, similar to applying a bandage over a sprain. Do not apply a tourniquet, or cut or suck the bite. Get the victim medical help as soon as possible so that antivenene can be given if necessary.

Travelling with Children

» Consider giving children the BCG vaccine for tuberculosis if they haven't had it; for more info see the tuberculosis section earlier in this chapter.

» In hot, moist climates any wound or break in the skin may lead to infection. The area should be cleaned and then kept dry and clean.

» Avoid contaminated food and water. It may be helpful to take rehydration powders for reconstituting with boiled water. Also see the boxed text, Traveller's Diarrhoea, in this chapter.

» Encourage your child to avoid dogs or other mammals because of the risk of diseases. Any bite, scratch or lick from a warm-blooded, furry animal should immediately be thoroughly cleaned. If there is a possibility that the animal is infected with rabies, seek immediate medical assistance; for more information see the rabies section earlier in this chapter.

» For children and pregnant or breastfeeding women, double-check drugs and dosages prescribed for travel by doctors and pharmacists, as they may be unsuitable. Some information on the suitability of drugs and recommended dosage can be found on travel-health websites in this chapter.

Women's Health

Contraception The **International Planned Parenthood Federation** (www.ippf.org) can advise you about the availability of contraception in Turkey and other countries. Pharmacies stock *ertesi gün hapı* (morning after pill).

Pregnancy Take written records of the pregnancy and your blood group, which will be helpful if you need medical attention (in Turkey you have to pay for blood infusions unless a friend supplies blood for you). Antenatal facilities vary greatly in Turkey so think carefully before travelling to out-of-the-way places, bearing in mind the cultural and linguistic difficulties, not to mention poor medical standards you might face if health care is needed.

Sanitary pads Fairly readily available, but tampons are not always available outside major cities and are expensive – bring some from home.

Language

WANT MORE?

For in-depth language information and handy phrases, check out Lonely Planet's *Turkish Phrasebook*. You'll find it at **shop. lonelyplanet.com**, or you can buy Lonely Planet's iPhone phrasebooks at the Apple App Store.

Turkish belongs to the Ural-Altaic language family. It's the official language of Turkey and northern Cyprus, and has approximately 70 million speakers worldwide.

Pronouncing Turkish is pretty simple for English speakers as most Turkish sounds are also found in English. If you read our col-oured pronunciation guides as if they were English, you'll be understood. The symbol ew represents the sound 'ee' pronounced with rounded lips (as in 'few'), and the symbol uh is pronounced like the 'a' in 'ago'. Note also that the Turkish r is always rolled and that v is a little softer than in English.

Word stress is quite light in Turkish, and generally falls on the last syllable of the word. In our pronunciation guides the stressed syllables are in italics.

BASICS

Hello.
Merhaba.   mer·ha·ba

Goodbye.
Hoşçakal.   hosh·cha·kal
(said by person leaving)
Güle güle.   gew·le gew·le
(said by person staying)

Yes.
Evet.   e·vet

No.
Hayır.   ha·yuhr

Excuse me.
Bakar mısınız.   ba·kar muh·suh·nuhz

Sorry.
Özür dilerim.   er·zewr dee·le·reem

Please.
Lütfen.   lewt·fen

Thank you.
Teşekkür ederim.   te·shek·kewr e·de·reem

You're welcome.
Birşey değil.   beer·shay de·eel

How are you?
Nasılsınız?   na·suhl·suh·nuhz

Fine, and you?
İyiyim, ya siz?   ee·yee·yeem ya seez

What's your name?
Adınız nedir?   a·duh·nuhz ne·deer

My name is ...
Benim adım ...   be·neem a·duhm ...

Do you speak English?
İngilizce   een·gee·leez·je
konuşuyor   ko·noo·shoo·yor
musunuz?   moo·soo·nooz

I understand.
Anlıyorum.   an·luh·yo·room

I don't understand.
Anlamıyorum.   an·la·muh·yo·room

ACCOMMODATION

Where can I find a ...?	Nerede ... bulabilirim?	ne·re·de ... boo·la·bee·lee·reem
campsite	kamp yeri	kamp ye·ree
guesthouse	misafirhane	mee·sa·feer·ha·ne
hotel	otel	o·tel
pension	pansiyon	pan·see·yon
youth hostel	gençlik hosteli	gench·leek hos·te·lee

How much is it per night/person?
Geceliği/Kişi   ge·je·lee·ee/kee·shee
başına ne kadar?   ba·shuh·na ne ka·dar

Is breakfast included?
Kahvaltı dahil mi?   kah·val·tuh da·heel mee

Do you have a ...?	... odanız var mı?	... o·da·nuz var muh
single room	Tek kişilik	tek kee·shee·leek
double room	İki kişilik	ee·kee kee·shee·leek

air conditioning	klima	klee·ma
bathroom	banyo	ban·yo
window	pencere	pen·je·re

DIRECTIONS

Where is ...?
... nerede?   ... ne·re·de

What's the address?
Adresi nedir?   ad·re·see ne·deer

Could you write it down, please?
Lütfen yazar   lewt·fen ya·zar
mısınız?   muh·suh·nuhz

Can you show me (on the map)?
Bana (haritada)   ba·na (ha·ree·ta·da)
gösterebilir   gers·te·re·bee·leer
misiniz?   mee·seen·neez

It's straight ahead.
Tam karşıda.   tam kar·shuh·da

at the traffic lights
trafik   tra·feek
ışıklarından   uh·shuhk·la·ruhn·dan

at the corner	köşeden	ker·she·den
behind	arkasında	ar·ka·suhn·da
far (from)	uzak	oo·zak
in front of	önünde	er·newn·de
near (to)	yakınında	ya·kuh·nuhn·da
opposite	karşısında	kar·shuh·suhn·da
Turn left.	Sola dön.	so·la dern
Turn right.	Sağa dön.	sa·a dern

EATING & DRINKING

What would you recommend?
Ne tavsiye   ne tav·see·ye
edersiniz?   e·der·see·neez

What's in that dish?
Bu yemekte neler var?   boo ye·mek·te ne·ler var

I don't eat ...
... yemiyorum.   ... ye·mee·yo·room

Cheers!
Şerefe!   she·re·fe

To get by in Turkish, mix and match these simple patterns with words of your choice:

When's (the next bus)?
(Sonraki otobüs)   (son·ra·kee o·to·bews)
ne zaman?   ne za·man

Where's (the market)?
(Pazar yeri) nerede?   (pa·zar ye·ree) ne·re·de

Where can I (buy a ticket)?
Nereden (bilet   ne·re·den (bee·let
alabilirim)?   a·la·bee·lee·reem)

I have (a reservation).
(Rezervasyonum)   (re·zer·vas·yo·noom)
var.   var

Do you have (a map)?
(Haritanız)   (ha·ree·ta·nuhz)
var mı?   var muh

Is there (a toilet)?
(Tuvalet) var mı?   (too·va·let) var muh

I'd like (the menu).
(Menüyü)   (me·new·yew)
istiyorum.   ees·tee·yo·room

I want to (make a call).
(Bir görüşme   (beer ger·rewsh·me
yapmak)   yap·mak)
istiyorum.   ees·tee·yo·room

Do I have to (declare this)?
(Bunu beyan   (boo·noo be·yan
etmem) gerekli mi?   et·mem) ge·rek·lee mee

I need (assistance).
(Yardıma)   (yar·duh·ma)
ihtiyacım var.   eeh·tee·ya·juhm var

That was delicious!
Nefisti!   ne·fees·tee

The bill/check, please.
Hesap lütfen.   he·sap lewt·fen

I'd like a table for ...	... bir masa ayırtmak istiyorum.	... beer ma·sa a·yuhrt·mak ees·tee·yo·room
(eight) o'clock	Saat (sekiz) için	sa·at (se·keez) ee·cheen
(two) people	(İki) kişilik	(ee·kee) kee·shee·leek

Key Words

appetisers	mezeler	me·ze·ler
bottle	şişe	shee·she
bowl	kase	ka·se
breakfast	kahvaltı	kah·val·tuh
(too) cold	(çok) soğuk	(chok) so·ook

Signs

Açık	Open
Bay	Male
Bayan	Female
Çıkışı	Exit
Giriş	Entrance
Kapalı	Closed
Sigara İçilmez	No Smoking
Tuvaletler	Toilets
Yasak	Prohibited

English	Turkish	Pron
cup	fincan	feen·jan
delicatessen	şarküteri	shar·kew·te·ree
dinner	akşam yemeği	ak·sham ye·me·ee
dish	yemek	ye·mek
food	yiyecek	yee·ye·jek
fork	çatal	cha·tal
glass	bardak	bar·dak
grocery	bakkal	bak·kal
halal	helal	he·lal
highchair	mama sandalyesi	ma·ma san·dal·ye·see
hot (warm)	sıcak	suh·jak
knife	bıçak	buh·chak
kosher	koşer	ko·sher
lunch	öğle yemeği	er·le ye·me·ee
main courses	ana yemekler	a·na ye·mek·ler
market	pazar	pa·zar
menu	yemek listesi	ye·mek lees·te·see
plate	tabak	ta·bak
restaurant	restoran	res·to·ran
spicy	acı	a·juh
spoon	kaşık	ka·shuhk
vegetarian	vejeteryan	ve·zhe·ter·yan

Meat & Fish

English	Turkish	Pron
anchovy	hamsi	ham·see
beef	sığır eti	suh·uhr e·tee
calamari	kalamares	ka·la·ma·res
chicken	piliç/tavuk	pee·leech/ta·vook
fish	balık	ba·luhk
lamb	kuzu	koo·zoo
liver	ciğer	jee·er
mussels	midye	meed·ye
pork	domuz eti	do·mooz e·tee
veal	dana eti	da·na e·tee

Fruit & Vegetables

English	Turkish	Pron
apple	elma	el·ma
apricot	kayısı	ka·yuh·suh
banana	muz	mooz
capsicum	biber	bee·ber
carrot	havuç	ha·vooch
cucumber	salatalık	sa·la·ta·luhk
fruit	meyve	may·ve
grape	üzüm	ew·zewm
melon	kavun	ka·voon
olive	zeytin	zay·teen
onion	soğan	so·an
orange	portakal	por·ta·kal
peach	şeftali	shef·ta·lee
potato	patates	pa·ta·tes
spinach	ıspanak	uhs·pa·nak
tomato	domates	do·ma·tes
watermelon	karpuz	kar·pooz

Other

English	Turkish	Pron
bread	ekmek	ek·mek
cheese	peynir	pay·neer
egg	yumurta	yoo·moor·ta
honey	bal	bal
ice	buz	booz
pepper	kara biber	ka·ra bee·ber
rice	pirinç/pilav	pee·reench/pee·lav
salt	tuz	tooz
soup	çorba	chor·ba
sugar	şeker	she·ker
Turkish delight	lokum	lo·koom

Drinks

English	Turkish	Pron
beer	bira	bee·ra
coffee	kahve	kah·ve
(orange) juice	(portakal) suyu	(por·ta·kal soo·yoo)
milk	süt	sewt
mineral water	maden suyu	ma·den soo·yoo
soft drink	alkolsüz içecek	al·kol·sewz ee·che·jek
tea	çay	chai
water	su	soo
wine	şarap	sha·rap
yoghurt	yoğurt	yo·oort

EMERGENCIES

Help!
İmdat!   eem·dat

I'm lost.
Kayboldum.   kai·bol·*doom*

Leave me alone!
Git başımdan!   geet ba·shuhm·*dan*

There's been an accident.
Bir kaza oldu.   beer ka·za ol·*doo*

Can I use your phone?
Telefonunuzu   te·le·fo·noo·noo·*zoo*
kullanabilir miyim?   kool·la·*na*·bee·leer mee·*yeem*

Call a doctor!
Doktor çağırın!   dok·*tor* cha·uh·ruhn

Call the police!
Polis çağırın!   po·*lees* cha·uh·ruhn

I'm ill.
Hastayım.   has·*ta*·yuhm

It hurts here.
Burası ağrıyor.   boo·ra·*suh* a·ruh·yor

I'm allergic to (nuts).
(Çerezlere)   (che·rez·le·*re*)
alerjim var.   a·ler·*zheem* var

SHOPPING & SERVICES

I'd like to buy ...
... almak istiyorum.   ... al·*mak* ees·*tee*·yo·room

I'm just looking.
Sadece bakıyorum.   sa·de·je ba·*kuh*·yo·room

May I look at it?
Bakabilir miyim?   ba·*ka*·bee·leer mee·*yeem*

The quality isn't good.
Kalitesi iyi değil.   ka·lee·te·*see* ee·*yee* de·*eel*

How much is it?
Ne kadar?   ne ka·*dar*

It's too expensive.
Bu çok pahalı.   boo chok pa·ha·*luh*

Do you have something cheaper?
Daha ucuz birşey   da·*ha* oo·*jooz* beer·*shay*
var mı?   var muh

There's a mistake in the bill.
Hesapta bir   he·sap·*ta* beer
yanlışlık var.   yan·luhsh·*luhk* var

Question Words

How?	Nasıl?	na·*seel*
What?	Ne?	ne
When?	Ne zaman?	ne za·*man*
Where?	Nerede?	ne·re·de
Which?	Hangi?	han·gee
Who?	Kim?	keem
Why?	Neden?	ne·den

ATM	bankamatik	ban·ka·ma·*teek*
credit card	kredi kartı	kre·dee kar·*tuh*
post office	postane	pos·*ta*·ne
signature	imza	eem·*za*
tourist office	turizm	too·*reezm*
	bürosu	bew·ro·*soo*

TIME & DATES

What time is it?	Saat kaç?	sa·*at* kach
It's (10) o'clock.	Saat (on).	sa·*at* (on)
Half past (10).	(On) buçuk.	(on) boo·*chook*

in the morning	öğleden evvel	er·le·*den* ev·vel
in the afternoon	öğleden sonra	er·le·*den* son·ra
in the evening	akşam	ak·*sham*
yesterday	dün	dewn
today	bugün	boo·*gewn*
tomorrow	yarın	ya·*ruhn*

Monday	Pazartesi	pa·zar·te·see
Tuesday	Salı	sa·*luh*
Wednesday	Çarşamba	char·sham·ba
Thursday	Perşembe	per·shem·be
Friday	Cuma	joo·ma
Saturday	Cumartesi	joo·mar·te·see
Sunday	Pazar	pa·zar

January	Ocak	o·jak
February	Şubat	shoo·bat
March	Mart	mart
April	Nisan	nee·san
May	Mayıs	ma·yuhs
June	Haziran	ha·zee·ran
July	Temmuz	tem·mooz
August	Ağustos	a·oos·tos
September	Eylül	ay·lewl
October	Ekim	e·keem
November	Kasım	ka·suhm
December	Aralık	a·ra·luhk

TRANSPORT

Public Transport

At what time	... ne zaman	... ne za·man
does the ...	kalkacak/	kal·ka·jak/
leave/arrive?	varır?	va·ruhr
boat	Vapur	va·poor
bus	Otobüs	o·to·bews
plane	Uçak	oo·chak
train	Tren	tren

Numbers

1	bir	beer
2	iki	ee·kee
3	üç	ewch
4	dört	dert
5	beş	besh
6	altı	al·tuh
7	yedi	ye·dee
8	sekiz	se·keez
9	dokuz	do·kooz
10	on	on
20	yirmi	yeer·mee
30	otuz	o·tooz
40	kırk	kuhrk
50	elli	el·lee
60	altmış	alt·muhsh
70	yetmiş	et·meesh
80	seksen	sek·sen
90	doksan	dok·san
100	yüz	yewz
1000	bin	been

Does it stop at (Maltepe)?
(Maltepe'de) (mal·te·pe·de)
durur mu? doo·roor moo

What's the next stop?
Sonraki durak son·ra·kee doo·rak
hangisi? han·gee·see

Please tell me when we get to (Beşiktaş).
(Beşiktaş'a) (be·sheek·ta·sha)
vardığımızda var·duh·uh·muhz·da
lütfen bana lewt·fen ba·na
söyleyin. say·le·yeen

I'd like to get off at (Kadıköy).
(Kadıköy'de) inmek (ka·duh·kay·de) een·mek
istiyorum. ees·tee·yo·room

I'd like a ... ticket to (Bostancı).	(Bostancı'ya) ... bir bilet lütfen.	(bos·tan·juh·ya) ... beer bee·let lewt·fen
1st-class	Birinci mevki	bee·reen·jee mev·kee
2nd-class	İkinci mevki	ee·keen·jee mev·kee
one-way	Gidiş	gee·deesh
return	Gidiş-dönüş	gee·deesh·der·newsh

first	ilk	eelk
last	son	son
next	geleçek	ge·le·jek

I'd like a/an ... seat.	... bir yer istiyorum.	... beer yer ees·tee·yo·room
aisle	Koridor tarafında	ko·ree·dor ta·ra·fuhn·da
window	Cam kenarı	jam ke·na·ruh

cancelled	iptal edildi	eep·tal e·deel·dee
delayed	ertelendi	er·te·len·dee
platform	peron	pe·ron
ticket office	bilet gişesi	bee·let gee·she·see
timetable	tarife	ta·ree·fe
train station	istasyon	ees·tas·yon

Driving & Cycling

I'd like to hire a ...	Bir ... kiralamak istiyorum.	beer ... kee·ra·la·mak ees·tee·yo·room
4WD	dört çeker	dert che·ker
bicycle	bisiklet	bee·seek·let
car	araba	a·ra·ba
motorcycle	motosiklet	mo·to·seek·let

bike shop	bisikletçi	bee·seek·let·chee
child seat	çocuk koltuğu	cho·jook kol·too·oo
diesel	dizel	dee·zel
helmet	kask	kask
mechanic	araba tamircisi	a·ra·ba ta·meer·jee·see
petrol/gas	benzin	ben·zeen
service station	benzin istasyonu	ben·zeen ees·tas·yo·noo

Is this the road to (Taksim)?
(Taksim'e) giden (tak·see·me) gee·den
yol bu mu? yol boo moo

(How long) Can I park here?
Buraya (ne kadar boo·ra·ya (ne ka·dar
süre) park sew·re) park
edebilirim? e·de·bee·lee·reem

The car/motorbike has broken down (at Osmanbey).
Arabam/ a·ra·bam/
Motosikletim mo·to·seek·le·teem
(Osmanbey'de) (os·man·bay·de)
bozuldu. bo·zool·doo

I have a flat tyre.
Lastiğim patladı. las·tee·eem pat·la·duh

I've run out of petrol.
Benzinim bitti. ben·zee·neem beet·tee

GLOSSARY

Suffixes in brackets are a form of the word you may hear in conversation.

acropolis – hilltop citadel and temples of a classical Hellenic city
ada(sı) – island
agora – open space for commerce and politics in a Graeco-Roman city
Anatolia – the Asian part of Turkey; also called *Asia Minor*
arabesk – Arabic-style Turkish music
arasta – row of shops near a mosque, the rent from which supports the mosque
Asia Minor – see *Anatolia*

bahçe(si) – garden
banliyö treni – suburban train lines
bedesten – vaulted, fireproof market enclosure where valuable goods are kept
belediye – municipal council, town hall
bey – polite form of address for a man; follows the name
bilet – ticket
bouleuterion – place of assembly, council meeting place in a classical Hellenic city
bulvar(ı) – boulevard or avenue; often abbreviated to 'bul'

cadde(si) – street; often abbreviated to 'cad'
cami(i) – mosque
caravanserai – large fortified way-station for (trade) caravans
çarşı(sı) – market, bazaar; sometimes town centre
çay bahçesi – tea garden
çayı – stream
çeşme – spring, fountain

dağ(ı) – mountain
deniz – sea

dervish – member of Mevlevi Muslim brotherhood
dolmuş – shared taxi; can be a minibus or sedan
döviz (bürosu) – currency exchange (office)

emir – Turkish tribal chieftain
eski – old (thing, not person)
ev pansiyonu – private home that rents rooms to travellers
eyvan – vaulted hall opening into a central court in a *medrese* or mosque; also balcony

fasıl – Ottoman classical music, usually played by gypsies

GAP – Southeastern Anatolia Project, a mammoth hydroelectric and irrigation project
geçit, geçidi – (mountain) pass
gişe – ticket booth
göl(ü) – lake
gület – traditional Turkish wooden yacht

hamam(ı) – Turkish bathhouse
han(ı) – caravanserai
hanım – polite form of address for a woman
haremlik – family/women's quarters of a residence; see also *selamlık*
heykel – statue
hisar(ı) – fortress or citadel
Hittites – nation of people inhabiting Anatolia during 2nd millennium BC
hükümet konağı – government house, provincial government headquarters

imam – prayer leader, Muslim cleric
imaret(i) – soup kitchen for the poor, usually attached to a *medrese*

indirim – discount
iskele(si) – jetty, quay

jandarma – gendarme, paramilitary police force/officer
jeton – transport token

kale(si) – fortress, citadel
kapı(sı) – door, gate
kaplıca – thermal spring or baths
Karagöz – shadow-puppet theatre
kaya – cave
KDV – *katma değer vergisi,* Turkey's value-added tax
kebapçı – place selling kebaps
kervansaray(ı) – Turkish for *caravanserai*
keyif – relaxation (refined to a fine art in Turkey)
kilim – flat-weave rug
kilise(si) – church
köfteci – *köfte* (meatballs) maker or seller
konak, konağı – mansion, government headquarters
köprü(sü) – bridge
köşk(ü) – pavilion, villa
köy(ü) – village
kule(si) – tower
külliye(si) – mosque complex including seminary, hospital and soup kitchen
kümbet – vault, cupola, dome; tomb topped by this

liman(ı) – harbour
lokanta – eatery serving ready-made food

mağara(sı) – cave
mahalle(si) – neighbourhood, district of a city
medrese(si) – Islamic theological seminary or school attached to a mosque
mescit, mescidi – prayer room, small mosque
Mevlâna – also known as Celaleddin Rumi, a great mystic and poet (1207–73),

founder of the Mevlevi whirling *dervish* order

meydan(ı) – public square, open place

meyhane – tavern, wine shop

mihrab – niche in a mosque indicating the direction of Mecca

milli parkı – national park

mimber – pulpit in a mosque

minare(si) – minaret, tower from which Muslims are called to prayer

müze(si) – museum

nargileh – traditional water pipe (for smoking); hookah

necropolis – city of the dead, cemetery

oda(sı) – room

odeon – odeum, small classical theatre for musical performances

otobus – bus

otogar – bus station

Ottoman – of or pertaining to the Ottoman Empire which lasted from the end of the 13th century to the end of WWI

pansiyon – pension, B&B, guesthouse

paşa – general, governor

pastane – pastry shop (patisserie); also *pastahane*

pazar(ı) – weekly market, bazaar

peribacalar – fairy chimneys

pideci – pide maker or seller

plaj – beach

PTT – Posta, Telefon, Telegraf; post, telephone and telegraph office

Ramazan – Islamic holy month of fasting

saat kulesi – clock tower

şadırvan – fountain where Muslims perform ritual ablutions

saray(ı) – palace

sedir – bench seating that doubled as a bed in Ottoman houses

şehir – city; municipality

şehir merkezi – city centre

selamlık – public/male quarters of a residence; see also *haremlik*

Seljuk – of or pertaining to the Seljuk Turks, the first Turkish state to rule Anatolia from the 11th to 13th centuries

sema – *dervish* ceremony

semahane – hall where whirling *dervish* ceremonies are held

serander – granary

servis – shuttle minibus service to and from the *otogar*

sinema – cinema

sokak, sokağı – street or lane; often abbreviated to 'sk'

Sufi – Muslim mystic, member of a mystic (*dervish*) brotherhood

tabiat parkı – nature park

tavla – backgammon

TC – Türkiye Cumhuriyeti (Turkish Republic); designates an official office or organisation

TCDD – Turkish State Railways

Tekel – government alcoholic beverage and tobacco company

tekke(si) – *dervish* lodge

tersane – shipyard

THY – Türk Hava Yolları, Turkish Airlines

TML – Turkish Maritime Lines

tramvay – tram

TRT – Türkiye Radyo ve Televizyon, Turkish broadcasting corporation

tuff, tufa – soft stone laid down as volcanic ash

türbe(si) – tomb, grave, mausoleum

valide sultan – mother of the reigning sultan

vezir – vizier (minister) in the Ottoman government

vilayet, valilik, valiliği – provincial government headquarters

yalı – grand waterside residence

yayla – highland pastures

yeni – new

yol(u) – road, way

behind the scenes

SEND US YOUR FEEDBACK

We love to hear from travellers – your comments keep us on our toes and help make our books better. Our well-travelled team reads every word on what you loved or loathed about this book. Although we cannot reply individually to postal submissions, we always guarantee that your feedback goes straight to the appropriate authors, in time for the next edition. Each person who sends us information is thanked in the next edition – and the most useful submissions are rewarded with a free book.

Visit **lonelyplanet.com/contact** to submit your updates and suggestions or to ask for help. Our award-winning website also features inspirational travel stories, news and discussions.

Note: We may edit, reproduce and incorporate your comments in Lonely Planet products such as guidebooks, websites and digital products, so let us know if you don't want your comments reproduced or your name acknowledged. For a copy of our privacy policy visit lonelyplanet.com/privacy.

OUR READERS

Many thanks to the travellers who used the last edition and wrote to us with helpful hints, useful advice and interesting anecdotes:

A Roberta A Acquaviva, Tahsin Acer, Selda Adalar, Adam, Mary Adam, Robyn Adams, Turkan Adatepe, Joel Adcock, Katrien Adriaensen, Yossef Aelony, Cristina Agdiniz, Rupal Agrawal, Levent Akad, Ria Akay, Umut Akdemir, Carrie Akkelle, Hylke B Akkerman, Gerard Akse, Catherine Allen, Noah Allington, Sellwood Almond, Livia Alvarez Almazan, Laura Ambrey, Diana Amith, Yassine Amnay, Phil & Hilary André, Christy Anderson, Chris Andrews, Estela Aparisi, Kathy Arici, Zeynal Arslan, Mustafa Askin, Andy Aten, Mehmet Ates, Geoffroy Aubry, Christian Audet, Gaynor Austen, Ibrahim Aydemir, Elif Aytekin **B** Alexandra Babynec, Bonita Backhouse, Karen Bacon, Howard Bade, Sandeep Bagchee, Ibrahim Bagci, Charles Bagley, Ann Baker, Cagla Balcilar, Olaf Ballnus, Christoph Balmert, Lee Banner, Susan Barlow, Jennie Barry, Rosa Barugh, Elodie Bauguen, Martin Baumann, Agnes Bayatti-Ozdemir, Gary Beckman, Greg Beiter, Ertugrul Bekler, Adam Benbrook, Antonella Benvegna, Adam Berg, Francisco Berreteaga, Bettina Bert, R Bevelacquy, Leslie Bialik, Douwe-Klaas Bijl, Tom Billings, Steve Bilton, Kashi Bilwakesh, Salih Birbilen, Orçun Birol, Anne Bishop, Steven Bland, Richard Bloomsdale, Fred Blouin, Sarah Boddington, Linda Bolt, Christopher Booksh, Charlÿe Bosgra, Rosa Bosio, John Bosman, Bülent Boyaci, Flo Boyko, Kubra Boza, Yunus Bozkus, Erin Brady, Alexander Brandt, Stella Brecknell, Mark Breedon, Jill Breeze, Isabelle Breton, Bettina Breuninger, Andrea Brewer, Christian Brockhaus, Daniel Broid, Sergey Broude, John Brozak, Sammie Buben, Pieter Buijs, Victoria Burke, Bobby Burner, Chris Burns, Kent Buse, Graham Butterfield **C** Marina C Murray Cain, Rema Calauor, Seyit Can, Serena Cantoni, Ryan Cardno, Kim Carey, Martinez Carlos, Linda Carlton, Julie Carson, Sonja Carter, Sarah Cartwright, Natalia Carvajal, Bee Castellano, Gilles Castonguay, Tugba Cavusoglu, Matej Cebohin, Marco Cencini, Duygu Cenesiz, Irfan Cetinkaya, Irfan Çetinkaya, Andrew Chapman, Joanne Chatfield, Yvonne Cheung, Susan Christie, Vicki Chu, Ilya Chubarov, Huseyin Cicek, Refik Çiftçi, Francesco Cisternino, Jack Clancy, Sue Clarkson, Fatma Çolakoglu, Lisa Cole, Angela Coleman, Helena Colliander, Heather

Collins, Ben Connell, Sarah-Jane Cooper, Tunahan Corut, Paul Corvi, Alexandre Couture Gagnon, Lorena Covanni, Sarah Cross, Melissa Crumpler, Majatta Cunynghame, Dianne Currie, Michael Dallin, Jo David, Josephine David & Mark Breedon **D** Alexander De Jaeger, Annamaria De Crescenzio, Bianca De Vos, Helen De Munnik, Karin De Boer, Michiel De Graaff, Peter Debruyne, Mauricio Del Razo, Victor Del Arco Cristià, Anna Delinikola, Ediz Demiralp, Chris Derosa, Bert D'Hooghe, Lynn Dickhoff, Paula Dickson, Martın Dion, Alison Diskin, Martina Doblin, Ahmet Dogan, James Donald, Pauline Dong, Dee Doutch, James Down, Michael Doyle, Erik Du Pon, Rob Dubin, Dudley Mcfadden, Julien Dumoulin-Smith, Kiril Dunn, Mary Dunn, Eileen Dyer **E** Gary Edwards, Alexander Eichholz, Trym Eidem Gundersen, Erdjan Eker, Sina Elle, Katherine Ellis, Sara Emery, Martin Engstrom, Cagla Erdogan Ruacan, Firat Erel, Izi Ersonmez, Rabiya Ertogdu, Tayfun Eser, Tayfun Eser, Dursun Esmeray, Jasmine Evans, Jeremy Evans, Michael Evans, Rigmor & Joergen Eybye **F** Dan Faden, Hallie Fader, Jackie Farquhar, Rob Farrington, Sophie Feather-Garner, Adam Federman, Rachel Fentem, Alberta Ferligo, Diego Fernandez Belmonte, Lee Ferron, Gianni Filippi, Moira Findlay, Laura Fine-Morrison, Elke Flemming, Margot Fonteyne, Alexa Forbes, Joey Fowler, Christopher Fox, Mateusz Franckiewicz, Sandra Frank, Amber Franklin, Dario Freguia, Gerry Fuller, Thomas Furniss **G** Cheryl G Paul Gabriner, Phil Gaffey, Ruth Gallant, Scott Gavens, Freek Geldof, Stephanie Geller, Mr Gergely, Paola & Luca Giacometti, Sandy Gibbs, Anina Gidkov, John Gilchrist, Selen Gobelez, Louisa Gokkaya, Julian Gonzalez, Carmelita Görg, Pıerre Gourteau, Ozge Gozke, David Graham, Stefano Grando, Maria Grazia Vanaria, Stephanie Green, James Grieve, Maxmilian Grillo, Melissa Grima, Megan Grover, Leif Jr Gulddal, Arnold Guinto, Dilay Gulgun, Furkan Gun, Alastair Guthrie **H** Rana Haddad, Craig Hadley, Avgusta Hajicosta, Zelda Hall, Spence Halperin, Jane Hamilton, Dik & Sinclair Harris, AJ Hartman, Diana Hartshorn, Jennifer Hattam, Olaf Hauk, Aran Hawker, Tom Haythornthwaite, Rachel Heatley, Angela Heidemann, Karl-Wilhelm Heinle, Kees Hemmes, Kate Hendry, Stein Henrik Softeland, Gilles Herve, Claire Heywood, Jeffrey Hibbert, Mike Hill, Adele Hogg, Christine Hoier, Richard Holland, Jenny Hope, Sonya Hope, Joe Horacek, Tim Hoskins, John Howell, Stephen Howse, Karine Hueber, David Hughes, Becky Hunter-Kelm **I** Ted Ibrahim, Tolga Ilgar, Artar Inciduzen, Klaus Inhuelsen, Karina Ioffee, Ruth Isaacs **J** Terry Jack, Erdmute Jahn, Kaj Jalving, Catherine James, David Janssen, Jared, Anthony Jenkins, Denise Jensen, Jo, John, Craig Johnston, Grey Johnston, Louanne Jones, Ildiko Jordaki, Annika Joseph, Rosalie Justus **K** Erdal Kahya, Orhan Kalender, Susan Kambouris, Jorrit Kamminga, Edmond Kannchen, Kubilay Karabulut, Hallie Keel, Geoff Kelsall, John Kent, Malcolm Kent, Madaline Keros, Nader Khalili, Chris Khoo, Burcu Kiliç, Stephen Killeen, Cameron King, Kevin Kingma, George Kingston, Cigdem Kiray, Martha Kirmaz, Alan Kirschbaum, Judy Kleiman, Ashely Knight, Gordon Knight, Burakhan Kocaman, Diana Koether, Kristian Kofoed, Ildi Kohles, Benjamin Kohlmann, Burcu Kök, Lauren Koopman, Allison Koslen, Melle Koster, Renee Kovacs, Malgorzata Kowalew, Marko Krajina, Katrin Kröger, Christian Kukkula, Gürol Kutlu, Tom Kyffin, Martina Kyselova **L** Kim Ladone, Ian Laing, Sukhjit Lalli, Lewis Lamb, Tess Lambourne, Peter Lang, Ashley Lee, Jay Lee, Mike Lee, Audun Lem, Lionel Leo, Maria Letizia Cagnacci, Bev Lewis, Nick Lewis, Ian Lincoln, Sean Ling, Alona Lisitsa, Alannah Little, Erika Lo, David Locke, Laynni Locke, Steve Locke, Katie Lord, Paolo Lorenzoni, Sam Lovell **M** Josh Mackenzie, Edit Madaras, John Mahon, Lloyd Malin, Eldar Mamedov, Guy Mander, Michael Mann, Juliana Manoliu, Francesca Marini, Andre Marion, Y Selvihan Matthaei, Ah McAdam, Margaret McAleese, Jennifer McCarter, Amber McClure, Lyle McClure, Warren McCulloch, Ruth McDonald, Andrew McLean, Eoghan McSwiney, Janice Meier, Susan Meierhans, Steven Meiers, Val Menenberg, Rod Mepham, Gerald Meral, Olivier Meunier, Corrie Meus, Laura Miguel, Jason Milburn, Craig Miller, Janelle Miller, Sheila Miller, Ashley Milne-Tyte, Thomas Mira Y Lopez, Jordan Mitchell, Monika Moesbauer, Dennis Mogerman, Lorraine Montgomery, Ignacio Morejon, Janet Morrissey, David Motta, Robert Motta, Caroline Moulton Ratzki, Mitja Mueller, Catherine Murphy, Rita Mushinsky, Matt, Michela, Milos **N** Chris Nash, Holly Nazar, Andronikos Nedos, Paolo Neri, Emily Neumeier, James Newman, Kien Ngo, Thao Nguyen, Dylan Nichols, Daryle Niedermayer, Jessica Norcini, Anissa Norman, Aidan Norton **O** Denise O Riley, Rafa Ocón, Colette O'Connor, Oezen Odag, Kateena O'Gorman, Nida Ogutveren, Greg O'Hern, Gunes Oktay, Saban Olcer, Dervis Ölmez, Deirdre O'Reilly, Nadi Otlu, Funda Ozan, Kutay Ozay, Yilmaz Özbay, Ayfer Ozcan, Sevket Ozdemir, Mo Ozer, Cüneyt Özkan, Kemal Ozkurd, Erkan Ozsu **P** Denis Pacquelet, Rolf Palmberg, Michelle Parlevliet, Lisa Parolini, Kellene Parra, Alia Parrish, Vish Patel, Trent Paton, Alja Pavletic, David Pawley, Amanda Pearson, Rui Pedro, Jo Peeters, Ana Peralta, Paul Pesie, Simon Peters, Niklas Petersen, Johan Petersman, Sonia Petrich, Beate

Philipp, Penny Phillips, Megan Philpot, Andrew Phippard, Susan Pike, Vivian Pisano, Boizen Platon, Jim Pleyte, Jan Polatschek, James Pollicott, Jeffrey Polovina, Christy Pomeranz, Ben Potter, Hélène Potvin, Christine & Mike Poznanski, Rossana Pozzati, Brad Prestipino, Silvia Primerano **R** Peter Radford, Roxanne Rahim, Ruba Rahman, Boyden Ralph, Uday Ram, Chas Rannells, Gaye Reeves, Daniel Rellstab, Tanja Remec, Keith Resnick, Julie Reynolds, Claudio Riccio, Leona Riegle, Heather Riggin, Ale Rincon, Helen Ripley, Narelle Ritchie, Aaron Robertson, Gulsah Robertson, Gina Robinson, Katie Robinson, Norm Robinson, Maiza Rocha, Rodriguez, Joshua Rogers, Kyle Rogerson, Xavier Roman, Thomas Ropars, Rami Rosenbaum, Annie Rousseau, Selin Rozanes, Edoardo Rubbiani, Karen Rutter **S** Ortal-Paz Saar, Maria Sachocos, Ali Safak, Melih Saglambasoglu, Bulent Sahin, Sayim Sahin, Berrin Sakman, Emilio Salami, Lyn Salisbury, Brianne Salmon, Taylan Sargin, Der Sarkissian Anouche, Olivier Savary, Joan Scapetis, Els Schep, Dick Schilp, Lauren Schlanger, Manuela Schliessner, Daniel Schmidt-Loebe, Claudia Schnellinger, Siegfried Schwab, Duncan Scudamore, Nicholas Scull, David Sears, Robert Sears, Paul Seaver, Mehmet Segil, Figen Semerciyan, Ramazan Serbest, Lori Shapiro, Akbar Sharfi, Sue Sharp, Trish Shea, Jenny Sheat, Kirsty Shepherd, Tory Shepherd, Jenni Sheppard, Rachel Sheppard, Timothy Silvers, Paul Simon, John Singh, Ellen Sitton, Ben Skinner, Alena Slavikova, Tom Smallman, Britt Smith, Colleen Smith, Val Snedden, Renee Snyder, Maria Soledad Rueda, Sabrina Spies, Silvia Spies, Eckart Spindler, Jaap Sprey, John Springborn, Branislav Srdanovic, Aarthi Srinath, Ioannis Staikopoulos, Paul Stamatellis, Bruce Stanger, Robert Stanton, Sandra Stanway, Sarah Steegar, Margaret Steel, Sam Steele, Clifford Stein, Jozef Steis, Joanne Steuer, Stan Steward, Taryn Stewart, Jody Steyls, Renske Stichbury, Chantal Stieber, Tom Stockwell, Mirjam Stoll, Lei Sun, Jesse Sutton, Monique Sweep, Frank & Linda Szerdahelyi, Patricia Szobar **T** Lindsay Tabas, Kristina Täht, Yuki Tanaka, Erach Tarapore, Nes Tarjan, Robert Tattersall, Alessandro Tavano, Lucy Taylor, Susan Taylor, Outger Teerhuis, Miia Teir, Philip Tervit, Sebastian Teunissen, Jon Thomas, Anne Thompson, Gordon Thompson, Panom Thongprayoon, Jerry Tilley, Tim Bewer, Zeynep Tiskaya, Ted Todd, Karina Tokur, Cristian Tolhuijsen, Müjde Tosyali, Agnes Toth, Alan Tourle, Edward Trower, Maya Tsukernik, Carley Tucker, Fatih Türkmen **U** Gino Uguccioni, Suat Ulusoy, Yorukhan Unal, Jayda Uras, Cagri Uyarer **V** Anja Van Heelsum, Hanny Van Den Bergh, Jeannette Van Eekelen, Marianne Van Der Walle, Ronald Van Velzen, Ruben Van Moppes, Steven Van Renterghem, Tom Van Buitenen, Wim Van Der Sluijs, Paula Vandalen, Paola Velasquez, Savin Ven Johnson, Michele Volpi, Joachim Von Loeben, Beryl Voss, Simon Vuuregge **W** JP Waelter, Birgit Wagner, Robert Walker, Wendy Walsh, Mei Wang, Tom Weaver, Antje Weber, Pieter Weeber, Jason Weetman, Edward Wendt, Michael Wenham, Sibylle Wensch, Bill White, Helen Wienand, Nancy Wigglesworth, Maggy Wilcox, Kevin Wilkinson, Jo Williams, Sue Willingham, Brian Willis, Alison Willmott, Natashar Wills, Sean Windsor, Katarzyna Winiarska, Gordon Winocur, Chris Winters, Anna Wittenberg, Sarah Wolbert, Otto Wolkerstorfer, Celena Wong, Nicola Woodcock, Michael Woodley, Alison Woods, Mirjam Wouters, Stefan Wuelfken **Y** Deborah Yagow, Mary Yang, Elif Yenici, Ugur Yenici, Karen Yeung, Natalia Yialelis, Mehmet Yildirim, Sakir Yilmaz, Ian Young, Veysel Yuce, Renan Yücel **Z** Thelma Zarb, David Zaring, Mark Zekulin, Mark & Jolee Zola, Mengmeng Zong, Anne Zouridakis, Manuele Zunelli

AUTHOR THANKS

James Bainbridge

A hearty çok teşekkür to the innumerable folk who helped me in İstanbul and while on the road: Selcuk Akgul, Yener and friends, Leyla Tabrizi, Funda Dagli, Pat, Ekrem and the Kelebek posse in Göreme, Ece in İzmir, Ziya, Bill and the gang in Eceabat, Melek Anne and Café Pena in Edirne, Lütfi et al in Behramkale, Annette in Ayvalik, Mustafa in Bergama, Remzi in Foça and Talat in Alaçatı. Imogen, Cliff and my fellow authors have been journalist- and editor-shaped rocks. Cheers to Jen for teaching me backgammon, and dankie to Leigh-Robin for coming on the adventure.

Brett Atkinson

Thanks especially to the warm and welcoming Kurdish people of southeastern Anatolia. Special thanks to Selin, Alison, and Jale for their friendship and support for a Kiwi a long way from home, and to all the other travellers I met on the road. Cheers to fellow scribes James Bainbridge and Virginia Maxwell for a great night out in İstanbul, to commissioning editor Cliff Wilkinson in London, and to the hardworking editorial and cartography team at the Melbourne Lonely Planet mothership.

Jean-Bernard Carillet

Many thanks to Celil and Osman, my guardian angels, who went out of their way to help me when my car broke down in the steppe. I'm also indebted to Zafer, Necmettin,

Cumhur, Bülent, Ebubekir, who shared their knowledge with me. Coordinating author extraordinaire James Bainbridge deserves a pat on the back for his patience and tenacity. Many thanks also to Brett Atkinson and Will Gourlay. At Lonely Planet, special thanks to Cliff for his careful supervision, style-guru Laura, and the carto and production team.

Steve Fallon

A very special çok teşekkürler to oracle Jayne Pearson in Kaş and my partner and loyal travelling companion, Mike Rothschild. Others who provided assistance along the way include Mehmet Acar in Marmaris; Carrie and Şaban Akkelle in Çıralı; staff at the Arsuz Otel in Arsuz (Uluçınar); Phil Buckley in Kaş; İlknur İdrisoğlu in Dalyan; Yakup Kahveci in Kızkalesi; Sibel Romano in Reşadiye; Nermin Sümer and Aziz Tankut in Antalya; Emrah Tag in Side; and İrfan and Saffet Tezcan in Kaleköy (Kekova). In London, thanks to Ceyda Sara Pekenc and staff at Redmint Communications.

Will Gourlay

Thanks to Clifton Wilkinson for getting me on board the Turkey team again, and thanks to Anna and the inhouse editorial team at Lonely Planet. In Turkey, Pat Yale has again been a great source of information as well as sharing inspiring tales of Easter services in Mardin et al. Finally, thanks to Claire, Bridget and Tommy, still my all-time favourite Turkey travel companions. Let's do it all again, soon.

Virginia Maxwell

Many thanks to Pat Yale, René Ames, Tahir Karabaş, Eveline Zoutendijk, Saffet Tonguç, Ercan and Şenay Tanrıvermiş, Ann Nevens, Jennifer Gaudet, Özlem Tuna, Shellie Corman, Mehmet Umur, Emel Güntaş, Faruk Boyacı, Özen Dalgın, Selin Rozanes, Necdet and Ayse Bezmen, Atilla Tuna, and the many locals who shared their knowledge and love of the city with me. Thanks also to fellow authors James Bainbridge, Brett Atkinson and Steve Fallon.

Brandon Presser

A heartfelt çok teşekkürler to Haldun, Uğur and Damla (dondurma!), Muge, Figen (my Turkish Maman) and Nirvana, Angela, Selim and Tamera, Sinem, Kerim, Cumhur, Mehmet, Murat, the prodigal Barbarbos musketeers, and my lovely travel companions Yağmur and Justine. A huge thank you to everyone in Lonely Planet–land, especially Cliff, James and Imogen. And, on what has been dubbed 'the trip of losing things', I'd like to thank Joanne for making sure that I didn't lose my mind.

Tom Spurling

In Göreme, a debt of gratitude to Mustafa at Heritage Travel and Ali at Kelebek. Thanks as always to Pat Yale for the beginnings. Love

THIS BOOK

This 12th edition of Turkey was researched and written by the estimable author team of James Bainbridge (coordinating author), Brett Atkinson, Jean-Bernard Carillet, Steve Fallon, Virginia Maxwell, Brandon Presser and Tom Spurling. Will Gourlay wrote History, The Arts, Architecture and The People. The Health chapter is based on original research by Dr Caroline Evans. Tom Brosnahan researched and wrote the first five editions of Turkey. The 11th edition was written by James Bainbridge (coordinating author), Brett Atkinson, Jean-Bernard Carillet, Steve Fallon, Joe Fullman, Will Gourlay, Virginia Maxwell and Tom Spurling. This guidebook was commissioned in Lonely Planet's London office, and produced by the following:

Commissioning Editors Glenn van der Knijff, Clifton Wilkinson

Coordinating Editor Anna Metcalfe

Coordinating Cartographer Dianna Duggan

Coordinating Layout Designer Kerrianne Southway

Managing Editors Imogen Bannister, Bruce Evans

Managing Cartographers Shahara Ahmed, Herman So

Managing Layout Designer Indra Kilfoyle

Assisting Editors Janet Austin, Susie Ashworth, Carolyn Boicos, Jessica Crouch, Jocelyn Harewood, Lesley McCave, Alan Murphy, Joanne Newell, Susan Paterson, Kirsten Rawlings

Assisting Cartographers Enes Basic, Ildiko Bogdanovits, Csanad Csutoros, Xavier Di Toro, Jennifer Johnston, Andy Rojas, Amanda Sierp

Assisting Layout Designers Jacqui Saunders

Cover Research Aude Vauconsant

Internal Image Research Sabrina Dalbesio

Language Content Annelies Mertens, Branislava Vladisavljevic

Thanks to Mark Adams, Elisa Arduca, Imogen Bannister, David Connolly, Stefanie Di Trocchio, Janine Eberle, Joshua Geoghegan, Mark Germanchis, Chris Girdler, Michelle Glynn, Jocelyn Harewood, Lauren Hunt, Paul Iacono, Laura Jane, David Kemp, Lisa Knights, Nic Lehman, Shawn Low, Katie Lynch, John Mazzocchi, Wayne Murphy, Trent Paton, Adrian Persoglia, Piers Pickard, Lachlan Ross, Michael Ruff, Julie Sheridan, Laura Stansfeld, John Taufa, Sam Trafford, Juan Winata, Emily Wolman, Nick Wood

to Ruth for the carpet and for taking care of Lucy. In Ürgüp, there's only one Esbelli and only one Suha! In Tokat, thanks to Tügce. In Ankara, thanks to Helen Mary for joining the party. In Safranbolu, cheers to the Gül Evi crew. In İstanbul, well done Dodger for surviving the brutal man love. In Lonely Planet–land, thanks to James, Cliff, the editors, cartographers and the publishing team for your brilliant work. And to Lucy and Oliver... we did it!

ACKNOWLEDGMENTS

Climate map data adapted from Peel MC, Finlayson BL & McMahon TA (2007) 'Updated World Map of the Köppen-Geiger Climate Classification', Hydrology and Earth System Sciences, 11, 163344.

Cover photograph: Kaputaş cove and beach, Kalkan, Antalya, Turkey/Izzet Keribar, LPI. Many of the images in this guide are available for licensing from Lonely Planet Images: www.lonelyplanetimages.com.

ACKNOWLEDGMENTS

NOTES

index

how to use this book

These symbols will help you find the listings you want:

- ◉ Sights
- ✦ Activities
- ⬤ Courses
- ☞ Tours
- ⚑ Festivals & Events
- ⊫ Sleeping
- ✕ Eating
- ◗ Drinking
- ☆ Entertainment
- 🔒 Shopping
- ⓘ Information/Transport

Look out for these icons:

- TOP CHOICE — Our author's recommendation
- FREE — No payment required
- ⬛ — A green or sustainable option

Our authors have nominated these places as demonstrating a strong commitment to sustainability – for example by supporting local communities and producers, operating in an environmentally friendly way, or supporting conservation projects.

These symbols give you the vital information for each listing:

- ☏ Telephone Numbers
- ⊙ Opening Hours
- ℗ Parking
- ⊖ Nonsmoking
- ❄ Air-Conditioning
- @ Internet Access
- ☎ Wi-Fi Access
- ☒ Swimming Pool
- ✔ Vegetarian Selection
- 🍴 English-Language Menu
- ♠ Family-Friendly
- 🐾 Pet-Friendly
- ▯ Bus
- ⬇ Ferry
- Ⓜ Metro
- Ⓢ Subway
- ⊖ London Tube
- ▯ Tram
- ▯ Train

Reviews are organised by author preference.

Map Legend

Sights
- ◐ Beach
- ◓ Buddhist
- ✖ Castle
- ✚ Christian
- ◉ Hindu
- ● Islamic
- ✡ Jewish
- ❶ Monument
- ▦ Museum/Gallery
- ✪ Ruin
- ◒ Winery/Vineyard
- ◉ Zoo
- ◉ Other Sight

Activities, Courses & Tours
- ◌ Diving/Snorkelling
- ◍ Canoeing/Kayaking
- ◌ Skiing
- ◍ Surfing
- ◌ Swimming/Pool
- ◍ Walking
- ◌ Windsurfing
- • Other Activity/Course/Tour

Sleeping
- ◌ Sleeping
- ◍ Camping

Eating
- ◍ Eating

Drinking
- ◌ Drinking
- ◌ Cafe

Entertainment
- ◌ Entertainment

Shopping
- ◌ Shopping

Information
- ◎ Post Office
- ❶ Tourist Information

Transport
- ◔ Airport
- ⊗ Border Crossing
- ◉ Bus
- ⊷ Cable Car/Funicular
- ◌ Cycling
- ◌ Ferry
- Ⓜ Metro
- ◉ Monorail
- ℗ Parking
- Ⓢ S-Bahn
- ◉ Taxi
- ◆ Train/Railway
- ◌ Tram
- ⊙ Tube Station
- Ⓤ U-Bahn
- • Other Transport

Routes
- Tollway
- Freeway
- Primary
- Secondary
- Tertiary
- Lane
- Unsealed Road
- Plaza/Mall
- Steps
- Tunnel
- Pedestrian Overpass
- Walking Tour
- Walking Tour Detour
- Path

Boundaries
- International
- State/Province
- Disputed
- Regional/Suburb
- Marine Park
- Cliff
- Wall

Population
- ◯ Capital (National)
- ◉ Capital (State/Province)
- ● City/Large Town
- ● Town/Village

Geographic
- ◌ Hut/Shelter
- ◌ Lighthouse
- ◌ Lookout
- ▲ Mountain/Volcano
- ◌ Oasis
- ◌ Park
-)(Pass
- ◌ Picnic Area
- ◌ Waterfall

Hydrography
- River/Creek
- Intermittent River
- Swamp/Mangrove
- Reef
- Canal
- Water
- Dry/Salt/Intermittent Lake
- Glacier

Areas
- Beach/Desert
- + + + Cemetery (Christian)
- × × × Cemetery (Other)
- Park/Forest
- Sportsground
- Sight (Building)
- Top Sight (Building)

Virginia Maxwell

İstanbul After working for many years as a publishing manager at Lonely Planet's Melbourne headquarters, Virginia decided that she'd be happier writing guidebooks than commissioning them. Since making this decision she's covered nine countries for Lonely Planet, most of them around the Mediterranean. Virginia knows Turkey well, and loves it with a passion. As well as working on the previous three editions of this country guide, she is also the author of the İstanbul City Guide and İstanbul Encounter pocket guide and writes about the city for a host of international magazines and websites.

Read more about Virginia at:
lonelyplanet.com/members/virginiamaxwell

Brandon Presser

Ephesus, Bodrum & the South Aegean, Western Anatolia After earning an art history degree from Harvard University and working at the Louvre, Brandon swapped landscape canvases for the real deal and joined the glamorous ranks of eternal nomadism. Today, Brandon is a full-time travel writer – he's written 20 Lonely Planet titles, from Iceland to Thailand and many 'lands' in between. For this assignment Brandon travelled from the cold and clear Aegean seas to the dusty backroads of Anatolia; his Turkish adventure will forever remain a cherished memory.

Read more about Brendon at:
lonelyplanet.com/members/brandonpresser

Tom Spurling

Ankara & Central Anatolia, Cappadocia Tom Spurling first travelled to Turkey in 2003 to spend the low season in Olympos while waiting for the high season in Olympos. For the previous edition of Turkey, he researched the Mediterranean with his pregnant wife and her all-day sickness. For this edition they returned with baby Oliver who was particularly inspired by the Hittite ruins of central Anatolia. When not travelling Tom lives in Melbourne and teaches high school boys to make the most of their holiday time.

Read more about Tom at:
lonelyplanet.com/members/tomspurling

Will Gourlay

History, The Arts, Architecture, The People A serial visitor to Turkey, Will first arrived in İstanbul almost 20 years ago. His first lengthy foray took him through Southeast Anatolia and into Syria. He returned soon after to teach for a year in İzmir, where he learned the delights of İskender kebap and the perils of rakı. Recent trips have been with his wife and children, all of whom are becoming as obsessed with Turkey as he is. Will is now undertaking doctoral research into Turkish culture and society.

OUR STORY

A beat-up old car, a few dollars in the pocket and a sense of adventure. In 1972 that's all Tony and Maureen Wheeler needed for the trip of a lifetime – across Europe and Asia overland to Australia. It took several months, and at the end – broke but inspired – they sat at their kitchen table writing and stapling together their first travel guide, *Across Asia on the Cheap*. Within a week they'd sold 1500 copies. Lonely Planet was born.

Today, Lonely Planet has offices in Melbourne, London and Oakland, with more than 600 staff and writers. We share Tony's belief that 'a great guidebook should do three things: inform, educate and amuse'.

OUR WRITERS

James Bainbridge

Coordinating Author; Thrace & Marmara, İzmir & the North Aegean The last few years have been all about Turkey for James. While coordinating the previous edition of *Turkey*, he researched Cappadocia and Central Anatolia, then wrote up his kebap-stained notes at home in Hackney, a Turkish enclave of London. For this edition he moved to İstanbul. When he hasn't been learning to love suffixes on a Turkish course, or sitting among Mac-toting artists in Cihangir's trendy cafes, he has written about the city for worldwide publications. James' travel writing on Turkey, and other countries from India to Ireland, has appeared in a dozen Lonely Planet guidebooks and publications including the *Times* and the *Guardian*.

Brett Atkinson

Black Sea Coast & the Kaçkar Mountains, Southeastern Anatolia Since first visiting Turkey in 1985, Brett Atkinson has returned regularly to one of his favourite countries. Highlights have included ballooning in Cappadocia, discovering the poignant remains of Ani and Afrodisias, and honeymooning with Carol in İstanbul. For this research trip he visited southeastern Anatolia for the first time, and the region's stunning scenery, Kurdish culture, and excellent food didn't disappoint. Brett has written about over 40 different countries as a guidebook author and travel writer. See www.brett-atkinson.net.

Jean-Bernard Carillet

Northeastern Anatolia A Paris-based journalist and photographer, Jean-Bernard has a passion for remote corners and adventure-laden regions – small wonder then that he keeps returning to northeastern Anatolia. He has clocked up five trips there, and each time the area has woven its spell on him a little more (despite a couple of major rental car breakdowns). Seeking out churches and castles of yore lost in the steppe or perched on cliff tops, climbing majestic summits (including Mt Ararat), hiking in the Kaçkars, rafting the Ispir River – he can't think of a better playground.

Steve Fallon

Antalya & the Western Mediterranean, Eastern Mediterranean Owning a house in Kalkan and being on first-name basis with most of the Turkish Airline in-flight staff currently flying between London and Dalaman, Steve considers Turkey a second home. This assignment took him from the hotspots of Marmaris to the hotchpot that is Hatay where he discovered the joys of fresh thyme salad, castles that walk on water and early Christianity. And although *Türkçe'yi hala mağara adamí gibi konuşuyor* (he still speaks Turkish like a caveman), he says only nice things in his new favourite language.

Read more about Steve at:
lonelyplanet.com/members/stevefallon

OVER PAGE MORE WRITERS

Published by Lonely Planet Publications Pty Ltd
ABN 36 005 607 983
12th edition – March 2011
ISBN 9781741797244
© Lonely Planet 2010   Photographs © as indicated 2010
10 9 8 7 6 5 4 3
Printed in China